MODERN REAL ESTATE

FOURTH EDITION

CHARLES H. WURTZEBACH
THE PRUDENTIAL REALTY GROUP

MIKE E. MILES
**UNIVERSITY OF NORTH CAROLINA
AT CHAPEL HILL**

JOHN WILEY & SONS, INC
NEW YORK ■ CHICHESTER ■ BRISBANE ■ TORONTO ■ SINGAPORE

Acquisitions Editor   John Woods
Production Manager   Joe Ford
Designer   Maddy Lesure/Carolyn Joseph
Production Supervisor   Elizabeth Austin
Copy Editor   Marjorie Shustak
Cover Photograph   Norman McGrath

Recognizing the importance of preserving what has been written, it is a policy of John Wiley & Sons, Inc. to have books of enduring value published in the United States printed on acid-free paper, and we exert our best efforts to that end.

Library of Congress Cataloging in Publication Data:

Wurtzebach, Charles H.
    Modern real estate / Charles H. Wurtzebach, Mike E. Miles. — 4th
ed.
        p.   cm.
    Includes index.
    ISBN 0-471-52591-X
    1. Real estate business.   2. Real estate business—United States.
I. Miles, Mike E.   II. Title.
HD 1375.W873   1991
333.33′0973—dc20   90-48555
                                                              CIP

Printed in the United States of America

10 9 8 7 6 5 4 3 2 1

$\mathcal{P}$ REFACE

The past two decades have been marked by a significant increase in the recognition given real estate both as a major investment vehicle and as a vital productive factor in our economy. This recognition has led to the acceptance of real estate as a field of study requiring both academic preparation, as evidenced by growth in college and university real estate programs, and practical experience. New educational programs sponsored by various professional real estate associations attest to the vigor with which the industry is promoting formal training both before and during a professional career.

This book is for individuals taking the Principles of Real Estate course at the college or university level. It also provides useful background reading for those entering careers in real estate and related industries without the benefit of formal real estate education. Additionally, individuals entering real estate-related careers, such as architecture, who lack a business background, will find *Modern Real Estate* a valuable source of information in a broad range of real estate areas.

As a classroom text, the book assumes some previous or concurrent exposure to the standard "core" business courses. Drawing on the student's general business background, the book examines the unique features of real estate with a focus on *action* and *decision making*. The book concentrates on the "why" of decisions and the interrelationship among the key decision makers in the industry.

As the real estate business becomes more sophisticated, the real estate professional must make greater efforts to understand the essential workings of all aspects of the industry in order to make correct decisions in his or her specialized area. For example, the better sales associate is the one who knows real estate financing, law, and construction fundamentals as well as the fine details of real estate marketing. *Modern Real Estate* describes the workings and theoretical underpinnings of the major fields within the real estate industry and clarifies the linkages and relationships of the different fields. In doing this, the book offers a survey of the real estate industry that molds an academic perception with guides for practical decision making. With this overview, the student may proceed in future study to develop expertise in any of the many specialty areas that make up the real estate industry.

Part 1 acquaints the student with the *spatial element* and the *interdisciplinary* nature of the real estate industry. The place of real property in the American economic system is traced. The theme or unifying concept of the book is portrayed as the "real estate game." The reader learns the definition of a "winner" and is introduced to the players and their respective roles in the real estate marketplace. With this macroeconomic introduction as a basis, certain theories from regional and urban economics are analyzed to clarify the spatial element in real estate decisions. Consideration of the physical side of constructed space and our interaction with the spacial environment complete the analytical framework.

Part 2 introduces the student to the basic concepts of the American legal system and the essentials of real estate law that make up the formal rules of the real estate game. The legal concepts with which the real estate decision maker deals are explained.

Part 3 is a straightforward presentation of real estate appraisal with an emphasis on what produces *value*. The practical dimension of regional and urban economics is shown in the appraisal process, which itself is a link to the investment section.

Part 4 begins by briefly discussing the basics of marketing in general, and then moves to the unique aspects of real estate marketing. Brokerage is covered in Chapter 10, with the process of marketing the single-family home distinguished from the marketing and leasing of income properties. Appendix 10A gives the details of a real estate closing, and appendix 10B contains the Realtor Code of Ethics. The increasingly important field of asset management is the subject of Chapters 11 and 12. First the basics of property management are covered, then the additional considerations of institutional and corporate owners.

Part 5 first reviews the U.S. financial system and identifies the lending institutions that finance real estate. Financing mechanics from the borrower's perspective are covered first; then lender underwriting criteria and loan analysis are presented. The more complex operations of the secondary mortgage market are covered in Chapter 16.

Part 6 on taxation begins with a brief summary of income and property taxation and emphasizes real estate's unique position. The reader is then introduced to the major provisions of the Internal Revenue code specifically affecting real estate. This edition includes the significant tax law changes called for in the 1986 Tax Reform Act as well as the necessary historical perspective to fully appreciate the tax environment entering the 1990's. (Should any of the more significant currently proposed tax law changes be enacted, Wiley will provide a short paperback update.)

Part 7 on investment brings together the previous material in a real estate investment model. The unique features of real estate are highlighted, this time in a risk-return framework. Chapter 20 reviews the principles of investment analysis. Chapter 21 develops the discounted cash-flow model that is an extension of our original definition of winning the real estate game. Chapter 22 covers the more advanced material involving real estate decision making in a "portfolio" framework. Finally, Chapter 23 examines the various ways in which the "bundle of rights" is packaged to suit different investors. This chapter deals with the emergence of real estate investment managers in the context of the theory developed in Chapters 20–22.

Part 8's topic is the asset creation side of the real estate industry: real estate development. The description of the development process, in Chapters 24 and 25, integrates material from previous parts on law, appraisal, marketing, finance, and investment. Chapter 26 presents a methodology for market and economic feasibility analysis, completing the presentation of the dynamic side of the real estate investment model.

Part 9 deals with public policy. In Chapter 27 we examine the very extensive role of government in real estate. In Chapter 28 we look at the long-term trends in the industry that have motivated, and have been motivated by, government's role. Chapter 29 covers several topics that we expect will be increasingly important in the years to come. In this way, our introduction to the real estate industry concludes with an "eye to the future," which is an essential part of good decision making.

Compound interest tables, a glossary, and an index provide comprehensive aids in understanding and using the concepts introduced in this book. Suggested readings and references are given at the end of each Part.

In total, the book gives sufficient depth and breadth to allow the reader to claim a general understanding of "the industry." If the reader plans detailed subsequent study in a particular area or if time is limited, certain chapters may be omitted with no loss of continuity. The more advanced chapters are Chapter 12, Asset Management: The Institutional and Corporate Perspective; Chapter 16, The Secondary Mortgage Markets; Chapter 19, Tax Credits, Installment Sales, Like-Kind Exchanges, and Other Considerations; Chapter 22, Real Estate and Modern Portfolio Theory; Chapter 23, Institutional Real Estate Investment; Chapter 26, Land Use Feasibility Analysis; Chapter 28, Long-Term Trends in Urban Structure and Land Use; and Chapter 29, New Ways to Play the Real Estate Game. If these chapters are left as "suggested future reading," the book will help any beginning student. Including all these chapters in a one-semester course constitutes a highly rigorous introduction to real estate.

We are happy to note that both men and women are active and successful in the real estate profession. It is gratifying to observe that women are entering the field in increasing numbers and assuming major decision-making roles. However, if every sentence in this book used "he or she," "him or her," and "his or hers" when referring to the real estate profession, the book would become difficult to read. Therefore, for ease of expression, "he," "his," and "him" are used in some places and "she," "hers," and "her" in others, and these refer to both female and male real estate professionals.

ACKNOWLEDGMENTS

It would be impossible to recognize and thank all the individuals who have contributed to the development and preparation of this fourth edition. Our indebtedness extends to family, former students, and colleagues in academia and business.

We are particularly indebted to the contributions made by the following colleagues and friends who offered insight and suggestions throughout the evolution of this book: the late James A. Graaskamp, University of Wisconsin-Madison; Michael A. Goldberg, University of British Columbia; William B. Brueggeman, Southern Methodist University; Steve Sears, Texas Tech University; Terry Grissom, Texas Real Estate Research Center; Fred E. Case, University of California, Los Angeles; Kenneth M. Lusht, Pennsylvania State University; Raymond W. Lansford, University of Missouri, Columbia; Wallace F. Smith, University of California, Berkeley; Howard H. Stevenson, Harvard University; Harold A. Lubell, Assistant Attorney General of New York in charge of the Real Estate Financing Bureau; F. L. Wilson, Jr., Dickenson-Heffner, Baltimore, Maryland; Charles B. Akerson, Akerson Valuation Company, Boston, Massachusetts; Bill Poland, Bay West Development, San Francisco, California; John Hemphill, Vacation Resorts, Aspen, Colorado; Norman G. Millier, University of Cincinnati; Donald W. Bell, University of Hawaii; Roger R. Sindt, University of Nebraska; Karl L. Guntermann, Arizona State University; Thomas P. Boehm, University of Tennessee; Kerry D. Vandell, University of Wisconsin-Madison; Tom McCue, DePaul University; Marc T. Smith, Temple University; Douglas Bible, Louisiana State University; Eugene H. Fox, Northeast Louisiana University; Roger Cannaday, University of Illinois; and William Landgon, Florida State University.

Our special thanks in this edition go to David J. Hartzell, University of North Carolina at Chapel Hill, who did the rewrite of Chapter 16; David Shulman and all of the Salomon Brothers research team who are quoted extensively throughout the text; Jim Bichsel, executive director of the North Carolina Association of Realtors, for his help with the brokerage section; Paula Shanley and Anatole Pevner of Prudential Real Estate Investors, Inc., who handled drafting and researching important sections of the text; and most importantly, Ginger Travis, our in-house editor through all four editions. She never got rich in real estate, but we love her anyway.

CHARLES H. WURTZEBACH
MIKE E. MILES

Newark, New Jersey
Chapel Hill, North Carolina

$\mathcal{B}$ RIEF CONTENTS

PART 4   **MARKETING, BROKERAGE, AND MANAGEMENT**

PART 5   **REAL ESTATE FINANCE**

PART 6   **TAXATION**

$\mathcal{C}$ONTENTS

5 TRANSFERRING REAL ESTATE INTERESTS 122

PART 3   VALUATION AND THE APPRAISAL PROCESS

6 PRINCIPLES OF VALUATION 161

7 THE SALES COMPARISON APPROACH AND THE COST APPROACH 181

11 ASSET MANAGEMENT: THE PROPERTY MANAGEMENT PERSPECTIVE   302

12 ASSET MANAGEMENT: THE INSTITUTIONAL AND CORPORATE PERSPECTIVES   329

PART 5   REAL ESTATE FINANCE

13 THE FINANCIAL SYSTEM AND REAL ESTATE FINANCE   367

PART 6   TAXATION

17   INCOME AND PROPERTY TAXATION   497

18   REAL ESTATE INCOME TAX DEDUCTIONS   520

26 LAND USE FEASIBILITY ANALYSIS   677

PART 9   PUBLIC POLICY AND PROSPECTS
FOR THE FUTURE

27 GOVERNMENT INVOLVEMENT   709

P A R T 1

THE ANALYTICAL
FRAMEWORK

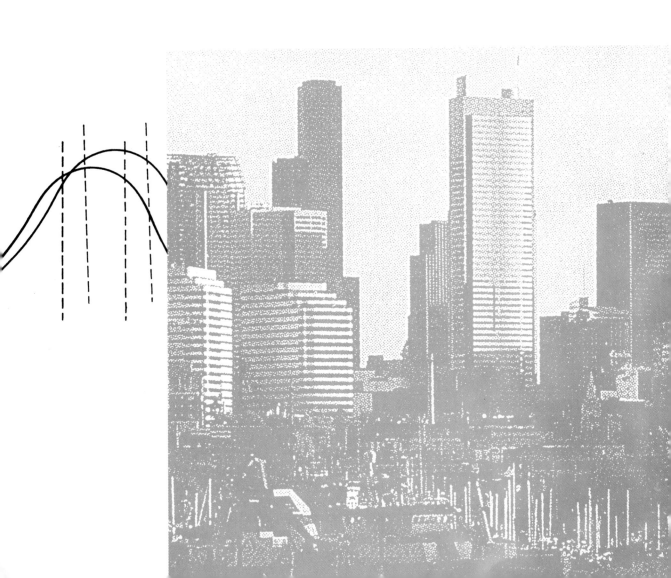

$\mathcal{T}$HE AMERICAN REAL ESTATE INDUSTRY: AN OVERVIEW

The real estate industry can be viewed as a market-oriented game—a game in the sense that it has players, rules, and a way to determine a winner. This view is developed throughout the book, as are these related observations: (1) In real estate markets, as in all business, *change* is constant; (2) the "rules of the game" are also ever-changing; and (3) the winner of the game usually is the person who can anticipate *future* change and act on the opportunity it presents.

REAL ESTATE AS A MARKETPLACE GAME

The real estate game analogy can lead in several directions. In the most obvious direction, the winner of the game is the player who ends up with the most chips (i.e., the one who gets the money). In pursuit of the chips, as in most games, players must act in accordance with previously defined rules. A whole host of both formal legal rules and less formally defined social values set limits on the real estate professional's actions. However, unlike a parlor board game (Monopoly® comes to mind), the real estate marketplace has rules that change *during the game*. In addition, players enter and leave during the game, creating dynamic market conditions. In the real estate game, players include some consumers, some professional suppliers, and some sources of investment capital—each with a different role and a different strategy for "winning the game." In all cases, however, the game centers around a physical product, a point that we also highlight throughout the text.

The game begins with a physical product that produces value. Most typically, *value is a function of expected future cash flows.* The players must understand the physical asset and various market forces that affect the amount of these expected cash flows. However, even in playing the game to get the chips, the player must recognize many important externalities (i.e., the positive or negative effects, or both, on surrounding land parcels). Throughout the text, we intertwine public policy concerns with the individual player's objective to win the game within the constraints of the marketplace. It is in this marketplace that players play to win and, it is hoped, the public is served.

THE REAL ESTATE MARKETPLACE

The real estate marketplace actually consists of a very large number of separate markets differentiated by (1) geographic location (neighborhood, city, and region and, in some cases, national boundaries or international groupings) and (2) type of real estate (single-family homes, office buildings, industrial properties, etc.). Indeed, since each parcel of property has a unique location that cannot be duplicated, it might almost be said that an infinite number of markets exist. Certain national markets (such as the financial markets) have a strong impact on all geographic and property-type markets, but real estate is still best understood as a collection of differentiated markets, for example, the upscale resort market in Tucson, Arizona, or the high tech industrial park market along route 128 in Boston. Real estate markets are the arenas in which the players (described later) carry out the activities that constitute the real estate game.

After the future cash flow expected to be generated by the physical asset is estimated, various claims on that cash flow must be considered. The most obvious claim is that of the many parties who make the asset continue to produce cash flow. These include a whole host of professionals whose claim is usually summarized under the accounting term "operating expenses." Rents paid by tenants less operating expenses leave net operating income.

Perhaps the largest claim on the net operating income is that of the lender (or lenders). This player, usually a financial institution, and its role are studied in detail in Part 5. Another large claimant is the federal government, which takes a share designated as income taxes. The rules for determining the extent of this share and investor's interest in creating "tax shelter" are studied at length in Part 6.

The residual or remaining portion is termed the equity cash flow. From a real estate investor's standpoint, winning the game involves maximizing this residual share as well as the likelihood of receiving this share. Players must forecast the future residual equity cash flow and the risk of not receiving it in order to determine value. Furthermore, the timing of the future cash flow is also a critical element as will be pointed out in both Parts 5 and 7. Different players may place a different value on a property's stream of income based on different goals and objectives. For example, a pension plan may prefer long-term capital appreciation whereas a retired individual may focus on current cash flow.

To summarize, analyzing real estate takes the form of a *model* in which the analyst does the following:

■   Estimates the net operating income (estimated gross revenue less estimated operating expenses) for a particular real estate project in a particular marketplace.

■   Deducts claims by lenders (interest and principal payments), government (taxes), and others that have priority over the equity claim.

■   Estimates the residual cash flow that belongs to the equity owner (the investor).

Applying the model to real-life situations can be a complex high-stakes endeavor as illustrated in Box 1-1. Still, behind the headline-making decisions lies a great deal of hard analysis, and that is what this text is about.

REAL ESTATE AS MORE THAN JUST A GAME

It must be stressed that there is harmony between playing to win and the successful working of our economy. This is merely another way of stating the basic philosophic premise of Adam Smith in his book, *The Wealth of Nations.* Smith, the eighteenth-century English philosopher-economist, stated that the self-interested dealings of buyers and sellers operating in the marketplace yield the best overall results for society as a whole. He wrote that the invisible "guiding hand" ensures that entrepreneurs working for their own individual benefit will unknowingly also be working to achieve the best possible outcome for the entire society. Markets can, of course, break down, and such breakdowns are frequently cited as the justification for government intervention. In fact, the U.S. real estate market is highly affected by government influences. For example, tax incentives and interest rate subsidies stimulate investment, while local zoning ordinances may limit development. In our mixed economy, "the guiding hand" belongs not only to entrepreneurs, but also to lobbyists, legislators, regulators, citizens' groups, and a host of others. Throughout the text we stress the interaction in the marketplace between the various players, including governments, as the key factors affecting value.

Another point to be made about real estate not being just a game is that the players, through their actions, affect a great many important areas of our national life that are not merely "economic." Private development's effect on the physical environment is the most dramatic example; others include the social implications of tax policy, urban and suburban development, and methods of transport. As a result, as is seen in Part 9, society, through government, periodically changes the rules of the game in an effort to make sure that the "guiding hand" continues to work—in both economic

1-1

**NEW YORK
LAND PRICE
BREAKS
RECORD, YET
HURDLE
REMAINS**

Just a few years ago, $2,000 a square foot for a New York City building site seemed like real estate's impossible dream. Now that mark has been far surpassed by a partnership that has agreed to pay about $4,000 a square foot for a midtown site.

For $4,000, you could buy several acres of Midwest farmland. And though Equitable Life Assurance Society has paid about $2,000 a square foot for a site, another developer, Cadillac Fairview Urban Development Inc., forfeited a $21 million downpayment a few years ago rather than pay $1,964 a square foot for a New York site. (The property later sold for $1,571 a foot.)

The partners in the $4,000-a-foot transaction are G. Ware Travelstead, formerly a North Carolina developer; First Boston Real Estate and Development Co., an arm of the big investment banker, First Boston Inc.; and Solomon Equities Inc.

Mr. Travelstead, who is also chairman of First Boston Real Estate, acknowledges that it's a record price but downplays the significance. What matters, he says, is how large a building can be built on the site, which is on Fifth Avenue at 56th Street. The larger the building, the less the land costs are as a percentage of total cost. To offset the high land costs, the partners are paying $15.7 million for the unused development rights of a neighboring church. That will permit construction of a 450,000-square-foot building, larger than the zoning ordinarily would permit.

The bigger building means the land cost per square foot of building is $136. Mr. Travelstead says, "Before we started, I said that if (the site) costs less than $170 a buildable square foot, the project will work economically." John Healy, senior vice president of BA Appraisals Inc., agrees that the price is "not that nasty" because of the extra space and, he adds, "they've got a super location."

Beyond the impressive price, the transaction is further evidence of First Boston Inc.'s emergence as a real estate developer under Mr. Travelstead's guidance. Its real estate portfolio now includes an interest in about four million square feet of real estate. Besides the Fifth Avenue building, First Boston and Mr. Travelstead plan to put up a 1,080-foot office building, the third tallest in New York, on Madison Avenue between 46th and 47th streets.

In that project, too, unused development rights are important. The rights, totaling 1.5 million square feet, are being transferred from Grand Central Terminal. Mr. Travelstead won't say what is being paid for the rights, but Mr. Healy of BA Appraisals says the word in real estate circles is that First Boston will pay between $40 and $55 a square foot, depending on how much of the development rights it uses.

Source: Robert Guenther, *The Wall Street Journal,* January 23, 1985, p. 35.

and noneconomic areas. When the rules are changed, private rights often give way to public rights, and the stresses involved in this "taking" may test the belief in democracy of those individuals who are adversely affected. (See Box 1-2.)

Philosophy is part of the basis of economics and therefore has a place in the analytical framework of the real estate industry. It is a critical element in building a winning strategy for the real estate game. Without it, we would not be able to understand changing public policy, which helps determine the rules of the game.

REAL ESTATE DEFINED

Property refers to things and objects capable of ownership—that is, things and objects that can be used, controlled, or disposed of by an owner. Real property (and real estate, which is treated as synonymous) consists of physical land plus structures and other improvements that are permanently attached.

In a more technical sense, real property refers to the legal rights, interests, and benefits inherent in the ownership of real estate. Put another way, one owns not land as such, but a bundle of rights to use and dispose of land and its improvements subject to various restrictions.

1-2
AIR TRAFFIC AND PRIVATE PROPERTY

Under English and American common law, ownership of real estate traditionally included ownership of the air space "to the heavens." Consequently, when airplane traffic began early in this century, some landowners sued for damages for invasion of air space (*trespass*). The courts had little difficulty in "reinterpreting" the common law to mean that ownership of air space extended only to a height that the landowner could reasonably anticipate making use of (to put up a building, for example). In this situation, limiting private rights for the benefit of the public seemed wholly justified.

But as years passed, a more serious issue arose. Owners of homes and businesses near airports complained that the noise of arriving and departing airplanes diminished the usability of their property. (In one famous case, the owner of a mink ranch claimed his animals could not breed.) These owners sued for damages.

Although most courts have ruled that just as in the preceding situation, private use must yield to the paramount public right, some cases have gone in favor of the landowner. Factors that courts have considered include (1) the number of landowners affected (and the consequent burden on the public purse if damages were to be granted), (2) whether property was acquired before or after the noise problem began, and (3) the degree of interference created by the air traffic.

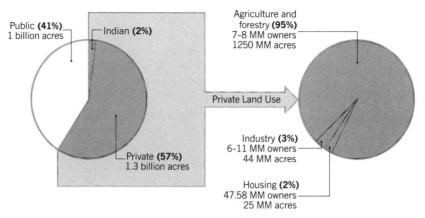

FIGURE 1-1   *U.S. land ownership*

Society, through the legislatures and the courts, defines the bundle of rights and can change the definitions from time to time. For example, zoning land for residential use eliminates the landowner's right to put a factory on the site. This general subject is discussed in detail in Parts 2 and 9. There are many claims on real estate, for example, the government's claim to taxes and a lender's claim to interest on and repayment of a loan. The residual claim—property ownership—confers the right to receive the cash flow from property subject to any prior claims.

THE VOLUME OF LAND IN THE UNITED STATES

A familiar phrase, often attributed to Richard Ely, is "under all is the land." That certainly is a literal statement of fact. Just how much land is there in the United States? There are approximately 2.3 billion acres. An acre is 43,560 square feet or 4,860 square yards. A rectangular parcel of land 210 feet by 207 feet is approximately 1 acre, and there are 640 acres in a square mile. A single-family house in an urban area can be put on a site as small as one-eighth of an acre. A large shopping center might take up 40 to 100 acres or more. With more than 2 billion acres available, there has never been, nor is there ever likely to be, an absolute shortage of land. However, well-located land definitely is in short supply in many places. What makes land well located is a key part of understanding the real estate industry.[1]

In terms of ownership, the federal government owns about 33 percent of the total acreage in the United States. (Because a large portion of this land is located in Alaska and other remote areas, the value of federal

---

[1] *A similar argument can also be made for agricultural land. There is no shortage of land that may legally be farmed, but there may be shortages of highly productive land.*

land is much less than 33 percent of the total.) State and local governments own another 8 percent, with Indian tribal lands accounting for 2 percent. Of the remaining land, 3 percent is classified as urban (i.e., developed or imminently developable land). This leaves 54 percent of the total acreage as privately owned rural land (Figure 1-1).

FEATURES OF THE REAL ESTATE ASSET

The chief characteristic of the real estate asset is its association with *land*. All the features that distinguish real estate from assets that are not real estate flow from this association. These features fall into two main categories: (1) physical and (2) economic.

PHYSICAL FEATURES

Real estate has three physical features.

❏ **IMMOBILITY.** Real estate is fixed in location and cannot be moved.[2] Therefore, it is at the mercy of the environment around it. One consequence of real estate's immobility is that real estate markets are primarily local, or, to put it another way, no national market exists for real estate as it does for most manufactured or farm commodities.[3] However, for some properties, the market may be local, national, or international, depending on the use and property rights involved. For example, interests in single-family houses are generally traded locally, whereas investment interests in many downtown office buildings are traded in international markets—for example, Japanese buyers of American office buildings.

❏ **UNIQUE LOCATION (heterogeneity).** Because land is immobile, it follows that every single parcel of real estate has a location that cannot be duplicated. Every parcel of real estate, being unique, is therefore heterogeneous or one of a kind. By comparison, commodities, such as grain or coal, or intangibles, such as shares of stock in General Motors Corporation, are exactly alike and are called **fungibles;** it makes no difference to the purchaser which particular one of a group of equal quality is obtained.

Heterogeneity implies that you do not have the perfectly competitive market situation that would necessarily provide an efficient allocation of resources. In addition, this heterogeneity and the small number of sales

---

[2]*One does hear, from time to time, of homes or other improvements affixed to land being severed and relocated. However, between the time of severance and reattachment, these technically become personal rather than real property.*

[3]*There is a well-established and active national market for the purchase and sale of mortgages—called the secondary mortgage market—but that is primarily a financial rather than a real estate market.*

as a proportion of the market at a given point in time imply a lack of information by buyers and sellers. Consequently, this market requires professionals such as brokers and appraisers to provide the information required to make the market function. In addition, the fixed location implies that **externalities** are going to play an important role in determining real estate value. This is not true for most other commodities. Consequently, we observe laws (e.g., zoning ordinances) and contractual arrangements (e.g., restrictive covenants) that exist only in the real estate market. Furthermore, public **infrastructure** (e.g., roads and utilities) can have a significant impact on value because these services are themselves location-specific.

❏ **INDESTRUCTIBILITY.**   The third physical feature of the real estate asset is that the land component, both as a physical asset and as the object of legal interests, is viewed as indestructible. Land may be mined, eroded, flooded, or desolated; nevertheless, the designated location on the earth's surface remains forever.

ECONOMIC FEATURES

If we turn next to the economic features of real estate, it can be seen that they generally parallel the physical features.

❏ **SCARCITY.**   Because every location is unique, only certain parcels can satisfy the requirements of a particular project or investment. So even though no absolute shortage of land exists in the United States, land for a particular purpose at a particular time and place may be quite scarce. The preference of a purchaser for a particular location is critical in determining the value of real estate. One site, because of its relationship to places of employment, shopping, transportation, schools, and even to the properties immediately surrounding it, can command a much higher price than land with similar physical or topographical features but with a slightly different location.

❏ **LONG ECONOMIC LIFE.**   Although improvements and additions to land are not indestructible in the sense that land itself is, they do normally have long useful lives. For example, some homes built at the time of American independence are still habitable. Of course, they have been remodeled and modernized, with new heating, plumbing, and electrical systems, but the original structure remains. This relative immunity of well-maintained structures against physical deterioration leads to an interesting phenomenon—the fact that buildings rarely fall down but are more often torn down because a new use will make the site more productive and hence more valuable.

❑ **MODIFICATION.**   The economic concept of modification focuses on the impact of development on the total value of a parcel—reflecting the fact that existing or potential future development can have a significant impact on value. More particularly, it can often be seen that development has a synergistic impact on property value. For example, the market or investment value of a completed project will normally be greater than the total of the individual costs of the land, labor, materials, and fair investment return necessary to develop the project. Conversely, modification (development) does not guarantee the **synergistic** value impact. If an incorrect or poor decision is made, the developed value may be well below the cost.

❑ **SITUS.**   The fourth important economic feature of land is its **situs,** that is, its interaction with the uses of surrounding land parcels. You may think of situs as another word for setting. The term also includes in its meaning the *influences* of the setting on the site. The simplest illustration of situs is shown in the accompanying street map. The residential homes located on lots A and B are identical, but B has a higher value because of the negative interaction of the noisy street and the residential use of lot A.

As we will see throughout the text and particularly in Chapter 22, the unique features or differences in the real estate asset make the real estate market (or markets) different. There tend to be a smaller number of potential buyers and sellers for any given property type and location. Information about properties is often difficult to obtain, expensive, and incomplete. In contrast to the stock market, financing is typically property-specific and of greater importance in valuation. In total, these differences make the real estate markets less "efficient" than their stock market counterparts in the sense that it is more likely that the price of the real estate asset may deviate from its true value. This can be a complex and difficult concept. For now, you need remember that the tendency toward inefficiency can create wonderful opportunities for the

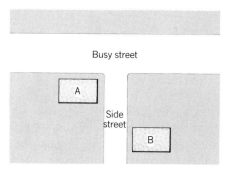

Busy street

Side
street

player who is "better at the game." As we move through the text, we will explore what it takes to be "better."

A preference to live in the northwest quadrant of a city or the emerging desire of many to move back to the city rather than out of it are examples of the situs phenomenon. The result will surely affect the economic value of the site even if identical improvements are available in some other neighborhood or area. As a consequence, land values on one side of town may be twice as high as those elsewhere in the city. In such cases, the economic difference can be attributed only to varying user tastes and preferences.

FEATURES OF THE REAL ESTATE MARKETPLACE

The real estate marketplace is different from many other markets in several ways. These differences are the result of the value of individual parcels, government's role in the marketplace, and the way in which people perceive the asset and what they expect from it.

❑ **UNIT VALUE.**   From both a physical and financial point of view, real estate tends to have great value. Because of the large dollar expenditure usually needed to acquire real estate, debt financing frequently plays an important role. Even when institutional investors acquire properties on an all-cash basis, the large-dollar-expenditure effect is still at work. Thus, financial institutions, government regulations of the financial markets, and federal government monetary and fiscal policies may have a more pronounced impact on real estate than on other commodities.

❑ **GOVERNMENT INTERVENTION.**   There tends to be more government intervention in the form of taxation, development incentives, and regulations governing the use and transfer of real property than in most other markets. Although we use the same tools to evaluate real estate that would be used to evaluate other assets, the unique institutional framework within which real estate decisions must be made makes real estate worthy of separate analysis.

❑ **PERCEPTIONS.**   Consider first the question of home ownership. One's home always represents both an investment and a use; home ownership gives one shelter, status, and an investment. But in the past few years, the investment aspect of home ownership has become much more important. Clearly, this has been due to the effectiveness of private homes as a hedge against inflation. (See Box 1-3.)

In the 1970s, home prices increased significantly faster than the general rate of inflation and offered a much better return to the individual investor than other common forms of investment. But during the 1980s, many homeowners experienced a roller-coaster value effect. For

1-3
HOMEOWNERS'
ATTITUDES

In spite of the difficult economic conditions and high interest rates of the 1980s, owning their own home remained a major ambition of most U.S. families, according to a survey by Louis Harris for the Federal National Mortgage Association. The survey was based on representative nationwide samples of homeowners and nonhomeowners. Of this group, 71 percent felt their next residence would be one they owned, and 79 percent preferred the single-family detached home to other alternatives. Other findings included the following.

Among homeowners, 40 percent said the main incentive behind ownership was the home's investment value, and 35 percent said the main incentive was the desire to put down roots in a community. Among nonhomeowners, 59 percent said housing prices were the main reason they had not bought a home; 36 percent cited high interest rates as the main disincentive.

The proportion of people expecting to move suggested that mobility will decline from the high levels of the late 1970s. People who did plan to move cited traditional reasons—need for more space, relocation caused by employment or retirement, desire to live in a better neighborhood, and, for nonhomeowners, desire to own a home. Of the 71 percent who said they expected to own their next home, most planned to finance the downpayment through sale of property or savings. In spite of poor market conditions at the time of the survey, most homeowners said they did not expect to have "a lot of trouble" selling the homes they currently owned.

Not surprisingly, most respondents (72 percent) were familiar with the traditional fixed-rate mortgage; however, 42 percent were also aware of newer mortgage types, although most were uncertain exactly how they worked. A large majority (78 percent) said they preferred to be able to choose among a variety of mortgage options.

example, during the mid-1980s home values in the Northeast far exceeded the national average after oil prices peaked in 1982, fell precipitously through the rest of the decade, and dragged down housing values elsewhere, particularly in the Southwest. At the same time the extraordinary bull market experienced by Wall Street fueled optimism and pushed up incomes. The result was rapidly rising home prices in the New York metropolitan area. However, by the end of the decade the market was beset by increased risk on Wall Street (remember October 1987) and recession fears. These fears contributed to falling home prices in some markets over the last few years of the decade. Whether the leveling of home prices in the late 1980s will change the "perception of the 1990s" is not yet clear. It is safe to say, however, that home buyers are willing to pay ever larger portions of their total income to carry a house. Until fairly recently, it was taken as an article of faith by many lenders that no more than 25 percent of a family's income should go for housing or rental costs. This rule has become obsolete, at least in connection with home ownership. This is true even though more women than ever are entering the work force, and their pay is now counted as part of the family income.

A study of housing costs by the U.S. League of Savings Association indicated that, throughout the United States, 30.5 percent of all homeowners spend more than 25 percent of their income to carry their own homes. Home ownership costs generally are considered to include (1) mortgage payments covering interest and amortization, (2) real estate taxes, and (3) insurance premiums. Although it is true that, in older European societies, even greater proportions of total income are spent on shelter, nevertheless the sharp upsurge in housing costs in the United States is a source of concern to many analysts.[4]

Investors in income property also have experienced a change in their perception of real estate. In the 1970s and the early 1980s, tax ramifications dominated many investment decisions. The game then was as much or more tax shelter as it was real estate. More recently, economic feasibility and prospective value appreciation have assumed the forefront of investment consideration. This shift has been caused primarily by tax reform.

❏ **EXPECTATIONS.**   It seems fair to say that traditionally most people expect continued appreciation in real estate values. As already noted, this is a prime reason for the increased desire for home ownership by the general public. The same expectation on the part of income property investors can be inferred from their willingness to buy property at prices that will restrict them to a relatively small and, in some cases, negative annual cash flow.

On the other hand, "no tree grows to the sky." In retrospect, it is difficult to believe that farmland prices could continue to rise as fast as they did in the 1970s without a concomitant increase in the prices received by farmers for their crops. In fact, the first half of the 1980s saw a significant decline in farmland prices in many areas. In any market, expectations of continued price increases work only for a while; the point finally comes when investors see that there is no longer economic logic behind the price increases, and prices cease rising and either stabilize or decline.

Another way of stating this is to say that the "greater fool" theory of investing works only for a limited time. Under this theory, investors

---

[4]*Note that utility costs, real estate taxes, and insurance premiums have also been increasing in recent years. Increases in these costs have contributed greatly to the inability of many Americans to attain home ownership.*

justify purchases at a high price because subsequent resales can be made to an even greater fool at an even greater price. Ultimately, when no greater fool can be found, prices stop rising.

People have also come to expect rapid change in many of the fields associated with real estate, notably government regulation, the financial markets, and particularly the tax laws. The impact of this expectation of change will be an important element in the investment model developed in Part 7. The high number of farm foreclosures in the 1980s suggests at least a temporary halt in the long period of rapid appreciation.

❑ **PSYCHIC INCOME.**   It is clear that satisfaction derived from the ownership of real estate is often nonpecuniary in nature. Examples of such **psychic income** abound in the marketplace. In the housing sector, this phenomenon is known as "keeping up with the Joneses" or is expressed as "pride of ownership." Such utility derived from ownership represents a return to homeowners and, as such, affects the price they are willing to pay. Investors, too, derive psychic income from their ownership share (however small) in a prestigious building such as the Empire State Building in New York City. Users may pay a premium rent for the "right address," whether residential or commercial.

REAL ESTATE AND THE GENERAL ECONOMY

Before we move to a further study of the real estate industry itself, this unique asset should be viewed in the context of the overall economic life of the nation.

GROSS NATIONAL PROFIT

One way to do this is to look at gross national product (**GNP**)—the value of all goods and services produced in the country. GNP is now running at over \$4.9 trillion a year—roughly \$19,750 per person.[5] Of this total, individuals consume about 64 percent, the government purchases another 21 percent, and the private sector invests 15 to 16 percent. This reinvestment must be noted because it determines the nation's productive capacity in the future. Private investment *first* must be sufficient to provide for replacement of existing depreciated assets and *second* must provide for new investments if the nation's productive capacity is to improve (i.e., if society's wealth is to increase).

From a real estate standpoint, it is interesting to note that over half of annual domestic private investment is in real property assets, and over half of this (one-quarter of the total) is usually in residential housing. Remember that these figures do not include governmental investment in

---

[5]Survey of Current Business, *United States Department of Commerce, Bureau of Economic Analysis (monthly).*

real property. In short, the investment factor in GNP is a key figure, and real estate is the largest component of gross private domestic investment.

NATIONAL INCOME

A second way to get a feel for the relative importance of the real estate industry is to look at national income. National income is essentially GNP minus depreciation and indirect business taxes. The components of national income are as follows.

- *Compensation of employees,* which represents about 73 to 77 percent of the total and has been increasing over the past two decades.

- *Corporate profit,* which today represents about 6 to 8 percent of the GNP and has been decreasing over the past two decades.

- *Proprietors' income,* which represents about 5 to 8 percent of the total and has also been decreasing.

- *Rent,* which is about 1 to 2 percent and decreasing.

- *Interest,* which is about 8 to 11 percent and increasing.

There is an interesting relationship between the last two items. Three decades ago, rent was nearly three times interest, whereas today interest is four times rent. Why has this happened? One reason is that interest rates have risen more rapidly than rents (and there are several causes for this increase). Another is that over the past quarter century borrowed capital has increased as a percentage of the total financing for real estate investment. For both reasons, more of total cash flow is going to lenders. This means lenders have gradually been obtaining a more active voice in decision making in the real estate industry. (Total mortgage debt now exceeds $2 trillion and represents about 30 percent of the total funds raised in the United States each year.)

EMPLOYMENT

Another way to come to grips with the scope of the real estate industry is to look at national employment figures. Approximately 110 million workers are employed in the United States. Of these, 1.4 million were classified as being in the real estate business, with another 5.3 million being employed in construction, which, for the purpose of this book, is part of the real estate industry. Thus, about 6 percent of employment is represented by real estate. This is an impressive figure and indicates that the creation of new jobs is one reason why government at all levels is continually interested in new construction of real estate projects.

An interesting sidelight to the total employment figures deals with the number of people actively marketing real estate. In 1969, fewer than 100,000 persons were entitled to be designated **Realtors**® (a designation limited to members who have satisfied specified requirements of the National Association of Realtors (NAR), the leading real estate trade association in the United States).[6] This figure rose to nearly 800,000 in 1981. (The 1982 figure was around 650,000 with the dramatic reduction a result of the recession.) The membership as of October 1989 was 819,926. This tremendous rise in the number of people involved in the service functions associated with real property illustrates the extraordinary growth in real estate transactions in that period as well as the increased interest in real estate by people throughout the country.

IMPORTANCE FOR DECISION MAKING

Why are such matters of macroeconomics important to microlevel decision making? Even though the real estate game is primarily played in an array of local markets, the industry is always affected by national economic conditions—sometimes dramatically. The extent of this impact varies from market to market, whether defined by geography or property type. Certainly, the price of construction materials is influenced by national conditions; so is the price of money (interest), and this often is the most important cost of all. Labor tends to be more of a localized phenomenon (because people really are not as mobile as many economics texts assume), but nevertheless it remains subject to trends within the national economy—witness regional population shifts to the Sunbelt that occurred in the 1970s.

Real estate also has a significant impact on the macroeconomy. The construction industry, in its broadest definition (which includes the construction of industrial plants, highways, and other public facilities as well as homes and commercial properties), is larger than any other industry, accounting for almost 10 percent of the GNP. (In dollar terms, around $386 billion of new construction was completed in 1988.) The real estate industry is a major source of employment; a voracious user of capital; and, insofar as housing is concerned, a provider of one of the basic necessities of life. Consequently, government at all levels has assumed a major role in real estate.

Since the Housing Act of 1948, which set forth the goal of "a decent home and suitable living environment for all Americans," the federal government has been an active, even aggressive, player in the real estate game. A major cabinet-level department, the U.S. Department of Housing and Urban Development (**HUD**), is totally devoted to real estate

---

[6]*In the early 1970s, sales associates became eligible for the title Realtor Associate. Accordingly, the Realtor ranks immediately increased by about 450,000 and then grew more gradually.*

issues, with many other departments devoting a significant portion of their time to real estate. Furthermore, local governments are even more involved in real estate matters from land use regulation to real property taxation. The multifaceted role of government in real estate is developed throughout this book until, in Part 9, the logic behind governmental involvement is studied so that future changes in its role can be anticipated.

REAL ESTATE AND WEALTH

In 1985, Roger G. Ibbotson, Laurence B. Siegel, and Kathryn S. Love published an article entitled "World Wealth: Market Values and Returns" in the fall issue of the *Journal of Portfolio Management*. Since then, their work has been widely quoted in the investment community, which has a vital interest in both U.S. and worldwide allocation of wealth among different groups of assets. This work is summarized in Figures 1-2 and 1-3. It clearly shows the dominant position of real estate in terms of both total wealth and "investable" wealth.

We argue in this text that real estate trades in a variety of markets. Single-family dwellings and small and medium-sized commercial properties tend to trade in local markets. Larger commercial properties tend to

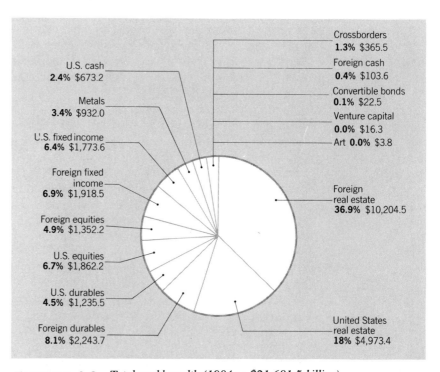

FIGURE 1-2   *Total world wealth (1984 = $21,681.5 billion)*

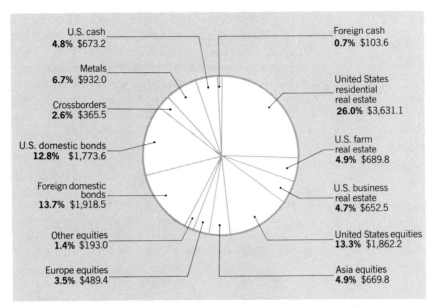

F I G U R E 1-3 *Worldwide investable wealth (1984 = $13,954.1 billion)*

trade in national and international markets. Therefore, national and international economic trends definitely affect real estate values. If we look at the allocation of world wealth, it is clear that real estate affects many, if not most, of the world's economic activities by virtue of its collective size. This effect is viewed here from a financial perspective. Possibly even greater effects are seen in the physical and social dimensions of our lives.

REAL ESTATE DEMAND AND SUPPLY

As we return from the world of macroeconomics, it should be understood that the equity investor's return depends primarily on the price that can be obtained for the product sold, which is **space**—more accurately, space-over-time with certain associated services. For example, the indoor tennis club sells space per hour; the motel, space per day; and the apartment building, space per month or year (all these being designated as rental space). The home builder, on the other hand, sells space subject to no time limit.

The price that can be charged for space is a function of the same three elements that set any other type of price: (1) demand, (2) supply, and (3) public policy restraints.

In addition to the space market, an increasingly important real estate "capital market" developed in the 1980s. Now an international market, the real estate capital market emerged after the mid-1970s to provide an effective mixed asset portfolio diversifier, that is, an addition to portfolios containing stocks and bonds. Suddenly, in the 1980s real estate investment decisions were being made with consideration not only to space markets, but also to capital markets. This meant that institutions began to compare real estate returns to returns that could be earned on alternative asset classes. As a result, institutional investors became willing to accept lower real estate returns than previously acceptable because yields on stocks and bonds had declined. The portfolio impact on real estate investment decision making is discussed in detail in Part 7.

DEMAND

Only **effective demand** is relevant. That is, potential users of proposed space not only must exist, but they must also have the purchasing power to acquire (through purchase or lease) the desired space-over-time plus associated services. This is true of demand for any product.

But real estate is more complicated because is it *both* a capital good and a consumer good. For-sale housing (a single-family house, condominium, or cooperative unit) is a consumer good—it is sold directly to the occupant-user. It is also the largest investment asset of many homeowners. Most other kinds of real estate—income properties—are owned by investors who then sell space (via a lease or other means) to the final consumer. It may be said that the entire building is a capital good, intended to produce income, but the individual units of space within are the consumer goods, intended for actual occupancy and use.

In the final analysis, real estate will be profitable only to the extent the space available is occupied and paid for, whether outright (through purchase) or from period to period (through rent). Thus, a developer should make careful market studies to ascertain the probable extent of effective demand for the space when it is expected to be ready. This is not always done properly. One trouble with market studies can be that four developers simultaneously identify a demand for, say, a 100-unit project, and each builds a project so that 400 units swamp the market. Real estate market analysis is far from a precise science, as is discussed in Part 8.

SUPPLY

The key to analyzing real estate supply is an awareness of the ability of a constructed asset to satisfy needs—that is, attention must be paid to the utility derived from the asset. Three special factors are involved when supply of real estate is discussed: (1) time, (2) place, and (3) substitution.

❑   **TIME.**   The long construction period for real estate means that supply often lags behind demand. This affects the marketplace in both expansionary and contracting phases of the business cycle. During periods of expansion, supply lag means that demand is unsatisfied, so prices and rentals rise. During periods of contraction, supply lag (the inability of producers to stop work on a project under construction) results in an oversupply of space. For-sale units remain unsold, and vacancies in rental properties are high (Figure 1-4).

❏ **PLACE.** As already noted, one of the unique characteristics of real estate is its fixed location. New supply can only be created by (1) new construction or (2) substitution at the particular location; it cannot be transferred from elsewhere as, for example, oil, grain, or capital may be.

❏ **SUBSTITUTION.** To some degree, one kind of real estate may be converted to another in order to meet shifts in demand. For example, the demand for owned (compared to rented) residential units has been quite high in recent years as individuals seek to take advantage of the considerable tax benefits of home ownership, as well as its general ability to appreciate. This has resulted in the conversion of rental apartments to condominiums in many parts of the country. An even more striking example is the conversion of unused commercial or loft space in many cities into residential properties owing to the increased effective demand for housing. Substitution often meets with obstacles in the form of zoning laws, building codes, and tenant-protection legislation. Such legislation often seeks to slow down the conversion of rental properties to condominiums in the interests of tenants who may lack the capital to purchase their residential units.

PUBLIC POLICY

In addition to basic supply and demand considerations, a third factor is important in real estate pricing. This is the impact of government reg-

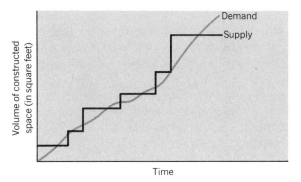

FIGURE 1-4 *Construction supply and demand*

ulation, which expresses public policy on new development and redevelopment. The regulation of land development in the interest of environmental protection is a good example.

Much regulation on the local level, though purportedly aimed at protecting the environment, may actually seek to slow down or even prevent growth in order to preserve the style of living preferred by the existing residents. Whatever the motive, these restraints can effectively limit or encourage additions to supply.

In the interests of providing adequate housing for those otherwise unable to afford it, government at all levels has made available a large number of programs to subsidise, insure, or directly finance new and rehabilitated housing. In addition, the government plays a vital role in providing the infrastructure (roads, sewer and water facilities, schools, etc.) that is the necessary preliminary to new development. The relationship among the government's roles as regulator, supplier, and user of real estate as well as the policy implications of the governments's role—what type of activities should be encouraged and who should pay the cost—are discussed further in Parts 6 and 9.

MARKETPLACE INDIVIDUALS AND INSTITUTIONS

An essential part of our analytical framework for real estate decision making is an understanding of the players in the marketplace and their motivations. The real estate markets are the arenas in which the market-oriented game is played out. Who then are the groups of players who participate in the various real estate markets, which, in turn, have such a pronounced influence on the national economy and life-styles in general?

To answer this question, we must identify the players, the reasons they participate in the marketplace, and the ways they play. Throughout this introduction to the real estate industry, *why* is the key question—why do they play and what are the stakes? It is the key to understanding the descriptive material and furthermore the key to projecting changes in the future.

The framework of judging winners based on residual value is implicitly a forward-looking or futuristic framework. First, an understanding of the investor's reasons (an investment strategy) for investing in real estate must be understood. Second, individual projects that will meet the investment strategy must be identified. Then, a projection of probable future events that will affect operating cash flows and, consequently, residual value must be made. When these are completed, the individual players in the marketplace and their role in the creation of cash flows should be clear. Going through this process shows how the players affect the overall "bottom line" and what compensation they expect in return for their efforts.

THE PARTICIPANTS

There are several broad categories of participants, each including both individuals and institutions (Figure 1-5).

- *The users,* those demand-oriented consumers, including owner-occupants and tenants.
- *The suppliers,* including construction workers, architects, engineers, surveyors, developers, and investors.
- *Federal, state, and local government,* along with their respective agencies, and the courts, which are the final arbitrators among the participants.
- *Associated professionals,* independent of users, suppliers, and government but critical to the operation of the real estate markets.

We'll look at these players in more detail below.

THE USERS

On the demand side of the pricing equation are the users of real property. The users enjoy the benefits that are in essence the socially defined rights conveyed in real property ownership (See Box 1-4.)

Users are represented by both owner-occupants and **tenants.** They include (1) individuals, (2) private and public institutions, and (3) governmental units. Furthermore, their motivation or need for real estate

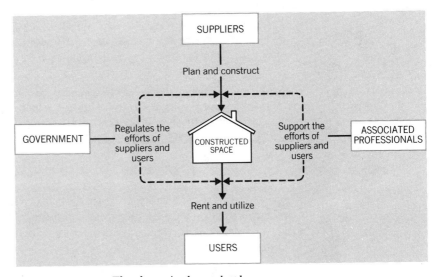

FIGURE 1-5 *The players in the marketplace*

**1-4
POPULATION
AND LONG-
TERM DEMAND
TRENDS**

Ultimately, all real estate demand is related to people. It is people who use real estate for living, working, storing goods, recreation, and finally, interment. So when demand for real estate is discussed, insight can be gained by looking at population trends.

The last detailed census, in 1980, showed a population of 226.5 million in the United States. By 1990, over 250 million people inhabit our nation—an increase of about 8 percent in the period from 1980 to 1990.

To illustrate how the population profile affects real estate, consider the 20- to 29-year-old age group. This group included 31 million people in 1970, jumped to almost 41 million in 1980, and declined to 38 million by 1990.

Why the big jump between 1970 and 1980? It reflects the baby boom that occurred after World War II, particularly in the five-year period from 1950 to 1955. Since this is the age group that normally forms most new households, its members constitute the main demand for apartment units and first houses. It is not surprising that the decade of the 1970s was very strong for residential building. During the 1980s, the 20- to 29-year-old group did not grow and so did not generate increased demand for starter homes. (However, the 30- to 39-year-old group, also important in "move up" home buying, increased substantially in the 1980s, for it contained the baby boom generation.)

Consider next the sharp growth in the 65-year-and-over group. The number of senior citizens increased considerably in the 1970s and grew by another 20 percent in the 1980s. This is one reason real estate developers anticipate sharply rising demand for retirement communities and congregate housing facilities (living units with private accommodations and central dining rooms) as well as for medical and nursing facilities. The members of this age group who live in their own homes will want small and compact housing units near public transportation and convenient to shopping and recreational facilities.

Not only do space users change over time in total numbers and ages (and consequently desires), but they may also move geographically. In the recent past, many people have migrated to the Sunbelt, and businesses have been increasingly willing to decentralize their manufacturing operations.

services varies considerably. Investors are also critical to demand as intermediaries seeking an outlet for their funds and a return that is a function of users' demand for space (i.e., the rent which the property can command).

OWNER-OCCUPANTS.   Owner-occupants include, first of all, *homeowners,* both primary residence owners and owners of second homes.

As noted earlier, a home has come to be seen as more than simply a way to provide shelter. It expresses aspects of personal ego and social status, as evidenced by psychic income, as well as serving as an investment. Also classified as owner-occupants are *business owners*, both proprietary and corporate. These individuals and institutions often own the offices, shops, and plants in which they produce and market the nation's goods and services. *Government* itself, at the federal, state, and local levels, as well as supporting agencies, very often owns its own offices. And finally, within the owner-occupant category are *churches and other civic groups* that own not only their primary structure, but also other property used in some way to further the goals of the particular group. Each of these groups can be further stratified by income level as well as social and cultural background.

TENANTS.   Although roughly two-thirds of the nation's residential stock is owner-occupied, tenants represent a very significant factor on the user, or demand, side. Single- and multifamily rental housing is the largest component of the housing stock in larger metropolitan areas, particularly in older cities. There are also business tenants, both large and small, proprietary and corporate, which lease rather than own. In many cases, government is also a tenant rather than an owner. A consideration of leisure activities demonstrates that almost the entire population at some time has been a tenant of a hotel, motel, or vacation unit.

THE SUPPLIERS

In the context of the overall importance of the real estate market, it is relevant to note that almost every facet of our life-style is influenced by how real property is developed and used. In other words, the demands of the users, as satisfied by the suppliers, have a pronounced impact not only in the immediate future, but also in the distant future.

John Portman, creator of the "Hyatt Hotel Look," discusses the need for the supply side to produce space that is oriented to the individual and the satisfaction of that individual's needs. This concept of satisfaction goes beyond a purely spatial dimension to consideration of the individual's psychological well-being (See Chapter 3 for a fuller discussion.)

On the supply side, the chief characteristic of the real estate industry is the relatively long lead time required for supply to adjust to demand. This is because of the nature of the construction process. The response time is considerable even when construction is completed on schedule. Add to this the nature of development, which includes delays related to weather problems, material and labor shortages, strikes, and governmental regulatory action, and the response time can become even longer.

DEVELOPERS, SURVEYORS, ARCHITECTS, AND ENGINEERS. The **developer** is the prime mover of the supply side, functioning as the quarterback of the development process. He is the entrepreneur who puts together the various input factors required to satisfy effective demand. The first professionals used by developers generally are **surveyors,** who are involved not only in defining the boundaries of the land originally acquired by the developers, but also later in the process by showing the location of the proposed improvements on that land in a manner suitable for construction. Next come the **architects,** who design the project to meet the specifications laid out in a general form by the developers. Given the physical constraints of the particular site as identified by the surveyors, the architect in many cases will go beyond the design role and become involved in the construction supervision process. As part of the design function, the architect will typically employ engineering experts. The **engineers** will be responsible for assuring the structural soundness of the project designed by the architect.

Collectively, the surveyors, architects, and engineers provide the plans and specifications that translate the developers' requests into a usable plan for the general contractor. Note that, on large projects, the architectural supervision role has often been transferred to a construction manager, whose function is explained in greater detail in Part 8.

GENERAL CONTRACTORS AND SUBCONTRACTORS. The **general contractor** (GC) is the focal point of the 5-million-worker construction industry. GCs can range in size from the giants who command national and even international reputations, such as Brown and Root, to individual home builders, who perform the same function on a smaller scale.

The GC groups and coordinates the activities of the workers who actually build each different segment of a particular project. The typical real estate construction job would involve the following elements.

- One set of **subcontractors** doing the excavation work.
- Another set of subcontractors doing the concrete work.
- A rough carpentry group.
- A finish carpentry group.
- Electricians.
- Plumbers.
- Roofers.
- Assorted suppliers of mechanical appliances that become fixtures in the completed structure.

It is the GC's job to schedule each of these tasks so that the workers arrive on the site and accomplish the various tasks in such a manner that the overall work flow is completed efficiently and on schedule. It is also the GC's job to see that the subcontractors arrive on site when needed with a clear description of what they are to do.

The GC signs a contract with the developer to build the project according to the plans and specifications of the architect. The work is then subcontracted to different construction workers or construction companies, who perform the actual construction tasks. In some instances, especially with larger firms, the general contractor will specialize in one or more construction tasks and subcontract the rest.

INVESTORS.   Directly connected with user-oriented demand is investor demand. The connection is direct because investors are looking for cash flow from their investments, and the cash flow from any real estate project is a function of user demand. However, to understand the operations of the various real estate markets, initially it is important to look at investors as a separate group.

Investors are represented by individuals and institutions that provide the capital necessary for the purchase or development of a particular real estate project. They may take the position of either an equity investor or a lender. In either case, the funds they provide contribute to actualizing the effective demand for specific types of real estate projects.

❏ **INDIVIDUALS.**   Within this investor group are individuals investing in rental property as well as raw land. Although initially their portfolios may be rather small, in numerous cases creative financing, knowledge, and personal drive have been used to amass large fortunes through real estate investment. In addition to individuals, investor groups provide both equity and debt capital. Such investor groups spread risk and allow for the concentration of large-scale amounts of equity capital. In this way, larger properties can be acquired and managed centrally, taking advantage of tax laws to minimize the taxable income of the participants in the investor group.

❏ **CORPORATIONS.**   Corporate users can also be considered investors. Corporations have come to own real property, not only in order to provide the space they need for their primary activity, but also to provide for corporate growth planning and, in some cases, to take advantage of the pure investment attractiveness offered by real property.

Thoughtful observers of the corporate scene have suggested that the position of chief financial officer may soon be replaced by two positions. The first, the financial vice president, will handle the firm's short-term financial position, and the second, the fixed asset officer, will handle all property financing, leasing, and management. Regardless of the particular organizational structure, major corporations are becoming increasingly aware of the importance of their real estate assets and are seeking to ensure active management of these assets by moving more aggressive executives to real estate positions.

❏   **INSTITUTIONAL INVESTORS.**   The growing role of institutional investors, both foreign and domestic, was one of the most significant trends in the real estate marketplace during the 1980s. Active as lenders as well as equity investors, banks, pension funds, and life insurance companies have greatly expanded their impact. As we enter the 1990s, many observers believe that institutional investors will come to dominate the real estate investment markets. The dominance of institutional investors, if it happens, will further reduce the characterization of the real estate marketplace as the last bastion of the entrepreneur. The important role of institutional investors is discussed more fully in Parts 5 and 7.

THE GOVERNMENT

As stressed throughout this study of the real estate industry, government is a key factor. At this point, it is appropriate to note the role of government as a partner to the industry in providing the total package of benefits offered by real estate development. Government at all levels affects the value and use of land almost as much as developers do. Federal, state, and local governments do this by providing the infrastructure—the roads, utilities, and so on—that complements constructed property. Government decisions on the extent and location of supporting infrastructure have a great influence on the nature and scope of development.

FEDERAL GOVERNMENT.   The federal government is a tremendously important factor in real estate markets, first of all because it owns one-third of the total acreage in the 50 states. In addition, federal facilities—particularly military installations—have a dramatic impact on surrounding development. This impact can be identified by the effect of federal facilities on the economic base of the community in which they are located. Such elements as housing patterns, commercial services, and entertainment represent areas on which the impact is most visible.

The federal government also has a series of regulatory programs, most notably in the environmental area, which affect private development. One result of such programs has been an increase in the time and cost associated with planning a development and obtaining federal government approval. In addition, a series of federal government programs support and finance a state government role in land use planning.

Through the Department of Housing and Urban Development, the federal government supports housing and related urban development programs. (See Part 9.) Through secondary market operations, several federal agencies support the flow of funds into housing. Thus, by ownership, regulation, and support, the federal government is a prime influence on the real estate industry.

STATE GOVERNMENT.   The state government, often in conjunction with the federal government, provides a good deal of the regional infrastructure necessary for real property development. State government also handles the location of state government facilities (such as prisons, universities, and office buildings) that have a significant impact on development in given regions.

State governments have traditionally passed most of their regulatory role on to local governments through local government enabling statutes. However, this can vary considerably from state to state. In some instances (notably California), state governments have implemented a significant amount of legislation affecting particularly coastal development, whereas in others (e.g., Texas), relatively little legislation has emerged. Throughout the last decade, a trend toward greater land use planning at the state level has developed.

LOCAL GOVERNMENT.   Local government is extremely important because it is local government that has the power—or that most often uses the power—to tax real property. Furthermore, through the power of eminent domain, local government can condemn land for public use. A local government is also the government unit most likely to exercise the police powers (the power of government to preserve the health and well-being of the citizenry) through zoning, subdivision ordinances, and building codes. Many local governments have recently developed master plans or growth management plans in an effort to respond to urban growth. Local government is also responsible for recordkeeping, which, as seen in Part 2, is a very important function. And, as mentioned at the federal and state levels, the provision of infrastructure is a major role of local government as is facility location.

Just as in the private sector, individuals carry out each of these government functions. The number of government sector real-estate-related careers has grown as the functions of government have expanded. Part 9 presents a closer and more detailed discussion of working with, in, and for the government. However, even at this early point, it should be obvious that government is almost always your partner when playing the real estate game successfully. Like any partnership, it is important to work at the relationship.

THE COURTS.   The courts have come to play an increasingly important role in real estate markets as the final arbitrators of disputes.

Essentially, the courts refuse to allow one individual or institution to burden the property of another unduly. This concept, which evolved over several centuries in both English and American law, has led to the development of certain preplanning activities designed to avoid the heavy cost of later litigation. Such preplanning is the basis for zoning and subdivision ordinances, both of which have become crucial instruments of local government regulation. In Part 2, the focus is on law and the courts' recent interpretations of the law as they constitute the rules of the game in the real estate industry.

ASSOCIATED PROFESSIONALS

Working with users, suppliers, and government are a host of associated professionals who make possible the activities that occur in the various real estate markets. These professionals provide services that make up an important part of the actual day-to-day activity in the real estate market. In most instances, they provide staff support and input for users, suppliers, and government. As such, the role of the associated professionals is to assist in policy formulation and decision making. They do not generally make line decisions, but they have a significant effect on what decisions are ultimately made and implemented.

The following is a list of the associated professionals who assist real estate decision makers. Each of these groups is discussed throughout the text.

Attorneys	Real estate appraisers
Title examiners	Real estate consultants and counselors
Land planners	
Marketing agents and brokers	Accountants
Property managers	Insurance agents
	Lenders

REAL ESTATE EDUCATION

No overview of the participants in the real estate marketplace would be complete without a brief discussion of real estate education and management decision making in the industry. The recent past has seen tremendous growth in interest in real estate education. This is due to a variety of factors, including the prosperity of the industry and the increasing complexity of the real estate decision-making process. In addition, license regulation and related private sector designations have become more prevalent and more rigorous in the recent past, increasing the demand of those in the industry for higher levels of education. Finally, and possibly most important, the nation has come to realize that its physical resources are neither inexhaustible nor indestructible.

Finite resources imply a need to relate use and development of real property assets with the general goals of the society as a whole. Or, alternatively stated, real estate decision making involves certain externalities that must be monitored to ensure that the individual pursuing his or her enlightened self-interest (winning the game) is functioning in a manner consistent with the general well-being of society as a whole.

The response to the recent growth of interest in real estate education has come from several groups of institutions. Universities have offered undergraduate, master, and doctoral programs in the real estate field. Colleges have moved toward undergraduate programs—or at least elective courses—focusing on the industry. Many community colleges now offer two-year associate degree programs in real estate. In addition to these full-time academic programs, the same institutions have provided a series of continuing education offerings to help those already engaged in the industry improve and develop their skills.

Professional associations have also been very active in promoting real estate education. The National Association of Realtors®[7] through its various subsidiaries offers several series of courses leading to such well-known designations as the MAI and the CCIM. State Realtor® organizations also offer courses leading to the Graduate Realtors Institute (GRI) designation. The Society of Real Estate Appraisers (SREA designation)[8], the Mortgage Bankers of America[9], the Urban Land Institute[10], the Lincoln Institute for Land Policy[11], and the Urban Institute[12] offer courses and publications. In addition, state and national bar associations[13] and CPA associations[14] offer specific real estate courses. Finally, certain proprietary schools have been established to teach specific subjects within the industry. (Such schools are most significant in the brokerage licensing field.)

Individuals involved in teaching any of these types of real estate education may become members of the National Association of Real Estate Educators[15] or the related state-level association. There is also the National Association of Real Estate License Law Officials[16] for those who regulate both the teaching and licensing of real estate professionals.

[7]*430 North Michigan Avenue, Chicago, Ill. 60611–4088.*

[8]*645 North Michigan Avenue, Chicago, Ill. 60611.*

[9]*1125 15th Street, N.W., Washington, D.C. 20005.*

[10]*1090 Vermont Avenue, N.W., Washington, D.C. 20005.*

[11]*26 Trowbridge Street, Cambridge, Mass. 02138.*

[12]*2100 M Street, N.W., Washington, D.C. 20037.*

[13]*National Bar Association, 1773 T Street, N.W., Washington, D.C. 20005.*

[14]*1211 Avenue of the Americas, New York, N.Y. 10036–8775.*

[15]*510 N. Dearborn Street, Chicago, Ill. 60610*

[16]*2580 South 90th Street, Omaha, Neb. 68124.*

SUMMARY The general overview in this chapter forms the basis of a decision-making framework that is completed in the next two chapters. This overview has identified all the key concepts to be developed in more depth throughout the book in the course of carrying out two objectives: (1) describing how the real estate industry operates and (2) analyzing the decision-making process utilized by the major participants.

The emphasis throughout is on understanding why real estate players play the way they do, why real estate institutions function as they do, and why the real estate markets price assets as they do. Thus, purely descriptive material is kept to a minimum, and examples and illustrations are drawn from real life to highlight the practical considerations that affect decision making.

The real estate marketplace gathers together a wide variety of individuals, institutions, and government units with varying resources, skills, and objectives. In view of the enormous importance of real estate in the political, economic, and social life of the nation, this is not surprising. The real estate decision maker must have a clear understanding of the demand and supply considerations arising from the relationships among these groups that affect real estate markets. Only when all participant roles in the marketplace are viewed in their proper perspective can effective analysis for real estate decisions occur.

IMPORTANT TERMS

Architect	Infrastructure
Developer	Investor
Effective demand	Psychic income
Engineer	Realtor
Externalities	Situs
Fungibles	Space
General contractor	Subcontractor
GNP	Surveyor
Heterogeneity	Synergistic
HUD	Tenant

REVIEW QUESTIONS

1.1 Differentiate between real and personal property.

1.2 Why can it be said that although there is no absolute shortage of land in the United States, good properties are hard to locate?

1.3 List and define the key physical and economic characteristics of land.

1.4   Why should real estate analysts focus on effective demand when analyzing a real estate market?

1.5   How might the concept of psychic income affect an owner's valuation of a single-family dwelling?

1.6   To what can real estate supply lag be attributed?

1.7   How can real estate be both a capital and a consumer asset?

1.8   What are the four categories of real estate participants?

1.9   What factors cause real estate to adjust slowly to changes in demand?

1.10   How much of the nation's residential housing stock is owner occupied?

*R*EGIONAL AND URBAN ECONOMICS

The productivity of real estate is based on a combination of its locational, physical, and legal attributes. The ability to analyze the impact of location on land use decisions is the first and most important skill in the real estate game. Location is much more than just the positioning of various points on the surface of the earth. Locational analysis identifies social, economic, institutional, legal, and physical phenomena as they relate to a specific land parcel. The ability to relate this eclectic group of topics to a specific parcel of land requires a logical process. The techniques and theories to achieve this analytical process from a business perspective are found in the academic disciplines of regional science, urban economics, and urban land economics. Each of these disciplines is concerned with the economic determination of land use. Use is one of the central premises of value, and value is the bottom line of the real estate game.

SPATIAL ECONOMICS IN REAL ESTATE ANALYSIS

In this chapter we discuss the evolution of thought and the major techniques associated with economic development and location that are collectively known as regional economics. We then move to urban economics and neighborhood and district dynamics and begin to consider the host of social issues associated with land use decisions. In Chapter 3 the analytical framework for real estate decision making is completed with a discussion of the theoretical approaches for determining the economic value of a specific site. Here we also consider what the limitations of social and economic theory are and how economic theory can be used to assist a real estate decision maker in carrying out a project.

This is not an economics text, yet we borrow central concepts from several urban and regional economics texts.[1] If we hit only the high

---

[1]*See the reading references at the end of Part 1 for a listing of these texts.*

points and move rapidly, we easily lose track of the objective. Please make no mistake about our intent; we are trying to improve our decision-making ability. Because location is the chief distinguishing characteristic of real estate, it is central to our analytical framework. We use theory only as it helps us organize data and forecast trends. There is a great deal of spatial data available. The winning players are those who can interpret this historical information and develop forecasts about the future. At a microlevel, this boils down to forecasting the net operating income of property, that is, the bricks and mortar productivity of the real estate asset. As we move through the text, we will add tax and financing considerations, but the most important item is the forecast of net operating income.

Real estate analysts naturally start by looking at the operating history of the property they are trying to value, for example, a small medical office building. As we will see in some detail in Part 4, they then collect "comparable" information on similar properties to obtain a current feel for the particular market. Next the analysts project trends in the market, and finally they reconcile the history, comparables, and trends in forecasting the net operating income. Why do we study regional and urban economics? Because it helps us project trends. This is the most difficult part of forecasting, and accurate forecasting is the most important element in winning the game.

Because forecasting is critical to the successful player, we will not conclude our treatment in this section. In Part 4 on marketing and Parts 8 and 9 on development and public policy, we continue what is begun in Part 1. Here we develop the analytical framework; in future parts, we add taxes and financing, and so on.

Table 2-1 is a guide to using Chapters 2 and 3. If you are beginning to feel as though you are losing sight of the forest because of the trees, remember our objective, and check this table to see where you are in the development of the analytical framework.

After a brief consideration of points I and II, we focus on the questions that are asked in point III. Forecasting may well be more an art than a science; yet, in real estate, there is a logical way to proceed.

NEVER START TOO NARROW

Although real estate typically trades in a local market, certain national and even international influences cannot be ignored. The Federal Reserve's monetary policy and tax policy as administered by the Treasury Department are important national factors that influence all real estate decisions. Yet the winning player takes an even broader view to avoid making an error of omission. (We will give you an example of such an error shortly.)

TABLE 2-1.   A FRAMEWORK FOR FORECASTING

1. *Never start too narrow.* There really is a worldwide perspective from which to view the local duplex, and it may not be totally economic.

2. *Only a fool skips the legwork.* Review the property's operating history, gather the comparables, and check in with local government.

3. *"Why" is the key to the future.* Try to understand the history in order to predict the future.
   a. What motivates a regional economy?
   b. How do industries choose a regional location?
   c. What tools are helpful in analyzing regional growth?
   d. What is unique about an urban economy?
   e. How do cities grow?
   f. Why do urban areas grow?
   g. How is rent determined?
   h. How do surrounding land uses affect rent?
   i. How do land uses and rents change over time?
   j. How can creativity be used to take a possible step beyond the limits of existing trends?
   k. So what number do you use?

Shelter is one of our basic needs, but so are food and clothing, both of which come from the land. Comparing the world's productive land resources with the world's population, we can easily see problems of an incredible magnitude on the horizon.[2]

Do these issues really affect the valuation of a local duplex? Absolutely! Immigration is rapidly changing the face of urban America. If you want to forecast the rent, you have to determine the socioeconomic characteristics of the likely tenants. Life-style, desired amenities, and ability to pay rent vary dramatically across groups.

Is it just New York City? Certainly not! When Mexico devalued the peso in the early 1980s, retail stores in San Diego went broke, and condominiums sat empty at Disney World in Orlando. Why? Because the buying power was no longer coming across the border.

Real estate is an interdisciplinary field. Everything from studying freshman economics to reading the sports page may be useful. In this text we focus on what is unique about real estate. Still, if the analyst does not start with a very broad view of locational change, the best detailed analyses lose to an overriding demographic trend. What was that error of omission mentioned earlier? Buying a shopping center in El Paso in 1981. The history looked good, and comparable properties were doing

---

[2]*For a more complete treatment of these issues, see Raleigh Barlowe's* Land Resource Economics *(Englewood Cliffs, N.J.: Prentice-Hall, 1978).*

well. However, the tenants' customers were Mexicans, and when the peso was devalued, they quit buying.

ONLY A FOOL SKIPS THE LEGWORK

After you look at the big picture, the next step is to examine the property's operating history carefully. You should also check to see how similar properties are doing and ask city planning officials about regulatory and infrastructural (streets and utilities) changes. This information is the foundation from which to project trends and eventually make forecasts. Checking the history and the comparables is not as simple as it sounds, and in several subsequent parts of the book we will deal extensively with these issues. Finally, in Chapter 26, we will bring it all together in a complete feasibility analysis.

"WHY" IS THE KEY TO THE FUTURE

At this point, we are still establishing the basic analytical framework. Consequently, the rest of Chapters 2 and 3 will deal with real estate's most distinguishing characteristic, location, and how the decision maker can develop an ability to forecast spatial trends. This is essentially a process of understanding why things have happened the way they have in the past and then determining whether they are likely to continue to happen that way in the future—and if not, what will happen.

WHAT MOTIVATES A REGIONAL ECONOMY?

Economics is the study of the production, distribution, and allocation of scarce resources. Regional economics is the study of the **spatial order of the economy.** It is the study of the geographic allocation of *resources*. It is also concerned with where *activities* are or will be located. Regional economic theories tie together vast quantities of factual data, enabling the analyst to describe the origins of the location of cities, as well as relate and measure the economic activity within a given area. These descriptive and analytical abilities enable us to identify the critical variables that influence the location of activities on the **spatial plane.** Furthermore, they allow us to isolate the effect of changes in critical variables. With an understanding of the logical effect of different kinds of changes, the analyst's predictive abilities are improved. As the location preferences of individuals, firms, industries, and institutions change, the demand for land in any one area, at a specific time, is correspondingly altered. The productivity of different properties and hence their relative advantage also change over time. The effect is an alteration in land use patterns and real estate values.

Physical, social, and political relationships do matter in real property analysis. Distance, geography, and **topography** all are important, as is climate. Soils are of crucial importance in agriculture and extractive industries; their load-bearing capacity and related characteristics are relevant whenever construction is contemplated. The manufactured environment (e.g., roads, airports, and railroads) as well as political boundaries have a significant influence on land use and value.

TRANSPORTATION AND LOCATION

Businesses and households locate where they can gain more than they can elsewhere. Businesses provide goods and services to households, and they profit by providing the goods people want at attractive prices. In this regard, proximity to markets is often a crucial determinant of costs and hence profitability. At the same time, households locate in relation to services and jobs, and to achieve an optimal set of housing **amenities.** (Amenities here refers to that large set of not necessarily economic benefits—e.g., living one block from a new, high-quality, public tennis court.)

Business location decisions can be categorized as either materials-oriented or market-oriented. In manufacturing terms, firms characterized as weight-losing processes tend to locate near their source of raw materials. Firms that experience a weight-gaining process tend to locate near their markets. Service firms, in contrast to manufacturing firms, are market-oriented and locate to serve the customer.

The weight-losing process, in part, explains why lumber mills and paper companies' pulp mills are located near the forests of the Pacific Northwest. Similarly, the location of the city of Birmingham, Alabama, is adequately explained by the convenience of having strong veins of coal and iron ore located in the same area. On the other hand, the weight-gaining process explains the predominance of local and regional breweries throughout this nation. But industries do not always locate next to raw materials or markets. Depending on demand and cost relationships, they may maximize their position by locating in between. However, the key determinants are still weight and cost of transportation.

As the U.S. economy moves toward an increasingly information- and services-based economy, the definition of location is being given greater attention. For example, advances in technology have reduced the need for back-office operations to be located in downtown central business districts. Many companies (for example, banks, brokerages, and insurance companies) have moved clerical back-office operations to suburban areas where typically office rent is cheaper, wages are lower, and commuting time is greatly reduced. The point to remember here is that information-based jobs are not tied to manufacturing processes. As a result, the cost of doing business issue and the employees' quality of life concerns help to redefine the economic concept of location.

LOCATION AND THE ECONOMIC BASE

Regional economics is concerned with the location of individual producers, firms, and so on. It is also concerned with the structure of regions in terms of the hierarchy and systems of cities, industrial location patterns, and land use. Consequently, regional economics also has to do with regional accounts (economic statistics on a particular region), development, and growth. Consideration of the latter topics aids in trade and income analysis. The trade and income of a region direct the activities of an area and its economy. These factors directly influence the nature and strength of the various real estate markets. For example, the abundance of resources enhances the economic base of the Sunbelt and western states, and this has attracted other economic activities that have directly increased the competition for space in many communities. The resulting increase in the Sunbelt's land prices may one day make other areas more attractive owing to the relatively lower price of land.

To take one example of a critical national resource and its impact "regionally" on certain segments of the market, it is readily apparent that the major consumer of office space in Houston, Tulsa, Denver, Casper, and Calgary has been the oil industry. In the late 1970s, these oil cities boomed with the expectation of continued increases in the price of oil. By the mid-1980s overbuilding, high vacancy, and resulting lower values were the common story. The resources and activities of an area are extremely significant to different segments of the real estate market, and numerous forces interact to determine the demand for space.

Surrounding economic activity may well be the single most important determinant in setting land value and influencing land use decisions. This is so because land *values* depend on land *use;* and the uses in demand for housing, commercial, and industrial real estate almost always involve land close to economic activity. It follows that changes in economic activity can significantly affect land use decisions. For example, the construction of the Alaskan pipeline represented a major stimulus to the economic activity of affected regions in that state. The resulting impact on land use decisions and value was also significant. On the other hand, the closing of a manufacturing plant or a military base can have a devastating impact on surrounding property values.

There are exceptions to the simple proximity of economic activity stimulating land use and land value, but they are the result of special circumstances. Thus, a gold mine has value, even though it is located in the midst of a desert, because its use value arises from the mineral deposits there. A resort located in an exotic and inaccessible area also has value precisely because it is not near other activities. Here the **use effect** derives from the very isolation of the location.

Beyond the direct physical and economic factors of a particular region, cultural characteristics may also be significant. Clearly, residents of the San Francisco Bay area find a quality of life in that area that arises from more than the purely physical characteristics of the region and that induces them to pay more for real estate than could be justified by strictly economic measures.

PRAGMATIC ORIGIN

Regional economics is distinguished by its pragmatic origin—that is, its concepts have grown from practical experience and what individuals have seen around them. **Regional economics** may be defined as a discipline devoted to explaining dynamic economic activity within a spatial context.

Regional growth analyses, or *models,* were first used to help determine where the government should provide certain public services. Inherent in these early models was a political element; cultural and non-economic factors were considered along with the physical characteristics of the particular region. Subsequently, industrial location models were developed and were even more pragmatic. Regional economists used these models to assist businesses seeking optimal locations for new facilities. The products of these private-sector studies were *pro forma locations.* These pro forma locations can be viewed as a type of regional economic study with a business orientation.

INTERDISCIPLINARY FLAVOR

As should be clear from its definition, regional economics is not limited to a mechanistic "balance sheet" description of a particular region at one moment in time. Politics, social factors, and cultural amenities all will have a long-term impact on a region. Because the real estate asset is fixed in location with improvements having a long economic life, regional changes eventually will affect the residual cash flow of the individual real estate project. Therefore, the interdisciplinary approach of regional economics is consistent with our analytical framework, which considers all influences on the residual cash flow. Unlike Parker Brothers' popular real estate game Monopoly®, players in the real world's real estate game must consider a complex and dynamic set of social factors as well as immediate cash flows.

IMPORTANCE OF REGIONAL ECONOMICS

From what has been already said, it should be clear why the analyst must carefully examine all surrounding influences when seeking to determine the value of real property. In particular, attention should be paid to expected future trends in light of the long life of the real estate improvement and the inability to move real estate to a different location.

For example, the regional analyst will seek to identify **external economies** (benefits) that arise because similar and supporting facilities are near the property in question. This factor is referred to as *benefits from agglomeration*. A classic illustration of **agglomeration** on the output side is "new car row," the street in any city on which several car dealerships are located. Potential buyers can shop more efficiently because of the concentrations of related activities such as repair shops, tire dealers, muffler houses, and so on, located in the same area to profit from the heavy consumer traffic. On the input side, California's Silicon Valley shows producers the benefits to be gained by locating related products in the same region.

The analyst also will note **external diseconomies**—that is, negative influences—from the nearness of dissimilar activities or uses that are not compatible with the property in question. Both these positive and negative factors will affect the cash flow of income properties and the sale prices of owner-occupied, single-family homes.

HOW DO INDUSTRIES CHOOSE A REGIONAL LOCATION?

Although this book focuses on the real estate industry rather than regional or urban economics, a brief introduction to the major industrial location theories that have evolved over the past 150 years will cast light on the sources of real estate value. Industries provide jobs that create a need for residential and commercial development. Hence, an understanding of industrial location is basic to predicting a host of related rent levels.

VON THÜNEN: HIGHEST AND BEST USE

Johann von Thünen is often cited as one of the first regional economists. His *Isolated State* (1826)[3] sought to explain agricultural locations in Germany and became the first serious attempt to incorporate the spatial element in pragmatic economic thought.

Von Thünen assumed a central town as the sole market center, surrounded by a flat, featureless, homogeneous plain with no transportation advantages (save distance) and of equal fertility. The wilderness at the edge of this market area could be cultivated if necessary, and farmers tried to maximize profits in the context of a given demand and fixed coefficients (costs) of production. These assumptions (which clearly are never met in real-life situations) led to an explanation of land use by a rent gradient that put high-intensity crops (density of yield per acre) near the center along with higher priced crops and crops necessitating heavier transportation costs. His work first gave expression to what has

[3]*For an English translation, see Peter Hall, ed.,* Von Thünen's Isolated State *(London: Pergamon Press, 1966).*

become the **highest-and-best-use principle**—that land use will be economically determined in the marketplace by the ability of user groups to pay rent for the land. In an agricultural setting, this involves (1) yield per acre, (2) price of crops, and (3) cost of transporting the crops.

WEBER: BUSINESS LOCATION DECISIONS

Alfred Weber, in his *Location of Industry* (1909)[4], transferred many of Von Thünen's ideas to a consideration of business location decisions. To Von Thünen's assumptions, he added scattered "deposits" of natural resources and labor. His results extended earlier work by showing that businesses locate to minimize both transportation costs to market and the transportation cost of moving the factors of production (materials and labor) to the plant site.

LOSCH: SPATIAL ELEMENT OF CONSUMER DEMAND

August Losch, in the *Economics of Location* (1939)[5], assumed uniform population distribution (consumers) and showed that the market penetration of a firm (based solely on price) can be explained by the spatial element. In other words, the plant located closest to the consumer would be able to offer that consumer the lowest price owing to lower transportation costs and therefore dominate the market. This was a twist on Weber, moving from one market center to describe demand as well as supply on a spatial basis.

HOOVER: THE ROLE OF INSTITUTIONAL FACTORS

Edgar M. Hoover, in his *The Location of Economic Activity* (1948),[6] moved beyond a consideration of direct costs and incorporated **institutional factors** in his regional analysis. He noticed that political boundaries were important and opened the door for considering all the cultural and psychological characteristics of a region as well.

ISARD: A FORMAT FOR DECISION MAKING

In *Location and Space Economy* (1956), Walter Isard[7] borrowed from previous writers and refined their ideas into a straightforward format for

---

[4]*Alfred Weber,* Theory of the Location of Industries *(Chicago: University of Chicago Press, 1929).*

[5]*August Losch,* The Economics of Location *(New Haven: Yale University Press, 1954).*

[6]*Edgar M. Hoover,* The Location of Economic Activity *(New York: McGraw–Hill, 1948).*

[7]*Walter Isard,* Location and Space Economy *(New York: Wiley, 1956).*

industrial location. He postulated that industries would make location decisions based on the costs, revenues, and personal factors associated with alternative locations. Under costs, he focused on transfer of inputs, transfer of outputs, and such local costs as available labor and utilities. In the revenue area, he talked about market control through location. Finally, under personal factors, he included the whole spectrum of interdisciplinary concerns about life-style in a particular location.

Our goal is to use Isard's format to move beyond the restrictive assumptions of earlier writers while still drawing useful material form their insights. The major considerations noted earlier seem obvious with hindsight (even though they are often very difficult to apply and reduce to dollars and cents). However, throughout the book, examples are noted of serious errors resulting from a failure to integrate fully these simple concepts in the analysis of real estate projects. Note at this juncture that Isard's format is forward looking. The "why" must be put into the past so that it may help us predict the future. (See Box 2-1.)

WHAT TOOLS ARE HELPFUL IN ANALYZING REGIONAL GROWTH?

Over the years, some practical tools for analysis have been developed from the theories about regional growth and industrial location that were previously sketched. Although the results obtained from using these tools are often imprecise, they do emphasize the key factors that should influence the decision maker in real estate and urban planning.

THE EXPORT BASE MULTIPLIER

The **export base multiplier** is used to project the number of new jobs that will be generated by certain types of new industry that locate within the region. We arrive at the multiplier as follows. All outputs in the region are divided into *basic* and *nonbasic* categories. Essentially, all goods and services that are sold outside the region (*exports*) are considered basic, and all others are considered in the nonbasic category. The *multiplier* is simply the ratio of jobs (or income) in the whole region (basic plus nonbasic) to jobs (or income) in the basic industries. When a new export industry moves to the region, the number of jobs generated there will be a product of the number of jobs in the new industry times the multiplier.

This is a very quick and easy approach and is often the basis of "chamber of commerce" estimates. However, the method is not without faults. The multiplier is a crude measure and changes over time. Classification of basic industries is difficult, and an unusual base year will distort the results. Finally, on a more theoretical basis, this approach is flawed because clearly the world economy grows with no exports—so why must the regional economy have exports to have growth?

Export base projections are common in the real estate markets and can be both interesting and informative. However, they are generally not

2-1

**LOS ANGELES'
GROWTH
DIFFERS FROM
THAT OF OTHER
MAJOR CITIES**

Los Angeles has always danced to a slightly different tune than the rest of the United States. So it shouldn't be surprising to note that when it comes to employment growth, the city is somewhat unique.

Skyscrapers shot up in downtown Los Angeles throughout the 1980s. But the projected employment growth of the residents of Los Angeles County lags that of other major U.S. markets. Current forecasts of employment growth indicate that over the next five years Los Angeles' employment growth rate should approach 1.36 percent while that of other major markets will grow at a 1.67 percent rate.

If employment growth is slow relative to that of other markets, why all the downtown development? First, during the 1980s Los Angeles attracted the major financial institutions that have made the city the financial gateway to the Pacific Basin. As a result, employment within the city shifted toward financial services and slightly away from traditional manufacturing jobs. This shift increased the demand for downtown office space and stimulated new development. As in all other major U.S. cities, the current question revolves around estimating the strength of this shift to financial services. Have developers brought too much space to market? The answer is probably yes—at least the level of necessary new space in the 1990s will not match the needs of the 1980s—if employment growth follows current forecasts, which are lower than the 1980 experience.

We can understand how an individual real estate investment will perform by understanding the dynamics of market growth. In the case of Los Angeles, although growth in employment has declined, a shift in the composition of that employment has had a dramatic effect on the market.

suited to serve as the sole basis for estimating market demand in a more refined real estate analysis.

Beyond the export base multiplier, several other common short-cut classification aids are available. Variations of the **location quotient** express a region's percentage of jobs in any given industry as the numerator of a ratio whose denominator is the national percentage of jobs in the given industry. Thus, regions with location quotients greater than one are said to reflect concentrations of the particular activity, and their local economies will be more affected by the fortunes of the particular industry. For example, California would have a high location quotient for aerospace activities, whereas Ohio would have a low location quotient for oil exploration. An example of a location quotient formula is

$$\text{Location quotient} = \frac{\% \text{ of region's jobs in industry}}{\% \text{ of nation's jobs in industry}}$$

SHIFT SHARE

Shift share analysis is a similar approach to analyzing a region's growth. It measures the region's industry by two standards.

❑ **INDUSTRY MIX.**   For each regional industry, the location quotient is determined in the manner just described. The industry's national growth rate is also established. The region will have a favorable "mix" if its industries with location quotients greater than one are also fast growing nationally. In other words, the region has more than its share of employees in industries that are growing rapidly.

❑ **COMPETITION.**   Here a ratio is established for each regional industry between the region's and the nation's growth rate in the industry. The region will enjoy a favorable competitive position in any industry in which its growth is more rapid than the national growth. The shift share technique is a quick way to look at a region and analyze the characteristics of its growth. Like the location quotient and export base multiplier, it is a useful tool but is not the primary element in a complete market analysis.

INPUT/OUTPUT ANALYSIS

Input/output analysis is a matrix (tabular) approach to understanding a regional economy. The rows and columns of the various tables have identical headings representing the major industries in that region plus an export category. After a series of transition matrices, the final input/output matrix shows how an additional dollar spent in any one industry will affect sales in each of the other industries.

Input/output tables (matrices) can be very useful in anticipating derivative regional growth. They tend to be very detailed and intuitively appealing. However, they suffer from certain data limitations. First, the information is suspect because of possible deficiencies in collection procedures. And, more important to the real estate analyst who uses the past only to predict the future, the data are usually several years old before they are published.

The theories of regional growth and industrial location discussed in the early part of this chapter are descriptive in nature. The tools previously described represent an attempt to move beyond description to prediction. Unfortunately, they are usually too simple to be more than a starting point in serious real estate analysis. Still, these theories provide a useful framework for analysis. As an explanation of why real estate markets operate in a particular way, the descriptive nature of such theories can provide a useful check or safeguard. To be successful, this historically determined framework must be expanded to encompass dynamic considerations based on the "why" of past experience in order to project future residual cash flows as the model requires.

THE RELATIONSHIP OF REGIONAL AND URBAN ECONOMICS

The analytical tools of regional economics are also employed in the analysis of urban areas. In fact, the topics of regional economics are strongly related to the study of urban economics. Both areas of study are concerned with spatial economics and location analysis. Both are involved in the relationship of population concentrations to one another and the causes and direction of growth and development. In terms of theoretical development (and application), regional economics differs from urban economics only in the size of the spatial area considered. **Urban economics** deals with the urban complex whereas regional economics is concerned with counties, states, and broad economic areas such as the southeastern United States.

Because a city or urban area is not always a clearly identifiable economic entity, the Bureau of the Census uses Metropolitan Statistical Areas (**MSAs**) to define urban concentrations. The **MSA** delineation is also useful because of the interrelationship of an urban area with its hinterland included in the MSA. (The **hinterland** is the area surrounding the urban concentration that makes up the market for the services offered at the central location.) Using the MSA, the analyst has a better measure of the area of economic activity and is, consequently, able to make better decisions than if he were to rely solely on "city" statistics.

In summary, the major difference between regional economics and urban economics is that regional economics can deal with any sized spatial unit—the Rocky Mountain states, Utah, northwestern Utah, for example—whereas urban economics concentrates on the spatial unit termed a city or metropolitan area. In concentrating on the city or metropolitan area, the urban economist can identify the most important variables of problem situations that are witnessed in the daily operation of activities occurring over a citywide basis.

WHAT IS UNIQUE ABOUT AN URBAN ECONOMY?

Like regional economics, urban economics is a macrolevel discussion of spatial economics. Like regional economics, urban economics has its origins in the neoclassical school of economics. It applies the conventional wisdom of economics to the city or metropolitan area. (Henceforth, we will use simply city.) The city in urban economics is treated as an economic organism or entity much as traditional economics analyzes the firm or an industry. Unfortunately, the city is not as pure an economic organism as the firm or an industry.

As an economic entity, the city is both a producer and consumer. The city consumes and utilizes labor, capital, land, and entrepreneurial input. It produces services and durable products such as the public infrastructure. This public infrastructure is the street and utility network that gives structure to the city. It represents the public capital investment of a community.

Urban economics is significant to the study of real estate for several reasons. It identifies (and affords methods of analysis to study) the economic activities that occur within the urban complex. The economic activities of a city help identify the economic participants of an area. Because all economic activity must occur within a spatial dimension, the real estate analyst is able, on a macrolevel, to identify sources of demand for current space. More important, the potential for future demand can be identified.

Urban economics explains the underlying analytical premise for real estate market analysis. (The linking of market activity to real estate use/demand will be more obvious with the introduction of urban land economic concepts, which follows shortly.) Urban economic principles provide a macroperspective of real estate influences if we follow the late Professor James A. Graaskamp's lead and view the city as a **terrarium** or laboratory in which individual real estate decisions are made. The individual real estate investment decision should respond to the economic, physical, social, legal-political, institutional, and environmental forces that form the markets in which people operate. These forces are broad and often ambiguous. Still, while analytically viewing the environment at a point in time within the macrocontext of the city, we can liken our observation to that of looking into a terrarium. By using the analytical tools of the urban economist, we can begin to observe the patterns of urban growth and the variables that explain the logic of location within the terrarium.

LOCAL ECONOMY

Wilbur Thompson[8] stated that the economy of a city can be measured or evaluated by three basic indices of economic welfare.

1. *Affluence:* expressed as a high and rising level of income, measured in money terms first but translated into real terms by taking full account not only of local differences in the cost of living, but also, and perhaps more important, local differences in the range of goods and services available.

2. *Equity:* expressed as a "fair" distribution of income, considering both the distribution of earned income under a free-market price system and the redistribution of income effected by government taxes, services, and transfer payments. As noted in Chapter 1, the free market can break down, leading to government intervention to provide what society determines to be "equity."

---

[8]*Wilbur R. Thompson,* Urban Economics *(Baltimore, Md.: Johns Hopkins University Press, 1965).*

3. *Stability:* expressed in terms of seasonal, cyclical, and growth stability. The problem is both maintaining employment and income and achieving efficiency in the use of resources (e.g., avoiding peak congestion and off-peak idle capacity).

These three indices form the basis for the economic study of cities. Economic conditions in a city support the economic health of its various real estate markets. The regional and urban economic tools of economic base, location quotients, shift share analysis, and input/output tables are quantitative methods of analyzing and stating the comparative strengths and weaknesses of a community. In total, these economic strengths or weaknesses provide a current macro perspective of a local real estate market. The current economic conditions of the city also give rise to projections of the direction of growth or decline, or both. The patterns of growth in a metropolitan area enable the student of real estate to make projections of future land use patterns. These uses of land will influence the current and future value of the real estate.

In viewing both the structure and growth patterns of a city (to project land markets accurately), we can distinguish major differences between cities. These differences relate to the regions of the country in which the cities are located and the ages of the cities. Size, race, culture, topography, and a host of other factors further distinguish the different cities.[9]

TRANSPORTATION

In an economic context, a city's structure is often explained by transportation costs as such costs relate to the activities that result in the original city's development according to a resource or market orientation. Unlike the cities of Birmingham and other resource-related communities, cities such as New York City, Chicago, Atlanta, Houston, and San Francisco have grown up at **transshipment points.** Transshipment points (also known as break-in-bulk points) are where transportation modes change, for example, the transfer of goods from ships to railways or trucking facilities. New York, Chicago, and Houston are classic cases.

Cities such as Houston, Atlanta, and Chicago represent a combination of transshipment points and market or resource-oriented activities. Chicago handles the shipment of agricultural resources to market from dispersed production centers. Dallas and Atlanta represent the distribution centers from which goods are transferred, warehoused, and then dispersed to subregions of the country.

---

[9]*See Edgar Hoover and Raymond Vernon,* Anatomy of a Metropolis *(Cambridge, Mass.: Harvard University Press, 1959), for a further discussion of these factors.*

THE MONONUCLEAR CITY

Intercity and regional transportation facilities and associated economic activities of a community are the basis of the **mononuclear theories of urban structure.** On a macroeconomic level, we can use the mononuclear concept of a city to see growth characterized as decentralization. James Heilbrun[10] states that the decentralization characteristic of urban growth can be explained by the overflow effect and the automobile effect.

Heilbrun describes the overflow effect by illustrating the central city with fixed boundaries enjoying continuous population growth such that vacant land within its boundaries eventually is used up. Even though this growth results in higher density, ultimately some of the metropolitan population will spill over into the suburbs. In the initial stages of growth, the suburban ring is composed of scattered suburbs and satellite cities. Growth in the suburban ring is slow at first because development is still possible, economically and physically, within the central city boundaries. As the economic capacity of the central city is approached, the suburban population will eventually outgrow the central city.

The overflow effect was graphically illustrated in Heilbrun's original depiction, which suggests that cities with the densest central city development also have statistically experienced the greatest ring area growth.

Heilbrun further notes that the cities with the densest central city occupancy are also the cities of the North and East; the cities of the South and West are characterized by less central city density. This is explained partly by the transportation patterns that dominate the urban structure during periods of growth. The eastern cities were often founded at transshipment points. Intercity travel was concentrated in public rail and water facilities. In the formative days of the older eastern cities (primarily the eighteenth and nineteenth centuries), private intracity transportation was represented by "hoof and foot" travel.

Horse-drawn wagons and manual labor transferred goods from rail and water facilities to the warehouse and retail operations. The economic and physical cost of intraurban transportation helped create constricted central cities. Because urbanization and industrialization were predominant in the North and East in the early development of this country, the age of the cities, in part, explains the density and ring development of the Northeast.

Urban economists explain the state of the newer cities often observed in the West and South (e.g., Denver and Atlanta) by the automobile effect. Younger cities tend to be much less densely populated than older cities, as measured by inhabitants per square mile, because the automobile permitted people to settle both farther apart and horizon-

[10]James Heilbrun, Urban Economics and Public Policy *(New York: St. Martin's Press, 1974).*

tally rather than vertically on the land. (The automobile effect is also useful because the overflow effect alone does not account for the decline in population experienced by so many central cities in recent years.) The automobile effect is characteristic of the impact of the change in transportation technology on the structural pattern of cities. Older cities illustrate the influence of "hoof-foot" transportation by a more compact central city and denser architectural development than is witnessed in younger cities. Physical examples of the antiquated transport system are narrow streets, narrow lots and commercial buildings, three-story warehouses in the **CBD** (central business district), and a mononuclear structural framework for the community.

RAIL TRAVEL

Rail travel, in the form of streetcar and subway facilities, revolutionized intracity travel. Such rail travel has natural limitations, however. Service is constrained to points along the right of way, and the physical capital investment in rail facilities is massive. The economic effect of these limitations is to restrict the number of routes to those with sufficient projected customer usage to establish economic feasibility. Consequently, intracity rail transportation has further contributed to a mononuclear city, with dense inner-city development, the need for vertical development, and the occupancy of vertical space by service activities. The placement of the stationary rail systems, radiating out of the nucleus of the city, can be witnessed in a radial or axial structural pattern for many cities. The city's placement of these facilities thus predetermines future growth.

These facilities can also retard growth by limiting the alternative sites for development to those with ready access to mass transit. Unfortunately, the diseconomies of intracity mass transit in cities with less dense concentrations have caused problems in such younger cities as Houston. Although many commuters in San Francisco and Atlanta enjoy BART and MARTA, experience has shown that neither system is cost-justified. Similarly, the metro in Washington, D.C. is beautiful, but it is probably the last major new system that the United States will see for some time.

THE AUTOMOBILE

Observation of the older cities illustrates that the mode of transportation available in an earlier formative period was animal or rail. Because these forms of transportation best served a centralized city, cities tended to grow in a centralized pattern. Economic activities benefited from the availability of rail and proximity to other activities, and, as a result, the economics of agglomeration encouraged further centralized growth.

Robert Haig,[11] author of *Major Economic Factors in Metropolitan Growth and Arrangement,* called this self-reinforcing congested growth "friction of space." Only major technological development could alter the physical forms and social institutions that dictated the mononuclear structure of older cities. The development of the combustion engine was such a major technological development.

The automobile enabled people and their economic activities to escape the constraints of capital fixity (i.e., rail lines). The automobile also provided cheaper and more efficient transportation than that afforded by animal muscle so that more people could afford to go a longer distance, faster. In the 1920s, city structure became more fluid and the automobile combined with the overflow effect to create the phenomenon of **suburbanization.** Some suburbanization was noted in the 1890s with the advent of "streetcar suburbs," but the major move came as a result of the automobile.

From a real estate perspective, the automobile generated both positive and negative effects. Some positive effects included (1) more land availability, facilitating horizontal building, which is cheaper per unit; (2) the movement of economic activity other than residential to the urban fringe (i.e., warehousing, manufacturing, retailing, and so on); (3) an increase in alternative land sites for development; and (4) the decentralization of jobs. Negative real estate effects of the automobile included (1) air pollution; (2) urban sprawl; (3) unrelated land uses, which can result in undesirable growth patterns and loss of amenities to many; and (4) higher costs of providing government services to those more remote areas.

A consideration of the spatial dimension introduces transportation as a fifth factor of production (beyond land, labor, capital, and entrepreneurship). Transportation cost is important in many economic activities because it is a variable in the location decision. Based on the five factors of production viewed in a spatial environment, we will establish a forward-looking approach to location analysis. Note that urban concentrations develop within regions. It is now time to study these urban concentrations and try to establish the "whys" behind urban growth patterns. Again if we understand the "whys," an accurate projection of what will go on around a real estate site in the future can be made. Given the real estate project's long life and the significant possibility of positive and/or negative externalities, we see that projection of urban growth patterns is a critical element in successful real estate analysis.

HOW DO CITIES GROW?

Following the same pattern used in the study of regional economics, we will examine the historic evolution of descriptive urban models before we turn to the "whys" of urban dynamics.

[11]*Robert Murray Haig,* Major Economic Factors in Metropolitan Growth and Arrangement *(New York: Arno Press, 1974).*

CONCENTRIC CIRCLE THEORY

In *The City* (1925), Ernest Burgess[12] suggested a **concentric circle theory** to describe urban growth patterns. Remember that Burgess was writing in the early 1920s, and at that time what he saw in most cities was a clearly distinguishable central core. He labeled this core the *central business district* (CBD) and postulated that it typically contained large office buildings, well-established retail stores, government buildings, and so on.

This CBD was the most intensively used space and therefore the most valuable land in the city. Around this CBD spreading out equally in all directions, Burgess saw a second circular area, which he labeled the *zone of transition*. Located in this area were some low-income dwelling units, some nightclubs, some light manufacturing, and the commercial activities that could not justify space in the CBD. Moving out to a third concentric circle, Burgess saw a *zone for worker homes*. These were the citizens who worked in the manufacturing areas in the zone of transition as well as the CBD. Very often the structures in this zone were large older homes that over time had been converted to multifamily units. They were not the slums seen in parts of the zone of transition, yet they were clearly lower or working-class dwelling units. A fourth concentric zone included *the middle-class and some high-income units*. Here, Burgess saw the very wealthy and the middle class in both single- and multifamily homes. Even at this early date, he started to notice some entertainment and some commercial establishments appearing in this zone near higher income consumer groups. The fifth and final circle in Burgess's theory was the *commuter zone*. It was comprised of scattered dwelling units for workers who were willing to commute long distances for the privileges of less urbanized living. (See Figure 2-1.) The driving force in this theory is a continuous migration. As the wealthy move to new homes that better meet their changing needs, the slightly less well off move into their former neighborhood. As this process (known as **filtering**) continues, subsequent economic levels move up the scale. As we will see later in this chapter, the logical conclusion of this age- and income-induced filtering is a "hollow shell."

AXIAL THEORY

In 1925, Burgess's concentric circle theory seemed a reasonable description of many urban concentrations. However, soon after his publication, several other authors began to describe what has come to be known as the **axial theory** of urban growth. The axial theory is a direct takeoff on Burgess but picks up on an important factor affecting urban growth that Burgess ignored: transportation axes or arteries.

The axial theory begins, as did Burgess's concentric circle theory,

[12]*Ernest Burgess,* The City *(Chicago: University of Chicago Press, 1925).*

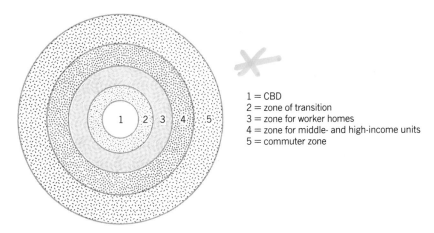

1 = CBD
2 = zone of transition
3 = zone for worker homes
4 = zone for middle- and high-income units
5 = commuter zone

F I G U R E 2-1   *Concentric circle theory*

with a CBD, which is still the most intensively used land, the most valuable land, and the land supporting the largest buildings. Here again, around the CBD are several zones. Depending on the particular author's interpretation, these zones parallel to a greater or lesser degree Burgess's zones. In other words, beyond the CBD, there is a transition zone that encompasses light manufacturing operations and some worker housing. Beyond this come the rest of the worker homes and eventually upper class homes, subdivisions for the middle class, and finally a commuter zone. What distinguishes the axial theory from the concentric circle theory is that these zones do not radiate in concentric circles from the CBD. It is not *distance* to the CBD that is the key but rather *commuting time* to the CBD. Thus, the axial theory develops growth patterns around the major transportation arteries to the CBD. Remember that in the 1930s and 1940s, most workers still did not own cars and commuted to their jobs via public transportation. Therefore, the development beyond the CBD tended to cluster around the sources of existing transportation. By focusing on transportation, the axial theory was a logical and useful extension of the concentric circle theory. (See Figure 2-2.)

SECTOR THEORY

In the 1930s, Homer Hoyt[13] developed what is known as the **sector theory.** This theory attempts to explain residential concentrations around the CBD. While studying residential concentrations, Hoyt was the first to notice that the pattern of activity within the CBD in some

[13]*Dr. Hoyt was one of the great figures in urban economics. Several of his works are important readings for the serious real estate analyst. We suggest* The Structure and Growth of Residential Neighborhoods in American Cities *(Washington, D.C.: FHA, 1939) and* The Changing Principles of Land Economics *(Washington, D.C.: Urban Land Institute, 1968).*

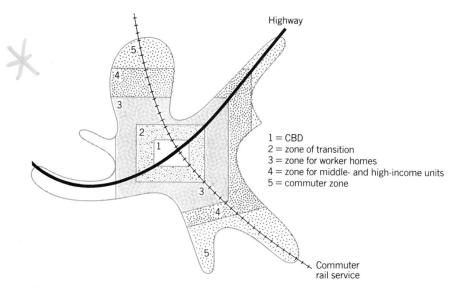

1 = CBD
2 = zone of transition
3 = zone for worker homes
4 = zone for middle- and high-income units
5 = commuter zone

FIGURE 2-2   *Axial theory*

cities was changing dramatically. Essentially, Hoyt noted that various groups in the social order tended to be segregated into rather definite areas according to their self-perceived social status. Naturally, there were several exceptions to this rule, but the casual observer would clearly note it in most areas. In other words, where the axial theory stated that like-income groups would locate like-commuting times from the CBD, Hoyt said that this was not the total picture. Cultural as well as economic factors would result in clustering at logical distances from major transportation routes. Quite naturally, higher income groups lived in homes that commanded the highest prices, and lower income groups lived in lower priced dwelling units. (See Figure 2-3.)

In Hoyt's work, the lower priced units were located near the CBD and tended to expand out from the central city as the city grew. For Hoyt, the basic principle of American cities (distinguishing them from most European cities) was that American cities grew by erecting new buildings at the periphery rather than in the CBD. Based on this observation, Hoyt began to notice what he termed a **hollow shell effect** in certain central cities. Up to this time, the CBD had always been the most valuable area within the city. Consequently, the property constructed on the land in this area was generally the most valuable property in the city. However, during this period of history, the pattern was changing. For several reasons, certain areas within the central city were beginning to decay. Money was being spent at the periphery; the wealthy were moving out. As they moved out, the lower income groups were moving into lower-middle-class neighborhoods, the lower-middle class moved into the middle-class homes, and the middle class moved into the upper-

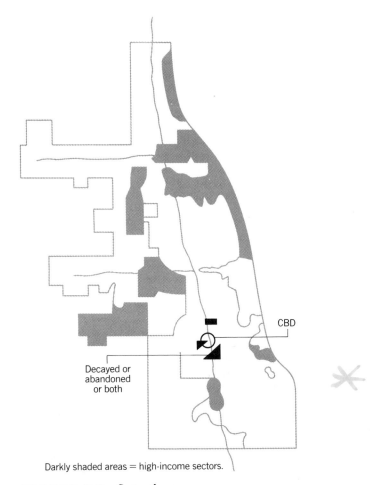

Darkly shaded areas = high-income sectors.

FIGURE 2-3 *Sector theory*

middle-class homes. All this had a filtering effect that left the poorer residents in the oldest and most functionally obsolete houses. Add to this the lower level of maintenance necessitated by relative poverty, and the older areas in and directly adjoining the CBD began to show a "hollow shell" effect. Thus, in Figure 2-3 the decayed or abandoned areas began to appear at the same time that other parts of the city, more distant from the CBD, were developing nicely.

MULTIPLE NUCLEI THEORY

In the 1940s Chauncey D. Harris and Edward L. Ullman[14] developed a new twist on the sector theory. Their **multiple nuclei theory** consisted of

[14]See Ronald R. Boyce, ed., Geography as Spatial Interaction (Seattle: University of Washington Press, 1980).

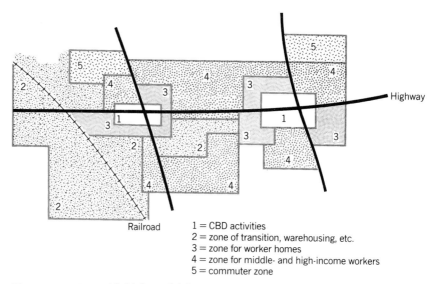

1 = CBD activities
2 = zone of transition, warehousing, etc.
3 = zone for worker homes
4 = zone for middle- and high-income workers
5 = commuter zone

FIGURE 2-4 *Multiple nuclei theory*

describing new urban centers within the residential concentrations created by the purchasing power and job requirements of those living in the residential area. In other words, as homogeneous income groups clustered together, certain services were demanded, and mini-CBDs developed to provide those services. Certain groups profited economically from locating together outside the urban core. Coupled with many social factors, this outside activity collectively caused the CBD to lose its position as the sole focal point within the urban concentration. Activity centers developed outside the CBD because of the advantages of agglomeration, specialization, and the desire to escape certain negative externalities. These smaller focal points, or *nuclei*, developed in the residential areas surrounding the old CBD, which was itself now partially decaying. (See Figure 2-4.)

SUMMING UP WITH AN EXAMPLE

All four of these theories are logical. In fact, in perspective, we see that their supposed insights are quite obvious. Nevertheless, we can still draw very useful conclusions from these simple descriptive urban models.

For example, the Dallas–Fort Worth area in the early 1970s was a hotbed of land speculation. The two Texas cities are approximately 30 miles apart, and it seemed logical to assume that they would eventually grow together to be one city. (See Figure 2-5.) To some extent, a similar development pattern had been seen earlier in the Boston–Washington, D.C., corridor and was clearly apparent between San Francisco and San Jose as well as between Los Angeles and San Diego. The prevailing forecast was for this same phenomenon to happen in this rapidly growing southwestern area.

The Dallas–Fort Worth airport (when constructed, it was the largest in the world) was located between the two cities. The Texas Rangers and Dallas Cowboys both located their respective baseball and football stadiums at intermediate points between the two cities. Major recreational facilities, such as Six Flags Over Texas, located in the area. In the small municipalities that controlled the area, development enthusiasm seemed unbounded. Syndicators bought parcels of land and (through investment packages that will be described later in this book) made these parcels particularly attractive to potential investors. The syndicators were able to organize partnerships to buy from other partnerships and sell to still other partnerships, with each group recognizing tremendous profits (at least on paper).

In mid-1970, as the real estate industry experienced a severe slowdown, these land ventures fell on difficult times. Foreclosures "fell through" several layers of partnerships. What happened was that Partnership C would foreclose the property (taking it over by bidding it in at the foreclosure auction) when the group to which it had sold defaulted on its note. The result was that Partnership C would itself lose the land

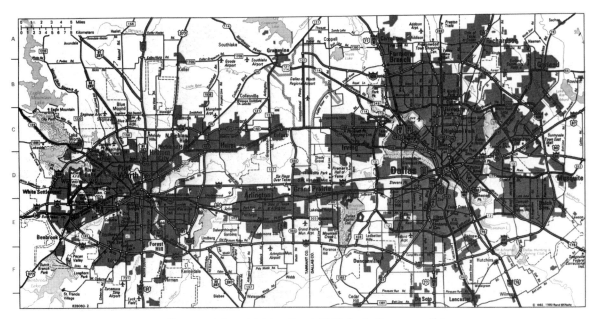

Source: ©Copyright by Rand McNally & Company, R.L. 83-5-100.

FIGURE 2-5   *Dallas-Fort Worth, Texas, map*

when it could not pay its own note to Partnership B, which had originally sold it the land.

How could the simple urban models just described have helped avert the Dallas–Fort Worth fiasco? If we remember the seemingly simple concentric circle theory, we would realize that for Dallas and Fort Worth to grow together into a city whose center was located midway between the two existing cities, a total population greater than that of New York City would be required. Certainly, all the land between the two cities would not be developed in the near future. Looking to the axial theory and growth in transportation patterns for an explanation, we would realize there was still an incredible abundance of land. Using the sector theory, we would have noticed that only certain parts or sectors of this land would be developed with high-income property, which would, in turn, generate high land values and consequently high profits for land investors. The multiple nuclei theory takes this one step further and suggests that there would be only certain smaller commercial concentrations within the residential concentrations between these two cities. Although these four theories seem quite simple, millions and millions of dollars would have been saved had investors been reflective enough to use logical insights derived from these descriptive models to understand the real estate markets in which they were investing.

By 1975, the bubble had burst, and economic logic again came to dominate land pricing. With the return to economically justifiable prices, many speculators were wiped out. Although particular real estate markets may in some sense feed on themselves (relying on the "greater fool" theory), the sophisticated analyst realizes that, in the long run, prices must be economically justified. Today Las Colinas is a major new business center near the Dallas–Fort Worth airport. Prosperous and growing, it has a total size that is still small in relation to the total land area of the midcities.

WHY DO URBAN AREAS GROW?

Descriptive models are useful only as aids in predicting the future. In the example of Dallas–Fort Worth, the results clearly suggest that the serious analyst should go beyond these models and ask "why" cities grow. Harry Richardson,[15] in his classic text, *Regional Economics*, cites several possible hypotheses. He begins with Walter Christaller's central place theory,[16] which postulates that a city grows because of the demand for services from what Christaller termed the hinterland or surrounding areas. Christaller developed a hexagonal model (not totally unlike Von

[15]Harry Richardson, Regional Economics (*Champaign-Urbana: University of Illinois Press, 1979*).

[16]*Christaller's work is an extension of the work of Von Thünen and Losch as described earlier in the chapter. See Walter Christaller,* Central Places in Southern Germany (*Englewood Cliffs, N.J.: Prentice-Hall, 1966*).

Thünen's model) with the nature of the urban concentrations described by the size of the areas they serviced. Certain goods have to be supplied at fairly local levels; grocery stores are an example. Other services could be supplied by more distant and more concentrated urban areas. The types of services involved here would include universities, manufacturing plants, and so on. Cities such as New York could be explained as providing a set of financial services to the nation as a whole.

Christaller's approach was a starting point, and Richardson goes on to examine other theories. The economic base theory (discussed earlier in the regional economics section) can be used to describe urban growth. A human ecological approach explains city growth based on various needs for human interaction. A takeoff on this is the information theory, which postulates that cities grow in order to provide information flows. (Again, New York City is a good example.) Some theories even argue that once population concentrations reach a certain minimum size, growth is locked in, in a ratchetlike manner.

Some combination of these theories must be used to explain why cities grow the way they do and why we have competition for location within a city. What will this competition do to the price of land and to the development of surrounding land parcels?

2-2
FAST GROWING
METRO AREAS

Boulder, Colorado, and Du Page, Illinois, are the only major urban markets outside the Sunbelt and California in a recent ranking of the ten fastest growing metropolitan markets in the United States, based on data provided by NPA Associates, Inc.

At the top of the list is Anaheim, California. While it isn't easy to get a statistical handle on local economic growth, employment forecasts are widely considered the best indicator of near-term economic growth. But real estate analysts should be wary of making decisions based on forecasts that exceed five years. This is because most forecasters merely extrapolate near-term trends in order to estimate longer term forecasts.

Here's our best guess as to the ten fastest growing urban markets in 1988–93, based on average annual percentage growth in total employment. Our estimate of the average yearly job growth rate for all urban areas is 1.67 percent.

Anaheim, Calif.	4.2%	Ft. Lauderdale, Fla.	3.5 %
West Palm Beach, Fla.	4.1%	Oxnard-Ventura, Calif.	3.5 %
Orlando, Fla.	3.8%	Las Vegas, Nev.	3.4 %
Boulder, Colo.	3.6%	Phoenix, Ariz.	3.3 %
Du Page, Ill.	3.5%	Santa Rosa, Calif.	3.24%

There is no complete model to offer as a substitute for the "why" theories previously suggested. However, some additional factors quite clearly affect the way cities grow. (See Box 2-2.)

OTHER FACTORS IN URBAN DYNAMICS

The story of cities—their origin, growth, and decline—is a fascinating one, combining, as it does, elements of geography, trade, sociology, economics and culture. History itself can influence urban dynamics. Both Boston and Philadelphia offer clear evidence of how historic areas can influence urban development patterns.

Legend can also be a factor. At a certain point in time, critical events may occur that cause residents to believe that one part of a city is superior to another. Legend has it that when Stephen F. Austin's troops were camped on the Colorado River during the war with Mexico, a group of his soldiers became ill with a highly contagious disease. To isolate these troops, he sent them south of the river and successfully avoided contaminating the entire army. Ever since then, the city (which has come to be known as Austin, Texas) has had its more expensive development north of the river.

The city of Austin is not alone in having a northwest orientation. The majority of American cities have tended to develop the more expensive residential communities on the northern and western sides. Although there are notable exceptions—Jacksonville, Florida; Tulsa, Oklahoma; Charlotte, North Carolina; Tampa, Florida; Charleston, South Carolina; Dayton, Ohio; and St. Louis, Missouri among them—there is a certain tradition that northwest is best. This may well be irrational legend. Or the tradition may have something to do with the fact that in the Northeast the prevailing winds are from the north. As some early American cities developed with industry in the CBD, the prevailing winds kept any unpleasant odors away from the northern part of town. Whatever explanation seems most believable (or enjoyable), legend and tradition play a part in the real estate game.

Changing racial and ethnic patterns are important in understanding urban dynamics. Filtering, whereby better homes are continually filtering down to owners with lower incomes, with the very wealthy building new homes and so triggering the process, can affect urban dynamics. Racial patterns are slightly different. Racial and ethnic concentrations can create some of the more beautiful and interesting sections of a city. On the other hand, changing racial and ethnic patterns, when coupled with income disparity, have been identified by some as the causes of the growth of slums and blight in previously healthy neighborhoods.

Migration is another important element in many cities. In faster growing sections of the country, particularly in the Southwest and West, migration to the region explains a large part of the growth of certain cities. If migration can be tied to particular industries, then in some sense residential development and consequent commercial activities can be explained. In other cities, especially port or border cities, migration is significantly composed of illegal aliens, and real estate markets adapt to provide the services that this group is able to support financially. Consider the impact of recent Latin immigration in southern California or the impact of earlier Oriental immigration to the San Francisco area.

The list of considerations in this interdisciplinary field is almost endless. A growing awareness of the importance of energy makes certain areas more attractive than others. In fact, as the price of gasoline once again starts to rise, locations with easier access to mass transit become more attractive than areas serviced by the private automobile. Crime is also a factor, particularly after some of the precedent-setting landlord liability cases in the Washington, D.C., courts. The changing concept of the modern family, unmarried couples living together, higher divorce rates, smaller families, and starting families later all have a dramatic impact on real estate development. Technological change is important, as are new patterns of leisure-time use, population growth, social ideals, quality of television, air conditioning, and even changing weather patterns. Adding increasing complexity to the analysis is the accelerating rate of change. Remember that the real estate asset has a long economic life in a fixed location. The faster the rate of change, the more important consideration of future trends becomes to the real estate analyst. *Only after analyzing all of the relevant market factors can we make projections of residual cash flows. (Remember that the microdefinition of winning is tied directly to projected cash flows.)*

How Regional Theory and Urban Economic Theory Are Used

For the real estate analyst, the study of regional and urban economics must be put into the proper perspective. This requires that the topics and ideas presented in these sections be evaluated on the basis of how such theory can assist the real estate decision maker. Clearly, regional and urban development affects the marketplace and, as such, is not itself at issue. However, applying or using theory in the analysis of a specific localized real estate market is another matter. What the analyst needs is to be able to draw analogies from regional and urban economic theory that help to explain activity, current and future, occurring in a specific market.

Regional and urban economic theories are important to the real estate analyst because such theories firmly fix the spatial dimension of the real estate marketplace. This spatial dimension concept includes the impact of many factors on a particular site. Employment opportunities, transportation, public services, climate, entertainment, and educational facilities are among the factors that affect the evaluation of a particular site by the marketplace. These factors determine how the site fits into the surrounding regional and urban economic scenes. Demand for (and hence value of) a particular site can be critically related to how it fits into the spatial setting. This includes both how the site is affected by surrounding activity (**location effect**) and how the site itself (**use effect**) affects surrounding activity.

For example, the development of a regional economy can be profoundly affected by climate. In the case of Florida, land use decisions are materially affected by climatic characteristics. The growth and development of a tourism-dominated economic base is largely a function of the climate. Consequently, land use decisions are significantly affected by how the site fits into the economic activity of the area. Beachfront property would be more valuable than some central city areas, for example.

How the site affects surrounding uses within the spatial context can also be exemplified by the impact of regional shopping centers. Such a center serves as a magnet for many other uses (e.g., office and light commercial development). The opportunity to take advantage of the traffic generated by the center can make other developments feasible, whereas without the presence of the shopping center they could not be justified.

LOCATION ANALYSIS

Analysts have relied on the relationships suggested by regional and urban economic theories to develop the quantitative tools useful in location analysis. Real estate analysts can use some of these tools (e.g., export base multipliers, location quotients, and shift-share analysis) to project future economic activity in an area. As markets change, it is important to be able to forecast future trends, and these tools can give a quick first approximation.

For example, the location of a new manufacturing plant may have considerably more impact on an area than merely an increase in employment. The type of employees required makes a great deal of difference. If local skills satisfy the new labor demand, the effect on the economy will be considerably different than if new skills must be attracted to the community. In the prior case, unemployment would fall, some shifting might occur in the housing market, and the demand for city services would be only slightly affected. If new skills in employees are required by the new manufacturing plant, the resulting in-migration will increase the demand for housing and city services, but the level of unemployment might not be materially affected.

GOVERNMENTAL POLICY DECISIONS

Based on regional development patterns, certain urban concentrations develop. As cities grow and change, many government policy decisions must also be made. These policy decisions can materially affect land use decisions and future growth. Because real estate decisions are highly influenced by government policy, it is critical that real estate analysts recognize the dynamic role of government as regional and urban economic conditions change.

Descriptive urban models can be useful in identifying the forces that shape the internal structure of cities. This structure refers not only to the spatial development of cities, but also to their social, political, and cultural characteristics. The real estate analyst can utilize urban models in understanding and anticipating government policy as it relates to city growth and development; in many cases, government policymakers are using the same models. (Part 9 deals extensively with the role of government and the public–private interface.)

SUMMARY The fixed location and long economic life of improved real estate represent unique asset characteristics. Location fixes a site within a regional and/or urban market. The long economic life of improvements necessitates a clear understanding of dynamic market factors affecting a site over the long run. As a result, the spatial characteristics of the real estate plus specific site improvements define or identify specific markets. The market of a particular site can be examined in terms of how the site affects surrounding parcels (use effect) and how surrounding activity affects the site (location effect). As all markets are somewhat different, the real estate analyst must understand the region and the city in order to develop a coherent framework for real estate analysis.

Regional and urban economics provide useful tools for focusing on the important spatial element of real estate markets. The pragmatic origin and development of regional and urban economic theory provide tools that the real estate analyst can use to evaluate the location effect. This requires an interdisciplinary approach that accurately evaluates both positive and negative externalities. Evaluation of the impact of these externalities is important in projecting residual cash flows over time for any particular project.

Finally, it is important to remember that the real estate market is governed by a set of socially defined rules. The rules of the game can be changed if society's best interest is not being served. Local, state, and federal government policy decisions represent the mechanism society has chosen to implement such change. Therefore, in developing an analytical framework for the analysis of real estate decisions, we must evaluate regional and urban economic considerations within the context of a dynamic marketplace and society's best interest.

IMPORTANT TERMS

Agglomeration

Amenities

Mononuclear theories of urban structure

Axial theory

CBD

Concentric circle theory

Export base multiplier

External economies
 (diseconomies)

Filtering

Highest-and-best-use principle

Hinterland

Hollow shell effect

Input/output analysis

Institutional factors

Location effect

Location quotient

MSA

Multiple nuclei theory

Regional economics

Sector theory

Shift share

Spatial order of the economy

Spatial plane

Suburbanization

Terrarium

Topography

Transshipment points

Urban economics

Use effect

REVIEW QUESTIONS

2.1   Why can regional and urban economics be called economics with a spatial dimension?

2.2   What is the difference between the use effect and the location effect as they affect the value of a site?

2.3   In reference to the export base multiplier, how is the output of a region divided between basic and service categories?

2.4   Name three identifying features of a city.

2.5   How did the axial theory expand on the concentric circle theory of urban land development?

2.6   Explain the sector theory.

2.7   How can legend play a role in the pattern of a city's development?

2.8   Briefly discuss Von Thünen's explanation of agricultural locations.

2.9   What are the basic differences between regional and urban economics?

2.10   What are the possible uses of a descriptive urban model?

S PATIAL ECONOMICS: RENT, SITUS, AND SUCCESSION THEORY

In Chapter 2 we looked at the major forces that shape a city's structure and growth. The chapter concluded with four urban growth models. These models suggest the general patterns of how a city develops but stop short of predicting the use or economic value of a specific parcel of land. To fill this gap, urban *land* economists (distinct from urban economists) have developed theories about the dynamics of *specific* urban sites. This chapter highlights three of their theories: rent, situs, and land use succession.

Theories are useful to all types of real estate players; after all, theories help us explain and organize facts so that we can make decisions. However, in the end not even the most sophisticated theories completely explain the rich complexity of our cities. We conclude chapter 3 by discussing the limitations of urban theory in relation to the actual land development and redevelopment process. The failure of theory to account for all the changes introduced by imaginative individuals is illustrated with two examples of America's leading developers. John Portman and James Rouse broke from the mold. Rather than react to the market forces described in Chapter 2, they have created new products to capture new markets. We urge you to seek this same kind of creativity; yet, even if you have this potential, you will still need the analytical framework developed here as a basis from which to exercise your creativity.

We begin by briefly introducing the theories. Theories of urban structure show the link between urban economics and urban land economics. Urban economists examine the distribution of economic activities within the urban complex. Urban land economists examine *the distribution of land among economic activities* within the urban complex and the substitution of other factors of production for land.

HOW RENT IS DETERMINED

Early rent theorists analyzed a city's structure from a classical economic perspective wherein the basic land use is agricultural. **Rent theory** had two major parameters: (1) land value or site rent and (2) transportation cost. **Site rent** was defined as the rent paid for a site under a specified use less the rent it could command in an agricultural use. This work extended the ideas of Von Thünen (discussed in the preceding chapter) to the urban landscape.

Early rent theorists were most concerned with regional growth, the hierarchy of cities within a region, and applications to regional markets. Later economists such as William Alonso and Richard Muth[1] went beyond the earlier work and used rent theory to explain urban structure.

ALONSO AND MUTH: URBAN LAND MARKETS

In *Location and Land Use,* Alonso states that urban sites are composed of both land and location. Alonso's model considers residential, business, and agricultural land uses within the Von Thünen framework. Alonso's work emphasizes the tradeoff of site rent for transportation cost in the decisions of individuals about where to locate within the city.[2]

Following Alonso's model, a household's entire annual shelter expenditure can be allocated between transportation cost and site rent. Site rent is highest at the CBD and will decrease as distance from the CBD increases. Transportation costs, on the other hand, are cheapest near the CBD and will increase with distance from the CBD. The curve of site rents, an economic map of a community, is called a **bid rent curve**.[3] Figure 3-1 explains why development is more dense in the center of a city and less dense around the fringes. As one moves out from the CBD, more land can be consumed because of the lower site rent per unit. In the past, this model has been used to explain the distribution of income groups within a city. The wealthier live on the fringe, consume more units of land (even though it costs less per unit), and benefit from the

[1]William Alonso, "Location Theory," in John Friedmann and William Alonso, eds, Regional Development and Planning (Cambridge, Mass.: MIT Press, 1964); Richard R. Muth, Cities and Housing: The Spatial Pattern of Urban Residential Land Use (Chicago: University of Chicago Press, 1969). In several scholarly articles, these authors developed the first formal economic models of residential location, applied Hoover's and Vernon's theories to the city and residential location, and moved urban economic thinking to a new level.

[2]Assumptions of the Alonso model: (1) The city is a flat plain; (2) residential land use is a focus; (3) all production and distribution activity in the community takes place at a single point, the central business district (CBD); (4) cost of building and maintaining houses (short run excluded) is constant throughout the city; (5) population is socially homogeneous and of the same income level; and (6) site rent rather than land value is the basic measure. (Rental markets are assumed to be more knowledgeable than purchasing markets in real estate because participation is more widespread and transactions are more frequent.)

[3]This discussion is taken directly from Muth. The serious student will find in Muth's work (footnote 1) a way to incorporate transportation cost change and technology of production change into the rent estimation.

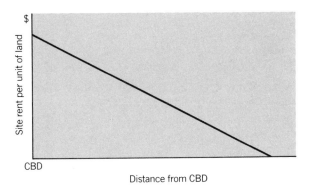

FIGURE 3-1   *Bid rent curve: demand view*

amenities that the consumption of more land affords. They choose to incur more travel expense because they are financially capable of absorbing the daily cost of transportation to a job in the central city. The poor cannot absorb these daily costs of transportation and so are forced to live near their work. Because the site rent is greater near the center of the city, to afford the rent more people must occupy less horizontal space and, consequently, are stacked vertically. The result is that the central city is more densely settled, since the poor have less freedom of movement than the wealthy. North American cities are characterized by the "**prisoner's dilemma**": the poorest people live on the most expensive land and cannot afford to escape. Parts of Manhattan Island are a classic example. Midtown has some of the highest rents in the world; yet, in parts of Harlem and the Bronx, the very poor live packed together, financially unable to move out and commute in from any other location.

Alonso's model focuses on demand. Muth, Edwin Mills,[4] and George Stigler, among others, contribute the supply side of rent theory. Muth and others assert that the cost of constructing housing is the primary force determining urban population density. They imply that because land prices are higher near the center of the city, builders substitute capital for land, building vertically on a site. Stigler adds that building costs decline much less than land prices, if at all, as one moves out from the CBD. As a result, larger quantities of land are used relative to buildings as one moves away from downtown. Thus, density decreases as distance from the CBD increases. A supply-side view of the bid rent curve as held by Muth is shown in Figure 3-2.

The shape of the bid rent curve has been altered from a linear relationship per Alonso's model to an inward-sloping curve posited by Muth. The physical structure of some cities, especially older cities in the

[4]*Edwin S. Mills,* Studies in the Structure of Urban Economy *(Baltimore, Md.: Johns Hopkins University Press, 1972).*

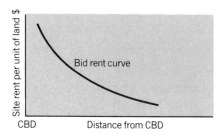

FIGURE 3-2 *Bid rent curves including the supply view*

Northeast and Midwest, supports explanations of value based on distance from the city center as reflected in transportation costs, building costs, and capital substitution.

In Chapter 2 we noted that many cities of the West and South are better described by the multiple nuclei model than by the concentric circle model. How does the multiple nuclei model fit with rent theory? The center of each nucleus is a focal point comparable in many respects to the CBD in the concentric circle and axial theories. As in those theories, site rent should decline as distance from the center of each nucleus increases. That point outside the center at which the site rent of one nucleus (neighborhood) is equal to the site rent of another nucleus establishes the boundary between the two nuclei (neighborhoods) (see Figure 3-3).

Points A and B are the centers, or economic focal points, of a city's neighborhoods. Points D and E represent the economic boundaries of neighborhoods. The peak points of each neighborhood collectively represent the metropolitan bid rent curve. The multiple nuclei model helps explain a metropolitan area like Houston, which as a CBD competing with important outlying retail and office centers such as Greenwood Plaza and the Galleria area. In later chapters, we use the multiple nuclei

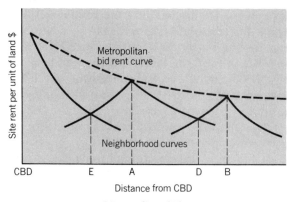

FIGURE 3-3 *Metropolitan bid rent curve*

concept to establish the market trade areas for parcels of real estate and other products.

Theories of urban structure provide a large-scale perspective on land markets. Such models do not, however, address other complex environmental influences that determine where and why activities locate as they do. Urban land economists have developed a concept known as **situs theory** to account for some of these influences.

HOW DO SURROUNDING LAND USES AFFECT RENT?

Richard B. Andrews,[5] a premier urban land economist, has broadly defined **situs** as "the total urban environment in which a specific urban land use on a specific land parcel functions and with which it interacts at a specific time."

The *use* of a specific parcel of land is distinct from the land parcel itself. Land is a physical thing bound by legal rights. Not only does an individual parcel of land have its own physical and legal attributes, but it is also surrounded by other parcels of land with their own characteristics. The setting created by surrounding land has an effect on any individual parcel of land. Surrounding land use is a key variable for analysis in the *situs,* or setting, of any individual parcel. A particular use may be appropriate on a given site because of that use's relationship to other nearby uses.

For a parcel of land to have economic significance, it must be defined in terms of a specific use. The aggregation of individual land uses establishes the character of the urban environment. For example, think of Youngstown, Ohio, and the implications of being a steel manufacturing town—in contrast to Palo Alto, California, a university town near Silicon Valley, a center of the microelectronics industry in the United States. The total environment determines the relationship among uses and the relationship of the environment to any particular site's use. Physical characteristics like the location, configuration, and topography of any individual parcel then become constraints on the most likely use indicated by factors external to the site. The importance of situs theory is its insistence that a piece of land does not exist in isolation; rather, its likely use and economic value are inextricably linked to its surroundings.

The analysis of situs can be organized around three considerations: activities, associations and accessibility, and environment.

ACTIVITIES

The use of a parcel of land is an economic activity. An **establishment** is the urban land economists' term for the basic unit of land use. An estab-

---

[5]*Richard B. Andrews,* Urban Land Economics and Public Policy *(New York: Free Press, 1971).*

lishment consists of individuals or groups occupying recognizable places of business, residence, government, or assembly. However, the concept of an establishment is complicated because many establishments may include a variety of functions, and the various functions of a single establishment may require different site attributes. For example, take an industrial firm. Management needs information and personal business contacts; these needs may dictate one type of site, whereas the warehouse and distribution functions of that same firm require low-cost space and good access to transportation routes. Robert M. Haig recognizes this issue with the notion of a "packet of functions."[6] He asserts that each function of an establishment is best served in a different location. Executive-level management might best be situated in office facilities in the inner city, whereas warehousing could be located in industrial parks on the urban fringe near interstate highway or rail facilities, or both.

The lesson for the real estate analyst is that by identifying the activities conducted by a business, one can locate sites appropriate to the functions of each department. Understanding functions facilitates understanding site needs, which in turn leads to identification of the necessary major linkages in a given area. A **linkage** is a relationship between establishments that results in the movement of people or goods. Identifying these linkages and relating them to the business activity seeking a site are obviously important determinants of the rent expected from development on the site.

ASSOCIATIONS AND ACCESSIBILITY

Situs analysis tries to identify not only activities within establishments, but also the relationship between various establishments. Establishments in an area may be competitive as well as complementary, depending on the economic activity. For example, notice the proximity of automobile dealerships to one another in any given community. Why do competitors locate along "automobile rows"? A major reason is that an automobile is a durable good and people will shop to make comparisons between alternatives. When a comparative shopping trip is in progress, it behooves dealers to make the trip convenient. Why do fast-food services tend to group together? Fast-food services are selling convenience. Convenience often leads to impulse buying and not comparative shopping behavior. Again, the key word is convenience. Auto dealers and fast-food restaurants seek direct proximity to markets they serve, both offering convenience in different ways to purchasers in hopes of maximizing sales. These are examples of output-side **agglomeration economies.**

An interesting example of convenience to both a stationary and a

---

[6]*Robert M. Haig,* Major Economic Factors in Metropolitan Growth and Arrangement *(New York: Arno Press, 1974).*

mobile market is best illustrated by the Hungry Mile Drive of West Lindsey Street in Norman, Oklahoma. The Hungry Mile is situated between the campus of the University of Oklahoma and the I-35 interchange. The major linkages are the interstate highway interchange and the university. The stationary linkage is the campus with a student population generating demand for fast food. The mobile linkage is the automobile traffic on the interstate, which is tied in to the campus by West Lindsey Street.

Complementary land use associations refer to those associations between sites that support one another. Complementary associations are obvious in instances of a cannery or bottling plant locating next to a brewery, or a bookstore near a university campus.

It is important to recognize land use associations because real estate uses at any one site are linked to the activities occurring elsewhere in their locale. These relationships can be competitive or complementary. If a use in the area goes out of business or if a residence is converted from a single-family home to a boarding house, there is a break in existing neighborhood associations. (The analogy can be made to a break in an ecological chain.) In real estate analysis, it is important to recognize fully the connection of one site to all others and to be aware that the stability of one site is associated with the stability of others. Positive associations enhance expected rent, but a break in important associations can materially reduce a tenant's prospects and consequently expected rent. For example, when a high-fashion women's clothing store leaves a strip shopping center, the adjacent lingerie store is probably doomed.

ENVIRONMENT

We have noted that the activities on one site and that site's associations with, and accessibility to, activities on other sites are of vital importance to the location decision. The total environment in which activities and movement between activities occur is also important. Neighborhoods of a city evolve out of the needs and abilities of a wide range of users. These users may have different preferences for the physical, social, economic, and institutional environment.

Obviously, the physical environment has much to do with the attraction of particular uses to certain neighborhoods of a city. For example, industrial, commercial, and certain institutional uses are likely to be attracted, because of cost, to sites on flat terrain in a community. But residential and other institutional facilities are often attracted to rolling or hilly sections because of the elevation and good views they offer.

Social environments can be important to some location decisions, especially residential ones. Generally, single-family residential neighborhoods within a city illustrate homogeneity in housing size and price.

Residential neighborhoods illustrate the tendency for similar income or occupational groups to live together.[7]

The economic environment of an area both acts on and is created by establishments predominant in the area. The economic environment of an area is the sum of the individual activities as they link to one another. In this sense, the recognition of activities and associations among them aids in understanding the local company.

All three elements involved in the concept of situs clearly show that location of land uses is more than just a function of physical geography. Location reflects the complex arrangement of economic activities using finite spatial resources. As a tool to explain why specific uses locate on specific land parcels, situs theory is a building block for all areas of study that deal with spatial economics. It was probably best summarized by Richard Ratcliff as follows.

> The essence of location derives from one of the elemental physical facts of life, the reality of space. We cannot conceive of existence without space; if there were no such thing, all objects and all life would have to be at one spot. If this happened to be the case, real estate would have no such quality as location; all real estate would be in the same place, equally convenient to every other piece of real estate and to every human activity and establishment. But under the physical laws of the universe, each bit of matter—each atom, molecule, stone, dog, house, and man—takes up space at or near the surface of the earth. As a result, no two objects can be at the same place at the same time. Necessarily, then, all people, animals and objects are distributed in a spatial pattern.[8]

What can real estate users, investors, developers, and lenders do with situs theory? They can identify or create opportunities for natural spatial monopolies. On a smaller scale, they can better identify sites of less risk or of greater advantage within local markets. Principally, they can use situs theory as a tool to avoid overlooking the interdependency of a specific site and its total environment and, with knowledge of this interdependency, better evaluate risk and opportunities for gain.

Although a site within a neighborhood within a city can be viewed at a particular point in time like a still photograph, that photograph of a moment contains the flow of time past. Situs is not static. It captures the accumulation of past land use patterns and relationships that may still be in flux. Sometimes the rate of change is minute. Nevertheless, change is virtually always taking place in the environment. The ability to identify

---

[7]There are notable exceptions. Such communities as Oak Lawn in Dallas are known for their heterogeneity, but they are clear exceptions to the general tendency.

[8]Richard U. Ratcliff, Real Estate Analysis (New York: McGraw–Hill, 1961), p. 62.

change is extremely important to real estate participants. The investor, the developer, and the lender should all perceive a site in the context of a moving picture. Aiding this perspective, urban land economics has another tool to account for change over time: land use succession theory.

HOW DO LAND USE AND RENTS CHANGE OVER TIME?

Land use succession theory is based on the premise that real estate, though physically fixed, is economically flexible. A biological analogy is useful here. Like a living organism, a site, a neighborhood, or a segment of a city may go through states of a life cycle. For example, a particular residential area may be viewed as the new, more modern, and desirable area of the city to live in. As it is new, it is only partially developed and still has the capacity to grow. The stages in the life cycle of a new neighborhood are shown in Figure 3-4.

The first phase is characterized by rapid growth. This stage is illustrated by the segment of the curve rising at an increasing rate. Over time, vacant lots are improved with houses, and the potential for growth slows down. This stage is illustrated on a continuum by the section of the curve rising at a decreasing rate. As nearly all the vacant land is built on and as the structures (and family cycles) mature, so the neighborhood enters into a stage of maturity. The maturity phase is illustrated by the nearly flat segment of the continuum at its peak and usually lasts for an extended, sometimes indefinite period.

In some situations, as buildings in the area begin to age, maintenance may be deferred. Older designs and materials may no longer suit current market preferences and so may introduce functional obsolescence. External competition from newer subdivisions may siphon off potential buyers that previously would have desired to live in the subject

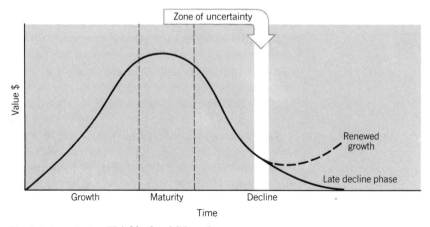

FIGURE 3-4 *Neighborhood life cycle*

neighborhood. From one or more of these occurrences the neighborhood may slip into an accelerating stage of decline.

The decline phase may not be terminal. Rather than continue indefinitely to decline, a site and its neighborhood can enter what Richard Andrews terms the zone of transition. Andrews says that the question in the zone of transition is whether decline will continue with a flattening of the curve—termed the late decline phase—or whether the forces of land use succession will prevail and an upturn of values will occur through new growth and renewal.

The late decline phase is apparent across the country in cities where buildings have been abandoned by owners. The South Bronx area of New York City is a notorious example of the late stage of decline.

Renewed growth can be set off by increased demand for existing properties with the same use. Atlanta witnessed such a renewal in the early to mid-1970s in both Peachtree Hills and Inman Circle. Peachtree Hills is an area of older small houses near the inner city. Initially, young middle-class couples saw this area as a desirable alternative to more expensive housing in the suburbs. The result was that as more couples bought and improved their 1940-vintage housing, the value of all the improvements in the area began to increase. The same phenomenon occurred in Inman Circle, an area of early 1900s houses. Much of the housing stock was totally dilapidated. The neighborhood was surrounded by a slum. As initial units in Inman Circle were renovated, other buyers began to move in, attracted in part by the inner-city location and the charm of older architecture. The result in both cases was that latecomers had to pay higher prices as the renewal accelerated. The lesson of land use succession is that timing is very important in real estate decision making.[9]

An alternative occurrence in the renewed growth phase is for different land uses to begin to compete for sites in a given area. This trend is often observed in the encroachment of commercial facilities into a residential area. One example is the conversion, or removal, of old houses for office use on Guadalupe Street between Seventh and Tenth streets in Austin, Texas. Another is the conversion of transient hotels to owner-occupied condominiums in Miami Beach as tourism has declined. In Hawaii some hotels changed to condominiums and remained hotels, showing that ownership as well as use may change.

In general, land use succession has two sources. First, a change in land use can take place as the result of competition from outside, as when an oil company outbids a residential purchaser for a home. Second, if a building no longer has the attributes desired in the market

[9]Obviously, **gentrification** is more widespread than Atlanta. The general movement initiated by increased energy costs, higher new home prices, etc., can be seen throughout the country.

F I G U R E 3-5   *The look of land use succession: Raleigh, North Carolina*

because of changes in design or in buyer perceptions, a shift to another use may take place.[10]

Land use succession theory can be understood in conjunction with situs theory. In situs theory, if a linkage is altered, the entire neighborhood may change. For real estate this change can be as slight as the renting of one house in a previously 100 percent owner-occupied neighborhood. It may be the construction of a high rise in an area of low-rise buildings, precipitating the construction of a series of high-rise buildings. The interrelationship of politics, law, social values, and economics cannot be dismissed as superficial in its effect on land use and location decisions. We discuss these issues shortly.[11]

The most obvious place to see land use succession, for most of us, is downtown. Buildings like the one shown on the left in Figure 3-5 are a familiar sight in the central business district of many cities. Built in the late nineteenth and early twentieth centuries, now obsolete commercial buildings like the one shown here typically were solid brick masonry with wood roof and floor structures, were two to three stories high (with no elevator), and were long and narrow (because of competition for street

[10]*Today most urban land economists believe that age per se is not the dominant force; rather, they think that certain macroforces (such as transportation changes, changes in taste, etc.), combined with aging, explain neighborhood change and that* **regeneration** *is more likely than previously thought.*

[11]*Students interested in neighborhood succession may want to explore expanded discussions of household expectations, the arbitrage process, and filtering. Helpful readings in this area are (1) James T. Little, "The Dynamics of Neighborhood Change," in Donald Phares,* A Decent Home and Environment *(Cambridge, Mass.: Ballinger Publishing Co., 1977), and (2) C. L. Levin et al., "Neighborhood Change in the Seventies: Summary and Policy Implications," a working paper from the Institute for Urban and Regional Studies, Washington University, St. Louis, Missouri 63130.*

frontage). Today in their decline these old downtown store buildings are often occupied only on the ground floor and sometimes only in the front half. Tenants in unrenovated old store buildings like these usually pay low rent (sometimes $1 per square foot or less per year) and operate small businesses patronized by low-income, inner-city residents. The building on the left in Figure 3-5 is in the heart of the central business district of Raleigh, North Carolina, located on Fayetteville Mall (formerly Fayetteville Street).

One block away on Fayetteville Mall, the building pictured on the right in Figure 3-5 typifies the renewal of old downtown properties. In Raleigh, although retail use declined in the CBD, demand for office space grew around the core of government buildings, the courts, and the major banks (see Figure 3-6). In the 1970s and early 1980s, law firms and other private investors began purchasing old commercial buildings for conversion to offices. Conversion typically requires new heating and air-conditioning systems; additional plumbing; modern floor, ceiling, and wall coverings; and fire exits. Structural work may range from moving interior partition walls to replacing roof and floor systems.

In many cities, as in Raleigh, North Carolina, the downtown nucleus of established government offices, courts, and financial institutions is the magnet pulling more new offices, hotels, and convention centers to the CBD. To make way for big new developments, many of the old, obsolete structures are demolished. Along with large new structures, some older buildings are renovated and/or converted. At its best, the mixture of old and new can make downtown more vibrant and exciting. Often renewal is accompanied by the return migration of middle-class professionals to older inner-city residential neighborhoods convenient to work and to cultural activities.

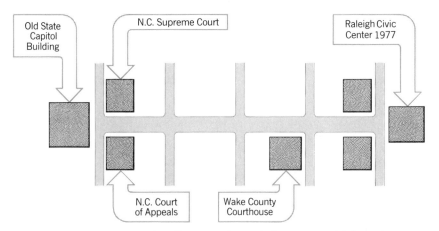

FIGURE 3-6   *Magnets for office space demand: downtown Raleigh, N.C.*

CREATIVITY—A POSSIBLE STEP BEYOND THE LIMITS OF EXISTING TRENDS: THE EXPERIENCE OF TWO DEVELOPERS

Rent, situs, and land use succession theories all help to explain the structure of cities and the reasons particular uses end up on particular sites, resulting in value. In economics, choices like land use and location decisions are presented as logical outcomes following a host of assumptions. In real life, theories help the analyst understand complex interrelationships in a variety of ways. For example, an analyst may be trying to estimate the value of a developed property, using past financial statements (probably unaudited and possibly incomplete); theory is a testing tool with which the analyst questions the *logic* underlying those historical numbers in the marketplace. When the analyst looks at properties similar to the subject, trying to arrive at a value estimate of the subject based on comparable rents or selling prices, theory again helps the analyst put a value on differences in location. These differences, when quantified, can be used as adjustments to comparable rents or selling prices to indicate the value of the subject. Finally, theory is very useful when an analyst seeks to project future responses to trends observed today in the market.

Still, players should not use theories about land use in a way that stifles creativity. Theories are rational, but intuition and creativity are not. Two developers whose work went beyond theories are discussed next. Each had his own ideas about using urban space and was strong enough to turn the ideas into bricks and mortar. Let us first consider as background some classical notions about the motives of developers and their place in the market.

Although economists have revised the original classical economic model as propounded by Adam Smith in the eighteenth century, many of its precepts and assumptions have been carried through to the present day, especially in the form of the images, created by the popular press and politicians, of "capitalism" or the "free enterprise system." Remember that from the beginning Adam Smith's theory was a simplification of reality and that, in fact, a pure capitalistic system never existed, nor has any other "pure" economic system. The continued tinkering with the rules as applied to urban land highlights the difficulty of adequately explaining all the diverse forces that create the urban mosaic.

In theory, in a capitalist system a developer is motivated by profit. The profit motive, however, is tempered by the Judeo-Christian ethic of stewardship. This ethic is the major justification for the existence of private property.[12] In addition, again in theory, the developer is disciplined by the marketplace, based on the assumptions of an informed, sovereign consumer; full employment; and an acceptable distribution of

---

[12]*The student of comparative religions and philosophy will note that similar justifications for private property exist in most of the world's major religions. The important point for the real estate analyst is that society has control and decides on a particular system or version of "private property." If the system ceases to serve the society, it will be changed or replaced.*

income, mobility of resources, and a limited government to arbitrate disputes and provide for the health and safety of the citizens of a community.

The reality of real estate development, particularly in recent years, violates many of the assumptions of classical capitalism. Although developers continue to be motivated by profit—critics might say greed—many of the checks in the system have disappeared—if they ever existed to begin with. By way of illustration, again let's consider the central business district of almost any large, older American city in the decline stage. In many instances, large pockets within the CBD were allowed to deteriorate, documenting that the stewardship function was subordinated to the economic idea that profit must be sufficient to offset the risks of development or redevelopment. The risk in doing downtown development increased primarily because the assumptions of full employment and an acceptable income distribution were violated. The urban poor often were concentrated in and around the city centers. These citizens, unable to participate fully in the capitalist system, understandably sought government redress of their ills. (The level of success achieved by government programs is considered in Part 9.)

Furthermore, although CBDs usually have many property owners, the major holdings tend to be concentrated in the hands of a few major financial institutions and wealthy individuals. Real estate markets are inefficient compared to other economic markets because of some of their unique characteristics, particularly the large unit size of individual properties and the complex information required to play the real estate game. As a consequence, the classical tenets of capitalism do not always operate to protect the public interest or to ensure the continued vitality of the heart of a city, the CBD.

Owing to some of the recognized limitations of the capitalistic system, the role of government (municipal, state, and federal) has greatly expanded in many cities: as a regulator of real estate activities, as an agent to redress social inequities and problems, as a police force to deal with increasing problems of crime, as a force attempting to revitalize the economics of the downtown, and as a landowner in its own right. These functions of government are far more extensive than those set out in classical economic theory as necessary in a healthy capitalist system. Collectively, these roles of government represent the emergence of the political system as a powerful force that creates rules under which the economic system operates.

Two of America's most successful developers of downtown areas, James Rouse and John Portman, have recognized the limitations of the economic system, which basically assumes a large number of small-scale developers mechanistically responding to signals in the marketplace, and have boldly forged their own roles in the mixed economic-political marketplace that exists in many large American cities today. The activities of

Rouse and Portman are summarized to illustrate that a group of developers emerging in large cities and small towns throughout the nation are using vision, ingenuity, and innovative financing in cooperation with the political system to alter historic patterns of urban development. Although some observers might argue with the results, there is little doubt that creative endeavors are reshaping our cities.

JAMES ROUSE

A native of Maryland, James Rouse became active in urban issues in the early 1950s, serving on a variety of local housing and planning boards in Baltimore and nationally with various federal agencies. Rouse's initial financial successes, however, were in mortgage banking and development of many regional shopping malls, primarily in suburban areas. During the social upheaval of the late 1960s, Rouse became aware that the economic system that had allowed real estate development firms like the Rouse Company to prosper was the same system that had permitted the decay of urban areas. And so, beginning with the planned new community of Columbia, Maryland, the Rouse Company took the new approach of designing and developing projects to meet what it saw as the spatial needs of human beings instead of simply submitting to the impersonal economic forces that had led to suburban concentrations typical of much of America's manufactured landscape.

Over the past two decades, Rouse has continued to practice his philosophy, with increasing emphasis on the potential of downtowns to enrich human life. In a *Time* magazine cover story he said, "The only legitimate purpose of a city is to provide for the life and growth of its people." To which he added, "Profit is the thing that hauls dreams into focus."[13]

The physical expression of his beliefs is a series of projects the Rouse Company has undertaken, with political and financial support from a number of cities, to create imaginative, festive, urban marketplaces that attract people back downtown. These markets are also designed to serve as a catalyst for other downtown development where traditional economic analysis might suggest none was justified. Baltimore's Harborplace, Boston's Faneuil Hall (see Figure 3-7), and Philadelphia's Gallery at the Market East are just a few examples of successful downtown projects developed by the Rouse Company.

James Rouse has retired as president of the Rouse Company and has established a smaller company, Enterprise Development, to pursue similar but smaller projects in conjunction with local developers. He "won the game" in real estate development and can now choose to play only in

---

[13]Michael Dewarest, "He Digs Downtown," Time, August 24, 1981, pp. 42–52.

FIGURE 3-7   *Faneuil Hall, Boston*

the most creative and challenging markets. Rouse is not bound by market studies of what is; rather, he seeks to determine what can be.

Waterside, an urban marketplace planned for the waterfront of Norfolk, Virginia, is the new company's first major project. It is innovative in that the city not only will absorb a great deal of the up-front costs and risks of the project, but will also earn a percentage of any profits. In effect, government itself becomes a player in the capitalistic game of real estate development. Such an incentive may be what cities need to make them work again.

JOHN PORTMAN

Whereas Rouse has created vibrant new marketplaces in old cities and has induced cities to participate as entrepreneurs, John Portman has presented a new view of constructed space. Beginning as an architect, Portman had a view of "space for people," unencumbered by restrictive traditions. When others refused to give physical reality to his ideas, he became a developer and created the space himself. Portman is famous for his hotels, which are dramatic, self-contained, and entertaining—among them the Hyatt Regency and Peachtree Center Plaza in Atlanta, the Hyatt Regency O'Hare in Chicago, and the Hyatt in San Francisco. His hotel interiors were revolutionary in that lobbies sometimes were as high as the building itself, giving the impression of vast open space exposing levels of diverse activities (bars, restaurants, glass elevators, the hotel lobby), all of which is on view as if in some gigantic ant colony. Portman proved that exciting design can create a market for space.

Interestingly, Portman is sometimes criticized today for his self-contained, inward-looking structures, which supposedly ignore the impact of the structure on the larger urban area. In particular, the high-rise Renais-

FIGURE 3-8 *Renaissance Center, Detroit*

sance Center (see Figure 3-8) in Detroit with its offices and stores has been cited as not conforming with the low-income population surrounding it. Perhaps someday we will see a developer of sufficient vision and talent to do for large urban areas what Portman has done for interior structural design. The technological capacity for three-dimensional, computer-aided architectural design is still relatively new, and the 1990s may well witness new forms in human interaction with constructed space.

SUMMARY Economics can be viewed as the science which studies human behavior as a relationship between ends and scarce means which have alternative uses. Lifetime students of real estate will find that the central premise of most real estate decisions will be deciding between alternative uses or investments. A good grasp of economics provides analytical tools useful in real estate analysis.

Spatial economics is economics applied to defined spaces, for example, to regions of a country, cities, neighborhoods, and, ultimately, individual parcels of land. Regional and urban economics are useful to real estate participants—investors, developers, lenders, planners—as a way of understanding economic forces at work in a given territory. Most analysts want to predict what will happen over some future period in relation to proposed investments. Identifying economic cycles and trends in the relevant area is one step in making decisions as to how to allocate resources. These are decisions that affect us all, from the small scale—whether to buy ten shares of common stock in a publicly traded home-building company or put the same amount in a money market fund—to the large scale—whether to vote yes to a multimillion dollar bond issue to expand a regional airport.

In focusing on places, regional and urban economics highlight a fifth factor of production—transportation, or the cost of movement. This factor and the other four (land, labor, capital, and management skill) combine to create the built environments we know, particularly the cities.

Urban land economics takes the study of defined spaces down to individual land use decisions. The three theoretical building blocks of urban land economics are rent, situs, and succession theories. With regard to rent theory, in urban economics the emphasis is on total economic activity in the urban framework. In urban land economics, the emphasis is on the aggregated allocation of land to various uses in a city. Situs theory has a microfocus. It views the relationship of a specific land use on a specific parcel of land to the total urban environment. This approach is broad but narrowly focused. Situs theory is an approach that can link all the various disciplines of spatial economics. It also provides an organized approach to analyzing individual real estate decisions.

Economic forces are dynamic, not static, and land use succession theory emphasizes change as it occurs in the life cycle of neighborhoods. It is to the advantage of real estate participants to recognize change at all levels of the economy, from the national to the city to the neighborhood level, and to be able to relate signs of change to decisions about specific pieces of real estate. The point is obvious; but opportunities are often overlooked, and risks go unrecognized when people fail to notice the small signs of change taking place around them. Situs theory draws attention to the link between a piece of real estate and its environment; land use succession theory adds emphasis on change within neighborhoods.

Because real estate is inherently site-specific, with each site possessing many unique attributes, no theory can capture the full range of forces that gives an urban site its value. The use of economic theories and models in isolation from other social, demographic, historical, geographic, and political influences gives a useful though incomplete view of real estate dynamics.

In recent years, the role of government in real estate has grown significantly, particularly in inner cities, adding another factor to decision making. It is important to remember that the real estate market is governed by a set of socially defined rules. It should also be recognized that the rules of the game can be changed if society's best interests are not served. Local, state, and federal government policy represent the political mechanism for enforcing change.

In this regard, what are appropriate public policy goals? Should government support (1) maximization of business profits, (2) maximization of real incomes, (3) improvement in the quality of life, or (4) re-distribution of income (wealth), or a combination of these? Are these various goals inherently contradictory? We return to these questions in Part 9. Let us note here at the end of our discussion of economic forces that politics, law, and social values are all expressed in our economic system. Real estate decision makers should never ignore them. Perhaps in a world where the rules are changing, developers gifted with the insight and persistence to account for public policy objectives, rather than to respond only to market demands, will have the greatest creative opportunity to enhance the value of urban space. A few ideas to stimulate your creativity are presented in Box 3-1.

3-1
MARKET SHIFTS
IN THE 1990S

The domestic real estate revolution of the 1980s took place in the areas of portfolio analysis and asset management. However, dramatic changes in the flow of capital into real estate throughout the world will make "globalization" the watchword of the 1990s. This trend has become apparent in the last five years and will continue to be a major force in the marketplace through the 1990s. Here's one view of a few of the positives and negatives which U.S. investors seeking to expand in Europe will face:

Positives

- The European economy is large and growing.
- Europe is where the United States was 20 years ago in terms of a structural shift from manufacturing to service.
- European markets aren't overbuilt, and strict land use regulations should keep that from happening.
- U.S. developers may have something to offer the market: closer attention to tenant services, quality product, and especially higher construction technology.
- U.S. investors are comfortable with innovative financial structures and can bring this creativity to the marketplace.

Hurdles and Hassles

- The ability to get control of sites and win development approval is even more critical in Europe than in the United States.
- The approval process is long, arduous, and very expensive.
- Sites are very rare.
- Although no one wants to talk about them, political payoffs and other extraordinary costs to intermediaries are not uncommon.

■ Cultural and language barriers are very high.

■ Legal, accounting, tax, and currency costs and risks present massive barriers to successful development.

■ Labor costs are high, and unions are very strong.

Source: "Emerging Trends in Real Estate: 1990," by Real Estate Research Corporation, 72 West Adams, Chicago, Ill. 60603.

IMPORTANT TERMS

Agglomeration economics

Bid rent curve

Complementary land use associations

Establishment

Gentrification

Land use succession theory

Linkage

Prisoner's dilemma

Regeneration

Rent theory

Site rent

Situs

Situs theory

REVIEW QUESTIONS

3.1   Distinguish between urban economics and urban land economics.

3.2   Define situs. Why does "environment" refer to more than just physical surroundings?

3.3   What does rent theory seek to explain? What are the shortcomings of rent theory?

3.4   How does the idea of a life cycle relate to land use succession theory?

3.5   In the central business district, a 90-year-old, three-story brick store building, currently with only the ground floor rented, is purchased by two accountants and an attorney who intend to remodel it completely for offices. At what stage is this structure in its life cycle?

3.6   Of rent theory, situs theory, and land use succession theory, which gives the most recognition to change taking place in the environment? To the structure of cities? To groups of similar land uses?

3.7   An investor considers buying into a syndicate that will own a 60,000-square-foot warehouse in a new industrial park. What does situs theory offer to help the investor make a decision?

3.8 How can land use succession theory be used by the investor in Question 3.7?

3.9 In what ways does government (city, county, state, or federal) interact with land use in the central business district of our cities, particularly older cities?

3.10 Of the three major theories of urban space, which comes closest to explaining the downtown developments of John Portman and James Rouse? In what ways do the theories fail to explain these two visionary developers?

REFERENCES

Alonso, William. "Location Theory." In John Friedmann and William Alonso, eds., *Regional Development and Planning, A Reader*. Cambridge, Mass.: MIT Press, 1964, p. 83.

Arnold, Alvin L., and Jack Kusnet. *The Arnold Encyclopedia of Real Estate*. Boston: Warren, Gorham and Lamont, 1978.

Barlowe, Raleigh. *Land Resource Economics*. 4th ed. Englewood Cliffs, N.J.: Prentice Hall, 1985.

Bish, Robert L., and Hugh O. Nourse. *Urban Economics and Policy Analysis*. New York: McGraw–Hill, 1975, Chaps. 3 and 4.

Corgel, John B., and Halbert C. Smith. *Real Estate Perspectives*. Homewood, Ill.: Irwin, 1987.

Daniel, Helen I., and Ronald K. Wills. *Case Studies in Real Estate*. Englewood Cliffs, N.J.: Prentice Hall, 1990.

Ely, Richard T., and George S. Wehrwein. *Land Economics*. Madison: University of Wisconsin Press, 1964, Chaps. 2 and 3. (Originally published by Macmillan, 1940.)

Ficek, Edmund F., Thomas P. Henderson, and Ross H. Johnson. *Real Estate Principles and Practices*. 4th ed. Columbus, Ohio: Merrill, 1987.

Greer, Gaylon E., and Michael D. Farrell. *Contemporary Real Estate: Theory and Practice*. Hinsdale, Ill.: Dryden Press, 1983.

Haggett, Peter. *Locational Analysis in Human Geography*. New York: St. Martin's Press, 1966.

Heilbrun, James. *Urban Economics and Public Policy*. 3rd ed. New York: St. Martin's Press, 1987.

Hines, Mary Alice. *Principles and Practices of Real Estate*. Homewood, Ill.: R. D. Irwin, 1976.

Hoover, Edgar M. *The Location of Economic Activity*. New York: McGraw–Hill, 1963.

Institute for Business Planning Research and Editorial Staff. *Real Estate Deskbook*. 5th ed. Englewood Cliffs, N.J.: Institute for Business Planning, 1977.

Lawrence, Richard L. *The Selection of Retail Locations*. New York: McGraw–Hill, 1958.

Levine, Mark Lee. *Real Estate Fundamentals*. St. Paul, Minn.: West Publications, 1971.

Mandelker, Daniel R. *Managing Our Urban Environment: Case, Text and Problems*. 2nd ed. New York: Bobbs–Merrill, 1971.

Mills, Edwin, and Bruce Hamilton. *Urban Economics.* 4th ed. Glenview, Ill.: Scott, Foresman and Co., 1989.

Nourse, Hugh O. *Regional Economics.* New York: McGraw–Hill, 1968, Chap. 4.

Pearson, Karl G., and Michael Litka. *Real Estate Principles and Practices.* 3rd ed. Columbus, Ohio: Grid Inc., 1980.

Ratcliff, Richard U. *Real Estate Analysis.* New York: McGraw–Hill, 1961.

Richardson, Harry W. *Urban Economics.* Hinsdale, Ill.: Dryden Press, 1978.

Ring, Alfred A., and Jerome Dasso. *Real Estate: Principles and Practices.* 11th ed. Englewood Cliffs, N.J.: Prentice Hall, 1989.

Shenkel, William M. *Modern Real Estate Principles.* Dallas, Tex.: Business Publications, 1980.

Sirmans, C. F., and James B. Kau. *Real Estate.* New York: McGraw–Hill, 1985.

Smith, Wallace F. *Urban Development: The Process and the Problems.* Berkeley: University of California Press, 1975, Chaps. 3 and 6.

Unger, Maurice A., and George R. Karvel. *Real Estate: Principles and Practice.* 7th ed. Cincinnati, Ohio: South-Western, 1983.

United Nations. *Demographic Yearbook.* New York: United Nations, current years.

United Nations. *The World Population Situation in 1970–1975 and Its Long-Range Implications.* United Nations Department of Economic and Social Studies Report No. 56. New York: United Nations, 1974.

Wofford, Larry E. *Real Estate.* 2nd ed. New York: Wiley, 1986.

World Population Growth and Response 1965–1975: A Decade of Global Action. Washington, D.C.: Population Reference Bureau, 1976.

Yeates, Maurice. *The North American City.* 4th ed. San Francisco.

PERIODICALS

American Real Estate and Urban Economics Association Journal
International Real Estate Journal
The Journal of Real Estate Research
Real Estate Forum. New York: Real Estate Forum, Inc. (monthly)
Real Estate Issues. Chicago: National Association of Realtors (semiannually)
Real Estate Review. Boston: Warren, Gorham and Lamont (quarterly)

NEWSLETTERS

Real Estate Newsline, Los Angeles, Calif.: Leventhal and Company (monthly)

Recent Research Results. Washington, D.C.: U.S. Department of Housing and Urban Development (monthly)

NEWSPAPERS

Every major business publication (*Wall Street Journal, Newsweek, Barron's,* etc.) deals with real estate, as do all local newspapers. Given the importance of real estate and its interdisciplinary nature, it is hard to read anything that doesn't provide some kind of insight into the industry.

THE LEGAL ENVIRONMENT

R EAL ESTATE INTERESTS AND FORMS OF OWNERSHIP

In Part 1, we viewed real estate in an economic context. The central question there was how value in real estate is created, and the conclusion was that a key element in valuing real estate is its location. More precisely, real estate has value because of the uses to which it can be put, and its location is the critical element in determining those uses.

In Chapter 3, we illustrated the all-important role of government, with a focus on the dynamic connection between urban land economics and the rules of the game. We saw that the rules are changing even faster and that the impact of changing rules on value can be very dramatic. With this perspective clearly in mind, we are ready to examine the traditional basic elements of real estate ownership (Chapter 4) and real estate conveyance (Chapter 5).

In this chapter, we approach the question of use, which was so central to Chapters 1–3, from a slightly different perspective. We now inquire into the mechanics by which interests in land can be created and transferred. These are the formal rules of the game and, consequently, an important part of the framework for decision analysis.

Real estate law is discussed not from the point of view of the attorney, because that is not the focus of this book, but rather with two other objectives in mind:

- To explain basic legal concepts relating to land ownership and transfer that should be understood by a business person or investor who is negotiating a real estate transaction or facing a decision about how to use or dispose of real estate;

- To illustrate some of the unique investment advantages of real estate—in particular, the ability to divide a parcel of real estate into a number of separate physical and legal interests, each attractive to a different participant in the investment process.

As the subjects in this chapter and the next are discussed, it will be apparent that the features that make real estate a unique asset—its fixed location and its long life—are also the critical elements in determining its legal characteristics.

This chapter is divided into three parts. First, we examine real estate itself to determine precisely what is owned in a physical sense. Next, we identify the different types of legal interests that can exist in a parcel of real estate. Finally, we discuss the kinds of entities that are utilized in the ownership of real estate interests.

In both Chapters 4 and 5, our goal is not to train a lawyer. These chapters provide a survey of the issues covered in statutory and case law that are relevant for the real estate decision maker. This is the amount of law you need to know to think as a player and to *use legal counsel effectively*.[1]

Remember as you read the next two chapters that (1) real estate law has evolved over a long period of time, and (2) unlike the Uniform Commercial Code which governs commercial transactions throughout the country, each state has its own real estate rules, and the differences among states can be significant. In this text, we focus on the rules dealing with the major issues common to all or at least many states. Where the evolution is still in process, we examine the relevant history. Where rules vary dramatically from state to state, we note the major differences. Still, this is a general introduction, and many of the more successful players of the real estate game have chosen to supplement this text with a real estate law course in the state where their activities are concentrated.

PHYSICAL INTERESTS IN REAL ESTATE

First, let's look at real estate itself, that is, the physical asset. A parcel of real estate consists of land plus whatever grows on the land (e.g., crops) plus whatever is permanently attached to the land (e.g., a building). In addition, a parcel of real estate includes all the space *above* and *below* the surface of the earth.

In legal parlance, property is the collection of jural relations that exists among people with regard to things. In our language, it is the set of rules that deals with ownership.

It is important to distinguish between **real property** and **personal property.** Real property, as noted earlier, is the land and all things attached to the land in a manner indicating that the intent was to make the attachment permanent. Personal property, on the other hand, is everything else that can be owned. Therefore, your car is personal property. When personal property (such as a roll of carpet) is permanently at-

---

[1] *If you wish to pursue any particular interest in greater detail, extensive references are provided at the end of this part.*

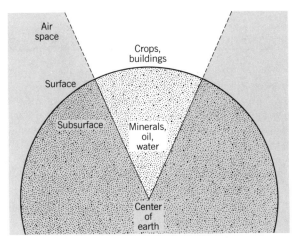

F I G U R E 4 - 1   *The three levels of real estate*

tached to a building (wall-to-wall carpeting is installed), it is called a **fixture** and becomes part of the real property.

So a parcel of real estate really consists of three different physical levels (see Figure 4-1).

■   A designated portion of the earth's surface with its crops and attachments (see page 132 for a discussion of how the earth's surface is measured). When the land borders natural waters, certain water rights may be acquired.

■   Above-surface space (i.e., **air space**) extending from the surface of the earth to some distance in space.

■   Subsurface space within an area circumscribed by lines drawn from the surface boundaries of the land to the center of the earth (the subsurface space forming an inverted cone).

Each of these physical interests may be utilized or possessed separately from the others. For example, X owns all the physical interests in a parcel of real estate called Blackacre. He may transfer to Y certain rights to possess or use the space beneath the surface of Blackacre (i.e., the subsurface rights), and he may transfer to Z ownership of the space above the surface of Blackacre (i.e., the air space). (See Boxes 4-1 and 4-2.)

WATER RIGHTS

Ownership of land bordering natural waters (lakes, rivers, or oceans) may or may not extend to land under the waters and may or may not

4-1

SUBSURFACE RIGHTS

Why would a person want *subsurface rights* in real estate that are separate and distinct from surface rights? One reason would be to remove minerals such as coal, oil, or gas. Another would be to put something such as a pipeline or subway under the ground. The general rule is that the owner of subsurface rights in land may remove anything from it that he wishes, subject to the following restrictions:

- Any limits imposed under an agreement with the owner of the surface rights.

- Government regulations with respect to zoning and mining practices (e.g., laws barring strip mining).

- Limitations imposed by the common law (e.g., the rule that land may not be excavated to the point of depriving adjacent properties of their natural support, which might cause buildings on those properties to collapse).

include the right to use the waters. The rules are complicated and vary in different parts of the country, summarized as follows.

❏ **RIPARIAN RIGHTS.**   The rights of an owner whose land borders a river, stream, or lake are governed in some states by the common-law doctrine of **riparian rights.** The doctrine of riparian rights permits the owner to use the water as he sees fit, subject only to the limitation that the owner may not interrupt or change the flow of the water or contaminate it. If the river, stream, or lake is nonnavigable, the owner of bordering land has title to the land under the water to the center of the waterway. However, in the case of navigable waters, the landowner's title runs only to the water's edge, with the state holding title to the land under the water. The reason for the distinction is that a navigable waterway is considered the same as a public highway.

❏ **PRIOR APPROPRIATION.**   On the Pacific coast and in western states where water is scarce, the common-law doctrine of riparian rights has been replaced by legislative law establishing the rule of **prior appropriation.** Under this rule, the right to use natural water is controlled by the state rather than by a landowner (except for normal domestic use). In prior appropriation states, the first user has priority but must obtain a permit from the state on showing of a need for the water. Title to the land under the water is generally subject to the same rules as in riparian rights states.

4-2
USING AIR SPACE

The right to use air space (air rights) is especially valuable in prime downtown locations where space is very expensive. In such areas, air rights may be available above railroad rights-of-way, highways, school buildings, post office buildings, and other low-rise structures. One of the most dramatic examples of the use of air space is the Pan Am Building in New York City. The Penn Central Railroad originally owned all the physical interests at that location; it utilized the subsurface to operate trains and the surface (plus a limited amount of air space) for Grand Central Terminal. It leased all the remaining air space for 99 years to a development company that built the Pan Am Building. A necessary part of the lease of the air space included "support rights," which permitted the developer to place columns on the surface and subsurface that support the building.

When a municipal zoning ordinance prohibits buildings above a designated height, air space above the zoning ceiling will have no economic value. However, in order to encourage construction, some municipalities permit a developer to "transfer" air rights from one location (where additional construction would be permitted) to another (where it would not). In this way, desirable space can be developed even though overall building density in the neighborhood or municipality remains within permitted levels. Air rights eligible for transfer are known as "transferable development rights" or TDRs.

Note that an owner of real estate does not have *exclusive* control of the air space above the land parcel. Airplanes, for example, are not "trespassing" when they cross air space sufficiently far above the earth. However, when air traffic causes damage to the surface, the landowner may be entitled to damages. Consider the following story reported by United Press International on March 26, 1982.

Jet's Boom Kills Pigs; $26,000 is Awarded

DELANO, Tenn., March 26 (UPI)—Betty Davis reluctantly accepted a $26,000 settlement in her suit charging that a low-flying Air Force Phantom jet cracked a sonic boom over her farmhouse, hammering the fillings out of her teeth, killing 61 pigs, and blowing her home off its foundations.

Mrs. Davis, whose family had demanded $2 million in damages from the Air Force, accepted the out-of-court settlement Thursday but said what she really wanted was never to see another low-flying Phantom jet again.

❏ **LITTORAL RIGHTS.** A special doctrine applies to land that borders large lakes and the oceans. Referred to as **littoral rights,** ownership of such land permits use of the waters without restriction; however, title extends only to the mean (average) high-water mark. All land on the waterside of this mark is owned by the government.

LEGAL INTERESTS IN REAL ESTATE

Real property—that is, the physical entity itself—is comprised of the three separate facets of surface, subsurface, and air space. The individual may have an ownership interest in any of these, in two out of three, or in all three. But of just what does ownership consist?

OWNERSHIP AS A BUNDLE OF RIGHTS

In Anglo-American law, real estate ownership is most often viewed as consisting of a "**bundle of rights.**" This includes the rights of (1) **possession,** (2) **control,** (3) **enjoyment,** and (4) **disposition.**

- The *right of possession* refers to occupancy and includes the right to keep out all others.

- The *right of control* deals with the right to alter the property physically.

- The *right of enjoyment* protects the current owner from interference by past owners or others.

- The *right of disposition* permits conveyance of all or part of one's bundle of rights to others.

All these rights are subject to limitation or restriction by governmental action. (See Part 9 for a discussion of zoning.) They are also subject to restrictions created or agreed to by prior owners that are binding on their successors. For example, owners in a residential community may desire that no parcel of land be used in the future for a commercial enterprise. Provided they comply with the legal rules, they can restrict future use of the land within reasonable limits.

The bundle of rights that constitute real estate ownership can be divided in a surprising number of ways. In general, these ownership rights can be classified into three major categories: (1) freehold estates, (2) possessory estates, and (3) nonpossessory interests. (See Figure 4-2.) These three general categories are described in the paragraphs that follow.

FREEHOLD ESTATES

Freehold (ownership) **estates** represent the highest quality of rights associated with real property under our legal system. In general, the holder of such an estate may exercise the full bundle of rights that relate to real property, subject always to overriding public policy as expressed in statute law, court decisions, and governmental regulation. The freehold category includes three significant types of estates: (1) **fee simple,** (2) **defeasible fees,** and (3) **life estates.**

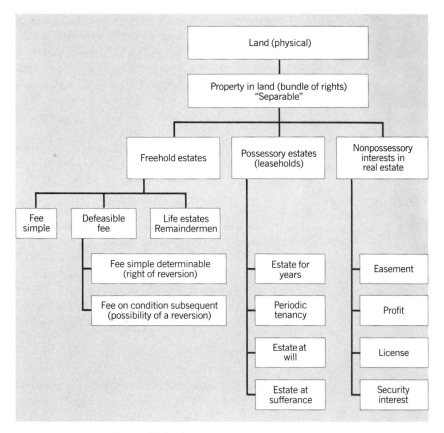

FIGURE 4-2 *Estates in land*

FEE SIMPLE ABSOLUTE

The most straightforward estate in land is known as the *fee simple absolute* or *fee simple,* and is often referred to simply as a *fee.* Fee simple ownership represents the most complete form of private property ownership recognized by our law. A fee simple interest creates an absolute and complete right of ownership for an unlimited duration of time with an unconditional right of disposition and use (i.e., the complete bundle of rights). Consequently, fee simple ownership is the most desirable interest in land. A fee simple interest may be transferred by using the words "to X, his heirs and assigns" in the instrument conveying the interest.

DEFEASIBLE FEES

A special kind of freehold interest, seen infrequently today, is the *defeasible fee,* that is, a fee simple subject to being defeated or terminated.

This type of interest is also known as a *qualified fee*. In plain terms, this is a fee simple interest subject to certain conditions that, if not met, will cause the owner to lose his interest in the property. The conditions may be permanent, or they may continue for a specified number of years. The origin of defeasible fees goes back to the early English common law when land was virtually the sole significant source of wealth. By tying up land with defeasible fees (and other devices), large landholders sought to ensure that the land would remain in certain uses or "within the family" for generations to come—which, in fact, often has been the case.

Two kinds of defeasible fees are (1) **fee simple determinable** and (2) **fee on condition subsequent.**

❏ **FEE SIMPLE DETERMINABLE.**   A fee simple determinable is fee simple ownership that automatically will terminate on the happening (or failure to happen) of a stated condition. Such a fee is usually expressed by a conveyance "to X, his heirs and assigns, *so long as they use the property for Y purpose.*" Provided that X does, in fact, use the property for Y purpose, he has all the bundle of rights associated with fee simple ownership (except, of course, the right to change the use). If the use is changed, X's title terminates, and the property reverts to the grantor or to his heirs if he is no longer living. (Thus, the grantor has a possibility of a reversion.)

A few years ago, the New York courts were faced with a case in which land had been conveyed about 90 years earlier to a municipality "so long as the land is used as a railroad station." The grantor had desired to provide a site for the commuter railroad and wished to ensure that the land would not be used for any other purpose. With changing times, the railroad discontinued service to the community, and the municipality sought to sell the land for another use. At that point, the heirs of the original grantor claimed that because the condition of use was no longer met, the land reverted to them. The court upheld their claim.

❏ **FEE ON CONDITION SUBSEQUENT.**   Just as with a fee simple determinable, a fee on condition subsequent creates an ownership interest that can be lost on the happening of a stated event or condition in the future. The typical phrasing in a conveyance of such a fee from Y to X would be "to X, his heirs and assigns, *but if* the land is used for the purpose of selling alcoholic beverages, Y may enter upon the land and regain title."

As in the case of a fee simple determinable, it is clear from such a conveyance that the bundle of rights associated with fee ownership is limited in one particular respect—the use to which the property may be put.

What is the difference between the two types of defeasible fees? In essence, it is a matter of the precise manner whereby title will be lost by an owner failing to comply with the condition. In the case of a fee simple determinable, title is automatically terminated when the condition is violated; by comparison, the grantor of a fee on condition subsequent must exercise his right of reentry before title is lost by the grantee. (Thus, he has a **right of reentry.**) These highly technical distinctions are normally of interest only to a real estate attorney; they are mentioned here to show that real estate is subject to legal rules that sometimes are centuries old and yet may still have relevance today.

The primary objection to defeasible fees is that they are *restraints on alienability* (transferability). Defeasible fees limit the transferability of real estate because a prospective purchaser, knowing he would lose the title if the condition were to be violated, would be reluctant to buy. Courts and legislatures care about free transferability because both economic and social development would be hindered if many parcels of real estate were tied up with ancient restrictions that prevented the most productive use of the property in today's world. Consider the parcel of real estate, referred to earlier, that could be used only as a railroad station even though no railroad continued to serve the particular community.

As a result of the dislike of defeasible fees, many state legislatures have passed laws providing that a defeasible fee automatically will become a fee simple after a certain number of years (e.g., 25 years) if it has not been terminated by that time. A court of law, called on to interpret a conveyance as either a fee simple or a defeasible fee, will favor the former interpretation because of the public policy against restraints on alienability.[2]

LIFE ESTATES

The life estate is an extremely common form of freehold estate and has a long history. (See Box 4-3.) In a life estate, the grantor conveys a fee simple interest to a grantee (usually a spouse or other family member) for a period measured by the lifetime of the grantee. A typical conveyance would be "to my wife X for her life and then to my son Y." In rare cases, the measuring lifetime may be that of a third party, for example, "to my son Y for the life of my wife X, and then to my daughter Z." As indicated by these conveyances, after the measuring lifetime has expired, title to the property automatically will go to another person. The subsequent interest is called a *remainder* (because it is what remains after the life interest expires), and the person who ultimately will receive it is called the **remainderman.** The person holding the life estate is the **life**

---

[2]*In older books, the fee tail is also mentioned at this point. Under a fee tail, which has been abolished in the United States, the property was always inherited by the elder male child. This feudal concept clearly would be detrimental to a "market" economy because it prevents transfers to those who may be better able to utilize property (both in their own and in society's interests).*

4-3 DOWER AND CURTESY RIGHTS (LIFE ESTATES)

Life estates were an early form of social security. When a landowner died in feudal England, his wife automatically received a one-third interest in all his real estate, whether or not such an interest was specifically conveyed to her by will. In this way, widows would not become a burden on the community. The life estate in feudal England was known as the *dower interest,* and the widow holding such interest was known as a *dowager,* a term that has come to mean an elderly lady of means. Under certain circumstances, a widower also had certain rights in his wife's estate. This was known as the *right of curtesy.*

The traditional concept of dower and curtesy has been abolished in almost all the United States and has been replaced in some states by a *homestead right* and in other states by a *statutory interest* (or statutory share). Under a homestead right such as that created by Florida law, a surviving spouse is entitled to a life estate in the couple's residence if title was held by the deceased spouse at his or her death and regardless of any other disposition made by the will of the deceased spouse.

Under the statutory interest approach, the surviving spouse has the right to claim an interest in the deceased spouse's estate even though the surviving spouse was cut out of the will or given less than a certain percentage of the estate. For example, the surviving spouse may be entitled to receive a one-third interest in all the property (real and personal) owned by the deceased at his or her death, regardless of any contrary provision in the will.

tenant, a term that can be confusing since it has nothing to do with a lease.

The life tenant may treat the property in all respects as would an owner in fee simple, subject only to two restrictions.

- *The life tenant must maintain the property in reasonably good condition in order to protect the interests of the remainderman.* The life tenant has a right to possess the property during the measuring lifetime but must act in a way to respect the future interests of the remainderman. For example, the family home that is left to the surviving spouse cannot be permitted to deteriorate to the point where it becomes uninhabitable and worthless to the remainder interest. Any act or omission by the life tenant that does permanent injury to the property or unreasonably changes its character or value constitutes *waste* and may be enjoined (prohibited) by a court as a result of a lawsuit brought by the remainderman.

- *Life tenants may convey the life interest to a third party but can convey no more than such interest.* Because a life estate is a freehold interest, it includes the right of disposition. However, no person can convey more than he or she owns. Consequently, the life tenant can sell only the life estate. Since the duration of a life estate is always unknown (because it will terminate on the death of a named person), it is not likely that anyone would pay a great deal for such an estate. For this reason, life estates normally are not used in commercial transactions.

Life estates are frequently described as freehold estates but not estates of inheritance. This is obviously so whenever the measuring life is that of the life tenant. Such an estate cannot be inherited by another since it will terminate on the death of the life tenant. But in the rare case where the measuring life may be of another person, the life estate will be inherited by the heirs of the life tenant.

POSSESSORY ESTATES: LEASEHOLDS

The holder of a freehold estate has *ownership* of the property. By comparison, the holder of a **possessory or leasehold estate** has *possession* of the property. Since possession is merely one of the bundle of rights associated with ownership, it is clear that when a leasehold interest is created, it represents a *separation* of the bundle of rights. The separation is into (1) a fee interest (the interest of the landlord, also called the *lessor*) and (2) a leasehold interest (the interest of the tenant, also called the *lessee*). The two interests in the property exist simultaneously.

- The tenant has the right to possession of the property, subject to the terms of the lease and for the duration specified in the lease.
- The landlord retains all the other ownership rights plus the right to regain possession when the lease expires (the *right of reversion*).

The ability to divide real estate into a fee and a leasehold interest offers enormous flexibility in putting together a transaction among several parties. Probably the greatest master of the technique of "slicing up" a parcel of real estate into various interests was the late William Zeckendorf, Sr. At different times, Zeckendorf referred to his technique as the *Hawaiian technique* (he claimed he thought of it while fishing in that state) or the *pineapple technique* (the initial single ownership interest in a parcel of land could be sliced up into a number of interests, just as a pineapple could be sliced into a number of sections). Whatever he called it, Zeckendorf was able to create complicated real estate interests that resulted in developments that otherwise might never have been built. A notable example is the United Nations Plaza building adjacent to the United Nations in New York City. In this development, three different fee interests plus a leasehold interest plus five mortgage interests were carved out of a single parcel of land. (Box 4-4 describes how it was done.)

In midtown Manhattan, next to the United Nations, stands a single structure that consists of a 6-story office building on top of which rise two 32-story residential towers. Begun in 1964, the project is a classic illustration of the late William Zeckendorf's *pineapple technique.* The project was originated by Zeckendorf's company, Webb & Knapp, but when it began its slide into bankruptcy, development was taken over by Alcoa Associates, a joint venture between Alcoa and Canadian interests.

The best way to visualize the various interests created in the building is to follow the transactions as they occurred.

- *Three fee interests.* The developer (Associates) originally owned the property in fee simple. The first step it took illustrates the fundamental operating principle that Zeckendorf followed, which was to minimize or eliminate entirely the need for any of his own cash in the transaction. Associates created two cooperative housing corporations, each to own one of the 32-story towers to be constructed above the office building. Associates then sold a fee simple interest in air space to each cooperative corporation. At that point, three separate fee interests had been created in the parcel of real estate. The price received for the two air space parcels was $38 million.

- *Leasehold interest.* To further reduce its cash requirements, Associates sold its fee interest (consisting of the land plus sufficient air space for the office building) to Equitable Life Assurance Society for $12 million. Simultaneously, Associates leased back the identical space from Equitable for a term of 99 years. This transaction is known as a *sale-leaseback.*

- *Leasehold mortgage.* Associates then obtained a loan of $3.5 million from Equitable secured by Associates' leasehold interest. This type of loan is called a *leasehold mortgage.* How could the leasehold interest be security for a loan? Associates anticipated making a substantial profit from the difference between the rent it would collect from office tenants and the rental (the *ground rent*) it would have to pay Equitable. This flow of income (anticipated for 99 years) was adequate security for a 27-year loan.

- *Four fee mortgages.* Since it was not likely that the cooperative apartment units could be sold without substantial financing, Equitable agreed to provide first mortgage financing to each of the cooperative corporations, and Associates agreed to provide financing secured by second mortgages.

- *Total of nine interests.* A total of nine different interests were created. Of these, three were fee interests, one was a leasehold interest, and five were security (mortgage) interests, consisting of a leasehold mortgage, two first fee mortgages, and two second fee mortgages (all of the fee mortgages covering the air space fee interests owned by the cooperative corporations). Associates raised a total of $53.5 million by selling off the two air space fee interests and mortgaging its leasehold interest. This probably came close to paying for the original land cost plus the cost of putting up the 6-story office building. Associates ended up (for very little cash investment) holding a 99-year leasehold of an office building in the heart of Manhattan.

A *leasehold interest* is created by a **lease,** which is usually in writing but is sometimes oral. A lease is unique because it is both a *conveyance* (i.e., it transfers the right to possession of real estate) and a *contract* (i.e., it creates rights and duties between the landlord and the tenant).

A primary feature of leasehold interests is that they are never for a perpetual term. Consequently, it is convenient to categorize leasehold interests according to their duration. The four categories are

- Estate for years
- Estate from period to period (periodic tenancy)
- Estate at will
- Estate at sufferance

ESTATE FOR YEARS

By far the most common type of leasehold interest is the **estate for years.** This type includes all leases with a fixed term—whether a residential lease for one year or a ground lease for 99 years. An estate for years will expire automatically at the end of the period designated, at which time the tenant's right of possession ends and possession reverts to the landlord. The lease, however, may grant renewal options to the tenant that, if properly exercised, will continue the leasehold for another designated term.

ESTATE FROM PERIOD TO PERIOD

This type of leasehold estate, also very common, is most often used for residential and small commercial properties. An **estate from period to period** is created whenever the lease specifies the amount of rent for a designated period but does not state a specified term for the lease.

For example, if a lease provides that rent shall be paid at the rate of $100 per month, a *month-to-month tenancy* is created. The tenant is entitled to possession and is obligated to pay rent until either landlord or tenant gives notice of intention to terminate the lease. The time of such notice and the form in which it must be given are usually determined by statute (e.g., either party may terminate the lease on 30 days' written notice, delivered personally or sent by certified mail to the other). Because this type of estate cannot assure the tenant of possession for any lengthy period, it is not normally used where a tenant, such as a retailer, must spend substantial sums to prepare the premises for use.

ESTATE AT WILL

An **estate at will** (or tenancy at will) is created by an oral agreement between landlord and tenant to the effect that the tenant may occupy the premises as long as it is convenient for both parties. Estates at will can create problems for both parties since no written instrument specifies the amount of rent or the rights or responsibilities of either party.

ESTATE AT SUFFERANCE

This rather unusual form of leasehold estate exists when a leasehold interest, whether for years, periodic, or at will, expires or terminates without the tenant vacating the property. In other words, the tenant continues to hold the premises at the sufferance of the landlord; this estate is called an **estate at sufferance.**

In theory, the landlord may dispossess the tenant at any time. However, as in the case of an estate at will, the landlord may have to give a prior period of notice.

THE LEASE

As already noted, the lease instrument is both a conveyance of a real estate interest (a leasehold) and a contract between landlord and tenant. The lease should be in writing for several reasons. First, a written lease helps avoid misunderstandings. It is much easier to recall the specific understanding on a particular point when a lease is in writing. Commercial and office leases, which may extend for 25 or more years and involve cumulative rentals in the millions of dollars, may run to as much as 100 pages.

Second, a lease may have to be in writing to be legally enforceable. In most states, leases with terms exceeding a certain length will be enforced by the courts only if they are evidenced in writing.

The requirements of a valid lease include the following:

- Names and signatures of legally competent parties
- Description of premises
- Amount of rent
- Term of the lease
- Commencement and expiration dates
- Rights and obligations of the parties during the lease term

A typical lease will include provisions covering the following matters. What areas are to be maintained by the landlord and which by the tenant? Who will pay utilities? Who will pay for property insurance and property taxes? It is possible that, as costs increase, the tenant, pursuant to a lease clause, will bear the increase (an **escalation clause**). (See Box 4-5). What improvements and alterations does the tenant have the right

4-5
TYPES OF
RENTAL
PAYMENTS

To a business person or investor, the rent provisions of a lease are critical. Types and manner of rental payments are limited only by the ingenuity of real estate professionals. The most common types are these:

- *Gross rental (gross lease).* A gross rental is one that covers operating expenses as well as the landlord's profit. Under a gross lease, the landlord, not the tenant, pays the costs of operating the premises. An apartment house lease is an example.

- *Net rental (net lease).* A net rental is one that represents the landlord's return on his investment and does not include operating expenses, which are paid by the tenant separately. The net lease is typically used in commercial leases of freestanding premises (e.g., a building occupied by a single retail tenant such as a supermarket). The tenant pays all operating expenses, in addition to the net rental.

- *Flat (fixed) rental.* A flat rental is a rental that is fixed and unchanging throughout the lease term. At one time, flat rentals were common even for long-term commercial leases, but because of periodic dramatic increases in the rate of inflation, these are now rather uncommon. An apartment house lease typically calls for a fixed rental since the term is usually short.

- *Graduated rental.* A graduated rent is one that moves up or down in a series of steps during the lease term. A step-up rental involves an increase at each stage. A step-down rental involves a decrease in each stage.

- *Escalator (index) rental.* An escalator rental is a type of rental that moves up or down in accordance with an outside standard (e.g., the consumer price index) or an inside standard (e.g., operating costs of the particular property). Rental escalation has now become very common in office and commercial leases as a means of shielding the landlord against the effects of rapid inflation. Escalation clauses are also beginning to appear in apartment leases.

- *Percentage rental.* A percentage rental is an extremely common form of rental payment in retail store leases. The tenant normally pays a minimum fixed rent plus an additional rent equal to a percentage of sales over a fixed amount. The tenant's gross sales rather than net profits is almost always used as a standard in order to avoid disputes about how net profits are to be determined. In addition, gross sales are more likely to keep pace with inflation than are net profits. Consequently, a percentage rental based on sales is a better inflation hedge for the landlord than is one based on profits.

to make? What happens in the event that the tenant cannot pay? What happens if the property is condemned by the government under eminent domain? What happens at the end of the lease period? Does the tenant have the right to assign or sublease the premises? If so, at what price and under what terms?

CHANGING CONCEPT OF LEASES

The concept of a lease has changed in an interesting and dramatic way over the past 20 years. For centuries, the courts and legislatures always regarded a lease as primarily a conveyance, with the contractual aspect purely secondary. As a result, a very dim view was taken of tenant efforts to hold back rent when landlords failed to carry out their obligations, such as providing heat in the wintertime.

The courts' view was that rent was the consideration for the conveyance of the right to possession. Consequently, the rent had to be paid regardless of the landlord's failure to perform his contractual duties. The reason for this seemingly harsh view was that leases originally were primarily for farmland, where the farmer operated as a totally independent businessman, putting up his own house and farming the land as an entrepreneur—quite a difference from a tenant who lives in a studio apartment in a 25-story apartment house.

Over the past two decades, however, a very sharp shift has taken place toward emphasizing the contractual aspects of the lease. This is the legal rationale for such phenomena as *rent strikes,* where tenants hold back rent payments until landlords perform in accordance with the lease. In a broader context, this shift has been part of the consumer revolution wherein state and federal statutes protect the rights of purchasers and users of property.

NONPOSSESSORY INTERESTS

A third category of interests that can be created in real estate are designated **nonpossessory interests** or rights—that is, none of these rises to the "dignity" of an interest that carries with it ownership or possession. The four common types are (1) easements, (2) profits, (3) licenses, (4) and security interests (see Figure 4-2).

❑ **EASEMENTS.** An **easement** is an interest in real estate that gives the holder the right to use but not to possess the real estate. A common form of an easement is a right-of-way—that is, the right to cross over the land of another. Another is the electric utility or telephone easement, which permits a utility company to place poles at designated points on the land and run wires between them. Because an easement involves some restriction or limitation of the right of ownership, land subject to an easement is said to be *burdened* with an easement, and, to some extent, its value may be diminished.

There are two general types of easements. The first is the **easement appurtenant,** which attaches to the land and is not a personal right. The second type of easement is an **easement in gross,** which does not benefit a property. Instead, it benefits the individual or institution that owns it.[3]

Some real estate is subject to an easement that is unconnected with any other parcel of land, that is, an easement that is personal to the individual or institution benefiting from it. Electric utility and telephone easements are examples. Easements in gross usually are not assignable and terminate upon the death of the easement owner. For example, if the railroad closed a section of railway, the easement would no longer exist and the owner of the land could use it as he or she saw fit.

An easement may be created in several ways.

❏ **EXPRESS EASEMENT.** An **express easement** is created by a writing executed by the owner of the *servient tenement* (the property subject to the easement). The writing may be called a *grant of easement* or similar title.

Consider two plots of land adjacent to one another. The deed, or document of title, to lot A gives its owner the right to cross over lot B in order to reach a public highway. In this situation, ownership of A (called the *dominant tenement*) includes as one of the bundle of rights of owner-

---

[3]*The clearest distinction we have found between an easement appurtenant and an easement in gross is from the fifth edition of the South Carolina Real Estate Commission.*

In Figure A, Lot 3 has a 30-foot roadway easement across Lot 1. This easement is appurtenant to and passes with Lot 3 regardless of whether Lot 3 expressly transfers the easement when Lot 3, the dominant estate, is sold. It also binds whoever may buy Lot 1 in the future whether or not the deed to Lot 1 refers to the easement. A common example of an easement appurtenant is the right to travel over another's property, party walls, and shared driveways. In a condominium, the rights to walk over the parking, to have utility lines running through the walls, or to have a sewer pipe running beneath the land surface are also examples of easements appurtenant. An easement appurtenant exists if there are two adjacent tracts of land owned by different parties. The tract over which easement runs is known as the servient tenement; the tract that is to benefit from the easement is known as the dominant tenement.

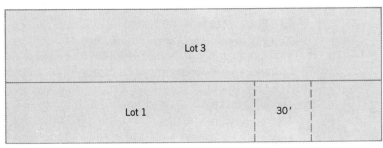

Highway

ship an easement appurtenant (i.e., an easement that accompanies ownership). B, which is burdened by the right of way, is the *servient tenement;* it is subject to an obligation that may or may not reduce its value in any significant way, depending on the location of the right of way and the use to which B is being put.

Remember, an easement appurtenant, being part of the bundle of rights of ownership, is not a personal right but attaches to the land (the legal phrase is *runs with the land*) and so is conveyed to subsequent owners of the dominant tenement.

Real estate may be subject to an express easement that is unconnected with any other parcel of land, that is, an easement personal to the individual or institution benefiting from it—in other words, an easement in gross. Electric utility and telephone easements would be an example. Other types of commercial easements in gross are railroad and pipeline rights of way. Thus, both an easement appurtenant and an easement in gross may be expressively created.

❏ **IMPLIED EASEMENT.**   An **implied easement** arises when the owner of a tract of land subjects one part of the tract to an easement (such as a right-of-way) that benefits the other part and then conveys one or both parts of the tract to other parties so that divided ownership results. In such a case, common law holds that an implied easement arises in favor of the *dominant tenement* and burdens the *servient tenement.*

❏ **EASEMENT BY NECESSITY.**   An **easement by necessity** is a special form of implied easement and arises when the owner of a tract subdivides or separates a part of the tract so that the severed part has no access to the outside world except across the balance of the tract. Under such circumstances and in order to permit the productive use of the isolated land, common law implies the right-of-way across the grantor's land to a public highway. Some states provide by statute that the owner of land lacking access to a public way may petition the courts to have a *cartway* condemned for his use. Again, the purpose is to encourage the development and use of land for the benefit of society in general. The concept is simple enough, but consider the problem raised in Box 4-6.

❏ **EASEMENT BY PRESCRIPTION.**   An **easement by prescription** arises when a stranger (i.e., one without ownership or possessory right) makes use of land for a prescribed period of time (e.g., 10 years) and does so openly and without pretense of having the true owner's consent. Under such circumstances, the use that was originally adverse (against the interest of the owner) may ripen into an easement that is recognized by law. This is similar to the process of acquiring title to land by adverse possession (discussed on pages 140–141). An example of a **prescriptive**

**4-6
RIGHT-OF-WAY
ACCESS
EASEMENT
DESTROYED
WHEN STATE
OPENS, THEN
CLOSES ROAD**

When an easement is created for a specific purpose, the easement will last only as long as the purpose remains in existence. But what if a lapsed purpose for an easement is revived? Should the defunct easement then return to life?

Landlocked Lot

In 1949, Richard and Elizabeth Duffell owned a lot in Montgomery, Alabama, that had no street access. At the time, the nearest street was Ann Street, but an extension of Spruce Street was planned that would bring it closer to the Duffells' lot than Ann Street. Their neighbors, the Bonners, accommodated the Duffells by selling them a 25-foot-right-of-way easement across their property. The deed of easement stated that "it is the purpose and intention hereof to provide a means of ingress and egress and space for water line and sewage to and from Ann Street or to and from the proposed extension of Spruce Street. . . ." The Spruce Street extension was completed in 1951, and use of the easement lying between Spruce and Ann streets was discontinued.

In the 1960s, Alabama began acquiring land in the area in connection with the construction of Interstate Highway 85. Spruce Street was closed to make way for an on-ramp. In order to regain local street access, Sasser, who now owned the Duffell property, sought the reactivation of the portion of the old easement running out to Ann Street.

Only One Easement

Unfortunately, Aronov, who now owned the Bonner property, had already leased the land over which the Ann Street portion of the easement ran. Aronov told Sasser to forget the easement, and litigation ensued. The trial court rejected Sasser's claim, and the matter went to the Alabama Supreme Court. There, the language of the easement was examined, particularly the stated purpose of providing ingress and egress "to and from Ann Street or to and from the proposed extension of Spruce Street." In the court's view, the use of the word "or" was evidence of an intent to create but one easement. These words plus the physical layout of the easement led the court to conclude that the easement was intended to provide access from the old Duffell property to the closest street.

Easement Extinguished by Halves

Sasser did not dispute the court's perceptions concerning the parties' intentions in creating the easement. He argued that there was nothing incompatible between these intentions and his claim that, when the Spruce Street extension was closed, an easement running out to Ann Street continued to exist. Against this argument, the court interposed the general rule to the effect that an easement given for a specific purpose terminates as soon as the purpose ceases to exist, is abandoned, or is rendered impossible of accomplishment. Upon completion of the Spruce Street extension, said the court, the purpose of the Ann Street portion of the easement ceased to exist, and that easement was forever extinguished. In like manner, once the Spruce Street extension was closed, the remaining portion of the easement was extinguished. [*Sasser* v. *Spartan Food Sys., Inc.,* 452 So. 2d 475 (Ala. 1984)].

Observation

If the purpose for which an easement is required may be accomplished in either of two ways, it is important, from the standpoint of the grantee, to word the easement to preclude the kind of one-two punch destruction of the easement seen here.

Source: Real Estate Law Report, published by Warren, Gorham, and Lamont (New York), 14:6 (November 1984), p. 1.

easement would be extended use by one neighbor of another neighbor's driveway, with the first neighbor openly claiming the "right" to such use.

PROFITS

A **profit** in land (technically known as *profit à prendre*) is the right to take a portion of the soil or timber or remove subsurface minerals, oil, or gas in land owned by someone else. A profit represents an interest in real property, and it must be in writing. The distinction between a profit and an easement is that an easement merely permits use of the property, whereas a profit involves a removal of part of the land. A profit may also be distinguished from a gas and oil or mineral *lease*. Such a lease requires the lessee to pay a royalty to the landowner calculated on the amount of natural resource taken.

LICENSES

A **license** is the right to go on land owned by another for a specific purpose. A license in most cases is merely a revocable privilege granted by the owner to another and does not represent an interest in real estate. Almost everyone frequently is a licensee. Whenever a ticket is purchased to attend a sports or other event in a stadium or hall, the individual is purchasing a license. Similarly, if the privilege of hunting or fishing on the lands of another is given, whether or not for a consideration, the hunter or fisherman is a licensee.

SECURITY INTERESTS

A final type of nonpossessory interest in real estate is the **security interest** (i.e., the interest of one holding a mortgage). Security interests are discussed in detail in Chapters 14 and 15. At this point, note only that the holder of a mortgage has a legal interest in real estate, but it will not develop into possession or ownership unless a default occurs under the terms of the mortgage (e.g., nonpayment of an installment when due), at which point the mortgage holder can exercise its rights to foreclose against the property. (The foreclosure procedure is covered in Part 5.)

LIENS AND DEED RESTRICTIONS

In some sense, liens and deed restrictions also create nonpossessory interests. The lien holder (lender) has certain rights, which are covered in detail in Part 5. Moreover, restrictions placed in a deed give certain rights to those who benefit from those restrictions, as explained further in Chapter 5.

FORMS OF OWNERSHIP

At this point, it should be clear that the following holds true.

- Real estate is really made up of three different elements: (1) *surface rights*, (2) *subsurface rights*, and (3) *air space* (called the *physical interests in real estate*).
- A variety of "shares" may be held in each of these physical interests in real estate, including (1) *ownership shares*, (2) *possessory shares*, and (3) *nonpossessory shares* (called the *legal interests in real estate*).

We will now discuss the five different ways of holding a legal interest in real estate (the five simple *forms of ownership*):

- Single ownership
- Tenancy in common
- Joint tenancy with right of survivorship
- Tenancy by the entirety
- Community property

Note that all but the first are known generally by the term *concurrent ownership* (i.e., ownership by more than one person). Concurrent ownership can be created because the bundle of rights is divisible. (See Figure 4-3.)

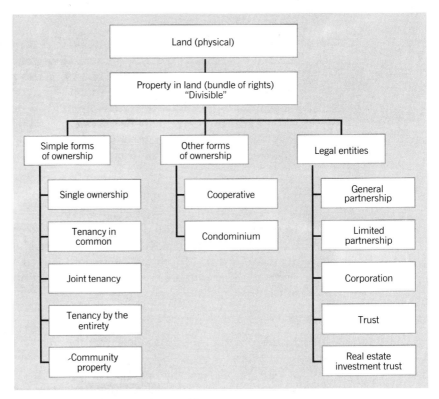

FIGURE 4-3   *Forms of ownership*

SINGLE OWNERSHIP

Single ownership of an interest in real estate is the simplest form of ownership, for no division of the bundle of rights is required. Residential properties and relatively small-scale business enterprises frequently are held by a single individual, whereas larger enterprises are frequently held by a single corporation or a single partnership. (Corporations, partnerships, and other vehicles for owning interests in real estate are discussed later in this chapter.) Overall, most real estate interests in the United States are held in single ownership.

TENANCY IN COMMON

The **tenancy in common** is the most frequently used form of concurrent ownership. When two or more persons hold as tenants in common (the term *tenants* as used here has nothing to do with a lease or leasehold interest), each has an individual interest in the entire property to the extent of his ownership share.

For example, three tenants in common will each own a one-third undivided share in the entire property rather than a specified one-third portion of the property. Although normally each tenant in common has the same share as his cotenants, this need not necessarily be the case; one of three cotenants may own a 40 percent undivided share, with each of the others owning 30 percent shares.

Each tenant in common may sell, mortgage, or give away his interest during his life and transfer it at death, just as though the entire property were owned in single ownership. The right of each tenant in common to possession of the property is subject to the right of his cotenants. Each has the right to an accounting of rents and profits (when the property produces income), and each is entitled to reimbursement by the others of monies he expends for necessary maintenance, repair, property taxes, and other expenses.[4] Any such reimbursement will be proportionate to each tenant's interest.

JOINT TENANCY

A **joint tenancy** is not the same as a tenancy in common; among other minor differences, one is very significant. The difference is the **right of survivorship,** which means that if any joint tenant dies, his interest automatically passes in equal shares to the remaining joint tenants.

For example, if A and B are joint tenants and A dies, title to her one-half undivided share automatically goes to B, who thereby becomes the sole owner of the property. If three joint tenants had owned the property and one died, each of the two survivors would take one-half of the deceased joint tenant's interest.

Because the survivorship feature runs contrary to the traditional pattern of devise and descent (inheritance), those wishing to enter into a joint tenancy must clearly specify this intent at the time they take title. Otherwise, a tenancy in common is presumed.

Although a joint tenant cannot devise his interest by will (since it passes automatically on death), he can sell or give away his interest during his lifetime, thus changing the joint tenancy to a tenancy in common.

TENANCY BY THE ENTIRETY

A **tenancy by the entirety** is a joint tenancy between husband and wife. The tenancy carries with it the same right of survivorship as a joint

---

[4]*Because each tenant in common owns an undivided interest in the property, difficult problems may arise when they disagree among themselves and wish to go their separate ways. Any tenant in common is entitled to begin a legal proceeding called an* action for partition. *If the property cannot be equitably divided, the court will order it to be sold, with the proceeds to be divided among the cotenants according to their interests.*

tenancy so that, on the death of either spouse, the survivor takes the entire estate. Unlike a joint tenancy, however, neither spouse can convey any part of the property during their joint lives unless the other spouse joins in the conveyance. In many states, any conveyance to a husband and wife is presumed to create a tenancy by the entirety. Thus, tenancy by the entirety acts to protect the rights of a surviving spouse in property owned during the marriage.

Property held under tenancy by the entirety is not subject to levy by creditors of only one of the owners. This feature was designed to protect the family from the business failures of one of the spouses. In the event the owners are divorced, the tenancy is destroyed and the divorced spouses become tenants in common.

COMMUNITY PROPERTY

The three types of concurrent ownership just described—tenancy in common, joint tenancy, and tenancy by the entirety—are derivations of English common law. The type of ownership known as **community property,** by contrast, derives from Spanish or French law and is now recognized by statute in eight states: Arizona, California, Idaho, Louisiana, Nevada, New Mexico, Texas, and Washington. In these states, each spouse is an equal co-owner of all the property acquired during the existence of the marriage as a result of the joint efforts of the spouses, and there is a presumption that all the property of husband and wife is community property. However, the spouses can, by mutual consent, convert community property into the separate property of either spouse.

Property is not considered community property if it was owned by either spouse before the marriage or acquired by either spouse during the marriage by gift, inheritance, or will. (Such separate property must not be commingled, or it will lose its ownership identity and become community property.) Community property statutes sometimes also provide that one-half the earnings of either spouse during the existence of the marriage belongs to the other spouse. This rule has been the basis of some celebrated proceedings between both married and unmarried couples in recent years.

On the death of a spouse **intestate** (i.e., without leaving a will), the surviving spouse may or may not take all the community property, depending on the statute of the particular state. Divorce ordinarily destroys the community property status, and, pending a divorce, separation agreements involving property settlements and reservations with respect to the future earnings of one or both spouses are usually made.

The effect of community property is similar (although the legal form is very different) to tenancy by the entirety. Both serve to protect the interest of the "uninformed" spouse. To ensure a good conveyance, both husband and wife must often sign the deed in a community property state, and both signatures are always required when the selling interest is owned by a tenancy by the entirety.

TWO SPECIAL FORMS OF OWNERSHIP

In addition to the ownership forms just described, two special types of ownership interests exist in real estate, the condominium and the cooperative corporation.

CONDOMINIUMS

As with community property, the **condominium** concept does not derive from English common law. Rather, it dates back over 2,000 years to Roman law, from which it has become a part of the civil law followed by most countries in Western Europe and South America. Although introduced into our country as recently as 1952 (in Puerto Rico), statutes authorizing condominium ownership now have been passed by every state and the District of Columbia.

Condominium (*codominion*) means common ownership and control, as distinguished from sole ownership and control. In a condominium project, each unit (e.g., apartment) is individually owned, whereas the general elements of the building (e.g., lobby, corridors, exterior walls) are commonly owned. Although by far most condominium projects are residential, the concept has been extended to commercial, industrial, and recreational projects.

To create a condominium, the owners of the property must file a declaration of condominium (or master deed) with the local land records office. The declaration includes a detailed description of the individual units in the property and of the common areas that may be used by all the owners. The declaration also sets forth the percentage of ownership that attaches to each individual unit. This percentage establishes the voting rights of each unit owner and each owner's contribution to the general operating expenses of the property.

Each owner of a condominium unit may sell or mortgage his unit as he sees fit. Property taxes are levied on each unit rather than on the entire project. The condominium unit owners constitute an owners' association and elect a board of directors, which is responsible for the day-to-day running of the condominium project.

We will return several times in the text to the condominium concept. Its popularity in recent years has led to new financing techniques and complex property management questions.

COOPERATIVE HOUSING CORPORATIONS

The essential element of a cooperative housing corporation (**cooperative**) is that ownership is in a corporation, the shares of which are divided among several persons. Each of those persons is entitled to lease a portion of the space by virtue of his or her ownership interest—that is, ownership and the right to lease and use the space are inseparable. Typically, a residential building is acquired by a corporation organized as a cooperative (as distinguished from a business corporation organized for profit). Each share (or specified group of shares) in the corporation carries with it the right to lease and use a designated apartment. Each shareholder executes a *proprietary lease* with the corporation, which is similar to a standard lease and pursuant to which the tenant-owner may occupy the designated unit.

Just as with a condominium, the cooperative project is run by a board of directors. Unlike a condominium, the project has a single owner—the cooperative corporation—which may mortgage the property (thus automatically providing financing for each apartment owner). The property is a single parcel for purposes of real estate taxation, and the taxes paid by the corporation are allocated among the various unit owners, as are all the common area and maintenance expenses of the building. Each owner then pays a monthly assessment (equivalent to rent) to cover the operating expenses and necessary repairs and replacements.

DIFFERENCE BETWEEN CONDOMINIUMS AND COOPERATIVES

A significant difference between a condominium and cooperative lies in the possible "snowball" effect if an individual owner defaults. In the case of a cooperative, default by a tenant-shareholder means that the remaining owners must assume his or her portion of real estate taxes, mortgage debt service, and common area expense. If a number of tenant-shareholders default, the burden on the remaining owners becomes correspondingly heavier, and a snowball effect may be created, causing more and more tenants to default. Precisely this kind of situation occurred during the depression of the 1930s, causing many cooperatives to fail.

By contrast, a condominium unit owner is responsible for his or her own mortgage financing and real estate taxes on the unit owned. Consequently, in the event of a default by a single-unit owner, only that owner's share of operating expenses (but not taxes or debt service) must be assumed by the remaining owners. As a result, a "snowball" is much less likely to occur in a condominium project—one obvious reason for the popularity of this form of ownership.

LEGAL ENTITIES FOR OWNING REAL ESTATE INTERESTS

The preceding section pointed out that a real estate interest may be held by one person (single ownership) or by several persons (concurrent ownership). This section considers what kinds of "persons," other than individuals, can own a real estate interest. The five types briefly discussed are

- The general partnership
- The limited partnership
- The corporation
- The land trust
- The real estate investment trust (REIT)

None of these vehicles for ownership (except for the last) is unique to real estate, being available for ownership of any kind of property. They are discussed here because real estate investors commonly use them to achieve additional flexibility in financing and managing real estate and in achieving the most desirable tax consequences.

Omitted from the list are two frequently used terms in real estate investing: **syndicate** and **joint venture.** The reason is that both terms merely refer to the general idea of group ownership. A syndicate may be made up of any number of investors from three to four to several hundred. Joint ventures generally describe a two-party relationship between a developer or operator and an institution that provides the financing (although sometimes more than two parties are involved).

WHY OWNERSHIP VEHICLES ARE USED

Before discussing the various types of ownership vehicles, we should say a word about the reasons for utilizing them. The major advantage they offer is the ability to pool capital contributions from a number of individuals. Another significant advantage is that these vehicles (except for the general partnership) insulate the individual investor from any liability for losses beyond the capital contributions the investor agrees to make. In addition, these vehicles provide a way for individual investors inexperienced in real estate to benefit from the expertise of professional developers and investors who undertake (for a portion of the return) the management responsibilities of the investment. Finally, as described in Part 6, these different ownership vehicles have different tax characteristics, which are important in structuring the ideal vehicle to accomplish a particular investment objective.

GENERAL PARTNERSHIP

The **general partnership** is a form of business organization in which two or more persons are associated as co-owners in a continuing relationship for the purpose of carrying on a common enterprise or business for a profit. An agreement of partnership (also called *articles of partnership*) defines the rights and obligations of each partner and sets forth how profits and losses are to be shared. Unlike a corporation, a general partnership requires no formal legal action or charter from the state in order to function. Once organized, however, a partnership must operate in accordance with legal rules that in most states follow a model known as the Uniform Partnership Act.

In the ownership or operation of real estate, a partnership has one overriding advantage over the business corporation. The partnership is not considered a tax entity apart from its members. As is discussed in Part 7, Investment Analysis, real estate investments may generate "tax losses" that can be used to offset other passive income[5] of the investor. Because a partnership is not a separate tax entity, such tax losses on real estate owned by a partnership can be "passed through" to the individual partners and used to offset their outside passive income. If a corporation is the owner, no pass-through can occur since the corporation is treated as an independent tax entity.

Another important distinction between a general partnership and the other forms of ownership entities is that each general partner is entitled to an equal voice in partnership affairs, in the absence of a provision to the contrary in the agreement of partnership. In the other ownership vehicles, management is concentrated in the hands of a few of the participants. Thus, the general partnership is appropriate when each participant wishes to have the right to join in management decisions. On the other hand, because all (or sometimes a majority) of the partners must agree to decisions in a general partnership, it is most suitable for relatively small and intimate groups of investors who are confident of their ability to work together.

The general partnership format does have certain disadvantages. The death of a general partner typically terminates the partnership and forces reorganization. More important, each general partner is liable for his or her partner's acts on behalf of the enterprise. The risk of loss is not limited in amount, and the liability may come as a result of one partner's actions completely independent of another's. If one partner signs a contract as a general partner, other partners are bound to honor that contract.

---

[5]*See Part 6 for a full explanation of the distinction between earned, portfolio, and passive income.*

LIMITED PARTNERSHIP

A **limited partnership** is a special type of partnership. It is composed of one or more general partners who manage the partnership affairs and one or more limited partners who are passive investors, who do not actively participate in the management of partnership affairs, and who, as a consequence, may legally limit their liability to the amount of cash actually invested (or to the amount they specifically promise to provide in the event they are called on to do so). By comparison, the general partner must assume full and unlimited personal liability for partnership debts.

The limited partnership is the most common form of organization used for real estate syndications since it combines for the limited partners the limited legal liability offered by the corporate form of organization with the tax advantages of the partnership form (i.e., the pass-through of losses). By using a limited partnership, real estate professionals may join the financial resources of outside investors with their own skills and resources and at the same time concentrate management in their own hands. Of course, there have been cases of a supposed "professional" fraudulently running away with the money. No ownership vehicle is foolproof, and personal ethics as well as the formal rules of the game are needed to ensure a game that benefits society.

A limited partnership is formed by a written agreement of partnership pursuant to a state statute. Most statutes are patterned after a model known as the Uniform Limited Partnership Act. Whereas a general partnership is an entity recognized by common law and can therefore come into existence independent of any statute, a limited partnership is a "creature of statute" and will not be given legal recognition unless an appropriate certificate of limited partnership has been filed with the appropriate state authority.

CORPORATION

A **corporation** is a separate legal entity—an artificial person—created in accordance with the laws of a particular state (the federal government not having the power to create business corporations). Thus, the corporation is an entity entirely distinct from its shareholders. Its charter may provide that it will have a perpetual life, and it operates through a board of directors elected by the shareholders. The major advantage of, and the original purpose for, the corporate form was to limit each shareholder's liability to the amount of his or her capital investment; a secondary purpose was to make shareholder interests freely transferable by means of assignable corporate shares. Both features made the corporation useful for aggregating investment capital.

The major disadvantage in using a corporation to own real estate is that the corporation is recognized as an independent entity for tax purposes. Thus, tax losses from corporately owned real estate may not be passed through to the individual shareholders but may be utilized only by the corporation itself. Because it may not have any other income against which the losses may be offset, the losses may be of no use. (As explained in Part 6, the 1986 tax law changes lessen this problem.) On the other hand, if the corporate real estate produces net income, a problem of double taxation must be faced. The corporation first must pay a corporate income tax on its net income. Then, to the extent the income is distributed in the form of dividends, the shareholders may pay a personal income tax on such income.[6]

In certain situations, it may be possible to use an **S Corporation.** As explained in Part 6, this corporate election allows the shareholders to be taxed directly as in a partnership. Congress intended the S Corporation for small operating businesses, and in real estate it is most often used by active players, not by investors.

TRUST

The **trust** is the least commonly used ownership vehicle, being somewhat cumbersome in its .organization and operation. Nevertheless, it remains popular in some parts of the country (where it is often known as a *land trust*). A trust is a legal relationship among three persons, normally established by a written agreement, in which

- A *trustor* or *creator* transfers legal title to real estate to

- A *trustee,* who holds the legal title with the responsibility of administering it and distributing the income for the benefit of

- One or more *beneficiaries* who hold beneficial or equitable title to the real estate.

For example, a group of investors may organize a land trust, with themselves as beneficiaries, naming a trustee (such as a trust company) that utilizes funds provided by the beneficiaries to buy a parcel of real estate and administer it for their benefit.

The great advantage of the land trust, which it shares with the partnership, is its ability to act as a conduit for tax purposes. Thus, if the real estate generates tax losses, these can be passed through directly to the

---

[6]*In the case of a small, closely owned corporation (known as a* close corporation), *the problem of double taxation often can be avoided by distributing corporate income to the shareholders in the form of salaries or other compensation. In this situation, the corporation may deduct the cost of such salaries and thus reduce its own income, although the shareholder-employees will be taxed on the income they receive.*

beneficiaries, but if the real estate produces taxable income, the trust avoids the double tax that results from use of the corporate form as long as it distributes the income.

Because legal title to the real estate owned by a trust is in the name of the trustee, transfers of title can be effected without disclosing the names of the beneficiaries or requiring their participation. In addition, any changes in the personal or business affairs of a beneficiary—such as business reverses or a divorce—have no effect on the title to the property owned by the trust (although the interest of the particular beneficiary may be affected).

To be distinguished from the land trust is the *personal trust,* which is a common means of holding property (real estate and otherwise) for the benefit of members of a family, particularly the spouse or children of a dependent. A trust may be set up by will (a testamentary trust) or may be set up during the lifetime of the trustor (an inter vivos trust, that is, one between living persons). In family estate planning, the trust is an extremely flexible instrument, and for this reason it is one of the most frequently used vehicles for controlling individual wealth.

REAL ESTATE INVESTMENT TRUST (REIT)

A special form of trust ownership is the **Real Estate Investment Trust** or **REIT,** which is wholly a creature of the Internal Revenue Code. REITs were set up as a parallel form of investment vehicle to common stock mutual funds, to permit small investors to invest in a diversified portfolio of real estate just as they could in a portfolio of common stocks in a mutual fund.

The major tax benefit of a REIT is that, as long as it distributes at least 95 percent of its net income to its shareholder-beneficiaries, it need not pay any income tax (although the individual shareholders must pay a tax on the dividends received). Thus, the problem of double taxation is eliminated. REITs are strictly limited by statute to the types of operations they may conduct. (More detail on REITs is provided in Parts 5 and 6.)

CURRENT TRENDS IN REAL ESTATE INTERESTS AND OWNERSHIP

Traditionally, the legal rules affecting rights in real property have changed very slowly. The major cause of this is the permanence of land and hence the long-term nature of interests in land. Courts and legislatures have hesitated to create new rules that might affect titles acquired many years ago or change the allocation of the bundle of rights created by long-standing leases or other agreements.

In the past quarter century, however, the pace of change in this area has speeded up a great deal. There are several reasons for this. One of the most important has been inflation, which has substantially changed the economic relationship between landlords and tenants and between developers and lenders. Another has been changes in the tax laws, which encourage new forms of investment techniques. Most important are those changes related to owner liability discussed in Chapter 28.

SUMMARY   This chapter should have amply demonstrated that it is no simple matter to answer the question, "Who owns the parcel of real estate known as 150 Main Street?" Three parallel lines of investigation must be followed to provide an adequate answer.

- *First,* we must determine if the physical real estate at 150 Main Street has been separated into different types of physical interests—that is, whether there has been a severance of air rights, surface rights, and subsurface rights or whether the physical interest remains a unified one.

- *Second,* we must determine if there is a single legal interest in the real estate (i.e., a fee simple absolute) or whether there has been a separation of legal interests, between a present and future fee interest; a fee and leasehold interest, by creation of a nonpossessory interest such as an easement or license; or any possible combination of the foregoing.

- *Third,* we must determine whether each legal interest in each physical interest in the real estate is owned by a single person (*in severalty*) or divided through some concurrent ownership form. In addition, different ownership vehicles are possible whether the real estate is owned in severalty or in some concurrent ownership form.

IMPORTANT TERMS

Air space	Joint tenancy
Bundle of rights	Joint venture
Community property	Lease
Condominium	License
Control	Life estate
Cooperative	Life tenant
Corporation	Limited partnership
Defeasible fees	Littoral rights
Disposition	Nonpossessory interest
Easement	Personal property
Easement appurtenant	Possession
Easement by necessity	Possessory or leasehold estate
Easement by prescription	Prescriptive easement

Easement in gross

Enjoyment

Escalation clause

Estate at sufferance

Estate at will

Estate for years

Estate from period to period

Express easement

Fee on condition subsequent

Fee simple

Fee simple determinable

Fixture

Freehold estates

General partnership

Implied easement

Intestate

Prior appropriation

Profit

Real Estate Investment Trust (REIT)

Real property

Remainderman

Right of reentry

Right of survivorship

Riparian rights

S Corporation

Security interest

Subsurface rights

Syndicate

Tenancy by the entirety

Tenancy in common

Trust

REVIEW QUESTIONS

4.1   What three types of physical interests in real estate can be owned?

4.2   Explain the difference between riparian rights and prior appropriation.

4.3   Name the four key rights associated with real estate ownership.

4.4   Why are defeasible fees looked on with disfavor by the courts?

4.5   What is the difference between a life estate and a fee simple absolute?

4.6   Define two types of leasehold estates.

4.7   Why does the view of a lease as a contract offer a rationale for rent strikes?

4.8   What is the difference between an easement and a license?

4.9   What might be the advantage of a joint tenancy over a tenancy in common?

4.10 What is a condominium, and how does it differ from sole ownership?

4.11 List the advantages and disadvantages of a partnership as compared to a corporation in the ownership of income-producing property.

4.12 What is the primary attraction of a real estate investment trust?

$\mathcal{J}$ RANSFERRING REAL ESTATE INTERESTS

Chapter 4 identified the various legal interests in real estate that can be created and separately owned. It is worth mentioning again that the numerous combinations that may be formed from these legal interests makes real estate an extremely flexible form of investment. This may seem strange since real estate as a physical asset is permanent and immobile. Actually, it is precisely because land has perpetual life and fixed location (and great economic value) that it is feasible for a number of separate investment interests to exist simultaneously in a single parcel.

In this chapter, we'll discuss the mechanics of transferring interests in real estate. The legal technicalities of real estate transfers (conveyance) lie in the domain of the real estate lawyer and so are not included here. But the real estate professional should understand the general rules and procedures of real estate transfers for at least three reasons.

The first is that in negotiating the terms and price of a transfer of a legal interest (as described in Chapter 4), the parties should understand existing or potential limitations on *title* that may affect the future usefulness of the property. Any existing limitations could adversely affect value.

The second reason is that some of the procedures described in this chapter are also investment techniques. For example, using an option to tie up land pending future development may be a much more efficient use of capital resources than would be an outright purchase.

Third, the flexibility of the real estate claim allows satisfaction of a diverse set of social needs in a capitalistic economy. If you want to make the city a better place for everyone to live, you need to understand how real property is owned and conveyed.

This chapter deals with four major subjects.

■ *The concept of title.* The bundle of rights involved in ownership is defined, and the extent to which such rights can be limited by private agreement or governmental action is explained.

- *Methods of transferring title.* The various ways, both voluntary and involuntary, by which title passes from one person to another are discussed.

- *Contract of sale.* The major provisions in the key instrument in the purchase and sale of real estate are explained.

- *Deeds.* The legal instrument that actually transfers title from one person to another is discussed.

THE CONCEPT OF TITLE

The term **title** is virtually synonymous with *ownership.* When used without limitation, title implies the highest degree of ownership that may exist—that is, ownership in fee simple absolute. Title may also be used in a more restricted sense—to indicate a form of ownership limited in duration or extent. For example, an individual owning a life estate or a fee simple determinable also has title, but the title is subject to the limitations inherent in these types of fee interests. Consequently, the statement "I have title to this land," does not convey sufficient information to a potential purchaser or other user of the land. It is necessary to determine the precise type of real estate interest held by the person claiming title.

Title is ownership, and ownership is a bundle of rights. The four major rights of ownership were identified in Chapter 4: (1) *possession,* (2) *control,* (3) *enjoyment,* and (4) *disposition.* The bundle of rights is not absolute. Rights may be limited or restricted by private agreements or by governmental regulation or statute. We describe the most important of these private and public limitations.

PRIVATE LIMITATIONS ON TITLE

First and most basic, title may be limited or restricted because of the *existence of leaseholds or nonpossessory interests in the property.* For example, the holder of a fee simple in real estate may have entered into a ten-year lease with a tenant. If the owner sells his fee simple interest during the ten years, the buyer takes title subject to the existing lease. If the owner had granted a right-of-way easement over the land to a third party, a buyer would take subject to the easement as well.[1]

Second, limitations may arise through *restrictive covenants or conditions* imposed by prior owners of the land that bind all successive owners. A **restrictive covenant** may cover such matters as (1) the minimum size of a building lot (e.g., the house must be on a one-acre lot), (2) setback requirements (e.g., a building must be at least 20 feet from the property

---

[1] *This assumes the buyer is told of these other interests or is otherwise aware of them, which is normally the case. If the buyer is totally ignorant of these other interests, some complicated legal questions may arise.*

line), and (3) uses to which the property may be put (e.g., residential only). However, the courts will not enforce racial, religious, and ethnic restrictions.

In order for a restrictive covenant to bind future owners of the property, the covenant must be written into the deed or be in a separate instrument that is entered on the public records (a subject discussed in the final section of this chapter). Such a covenant is said to *"run with the land."* Restrictive covenants, once created, may be terminated in a number of ways. The covenant itself may contain a time limit (e.g., 25 years). It may be terminated by the unanimous agreement of the property owners who benefit from it. Finally, if the covenant is violated repeatedly over the years with no attempt to enforce it, the court may throw out any subsequent action to enforce it on the ground that the covenant no longer has any legal effect. Courts tend to interpret restrictive covenants in a strict manner and to resolve questions against them because of the fundamental social policy in favor of the free and unrestricted use of land.

PUBLIC LIMITATIONS ON TITLE

Limitations on the bundle of rights that make up title or ownership may arise from an overriding public interest. Public controls generally fall into four groups: (1) common-law restrictions on property use, (2) police power, (3) eminent domain, and (4) property taxation.

❏ **COMMON-LAW RESTRICTIONS.** Over the centuries, the Anglo-American common law developed certain doctrines that restrict the use of private property in the interests of the general community. The most important of these is the **law of nuisance.** Nuisance, as a legal concept, refers to the use of one's property in a manner that causes injury to an adjacent landowner or to the general public. Conducting a manufacturing operation on one's land that creates noxious fumes or odors or operating a motorcycle track on land in a residential area are examples of legal nuisances that may be enjoined (barred) by a court of law.[2]

❏ **POLICE POWER.** **Police power** constitutes the inherent power of a government to enact laws that promote the public health, morals, safety, and general welfare. Under our federal system, police powers are exercised by the individual states rather than by the federal government.

---

[2]*A special application of the nuisance concept is the doctrine of* attractive nuisance. *This holds a landowner responsible for injury to children who may enter on the property and suffer injury as the result of a feature of the property that is both attractive and dangerous. An unfenced swimming pool is perhaps the most common example. Here the law imposes a restraint on the use of property in the interests of the safety of others.*

Although laws enacted under the police power can be very broad, they are not entirely without limitation. Under both federal and state constitutions, such laws must be nondiscriminatory and must operate in a uniform manner. The police power of a state may be delegated to its political subdivisions (e.g., county, city, or other municipality). For the real estate owner or developer, the most significant police powers are those that do the following:

- Regulate the use of land through zoning and subdivision ordinances.

- Create local building codes or standards.

- Seek to limit pollution by environmental controls (which may limit or bar the development of real estate).

- License professionals operating in the real estate industry.

An important point to note is that exercise of the police power does not impose an obligation on the state or local government to compensate the landowners for any loss of value—unlike a taking under eminent domain, discussed next. Thus, in many cases, it becomes critical to determine at what point the police power ends and the right of eminent domain begins.

For example, if the state bars *any* development of land in the interests of environmental control, so that the owner is unable to realize an economic return on his or her investment, has there been a legitimate exercise of the police power or a taking requiring compensation? As seen in Part 9, this issue remains one of the major areas of controversy in the field of real estate law.

❏ **EMINENT DOMAIN.**   The most extensive public limitation on title or ownership is the right to take private property for public use through the exercise of the power of **eminent domain.** This taking is known as a *condemnation;* whenever it occurs, the owner is entitled, by constitutional requirement, to proper compensation. This is usually based on the property's appraised value on the date of taking. Examples of public purposes for which property may be taken include construction of highways, schools, and parks.[3]

The power of eminent domain can be viewed from another aspect. By using this power to create highways, schools, and other public facilities included in the term *economic infrastructure,* governments strongly influence land use decisions. The growth of the suburbs following World War II, which constituted one of the most profound social revolutions in our history, had a direct correlation with the creation of the national highway system.

---

[3]*Another way for the state to acquire ownership is through the law of* **escheat.** *Under this provision of the law, if a person dies with no will and no heirs, his real property passes to the state.*

At times the city may have a choice when seeking to accomplish a public purpose such as low-density development. It would be cheaper, from the government's perspective, to "downzone" developed land so as to permit only light development. On the other hand, the property owner would prefer that the city condemn the land and pay for the right to restrict development. We will deal with this issue further in Part 9: for now Box 5-1 gives the Supreme Court's current position (or lack of a position) on when a city must compensate an owner for the effects of restrictive zoning.

❏ **PROPERTY TAXATION.**   As is discussed in detail in Chapter 17, real property taxes were one of the earliest methods of public finance and remain the primary source of funds for local governments today. **Real property taxation** represents a limitation on property use because any unpaid taxes constitute a lien (claim) against the real estate, taking priority over any private liens such as mortgages, and permitting the municipality to foreclose against the property if the taxes are not paid within a specified time (usually one to three years).[4]

Recall that in Chapter 3 we said government is "always your partner" in any real estate activity. Remember that the title limitations discussed above any dynamic, changing as society's needs change. Also changing over time are the positive contributions of government to the partnership, that is, the quality of roads, libraries, police protection, and so on. The dynamic nature of this partnership is one of the most challenging aspects of the real estate industry.

EXAMINING AND INSURING TITLE

Questions about title usually arise at the time property is sold; the buyer will not be willing to complete the transaction unless the buyer is assured that the seller's title is, in fact, what it is represented to be in the contract of sale. Normally, the buyer of real estate is entitled to receive **good and marketable title.** Such a title:

■ *Can be traced from the present owner backward in time through a series of previous owners until a point is reached at which the property was transferred from a sovereign government, the ultimate owner of all land.* This will be the federal government, a state government, King George III of England, or, in some states such as Louisiana and Texas, a French or Spanish sovereign.

---

[4]*A particular type of property tax is the* special assessment, *which a municipality levies against property within a specific neighborhood in order to pay for a local improvement (e.g., pavements, sewers, street lights) that is intended to benefit only the properties within the area rather than the entire community.*

■ *Is not subject to any defects or limitation except those specified in the contract of sale.* The contract normally specifies all known limitations on ownership—for example, utility easements, use restrictions, and the like. Since these limitations on title are beyond the power of the seller to eliminate, the buyer must accept them or decline to enter into the contract.

The buyer of real estate normally will verify or establish title by utilizing the services of (1) an attorney, (2) a title abstract company, (3) a title insurance company, or a combination of these to examine the land records to ascertain whether a good and marketable title can be conveyed.

The result of the examination will be an **abstract of title,** which provides a history of title to the property and lists all restrictions and limitations. In addition to those already mentioned (limited fee interest in the seller, restrictive covenants, etc.), these may include (1) tax liens (for unpaid property or income taxes), (2) mortgages, or (3) other claims. In addition, **mechanic's liens** (claims by persons who have performed work on the property and who have not been paid) may exist. Mechanic's liens can be particularly troublesome, for they may be filed after the work is done but are effective, when filed, as of the date the work began. Like problems with claims of short-term tenants whose leases are not recorded, the potential of mechanic's liens forces the examiner to examine the property physically as well as to study the abstract.

The buyer or his lawyer should carefully compare the abstract of title to the title promised by the contract of sale. If the comparison reveals defects, claims, or limitations not specified in the contract of sale, the buyer will not be required to go through with the transaction.

It is possible that a mistake may be made in preparing the abstract of title or that a defect in the title of the present owner may not be discoverable (e.g., a forgery in an earlier deed). To obtain protection against such mistakes or undiscoverable defects in title, the buyer may obtain title insurance from a **title insurance** company. Such insurance provides coverage against monetary loss to the buyer in the event title to the property is lost or limited for a reason not known at the time the buyer acquired his title.[5] The lending institution that provides the buyer with financing normally will require that its loan be protected by title insurance. (See Box 5-2).

[5]*Title insurance differs in one major respect from all other types of insurance. It provides coverage against loss due to a cause that has already occurred. All other insurance provides coverage against loss due to a future cause. This is one reason why payment for title insurance is by a single premium paid at the time of closing. It is important to note that title insurance protects the insured against loss only to the extent of the policy. If land is bought for $20,000 ($20,000 obtained in title insurance) and then a home for $80,000 is built, in the event of faulty title, the insurance pays only $20,000, not $100,000.*

Typically, we speak of owner's title insurance and lender's title insurance. The lender will usually require the latter in the amount of the mortgage loan. If the owner also wants protection for the downpayment amount, he or she must so specify and pay an additional premium.

5-1

AN UNEASY LOOK AT *FIRST LUTHERAN* AND *NOLLAN*

Summary

In two landmark rulings in 1987, the U.S. Supreme Court placed important restrictions on the power of local and state governments to regulate land use. In the first case, *First English Evangelical Lutheran Church of Glendale* v. *County of Los Angeles, California,* No. 85–1199 (*First Lutheran*), the Court ruled if a development moratorium on all use of a parcel of land constitutes a taking of property, government would be liable for compensatory damages.[a] In the second case, *Nollan* v. *California Coastal Commission,* No. 86–133 (*Nollan*), the Court restricted the ability of local and state governments to exact conditions on new developments in exchange for the appropriate permits.[b]

Both of these rulings were hailed by the development and owner communities in that they appear to herald a period of deregulation and higher profits for [the] land development industry. Although we agree in part in the short run, over the longer term we are more cautious. We believe that the two rulings will have at least two unintended consequences. First, supply constraints that kept vacancy levels at reasonable levels in growth-controlled areas could very well be removed. This weakening of controls will lower profits, not increase them. Second, it could ultimately lead to stricter controls of the traditional variety where a political consensus exists.

Background

In the late 1960s land use regulation began to expand dramatically. The process of zoning and rezoning land and receiving the appropriate development permits from the local government, which was once rather simple, became extremely complicated. In response to increased public concern about environmental protection, traffic, open space, and the fiscal impact of developments a panoply of regulation was introduced. These regulations are now most prevalent on the West and Northeast coasts and in upper-income suburban communities. They are least prevalent in the South.

Environmental impact reports became commonplace in many areas and governments began to exact conditions in exchange for development permits. These conditions range from reductions in density and height, to architectural review, impact fees on in-kind contributions for roads, sewers, flood control, schools, parkland, low-income housing, and day care. An impact fee can be viewed as an excise tax on land use changes and works to slow the supply of land to the market.

In the process of implementing these programs, local governments declared moratoria on development so that they could adequately plan for growth. In

[a]In *First Lutheran* the landowner was prohibited from developing land for a period of eight years because of the possibility of flooding.
[b]In *Nollan* a beach front property owner was required to dedicate a lateral easement to allow public access to the beach in front of the property as [a] condition to tearing down and rebuilding a single-family residence.

some cases these moratoria were thinly veiled measures designed to stop development. More often than not, the new plans significantly reduced the development of the land. The economic effect of all this regulation was to restrict supply, which then increased the value of already built properties and those properties that received the appropriate development permits. Undeveloped properties without permits were devalued. Put simply, local monopolies were created. Along the way a monopoly-entrenching "development facilitator" industry was created that to this day supports a retinue of lawyers, planners, consultants, lobbyists, and engineers.

With many real estate markets glutted, institutional investors have sought out zoning-induced, supply-constrained markets. Buildings in these markets are protected from the competition and thus tend to achieve higher rents and occupancy levels. The quasi-monopoly values are capitalized into building prices. Generally speaking, because these supply constrained markets are either in vibrant downtowns or upper income neighborhoods, they offer the added attraction of having a built-in base of executives and professionals from which to draw tenants and customers.

The Initial Impact of First Lutheran and Nollan

Into this complicated system of controls step the *First Lutheran* and *Nollan* decisions. The *First Lutheran* ruling will give governments pause before they put development moratoria into place. Prior to *First Lutheran* all the relief a landowner could obtain from a government was to get a declaration that the moratorium was unconstitutional. Now, if the moratorium is ruled a taking, the landowner can receive money damages for the loss of use as well. This puts the local treasury on the hook, and it will obviously limit the use of moratoria. Land now covered by moratoria will increase in value, but this could lower the value of nearby developable land.

Therefore, if landowners are threatened with a loss of development rights without an interim moratorium, they will "use them before they lose them." This will cause an onslaught of supply that will initially work to "*lower*" values in the aggregate, not raise them. History is replete with evidence of developers attempting to build in advance of stricter regulation. This result will hold in dense urban areas. In less dense rural and fringe areas, where land has already been subdivided, the *First Lutheran* ruling will allow property owners to rest easy in the thought that it will be very difficult for government to prevent the construction of, for example, a single-family house on an individual lot.

Nollan, on the other hand, strikes at the types of conditions and exactions a government can place on a development. The Court ruled that the power to deny creates the power to condition. There has to be a very direct nexus between the governmental purpose and the condition imposed. This ruling calls into question the use of annual caps on development and requirements for low-income housing and day care centers in connection with the construction of office buildings that have been imposed by several cities. It also may affect, depending on the project, the use of traffic mitigation and parkland fees as well. The question that future courts will have to decide is how close the nexus has to be between a development and the conditions required. *Nollan* will cause greater reluctance on the part of government to condition new development. This will lower the implicit tax burden on development and therefore increase the level of construction.

As a result of these two cases, governmental constraints on new development will be loosened. Over the past seven years these have been the only real restraints on development. Certainly, the availability of financing and high vacancy rates in the office sector have not. In a sense, strong land use regulations have protected developers from themselves. Now with these constraints weakening, the owners of existing buildings will find themselves faced with competition that they had not foreseen as regulatory barriers to entry are loosened. In highly regulated environments the market will tend to soften and the values of existing buildings will tend to fall.

The Longer-Term Consequences

Strange as it may seem the longer-term consequences may lead to even stricter land use regulation than we have now. The land use regulation that arrived in the 1970s did not appear in a vacuum. The political system reacted to public concerns, right or wrong, about the quality of the environment. Those concerns are not going to go away. Thus, if new development projects cannot be conditioned to meet public concerns on a case-by-case basis, all development could be significantly reduced in scope. This would happen through the process of wholesale "downzoning." For example, land zoned for 20-story buildings could be downzoned to four-story buildings. Any developer seeking a greater height would thus have to seek a special variance. In this way the governing body would meet the test of *First Lutheran* in that the land would have a use, and it would avoid the issues raised by *Nollan* by not allowing variances.

Before the champagne is uncorked, landowners and developers ought to carefully think through the forces that are about to be unleashed. People tend to forget that what is good for one landowner is not necessarily always good for an entire industry. Where land use regulation has been intense, market participants have been sheltered from competition. It is not a coincidence that the best real estate markets, such as those in California and the Northeast, are where land use regulation is most severe and, conversely, where there has been little or no regulation (Texas, Arizona, and the Southeast), markets are glutted.

Thus, we believe that *First Lutheran* and *Nollan* may lead to more uncertainty, rather than less. In areas with light regulation, regulation will probably remain limited. However, in areas of heavy regulation, investors face the risk that the regulatory environment could vary widely. This will depend on the attitude towards development of the local electorate and the political strength of the development community. Investing in supply-constrained areas has become riskier.

Source: Pamphlet by David Shulman, Salomon Brothers, Inc., dated July 27, 1987; Lot (8-24-76-54-118).

5-2
WHEN
INSURING TITLE
CAN PAY OFF

Title insurance can protect a property owner against different types of possible defects in his title (in addition to a prior forgery, the example mentioned in the text). For example:

- *Sale by minor.* A seller who is a minor at the time he executes a deed transferring title to real estate may be in a position to disaffirm the transfer when he reaches his majority. If the age of the seller was unknown to the buyer at the time of the transfer, the buyer's title insurance will protect him against possible loss of the property if the seller subsequently disaffirms the sale.

- *Missing heir.* Suppose a buyer purchases property from a widow, the only known heir of her husband who had died without leaving a will. Subsequently, a claim against the property is made by a man who was the son of the widow's husband by a former marriage. He had left home to make his own way in the world, and the widow had either not known of his existence or had failed to disclose it. Nevertheless, he is entitled to a share in his father's estate. The title company would be obligated to compensate the heir for this interest.

- *Death of seller.* An individual buys property from a representative of the owner who holds a power of attorney. The power is properly recorded, and a careful inspection shows it to be technically proper in all respects. It turns out, however, that the owner had died two days before the sale was made, a fact unknown to both her representative and the buyer. Since the power of attorney had expired with the owner's death, the transfer was void. The new owner's loss would be covered by title insurance.

- *Survey error.* When Ms. A. bought a home, she had a survey made that showed all buildings to be well within the boundaries of her lot. Subsequently, the adjoining property was placed on the market, and a survey made by its owner disclosed the fact that Ms. A's garage and driveway were partly built on the adjoining land. Ms. A's survey had been incorrectly made. Ms. A was forced to purchase a strip of land wide enough to bring her garage and driveway within her property boundaries. She would be reimbursed for this expense under a title insurance policy.

It is important to remember that tile insurance is, in fact, an insurance policy and that insurance policies may have exceptions. Ms. A would have been reimbursed in this case only as long as her title insurance policy did not have an exception reading "excepting any title deficiency that a current survey would have disclosed." As with most exceptions to insurance policies, the company will remove the survey exception clause—for a fee.

In addition to protecting a property owner against unknown prior defects in title, a title insurance policy can protect a buyer against known defects or potential claims. For example:

- *Possible right-of-way.* A buyer bought a vacant lot, intending to construct a large office building. Local residents had been in the habit of crossing over the property, and it was conceivable that a public right-of-way had come into existence. The buyer was unwilling to construct the building without protection against a future claim. The title insurance company, considering the extreme unlikelihood that a legal right-of-way existed, agreed to insure the title without qualification.

- *Type of deed.* A purchaser of property from a life insurance company insisted on a general warranty deed (see page 151). However, the insurance company was not permitted by its charter to execute such a deed. Instead, the parties shared the cost of a title insurance policy, which gave the purchaser the same protection.

LAND DESCRIPTION AND MEASUREMENT

We will take a moment here to explain how to measure the physical space to which title is held. How does a buyer determine precisely how much land is being purchased? How does an owner determine precisely what the boundaries are so that the extent of his exclusive rights of possession are known?

Land typically is described by surface measurements (see Table 5.1) with the property rights extending downward like an inverted cone to the center of the earth and upward "to the heavens." Surface measurements are usually by one of two means, metes and bounds or government survey.

❏ **METES AND BOUNDS.** Since colonial days it has been standard practice to identify the boundaries of property with certain landmarks such as Poland's Creek or O'Malley's Old Oak Tree. The system was refined by developing more enduring reference points, and the procedure is now called a metes and bounds description. Metes are measures of distance, and bounds are compass directions. Thus, as shown in Figure 5-1, a property's boundaries are sequentially described, starting at a well-defined beginning point (often a landmark such as a street intersection).

❏ **GOVERNMENT SURVEY.** The Continental Congress and the Congress of the United States strenuously debated boundary issues and in 1785 created the rectangular **survey** system as an improvement on the haphazard and at times cumbersome metes and bounds system. Since the original colonial states were already settled, the new system could be applied only to new territories still in the public domain. Today the rectangular survey or government survey system applies to Florida and all lands west of the Allegheny Mountains.

The government survey system divides large areas into 24 square-mile quadrangles, with north–south lines called meridians and east–west

TABLE 5-1 TABLE OF LAND MEASUREMENTS

LINEAR MEASURE		SQUARE MEASURE	
9.92 inches =	1 link	30¼ square yards =	1 square rod
25 links =	16½ feet	16 square rods =	1 square chain
25 links =	1 rod	1 square rod =	272.25 square feet
100 links =	1 chain	1 square chain =	4,356 square feet
16.5 feet =	1 rod	4,840 square yards =	1 acre
5.5 yards =	1 rod	640 acres =	1 square mile
4 rods =	100 links	1 section =	1 square mile
66 feet =	1 chain	1 township =	36 square miles
80 chains =	1 mile	1 township =	6 miles square
320 rods =	1 mile		
5,280 feet =	1 mile		
1,760 yards =	1 mile		

AN ACRE IS

- 43,560 square feet
- 165 feet × 264 feet
- 198 feet × 220 feet
- 5,280 feet × 8.25 feet
- 2,640 feet × 16.50 feet
- 1,320 feet × 33 feet
- 660 feet × 66 feet
- 330 feet × 132 feet
- 160 square rods
- 208 feet 8.5 inches square or
- 208.71033 feet square
- any rectangular tract, the product of the length and width of which totals 43,560 square feet

lines called parallels. Each quadrangle is further divided into townships (6 miles on each side containing 36 square miles). Townships are identified in reference to a baseline (parallel) and a principal meridian so that (see Figure 5-2) T3N, R2W is the third township north of the baseline and the second west of the principal meridian.

Townships are divided into 36 one-square-mile sections, which are numbered sequentially as shown in Figure 5-3. The sections are then subdivided into quarter sections and on down as shown in Figure 5-4.

DESCRIPTION BY LOT AND BLOCK NUMBER

Inside urban areas, smaller developed parcels are usually identified by reference to a plat whether the entire area is identified with metes and bounds (eastern United States) or government survey (western United

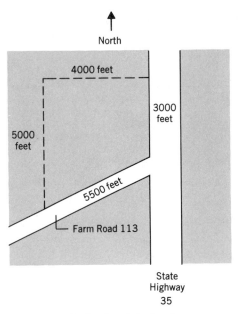

FIGURE 5-1 *Lacy's turkey farm*

Beginning at the intersection of the northern side of the Farm Road 113 right of way and the western side of the State Highway 35 right of way in Mason County, Idaho, and proceeding South 82 15 West [82 degrees and 15 minutes] for 5,500 feet to an iron pin, then due North 5,000 feet to an iron pin, then North 89 10 East to the westerly boundary of State Highway 35, and finally due South 3,000 feet to the point of beginning.

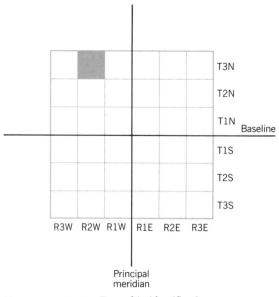

FIGURE 5-2 *Township identification*

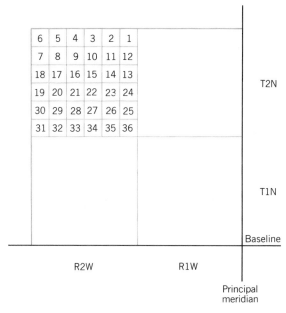

F I G U R E 5-3 *Sections in townships*

States). The subdivision developer's engineer prepares a **plat** (map), which is recorded at the courthouse or other depository of official documents. Once the plat is recorded, subsequent identification of property is by lot and block number as shown on the plat.

**TRANSFERRING
TITLE TO REAL
ESTATE**

One of the fundamental rights associated with real estate ownership is the right to transfer title to others. This right of transfer is virtually absolute. It is subject only to (1) the rule that a person cannot convey what he or she

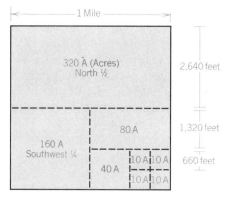

F I G U R E 5-4 *A section of land (640 acres)*

does not own (so that a person holding a life estate can convey only that interest and no more) and (2) statutory restrictions on the ownership of real estate. (For example, some states restrict ownership of farmland by aliens or corporations.)

Title to real property may be transferred in one of seven ways:

- Purchase and sale
- Inheritance
- Gift
- Foreclosure or tax sale
- Adverse possession
- Escheat
- Eminent domain

The first four of these are normally evidenced by a deed (or will), but the latter three are not.

PURCHASE AND SALE

By far the greatest number of property transfers are by sale for a consideration (price). Unlike the sale of personal property, the sale of real estate involves a rather complex process that may extend anywhere from 30 days to six months or more.

The large capital investment normally required is *not* the primary reason for the complexity of the real estate transfer process, although this is certainly part of the explanation. A more important reason relates to one of the unique features of real property: *its permanence.* A new automobile or a new oil tanker, when it comes from the hands of the manufacturer, has no history. It has not been possible, except perhaps in rare cases, for other claims to attach to the property or for any restrictions on the title to the property to have come into being.

But, as we have already seen, the matter is quite different in real estate. Every parcel of property does have a history—of transfers, financing, improvement, and claims of one kind or another. Consequently, a period of time must elapse to permit a buyer to properly examine the title to determine whether the seller can convey clear and marketable title. In addition, outside financing normally must be arranged, and this, too, takes time.

The essentials of the real estate sale process may be summarized as follows.

- *With respect to a designated parcel of land,* a buyer makes the seller an **offer of purchase,** or the seller makes the buyer an **offer of sale.**

This is often done through the use of real estate brokers. (The brokerage process is discussed in Chapter 10.)

■ *If the offer by one party is accepted by the other,* a meeting of the minds has occurred, which is evidenced by a written contract of sale. The contract is the crucial element in the real estate sale process, and it is discussed later in this chapter.

■ *After the contract of the sale is signed,* a period of time (the *contract period*) normally elapses before the actual transfer of title (the **title closing**). During this period, certain preclosing activities occur. The two most important are performed by the buyer: (1) examining the title to be sure the seller can convey what has been promised (discussed earlier) and (2) arranging any financing. In addition, a property survey may be necessary, and the seller must take any necessary steps to be sure the property conforms to the conditions set forth in the contract (e.g., that it be free of any tenants, that it be in good repair, etc.).

■ *The contract of sale normally will set a closing date,* at which time the buyer receives a deed evidencing title to the property in exchange for which the agreed-on price is paid to the seller. If the buyer has arranged financing, the lender or a representative may also be present at the closing to transfer the loan proceeds to the seller as part of the sales price. In consideration of the loan, the lender will receive a mortgage executed by the buyer whereby the property becomes security for the loan.

The type of closing described, in which the parties meet together to exchange instruments of conveyance and consideration, is the form usually followed in the eastern United States. In many western states, title is transferred by an **escrow closing.** A third party, such as a trust company or title company, is designated as an escrow holder; and the deed, consideration, loan proceeds, note, and mortgage as well as other necessary instruments are deposited with it as they are prepared or become available. When all the conditions of the contract of sale have been complied with, the escrow holder will redistribute the deposited instruments and cash to the appropriate parties and thus end the closing process. (Appendix A to Chapter 10 describes the closing process in detail.)

INHERITANCE

Second only to purchase and sale, the most common method of transferring title to real estate is as a result of the owner's death. The general term to describe such transfer is **inheritance,** which includes both a transfer by last will and testament (called a *devise*) or a transfer by the laws of intestacy—that is, where no will has been executed so that the owner dies intestate (called *descent and distribution*).

The subject of inheritance is a complex one that does not primarily concern us in this book. A few brief observations, however, will sum up the chief points that should be remembered.

- *Certain types of legal interests automatically expire at the death of the holder,* and, consequently, no transfer takes place. For example, a life estate measured by the holder's life expires by its own terms. In addition, an easement or license that is personal to the holder also does not survive the holder's death.

- *Legal interests held in concurrent ownership,* where a right of survivorship exists, pass automatically to the surviving owner and thus are unaffected by the provisions of the decedent's will or by state laws regarding descent and distribution. The two types of concurrent ownership that involve this right of survivorship are (1) joint tenancies and (2) tenancies by the entirety.

- *In most states, the right of a surviving spouse to share in the deceased's estate overrides a contrary provision in the will.* The specific share of a surviving spouse varies among the states.

- *Apart from these three exceptions,* legal interests in real estate may be transferred by will in any way and to whichever persons the decedent wishes. Property passing by will carries with it all the rights and privileges, as well as all the liens and encumbrances, that existed prior to the death of the owner. (See Box 5-3.)

- *When a decedent has made no will and so dies intestate,* property will *descend and be distributed* among the legal heirs of the decedent in accordance with the laws of the particular state in which the property is located. In general, these statutes provide that the property will be distributed among spouse and children if they survive and, if not, among collateral family members (e.g., parents, brother and sisters, and nephews and nieces).

GIFTS

Gifts among family members are more likely to involve transfers of securities than of land. However, gifts of real estate are not uncommon and often play an important role in family tax planning. The annual gift tax exemption allows a donor to make a gift of up to $10,000 each year to as many different persons as she wishes without being subject to any obligation for gift taxes. The two essential elements to make a valid gift are (1) the intention by the donor to make a gift and (2) delivery of the property constituting the gift. When the property itself is not capable of physical delivery, as in the case of real estate, delivery is made by means of a deed of gift.

5-3 HOW THE "STEPPED-UP" BASIS BENEFITS HEIRS	Under the federal tax laws, property that is transferred by inheritance rather than by gift carries with it a major tax advantage. The advantage is that inherited property takes as its cost basis for tax purposes the fair market value as of the decedent's death even if this value is higher than the original cost. For example, assume a decedent bought property ten years ago at a cost of $10,000 and held it until his death, at which time it was worth $50,000. The person receiving it from the estate would take as his cost basis the $50,000 market value rather than the original cost of $10,000. (In other words, the basis is stepped up.) If the property were subsequently sold for $75,000, the taxable gain would be only $25,000. Thus, as a result of the "stepped-up basis," no tax need ever be paid on the $40,000 appreciation that occurred during the decedent's lifetime.
	By comparison, if the decedent had made a gift of the property during his lifetime, the donee of the gift would be required to carry over the original cost of $10,000 as his basis for tax purposes.

FORECLOSURE SALE OR TAX SALE

A transfer of title to real estate as a result of mortgage foreclosure or failure to pay real estate taxes is an involuntary form of transfer—that is, against the will of the owner. A mortgage foreclosure is one of the remedies of a mortgage holder (*mortgagee*) in the event that the property owner (*mortgagor*) fails to pay installments when due or fails to comply with other provisions of the mortgage instrument. (As explained in Part 6, the mortgage is the instrument that "secures" the promise to pay with the real estate.)

In general, two types of foreclosure are utilized in the United States: (1) foreclosure by action and sale and (2) foreclosure under power of sale. When the secured interest is evidenced by a mortgage, the first type is used. A court action is commenced by the mortgagee, resulting in a decree of foreclosure and an order by the court that the real estate be sold. When the secured interest is evidenced by a deed of trust, no court action is needed; and the lender of his or her agent, pursuant to a power of sale in the deed of trust, may sell the property at public sale. In both types of foreclosure, the sale is not valid unless prior notice has been given both to the mortgagor and to the public. The intention is to realize a price as close as possible to the fair market value of the property. The proceeds of the sale are applied to payment of the mortgage debt (together with unpaid interests and costs), with the balance going to the property owner (or junior creditors, if any).

In order to avoid the expense and publicity involved in a foreclosure sale, a defaulting mortgagor will sometimes convey the property to the mortgagee by a *deed in lieu of foreclosure,* in consideration of which the mortgagee will cancel the balance of the debt.

In the event a property owner fails to pay real estate taxes for a prescribed period, usually several years, the municipality may file a tax lien against the property and enforce the lien by conducting a tax sale. Again, notice to the public is required so that some assurance exists that a price close to the fair market value is realized. Unpaid taxes are satisfied from the sale proceeds with the balance going to the property owner or to discharge outstanding mortgages.

ADVERSE POSSESSION

An unusual method of acquiring title to real estate is by **adverse possession.** This doctrine has its roots in the very early history of the English common law. An individual may obtain a valid title to a parcel of real estate by openly occupying the land and representing himself as its owner for a period of years. This period was originally 21 years but now varies from state to state.

For example, suppose A begins to farm a tract of land under an honest presumption of ownership—perhaps because it is adjacent to land that A *does* own or because A has a deed that appears to be genuine but that, in fact, has a forged signature. A farms the land, pays taxes on it, and represents himself as the owner for the period of years that the law of the state requires to obtain title by adverse possession. At the end of that period of time, A will have legal *title* to the land. If B, the true owner, then presents himself and seeks to eject A, A will have a good defense to the action. (See Box 5-4.)

If A wants to have a document establishing his title, he will have to bring a special type of legal proceeding—called an *action to quiet title.* The essence of this proceeding is publication of notice setting forth A's claim to title and notification to every individual who may have any claim to the land, as determined by an examination of pertinent legal records. If the court then finds that A has met the statutory requirement—generally stated as open and continuous possession under a claim of right for the statutory period—then A will have a judgment declaring him to be the owner of the land.

Note that adverse possession is closely related to a prescriptive easement (see p. 106). In both cases, the rights of one person in land are transferred to another. The justification for these rules lies in the public policy that land should be as productive as possible and that one possessing and using land for a long period of time should not be evicted in favor of a long-absent owner. In many states, two different statutory periods are specified for acquiring title by adverse possession. The shortest statutory period is available to the possessor of land who claims under

5-4
BOUNDARY
DISPUTES AND
ADVERSE
POSSESSION

The doctrine of adverse possession—gaining title to land through possession rather than title—goes back many centuries in English history. During times when written records were often incomplete or destroyed, it was essential to have some means other than private battles to determine boundaries separating private landholdings. So the rule gradually evolved that possession under a claim of right for a period of time would determine title even against a written deed if the true title holder failed to assert his ownership—if he "slept on his rights."

The rule still applies in today's more settled times. In 1981, a New York court was faced with this set of facts. Mr. Rusoff bought a house in the suburbs in 1959 and immediately built a substantial wall along what he believed to be the north boundary of his property. He also planted bushes and trees along the boundary. It turned out that the wall actually enclosed two feet of the adjacent property owned by Mr. Engel. Neither Rusoff nor Engel realized this until years later, when a survey was taken after more than 15 years had passed (then the period of adverse possession in New York). After that time, Mr. Rusoff brought an action for a judgment determining him to be the owner of the land enclosed by the wall. Under the terms of the New York statute, title by adverse possession is gained when land is "cultivated or improved" or "has been protected by a substantial enclosure" for the necessary period of years. In addition, the possession of the land must be under a claim of right. The court ruled in favor of Mr. Rusoff.

a **color of title** (i.e., has a deed or other instrument that apparently conveys title but is, in fact, defective). The longer period to acquire adverse possession applies to persons who claim ownership but have no written instrument to support their claim. A final point about the statutory period is that it will not "run" in many states under certain specified conditions—for example, if the owner is a minor, insane, or in the military service.

ESCHEAT

The most unusual method of acquiring title to land is by **escheat.** Under this ancient common-law doctrine, if the owner of real estate dies without leaving a will and no heirs survive to inherit the property under the laws of descent and distribution, the state obtains title to the property. The original basis for the escheat doctrine was the feudal concept that ultimately the king owned all land. The feudal system of land ownership has long since been replaced by what is known as the **allodial system** (the current system described in this text). However, the doctrine of escheat remains, since on the death of an owner without a will or heirs, ownership of the real estate vests in the state.

EMINENT DOMAIN

The power of **eminent domain** has already been discussed as one of the public limitations on title. Since it is also a method of transferring title from private to public ownership, it is listed here as well. The price paid by the *condemning authority* (i.e., the government agency acquiring the land) normally is equal to the appraised value.

Compensation must be paid not only for land actually taken or utilized, but also for damages resulting from the taking. The two types of such damage are *severance damage* and *consequential damage. Severance damage* occurs when only a portion of property is taken. As a result, the remaining portion may lose much of its value, perhaps because it has a distorted or unusual shape, is not large enough to permit an economic use, or has lost access to highway or other desired location. In all these cases, the property owner must be compensated not only for the property actually taken, but also for the loss of value to the remaining property. *Consequential damage* is suffered when the property of one owner is taken by the government, and, as a result, damage is suffered by an adjoining owner. For example, property A is taken for a public use, as a result of which flooding occurs on adjacent property B. The owner of property B may be in a position to claim consequential damages for the taking.

PARTITION

When joint owners of real property wish to have separate property and they cannot agree among themselves to a division of the property, they can ask the court to help them. The judge may sell the property (partition sale) or divide it in an effort to be fair to all owners. The result of a court-ordered partition is another way to pass title.

ACCRETION

Over time rivers change their courses. When the river is a dividing line between two property owners, this can cause property ownership to change. If the change in course is sudden and dramatic, the adjoining owners draw a new boundary where the river used to be, and the only change is potential loss of dry land to the new river bed. On the other hand, if the change in the river's course is slow, the river remains the boundary, and one owner gains land through **accretion** while the other loses land.

CONTRACTS OF SALE

The **contract of sale** (also known as a *sales contract, agreement of sale,* and by a variety of other names) is the key instrument used in connection with the purchase and sale of real estate. The contract states the price of the property, the conditions involved in the transfer, and the rights and duties of each party. Once having signed the contract, each party is legally bound by it unless the other party consents to a change or modification.

The term "contract for deed" (also land contract or installment sales contract) is also a contract but has a special meaning. A contract for deed calls for a sale, with the deed not being given to the buyer until he or she has paid off a note to the seller. This instrument protects the seller since it is easier to cancel a contract for nonpayment than to foreclose under a mortgage or deed of trust.

The contract of sale does not itself transfer title; this is the function of the deed, which is discussed next.

ELEMENTS OF A CONTRACT

A contract is essentially an exchange of promises or an exchange of a promise (by one party) for performance of an act (by the other party). All contracts—whether for transfers of real estate, brokerage services, or any other purpose—can be classified in certain ways and have certain essential elements.[6]

❑ **MUTUAL AGREEMENT.** A contract requires a "meeting of the minds" by the parties concerning the substance of the agreement. This mutual agreement is normally manifested by the procedure of *offer* and *acceptance.*

An **offer** is a statement by one party of willingness to enter into a contractual arrangement. An offer must (1) be definite and certain, (2) define the precise subject matter of the proposed contract, and (3) be communicated by the offeror (the one making the offer) to the offeree (the recipient of the offer).

---

[6]*Contracts can be classified as (1) bilateral and (2) unilateral.*
By far the most common type, a bilateral *contract is one in which promises are exchanged. For example, A says to B, "I will pay you $10,000 for 150 Main Street." B says to A "I agree." This example is of an* oral bilateral *contract. If the promises were reduced to writing, it would be a* written bilateral *contract. Furthermore, it is an* express *contract because the promises are spelled out in words (whether spoken or written). There are circumstances where promises can be inferred by circumstances or by the actions of the parties. Such an* implied *contract is just as enforceable as an express contract, although it is much harder to prove. It is difficult to visualize a situation where an implied contract to sell land could arise.*
A unilateral contract *involves the exchange of a promise for an actual performance of an act. For example, A says to B, "I will pay you $50 if you will pace off the boundaries of this land." B says nothing but proceeds to perform the requested act. Upon B's performance, a binding unilateral contract has been entered into and A must pay B $50.*

Once the offeree has received an offer, the offer remains open and capable of being accepted until (1) it expires by its own terms, (2) the offeree rejects it, or (3) the offeror revokes it. An offer can also be canceled by the destruction of the subject matter (as where a building is destroyed by fire) or by circumstances that make the proposed contract illegal.

Acceptance of an offer occurs when the offeree, by word or deed, clearly manifests his or her intention to accept. The acceptance must (1) be positive and unequivocal, (2) conform precisely to the terms of the offer, and (3) be communicated to the offeror within the permissible time period.

An offeree may neither accept nor reject an offer but instead may make a **counteroffer.** Then it is up to the original offeror to decide to accept, reject, or make yet another counteroffer. And so the procedure will continue until a final rejection or acceptance has taken place.

❏ **REALITY OF ASSENT.** The assent of a party is real when it is given freely and with full knowledge of the circumstances affecting the agreement. When assent is not freely given, the contract may be invalid (i.e., not binding), depending on the cause. Four such cases are fraud, mistake, duress, and undue influence.

Fraud is the intentional misrepresentation of a material fact in order to induce another to part with something of value. It clearly indicates an absence of real assent by the defrauded party. To constitute fraud, there must be a misrepresentation of a fact, not merely an opinion (so-called **puffing**). The misrepresentation must also be material (i.e., significant or substantial), and it must be made with the intention that the other party rely on it to his detriment.

Mistake may or may not be grounds for holding a contract invalid. Mistakes of law (i.e., not understanding the legal consequences of an action) normally are not enough to excuse someone from complying with a contract. Mistakes of fact (e.g., how much acreage is included in a parcel of land) may or may not justify a cancellation (*rescission*) of a contract, depending on how material the mistake is and whether the other party should have realized a mistake was being made.

Duress is the obtaining of consent by the use of force or the threat of use of force.

Undue influence is the use of improper or excessive persuasion by one in a confidential relationship to another.

❏ **LEGAL CAPACITY TO CONTRACT.** A valid contract also requires that each party have the legal capacity to enter into a contractual relationship. *Legal capacity* means the ability to reason and understand the significance of an agreement.

Minors (children under the age of 18 or 21, depending on the particular state) generally lack legal capacity to enter into a contract except contracts for necessaries (e.g., contracts or purchases of food, medicine, clothing, etc.) Essential housing is usually considered a necessity as well, and so a minor may be held liable for the reasonable value of residential property occupied by the minor. If the contract is not for a necessity, the minor has the right to disaffirm the contract on reaching majority. This type of contract is called *voidable* because it is considered to be valid until the minor takes steps to disaffirm his obligations. Insane, incompetent, and at times intoxicated persons are not legally competent to enter into a contract.[7]

❏ **CONSIDERATION.**   Consideration for a promise or for performance is that which is given in exchange for it. The concept of consideration is fundamental to the Anglo-American idea of a contractual relationship. Except in rare instances, a promise unsupported by consideration from the other party cannot be enforced.

In general terms, consideration can include anything that constitutes a detriment to the *promisor* (the one making a promise) or a benefit to the *promisee* (the one to whom the promise is made). If A promises to pay B $10, that is consideration because B benefits. If A promises to refrain from doing something that is otherwise a matter of right (such as putting a building of more than six stories on his land), that also is consideration. It is important to note that the law does not look to the adequacy of the consideration but merely whether consideration was actually bargained for. Thus, past consideration (payment for an obligation already owed) cannot be consideration for a new contract. Similarly, illusory promises are not good consideration.

❏ **LEGALITY OF THE TRANSACTION.**   A contract will be enforceable only if the purpose is legal. A contract to buy or sell real property for an illegal purpose (e.g., gambling in a state that bars this activity) would be void and unenforceable.

❏ **CONTRACT IN WRITING.**   A final requirement for certain types of contracts is that they must be in writing in order to be enforceable. This requirement originally was imposed by an English statute, the *Statute of Frauds,* enacted in 1677. Its purpose was to prevent many fraudulent claims that were based on alleged oral promises or agreements. All American states have statutes modeled after the original Stat-

---

[7]*Until fairly recently, married women often lacked the right to own real estate as well as to exercise other legal rights. But by enactment of laws protecting married women's rights in virtually all states, these common-law disabilities have been eliminated so that a married woman now occupies the same legal status as her husband.*

ute of Frauds, and they are known by that name. For the purposes here, there are two significant types of agreements to which statutes of fraud apply.

- All contracts for the sale and purchase of real estate.
- All leases of real estate for a term exceeding a specified period (more than one year in most states).

Note that the statute of frauds will be satisfied as long as the person against whom the contract is sought to be enforced has signed it. It is not necessary that the person seeking to enforce the contract has signed it.

Generally, the writing must contain the following information:

- The identity of the parties.
- The identification of the subject matter of the contract.
- The consideration.

The writing need not be designated a contract. Any written memorandum will suffice to satisfy the statute, provided it contains the requisite information.[8]

KEY PROVISIONS OF THE CONTRACT

With this general background in mind, let us review the major provisions in a typical real estate contract. (Sometimes an option agreement precedes the contract of sale—see Box 5-5.) Preparation of a contract is normally the work of an attorney. However, the real estate decision maker should have sufficient background to understand the substance of an agreement and be alert to possible business or investment decisions that must be made in connection with certain provisions.

❑ **DATE OF AGREEMENT.**   The agreement should be dated because some provisions may contain time periods that refer to the date of execution of the contract. In addition, some states require local real estate contracts to be dated.

---

[8]*An important exception to the writing requirement of the Statute of Frauds is that an oral contract can be enforced where substantial* part performance *has occurred. Although the various states do not agree on precisely what constitutes substantial part performance, the acts most commonly relied on in the case of real estate are (1) total or part payment of the purchase price, (2) delivery of possession of the property to the buyer, and (3) improvements made on the property by the buyer. The reason these acts make a writing unnecessary is that it is unlikely that any of these acts would be performed if the parties had not reached a contractual agreement concerning sale of the property.*

5-5
USING OPTIONS

A *purchase option* is the right to buy a specified parcel of real estate from the owner at a specified price within a designated period. (Similarly, a sale option is the right to sell real estate while a lease option is the right to lease real estate.) For example, S owns 150 Main Street. S (as *optionor*) gives an option to J (as *optionee*) under which J may elect within the next 30 days (the *option period*) to buy 150 Main Street for $10,000. J Gives S cash to bind the option; the cash might equal 1 or 2 percent of the sales price.

If J decides not to buy the property within 30 days, S keeps the cash for his willingness to keep the property off the market for that time. If J decides to buy the property within 30 days, the parties enter into a formal contract of sale. (Ideally, J will want the form of contract agreed to at the time he is given the option in order to avoid the need to negotiate if he decides to exercise the option.)

As noted in Part 8, an option is a useful way to tie up land without committing substantial capital. Options may take a number of forms, each suitable for a different type of transaction. Some of the most common forms are as follows.

- *Fixed option.* This is the simplest form of option, entitling the optionee to buy the property at a fixed price during the option period.

- *Step-up option.* This type of arrangement is used in long-term options; the purchase price of the property increases by steps periodically throughout the option period. In the case of a renewable option, the step-up will frequently occur at the time of renewal.

- *Rolling option.* These options are most commonly used by subdividers of raw land. The option covers several contiguous tracts. The developer buys and subdivides one tract and, if it proves profitable, he can then acquire the next tract. Thus, the option "rolls" from one tract to another. Usually, the price steps up as each tract is acquired, thus permitting the landowner to share in the increased value of the property as it is built up. In addition, the landowner spreads his gain over a period of years and so is not required to report it at once.

- *Full-credit option.* Here the price for the option is fully credited against the purchase price of the property if the option is exercised.

- *Declining-credit option.* As an inducement to the optionee, the percentage of the option price that may be credited against the purchase price of the property declines as time goes by.

In addition to tying up property with minimum capital, options permit speculation in property with only a very small cash outlay. For example, a speculator might pay $1,000 for an option to buy real estate at $50,000. Within the option period (say, six months), the value of the real estate rises to $60,000. The optionee can sell his option to a third party for $10,000, who can then purchase the property for $60,000 ($10,000 for the option plus $50,000 paid to the seller of the real estate). The optionee has made a profit of $9,000 on his $1,000 investment.

❏ **NAMES AND CAPACITY OF PARTIES.**   The parties should be identified by name and, if other than individuals, by type of organization (e.g., corporation or partnership).[9]

❏ **DESCRIPTION OF PROPERTY AND INTEREST CONVEYED.** Any description of the property is sufficient provided it, in fact, accurately defines the parcel of real estate being conveyed. If the seller has less than a fee simple interest, this should be specified.

❏ **CONSIDERATION AND MANNER OF PAYMENT.**   In most cases, the consideration paid for the real estate will be money. When money is the consideration, it normally will be paid in two installments: (1) The escrow or downpayment (frequently, 10 percent of the total price) and (2) the balance at the closing of title. To the extent that the buyer takes over an existing mortgage on the property, the cash to be paid will be reduced by that amount. (See Box 5-6.)

❏ **CONDITIONS OF SALE.**   Frequently, the sale will be subject to specified conditions, with one party (usually the buyer) or both parties entitled to cancel the contract if the conditions are not satisfied.

❏ **STATE OF TITLE; TYPE OF DEED.**   Since no title is "perfect," the contract will specify precisely what defects and limitations the buyer is obligated to accept. In addition, the form of deed will be specified.

❏ **PERSONAL PROPERTY.**   Frequently, a sale of real property is accompanied by the sale of related personal property, such as the furnishings in a motel or the carpets and blinds in a private home. A list of personal property to be conveyed should be attached to the contract.

❏ **RISK OF LOSS.**   During the contract period (between the signing of the contract and the closing of title), the property might be destroyed or damaged by fire or other cause. Who bears the risk of loss? Most states have a statute that spells out where the risk lies (usually on the seller). If the parties wish a different result, the contract should so provide. (Note that the party assuming the risk can be protected by purchasing insurance.)

---

[9]*In any case where an individual party is not acting on her own behalf (e.g., an agent for a principal or an individual for an organization), such individual should establish her authority to act. An agent can bind his principal in a real estate contract only when the agent's authority is in writing. A general partner has the authority to bind the partnership, but it must be clear that he is, in fact, a general partner. A corporate officer may bind the corporation if he has actual authority or apparent authority (i.e., circumstance makes it appear as if he has authority). To be on the safe side, however, a corporate officer should produce a resolution of the board of directors authorizing the purchase or sale.*

5-6
AN "UNDER THE TABLE" DEAL FALLS THROUGH

Sometimes, buyers and sellers of real estate are tempted to pass a portion of the price "under the table" in order to reduce the seller's tax liability. But this sort of illegality can backfire. Here is an actual case involving the sale of six acres of waterfront land in the town of Southhampton, New York. The seller's price was $180,000. The buyer refused to pay that price but came back with a counteroffer that he claimed would net the seller the equivalent of $180,000 on an after-tax basis.

His proposal was to have the contract specify a purchase price of $120,000. The buyer would sign a side agreement obligating himself to pay an additional $40,000 in cash. If the seller failed to report the cash payment, his tax savings would enable him to end up with virtually the same after-tax proceeds that he would have received if no price concession had been made to the buyer.

The seller agreed, and the contract of sale and side agreement were signed. The buyer gave a $10,000 deposit by check, which contained a notation that the total price was $120,000 (not $160,000). The seller showed the papers to his attorney, who refused to take part in the transaction. The seller then refused to go ahead. He also declined to return the $10,000 downpayment.

The buyer began an action to compel the seller to go through with the deal. The court applied the ancient (but still applicable) common-law doctrine of "clean hands." This bars relief to a plaintiff who himself is a wrongdoer. In this case, a comparison of the notation on the check (that the purchase price was $120,000) with the contract and side memorandum (indicating a total price of $160,000) showed that both parties had participated in a plan to evade taxation. Result: the complaint was dismissed, and the purchaser, who cooked up the scheme, was out $10,000.

❏ **DATE AND PLACE OF CLOSING OF TITLE.** The contract will often specify the date and place when the actual closing of title will take place. This should be set far enough ahead so that reasonable time is given for the performance of any conditions that must be satisfied. Normally, either party is entitled to one (or possibly several) adjournments of the closing. However, if the contract specifies that *time is of the essence,* then it is understood that the closing date is firm and no adjournments will be permitted without penalty to the delaying party.

❏ **DEFAULT PROVISIONS.** In practice, real estate contracts normally contain provisions covering possible defaults by either party. When the buyer defaults, the contract may provide that the seller is entitled to keep the downpayment as liquidated damages but has no further claim against the buyer for the balance of the purchase price. On the other hand, in the event of a default by the seller, the buyer may be entitled only to receive back any downpayment (plus reimbursement for certain specified expenses, such as title examination) and have no further remedy against that seller.[10] In any case, the contract should clearly state the intent of the parties with regard to default.

❏ **SIGNATURES.**   Finally, the contract must be signed by all parties to it. Recall that, under the statute of frauds, the contract will not be enforced against one who has not executed it.

It is worth repeating that the real estate contract of sale is the most important instrument in a real estate transaction because it establishes the framework in which the transaction will take place. Both statutory law and common law do provide a set of rules for settling disputes between parties to a real estate agreement, but most of these can be overridden by a provision in the contract itself. So it is up to the real estate decision maker and his or her professional counsel to be sure that the contract achieves the desired objectives and provides protection against possible risks.

DEEDS AND THEIR RECORDATION

In virtually all cases, title is evidenced by a written instrument called a **deed.** There are three questions to be answered about deeds.

- What makes a deed valid?
- What are the various types of deeds?
- Why are deeds recorded?

ELEMENTS OF A VALID DEED

A deed must (1) be in writing, (2) identify the person or persons to whom title is conveyed (the grantee or grantees), (3) identify the property being conveyed, and (4) be signed by the person or persons making the conveyance (the grantor or grantors).

---

[10]*In the case of a contract for the purchase of real estate, a default by the purchaser normally will consist of his or her failure to pay the full purchase price at the time set for the closing of title. In such event and absent any contrary provision in the contract, the seller may sell the real estate elsewhere and seek damages against the defaulting purchaser equal to the difference between the contract price and the price received by the seller in the substitute transaction. If the seller defaults, by being unable or unwilling to convey title to the real estate in the form set forth in the contract, the purchaser (absent any provision in the contract to the contrary) normally is in a position to seek specific performance of the contract—that is, the purchaser may seek a judgment by a court requiring the seller to convey the contracted real estate. The purchaser is not limited to an action for money damages because every parcel of real estate is deemed unique by virtue of its unique location; thus, monetary damages do not always represent adequate compensation to the purchaser.*

If more than one grantee is named, the nature of their concurrent ownership should be specified (e.g., tenants in common or joint tenants with right of survivorship). The grantees must be legally capable of holding title, and the grantors must have the legal capacity to convey title; if they are doing so on behalf of an artificial person, such as a corporation or partnership, they must have the authority to act on its behalf.

❑ **WORDS OF CONVEYANCE.**   The deed must contain words of conveyance—that is, language that makes clear the intention to transfer title. An example is "the said grantor does hereby grant and convey to the said grantee. . . ."

❑ **CONSIDERATION.**   In addition, common law required the deed to recite the payment of consideration, although the amount was irrelevant. Many states have passed laws eliminating this requirement, but most deeds do use language such as "in consideration of one dollar in hand paid, the receipt and sufficiency whereof is hereby acknowledged. . . ." The parties will not wish to specify the exact purchase price since the deed almost always will be recorded and thus open to public view.

❑ **DELIVERY.**   Finally, a deed must be delivered in order for the transfer of title to be effective. The most common form of delivery is directly to the grantee. But delivery may be effective if the deed is given to an agent of the grantee, is given to the local records office for recording, or is otherwise transferred under circumstances making clear the grantor's intention to complete the transaction. However, when a grantor signs a deed and then retains possession of it, no transfer of title has occurred.

TYPES OF DEEDS

Deeds come in several different categories. The principal distinction among them relates to the precise responsibilities that the grantor assumes in connection with the conveyance. These responsibilities are called *warranties*. A warranty combines a representation that a certain state of facts is true and the responsibility to make good any damages if the facts turn out to be otherwise.

❑ **GENERAL WARRANTY DEED.**   This deed includes the broadest warranties by the grantor and so would be most preferred by the grantee. Although the precise warranties in such a deed depend on the law of the particular state, **general warranty deeds** usually contain four basic covenants.

- The *covenant of seisin,* by which the grantor represents that he or she, in fact, owns the property.

- The *covenant of the right to convey,* by which the grantor represents that no obstacle exists to a transfer of the property.

- The *covenant against encumbrances* (i.e., a representation that no claims exist against the property other than those specified in the deed or contract).

- The *covenant of quiet enjoyment,* by which the grantor represents that no person with a superior right to the property can interfere with the grantee's use or possession of the property.

❑ **SPECIAL WARRANTY DEED.**   This is exactly the same as a general warranty deed with one important distinction: the grantor will be liable for breach of warranty only if the cause arose through the grantor's own act or during his period of ownership. The grantor thus disclaims any responsibility for defects that arose before he became the owner. A **special warranty deed** is commonly given by a bank trust department. The bank wishes to avoid responsibility for any defects that originated prior to the bank's ownership (as trustee).

❑ **QUITCLAIM DEED.**   Although this deed, too, can effectively convey title, it is normally used as a means of surrendering a claim to property that may or may not be valid. In effect, the grantor under a **quitclaim deed** says: "I don't know if I own this property, but if I do, I convey to you whatever rights I may have." This type of deed is also used to correct an error made in an earlier conveyance.[11]

The quitclaim deed is very important in clearing "clouds on title." For example, Harry had two sons, Fred and Grover. Fred stayed home to take care of Harry in his old age while Grover became a dentist. All three agreed that Fred should have the small family farm when Harry died; however, Harry never executed a will.

Upon Harry's death, Fred chose to sell the farm and move to the city. When the prospective buyer's attorney "checked the title," he found that Fred and Grover had equal claims under the state's descent and distribu-

---

[11] *In addition to the categories just distinguished, deeds are often known by the name or authority of the person executing them. Thus, an* executor's deed *is made by the executor of an estate (and the grantee is put on notice that he must be sure of the executor's authority to make the conveyance). A* sheriff's deed *conveys property sold at a sheriff's sale following foreclosure proceedings, and a* tax deed *follows a forced sale for failure to pay real estate taxes. The term* judicial deed *is often used to describe any deed from a sale resulting from a judicial proceeding. Most of these deeds are without covenants, but this is not invariably so.*

tion laws. Grover was unwilling to sign the general warranty deed called for in the contract of sale because he felt he had no right to the property, and he also didn't want to make the promises inherent in the general warranty deed.

The buyer's lawyer held up the sale because Fred could not show "good and marketable title." Grover then gave Fred a quitclaim deed (which contained no warranties). This was recorded and cleared the cloud on Fred's title, allowing him to convey successfully to the buyer.

RECORDING DEEDS

As noted previously, title effectively passes to the grantee once the deed has been delivered to and accepted by the grantee. In practice, however, the grantee will take one further step—and is well advised to take it as quickly as possible. This step is to bring the deed to the local land records office and have it "recorded."[12] A photocopy is made of the deed and is filed in a record book, which is tied to an indexing system so that ownership claims become public knowledge. By thus making it relatively easy for title holders to be identified, the recording system is considered to "put the world on notice" that the property described in the recorded deed is owned by the individual named there (the owner of record).

Most recording statutes generally have the following features.

- They do not affect the validity of the deed between the grantor and grantee; they merely determine the outcome if more than one deed is given to the same property.

- The deed cannot be recorded until it is acknowledged—that is, the person signing the deed must acknowledge his or her signature before a notary public or commissioner of deeds.

- Whether the deed itself or a memorandum of deed is recorded, sufficient information must be placed on record so that the parties and the property can be identified.

CONSTRUCTIVE NOTICE

Not only deeds but also mortgages, leases, contracts of sale, mechanic's and tax liens, restrictive convenants, and other matters pertaining to land may be recorded. In this way, protection against fraudulent acts is afforded to anyone having an interest in real estate, for anyone dealing with land is deemed to know any fact that has been spread on the public

---

[12]Note that all land records are recorded in the local office where the land is located, not in the land office nearest to the owner.

record. A person is said to have *constructive notice* of such information, whether or not the person has actual notice of it. Again, all these recorded instruments become part of the abstract (history) of title.

The history of recording statutes is an interesting one but can only be given briefly here. Under early law, the rule was "first in time, first in right." If T sold property to D on Monday and then sold the same property (fraudulently, of course) to H on Wednesday, D had the better title. Recording statutes were passed to reduce the possibility of these double sales. The first recording statute in this country was a 1640 law in the Massachusetts Bay Colony; over the years, all states have passed these statutes, which differ in certain significant ways. Most statutes say that "first to record, first in right." So, in the example given, if H (the second grantee) raced to the courthouse ahead of D and recorded a deed first, H would keep the property. (D, of course, would have a claim against T if T could be found.) Therefore, this statute is called a *race-type statute.*

Another type says that if the first grantee fails to record before the second conveyance is made and the second grantee did not know of the first conveyance, the second grantee is the title holder. Thus, in the example, if D failed to record the deed before Wednesday, when the second conveyance was made to H, and H was ignorant of the deed to D, H is the title holder. This type of statute, called a *notice-type statute*, again penalizes the original grantee if he fails to act promptly.

SUMMARY

The material contained in this and the prior chapter constitutes the legal rules by which the real estate game is played. It is important that the real estate decision maker have knowledge of this legal environment in order to be able to know the right questions to ask, to be able to negotiate business aspects of a transaction, and to use the services of legal counsel effectively. These rules change over time as society finds better ways to serve its needs. Forecasting changes in the rules can be a critical element in winning the game, so we will return to this subject in Chapters 28 and 29.

In this chapter, we discussed the "nuts and bolts" of real estate conveyancing. First, title and ownership were analyzed, and the private and public limitations on ownership were described. Private limitations may exist because other persons have some of the bundle of rights in the particular property or because of restrictive covenants or conditions imposed by prior owners. Public limitations on title arise by virtue of restrictions created by the common law, police power, eminent domain, or as a consequence of property taxation.

Next, the methods of transferring title to real estate were discussed. Of the seven ways of transferring title, purchase and sale is by far the most important method, although transfers by inheritance or by gift also are common. Other methods include the foreclosure sale, adverse possession, escheat, and eminent domain.

Whenever title is transferred by purchase and sale, the primary instrument is the contract of sale. A valid and binding contract must meet certain requirements and normally contain certain key provisions. The contract of sale will result in a closing at which time a deed, evidencing the formal transfer of title, will be exchanged for cash or other consideration paid by the purchaser. Deeds are normally recorded in a public records office in order to put the world on notice that title to the particular property has been transferred and is now owned by the individual named in the deed (the owner of record).

IMPORTANT TERMS

Abstract of title	Mechanic's lien
Accretion	Offer
Adverse possession	Offer of purchase
Allodial system	Offer of sale
Color of title	Plat
Contract of sale	Police power
Counteroffer	Puffing
Deed	Quitclaim deed
Eminent domain	Real property taxation
Escheat	Restrictive covenants
Escrow closing	Special warranty deed
Fraud	Survey
General warranty deed	Title
Good and marketable title	Title closing
Inheritance	Title insurance
Law of nuisance	

REVIEW QUESTIONS

5.1   Why should a real estate investor or advisor be familiar with the rules regarding real estate transfers?

5.2   In what sense is a restrictive convenant a limitation on title? Give an example.

5.3   List and define the four types of public limitations on title.

5.4   What are the two major requirements for good and marketable title?

5.5   Explain how a parcel of land is described under (1) the metes and bounds system and (2) the government survey system.

5.6   What are the two most common methods of transferring title to real estate?

5.7   Name the six essential elements for a valid contract to convey real estate.

5.8   What is one major advantage of a purchase option over an actual purchase of real estate?

5.9   Explain the difference between a general and special warranty deed.

5.10   What is the primary purpose of recording a deed of real estate?

REFERENCES   American Law Institute, *Restatement of the Law, Torts,* A.L.I., 1934–39; and *Restatement of the Law, 2d Torts.* A.L.I. 1965–79. Updated by supplements.

American Law Institute. *Restatement of the Law of Property,* A.L.I., 1936–44; and *Restatement of the Law, Property 2d,* A.L.I. 1977–83. *Restatement 2d* deals entirely with landlord–tenant law and the law of donative transfers. Updated by supplements.

Barrow, Paul. *Federal Regulation of Real Estate: The Real Estate Settlement Procedures Act.* 2nd ed. Boston: Warren, Gorham, and Lamont, 1983.

Bergin & Haskell. *Preface to Estates in Land and Future Interests.* 2nd ed. Foundation Press, 1984.

Bosselman, Fred P., Duane Ferner, and Tobin M. Richter. *Federal Land Use Regulation.* New York: Practicing Law Institute, 1977.

Browder, Olin L. *Basic Property Law.* 4th ed. St. Paul, Minn.: West, 1984.

Clurman, David. *The Business Condominium: A New Form of Business Property Ownership.* New York: Wiley, 1973.

Clurman, David, and Edna L. Hebard. *Condominiums and Cooperatives.* New York: Wiley, 1970.

Corley, Robert N., Peter J. Shedd, and Charles F. Floyd. *Real Estate and the Law.* New York: Random House, 1982.

Cunningham, Stoebuck & Whitman. *The Law of Property.* St. Paul, Minn.: West, 1984.

Everhart, Marion E. *Everhart on Easements.* St. Paul, Minn.: Todd, 1981.

Fishman, Richard P. *Housing for All Under Law: New Directions in Housing, Land Use, and Planning Law.* Chicago: American Bar Association, Advisory Commission on Housing, 1983.

French, William B., and Harold F. Lusk. *Law of the Real Estate Business.* 5th ed. Homewood, Ill.: Irwin, 1984.

Friedman, Milton. *Contents and Consequences of Real Property.* 3rd ed. New York: Practicing Law Institute, 1975.

Haar, Charles M. *Land Use Planning.* Boston: Little, Brown, 1980.

Jacobus, Charles. *Real Estate Law.* Englewood Cliffs, N.J.: Prentice-Hall, 1985.

Kratovil, Robert. *Modern Mortgage Law and Practice.* 8th ed. Englewood Cliffs, N.J.: Prentice-Hall, 1983.

Lynn, T. S., H. F. Goldberg, and D. S. Abrams. *Real Estate Limited Partnerships.* New York: Wiley, 1977.

Moynihan. *Introduction to the Law of Real Property.* 2nd ed. St. Paul, Minn.: West, 1987.

Prosser and Keeton on the Law of Torts. 5th ed. St. Paul, Minn.: West, 1984.

Protective Covenants. Arlington, Va.: National Association of Industrial and Office Parks/Educational Foundation, 1985.

Reilly, John W. *Language of Real Estate.* 3rd ed. Chicago: Longman Financial Services Institute, 1988.

Reilly, John W. *The Language of Real Estate in Hawaii,* Honolulu: Edward Enterprises, 1975.

Rohan, Patrick J., and Michael P. Sanchirico. *Homeowner Associations and Planned Unit Developments Law and Practice.* Albany, N.Y.: Matthew Bender and Co., 1986.

Rose, Jerome G. *Legal Foundations of Land Use Planning: A Textbook/Casebook.* Piscataway, N.J.: Center for Urban Policy Research, 1981.

Schoshinski. *American Law of Landlord and Tenant.* Lawyer's Cooperative, 1980.

U.S. Department of HUD. *Cooperative Conversion Handbook.* Washington, D.C.: U.S. Department of HUD, 1980.

Warner, Raymond. *Real Estate Closings.* 2nd ed. New York: Practicing Law Institute, 1988.

Webster's Real Estate Law in North Carolina. 3rd ed. Charlottesville, Va.: Michie, 1988.

Zerner, Robert V., et al. *Guide to Federal Environment Law.* Washington, D.C.: Bureau of National Affairs, 1988.

PERIODICALS

Ecology Law Quarterly. Berkeley: School of Law, University of California (quarterly).

Land Use Law and Zoning Digest. Chicago: American Planning Association (monthly).

National Property Law Digest. Washington, D.C.: National Property Law Digest (monthly).

Real Estate Law Journal. Boston: Warren, Gorham, and Lamont (quarterly).

Real Property, Probate, and Trust Journal. Chicago: American Bar Association (quarterly).

P A R T 3

VALUATION AND THE APPRAISAL PROCESS

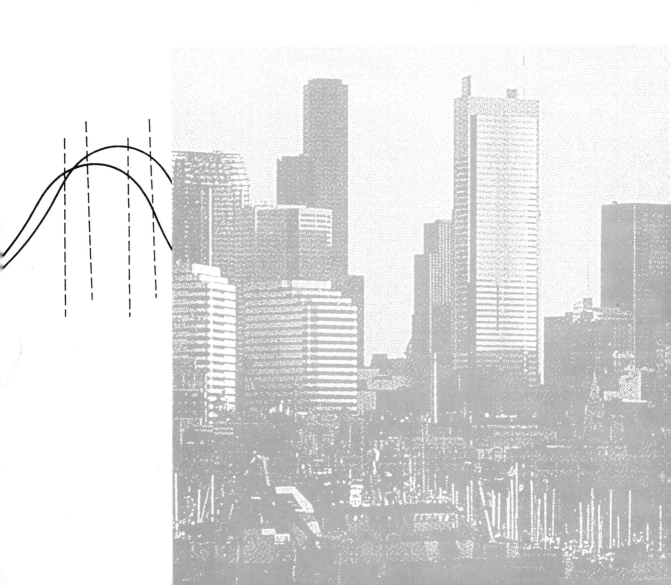

*P*RINCIPLES OF VALUATION

In Part 1, we described real estate in physical and economic terms, and identified the features that make it desirable in the marketplace. Recall that the unique features of a parcel of real estate are its location and its perpetual life in that location. Urban and regional demographics as well as the physical characteristics of all construction on and around the parcel determine the property's ability to satisfy market demand. Various ways to own and transfer property were defined in Part 2. In Part 3, we examined the marketing of real estate, looking at the determination of consumer needs and the process by which real estate (space-over-time with certain services) is sold. Building on this foundation,[1] we are now ready to consider the subject of real estate valuation and to seek answers to two particular questions.

- Can the specific elements or factors that contribute to the value of a parcel of real estate be identified?

- What methods are used to arrive at a valuation figure for a parcel of real estate (the process known as **appraisal**)?

This chapter deals generally with the answers to the first question, and Chapters 7 and 8 discuss the three traditional methods used by appraisers in the valuation process (i.e., the sales comparison, cost, and income methods). At the outset, it should be emphasized that the concept of value is a complex one since values will differ depending on the

---

[1] *The history of appraisal thought is too extensive even to cover briefly in an introductory text. Still, a few names must be mentioned. The foundation is in the classical economists—Smith, Ricardo, Malthus, Marx, Mill, and Marshall. This thought was continued by the urban, regional, and urban land economists cited in Part 1. Great contributions in specific appraisal applications have come from John Zangerle, Frederic Babcock, Robert Fisher, Paul Wendt, Leon Ellwood, Richard Ratcliff, William Kinnard, and James Graaskamp, among others. The works of these gentlemen and of their many younger contemporaries are cited in the references at the end of Part 4.*

assumptions of the person making the valuation and the context in which the appraisal is made. Owners of real estate, using different assumptions, have been known to argue *simultaneously* for a higher valuation (in a condemnation proceeding to determine the compensation to be paid by the municipality) and for a lower valuation (in a property tax-reduction proceeding, in which the owner seeks to lower the assessment placed on the property).

Still, a number of empirical rules have been sufficiently tested by experience so that they are entitled to be called concepts or principles of valuation. Perhaps the most complete expression of the appraisal "body of knowledge" is found in *The Appraisal of Real Estate,* ninth edition, by the American Institute of Real Estate Appraisers. In this section we drew heavily from that source to present the basic principles of valuation.

"An appraisal is an unbiased estimate of the nature, quality, value, or utility of an interest in, or aspect of, identified real estate and related personalty."[2] An appraisal is based on selective research into appropriate market areas; assemblage of pertinent data; the application of appropriate analytical techniques; and the knowledge, experience, and professional judgment necessary to develop an appropriate solution to a problem. In other words, an appraisal is first and foremost an *opinion.* It is based on the analysis of facts but is itself an opinion. It is an opinion of the value of a specific ownership claim (Part 2) based on the future benefits expected to accrue to the owner of the claim. The appraisal is of a specific property as of a specific date.

REASONS FOR AN APPRAISAL

An appraisal may be sought for a number of different reasons, discussed as follows.

PROPERTY TAXES

Perhaps the most common reason for appraisals is for local governments to prepare assessments rolls in connection with levying property taxes. These taxes are typically based on the current fair market value of real estate within the taxing district.

LOAN PURPOSES

Probably the next most frequent use of an appraisal is to establish the value of a parcel of real estate that is to serve as collateral for a loan. Either because of statutory restriction or internal policy, a lending in-

---

[2]The Appraisal of Real Estate, *9th ed. (Chicago: American Institute of Real Estate Appraisers, 1987), p. 11.*

stitution normally will not lend in excess of a specified percentage of value (called the *loan-to-value ratio*).

For example, a lender may be unwilling to lend more than 75 percent of the appraised value of an office building. Alternatively, some lenders may be willing to lend a higher percentage of value, provided the borrower is willing to pay a somewhat higher interest rate to compensate for the extra risk. In either situation, an independent determination of value is necessary.

OTHER PURPOSES

Appraisals are frequently required by insurance companies in connection with the adjustment of a loss resulting from fire or other casualty. In addition, when private property is taken under the power of eminent domain and the municipality and owner are unable to agree on what is fair compensation, testimony by appraisers is a crucial element in the condemnation proceeding to determine the amount to be paid for the real estate.

When a person dies owning real estate, an appraisal normally is required in connection with the determination of estate tax. Separation or divorce agreements frequently require appraisal of property owned by either or both spouses. In some ground leases, where vacant land is leased for a long period of time to a developer who builds an improvement, the ground rental may be subject to adjustment at periodic intervals based on a reappraisal of the land. And, in many sales transactions, the purchaser seeks an independent appraisal as an aid to determining the price to be paid. All these reasons are summarized in Table 6-1.

CHARACTERIS-TICS OF VALUE   Real property values are affected by four characteristics. All are necessary, in varying degrees, for value to be present, and none alone is sufficient to create value. The four characteristics are (1) utility, (2) scarcity, (3) effective demand, and (4) transferability.[3]

❑ **UTILITY.**   Utility can be viewed as the ability of a good or service—in this case, real property—to satisfy a need. The degree to which a property satisfies particular needs is highly affected by the characteristics of the property and the purpose for which it is being used.

---

[3] *In the ninth edition of* The Appraisal of Real Estate, *characteristics are listed as "factors." Factors of value are shown in four parts as utility, scarcity, desire, and effective purchasing power. Transferability is dropped as a factor. We prefer the traditional listing and have continued it in this edition of* Modern Real Estate. *If you sit for an appraisal examination given by the American Institute, remember the distinction.*

TABLE 6-1   POSSIBLE REASONS FOR AN APPRAISAL

1. Transfer of ownership
   a. To help prospective buyers set offering prices.
   b. To help prospective sellers determine acceptable selling prices.
   c. To establish a basis for real property exchanges.
   d. To establish a basis for reorganization or merging the ownership of multiple properties.
   e. To determine the terms of a sale price for a proposed transaction.

2. Financing and credit
   a. To estimate the value of the security offered for a proposed mortgage loan.
   b. To provide an investor with a sound basis for deciding whether to purchase real estate mortgages, bonds, or other types of securities.
   c. To establish the basis for a decision regarding the insuring or underwriting of a loan on real property.

3. Just compensation in condemnation proceedings
   a. To estimate market value of a property as a whole—that is, before the taking.
   b. To establish the market value of the remainder after the taking.
   c. To estimate the damages to the property.

4. Tax matters
   a. To estimate assessed value.
   b. To separate assets into depreciable (or capital recapture) items such as buildings, and nondepreciable items such as land, and to estimate applicable depreciation (or capital recapture) rates.
   c. To determine gift or inheritance taxes.

5. Investment counseling and decision making
   a. To set rental schedules and lease provisions.
   b. To determine feasibility of a construction or renovation program.
   c. To help corporations or third parties purchase homes for transferred employees.
   d. To serve the needs of insurers, adjusters, and policyholders.
   e. To facilitate corporate mergers, the issuing of stock, or the revision of book value.
   f. To estimate liquidation value for forced sale or auction proceedings.
   g. To counsel clients on investment matters, by considering their goals, alternatives, resources, constraints, and timing.
   h. To advise zoning boards, courts, and planners, among others, on the probable effects of proposed actions.
   i. To arbitrate between adversaries.
   j. To determine supply and demand trends in a market.
   k. To determine the status of real estate markets.

Source: The Appraisal of Real Estate, *9th ed. (Chicago: American Institute of Real Estate Appraisers, 1987), p. 10.*

❑ **SCARCITY.**   **Scarcity** refers to the relative availability of a particular good or commodity. In the case of real property, the value characteristic of scarcity is probably more affected by the state of building technology and by location than by mere quantity. Land need not be scarce in an absolute sense in order to have value, but its value is highly affected by the scarcity of certain property types (uses) within a given area.

❑ **EFFECTIVE DEMAND.**   In order for real property to have value, **effective demand** for the property must exist. As noted in Part 1, effective demand is the desire (need) for an economic good coupled with the buying power or ability to pay for that good. Desire alone is not sufficient; many people would like to live in a $300,000 house, but few have the ability to pay for such a house.

❑ **TRANSFERABILITY.**   **Transferability** refers to the absence of legal constraints on the owner's right to sell or convey his or her property rights to another. If the legal interest associated with the ownership of real property cannot be conveyed, its value in exchange will be nonexistent, whatever its value in use to the owner.

FORCES AFFECTING VALUES

Real estate will have value provided it is useful, scarce, and transferable and provided there is effective demand for it. In general, four primary "forces" influence real estate values: (1) physical-environmental, (2) economic, (3) social, and (4) governmental. Together, they interact and create the environment and the marketplace within which real property is owned, used, and transferred.

❑ **PHYSICAL-ENVIRONMENTAL FORCES.**   The physical forces that influence real property site values include location, size, shape, area, frontage, topsoil, drainage, contour, topography, vegetation, accessibility, utilities, climate, and view. The values of structures are determined by construction quality, design, adaptability, and harmony with their surroundings. Each of these physical characteristics can play a major role in determining how a particular parcel may be utilized. The use to which a parcel is put, in turn, materially affects the benefits that accrue to the owner and, thus, the property's value.

❑ **ECONOMIC FORCES.**   Economic forces influencing the value of real property reflect how the property interacts or fits within the economy of the region and neighborhood. Such factors as community income, the availability and terms of mortgage credit, price levels, tax rates, and labor supply represent economic forces affecting property values.

❏ **SOCIAL FORCES.** Social forces such as attitudes toward household formation (living alone or with others, having children, etc.), population trends, neighborhood character, architectural design, and utility have an impact on value. Unlike physical and economic forces, social forces are more subjective in nature and are therefore sometimes difficult to interpret.

❏ **GOVERNMENTAL FORCES.** Governmental forces include the impact of local, state, and federal governments and are collectively referred to as *public policy*. Examples of governmental forces that affect value include zoning and building codes, real property taxation, public housing, and police and fire protection. The role or impact of governmental decisions on market value cannot be ignored.

All these forces are dynamic or changing over time—even the physical forces. The framework in this book is forward-looking, requiring the decision maker to estimate the impact of these forces over the life of the subject property.

VALUE, PRICE, AND COST

The terms *value, price,* and *cost* are frequently used in relation to real estate decision making. As far as real estate appraisal is concerned, it is of critical importance that these terms be differentiated. Value, price, and cost are different concepts, and the real estate decision maker should use these terms only within their proper definition.

VALUE

According to its objective definition, **value is the power of a good or service to command other goods or services in the marketplace.** In a very simple barter economy, value can be determined by following this definition literally. For example, A may offer a dozen bananas in the market and see what response he receives from B who may offer him goods or services in exchange (See Box 6-1.)

In our modern economy, the process of determining value is somewhat more complicated. When we talk about a *capital asset* (i.e., something that produces income, such as an office building), it is common to define value as the *present worth of the future cash flow.* If the office building is expected to produce $10,000 of cash flow every year in perpetuity, the value of the office building will be equal to the value today of the right to receive these future annual cash flows.

Although this financial concept of value is more useful than the simple definition given earlier, it has some weaknesses when applied to real estate. Two are that (1) not all property generates a periodic cash flow (e.g., raw land) and (2) some benefits associated with property ownership are nonpecuniary in nature (e.g., the benefits of living in

6-1
MARKET VALUE

Market value is the major focus of most real property appraisal assignments; developing an estimate of market value is the purpose of most appraisal assignments. Most definitions of market value are based on a decision by the California Supreme Court in an eminent domain case (*Sacramento Railroad Company* v. *Heilbron,* 156 Calif. 408, 1909). That definition reads as follows.

The highest price estimated in terms of money which the land would bring if exposed for sale in the open market, with reasonable time allowed in which to find a purchaser, buying with knowledge of all the uses and purposes to which it is adapted and for which it is capable.

There are two other widely accepted definitions.

The price at which a willing seller would sell and a willing buyer would buy, neither being under abnormal pressure.

The price expected if a reasonable time is allowed to find a purchaser and if both seller and prospective buyer are fully informed.

Fundamental assumptions and conditions are presumed in the definition of market value. They are as follows.

1. Buyer and seller are motivated by self-interest.
2. Buyer and seller are informed and are acting prudently.
3. The property is exposed for a reasonable time on the open market.
4. Payment is made in cash, in its equivalent, or in specified financing terms.
5. Specified financing, if any, may be the financing actually in place or on terms generally available for the property type in its locale on the effective appraisal date.
6. The effect, if any, on the amount of market value of atypical financing, services, or fees shall be clearly and precisely revealed in the appraisal report.

Source: The Appraisal of Real Estate, 9th ed. (Chicago: American Institute of Real Estate Appraisers, 1987), pp. 15–20.

one's own home). So real property value might be defined as the present worth of *all* future benefits.

PRICE

Price is the amount of money that is actually paid, asked, or offered for a good or service. As such, price represents two people's estimates of value in terms of money. Such an estimate may be greater than, equal to, or less than the "objective value" of the good or service in question.

In real estate transactions, one of the major factors that causes the price of a particular parcel to differ from its "objective value" is the type of financing that may be available. A property that is worth $X on the assumption that customary financing will be available might well be worth as much as $X plus $Y if the seller is willing to take back a mortgage equal to the full price so that the buyer need not put up any cash equity at all. In addition, price may vary from value because of the lack of negotiating skills by either buyer or seller, because of unwarranted optimism by the buyer or pessimism by the seller, or because either party is operating under unusual constraints.

A good example of the last is the urgency felt by many foreigners to move capital out of their own country to the United States. The United States is regarded as one of the most stable societies in the world and one that continues to offer opportunities to private capital. In such circumstances, a buyer may be willing to pay a price above the value that may be put on the property by an independent appraisal. One might say that, in this situation, the value in use exceeds the objective value. The same would be true of the old family home or the dilapidated but still popular college beer joint.

Cost

The **cost** of a particular commodity is a historical figure, a price paid in the past, or the cost to construct a building today. A property's cost may have little or no effect on its value today.

Value, price, and cost might possibly be equal for a new property, but this would be the exception rather than the rule. Value in exchange or objective valuation requires the interaction of buyers and sellers. Therefore, the forces at work in the marketplace that influence value and the characteristics of value previously discussed must be understood in order to develop an appropriate model for real property valuation. Clearly, the decision maker must know value in order to avoid paying too much for an existing property or building a new property that cannot be cost-justified.

VALUE INFLUENCES AND PRINCIPLES　On the basis of many years of experience, appraisers have developed certain value influences and principles of value that represent a crystallization of their understanding of how the real estate marketplace operates. The brief descriptions of the ten concepts that follow are drawn from *The Appraisal of Real Estate*.

ANTICIPATION

As an influence on value, the concept of anticipation embodies a point of view that is obvious enough. An estimate of value should always be based on future expectations (**anticipation**) rather than past performance.

This is not to say that the past may not be a good forecaster of the future or that the past financial history of an investment should not be studied carefully. The concept we intend to emphasize is that because of the anticipated long life of improved real estate, the appraiser must never forget that the concern is with *future* productivity and not simply with historic data.

During the 1970s, many apartment house investments turned out badly when fuel costs increased sharply. Because leases did not so provide, these costs could not be passed along directly to tenants. This turned positive cash flows into losses. Perhaps the sharp increases could not have been anticipated. Nevertheless, this is a dramatic illustration of the importance of anticipating and projecting regional and urban trends, as discussed in Part 1.

CHANGE

The concept of **change** is, in one sense, merely a specific application of the concept of anticipation. The emphasis here is on the identification of trends that affect the subject property and that will cause foreseeable consequences.

Change is inevitable and is seen in all the forces affecting value. Because the physical-environmental, economic, social, and governmental factors affecting an individual property are changing, an appraisal estimate of value is valid only at the time specified by the appraiser.

SUPPLY AND DEMAND

In a completely free economy, the interaction of **supply and demand** would be the sole determinant of value. In our partially free economy, governmental influences are often as important in establishing a complete pricing model. In any case, demand must be backed by purchasing power in order to be effective, and supply must provide utility satisfaction in order to attract effective demand.

COMPETITION AND EXCESS PROFIT

The concept of competition and excess profit expresses a principle of a free enterprise system: abnormal profits cannot be expected to continue indefinitely into the future. In other words, unless monopoly profit is protected by unique location, governmental regulation, or some other factor, **competition** will be generated which in time will reduce the abnormal profit from the subject property to a normal range. For example, the first hotel with a glass elevator attracted a flood of customers and, for a time, generated extraordinary cash flows. However, once competition picked up the idea and built similar elevators, the cash flows were reduced to a more normal level.

SUBSTITUTION

The concept of **substitution** states that when two parcels of property have the same utility, the property offered at the lower price will sell first. This concept is crucial in two of the three appraisal approaches. In the *sales comparison approach* (in which properties are compared), one issue is whether, in fact, the various properties have the same utility. In the *cost approach,* the concept of substitution explains why a buyer would not pay more for an existing improvement on real property than the cost to the buyer to build the improvement new.

The principle of substitution is very close to the "opportunity cost" idea developed in your basic economics course. At times, value can be estimated from the cost of opportunities foregone.

SURPLUS PRODUCTIVITY AND BALANCE

Of the four factors of production, land is assumed to be the last one to be paid. This is so because it plays a passive role, and a return must first be paid to the other three factors—capital, labor, and entrepreneurship—in order to induce them to utilize the land. Consequently, the return to land is **surplus productivity** in the sense that it is the residual return after payments to the other three factors.

Related to the concept of surplus productivity is the concept of **balance,** which says that the overall return will be highest (and, consequently, the return on the land will be highest) when the optimum balance is struck among the various factors of production.

For example, consider the case of a man and wife who operate a fast-food restaurant as a "mom and pop" operation. They purchase the land, construct the improvements, and work 12 hours a day, 7 days a week. At the end of their first year in operation, they have a nice profit. But what is earning a return?

■ *First,* the couple must pay themselves salaries for their labor.

■ *Second,* a portion of the profit must be set aside as a return *of* investment (representing the depreciation of the improvements), and an additional portion properly represents a return *on* the investment in the improvements.

■ *Third,* a part of the return goes for coordination (i.e., the management or entrepreneurial function).

■ *Finally,* the balance, if indeed anything is left, represents a return on the capital invested in the land. At times, it may turn out that there is *no* surplus productivity and that the land in that particular use is in fact earning no return at all.

CONFORMITY

The concept of **conformity** suggests that maximum value accrues to a parcel when a reasonable degree of social and economic homogeneity are present in a neighborhood. This is not to say that monotonous uniformity is rewarded above all else. Rather, it illustrates the sector theory of urban growth (see Chapter 2) and the fact that economic or psychological benefits arise from grouping reasonably similar activities. Zoning laws are a partial recognition of this concept.

CONTRIBUTION

The concept of **contribution** is an application of the law of marginal utility. The concept says that changes in an existing improvement or in a portion of an improvement can be justified in a financial sense only if the increase in cash flow represents a fair return on the additional investment.

For example, suppose the owner of an office building is considering replacing the manned elevators with automatic ones. There will be an initial capital investment, but once the change is made, operating expenses will decline because fewer employees will be needed. The concept of contribution addresses the impact on value of increasing the net operating income (NOI) relative to the cost of doing so.

EXTERNALITIES

The principle of **externalities** suggests that positive and negative economies can be generated by factors external to a specific property. For example, locating a residential subdivision directly downwind from a municipal landfill (garbage dump) can have a negative impact on the value of the subdivision and the homesites within it. Conversely, the location of a retail site within easy access to a major thoroughfare can certainly enhance the value of the site.

The impact of location in an economic sense on the value of a given parcel means that real estate is probably affected more by externalities than is any other asset. Furthermore, because many individuals and entities own real estate, any one owner is likely to be affected, positively or negatively, by adjacent or surrounding landowners.

The principle of externalities is a direct application of the situs concept developed in Chapter 3 and is critically important to a complete appreciation of the principles of anticipation and change.

HIGHEST AND BEST USE

The best known and most quoted principle of real estate valuation is that of **highest and best use,** a concept that can be traced back to Johann von Thünen, whose theories are briefly noted in Chapter 2. The essence of this concept is that land is valued on the basis of the use that, at the time the appraisal is made, is likely to produce the greatest return. Put another way, the highest and best use of land is the use that produces, according to the concept of surplus productivity and balance, the highest residual return to the land. The highest and best use must be legally, physically, and economically logical over the foreseeable future and must take into consideration all relevant risks.

The highest and best use of a parcel of land is likely to change over time. A retail site away from the central business district (CBD) may be suitable today for only a small grocery store. However, if the city grows in that direction, the highest and best use of the site will change, justifying increasingly large structures as time passes.[4] (See Boxes 6-2 and 6-3.) Government must respond to such urban growth with changes in the level of infrastructure and zoning if the economically justified, more intensive use is to be physically and legally possible.

THE MEANING OF MARKET VALUE

To this point, we have attempted to isolate the various aspects of value and to distinguish value from other related concepts such as cost and price. For the remainder of the chapter, we will focus on the process by which an appraiser arrives at a figure representing estimated value.

First, just what the final appraisal figure represents must be defined. What can be used as a working definition of *value*? Depending on the reason for the appraisal, the definition may vary. It is possible that an appraiser may be asked to estimate *going concern value* (the value of a business that anticipates continuing in operation), *liquidation value* (the value of the separate assets of a business that is being terminated), *value*

---

[4]On the other hand, an additional factor must be included in the highest and best use equation for land already developed. That extra factor is the cost of demolishing the existing improvement. Thus, the highest and best use of vacant land might be a 20-story office building. But if the land already is improved with a 10-story building, the cost of demolishing the existing structure may be so great that the highest and best use (from the point of view of return of investment) remains the present use rather than a taller building.

6-2 HIGHEST AND BEST USE: A CONCEPT	Highest and best use is defined as

> *The reasonably probable and legal use of vacant land or an improved property, which is physically possible, approximately supported, and financially feasible, and which results in the highest value.*

The definition applies specifically to the highest and best use of land or improved property. When a site contains improvements, the highest and best use may be determined to be different from the existing use. The existing use will continue unless and until the land value in its highest and best use exceeds the sum of the entire property in its existing use and the cost to remove the improvements.

The definition implies that the contributions of a specific use to community development goals and the benefits of this use to individual property owners are taken into account in determining the highest and best use. An additional implication is that the appraiser's judgment and analytical skills determine the highest and best use. The use is determined from analysis and represents an opinion, not a fact to be found. In appraisal practice, the concept of highest and best use represents the premise on which value is based. In the context of *most probable selling price* (market value), another appropriate term to reflect highest and best use would be *most probable use.* In the context of investment value, an alternative term would be *most profitable use.*

The definition indicates that there are two types of highest and best use. The first type is highest and the best use of land or a site as though vacant. The second is highest and best use of a property as improved. Each type requires a separate analysis. Moreover, the existing use of a site may or may not be different from its highest and best use.

Source: The Appraisal of Real Estate, 9th ed. (Chicago: American Institute of Real Estate Appraisers, 1987), p. 269.

in use (the value a specific property has for a specific use), *investment value* (the value of an investment to a particular investor based on his or her unique investment requirements), *assessed value* (value according to a uniform schedule for tax rolls in ad valorem taxation), or *insurable value.* Most frequently, however, the appraiser seeks to determine *market value.*

Market value as defined in this text is the logical extension of the arguments developed in Box 6-1.

Recall that value exists when a scarce good satisfies the needs of those able to trade other resources to obtain the particular good. Our

6-3

HIGHEST AND BEST USE: AN EXAMPLE

The highest and best use for a piece of property can sometimes reside in the eye of the beholder. Marvin Davis chose land development over filmmaking for Twentieth Century Fox Film Corporation's 63-acre studio site in Los Angeles. The choice made sense for Davis, an oilman and veteran of Denver real estate development, who bought the film company in June 1981. The value of the land is estimated at $500 million, thanks to the Los Angeles real estate boom, and Davis figured that high-rise office buildings were more likely than films to enhance that value.

Six other major movie studios, though, are sitting on big chunks of Los Angeles land worth far more now at market than on the companies' balance sheets. Are these companies so rich that they can ignore an undervalued asset?

Not at all, but at the moment most studios think their real estate empires should remain in the movie and TV business—a business whose future they believe is bright. With a limited number of available studios and rising demand for their use, movie people see studios as assets that can produce profit if rented out or save costs if used for their own company's films and television series.

Source: Adapted from William Harris, "Someday They'll Build a Town Here, Kate." Adapted by permission of *Forbes* Magazine from the October 26, 1981, issue, pp. 135–139.

definition of market value, however, goes beyond the straightforward economic definition. It is the highest price estimated in terms of cash, not trades, and includes a normal amount of debt financing at a market interest rate. This is an important distinction because the purchase of real property usually requires financing. Particularly advantageous financing terms included in the offer to sell can affect the sales price of the property. Consequently, the appraiser seeking to determine market value typically estimates value based on the most likely (or a market-determined) debt level and interest rate.

The phrase *reasonable time* means that real property is not a perfectly liquid asset and that to obtain the highest price may require more than a few days or a few weeks, depending on the particular type of property. Finally, from the land bubble example in the Dallas–Fort Worth area described in Chapter 2, note that an appraisal is an estimate of the *present worth* of future benefits or interest. As long as this definition is kept in mind, the appraiser avoids being caught in a speculative aberration.

As the three approaches to value are explored, the possibility of being caught in a market where the greater-fool theory is alive and rampant is lessened if the analyst reflects on the underlying economic logic supporting a market value conclusion.

THE VALUATION PROCESS

The steps in the valuation process can now be outlined. This process is not merely the technical agenda followed only by a professional appraiser. It is the analytic process that any experienced investor will go through when looking at properties. The formal valuation process consists of seven steps as illustrated in Figure 6-1.

DEFINITION OF THE PROBLEM

As Figure 6-1 indicates, defining the appraisal problem sets the stage for the actual appraisal.

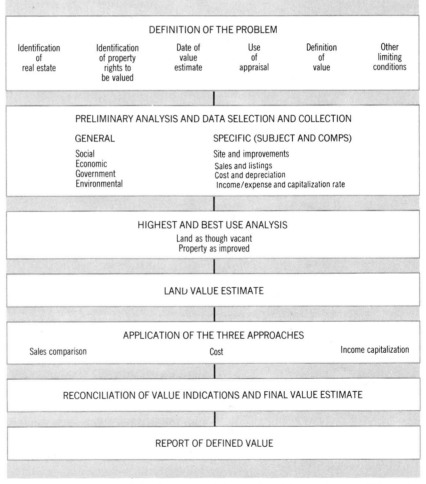

FIGURE 6-1   *The Valuation Process [Source: "The Appraisal of Real Estate," 9th ed.* (Chicago: American Institute of Real Estate Appraisers, 1987), p. 63.]

- *The particular parcel of real estate must be identified,* using one of the forms of legal description previously discussed.

- *Then the particular legal rights or estates to be appraised must be identified.* Is the appraiser to value a fee interest, a life estate, or a long-term leasehold?

- *The date of valuation is also important,* for an appraisal describes and values real estate as of a precise moment in time. This is a particularly crucial factor in condemnation proceedings, since the land taken is valued as of the date of taking. (Consider the importance of setting the date of valuation in connection with recent Indian claims for compensation for land taken many generations ago.)

- *A clear understanding must exist both as to the purpose or objective of the appraisal and the type of value sought.* We have already noted that market value is normally the standard of value, but, on occasion, the issue may be the insured value of property, the liquidation value of a business, or something else.

- *Finally, any limiting conditions must be clearly stated.* These would include any assumptions the appraiser makes that significantly affect value.

PRELIMINARY ANALYSIS, DATA SELECTION, AND COLLECTION

The preliminary survey and appraisal plan constitute the logistics of the appraisal process. The appraiser defines the data that will be needed and the sources of that data. Based on this information, personnel needs are estimated, a time schedule is established, and, in a more complex appraisal, a formal flow chart of the activities is prepared.

All relevant data affecting a property are considered in a sound appraisal. The pool of information generally will fall into two categories: (1) that relating to the environment in which the property is located (general market data) and (2) that relating to the property itself (specific site data).

❑ **GENERAL MARKET DATA.** In the first category, social, economic, and political characteristics of the region, city, and neighborhood are included. Remembering the principle of anticipation, the appraiser will concentrate on identifying the trends that are expected to continue in the future. A continuing question will be how data about the past relate to a projection of the expected economic life of a particular property. In this analysis, the tools developed in Chapters 2 and 3 are particularly relevant.

❏ **SPECIFIC SITE DATA.**   The second category of data involves the property itself. The physical site is inspected, and the improvements are examined to determine the extent of depreciation and the ability of the improvement to carry out its present or intended use.

The appraiser will also seek complete financial and operating information about the property, as well as comparative market information. "Comparables" are used in all three approaches to value. Depending on the nature of the subject property, comparable property information includes sales data, rental rates, and operating expense figures as well as physical and locational characteristics of properties used in the comparison process. (A detailed description of feasibility analysis is presented in Part 8.)

HIGHEST-AND-BEST-USE ANALYSIS

In the case of vacant land, the appraiser is free to consider any reasonable potential use. In the case of property already improved, the appraiser must consider reasonable alternative uses in light of the existing use, its prospective returns, and the cost of demolition. In some cases, an "interim use" may be specified if the appraiser feels that at a foreseeable future date (but not currently) the market will support more intensive use of the land.

LAND VALUE ESTIMATE

The land value is often estimated separately and apart from the value of any structures. Usually, the land value is established by using the market data (comparative) approach presented in Chapter 7. The land value may also be estimated by anticipating development or redevelopment. In this procedure, the anticipated combination of structure and land is valued, and the cost of construction is subtracted to leave the land value.

APPLICATION OF THE THREE APPROACHES

It should now be apparent that property appraisal is an art, not a science. An estimate of value is never spoken of as scientific fact, but rather as an opinion.

For this reason, an appraiser normally will not follow a single path toward a value conclusion. Over the years, three separate approaches have been developed: (1) the **cost approach,** (2) the **sales comparison** (or market data) **approach,** and (3) the capitalization or **income capitalization approach.**

Each of these approaches is discussed in some detail in the following chapters. At this point, we note only the essence of each method.

- *The cost approach* relies on the principle of substitution. It says that one should pay no more for an existing building than an amount equal to the cost of replacement.

- *The sales comparison approach* also relies on the principle of substitution, saying that a property is worth approximately the same as another property offering similar utility (a similar stream of benefits).

- *The income capitalization approach* states that the value of property is the present worth of future cash flows that the property is expected to generate (e.g., a property is worth X times its annual net or gross operating income).

RECONCILIATION OF VALUE INDICATIONS AND FINAL VALUE ESTIMATE

The fifth step in the appraisal process is a reconciliation of the value estimates derived from the three different approaches to value. The reconciliation is *not* a simple average of the three results. Depending on the nature of the property and the objective of the appraisal, one approach will appear to be more appropriate than another, and experienced appraisers will meld the results of the three approaches. (See Box 6-4.) The end of the appraisal process is an estimate of the property's value as of a particular date.

6-4
RECONCILIATION IS NOT ADDITION

An investor in Ann Arbor, Michigan, hired an appraiser to evaluate two adjoining tracts of land that were offered for sale at an aggregate price of $3 million. The appraiser, relying on the sales comparison and land residual approaches (a variation of the income capitalization method), ended up with an estimate of $2.5 million for the two tracts, together.

The investor mistakenly assumed that the market data approach was used on one tract and the land residual approach on the other, giving a *combined* value of $5 million for the two tracts. He snapped up the properties at the asking price, believing he had a bargain, but eventually regretted that he had not more fully understood the appraisal process.

REPORT OF DEFINED VALUE

Normally, the professional appraiser will write a formal appraisal report setting forth the six steps just described. This report is the justification and evidence of the final opinion of value rendered by the appraiser.

For larger properties, the final report will be an extensive narrative. For smaller residential properties, a standard form report will be used, as shown in Chapter 7. If a client wants an opinion without a formal report, the appraiser may prepare a letter report at a lower cost to the client.

SUMMARY   Appraisal is the formulation of an opinion of value—most often an opinion of market value. This opinion is derived by analyzing the forces influencing value and utilizing the ten concepts of value through the valuation process described in this chapter.

Even the income approach to value does not represent a completely objective assessment but rather requires many subjective judgments by the appraiser. Appraisal is a way to approach value that includes all the market and property considerations that are part of our framework for analysis. However, the appraisal process is geared to a market consensus and not to the unique situation of an individual investor. In later chapters, we present a more individualized and flexible approach to investment analysis.

In this chapter, we have covered the appraisal process as it has evolved in practice. This process is not without criticism. Ratcliff, Graaskamp, and others cited in the references at the end of this Part have attacked the traditional process and suggested major changes.

IMPORTANT TERMS

Anticipation	Income capitalization approach
Appraisal	Market value
Balance	Price
Change	Sales comparison approach
Competition	Scarcity
Conformity	Substitution
Contribution	Supply and demand
Cost	Surplus productivity
Cost approach	Transferability
Effective demand	Utility
Externalities	Value
Highest and best use	

REVIEW QUESTIONS

6.1 How might an appraisal designed to estimate market value differ from one designed to estimate value for fire insurance purposes?

6.2 Assume you are interested in buying a property and discover the owner has a life estate interest. How might this discovery affect your offering price?

6.3 What are the critical differences among value, price, and cost with respect to their use in real estate decision making?

6.4 How might the concept of increasing and decreasing returns affect the value of a 1,000-unit mobile home park?

6.5 Define market value as it should apply to real estate appraisal.

6.6 What is meant by the term *highest and best use* as it is applied to real estate?

6.7 Why is the date of valuation crucial when appraising condemned property (eminent domain)?

6.8 What should be included in the site analysis portion of the appraisal process?

6.9 Would you maintain that an estimate of market value is an opinion or fact? Why?

6.10 How should the three estimates of value be reconciled to result in final estimate of value?

*T*he Sales Comparison Approach And The Cost Approach

The basic concepts of value described in the previous chapter find concrete expression in the three approaches to value: the sales comparison approach, the cost approach, and the income capitalization approach. The first two, discussed in this chapter, correspond more or less closely to practices most people follow in making judgments about any kinds of value. The third method, the income capitalization approach, requires a more detailed explanation, to which Chapter 8 is devoted.

THE SALES COMPARISON APPROACH

Of the three basic approaches to value, the **sales comparison** (or market comparison) **approach** is most easily grasped by the newcomer to real estate because it is related to the comparison shopping most of us do when purchasing a new automobile, a new suit, or products in the local supermarket.

The theory of comparable sales analysis is based on the assumption that the market value of a property (the **subject property**) bears a close relationship to the prices of similar properties that have recently changed hands. Because no one property is exactly like another and the passage of time affects values (including the value of the dollar), the analyst's goal is to find properties that resemble the subject property *as closely as possible* and then to make appropriate adjustments to reflect whatever differences exist (including those relating to the time and terms of sale).

It is apparent that the sales comparison approach lends itself best to situations where very similar properties are bought and sold on a relatively frequent basis. Single-family dwellings and raw land often represent such markets, and it is with such properties that the sales comparison approach is most successful.

The sales comparison approach relies the most heavily on the principles of substitution, supply and demand, externalities, and contribution. The comparison shopping analogy used earlier is a direct application of the substitution concept, which works in a market where price is a function of the interaction of supply and demand. The sales adjustments made in the market data approach are for various externalities as well as physical differences, with the magnitude of the physical differences resting on the contribution concept.

STEPS IN THE SALES COMPARISON APPROACH

A straightforward outline of the steps involved in the sales comparison approach is as follows.

- First, comparable properties that recently have traded are located.

- Second, the key features or characteristics of the subject and the comparable properties are identified.

- Third, the sale price of each comparable property is "adjusted" to reflect the differences between the comparable property and the subject property. (In effect, the price for the subject property is estimated by considering the differences between them.)

- Fourth, a judgment about the market value of the subject property is reached through a consolidation process that weighs the adjusted prices of the comparable properties.

FINDING COMPARABLES

The first step in applying the sales comparison approach is finding **comparable properties.**[1] The reliability of the sales comparison approach is a direct function of the comparable sales used in the analysis.

Suppose A is seeking to value a three-bedroom, two-bath, all-brick home at 411 Yorktown Street. A discovers that five other three-bedroom, two-bath, all-brick homes on similar lots located on Yorktown have sold in the past three months for $87,500. It is not difficult to conclude that the value of the subject property is very close to $87,500. On the other hand, a ranch house, located in Montana, with 12 bedrooms and 1 bath, which is 30 miles from the nearest house, is more difficult to evaluate by the sales comparison approach.

Not surprisingly, nearly all appraisals fall somewhere between these two extremes. The task of the appraiser or analyst is to find similar properties *whose sales terms can be verified* to use as comparables in judging the market value of the subject property. In choosing comparables, the appraiser must have a clear idea in mind of what constitutes an accept-

---

[1]*This is actually part of the preliminary analysis and data selection and collection that make up stage two of the overall valuation process as described in Chapter 6.*

**7-1
CHOOSING
VALID
COMPARABLES**

"They're Having a Sale in Orlando, Florida and What They're Selling Is Orlando." This story was reported in *The Wall Street Journal* on March 14, 1975. The Orlando area experienced significant overbuilding during the 1974–75 period, and some people feel that a misuse of the sales comparison approach was largely responsible. In the *Journal* article, Robert N. Gardner, an executive with Condev Corporation, a real estate development firm, says:

> We were so busy building apartments that everyone was unaware that a lot of people who were in the apartments were construction workers who were coming in to build more new apartments. No one knew what anyone else was doing and the real estate investment trusts were throwing money in every direction.

What happened was that many properties used as comparables in appraisals were tenanted by transient construction workers or were owned (as condominium units) by speculators holding for resale. As soon as demand showed signs of turning down, the cycle reversed and the result for Orlando investors was a very drastic drop in occupancy rates.

able comparable. In addition, the characteristics of the comparable that differ from the subject property must be identifiable, and they must be of a kind that can be "priced" with a reasonable degree of certainty.[2] Under normal circumstances, it is desirable that four to seven comparable properties be located. (See Box 7-1.)

Remember that property differences can be either positive or negative. That is, each comparable property normally will have some features that make it worth more than the subject property and some deficiencies that make it worth less.

IDENTIFYING CHARACTERISTICS OF VALUE

The appraiser or analyst must next identify the major characteristics of the subject and the comparable properties that determine its value. On this basis, the appraiser will determine which properties are comparable to the subject and then check the comparables for additional characteristics that affect their value. These **characteristics of value** can be divided into two broad classifications: (1) property characteristics and (2) nonproperty characteristics.

[2]*A property with unique historical or cultural associations or with sole access to an adjacent body of water will not normally be a suitable comparable.*

❏ **PROPERTY CHARACTERISTICS.**   The **property characteristics** are essentially physical items. The significant ones are (1) location, (2) size of the land parcel, (3) size of constructed space, (4) type of construction, and (5) quality of construction. The terrain of the site; the design, age, condition of the improvement; and the interior configuration are also relevant items. When the property is a residence, consideration should be given to such outdoor amenities as tennis courts and swimming pools as well as to special features of the house, such as fireplaces, elaborate interior features, or any other major element of difference between the subject property and the comparable property.

❏ **NONPROPERTY CHARACTERISTICS.**   In addition to physical characteristics, certain **nonproperty characteristics** are important in utilizing the sales comparison approach. The chief nonproperty characteristics include the following.

- *Verified sales price.* Since the sales comparison approach adjusts comparable selling prices to make them similar to the subject, this method relies heavily on a verified sales price. In most cases, verification is based on information provided by real estate brokers and other appraisers.

- *Date of sale.* The elapsed time since a comparable property has been sold may be important if either the national or local economy has been experiencing significant inflation. In the mid-1980s, accelerating financial services employment growth in New York created a situation in which elapsed time of as little as six months pushed the current market value of the comparable property several percentage points above its sale price.

- *Financing Terms.* Since real property is usually purchased with the use of borrowed funds, the financing terms are particularly important. A property that has unusually attractive financing will command a better price than an identical property without such financing.

Consider again the example of the home on Yorktown Road. If the subject home was financed with a 7 percent interest rate loan that could be assumed (taken over) by a new purchaser despite much higher current rates, and the comparable homes had 10 percent loans of equivalent amounts, the prices of the latter properties would have to be adjusted to reflect the less advantageous financing.

- *Unusual conditions of sale.* Finally, any special conditions of sale must be taken into account. This is particularly important in sales that are not at *arm's length* (i.e., sales between persons who are not strangers to one another, as by a father to a daughter or between business associates).

For example, if a condition of one particular sale is that the seller can continue to use the property for six months without payment of any rent or that the property is to be repaired by the seller subsequent to the sale, these items must be accounted for in the adjustment process. (See Table 7-1.)

❏ **SOURCES OF INFORMATION.** The sources of information on comparable properties will vary depending on the nature of the property being appraised. The most common source of data for a single-family residence in a metropolitan area is the local multiple listing service. This joint brokerage facility will be explained more fully in Part 4. Although the format varies from city to city, Figure 7-1 is typical. When a property is listed for sale, the detailed information specifying terms of the offer to sell are provided as shown on the left-hand side of Figure 7-1. When the property sells, the additional data shown on the right are provided.

Another good source of information is the county courthouse. As noted in Part 2, deeds are "recorded" after most sales, and this is a public record. That is, anyone may obtain access to the information. In some states, such as Oregon, recorded deeds must contain the sale price. In other states, tax stamps must be affixed to recorded deeds, indicating the amount of new money involved in the transaction. Although these records are incomplete from the appraiser's perspective, they (at the very least) provide evidence that a transaction has occurred. The appraiser can then proceed to collect additional information from those involved, that is, from the buyer, seller, broker, and possibly the lender.

ADJUSTING THE PRICES OF COMPARABLE PROPERTIES

The next step is to adjust the prices of the comparable properties to reflect the differences between each of them and the subject property. Where the comparable property lacks an element of value possessed by the subject property, the value of that particular element is *added* to the sale price of the comparable. Where the comparable has a feature that is not present in the subject property, the value of the feature is *subtracted* from the sales price of the comparable.

By this process, the subject property is given a value (vis-à-vis each comparable) so that, in theory at least, the person who bought the comparable property would have been willing to buy the subject property at the given value.

The actual adjustments can be made by (1) unit of comparison (e.g., an adjustment per square foot), (2) dollar adjustments (e.g., a lump-sum

---

TABLE 7-1   COMPARABLES USED IN THE SALES COMPARISON APPROACH

Subject Property

The subject is a single-family dwelling located at 10 Stoney Creek. It has 2,811 square feet, four bedrooms, two baths, double garage, two living areas, no pool, central air and heat, no fireplace, and above-average landscaping with no fence. The property consists of 5.33 acres in a subdivision of similar lots.

Comparable 1

Located on a 4-acre lot 1,500 yards down Stoney Creek. It has 2,500 square feet, four bedrooms, two and one-half baths, double garage, two living areas, no pool, central air and heat, a fireplace, above-average landscaping, and a fully fenced yard. It sold nine months ago with market financing for $163,350.

Comparable 2

Located across the street from the subject on a 5-acre lot, this property has 2,800 square feet, four bedrooms, two baths, double garage, two living areas, no pool, central air and heat, no fireplace, poor landscaping, and a fully fenced yard. This comparable sold last week for $190,350, but the seller gave the buyer a loan over and above the normal financing available at an attractive interest rate. (In the jargon, the seller took back a second.)

Comparable 3

This property is located about a mile from the subject on a 3-acre lot near a major expressway. It has 2,000 square feet, four bedrooms, one and one-half baths, double garage, one living area, no pool, central air and heat, no fireplace, excellent landscaping, and a fully fenced yard. It sold two months ago with market financing for $143,100.

Comparable 4

Located on a busy street behind the subject, this is a 6-acre corner lot. This comparable has 3,000 square feet, five bedrooms, two baths, double garage, two living areas, no pool, central heat but not air conditioning, a fireplace, above-average landscaping, and an unfenced yard. It sold last month with market financing for $174,150.

Comparable 5

This comparable is on a 5-acre lot one mile from the subject. It has 2,800 square feet, four bedrooms, two baths, double garage, two living areas, a pool, central air and heat, a fireplace, above-average landscaping, and a fully fenced yard. It sold three months ago for $189,000 with market financing.

Note: By subdivision ordinance, all homes are frame construction with minimum-quality standards, thus obviating the need for quality adjustments in the appraisal.

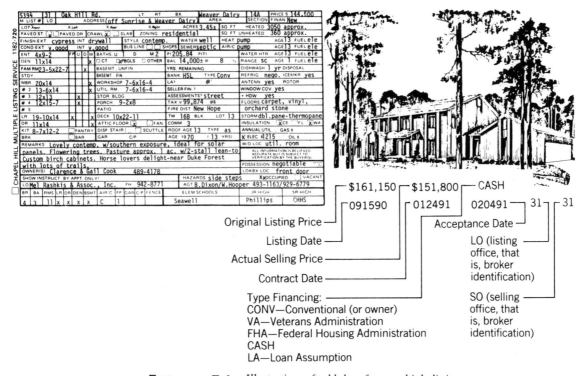

FIGURE 7-1 *Illustrations of sold data from multiple listings*

adjustment for a fireplace or central air conditioning), or (3) a percentage adjustment. The percentage adjustment is particularly useful in handling differences in timing of the sale.

10 STONEY CREEK

Consider the appraisal of 10 Stoney Creek, the subject property. Using the "sold" version of the multiple listing service, the appraiser locates five comparable properties in the same subdivision (see Table 7-1). The appraiser determines the primary physical characteristics of value for this locality and analyzes the comparables as shown in Table 7-2. The appraiser then confirms the terms of sale with one of the principals (buyer, seller, broker) and prepares the market comparable adjustments shown in Table 7-3.

The size of each of the adjustments is determined by the market. Ideally, the appraiser will use "paired sales" to obtain the actual figure. Under the paired-sales technique, the difference between two sales that

TABLE 7-2   MARKET COMPARABLE ADJUSTMENTS

Date of Sale
Values in the subject neighborhood have been increasing at 1 percent per month.

Financing Terms
The sales price of comparable 2 must be adjusted downward because it would be inflated by the value of the advantageous seller financing.

Location
The sale prices of comparables 3 and 4 must be adjusted upward, for the heavy traffic would have adversely affected their prices.

Lot Size
The sale prices of comparables 1 and 3 must be adjusted up for their smaller lot size, and the sales price of comparable 4 must be adjusted down since this property is larger than the subject.

Constructed Space
Comparables 1 and 3 are smaller than the subject, so their sale prices must be adjusted up; that of comparable 4 must be adjusted downward.

Number of Bedrooms
The appraiser determined that no adjustment for number of bedrooms was dictated by the market given the overall size adjustment.

Number of Bathrooms
The sale price of comparable 1 was adjusted down for the extra half bath, and that of comparable 3 was adjusted up since it had only one and one-half baths.

Living Areas
Comparable 3 was adjusted upward in price, for it had only one living area.

Pool
The sale price of comparable 5 was adjusted downward because it had a pool that the subject lacked.

Central Air and Heat
Comparable 4 was adjusted upward in price because it has no central air conditioning.

Fireplace
Comparables 1, 4, and 5 were adjusted downward in price for having this extra amenity, a fireplace.

Landscaping
The sale price of comparable 2 must be adjusted up because of its poor landscaping, and that of comparable 3 must be adjusted down for its excellent landscaping.

Fence
Comparables 1, 2, 3, and 5 were adjusted downward in price because they had a fence and the subject did not.

TABLE 7-3 THE SALES COMPARISON GRID

The grid format is an excellent way to display data collected under the sales comparison approach. The information that follows is derived from data set out in Table 7-1 as adjusted for all the reasons given in Table 7-2.

	SUBJECT	1	2	3	4	5
Nonproperty Characteristics						
Sale price	—	$163,350	$190,350	$143,100	$174,150	$189,000
Date of sale	—	14,700	—	2,860	1,740	5,670
Financing terms	Market	—	(5,400)	—	—	—
Conditions of sale	Normal	—	—	—	—	—
Property Characteristics						
Location	10 Stoney Creek	—	—	13,500	8,100	—
Lot size	5.33 Acres	6,750	—	10,800	(5,400)	—
Structure Size (square feet)	2,812	2,000	—	5,400	(1,300)	—
Number of bedrooms	4	—	—	—	—	—
Number of bathrooms	2	(1,350)	—	2,700	—	—
Garage	2	—	—	—	—	—
Living areas	2	—	—	2,700	—	—
Pool	No	—	—	—	—	(16,200)
Central air conditioning and heating	Yes	—	—	—	3,375	—
Fireplace	No	(2,000)	—	—	(2,000)	(2,000)
Landscaping	Above average	—	2,000	(1,000)	—	—
Fence	No	(1,350)	(1,350)	(1,350)	—	(1,350)
Adjusted Sale Price	—	$182,100	$185,600	$178,710	$178,615	$175,120
Indicated Market Value of Subject	$182,000					

After a close examination of the comparables, the indicated market value of the subject was determined by considering all five comparables but giving the most weight to comparables 2 and 5, which had the fewest adjustments.

are very similar except for one feature (say a pool) is used as the figure for this adjustment. The most common example of the paired-sales technique is in the time of sale adjustment. If the same house sells a second time six months after the first sale for 3 percent more, there is some indication that prices are rising at ½ percent per month.

Since it is difficult to find paired sales for all adjustments, a variety of other techniques are used. In larger markets with an extensive amount of data available, multiple regression can be very useful. In smaller markets, the appraiser will estimate the value of the characteristic being adjusted by using a combination of cost to install and desirability in the marketplace.

REACHING A CORRELATION OF VALUE

The final step in the sales comparison approach is to reach an opinion of value for the subject property based on the adjusted sale price of all the comparables. Most professional appraisers eliminate any sales prices that vary widely from the others in the group. They do so on the assumption that some element of comparison has been missed or that these particular properties have unique features that make them inappropriate as comparables.

The remaining adjusted sale prices are evaluated and correlated to produce a final indication of market value of the subject property. In the correlation process, the appraiser may give more emphasis to the properties that most closely resemble the subject property.

THE COST APPROACH

The **cost approach** to value states that the value of a property is roughly equal to (1) the cost of reproducing the property minus (2) a figure that approximates the amount of value of the property that has been "used up" in the course of its life (i.e., a figure representing its lessened productivity). In short, a property is worth its reproduction cost minus accrued depreciation plus land value. By contrast, the sales comparison approach states that the worth of a property is equal to the price an informed purchaser would pay for it; the income approach says that the worth of a property is equal to the present value of the anticipated stream of future benefits.

PRINCIPLES OF VALUE

Although the definition of the cost approach given in the previous paragraph is not controversial in a theoretical sense, the application of this method can be very controversial indeed. Some of the controversies are indicated in the course of this chapter. Several of the ten principles of value set forth in Chapter 6 are involved in the cost approach, particularly the principles of anticipation, substitution, change, increasing and decreasing returns, and highest and best use.

STEPS IN THE COST APPROACH TO VALUE

Four steps are involved in the cost approach to value.

- First, an estimate is made of the cost to reproduce the existing improvements.

- Second, an estimate is made of the dollar amount of **accrued depreciation** that has occurred during the life of the improvements. The accrued depreciation is deducted from reproduction costs to show the depreciated cost of the improvements.

- Third, the estimated value of the land (site value) is arrived at by using the market data approach.

- Fourth, an opinion of value is arrived at by adding the site value to the depreciated cost of the improvements.

REPRODUCTION AND REPLACEMENT COST

An important distinction exists between reproduction cost and replacement cost. **Reproduction cost** refers to the cost at today's prices to build an exact replica of the structure being valued. Reproduction cost assumes that the same quantity and quality of material and labor is utilized as when the structure actually was built. In short, reproduction denotes the same structure in replica. By comparison, **replacement cost** denotes the cost of replacing an existing building with one of equal utility, although the same materials or the same design may not be used, reflecting changes in technology, design, building techniques, and cost.

REPRODUCTION COST NEW

Although it might appear that replacement cost should be used in the cost approach to value, the concept of **reproduction cost new** represents the true theoretical foundation for the cost approach because it relates directly to the accrued depreciation that is estimated in the next step in the process. Consequently, most of the discussion that follows is designed to estimate reproduction cost new. This estimate of reproduction cost must reflect *all* ingredients of cost to the typical purchaser, but there are several alternative methods of cost estimation. Generally, an appraiser or analyst will use either one of these methods or one of several published construction cost services.

TRADE BREAKDOWN OR BUILDER'S METHOD

The trade breakdown or builder's method of estimating reproduction cost is a recommended method when preparing the demonstration appraisal report required for designation by the American Institute of Real Estate Appraisers (AIREA). This method most nearly represents the thinking of residential building contractors and can readily be understood by both appraiser and investor. The method does require a knowledge of the major components of the structure and expresses cost on a square-foot or percentage of total cost basis. (Certainly, a working knowledge of structural components is fundamental to the entire appraisal process.)

In the trade breakdown or builder's method,

  Direct costs (labor, materials, equipment, and subcontractors' fees) are added to

 Indirect costs (financing charges, selling costs, insurance premiums, permit and license fees, survey costs, architectural and legal fees, and builder's profit and overhead) to arrive at

■ Estimated reproduction cost new of the improvements on the site.

QUANTITY SURVEY METHOD

A more elaborate approach to estimating reproduction cost involves a complete building cost estimate by a contractor involved in the particular kind of construction in the area. The quantity survey method requires a complete itemization of all prices for materials, equipment, and labor, plus a complete list of all overhead price items plus profit. The cost of such an estimate, however, normally exceeds what an investor or purchaser is willing to pay, and so this method is not used frequently.

COMPARATIVE UNIT METHOD

A much more simplified approach is the comparative unit method. Here, an estimate of reproduction cost per square foot is derived by dividing the total known cost of similar structures by the total square footage of those structures. The resulting standard or comparative unit of cost is then applied to the subject property. This approach is acceptable only for preliminary or cursory appraisals rather than in-depth analyses.

❑ **CONSTRUCTION COST SERVICES.** Published cost services provide estimates of reproduction cost for typical structures and are useful timesaving devices. These services also provide localized indices to

TABLE 7-4 REPRODUCTION COST FROM MARSHALL AND SWIFT FOR 10 STONEY CREEK	
By means of the illustrated selection chart provided by Marshall and Swift, it is determined that the subject property is a class D very good single-family residence.	
Construction Costs	
Cost per square foot on interior space $69.12[a] × 2,811 ft.	$194,300
Garage	12,000
Built-in range	1,125
Total Cost	$207,425
Multipliers	
Current cost[b] 1/90	1.02
Local—Raleigh, N.C.	0.87
Combined	0.88
Current, Local Reproduction Cost ($207,425 × 0.88)	$182,534

[a]*Using the calculator section of Marshall and Swift, the appraiser includes in this square-foot cost all costs other than land and site preparation.*

[b]*These multipliers are updated monthly.*

take into consideration varying costs throughout the country. Probably the most used service is offered by Marshall and Swift Company of Los Angeles, California. The various services identify the costs of the major components of structures and provide adjustments for inflation and for different geographic areas of the country. (See Table 7-4.) Being out-of-date and not specific enough for a particular submarket are some of the possible drawbacks of such services.

ESTIMATING ACCRUED DEPRECATION

The use of the term "depreciation" is pervasive in real estate. It is meant here as an appraisal or valuation concept, and it is met again in later chapters as an accounting concept and then as a tax concept. As used here, *depreciation* refers to reduction in the value of buildings or improvements as a result of physical, functional, or economic factors.[3]

Accrued depreciation is a measure of the loss in utility of the subject property in its present condition, from all forms of depreciation, as

[3]*Land does not depreciate in an appraisal, accounting, or tax sense. The reason is that land has perpetual life, and the "bundle of rights" that constitutes the legal concept of ownership also goes on forever.*

compared with its condition as a totally new improvement representing the highest and best use of the site. To the extent that improved real estate loses utility (i.e., suffers depreciation), it has suffered a decline in value from its *reproduction cost new*. (Remember that a declining building value is not inconsistent with rising real estate values as long as the land component's increase exceeds the building component's decrease.) Therefore, after the accrued depreciation suffered by an improved parcel of real estate is estimated, the amount of such depreciation is subtracted from reproduction cost new to arrive at the present depreciated cost of the improvements.

The appraisal process recognizes three different types of depreciation: (1) physical, (2) functional (functional obsolescence), and (3) external (economic location obsolescence).

PHYSICAL DEPRECIATION

Physical depreciation is the kind of "using up" of an improvement that is easiest to understand. It is the loss of value suffered by improvements resulting from wear and tear, disintegration, and the action of the elements. All man-made improvements suffer physical depreciation, although it may be very gradual, particularly in the early years of use.

❏ **CURABLE PHYSICAL DEPRECIATION.**   Physical depreciation may either be *curable* or *incurable*. Curable physical depreciation is also known as *deferred maintenance* because the primary cause of such depreciation is the failure of the owner to maintain the property on an ongoing basis. Such depreciation is called **curable depreciation** because the cost of eliminating or correcting it is less than or equal to the value that will be added to the property as a result. Most items of "normal" maintenance come under this heading.

Examples of curable physical depreciation include replacing broken windows, painting the exterior and interior of the house, and cleaning and making minor replacements to the furnace. In all these cases, the cost to cure is relatively small and is undoubtedly justified (in an economic sense). (See Table 7-5.)

❏ **INCURABLE PHYSICAL DEPRECIATION.**   The other type of physical depreciation is that which is incurable. The term "incurable" does not refer to the impossibility of curing the defect, for virtually any physical defect can be repaired or replaced, but to the lack of economic justification in doing so. Physical depreciation is considered **incurable depreciation** if the cost to cure or correct the physical defect is greater than the value that will be added to the property as a result. For example, it would be illogical to replace a five-year-old roof that was capable of

TABLE 7-5 CURABLE PHYSICAL DEPRECIATION: 10 STONEY CREEK	
1. Crayon on walls—children's bedroom: paint room	$150
2. Broken tile—kitchen: replace	80
3. Torn screen—playroom: replace	50
Total physical curable depreciation	$280

lasting another ten years. However, the five-year-old roof is less valuable than a brand-new one. (See Table 7-6.)

FUNCTIONAL DEPRECIATION (FUNCTIONAL OBSOLESCENCE)

Functional depreciation is the loss of value suffered by real estate because buildings or improvements do not provide the same or as efficient utility as a new structure. Functional depreciation represents the impact of changes in building technology and consumer tastes and preferences on the value of improvements.

TABLE 7-6 INCURABLE PHYSICAL DEPRECIATION: 10 STONEY CREEK

SHORT-LIVED ITEMS	COST (PART OF HARD CONSTRUCTION COST)	ORIGINAL EXPECTED LIFE (YEARS)	REMAINING EXPECTED LIFE (YEARS)	PERCENTAGE DEPRECIATION	DEPRECIATION
Roof	$ 10,000	12	9	25	$ 2,500
Heating and air conditioning	10,000	15	12	20	2,000
Water and plumbing	4,725	20	16	20	945
Interiors (composite to simplify presentation)	22,950	6	5	16.6	3,800
Total short-lived items	$ 47,675				$ 9,345
Long-lived items[a]	$134,859	50	40	20	26,971
Total incurable physical depreciation					$36,316

[a]Total reproduction costs (from Table 7-4) $182,534 less short-lived items of $47,675 equals $134,859.

Another term for such depreciation is *obsolescence*. Just as with physical depreciation, functional obsolescence may either be curable or incurable. Again, the use of these terms does not refer to the absolute ability to cure but rather to the economic justification.

❏ **CURABLE FUNCTIONAL OBSOLESCENCE.** A good example of curable functional obsolescence is lack of a modern kitchen in a residence. Many individuals will not buy an old house with a kitchen that has not been modernized or will reduce their offer by the cost of a new kitchen. Consequently, the owner of a house who installs a new kitchen might well anticipate recouping the investment upon sale. Other examples of curable functional depreciation include lack of air conditioning in office or commercial space, and outmoded storefronts.

The amount of curable functional depreciation from which a property suffers is equal to

■ The cost to cure, minus

◢ Physical depreciation previously deducted

The reason for this second step is that, in the valuation process, the physical depreciation of the particular component has already been deducted. In order to avoid double counting, we must net out this depreciation factor from the computations. Note that if replacement cost rather than reproduction cost is used, excess or superadequate items may be neglected. However, the result will not be as precise. (See Table 7-7.)

❏ **INCURABLE FUNCTIONAL OBSOLESCENCE.** Incurable functional obsolescence is, again, a measure of the reduced ability of a structure or one of its components to perform with the same utility as when new. The cost of curing or correcting the defect, however, is more than the value increment that would result. Consequently, the depreciation is deemed incurable.

For example, a four-story private residence that might otherwise be

---

TABLE 7-7 CURABLE FUNCTIONAL OBSOLESCENCE: 10 STONEY CREEK

No electric outlet in second bath

Cost to install $180.00

Note: Because this item is new, no netting of previously taken physical depreciation is required.

suitable for a multitenant building has a large, winding staircase; in a modern structure, the staircase would be replaced by an elevator. The cost of installing one, however, is not justified by the value added to the property. An office building built many years ago with high ceilings and wide corridors offers amenities that cannot be provided today because of high costs and is another example of incurable obsolescence. The owner of such a building would probably decide against lowering the ceilings and narrowing the corridors in order to create more rental space because the additional rental income would not represent a satisfactory return on the additional investment that would be required. Note that in both cases, the presence of incurable depreciation does not mean that the property is not a good investment. It may well be a good investment, provided the price reflects the depreciation that acts to reduce the future flow of income.

To approximate the amount of incurable functional obsolescence, the appraiser or analyst most often relies on the income approach to value. An estimate is made of the lower rent that the improvement will command owing to the incurable depreciation, and this rent loss is capitalized by a process that is explained in the next chapter dealing with the income approach to value. (See Table 7-8.)

EXTERNAL DEPRECIATION

The final form of depreciation is termed **external depreciation** (sometimes known as *economic* or locational *obsolescence*). It is a measure of the diminished utility, and hence diminished value, of improved real estate owing to negative environmental forces in the surrounding area. It directly reflects the importance of the spatial element (location) in real estate valuation.

Note the significant difference between this type of depreciation and the other two. With physical and functional depreciation, value is lost through the condition of the subject property itself, whereas in external depreciation, utility is lost through the relationship of the subject property to its surroundings. It is obvious that external depreciation is almost always incurable since the property owner is not in a position to control conditions external to the property. (See Box 7-2.)

TABLE 7-8 INCURABLE FUNCTIONAL OBSOLESCENCE: 10 STONEY CREEK	
No built-in dishwasher (and no kitchen location suitable)	
Cost measure-estimate of lost value	$600.00

7-2
INSTANT
ECONOMIC
OBSOLESCENCE:
THE TIME
FACTOR

Recently, a very astute investment group formed a partnership to invest in a planned bulk warehouse distribution site. The partnership borrowed funds and constructed a high-quality warehouse as planned. According to the cost approach to value, the warehouse was worth $4.7 million. Once completed, the investment partnership found that they could not lease the warehouse at rental levels sufficient to justify what they thought to be the fair value, the $4.7 million cost. The building had legitimately cost that amount and, being new, had no physical deterioration, either curable or incurable. Furthermore, the group had researched the warehouse market, and the warehouse showed no signs of either curable or incurable functional obsolescence.

Where had the group made a mistake? It had valued the site at its highest and best use, which the group took to be a warehouse. In the long run, the site *was* best suited for a warehouse, but the market would not absorb the additional warehouse space for some years. Consequently, to value the project by using the cost approach to value, the group should have shown a value reduction to reflect the fact that the space could not be fully occupied for the first few years of the project's existence—that is, there should have been recognition of economic obsolescence to reflect the fact that the site could not for a number of years support a warehouse.

Note: The example shows that pro forma appraisals of planned projects can be more difficult than appraisals of existing properties.

As with the other types of incurable obsolescence, economic loss is approximated by setting a value on (capitalizing) the lessened rent that can be anticipated because of the negative economic factors. For example, a zoning change may permit commercial or industrial uses in a formerly residential neighborhood, with the result that an apartment building must drop its rental rates to attract tenants.

DETERMINING DEPRECIATED COST

After completion of the two initial steps in the cost approach, the total accrued depreciation arising from all three types of depreciation is added up, and that figure is subtracted from reproduction cost new. The resulting figure is the present depreciated cost of the improvements on the land.

The problem of valuing the land, which so far has not been considered, remains to be solved.

VALUING THE SITE

The most commonly used method is the *sales comparison approach,* which was discussed earlier in the chapter. In other words, the appraiser or analyst asks the question, "What have comparable undeveloped parcels of property sold for in this approximate location in the recent past?"

It should be more and more evident that the three approaches to value are closely interrelated; and all deal with identical data, similar logic, and, in many cases, the same mechanics.

OPINION OF VALUE

The opinion of value is the fourth and final step in the cost approach. In the second step, accrued depreciation is subtracted from reproduction cost new to yield the present depreciated cost of the improvements. Now the value of the site is added, which is determined in accordance with one of the methods just described, to arrive at an estimate of value for the entire parcel.

The cost approach to value is most reliable when a property is relatively new and accurate estimates of construction costs can be made. Furthermore, a newly improved property will normally have suffered less depreciation of all types. (See Table 7-9.)

REPORTING THE OPINION OF VALUE ON A SINGLE-FAMILY PROPERTY

Figure 7-2 presents the appraisal of 216 Graystone Drive on the standard Federal National Mortgage Association (FNMA) Form, Uniform Residential Appraisal Report. This appraisal form is the typical final product of an appraisal of a single-family dwelling. The specific contents of the appraisal report include many items that have not been dealt with in detail in this chapter. However, it is important to understand and appre-

---

TABLE 7-9 COST APPROACH: VALUE CONCLUSION

Reproduction Cost		$182,534
Depreciation		
Physical curable	280	
Physical incurable	36,316	
Functional curable	180	
Functional incurable	600	
Economic (none)	0	
Total Depreciation		(37,376)
Site Value (Market Data Approach)		40,000
Total		$185,158
Rounded		$185,150

Property Description & Analysis   **UNIFORM RESIDENTIAL APPRAISAL REPORT**   File No. _____

SUBJECT

Property Address	216 Graystone Drive	Census Tract 118	LENDER DISCRETIONARY USE
City	Chapel Hill	County	State NC	Zip Code 27514	Sale Price $
Legal Description	Lot 29, Section 9, Coker Woods West, Plat Book 30, Pg. 125	Date
Owner/Occupant		Map Reference 7/29B/25	Mortgage Amount $
Sale Price $	Date of Sale	PROPERTY RIGHTS APPRAISED	Mortgage Type
Loan charges/concessions to be paid by seller $		X Fee Simple	Discount Points and Other Concessions
R.E. Taxes $	Tax Year	HOA $/Mo.	Leasehold	Paid by Seller $
Lender/Client Carolina Savings and Loan		Condominium (HUD/VA)	
		De Minimis PUD	Source

NEIGHBORHOOD

LOCATION		Urban	X Suburban	Rural	NEIGHBORHOOD ANALYSIS	Good	Avg.	Fair	Poor
BUILT UP	X	Over 75%	25-75%	Under 25%	Employment Stability	X			
GROWTH RATE		Rapid	X Stable	Slow	Convenience to Employment	X			
PROPERTY VALUES	X	Increasing	Stable	Declining	Convenience to Shopping	X			
DEMAND/SUPPLY		Shortage	X In Balance	Over Supply	Convenience to Schools	X			
MARKETING TIME		Under 3 Mos.	X 3-6 Mos.	Over 6 Mos.	Adequacy of Public Transportation	X			

PRESENT LAND USE	%	LAND USE CHANGE	PREDOMINANT	SINGLE FAMILY HOUSING			Recreation Facilities	X			
				PRICE $ (000)	AGE (yrs)		Adequacy of Utilities	X			
Single Family	80	Not Likely	X OCCUPANCY				Property Compatibility	X			
2-4 Family		Likely	Owner	X	190	Low	3	Protection from Detrimental Cond.	X		
Multi-family		In process	Tenant					Police & Fire Protection	X		
Commercial		To:	Vacant (0-5%)		350	High	3	General Appearance of Properties	X		
Industrial			Vacant (over 5%)			Predominant		Appeal to Market	X		
Vacant	20				225 - 250						

Note: Race or the racial composition of the neighborhood are not considered reliable appraisal factors.

COMMENTS: The subject property is located in Coker Woods West subdivision on the northern side of Chapel Hill. The location is convenient to shopping and employment centers. Pride of owner-ship and re-sale values have historically been good in the area. Schools and parks within walking distance.

SITE

Dimensions	164.90' X 223.17' X 81.66' X 238.20'		Topography	Good-gentle sloping
Site Area	28,400 +/- sq.ft.	Corner Lot No	Size	Typical
Zoning Classification	Residential	Zoning Compliance Yes	Shape	Rectangular
HIGHEST & BEST USE: Present Use		Other Use	Drainage	Positive from House

UTILITIES	Public	Other	SITE IMPROVEMENTS	Type	Public	Private	View	Good-wooded lot
Electricity	X		Street	Asphalt	X		Landscaping	Good
Gas			Curb/Gutter	Concrete	X		Driveway	Concrete
Water	X		Sidewalk	Concrete	X		Apparent Easements	None Adverse
Sanitary Sewer	X		Street Lights		X		FEMA Flood Hazard Yes* No X	
Storm Sewer	X		Alley				FEMA* Map/Zone	

COMMENTS (Apparent adverse easements, encroachments, special assessments, slide areas, etc.): No apparent adverse easements, encroahments, or other adverse conditions. Routine utility easements are present.

IMPROVEMENTS

GENERAL DESCRIPTION		EXTERIOR DESCRIPTION		FOUNDATION		BASEMENT		INSULATION	
Units	1	Foundation	Brick&Block	Slab		Area Sq. Ft. No		Roof	
Stories	2	Exterior Walls	Masonite	Crawl Space	Yes	% Finished 0		Ceiling	X
Type (Det./Att.)	Det.	Roof Surface		Basement	No	Ceiling		Walls	X
Design (Style)	Traditional	Gutters & Dwnspts.	Galvanized	Sump Pump	No	Walls		Floor	X
Existing	Yes	Window Type	Wood	Dampness	No	Floor		None	
Proposed	No	Storm Sash	No	Settlement	No	Outside Entry		Adequacy	X
Under Construction	No	Screens	Yes	Infestation	No			Energy Efficient Items:	
Age (Yrs.)	4	Manufactured House	No						
Effective Age (Yrs.)	3-4								

ROOM LIST

ROOMS	Foyer	Living	Dining	Kitchen	Den	Family Rm.	Rec. Rm.	Bedrooms	# Baths	Laundry	Other	Area Sq. Ft.
Basement												
Level 1	X	X	X	X		X			.5	X	BKFT	
Level 2								4	2			
									2			

Finished area above grade contains: 9 Rooms; 4 Bedroom(s); 2.5 Bath(s); 2488 Square Feet of Gross Living Area

INTERIOR

SURFACES	Materials/Condition	HEATING		KITCHEN EQUIP.		ATTIC		IMPROVEMENT ANALYSIS	Good	Avg.	Fair	Poor
Floors	Hardwood	Type	FWA (HP)	Refrigerator		None		Quality of Construction	X			
Walls	Drywall	Fuel	Electric	Range/Oven	X	Stairs	X	Condition of Improvements	X			
Trim/Finish	Good	Condition	Good	Disposal	X	Drop Stair		Room Sizes/Layout	X			
Bath Floor	Ceramic	Adequacy	Good	Dishwasher	X	Scuttle		Closets and Storage	X			
Bath Wainscot	Ceramic	COOLING		Fan/Hood	X	Floor	X	Energy Efficiency	X			
Doors		Central	Yes	Compactor		Heated		Plumbing-Adequacy & Condition	X			
		Other		Washer/Dryer		Finished		Electrical-Adequacy & Condition	X			
		Condition	Good	Microwave	X			Kitchen Cabinets-Adequacy & Cond.	X			
Fireplace(s) Family Rm # 1		Adequacy	Good	Intercom				Compatibility to Neighborhood	X			

AUTOS

CAR STORAGE:	Garage	X	Attached	X	Adequate	X	House Entry	Appeal & Marketability	X			
No. Cars 2	Carport		Detached		Inadequate		Outside Entry	Estimated Remaining Economic Life	50-55	Yrs.
Condition Good	None		Built-In		Electric Door		Basement Entry	Estimated Remaining Physical Life		Yrs.

COMMENTS

Additional features: Entrance Stoop - 4',9" X 10'1", 10"X 6'5", 5'X5' 6". Brick Patio off Family room - 11' 10" X 14'3".

Depreciation (Physical, functional and external inadequacies, repairs needed, modernization, etc.): None

General market conditions and prevalence and impact in subject/market area regarding loan discounts, interest buydowns and concessions: Good Market Conditions

Freddie Mac Form 70 10/86 12Ch. CL.   Forms and Worms Inc.,* 315 Whitney Ave.,* New Haven, CT 06511 1(800) 243-4545   Item #111710   Fannie Mae Form 1004 10/86

FIGURE 7-2 *FNMA uniform residential appraisal form*

Valuation Section   **UNIFORM RESIDENTIAL APPRAISAL REPORT**   File No.

Purpose of Appraisal is to estimate Market Value as defined in the Certification & Statement of Limiting Conditions.

COST APPROACH

BUILDING SKETCH (SHOW GROSS LIVING AREA ABOVE GRADE)
If for Freddie Mac or Fannie Mae, show only square foot calculations and cost approach comments in this space

Measurements		No. Stories		Sq. Ft.
14'3" X 20' 10"	X	1	=	297
30'2" X 36' 1"	X	2	=	2177
(10" X 6'5")	X	1	=	(5)
2'8" X 7'3"	X	1		19
Total Sq. Ft.				2,488

ESTIMATED REPRODUCTION COST-NEW-OF IMPROVEMENTS:

Dwelling 2488 Sq. Ft. @ $ 60	= $ 149,280
Sq. Ft. @ $	=
Extras Attic	= 6,000
	=
Special Energy Efficient Items	=
Porches, Patios, etc. Stoop/81;Patio/169	= 3,150
Garage/Carport 545 Sq. Ft. @ $ 30	= 16,350
Total Estimated Cost New	= $ 174,780

	Physical	Functional	External	
Less				
Depreciation	6,000	-0-	-0-	= $ (6,000)

Depreciated Value of Improvements .... = $ 168,780
Site Imp. "as is" (driveway, landscaping, etc.) = $ 2,000
ESTIMATED SITE VALUE .... = $ 70,000
(If leasehold, show only leasehold value.)
INDICATED VALUE BY COST APPROACH ...... = $ 240,000

(Not Required by Freddie Mac and Fannie Mae)
Does property conform to applicable HUD/VA property standards?   [X] Yes [ ] No
If No, explain: _____

Construction Warranty [ ] Yes [X] No
Name of Warranty Program _____
Warranty Coverage Expires _____

SALES COMPARISON ANALYSIS

The undersigned has recited three recent sales of properties most similar and proximate to subject and has considered these in the market analysis. The description includes a dollar adjustment, reflecting market reaction to those items of significant variation between the subject and comparable properties. If a significant item in the comparable property is superior to, or more favorable than, the subject property, a minus (–) adjustment is made, thus reducing the indicated value of subject; if a significant item in the comparable property is inferior to, or less favorable than, the subject property, a plus (+) adjustment is made, thus increasing the indicated value of the subject.

ITEM	SUBJECT	COMPARABLE NO. 1		COMPARABLE NO. 2		COMPARABLE NO. 3	
Address	216 Graystone Drive	109 Graystone Dr.		204 Summerwood Drive		223 Graystone Dr.	
Proximity to Subject		Subject S/D		Subject S/D		Subject S/D	
Sales Price	$ 250,000		$ 249,750		$ 252,875		$ 247,145
Price/Gross Liv. Area	$ 100.48	$ 97.75		$ 87.50		$ 118.25	
Data Source	Inspection	Inspection		Inspection/MLS		Inspection/MLS	
VALUE ADJUSTMENTS	DESCRIPTION	DESCRIPTION	+ (–)$ Adjustment	DESCRIPTION	+ (–)$ Adjustment	DESCRIPTION	+ (–)$ Adjustment
Sales or Financing Concessions							
Date of Sale/Time	4/10/90	12/15/89	5,200	3/6/90	-0-	3/25/90	-0-
Location	In town	In town	-0-	In Town	-0-	In town	-0-
Site/View	Good	Good	3,500	Good	-0-	Average	8,000
Design and Appeal	Traditional	Traditional	-0-	Traditional	-0-	Traditional	-0-
Quality of Construction	Good	Good	-0-	Good	-0-	Good	-0-
Age	4 Years	New	(6,000)	4 Years	-0-	New	-0-
Condition	Good	New	-0-	Good	-0-	New	-0-
Above Grade	Total Bdrms Baths	Total Bdrms Baths		Total Bdrms Baths		Total Bdrms Baths	
Room Count	9 4 2.5	8 3 3	(1,000)	9 4 3	(1,500)	12 4 3.5	(2,500)
Gross Living Area	2488 Sq. Ft.	2555 Sq. Ft.	(3,000)	2890 Sq. Ft.	(18,000)	2090 Sq. Ft.	18,000
Basement & Finished Rooms Below Grade	None	None	-0-	None	-0-	Finished/1040	(26,000)
Functional Utility	Average	Average	-0-	Average	-0-	Average	-0-
Heating/Cooling	Central	Central	-0-	Central	-0-	Central	-0-
Garage/Carport	Garage/545	Garage/572	-0-	Garage/272	6,000	Garage/484	1,300
Porches, Patio, Pools, etc.	Stoop/81 Patio/169	Stoop Porch/318	(1,500)	Stoop/50 Deck/270	4,000	Stoop Deck/264	4,000
Special Energy Efficient Items	Ins Glass Full Ins. Zoned Heat Pump	Equal	-0-	Equal	-0-	Equal	-0-
Fireplace(s)	One	Two	(2,000)	One	-0-	Two	(2,000)
Other (e.g. kitchen equip., remodeling)	Range, DW, HF,Micro,DSP	Same & Fence	(2,000)	Same, No Micro	750	Same & Fence	(2,000)
Net Adj. (total)		+ [X] –$ 6800		+ [X] –$ 8,750		+ [X] –$ 7,200	
Indicated Value of Subject			$ 242,95		$ 244,125		$ 239,945

Comments on Sales Comparison: _All comparables are sales in the subject subdivision and are similar in design and market appeal to the subject property. Comparable #2 is most similar to the subject property and has been given greatest consideration._

INDICATED VALUE BY SALES COMPARISON APPROACH .... $ 245,000
INDICATED VALUE BY INCOME APPROACH (If Applicable) Estimated Market Rent $ _____ /Mo. x Gross Rent Multiplier _____ = $ N/Z
This appraisal is made [X] "as is" [ ] subject to the repairs, alterations, inspections or conditions listed below [ ] completion per plans and specifications.
Comments and Conditions of Appraisal: _____

RECONCILIATION

Final Reconciliation: _Greatest consideration has been given to the conclusion of the Market Data Analysis. This value is well supported by the Cost Approach. Houses not typically rented in this market; therefore, Income Approach not used._

This appraisal is based upon the above requirements, the certification, contingent and limiting conditions, and Market Value definition that are stated in
[X] FmHA, HUD &/or VA instructions.
[ ] Freddie Mac Form 439 (Rev. 7/86)/Fannie Mae Form 1004B (Rev. 7/86) filed with client _____ 19 ___ [ ] attached.
I (WE) ESTIMATE THE MARKET VALUE, AS DEFINED, OF THE SUBJECT PROPERTY AS OF April 30 1990 to be $ 245,000
I (We) certify: that to the best of my (our) knowledge and belief the facts and data used herein are true and correct; that I (we) personally inspected the subject property, both inside and out, and have made an exterior inspection of all comparable sales cited in this report; and that I (we) have no undisclosed interest, present or prospective therein.

Appraiser(s) SIGNATURE _____   Review Appraiser SIGNATURE _____   [X] Did [ ] Did Not
           NAME _____   (if applicable) NAME _____   Inspect Property

Freddie Mac Form 70 10/86   .2Ch   Forms and Worms Inc.,* 315 Whitney Ave., New Haven, CT 06511 1(800) 243-4545   Fannie Mae Form 1004 10/86

FIGURE 7-2 *(cont.)*

ciate the amount of detailed information that is included in any appraisal. In addition to the form itself, it would be typical for the appraiser to attach a building sketch, location map, photograph addendum, definition of market value employed, and a certification and statement of limiting conditions.

SUMMARY   Many appraisers consider the sales comparison approach to be the most sensible method of estimating market value. Even to the experienced appraiser, it often seems the most logical approach when sufficient data can be obtained. It is the approach used most heavily in appraisals of single-family homes and raw land.

The steps involved in the sales comparison approach include the (1) location of comparable properties, (2) identification of value characteristics, (3) adjustment of differences in value characteristics, and (4) final correlation of value. Each of these steps requires a knowledge of the sources of data and experience in making value judgments.

Any value conclusion reached by the sales comparison approach should be carefully cross-checked. One way of doing so is by looking at the underlying economics. Specifically, in the valuation of a single-family home, if the rent that could be obtained from a tenant does not justify the value under the sales comparison approach, any excess value must be sustained as arising from the "psychic income" associated with home ownership.

The cost approach to value relies on several of the basic principles set out in Chapter 6. Perhaps the most obvious one is the principle of substitution, which states that a property's value will be no greater than the cost to reproduce improvements that generate the same stream of utility. That is, no one will pay more for existing property than the cost for new construction on a comparable site. Thus, the cost approach is sometimes useful in setting a ceiling on value.

Under the cost approach, reproduction cost new of the improvements, less all elements of accrued depreciation, is added to the site value to obtain an estimate of total value. The cost approach is most reliable when accurate construction cost figures are available and little depreciation is involved. The approach is very often used for valuing new properties that do not produce income and have few comparables—in other words, in situations in which the sales comparison and income capitalization approaches are difficult to apply.

Many practicing appraisers use the form designed by the Federal Home Loan Mortgage Corporation and the Federal National Mortgage Association[4] for residential appraisals. As you can see in Figure 7-2, this

---

[4]*The operation of these two institutions will be explained in Part 5, Real Estate Finance.*

form captures all the highlights of the sales comparison and cost approaches presented in this chapter.

With the general understanding of the appraisal process and appraisal methodology gained in the last two chapters, you should be able to appreciate why this condensed form contains the information it does. In today's modern appraisal office, comparable property data are computerized, and word processors produce these form reports in a highly efficient manner. However, the opinion of value is still only an opinion and no better than the judgment of the appraiser behind the opinion.

IMPORTANT TERMS

Accrued depreciation
Characteristics of value
Comparable properties
Cost approach
Curable depreciation
External depreciation
Functional depreciation
Incurable depreciation

Nonproperty characteristics
Physical depreciation
Property characteristics
Replacement cost
Reproduction cost
Reproduction cost new
Sales comparison approach
Subject property

REVIEW QUESTIONS

7.1   When implementing the sales comparison approach, on what basis should an appraiser identify comparable properties?

7.2   What are the most common nonproperty characteristics of a single-family comparable?

7.3   When estimating value by the sales comparison approach, the appraiser must determine what the dollar amount of the adjustment is and if the adjustment is a negative or positive amount. Explain the process used by the appraiser to determine these factors.

7.4   If a father sold a property to his daughter just before his death, how should the reported sales price be adjusted in the sales comparison approach?

7.5   What real estate property types might be most accurately appraised by using the sales comparison approach?

7.6   Differentiate between the concepts of reproduction cost new and replacement cost as they are used in the cost approach.

7.7   Outline the general steps in the cost approach to value.

7.8   What methods might an appraiser utilize to estimate reproduction cost new?

7.9   Discuss the differences between curable and incurable physical depreciation. What form of depreciation is always incurable?

7.10   As the sales comparison approach is normally relied on in valuing the site in the cost approach, what important property characteristics might be utilized?

THE INCOME CAPITALIZATION
APPROACH TO VALUATION

The key to understanding the income approach to valuing real estate lies in understanding the relationship between a stream of income and value. In essence, an investor who buys real estate (or stocks, bonds, or other income-producing property) really is buying a *future flow of income*—that is, a future stream of benefits. If this is so, it follows that the present value of a parcel of property can be estimated by the following.

- Projecting the amount, certainty, and length of a future flow of income.

- Placing a dollar valuation on the future flow of income—by, as appraisers say, applying an appropriate capitalization rate.

The process can be stated more precisely this way. $MV = \dfrac{NOI}{R}$

> *The market value (V) of property equals its stabilized **net operating income** (NOI) divided by an appropriate market **capitalization rate (R)**, or V = NOI/R.*

Although the logic of using the income approach for appraising income-producing property is impeccable, a great deal of talent and experience are required in estimating stabilized NOI. This is the "true" earning capacity of the property uninfluenced by extraordinary or nonrecurring factors. In addition, several subtleties are involved in deriving the appropriate capitalization rate. These matters are discussed in greater detail in this chapter.[1] (See Box 8-1.)

---

[1] *Income capitalization has been around a long time. The great Von Zanthier used it to establish a "Meisterschule" for forestry valuation in 1764. See Filbert Roth,* Forest Valuation *(Ann Arbor, Mich., George Wahr, Publisher, 1926).*

8-1
THE MORE
GENERAL
VALUATION
MODEL

The formula $V = NOI/R$ is a simplified version of the discounted cash flow model, which is the basic tool we will develop in Parts 5 and 7. That more general value equation is

$$V = \sum_{t=1}^{N} \frac{NOI_t}{(1 + r)^t} + \frac{\text{Proceeds from sales}_t}{(1 + r)^t}$$

Where r is the required return, which is similar, but not identical, to R.

With this formula, the income approach to value states that market value is the present value of future benefits. For an income-producing property, the stream of future benefits is the annual cash flow over a projected holding period plus the residual cash flow from sale of the property at the end of that holding period.

THE CONCEPT OF STABILIZED NET OPERATING INCOME

One of the major difficulties in real estate financial analysis is the lack of uniform terminology. Sometimes the same term has different meanings; sometimes several terms are used to refer to the same thing. In this book, financial terms are given very specific meanings, and it is important, when you are using other sources or analyzing particular real estate transactions, to be sure that the same terms are similarly defined.

NET OPERATING INCOME

One of the most frequently used terms in real estate financial analysis is NOI. This is defined as the balance of cash remaining after deducting the operating expenses of a property from the gross income generated by the property.

There are two important points to remember about NOI.

■ In a determination of NOI, debt service on any existing or projected mortgages is ignored, for NOI is intended to demonstrate the earning capacity of the real estate exclusive of any financing.

■ In a determination of NOI, historic accounting depreciation deductions are ignored; only cash expenses for operating the property are considered.

❏ **GROSS RENTAL RECEIPTS.**   The first step in deriving NOI is to estimate **gross rental receipts (GRR).** (See Table 8-1.) GRR reflects the

TABLE 8-1   DERIVING NET OPERATING INCOME

1. Gross rental receipts
    + Nonrental income
    Potential gross income

2. Potential gross income
    − Vacancy and credit loss
    Effective gross income

3. Effective gross income
    − Operating expenses
    Net operating income

appraiser's estimate of what rental income would be if the property were 100 percent occupied for an entire 12-month period. In deriving GRR, the appraiser relies on three major sources: (1) the records of the subject property, (2) comparables, and (3) trends in the marketplace. (See Chapters 2 and 3.) The property records (where possible, signed leases and audited financial statements) will indicate the present rent roll and the total rent currently being received. However, rents currently being paid under existing leases (called *contract rents*) may not represent *market rents*. Market rents may be higher or lower than contract rents because market conditions may have changed since the leases were signed and rents were fixed. It is necessary, therefore, to determine the current market rental value of the space in the subject property.

Where the contract rent and market rent differ, the appraiser must decide which to use in the projected operating statement. If tenants have very short-term leases, it is likely that, within a fairly brief period, contract rents will move up or down toward current market rents as the current leases expire. On the other hand, if the building is occupied by a single tenant who has a lease for 25 or 50 years, current market rentals mean little in evaluating the future rental stream. Usually, since terms fall somewhere between these extremes, the analyst prepares a **lease expiration schedule,** showing when each lease expires, and constructs a future rental stream to reflect these expirations. As mentioned earlier, the figure for GRR will include the rental expected from *all* space in the building, whether or not it is vacant at the present time. A provision for vacancies is introduced in the calculation of effective gross income.

❏ **POTENTIAL GROSS INCOME.**   After arriving at a figure for GRR, the analyst must ascertain any additional income earned from sources other than rent. Examples of these are: (1) automatic washers and dryers in the laundry room, (2) vending machines, (3) parking fees,

(4) swimming pool, and (5) other amenity fees. The GRR plus other income represents the property's **potential gross income (PGI).**

❏ **EFFECTIVE GROSS INCOME.**   The next step in determining NOI is to calculate the **effective gross income (EGI),** which is arrived at by subtracting from PGI a figure representing **vacancy and collection (or credit) loss.** The vacancy expense, which is calculated as a percentage of GRR (frequently ranging between 7 and 15 percent of GRR) reflects the experience of the subject property or of comparable properties in the area and also projected trends in the marketplace.

Collection loss expense, also expressed as a percentage of GRR, reflects unpaid rent as well as uncollectible bad checks. Subtracting vacancy and collection loss from GPI results in EGI.

❏ **OPERATING EXPENSES.**   The final step in calculating NOI is estimating and deducting **operating expenses.** As already noted, these are expenses directly related to the operation and maintenance of the property. They do not include debt service or depreciation. Typical operating expenses include the following items.

- Real estate taxes (not last year's but next year's)[2]
- Payroll
- Maintenance and repair (M&R)
- Fire and hazard insurance premiums
- Utility costs
- Management fees
- Supplies
- Replacement reserve

After operating expenses are deducted from effective gross income, the resulting figure is NOI.

STABILIZED NET OPERATING INCOME

The initial derivation of an NOI figure will be based on the financial records of the property. Since the focus here is not on a historical record but on a projection of future income, it is necessary to exclude unusual or nonrecurring items of income and expense as well as eliminate distortions that may have been introduced into the financial statements, inad-

---

[2]In the more generalized discounted cash flow formulation, taxes (and all operating expenses) would be estimated for each year of the holding period.

vertently or otherwise, by the present owner. The result is a **stabilized NOI** figure, often called *stabilized net.*

The purpose of the stabilization process is to show, to the extent possible, the true future earning power of the property. One traditional approach to reaching a stabilized NOI figure is simply to average income and expenses for the past several years. Thus, for example, a five-year average would be shown as five-year stabilized net.

During a period of rapid inflation or significant economic change, however, this approach may not be adequate. A better way to arrive at a stabilized NOI is to analyze the operating statement for the past two or three years, make appropriate adjustments, and then further adjust the figures to reflect foreseeable future changes (e.g., a proposed increase in the property tax rate). (See Box 8-2.)

A property's current NOI, as shown on its financial statement, can diverge from the property's true stabilized NOI in several ways, including (1) lease concessions, (2) deferred maintenance, (3) needed capital improvements, and (4) inadequate reserves, which are discussed next.

8-2
INCONSISTENT REVENUE AND EXPENSE ESTIMATES

Recently, a major East Coast financial institution made a construction loan on the Brandywine Apartments to be built in East Lansing, Michigan. In convincing the institution to make the construction loan, the developer showed a projected value based on the income approach to value. At the date he made the loan request, he was careful to document his expense projections. In fact, they were the exact expenses for a similar apartment project in East Lansing in the preceding year.

The developer then projected income for the first year of operation. He subtracted the expenses from the projected income to arrive at the NOI figure, which was capitalized to determine value. Once the project was completed, the developer sought permanent financing. Potential permanent lenders used the income approach to determine the value of the collateral. They did not, however, make the mistake of using next year's revenues with last year's expenses. Consequently, their value projection used lower NOI and a lower overall project value.

With this lower value, they were not willing to make a loan large enough to cover the entire construction loan made by the East Coast lender. With no possibility of getting out of the Brandywine project except by partial payment plus a second lien position, the East Coast lender reluctantly took back a second mortgage.

Simple errors (in this case the construction lender's failure to analyze fully the original appraisal) can be costly.

❑ **LEASE CONCESSIONS.**   An owner's financial statement may accurately show GRR currently being collected. However, in order to fill up a new building or survive a period of market weakness, the owner may have granted **lease concessions** that have not yet been fulfilled. For example, every tenant may be entitled to one rent-free month for each year of the lease. Some tenants may have step-down renewal options, giving them the right to renew at a lower rental in the future. In these unusual cases, future rental income will be less than at first appears.

❑ **DEFERRED MAINTENANCE.**   A property may show a healthy NOI along with a very low figure for maintenance and repair. It may turn out that the building suffers from **deferred maintenance** (which was identified in Chapter 7 as a form of physical depreciation). Here the true return from the property is not only less than appears, but a new owner must also spend additional funds to restore the property to optimum operating condition.

❑ **NEEDED CAPITAL IMPROVEMENTS.**   The owner may have postponed making needed capital improvements. Although this inadequacy will not be reflected in the operating statements as such, it does mean that a new purchaser will be required to provide additional capital for the necessary improvements, thus reducing the return on his investment.

❑ **INADEQUATE REPLACEMENT RESERVES.**   When personal property is a significant factor, as in the case of motels, adequate cash reserves should be maintained to replace short-lived items (e.g., furniture, carpets, etc.). Once again, to the extent that **replacement reserves** are inadequate, the indicated NOI is too high. In addition, the new owner will have to build up the reserves as soon as he or she takes title. We do not mean to imply that most owners keep a bank account labeled "replacement reserves" and turn it over to the buyer at the time of sale. We do mean that replacements are a real cost, and underestimating them can cause an analyst to overestimate NOI correspondingly and consequently overvalue the property.

After considering these potential problem areas, the appraiser has only one major concern left in projecting *stabilized NOI*. That concern is the potentially uneven impact of inflation. Lease provisions may call for tenants to cover part of any operating expense increase, to pay higher rent if inflation (as expressed as a rise in the consumer price index) is experienced, or to pay a percentage rent (defined in Chapter 4), or a combination of these. Depending on the specific lease provisions, inflation may affect the NOI of two buildings, which are physically very similar, in very different ways.

Since inflation is also a problem in determining the capitalization rate, we will postpone further discussion of this issue until the end of the chapter. At this point, however, it is important that you appreciate the difficulty of estimating the stabilized NOI in situations involving complex lease provisions and uncertain rates of inflation.

DERIVING A CAPITALIZATION RATE

Having arrived at a stabilized NOI figure for the property in question, the appraiser has accomplished the first step in applying the income approach to value. The second step is calculating the appropriate **capitalization rate.** *Capitalization* is the process of converting a future income stream into a present value. The capitalization rate is the percentage rate by which the future income stream is divided to arrive at a single figure that represents present value. For example, a capitalization rate of 10 percent applied to an annual income of $1,000 gives a present value of $10,000 ($1,000 ÷ 0.10 = $10,000).

Capitalization rates vary among particular types of investments and from one period of time to another. Higher capitalization rates (expressed as a percentage) are utilized when NOI is more speculative, that is, riskier, or when higher inflation is anticipated. The converse is also true. Lower capitalization rates are utilized for projects generating a more secure NOI or for times when significant inflation is not anticipated.

Important factors in choosing a capitalization rate are listed as follows.

- Type of property (e.g., apartment building, office building, etc.).
- Location (in the main business district, a few feet may make one location better than another).
- Age (the older the building, the less future income can be derived from it in its present state).
- Quality of the tenancies (e.g., holding tenant quality constant, a long-term lease usually means more secure NOI than a short-term lease).

FOUR ELEMENTS OF A CAPITALIZATION RATE

From a theoretical standpoint, the capitalization rate has four separate elements.

- Real return
- Inflation premium
- Risk premium
- Recapture premium

❑ **REAL RETURN.** A person invests capital only if there will be compensation for deferring immediate consumption. Even if the investment involves no risk and even if the price level remains stable, the return will still be sought. Thus, the central element in any return calculation is the real return.

The **real return** required by investors and lenders can be estimated by looking at the traditional relationship between risk-free 90-day Treasury bills and the rate of inflation over the past two decades. Various researchers have put this difference (i.e., the real return) at 2 to 3 percent annually.

❑ **INFLATION PREMIUM.** Investors have come to expect a decline in the value of the dollar over time—that is, they assume an inflationary economy. Expecting inflation, the investor requires the return from any perspective investment to go beyond the real return and give an additional return to compensate for future inflation. Put another way and perhaps more logically, the investor wants to receive back the number of dollars that gives the same purchasing power as the dollars he or she originally invested. In a period of inflation this requires more dollars to be returned than were invested.

When an analyst or appraiser is constructing a capitalization rate, a judgment must be made as to the expected rate of inflation during the holding period of the asset that is being valued. Obviously, this may be an extremely difficult judgment to make. One guideline in estimating the combined real return and **inflation premium** expected by investors is the current rate on Treasury bonds having a maturity equal to the projected holding period of the subject property. Treasury bonds are used because the return on such bonds is made up almost wholly of the required real return plus inflation premium (i.e., there is virtually no risk except the risk of underestimating inflation). Subtracting 2 to 3 percent (real return) from this Treasury rate gives the composite market expectation about inflation.

❑ **RISK PREMIUM.** Unlike Treasury bonds, real estate projects carry risk, which may be substantial. The investor recognizes this risk and requires compensation for it through an expected return higher than that paid on riskless or lower risk investments.

Just how large the **risk premium** should be is the subject of endless professional and academic debate. This topic is discussed, and a straightforward approach to choosing a risk premium is suggested in Chapter 20. At this point, it is appropriate to say that the riskier the project, the higher the risk premium and consequently the higher the capitalization rate.[3]

---

[3]*Note that the sum of the real return, the inflation premium, and the risk premium is often referred to collectively as the discount rate or the required rate of return on capital.*

TABLE 8-2 RECAPTURE PREMIUM: STRAIGHT LINE VERSUS SINKING FUND		
	STRAIGHT LINE (%)	SINKING FUND (%)
Real return	2.0	2.0
Inflation premium	6.0	6.0
Risk premium	2.0	2.0
Recapture premium	3.3	0.6
Capitalization rate	13.3	10.6

Note the impact of using the straight-line method or the sinking fund method on the capitalization rate. Assume a 30-year economic life.

❑ **RECAPTURE PREMIUM.**   If an investment were to produce income in perpetuity, the three elements already mentioned would be sufficient to make up the capitalization rate. Improved real estate usually has a long economic life, but it cannot have an infinite life.[4] Consequently, the investor requires not only a return *on* invested capital (the first three factors above), but also a return *of* invested capital. Thus, an element representing recapture of investment must be included in the capitalization rate.

The **recapture premium** can be calculated by using either the straight-line or sinking fund method. If, for example, a project were expected to last 50 years, the straight-line recapture premium (calculated with respect to the value of the improvements) would be 2 percent a year (50 years × 2 percent per year = 100 percent over the 50-year economic life).

A more theoretically acceptable approach is to use a **sinking fund concept.** This concept introduces the element of interest that will be earned on the capital recouped each year during the period. Thus, the investor can receive something less than 2 percent each year and still recover an entire investment over the 50-year period because interest will be earned (or some other return) on the money received in years 1, 2, 3, and so on, compounded up to year 50.

The major distinction between the straight-line and sinking fund methods is that, under the straight-line method, reinvestment is *not* assumed. In the sinking fund method, reinvestment of the recaptured capital is assumed to produce a return, which can be calculated in one of several different ways. (See Table 8-2.)

---

[4]The land *element in a property investment does have perpetual life, but the improvements will depreciate over a specific period of time.*

The astute reader will have noticed a potential inconsistency at this point in estimating stabilized NOI and the capitalization rate. Inflation must be handled in a consistent manner in both cases. If stabilized NOI is unaffected by inflation, the foregoing calculation of a capitalization rate, using expected future inflation as one component, is correct. However, to the extent that stabilized NOI increases with inflation, an inflation premium in the capitalization rate is inappropriate. If, for example, lease provisions provided that NOI would increase exactly with inflation, no inflation component should be included in the capitalization rate.

BAND OF INVESTMENT APPROACH

One well-known approach in determining the capitalization rate is the **band of investment approach.** This approach is similar to the weighted average cost of capital concept used in corporate finance. In this approach, the appraiser or analyst calculates the most probable mortgage interest rate that will be utilized for financing the property as well as the rate of return sought on the equity investment. Each of the rates is weighted by the proportion of total value it represents to determine the capitalization rate. In a typical case, the mortgage rate might account for 75 percent of the total value (this being a common loan-to-value ratio), whereas the equity rate would represent 25 percent of the investment. (See Table 8-3.)

Although the band of investment approach is at first appealing, one quickly notices that the appraiser must still estimate the debt and equity rates. The debt rate is usually obtainable from the capital markets, but the estimation of an appropriate equity rate is much more difficult. Consider, for example, the difference between the impact of taxation on a taxable and nontaxable investor's (Part 6) required return.

TABLE 8-3   BAND OF INVESTMENT APPROACH

Debt	75% of total value
Interest cost	12%, 30 yr, mortgage constant = 0.124144
Equity	25% of total value
Equity rate	9%
Debt portion	$0.75 \times 0.124144 = 0.093$
Equity portion	$0.25 \times 0.09 \quad = \underline{0.023}$
Capitalization rate	0.116 or 11.6%

USING COMPARABLES

In the world of the practicing appraiser, the capitalization rate is often derived from the marketplace by using a comparable sales approach (largely because of the difficulties with the theoretical approach and band of investment approach just described). In other words, the appraiser finds sales of similar properties. For these properties, the stabilized income and the sale price are determined.

Based on these comparable sales, the capitalization rate is calculated. For example, if a sale price of $100,000 is associated with a $10,000 NOI, the capitalization rate is 10 percent ($10,000 ÷ $100,000 = 10%). This capitalization rate is known as the **overall capitalization rate (OAR)** and is the cap rate used most frequently in practice. The OAR is often called the overall rate of return because it includes a return "on" and a return "of" capital. (See Table 8-4.)

Thus, in a manner similar to the market data approach, an appropriate overall capitalization rate for the particular property being appraised is derived from the marketplace. However, while this is a practical way to calculate the capitalization rate, it should always be checked by the theoretical approach suggested above in an effort to justify the market value on an economic basis. (See Box 8-3.)

GROSS INCOME MULTIPLIER APPROACH

The **gross income multiplier (GIM)** is a rule of thumb method of arriving at an indication of value. It involves multiplying effective gross income (rather than NOI) by a factor that varies according to the type of property and its location.[5]

For example, an apartment building in a particular neighborhood may be valued at "six times annual gross." Thus, if its EGI for one year amounted to $100,000, the value would be taken as $600,000. This approach also can be used to establish a rule-of-thumb rental for a private home where fair market value is known. For example, the monthly rental of a private home in a particular area might be 1 percent of the fair market value. Thus, if the value is $60,000 (established by the sales comparison approach), the rental will be $600 per month.

As with all rules of thumb, the multiplier method should be used with caution, if at all. If all properties of a particular type had similar operating expenses and were identical in all respects except for the amount of rental income, the multiplier approach could be used with confidence. Obviously, this is not often the case. The danger in the use of

---

[5]*Some analysts prefer to use potential gross income or gross rental income in the multiplier. Any of the three is acceptable as long as it is clearly labeled and the comparables are extracted from the market by using the same measure.*

TABLE 8-4   INCOME APPROACH: AN OFFICE BUILDING EXAMPLE (41,520 SQ FT)

Net Operating Income Schedule

Gross rental receipts		$523,467
Plus nonrental income (parking)		10,450
Potential gross income		533,917
Less vacancy and credit loss @ 7%		(37,374)
Effective gross income		496,543
Less operating expenses		
Real estate taxes	$24,950	
Real estate insurance	3,500	
Property management	24,860	
Utilities	29,000	
Janitorial	14,500	
Elevator maintenance	3,000	
Maintenance personnel	4,000	
Repairs and supplies	5,500	
Advertising and leasing	6,000	
General and administrative	3,000	
Reserves for replacements	5,000	
Total operating expenses		(123,310)
Net Operating Income		$373,233

Capitalization Rate—Band of Investment Approach

Debt	75% of total value
Interest cost	12%, 30-year amortization, annual mortgage constant = 0.124144
Equity	25% of total value
Equity rate	9%
Debt portion	0.75 × 0.124144 = 0.0931
Equity portion	0.25 × 0.09 = 0.0225
Capitalization rate	0.1156 or 11.6%

Value

Stabilized net operating income	$ 373,233
Capitalization rate	11.6%
Value ($373,233 ÷ 0.116)	$3,217,525

<table>
<tr><td>

8-3
EXAMPLE
OF INCOME
APPROACH
TO VALUE
FOR SMALL
RESIDENTIAL
PROPERTY

</td><td>

The following income approach to value example presents the valuation of a residential duplex.

Subject Property

The subject is a duplex located at 5811 Pine Street. Each of its two units contains 1,150 square feet, two bedrooms, two bathrooms, combined kitchen–dining area, living room, carport, and patio.

Comparable 1

Located across the street from the subject, each unit in this duplex rents for $440 per month. It is slightly smaller than the subject. Each unit contains 1,075 square feet, two bedrooms, one and one-half bathrooms, combined kitchen–dining area, living room, carport, and patio. Comparable 1 is the same age and condition as the subject and was purchased for $105,600 two months ago.

Comparable 2

Located five blocks from the subject in a slightly nicer area, each unit in this triplex rents for $460 per month. The three units each contain 1,100 square feet, two bedrooms, two bathrooms, combined kitchen–dining area, living room, carport, and patio. Comparable 2 was purchased for $173,880 four months ago.

Comparable 3

Located three blocks away in a neighborhood comparable to the subject, this duplex contains a floor plan that is identical to the subject. Built during the same year as the subject, each unit is currently rented for $450 per month. The current owners recently rejected an offer to buy the property for $102,600.

</td></tr>
</table>

Net Operating Income

Potential gross income	$10,800
$450 per unit per month	
Vacancy and credit loss	(540)
Effective gross income	10,260
Operating expenses	(2,700)
Net operating income	$ 7,560

Capitalization Rate

Theoretical approach	
Real return	3.0%
Inflation premium[a]	2.6%
Risk premium	2.0%
Recapture (sinking fund)	0.5%
	7.65%

OAR approach: Comparable	Sales Price	NOI	OAR
1	$105,600	$ 7,390	7.0%
2	$173,880	$11,590	6.67%
3	$102,600[b]	$ 7,560	7.37%
	Say 7.5% for Subject		.0702

GIM approach: Comparable	Sales Price	GRR	GIM
1	$105,600	$10,560	10.0
2	$173,880	$16,560	10.5
3	$102,600[b]	$10,800	9.5
	Say GIM = 10X for Subject		

Value	
Theoretical approach	$ 98,850 98823.52
OAR approach	$100,800
GIM approach	$102,600
Say	$100,500

[a]From the capital markets the long-term inflation expectation is 6½%. The appraiser expects net operating income increases to cover 60% of inflation. Thus 40% of 6½% should be included in the capitalization rate.

[b]Offer rejected.

this approach is that unique features of the particular building being considered, whether good or bad, are not given proper weight.

PROBLEMS WITH SIMPLE CAPITALIZATION

TAX CONSIDERATIONS

A capitalization rate determined from the marketplace embodies a particular set of tax considerations, which reflect the tax position of whatever type of investor dominates the particular market. Obviously, these tax considerations may not be those of a specific investor who is seeking to evaluate a property. So although it is appropriate for an appraiser seeking a value that has general validity to use a market-established capitalization rate, the person about to make a decision in a particular investment situation should always develop an investment model incorporating income tax considerations, as is discussed in Part 7.

RECOGNIZING APPRECIATION OR DIMINUTION OF VALUE

One of the most basic problems with the simple formula $V = NOI/R$, as well as with all the variations mentioned so far, is the failure to account for appreciation or diminution of value in the property over the assumed period of ownership. In periods of rapid price changes, this can be an important factor in an investor's calculations. Witness the rapid inflation of the 1977–82 period, during which real estate in general increased sharply in price. Even though future value changes obviously are speculative, is there a way to consider them in an estimate of value?

There is such a method, representing a more sophisticated twist on the income approach to value. It is known as the **Ellwood technique,** named after the late L. W. (Pete) Ellwood, one of the deans of the appraisal profession. Although this technique goes beyond the scope of the investigation in this book, we should be aware that the Ellwood tables do account for appreciation and diminution of value as well as for loan amortization. (See Box 8-4.) Still, even the Ellwood tables leave some-

---

8-4
**ELLWOOD
FORMULATION**

L. W. Ellwood, author of the *Ellwood Tables,* was the first to develop a practical conclusion and to promulgate the concepts of mortgage-equity analysis within the area of real property valuation.[a] The original Ellwood equation for the overall capitalization rate is

$$R_O = Y_E - MC^{+\text{dep}}_{-\text{app}} \, 1/S_n$$

where

Y_E = equity yield rate

M = ratio of mortgage to value

C = mortgage coefficient[b]

$1/S_n$ = sinking fund factor at equity yield rate for the ownership projection period

dep = depreciation in property value for the projection period

app = appreciation in property value for the projection period

Although the *Ellwood Tables* provided precalculated mortgage coefficients (C) for many combinations of equity yield rates (Y_E) and various mortgage terms, the mortgage coefficients are no longer required or particularly useful since the advent of hand-held calculators.

The Ellwood formula assumes a level income flow; overall property value may be assumed to increase, decrease, or remain stable. If the income flow is not level, the formula *must* be modified to reflect the effect of changing income streams. This is accomplished by using the *J*-factor. When it is assumed that there is level income and no change in value, the derived rate is known as the *basic capitalization rate* (*r*). This rate reflects the effect of financing and is developed as follows:

$$R_o = Y_E - MC$$
$$RO = r$$
$$r = Y_E - MC$$

Thus, the basic capitalization rate is a building block to develop overall capitalization rates with additional assumptions. For example, when there is a change in value, the formula is

$$RO = r - \Delta_o\, 1/S_n$$

In current symbols, the equation is restated as

$$RO = Y_E - M(Y_E + P\, 1/S_n - R_M) - \Delta_o\, 1/S_n$$

where

P = ratio paid off (mortgage)[c]

ΔO = change (in total property value)

R = mortgage capitalization rate (mortgage constant)

[a]L. W. Ellwood, *Ellwood Tables for Real Estate Appraising and Financing,* 4th ed. (Cambridge, Mass.: Ballinger, 1977).

[b]The mortgage coefficient C may be computed using the formula $C = Y_E + P1/S_n - R_M$.

[c]The ratio of mortgage paid off may be computed using the formula $P = (R_M - i)/(R_{MP} - i)$ where R_M = the mortgage capitalization rate for the full amortization term, and R_{MP} = the mortgage capitalization rate for the projection period.

Source: The Appraisal of Real Estate, 8th ed. (Chicago: American Institute of Real Estate Appraisers, 1983), pp. 426–428.

thing to be desired in terms of their treatment of the time value of money and the special tax considerations applicable to some investors. Ten years ago you would have had to learn to use the Ellwood formula. With today's business calculators and microcomputers to do the math, it is easier to use discounted cash flow. If you decide that Part 7 is tough, look back at Box 8-4 and remember how tough it might have been.

DISCOUNTED CASH FLOW

In the simple appraisal formulations illustrated in this chapter, several divergent influences (inflation, tax shelter, neighborhood decline, leverage, and many more) are subsumed in two estimates: stabilized NOI and the capitalization rate. The Ellwood technique allows recognition of uniform appreciation and loan amortization but is still quite restrictive. Today appraisers are turning to a full discounted cash flow analysis for complicated income property appraisals. The discounted cash flow approach, built on the concepts covered in this chapter, is the focus of Chapter 21.

SUMMARY   In this chapter, we analyzed the simplified formula for the income capitalization approach to value. We also mentioned some of the more sophisticated variations used by professional appraisers and analysts. The two major elements noted were (1) estimation of stabilized NOI and (2) selection of the appropriate capitalization rate. Both require experience and knowledge. The ability to accurately estimate NOI is the real test of one's familiarity with the market.

Of the three approaches to value, the income approach is the most similar to the analytical framework for determining the "winner of the game." However, remember that the income approach, as well as the two others, is a generalized estimate of value, as distinguished from a value conclusion that is relevant to a particular investor who must judge an investment in the context of his or her own financial, tax, and investment circumstances.

When reviewing the three approaches to value, remember that step 5 in the appraisal process (as described in Chapter 6) is the reconciliation of the various value conclusions reached. The professional appraiser or analyst never takes a simple average of the three value conclusions. For any particular appraisal, one approach may be more appropriate than another and so be deserving of more weight.

The cost approach is useful in valuing properties that do not generate measurable income and have few comparables (e.g., the new city library). The sales comparison approach is the most useful when a substantial number of truly comparable properties that have sold recently can be located. The income approach is most logical when evaluating income-producing property, for here the investor is really buying a future flow of income.

The most difficult part is estimating NOI; it may be more of an art than a science, requiring a feel for all the elements of value covered in Parts 1, 2, and 3.

The 1980s placed tremendous pressure on the traditional appraisal process. The influx of institutional investors (Chapter 23) has necessitated far more frequent appraisals of large commercial properties. As accounts use appraisers' opinions of value to provide return data to Wall Street analysts, more problems become apparent in certain applications of the traditional approaches. The basic concepts covered in this part are sound. However, naive application of the three approaches can cause serious problems on larger properties. The appendix to Chapter 23 discusses applying the income approach to value (the discounted cash flow version) to complex valuation situations. We suggest you read it quickly now to get a feel for the problems involved and then return for a more detailed reading after you study Part 7. Major property valuation is a complex and exciting challenge. We hope you enjoy the brief introduction in Appendix 23A.

| 8-5 1991 WILL BE A BIG YEAR FOR APPRAISAL FIRMS | In 1991, the two largest appraisal trade organizations—The American Institute of Real Estate Appraisers (MAI highest designation) and The American Society of Real Estate Appraisers (SREA highest designation)—are scheduled to merge. The new combined organization—The Appraisal Institute—should be more powerful and better able to improve the quality of the appraisal product through professional education and self regulation (like the American Institute of Certified Public Accountants).

Also in 1991, the appraisal sections of the Financial Institutions Reform, Recovery, and Enforcement Act (1989) will be felt in the market place. Among other things, this will require state licensing of appraisers much like the states license real estate brokers and sales persons (Part IV). Thus by the end of 1991, professional appraisers will be both designated (by their trade organization) and certified (by the state). |
|---|---|

IMPORTANT TERMS

Band of investment approach
Capitalization rate
Deferred maintenance
Effective gross income (EGI)
Ellwood technique
Gross income multiplier (GIM)
Gross rental receipts (GRR)
Inflation premium
Lease concessions
Lease expiration schedule
Net operating income (NOI)

Operating expenses
Overall capitalization rate (OAR)
Potential gross income
Real return
Recapture premium
Replacement reserves
Risk premium
Sinking fund concept
Stabilized NOI
Vacancy and collection (or credit) loss

REVIEW QUESTIONS

8.1   What is the distinction between gross rental receipts and gross effective income?

8.2   Why should an appraiser make sure stabilized NOI is being used in the income approach?

8.3   How would the existence of long-term leases from high-quality tenants affect the capitalization rate associated with an office building?

8.4   Differentiate between a return *on* capital and a return *of* capital.

8.5   From a theoretical point of view, why might the sinking fund method of calculating the recapture premium be more acceptable than the straight-line method?

8.6   How is the gross income multiplier used to estimate market value?

8.7   When must the appraiser make sure he or she uses the market rent when appraising an income property?

8.8   How will the preparation of a lease expiration schedule aid the appraiser in accurately estimating an appropriate stabilized NOI?

8.9   Should property management fees be included in the operating expense statement when the property owner is assuming management responsibility? Why or why not?

8.10 Why might an appraiser find the interest earned on U.S. Treasury bonds helpful in estimating a capitalization rate?

REFERENCES   BOOKS

Akerson, Charles B. *Capitalization Theory and Techniques: Study Guide.* Chicago: American Institute of Real Estate Appraisers, 1984.

Albritton, Harold D. *Controversies in Real Property Valuation: A Commentary.* Chicago: American Institute of Real Estate Appraisers, 1982.

American Association of State Highway Officials. *Acquisitions for Right of Way.* Washington, D.C.: 1962.

American Institute of Real Estate Appraisers. *Reading in Real Property Valuation Principles.* Vol. 1. Cambridge, Mass.: Ballinger Publishers, 1977.

American Institute of Real Estate Appraisers. *The Appraisal Journal Bibliography, 1932–1969,* Chicago; 1970. *The Appraisal of Rural Property.* Chicago: 1983. *Condemnation Appraisal Practice,* Vol. 2. Chicago: 1973. *Guidelines for Appraisal Office Policies and Procedures.* Chicago: 1981. *Readers' Guide to the Appraisal Journal, 1970–1980.* Chicago: 1981. *Readings in the Appraisal of Special Use Properties.* Chicago: 1981. *Readings in Highest and Best Use.* Chicago: 1981. *Readings in the Income Approach to Real Property Valuation.* Chicago: 1977.

Readings in Market Value. Chicago: 1981. *Readings in Real Estate Investment Analysis.* Chicago: 1977. *Readings in Real Property Valuation Principles.* Chicago: 1977. *Real Estate Appraisal Bibliography.* Chicago: 1973. *Real Estate Appraisal Bibliography, 1973–1980.* Chicago: 1981.

American Institute of Real Estate Appraisers. *The Appraisal of Real Estate.* 9th ed. Chicago: American Institute of Real Estate Appraisers, 1987.

Andrews, Richard N. L. *Land in America.* Lexington, Mass.: D. C. Heath, 1979.

Babcock, Frederick M. *The Appraisal of Real Estate.* New York: Macmillan, 1924.

Babcock, Frederick M. *The Valuation of Real Estate.* New York: McGraw–Hill, 1932.

Bloom, George F., and Henry S. Harrison. *Appraising the Single Family Home.* Chicago: National Association of Realtors, 1978.

Bonright, James C. *The Valuation of Property.* Vol. 1. Charlottesville, Va.: Michie Co., 1965.

Boyce, Byrl N., ed. *Real Estate Appraisal Terminology.* Rev. ed. Chicago: American Institute of Real Estate Appraisers and Society of Real Estate Appraisers, 1981.

Colean, Miles L. *Renewing Our Cities.* Millwood, N.Y.: Kraus Reprint and Periodicals, 1975.

Conroy, Kathleen. *Valuing the Timeshare Property.* Chicago: American Institute of Real Estate Appraisers, 1981.

Dilmore, Gene. *Quantitative Techniques in Real Estate Counseling.* Lexington, Mass.: D. C. Heath, 1981.

Dombal, Robert W. *Residential Condominiums: A Guide to Analysis and Appraisal.* Chicago: American Institute of Real Estate Appraisers, 1976.

Doran, Herbert B., and Albert G. Hinman. *Urban Land Economics.* New York: Macmillan, 1928.

Eaton, James D. *Real Estate Valuation in Litigation.* Chicago: American Institute of Real Estate Appraisers, 1982.

Ellwood, L. W. *Ellwood Tables for Real Estate Appraising and Financing.* 4th ed. Chicago: American Institute of Real Estate Appraisers, 1977.

Ely, Richard T. *Property and Contract in Their Relation to the Distribution of Wealth.* New York: Macmillan, 1914.

Ely, Richard T., and Edward W. Morehouse. *Elements of Land Economics.* New York: Macmillan, 1924.

Ely, Richard T., and George S. Wehrwein. *Land Economics.* New York: Macmillan, 1940.

Epley, Donald R., and James H. Boykin. *Basic Income Property Appraisal.* Reading, Mass.: Addison–Wesley, 1983.

Fisher, Ernest M. *Advanced Principles of Real Estate Practice.* New York: Macmillan, 1930.

Fisher, Ernest M. *Principles of Real Estate Practice.* New York: Macmillan, 1923.

Fisher, Ernest M., and Robert Fisher. *Urban Real Estate.* New York: Holt, 1954.

Foreman, Robert L. *Communicating the Appraisal: A Guide to Report Writing.* Chicago: American Institute of Real Estate Appraisers, 1982.

Friedman, Edith J., ed. *Encyclopedia of Real Estate Appraising.* 3rd ed. Englewood Cliffs, N.J.: Prentice-Hall, 1978.

Friedman, Jack P., and Nichols Ordway. *Income Property Appraisal and Analysis.* Reston, Va.: Reston, 1981.

Garrett, Robert L., Hunter A. Hogan, Jr. and Robert M. Stanton. *The Valuation of*

Shopping Centers. Chicago: American Institute of Real Estate Appraisers, 1976.

Gibbons, James E. *Appraising in a Changing Economy: Collected Writings.* Chicago: American Institute of Real Estate Appraisers, 1982.

Gimmy, Arthur E. *Tennis Clubs and Racquet Sport Projects: A Guide to Appraisal, Market Analysis, Development and Financing.* Chicago: American Institute of Real Estate Appraisers, 1978.

Graaskamp, James A. *A Demonstration Case for Contemporary Appraisal Methods.* Madison, Wis.: Landmark Research, Inc., 1977.

Grebler, Leo. *Experiences in Urban Real Estate Investment.* New York: Columbia University Press, 1955.

Harwood, Bruce. *Real Estate Principles.* 4th ed. Englewood Cliffs, N.J.: Prentice-Hall, 1986.

Heurer, Karla L. *Golf Courses: A Guide to Analysis and Valuation.* Chicago: American Institute of Real Estate Appraisers, 1980.

Hoagland, Henry E. *Real Estate Principles.* New York: McGraw-Hill, 1940.

Hoover, Edgar M. *The Location of Economic Activity.* New York: McGraw-Hill, 1963.

Hoyt, Homer. *According to Hoyt.* Washington, D.C.: 1966.

Hoyt, Homer. *One Hundred Years of Land Values in Chicago.* Salem, N.H.: Ayer Co., 1970.

Hurd, Richard M. *Principles of City Land Values.* Salem, N.H.: Ayer Co., 1970. (First published 1903. See especially p. v.)

International Association of Assessing Officers. *Assessing and the Appraisal Process.* 5th ed. Chicago: 1974.

International Association of Assessing Officers. *Property Assessment Valuation.* Chicago: 1977.

Isard, Walter. *Location and Space Economy.* New York: MIT and Wiley, 1956.

Kahn, Sanders A., and Frederick E. Case. *Real Estate Appraisal and Investment.* 2nd ed. New York: Ronald Press, 1977.

Kinnard, William N., Jr. *Income Property Valuation: Principles and Techniques of Appraising Income-Producing Real Estate.* Lexington, Mass.: D. C. Heath, 1971.

Kinnard, William N., Jr., and Byrl N. Boyce. *An Introduction to Appraising Real Property.* Chicago: Society of Real Estate Appraisers, 1978.

Maisal, Sherman J., and Stephen E. Roulac. *Real Estate Investment and Finance.* New York: McGraw–Hill, 1976.

Miller, George H., and Kenneth W. Gilbkeaw. *Residential Real Estate Appraisal.* Englewood Cliffs, N.J.: Prentice-Hall, 1980.

National Association of Independent Fee Appraisers. *Income Property Appraising.* St. Louis, Mo.: National Association of Independent Fee Appraisers, 1982.

National Association of Independent Fee Appraisers. *Principles of Residential Real Estate Appraising.* St. Louis, Mo.: National Association of Independent Fee Appraisers, 1982.

National Association of Real Estate Appraisers. *Reviewer's Guide.* Vol. 1. St. Paul, Minn.: Todd Publishing, 1981.

Park, R. E. *The City.* Chicago: University of Chicago Press, 1984.

Ratcliff, Richard U. *Modern Real Estate Valuation: Theory and Application.* Madison, Wis.: Democrat Press, 1965.

Ratcliff, Richard U. *Urban Land Economics.* New York: McGraw–Hill, 1949.

Reynolds, Judith. *Historic Properties: Preservation and the Valuation Process.* Chicago: American Institute of Real Estate Appraisers, 1982.

Ring, Alfred A., and James H. Boykin. *Valuation of Real Estate.* Englewood Cliffs, N.J.: Prentice-Hall, 1986.

Rohan, Patrick J., and Melvin A. Reskin. *Condemnation Procedures and Techniques: Forms.* Albany, N.Y.: Matthew Bender (looseleaf service).

Rushmore, Stephen. *Hotels, Motels, and Restaurants: Valuations and Market Studies.* Chicago: American Institute of Real Estate Appraisers, 1983.

Rushmore, Stephen. *Valuation of Hotels and Motels.* Cambridge, Mass.: Ballinger, 1982. 120 pp.

Seldin, Maury. *Real Estate Handbook.* 2nd ed. Homewood, Ill.: Dow Jones-Irwin, 1989.

Seldin, Maury, and Richard H. Swesnick. *Real Estate Investment Strategy.* 3rd ed. New York: Wiley, 1985.

Shenkel, William M., and Jerry D. Belliot. *Real Estate Appraisal.* 2nd ed. New York: McGraw-Hill, 1978.

Smith, Halbert C. *Real Estate Appraisal.* Columbus, Ohio: Grid Publishing, 1987.

Smith, Halbert C., Carl J. Tschappat, and Ronald W. Racster. *Real Estate and Urban Development.* Homewood, Ill.: Irwin, 1981.

Society of Industrial Realtors. *Industrial Real Estate.* 4th ed. Washington, D.C.: Society of Industrial Realtors, 1984.

Suter, Robert C. *The Appraisal of Farm Real Estate.* Danville, Ill.: Interstate, 1980.

Unger, Maurcie A. *Elements of Real Estate Appraisal.* New York: Wiley, 1982.

Von Thünen, Johan Heinrich, *Der Isolierte Staat.* Jena Gustav Fisher, 1910.

Weber, Alfred. *Theory of the Location of Industry.* Carl Joachim Friedrich, ed. Chicago: University of Chicago Press, 1929.

Weimer, A. M., Homer Hoyt, and George F. Bloom. *Real Estate.* 8th ed. New York: Wiley, 1982. 1st ed., New York: Ronald Press, 1939.

Wendt, Paul F. *Real Estate Appraisal Review and Outlook.* Athens: University of Georgia Press, 1974.

Williams, Martha R., and William L. Ventolo, Jr. *Fundamentals of Real Estate Appraisal.* 2nd ed. Chicago: Real Estate Education Co., 1980.

Wolf, Peter. *Land in America: Its Value, Use, and Control.* New York: Pantheon, 1981.

BUILDING COST MANUALS

Boeckh Building Valuation Manual, 3 vols. Milwaukee: American Appraisal Co., 1967. Vol. 1: Residential and Agricultural; Vol. 2: Commercial; Vol. 3: Industrial and Institutional. 1967 cost database; wide variety of building models; built up from unit-in-place costs converted to cost per square foot of floor or ground area. Boeckh Building Cost Modifier, published bimonthly for updating with current modifiers.

Building Construction Cost Data. Duxbury, Mass.: Robert Snow Means Co. (annually). Average unit prices on a variety of building construction items for use in making up engineering estimates. Components arranged according to uniform system adopted by American Institute of Architects, Associated General Contractors, and Construction Specifications Institute.

Dodge Building Cost Calculator and Valuation Guide. New York: McGraw-Hill Information Systems Co. (looseleaf service; quarterly supplements). Building costs arranged by frequently occurring types of sizes of buildings; local cost modifiers and historical local cost index tables included. Formerly *Dow Building Cost Calculator.*

Marshall Valuation Services. Los Angeles: Marshall and Swift Publication Co. (looseleaf service; monthly supplements). Cost data for determining replacement costs of buildings and other improvements in the United States and Canada; includes current cost multipliers and local modifiers.

Residential Cost Handbook. Los Angeles: Marshall and Swift Publication Co. (looseleaf service; quarterly supplements). Presents square-foot method and segregated-cost method; local modifiers and cost trend modifiers included.

SOURCES OF OPERATING COSTS AND RATIOS

Building Owners and Managers Association International. Downtown and Suburban Office Building Experience Exchange Report. Washington, D.C.
Annually, since 1920; analysis of expenses and income (quoted in cents per square foot); national, regional, and selected city averages.

Dun and Bradstreet. *Key Business Ratios in 125 lines.* New York.
Annually; balance sheet, profit-and-loss ratios.

Institute of Real Estate Management. Income/Expense Analysis: Apartments, Condominiums & Cooperatives. Chicago.
Annually, since 1954; data arranged by building, then by national, regional, metropolitan, and selected city groupings; operating costs per room, per square foot, etc. Formerly Apartment Building Experience Exchange.

Institute of Real Estate Management. Income/Expense Analysis: Suburban Office Buildings, Chicago.
Annually, since 1976; data analyzed on basis of gross area, gross and net rentable office areas; dollar-per-square-foot calculations; national, regional, and metropolitan comparisons and detailed analyses for selected cities.

Laventhol and Horwath. *Lodging Industry.* Philadelphia.
Annually, since 1932; income, expense, and profit data; includes historical trend tables.

Laventhol and Horwath and National Restaurant Association. *Tables-Service Restaurant Operations.* Philadelphia.
Annually, since 1976; income-expense data and operating ratios; superseded the Laventhol and Horwath Restaurant Operations report that began in 1959.

National Retail Merchants Association, Controllers' Congress. *Department Store and Specialty Store Merchandising and Operating Results.* New York.
Annually, since 1925; merchandise classification base used since 1969 edition (1968 data); geographical analysis by Federal Reserve districts. Known as the "MOR" report.

National Retail Merchants Association. *Financial and Operating Results of Department and Specialty Stores.* New York.
Annually, since 1925; merchandise classification base used since 1969 edition (1968 data); geographical analysis by Federal Reserve districts. Known as the "MOR" report.

National Retail Merchants Association. *Financial and Operating Results of Department and Specialty Stores.* New York.

Annually, since 1963; data arranged by sales volume category. Known as the "FOR" Report.

Pannell, Kerr, Forster. *Clubs in Town & Country.* New York.

Annually, since 1953; income-expense data and operating ratios for city and country clubs; the geographical data given are listed according to four U.S. regions.

Pannell, Kerr, Foster. *Trends in the Hotel-Motel Business.* New York.

Annually, since 1937; income-expense data and operating ratios for transient and resort hotels and motels; the geographical data given are listed according to five U.S. regions.

Robert Morris Associates. *Sources of Composite Financial Data—A Bibliography.* 3rd ed. Philadelphia:

An annotated list of 98 nongovernment sources; arranged in manufacturing wholesaling, retail, and service categories; subject index to specific businesses, publishers' names and addresses given for each citation.

Urban Land Institute. *Dollars and Cents of Shopping Centers.* Washington, D.C.: 1990.

First issued in 1961; revised every three years; income and expense data for neighborhood, community, and regional centers; statistics for specific tenant types given.

PERIODICALS

The Appraisal Journal. American Institute of Real Estate Appraisers. Chicago.

Quarterly. Oldest periodical in the appraisal field, published since 1932; technical articles on all phases of real property appraisal; section on legal decisions included as regular feature. Consolidated index covering 1932–69 available.

Appraisal Review Journal. St. Paul, Minn.: National Association of Review Appraisers (three times a year).

The Real Estate Appraiser. Society of Real Estate Appraisers, Chicago.

Bimonthly. Technical articles and society news; section on legal cases included as regular feature. Consolidated bibliographies for 1935–60 and 1961–70 available. Previously published as *The Review* and as *Residential Appraiser.*

Survey of Buying Power. Sales Management, New York.

Annually. Population totals and characteristics, income and consumption data presented in various categories: national, regional, metropolitan area, county, city; separate section of Canadian information. A source for population estimates between the decennial United States censuses.

NEWSLETTERS

Briefs. Chicago: Society of Real Estate Appraisers (monthly).

1990 Publications Catalog. Chicago: American Institute of Real Estate Appraisers (annually).

MARKETING, BROKERAGE, AND MANAGEMENT

$\mathcal{M}$ARKETING

The marketing function, broadly defined, is (1) anticipating, and sometimes even creating, society's needs, then (2) producing and/or distributing goods and services to satisfy those needs, and, finally, (3) convincing society that those goods and services do in fact satisfy its needs.[1] For the average business, marketing boils down to this: "It's not worth anything if it can't be sold."

In real estate, the product sold is space (over time with certain services). The person who buys or rents space wants to use it (e.g., a family buying a house or a retailer renting a store), wants to hold it as an investment and lease it out to others to use (e.g., an investment group buying an office building), or wants to use the land to produce food and fiber (e.g., farmers).

In this chapter, we introduce some general concepts involved in marketing real estate and consider some techniques used to market particular types of properties. Other aspects of the broad **marketing function** are discussed in appropriate chapters throughout the book, particularly demand analysis in Part 8. In Chapter 10, the mechanics of brokerage are covered (drawing heavily on the legal framework for a real estate conveyance as described in Chapter 5). Thus, Chapter 9 covers the entire marketing process, and Chapter 10 deals with the specific mechanics of brokerage—first the overview and then the operations. (Appendices 10A and 10B describe the mechanics of a real estate closing and the Realtor Code of Ethics which represents the standards that "most" real estate persons have "pledged" to abide by.) Finally, Chapters 11 and

---

[1]*Some version of this broad definition can be found in every marketing principles text. It is important for the student to begin with such a broad definition; a broad view is critical to a full appreciation of the development process covered in Part 8. See Philip Kotler,* Marketing, *6th ed. (Englewood Cliffs, N.J., Prentice Hall, 1988), or E. Jerome McCarthy and William Perreault,* Basic Marketing, *10th ed. (Homewood, Ill.: Irwin, 1990).*

12 deal with asset management, the ongoing management associated with the use of real estate (i.e., the service element associated with the sale of space).

Remember, business decisions should be *integrated* in the sense that there are no strictly financial or marketing problems—only financial and marketing dimensions—to general business problems. This part of the book is a direct extension of the regional and urban land economics theory covered in Part 1. The things being marketed are the legal interests discussed in Part 2. After a detailed consideration of financing, taxes, and investment, we will return to the market as a major dimension of the development process in Part 8. Real estate is truly the home of the interdisciplinary generalist.

In terms of the number of real estate careers, marketing is second only to construction. The best paying jobs are marketing jobs that require a comprehensive understanding of all the elements of real estate decision making. The top people at Coldwell Banker, Cushman and Wakefield, Richard D. Ellis, Arthur Rubloff, or any of the leading regional brokerage firms are major players in the game and enjoy the benefits of winning.

TYPES OF REAL ESTATE MARKETING ACTIVITIES

The entire marketing function can be broken down into three separate steps. The three steps are listed as follows, with the terms in parentheses used in the real estate context.

- Market research (market study)
- Market analysis (feasibility study)
- Marketing plan (marketing study)

MARKET RESEARCH

For marketing in general, market research means collecting all relevant data pertaining to the product or service being studied. Often a distinction is made between primary and secondary data. **Primary data** are developed directly by the market researcher, for example, by conducting surveys or making personal observations. **Secondary data** are gathered from existing studies, for example, census figures and trade association data. Obviously, the first type of data is more valuable but also more difficult to collect and hence more expensive. The latter type of data is much more available, but it is more likely to be dated or not directly relevant to the specific use of the particular location of interest to the analyst, or both. Census data are a classic example of secondary data. Often they are very useful, yet they must be updated, and adjustments must be made because census tracts do not perfectly coincide with the area of interest to the analyst.[2]

In real estate, a **market study** typically analyzes general market demand for a single type of real estate product (e.g., apartments, shopping centers, or office space) at a particular location. The market study considers both the present *and future* demand for the particular type of land use as well as the present and future supply of *competitive facilities.* An example would be a study of the demand and supply of office space in downtown Detroit over the period of the next 48 months. Just as with any market research project, a real estate market study will depend both on primary and secondary data.

Normally, a market study ends with the creation of an **absorption schedule.** Such a schedule shows the time required for the market to absorb the expected supply of a particular type of real estate space that will be offered in the near future, as well as the expected price range for the space. For example, a market study may project 2 million square feet of office space coming to market over the next 24 months, with all of it capable of being leased at a rental range of $12 to $15 per square foot. As Part 9 shows in some detail, the high-quality market study contains an absorption schedule for the particular product. That is, the general market absorption schedule is further refined for the features, functions, and benefits of particular products. The time and price prediction includes such important cash flow items as free rent and tenant improvements.

For example, consider the components of a market study for a potential hotel. The analyst will begin with a consideration of national, state, regional, and local trends relevant to the particular type of hotel (business, nonbusiness travel, destination, resort, etc.). Population, household, economic, and other dimensions of these trends will be considered and related to the proposed project. The sources of demand and trends in demand will be specifically enumerated. Competition, both existing and potential, will be analyzed. All this information will be reduced to an estimate of room-night demand at a given rate with appropriate adjustments for the particular hotel's amenities and for seasonality and weekend effects. This is the bottom line, the hotel version of an absorption schedule.

---

[2]*Several "real estate specific" secondary sources have arisen over the last decade. Large brokerage firms such as Coldwell Banker and Richard Ellis publish vacancy rates in markets where they operate. Independent newsletters are also available summarizing recent sales and financings.*

Probably the most important recent development has been the emergence of state "Real Estate Research Centers." California, Connecticut, Ohio, Illinois, and Texas have large centers, as do Wharton, MIT, NYU, and USC. These centers, along with smaller centers in several other states, produce a series of research monographs as well as regular publications, television spots, and radio commentaries.

MARKET ANALYSIS

Once having obtained as much market data as possible, the marketing specialist will analyze the data and interpret the results to determine whether a proposed product or service can in fact be sold successfully (i.e., to return a satisfactory profit to the seller). Thus, market analyses nearly always involve computing likely rates of return on investment for a particular product. A market study may indicate that a product or service can be sold, but the market analysis may indicate that the sale is not feasible, because it will not return a satisfactory profit.

In the case of real estate, the specialist performs the **feasibility study** to determine whether a specific real estate project can be carried out successfully in a financial or investment sense. For example, the absorption schedule might indicate that a particular amount of square footage proposed to be developed at a given site might be rented quickly at certain rent levels. However, construction costs, time lag, and all other risks involved in purchasing and developing the site might reduce the projected profitability below acceptable levels. Both market and feasibility studies for real estate are considered in detail in Part 8, which covers real estate development.

MARKETING PLAN

The final step, following the market research and market analysis, is the marketing plan—the course the particular company will follow in selling its goods or services. Many companies prepare both long-range and short-range marketing plans; the former is really a general framework for the company's activities in the future, and the latter is a more specific program for selling goods or services in the context of the current economic picture. Later in this chapter and in the next chapter, we deal with the various marketing techniques that can comprise a marketing plan.

In the case of real estate, a **marketing study** is usually a short-term program devoted to selling or leasing space in the particular project that is the focus of the study. Sometimes, however, as in the case of a large residential subdivision that may be developed in stages, both a short-range and long-range marketing study may be prepared. In addition, the marketing of rental properties is a continuing process. In the case of motels, hotels, and other hospitality facilities, marketing is done virtually continuously because space must be sold each day.

ELEMENTS OF A MARKETING PLAN

A marketing plan or marketing strategy may be an elaborate blueprint for the sale of millions of dollars' worth of homes, condominiums, or commercial space over a period of years, involving the expenditure of hundreds of thousands of dollars. At the other extreme, it may be prepared by a property owner who scratches some ideas on the back of an envelope. But all these marketing plans should have some elements in common.

(Note that the raw material for the marketing plan comes largely from the feasibility study, which itself drew heavily from the marketing study. Note also that all three are interactive: for example, adding some additional features—and increasing the costs shown in the feasibility— will usually have a positive impact on the absorption schedule. Similarly, increasing the money spent on advertising—part of the marketing plan—can also have a positive impact on absorption. Because of these interrelationships, most analysts combine the three studies in a series of compatible computer spreadsheets.)

❏ **FIRST,** marketing strategy involves defining the objective. Is the goal to rent a single-family house, sell 150 projected homes in a new subdivision, lease apartments in a new building, or sell a distressed property that is on the verge of bankruptcy?

❏ **SECOND,** is the goal of the marketing plan strictly profit maximization in the shortest possible time, or does the seller have some form of residual interest in the property? For example, the seller may be given a long-term management contract by the buyer or buyers, or the seller may retain a share in ownership through a joint venture with other parties. Sometimes the seller/developer may have goals in addition to realizing a profit; for example, a business firm may finance a residential project in order to provide housing for its workers.

❏ **THIRD,** the potential pool of tenants or buyers must be identified. This information can normally be drawn from the feasibility study (previously discussed) and is a refinement of the absorption schedule previously described. The marketing plan must specify the rent or price levels that are projected to attract tenants or purchasers. The result of this identification of tenants/buyers and rent/price levels is the definition of a primary geographic market that will be the focus of the marketing strategy. The primary market can be the immediate neighborhood, the metropolitan area, the entire state, or the nation (as in the case of sales of building lots or raw land in a national resort area). This process of **market segmentation** is critical for the remainder of the marketing plan because the plan is largely a function of the needs, desires, and characteristics of the defined market segment.

❏ **FOURTH,** a list of the **marketing techniques** that will be utilized must be compiled, as in the following list:

■ A sign at the property, often the only marketing aid needed when demand is very high.

- Classified or space advertisements in local newspapers (see Box 9-1).
- Billboards.
- Printed brochures.
- Radio or television time.
- Direct mail.
- "Cold" canvassing (i.e., contacting all the individuals in a neighborhood by telephone or door-to-door solicitation).

Whatever the marketing techniques used, sales personnel will play an important role in the marketing process. The salespeople may be employees of the seller or developer working at the site or may be independent agents working on commission. (Chapter 10 discusses the brokerage function in detail.)

In choosing the particular marketing techniques to be utilized, the seller or the seller's agent must bear two important considerations in mind. One is the financial resources available for marketing. (These were part of the costs shown in the feasibility study.) Marketing is a necessary and often significant cost of delivering the product (space over time) to users, but money for it is not unlimited. The other is the **sales** or **leasing schedule,** which is necessary for the project to succeed financially. This schedule, relevant only in the case of a large marketing program and partially derived from the general market absorption study referred

---

9-1
WHAT SHOULD A CLASSIFIED ADVERTISEMENT FOR A RESIDENTIAL PROPERTY CONTAIN?

The Realtors National Marketing Institute, an affiliate of the National Association of Realtors®, reports what buyers say they want to read about the following in a residential property advertisement.

INFORMATION	PERCENTAGE
Geographic area	67
Price and terms	66
Number of bedrooms	58
Condition of property	55
Convenience to schools	52
Convenience to shopping	45
Convenience to churches	45
Number and size of closets	42
Size of lot	38
Number of bathrooms	36
Taxes	34

to earlier in this chapter, is simply the projected rate at which the particular property for sale or lease can be marketed in a given locality (e.g., six single-family homes in a specific subdivision can be sold each month).

The sales or leasing schedule is important because the longer it takes to market the properties, the higher will be carrying costs such as interest, real estate taxes, and selling costs. Aggressive marketing can usually increase the absorption rate somewhat. However, basic factors determining demand will put limits on any increase, at least in the absence of substantial price concessions that the developer will seek to avoid, except in extreme cases. Still, the objective is to trade off optimally (1) the cost of the marketing plan, (2) the length of the sales or leasing schedule, and (3) the risk of failure. Item 3 is usually inversely related to items 1 and 2; that is, the more you cut costs and assume rapid leasing, the riskier your plan.

MARKETING RESIDENTIAL PROPERTIES

The overwhelming percentage of marketing transactions in real estate involves the sale or rental of residential space, whether single-family houses, condominiums, or apartment units. Most of these transactions ultimately are consummated by a broker working with an individual seller and an individual buyer. (The role of the broker is discussed in detail in Chapter 11.) At this point, we consider generally the marketing approach used in connection with the various types of residential properties.

NEW SINGLE-FAMILY HOUSES

Each year, around 1 million new single-family homes are built in the United States. Although in any given year, sales may be somewhat above or below this number, it is obvious that developers must make a tremendous marketing effort to dispose of the annual inventory. A marketing plan for a new residential subdivision encompasses the following steps.

❏ **EVALUATING THE SITE.** The very first step is to evaluate the desirability of the location. In the case of one-family houses, proximity to schools, shopping, and transportation to work are essential. In fact, all the considerations enumerated by the urban land economists in Chapter 3 are important. The size, shape, and topography of potential lots are major factors, as is proximity to busy streets. The availability of all utilities and public services must also be considered.

❏ **CONSIDERING THE SIZE AND DESIGN OF HOUSES.** Home styles vary among different parts of the country, for different income groups, and at different periods of time. Space considerations obviously are important, for the larger the house, the more expensive it will be. If the builder decides to offer less space, his decision about whether to reduce the number of rooms, the size of rooms, and so on, may have a strong influence on the market segment to which the house will appeal. (See Box 9-2.)

❏ **CHOOSING MARKETING STRATEGIES.**   The potential market for the new homes already will have been identified in the feasibility study. The builder chooses the location, style, and size of the homes in terms of a particular market segment: young married couples without children, already-established families, or older couples whose children have left home (the "empty nesters"). At this stage, a specific marketing strategy must be developed for successfully reaching the target group. For example, most first-time homebuyers will be presently living in rental projects nearby. Therefore, fliers focusing on the benefits of home ownership delivered to apartment projects in the area may be the most cost-effective way to reach potential buyers. Established families are likely to own a home and be "trading up." Since they are more spread out geographically and already know the benefits of home ownership, a different marketing strategy should be chosen.

❏ **PREPARING PUBLICITY AND ADVERTISING.**   The fourth step in the marketing plan is to prepare an advertising and publicity campaign. This involves preparing a detailed brochure that can be given out at the site, classified and space advertising in local newspapers, and possibly a radio and TV campaign.

❏ **SELECTING AND/OR TRAINING A SALES FORCE.**   Finally, the sales force, which will deal with prospective buyers and "close" the sale, needs to be retained. In larger developments, a permanent staff may be hired and trained. In other cases, it may be more cost-effective to

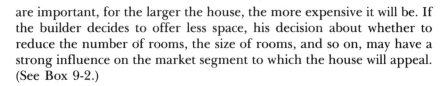

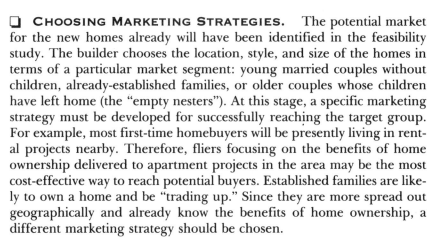

9-2
HOUSING
DEMOGRAPHICS
ARE CHANGING

There are now over 250 million Americans, of whom 13 percent are black, 8 percent Hispanic, and 3 percent Asian. Overall, the number of householders under 25 dropped 30 percent during the 1980s, while the high-income group (age 35 to 40) grew by over 30 percent.

The number of households grew 70 percent faster than the number of people over the 1980s as more people were living alone for various reasons. The number of married couples with children living at home dropped to 31 percent of the population, while female head of household was the fastest growing category, up 36 percent in the last decade.

"list" the properties with independent "brokers" and pay for the sales effort strictly on a commission basis as explained in Chapter 10.

RESALES OF SINGLE-FAMILY HOUSES

Although a large number of new homes are sold each year, the number of annual resales of existing homes is much larger. For example, in the 1980s approximately twice as many resale transactions took place as new home sales.

The great majority of resale transactions are consummated through real estate brokers, who find their major source of commissions in this type of marketing. Unlike the sale of a large number of homes in a residential subdivision, the sale of an existing house calls for a much more individual relationship between agent and owner. Thus, it is more appropriate to discuss this type of transaction in Chapter 10, on brokerage.

CONDOMINIUM PROJECTS

Condominiums have grown rapidly as a form of housing because they combine the status of ownership and tax advantages with "maintenance-free living." Cooperative ownership, in those areas of the nation where it is popular, offers some of the same advantages.

Marketing both types of housing is essentially the same as marketing new single-family homes. The major difference is that the condominium buyer is often much less aware of the legal aspects of condominium living. Therefore, it is important that the agent or salesperson make clear that the owner of a condominium unit has a close relationship with co-owners because of the joint ownership of common areas and the need to manage the entire project in the interests of all. As we mentioned in Part 1, there has been a trend toward condominiums in several markets. However, as shown in Box 9-3, not all the condominium developers did a good job on their market studies.

APARTMENT RENTALS

The final major category of marketing residential space is the leasing of units in rental buildings. Since this is often the function of the property manager, discussion of this form of marketing is deferred until Chapter 8.

INCOME PROPERTIES

Marketing income properties involves two quite different types of transactions. The first is the *sale* of an income property (office building, apartment building, or shopping center, etc.) to investors who expect to hold the property for rental income or to space users who prefer to buy

**9-3
CONDOMINIUM
MARKET
SOFTENS AS
SUPPLY
INCREASES**

In early 1985, condominiums were the Sunbelt's softest sector, according to *Housing Markets*. The production of condominiums surged in the recent past in most southern and western markets, just in time to meet shrinking demand. Completions of condominiums increased in 1984 by more than 100,000 to a 10-year high of more than 227,000; however, most of that increase was not absorbed. The softness was largely concentrated in stacked condominiums—units in mid-rise buildings. Town houses, patio-homes, and detached condominiums continued to sell well.

The weakness of the market began with resales, many of them investor-owned units; it has proved difficult to sell units in buildings that are heavily rented. Sellers cannot provide the aggressive financing that made it easy for them to buy; and many of the original buyers have moved on. During this same period, in many markets—such as Atlanta, Phoenix, Dallas, and Florida—a buyer paid the same price for a stacked condominium unit as for a cluster house only a few miles farther out. Finally, the supply of stacked units was overwhelming. Between 1980 and 1984 about 600,000 came on the market, more than twice as many as in the previous five years, and another 250,000 were created through conversion. The production of fourplex, town house, and single-family-type condominiums did not increase nearly as rapidly.

This pattern is not uniform. In most eastern and midwestern markets, the production of a variety of condominiums held its own. These units were geared mostly to empty nesters, the stacked product did not dominate, and presales precluded overbuilding. In the hot New York and Boston markets, conversions, new-unit sales, and resales were all doing well. High-rise condominiums were selling readily in Manhattan and San Francisco, but in most places the market for them tended to be even softer than that for low-rise units.

Source: U.S. Housing Markets, April 26, 1985; the Lomas and Nettleton Company, 404 Penobscot Building, Detroit, Mich. 48226.

The 1990s Perspective: Today, most forms of real estate are "oversupplied." However, the stacked condominium continues to do worse than any other form of residential property, particularly in the Sunbelt. Obviously, this market segment was, and continues to be, smaller than developers thought.

rather than rent space needed to carry on their trade or business. The other type of transaction is *rental* of space in an income property, almost always to space users such as business tenants, retail operations, or service firms.

SALES

The purchaser of an income property typically is more sophisticated than the single-family buyer, and tax consequences become much more important in this type of transaction. Because the market for income properties—particularly large ones—is much smaller than for residential ones, the income property agent often will use a "rifle approach" rather than a "shotgun approach" in seeking out prospects. Still, the basic principles of marketing apply just as well to the sale of a multimillion-dollar office building or shopping center as they do to the sale of a single-family home.

TYPES OF PURCHASER. Purchasers of income properties can be grouped into three general categories. The first is the individual or small business firm seeking a property for use in a trade or business. The agent performs much the same function in this type of transaction as in the sale of a residential property except that a much more detailed knowledge of the buyer's *operations* is usually required (i.e., how the space will fit his or her physical/logistical operations).

Next is the institutional purchaser seeking to develop a portfolio of income properties. Examples of this type of purchaser include (1) life insurance companies, with large real estate equity interests as well as mortgage portfolios; (2) real estate investment trusts (REITs), which hold real estate just as mutual funds hold common stocks; (3) large public partnerships, which syndicate interests in real estate to hundreds or even thousands of individual investors; and (4) pension funds.

These clients are generally looking for relatively safe investments and often are more interested in cash flow than in tax shelter. Here the agent must know the client's *investment* needs and present the transaction in a fairly sophisticated manner. These institutions are generally conservative and typically use agents whose personal manner corresponds to this conservative bias. (See Chapter 13 for more detail.)

Finally, and falling somewhere between the first two categories, are individuals and smaller syndicates that are made up of a number of investors, frequently local professionals and businesspeople, who wish to own one or more properties for investment purposes. Frequently, the agent herself may be a member of such a syndicate, sometimes acting as the general partner responsible for choosing and managing the properties of the syndicate. In such situations, tax considerations are often very important. Some of the clients will be very sophisticated in financial affairs, and others will be relatively naïve; the agent must present the transaction accordingly.[3,4]

---

[3]*In the recent past, various efforts have been made to establish a real estate exchange similar to the stock exchanges. One such exchange is the American Real Estate Exchange (AMREX). AMREX conducts sessions in various cities around the country at which information about various properties is flashed on screens around the room. An interested purchaser then goes to a table on the exchange floor, where he or she is put in touch with the seller with whom private negotiations may take place.*

[4]*Several related topics are covered regularly in* Real Estate Issues, *a quarterly publication of the American Society of Real Estate Counselors, 430 North Michigan Avenue, Chicago, Ill. 60611.*

RENTALS

Marketing strategies to rent space in an income property will depend largely on the type of tenant that is required. (See Box 9-4.) When retail space is to be leased, the broker must determine the kinds of retail operations that might be suitable and make an effort to contact or locate business concerns within the area that might be interested in moving or expanding to a new location.

In the case of an office property, the prospective market is much broader, for an office tenant is much less likely to require a precise location than a retail operation. Put another way, office space is much more **fungible** than retail space, where even a difference of a few feet may be important. In the office building situation, the quality of the constructed space is more likely to be able to offset a modest locational

9-4
LOCATING
PROSPECTIVE
TENANTS

The agent can use the following techniques to develop a pool of prospective tenants.

- *Door-to-door canvass.* Representatives of the developer may seek to contact personally every office tenant in every building around a new project, seeking any indications of interest in new space.

- *Telephone canvass.* Alternatively, the agent may, by using a reverse telephone directory, call every office tenant within the vicinity. If the call evinces any interest by the prospect, a followup meeting is arranged.

- *Distant prospects.* Demand for space may also come from areas outside the local market. This requires that the successful agent have extensive contacts that can be utilized for this type of marketing.

- *Letter of intent.* A prospect who shows any interest in new space is asked to sign a **letter of intent** that states, in effect, that "I have some interest in X square feet at $Y per square foot, and I sign this letter with the understanding that it is in no way legally or morally binding." The purpose of the letter is twofold: (1) the prospect has made some commitment, however minimal, toward considering a move when the space is available; and (2) these letters constitute some evidence of demand for space that may have some effect in connection with negotiations to obtain financing for the project.

- *The space study.* When a letter of intent has been obtained, the agent may offer to make a study of the prospect's current space. The objective is to present both the prospect and the developer with a clear picture of the space requirements and so make negotiations more fruitful for both sides.

9-5 MOST EXPENSIVE RETAIL AREAS	When you think of the nation's priciest retail streets, does New York's Columbus Avenue—the neighborhood where the play *West Side Story* was set—come to mind? Probably not, but a survey by Garrick-Aug Associates Store Leasing, Inc., suggests that this yuppie mecca ranks among the streets with the nation's highest retail rents. Here are the top 10.

CITY—STREET	RENT PER SQUARE FOOT
New York—Fifth Avenue	$150–$383
New York—Madison Avenue	$150–$250
Beverly Hills—Rodeo Drive	$150–$200
Chicago—Michigan Avenue	$100–$150
San Francisco—Union Square/Post Street	$100–$125
San Francisco—Sutter Street	$100–$125
Palm Beach, Fla.—Worth Avenue	$75–$100
Washington, D.C.—Connecticut Avenue	$75–$100
New York—Columbus Avenue	$75–$100
Boston—Newbury Street	$75–$100

Source: The Wall Street Journal, July 17, 1985, p. 31.

disadvantage. Conversely, the retailer demands a location that is convenient (in every sense of the word) to trade clients. Ever wonder where the nation's most expensive retail areas are? (See Box 9-5.)

SPECIAL PROPERTIES

Some types of property are handled by specialists because they require special know-how on the agent's part or because only a limited market exists for the property. The selling fee or commission in these situations is often negotiated for each particular transaction in recognition of the marketing expertise required and because of the extra time, effort, and expense usually involved. Some of the unique aspects of marketing specialized properties are discussed in Box 9-6.

VACATION HOMES AND BUILDING LOTS

The second-home market has experienced periods of extremely rapid growth. Many second-home projects are sold in the same manner as any residential subdivision. However, because resort areas draw on a much larger market area (perhaps the entire world), advertisements in national or regional media often are used. More significantly, buyer motivation usually is a combination of personal (vacation) use and investment for

9-6
DIFFERENT
APPROACHES
TO MARKETING

Sometimes, a property comes to market that is unique in some way. A consideration of the marketing alternatives open to the seller tells a lot about how real estate is marketed.

Wide Distribution Through Real Estate Brokers

At first blush, listing the property with as many real estate brokers as possible would seem to have merit. However, this method probably is undesirable. Wide circularization of a property's availability tends to tarnish its image; in addition, the seller may find himself inundated with offers that bear no relationship to the true value of the property but that impose an administrative burden. Finally, most of the brokers receiving the property for listing would be either unable or unwilling to take the time and effort to analyze and understand a complex parcel, its problems, and its potentials.

Auction

An auction is ill-suited to selling a unique parcel for most of the reasons just given. The property's potential is not likely to be adequately described in a printed preauction publicity piece. Furthermore, although auctions are popular for the sale of other types of investment property (e.g., fine art, jewelry), they are often associated in the real estate field with distressed properties and so could easily tarnish the image of a top-quality parcel.

Sealed Bids

In connection with the sale of a unique and complex property, the essence of a good marketing plan is to attempt to eliminate or minimize the uncertainties and unknowns involved. In this way, the buyer is less likely to feel it necessary to keep a substantial cash reserve, that is, lower his offering price. In order to eliminate or minimize the uncertainties, however, the seller must make himself available for discussions and negotiations with potential buyers. Because a **sealed-bid procedure** forecloses the opportunity for discussion, it is not suitable at the beginning of a sales campaign for a unique parcel. On the other hand, a modified sealed-bid process may be the only equitable method of bringing a long sales campaign to a close, when a number of qualified buyers indicate they are prepared to make a serious offer.

Direct Offering to Principals

If the seller of the unique property or her representative has personal relationships or knows of the major investors qualified to take over the property, direct contacts with the principals may be worthwhile. This procedure allows the seller to measure the depth and extent of interest among these qualified buyers while retaining complete knowledge of and control over negotiations.

> **Limited Distribution to Brokers**
>
> A final marketing method is to contact and meet with a carefully selected list of brokers known for their ability to bring together buyers and sellers of prime properties similar to that being offered. This approach may be used after or concurrently with an initial period during which the seller seeks to make offers directly to principals.
>
> For large properties, the major investment banking firms (e.g., Salomon, Goldman Sachs, Morgan Stanley, etc.) are logical brokers. They have the global contacts, but their services are not inexpensive.

potential appreciation in value. Consequently, in this type of selling, the educational function of the agent is very important.

An even more specialized type of selling is required when "**time sharing**" is utilized. Under this system, one may purchase a specific "time slice" (e.g., the first two weeks in July) instead of buying the entire unit. Thus, a single unit may have as many as 25 different owners (with two weeks set aside each year for maintenance and repair). The great advantage of a time share is the much smaller investment required. In addition, several exchange services are available whereby the owner of a time share may exchange it for a stay at a different resort that is a member of the service.

FARMS AND RANCHES

Farm and ranch brokerage is an important specialty because of the large amount of farm and ranch property in the United States and its importance in the overall economy. The agent must understand such subjects as agricultural productivity, the cattle cycle, water rights, and pasture rights. The production function of the land is more complex than simply supporting a structure in a fixed location. The potential farm purchaser wants to know what it can produce, that is, what return he can expect, and this necessitates specialized knowledge on the part of the sales agent.

Marketing can be expensive because it takes a considerable amount of time for the sales agent to become fully acquainted with all the "features, functions, and benefits" of an operating farm or ranch. Furthermore, properties are not clustered together in an urban area. Showing a farm to a prospect takes considerable time, and getting to the second farm to be shown may take even longer.

DISTRESSED PROPERTIES

The term *distressed properties* is used to describe projects in trouble: for example, a for-sale project in which the developer is having difficulty with sales or any income property that is failing to show a positive cash flow or that has already been foreclosed by an unpaid lender. The object in such cases is either to sell the property as quickly as possible or mount a crash effort to fill up vacant space and put the property in the black. (See Box 9-7.)

Agents dealing with distressed properties often need special skills, particularly in mass merchandising techniques. For example, an auction is sometimes used to dispose of unsold units in a condominium; although buyers may obtain bargains, the ending of the developer's carrying charges for construction loan interest and real estate taxes may make this his best alternative. Legal skills also are important both in dealing with foreclosure and handling disgruntled tenants. In Part 9, we will deal with the most massive and most challenging distressed property sale of all time, and *you* as a taxpayer are one of the owners. Since dealing with the portfolio of the Resolution Trust Corporation (the former investments of

---

9-7
MARKETING
DISTRESSED
PROPERTIES

Here are three actual examples of how creative thinking can help a property in trouble.

- *Lower carrying costs.* An agent was asked to suggest ways of saving a condominium project that was selling at the rate of three units per month, with overhead and carrying charges gradually wiping out the builder's equity. Applying the principle that the buyer worries more about carrying costs than ultimate price, the agent increased the price by $2,000 and cut the mortgage interest rate by 3 percent. This jumped unit sales to 10 per month, an absorption rate that enabled the builder to get out whole.

- *Build up equity.* In another case, a consultant was retained by a lender worried about slow sales in a new condominium project. Believing that the problem lay in the 20 percent down requirement, the consultant suggested that buyers be permitted to take possession upon signing a contract, paying only a monthly charge equal to debt service under the mortgage. However, the initial monthly payments went toward the required 20 percent downpayment; this usually required some time after which the permanent loan was funded and the monthly charge went to service the loan. During the buildup period, the developers paid the real estate taxes and the maintenance fees. As a result, the condominium project was a success.

- *Redesign units.* In yet another case, a three-bedroom town house project was drawing interest from young families and singles who found the units too large. A wall was removed, turning two bedrooms into a large bedroom suite. The project sold out at the same price within six weeks.

now failed savings and loans) has many dimensions, it is appropriately deferred to the final part of this book.

**PROFESSIONAL
SELLING HAS
COME OF AGE**

In previous editions of this book, we ended the marketing study section with a comment on the importance of selling. But today, with the over-built conditions in nearly every market, such brief coverage is inadequate. We didn't figure this out by ourselves; we were continually reminded of it by the leading professionals we met. While they had many different personal styles, the winners could all sell.

Inaccurate or insufficient market studies and less than rigorous economic analysis (in the feasibility study) can doom even the greatest salesperson. However, wonderful study and analysis will be wasted if no one can sell. All the tools listed above as considerations in the marketing plan are important, but so is personal professional selling.

In most of this chapter, we have simply reminded you of basic marketing principles that you learned in earlier courses. Here we take a little more time with what is *academically* a very soft subject. Why? First, it is crucially important; and second, it usually isn't covered anywhere else in a college curriculum. (We are indebted in Kurtz, Dodge, and Klompmaker for several of these ideas.)[5]

WHAT IS PROFESSIONAL SELLING AND HOW DOES IT FIT INTO THE BROAD DEFINITION OF MARKETING?

Professional selling involves dealing professionally with the interpersonal persuasive process that influences a business decision. Whose decision? Your client, your lender, your government sector partner, even the members of your own company.

There is a dynamic tension between meeting the needs of the customer (remember the broad definition of marketing: anticipate the need, produce the good or service, and then convince the customer your good or service does meet his need) and your own need *not to cut the rent* (or give away too many dollars of tenant improvement, etc.). In a capitalistic society, you only get to keep meeting the client's needs in the long run if you make a profit.

In real estate there is a clear *selling spectrum* as the selling process moves from initiation through capture to maintenance. In implementing the marketing study, it is critically important to have the right skills at the right point in the spectrum. A detail-oriented lawyer might have a great deal of trouble in the initiation phase, which is oriented toward demand creation. And she might be overpriced (i.e., would be paying for the

[5]*David Kurtz, Robert Dodge, and Jay Klompmaker,* Professional Selling, *5th ed., Plano, Tex.: Business Publications, Inc. 1988.*

wrong skills) as well. However, these same skills are needed at the end of the capture phase (i.e., approaching closing). What do you need in the ongoing service selling which constitutes the maintenance phase? Customer relations skills, as described in Chapter 11, are a primary requisite of the successful property manager.

Once the right skills are in the right place in the selling spectrum, we must match the compensation arrangement to the responsibilities to assure goal congruence between the marketing plan and the individual salesperson's objectives. (That is, the proper compensation plan seeks to equate the organizational objectives as one level with the individual sales person's objectives as another level.) In real estate, commission-based compensation dominates in the middle of the spectrum, with some finders' fees at the front end and salary plus bonus typical in the maintenance phase.

Next, what are the goals of the client, both the organization and the individual decision maker? At both levels, the famous Maslow hierarchy of needs shown in Figure 9-1 is a useful analytical tool. You sell different features, functions, and benefits in different ways depending on the buyer's position in the hierarchy. An individual decision maker who is very insecure in her job will respond more favorably to safety offered by your product (the same space over time with associated services that the competition has), whereas the buyer (again, both organizations and individual decision makers) seeking esteem may look more favorably on high tech features of the building and more striking architecture.

As part of the marketing plan, the goals of your organization and market realities (as collectively laid out in the feasibility study) must be communicated to the marketplace. You must be aware of your image in the market and establish a message that is logically consistent with this

FIGURE 9-1 *Abraham Maslow's hierarchy of human needs (adapted from several publications by the authors)*

image. (For example, a house builder famous for custom-built homes shouldn't simply start advertising affordability.) Some logical connection must be made in the consumer's mind between where you have been and what product you now wish to sell.

In addition to knowing both the receiver and the sender, another ingredient in the successful message (be it television, radio, or word of mouth) is anticipation of *interference*. Anticipate problems and structure the initial message to begin dealing with the problem. Furthermore, design a feedback mechanism in the process so that the message can be adjusted as new interference is detected. For example, stacked condos have a weak reputation in the South and Midwest. If you are building this type of product, your marketing message should deliver a rebuttal to the commonly held perception of low to negative appreciation in this property type.

❏ **ADVANCE PREPARATION.**   Prior to initiation of contact if possible, and certainly before the capture phase of the selling process, detailed preparation of the sales agent is needed. Beyond overall knowledge of the industry and market (which must be continually updated), the sales agent uses the feasibility study. It describes the product and the intended market niche (the target buyer).

Next, sales leads must be identified as *prospects* and these prospects *qualified. Prospecting*, the search for prospectors from leads, can take considerable time. Consider an upper end retirement development in Hawaii. Leads come from everything from country club membership rolls to corporate annual reports which usually announce retirements. Leads are found for this type of property throughout the United States and the entire Pacific rim. Through some combination of the sources listed in Figure 9-2, the vast number of leads must be reduced to a manageable number.

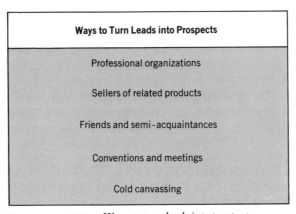

Ways to Turn Leads into Prospects

Professional organizations

Sellers of related products

Friends and semi-acquaintances

Conventions and meetings

Cold canvassing

F I G U R E **9-2** *Ways to turn leads into prospects.*

Working with the prospects list, the sales agent seeks to qualify the most likely prospects. This involves (1) determining (given the product marketed) what constitutes a qualified prospect and how to measure qualification; (2) determining if the prospect possesses these qualities; (3) determining which prospects can afford the product; and (4) deciding what level of effort a qualified prospect warrants.

The data on each qualified prospect are matched to the marketing tools listed in the marketing plan. Real estate sales agents seek to know their product from the perspective of how the qualified prospect will use it. Next, sales agents must arrange the interview. Cold calls are tougher in real estate. Even the best video doesn't capture all of a property's *situs*. Thus, promotional events such as tennis tournaments, for example, as in the case of the high-end Hawaii resort, are often justified.

❑ **MAKING THE PLAY.**   At this point, you believe that your product satisfies the prospect's needs and that the prospect can afford the product. Now the message must (1) be understandable; (2) be of positive value to the prospect (tell him something he doesn't already know); (3) mesh the product's features, functions, and benefits to the buyer's goals; and (4) motivate the buyer to move as expeditiously as possible toward a contract of sale.

Some sales agents concentrate on emphasizing need satisfaction. Others prefer an interactive approach that allows the sales agent to move easily between level 1 (the buying organization's needs and the physical product itself) and level 2 (the particular decision maker's needs in the transaction). Still others emphasize the stimulus-response approach: "Boston Consulting has the top floor of the First National Building. It's a very prestigious view. Of course, you—Bain Consulting—will look down on them from our new property." Most sales agents use a combination or balanced approach adjusted to each individual sales opportunity.

Demonstrating the real estate product is often accomplished by video. Unfortunately, a high-quality video is not inexpensive; hence, a "general-purpose" video is often used. This alternative is quite acceptable as long as the entire sales presentation doesn't sound canned. With such a high ticket item as real estate, the sales presentation is usually individually tailored to fit the buyer.

Be prepared for questions; they are often a sign that the prospect is interested. Through anticipation, know when to use (1) counter questions; (2) testimonials; (3) shift (i.e., "Yes, but . ."), or (4) direct rebuttal.

❑ **CLOSING AND CONTINUING TO SELL.**   The closing has always been the goal, and the sales agent needs to move there as expeditiously and *inexpensively* as possible once the prospect is motivated to action. The first step is to *ask for the sale*. This can be done directly, by assumption (here are your closing costs) or even on a trial basis (i.e., when do you want to move in?)—but it must be done.

Immediately after the buyer's decision, the sales agent should begin the support/facilitation role that she will maintain until closing. Remembering the selling spectrum, the skills now needed are time and people management. (Appendix 10B deals with several "typical" real estate situations.)

During contract negotiations and during the period from contract to closing, it is quite easy to "give away the store." Tenant improvements, free rent periods, and expense pass-through provisions are critically important to the owner's bottom-line cash flow. The selling continues right on through the closing when the lawyer's skills (and the bulldog's attitude) suddenly become more important.

Remember, you are ethical, and you are in the business for the long run. Those who are competent, tough, and fair tend to get the referrals.

SELLING IN PERSPECTIVE

Personal, professional selling isn't largely an "academic skill" because it's not easy to teach in a classroom. However, reflection on the key points mentioned here will help you refine the talents you learned in a lifetime of getting ready for Saturday night.

SUMMARY   The composite market function in the real estate industry is very broad, ranging from preliminary market research and feasibility studies to "face-to-face" dealings with the purchaser. In this chapter, marketing has been discussed in a general way, with the intention being to introduce the major concepts and considerations in this area.

Although the sales function varies widely depending on the type of property, all require that the effective broker or salesperson have a good overall understanding of the product, an in-depth knowledge of the marketplace, and a good feeling for the objectives of the prospective purchaser.

Recall that in Part 1 we stressed that value was a function of expected future benefits and that, consequently, forecasting was tremendously important. A specific discussion of brokerage and the mechanics of the marketing of real estate (i.e., selling space over time with certain services) follows in Chapter 10 with asset management covered in Chapters 11 and 12. However, before we leave the broad marketing function, reflect for a moment on the importance of anticipating what is going to happen in the marketplace. As food for thought, Box 9-8 reproduces thoughts from *Land Use Digest*. This monthly publication of the Urban Land Institute is an excellent way for the real estate professional to keep abreast of new thoughts and recent research.

9-8

A TYPICAL ISSUE OF *LAND USE DIGEST*

U.S. Economic Growth

The driving force behind U.S. economic growth over the past few years has been trade. With the lowered value of the dollar, exported American goods are less expensive for foreign consumers, while foreign imports are more expensive for shoppers here. Regional economies with a relatively high proportion of employment bases composed of goods and services that are exported have fared better in recent years than those with a low proportion, and will continue to see strong growth into the next decade, according to a report in *Professional Builder.* While other factors contribute to economic performance, a strong export base seems to be an important contributor. (*Professional Builder,* October 1989; Cahners Publishing Co., Cahners Plaza, 1350 E. Touhy Avenue, Des Plaines, Ill. 60018; 312–635–8800)

Hurricane Hugo and the San Francisco Earthquake

Hurricane Hugo and the San Francisco earthquake, nature's one-two punch this fall [1989], have had a major impact on real estate in the cities affected, but the repair and rebuilding processes reflect some very different concerns. In Charleston, South Carolina, one of several cities still reeling from the hurricane's effects, many homeowners may find they will be allowed to rebuild their beachfront homes only if the property is located 20 feet inland or 40 times the annual beach erosion rate—whichever is greater—from the crest of the primary oceanfront dune, under provisions of the state's Beachfront Management Act of 1988. For damaged buildings within the no-construction zone, the law assigns percentages to structural systems within a house; the building must be at least 33 percent intact after a storm or it cannot be rebuilt. In San Francisco, the overall effects of the earthquake are expected to be small, with affordable housing perhaps the major market element disturbed. Older, unreinforced masonry buildings in San Francisco and Oakland, many of them sites of less costly housing, were hit hard, according to early reports. (*Washington Post,* October 21, 1989; Washington Post Co., 1150 15th Street, N.W., Washington, D.C. 20071; 202–334–6000. *ENR,* September 28, 1989; McGraw–Hill, Inc., 1221 Avenue of the Americas, New York, N.Y. 10020; 212–512–2000)

New Convention Facilities

Seventeen new convention facilities are planned or under construction, and 30 more centers are planning or completing expansions, according to *Tradeshow Week* magazine, which also predicts an annual 4.6 percent growth in the number of centers in the United States and Canada. This rate of growth would result in an increase in the number of major convention centers—those having more than 25,000 square feet of prime space—from a total of 320 in 1989 to 434 in 1995. In anticipation of an increase in the size and number of trade shows, eight of the 17 new centers contain more than the industry average of 165,000 square feet, while 12 of the 30 additions contain 150,000 square feet or more. Among the locations adding new centers are Minneapolis, where the new 800,000-square-foot center will replace a facility with a 100,000-square-foot exhibit hall; and San Diego, where a $115 million, 500,000-square-foot center is slated to open later this year. (*Building Design and Construction,* September 1989, Cahners Publishing Co., Cahners Plaza, 1350 E. Touhy Avenue, Des Plaines, Ill. 60018; 312–635–8800)

Cleveland Builders Fighting Impact Fees

The Building Industry Association of Cleveland and Suburban Counties is preparing to do battle over local governments' intentions to levy impact fees for nondevelopment construction. The city of Orange is expected to impose a $750 impact fee—to be used for recreation—on all new homebuilding permits, making it one of the first localities in the area to levy such charges. Should this come to pass, the BIA is poised to challenge the city's right to charge such a fee, according to BIA's Timothy Grendell. (*Economic Growth Report,* October 4, 1989; CD Publications, 8204 Fenton Street, Silver Spring, Md. 20910; 301–588–6380)

GE: Bringing Affordable Housing to Life

General Electric Capital Mortgage Insurance Companies has launched a Community Home Buyer's Program to provide homebuyer counseling, mortgage financing based on flexible underwriting criteria, and home inspection assistance to qualified buyers. Under this program, low- and moderate-income households will be able to finance fixed-rate 15- and 30-year mortgages with downpayments as low as 5 percent. Initially, 50 leaders are expected to participate. Nearly $500 million in financing is available so far, or enough to cover the purchase of about 10,000 residences. The maximum loan amount will be based on the buyer's income; the highest income served will be about $32,000 annually, enough to purchase a $75,000 home. (*NAHRO Monitor,* September 30, 1989; National Association of Housing and Redevelopment Officials, 1320 18th Street, N.W., Washington, D.C. 20035; 202–429–2960)

The Auto Service Center: Addressing Some Special Issues

The automobile service center, a one-stop center for automobile care needs—from car washing to major repairs to ancillary services such as alarm or cellular phone installations—is a relatively new concept in real estate development that appeals to consumers who, in general, are holding on to their cars longer; to retailers who can capitalize on the dynamics of several related tenants in one location; and to developers, who must maintain its neat and clean appearance to be aesthetically appealing; and managers must ensure that tenants comply with environmental laws, especially those regulating hazardous substance usage, storage, and disposal. (*Journal of Real Estate Development,* Summer 1989; Federal Research Press, 210 Lincoln Street, Boston, Mass. 02111; 617–423–0978)

Investing in Apartment Complexes

The popularity of apartment complexes among institutional investors seems to be a result of a market driven more by demand than capital: high vacancy rates of the early 1980s have been mitigated by a significant drop in the construction of new units since the middle of the decade. To be considered of institutional quality, an apartment complex should offer construction and features equal to those found in the market's best properties. It should also be located in a growing middle- to upper-income area that demands high-quality units and is in relative balance with regard to supply and demand. (*Real Estate Report,* vol. 18, no. 4, 1989; Real Estate Research Corporation, 72 W. Adams Street, Chicago, Ill. 60603; 312–346–5885)

Pension Fund Investments in Real Estate

U.S. pension investors have committed an estimated $12.214 billion in new dollars to new property investments during the year ended June 20, 1989, according to a *Pensions & Investment Age* survey of 100 investment management firms. The survey found that tax-exempt real estate amounted to $113.413 billion as of June 30, up 19.9 percent from $94.579 billion the previous year. Tax-exempt equity real estate assets rose 24.3 percent to $90.145 billion; tax-exempt hybrid debt assets rose 17 percent to $17.875 billion; and tax-exempt mortgage assets fell 19.6 percent to $5.292 billion. The new money flowing into realty investments, added to the increase in value of existing property holdings, has increased the allocation to real assets as of June 30. The survey also found that tax-exempt portfolios typically contain the following property mix: office/commercial, 35 percent; retail, 21 percent; industrial, 21 percent; multifamily housing, 9 percent; hotel/resort, 2 percent; and other, 12 percent. (*Pensions & Investment Age,* October 2, 1989; Crain Communications, Inc., 740 Rush Street, Chicago, Ill. 60611; 312–210–0114)

Rationing of Building Permits to Control Growth

This controversial technique has had a very dramatic impact on housing prices in many localities, essentially accelerating the rise in housing prices and adversely affecting the affordability of housing. Some municipalities have taken steps to alleviate this difficulty. Key West, Florida's 1986 growth management ordinance establishes the number of dwelling units that still can be constructed before the island is completely built out and grants permits for either 7 percent of that number or 300 units per year. Colorado's permit allocation ordinance, first enacted in 1977, has had two major revisions that have transformed it from a merit-based system to one that grants applicants a proportional share of the available building permits. The city requires that 15 percent of the units being built be moderate-income units or that 7.5 percent be low-income units. At the option of the city's housing authority, the developer may be allowed to make a cash payment in lieu of constructing the required affordable units. Although the city has received applications for less than half of the 800 available allocations, the ordinance has eased the cyclical nature of the building business. Hilton Head Island, South Carolina, has imposed a six-year rate of growth schedule to coordinate the development of residential units with the development of the Cross Island Expressway, a controlled access route that will ease the strain on the only road that presently runs the length of the island. The city does not require the provision of affordable housing; rather, the zoning ordinance includes an affordable housing overlay zone that provides density bonuses and relaxes site development standards in exchange for the provision of low- and moderate-income units. To date, the overlay zone has not been used. (*Zoning News,* September 1989; American Planning Association, 1313 E. 60th Street, Chicago, Ill. 60637; 312–955–9100)

Cascades Town Center

Cascades Town Center, a streetfront, upper-end destination retail center under construction in Loudoun County, Virginia, will be the centerpiece of a new planned community 20 miles from the nation's capital. The 3,000-acre community will include 6,000 new homes for various income levels; four shopping centers geared to different regions and income levels within the complex; and athletic facilities, including several golf courses, 24 miles of jogging trails, three pools, 24 tennis courts, and a private country club. The Town Center will feature a farmers' market with an adjoining food court, as well as 4.4 million square feet of office space, 200 urban apartments, a 250-room hotel, and daycare facilities for children and for the elderly. Construction is by Kettler & Scott, Vienna, Virginia, which began building the retail and road network in fall 1988 and the golf courses in fall 1989. The residential portion is slated to be completed in six to eight years, and is expected to have an absorption rate of 1,000 units per year. (*China Store Age Executive,* October 1989; Lebhar-Friedman, Inc., 425 Park Avenue, New York, N.Y. 10022; 212–371–9400)

The Best Places to Do Business

Atlanta ranked number one in a survey of 404 chief executive officers queried by the Louis Harris organization for Cushman & Wakefield. While 38 percent of the respondents named Atlanta as their first choice, 29 percent named Seattle, last year's number 12 choice, as their second pick for this year. Overall, 22 of the top 31 cities received improved rankings over the last year, although four cities dropped from the top 10 list: Boston; Dallas/Fort Worth; Washington, D.C.; and Phoenix.

An analysis of the same 31 market areas conducted by corporate relocation consultants Moran Stahl & Boyer resulted in quite different ratings. Asked to consider such necessities as an adequately trained and sized labor market, an appropriately strong and diverse economy to withstand fiscal difficulties, infrastructure sufficient to keep pace with the region's growth, and an attractive quality of life, MS&B selected the Dallas/Fort Worth metroplex area as number one. (*Business Facilities,* October 1989; BusFac Publishing Co., 121 Monmouth Street, Red Bank, N.J. 07701; 201–842–7433. *Fortune,* October 23, 1989; Time Magazine Company, Inc., Time & Life Building, Rockefeller Center, New York, N.Y. 10020; 212–586–1212)

Land Acquisition Programs

Land acquisition programs are on the rise nationwide, as state and local governments move to buy property and development rights to preserve open space, provide more parks, and save farmland from urbanization. Private "land trusts" have been growing throughout the 1980s, but the entry by government agencies is relatively new. Interest in the Northeast has been intense, where states and localities have committed over $1 billion in public funds to such programs, including Vermont's new $3 million housing and land conservation program and Suffolk County, New York's $300 million commitment to preserving watersheds. California's Proposition 70, a $770 million land acquisition bond issue that was passed last year, included $63 million earmarked for the purchase of agricultural property rights. In Illinois, Libertyville Township has acquired more than 700 acres of land through an open-space district. (*California Planning and Development Report,* September 1989; Torf Fulton Associates, 1275 Sunnycrest Avenue, Ventura, Calif. 93003; 805–642–7838)

Advantages of the Suburbs

Suburban office building advocates have long pointed to two major advantages of locating in the suburbs: an improved quality of life and the less expensive costs of doing business outside the central business district. A recent survey conducted by the Metropolitan Consulting Group of Chicago finds that the cost gap is narrowing in many locations; in many markets the difference ranges from 5 to 9 percent. (*Real Estate Leasing Report,* October 1989; Federal Research Press, 210 Lincoln Street, Boston, Mass. 02111; 1–800–682–5759)

Source: Land Use Digest.

IMPORTANT TERMS

Absorption schedule	Marketing study
Feasibility study	Marketing techniques
Fungible	Primary data
Letter of intent	Sales or leasing schedule
Market segmentation	Sealed-bid procedure
Market study	Secondary data
Marketing function	Time sharing

REVIEW QUESTIONS

9.1   What specific information does an absorption schedule provide?

9.2   What is the critical difference between a market study and a feasibility study?

9.3   As an agent representing a seller, how might you advise your client as to presale fixups and repairs?

9.4   Why might the purchaser of an income property for investment purposes be more sophisticated than a single-family dwelling buyer?

9.5   Would you expect a retail tenant or an office tenant to be more concerned about the *exact* location when moving or expanding? Why?

9.6   What factors might affect a marketing campaign for vacation homes?

9.7   How might the concept of "time sharing" be utilized in marketing resort property?

9.8   List and explain the major elements of a marketing plan.

9.9   Identify some of the important information you would recommend be included in a classified ad for a single-family dwelling.

9.10 Why might an agent find it necessary to explain legal ramifications of condominiums when selling property in that ownership form?

BROKERAGE

Chapter 9 gave you the basic ideas for understanding the marketing of real estate. In this chapter, we focus on the *people* involved in real estate transactions—either the **principals** (buyers and sellers) or their **agents** (brokers and associated salespersons). The relationship between principals and agents is one of **brokerage,** and this chapter discusses how the brokerage function is carried out.

THE KEY ROLE PLAYED BY BROKERS

The term **marketing process** refers to the methods used to enable, assist, or encourage the sale of property and goods in the marketplace. (This follows directly from the marketing study outlined in the preceding chapter.) If marketing methods are examined strictly in terms of the people involved, three general types of transactions can be identified.

❏ **SALES BETWEEN PRINCIPALS DIRECTLY.** Mail order sales by companies selling their own products are the most important example of sales between principals in the general economy. In the real estate industry, sales between the seller and the buyer directly are fairly common in the resale of private homes. Residential real estate advertisements frequently specify "for sale by owner" or "principals only." Another area of direct selling in real estate is by developers of residential or resort projects who use an in-house sales staff.

❏ **SALES BY DEALERS.** Sales by dealers are by far the most common form of commercial transaction found in the general economy. A *dealer* performs an intermediary role between the producer of goods and the final consumer. In contrast to a broker, a dealer acquires title to goods to be sold. Most retailers are dealers. When it comes to big-ticket items, the automobile industry is the prime example of dealer-controlled commerce. Dealer sales in real estate are less common.

❏ **SALES BY BROKERS.** A broker is an intermediary or middleman who brings together buyers and sellers of the same commodity or product and who receives a commission for services. In most states, an individual must first pass a test for a salesperson's license and then work for a broker to gain experience before taking a second examination to obtain a broker's license. The distinction between a broker and a dealer is that the broker does not have title to the brokered goods or property. In real estate, brokers play the major marketing role.

SUITABILITY OF BROKERAGE FOR REAL ESTATE TRANSACTIONS

Why is the method of brokerage so suitable for real estate? The reasons lie in the nature of the real estate asset.[1]

❏ **HIGH COST.** Because a parcel of real estate generally costs a great deal to acquire, it is not feasible to sell most real estate through a dealer system. This would involve purchase by a dealer of a portfolio of real estate assets that would then be held for resale at a profit. In practice, the cost of carrying the inventory would be too high.[2] (See Box 10-1.)

❏ **UNIQUE ASSET.** Because real estate is immovable, each piece is unique; therefore, a parcel of property often must be seen or described to a very large number of people before a buyer for that precise parcel can be found. The property owner usually cannot sell the property personally for lack of a list of prospects or an office to which new prospects will be drawn. Brokers have both. Few owners have a current knowledge of the market, and selling even a home can be a major inconvenience. Again, the broker can be a cost-effective way to get the job done.

The nearest exception to the uniqueness of real estate is illustrated by mass-developed building lots or vacant land, and large residential subdivisions with a single builder constructing new homes that are prac-

---

[1]*Note that this enumeration parallels the discussion of the unique aspects of real estate in the analytical framework developed in Part 1.*

[2]*The one occasion when a dealership role often is assumed is when a lender acquires properties following defaults under mortgage loans. In these situations, the involuntary dealer normally is anxious to dispose of the properties as quickly as possible. Indeed, national banks that acquire properties through foreclosure proceedings are required by regulatory agencies to dispose of the property within a fixed period of time. Such property is listed separately on the bank's financial statement.*

Another example of a dealer-type transaction is the residential trade-in program occasionally utilized by the real estate brokers to encourage resales. Under these programs, the broker agrees to purchase the present residence of a person seeking a new home—usually a more expensive one to which he is "trading up." The broker normally will not take title to the old house until after it has been listed with the broker and offered on the market for a specified period of time, e.g., 90 days.

**10-1
CASH-AND-
CARRY HOUSE
SALES**

One of the most unusual techniques for marketing homes is that of a former California roofer named Tony J. Lozano, who acts as a dealer in homes.

Mr. Lozano buys one-family houses that otherwise would have to be demolished to make room for new buildings. He moves the houses to a 20-acre site that at any one time may have several dozen houses in all styles and designs. Potential buyers can browse at leisure; if they like a house and can negotiate a satisfactory price, Mr. Lozano's eight-man crew moves the house to the buyer's lot.

Mr. Lozano purchases the used houses for about $1,500 each, and it may cost up to five times that amount to move the house to Mr. Lozano's "store." He resells them for two to three times his cost, which means a good profit for him and still a bargain for the home buyers, who usually are blue-collar workers who have found themselves priced out of the conventional real estate market.

tically alike. It is precisely these types of real estate sales that are often done directly between buyer and seller rather than through brokers.

❏ **NEED FOR FINANCING.**   Most real estate purchases are financed in large part by third-party loans, typically from institutional lenders. Particularly in the residential market, the real estate broker performs an important function in keeping track of lending sources (often local banks or savings and loan associations, but national institutions as well; see Part 5) and knowing their specific requirements for mortgage loans.

❏ **COMPLEX AND DIFFICULT MARKET.**   Because of the uniqueness of every parcel of real estate, its high cost, its varied uses, and the need for outside financing in most cases, the marketing process is complex and difficult. Every transaction requires time-consuming face-to-face negotiation, as well as an understanding of legal documents, financial statements, and so on. A trained broker is in a position to provide the needed assistance to buyers as well as sellers. An important point to note is that the broker usually knows the prices of all recent sales in the neighborhood, and so is able to judge the value of the present property by applying the market data approach.

**DEFINING
BROKERAGE**

Just what is a **broker?** One statutory definition is that a *broker* is anyone "who, acting for a valuable consideration, sells, buys, rents or exchanges real estate or, in fact, attempts to do any of these things." Each of the 50 states has a statute requiring any person who performs a real estate

10-2 REAL ESTATE LICENSING EXAMINATIONS

The various states set their own requirements for obtaining a real estate broker's or salesperson's license. The applicant normally must pass a written examination and must have completed a specified course of study or a period of employment in a brokerage office or both.

In 1970, a movement began to develop a professionally prepared uniform examination that could be offered by any state. Such an examination, known as the *Real Estate Licensing Examination* (RELE), is administered by the Educational Testing Service (ETS) in Princeton, New Jersey, and is now used by over half the licensing jurisdictions in the United States.

The uniform test comes in two different versions: (1) for salesperson license candidates and (2) for broker license candidates. A separate portion of the RELE, known as the *State Test,* covers the laws, regulations, and practices unique to each jurisdiction and so differs in each state.

Even though a state uses the RELE, it still sets its own prelicensing requirements. For example, the applicant may be required to have a minimum number of hours of real estate instruction from a qualified school. Even through the Reagan years, the trend remained clearly toward tougher tests and more education and more experience. Both the real estate industry and consumers at large have an interest in the increased professionalism that can result from more stringent licensing requirements.

brokerage function to obtain a license from the state prior to receiving any commission or fee. The rigor of the licensing requirements varies dramatically, ranging from states such as California and Texas, with very strong licensing laws, to some others where licensing is little more than a formality. (See Box 10-2.)

Licenses usually are of two types: (1) the broker's license and (2) the salesperson's license. The broker's license permits the holder to carry on any brokerage activities independently. The salesperson's license permits the holder to render brokerage services only in association with a fully licensed broker. In such cases, the commission is paid to the broker who then divides the commission with the salesperson.[3] Consequently, the typical brokerage office involves one or more brokers who are principals in the firm together with a group of salespersons who work either as employees or more frequently as independent contractors.[4]

---

[3] *A broker cannot legally split a commission with an unlicensed person.*

[4] *The term* Realtor® *is often used synonymously with real estate broker. This is a misuse of the term* Realtor®, *which is a trademark designation for persons who are members of the National Association of Realtors® (NAR®), the leading brokerage association in the United States. (See Box 10-3.)*

10-3
NATIONAL
ASSOCIATION
OF REALTORS®

The real estate industry has a number of organizations operating at national, state, and local levels, which seek to promote high standards of conduct and to protect the interests of the public. By far the largest and best known of these is the National Association of Realtors® (NAR®), at one time known as the National Association of Real Estate Boards (NAREB).

The membership of NAR® consists of Realtors® and Realtor®-Associates and includes among its members real estate brokers, property managers, appraisers, and salespersons working in all areas of the real estate industry.

The NAR® functions through state and local real estate boards. The term Realtor®, which was adopted by the association in 1916 to identify its members, is a federally registered collective trademark. Only real estate brokers admitted to membership in state and local NAR® boards are permitted to use the trademark. Salespersons are admitted to Realtor®-Associate status.

The NAR® consists of a national office, 50 state associations, and more than 1,600 local boards. Its members subscribe to a strict code of ethics established by the association. The national association provides educational programs in various real estate specialities, public relations work, and research and legislative activities.

The national association authorizes the state associations to issue a certificate and the designation GRI (Graduate, Realtor®'s Institute) to those members who have demonstrated competency in the course material of the GRI program. The purpose of the program is to educate and train persons to function effectively in the brokerage business in which the primary activity is brokering single-family homes and in which occasional opportunities arise in auxiliary activities such as leasing and managing, and the sale of simple investment, commercial, and industrial units.

The NAR® has a number of affiliates (designated as Societies, Institutes, and Councils) that represent specialized activities in the real estate profession. These affiliates are briefly described as follows.

Institutes, Societies, and Councils

American Institute of Real Estate Appraisers: The American Institute of Real Estate Appraisers, founded in 1932, awards the MAI (Member, Appraisal Institute) and RM (Residential Member) designations. The nation's leading publisher of real estate literature, it is the only appraisal organization affiliated with the National Association of Realtors®. Members and candidates subscribe to a strict Code of Ethics and Standards of Professional Practice. Continuing education is encouraged through a certification program. The Appraisal Institute has 7,284 members; 7,447 MAI candidates; and 7,031 RM candidates.

A. Scruggs Love, Jr., San Antonio, Texas, President
Patricia J. Marshall, Mineola, New York, President-elect
Richard B. Gaskins, Executive Vice President (312) 329–8559

American Society of Real Estate Counselors: ASREC, the preeminent real estate counseling society, was formed to enhance the quality of advice available to the public on property matters. Competent, independent real estate advice and guidance is provided on a fee basis by Counselors who subscribe to a rigidly enforced Code of Ethics and Standards of Professional Practice. Members are qualified to use the designation CRE (Counselor of Real Estate). ASREC has 821 active members and 14 members emeriti.

James E. Gibbons, Garden City, New York, President
Eugene P. Carver, Los Angeles, California, President-elect
Lois Hofstetter, Executive Vice President (312) 329–8428

Institute of Real Estate Management: IREM was established in 1933 to advance professionalism in property management. It awards the Certified Property Manager® (CPM®) designation to property and asset managers who meet its standards of experience, education, and ethical conduct. IREM also awards the Accredited Management Organization® (AMO®) designation to property management firms, and the Accredited Residential Manager (ARM®) recognition award to on-site managers. IREM currently has approximately 8,800 CPM® members; 2,700 ARM® participants; and 545 AMO® firms.

Donald M. Furbush, San Francisco, California, President
John W. Magnuson, Tacoma, Washington, President-elect
Ronald Vukas, Executive Vice President (312) 661–1930

Real Estate Securities and Syndication Institute®: RESSI provides syndicators with tax updates, regulatory-legislative bulletins, organized industry representation and advocacy, association with industry leaders, and syndication courses and publications. Members can earn the professional designation of SRS (Specialist in Real Estate Securities). RESSI has 2,000 members, 190 designees, and 95 candidates.

Mark J. Sletten, SRS, Roseville, California, President
Richard Deagazio, Boston, Massachusetts, President-elect
David S. O'Bryon, Forum Executive Director (312) 670–6760

Realtors® Land Institute: RLI was established in 1944 as a trade association for urban and rural real estate practitioners. Members of the Institute specialize in such areas as subdivision development, real estate marketing, foreign investment, urban and investment land, farms and ranches, commercial and development properties, and residential sales. Members may earn the designation of Accredited Land Consultant (ALC).

Larry B. Caldwell, ALC, Ithaca, New York, President
Robert C. Meeks, Sylacauga, Alabama, President-elect
Linda Thompson, Executive Vice President (312) 329–8441

Realtors National Marketing Institute®: Through its three independent Councils, RNMI® promotes professional competence through education in residential brokerage and sales, commercial-investment real estate, and real estate brokerage management. The following professional designations are offered: CCIM (Certified Commercial Investment Member), CRB (Certified Real Estate Brokerage Manager), and CRS (Certified Residential Specialist). RNMI® has 34,239 members, with the Commercial-Investment Real Estate Council having 5,798 candidates and 2,699 CCIM designees; the Real Estate Brokerage Council having 2,708 general members and 6.051 CRB designees; and the Residential Sales Council having 3,222 candidates and 13,761 CRS designees.

David B. Doeleman, CRB, CRS, Portland, Oregon, President
Harold L. Kahn, Newburgh, New York, President-elect
Nanci Gentile, Executive Vice President, Administrative Services (312) 321–4411

Society of Industrial and Office Realtors®: The Society of Industrial and Office Realtors® is an international organization whose 1,800 members are specialists in a variety of activities, including the marketing of industrial and office properties. A professional affiliate of the National Association of Realtors®, SIOR is dedicated to the maintenance of high professional standards in the fields of industrial and office real estate.

Thomas W. Adler, Cleveland, Ohio, President
Mervyn E. Kirshner, Los Angeles, California, First Vice President
Don Wilkinson, Memphis, Tennessee, Second Vice President
Nancy Bryant, Executive Vice President (202) 383–1150

Women's Council of Realtors®:WCR is an organization that provides a referral network, programs and systems for personal and career growth, opportunities for increased productivity and financial security and development of leadership skills. WCR offers the Leadership Training Graduate (LTG) designation and the Referral and Relocation Certification (RRC). Founded in 1938, WCR is organized into 340 local chapters and 38 state chapters and has 18,800 members, 470 designees, and 175 candidates.

Terry Sullivan, Cedarburg, Wisconsin, President
Rosanna Sumner, Abilene, Texas, President-elect
Catherine Collins, Executive Vice President (312) 329–8480

Certain categories of individuals are exempt from the licensing requirements. Although these vary among the states, the most common are

■ Individuals acting on their own behalf.

■ Attorneys acting in the course of their law practice.

■ Court-appointed administrators, executors, or trustees.

- Public officials in the course of their official duties.

- Employees of regulated utilities acting in the course of the firm's business.

THE BROKER AS AGENT

In describing the legal position of the broker vis-à-vis the other parties to the transaction, the key term is *agent*. An *agent* is one who represents or acts for another person, called the *principal,* in dealing with third parties.

The agent is in a **fiduciary relationship** with a principal. An agent represents the principal and acts only with the principal's consent and is subject to his direction and control. Whatever business a person can transact for himself may be delegated by him to an agent.

Agents generally fall into two classes.

- **Special agents** are authorized to perform one or more specific acts for the principal and no others. Real estate brokers normally are special agents.

- **General agents** are authorized to conduct all the business, or a variety of transactions, for the principal within stipulated limits.

Creation of an agency is governed by the principles of contract law and may arise by written or oral agreement. However, most state statutes of frauds require the agent's authority to be in writing if a real estate contract or lease is involved. Less frequently, an agency relationship can be created by circumstances that give the agent justified reasons for believing the principal has created an agency. This is called **implied agency.** Finally, even when no express or implied agency actually exists, there may be an **apparent agency.** An apparent agency is created when the principal, by words or acts, gives third parties reason to believe that they may rely on someone as the agent of the principal.

An agency may be terminated by (1) expiration of the written agreement establishing the agency; (2) mutual consent of principal and agent; (3) revocation by the principal (except in certain cases where the agent has an interest in the transaction); or (4) operation of law, such as the death, insanity, or bankruptcy of either the principal or agent.

The principal in the agency relationship has many obligations, including these.

- Compensate the agent for services rendered.

- Reimburse, according to the listing contract, the agent for expenses incurred.

- Indemnify the agent for certain losses and liabilities incurred in the course of the agency.

The agent's chief duties are as follows.

- Loyalty to his or her principal.
- Obedience to the principal's instructions.
- Care in the performance of his or her duties.
- Accountability for the principal's money or property.
- Full disclosure to the principal of all material facts relevant to the purpose of the agency. (See Box 10-4.)

The specific methods for establishing the agent–principal relationship in real estate are discussed next.

LISTING AGREEMENTS

A **listing agreement** is often referred to simply as a *listing*. It represents a contractual relationship between the seller of property, who is the principal, and a real estate broker, who is the agent.

10-4
THE FIDUCIARY RELATIONSHIP

Real estate brokers are fiduicaries—that is, in a relationship of trust and confidence with their principal. As a consequence, brokers assume obligations that are not present in the normal arm's length business relationship.

Brokers have been held to have *breached* the fiduciary relationship to their clients for the following activities:

- *Secret profits.* If the broker stands to make any profit other than his commission, he must disclose the source of that profit to his principal or forfeit his commission, lose his profits, or be forced to pay both compensatory and punitive damages.

- *Undisclosed purchase for own account.* A broker must avoid an undisclosed dual agency for another or action for her own account. This might occur when a broker locates a property she feels is underpriced, buys it, and immediately sells it to an unsuspecting buyer–client for a profit.

- *Failure to disclose an offer.* A broker may be liable in damages if he fails to inform the seller of an offer to buy regardless of whether the broker profited from the concealment. A broker must also disclose to his principal any knowledge that a prospective purchaser may be willing to offer better terms than the submitted offer reflects.

- *Failure to disclose material information.* The broker must disclose all material matters within her knowledge. For instance, she must reveal any knowledge concerning recent sales of surrounding land, and whether the seller could obtain a greater profit by subdividing his property.

Approximately half of the 50 states impose a requirement (as part of their statutes of frauds) that a broker may not sue for an unpaid commission unless the agreement is in writing. In the remaining states, an oral agreement is enforceable; however, it is a good idea always to have a written agreement to lessen the chance that a misunderstanding can arise on either side.

A listing agreement normally will contain the following particulars.

- Names of the parties.
- Services to be performed by the broker (e.g., obtaining a buyer or tenant for the principal's property).
- Description of the property.
- Seller's asking price and other material terms of the sale.
- Amount of commission and terms on which it is to be paid.
- Duration of the agreement.
- Type of listing.
- Signatures of the parties.

TYPES OF LISTINGS

Three types of listing agreements generally are utilized in the real estate industry: (1) open, (2) exclusive agency, and (3) exclusive right to sell.

❑ **OPEN LISTING.** Under an **open listing,** the owner of property notifies the broker that it is being offered for sale at a specified price. It is understood that the broker will be entitled to a commission if—in a classic phrase used in the brokerage business—the broker procures a purchaser *ready, willing, and able* to purchase the property on the terms specified by the seller.

Generally, the courts have held a ready, willing, and able buyer does not have to be one who accepts every condition laid down by the seller, for it is normal to anticipate that a certain amount of good-faith bargaining will take place once a basic agreement as to price has occurred. It is conceivable that a broker may become entitled to a commission, having procured a ready, willing, and able buyer, even though no contract of sale, for any reason, ultimately is signed. To avoid this possibility, some sellers insist that the broker agree in advance that the commission will not be payable *unless and until* a contract of sale is signed or title to the property passes to the buyer.

The open listing agreement is an example of a *unilateral contract.* The consideration for the seller's promise to pay a commission is the performance by the broker of the requested service: procuring a buyer. Until the service has been performed, the seller is free to revoke an offer to pay a commission. The offer cannot, however, be revoked under conditions amounting to fraud. Such a situation is where the seller rejects a buyer introduced by the broker, revokes the listing, and then begins negotiations with the same buyer.

The seller may also list the property with many different brokers or sell the property directly since no liability to pay a commission will arise until a broker actually produces a buyer, at which point the remaining listings will be revoked.

❑ **EXCLUSIVE AGENCY.**   In an **exclusive agency,** one broker is given an *exclusive* on the property, and the seller agrees that if any other broker procures a buyer, the exclusive broker nevertheless will receive a commission. Thus, the seller can retain another broker only at the risk of paying a double commission. The seller, however, can sell the property personally without paying a commission to the exclusive broker.

An exclusive agency listing is a *bilateral,* rather than a unilateral, *contract*—that is, promises are exchanged, with the broker's promise considered to be an agreement to devote time and effort to selling the property. Consequently, the seller cannot revoke the listing at will and should have the agreement specify a term (frequently, 90 days). If the agreement fails to specify a term, the law assumes a *reasonable period,* which means that ultimately a court may have to be called on to decide when the listing ends.

A seller normally will agree to an exclusive agency for a property that is likely to be difficult to sell because of its location or condition, or because there is a dearth of buyers. In these cases, an effective selling job by the broker may require vigorous efforts to find prospects as well as expenses for advertising, the preparation of brochures, and the like. Understandably, a broker will be reluctant to expend time and incur costs without the protection of an exclusive agency.

❑ **EXCLUSIVE RIGHT TO SELL.**   An **exclusive right to sell** is exactly the same as an exclusive agency with one important exception: Even if the seller finds a buyer directly, a commission will be payable to the exclusive broker. Most courts will not recognize the existence of an exclusive right of sale unless the agreement specifically sets forth the broker's right to be paid under any circumstances.

An exclusive right to sell is sometimes required in order to use a multiple listing service. In such cases, where brokers share listings, the selling agent needs to be assured of compensation when working through a subagency agreement with the listing broker. (See Box 10-5.)

❑ **NET LISTINGS.**   The three previous types of listings are distinguished by when a commission is due; the net listing concept deals with the amount of the commission. The concept is a simple one. The

10-5
PROTECTING
THE BROKER

Seller Donahoe gave broker Calka an exclusive right of sale providing:

- *The seller would refer any prospective purchaser of whom he had knowledge during the term of the listing to the broker;*
- *In the event of sale by the seller during the term of the listing or within 12 months thereafter to any person with whom broker negotiated during the term, a commission would be payable.*

During the listing period, Vollmar approached the seller, Donahoe, and asked if it was his farm that was up for sale and the selling price. When told that it was $130,000, he stated he would not pay that much for a farm. However, he told Donahoe to contact him if Calka didn't sell the farm. Donahoe never advised Calka of this prospective purchaser. One day after the expiration of the listing, Donahoe and Vollmar reached an agreement at a price of $110,000. Calka then sued for his commission.

A Michigan court held that when Donahoe promised to refer any prospective purchaser to Calka, he was bound to do so. The court said that a "prospective purchaser" is not necessarily one who is willing to pay the asking price. He may be one who wants to bargain. The broker was entitled to negotiate with him in his efforts to make the sale. The failure of the seller to advise the broker of Vollmar's inquiry was a breach of the contract. Since the subsequent sale was consummated within the 12-month period stated in the contract, Calka would then have been entitled to his commission. The seller was required to pay Calka his commission.

owner requests a net amount, and the broker receives as a commission the amount by which the purchase price exceeds this net payment to the seller. Although net listings are popular with some owners, they tend to put the broker in a difficult position relative to the buyer and are illegal in some states.

MULTIPLE LISTING SERVICE

A **multiple listing service** (MLS) differs from the types of listing just described. MLS is the pooling of listings by a group of sales agents. In the most common situation, agents negotiate exclusive right to sell listings and then notify a central service group of the listings. This central service group periodically disseminates information about all listings available through the MLS. In this manner, any agent through subagency agreements can sell the listings of any other agent and be assured a portion of the commission as specified in the information disseminated. To the seller's benefit, MLS provides wider exposure of the property than would a single broker.

Multiple listing services exist in all large and most small cities. In the largest cities, the service is computerized, offering online access to the brokers. In small cities, the MLS produces a weekly or biweekly book containing all active listings. (See Figure 10-1 for an example of the information provided by the typical MLS.) In addition to active listings, most services also provide a record of sold properties and their sales prices. This information is helpful to brokers in advising their clients on current market prices. (More detail on this valuation aspect of the MLS service is provided in Part 3.)

From the perspective of a home buyer, the MLS arrangement can be misleading. Suppose the Whites go to Broker A, seeking assistance in finding a home. Through the MLS, Broker A finds several prospects and shows them to the Whites, and they select the Smith home. This home was listed by Broker B, who is clearly the Smiths' agent. The Whites naturally feel that Broker A is their agent because they sought him out and he has "been working with them." However, legally Broker A is sharing Broker B's commission and is thus a subagent of Broker B.

OBJECTIVES OF THE SALES AGENT

The vast majority of MLSs are sponsored by local boards of Realtors® and tend to be dominated by residential listings. The sales agent wants not only an exclusive right to sell but also a listing that *will* sell and, consequently, generate a commission. In this regard, price, terms, and seller motivation make up the listing triangle. Essentially, the more competitive the price, the longer the term of the listing (the amount of time in which the agent has a right to receive a commission for finding a buyer); and the greater the seller's motivation, the more likely the listing will generate a commission for the listing agent. If the sales agent spends time and money marketing a particular listing that expires without a sale, the agent loses both time and money. The seller, on the other hand, prefers a higher price and the freedom to terminate the listing quickly if the broker does not achieve the desired results. In practice, the two trade off their desires and find an acceptable middle ground.

OBTAINING LISTINGS

Obviously, the MLS process begins with a sales agent (broker or associated salesperson) obtaining a listing contract from a prospective seller. This agent or another agent may then sell the property with the commis-

Residential Form

73508	Add	3405 Suncrest Drive			$ 89,500
Legal	Lot 10	Block	E	Buckingham Ridge	Section 2
Bdrm. 3 or 4*	Baths 2	FPA No	Age 8	Yrs.	1st Lien $
LR 1 Den 1	Zoned A	Lot 70 × 180			Type CV P 397.00
Sep. Din. N	Liv. Din.	Faces E	Corner No		Yrs. Left 22 Int. 9%
Trees s	Sewage c	Street P	Pool Yes		Mortgage Franklin Savings
Const. Stone	Found. S	Blks. to Bus 1	Fence Privacy		Com't. Amt. $
Stories 1	Roof C				Type
Floors C/T	LD No	Elem. Pleasant Hill			How Sell C, A, CV
Air Cond. C	Heat C	Jr. Travis Hts.			Owner Carry No
Garage 2	C/P	Hi Sch. Crockett			Title Evid. TP at S
Wash Conn. Yes	DW Yes	TAX-City 479.65			Trans. Fee
Dryer Gx E	DSP Yes	Sch. 580.70			Area 6 WD
FP in SLA	R Bl	St. & C.			How Show CF-LB

Remarks Large, nicely landscaped lot with a 16' × 32' above ground pool.
   *Study off living room can be 4th bedroom. Beamed front room and master bedroom.
   Covered patio.

Occupant Mr. & Mrs. John White	Ph. 471-3268	Key LB Poss. Closing
Owner Same		Ph. 471-3268
Listor Bill Stanton		Ph. 542-0411
REALTOR Stanton Realty		Ph. 542-0410

FIGURE 10-1 *Sample of a multiple listing*

sion divided as explained below. The job of the listing agent is first to gain the confidence of the seller. The agent must then establish what can be done for the seller in marketing the property. The agent must show that it is good business to deal with an agent. Finally, the seller must be motivated to act—that is, to sign a listing agreement.

COMPENSATING THE BROKER

The broker is usually paid a **commission** based on some percentage of the final sales price (or total rentals in the case of a lease). To understand the commission arrangement adequately, we must answer four questions.

- Who pays the commission?
- How is the commission split?
- How much is the commission?
- When is the commission paid?

PAYMENT OF THE BROKERAGE COMMISSION

In the great majority of cases, the owner (seller) of the property retains the broker and has the obligation to pay the brokerage commission. It may sometimes happen, however, that the buyer enters into an agreement with the broker and promises to pay a commission. This might occur where the buyer is eager to obtain a particular parcel of property that is not currently on the market or where the buyer is seeking an unusual and difficult-to-find property.

THE AMOUNT OF THE BROKER'S COMMISSION

For many years, local real estate boards published a schedule of recommended commission rates for various types of transactions. Beginning in the 1970s, a series of federal antitrust complaints and legal proceedings resulted in the withdrawal of such schedules. Consequently, principals are free today to negotiate commissions.

As a matter of practice, many sellers tend to accept the "going rate" in the community. The commission rate today usually ranges between 5 and 7 percent in the case of residential properties. The same range may apply to income properties up to a specified amount of the sales price (say, the first $100,000), thereafter declining in stages as the price increases. A 10 percent or higher rate may apply to raw land where the purchase price is typically lower.

In income-producing as distinguished from single-family residential transactions, the commission often is directly related to the specific services rendered by the broker. The more valuable the broker's services, the higher the commission.

When dealing with brokers, remember that a broker must invest a good deal of time and effort in many transactions that never close and for which the broker receives no commission. Consequently, it becomes easier to understand the occasional "quick deal" that brings an immediate commission to the broker. Furthermore, the gross commission must often be divided among several different people, with each only receiving a small share of the total, some of whom will have incurred significant out-of-pocket expenses. At the same time, a hardworking and aggressive individual can earn a great deal of money as a broker. (See Box 10-6.)

WHEN THE BROKER'S COMMISSION IS PAID

In the absence of a specific agreement, the broker is legally entitled to a commission on procuring a ready, willing, and able purchaser, even though no final transfer of title ever occurs. It is obvious that interpreting "ready, willing, and able" in such situations can lead to disputes and litigation.

To avoid this type of controversy, most principals and brokers prefer to spell out in a written agreement the precise conditions on which, and the time when, the commission will be paid. For example, the agreement may provide that the commission will not be payable if title does not pass for any reason whatsoever. This is the language most favorable to the seller. The broker may object that if the transaction fails because of the willful default of the seller, the broker should not lose the commission, and the language may be amended accordingly. Other variations of the

---

10-6
COMMISSION
SPLITS

Assume that a 7 percent commission is earned on the sale of a $100,000 home, so that the total commission is $7,000. If the home was sold through a multiple listing service by a broker other than the listing broker, the commission must be divided between them.

Assume further, for the sake of simplicity, the split is 50–50, so that each broker receives $3,500. Within each firm, a further division may take place between the salesperson who listed or sold the property and the broker for whom the salesperson works. This split is usually set forth in an agreement between the salesperson and the broker.

If this split also is 50–50, then each salesperson (who either obtained the listing or brought about the sale) receives $1,750 (one-quarter of the commission), and each broker receives the same amount.

The broker's share must cover the cost of office operations, including rent, secretarial costs, and advertising. In addition, if the broker is a member of one of the franchise chains now operating, such as Century 21, Red Carpet, Better Homes and Gardens, or Electronic Realty Associates, a portion of the broker's share of the commission must go to the parent organization.

basic language can narrow or enlarge the possibility that the seller may have to pay a commission, notwithstanding failure of the transaction. Still, in most cases, the broker is not paid until a successful closing is held.

SELLING A RESIDENTIAL PROPERTY

We have defined a broker as one who brings together a buyer and a seller and who receives a fee or commission for acting as the agent of one of the parties (usually, the seller). This bare-bones definition must be clothed with much more detail if the broker's function is truly to be understood. Particularly in the case of residential real estate, both the buyer and seller are involved in one of the most important financial transactions of their lifetimes. In addition, the first-time buyer usually has no experience whatsoever in purchasing real estate and so is understandably cautious. What this means is that the real estate broker must seek to ascertain precisely what each party desires and then guide them through the negotiating process until a decision is reached. The process can be described in six steps.

❑ **LOCATING PROSPECTS.**   The process begins when a home is listed with a broker for sale.[5] The broker has other listings as well, plus a list of prospective buyers who have been inquiring about properties in the recent past. The mere act of listing the house by the seller exposes it to all of the broker's buying prospects (as well as the prospects of other brokers who are part of a multiple listing service or with whom the listing broker cooperates). In addition, the property will be brought to the attention of those persons contacting the broker during the listing period. Finally, the broker may pursue prospects either by advertising the property in local newspapers or by active solicitation of particular prospects. This last approach is likely to be used only for high-priced, "one of a kind" properties that are likely to appeal only to a small group of affluent buyers.

❑ **QUALIFYING PROSPECTS.**   Of the many persons to whom the property is shown or described, only a few are likely to be serious prospects. Such a prospect is one who qualifies in two ways: (1) his requirements match fairly closely the features of the property being offered, and (2) he is in a financial position to acquire the property, both in terms of the downpayment and the carrying costs.

Brokers play one of their most important roles in helping the buyer decide precisely what kind of property he or she wants. A prospective

---

[5]*The broker typically expends considerable effort to obtain listings. Obviously, the broker would usually prefer a listing that is (1) attractive to a wide market, (2) competitively priced, (3) owned by a principal anxious to sell, and (4) free of any title or structural defects. The broker would also like an exclusive right to sell agency over a substantial period of time to assure that his efforts result in a commission.*

buyer usually gives a fairly specific description of the kind of house being sought. However, the buyer (unless unlimited money is available) quickly realizes that a number of tradeoffs must be made in choosing a house. For example, is it worth accepting a lesser neighborhood in order to get a house with one more bedroom? And how much extra distance to public transportation will the buyer accept in order to get a somewhat larger lot? A broker's advice is often very valuable in helping the buyer recognize these tradeoffs and select the alternatives that best meet the buyer's objectives.

If the broker can find a property that meets the buyer's needs and create the atmosphere in which such an important "act of confidence" can take place, the buyer will commit to the purchase. It is thus the broker's role to meet the physical, financial, and psychological needs of the buyer. Once the buyer has made a decision about a property, the broker must then work with the buyer to see that financing needs are met. The broker will need to know which financial institutions in the area are making home mortgage loans and the requirements of each. Since the subject of residential loan analysis is discussed in detail in Chapter 15, it will not be elaborated here.

❏ **MAKING THE OFFER.** When a prospective buyer is prepared to make an offer to purchase a property, the broker must communicate it to the broker's client, the seller. Most often, the broker insists that the offer be in writing, both to avoid misunderstanding and to reduce the possibility of merely frivolous offers by buyers. Usually, the offer will be accompanied by a check for "earnest money." As the term indicates, this is intended to demonstrate the serious intentions of the buyer. The amount of the check may be $500 or a similarly small amount, and normally it will be returned to the buyer if no contract is negotiated.

The written offer takes a number of different forms in various parts of the country. In some places, it takes the form of a *receipt* for the earnest money given to the broker; the receipt also authorizes the broker to submit an offer to purchase the named property at a designated price. In other areas, *conditional binders* are used. The binder spells out the details of the offer but usually provides that the seller's acceptance of the offer will not automatically create a contract until the buyer has had a chance to consult an attorney or until other specified conditions are met. Increasingly, there is an effort to "put everything" into the offer. If the offer is complete, then it becomes the contract of sale when the other party accepts it. As we saw in Part 2, the contract of sale is the key document that drives the process through the closing. By putting everything into the offer, subsequent misunderstandings and extended after-the-fact negotiations are minimized. With extensive offers and counteroffers, the broker must be careful to assure that each is complete in case it is accepted and becomes the contract of sale.

❑ **RESPONDING TO THE OFFER.** In the normal situation (i.e., when the seller has listed the property with the broker), the seller is the broker's client to whom the broker's loyalty is owed. Consequently, the broker, on presenting the offer to his or her client, must make full disclosure of any other circumstances relevant to the seller's acceptance of the offer. For example, if the offer is at a price less than that asked by the seller and the broker believes the buyer is prepared to bid more, the broker should so advise the seller. If the seller likes the buyer's offer, the parties may proceed to negotiate the specific details of the transaction. If the seller declines to accept the offer but makes a counteroffer, the broker must return to the buyer and begin the process over again.

In the case of an MLS service, often two brokers are involved. In such cases the buyer's offer is transmitted to the "seller's" broker by the "buyer's" broker and then to the seller. The "buyer's" broker is usually "participating" in the selling broker's listing and is the subagent of the "seller's" broker.

❑ **HANDLING THE NEGOTIATIONS AND CONTRACT.** A "meeting of the minds" between buyer and seller—that is, an offer by the buyer that is orally accepted by the seller—is far from marking the end of the broker's role. In the great majority of cases, the next important step is to reduce the agreement to a written contract of sale, spelling out the exact obligations of each party. A wide variety of questions may have to be answered during this time. For example, what personal property will go with the house? How much time will the buyer have to arrange financing? Who will make repairs that become necessary between the contract and the closing of title? During this entire process, the broker acts as advisor to both parties (always remembering his primary duty of loyalty to his or her client, usually the seller). Personal ethics are an important part of the real estate game, particularly on the selling side.

❑ **CONTRACT PERIOD AND CLOSING.** The broker will continue his efforts during the contract period—the time between the signing of the contract and the closing of title. (Note that the broker may already have become entitled to his commission at the time the contract was signed; nevertheless, he normally will do what he can to be sure that the final closing occurs on schedule.) Perhaps the broker's major role during this time is to help the buyer arrange financing with a bank, savings and loan association, or other lender. In addition, if either party seems unwilling or unable to carry out a contract obligation, it is normally the broker who will try to find a satisfactory solution. Finally, the broker will often be present at the closing of title, and often at this time he will receive a check for his commission. (An example of a residential closing is given at the end of this chapter, with the mechanics covered in Appendix 10A.)

SELLING A COMMERCIAL PROPERTY Although most brokers deal in residential properties, a significant number specialize in commercial transactions, handling the sale of income properties or the lease of space in commercial buildings. The essential process of bringing buyer and seller together is the same whatever the type of property, but significant differences exist between residential and commercial sales. The most important of these are briefly summarized as follows.

❏ **TYPE OF PROPERTY.** Income properties come in a wide variety of types, including apartment buildings, office buildings, retail stores, shopping centers, hospitality facilities (hotels and motels), industrial properties, and raw land. Many brokers specialize in only one or two of these types; for example, some brokers specialize in hospitality facilities, and others limit themselves to dealing in undeveloped land. Even within property types, the successful broker must know the bottom line of current market trends.

❏ **TYPES OF BUYERS.** Whereas virtually all buyers of houses intend to reside in the homes themselves, buyers of income properties are investors who may have quite different objectives. Some investors seek a totally passive role. For them properties requiring a minimum of management (such as a warehouse net-leased to a tenant) are suitable. Others wish to play a more active or aggressive role; for them, an apartment house or office building may be more desirable. Finally, some properties (hospitality facilities, restaurants, indoor tennis courts) are as much businesses as real estate operations and require a more specialized type of management. The commercial broker must determine the precise objective of his client in order that time and effort not be wasted in showing unsuitable properties.

❏ **TYPE OF TRANSACTION.** Most commercial property transactions involve the lease of space rather than the purchase of entire buildings, and many brokers specialize in leasing transactions. (In the case of apartment buildings, a commercial broker normally will handle the purchases and sales, but leasing of individual apartment units is a function of the property manager.) Because a large office building or shopping center may involve dozens or even hundreds of leases, it is obvious that the leasing broker may have far more separate transactions (although at smaller commissions) than will the selling broker.

❏ **PROPERTY EXCHANGES.** In some markets, a number of transactions take the form of "tax-free exchanges." By a special provision of the Internal Revenue Code, direct swaps of certain types of investment properties permit the owners to defer tax that would otherwise be due on any appreciation in value. Exchanging is often a complex process, sometimes involving three, four, or more properties. (See Part 6 for the tax mechanics.)

❏ **SYNDICATION.**   A major source of equity capital for real estate in the middle 1980s was investment groups that utilized a partnership or other business entity (see Chapter 6) to pool their capital and acquire income property. In many smaller syndications, a real estate broker plays a central role, for it is she who has both the property listings and the contacts with investors. In organizing a syndicate, the real estate broker often wears two hats, acting as the syndicator (general partner) and handling the brokerage function. While tax law changes in 1984 and 1986 dramatically reduced the volume of tax-oriented syndications, many investment groups (both national and local) still buy real estate as described in Part 7.

THE CLOSING

As already noted, the culmination of the real estate marketing process comes with the closing of title, at which time the seller executes the deed that actually conveys title to the buyer in exchange for the balance of the purchase price. The balance of the price may be paid in one or a combination of several ways.

- In cash, either from the buyer directly or from a lending institution that has agreed to finance the purchase on the security of a mortgage.
- By the buyer agreeing to assume (take over) the future obligations on a mortgage already exiting on the property.
- By the buyer executing a purchase-money mortgage in favor of the seller, in exchange for which the seller will receive from the buyer a portion of the price in installments over a period of years.

The closing may consist of a face-to-face meeting of all the parties (including any lenders as well as the broker) or may utilize the escrow method, in which the parties deposit the various instruments and payments with an escrow holder (such as a trust company or title company) that will redistribute the deposits when all the conditions of the contract have been complied with.

The following example of a single-family closing illustrates the process and the types of problems that may have to be resolved before the transaction is finally completed. Closings of large commercial properties are considerably more complex than the example given here, but the essential problems are likely to be the same. Here in the body of the chapter we deal with the closing conceptually. With this background, you will be ready for the mechanics of a closing as presented in Appendix 10A.

INDIVIDUALS INVOLVED IN THE CLOSING

A single-family house closing requires the participation (although not necessarily the actual presence) of the individuals as shown in Table 10-1.

THE CLOSING PROCESS

Once all the documents have been produced at the closing and have been studied by the buyer and seller or their representatives, a precise computation must be made of the amount of cash and/or mortgages to be transferred. The required data include the purchase amount, the amount of any loans, loan charges, broker's commission, fees for title insurance, appraisal, survey, recording of instruments, tax stamps, and various other items depending on the state in which the transaction takes

TABLE 10-1 THE CLOSING: PARTICIPANTS AND THEIR FUNCTIONS

PARTICIPANT	CLOSING FUNCTIONS
Seller	Signs the deed; receives a check.
Buyer	Pays for the property; signs any mortgage; receives a key.
Lawyer	May handle closing. Drafts deed, note, mortgage, etc. Checks title records. Records deed, note, etc., after closing.
Title company	May handle all four functions attributed to the lawyer depending on the state. Issues an insurance policy written by an insurance company guaranteeing title.
Lender	Checks buyer's credit. Requires title check or title insurance or both. Discloses cost of financing to the buyer. Requires an appraisal to establish the value of the collateral (home). Makes the loan.
Listing broker	Obtains property listing from seller and negotiates sale.
Selling broker	Produces buyer and assists in negotiations.
Appraiser	Provides an estimate of the collateral's value for the lender. May assist the buyer or the seller in setting the price.
Surveyor	Ensures no encroachments (i.e., that the subject buildings and no others are located on the land described in the contract of sale).
Inspectors	May be used to ensure that the roof, mechanical systems, etc., are in working order before the closing.

place. Finally, an adjustment **proration**[6] must be made for payments (typically, real estate taxes and insurance premiums) that partly cover a period in which the seller was the owner and a period in which the buyer will be the owner. For the reader to get a sense of how these matters are handled, a sample closing is described in Box 10-7 and Box 10-8.

Considering the variety of items involved, as demonstrated in the example, closings frequently do not go smoothly. In fact, a recurring nightmare of the real estate broker (and the buyer and seller as well) is the closing that does not close. (As already noted, the real estate broker may have agreed that she will not be entitled to receive her commission until the transaction actually closes and title passes to the buyer.) An additional list of potential closing problems is found in Box 10-9. Working through the "why" behind each of these problems and understanding how these problems can be resolved constitute an excellent summary of the brokerage function and much of the legal material in Part 2.

SUMMARY

The brokerage process is particularly well suited for real estate transactions. Some reasons for this are the cost of real estate, its unique features, the need for financing, and the complex and difficult nature of the real estate market. Because of the importance of the brokerage function and the role of the broker as a fiduciary, all states require real estate brokers and salespersons to be licensed.

Brokers and clients are in the relationship of agent and principal; thus, each has specific duties and obligations toward the other. The most important are the broker's loyalty in representing a principal's interest and strict compliance with the principal's instructions.

The relationship between a broker and client is established by a real estate listing agreement. The agreement may take one of three forms: open listing, exclusive agency, and exclusive right of sale. In addition, brokers have established multiple listing services to assure the widest distribution of information among themselves of properties on the market.

Compensation of the real estate broker is usually in the form of a commission, payable either when the broker produces a purchaser ready, willing, and able to buy the listed property or when title to the property passes to a purchaser. In either case, the seller normally pays the commission. The commission frequently must be divided among several parties, including the listing broker, the selling broker, and the salespersons working for them who may have actually listed or sold the property.

The real estate conveyance culminates in the closing. Here legal requirements (see Part 2) are a significant part of the marketing process.

---

[6]As shown in the example that follows, a proration is simply a splitting of annual costs, usually on the basis of the date of closing. For example, property insurance is typically paid in advance. If the seller bought a one-year policy 72 days before the closing, then she is usually entitled to a payment from the buyer of $(365 - 72)$ divided by 365 of the annual premium.

**10-7
CLOSING
EXAMPLE**

You have had the dubious good fortune to list Mr. and Mrs. Verytight's home. A competitor had found a buyer, and you bring the offer to purchase to the Verytights. After courteously offering you half a glass of flat beer, Mrs. Verytight wants to know exactly how much cash everyone will receive, assuming they accept the offer and the closing goes according to schedule. The listing contract and offer to purchase provide the following information.

- The buyer claims to be ready, willing, and able to buy the Verytights' property.
- The closing is scheduled to take place at Last Hope Savings and Loan at 9:00 A.M. on March 5.
- Mr. Stuffy is the attorney who will represent the Verytights.
- Hold-On Title Guarantee Company will provide the title insurance, and the contract calls for the "survey exception clause" to be deleted.
- The buyer is authorized to inspect the property on March 4.
- The stated purchase price is $50,000, and the buyers have made the purchase contingent on receiving an 80 percent loan at market rates.
- The Verytights bought a three-year fire insurance policy costing $600 on January 1, which will be transferred to the buyers.
- All the kitchen appliances, the curtains, drapes, and lawn mower are included in the sale.
- In the prior year, city property taxes came to $480, county taxes to $150.
- A special assessment of $60 was made against the property on January 31 of this year to support a nearby recreational area. The assessment is payable $12 a year at the end of each year for the next five years.
- All utilities will be cut off by the Verytights on March 5.
- The Verytights owed $32,150 on a 9 percent first lien as of the end of February when they made their last payment.
- The buyer is expected to get a 9 percent loan and pay a one point origination fee at closing.
- The deed preparation will cost $20, the recordation $2.50. The sales commission is 6 percent, which will be split evenly between the selling and listing broker.
- The earnest money deposit of $500 is being held by the listing broker.
- The actual prorations will be based on a 360-day year and a 30-day month.
- The title insurance will cost $150.
- The appraisal will cost $100.
- The survey will cost $75.
- All costs are to be paid by the customary party.

Before arriving at the Last Hope Savings and Loan, please prepare a closing statement based on the preceding assumptions (then check yourself with Box 10-8). Next, solve the minor problems listed in Box 10-9.

10-8 BUYER AND SELLER CLOSING STATEMENT FROM 10-7

SELLER'S CLOSING STATEMENT	DEBIT	CREDIT	BUYER'S CLOSING STATEMENT	DEBIT	CREDIT
Purchase price		$50,000.00	Purchase price	$50,000.00	
Loan retired	$32,150.00		Lien assumed		$40,000.00
Prorations:			Prorations:		
Interest[a]	32.15		Property taxes[f]		112.00
Insurance[b]		564.45	Insurance[g]	564.45	
Special assessment[c]	2.13		Special assessment		2.13
Property tax[d]	112.00				
Other charges:			Cash charges and credits:		
Buyer's deed	20.00		Loan origination	500.00	
Revenue stamps	25.00		Appraisal	100.00	
Commission[e]	3,000.00		Survey	75.00	
	$35,341.28	$50,564.45	Title insurance	150.00	
Balance due seller		$15,223.17	Deed recordation	2.50	
			Earnest money		500.00
				$51,391.95	$40,614.13
			Balance due from buyer		$10,777.82

[a] $4/30 \times \frac{1}{2} \times \$32{,}150 \times 9\% = \$32.15$. This interest and the remaining principal balance will be paid to the appropriate lienholder.

[b] $\$600 - (64 \times \frac{3}{60} \times \frac{1}{3} \times 600) = \$564.45$. The Verytights get credit for the unused portion of the insurance policy.

[c] $64 \times \frac{3}{60} \times \$12 = \$2.13$. The Verytights must pay their portion of the assessment which will be paid by the new owner (buyer) on December 31.

[d] $\$630 \times \frac{64}{360} = \$112$.

[e] $1,500 to listing broker and $1,500 to selling broker.

[f] $\$630 \times \frac{64}{360} = \$112.00$.

[g] $\$200 \times \frac{236}{60} + \$400 = \$564.45$.

10-9 POTENTIAL CLOSING PROBLEMS	

10-9 POTENTIAL CLOSING PROBLEMS

- The buyer may request a postponement, but the seller may refuse because the contract specifies "time is of the essence."

- The buyer may tender a personal (rather than a certified or bank) check in payment of the price.

- The survey may reveal an apparent right-of-way easement over the land.

- A search of the land records may reveal unpaid taxes.

- The buyer's inspection may show the following:

  Apparent occupancy by persons claiming to be tenants or owners by adverse possession.

  Violations of the local building code.

  Evidence of new construction.

- The appraised value may be insufficient to support the loan requested by the buyer.

- The seller may wish to remain in occupancy for two weeks following the closing.

- The building may not be empty of furnishings or not "broom clean."

- There may be structural defects found by the consulting engineer.

- Government and/or financial institution red tape can cause critical delays.

Understanding the adjustments described Box 10-8, as well as the problems listed in Box 10-9, will help the reader to understand the important linkages in the real estate marketing process.

IMPORTANT TERMS

Agents

Apparent agency

Broker

Brokerage

Commission

Exclusive agency

Exclusive right to sell

Fiduciary relationship

General agents

Implied agency

Listing agreement

Marketing process

Multiple listing service

Open listing

Principals

Proration

Special agents

REVIEW QUESTIONS

10.1   In marketing real estate why do people rely on brokers?

10.2   Compare and contrast special and general agents. Of what type would you expect a real estate broker to be?

10.3   What is the nature of the relationship between a broker and a sponsored salesperson?

10.4   What is the broker's role as an agent of the principal?

10.5   How might an implied agency between a broker and principal be created?

10.6   What are the three types of listing agreements? How are they different?

10.7   How might participation in a multiple listing service enhance a broker's ability to market a property successfully?

10.8   When is a broker's commission earned? When is it usually paid?

10.9   How is the level or size of a real estate commission determined?

10.10   Under what circumstances might a listing salesperson receive a relatively small portion of a real estate commission?

$\mathscr{T}$HE CLOSING PROCESS

The closing concludes the real estate transaction; at this time title passes from the seller to the buyer. Real estate closings are usually conducted at the offices of either a title company or real estate attorney. The focus of the closing is allocating and distributing funds to the various parties in the transaction. In addition to the buyer and seller, real estate brokers, attorneys, lenders, title companies, pest inspectors, property inspectors, taxing authorities, and property and mortgage insurers may in some way all be involved in the closing. It is at this stage of the transaction that there are often disputes about which party is responsible for paying certain fees and charges. Since the responsibility for the payment of most fees is determined by the contract of sale, it is at closing that the strength of the sales contract is evidenced.

This appendix focuses on the provisions of two federal laws that must be followed—Regulation Z, which deals with truth in lending, and the Real Estate Settlement Procedures Act. At the end of this appendix we present a settlement guide and a sample closing statement. The purpose of this appendix is to familarize you with the closing process so that you can be a better decision maker, not to prepare you to become a closing officer.

TRUTH IN LENDING

Consumer concern over underlying mortgage terms and conditions spurred passage of the Consumer Credit Protection Act in July 1969. The main emphasis of the act was on complete and full disclosure. Included in the act was the Truth-in-Lending Act, which granted the Federal Reserve Board the power to implement its provisions. Using this power, the board established Regulation Z, which applies to anyone who grants credit in any form. Although it does not regulate interest rates, the regulation ensures that the costs of credit will be explicitly identified for consumers. Another major purpose of Regulation Z is to standardize credit procedures, thereby allowing consumers to shop around for the cheapest form of credit.

All credit for real estate is covered under Regulation Z when it is for an individual consumer.

EFFECTS OF REGULATION Z ON REAL ESTATE TRANSACTION.

❑ **DISCLOSURE.** The lender must disclose what the borrower is paying for credit, that is, the total cost, in annual percentage terms. The finance charge includes interest, loan fees, inspection fees, FHA mortgage insurance fees, and discount points. Other fees need not be included.

❑ **RIGHT TO RESCIND.** Regulation Z provides that the borrower shall have the right to rescind or cancel the transaction if it involves placing a second or junior lien against real estate that is to be a principal residence. The right must be exercised before midnight of the third business day following the transaction, which allows a three-day "cooling off" period during which the borrower can reassess the transaction.

❑ **ADVERTISING.** Real estate advertising is greatly affected by Regulation Z. It allows the use of general terms describing financing available; but, if any details are given, they must comply with the regulations. Any finance charge mentioned must be stated as an annual percentage rate (APR). If any credit terms are mentioned, such as the monthly payment, term of loan, or downpayment required, then all the following information must be given: cash price, annual percentage rate required, downpayment, amount, and due date of all payments.

❑ **EFFECT ON REAL ESTATE PERSONNEL.** Regulation Z does not indicate that brokers or salespersons should refrain from making direct contact with lenders on behalf of prospective purchasers. Of prime importance, however, is that the lender must be the one who decides if the loan should be made. The broker may not prepare or assist in the preparation of such an instrument as a loan application, note, mortgage, or land contract.

❑ **ENFORCEMENT OF REGULATION Z.** A lender who fails to disclose any of the required credit information can be sued for a specified portion of the finance charge. The lender, under some circumstances, may be fined up to $5,000 or sentenced to one year in jail, or both.

Figure A10A-1 illustrates a notice to the customer required by Regulation Z.

NOTICE TO CUSTOMER
as required by Federal Reserve Regulation "Z"   LOAN NO. _____

will lend to the borrower(s) in this transaction the amount below indicated. Interest computations on this amount will be at the contractual rate of
_____% on the outstanding balance. The **ANNUAL PERCENTAGE RATE** which includes with the contractual rate those costs listed
below as **PREPAID FINANCE CHARGE** is _____% and will begin to accrue on _____. Beginning on the
_____day of _____ 19_____ and due the _____ day of the month thereafter payments for Principal and Finance Charge,
will be due in _____ monthly installments of_____.

A.   **AMOUNT OF LOAN** committed in this transaction .... $_____

B.   Less **PREPAID FINANCE CHARGE** costs due at time of closing
    1. Loan Discount.. $_____
    2. Loan Processing Fee.. $_____
    3. Interest Thru .... $_____
    4. Private or F.H.A. Mortgage Insurance.............................. $_____
    5. _____ $_____
    6. _____ $_____
    7. _____ $_____
                   Total **PREPAID FINANCE CHARGE** $_____

C.   Equals **AMOUNT FINANCED** in this transaction... $_____

D.   Other costs not included in **FINANCE CHARGE:**   PAID BY CASH   PAID FROM LOAN PROCEEDS

    1. Title Insurance or Abstract .... $_____ $_____
    2. Opinion on Title .... $_____ $_____
    3. Appraisal .... $_____ $_____
    4. Credit Report.. $_____ $_____
    5. Survey... $_____ $_____
    6. Tax Escrow.. $_____ $_____
    7. Insurance Escrow .... $_____ $_____
    8. Hazard Insurance Premium............................. $_____ $_____
    9. Recording Fee.. $_____ $_____
    10. _____ $_____ $_____
    11. _____ $_____ $_____
               Total Charges Paid From Loan Proceeds $_____

E.   **NET PROCEEDS** .... $_____

F.   This Institution's security interest in this transaction is a _____ on property located at_____
    _____ also specifically described in the documents furnished for this loan.
    The documents executed in connection with this transaction cover all after-acquired property and also stand as security for future advances, the
    terms for which are described in the documents.

G.   Late payment formula:
    In event of default a late charge of .5% of the Principal and Interest payment will be charged for each installment not received by the
    Association within 15 days after the installment is due.

H.   Prepayment formula:
    When amount prepaid equals or exceeds 20% of the original loan, not more than 90 days interest on the amount prepaid may be charged
    beyond the date of payment.

I.   Rebate formula:
    None

J.   Miscellaneous disclosures:
    This Mortgage also secures the payment of any additional loans up to but not exceeding $5000.00 at the Mortgagee's option.

*K. **FINANCE CHARGE** includes:
    1. Total Prepaid Finance Charge (from B)................................. $_____
    2. Total Interest to be Earned over life of Loan......................... $_____
    3. _____ $_____
    4. _____ $_____
    5. _____ $_____
             Total **FINANCE CHARGE** $_____

    TOTAL PAYMENTS on this transaction (Principal and Interest) will be .... $_____

INSURANCE

PROPERTY INSURANCE: Property insurance, if written in connection with this loan, may be obtained by borrower through any person of his choice,
provided however, the creditor reserves the right to refuse, for reasonable cause, to accept an insurer offered by the borrower. If borrower desires property insurance to be obtained from or through the creditor, the cost will be $_____ for the_____ year term of the initial policy.   OTHER
INSURANCE: Credit life, accident, health or loss of income insurance is not required to obtain this loan. No charge is made for such insurance and No
such insurance may be provided unless the borrower signs the appropriate statement below. _____ is available at a cost of
$_____ for the _____ year term of the initial policy.   (TYPE OF INSURANCE)
I desire_____ insurance coverage.   I DO NOT desire such insurance coverage.

DATE _____ SIGNATURE _____   DATE _____ SIGNATURE _____

    I hereby acknowledge receipt of the disclosures made in this notice.

    BORROWER _____ DATE _____

BY_____
    BORROWER _____ DATE _____
* Not required for 1st mortgage purchase loans.

FIGURE A10A-1.   *Regulation Z statement*

THE REAL ESTATE SETTLEMENT PROCEDURES ACT OF 1974 (RESPA)

Few pieces of federal legislation in recent years have stirred as much controversy within the mortgage industry as has RESPA. The law was intended to help the consumer obtain residential mortgage financing and to minimize closing costs to the borrower by regulating the lending practices of the mortgage banking community. Although the act was passed in 1974 and was to go into effect on June 20, 1975, it generated so much confusion and controversy that Congress made significant changes effective in January 1976 and in June 1976. The following discussion relates to the act as amended.

RESPA applies to all settlements on loans for residential properties that are "federally related." The most important aspect of this statement is that the act applies to all loans secured by a first mortgage on single-family to four-family residential properties by any lender regulated by the federal government and even those whose deposits are insured by an agency of the federal government. Some other lenders are also covered by the act, but the preceding broad category includes the vast majority of residential mortgages made throughout the United States today. In all such mortgage settlements, the uniform settlement statement prescribed by HUD or its equivalent must be used (see Figures A10A-2 and A10A-3). The form is complex in comparison with closing statements previously used, and, in practice, brokers usually prepare their own closing statements to clarify the transaction for their clients.

PROVISIONS OF RESPA

- The lender must permit the borrower to inspect the closing statement one day prior to the closing. This statement must disclose the anticipated closing costs to the extent that they are known at that time; the costs are precisely determined at the time of closing.

- The lender must provide to the borrower a booklet titled "Settlement Costs" within three days after taking an application for a mortgage loan that is federally related, and the lender must also provide a good-faith estimate of the anticipated closing costs.

- Escrow account requirements by the lenders are regulated. Generally, the maximum that may be required is the sum of the amount that normally would be required to maintain the account for the current month plus one-sixth of the total estimated expenses for real estate taxes and insurance for the following 12-month period.

- Kickbacks and unearned fees are prohibited. Particular emphasis is placed on the relationship between the regulated lender and the title insurance companies. The lender may not, as a condition of the loan, specify the title insurer to be used.

A. U.S. DEPARTMENT OF HOUSING AND URBAN DEVELOPMENT SETTLEMENT STATEMENT	B. TYPE OF LOAN

B. TYPE OF LOAN

1. ☐ FHA   2. ☐ FMHA   3. ☐ CONV. UNINS.

4. ☐ VA   5. ☐ CONV. INS.

6. FILE NUMBER: 7. LOAN NUMBER:

8. MORT. INS. CASE NO.:

C. NOTE: This form is furnished to give you a statement of actual settlement costs. Amounts paid to and by the settlement agent are shown. Items marked "(p o.c.)" were paid outside the closing; they are shown here for informational purposes and are not included in the totals.

D. NAME OF BORROWER:	E. NAME OF SELLER:	F. NAME OF LENDER:

G. PROPERTY LOCATION:	H. SETTLEMENT AGENT:	I. SETTLEMENT DATE:
	PLACE OF SETTLEMENT:	

J. SUMMARY OF BORROWER'S TRANSACTION:		K. SUMMARY OF SELLER'S TRANSACTION:	
100. GROSS AMOUNT DUE FROM BORROWER		**400. GROSS AMOUNT DUE TO SELLER**	
101. Contract sales price		401. Contract sales price	
102. Personal property		402. Personal property	
103. Settlement charges to borrower (line 1400)		403.	
104.		404.	
105.		405.	
Adjustments for items paid by seller in advance		*Adjustments for items paid by seller in advance*	
106. City/town taxes to		406. City/town taxes to	
107. County taxes to		407. County taxes to	
108. Assessments to		408. Assessments to	
109.		409.	
110.		410.	
111.		411.	
112.		412.	
120. GROSS AMOUNT DUE FROM BORROWER		**420. GROSS AMOUNT DUE TO SELLER**	
200. AMOUNTS PAID BY OR IN BEHALF OF BORROWER		**500. REDUCTIONS IN AMOUNT DUE TO SELLER**	
201. Deposit or earnest money		501. Excess deposit (see instructions)	
202. Principal amount of new loan(s)		502. Settlement charges to seller (line 1400)	
203. Existing loan(s) taken subject to		503. Existing loan(s) taken subject to	
204.		504. Payoff of first mortgage loan	
205.		505. Payoff of second mortgage loan	
206.		506.	
207.		507.	
208.		508.	
209.		509.	
Adjustments for items unpaid by seller		*Adjustments for items unpaid by seller*	
210. City/town taxes to		510. City/town taxes to	
211. County taxes to		511. County taxes to	
212. Assessments to		512. Assessments to	
213.		513.	
214.		514.	
215.		515.	
216.		516.	
217.		517.	
218.		518.	
219.		519.	
220. TOTAL PAID BY/FOR BORROWER		**520. TOTAL REDUCTION AMOUNT DUE SELLER**	
300. CASH AT SETTLEMENT FROM OR TO BORROWER		**600. CASH AT SETTLEMENT TO OR FROM SELLER**	
301. Gross amount due from borrower (line 120)		601. Gross amount due to seller (line 420)	
302. Less amounts paid by/for borrower (line 220)	( )	602. Less reduction amount due seller (line 520)	( )
303. CASH (☒ FROM) (☐ TO) BORROWER		**603. CASH (☐ TO) (☐ FROM) SELLER**	

HUD 1A REV. 5/76 MID-WEST PRTG. CO.

FIGURE A10A-2.   *RESPA settlement statement, page 1*

L. SETTLEMENT CHARGES		PAID FROM BORROWER'S FUNDS AT SETTLEMENT	PAID FROM SELLER'S FUNDS AT SETTLEMENT
700.	TOTAL SALES/BROKER'S COMMISSION based on price $ @ % =		
	Division of commission (line 700) as follows:		
701.	$ to		
702.	$ to		
703.	Commission paid at Settlement		
704.			
800.	ITEMS PAYABLE IN CONNECTION WITH LOAN		
801.	Loan Origination Fee %		
802.	Loan Discount %		
803.	Appraisal Fee to		
804.	Credit Report to *		
805.	Lender's Inspection Fee		
806.	Mortgage Insurance Application Fee to		
807.	Assumption Fee		
808.			
809.			
810.			
811.			
900.	ITEMS REQUIRED BY LENDER TO BE PAID IN ADVANCE		
901.	Interest from to @ $ /day		
902.	Mortgage Insurance Premium for mo. to		
903.	Hazard Insurance Premium for yrs. to		
904.	yrs. to		
905.			
1000.	RESERVES DEPOSITED WITH LENDER FOR		
1001.	Hazard insurance mo. @ $ /mo.		
1002.	Mortgage insurance mo. @ $ /mo.		
1003.	City property taxes mo. @ $ /mo.		
1004.	County property taxes mo. @ $ /mo.		
1005.	Annual assessments mo. @ $ /mo.		
1006.	mo. @ $ /mo.		
1007.	mo. @ $ /mo.		
1008.	mo. @ $ /mo.		
1100.	TITLE CHARGES		
1101.	Settlement or closing fee to		
1102.	Abstract or title search to		
1103.	Title examination to		
1104.	Title insurance binder to		
1105.	Document preparation to		
1106.	Notary fees to		
1107.	Attorney's fees to		
	(includes above items No.:)		
1108.	Title insurance to		
	(includes above items No.:)		
1109.	Lender's coverage $		
1110.	Owner's coverage $		
1111.			
1112.			
1113.			
1200.	GOVERNMENT RECORDING AND TRANSFER CHARGES		
1201.	Recording fees: Deed $; Mortgage $; Releases $		
1202.	City/county tax/stamps: Deed $; Mortgage $		
1203.	State tax/stamps: Deed $; Mortgage $		
1204.			
1205.			
1300.	ADDITIONAL SETTLEMENT CHARGES		
1301.	Survey to		
1302.	Pest inspection to		
1303.			
1304.			
1305.			
1400.	TOTAL SETTLEMENT CHARGES (enter on lines 103 and 502, Sections J and K)		

The Undersigned Acknowledges Receipt of This Settlement Statement and Agrees to the Correctness Thereof

_____   _____
                Buyer   **Seller**

HUD 1B REV. 5/76 MID-WEST PRTG. CO.

FIGURE A10A-3. *RESPA settlement statement, page 2*

- The identity of the true borrower must be obtained by the lender, and the lender must make this information available to the Federal Home Loan Bank Board on demand.

- No fee may be charged by the lender for preparation of all the forms required by RESPA.

- The act requires the secretary of HUD to establish model land recording systems in selected areas of the country with the ultimate goal of establishing a uniform system that will presumably be less expensive than the system now in operation.

Although RESPA is directed at mortgage lenders, it obviously has an impact on all those engaged in the real estate business because of the industry's dependence on the availability of mortgage funds. Familiarity with the specified closing statement seems to be essential, if only for the purpose of being able to explain it.

SETTLEMENT (CLOSING) GUIDE

The following guide to the settlement proceedings in a real estate transaction does not list all the items one might encounter. Rather, it is designed to cover the items generally involved in a settlement. The debits and credits will vary for each individual transaction because many of the items are negotiable between seller and purchaser.

Certain bookkeeping practices must be understood in order to complete the settlement statement properly.

1. The term *debit* denotes something owed. This pertains to both the buyer's and seller's settlement statements.

2. The term *credit* denotes something that is receivable by either the buyer or the seller.

3. Because a double-entry accounting system is employed, the sum of the buyer's debits must equal the sum of the buyer's credits. The same must be true for the seller. Do not try to balance the buyer's statement with the seller's statement. Even though they appear on the same form, they are treated individually.

The order in which items appear on a settlement statement is reflected in Figures A10A-2 and A10A-3.

- *Purchase price.* The amount to be paid by the purchaser at settlement for the property is entered as a debit to the buyer. Since it is received by the seller, it is entered as a credit to the seller's statement. (lines 101 and 401)

- *Deposit.* The earnest money amount paid by the purchaser, which is used as part of the purchase price, should be entered as a credit to the buyer. No entry to the seller. (line 201)

- *Sales commission (broker's fee).* The fee charged by the broker for the sale of the property is an expense to the seller and should be debited. No entry to the buyer unless the buyer has agreed to pay the broker a fee to find a property. (lines 700–704)

- *New first mortgage.* If the buyer is obtaining a new loan to purchase the property, enter this amount as a credit since it is the means by which he or she is to pay the sales price. (line 202)

- *Assumed mortgage.* If the loan of the seller is being assumed by the buyer, enter this amount as a credit to the buyer and a debit to the seller. The amount is being used by the buyer to pay for the property to reduce the amount owed. The seller will use this amount to reduce the cash he or she will receive. In effect, the assumption is a credit for the buyer from the seller against the purchase price. (lines 203–209)

- *Pay existing mortgage.* The seller pays off the existing loan. This amount is debited to the seller, and the property may be transferred free and clear. (lines 504–509)

- *Second mortgage.* If a second loan is required to meet the purchase price by the buyer, enter the amount as a credit. No entry to the seller. (line 202)

- *Purchase money mortgage.* If the seller takes a purchase money mortgage for part of the sales price, enter the amount as a credit to the buyer against the sales price and as a debit to the seller against his or her cash receivable. (line 203)

- *Land contract.* If the seller sells the property under a land contract, enter the amount of the contract as a credit to the purchaser against the sales price and a debit to the seller against the cash to be received. (line 503)

- *Taxes in arrears, prorated.* If the taxes are not yet due and payable, prorate the annual amount of taxes including the day of settlement. Credit the purchaser and debit the seller. (lines 210–219, 510–519)

- *Taxes in advance, prorated.* If the taxes have been paid in advance, prorate the amount, including the day of settlement, and subtract it from the prepaid amount. The remainder should be debited to the buyer and credited to the seller. (lines 106–112, 406–412)

- Delinquent taxes. If taxes are delinquent, this amount should be charged to the seller. No entry to the buyer. (lines 510–519)

- *Fire insurance, canceled.* Credit the remaining premium balance to the seller. (line 1001)

- *Fire insurance, new policy.* Enter the cost of the new policy as a debit to the purchaser. (line 1001)

- *Fire insurance, assigned policy.* If the seller assigns the existing policy to the purchaser, prorate the premium and enter the remaining amount as a debit to the purchaser and a credit to the seller. (line 1001)

- *Interest in arrears.* If the loan is assumed or paid by the seller and interest is calculated in arrears, prorate to the date of closing the monthly interest and enter it as a debit to the seller. If the loan is assumed, enter the prorated amount as a credit to the buyer. (lines 808–811)

- *Interest on new loan.* Interest may be charged on a newly originated loan. Enter the amount as a debit to the purchaser. (lines 901–905)

- *Rent in advance.* Enter the prorated amount as a credit to the purchaser and a debit to the seller.

- *Rent in arrears.* If rent is collected in arrears, enter the prorated amount as a debit to the purchaser and a credit to the seller.

- *Title insurance, owner's policy.* Enter as a debit to the seller. (line 1110)

- *Title insurance, mortgagee's policy.* Enter as a debit to the purchaser. (line 1109)

- *Deed preparation.* Enter as a debit to the seller. (line 1201)

- *Abstract continuation.* Enter as a debit to the seller. (line 1102)

- *Opinion or examination of the abstract.* Enter as a debit to the purchaser. (line 1107)

- *Appraisal fee.* A negotiable item. It may be charged to the seller if requested by the purchaser, or charged to the purchaser if requested by the lending institution. (line 803)

- *Attorney fees, purchaser.* Debit the purchaser for any additional legal fees charged to him or her. (line 1107)

- *Attorney fees, seller.* Debit the seller for any additional legal fees charged to him or her. (line 1107)

- *Loan origination fee.* Debit the purchaser for the cost of originating the new loan. In the case of an assumption, a loan assumption fee may be charged. (line 801)

- *Conventional discount points.* Negotiable if charged. (line 802)

- *Recording, deed.* Debit to the purchaser. (line 1201)

- *Recording, mortgage.* Debit to the purchaser. (line 1201)

- *Escrow balance, assumed.* Debit to the purchaser and credit to the seller for the account balance. (lines 1001–1008)

- *Escrow payoff, existing loan.* Credit to the seller as an offsetting item to the loan balance. (lines 1001–1008)

- *Survey.* May be negotiable but generally charged as a debit to the purchaser. (line 1301)

- *Prepayment penalty.* Debit to the seller for prepaying loan balance. (lines 808–811)

- *Conveyance tax.* Debit to the seller. (line 1202)

- *Special assessments.* Negotiable. (lines 108, 408, 212, 512)

- *Settlement fees.* Negotiable.

- *Credit report.* Debit to the purchaser. (line 804)

- *Photo fee.* Debit to the purchaser. (line 1301)

- *Sale of chattels.* If bought by purchaser, debit to the purchaser and credit to the seller. Such items are sold under a separate bill of sale given by the vendor (seller) to the vendee (buyer). (lines 102 and 104)

- *Balance due from the purchaser.* The amount owed by the purchaser at settlement after subtracting the credits from his or her debits. Enter as a credit, since it is needed to balance the double-entry system. (line 300)

- *Balance due seller.* The amount received by the seller at settlement after subtracting the debits from the credits. Enter as a debit if the credits exceed the debits as a balancing item. Enter as a credit if the debits exceed the credits. (line 600)

The completed settlement statement is presented as Figures A10A-4 and A10A-5.

A.	U.S. DEPARTMENT OF HOUSING AND URBAN DEVELOPMENT SETTLEMENT STATEMENT	B. TYPE OF LOAN

B. TYPE OF LOAN

1. ☐ FHA   2. ☐ FMHA   3. ☐ CONV. UNINS.

4. ☐ VA   5. ☐ CONV. INS.

6. FILE NUMBER: 7. LOAN NUMBER:

8. MORT. INS. CASE NO.:

C. NOTE: This form is furnished to give you a statement of actual settlement costs. Amounts paid to and by the settlement agent are shown. Items marked "(p.o.c.)" were paid outside the closing; they are shown here for informational purposes and are not included in the totals.

D. NAME OF BORROWER:	E. NAME OF SELLER:	F. NAME OF LENDER:
Charles and Wilma Vance	Jack and Margaret Nickless	Anytown Savings & Loan

G. PROPERTY LOCATION:	H. SETTLEMENT AGENT:	I. SETTLEMENT DATE:
2785 Nulsen Drive Anytown, Texas	Safe Title Company — PLACE OF SETTLEMENT: Safe Title Company	September 30, 199X

J. SUMMARY OF BORROWER'S TRANSACTION:		K. SUMMARY OF SELLER'S TRANSACTION:	
100. GROSS AMOUNT DUE FROM BORROWER		400. GROSS AMOUNT DUE TO SELLER	
101. Contract sales price	$78,950	401. Contract sales price	$78,950
102. Personal property		402. Personal property	
103. Settlement charges to borrower (line 1400)	796.60	403.	
104.		404.	
105.		405.	
Adjustments for items paid by seller in advance		*Adjustments for items paid by seller in advance*	
106. City/town taxes to		406. City/town taxes to	
107. County taxes to		407. County taxes to	
108. Assessments to		408. Assessments to	
109.		409. Insurance	140
110.		410.	
111.		411.	
112.		412.	
120. GROSS AMOUNT DUE FROM BORROWER	$79,746.60	420. GROSS AMOUNT DUE TO SELLER	$79,090
200. AMOUNTS PAID BY OR IN BEHALF OF BORROWER		500. REDUCTIONS IN AMOUNT DUE TO SELLER	
201. Deposit or earnest money	1,000	501. Excess deposit (see instructions)	
202. Principal amount of new loan(s)	63,160	502. Settlement charges to seller (line 1400)	5,259.50
203. Existing loan(s) taken subject to		503. Existing loan(s) taken subject to	
204.		504. Payoff of first mortgage loan	57,897.85
205.		505. Payoff of second mortgage loan	
206.		506.	
207.		507.	
208.		508.	
209.		509.	
Adjustments for items unpaid by seller		*Adjustments for items unpaid by seller*	
210. City/town taxes to	510.03	510. City/town taxes to	510.03
211. County taxes to		511. County taxes to	
212. Assessments to		512. Assessments to	
213.		513.	
214.		514.	
215.		515.	
216.		516.	
217.		517.	
218.		518.	
219.		519.	
220. TOTAL PAID BY/FOR BORROWER	$64,670.03	520. TOTAL REDUCTION AMOUNT DUE SELLER	$63,667.38
300. CASH AT SETTLEMENT FROM OR TO BORROWER		600. CASH AT SETTLEMENT TO OR FROM SELLER	
301. Gross amount due from borrower (line 120)	79,746.60	601. Gross amount due to seller (line 420)	79,090.00
302. Less amounts paid by/for borrower (line 220)	(64,670.03)	602. Less reduction amount due seller (line 520)	(63,667.38)
303. CASH (☒ FROM) (☐ TO) BORROWER	$15,076.57	603. CASH (☒ TO) (☐ FROM) SELLER	$15,422.62

FIGURE A10A-4. *RESPA settlement statement, page 1 completed*

U.S. DEPARTMENT OF HOUSING AND URBAN DEVELOPMENT
SETTLEMENT STATEMENT
PAGE 2

L. SETTLEMENT CHARGES		PAID FROM BORROWER'S FUNDS AT SETTLEMENT	PAID FROM SELLER'S FUNDS AT SETTLEMENT
700.	**TOTAL SALES/BROKER'S COMMISSION** based on price $ 78,950 @ 6 % = $4,737		
	Division of commission (line 700) as follows:		
701.	$ to		
702.	$ to		
703.	Commission paid at Settlement		$4,737,00
704.			
800.	**ITEMS PAYABLE IN CONNECTION WITH LOAN**		
801.	Loan Origination Fee %	$631.60	
802.	Loan Discount %		
803.	Appraisal Fee to		100.00
804.	Credit Report to *		
805.	Lender's Inspection Fee		
806.	Mortgage Insurance Application Fee to		
807.	Assumption Fee		
808.			
809.			
810.			
811.			
900	**ITEMS REQUIRED BY LENDER TO BE PAID IN ADVANCE**		
901.	Interest from to @ $ /day		
902.	Mortgage Insurance Premium for mo. to		
903.	Hazard Insurance Premium for yrs. to		
904.			
905.			
1000.	**RESERVES DEPOSITED WITH LENDER FOR**		
1001.	Hazard insurance mo. @ $ /mo.	140.00	
1002.	Mortgage insurance mo. @ $ /mo.		
1003.	City property taxes mo. @ $ /mo.		
1004.	County property taxes mo. @ $ /mo.		
1005.	Annual assessments mo. @ $ /mo.		
1006.	mo. @ $ /mo.		
1007.	mo. @ $ /mo.		
1008.	mo. @ $ /mo.		
1100.	**TITLE CHARGES**		
1101.	Settlement or closing fee to		
1102.	Abstract or title search to		
1103.	Title examination to		
1104.	Title insurance binder to		
1105.	Document preparation to		
1106.	Notary fees to		50.00
1107.	Attorney's fees to		
	(includes above items No.:)		
1108.	Title insurance to		250.00
	(includes above items No.:)		
1109.	Lender's coverage $ 250.00		
1110.	Owner's coverage $		
1111.			
1112.			
1113.			
1200.	**GOVERNMENT RECORDING AND TRANSFER CHARGES**		
1201.	Recording fees: Deed $; Mortgage $; Releases $	25.00	7.50
1202.	City/county tax/stamps: Deed $; Mortgage $		
1203.	State tax/stamps: Deed $; Mortgage $		
1204.			
1205.			
1300.	**ADDITIONAL SETTLEMENT CHARGES**		
1301.	Survey to		75.00
1302.	Pest inspection to		40.00
1303.			
1304.			
1305.			
1400.	**TOTAL SETTLEMENT CHARGES** (enter on lines 103 and 502, Sections J and K)	$796.60	$5,259.50

The Undersigned Acknowledges Receipt of This Settlement Statement and Agrees to the Correctness Thereof

_____   _____
Buyer   Seller

HUD 1B REV. 5/76 MID-WEST PRTG CO

FIGURE A10A-5.   *RESPA settlement statement, page 2, completed*

REALTOR CODE OF ETHICS

CODE OF ETHICS, NATIONAL ASSOCIATION OF REALTORS®1

PREAMBLE

Under all is the land. Upon its wise utilization and widely allocated ownership depend the survival and growth of free institutions and of our civilization. The REALTOR® should recognize that the interests of the nation and its citizens require the highest and best use of the land and the widest distribution of land ownership. They require the creation and adequate housing, the building of functioning cities, the development of productive industries and farms, and the preservation of a healthful environment.

Such interests impose obligations beyond those of ordinary commerce. They impose grave social responsibility and a patriotic duty to which the REALTOR® should dedicate himself, and for which he should be diligent in preparing himself. The REALTOR®, therefore, is zealous to maintain and improve the standards of his calling and shares with his fellow REALTORS® a common responsibility for its integrity and honor. The term REALTOR® has come to connote competency, fairness, and high integrity resulting from adherence to a lofty ideal of moral conduct in business relations. No inducement of profit and no instruction from clients ever can justify departure from this ideal.

In the interpretation of this obligation, a REALTOR® can take no safer guide than that which has been handed down through the centuries, embodied in the Golden Rule, "Whatsoever ye would that men should do to you, do ye even so to them."

---

[1]*Where the word REALTOR® is used in this Code and Preamble, it shall be deemed to include REALTOR-ASSOCIATE.® Pronouns shall be considered to include REALTORS® and REALTOR-ASSOCIATES® of both genders.*

The Code of Ethics was adopted in 1913. Amended at the Annual Convention in 1924, 1928, 1950, 1951, 1952, 1955, 1956, 1961, 1962, 1974, 1982, 1986, and 1987.

Accepting this standard as his own, every REALTOR® pledges himself to observe its spirit in all of his activities and to conduct his business in accordance with the tenets set forth below.

ARTICLE 1

The REALTOR® should keep himself informed on matters affecting real estate in his community, the state, and nation so that he may be able to contribute responsibly to public thinking on such matters.

ARTICLE 2

In justice to those who place their interests in his care, the REALTOR® should endeavor always to be informed regarding laws, proposed legislation, governmental regulations, public policies, and current market conditions in order to be in a position to advise his clients properly.

ARTICLE 3

The REALTOR® should endeavor to eliminate in his community any practices which could be damaging to the public or bring discredit to the real estate profession. The REALTOR® should assist the governmental agency charged with regulating the practices of brokers and salesmen in his state.

ARTICLE 4

To prevent dissension and misunderstanding and to assure better service to the owner, the REALTOR® should urge the exclusive listing of property unless contrary to the best interest of the owner.

ARTICLE 5

In the best interests of society, of his associates, and his own business, the REALTOR® should willingly share with other REALTORS® the lessons of his experience and study for the benefit of the public, and should be loyal to the Board of REALTORS® of his community and active in its work.

ARTICLE 6

The REALTOR® shall seek no unfair advantage over other REALTORS® and shall conduct his business so as to avoid controversies with other REALTORS®.

ARTICLE 7

In accepting employment as an agent, the REALTOR® pledges himself to protect and promote the interests of the client. This obligation of absolute fidelity to the client's interests is primary, but it does not relieve the REALTOR® of the obligation to treat fairly all parties to the transaction.

ARTICLE 8

The REALTOR® shall not accept compensation from more than one party, even if permitted by law, without the full knowledge of all parties to the transaction.

ARTICLE 9

The REALTOR® shall avoid exaggeration, misrepresentation, or concealment of pertinent facts relating to the property or the transaction. The REALTOR® shall not, however, be obligated to discover latent defects in the property or to advise on matters outside the scope of his real estate license.

ARTICLE 10

The REALTOR® shall not deny equal professional services to any person for reasons of race, creed, sex, or country of national origin. The REALTOR® shall not be party to any plan or agreement to discriminate against a person or persons on the basis of race, creed, sex, or country of national origin.

ARTICLE 11

A REALTOR® is expected to provide a level of competent service in keeping with the standards of practice in those fields in which the REALTOR® customarily engages. The REALTOR® shall not undertake to provide specialized professional services concerning a type of property or service that is outside his field of competence unless he engages the assistance of one who is competent on such types of property or service, or unless the facts are fully disclosed to the client. Any person engaged to provide such assistance shall be so identified to the client and his contribution to the assignment should be set forth. The REALTOR® shall refer to the Standards of Practice of the National Association as to the degree of competence that a client has a right to expect the REALTOR® to possess, taking into consideration the complexity of the problem, the availability of expert assistance, and the opportunities for experience available to the REALTOR®.

ARTICLE 12

The REALTOR® shall not undertake to provide professional services concerning a property or its value where he has a present or contemplated interest unless such interest is specifically disclosed to all affected parties.

ARTICLE 13

The REALTOR® shall not acquire an interest in or buy for himself, any member of his immediate family, his firm or any member thereof, any entity in which he has a substantial ownership interest, property listed with him, without making the true position known to the listing owner, in selling property owned by himself, or in which he has any interest, the REALTOR® shall reveal the facts of his ownership or interest to the purchaser.

ARTICLE 14

In the event of a controversy between REALTORS® associated with different firms, arising out of their relationship as REALTORS®, the REALTORS® shall submit the dispute to arbitration in accordance with the regulation of their Board or Boards rather than litigate the matter.

ARTICLE 15

If a REALTOR® is charged with unethical practice or is asked to present evidence in any disciplinary proceeding or investigation, he shall place all pertinent facts before the proper tribunal of the Member Board or affiliated institute, society, or council of which he is a member.

ARTICLE 16

When acting as agent, the REALTOR® shall not accept any commission, rebate, or profit on expenditures made for his principal-owner, without the principal's knowledge and consent.

ARTICLE 17

The REALTOR® shall not engage in activities that constitute the unauthorized practice of law and shall recommend that legal counsel be obtained when the interest of any party to the transaction requires it.

ARTICLE 18

The REALTOR® shall keep in a special account in an appropriate financial institution, separated from his own funds, monies coming into his possession in trust for other persons, such as escrows, trust funds, clients' monies, and other like items.

ARTICLE 19

The REALTOR® shall be careful at all times to present a true picture in his advertising and representations to the public. The REALTOR® shall also ensure that his status as a broker or a REALTOR® is clearly identifiable in any such advertising.

ARTICLE 20

The REALTOR®, for the protection of all parties, shall see that financial obligations and commitments regarding real estate transactions are in writing, expressing the exact agreement of the parties. A copy of each agreement shall be furnished to each party upon his signing such agreement.

ARTICLE 21

The REALTOR® shall not engage in any practice or take any action inconsistent with the agency of another REALTOR®.

ARTICLE 22

In the sale of property which is exclusively listed with a REALTOR®, the REALTOR® shall utilize the services of other brokers upon mutually agreed upon items when it is in the best interests of the client. Negotiations concerning property which is listed exclusively shall be carried on with the listing broker, not with the owner, except with the consent of the listing broker.

ARTICLE 23

The REALTOR® shall not publicly disparage the business practice of a competitor nor volunteer an opinion of a competitor's transaction. If his opinion is sought and if the REALTOR® deems it appropriate to respond, such opinion shall be rendered with strict professional integrity and courtesy.

SSET MANAGEMENT: THE PROPERTY MANAGEMENT PERSPECTIVE

As the real estate game evolved in the 1980s, asset management became the key phrase. Asset management encompassed traditional property management as well as a new interest in fitting the operating strategy for a property to the owners' needs, particularly institutional and corporate owners. The marriage of traditional real estate operating management with portfolio and earnings per share considerations is young, but we look for innovations in this field to be a primary feature of the real estate industry in the 1990s, providing many if not most of the new jobs.

The foundation of asset management is property management, so that is where we begin in this first of two chapters devoted to the topic. In this chapter, we take a how-to approach, since the theory and tools of business management have likely been covered in your other courses. We will add the property dimension to management and perhaps will convince you that the real world doesn't offer many neat little financial problems, or marketing problems, or production problems. Rather, it offers *business* problems, most of which have a financial, marketing, and production dimension. Property management is very much a domain for the interdisciplinary generalist.

In the second chapter on asset management, Chapter 12, there is considerably more theory for two reasons: (1) the functional area theory (e.g., finance) is evolving to explain real estate applications, so your other course won't have covered it, and (2) a lot of the "how to" is still to come in the 1990s.

By now you know that the main product of the real estate industry is **space over time.** It comes in all forms: an apartment on a six-month lease, a beach resort time-share unit for two weeks a year, a department store in a regional shopping mall on a 30-year lease, an office condominium owned indefinitely, and a motel room off the interstate highway rented for one night. Most space, in order to have maximum value to its users, comes with **services**—utilities, maintenance, security, and someone in charge to collect the money and see that what needs doing gets done—property management, in other words.

Property management is the process of overseeing the operation and maintenance of real property to achieve the objectives of the property owner. Sometimes owners manage their own property, particularly small properties and particularly when they themselves occupy part of the space. But for larger properties or those whose owners live at a distance, management is usually performed by a paid property manager, either an individual or a management firm. There are exceptions, like industrial buildings on long-term leases, where tenants maintain the building, pay the taxes and insurance, and mail the owner a check each month. But most residential, office, retail, and many industrial properties offer services along with the space over time.

Property management has long been an underrated function in the real estate industry. The need for professional management did not become apparent until the depression of the 1930s, when numerous foreclosures revealed a pattern of management deficiencies. This oversight might seem strange, since running a large commercial or residential project in which hundreds or thousands of people reside or work is a highly challenging task, calling for training, good judgment, and a variety of technical skills. Traditionally, however, the emphasis in the real estate industry has been on the so-called permanent elements of the investment—good location, sound construction, and reasonable long-term financing—rather than on the day-to-day operation of the property. It has sometimes seemed as if a property owner, having made a very large investment in the permanent structure, assumed that the property would run itself with a minimum amount of supervision.

This concept of property management has changed substantially in the past decade. In an era of rising costs, it has dawned on owners that good property management is the major **controllable influence on residual cash flow** (i.e., the number of dollars that end up in the owner's pocket). It is true that both rent rates and operating expenses are largely shaped by market forces beyond the control of any one property owner (witness the very sharp rise in energy costs in the 1970s). But it is also true that comparable properties within the same geographic area often show significant variances in rental income and operating costs. Why? Close inspection often shows that "above-average" operating expenses and lower than average rent levels result from inadequate property management. (See Box 11-1.)

PROPERTIES REQUIRING MANAGEMENT

The level of management a property needs increases with the level of services and with the frequency that tenants turn over. Some examples of different managerial responsibilities and problems follow, organized by type of space.

11-1 IMPORTANCE OF PROPERTY MANAGEMENT	The classic mistake of the stock and bond investor moving into real estate involves underestimating the importance of management. Some investors have the feeling that real estate manages itself. A San Francisco real estate broker recently noticed a project that was on the market for $1 million. He knew how the property had been managed in the past and that the million dollar valuation was based on a capitalization of historic income figures. He borrowed money to buy the property. renegotiated certain leases, and established more efficient operating procedures. In six months he sold the property for $1.4 million based on the capitalized value of the new, higher net income. His contribution was management expertise.

RESIDENTIAL

To the extent that property management involves tenant relations, residential properties present the greatest challenge. The space leased by the residential tenant is "home," where the tenant and other family members spend a substantial amount of their free time and the rent for which may represent the tenant's largest single financial obligation. Consequently, the residential tenant expects a well-run property, with services and utilities available as promised at rents kept as low as possible (among other reasons, because residential rentals are not tax deductible as are business rentals). On the other side of the coin, one or two bad tenants in a project can be a continuing source of vexation to the property manager and to the other tenants.

The relatively short term of a residential lease means that the property manager is under continual pressure to maintain a high renewal rate in order to avoid vacated units that must be repainted, repaired, and re-leased in as short a time as possible. A property that is theoretically fully rented may, nevertheless, lose a substantial amount of rental income if turnover is very high and more than a few weeks elapse before each new tenant moves in.

Among the types of residential properties are (1) apartments, (2) condominiums and cooperatives, and (3) single-family homes.

APARTMENTS. The personal relationship between manager and tenant can be crucial to maintaining high occupancy. Turnover of tenants results in higher operating expenses and lower rentals collected. Asking fair rents and responding to tenants' needs (e.g., maintenance and repairs) are often the most important variables in successful apartment management.

CONDOMINIUMS AND COOPERATIVES.   The management of condominium and cooperative housing projects also presents some special problems. Although the general nature of the work to be done is very similar to that in other rental projects, the manager is dealing with a large number of owners (who may act like tenants) rather than with a single owner. Consequently, the manager is sometimes caught between owners arguing for major repairs to the building and owners seeking to hold down their expenses.

SINGLE-FAMILY HOMES.   The least involved form of residential management is the rental of single-family homes. The owner may have moved away for business or other reasons with the intention of returning at a later date to occupy the house or may be holding the property as an investment. In either case, the owner retains a local agent to collect rent, pay real estate taxes and debt service, and handle any problems that may arise. This type of management is frequently performed by real estate brokers, who charge a fee equal to a percentage of each month's rent.

OFFICE BUILDINGS

The property manager of an office building must be familiar with more complex lease provisions than those used for residential properties. For example, the office building tenant is very much aware of paying a rent rate measured by the square foot, and so the measurement of space becomes an important consideration. One frequently used measure is **rentable area** or rentable space. The manager must understand how to compute it. For example, are the bathrooms and hallways an added "load factor," with the tenant paying for her individual space plus her "share" of these common areas? Does the manager measure a tenant's space to the inside wall, the outside wall, or the center of the wall? In addition, **escalation and cost-of-living clauses** are common in office buildings and frequently are negotiated with each individual tenant. The answers are in the leases. The property manager must be enough of a lawyer to read them, enough of an engineer to be sure the services (e.g., elevators) work as promised, enough of a marketer to sell to the tenant on the quality of the services he provides, and enough of a financial accountant to report it all to the owner.

When leasing space, the property manager should bear in mind that the value of an office building is directly related to three interlocking elements: (1) the rent rate per square foot, (2) the quality of the tenancies, and (3) the length of the leases. The higher the rental rate, the higher the gross income. The more creditworthy the tenant, the more assured the owner may be that rents will be paid. Finally, the longer the lease term, the lower the risk of vacancies and turnover problems in the future. With longer term leases, it is more important to have appropriate escalation clauses or expense **pass-through** provisions, for the opportunities to increase base rent to cover increased operating costs are less frequent.

In office building management, service is particularly important. The property manager is responsible for making sure the premises are kept clean and secure, that elevators run reliably, that utilities work, and that the structure looks (and is) well maintained. To many office tenants, the amount of rent is secondary to the efficient provision of these services.[1] (See Box 11-2.)

Today's larger buildings are getting "smarter." They have computerized controls to handle heating and air conditioning loads to minimize energy consumption. Elevators are programmed to meet peak loads. The fire system is tied to the public-address warning system, sprinklers, and air pressure. Infrared sensors may turn lights on and off as they sense people entering and leaving rooms. Telecommunications using fiber optics can create data highways between distant locations either in concert with public telephone systems or independently. Telecommunications options are expensive and can be cost-justified only when operating management helps tenants ensure their full utilization.

RETAIL COMPLEXES

For larger retail complexes and particularly for shopping centers, competent property management is extremely important.

First, maintenance of the property itself requires substantial work. Each day large numbers of shoppers visit the premises, generating a great deal of rubbish and inflicting wear and tear on the improvements. Besides maintenance, daily security is an essential service.

Second, the property manager must keep alert to possibilities of making the premises more attractive and to the need to renovate and modernize selling areas. Fierce competition for retail business means constant efforts must be made to have customers return as often as possible. In addition, whenever new tenants lease space, renovation is required to suit the premises to the new user.

Third, the property manager performs an important function in obtaining a proper tenant mix for the retail complex. Too much competition among similar uses may mean business failures for the tenants and a negative cash flow for the landlord. Ideally, the various tenants should complement each other so that a shopper coming to one store will find related products or services in adjacent stores.

---

[1]*Operating statistics for office properties are maintained on a national level by the Building Owners and Managers Institute—see page 326.*

**11-2
TAKEOVER
LEASES AND
NONRAID
CLAUSES**

Leasing space in a soft market (one in which vacancy rates are high) can become extremely competitive, particularly in the case of office buildings. Office tenants, unlike tenants of industrial or retail space, do not usually invest large sums in fixtures or alterations and so may be induced to move to new space for a sufficient concession (typically better space at the same or a smaller rent). The leasing game heats up when large blocks of new space come onto the market either because a new building is completed or because a very large tenant vacates a space and leaves the area.

One technique used by a broker seeking to fill vacant space is the *takeover* lease (also known as the *back-to-back* lease). In this situation, a landlord anxious to fill up his building agrees to assume the remaining rent obligation of a tenant in another building if he will move. Obviously, the shorter the remaining term of the present lease, the more likely this approach will be used. The new landlord may be willing to take over a substantial rent obligation in order to capture a tenant, particularly in cases where the landlord must achieve a certain occupancy level in order to qualify for the full amount of his permanent financing.

Is there anything the tenant's present landlord can do to protect himself? One common method is the lease provision that the tenant may not assign or sublet to another without the landlord's consent. In consequence, the new landlord who wants to take over the lease will be unable to re-rent that space to another tenant and so must bear the entire cost of carrying the lease until its termination. The nonassignability clause may not fully protect the tenant's present landlord; many courts now interpret nonassignability clauses to permit assignments to new tenants as long as they are reputable and financially responsible. Further-more, the landlord of the new building may be so anxious to capture someone else's tenant that he may be willing to absorb the full cost of the unexpired lease.

Another deterrent the existing landlord may use is a **nonraid clause** in the lease. A nonraid clause treats any vacation of the premises by the tenant (even though he agrees to continue to pay rent) as a material breach, causing all unpaid rent to be immediately due and payable. This kind of clause is frequently used where the physical presence of a particular tenant is important (e.g., where the tenant is a well-known national firm). Acceleration of rent payments required by a nonvacation clause would make it necessary for the takeover landlord to pay a large sum up front in order to capture the tenant. An even more extreme form of a nonraid clause gives the landlord the right to an injunction prohibiting the tenant from moving out. However, there is no record of a court's ever having enforced such a provision.

One final question is whether the owner of a building can sue a raiding landlord for inducing the breach of a tenant's lease. In general, the answer is no; the new landlord is entitled to act in his own economic interests. However, if the raiding landlord acted fraudulently or maliciously (e.g., by claiming that the tenant's present building was in a dangerous condition), he might be liable for damages.

Finally, retail leases frequently contain **percentage rent** provisions by which the landlord is entitled to additional rent based on a percentage of gross sales over a specified minimum. The property owner must be prepared to negotiate the most favorable terms for the owner and also to ensure that percentage rents are correctly computed and paid as they come due.[2]

INDUSTRIAL

A more specialized type of management is involved with industrial property—that is, buildings that are used primarily for manufacturing or warehousing, and that may also include a limited amount of office space.[3] Much industrial property is either built or altered to meet the specific needs of a tenant who normally will sign a long-term lease (e.g., 10 to 20 years), enabling the landlord to recover the special costs involved. Such special-purpose buildings usually require only a minimal amount of management by the landlord since they are frequently leased on a net basis, with the tenant responsible for operating expenses, including real estate taxes and insurance.

On the other hand, some types of warehouse space are let on relatively short terms to more than one tenant. In this type of situation, the landlord may be responsible for maintenance and repair and must also anticipate the need to market the space at frequent intervals. One of the most important cash flow items of the late 1980s was the increasing cost of tenant alterations necessitated by tenant rollovers. In the 1990s, a critical property management function will be to service existing tenants and find the right new tenants with an eye to keeping down the cost of tenant improvements. In the increasingly competitive space markets—apartments, office, retail, and industrial—new leases usually provide for significant tenant improvements. Even on industrial properties, traditionally the type requiring the lowest tenant improvement, tenant improvements on a rollover can equal one year's gross rent. Consequently, keeping down rollovers (and therefore the cost of tenant improvements) is a primary objective of the cash flow-oriented owner.

HOTELS AND MOTELS

In the hospitality industry, service is crucial. This and the frequent turnover of guests (often daily) mean that hotels and motels require more

[2]The Dollars and Cents of Shopping Centers *is a good source of retail operating statistics. It is published by Urban Land Institute, 1200 18th Street N.W., Washington, D.C. 20036*

[3]*Two good sources of information on the management of industrial properties are the National Association of Industrial and Office Parks, 1215 Jefferson Davis Highway, Suite 100, Arlington, Virginia 22202 (publisher of* Development Magazine) *and Conway Data, Inc., 40 Technology*

constant management than any other category of space we have considered. In many cases, convention business is the major source of revenue. As a result, hotel and motel management includes food service and entertainment as well as the typical property management functions. Marketing is first in importance. The lease period is so short—one night—that management must find tenants for space vacated daily. Management skill creates value as much as does the physical property.[4]

HOSPITALS, REST HOMES, CONFERENCE CENTERS, AND OTHER SPECIAL-PURPOSE FACILITIES

Like hotels and motels, special-purpose facilities have a much higher proportion of service relative to space. These facilities often require very specialized management talent, frequently recruited from the professions involved. It is usually a matter of teaching real estate to a doctor or educator rather than the reverse. Consequently, several professional consultants serve these industries.[5]

PROPERTY MANAGEMENT FUNCTIONS

Having looked at how requirements for management vary by property type, we will now examine a manager's day-to-day duties in more detail. Like many working people, a property manager wakes up in the morning, dresses for work, eats breakfast, and drives to an office (either on or off the managed premises). Once there, what does he or she *do*? We will first list all of the functions and then cover the most important ones in greater detail.

MAKING A MANAGEMENT PLAN

As the agent of the property owner, the property manager is bound to carry out the owner's objectives. Making explicit those objectives is the first step in creating a **management plan.**

As we have seen, properties under paid management may be very small, or they may be multimillion-dollar complexes. A management plan can be equally simple or elaborate, as suits the scope of manage-

---

Park, Norcross, Georgia 30092–9934 (managers of the Industrial Developmental Research Council, an association of corporate and business development professionals, and publishers of Site Selection).

[4]*National hotel statistics are published annually by the accounting firm of Laventhol and Horwath, 1845 Walnut Street, Philadelphia, Pennsylvania 19103. The primary learning and resource center for the hotel industry is the School of Hotel Management at Cornell University. In addition, several of the larger chains (e.g., Holiday Inns) have extensive in-house educational programs for hotel management.*

[5]*Laventhol and Horwath publishes historical statistics and trend analysis for several special-purpose industries including life care and conference centers.*

ment and the market area of a property. Regardless of size, it is important to make a plan (which could range from a handwritten half page to 50 pages typed and bound, depending on the project). We will discuss the steps in making a plan for a larger project in this chapter. Here we should note that a management plan for any size property contains three points: (1) an analysis of the competitive environment, (2) an analysis of the property itself, and (3) enumeration of the owner's objectives and recommendations for achieving them.

MAKING A BUDGET

A manager collects money, pays the bills, and sends what is left to the owner—in millions or hundreds. A **budget** is essential for two reasons: (1) to regulate cash flow—that is, to make sure sufficient cash is on hand to meet obligations like taxes, mortgage payments, operating expenses, and special capital improvements (e.g., new roof) when needed; and (2) to measure performance—to act as a standard for measuring the manager's success in meeting objectives.

This topic, too, merits more attention and is discussed again later in the chapter.

SHOWING AND RENTING SPACE

Although marketing real estate is a function distinct from managing it, the two are often combined in the hands of the property manager or management firm. In the case of apartment buildings, the manager actually on the site (the **resident manager**) usually shows vacant apartments and may handle lease negotiations as well. In the case of commercial or office space, however, leasing is much more complex. Commercial leasing is often performed by specialists within a property management firm or may be handled by a separate brokerage firm. (See Box 11-3.)

Because of the importance of leasing and the expertise and special effort required to do it well, a property manager who handles the lease function often receives a commission over and above his regular management fee. The leasing function can be classified into three steps, all or some of which may be performed by the property manager or management firm.

❑ **SETTING RENTAL LEVELS.**   A **rent schedule** should be established with the objective of maximizing future rental income from the property. Setting rents is far from an exact science; it calls for the exercise of good judgment based on a knowledge of rent rates and available space in comparable buildings as well as the features, functions, and benefits of both the subject property and competing space. A technique

| 11-3 WHAT IS A RESIDENT MANAGER? | Many individuals begin a career in property management by becoming the on-site or resident manager. For all practical purposes, the two terms are synonymous.

A resident manager is an employee who oversees and administers the day-to-day building affairs in accordance with direction from the asset manager or owner. Resident managers, in general, have the greatest amount of day-to-day contact with the building's tenants. They also usually spend the greatest amount of time at the property. They may or may not supervise a maintenance staff, but they are directly responsible for managing the physical upkeep and maintenance of the property, as well as often leasing vacant units and collecting rents.

It is essential that resident managers possess a congenial personality. In most cases, they act as ambassadors of the management company and are the first, if not the only, company representative a prospective or current tenant deals with face-to-face. |

used by many professional property managers is the base-unit-rate approach. This involves choosing a standard unit in an apartment building (e.g., a two-bedroom apartment on the sixth floor) or a specified number of square feet in an office or commercial building. The base unit is assigned a rental figure derived from a study of the market with adjustments for differences between the particular property and its competition. (For example, a newer building normally commands higher rent for space than an older building, all other things being equal.) Within the particular building, rent rates will vary depending on the relative merits and deficiencies of each unit. For example, space on higher floors usually commands a premium over that on lower floors; upper floors offer the amenities of less street noise and a better view.

❏ **SOLICITING PROSPECTS.**   The second step in the leasing process is to advertise space in appropriate media (whether billboards, newspapers, radio, or television) and show space to prospective tenants. Although space is often shown in a perfunctory way, this task should properly be regarded as the time for intensive personal selling on the part of the leasing agent. To sell space effectively, the leasing agent must not only be familiar with every detail of the property being shown, but also should ascertain the precise needs and desires of the prospect as described in Chapters 9 and 10.

❏ **NEGOTIATING AND EXECUTING LEASES.**   Finally, the property manager will be involved, to a greater or lesser extent, in the negotiation and execution of the lease. In the case of an apartment project, where standard form leases are used and little negotiation normally occurs, the manager may perform the entire process. On the other hand, a long-term lease of several floors in a major office building will require the efforts of both legal counsel and the owner. Even here, however, the property manager plays an important preliminary role because of his initial contacts with the tenant.

COLLECTING RENT

The property manager is responsible for the *prompt* collection of rent and other payments due from tenants. When the rent is a fixed sum for the term of the lease, the task is simple. However, in many commercial buildings, a tenant's rent obligation may be made up of different items. For example, the tenant may pay a minimum rent that steps up at periodic intervals during the lease term, sometimes with some form of escalation rent (like increases tied to the Consumer Price Index) or with a percentage rent in the case of retail tenants. Tenants may also be liable for garage rentals or fees for specified services provided by the landlord. If additional rents and fees must be calculated by the landlord, they are not payable until bills have been prepared and rendered to tenants. Consequently, rent calculation and collection in a large income property can be complex and time consuming (See Box 11-4.)

MAINTAINING GOOD TENANT RELATIONS

Operating real estate is similar to every other business in one important respect: keeping the customer satisfied. It is true that a tenant signed to a fixed term cannot walk away from the property if she is poorly served, as can the customer in a department store. But every lease eventually comes up for renewal, and a high turnover can be a major operating expense. Furthermore, a building with a reputation for dissatisfied tenants will suffer in the marketplace. (See Box 11-5.)

In dealing with complaints from tenants, the property manager should be quick to cure deficiencies in services to which tenants are entitled. At the same time, one tenant should not be given favored treatment; other tenants will inevitably demand the same. The property manager must also use good judgment in enforcing the rules and regulations of the building (which often are incorporated into each lease). These rules and regulations can be quite detailed, particularly in the case of an interrelated operation like a shopping center. For example, the rules may specify whether a tenant is permitted to distribute handbills to shoppers, how loud music can be played by a record store, and how late stores must be open at certain times of the year like Christmas. Rules exist to

11-4

INCREASING RENTAL INCOME: SEVEN CASE HISTORIES

A property manager should always be alert to new ways of increasing rental income for the building. Improving building services (or remedying deficiencies in services) can justify higher rents. Increasing the amount of leasable space raises total rental revenues. Creating new types of uses for the building makes the space attractive to a wider range of tenants.

Here are seven actual cases in which ingenuity and alertness to opportunity produced more rent.

- *Lower-level discotheque.* A Cincinnati office building was fully rented except for basement space. The basement had one big advantage—an open floor area of 25,000 square feet. A disco owner was approached; at first he was hesitant because he desired windows and wanted his site to be visible. The building manager emphasized the excellent location in the heart of the city, near hotels and the convention center. The disco went in and was a huge success.

- *Shopping center college.* Walk-up space in older shopping centers is hard to rent because retailers usually insist on ground-level accessibility. A shopping center near New York City had such space available. The building manager converted 5,000 square feet into classrooms for a local college looking for space. Its attraction to the college was easy access by public and private transportation and plenty of free parking.

- *Increased security.* An office building in a less than prime location was 40 percent vacant; the reason appeared to be fear of crime in that neighborhood, particularly after dark. The manager induced the owner to make a relatively small investment in new locks for the building, increased lights for the parking area and entrance ways, and a security guard after 5:00 P.M. As a result, the vacancy rate was cut to 10 percent.

- *Additional rentable area 1.* In some commercial buildings, particularly those built or bought many years ago when space was relatively cheap, owners have kept desirable space for a management office. Income-minded managers have moved their offices to the basement or off the premises entirely in order to free the original space for rent.

- *Additional rentable area 2.* Older buildings constructed on corner plots often have entrances on two sides. This arrangement made sense when space was relatively cheap. In today's high-rent market, managers have discovered that closing up one entrance can convert common area to rentable area, creating valuable retail space without seriously inconveniencing tenants in the building.

- *Less is more.* Retailers have learned to operate with less space than previously in order to cut down on high total rent expense. Some alert property managers have offered tenants a rent reduction in exchange for recapturing a portion of their existing space. Tenants then enjoy higher sales per square foot on their remaining space, and the building manager creates more new rental units with a minimum amount of alteration and no new construction

■ *Minisuites.* Many business firms, particularly sales firms, require a base in a number of different locations. One Florida building devoted some space to minisuites, ranging in size from 50 to 400 square feet. Secretarial and answering services are provided on a pooling-of-costs basis. On a square-foot basis, minisuites usually command a premium rent rate.

minimize disputes among tenants as well as to maximize total shopping center sales for all tenants (and so increase percentage rents payable to the landlord). Deciding how strictly to enforce the rules is one of the most difficult jobs of the property manager. Authority, fairness, and diplomacy are all demanded by the work.

11-5
THE COST
OF TURNOVER

An income property with an extremely low vacancy rate may, nevertheless, have a very high *turnover* rate (new tenants coming into the building each year). This might occur, for example, when tenants were constantly leaving a badly operated building but were immediately replaced by new tenants seeking space in a tight market.

Is there anything wrong with this? Plenty. Turnover costs are much greater than most people realize. One real estate firm has calculated the average cost of turnover in an apartment project to be $400 per unit. First, the unit stops producing rent for at least a short period, from as little as two weeks to more than a month. Second, the apartment must be cleaned and often must be repaired and painted between tenants. Finally, the building management incurs higher overhead costs for personnel and advertising because of the constant need to find potential tenants, show the space, and negotiate leases.

In the case of an office building or commercial space, turnover costs can be much greater. Vacancies tend to be longer, so more rent is lost. Frequently, space must be altered—walls and electrical outlets moved, floors recarpeted—the cost of which may be all or partly borne by the landlord. In addition, use of an outside broker (a common occurrence) means a leasing commission must be paid. The result is that turnover costs for commercial space can add up to a year's rent or more.

It should be no surprise, then, that when it comes to his tenants, the successful property manager strives to keep them satisfied.

PAYING EXPENSES; KEEPING BOOKS AND RECORDS

The property manager must see to it that operating expenses, real estate taxes, insurance premiums, and mortgage payments are paid when due. Depending on the arrangement, a manager may be authorized to sign checks or may only prepare a list of payments for the owner's attention. The manager also keeps records of income and outlays and works with the owner's accountant in preparing annual financial statements and tax returns. The manager may also be responsible for reports required by government authorities.

ESTABLISHING MAINTENANCE SCHEDULES

Maintenance schedules specify the timing and amount of custodial services like cleaning common areas (as well as leased space when called for by the lease agreement), picking up garbage, removing snow and ice, and keeping up the parking area. Maintenance also includes making sure the building's operating systems are always functional. Tenants take for granted (rightly) their heating, ventilating and air conditioning, plumbing, and electrical service. The building manager is paid to take responsibility for keeping these systems running. In a larger property, one or more engineers may be permanently on the premises to look after mechanical equipment. In many buildings maintenance contracts are set up for heating and air conditioning equipment. Besides maintenance, the property manager is also responsible for inventory control, to ensure that cleaning supplies and other necessary items are on hand when needed. (In some establishments like hotels, inventory control is a highly specialized function that includes food and liquor.)

CONSERVING ENERGY

As recently as 10 or 15 years ago, energy in the United States was so cheap that virtually no thought was given to minimizing its use. Indeed, most rentals were on an "electricity inclusion" basis, that is, the landlord paid electrical charges no matter how much the tenant used. Needless to say, few leases are written that way today. (Certain kinds of office buildings are an exception.) When older leases come up for renewal, the landlord usually insists that electrical costs be paid by the tenant, either through a separate meter on the tenant's premises or by billing each tenant for a pro rata share of the total building cost. Alternatively, the costs of heating and cooling are often passed along to the tenant by escalation clauses in the lease that require each tenant to pay his or her pro rata share of cost increases above a base amount. This type of lease is common in multitenant buildings where separate meters are impractical.

Even when the landlord can pass on increases in energy costs to the tenants, a property manager should still strive for maximum energy efficiency. Otherwise, the tenants' costs will be higher than for comparable space in better managed buildings, and, to that extent, the manager's building will be less competitive in the marketplace. Striving for efficiency is especially important in older buildings where energy conservation played no role in the original building design.

The experience of recent years indicates that very substantial energy savings can be achieved with a few simple measures. One study showed that energy costs could be cut 20 percent if the following five steps were taken.

■ Regular inspection of building equipment to ensure efficient performance.

■ Careful timing of the heating-cooling system so that it operates at lower levels after working hours and on weekends.

■ Turning off all but the bare minimum of lights after work hours.

■ Careful monitoring of light during working hours so that excessively high levels of light are not supplied.

■ Minimizing the use of outside air (which must be heated in the winter and cooled in the summer).[6]

PROVIDING SECURITY

The increase in crime both against persons and property has made security a top demand by tenants of all types, whether residential, office, retail, or industrial. In addition, legislation and court decisions in many states have expanded the liability of a landlord for injury or property loss suffered by a tenant resulting from inadequate safety precautions or from the landlord's failure to repair doors, windows, or other points of access into the building or into individual rental units. The property manager has the difficult task of seeking to minimize the risk of crime while at the same time keeping operating cost increases to a minimum.

SUPERVISING PERSONNEL

Depending on size, a property may require none, one, or many employees for cleaning, maintenance, security, and other jobs. The proper-

---

[6]*If you are successfully integrating the material from the different chapters, this last point should have reminded you of a subset of the environmental issues. There is indeed a potential conflict between the desire to minimize energy costs and the problem of indoor air pollution. Managers do not want sick buildings either.*

ty manager normally determines the personnel requirements of the property and hires workers (within a budget approved by the owner). Depending on the terms of the management contract, wages and salaries are either paid by the property management firm (that then passes these costs along to the property owner) or are paid by the owner directly. A management firm handling a number of buildings around town normally finds it more economical to have its own staff service the buildings.

MAINTAINING PROPERTY INSURANCE

Adequately insuring a property—and doing so at the minimum cost—is important. Doing so requires a manager to keep up to date on the many types of insurance coverage available and to recommend appropriate insurers for the property. (This latter function is often performed by an insurance broker, who deals with the property manager or directly with the owner.) Finally, the property manager must investigate all accidents or claims for damages and see to it that reports are filed promptly with the insurer.

THE MANAGEMENT PLAN

At the beginning of the list of managerial functions, we noted the importance of preparing a management plan. It need not be long and complex. An acceptable management plan for a very small office building (say, 4,000 square feet) in a stable neighborhood with good occupancy could be written in a page or less. Though simple enough to be carried around in the manager's head, it would probably be worth the formality of writing down the plan for three reasons: (1) getting an explicit statement of the owner's objectives and assumptions cuts down on misunderstandings later (fewer instances of "But I thought you meant—"), (2) having something in writing in the file provides continuity if a property manager is transferred or leaves suddenly, and (3) the act of writing the plan down provides the framework and the discipline for thinking it through step by step.

For large, complex projects where nothing is left to chance, a carefully thought-out management plan is essential. We noted briefly that the three areas of analysis in a plan are the competitive environment, the property, and the owner's objectives.

REGIONAL AND NEIGHBORHOOD ANALYSIS

For the manager of a large, new income property such as an office building, the first step in preparing a management plan is to analyze the region and the neighborhood in which the property is located. The objective is to determine the precise niche the building can fill in its neighborhood and region—in particular, the types of tenants likely to be attracted and the level of rent they will be willing to pay. Regional and neighborhood analysis have been discussed theoretically in Chapters 2 and 3 and in a more practical way in Part 3 on appraisal. The point to stress about this analysis is that the property manager has to understand regional and neighborhood trends in relation to the building under management.

In any large urban area, changes are constantly occurring that create opportunities regardless of the economic climate or the cost of funds. Metropolitan centers operate as economic melting pots. Each is a meeting place of various industries experiencing different phases of economic growth and decay. At any one time, some industries are seeking new space while others are contracting and so making space available. These changing requirements create opportunities for new allocations of space. The property manager can play an important role in identifying changing trends and analyzing the impact on his or her building. There are several national publications that help the property manager see cross-regional comparisons that may be helpful in making local management decisions. (See Box 11-6.)

PROPERTY ANALYSIS

The second step is to study the property itself. There are four objectives.

- To know the physical condition of the building and (if it is an older building) the extent to which it suffers from the various types of depreciation discussed in Part 3.

- To measure with precision the amount of leasable space available in the building (as well as the gross area) and to prepare a building layout showing precisely where all space is located.

- To determine the tenant composition of the building (if already leased) and the exact amount of vacant space.

- To become familiar with the management procedures currently being followed.

This type of property analysis should be made whenever a manager is newly engaged, and whether or not the building is new or in use. The manager must know the product and its existing consumers. (See Box 11-7.)

OWNER'S OBJECTIVES AND MARKET ANALYSIS

We noted at the beginning of this chapter that real estate as a product is comprised of *space over time.* All buildings offer space over time; the

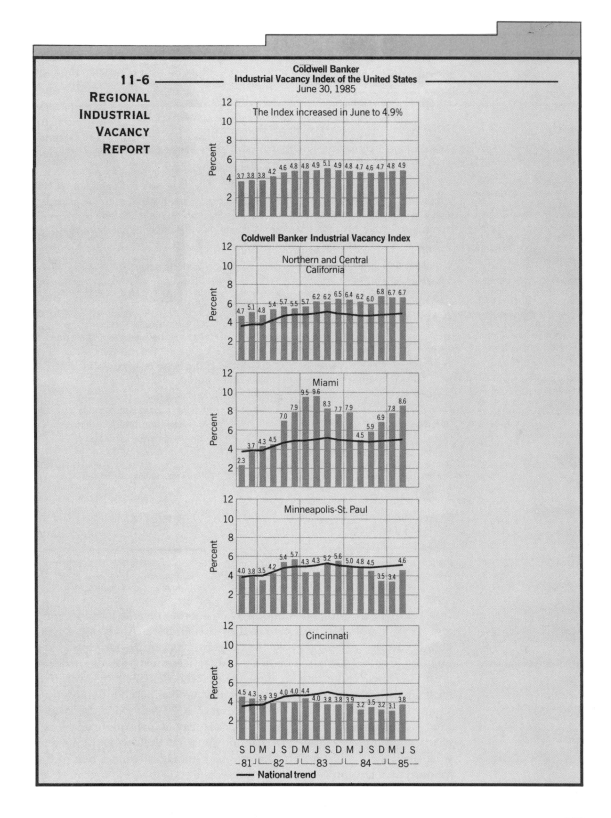

11-6
REGIONAL INDUSTRIAL VACANCY REPORT

Coldwell Banker
Industrial Vacancy Index of the United States
June 30, 1985

The Index increased in June to 4.9%

Coldwell Banker Industrial Vacancy Index

Northern and Central California

Miami

Minneapolis-St. Paul

Cincinnati

S D M J S D M J S D M J S D M J S
—81— —82— —83— —84— —85—
—— National trend

**11-7
CALCULATING
RENTABLE
AREA—FOR
OFFICE
BUILDINGS
BOMA
GUIDELINES
(BUILDING
OWNERS AND
MANAGERS
ASSOCIATION
INTERNATIONAL)**

A. Rentable Area—Multiple Tenancy Floor

The net rentable area of a multiple tenancy floor, whether above or below grade, shall be the sum of all rentable areas on that floor.

The rentable area of an office on a multiple tenancy floor shall be computed by measuring to the inside finish of permanent outer building walls, or to the glass line if at least 50 percent of the outer building is glass, to the office side of corridors and/or other permanent partitions, and to the center of partitions that separate the premises from adjoining rentable areas.

No deductions shall be made for columns and projections necessary to the building.

B. Rentable Area—Single Tenancy Floor

Rentable area of a single tenancy floor, whether above or below grade, shall be computed by measuring to the inside finish of permanent outer building walls, or from the glass line where at least 50 percent of the outer building wall is glass. Rentable area shall include all area within outside walls, less stairs, elevator shafts, flues, pipe shafts, vertical ducts, air-conditioning rooms, fan rooms, janitor closets, electrical closets—and such other rooms not actually available for the tenant for his furnishings and personnel—and their enclosing walls. Toilet rooms within and exclusively serving only that floor shall be included in rentable area.

No deductions shall be made for columns and projections necessary to the building.

Source: Quoted from BOMA, "Standard Method of Floor Measurement for Office Buildings," copyright 1977.

features that *distinguish* one building from another include location, rent, and services and amenities provided by the landlord. Analyzing a market, the property manager asks the question, "Given the location of the building, what rent levels, amenities, and services must I offer in order to attract tenants?" The answer depends on who demands space in that location and what existing or planned buildings compete for tenants (i.e., supply and demand). The other question is, "What does the owner want—maximum cash flow, prestige, or security of investment and long-term capital appreciation?" Depending on what the owner wants and what the market will support, the property manager reaches one of the following conclusions.

❏ **CONTINUING THE PRESENT USE.**   If analysis indicates that continuing the property's present use is the most likely road to achieving the owner's objectives and that substantial new investment in the property is not required, the property manager prepares a management program with an appropriate budget and a marketing plan.

❏ **REHABILITATION.**   If the property is suffering from curable physical depreciation (deferred maintenance), the property manager may propose a **rehabilitation** program, that is, a plan to restore the property to a satisfactory condition without changing its basic plan, style, or use. Rehabilitation could include painting, recarpeting, patching the parking lot, and replacing worn out gutters.

❏ **MODERNIZATION.**   Whereas rehabilitation cures physical depreciation, **modernization** cures functional depreciation. Modernization encompasses changes in style, design, and materials where changes are necessary to meet contemporary standards. Examples include installing central air conditioning in a retail store or office building, installing a modern kitchen in a residence, or adding amenities like a swimming pool to a motel. In general, modernization is justified from an economic point of view when anticipated increases in net operating income represent a reasonable return on cost.

When modernization involves changing the building's design, it is then known as *remodeling*.

❏ **CONVERSION.**   The most extreme change to a building is its **conversion** to another use. Conversion should always be considered as an alternative when a building returns insufficient cash flow owing to declining demand for the type of use it offers. Sometimes a decline in demand results from a change in neighborhood, as when a residential neighborhood gradually changes into a commercial one. (Local zoning ordinances, or their absence, will obviously have a powerful impact on such change.) Sometimes the change in demand results from trends nationwide. Once thriving commercial buildings in older central business districts across the country have declined in value and often stand vacant or only partly rented as a result of middle-class migration to the suburbs and the rise of regional shopping centers. Many former buildings in the inner city have been converted to professional offices, capitalizing on their proximity to banks, courts, and city government offices.

From an investor's point of view, conversion often has significant benefits over new construction. One is that older buildings frequently have extremely desirable locations. Another is that older buildings are often not only more soundly built but sometimes also offer unusual and attractive design features that can be turned into a competitive edge (like exposed brick walls and maple floors in old mill buildings converted to offices). Finally, an important impetus to conversion has been the trend toward preservation of historic buildings in general and in particular tax incentives (mainly tax credits) for modernizing many older buildings both with and without historic designation.

THE BUDGET   Whether a building is converted, rehabilitated, or kept in use as is, once operational it will require a **budget** as an essential part of its management program. The budget is an estimate of expected revenues and expenses for a fixed time period. It is used for two purposes: (1) to ensure that sufficient cash will be available for ordinary operating expenses as well as for capital replacements, mortgage amortization payments, and real estate taxes and (2) to act as a standard against which the performance of the property manager may be measured. Formats and line items vary, but the essentials of a budget are given in the following outline:

Gross Potential Income

(Less Vacancy and Collection Loss)

Gross Effective Income

(Real Estate Taxes)

(Fire and Extended Coverage Insurance)

(Utilities)

(Maintenance and Repair)

(Management)

(Reserve for Minor Replacements)

Net Operating Income

INCOME BEFORE DEBT SERVICE, INCOME TAXES, AND CAPITAL EXPENDITURES (NET OPERATING INCOME)

Estimated rental income is derived from the historical experience of the building as well as from market trends discerned by the property manager as discussed in Chapter 3 and again in the appraisal material. For example, if the current **market rent** for comparable space has risen above the **contract rent** currently being charged under existing leases, the property manager will project an increase in rental income as leases expire and space becomes available to re-rent. As noted earlier, the property manager is expected to keep current on rent levels charged for comparable space. (Note that the property manager, by virtue of his or her expertise, is an excellent source of information for a prospective purchaser establishing an investment *pro forma*.)

Expenses are sometimes divided between semifixed and controllable expenses. Semifixed expenses include real estate taxes, employment costs when fixed pursuant to a union contract, insurance premiums, and the like. (Note that these expenses still are often subject to some discretion. For example, real estate assessments can be challenged, and insurance premiums can be negotiated among different brokers. Nevertheless, for any given budget period they are usually fixed—thus, the term semifixed.) Controllable expenses are those over which the management has substantial discretion. Maintenance and repair (M&R) expenses are a good example, although here it should be noted that postponing such expenditures for any length of time can create serious operating deficiencies (the condition called deferred maintenance).

Net operating income, the income before debt service, income taxes, and capital expenditures, is what remains after estimated expenses are subtracted from projected rental income. Operating income as a percentage of gross income is a frequent yardstick for comparison among properties of the same type. (See Figure 11-1.)

PERFORMANCE MEASURE

When the period covered by the budget has actually elapsed, a comparison between the budget and the operating statement for that period shows whether there were significant variations and, if so, in what items. Often these variations are produced by circumstances beyond anyone's control. The burden, however, is on the property manager to explain why the budget has not been met. Very often, compensation of the property manager is tied to the budget. If the property manager "makes budget" or exceeds it, he or she may be entitled to additional compensation. Because the cost of management itself is one of the largest controllable costs in an income property, it is important that the owner be able to analyze the performance of the property manager.

A few years ago, most property records were on hand-kept ledgers, making periodic reports a time-consuming chore. Today property managers use microcomputers and enjoy the choice of several software packages designed specifically for various types of property management. (For more information on hardware and software options, check with the management associations listed at the end of this chapter.)

THE MANAGEMENT CONTRACT

An important aspect of the **management contract** to manage property is that it establishes an agency relationship between the manager and the owner. This agency relationship empowers the manager to perform duties with the assurance that as long as they are performed in good faith, the owner is legally bound by, and responsible for, the actions of the manager. As a result, it is important that the management contract be

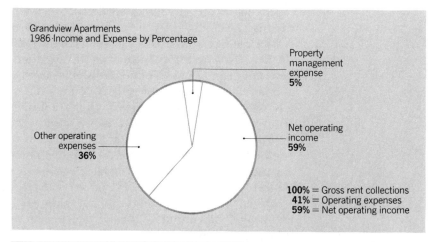

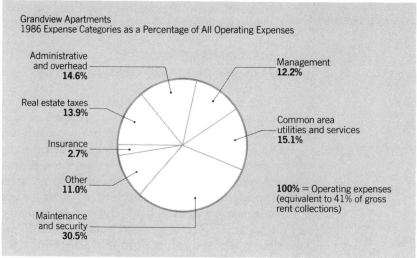

FIGURE 11-1   *Operating expenses*

carefully written and list the responsibilities and authority of the manager, including the following areas.

❑ **MANAGEMENT SERVICES.**   The manager is to be responsible for the physical condition of the property by preventing avoidable depreciation and tending to maintenance needs. The manager is also charged with collecting rent and other payments due the owner, providing utility and other services to the property users, and hiring employees and outside firms as necessary.

❑ **MANAGEMENT EMPLOYEES.**   The agreement may specify the number of employees and the job descriptions of each. The manager is to be responsible for the acts of each employee at the property site. Persons who handle money may need to be bonded.

❑ **AUTHORIZED EXPENDITURES.**   Expenditures by the manager should be limited to specified periodic charges, except in case of emergency. This protects the owner against large outlays without his or her knowledge or consent.

❑ **RECORDKEEPING AND NOTIFICATION.**   The agent is often expected to prepare an annual operating budget for each calendar or fiscal year and maintain financial records as the year progresses. The agent should inform the owner by a specified date each month of all collections and disbursements for the most recent period and should remit any balance due the owner.

❑ **INSURANCE COVERAGE.**   The agent's responsibility in this area should be spelled out.

❑ **ADVERTISING AND PROMOTION.**   Different properties require different degrees and types of advertising, and the management agreement should specify the agent's duties in this regard and who bears the cost of outside advertising.

❑ **DURATION OF THE CONTRACT.**   It is not a good idea for an owner to contract with a manager for an unspecified period. A definite period should be stipulated, with the contract then to continue until terminated by either party or extended for a defined period.

❑ **MANAGEMENT FEE.**   A property manager frequently works on a commission basis (e.g., 5 percent of gross income collected). However, a fixed fee may be payable, particularly when the management services require a relatively predictable amount of time (e.g., maintaining property records) and where an incentive for extraordinary effort is not deemed necessary by the owner. On the other hand, a service such as finding new tenants is one that calls for the exercise of discretion and good judgment and may involve intensive efforts. If a leasing commission is to be paid to the manager over and above the regular management fee, the contract should specify it. In addition, the manager may be entitled to fringe benefits and expense reimbursements.

ASSET/PROPERTY MANAGEMENT BECOMES MUCH MORE ENTREPRENEURIAL

As American industry in general has become more incentive-oriented, asset management is catching up with the other incentive-based real estate occupations (e.g., development and leasing). For example, Crow Companies residential group has made quality asset management a critical part of its long-term strategic plan. To attract and retain the best people, they offer the following program.

A talented, experienced manager will be assigned a market (e.g., greater Atlanta) with an exclusive on all Crow-owned properties. A management fee is paid to his group from these Crow properties which is just high enough to cover all the costs of the management operation. This manager's bonus is based on profits in his market.

The only way to make a profit is to (1) improve the operation of existing Crow-owned properties or (2) bring in new management business from other owners. If the manager becomes known as the best in the market, the number of properties under management increases and the manager's compensation can be every bit as attractive as that of a development partner.

MANAGEMENT ASSOCIATIONS

A number of professional and trade organizations exist in the field of real property management. The leading ones are described as follows.

INSTITUTE OF REAL ESTATE MANAGEMENT (IREM).

IREM[7] is an affiliate of the National Association of Realtors®. Individuals who seek to join must meet education and experience requirements. IREM offers two designations that are widely recognized in the real estate industry. A qualified individual may become a certified property manager (CPM) or accredited resident manager (ARM); a qualified management firm may be awarded the designation of Accredited Management Organization (AMO).

BUILDING OWNERS AND MANAGERS INSTITUTE (BOMA).

Operated by Building Owners and Managers Association International, the institute offers to those who successfully complete its management courses the professional designation of real property administrator (RPA). The Building Owners and Managers Institute specializes in office building management.

INTERNATIONAL COUNCIL OF SHOPPING CENTERS (ICSC).

ICSC specializes in retail property management and awards the designation of certified shopping center manager (CSCM) to those individuals who attend a series of courses and pass an examination.

---

[7]IREM *publishes* The Journal of Property Management *bimonthly. 430 N. Michigan Avenue, Chicago, Illinois 60611.*

SUMMARY   Property management is the foundation of asset management. It can often make a significant difference in the net cash flow from income property and consequently is an important variable when analyzing a property.

Management varies widely in its complexity based on the type of real estate and the size of the project. At one extreme, management of a single-family residence is least time consuming and complex and is often combined with the real estate brokerage function. At the other, property management in a large shopping center or office building is a full-time occupation. In hotels and motels, the service element is critically important and consequently makes good management even more valuable. Generally, the more services required and the more often space turns over, the higher the degree of management required.

The management contract is the key document defining the relationship between the managing agent and the property owner-principal. By virtue of the contract, the property manager acts as the owner's agent in satisfying the service demands of users (who lease space over time) and in seeing to it that the users perform their lease obligations, most notably the prompt payment of rent. Important steps in property management are preparing a management plan and preparing a budget.

IMPORTANT TERMS

Budget
Building Owners and Managers
  Association International
(BOMA)
Contract rent
Controllable influences on re-
  sidual cash flow
Conversion
Cost-of-living clause
Escalation clause
Institute of Real Estate Manage-
  ment (IREM)
International Council of Shop-
  ping Centers (ICSC)

Maintenance schedule
Management contract
Management plan
Market rent
Modernization
Nonraid clause
Pass-through
Percentage rent
Property management
Rehabilitation
Rentable area
Rent schedule
Resident manager
Space over time with services

REVIEW QUESTIONS

11.1   Why has property management often been an underrated function in the real estate industry?

11.2   What is the role of the management contract in specifying the relationship between the owner and the manager?

11.3   How are most property management fees determined?

11.4   List and discuss four important functions of the property manager.

11.5   What types of conflicts might arise between owners and managers of residential condominiums?

11.6   What is a nonraid clause? Under what conditions would it be included in the lease agreement?

11.7   Why is the tenant mix critically important to the successful management of a shopping center?

11.8   Would the lease associated with special-purpose industrial property tend to be long or short term? Why?

11.9   List and discuss some of the management activities associated with hotels and motels. Differentiate the management of a hotel from the management of a multitenant warehouse.

11.10   Why would a building be modernized by its owner? How is conversion different from modernization? When are changes like modernization or conversion justified?

ASSET MANAGEMENT: THE INSTITUTIONAL AND CORPORATE PERSPECTIVES

INTRODUCTION

The foundation of asset management (property management) was laid in Chapter 11; there we gave you the perspective of an individual property owner or a group of private investors in real estate. However, your understanding of asset management will be incomplete unless you are also familiar with the management goals and perspectives of two other very powerful players:

1. The institutional investor who manages a *portfolio* of properties to maximize returns and minimize *portfolio* risks.

2. The corporate owner, who manages real estate assets to achieve *corporate objectives*.

First, a property may be valued differently in a portfolio than in isolation. This is because whereas portfolio returns are simply a weighted average of the returns of the properties in the portfolio, portfolio risk is not usually a weighted average but depends on the covariance of the returns of the assets in the portfolio (as explained technically in Chapter 22). For this reason, institutional investment managers may employ leasing strategies that look suboptimal at the property level but are important to achieving overall portfolio objectives. Similarly, capital improvements may be accelerated or delayed based on portfolio needs. Second, in a corporate situation, earnings per share implications and corporate valuation methodologies may have an impact on how a property is managed. In both instances, the idea is to fit the management of the individual property to the client's needs as well as to marketplace and operating realities.

We begin this chapter with the portfolio concerns of institutional investors. As you read this material, please remember that such concerns are important for all types of investors, including lenders as indicated in

Box 12-1. The corporate perspective follows; it requires (beyond the appraisal material covered earlier in this text) some background in financial accounting and corporate finance. We recommend this background for all real estate players, along with architecture, engineering, sociology, political science, urban history, planning, marketing, and taxation; however, if financial accounting and corporate finance aren't your strong suit, you may want to skip Appendix 12. The concepts in the body of this chapter are essential, whereas the mechanics described in Appendix 12 are useful additions.

A BRIEF BACKGROUND ON INSTITUTIONAL REAL ESTATE INVESTMENT

In the early 1960s, European financial institutions were heavily involved in equity real estate investments and were developing considerable so-

12-1

STOCKS DROP SHARPLY ON REAL ESTATE FEARS

Fear of a bear market in real estate touched off a stock-market rout that drove prices of both big and little stocks sharply lower.

The Dow Jones Industrial Average tumbled 42.02 points to 2697.53, the first close below 2700 since late November. Over-the-counter stocks were hit even harder. The Nasdaq OTC Composite Index plunged 7.81 points, or 1.8%, to 436.03, the second biggest sell-off of the year after the Oct. 13 plunge.

The stock-market retreat sent some investors scurrying for the safety of government bonds, whose prices rose modestly. The yield on long-term Treasury bonds slid to the lowest level so far this year. Currency traders said the dollar's value yesterday reflected some of the stock market's woes, but the U.S. currency's moves weren't nearly as drastic as the stock market's plunge.

Analysts said a bearish article about real estate, both residential and commercial, in Barron's was the immediate cause of the stock market tumble. But they said it was merely the last straw in the mounting evidence that U.S. real estate is in trouble. New England banks have been suffering from bad real estate loans, the problems are spreading to the mid-Atlantic region, and even the superheated California market is showing signs of distress.

"The news has been getting progressively worse, and a lot of regional banks have high exposure to real estate and high-leverage transactions," said Kenneth Spence, director of the technical analysis group at Salomon Brothers. "We're seeing continued pressure on the financial stocks because of the deteriorating credit quality in those areas."

Source: The Wall Street Journal, Tuesday, December 19, 1989, p. C1, by Douglas R. Sease and Craig Torres, staff reporters of *The Wall Street Journal.*

<table>
<tr><td>

12-2

THE REASONS YOU DO NOT NEED (AND ARE NOT LIKELY TO DEVELOP) A GENERALIZED PARADIGM FOR REAL ESTATE

</td><td>

I. The local orientation of the markets.

II. The infrequent trading of individual properties.

III. The uniqueness and lack of comparability of individual assets.

IV. The importance of tax and financing considerations.

V. The relative lack of sophistication of investors.[a]

[a]Roulac (S. E. Roulac, "Can Real Estate Returns Outperform Common Stocks?," *Journal of Portfolio Management* (Winter 1976): 26–43) notes that securities markets became more efficient as institutional investors increased their level of participation and that increased efficiency should also come to the real estate market as these participants become more active.

</td></tr>
</table>

phistication. Here at home, things were simpler. U.S. institutions tended to stay with investments they were comfortable with, which did not include the real estate asset class dominated as it is by asymmetric information and heterogeneous products. As Steven Roulac later summarized, "real estate is inherently different" (see Box 12-2) and therefore is not likely to be understood as academics are coming to understand stocks and bonds. This left investment in real estate to individuals, who intuitively recognized the benefits of this asset class and did not require mathematical proof.

The young person directly out of an MBA program and in his first real estate position was counseled by the wise old master player: "Son, there are people who know real estate and people who don't know real estate." "But sir," replied the new initiate to real-world real estate, "what does it mean to 'know real estate'?" "Son, that comment implies that you don't know real estate and that's why we're letting you go."

This rejection was difficult to understand for the young person who had been taught mean-variance theory in school. He knew that investors wanted more return (a higher mean expected return) and less risk (a lower variance of expected mean returns). In fact, if the young person had gone to a leading institution, he would also have learned about Bill Sharpe, the patron saint of asset pricing, whose work developed mean-variance theory into the capital asset pricing model (CAPM)—the partially discredited (but still reigning) financial market paradigm.[1] Surely,

---

[1]*While Richard Roll's 1978 work has shown the CAPM to be "untestable" and numerous anomalies have been discovered, the only competing paradigm, Steven Ross's arbitrage pricing theory, is itself wanting in several respects (with regard to testability and practical application) and has failed to supplant the CAPM as the reigning capital market pricing paradigm. In fact, the current academic interest in option pricing theories can be traced in large part to the absence of a general market model that is not laden with anomalies.*

real estate was just one more asset that competed with stocks and bonds for the investor's attention.

Chapters 22 and 23 detail the math as well as the empirical evidence that has evolved over time as modern portfolio theory has been brought to bear on real estate. The bottom-line conclusion is that the real estate asset is a major part of the institutional investor's portfolio, and yet it is a unique part. Although real estate is one of the major capital market investment opportunities, it cannot, nor should be, treated exactly like a stock or a bond.

Because real estate is part of the institutional investor's portfolio, real estate investments are purchased to perform in a certain way. That is, they are purchased with the anticipation that they will add to the portfolio's expected return and the risk associated with that associated return. Certainly, all real estate is not alike, and investment managers have been very creative in segmenting the real estate market to produce subsets of the overall asset class. These different subsets within the real estate asset class have different performance characteristics relative to the rest of the real estate industry and to the stocks and bonds that investors currently hold in their portfolios.

Box 12-3 shows ten categories that one author has suggested to illustrate the range of possibilities for subsets within the real estate asset class. Each category is different from the other, having a different expected variance in returns and a different covariance of those returns with stocks and bonds. We include this illustration not because we believe it is the right categorization of the real estate asset, but because it indicates how people are thinking in the marketplace. The overall real estate markets are being segmented so as to produce groupings of real estate that have attractive characteristics when combined with a stock and bond portfolio.

Our interest here, however, is not in the financial aspects of why institutional investors want to hold real estate. This is a topic for Part 7. Rather, our concern here is with understanding how the desire of institutional investors to own real estate affects the basic property management functions described in Chapter 11.

CHANGES BROUGHT TO PROPERTY MANAGEMENT BY INSTITUTIONAL INVESTORS

Institutional investors have what are known as asset managers. Thus, an individual working for a large life insurance company, an "asset manager," is often charged with managing the property managers, who in fact manage the individual properties. Asset managers are typically MBAs or well-trained undergraduates who have not only expertise in real estate but also general training in all the major business disciplines—finance, marketing, production, and management. Asset managers make sure that the property managers manage the properties in such a way that collectively they fulfill the portfolio needs of the institutional investors.

12-3 AN EARLY LOOK AT NEW DIVERSIFICATION STRATEGIES	REAL ESTATE INVESTMENT STRATEGIES
CATEGORY NAME	DISTINGUISHING CHARACTERISTICS
*Oil sensitive	All properties located in Texas, Louisiana, Oklahoma, and Colorado.
*Trade deficit reduction expectation	Industrial properties (both warehouse and industrial-office-showroom) in counties with a greater than average concentration in manufacturing income on the logic that something other than services must be exported some day.
*Players' world	Properties that are not in the CBD, are less than five years old, are in counties with faster than median growth, and are not industrial warehouse on the logic that the "big pops" for new participants draw the "players" to their properties.
*Life-style play	Garden Office Buildings (both office, three stories or less, and industrial-office-showroom) in counties with populations under 1 million. Everyone wants to live in a "human scale."
*Distribution	Industrial buildings (warehouse) located within one mile of the interstate highway in counties with above-mean wholesale income.
*Yuppieland	All retail with less than 250,000 square feet in counties with income per capita greater than average—the logic that the "me" generation shops in specialty malls.
*Tomorrowland	All properties located in greater Los Angeles.
*New South	All properties in Atlanta, Charlotte, and Raleigh–Durham.
*Government based	All office and industrial-office-showroom properties located in counties where government income per capita is above average.
*Zoning protected	All properties in Boston and San Francisco where zoning has *for several years* reduced overbuilding by constraining supply.

From the beginning, institutional investment requires more reporting. The budgets described in the preceding chapter are typically more exacting when an institutional investor is involved. They are also consistent across properties so that the individual budgets may be easily aggregated at the portfolio level. These budgets are not only used for planning, but are also used both at the property and particularly at the portfolio level for evaluating performance over time.

With a detailed budget available at the portfolio level, repairs for individual properties may be planned so as to have the optimal effect at the portfolio level. For example, if the portfolio's objective is to minimize the variance of return, then repairs are often spread over time between the different properties so that not all repairs are being done in any particular quarter.

On the marketing side, it is now quite common for the asset manager to tell the individual property manager (or leasing agent) who is handling the property to focus on certain types of tenants. Often at the portfolio level, diversification is desired by type of tenant. Thus, prospective tenants are categorized by SIC (standard industrial classification) code, and the asset manager assures that the ongoing leasing at the different properties produces not all lawyers or all bankers but the desired mix across types of tenants.

The length of leases and renewal options are also tailored to achieve the desired portfolio result. If the particular portfolio of real estate assets is intended to provide inflation protection for the institutional investor, then the asset manager may direct the individual property manager to structure new leases accordingly. Hence, the lease negotiated at the local level may give away something in terms of current rent per square foot in order to obtain a CPI (Consumer Price Index) escalator provision. How is this different from individual ownership of the real estate? In the individual's situation, the owner typically looks to the tenant to see what the tenant needs and then determines the lease structure that will provide the highest present value for the property individually. With institutional investors, the lease that appears optimal at the property level may sometimes not produce the highest present value to the overall portfolio. Hence, leases are negotiated which in isolation do not appear to be optimal given market conditions and tenant desires. It is the asset manager's job to fit those market conditions and particular tenant desires to the needs of the institutional investor.

With institutional investors, more money is usually available for major repositionings when such repositionings appear attractive. Relative to individuals, institutions have deep pockets. For example, when an individual investor owns a shopping center, it may be difficult to reposition by buying out one of two weak anchor tenants and spending a great deal of money at the same time to refurbish the exterior appearance. However, institutional investors usually don't have this liquidity problem. If it makes good financial sense to buy out a weak tenant or spend more money on the exterior, the cash is generally available.

Another difference between traditional property management and asset management involves tenant relations. Recall that in Chapter 11 we talked about the importance of the property manager staying close to the tenants and knowing how the space over time with associated services was meeting their needs. This is, of course, still important if the property is one of many in an institutional investor's portfolio. However, in the portfolio case, not only can the individual property manager stay in close contact with the tenant in the building, but also the asset manager can maintain a macrolevel relationship with the individual store manager's boss or boss's boss. Thus, if Prudential owns an office building, the asset manager will be sure that the property manager is talking directly with the tenant in the building. At the same time, the asset manager will ensure that someone from the Prudential will call on the home office of that same tenant. Thus, the local property manager may be calling on the AT&T office manager, while another representative of the Prudential is calling on the home office of AT&T to determine the global space needs of the corporation. With institutional investment, it is possible to touch the tenant not just in the space, but in the home office of the tenant as well.

Institutional investment has also brought a quicker sharing of successes in one part of the country with other parts of the country. Because institutional investors tend to be more diversified geographically, they are in constant touch with different markets. When a new advertising strategy works or a new way is found to provide better security, these innovations tend to spread very rapidly. With an investment manager managing property managers in many regions, it is easier to effect change when new opportunities are seen.

Finally, it's important to note that with institutional investment, everything becomes more public. Traditionally in real estate, transactions were conducted by individuals and were not "public" (except insofar as deeds were recorded and, in some places, recorded deeds were summarized in the local newspapers). Although institutional investors do not broadcast their transactions, and there is not the kind of reporting required of corporations by the Securities and Exchange Commission, it is true that institutional investors have far more public disclosure requirements than individual investors do. Thus, one benefit of institutional investment is an outflow of more accurate and more detailed information about real estate transactions, which enables all of us to learn more about how real estate operates as both an investment and as a major component of wealth in our society.

THE CORPORATE PERSPECTIVE

History is a good starting point. In June 1988, the market capitalization of listed securities in the United States was approximately $2.3 trillion,[2] with real estate believed to comprise over 25 percent of that value.[3]

[2]*Market capitalization from* Anatomy of World Markets, *Goldman Sachs, September 1988.*

[3]*Zeckhouser and Silverman (S. Zeckhouser and R. Silverman,* Harvard Real Estate Survey *(National Association of Corporate Real Estate Executives, 1981) surveyed major American corporations concerning their real estate holdings and found that buildings and land owned by corporations that were not primarily in the real estate business typically accounted for 25 percent or more of the firm's assets. Veale updated this survey in 1987 and concluded that very little had changed in the six years since the Zeckhouser and Silverman study.*

Although real estate plays an important role on the corporation's balance sheet, the researchers Zeckhouser and Silverman found that only 40 percent of American firms clearly and consistently evaluate the performance of their real estate and only 20 percent manage their real estate for profit (i.e., try to match or exceed the rate of return they could achieve through alternative investments). Instead, corporations have traditionally treated real estate as a necessary cost of operations and, after careful analysis of the initial lease versus buy decision, have entered purchased real estate on the firm's balance sheet and thereafter largely ignored it. Given the magnitude of corporate real estate in both absolute and relative terms, the lack of management attention has been (and to a considerable extent continues to be) a serious problem.

The normal sequence of events involved in a corporate real estate decision is as follows:

1. The corporation decides on a need for additional space. This is usually *part* of a larger capital budgeting decision tied to *operations*. Traditionally, this operating decision is itself separate from the related financing decision.

2. The space need is passed on to the corporation's real estate group for implementation. In corporations with higher level estate officers, the real estate group has been actively involved in the spacial aspects of the original capital budgeting decision.

3. Major builder/developers and/or real estate brokers are contacted about the need, and these professionals are hired to perform their service. This involves an investment decision (via discounted cash flow analysis), but with a focus on flexibility and the residual position of the corporate investor. Important spin-off issues involve reputation, major client relations, and potential peripheral development profits.

4. Either the real estate professional or the corporation brings in an investment banking firm to advise on financing. There are a few basic alternatives with innumerable bells and whistles as shown in Box 12-4.

5. The group then selects a financing alternative that best meets all *stated objectives*. Inevitably, without the kind of model described in Appendix 12A, this final selection will be an apples versus oranges comparison with no good way to price alternative risks or to adjust alternative costs.

6. The real estate is then entered on the firm's balance sheet and largely ignored.

Box 12-5 lists some of the possible objectives a corporation might pursue through the more exacting management of its corporate real estate after

12-4	TYPE OF INSTRUMENT	ACTIONS	KEY ISSUES
FINANCING ALTERNATIVES	1. Conventional-investor owned, corporate leasee, a bank construction loan, insurance company permanent financing	Swap for fixed rate prefund permanent, joint venture equity with tenant or long-term lender	Length of lease, maturity of debt
	2. Special-purpose corporation for financing, ownership flexible, but the corporation takes the risk through a master lease	Rate commercial paper or domestic bond depending on maturity preference (backed by AAA letter of credit), privately placed lease payment bonds, construction period tranches	Long-term financial and operating flexibility
	3. Some form of zero coupon used to advance the realization of the expected appreciation	Combine lease payment bond with first mortgage	Size of residual and related risk
	In all the basic approaches:		Returns (and risks) to all three participants considering both current results and the expected residual values

the initial acquisition and financing decision. As real estate moves into the mainstream of corporate financial management, a vehicle is needed for the systematic pursuit of these objectives. This point is especially relevant today since firms now enjoy additional flexibility in managing their real estate holdings owing to (1) the creation of new financial instruments tailored to real estate and (2) the increased liquidity created by the presence of more institutional and foreign buyers in the market.

With increased flexibility, the well-managed firm should view real estate decisions from a combined capital budgeting and corporate financing perspective *on an ongoing basis*. As part of this endeavor, here we identify the potential gains from more active management of real estate and highlight some of the problems and issues. A formal model of the corporate real estate decision process is presented in Appendix 12.

12-5 OBJECTIVES OF CORPORATE REAL ESTATE MANAGEMENT[a]	1. Cash generation (but the related costs are, again, in apples and oranges unless a formal model is used).
	2. Takeover prevention (real estate-financed to real estate-motivated takeovers must be considered).
	3. More effective utilization of the tax laws.
	4. Minimizing agency cost (shareholder/bondholder and shareholder/manager).
	5. The use of real estate financing as a market signal.
	6. Playing the local real estate market by using the comparative advantage generated by the corporation's long-time horizon.
	7. Maintaining flexibility given the firm's current and expected space needs. Flexibility is an important consideration while pursuing Objectives 1–6.

[a]Objectives beyond the obvious desire to maximize the value of the firm.

The interaction of real estate with many aspects of the firm's operations and financing decisions creates a level of complexity which requires careful analysis. Our initial approach to the task is to develop the logic for a "holistic" corporate valuation model.

THEORETICAL SUPPORT FOR A CORPORATE REAL ESTATE VALUATION MODEL

Lack of active management of real estate assets, along with changes in the environment surrounding corporate-owned real estate, may result in significant value that is undetected by managers and investors alike. The potential hidden value in real estate is a function of (1) changes in capital market conditions, (2) changes in the firm's prospects, (3) changes in how the firm uses its real estate, (4) tax and accounting changes, and (5) changes in factors affecting the firm's agency costs. Specifically, changes in the capital markets affect real estate values via changes in market capitalization rates on real estate relative to those of other assets.[4] Changes in a firm's operating prospects resulting either from changes in return prospects or changes in risk exposure have a similar impact. The

---

[4]If required returns on real estate fall relative to required returns on other assets (as they have over the past several years due to an increased demand for investment-grade real estate by foreign and institutional investors), firms may find superior alternative investments.

expected return on real estate may justify ownership (as opposed to leasing) of real estate in periods when the firm's operating prospects are poor, but this relationship can reverse itself when the firm's prospects improve. The magnitude of the value increment created by changes in the use of a firm's real estate obviously depends on how much value the new use adds to the property. Changes in tax laws in 1984 and 1986 (which are discussed in more detail in Chapters 17–19) had a major impact on real estate values, and recent accounting changes embodied in the Financial Accounting Standards (FAS) No. 94 and No. 98 have added to this impact.[5]

The potential to increase the firm's value (in addition to the threat of takeover) suggests that firms should consistently review the performance and value of their real estate. Appraisal models of real estate value have been around for a long time as shown in Chapters 10–12, and these models do a satisfactory job of determining the market value of real estate *in isolation*. Knowing the value of real estate in isolation is not sufficient, however. A corporation must understand how its real estate holdings are affecting its *total* market to determine the best way to utilize this asset, and this requires a valuation model of real estate *within* the corporate setting. (For an examination of that valuation model, see Appendix 12.)

WHAT DOES THE HEIGHTENED CORPORATE AWARENESS IMPLY FOR THE MANAGEMENT OF THE REAL ESTATE ASSET?

First, heightened corporate awareness implies that a major new career path exists in corporate America. Corporations need asset managers who see things from the user's perspective. Just as institutional investors need asset managers to coordinate basic property management with their portfolio needs, corporate America needs asset managers to coordinate basic property management functions with the user's need to fulfill space requirements at the lowest net cost. From the corporate perspective, the asset manager must know accrual accounting in directing the on-site property manager, and he or she must have a system that brings the budget at the property level all the way through to its impact on the corporation's earnings per share, just as the budget in the institutional investor's case had to work its way all the way through the property's portfolio impact.

Corporate incentive systems will now have an impact on how the real estate asset is financed and on the timing of how it is managed. As we

---

[5]*FASB No. 94 requires consolidation of most real estate subsidiaries, potentially causing a major change in the firm's debt/equity position. FASB No. 98 curtails the use of sale–leaseback transactions by limiting the ability of a corporation to retain control of real estate while receiving off-balance-sheet treatment for the asset—unless the buyer has truly assumed the major risk position. These accounting changes, coming on the heels of the 1984 and 1986 tax law changes, clearly have the potential to affect the optimal structure of many corporate real estate financings.*

argued in the preceding section, the corporate fixed asset manager must look at the corporation's space needs and come up with an optimal financing plan. The corporation's space needs can at times be best met by leasing and at other times by ownership. Leveraging either position may sometimes be appropriate. Certainly, if the corporation owns the space, the timing of major repairs and extensive renovations will have to be sensitive to earnings per share. This is completely analogous to the institutional investor timing certain property-level functions to fit portfolio needs.

The IBM model may become common for many corporations. IBM in its major office towers has followed a policy of owning half of the building (jointly with a development partner) and occupying half of the same building. This is an effective way to provide for needed corporate space while at the same time making a real estate investment. As the major user of the space, IBM's investments are never vacant, and IBM can time the sale of the project to maximize proceeds. As the 1980s closed, we saw this strategy work very effectively in the Atlanta market, where the IBM office tower (50 percent owned and 50 percent occupied by IBM) was sold when IBM felt the market had peaked and when the company could use the related earnings.

In a world where most real estate product is oversupplied, it is only natural that the institutional investor will look to the corporation as a source of "occupied" investment real estate. Similarly, in a world that is ever more competitive, corporations will look to institutions to finance their real estate to lower overall financial costs. Thus, a natural marriage can be expected between the institutional investor, who may wish to own more equity real estate to maximize its portfolio position, and the corporation, which is often the end user of the space and which must provide itself with space at the lowest possible cost.

If such a marriage is to occur, then both construction and on-site property management must be more flexible. The corporation will often find that the institution does not want to own a huge project in one place and that building two or three more market-sized buildings will allow it to finance the properties more easily. Similarly, manufacturing space needs to be tailored to a more general audience, that is, be less specialized and more flexible, if this new source of financing is to be used. Clearly, much corporate physical space is special-purpose and doesn't fit this model. However, much more space could be made "market sensitive" to allow the corporation more financing flexibility. The asset manager is the one who must ensure that the on-site property management is capable of providing what the corporation needs from general-purpose space. As a corporation seeks to maximize financial opportunities by using more general-purpose space, the property management job becomes more complex. (See Box 12-6.)

12-6

THE ROLE OF THE REAL ESTATE PROFESSIONAL IN CORPORATE PLANNING AND STRATEGY IMPLEMENTA-TION

Although the corporate real estate manager's function is frequently considered a "piece of cake," his [or her] position has significant challenges and opportunities. In addition to being a good "business man or woman," the manager must also be thoroughly knowledgeable in real estate as a business and understand how it affects corporate needs and requirements. Many companies do not recognize the profit potential in their real estate assets. In the past, most have considered real estate only a necessity in carrying out their basic business rather than as an opportunity in itself to maximize the return on these assets while still meeting basic corporate requirements.

Historically, the job of the corporate real estate manager was to negotiate the purchase or sale of properties and the leasing or subleasing of space requested by corporate or operating division managements. Today it is becoming increasingly apparent that real estate planning should be an integral part of overall business planning because lead times are long. Research has shown that even something as simple as leasing office space can take as long as 18 months from identifying the needs to occupying the space if the location has to be established and extensive renovation is required. Total property development, when rezoning is required, can take as long as four years before the building is ready for occupancy.

The corporate real estate department needs to be involved in the strategic and corporate planning processes in order to minimize delays and maximize profit opportunities. Timely actions must be taken so that the facilities required will be ready when needed. Actions should be deliberate and not afterthoughts. If it subsequently turns out that the facility is not required, good facility decisions can usually be reversed, frequently at a profit.

Today the corporate real estate manager has four functions: (1) planning, as it relates to corporate business plans; (2) consulting, to provide the real estate expertise required to meet corporate objectives; (3) either coordinating or implementing real estate decisions taken by the corporation; and (4) acting as steward for the corporation's real estate assets once they have been acquired.

The planning process should begin with close cooperation with the various operating divisions to help project the facilities required by their business plans. These groups need to quantify how much space and what kinds of spaces are needed, both initially and in the future. This requires knowing how new technology affects the numbers of people and the facilities themselves. The business planners also need to appreciate the costs and extra time required to provide such special facilities as laboratories, clean rooms, and environmental controls. Furthermore, to be able to evaluate the economics of their various alternatives, these divisions need information on the availability and cost of labor, utilities, transportation, parking, housing, schools, and so on. Plans for acquiring new space should be circulated through the corporation to ensure that there are not already other company facilities that could satisfy the projected needs. This, in turn, requires an inventory and an analysis of all existing corporate facilities.

In helping to integrate divisional plans into the overall corporate plan, the corporate real estate manager should serve as the corporate planners' real estate consultant. He or she advises on the characteristics and trends of the various real estate markets in which the corporation either operates or wishes to operate in the future. He should also provide expertise on such things as lease versus buy–build decisions, the intricacies of projected cash flows, and the probable residual values of the various corporate real estate assets involved.

Once the corporate plan has been approved, the role of the corporate real estate manager shifts to implementation and coordination of the various activities required. As the implementer, the real estate manager carries out his traditional function as negotiator for the purchase or leasing of facilities. As such, he must be knowledgeable in real estate finance, tax, and law. He must know what each local market offers in terms of rent abatement, tenant allowances, free parking, rent escalation, and so on. Another example of this type of activity is the handling of partially utilized or **surplus facilities.** Depending on corporate objectives and the relative economics, it may be preferable to lease the building rather than sell it. When a facility is partially occupied, it may be advantageous to sell the building to another party with the provision of leasing back the space currently required.

There are also the purchase and sale of land. When acquiring property for projected or immediate company needs, the corporate real estate manager must realize that such purchases should often be handled through a "secret agent." The various sellers may inflate land costs when the buyer is known to them. It may prove profitable to assemble and rezone a larger amount of land than the company needs for itself. By such an **assemblage,** the basic value of the raw land can frequently be doubled, even without further improvements.

When it comes time to dispose of the surplus portion of the property, the real estate manager must also be knowledgeable in a number of specialized areas. He must recognize that, in order to protect his long-term capital gain on the improved property, he cannot sell it in small parcels without being considered a "dealer" and subject to ordinary income tax. He must also be familiar with the advantages of 1031 exchanges and installment sales aimed at deferring income taxes.

As a coordinator, the corporate real estate manager is frequently involved with the master planning of the building site, the design of the building and its construction, or the design and fit-out of an existing building. He must know how to work with architectural and engineering firms who do the site master planning and building design. He must coordinate the work of the various contractors in the field during the construction of the facility. The local project manager is responsible for handling the many problems encountered each day, but it is the responsibility of the real estate manager to handle those of a broader corporate nature. Both are responsible for the overall project budget and seeing that it is not overrun.

Finally, there are the corporate real estate stewardship function and the necessary auditing that it requires. The real estate manager must stay up to date on the activities at the various operating divisions and keep abreast of changes in their projected requirements, both increases and decreases.

Today the corporate real estate manager is recognized as having many functions to perform. He or she must be a true professional and not just someone who has been given a temporary assignment on the way to another job in the company. There will be increasing pressure to use corporate real estate assets as efficiently as possible. Many companies have closed outmoded plants and sold them, and others are thinking of selling existing facilities and leasing them back as a means of raising working capital. Others realize that there may be a new boom in real estate and, with it, the need to be able to turn their real estate assets into cash or to make other advantageous deals.

Source: Business Space Resources Ltd., Seattle, Washington.

SUMMARY

In Chapter 11, we looked at the basic property management functions. In Chapter 12, we have looked at two major players in the real estate game who affect how a property is managed. Nothing in this chapter changed the basic logic of Chapter 11. It is still critically important to manage well so that the space over time with certain services provides what tenants need. What we have shown here is that asset management goes a step beyond, to adjusting the on-site property management so that the property performs well for an owner who holds this property as one in a portfolio.

From the user's side, asset management is also necessary. Corporations have new opportunities to use their real estate, which requires that on-site design and property management be adjusted if the corporation is to achieve the maximum possible return from its real estate.

IMPORTANT TERMS

Agency cost
Assemblage
Asset management
Capital budgeting
Capital markets
Corporate financing
Corporate owner
Diversification strategies
Frank Russell Company (FRC)
Incentive systems
Institutional investor

Investment banking firm
National Council of Real Estate
    Investment Fiduciaries
    (NCREIF)
Portfolio returns
Portfolio risk
Securities and Exchange
    Commission
Standard Industrial Classification
    (SIC)
Surplus facilities
Takeover

REVIEW QUESTIONS

12.1   What is asset management?

12.2   How do you define portfolio risk?

12.3   How do agency costs affect corporate asset management?

12.4   Who are the larger U.S. (global) institutional investors?

12.5   How are corporate financing and corporate capital budgeting related in a real estate context?

12.6   How have recent tax law changes affected institutional real estate investment?

12.7   How can real estate assets be used in corporate takeovers?

12.8   What is the purpose of NCREIF?

12.9   What do investment bankers typically do for the corporate real estate officer?

12.10 What are the primary responsibilities of the corporate real estate officer?

CORPORATE VALUATION OF REAL ESTATE[1]

Techniques for valuing real estate separately from the remaining assets of the firm—the normal appraisal process—are well known. To value real estate within the context of the firm as a whole (and thereby properly account for interactions between real estate valuation, accrual accounting, and corporate valuation parameters) requires a comprehensive corporate valuation model that explicitly recognizes (and separately values) a firm's real estate holdings. Figure A12-1 presents the basic structure of such a model.

Valuing a corporation in this manner exposes the interactions of the corporation's real estate holdings with the firm's overall financial structure. Real estate is shown to affect the cost of equity, cost of debt, debt capacity, systematic risk, and the book to market value ratio of the corporation. While it is not always obvious what the direction or magnitude of the changes in these attributes will be, this model clearly points out the minimum information that the market needs to value a firm independent of its real estate holdings.

BASIC DCF METHODOLOGY

Valuing an unlevered flow using the discounted cash flow (DCF) methodology is straightforward: cash flows expected in the future are discounted at a rate that reflects both the time value of money and the operating or business risk of the flows.[2] When leverage is introduced, the

---

[1]This material is taken from an article "Modeling the Corporate Real Estate Decision" by Mike Miles, John Pringle, and Brian Webb. The Journal of Real Estate Research, *Volume 4, Number 3, Fall 1989.*

[2]There are at least four different ways to apply standard discounted cash flow techniques to the valuation of either financial or real assets. Each of these approaches uses a different discount rate applied to a different stream of cash flows. The most widely used by corporate America in the evaluation of capital investments is the weighted average cost of capital (WACC) approach. WACC values operating cash flows at a calculated discount rate and then subtracts the value of debt to determine the

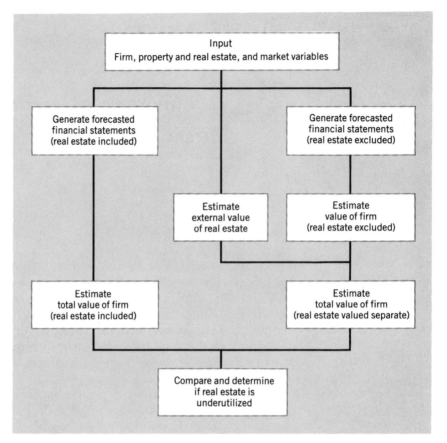

FIGURE A12-1   *Model of Corporate Valuation with Real Estate Explicitly Considered*

valuation problem becomes more complex, for the process must then account for financial leverage and interest deductibility in addition to operating risk.

When a firm owns real property, valuation takes on yet another degree of complexity as real estate is different than other corporate assets from an accounting tax, and appreciation/depreciation aspect.

market value of equity. A second methodology is called the equity-residual (ER) approach. This technique has been used in evaluating firms as well as individual projects. Under the ER methodology, the net cash flows to equity are valued after all debt service is subtracted. Two other approaches are less widely used. These are Stewart Myers' adjusted present value approach and a variation on the WACC technique suggested by Arditti and Levy. The WACC approach is described and utilized here. See any standard finance textbook for derivation of, and examples of the use of, the WACC methodology. For a technical discussion and critique of the strengths and weaknesses of WACC, see Myers (S. Myers, Interactions of Corporate Financing and Investment Decisions—Implications for Capital Budgeting, Journal of Finance *(March 1974), 1–25) and Miles and Ezzell (J. A. Miles and J. R. Ezzell, The Weighted Average Cost of Capital, Perfect Capital Markets and Project Life: A Clarification,* Journal of Financial and Quantitative Analysis *(September 1980), 719–30). See Chambers, Harris, and Pringle for a detailed conversion of the four methods.*

In recognition of the potential for hidden value in company-owned real estate, a thorough financial analysis must specifically address the individual value of the firm's real estate and incorporate the financing alternatives inherent in the real estate. This is of particular importance because the degree of financial latitude implicit in real estate is different from one firm to another. The next part of this section expands on this notion by separating the value of the firm into two distinct components: the value of the operating cash flows and the value of the real property. Each of these components is independently evaluated with consideration given to whether their separation substantially alters the riskiness of either in isolation. Unless you are a rather unusual human being, you are going to find the next few pages "heavy." Read them looking for two things: (1) how finance people value assets (it will make the real estate valuation methodologies developed in this text look simple and intuitively appealing), and (2) how a corporate chief financial officer whose bonus was driven by such concerns might make "unusual" decisions.[3] If you like this kind of number crunching, then follow the footnotes. They will give you enough references to model your favorite corporation's real estate decisions.

VALUING A FIRM

Consider the following hypothetical example in which privately held Alpha Manufacturing Company is being evaluated as an acquisition target by Omega Corporation. The problem at hand is to determine the value to Omega of Alpha's equity.[4]

A check of beta coefficients for comparable public companies might suggest a relevant market beta for Alpha.[5] Using publicly available data (as shown in the Atlantic Richfield example that follows) for the bond rate and market risk premium yields an equity capitalization rate for Alpha, as follows:[6]

$$K_e = \text{Risk-free rate} + \text{Market risk premium} \times \text{Beta}$$

[3]*The finance literature refers to the problem of corporate managers acting in less than the shareholders' best interest as "agency cost." Several useful references are found in this Appendix.*

[4]*For simplicity, it is assumed that there will be neither positive operating synergies in the combined firm (such as those that might result from previously overlapping distribution systems) nor negative organizational reactions to a merger (culture clashes, for example).*

[5]*Betas for many public companies can be obtained from the Value Line Investment Survey. The market portfolio used by Value Line in calculating its beta coefficients contains firms with financial leverage in their capital structures. For reasons of consistency, levered betas and levered market risk premiums are assumed throughout this Appendix.*

[6]*This presentation used the capital asset pricing model which has been the primary model in corporate finance textbooks since the early 1970s. It has come under increasing criticism from academics (see Roll, 1977) and recently has been seriously questioned in regulatory rate of return testimony (see ATT Divestiture FCC Docket 84–800). A more forward-looking alternative is to estimate the risk premium from a composite of analysts' forecasts (see Harris, 1986). Since derivation of the proper cost of capital is not the primary concern here, the CAPM methodology is followed. Note, however, that the use of analysts' forecasts to determine K_e is perfectly consistent with this overall presentation and would have no effect on the results shown later in this Appendix beyond the implications of using a different K_e.*

Assuming that Omega's management has determined the appropriate financing mix for the acquisition,[7] the weighted average cost of capital (WACC) is easily calculated using an estimate of the forward tax rate (T).

The WACC takes into account three factors: operating risk, financing mix, and tax deductibility of interest. Since financing mix and interest deductibility are accounted for in the discount rate, the WACC should be applied to Alpha's expected after-tax *operating* cash flows for a period of years, with interest excluded completely.

The terminal value for the cash flow stream must also be calculated.[8] The nominal perpetuity approach to estimating terminal value is straightforward and is the method normally used.[9] Starting with expected earnings before interest and taxes (EBIT), in the final year of the estimated period, we first multiply by 1-T to account for the tax liability on the operating flow. Assuming (1) that the flow is a perpetuity in nominal terms, (2) that depreciation is reinvested to cover capital expenditure requirements, and (3) that there is no additional investment in working capital, then cash flows from operations for all future years will be constant. Valuing this flow at the WACC gives a terminal value for the operating flows.

After using the WACC to discount the operating flows, Alpha's interest-bearing debt at time *t* must be subtracted to determine the equity value of the firm. Note that the *market value* of the debt, rather than its book value, should be subtracted.

VALUING THE REAL ESTATE OPTION

A look at Alpha's fixed assets might reveal that the firm owns its headquarters building. By looking first at the office building as a separate asset and valuing it in an unlevered state, we begin to see the potential for hidden value in the real estate. It is hidden not because it is hard to find on the balance sheet, but because its effect is not specifically considered in the firm valuation methodology outlined in the previous section. In fact, most financial analysts estimating a firm's earnings do not consider operating or financing options inherent in the firm's real estate,

---

[7]For a theoretical discussion of optimal capital structure, see Copeland and Weston (T. E. Copeland and J. F. Weston. Financial Theory and Corporate Policy. Reading, Mass.: Addison-Wesley, third edition 1988). In practical terms, the optimal capital structure is a function of the tradeoff between the lower after-tax cost of debt (interest, unlike dividends, being tax deductible) and the increased risk of insolvency as the required debt service payment is increased with increased debt. Theoretically, the value of K_d used to calculate the WACC should be the interest rate applicable to Alpha.

[8]For a practical application of this discussion of terminal values, see Table A12-3.

[9]To treat the terminal flow as a perpetuity in real terms raises some potentially tricky questions in dealing properly with debt flows.

mainly because they do not have access to the necessary information. This would not be a serious problem if all firms had the same proportionate option, but clearly, that is not the case. Some firms have great flexibility in their real estate, whereas others have practically none.

The estimated future sale price might be derived by capitalizing (more detail is found in Chapters 6–8) the last-year net operating income (NOI). Note that NOI is defined here as EBDIT (earnings before depreciation, interest, and taxes). The capitalization rate is empirical and not derivable theoretically. It is simply the typical ratio of NOI to market value for a local sample of real estate sales.

It should be noted that the general-purpose nature of the office building in this example greatly facilitates a transaction. With special-purpose buildings, an outside investor is less likely to see any appreciation potential.[10]

The operating flows are discounted at the required pretax return for unlevered real estate. This rate can be estimated from the mean DCF return actually realized on large national samples of properties. It can be calculated by relating ending market value plus cash flows received to beginning market value. Such a rate is analogous to the Ibbotson–Sinquefield data on common stock returns, both in its method of computation and in that it is post-corporate (nonexistent in this case), pre-personal tax. This rate will exceed the NOI capitalization rate for the same reason that market-required rates of return on common stocks typically exceed earnings/price ratios. That is, the capitalization rate is an earnings multiplier, whereas the discount rate is a total return figure.[11]

Note carefully that the discount rate is derived from *historical data*.[12] Using this figure requires the same leap of faith required to use the Ibbotson–Sinquefield data—namely, an assumption that market risk premiums will remain about the same in the future as in the past. It may often be advisable to adjust the historical data up or down to reflect current conditions; or, as in the corporate situation, we could use analysts' forecasts of future real estate returns such as those now available from both Salomon Brothers and Goldman Sachs.

---

[10]*If a refinancing is undertaken using special-purpose real estate, then the investor will be relying heavily on the corporate seller's promised lease payments. This presents difficult problems from valuation and tax standpoints. From the valuation perspective, an appraiser would have to estimate a residual value at the end of the lease period, which could prove difficult if the next most logical use were not readily apparent.*

[11]*As a comparison, in December 1987 the market RRR on the Standard and Poor's 500 stock index was about 14.5 percent (long-term government rate of 8.0 percent plus Ibbotson average historic risk premium), whereas the earnings/price ratio was 6 to 7 percent. The RRR includes an expected growth component, whereas the e/p ratio does not.*

[12]*The Russell-NCREIF Property Index returns, which are often used to estimate total returns for real estate, do involve the use of appraisals. For an empirical comparison of these figures with corresponding sales prices, see Cole, Guilkey, and Miles (R. Cole, D. Guilkey, and M. Miles. An Assessment of the Reliability of Commercial Appraisals.* Appraisal Journal *(July 1986) and Appraisals, Unit Values, and Investor Confidence in Real Estate Portfolios.* Real Estate Review *(Winter 1987)).*

Regardless of whether the buyer finances the purchase in some part with a mortgage, the corporation's capital structure will be affected by any real estate disposition. Since the real estate previously served as indirect collateral for corporate debt, it is logical to assume that part of the proceeds from sale will be used to reduce corporate debt. We could assume that the market values the real estate at its current value and that the firm is at its optimal debt ratio. In this case, we would reduce the corporate debt by the appropriate amount of mortgage debt (the optimal financing ratio for the property standing alone, for example, 80 percent of the market value of the real estate) and continue to use the original weighted average cost of capital.

Alternatively, if the market were totally ignorant of the real estate's value, we might reduce corporate debt by the book value change times the target percentage debt in the capital structure. In a world of imperfect information (i.e., the market does not have sufficient information to price the real estate), corporate debt might be reduced by the market value (rather than book) of the real estate times the target percentage debt in the capital structure. This intermediate position parallels the typical corporate loan which requires a prorated debt reduction upon the sale of any major asset.

OPERATING FLOWS WITHOUT REAL ESTATE

Having valued the real estate to a potential buyer,[13] consider now the valuation of Alpha's operating flows with the real estate removed. If the real estate is separated from the company, the firm's operating flows are altered significantly. Specifically, when the real estate is removed, the firm:

- Loses rental income.
- Is relieved of all operating expenses associated with the real estate.

---

[13] *This real estate analysis makes a number of simplifying assumptions in order to facilitate the presentation of the main issues. This illustration assumes that all rents are at current market rates for both premium (executive) and lesser (clerical) office space. Also ignored is the possibility of long-term leases whose payoffs might complicate a restructuring, as well as all the many important lease terms that can alter net rent over the years. Conceptually, these complications are not difficult, but the level of detail in the cash flow computations and financial reporting can be quite extensive. They can be very material and should clearly be included in any specific application of this methodology.*
From a tax standpoint, the problem has been made doubly difficult by the Tax Reform Act of 1984. Under the "original issue discount" rules, the buyer's basis cannot be inflated with artificially high lease payments or artificially low interest rates. For example, the IRS will not allow a firm to deduct above-market lease payments and then have the investor take higher depreciation writeoffs from the higher tax basis in the building, with that higher basis substantiated by the present value of the above-market lease payments.

- ■ Is relieved of all depreciation expense associated with the real estate.

- ■ Must now pay rent at market rates for its employees who remain in the building.[14]

Revised WACC cash flows are calculated by starting with the revised EBIT and adjusting for depreciation, capital expenditures, change in working capital, and interest earned on investment of the cash netted from sale. Next, the revised operating flows of the company with real estate removed are valued. Caution is warranted here. Separating the real estate from the firm might significantly change the riskiness of the firm. If the real estate involved secure long-term leases, and operating expenses were subject to little uncertainty, the real estate flows might be less risky than the firm's operating flows. Pulling out the real estate flows would cause the firm's beta to rise. On the other hand, if leases were not long term and if uncertainty were high regarding local market supply and demand conditions, the real estate flows might be more uncertain than the operating flows.[15]

Original unlevered cost of equity (K_o) is the starting point.

$$K_o = K_d + [K_e - K_d] \frac{E}{E + D\,(1 - T)}$$

Using a revised target debt ratio, with a resulting level of debt (D^*) and equity (E^*), after the real estate sale and corresponding loan payoff, the revised K_e and K_w are

$$K_e^* = K_d + [K_o - K_d] \frac{E^* + D^*(1 - T)}{E^*}$$

$$K_w^* = W_d^* K_d (1 - T) + W_e^* K_e^*$$

From these, the revised terminal value and the present values of the total cash flows are calculated. Finally, to arrive at a total value for the firm, the net cash realized from the real estate sale and assumed to be paid out as a dividend must be added back. This cash dividend can be estimated as follows:

Cash dividend = Market value of real estate − Tax − (Market value of real estate × Target Debt %)

[14]*If the corporation chooses to move a less visible group to cheaper space, that is, to combine financial strategy with a real operating move, the value of the cash flows without real estate would obviously rise.*
[15]*To infer an unlevered equity rate, K_o, from observable, K_e and K_d, there are at least four possible valuation models. The formula shown is based on MM (1963). See Harris and Pringle (R. S. Harris and J. J. Pringle. Risk-Adjusted Required Rate of Return—Extensions from the Average-Risk Case.* Journal of Financial Research *(Fall 1985)) for a fuller discussion.*

SUMMARY MODEL OUTPUT

When the real estate is sold, the firm immediately captures both the income and appreciation components of value inherent in the real estate asset. Since traditional accounting, on which WACC is based, recognized only the income side of real estate value, the firm might appear to be more valuable after the sale. If the analysis extended over a long period of time (say 50 years), however, the difference would disappear as the firm experienced higher rent expense (and less rent income) as the long-term cost of recognizing the real estate's appreciation at the front end.

In "perfect" capital markets, there would be no change in value resulting from the separation except where the separation was (1) accompanied by an operating change such as a move of some workers to cheaper space or (2) a more advantageous set of tax rates were encountered as a result of the separation.[16] The argument here centers on information, not market efficiency. The information available to analysts is insufficient-to properly value the appreciation component of the real estate return.

USING THE PARADIGM

The preceding model is no more than a combination of well-known accounting, finance, and real estate methodologies. It is a challenging task because it requires an explicit combination of accrual accounting, actual after-tax cash flows, and finance theory. (Traditionally, most analysts have focused on only one of these three areas at a time and hence have ignored difficulties in the interfaces.) It is useful in practice because it facilitates sensitivity analysis on key variables. The completeness of the model allows a holistic view of corporation finance that is not possible with any of the three methodologies in isolation. As market conditions change, the model helps the corporate financial officer continually re-evaluate the firm's capital structure, particularly the real estate component, to maximize shareholder value.

APPLICATION OF THE EXPANDED MODEL USING PUBLICLY AVAILABLE DATA

The above analysis indicates that when real estate comprises a significant portion of the firm's assets and has more potential for real capital gains than most other corporate assets, it is important for corporations to value their real estate independently. To value the remainder of the firm independent of its real estate holdings requires the removal of all cash flows and financing related to these assets. The most enlightening aspects of valuing a corporation in this fashion are the observed interac-

---

[16]A loose translation of Miller (M. Miller. Debt and Taxes. Journal of Finance (May 1977), 261–75) might even argue that rates of return would adjust to eliminate the potential tax benefit.

tions of the corporation's real estate holdings with the overall financial structure of the firm. (Tables A12-1 through A12-5 present the application of data from Atlantic Richfield to the model. Table A12-6 then presents in condensed form the results of similar analysis for Exxon, International Paper, and Time Incorporated. All these firms, like Atlantic Richfield, experienced a major real estate restructuring in the past two years.

Specifically, Table A12-1 presents the necessary variables for corporate valuation when real estate is to be considered independently in a real-life situation. Panel A of the table displays general firm variables, with Atlantic Richfield's 1986 data obtained from the firm's annual report,[17] and projections on most financial variables for the following four years (1987–1990) obtained from the *Value Line Investment Survey*.[18] Information on the real estate is presented in panel B, as obtained from the report of the real estate's sale in *The Wall Street Journal*, private surveys of local brokers, and/or the authors' estimates. Panel C displays general capital market variables that are required for the valuation analysis. These are obtained from *The Wall Street Journal, Value Line,* and estimated company annual reports. Finally, panel D discusses some of the key underlying assumptions of the model.

Table A12-2 presents expected financial statements (based on the data in Table A12-1) for Atlantic Richfield, with real estate included in the estimates. Table A12-3 presents these same expected financial statements, with real estate omitted from the balance sheet and its effect on the financial and operational aspects of the firm removed from the income statements. Table A12-4 looks at estimates of the independent values of the real estate to both a tax-exempt and a taxable investor. This analysis requires substantially more information than is publicly available for properties that have not recently been sold. To obtain the necessary information for this analysis, only corporations that had recent major real estate transactions (like Atlantic Richfield) were selected for this study, and only the specific property sold (instead of all real estate as would be desirable) were analyzed. Although market transaction prices are available on the properties analyzed here, making this analysis unnecessary, Table A12-4 indicates how real estate that has not recently been sold can be evaluated by internal management using standard discounted cash flow methods.

Table A12-5 presents the estimates of the value of Atlantic Richfield both with and without its real estate. Note that given the set of circum-

---

[17]*The compact disk data service DATEXT is the source for the annual reports.*

[18]Value Line *does not supply information concerning a firm's short-term interest-bearing debt, or the division of working capital into current assets and current liabilities. Information concerning non-operating income and expenses are only reported as special information and not on a consistent basis. Actual values for these variables were obtained for 1986 from the annual reports and projected into the future by the authors.*

TABLE A12-1 VALUATION VARIABLES FOR ATLANTIC RICHFIELD, 1986–90

PANEL A: FIRM VARIABLES	1986	1987	1988	1989	1990
Sales ($MM)	14,993.0	16,000.0	17,377.9	18,874.5	20,500.0
Annual sales growth	−0.333	0.067	0.086	0.086	0.086
Operating margin	0.209	0.215	0.205	0.205	0.205
Depreciation ($MM)	1,646.0	1,630.0	1,745.0	1,868.2	2,000.0
Nonoperating income	781.0	781.0	781.0	781.0	781.0
Coupon rate on corporate debt	0.113	0.113	0.113	0.113	0.113
Market rate on corporate debt	0.093	0.093	0.093	0.093	0.093
Corporate tax rate	0.528	0.460	0.380	0.380	0.380
Capital gains tax rate	0.280	0.380	0.380	0.380	0.380
Net profit ($MM)	615.0	910.0	993.7	1,085.2	1,185.0
Current assets/sales	0.316	0.316	0.316	0.316	0.316
Book value of land & real estate ($MM)	130.0	120.0	110.0	100.0	90.0
Depreciation of real estate ($MM)	10.0	10.0	10.0	10.0	10.0
Working capital ($MM)	993.0	1,000.0	1,091.4	1,191.1	1,300.0
Long-term debt ($MM)	6,969.0	5,800.0	6,085.7	6,385.5	6,700.0
Other long-term liabilities ($MM)	5,626.0	5,626.0	5,626.0	5,626.0	5,626.0
Net worth ($MM)	5,259.0	5,450.0	5,740.9	6,047.3	6,370.0

PANEL B: REAL ESTATE VARIABLES	1986	1987	1988	1989	1990
Square footage owned	1,200,000	1,200,000	1,200,000	1,200,000	1,200,000
Market rent per sq. ft.	34.50	35.54	36.60	37.70	38.83
Rent per sq. ft. (leased space)	43.00	44.29	45.62	46.99	48.40
% Change in market rent	0.03	0.03	0.03	0.03	0.03
Vacancy and collection losses (% of gross income)	0.05	0.05	0.05	0.05	0.05
Operating exp. (% gross inc.)	0.45	0.45	0.45	0.45	0.45
% Building occupied by firm	0.80	0.80	0.80	0.80	0.80
Life of building to new investor	31.5	31.5	31.5	31.5	31.5
Land market value ($MM)	110.00	110.00	110.00	110.00	110.00
Mortgage interest rate	0.0975	0.0975	0.0975	0.0975	0.0975
Mortgage term (yrs.)	30	30	30	30	30
Maximum loan to value ratio	0.80	0.80	0.80	0.80	0.80
New investor personal tax rate	0.35	0.35	0.35	0.35	0.35
Transaction cost of sale (%)	0.08	0.08	0.08	0.08	0.08
Capitalization rate for NOI	0.1025	0.1025	0.1025	0.1025	0.1025
Req. return on unlevered R.E.	0.1350	0.1350	0.1350	0.1350	0.1350
New investor's levered req. ret.	0.1723	0.1723	0.1723	0.1723	0.1723

PANEL C: VALUATION VARIABLES	1986	1987	1988	1989	1990
20-yr. U.S. bond rate (Rf rate)	0.085	0.085	0.085	0.085	0.085
Stock market return	0.145	0.145	0.145	0.145	0.145
Firm's beta	1.0	1.0	1.0	1.0	1.0

PANEL C: VALUATION VARIABLES	1986	1987	1988	1989	1990
Firm's debt ratio	0.520	0.520	0.520	0.520	0.520
Cost of debt	0.044	0.050	0.058	0.058	0.058
Cost of equity	0.145	0.145	0.145	0.145	0.145
Weighted average cost of capital	0.092	0.096	0.100	0.100	0.100

PANEL D

WACC versus Equity Residual Method: Valuing an unlevered cash flow using basic discounted cash flow methodology is straightforward: cash flows expected in the future are discounted at a rate that reflects the time value of money and the operating risk of the flows. When leverage is introduced, the valuation problem becomes more complex as the process must account for financial leverage and interest deductibility as well. The two most commonly used approaches to this problem are the weighted average cost of capital (WACC) approach and the equity residual (ER) approach. Under ideal conditions (where debt can be continuously adjusted so that it remains a constant percentage of the cash flows to be received), the two methodologies yield the same result. Under normal conditions, however, the two methodologies may yield substantially different results.[a] In light of the typical corporate situation of fairly decentralized investment decision making, but centralized financing, the WACC methodology will be used here. This methodology assumes a constant financing ratio rather than estimating specific amortization schedules for each project as the ER methodology requires. The cost of equity is estimated as the risk-free rate of return over the relevant time period (as measured by the 20-year Treasury bond rate), plus the market risk premium (6% over this time period) adjusted for the specific risk of the firm (estimated by the *Value Line* reported beta for the firm). The cost of debt is estimated as the holding period return on the corporation's bond issue with approximately 20 years to maturity, and relative weights are estimated by the current market value of equity and book value of debt.

Expost Versus Ex ante Risk Premiums: This analysis uses the capital asset pricing model (CAPM) to determine appropriate risk premiums for the individual firms. The CAPM has come under increasing criticism from academics and recently has been seriously questioned in regulatory rate of return testimony (see ATT Divestiture FCC Docket 84–800). A more forward-looking alternative is to estimate the risk premium from a composite of analysts' forecasts. Because derivation of the proper cost of capital is not the primary concern of this discussion, the CAPM methodology is followed despite questions of its accuracy.

Terminal Values: Both the WACC and the ER methodologies require estimates of future cash flows for some time into the future, followed by an estimate of the terminal value of the project (or in this case, the firm). The following analysis estimates annual cash flows for four years and then estimates a terminal value for the firm. Terminal values may be estimated by discounting an asumed perpetual cash flow at a nominal or real rate of return. In an inflationary world, it is not certain whether cash flows assumed constant into perpetuity should be considered real or nominal cash flows. Research comparing terminal value capitalization rate assumptions and the actual total market value of the firm suggests that an average of the two best approximates the real world situation. Starting with the ending year projections of cash flows, multiplying this figure by 1 minus the tax rate to account for the tax liability, assuming depreciation is reinvested to cover capital expenditure requirements and that there is no additional investments in working capital, and valuing this cash flow at the appropriate rate yields a terminal value for the firm.

[a]*For a thorough discussion of the issues that differentiate these two methodologies, see Salomon Brothers [12].*

TABLE A12-2   EXPECTED FINANCIAL STATEMENTS FOR ATLANTIC RICHFIELD, 1986–90 (REAL ESTATE INCLUDED)

PANEL A: BALANCE SHEET	1986	1987	1988	1989	1990
Current assets	4,743.00	5,061.56	5,497.47	5,970.91	6,485.13
R.E. (single property)	130.00	120.00	110.00	100.00	90.00
Fixed assets	16,731.00	15,756.00	16,251.17	16,767.58	17,306.00
Total assets	21,604.00	20,937.56	21,858.64	22,838.49	23,881.13
Current liabilities	3,750.00	4,061.56	4,406.07	4,779.77	5,185.13
Long-term debt	6,969.00	5,800.00	6,085.70	6,385.47	6,700.00
Other long-term liabilities	5,626.00	5,626.00	5,626.00	5,626.00	5,626.00
Total liabilities	16,345.00	15,487.56	16,117.77	16,791.24	17,511.13
Net worth	5,259.00	5,450.00	5,740.87	6,047.25	6,370.00
Total liabilities + net worth	21,604.00	20,937.56	21,858.64	22,838.49	23,881.13

PANEL B: INCOME STATEMENT	1986	1987	1988	1989	1990
Sales	14,993.00	16,000.00	17,377.93	18,874.52	20,500.00
CofGS and operating expenses	11,853.00	12,560.00	13,815.45	15,005.24	16,297.50
EBDIT	3,140.00	3,440.00	3,562.48	3,869.28	4,202.50
Depreciation	1,646.00	1,630.00	1,745.03	1,868.17	2,000.00
EBIT	1,494.00	1,810.00	1,817.45	2,001.11	2,202.50
Other income (expenses)	781.00	781.00	781.00	781.00	781.00
Interest expense	972.00	905.81	995.66	1,031.86	1,072.21
EBT	1,303.00	1,685.19	1,602.79	1,750.25	1,911.29
Taxes	688.00	775.19	609.06	665.10	726.29
Net income	615.00	910.00	993.73	1,085.15	1,185.00

PANEL C: FINANCIAL STATISTICS	1986	1987	1988	1989	1990
Return on assets	0.028	0.043	0.045	0.048	0.050
Return on net worth	0.117	0.167	0.173	0.179	0.186

stances relevant to the 1986 time period, Atlantic Richfield's value is maximized by selling the real estate. This result is not obvious from casual observation, as removing the real estate from the financial statements affects many aspects of the firm's financial operation—including the firm's cost of capital, debt capacity, and systematic risk—as well as its operating revenues and expenses.

The model of firm valuation examined here integrates real estate valuation, accrual accounting, and firm valuation in a consistent theoretical framework. Although this general model can provide a guideline

TABLE A12-3   EXPECTED FINANCIAL STATEMENTS OF ATLANTIC RICHFIELD, 1986–90 (WITHOUT REAL ESTATE)

PANEL A: BALANCE SHEET	1986	1987	1988	1989	1990
Current assets	4,743.00	5,061.56	5,497.47	5,970.91	6,485.13
Fixed assets (less real estate)	16,731.00	15,876.00	16,361.17	16,867.58	17,396.00
Land and real estate	130.00				
Total assets	21,604.00	20,937.56	21,858.64	22,838.49	23,881.13
Current liabilities	3,750.00	4,061.56	4,406.07	4,779.77	5,185.13
Long-term debt	6,969.00	5,800.00	6,085.70	6,385.47	6,700.00
Other long-term liabilities	5,626.00	5,626.00	5,626.00	5,626.00	5,626.00
Total liabilities	16,345.00	15,487.56	16,117.77	16,791.24	17,511.13
Net worth	5,259.00	5,450.00	5,740.87	6,047.26	6,370.00
Total liabilities + net worth	21,604.00	20,937.56	21,858.64	22,838.49	23,881.13

PANEL B: INCOME STATEMENT	1986	1987	1988	1989	1990
Sales	14,993.00	16,000.00	17,377.93	18,874.52	20,500.00
Original EBIT	1,494.00	1,810.00	1,817.45	2,001.11	2,202.50
Lost rent		10.10	10.40	10.71	11.03
Operating expenses saved		19.19	19.76	20.36	20.97
Lease payment		42.52	43.79	45.11	46.46
Depreciation saved		10.00	10.00	10.00	10.00
Revised EBIT	1,494.00	1,786.57	1,793.02	1,975.65	2,175.97
Other income/expenses	781.00	781.00	781.00	781.00	781.00
Interest expense	972.00	905.81	995.66	1,031.86	1,072.21
PBT	1,303.00	1,661.76	1,578.35	1,724.79	1,884.76
Tax	688.00	764.41	599.77	655.42	716.21
Net income	615.00	897.35	978.58	1,069.37	1,168.55
Gain from sale of RE		33.48			
Revised net income	615.00	930.83	978.58	1,069.37	1,168.55

PANEL C	FINANCIAL STATISTICS				
ROA	0.028	0.044	0.045	0.047	0.049
RONW	0.117	0.171	0.170	0.177	0.183

TABLE A12-4 ESTIMATED VALUE OF ATLANTIC RICHFIELD'S REAL ESTATE, 1987–90 (SOLD 11/25/86 FOR $200M)

PANEL A VALUE TO TAX-EXEMPT INVESTOR				
CASH FLOWS FROM REAL ESTATE	1987	1988	1989	1990
Gross income (maximum)	42.64	43.93	45.24	46.60
Vacancy and collection loss	2.13	2.20	2.26	2.33
Gross income (expected)	40.51	41.73	42.98	44.27
Operating expenses	19.19	19.76	20.36	20.97
Net operating income	21.32	21.96	22.62	23.30
Terminal value of real estate:				227.30
Ending year NOI/req. ret. on NOI				
Total cash flow from real estate	21.32	21.96	22.62	250.60
Present value of unlevered real estate	202.31			

PANEL B: VALUE TO TAXABLE INVESTOR				
ANNUAL AFTER-TAX CASH FLOWS	1987	1988	1989	1990
Net operating income	21.32	21.96	22.62	23.30
⟨Interest⟩	15.78	15.68	15.57	15.45
⟨Depreciation⟩	2.93	2.93	2.93	2.93
Taxable income	2.61	3.35	4.12	4.92
⟨Taxes⟩	0.91	1.17	1.44	1.72
⟨Principal payment⟩	1.03	1.13	1.24	1.36
Depreciation	2.93	2.93	2.93	2.93
Cash flow after tax	3.60	3.98	4.37	4.77
Terminal value				227.30
Less ending period loan balance				157.08
Less tax on sale				12.85
Terminal value cash flow				57.37
Total cash flow after tax	3.60	3.98	4.37	62.14
Present value of levered real estate	41.58			
Debt on real estate	161.85			
Total value of real estate	203.42[a]			

[a] *In this case the value appears to be greater to the taxable investor. This result will vary, particularly with changes in the level of pension fund interest in real estate (causing the discount rate in Panel A to change), changes in tax laws, and changes in mortgage interest rates.*

TABLE A12-5 ESTIMATES OF ATLANTIC RICHFIELD VALUE, 1987–90 (WITH AND WITHOUT REAL ESTATE)

PANEL A VALUE WITH REAL ESTATE INCLUDED				
TOTAL CASH FLOW	1987	1988	1989	1990
Earnings before interest & tax[a]	2,591.00	2,598.40	2,782.10	2,983.50
⟨Tax on EBIT⟩	1,191.86	987.39	1,057.20	1,133.73
Depreciation	1,630.00	1,745.03	1,868.17	2,000.00
⟨Capital expenditures⟩	645.00	2,230.20	2,374.58	2,528.42
⟨Change in working capital⟩	7.00	91.39	99.75	108.86
Net operating cash flows	2,377.14	1,034.45	1,118.74	1,212.49
Terminal value of the firm				
Perpetuity—ending year EBIT $(1 - T)/Kw$				26,231.7[c]
Total cash flow	2,377.14	1,034.48	1,118.75	27,444.1
Present value (discounted at Kw)	22,639.6			
Less beginning period debt	6,969.0			
Present value of equity	15,670.6			

PANEL B VALUE WITH REAL ESTATE VALUED SEPARATELY				
TOTAL CASH FLOW	1987	1988	1989	1990
Earnings before interest and tax	2,567.57	2,574.02	2,756.65	2,956.97
⟨Tax on EBIT⟩	1,181.08	978.13	1,047.53	1,123.65
Depreciation	1,620.00	1,735.03	1,858.17	1,990.00
⟨Capital expenditures⟩	635.00	2,220.20	2,364.58	2,518.42
⟨Change in working capital⟩	7.00	91.39	99.75	108.86
Net operating cash flows	2,364.49	1,019.33	1,102.96	1,196.04
Gain from sale of real estate	33.48[b]			
Terminal value of the firm:				
Perpetuity—ending year EBIT $(1 - T)/Kw$				26,295.5
Total cash flow	2,397.97	1,019.33	1,102.96	27,491.5
Present value (discounted at Kw)	22,713.5			
Less beginning period debt	6,969.00			
Present value of equity	15,744.5			

[a]Operating earnings before interest and taxes plus other income.
[b]The gain from the sale of real estate is based on the actual market transaction as reported in The Wall Street Journal, *November 20, 1988.*
[c]Panel D of Table A12-1 explains the real vs nominal rate issue on the perpetuity. See page 351 for calculation of the revised costs of debt and equity. The 26,231.7 shown above is the average of the value assuming a real perpetuity (33,888.4) and assuming a nominal perpetuity (18,574.9).

TABLE A12-6   VALUE OF SELECTED CORPORATIONS (WITH AND WITHOUT REAL ESTATE HOLDING) (MILLIONS OF DOLLARS)

FIRM	REAL ESTATE OWNED	REAL ESTATE SOLD AND LEASED BACK	DIFFERENCE
Atlantic Richfield	15,670.6	15,744.5	⟨73.9⟩[a]
Exxon	54,513.8	54,517.7	⟨ 3.9⟩
International Paper	3,162.4	3,230.3	⟨67.9⟩
Time Inc.	4,731.9	4,756.6	⟨24.7⟩

[a]*While the differences are large absolute numbers, they are small percentages of overall firm value. For perspective, the average difference in value is less than 1 percent of total value, while the market value of these firms differs from the theoretical value (model estimates) by an average of 14.66 percent. Hence, the magnitude of the real estate card is often dwarfed by potential valuation errors. This only indicates the importance of the kind of detailed evaluation of each property that is possible only with inside information (e.g., lease provisions). Even with better internally available data, financial valuation models are not perfect, and differences between theoretical and market prices may still be larger than the "real estate card." However, if the theoretical model generates values that are comparably biased for the firm with and without its real estate holdings, the difference may still be an accurate estimate of the magnitude of the "card."*

for all firms, every corporate situation is unique and consideration must be given to the idiosyncrasies of each firm. To illustrate, Table A12-6 shows the results of similar analyses of real estate transactions of four corporations: Atlantic Richfield with a $200 million sale, Exxon with a $305 million sale, International Paper with a $118 million purchase, and Time Incorporated with a $118 million sale. Relevant information for estimating the value of real estate was very difficult to obtain—even for real estate that recently sold. Similar public information is nearly nonexistent for real estate that has been held by the same corporation for any significant period.

The analysis presented here is based exclusively on public information and is for illustration purposes only. Application of this methodology in practice relies on superior internal forecasts and records available only to management. The fact that management alone typically has access to this information gives rise to the agency issues discussed in Miles, Pringle, and Webb (1989). This work shows that interesting agency issues derive from the interplay of three factors: underutilized real estate; the asymmetric information sets in the hands of management versus the markets; and management compensation plans that may exacerbate conflicts of interest.

WHAT DID ALL THOSE NUMBERS REALLY MEAN?

Many corporations have the opportunity to increase their profitability through more effective management of their real estate. This entails evaluating real estate on an ongoing basis using an approach that treats the interactions of real estate with the capital structure, debt capacity, cost of capital, and the overall operations of the firm. Real estate values so determined must be regularly compared to the external market value of the real estate in its highest and best use to determine whether it is being efficiently utilized.

Managers who evaluate their real estate and determine it to be undervalued have considerable flexibility in their actions. The market in general does not have the information to recognize underutilization, and the cost of obtaining the necessary information across a wide range of firms is often prohibitive.

Increased interest in real estate on the part of institutional investors adds another dimension to the problem. As pension funds and insurance companies become more active in this market, companies may find it increasingly attractive for others to own the real estate they occupy. Now, more than ever it is important for firms to view real estate as an asset that can and should be actively managed to achieve corporate goals.

REFERENCES   BOOKS

Aap, John M. *Handbook for Real Estate Market Analysis.* Englewood Cliffs, N.J.: Prentice-Hall, 1987.

American Society of Real Estate Counselors, books and booklets. Chicago: *Real Estate Counseling: A Professional Approach to Problem Solving, Office Buildings: Development, Marketing, and Leasing, Land Use Perspective, The Real Estate Counselor, Some Counseling Aspects in Condominium Development, The Internal Rate of Return in Real Estate Investments.*

Arnold, Fayette F., III. *Reviewing Condominium Projects.* St. Paul, Minn.: Todd, 1982.

Atkinson, H. G., and P. E. Wagner. *Modern Real Estate Practice: An Introduction to a Career in Real Estate Brokerage.* Homewood, Ill,: Dow–Jones–Irwin, 1974.

Bates, Dorothy R. *How to Run a Real Estate Office.* Reston, Va.: Reston Publishing Co., 1981.

Bayliss, Walter. *You Can Win the Real Estate Game: A Success Guide to Sales, Listings, and Time Management,* Reston, Va.: Reston Publishing Co., 1979.

Berman, David S. *How to Organize and Sell a Profitable Real Estate Condominium.* Englewood Cliffs, N.J.: Prentice-Hall, 1972.

Berston, Hyman M. *California Real Estate Principles.* Homewood, Ill.: Dow–Jones–Irwin, 1987.

Brown, Donald R., and Wendell G. Matthau. *Real Estate Advertising Handbook.* Chicago: Realtors National Marketing Institute, 1982.

Burke, D. Barlow, Jr. *Law of Real Estate Brokers.* Boston: Little, Brown, 1982.

Carpenter, Horace, Jr. *Shopping Center Management: Principles and Practices.* New York: International Council of Shopping Centers, 1978.

Case, F. *Real Estate Brokerage: A Systems Approach.* 2nd ed. Englewood Cliffs, N.J.: Prentice–Hall, 1982.

Cyr, John E. *Training and Supervising Real Estate Salesmen.* Englewood Cliffs, N.J.: Prentice–Hall, 1973.

Downs, James c., Jr. *Principles of Real Estate Management.* 12th ed. Chicago: Institute of Real Estate Management, 1980.

Fischer, Frederick. *Broker Beware: Selling Real Estate Within the Law*. Reston, Va.: Reston Publishing Co., 1981.

Fletcher, David R. *Condominium Sales and Listings*. Reston, Va.: Reston Publishing Co., 1982.

Foster, Ray. *Sensible Real Estate Selling Skills*. Reston, Va.: Reston Publishing Co., 1981.

Gale, Jack L. *Commercial/Investment Brokerage: An Introduction with Case Studies*. Chicago: Realtors National Marketing Institute, 1979.

Gilligan, Gerald S. *A Price Guide for Buying and Selling Rural Acreage*. New York: McGraw–Hill, 1976.

Halper, Emanuel B. *Shopping Center and Store Leases*. New York: Law Journal Seminars Press, 1981.

Hanford, Lloyd D., Sr. *The Property Management Process*. Chicago: Institute of Real Estate Management, 1972.

Ingerbresten, Mark. *Managing the Office Building*. Rev. ed. Chicago: Institute of Real Estate Management, 1985.

Institute of Real Estate Management. *Forms for Apartment Management*. Chicago: National Association of Realtors.

Institute of Real Estate Management. *Income and Expense Analysis: Office Building*. Washington, D.C.: Institute of Real Estate Management, 1990.

Institute of Real Estate Management. *Income and Expense Analysis: Apartments*. Washington, D.C.: Institute of Real Estate Management, 1990.

Institute of Real Estate Management. *Managing the Office Building*. Chicago: Institute of Real Estate Management, 1981.

Institute of Real Estate Management. *Managing the Shopping Center*. Chicago: Institute of Real Estate Management, 1983.

Institute of Real Estate Management. *Marketing and Learning Office Space*. Washington, D.C.: Institute of Real Estate Management, 1979.

Institute of Real Estate Management. *The Resident Manager*. Chicago: Institute of Real Estate Management, 1973.

Jaffe, Austin J. *Property Management in Real Estate Investment Decision-Making*. Lexington, Mass.: Lexington Books, 1979.

Kelley, Edward N. *Practical Apartment Management*. Chicago: National Association of Realtors, 1981.

Kusnet, Jack, and Robert Lopatin. *Modern Real Estate Leasing Forms*. Boston: Warren, Gorham, and Lamont.

Kyle, Robert C., and Floyd M. Baird. *Property Management*. Rev. ed. Chicago: Longman Financial Services Institute, 1987.

Levine, Mark Lee. *Landlords' and Owners' Liability*. Chicago: National Association of Realtors, 1979.

Lindeman, Bruce. *Real Estate Brokerage Management*. Reston, Va.: Reston Publishing Co., 1981.

Marcus, Bruce W. *Marketing Professional Services in Real Estate Advertising, Promotion, Public Relations*. Chicago: Realtors National Marketing Institute, 1982.

Marcus, Bruce W. *Marketing Professional Services in Real Estate, Advertising, Promotion, Public Relations*. Chicago: Realtors National Marketing Institute, 1981.

Market Profiles. Washington, D.C.: Urban Land Institute, Annual.

Mayer, Albert J., III. *Readings in Management for the Real Estate Executive*. Chicago: Realtors National Marketing Institute, 1978.

Messner, Stephen D. *Marketing Investment Real Estate.* Chicago: Realtors National Marketing Institute, 1982.

National Association of Realtors. *Existing Home Sales Series.* Chicago: Economics and Research Division, 777 14th Street, N.W., Washington, D.C. 20005 (annually, with monthly updates).

National Association of Realtors. *Spring Real Estate Market Report.* Washington, D.C. (annually).

National Institute of Real Estate Brokers. *Home Trade-in Handbook.* 155 East Superior Street, Chicago, Il. 60611.

1990 Boma Experience Exchange Report. Washington, D.C.: Building Owners and Managers Association International, 1990.

Protective Covenants. Arlington, Va.: National Association of Industrial and Office Parks/Educational Foundation, 1985.

Real Estate Brokerage: Income, Expense, and Profits. Washington, D.C.: National Association of Realtors, 1981.

Realtors National Marketing Institute. *Real Estate Advertising Ideas. Real Estate Office Management (1975). Selling Commercial Real Estate. Managing a Commercial Office Investment. Conversion and Marketing of Older Properties.*

Realtors National Marketing Institute. *Real Estate Salesmen's Handbook.* Chicago.

Realtors National Marketing Institute, 430 N. Michigan Avenue, Chicago, Ill. 60611. Several courses on different real estate topics.

Roberts, Duane F. *Marketing and Leasing of Office Space.* Rev. ed. Chicago: Institute of Real Estate Management, 1986.

Rosenberg, Jenny M. *Dictionary of Business and Management.* New York: Wiley, 1978.

Scavo, Janet. *The Condominium Home: A Special Marketing Challenge.* Chicago: Realtors National Marketing Institute, 1982.

Shenkel, William M. *Modern Real Estate Management.* New York: McGraw–Hill, 1980.

Taylor, Arlie L. *Owner's Guide for Monitoring a Motor Hotel Investment.* Dallas: Hospitality Media, 1981.

Walters, David W. *Real Estate Exchanges.* New York: Wiley, 1982.

Walters, William, Jr. *The Practice of Real Estate Management for the Experienced Property Manager.* Chicago: IREM, 1979.

Worldwide Lodging Industry: Annual Report on International Hotel Operations. New York: Horwath and Horwath International and Laventhol and Horwath (annually).

PERIODICALS AND NEWSLETTERS

Advertising Age. Chicago: Crain Communications, Inc. (weekly).

AMO Perspectives. Chicago: Institute of Real Estate Management (quarterly).

Building Owner's and Manager's Association International. Washington, D.C. (monthly).

Commercial Investment Journal. Chicago: Realtors National Marketing Institute.

Existing Home Sales Series. Washington, D.C.: National Association of Realtors (monthly).

Hotel Industry Insights. Lexington, Mass. (quarterly).

Journal of Property Management. Chicago: Institute of Real Estate Management (bimonthly).

Naiop News. Arlington, Va.: National Association of Industrial and Office Parks (quarterly).

National Trend of Business Economy/Limited-Service Lodging Industry. Laventhol and Horwath (monthly).

Real Estate Today. Chicago: National Association of Realtors (monthly).

Shopping Centers Today. New York: International Council of Shopping Centers (monthly).

Trends of Business in the Lodging Industry. Philadelphia: Laventhol and Horwath (monthly).

SECTION ON LICENSE PREPARATION

Danks, Laurence J. *Passing the Real Estate Salesperson's Examination.* Reston, Va.: Reston Publishing Co., 1981.

Ellis. *Guide to Real Estate License Examinations.* 3rd ed. Englewood Cliffs, N.J.: Prentice-Hall, 1983.

French, William B., Stephen J. Martin, and Thomas E. Battle III. *Guide to Real Estate Licensing Examinations.* Boston: Warren, Gorham, and Lamont, 1980.

Galaty, Fillmore, Allaway, and Kyle. *Modern Real Estate Practice.* 9th ed. Chicago: Real Estate Education Co., 1982.

Narello (National Association of Real Estate License Law Officials). *Guide to Examinations and Careers in Real Estate.* Reston, Va.: Reston Publishing Co., 1979.

National Association of Real Estate Law Officials. *Guide to Examinations and Careers in Real Estate.* Reston, Va.: Reston Publishing Co.

Sager, Lawrence. *Guide to Passing the Real Estate Exam.* Chicago: Real Estate Education Co., 1982. Designed for the ACT-style exam.

Smith, Douglas, and John Gibbons. *Real Estate Education Company Real Estate Exam Manual.* 2nd ed. Chicago: Real Estate Education Co., 1981. Designed for the ETS-style exam.

Tosh, Dennis, and Nicholas Ordway. *Real Estate Principles for License Preparation.* 4th ed. Englewood Cliffs, N.J.: Prentice Hall, 1988.

PART 5

REAL ESTATE
FINANCE

$\mathcal{T}$HE FINANCIAL SYSTEM
AND REAL ESTATE FINANCE

Real estate finance should be understood as part of the overall financial system. In this chapter we develop a simple model of a financial system that illustrates how the U.S. system and most market economies function; then we show how real estate finance fits in this model. In Chapter 14 we examine the effect of financing on equity (or residual) cash flows. We show how financing fits in the game analogy as a prior claim on net operating income affecting both the actual return to equity and the riskiness of that return. In Chapter 15 the lender's perspective is presented, that is, what types of loans are made and why. Finally, in Chapter 16 we consider the government's role in real estate finance with regard to mortgage insurance and secondary mortgage markets.

AN INTUITIVE MODEL OF THE OVERALL FINANCIAL SYSTEM

As you may recall from your first economics course, the total tangible investment made by the entire global economy in any period must equal total savings during that same period. In other words, as a group, we can invest only what we do not immediately consume. Total production less consumption (food, clothing, shelter, and parties) and government purchases of goods and services is the amount saved in the economy, and savings is what gets invested in tangible assets. In an ideal world (and usually even in this one) investment provides a better future by increasing the stock of assets (roads, buildings, an educated population, etc.):

$$\text{Production} - \text{Private consumption} - \text{Government} = \text{Investment}$$

Although this equation works for the economy as a whole, the financial system allows individuals (1) to save more in any period than they themselves want to invest in tangible assets or (2) to invest more in tangible assets than they have in personal savings (i.e., to borrow). In the financial system, individual savers' funds are thereby *aggregated* and then *allocated* to tangible investments. The intermediaries between the savers and the investors are the *capital markets,* where a variety of players perform the aggregation and allocation functions. (See Table 13-1.)

These functions are critically important to our economy, for only if we collectively save can we collectively invest. Furthermore, only if we as a nation invest in the most productive tangible assets can we have the greatest economic opportunities tomorrow. If we do not invest in the most productive tangible assets (those most likely to provide cost-efficient satisfaction of consumer desires), the pie will be smaller tomorrow than it might have been, and as a group we will be worse off.

How do the capital markets allocate funds to investments? They do so on the basis of *expected return and expected risk.* The future is uncertain, yet we form expectations about the productivity of any particular tangible asset. The capital markets allocate savings first to those tangible assets with the highest expected return and the lowest expected risk.

Why do they allocate on these criteria? The markets represent individuals. And a high return with low risk is precisely what individual savers want. Since savers' desires drive the financial system, let us begin by looking at the major groups of savers.

SAVERS

Some individuals save. The authors have always wanted to be savers. However, because students insist on buying used books, the authors'

TABLE 13-1   THE CAPITAL MARKETS IN THE UNITED STATES FINANCIAL SYSTEM

SAVERS	CAPITAL MARKET PLAYERS	INVESTORS
Individuals	Commercial banks	Government
Businesses	Bank trust departments	Businesses
Life insurance companies	Savings and loans	Individuals
Pension funds	Mutual savings banks	
	Credit unions	
	Life insurance companies	
	Real estate investment trusts	
	Mortgage bankers	
	Investment bankers	
	Venture capitalists	
	Investment managers	
	Syndicators	
	Government[a]	

[a]*Facilitator, regulator, and occasionally even lender.*

income (a measure of their productivity) seldom exceeds their consumption, and there is nothing left to save. Fortunately, other individuals are more prosperous (or at least more thrifty); collectively, Americans save about 5 percent of their income.[1]

Businesses also save, particularly since the Tax Reform Act of 1981 lowered the effective corporate tax rate (details in Part 6). Whenever a business has more cash flow than it needs for operations and dividends, it has savings that can be used for new investment.

In total, Americans personally consume about 63 percent of the GNP; government takes another 21 percent. This leaves about 16 percent as private domestic savings. Interestingly, neither individual savings nor business savings represent the major portion of total private domestic savings. Larger than direct savings is the buildup of reserves (i.e., savings) in life insurance companies and pension funds. These two reserves are another way that individuals (often with the help of businesses) save.

Today over two-thirds of the trades on the New York Stock Exchange are by institutional investors, mainly on behalf of life insurance companies and **pension funds.** The Department of Labor estimates that by 1995 total pension fund assets will have grown to nearly $3.0 trillion, making pension funds the largest and fastest growing source of savings in the economy. (Notice that even in this capitalistic system, the workers own a big piece of the pie.)

To the real estate analyst, understanding how savers drive the financial system is critically important. All savers want high return and low risk, but certain groups of savers have additional objectives and restrictions that are reflected in the capital markets. Only by understanding what savers want can the analyst fully comprehend what the players in the capital market are trying to achieve and, in the process, get the best possible financing (a major objective of the game).

Before we look at the players in the capital markets, let us quickly identify the other users, besides real estate investors, of the total savings pool—that is, the competitors for savers' dollars. Understanding the competition for funds is also very important to winning the real estate game.

INVESTORS IN TANGIBLE ASSETS

Savers "invest" their funds but not always in tangible assets. Often they go to the capital markets and buy a bank CD, a share of corporate stock, or an interest in a real estate limited partnership. In doing so, they are not making the final investment. Rather, they are investing *through* the capital markets where their savings (now called investments) are aggre-

---

[1]*The percentages shown in this section are derived from data available in* The Survey of Current Business *(U.S. Department of Commerce) and the* Federal Reserve Bulletin, *both monthly publications. The percentages vary slightly from year to year, with the figures shown here representative of the past five years.*

gated and allocated to those who want to invest in tangible assets—roads, buildings, equipment, and so on.

The biggest investor in tangible assets is the U.S. government. The largest part of this expenditure is financed by tax revenues. However, at the federal and some state levels, tax revenues have recently been insufficient to cover total government expenditures. One result is our familiar federal deficit, which must be financed by borrowing from savings. Because the U.S. government is the lowest risk borrower (money is worthless if our government folds), it gets whatever it needs from the savings pool first. Although the annual savings pool is quite large, the federal deficit exceeds $100 billion per year as we enter the 1990s.

After the government is financed, there is considerable competition for the remaining savings. Potential borrowers argue that they are in the low-risk category in an effort to obtain the funds they need at as low a rate as possible.

Major corporations (some of whom are savers at times) are major users of funds (investors in tangible assets). The chief financial officer of General Electric (GE) is really a purchasing agent standing between the corporation and the capital markets. His job is to buy (i.e., borrow) the money GE needs for growth and modernization at the lowest possible cost. (The cost of borrowed funds is the interest rate.)

Individuals also compete for funds in the capital market. Real estate developers, often through syndicators, must find the funding to finance the office buildings, shopping centers, and homes of tomorrow. Although some funding will come from equity sources, most of it comes from mortgage financing, which now accounts for nearly 30 percent of all annual borrowing. The total mortgage debt outstanding is over $3 trillion. And as shown in Box 13-1, more than half the mortgage debt has gone into housing.

Now that we know some of the competitors for savers' dollars, let us consider the players in the capital markets. We will focus on those most important to the real estate industry.

13-1 MORTGAGE DEBT OUTSTANDING	BY USE		BY FINANCIAL INSTITUTION	
	One-to four-family homes	66%	Commercial banks	21%
	Multifamily housing	9%	Savings institutions	29%
	Commercial	22%	Life insurance companies	7%
	Farm	3%	Federal and related agencies	6%
			Individual and other	11%
			Mortgage pools	26%

THE CAPITAL MARKETS

As we have already seen, one role of the **financial system**[2] is to gather or mobilize capital from many small (and some large) savers and allocate that capital to individuals and organizations who need it for investment in tangible assets and who are prepared to pay for it. The middlemen between the savers and the borrowers are **financial institutions** and other **intermediaries.** These are key players. Their activities of gathering and allocating capital, in a variety of **financial markets,** are the hub of our financial system (see Table 13-1).

Within the capital markets, priorities for allocating funds are determined on the basis of a pricing structure usually expressed in terms of interest rates and required returns. (Think of the "price" of your school loan, car loan, or credit card.) The rates at any given time are determined by the supply of, and demand for, funds within certain categories. These categories are usually classified according to the risks assumed by the lender and the length, or **maturity,** of the investment. For example, short-term (30-day) loans to creditworthy corporations are in a lower risk category than long-term (30-year) mortgage loans on beach property.

All rates are significantly affected by the degree of inflation or deflation in the general economy. Put another way, if inflation is running at a high rate, a large **inflation premium** will be built into all rates to reflect the erosion of capital, that is, the loss of its purchasing power over the term of the investment. (See Box 13-2 for a global perspective on the role of inflation in real estate finance.)

FINANCIAL INTERMEDIARIES

When a Treasury note is purchased directly from a Federal Reserve bank, the government is borrowing directly from the saver without any financial middleman. Similarly, when the seller of a single-family home accepts the buyer's mortgage note for a portion of the purchase price (a **purchase money mortgage**), no intermediary is involved. But these cases are exceptions to the general rule that financial markets normally use a *financial intermediary* to channel savings into investments. The middlemen receive and repackage capital, tailoring the size, term, and rate of loans and the rate and terms on savings to meet the needs of both savers and borrowers.

Some of the more important financial intermediaries are shown in Table 13-1. Together they manage an enormous pool of capital, which they place with investors—largely as loans. In this endeavor, each intermediary tries to make loans that are compatible with the kinds of capital they raise. For example, institutions with short-term liabilities (demand

---

[2]*The student with a considerable background in finance may skip directly to Appendix 13, which translates basic finance jargon into a real estate context.*

<table>
<tr><td>

13-2

WHAT CAN HYPER- INFLATION DO TO REAL ESTATE FINANCE?

</td><td>

In considering how a nation handles the financing of its real property, think about the problems created by hyperinflation. In 1989, Argentina had inflation rates ranging up to 100 percent a month. For those of you who have trouble with compounding, that comes to somewhere around 1 million percent per year. Obviously, this creates problems when we talk about the components of interest: a real return of 3 to 4 percent plus an inflation premium of 1 million percent and maybe a few hundred thousand percent for misestimating the inflation risk premium. Clearly, what works here in the United States won't work there. Yet Argentines have the same need for shelter that we have.

Since not everyone in Argentina can afford to pay cash for a home, there must be some way to finance homes. There must also be some way to finance the hotels and office buildings, and yet what works here won't work there.

One concept that has worked well in Argentina is financing by the condominium concept. As we described in Chapter 5, the condominium is a popular form of ownership, which in the United States is financed much as other real estate interests are financed. In Argentina, there is a twist. When you want to build something new, you don't sell all the condominium units to end users. You use some units to pay for the product; all the people producing the product get their share of the units. Since no bank credit is available for development financing, the electrical subcontractor gets two units, the plumbing subcontractor one unit, and so on, all the way on down the line. The legal interest of the condominium replaces, albeit in a much less efficient manner, the financing we use in this country.

Remember, finance is terribly important to real estate, but real estate is more important to people than finance is to real estate. Consequently, the real estate that people need will be built even when the most efficient finance possibilities don't exist.

</td></tr>
</table>

deposits of commercial banks) dominating their portfolio will tend to prefer short-term real estate loans, notably construction loans. Conversely, institutions with long-term liabilities (life policies of life insurance companies) tend to prefer longer term loans. For both, the idea is to match the maturities of their assets (loans) to their liabilities (deposits).

FINANCIAL MARKETS

Loans are originated (created) in many ways and in various places, to-gether known as the **primary financial market.** A business firm that raises capital by selling newly issued securities to the general public is raising capital in the primary market. So is the U.S. government when it sells a new issue of Treasury bonds. And so is a savings and loan association (S&L) when it agrees to finance the purchase of a home with a first mortgage loan. In all these instances new debt is being created.

Once debt has been created, units of debt, represented by bonds, deed of trust notes, notes and mortgages, and so on, may be traded in the **secondary financial markets.** The major secondary markets (for both common stock and bonds) include the (1) New York Stock and Bond exchanges, (2) American Stock and Bond exchanges, (3) regional exchanges, and (4) over-the-counter (OTC) markets. Short-term debt instruments—such as U.S. Treasury bills and commercial paper issued by large corporations—are traded in the *money market,* which is a conceptual, rather than a geographic, designation.

Before World War II, only a limited secondary market existed for real estate debt instruments, that is, mortgages. In recent years, however, a very active **secondary mortgage market** has developed. It broadened the capital pool for financing real estate, making it possible, for the first time, for many new types of savers and financial intermediaries to invest (lend) in real estate. Furthermore, the secondary mortgage market facilitates interregional credit flows, thereby creating a more efficient market. Finally, many traditional real estate lenders are able to make more real estate loans because of the liquidity provided by the secondary mortgage market. Selling loans replenishes lenders' funds, and they lend again. Thus, the secondary mortgage market expands the supply of funds to the primary mortgage market. (This subject is discussed in detail in Chapter 16.)

THE GOVERNMENT'S REGULATORY ROLE

A number of federal agencies are closely involved with the financial system and the financial markets. Their objectives may generally be described as the enhancement of an orderly financial system that promotes overall economic growth without unduly restricting individual freedom.

❏ **FEDERAL RESERVE SYSTEM.** The central banking system of the United States, the **Federal Reserve System (FRS),** is charged with overall monetary policy and related commercial bank regulation. An extensive discussion of the Federal Reserve System goes beyond the scope of this book, but the reader should remember that Federal Reserve policy affects both the overall money supply and rules under which financial intermediaries operate. The Federal Reserve System has a significant effect on the real estate industry in that its monetary policy often influences the cost and availability of credit.

❏ **FEDERAL DEPOSIT INSURANCE CORPORATION (FDIC).**
The FDIC, an independent executive agency, originally established in 1933, has the function of insuring the deposits of all commercial banks entitled to federal deposit insurance. The FDIC insures deposits up to $100,000 per account. The agency also has examination and supervisory powers over insured banks.

❏ **COMPTROLLER OF THE CURRENCY.**   The office of Comptroller of the Currency was created in 1863 as a part of the national banking system. Its most important functions relate to the organization, chartering, regulation, and liquidation of national banks.

❏ **FEDERAL HOME LOAN BANK SYSTEM (FHLBS).**   The FHLBS was established in 1932 to provide a permanent system of reserve credit banks for eligible thrift institutions, such as S&Ls, engaged in long-term home mortgage financing. Over the years, its functions expanded to the point where it constituted a number of separate federal agencies and federally sponsored organizations. The central agency in the group remained the Federal Home Loan Bank Board (**FHLBB**). It supervised 12 Federal Home Loan Banks, each located in one of the 12 regions into which the nation is divided. Savings associations holding 98 percent of the assets of the industry belonged to the FHLBS.

One of the FHLBB's major functions was to provide supplemental mortgage credit (liquidity) by advancing funds to its members to assist them in meeting heavy or unexpected withdrawals. In addition, the FHLBB chartered federal savings associations and had jurisdiction over state savings associations that are members of its affiliated agency, the Federal Savings and Loan Insurance Corporation (**FSLIC**). (Another affiliated agency, the Federal Home Loan Mortgage Corporation[**FHLMC**], provides liquidity through secondary mortgage market operations, as described in Chapter 16.)

The 1980s witnessed major changes in the regulation of financial institutions. these changes altered and continue to alter the structure of the financial system. The Depository Institutions Deregulation and Monetary Control Act of 1980[3] stimulated new competition between the different types of financial intermediaries by eliminating regulatory distinctions. Subsequently, the Garn–St. Germain Act of 1982 further hastened deregulation. Although the specifics of both pieces of legislation go well beyond the scope of an introductory text, Box 13-3 provides a summary and the major implications of the Garn–St. Germain Act.

Deregulation of financial institutions spawned a period of speculation by many of the nation's savings and loans. During this period, a flaw

---

[3]*Public Law 96-221—March 31, 1980. Chapters 9–12 of the Report of the President's Commission on Housing present an excellent summary of the issues involved and the expected impact on housing finance.*

13-3
SUMMARY AND IMPLICATIONS OF THE GARN–ST. GERMAIN DEPOSITORY INSTITUTIONS ACT OF 1982

FEDERAL RESERVE BANK OF ATLANTA
OFFICE CORRESPONDENCE
October 13, 1982

TO: Mr. Donald L. Koch
FROM: B. Frank King, David D. Whitehead and Larry Wall
SUBJECT: The Garn–St. Germain Act

This is our first cut at the major implications for financial structure, safety, and efficiency of the Garn–St. Germain Act. The implications that we find do not generally seem dramatic. Rather, the bill makes marginal changes that will play out over time.

In its most important features, the Act

1. Bails out thrifts with an exchange of paper, greater powers for the FSLIC, and the possibilities of interstate and interindustry mergers but leaves the insuring agencies with greater risk of losses from failures and tempts them to carry troubled institutions beyond the point where insurance losses would be least. The bailout provisions have a three-year life.

2. Establishes a new account to compete with money funds. The account as envisioned by the conference and the rumored DIDC concensus has a relatively high minimum. Deposit insurance may not overcome its disadvantages, but it will attract funds from money market mutual funds if confidence in the financial system is shaken.

3. Gives thrifts more powers. Aggressively used, these would have important impacts on commercial banks. There is considerable reason to doubt if the powers will be used aggressively.

4. Opens the door for limited interstate and interinstitutional acquisitions of depository institutions. The thrift bailout will limit the need for these, and the insurors' attitudes will greatly influence the number of such acquisitions. The import of this part of the Act is that it gives another boost to interstate banking; however, it may make bank holding company acquisition of healthy S&Ls more difficult.

5. Kills the time and savings deposit interest rate differential two years early.

In terms of the Act's impact on important groups:

■ The public gets a little interstate banking, more secure thrifts, more potential providers of business services, more providers of money market accounts, fewer property and casualty insurance competitors over the long haul.

■ Banks get an instrument to compete with MMMFs, a small interstate opportunity, elimination of the interest differential vis-à-vis thrifts, more competitors for commercial business, continuing property and casualty insurance limitations, less likelihood of acquiring healthy S&Ls, more flexibility in FDIC bailouts.

- Thrifts get bailed out, the same new money fund account powers as banks, new business deposit and lending powers, and interstate opportunities.

in the regulatory process became much more evident. Unlike the commercial banking system, which is regulated by the Federal Reserve, the Comptroller of the Currency, and the Federal Deposit Insurance Corporation, the savings and loan industry always enjoyed a closer relationship with its regulatory body. Thus, the Federal Home Loan Bank Board was as much a champion of the savings and loans as a regulator.

The closeness of the S&Ls with this regulator, coupled with the investment opportunities newly possible under deregulation and the considerable political clout of S&Ls with Congress, resulted in rather lax regulation. Over the 1980s, many savings and loans entered into very speculative real estate development and investment activities, and even into such vehicles as junk bonds. As the Bush administration assumed the White House, it was clear that the savings and loan industry was collectively bankrupt and that in aggregate it was in the hole between $150 billion and $200 billion. Since the majority of the deposits in the savings and loans were guaranteed by the FSLIC, the American taxpayer ultimately stands behind the deposits. Thus, this $150 billion to $200 billion deficit is a major national problem.

Table 13-2 shows that the problem is concentrated in some of the faster growing states and in the oil patch. Nonetheless, the problem is national in scope. The amount of dollars is so significant that Congress has established the **Resolution Trust Corporation (RTC).** The RTC is charged with managing the workout of this disaster, with the insurance function passing from the now eliminated FSLIC to the FDIC. In addition to tighter insurance control, new legislation requires that the savings and loans have greater capital if they participate in riskier lending and investment activities. This concept, known as the risk-based cost of capital, will require most of the savings and loans to increase their capital and, along with it, their long-term viability. However, as we enter the 1990s, it appears that many, if not the majority, of the nation's savings and loans are so far below the required capital level (under the risk-based cost of capital rules), and their prospects so meager, that they will be unable to raise the required capital. A large number of people now believe that the savings and loan industry, which has existed in this country for decades, is a thing of the past. Certainly, several of the larger and stronger S&Ls will evolve into major banklike financial institutions.

TABLE 13-2 U.S. THRIFT INSTITUTIONS: DISTRIBUTION OF ASSETS IN SELECTED STATES BY CAPITAL CATEGORY

ASSET DISTRIBUTION AS OF 6/30/89	INSTITUTIONS IN RTC	TANGIBLE INSOLVENT NOT IN RTC	TANGIBLE SOLVENT FAILING LEVERAGE RATIOS	TANGIBLE SOLVENT FAILING RISK-BASED CAPITAL GUIDELINES	INSTITUTIONS IN CAPITAL COMPLIANCE	TOTAL ASSETS (BILLION $)	TOTAL INSTITUTIONS
California	4.6%	1.2%	15.5%	33.2%	45.4%	$402.38	190
Florida	5.1	24.5	22.9	14.2	33.4	88.28	145
Georgia	6.7	16.5	6.5	3.8	66.4	20.25	70
Illinois	4.4	29.8	13.2	6.0	46.6	65.56	243
Indiana	0.6	3.0	15.7	19.4	61.2	13.87	102
Louisiana	18.3	25.1	8.7	7.5	40.4	14.96	93
Maryland	6.8	7.6	30.1	20.8	34.7	24.04	102
Missouri	8.3	15.9	30.1	4.8	40.8	24.34	80
New Jersey	1.1	13.4	40.5	3.6	41.3	55.20	132
New York	0.0	58.3	6.0	7.9	27.8	59.92	86
North Carolina	1.9	6.1	6.5	20.1	65.5	21.50	132
Ohio	3.7	11.6	23.6	15.0	46.1	52.02	220
Pennsylvania	11.5	22.6	5.7	9.6	50.6	46.56	165
Texas	26.9	23.6	37.4	3.8	8.2	100.91	204
Virginia	0.1	11.8	8.5	20.0	59.6	31.26	64
Wisconsin	1.5	0.0	3.6	17.0	77.9	17.09	70

Sources: Office of Thrift Supervision & U.S. League of Savings Institutions Research Department; Stan Ross, ed., "FIRREA Aims to Make Housing Available to Low-Income Persons," Real Estate Newsline—Special Issue, Vol. 6, No. 9 (September 1989).

However, it is quite possible that a majority of the savings and loans will no longer exist by the time the next edition of this text comes out.

LENDING INSTITUTIONS

Financial institutions generally specialize in one or more areas of real estate finance. To obtain the best loan, the borrower should know the type of institution that prefers to make the type of loan he or she wants.

As we look at the different loan originators in the next few pages, keep a few ideas in mind.

- The institution is trying to get the maximum return for the least risk. Lenders' revenues come from (1) the stated interest rate, (2) front-end fees called "points" (see Chapter 15), (3) provision of related services such as mortgage life insurance, and (4) any "other business" that comes to the institution because it made a particular loan.

- Institutions prefer loans that fit their liability structure, that is, loans that have similar maturities to their source of funds. Savers are the institution's source of funds, and different institutions cater to different groups of savers.

- The institution's self-image, as well as its management's attitude, is important. Some lenders avoid making certain types of loans because they lack experience. Others have an ego commitment to certain types of projects such as downtown revitalization.

- The institution's contact with and knowledge of the different segments of real estate markets (by type of property and location) affect the types of loans the institution makes. Each institution's lending policy is a function of the segment of the industry it understands.

- Government regulation has an important effect on the portfolios of financial institutions. These regulations range from ceilings on loan-to-value ratios to the allowable percentage of certain types of loans in the institution's portfolio.

PLAYERS IN THE CAPITAL MARKETS

INDIVIDUALS

Individuals can provide both equity and debt financing. As lenders, individuals can make loans directly or through financial intermediaries. When they lend through financial intermediaries, they place money with an institution, such as a commercial bank. The institution then aggregates several individual savers' deposits and originates loans that match the risk and maturity of the deposits. When mortgage markets are "tight," that is, when the financial intermediaries experience a net outflow of funds, individuals selling their homes are often forced to provide seller financing. In so doing, they collectively become a large direct source of mortgage credit.

COMMERCIAL BANKS (CBS)

Commercial banks are the largest financial intermediary in the U.S. financial system. They are regulated by federal or state governmental agencies or both. They are also the primary means by which the Federal Reserve carries out its responsibilities for monitoring the nation's money supply. (Federally chartered commercial banks are required to belong to the Federal Reserve System and to the Federal Deposit Insurance Corporation.) Traditionally, the commercial banks' sources of funds are dominated by short-term savings deposits and checking accounts. Consequently, their assets are concentrated in short-term loans to businesses for operations and for receivables financing. When making real estate loans, commercial banks emphasize construction and development loans and less frequently make long-term loans. Government regulations limit loan-to-value ratios and limit real estate loans to a stated percent of equity capital. As a result, mortgage loans make up only about 15 to 20 percent of most commercial banks' portfolios.[4]

Bank holding companies have grown in both size and scope in recent years. Through these holding companies, commercial banks are able to offer borrowers a range of services that go beyond the services traditionally provided by smaller commercial banks. Consequently, the nation's money center bank holding companies can offer the full spectrum of real estate financing.

BANK TRUST DEPARTMENTS

Commercial banks usually have a trust department. In the past, trust departments tended to handle individual estates and were not the most dynamic part of the bank. More recently, however, larger bank trust departments have managed a sizable portion of the growing pension fund reserve pool. In this capacity, they select, acquire, and monitor portfolios of stocks, bonds, and real estate. This is a lucrative business and is much more aggressively managed than the traditional trust department operation. Since, by law, the trust department must be completely independent of the commercial banking function in the bank, it is possible for a real estate developer, for example, to be turned down for financing by Bank of America's commercial group and receive financing from Bank of America's trust operation on the same project.

---

[4]*A notable exception would be Hawaiian commercial banks, mortgage loans dominate their portfolios.*

SAVINGS AND LOAN ASSOCIATIONS (S&Ls)

S&Ls are not as large in total assets as commercial banks, and they are shrinking. However, their loans are concentrated in the real estate industry, and they are the nation's largest mortgage lender. S&Ls draw on savings accounts and certificates as their primary source of funds. They were traditionally regulated by the Federal Home Loan Bank Board (FHLBB) if federally chartered, or by state agencies if they operated under a state charter. Agencies regulate the types of loans the S&Ls can make, the maximum interest rates they can pay on savings accounts, and their geographical lending limits. Because savings accounts (time deposits) are more stable than demand deposits, S&Ls have traditionally made longer term loans, primarily single-family mortgages in their local market.

Until the early 1980s, S&Ls were restricted by the so-called regulation Q ceilings from paying high rates of interest on savings deposits. When interest rates on alternative uses of the saver's dollar, such as government T-bills, rose above these ceilings (as they did in 1966, 1969, 1974, and 1979), many savers were induced to forgo the convenience of the S&L for the higher yield available on direct investment in debt instruments like T-bills.

Withdrawing funds from savings to invest directly in other debt instruments was called **disintermediation** because funds ceased to flow through the intermediary. Disintermediation caused problems for both S&L managers and the home-building industry. S&L managers were forced to look to the FHLBB to handle liquidity problems when they could not liquidate their long-term investments fast enough to satisfy depositors' withdrawal requests. Would-be home buyers were unable to find financing, for the S&Ls had no new money to lend, and, as a result, home builders were out of work.

As shown in Box 13-4, S&Ls were given new freedoms, on both the asset and liability sides, to prevent disintermediation. On the liability side, they could pay higher rates to attract savers' deposits even during periods of high interest rates. However, money market certificates offer only a partial solution to disintermediation. The major reason is that many S&L depositors immediately switch (within the S&L) to the new, higher yielding certificates (this is called **internal disintermediation**)— thereby placing the S&L in the unfortunate position of paying higher rates to keep existing deposits (liabilities) while their existing loans (assets) continue to yield the same rate of interest as before. Obviously, paying more for funds than they receive on loans is not a viable long-term strategy for S&Ls.

On the asset side, S&Ls were also given greater flexibility. As a result, some diversified into consumer lending, commercial real estate lending, and construction or development lending. Again, the solution has caused

13-4
SAVINGS AND LOAN COMPETITION IN THE 1980S: A PROPHECY AT THE BEGINNING OF THE DECADE

The 1980s will be the decade of challenge for S&Ls. Financial institutions at the end of this decade will bear little, if any, resemblance to those currently in existence.

The future will be more dynamic and demanding and will be characterized by

- More intense competition for funds. S&Ls will compete for funds not only with other depository institutions, but increasingly with nondepository institutions with large bases of retail customers and national distribution capabilities (like Sears) and with other innovative financial institutions that want to capitalize on their competitive strengths to market new financial services.

- The battle for funds in the 1980s will focus on rates paid for funds. With the increased availability of credit in a more homogeneous national market, institutional loyalties will be weakened, and money will flow to the highest bidders. High rates of inflation have made consumers more yield-conscious and more willing to incur higher risks in achieving higher yields.

- A blurring of institutional distinctions. The entry of new multipurpose institutions into the consumer financial services market will obliterate the traditional distinctions among various financial institutions. Consequently, there will be a substantial homogenization of the services provided by depository and other financial institutions. Finally, there will be a significant consolidation between various financial institutions in the future. Thus, there will be fewer, but larger, S&Ls in the future. The pressure to achieve the greater efficiencies and operating advantages accruing to larger-sized organizations will bring about consolidation within the S&L industry and other sectors of the financial services markets. The earnings problems of depository thrift institutions and the relaxation of statutory and regulatory impediments to geographic expansion will hasten consolidation.

Finding ways to respond creatively to these changes will be the primary challenge facing S&Ls in the 1980s. The formula for S&Ls' success in the 1980s will be

- The ability to attract savers' funds by offering competitive rates.
- The ability to offer a wide array of new services at competitive prices.
- The ability to manage interest margins and hedge lending-investing risks.
- The ability to generate new sources of noninterest income.
- The ability to improve earnings through greater efficiencies and cost reductions.

This transition will not be easy. S&Ls will have to broaden their asset base, change their pricing practices, increase the efficiency of their operations, and position themselves to deal with continued rate volatility. These changes will be uncomfortable, but, for S&Ls, survival is the issue of the 1980s.

Source: Richard G. Marcis, "Savings & Loan Planning for the New Competitive Environment," *Federal Home Loan Bank Board Journal* 14:7 (July 1981): 13.

new problems. As S&Ls moved into new fields, they were forced to compete with other financial institutions that had more experience and well-established contacts. By 1986, many S&Ls were again in serious trouble. This time the cause was not disintermediation but rather bad loans in types of real estate new to S&Ls.

As described earlier in the regulatory section, the problem of bad loans became so severe that it precipitated a major national crisis. The result has been the nearly complete dismantling of the entire Federal Home Loan Bank Board group; oversight responsibility for the problem properties has been shifted to the Resolution Trust Corporation and ongoing monitoring of savings and loan operations to the FDIC. In 1990, the situation remains so fluid that it is not useful to describe in detail all the new structures that are being put in place. With a problem of this magnitude, it will take at least a decade for the institutions, and their regulators, to sort out the problems.

Any student of the real estate industry must understand the potential impact of this crisis on many facets of the real estate industry. The Resolution Trust Corporation already (in 1990) has such a huge portfolio of problem loans assumed from defunct savings and loans that it is the nation's largest real estate owner. In the final section on trends, we project that the RTC's activities will create more real estate jobs than any other single institution or development in the 1990s. As Box 13-5 indicates, it will take a great deal of talent to manage the workout of all the troubled savings and loan properties. More importantly, how these properties are brought to market will have tremendous impact on surrounding properties and the rents they are able to charge. The magnitude of the problem is so great, particularly in Texas, Louisiana, and Arizona, that no new development can proceed without the developer's prudent consideration of what may emerge from the RTC's portfolio.

MUTUAL SAVINGS BANKS

Mutual savings banks are similar to the traditional S&Ls. Mutual savings banks exist in only 20 states, all but 2—Oregon and Washington—in the Northeast and Middle Atlantic regions. Savings banks originated in the nineteenth century to encourage thrift among working people. At that

**13-5
S&L SALE:
FIRST WAVE
HITS MARKET**

Washington—Interested in buying a karate studio in Greta, La.? How about a mortuary in Tyler, Tx., or an airport in Colorado Springs?

Today, a new government agency, the Resolution Trust Corp., will deliver to Congress its list of the real estate held by hundreds of sick savings and loans seized by the RTC—some 30,000 properties in all.

The four-volume list will provide the first opportunity for real-estate speculators, local housing agencies and other bargain hunters to glimpse the government's sprawling S&L property holdings.

Publishing the list is the first major step in the biggest real-estate marketing spree since the Homestead Act of westward-ho days. The RTC's three-man public-affairs department already has stacked up 22,000 letters of inquiry, "and we quit counting the phone calls," a spokesman says.

The RTC can only hope demand will be as broad as the range of property. The list stretches from a 316-square-foot condominium in Osage Beach, Mo., to a plot of undeveloped land spanning 744,000 acres of Port Orchard, Wash.

Hotels run the gamut from the Heart Break Hotel in Bowers Beach, Del., listed at $60,000, to the $75 million Hyatt Grand in Indian Wells, Calif. Also up for grabs are 50 restaurants, a dozen golf courses, a half-dozen churches, several private hospitals, dozens of marinas, and odds and ends such as a bingo parlor in Gonzales, La.

"The myth, as far as we are concerned, is that it is all junk," an RTC official says. "It's not." Consider all those single-family homes priced to sell, for instance, or those beachfront condominiums in North Carolina.

But matching buyers and sellers on this scale will be the biggest challenge of resolving the S&L crisis. Just compiling the list of what is available was time-consuming and costly, with loan files at hundreds of S&Ls being scanned for specific information that was entered into a gargantuan database at the RTC. "It was a little like the moonshot," says Tom Horton, the RTC's deputy in charge of asset disposal.

Under the law, the RTC also must separate the low-cost real estate to give public agencies and non-profit groups the first chance to bid. And from Washington as well as regional offices in Denver, Dallas, Atlanta, and Kansas City, the agency must keep tabs on the hundreds of private-sector firms that will manage and market the properties until they are sold.

Moreover, the agency will have to cope with the complexities of comparing bids for individual properties with bids for the S&Ls carrying the real estate in their portfolios. "They are going to need databases that they haven't created yet," says Karen Shaw, a banking consultant at the Institute for Strategy Development here.

In comparison with sweetheart sales that plagued a predecessor agency called the Federal Asset Disposition Association, the RTC claims bidding will be opened up as widely as possible. It will sell the four catalogs of properties for $50 each, or smaller volumes of just residential, commercial, or land properties for $10 or $15.

It also hopes to slice up the data it has collected to suit buyers looking in particular regions, beginning with a 500-page report that includes Houston, Dallas, and San Antonio properties. All lists will be updated every six months and be distributed to some libraries, with a toll-free number to call to find the nearest participating library.

"These lists are only the starting point," says Elaine Richardson, an official in the marketing department of the RTC. Indeed, the lists contain only the bare-bone vitals on individual assets—address, square footage, number of rooms, condition, list price and someone to contact. Some offer much less in the way of information, such as a listing for one acre of commercial real estate at 23426 Brush Pines in Magnolia, Tx., with not so much as a contact listed.

The RTC, created by the S&L bailout law passed in August, has only just begun considering how to market the real estate included in the list. At the moment, it's planning marketing the old-fashioned way, such as open-air auctions, newsletters and regional and national advertising. It's also kicking around display ads along the lines of "condo deals of the month," and running lists in banking and real-estate trade publications.

FOR SALE: RTC ASSETS

NUMBER OF INDIVIDUAL PROPERTIES AVAILABLE TO BUYERS

Residential, single family:	11,918
Residential, other:	14,895
Commercial:	2,516
Raw Land:	794

But the agency also will employ more sophisticated marketing. The RTC plans, for example, to use a AA Direct Marketing Corp., a unit of AMR Corp., to operate a 900 telephone line to the RTC asset-disposal section. The RTC says the initial three-month contract is valued at roughly $138,000.

Also planned, though not yet available, is a service that would allow buyers to use their personal computers to scroll through a database by region or type of real estate. The agency also will distribute the information on computer diskettes and laser disks, which are widely used by the real-estate industry.

The list released today is only the first wave. It includes only real estate that was seized with the 283 S&Ls under RTC control by Sept. 30—not the properties in the S&Ls taken over since then, and not the tens of thousands of properties still in the midst of foreclosure actions or held by S&L subsidiaries. Within a few years, the agency expects to control some $180 billion in real estate, as well as $120 billion in loans and securities.

Many people in the real-estate and thrift industries are skeptical that marketing on such a scale is possible. "They can write a newsletter, but how do they know who to send it to?" says Ray Sculfort, general manager of PaceLine National Management, a real-estate management firm.

"The advantage of public advertisements is that they open the bidding and avoid the mysteries of inside baseball," says Ms. Shaw, the Washington consultant. "The disadvantage is that the still-small staff is deluged by 22,000 letters, and probably only 1% are serious."

Source: Paulette Thomas, "S&L Sale: First Wave Hits Market," *The Wall Street Journal,* Tuesday, January 2, 1990, page B1.

time, the main population centers were in the northeastern United States. Population growth in other parts of the country coincided with the development of S&Ls, which came to dominate most of the country.

The term *mutual* indicates that savings banks are owned and operated by their depositors and are managed by a board of trustees. They are nonprofit institutions. S&Ls, by comparison, may be either mutual (about 70 percent) or stock (30 percent)—that is, owned by depositors or by shareholders.

CREDIT UNIONS

Credit unions are small savings and lending organizations set up to benefit members of a particular group, usually an individual business. Credit unions are the most numerous of the financial intermediaries; however, their very small individual size means that their aggregate deposits are relatively small. Nevertheless, from a real estate perspective, credit unions can be a good source of mortgage financing for home ownership or home improvement. Credit unions are regulated by the National Credit Union Administration in Washington, D.C., and are organized politically through their trade association in Madison, Wisconsin.

LIFE INSURANCE COMPANIES (LICs)

LICs provide financial security for policyholders. The premiums the companies collect are used largely to maintain reserves from which benefits are paid. These reserves constitute large pools of capital that must be invested. Since the inflows of funds, as well as the demands on these funds, are fairly stable over time, the LICs can make long-term mortgage loans. In fact, LICs are the major long-term lenders on many commercial and industrial properties. These loans have maturities similar to those for single-family loans, but there is neither mortgage insurance nor an active secondary market (i.e., there is less liquidity). Moreover, unlike

CBs and S&Ls, LICs are not geographically dispersed throughout the nation; rather, they are concentrated in a few centers. Because they cannot afford to make a large number of small loans throughout the nation, the asset structure of LICs consists primarily of large long-term commercial loans.[5]

Life insurance companies were among the first financial institutions to offer real estate investment management to pension funds. Today not only do they handle their own real estate investments, but they are also, as fiduciaries, the largest manager of equity real estate investments for pension funds. (More detail on this business is provided in Part 7.) Prudential Insurance, for example, is one of the nation's largest real estate investor–managers with over $40 billion in investments under management.

REAL ESTATE INVESTMENT TRUSTS

Real estate investment trusts (**REITs**) were established by legislation in the early 1960s. They are essentially corporations that pay no corporate taxes if they follow strict investment regulations. Recognizing the large capital necessary to make a real estate investment and the limited resources of the small investor, Congress saw REITs as a way to group small investors so that they could take advantage of the benefits of real estate investments.

REITs sell beneficial shares that are traded on the stock markets much like corporate common stock. In the past, many of them chose to leverage their position by borrowing on a short-term basis from commercial banks. These short-term loans were thought to be safe for the bank because of the cushion created by the REITs' equity capital as well as by the diversity of loans or equity interests held by the trusts (the trusts' assets). The exact makeup of a REIT's portfolio varies, depending on the management philosophy of the trustees. Some of the trusts are very conservative, making only first lien loans on fully leased high-grade properties. Others, seeking higher returns, are involved in much riskier land development and second lien financing.

REITs suffered a terrible beating in the mid-1970s (see Box 13-6), but in recent years they have made a dramatic comeback. Since the mid-1970s, their returns have been very attractive,[6] and they are now viewed as an appropriate ownership vehicle for individual retirement accounts and other small pension funds. When the Rockefeller family decided to sell the famous Rockefeller Center Complex in midtown Man-

---

[5]*Life insurance companies do hold substantial portfolios of single-family mortgage loans, but they typically are originated and are serviced by mortgage bankers whose position is explained shortly.*
[6]*Figures on REIT performance are available from the National Association of REITs in Washington, D.C.*

**13-6
HOW REITs
FELL INTO
TROUBLE**

Many REITs borrowed on a short-term basis, hoping that financial leverage would improve the return to their equity holders. They borrowed from the commercial banks at rates varying with prime. The most adventurous of them then made construction loans also tied to prime, but at four and five points over the prime rate. It looked like a money tree, and the REITs quickly became the darlings of Wall Street. Upside financial leverage meant even greater percentage returns to equity.

However, by 1974, real estate development was in serious trouble. The REITs found that they had the weakest loans. Since they charged the highest rates, developers with better projects went to a lower cost source of financing. The high-cost REIT loans were taken by developers involved in riskier projects. During the recession, demand for space dropped. At the same time, serious supply shortages arose because of the Arab oil embargo. Furthermore, sources of long-term credit (which would be used to pay off the short-term construction loans) dried up as disintermediation occurred in the real estate financial markets. All these factors collectively made developers unable to repay loans made by the REITs.

What had looked like a money tree turned out to be a money sink. When developers were unable to pay, the REITs had difficulty repaying their loans to commercial banks. On the one hand, the REITs could not afford to leave a project half-finished; and on the other, they could not find the money to complete the projects. As the REITs scrambled for cash to complete what had now become unfortunate development experiences, the banks tightened the credit reins. After a substantial grace period (a period of time to solve their own financial problems), the REITs came to recognize that the collateral for their loans—that is, the partially completed development projects—were in many cases not worth as much as the debt owed the REITs or the REITs' corresponding obligations to the commercial banks. In the late 1970s, many of the early REITs traded their development and construction loans to commercial banks for debt reductions and generally tried to work themselves out of the real estate lending business.

hattan in 1985, they chose a complex version of a REIT as the ownership vehicle.

MORTGAGE BANKERS

Another major originator of mortgage loans is the **mortgage banker.**[7] The mortgage banker differs significantly from other lenders in that it is

[7]An expanded discussion of the role of the mortgage banker is presented in Chapter 16 on secondary mortgage markets.

not a depository institution. The mortgage banker typically makes loans and then resells these loans to a permanent lender. Its function is to originate and service loans in markets where certain permanent lenders cannot operate efficiently. The most common example is found in single-family lending with life insurance companies serving as the final lender. Remember that the life insurance company is not located in the local market as is the S&L; therefore, it needs someone local to originate the loans and to service the loans (collect principal, interest, insurance, and tax payments). The mortgage banker serves this function.

Essentially, the mortgage banker borrows from a commercial bank through what is referred to as a warehousing line of credit and uses these funds to originate individual mortgage loans. Once a package of mortgage loans has been originated, this entire package is sold to an institutional investor such as a life insurance company. The package of loans is a large enough investment to interest the life insurance company, and the mortgage banker will continue to service these loans, eliminating the need for the life insurance company to have a local office. The mortgage banker earns a fee for originating the loan and charges a fee to service the loan for the life insurance company. The origination fee typically represents 1 percent of the mortgage amount, and the servicing fee will normally run from one-fourth to three-eighths of 1 percent of the outstanding loan balance. Mortgage bankers are typically very flexible and change the exact product being offered to meet both the needs of borrowers and the needs of those who invest in mortgages. As shown in Box 13-7 mortgage bankers definitely move to the market and expand their offerings as mortgage technology evolves.

Mortgage bankers should not be confused with **mortgage brokers.** Mortgage brokers help only to originate loans and do not service them. Most mortgage brokers bring large commercial borrowers and lenders together and are not active in the single-family mortgage market; they receive an origination fee for bringing the borrower and lender together.

INVESTMENT BANKERS

Investment bankers have traditionally been involved in the initial placement (primary market) of securities. Whether taking a company public with its first public stock issue or underwriting additional issues of debt or equity, investment banking is high-level finance. A corporate finance position with one of the country's leading investment banking firms is still "the" placement for a new MBA.

The national investment banking firms moved heavily into real estate in the late 1970s and 1980s. Salomon Brothers led the way in securitizing residential mortgages, with First Boston, Goldman Sachs, Morgan Stanley, Merrill Lynch, Shearson, and others bringing on an array of

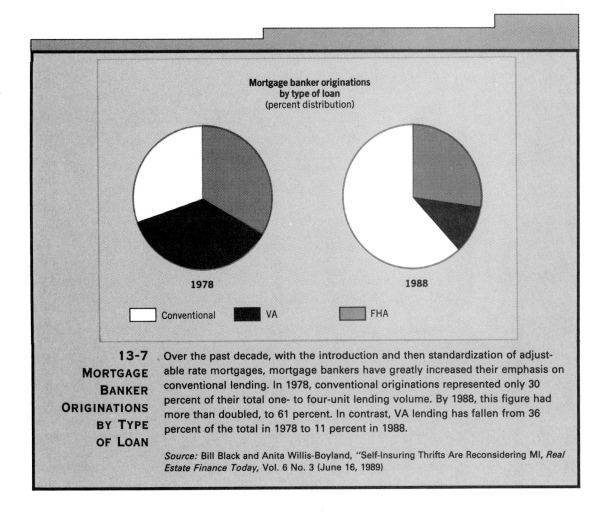

13-7
MORTGAGE
BANKER
ORIGINATIONS
BY TYPE
OF LOAN

Over the past decade, with the introduction and then standardization of adjustable rate mortgages, mortgage bankers have greatly increased their emphasis on conventional lending. In 1978, conventional originations represented only 30 percent of their total one- to four-unit lending volume. By 1988, this figure had more than doubled, to 61 percent. In contrast, VA lending has fallen from 36 percent of the total in 1978 to 11 percent in 1988.

Source: Bill Black and Anita Willis-Boyland, "Self-Insuring Thrifts Are Reconsidering MI, *Real Estate Finance Today,* Vol. 6 No. 3 (June 16, 1989)

new financing products. In Chapter 16, we will look at the original securitization of the residential mortgage instrument, and in Chapters 22 and 23, we will examine some of the more recent commercial mortgage instruments. At this point, it is important to understand that the investment banker is a primary innovator in the system. Investment bankers find new needs and new ways to fill these needs. Thus, their particular function changes over time. They originally entered the real estate market by helping securitize the residential mortgage. Then for a period in the mid-1980s, their major concentration was on securitizing the commercial mortgage. Today, the bulk of their activities involve high-level brokerage of "trophy properties" and international sourcing of debt financing.

VENTURE CAPITALISTS

The venture capitalist takes an entrepreneur from "an idea in a garage" to the initial public offering, that is, to the investment banker. By providing both funding and management assistance, the venture capitalist is critical in helping new businesses grow. Venture capitalists usually deal with real estate only to the extent that the new company needs space. They are not yet a significant player in real estate finance. However, while most venture capitalists have chosen to avoid the real estate field, we will show that a venture capital period now characterizes most real estate development. This change has occurred because regulation has significantly lengthened the amount of time between the development idea and the initiation of construction. The kind of financing needed to do the land feasibility and design studies is much like venture capital in the sense that the money must be expended without anything really tangible to show for the investment. Just as the venture capitalist financing a new business is forced to rely on inventory and receivables in a fledgling enterprise, the developer, rather than invest in land and bricks and mortar, is now investing in plans that as an investment are every bit as risky as the business start-ups funded by traditional venture capital. Since the risk is high, so is the required return, as we will show in more detail in Part 8.

INVESTMENT MANAGERS

A few specialized individuals and firms provide investment management services that compete with those offered by bank trust departments, insurance company separate accounts (fiduciary accounts), and investments bankers. In real estate, there are several well-known investment managers including Rosenberg Real Estate Equity Fund; Trust Company of the West; AEW—State Street; and JMB. These professionals manage pension and other funds invested in real estate assets. As explained in detail in Chapters 22 and 23, this group uses all the tools of modern portfolio theory along with the real estate fundamentals explained in this text.

SYNDICATORS

The press has had many negative things to say about syndicators. Allegations of abuses stem from the size of fees taken for "packaging" investments as well as from borderline tax shelters.

Although there have undoubtedly been serious abuses in some heavily tax-sheltered syndications, the principle of syndication is both simple and socially productive. The idea of syndication is to make ownership of

<table>
<tr><td>

13-8

THE INTERRELATED NATURE OF REAL ESTATE FINANCE AND THE AMERICAN FINANCIAL SYSTEM: AN EXAMPLE

</td><td>

The massive savings and loan problem has spawned and will continue to spawn a great deal of legislation. One of the first new legislated requirements that is having immediate impact is risk-based cost of capital, and one institution among the many affected by it is Great Western.

Unlike many savings and loans, Great Western is a large institution with a national presence. Headquartered in California, the company has offices in over 20 states and will originate something over $10 billion in mortgage loans in 1990. Great Western is not one of the insolvent savings and loans we have talked about, but one of a select group of mega-financial institutions that starts with a savings and loan. (On the commercial banking side an even larger example of a major financial institution would be Citicorp, which itself, as we have said in the text, handles more mortgage loans than any other primary mortgage lender.)

Although Great Western Financial does not have the acute problem faced by many savings and loans, it is of course impacted by the new risk-based cost of capital concept. Essentially, this legislation requires banks to have more capital for riskier types of lending than for less risky types of lending. Traditional single-family mortgage lending would be one of the less risky types of activity. However, it is not as simple as mortgage lending and nonmortgage lending. As we have stressed throughout the book, different kinds of mortgage loans carry various levels of risk. As will be pointed out in Chapter 16, a host of real estate market mechanisms, some federal and some private, insure (and thus make less risky) mortgage loans. One of the largest private mortgage insurers is General Electric Corporation through its finance subsidiary.

With the new risk-based cost of capital, it suddenly makes financial sense for Great Western to buy the services of General Electric to guarantee certain pools of loans so that Great Western's investment in this pool will be considered less risky and consequently Great Western can utilize its capital in other areas, that is, tie up less capital in this type of lending. Although the details of secondary market operations and mortgage insurance are deferred until Chapter 16, it is important in your first look at real estate finance to understand the related nature of the marketplace. As marketplace changes necessitate new legislation, they also create opportunities for new business relationships. In this case, one of the nation's largest manufacturing companies is providing insurance to a large lender so it will be able to make more loans.

</td></tr>
</table>

a large property accessible to smaller investors. All other things being equal, access by more investors improves market efficiency and makes life better.

Syndicators are a group of middlemen who make a profit by efficiently aggregating and allocating savings. Historically, they have organized as limited partnerships for the tax reasons discussed in Part 6, but they also use other forms such as the real estate investment trust. As we enter the 1990s, the big syndication firms of the 1980s are almost universally going through very tough times. The combination of tax law reform, overbuilding throughout the real estate industry, and their own errors has cast these firms' futures in serious doubt. While some form of syndication will probably continue (syndication has been around since the Middle Ages), the go-go era spawned by the 1981 Reagan tax cuts undoubtedly ended with the bankruptcy of VMS Realty in 1990.

FINANCIAL SUPERMARKETS

Supermarkets? With the emphasis on deregulation in the Reagan years, several of the capital market players have moved aggressively into areas formerly considered "other people's turf." Prudential Insurance now makes residential loans by telephone; wants to be your banker, stockbroker, insurance agent, single-family residence broker, and appraiser. Citibank wants even more, and both want to operate nationwide. Only time will tell whether economies in joint operation are sufficient to overcome the advantages of traditional specialties. It certainly is a brave new financial world.

GOVERNMENT AS A LENDER

In addition to the private institutions just mentioned, the federal government is an important player in real estate finance. As we noted earlier, the Federal Reserve regulates and provides credit to various loan originators. In addition, the federal government makes direct loans through several agencies, as explained in Part 9.

GOVERNMENT AS FACILITATOR IN REAL ESTATE FINANCE

MORTGAGE INSURANCE PROGRAMS

A special feature of real estate debt financing is the availability of mortgage insurance to protect lenders against losses on defaulted loans. Mortgage protection is available through government programs (**FHA** loan insurance or Veterans Administration [**VA**] loan guarantees) or from private mortgage insurers.

All the programs insure single-family home loans; the FHA programs extend to multifamily units as well as to single-family homes. The basic objective of all programs is to encourage private lenders to make loans that might otherwise be rejected because of geographical diversity or high loan-to-value ratios.[8] Mortgage insurance causes more funds to flow into mortgage finance.

LIQUIDITY AND THE SECONDARY MARKET

The mortgage lender is also concerned with the liquidity of its loans. Even if loans are safe (i.e., the collateral-borrower characteristics and mortgage insurance are sufficient to guarantee that the lender will not lose principal), it is still possible for the lender to have a liquidity problem. When financial institutions experience an outflow of deposits, they must be able to liquidate assets to meet the claims of their depositors or policyholders. The liquidity needs of different financial intermediaries vary, based on the volatility of their fund sources. For example, CBs have greater liquidity needs than LICs.

To meet lenders' liquidity needs, several government agencies have been established. Among these are the Federal National Mortgage Association (**FNMA** or Fannie Mae), the Government National Mortgage Association (**GNMA** or Ginnie Mae), the Federal Home Loan Mortgage Corporation (**FHLMC** or Freddie Mac), and the Federal Farm Loan Mortgage Corporation (FFLMC or Farmer Mac). These government and quasi-government agencies either provide or facilitate a secondary mortgage market where mortgage loan originators may sell loans when they need liquidity. Besides these government agencies, stockbrokers are active in marketing real estate-related debt instruments in the secondary market. In fact, some of these instruments are now traded in the futures and options markets. There is also a private secondary market where some financial institutions buy mortgages from originators and "securitize" them for sale to investors. (See Chapter 16 for a full discussion of the secondary mortgage markets as well as the various forms of insurance that facilitate their operation.)

CONSUMER PROTECTION

In the 1960s, consumer groups in the United States began a major effort to educate consumers in economic and commercial affairs and to pass legislation protecting consumers from fraud. This movement, called by some the "consumer revolution," has had a major impact on business transactions in this country. We have already shown you a legal example. In discussing real estate leases in Chapter 4, we pointed out that courts have moved toward viewing leases as contracts rather than conveyances

---

[8]*The use of private mortgage insurance allows regulated financial intermediaries to go beyond the standard 75 to 80 percent loan-to-value ceiling.*

because the concept of a contract provides greater protection for tenants. In Part 4, on marketing, the closings appendix covers truth in lending and the Real Estate Settlement Procedures Act. Several other consumer protection issues are covered in Part 9. (See also Box 13-9.)

In real estate lending, a major consumer issue has been **redlining.** In the 1970s, the federal government determined that the nonavailability of mortgage credit could lead to the decline of a neighborhood. It further noted that some lending institutions, to avoid what the institutions considered undue lending risks, were "redlining" certain neighborhoods, refusing to consider any loans within the redlined area. These areas were often declining central city neighborhoods with high concentrations of blacks, Hispanics, and other minorities. Race was an important ingredient in the problem of "lender-pushed urban decay." Legislation now outlaws redlining. In addition, the Federal Reserve is exerting pressure on commercial banks to make loans in "all" their lending areas before the bank can expand to new markets. Private mortgage lenders have also found it to their advantage to help the consumer (see Box 13-10).

Up to this point we have looked for the most part at the players in real estate finance. Now, for a few pages, we will look at the process.

THE FINANCING CYCLE

We will conclude our macroeconomic overview of real estate financing by classifying real estate loans according to the time the loan is made, in a sequence that begins with the acquisition of raw land and ends with a fully developed property ready for use or sale. The object of this discussion is threefold.

13-9
EQUAL CREDIT OPPORTUNITY ACT

In addition to the Truth-in-Lending Act (TiL), the Consumer Credit Protection Act (CCPA) also contains, as Title VI, the **Equal Credit Opportunity Act (ECOA).** This act prohibits discrimination in lending on the basis of sex, marital status, age, race, color, religion, national origin, or receipt by the applicant of public assistance.

Lenders must also consider permanent part-time earnings in evaluating an application for credit (sometimes an important consideration when a mortgage loan is being sought). The law prescribes in detail what questions may be asked or are prohibited on loan application forms. For example, in the case of a married couple, the lender may not inquire as to their childbearing plans.

The law is administered by the Federal Reserve Board, which has issued Regulation B to implement the law.

**13-10
GE'S
BORROWER
ASSISTANCE
PROGRAM: A
NEW WAY TO
KEEP MORE
DELINQUENT
BORROWERS IN
THEIR HOMES**

GE and you share a common goal: When a borrower becomes delinquent, we want to do everything possible to keep the family in the home. After all, *no one wins when a loan goes into foreclosure.*

Many delinquent families desperately want to keep their homes, but for some reason are temporarily unable to make the payments. That's where GE's Borrower Assistance Program can help.

Help Deserving Borrowers Stay in Their Homes

GE's Borrower Assistance Program is designed to help delinquent borrowers get back on their monthly payment schedules. For a qualified and deserving borrower, GE will advance funds to you or the servicer to bring the loan current, subsidize future payments or a combination of the two.

Easy Repayment Terms Help Borrowers—Which Helps You

Funds are advanced at *no interest cost.* The borrower repays the funds in easy monthly installments. Or, with servicer agreement, the funds can be deducted from a subsequent claim if the loan eventually goes into foreclosure.

In short, everyone wins. We make it easy as possible to keep the borrower in the home. And you continue to earn income on the loan, while preserving the borrower's dream of home ownership.

Investors Minimize REO Inventory and Reduce Losses

By reducing the likelihood of foreclosure on as many delinquent loans as possible, the investor will have fewer properties involved in foreclosure sales. And that means lower potential losses.

Services Reduce Collection Expenses

Because GE's Borrower Assistance Program can bring a loan current and provide for future payments, the servicer doesn't need to spend time and money collecting delinquent payments.

Everyone wins with GE's Borrower Assistance Program

The borrower stays in the home. The investor minimizes REO inventory and reduced potential losses. And the servicer reduces collection expenses.

Source: Internal GE publicity document reprinted with permission.

- To demonstrate the importance of financing at every stage of the real estate development process.

- To indicate how different sources of financing specialize in particular stages.

- To illustrate how loans at each stage are tailored, in their terms and interest rates, to reflect the lender's risks at each stage.

LAND ACQUISITION

The most common feature of land acquisition financing is the absence of institutional lenders. Institutions generally consider risk to be in inverse proportion to the cash flow from the property, because they consider the primary source of loan repayment to be the property itself. (See Box 13-11.) Since raw land generates no cash flow, loans to finance its acquisition are considered the most risky and frequently are avoided altogether or limited to a small percentage of an institution's loans, either as a matter of legal restriction or internal policy.

A common source of financing is a purchase money mortgage taken back by the seller of the land. In a land sale, the financing is extended because the seller often has no alternative if a buyer is to be found.

LAND DEVELOPMENT

Land development means preparing raw land for the construction of improvements. The process includes grading land where necessary; ob-

---

**13-11
RAW LAND
FINANCING**

Since land acquisition financing is relatively unavailable and costly, the developer must often have recourse to equity financing. One obvious source is the developer's own assets. Another frequent approach is to raise cash by a sale of interests to outside investors in a limited partnership in which the developer is the general partner.

The developer my avoid the need for any significant financing by entering into a joint venture with the landowner directly. The landowner contributes the land, and the developer contributes expertise and whatever small amount of cash is needed for primary expenses.

Yet another approach is to acquire the land under a long-term ground lease. This substitutes for an initial large capital outlay the obligation to pay a continuing ground rental for the term of the lease, which may run 99 years or more.

taining rezoning if required; and installing utilities, sewers, streets, and sidewalks. Although developed land (in the sense used here) creates no more cash flow than does raw land, it is nevertheless one step closer to the ultimate use and thus is somewhat easier to finance. Most development loans represent a first lien on the property, are short term, and the interest charged is usually tied to commercial banks' prime lending rate (1 to 4 points above the prime).

Development loans are usually made separately from construction loans when the raw land must be subdivided into smaller tracts or lots. The proceeds are disbursed in draws as the development progresses. The lender will allow release of specified tracts (lots) from the overall mortgage as development proceeds and the individual lots are sold to builders. When tracts or lots are released, the borrower must make a payment to the lender in exchange for the release. This **release price,** as it is called, is generally 10 to 20 percent greater than the proportional principal and interest associated with the released tract. This insures the lender of repayment with the sale of the choice lots and defers the developer's receipt of most of the profit until the development has been nearly sold out.

CONSTRUCTION

Real estate construction finance is a specialized process in which commercial banks play a dominant role. (At one time, REITs were a major player in the construction lending field, but this is no longer true.) The funds provided by the construction loan are used to pay for construction materials, labor, overhead, and related costs. The real estate is the collateral for the loan. The developer is sometimes required to post additional collateral, such as other real estate, securities, or possibly third-party guarantees.

Construction loans usually run from six months to two years, and, unlike most other types of loans, the actual loan funds are disbursed in stages (or draws) as construction proceeds. For example, 20 percent of the loan might be drawn down when the foundation is laid, the next 20 percent when the framing is completed, and so forth. In this way, the construction lender is assured that construction funds are being used for the intended purpose and, in the event of a default the value of the property will (the lender hopes) have been increased in an amount equal to the construction loan disbursements.

Construction lending is considered hazardous because construction itself is a risky form of real estate activity subject to numerous natural, economic, and political pitfalls. Therefore, the lender's return on construction loans is at the high end of the interest range. Typically, the borrower (developer) pays an initial loan fee plus an interest rate on the funds actually drawn down.

PERMANENT LOAN COMMITMENT.   The source of repayment of the construction loan is often the permanent loan. The construction lender, being a short-term lender, is often unwilling to contemplate the possibility that no permanent financing may be available when the construction is complete. To prevent this possibility, the construction lender usually requires the developer to obtain a **permanent loan commitment** as a condition to obtaining the construction loan. The commitment is an agreement by another lender (such as an S&L or LIC) to make the permanent loan provided the building is constructed in accordance with approved plans and specifications. This permanent loan commitment is often known as a **takeout commitment,** because it is the means whereby the construction lender will be taken out of the transaction when construction is completed.

In addition to the contract rate of interest, recent permanent loan commitments have often included an equity participation by the lender in addition to a fixed rate of interest. Participations allow the lenders to increase their yield by sharing in the before-tax cash flow (income participation) or capital gain (equity participation) of the project.

OWNERSHIP AND USE

The final stage in the real estate cycle begins when the property is put to use either by the owner or by tenants who have leased space. Now a lender can anticipate a long period of cash flow from the property to service a loan, and so it is at this point that a long-term (permanent) loan can be funded.

Usually a lender will already have committed itself to making the permanent loan. The developer needs only to provide to the permanent lender evidence of satisfactory completion, and the loan is disbursed (funded), most or all of it being used to pay off the construction lender.

Sometimes the permanent loan commitment will require not only that the improvements be completed, but also that a minimum rental level be achieved before the full amount of the permanent loan is funded.

Such a *rental achievement requirement* might provide that, on completion of the improvement, 70 percent of the permanent loan will be disbursed, with the balance of the permanent loan to be disbursed once 80 percent of the building is rented.

A loan containing this type of clause is called a *floor-to-ceiling loan* because it is disbursed in two stages. The purpose of the clause is to assure the lender that sufficient cash flow is forthcoming to service the loan before the entire amount is disbursed.

❏ **GAP FINANCING.**   Suppose the construction lender has insisted on a permanent (takeout) loan commitment equal to the full amount of the construction loan. If the best the developer can do is obtain a floor-to-ceiling loan, with the ceiling equal to the construction financing, a gap will exist if only the floor amount of the permanent loan is funded at the completion of construction.

To close this gap, the developer must obtain an additional loan commitment to provide **gap financing.** By this commitment, another lender agrees to provide a permanent second mortgage in the event the full amount of the permanent first mortgage is not advanced when construction is completed. As with most second mortgages, such an agreement will be more costly in terms of both interest and origination fees.

This is merely one example of the many financing variations that have been developed in the industry to meet specific situations. The varieties of financing techniques rival, if not exceed, the combinations of real estate interests that were discussed in Chapter 4. (See Box 13-12.)

Permanent financing of a newly completed real estate project is likely to go through a number of different modifications over the life of the project. The types of modifications include many possibilities. Among the more common possibilities are:

❑ **LIQUIDATION.**   The loan may be gradually amortized (paid off) during its term, eventually being liquidated in its entirety, at which point the owner's equity interest will equal the full market value of the property.

❑ **REFINANCING.**   Prior to the maturity of the original mortgage, the owner may (1) renegotiate its terms with the original lender, (2)

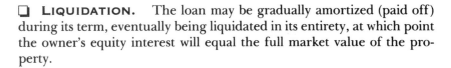
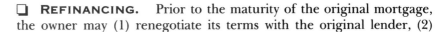

13-12 ANOTHER KIND OF HOUSING FINANCE	Although the American housing system seems normal, albeit complex, to most Americans, it is not the only way to finance housing. Singapore, for example, has had tremendous economic progress with one leader over the past 25 years. His vision of real estate ownership: every worker should own his own home. How does he make this possible? It is not with a Singaporian Fannie Mae or Freddie Mac; he simply passed a rule saying that every worker had to save 24 percent of his income and every employer had to put up an additional 12 percent, effectively meaning that every worker saves 36 percent of his income. This savings can be used only for specified expenditures—medical care, retirement, college for the children, or the home. We are told that in Singapore if you apply to buy too small a home, you are questioned. People know your salary, and they know you can afford a larger home because they know you have saved. This system is possibly a bit heavy handed, a bit "big brotherish," but it generates a tremendously high percentage of home ownership.

increase the loan amount, or (3) pay off the existing mortgage and obtain a new mortgage. All these are known by the term *loan refinancing*. In general, **refinancing** is done for one of three reasons: (1) to increase the property's sale potential by making the financing more attractive to a buyer, (2) to generate tax-free cash for the owner by increasing the existing debt, or (3) to decrease the existing debt so as to reduce the monthly debt service and increase the cash flow to the owner.

❏   **PREPAYMENT.**   Very often the owner of the property will sell it before the existing mortgage has been paid off. In such an event, the lender may call the loan,[9] or the new owner may wish to pay off the existing mortgage and arrange new financing.

We have looked at the financing cycle for real estate projects, and we have briefly introduced the U.S. capital markets with their extraordinary variety of players, working in a very sophisticated, innovative (and sometimes predatory) world. In the capital markets and in real estate, the 1980s were extremely tumultuous years for players of all kinds—extremely good for some (it was Donald Trump's big decade—he was barely known outside New York in 1980), and extremely bad for the syndicators, S&Ls, and some developers who lost their chips—not to mention the brokerage houses and investment banking firms that merged, folded, or laid off thousands of employees to survive. Before ending this chapter, it's worth pointing out how the turbulent 1980s changed our perception of the real estate game and what useful lessons can be derived.

THE GAME: LEVEL ONE AND LEVEL TWO

The real estate game is played on two levels. Level One of the game is about valuing the productive capacity of the property itself. At Level One, we try to determine how well the space over time, with associated services (i.e., the package being sold to the user of the real estate), serves the particular marketplace. How well it serves is determined by the rent it generates, and we have the tools to convert that expected rent to an estimate of value. This is valuation at Level One of the game, and most of this textbook is written about Level One.

At Level Two, we look at the many individual *players* of the game and evaluate the revenue not only to the project but also to the individual players. Why is this Level One/Level Two distinction important? When conflicting goals drive different players, the system can go haywire. Here is a current illustration. The United States is thought to have the most efficient capital markets in the world. How then could we have produced

[9]*In residential mortgages, such a lender "call provision on sale" is common. It is less common in commercial mortgages.*

the $150 billion savings and loan crisis? At Level One of the game, a vast number of projects were built that made no economic sense. In other words, no rational person would have expected the marketplace to pay enough rent for the space over time with associated services to justify the cost of the project. How could these projects have been built when at Level One they made no economic sense? If careful analysis had indicated that these properties would cost more than they were worth, then why did the savings and loans finance them? After all, the United States has lots of good financial analysts.

The answer lies in the Level One/Level Two distinction. As noted earlier in this chapter, public policy with regard to the savings and loan industry changed dramatically in 1980 and 1982. The savings and loans were in trouble at that time because they were lending long and borrowing short. They were borrowing from savers and lending on fixed-rate mortgages. When interest rates went up, their costs adjusted upward (they were flexible in the short term), but their revenues didn't because they lent long term with no short-term flexibility. The political fix to this problem was to allow S&Ls to enjoy the benefits of diversification across more types of investments and across more geographic regions. The logic behind this "solution" was that diversification reduced risk and would improve the savings and loans' position. This was fallacious logic, and the real reason behind the new initiative was the Congress's refusal to spend the money to fix the savings and loan problem that existed at the beginning of the 1980s. (Since many of the savings and loans were insolvent and the government insured depositors' funds, fixing the problem would have required a considerable infusion of cash from the federal government.) Congress gave savings and loan entrepreneurs something like a blank check. Owners of savings and loans could speculate with taxpayers' money, generating funds with high-yielding certificates of deposit, which were federally insured, and then making aggressive investments.

Look at Level Two of the game and think about the S&L entrepreneurs' position. Would they make low-risk investments or high-risk investments? Well, since many savings and loans were already slightly under water at the time entrepreneurs took them over (buying them cheap in a distressed condition), a low-risk investment would have been sure death. With a high-risk investment, they had at least a possibility that things would go well. So at Level Two it became quite clear what the entrepreneurs would want to do with the savings and loans—buy junk bonds and invest in speculative real estate. (In essence, "go for it.") They had very little to lose since the taxpayers were (and still are) footing most of the bill. This is an oversimplified explanation, but it makes the point. If you want to understand the savings and loan crisis, you can't do it exclusively at Level One (the real estate) but must look at Level Two (the players and the rules) as well.

At both Level One and Level Two, the structure of the game looks very similar. We begin by estimating revenues that can be generated from the marketplace, and we subtract the operating expenses necessary to provide the services that were promised to the marketplace. The result is a projection of net operating income, which (as we show in great detail in Part 7) can be translated into a cash flow and valued using the discounted cash flow method. The difference is that at Level One we value the rents to the building, and at Level Two we value the salaries, fees, bonuses, stock options, and other compensations that the individual players receive. In the savings and loan situation, the associations' position looked very risky as they moved into more speculative investments. However, the decision makers, the owners, had less to lose (the taxpayer had provided deposit insurance) and lots to gain (bonuses, stock options, dividends, etc.) if the speculations worked out well. In fact, since many of the more speculative real estate loans involved large "origination" fees that translated into immediate dividends for the S&L owners/entrepreneurs, many of these people won even if the investment didn't work out. Hence, the decisions that lost so much money for the associations (Level One) were really very rational for the owner/decision makers (Level Two).

It would be convenient to hang all the blame around the neck of Congress, the S&L lobbyists, and the S&L regulators; it is well known that tinkering with the system *always* has unforeseen results. But for the system to go so terribly wrong in this instance, other unforeseen events had to happen. One key event of the early 1980s was the bottom falling out of oil prices, dragging down local economies and thereby real estate markets all over the oil patch. Another was (1) the invention of junk bonds by Michael Milken at Drexel Burnham Lambert, (2) their ferocious use by the LBO (leveraged buyout) raiders of the 1980s, and (3) the propensity of S&Ls to invest in these instruments. None of the effects of these contributing factors could have been known in 1981 and 1982.

For the student of real estate and the aspiring player, the lesson from all this is to know the other players and try to ascertain their position. When public policy and economic forces induce conflicting goals among players, the result can be turbulence in the marketplace. To many, the S&L debacle has been a disaster; to a few, it presents opportunities. For those of us who aspire not to be victims, and in fact to win some chips, the obvious lesson is to look around and know what's going on—not just in our local markets with our local players, but nationally and globally. Remember, the overbuilding financed by the S&Ls ruined not just people directly involved but surrounding property owners as well when the oversupply caused rents to decline throughout the market.

In previous editions of this book, we chose to ignore the Level One/Level Two distinction, thinking that Level Two should be saved for a second course, possibly even a graduate course. However, with the increasing complexity of real estate markets, it becomes essential to understand this distinction in order to understand even the most basic transactions. This book remains essentially a Level One book, but for the interested student we will make allusions to Level Two where a Level Two explanation is the best way to understand the marketplace.

At both Level One and Level Two, there are formal rules to the game, and those are what we discussed in Chapters 4 and 5. Never forget, however, that the formal rules are only part of the total picture. Personal ethics and social mores make up the informal rules of the game, and the total structure of the game is a combination of both the formal and the informal rules. Finally, remember that the rules can and do change. When enough people object, public policy changes, and it can happen right in the middle of the game, affecting players (including the public) all the way up and down the line.

SUMMARY   A diverse group of financial intermediaries is involved in real estate lending. Government is not only a lender but also a regulator, insurer, and facilitator. The various lenders make different types of loans (different both in type of property and duration) based on their sources of funds, location, expertise, and regulatory constraints. Lenders' specialization is evidenced by the different points at which they participate in the real estate financing cycle. By knowing the players in the capital markets and their objectives, the real estate analyst is better able to obtain the right financing at the most attractive price.

IMPORTANT TERMS

Disintermediation	Gap financing
ECOA	GNMA
FDIC	Inflation premium
Federal Reserve System	Intermediary (financial)
FFLMC	Internal disintermediation
FHA	Maturity (of a loan)
FHLBB	Mortgage banker
FHLBS	Mortgage broker
FHLMC	Mortgage insurance
Financial institutions	Mutual savings bank
Financial markets	Pension fund
Financial system	Permanent loan commitment
FNMA	Prepayment (penalty)
FSLIC	Primary financial market

Purchase money mortgage
Redlining
Refinancing
REIT
Release price
Resolution Trust Corporation
(RTC)

Secondary financial markets
Secondary mortgage market
Takeout commitment
VA

REVIEW QUESTIONS

13.1   What is the role of financial intermediaries in bringing together savers and borrowers in the financial system?

13.2   Why is the secondary mortgage market important to real estate finance?

13.3   When evaluating financial institutions, how might you expect them to attempt to match their source of funds (liabilities) with their uses (assets)?

13.4   What has been the principle role of commercial banks in real estate lending?

13.5   What factors distinguish a mortgage banker from a mortgage broker?

13.6   How does the provision of mortgage insurance, private or government-sponsored, reduce the risk to real estate lenders?

13.7   What has been the thrust of consumer protection in the area of real estate lending?

13.8   Why doesn't the financing of raw land usually include a financial institution?

13.9   How does the repayment pattern of development loans differ from construction loans?

13.10 What is the purpose of a rental achievement requirement in a permanent loan commitment?

$\mathcal{F}$INANCE'S CONTRIBUTION TO THE BASIC REAL ESTATE VALUATION MODEL

1. *Capital markets* provide the global citizen with the opportunity to defer or advance consumption. As every basic economics text explains, this is one of the major benefits of a modern society.

2. *Interest rates,* as Irving Fisher first formally demonstrated, are the connecting link. The interest rate is the compensation to the individual who defers consumption and the cost to the other individual who accelerates consumption. The saver (deferrer) wants a real return, an adjustment for inflation, a premium for the fact that he or she may have misestimated what inflation will be, and a default risk premium.

3. *The spread* is the additional cost to the borrower (accelerator of consumption) above the interest rate paid to the saver. In the capital markets, a firm or individual (investment banker, venture capitalist, syndicator, commercial banker, etc.) plays a matchmaking role. First, the intermediary aggregates savers' funds and then allocates them to borrowers based on the *expected* risk and return of each prospective borrower.

    Spreads vary over time and over products and are quoted in different ways. In the mid-1980s, the spread over Treasury bonds on large investment-grade commercial mortgages was between 200 and 300 basis points, with the market controlled largely by life insurance company general accounts. Investment bankers saw an opportunity and began to securitize larger commercial loans at a spread of 150 basis points. This eventually forced life insurance companies to lower their margin (spread) on the best loans to around 125 basis points, which is the situation in 1990. With such a spread, investment bankers no longer have an incentive to securitize, as their cost of securitization exceeds 125 basis points. Thus, the market has remained with the life insurance companies but on a less profitable level.

4. *Agency cost* results when a Level Two player in the capital market does not have exactly the same goals and objectives as the saver he or she represents. Such situations have been well defined in corporate finance where the management of the corporation may act for the benefit of the equity holders at the expense of bondholders by paying out unusually high dividends or taking on riskier projects. The same kind of goal incongruence results from time to time in real estate situations. For example, in the syndication, the syndicator may profit from actions that don't perfectly match with the investor's objectives. As mentioned in the legal section; one objective of drawing the investment agreement is to try to achieve goal congruence between the operating party and the investor. Whenever this goal congruence is not achieved, there is an agency cost.

   Agency cost is reflected in a higher interest rate. The saver naturally wants additional compensation for the fact that the manager controlling the operation may not always act in his or her best interest. The greater the potential for the operating manager to act contrary to the investor's best interest, the greater the agency cost and the higher the interest rate.

5. *Market efficiency* in finance refers to the degree to which the price fairly reflects all that can be currently known about the prospective risk and return of any given investment. The closer the price is to what can be known, the more efficient the market. If a market is perfectly efficient, there is very little *comparative advantage* to the skilled player. Conversely, in less efficient markets, human capital can be very valuable and hence enjoys greater compensation.

6. *Information asymmetries* or differing expectations from the same information) explain many apparent market inefficiencies and, hence, the possibility for comparative advantage. Particularly in real estate investment, where a good bit of the action is in specific local markets, the cost of obtaining complete information often means that one player has greater information than another, and consequently more comparative advantage.

7. *Arbitrage theory* tells us that when there is a violation of the law of one price, someone will make a market in the exchange, and consequently the difference in price between two truly comparable items (i.e., after adjusting for all the differences in features, functions, and benefits) should be only the cost of making the market. From a real estate perspective, this tells us that the difference in price between a new modern building and a rehab building should be the cost of the rehab plus an entrepreneurial profit, which is consistent with the amount of time, expertise, and risk involved in the conversion.

8. Deviations from *the law of one price* can also be explained by information asymmetries. This creates particular problems for traditional appraisal theory (Part 3) which relies fundamentally on the law of one price. In addition to informational asymmetries, nonfinancial motivations for real estate investment and ownership can also explain deviation from the law of one price. To the extent that people enjoy owning a hotel because the maitre d' in the restaurant knows their name, and are willing to pay a little more than the cash flows justify for this ego rush, the traditional three approaches to value in appraisal theory will have problems.

9. All of the logic and mechanical tools of finance (Chapter 14) are important to the real estate analyst. Similarly, the institutional arrangements (Chapter 15) and government support activities (Chapter 16) are important to the player who wants to win this increasingly sophisticated game.

$\mathcal{F}$INANCING MECHANICS: THE BORROWER'S PERSPECTIVE

We presented an overall view of the financial system in Chapter 13. Now we focus on why the borrower wants to borrow and on the mechanics of figuring the cost to borrow. In Chapter 15, we will look at the other side of the financing picture—the lender's perspective and the different types of mortgage loans. Next, in Chapter 16, we examine what happens to loans after they are originated (i.e., when they are sold in the secondary mortgage market) and how the secondary market influences lenders' behavior in the primary market.

It is important for us to remember that **financing** divides the claims on a property's cash flow. When a project does not normally generate a cash flow (e.g., an owner-occupied, single-family dwelling), the owner makes the payments, and the property's financing establishes the priority of rights in the case of default. All the costs of a project must be financed through debt, equity, or some combination thereof.

THE RELATIONSHIP BETWEEN DEBT AND EQUITY FINANCING

When discussing financing, we refer to the entire right-hand side of the balance sheet, both debt and equity. The different financial instruments simply divide the cash flow generated by the left-hand side of the balance sheet (assets) among the different sources of funds represented by the right-hand side of the balance sheet. Each of the different suppliers of funds is willing to face certain risks and expects commensurate returns. As discussed in Chapter 13, the capital markets aggregate, then allocate, funds on this basis.

Figure 14-1 illustrates the fact that the **net operating income (NOI)** is essentially shared by the sources of financing.[1] In order for anyone to

---

[1]Today, in more complex commercial transactions, it is often difficult to draw a clear distinction between debt and equity financing. Lenders participate in cash flow, and one equity holder may lend his partner money. Still, it is instructive to begin the study of real estate finance by knowing the major

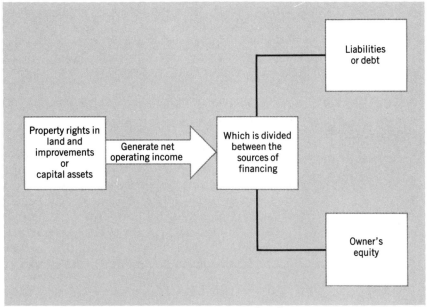

FIGURE 14-1 *How net operating income is shared*

convince the sources of financing to participate—that is, to invest in the project—the sources must feel that they are receiving a return that is commensurate with their risk. It is important that the sources of debt and equity financing understand one another's investment requirements because both sets of investor requirements must be satisfied for the project to be financed.

The NOI available to meet the total cost of financing the project is limited by the marketplace (i.e., by supply and demand). The level of gross rents is determined in the marketplace by tenants and landlords as they rent and offer to rent space. Generally, one landlord cannot increase rents by a significant amount above current market rents without experiencing a large increase in vacancy.

Similarly, a landlord cannot effectively cut operating expenses much below market levels without lowering the quality of the project. Certainly, quality property management can give one project a competitive edge, as explained in Chapter 11. Still, janitorial services require a certain amount of labor, and lights require electricity. Costs for these and other maintenance services are determined in the same fashion as are

differences between the two sides of the financing spectrum. In Part 7, we will show how the legal interests discussed in Part 2 can be used with the financing techniques discussed in this part to create a great variety of financing schemes with a myriad of claims somewhere between pure debt and pure equity.

rents; that is, both rents and operating expenses are constrained by supply and demand. Consequently, an investor cannot increase his or her rate of return by arbitrarily increasing rents or reducing operating expenses if a property is already efficiently managed.

THE BENEFITS AND COSTS OF FINANCING TO THE EQUITY HOLDER

As Modigliani and Miller showed in their classic 1958 article,[2] in a world of no income taxes and perfect markets, it does not matter whether one uses 10 percent debt or 80 percent debt. However, there are income taxes in this world, and markets are far from perfect. Today we observe a clustering of real estate debt-to-value ratios in the range of 70 to 90 percent. Since this empirically observed clustering is too great to have occurred by chance, there must be certain benefits to the investor from the use of debt financing. Furthermore, as most investors do not use 100 percent debt financing, there must be certain costs that eventually offset the benefits of debt, creating an optimal level of debt financing. (This level is analogous to an optimal capital structure in corporate finance.)

BENEFITS OF USING DEBT FINANCE

When the cost of debt financing (the interest rate) is lower than the return generated by the property (NOI divided by cost), then positive leverage is created. In such situations, the percentage return to equity is greater using debt than it is with no debt. (This important concept is illustrated with numbers later in the chapter.)

■ When an owner uses debt, the interest payments are tax deductible. Furthermore, the use of debt increases the tax basis beyond the equity investment, thus enhancing the tax shelter generated from depreciation. As discussed in Parts 6 and 7, these two facts allow the real estate owner who uses debt to reduce the government's share of the NOI.

■ The use of debt financing reduces the minimum investment necessary in any given project. Since investors have limited resources, a reduced minimum investment in one project allows them to spread their wealth over several investments, that is, to diversify. As we show in Part 7, diversification reduces portfolio risk, and lower risk means higher value.

■ Combining financing possibilities with the various forms of ownership (covered in Part 2), the decision maker can create new risk-

[2]F. Modigliani and M. Miller, "The Cost of Capital, Corporation Finance, and the Theory of Investment," American Economic Review (1958).

return opportunities, that is, new investments to fit specific investor needs. Flexibility to tailor the investment to suit the client further enhances the value of using debt financing.[3]

COSTS OF DEBT

When the prior fixed claim of debt is placed on a property, the variability of the cash flow to equity increases. (We will show you an example later in the chapter.) The increased variability means more risk; adding risk reduces value.[4] If the project's cash flow drops below the debt service amount, the investor may "lose control of the timing of the sale," that is, face foreclosure. This can be a very painful experience.

The financial institutions that aggregate savers' funds and then lend them to equity investors charge fees for their services. These charges, which are discussed in the Chapter 15, are generally paid by the borrower. Note that as you add debt to gain its advantages, you increase the risk to equity; this additional debt also increases the lender's exposure, causing the lender to increase his or her return (which is a cost to equity). Finally, the paperwork required in mortgage lending and the lender's time (as financial intermediary) must be compensated. Combining the cost of potential bankruptcy with all the costs of using a middleman,[5] we find that the incremental costs eventually outweigh the incremental benefits. Just before that point, the optimal percentage of debt financing is reached.

FINANCING COMPUTATIONS

Before we demonstrate with examples the benefits of debt financing to the equity investor, we should review several basic concepts and financial calculations. These concern the time value of money. Understanding the time value of money and its applications is a prerequisite for real estate decision making.

---

[3]*Although there are several reasons why the possibility of debt financing increases the value of real estate, this does not mean that borrowing $80,000 on a $100,000 property increases the value of the property. If it did, everyone would go out and buy properties and put debt on them. The potential benefits of using debt are already factored into the market value of the property, so that the property's value is independent of specific financing decisions. Naturally, a 3 percent long-term loan in a 12 percent market adds value, but that is the value of existing below-market financing, not of the decision to use debt.*

[4]*If the borrower is not personally liable for the debt, more debt does not necessarily mean more risk to the borrower. Without personal liability, the equity holder has limited downside risk, and more non-recourse debt reduces the magnitude of the downside because it reduces the amount of equity required.*

[5]*For those with a background in finance theory, there are very real information and agency costs in mortgage lending which also increase the borrower's costs. See M. Miles, J. Pringle, and B. Webb, "Agency Issues and Information Asymmetry in Corporate Real Estate,"* Industrial Development, *1990, for a fuller discussion of these issues.*

TIME VALUE OF MONEY

Simply stated, a dollar received today is more valuable than a dollar to be received in the future. A dollar received in the future is less valuable for three reasons.

❑ **OPPORTUNITY COST.** A dollar in hand today can immediately be invested and earn real interest (i.e., a real return over and above inflation without taking any risk). If the dollar is not to be received for one year, the real interest that could have been earned must be foregone. The foregone interest represents the **opportunity cost** associated with the receipt of a dollar in the future rather than today. Consequently, today's value—**present value**—of the dollar to be received in one year should be diminished by the amount of the opportunity cost. (We'll come back to this topic shortly.)

❑ **INFLATION.** Inflation reduces the value of the dollar. When price levels rise, more dollars are required to purchase the same amount of goods and services than previously. When a dollar is to be received in the future, its present value is diminished if inflation occurs before you get it. Conversely, if you borrow money today, dollars you use for future repayments will have less value than the dollars you borrowed should inflation occur in the interim.

❑ **RISK.** If a dollar is due you in the future, there is a possibility that the dollar will not be repaid or that the inflation premium has been misestimated. The risk of default and of misestimating inflation also diminishes the present value of the future dollar.

Note that the items just mentioned are three of the four components of the capitalization rate (income approach to value) and will be the components of the interest rate (the lender's perspective). They will also be the components of the equity discount rate (the equity required rate of return). However, as discussed in the introductory paragraphs to this chapter, the risk perspectives of debt and equity are different. In the income approach to appraisal, NOI was capitalized, and the risk premium was based on the overall riskiness of the project. At this stage of the financing discussion, we know that the lender has a prior claim and thus a less risky position. Conversely, the equity claim is riskier than the overall project risk precisely because of the lender's prior claim.

The concept of the time value of money is crucial to real estate analysis. Future cash inflows and outflows are evaluated by using **compounding** and **discounting.** Before going further, we will review the mechanics, including use of the compound interest tables at the end of the book.

COMPOUND INTEREST AND THE DISCOUNTING PROCESS

❑ **COMPOUNDING.**   Interest is payment for the use of money. **Compound interest** is no more than interest on interest, and the calculations for compounding are very straightforward. Suppose a savings association pays interest at the rate of 9 percent with the interest calculated once each year. Then a dollar invested (deposited) in a savings account yields $1.09 at the end of the year. It may therefore be said that, on the day it is deposited, the dollar's future value in one year is equal to

- Its present value ($1), plus
- The interest rate times the present value ($0.09)

To this point, simple interest has been described. However, in the second year of the deposit, 9 percent interest would be paid not merely on the $1 original deposit but also on the 9 cents earned as interest during the first year. Thus, the interest earned in the second year would amount to 0.0981 cents ($1.09 × 0.09 = 0.0981), or slightly more than eight-tenths of one cent more than the first year. This is an example of compound interest.

As a matter of practice, savings institutions have for many years compounded interest semiannually or quarterly, thus raising the effective annual interest rate by a small fraction. More recently, banks located where competition for funds is very great have been compounding interest daily. Compounded daily, an annual interest rate of 7.75 percent will actually pay 8.10 percent at the end of a full year, assuming the funds remain in the account during the entire period.

Compound interest can be calculated by painstakingly computing the interest at the end of every interest period (whether daily, monthly, quarterly, or otherwise) on the balance outstanding at that time. Another way to calculate the future value is to present the process mathematically.

The future, or compound, value is equal to the present value times one plus the interest rate raised to a power equal to the number of periods that the money is left in the savings account: $FV = PV (1 + r)^n$, Or see Table 14-1.

❑ **DISCOUNTING.**   **Discounting** is simply the reverse, or mathematical inverse, of compounding. In discounting, the **future value** is known, as is the interest rate and the term. The problem is to find the present value. Suppose a business associate promises to pay you $10,000 in one lump sum at the end of 10 years. The question is what you would pay your associate today (present value) for that promise. The answer is

---

TABLE 14-1   COMPOUND INTEREST (FUTURE VALUE) EXAMPLE

How much will $1,000 placed in a 9 percent *annual* compounding savings account be worth at the end of the third year?

I.   Hand computation FV = [PV × (1 + r) × (1 + r) × (1 + r)] or PV × (1 + r)^3

    $1,000   Initial principal
       9%   Annual interest rate
    $ 90   First-year interest

    $1,000 + $90 = $1,090   Principal during the second year
               9%   Annual interest rate
           $98.10   Second-year interest

    $1,090 + $98.10 = $1,188.10   Principal during the third year
                   9%   Annual interest rate
             $ 106.93   Third-year interest

    $1,188.10 + $106.93 + $1,295.03 Future value (end of third year)

II. From the compound interest tables FV = (1 + r)^n × PV
    A.   Compound interest factor (3 years at 9%—p. A-2, column 1) = 1.2950
    B.   Principal = $1,000
    C.   Future value = 1.2950 × $1,000 = $1,295.00

---

a function of your discount rate (interest rate) and how long you must wait for the payment (term). The formula for calculating present value of a single payment to be received in the future is an algebraic rearrangement of the compounding formula (see Table 14-2):

$$PV = FV \div (1 + r)^n$$

Interestingly, it is believed that the discounted cash flow (DCF) technique, so widely used in global commerce today, actually originated in real estate valuation. While it may not have been the first use of the technique, DCF was used early in the nineteenth century by German and Austrian foresters as seen in E. F. Von Gehren's "On Determination of the Money Value of Bare Forest Land" and M. Faustmann's "Calculation of the Value Which Forest Land and Immature Stands Possess for Forestry" (1849).

Table 14-2 suggests that if your discount rate were 9 percent you would pay your business associate $4,224.11 today for that promise. Stated another way, with a 9 percent discount rate you would be indif-

---

TABLE 14-2 DISCOUNTING (PRESENT VALUE) EXAMPLE

What is the value today of the right to receive $10,000 at the end of 10 years assuming a 9 percent annual discount rate?

I. Hand computation:

$$PV = \frac{FV}{(1 + r)^n} = \frac{\$10,000}{(1 + 0.09)^{10}} = \frac{\$10,000}{2.3673637} = \$4,224.11$$

II. From the Compound Interest Tables

    A. Annual PV factor (10 years at 9 percent, p. A-2, column 4) = 0.4224

    B. Future Value = $10,000

    C. Present value $10,000 × 0.4224 = $4224.00

---

ferent to receiving $4,224.11 today or the right to receive, 10 years from today, $10,000. Moreover, since discounting is the inverse of compounding, it can be seen that if $4,224.11 were deposited today earning 9 percent interest, the compound value would be $10,000 in 10 years.[6]

❏ **SERIES OF PAYMENTS.** The compounding and discounting formulas can be expanded to handle a series of payments or receipts as easily as a single payment or receipt. The examples in Tables 14-3 and 14-4 present the future value of a series of equal payments (compound **annuity**) and the present value of a series of receipts (discounted annuity).[7]

❏ **SINKING FUND ACCUMULATION.** To calculate the sinking fund method of recapture of capital (the fourth component of the capitalization rate in the income approach to value), you should determine how much must be set aside each period to accumulate a certain value. The **sinking fund accumulation** method is demonstrated in Table 14-5. The concept of the sinking fund can be used when an investor needs to determine how much must be set aside to replace fixtures that will wear out. For example, if the floor coverings in an apartment have a useful life of five years and are expected to cost $10,000, how much must be set

---

[6]*Today compounding and discounting are hardwired in inexpensive hand calculators, and nearly all personal computers have routines to calculate all the functions described in this chapter. Still, the beginner is well advised to start with the formulas and tables and obtain a thorough understanding of the mechanics before taking for granted the timesaving technologies.*

[7]*The formulas for the present value and future value of an annuity are*

$$PV = \frac{1 - (1 + i)^{-n}}{i} \cdot (\text{payment})$$

$$FV = (\text{payment}) \cdot \frac{(1 + i)^n - 1}{i}$$

TABLE 14-3   FUTURE VALUE OF AN ANNUITY

How much will $500 set aside each year accumulate to in 7 years if during the interim the funds can be invested at 12 percent compounded annually?

Amount of the annuity	$500
Term	7 years
Interest rate	12%
Annual annuity factor (p. A-5, column 2)	10.0890
Future value of the annuity ($500 × 10.0890)	$5,044.50

TABLE 14-4   PRESENT VALUE OF AN ANNUITY

What is the value today of receiving $500 a year for 7 years if the annual discount rate is 12 percent compounded annually?

Amount of the annuity	$500
Term	7 years
Interest rate	12%
Annual annuity factor (p. A-5, column 5)	4.5638
Future value of annuity ($500 × 4.5638)	$2,281.90

TABLE 14-5   SINKING FUND ACCUMULATION

How much must be set aside each period at 8 percent compounded monthly so that in 120 *months* $100,000 will accumulate?

Sinking fund period	120 months
Interest rate	8%
Monthly sinking fund factor (p. A-11, column 3)	0.005466
Amount to set aside each month ($100,000 × 0.005466)	$546.60

---

aside each *month* from income to replace the floor coverings? If we assume an 8 percent annual interest rate, it can be seen that each month $136.10 must be set aside to accumulate $10,000 (0.013610 × $10,000) in five years.[8]

---

[8]The sinking fund factor, that is, the amount to accumulate to a future value, is

$$\text{Sinking fund factor} = \frac{i}{(1 + i)^n - 1}$$

❏ **THE MORTGAGE LOAN CONSTANT** The lender will analyze the proposed financing from the perspective of risk and return. Lender return consists of interest and principal repayment. Interest represents a return *on* the lender's investment, whereas principal repayment represents a return *of* the investment capital. The total lender return (both "on" and "of") is represented by the debt service and is a function of the contract rate of interest and the maturity of the loan.

These two factors result in a **mortgage constant** (*K*), which represents the amount of debt service, expressed as a percent of the original loan, necessary to pay the contract rate of interest and the entire principal in equal periodic installments over the term of the loan. *K* is usually expressed as the percentage of the original principal that will be paid in regular installments. Thus, the debt service represents an annuity paid over the life of the loan. Each periodic payment consists of two parts: (1) interest for the preceding period on the outstanding amount of the loan at the beginning of the period and (2) partial payment of principal (**amortization**). (See Table 14-6).[9]

In the early years of a level, constant, amortizing loan, the largest proportion of the periodic payment is interest. However, as the loan principal is gradually reduced while the periodic payment remains constant, the amount of interest declines (since interest is calculated only on the outstanding balance). At the same time, the portion of the total payment going to amortize the loan principal gradually increases.

Without a full amortization schedule, the interest and principal components of any year's constant payment can be determined if the *mortgage loan constant* is known. This calculation is shown in Table 14-7.

Changes in either the term (repayment period) or the interest rate will change the mortgage loan constant. If the term remains the same, then

■ The higher the interest rate, the higher the constant.
■ The lower the interest rate, the lower the constant.

If the interest rate remains the same, then

■ The longer the repayment period, the lower the constant.
■ The shorter the repayment period, the higher the constant.

EFFECTIVE YIELD

The true or effective yield to the lender can be calculated using the Compound Interest Tables at the end of the book, as shown in Tables

[9]*In most single-family loans, the borrower pays principal, interest, property taxes, and insurance monthly—thus, the phrase PITI.*

TABLE 14-6   HOW TO DETERMINE MORTGAGE LOAN CONSTANT

What must a borrower pay each year on a $40,000 loan at 12% annual interest if the loan is to be amortized over 25 years?

I. *Annual Mortgage Loan Constant* (from the Compound Interest Tables):
    A. Loan amount = $40,000
    B. Interest rate (annual) = 12%
    C. Loan term = 25 years
    D. Mortgage constant factor (p. A-5, column 6) = 0.1275000
    E. Annual debt service ($40,000 × 0.127500) = <u>$5,100</u>

What would the *monthly* debt service be?

II. *Annual Mortgage Loan Constant* (from the Compound Interest Tables):
     A. Loan amount = $40,000
     B. Interest rate = 12%
     C. Loan term = 25 years or 300 months
     D. Factor (p. A-14, column 6) = 0.01053224
     E. Monthly debt service ($40,000 × 0.010532) = <u>$421.28</u>

Note: *The 12 monthly payments are less than the one annual payment as the borrower is reducing the principal in 12 steps during the year and thus pays less total interest (421.28 × 12 = $5,055.36 < $5,100.00).*

TABLE 14-7   THIRD-YEAR INTEREST CALCULATION

How much interest will the borrower pay in the third year on a $40,000, 12% interest, 25-year amortizing loan?

I. *Mortgage Loan Constant:*
    A. Loan amount = $40,000
    B. Mortgage constant factor (p. A-5, column 6) = 0.127500
    C. Annual debt service = $5,100 (40.000 (.1275))
II. *Third-Year Interest:*
     A. First-year interest = $40,000 × 12% = $4,800
         First year principal = $5,100 − $4,800 = $300
     B. Principal in second year = $40,000 − $300 = $39,700
         Second-year interest = $39,700 × 12% = $4,764
         Second-year principal = $5,100 − $4,764 = $336
     C. Principal in third year = $39,700 − $336 = $39,364
         Third-year interest = $39,364 × 12% = <u>$4,724</u>[a]

[a]*Clearly, this process would be very time consuming for the twenty-fifth year. It is shown here to illustrate the simplicity of the concept. In practice, actual calculations are done by using calculators or computers with preprogrammed routines.*

TABLE 14-8 YIELD CALCULATION WITH POINTS

A borrower has requested a $1 million loan at 11% for 20 years on a small motel that is expected to have an annual *net* operating income of $150,000 and is appraised at $1.2 million. The borrower has agreed to pay a four-point origination fee. What is the lender's effective yield?

I. *Mortgage Loan Constant:*
   A. Term = 20 years
   B. Interest = 11% annually
   C. Mortgage constant factor (p. A-4, column 6) = 0.125576
   D. Annual debt service ($1,000,000 × 0.125576) = $125,576

II. *Yield:*
   A. Cash advanced by lender = $1,000,000 − $40,000[a] = $960,000
   B. Annual debt service = $125,576
   C. Term = 20 years
   D. Factor ($960,000 ÷ $125,576) = 7.6448
   E. Yield determination
      1. Check each page in the Compound Interest Tables looking at column 5 (present value of an annuity) on the 20-year row.
      2. The 12% page (p. A-5, column 5) shows an approximately equal factor of 7.4694. Therefore, the effective yield of this loan is approximately 12% when repaid over 20 years.

[a]*Four-point origination fee.*

14-8 and 14-9. It should be noted that the effective pretax yield to the lender is also the effective pretax cost to the borrower. (Part 6 will add income tax considerations to the calculations). Determination of the lender's effective yield can also be achieved by calculating the internal rate of return. (This technique is presented in Part 7.) For now, we need emphasize only that the effective yield usually exceeds the contract rate of interest if an **origination fee** or **discount points**[10] are charged. Although beyond the scope of this text, early repayment and prepayment penalties may also increase the lender's effective yield and the borrower's effective interest cost.

The lender may go even further in seeking to enhance his or her return by asking for a "participation" in the income generated by the project. Although a complete evaluation of participating loans must await the development of investment material in Part 7, Table 14-9 presents an example.

[10]*An origination fee is an administrative charge made by the lender that is a direct cost to the buyer (see Table 14-8). Discount points involve adjusting the stated interest rate with an initial charge to effect a desired yield. (This will be explained later in this Part.)*

TABLE 14-9 YIELD CALCULATION WITH INCOME KICKER INTEREST

In the motel example in Table 14-8, assume that the lender will also receive 20% of *gross* income above $200,000. This "income kicker" is estimated to be about $18,000 per year. What is the effective yield including the kicker interest?

A. Cash advanced by lender = $960,000

B. Annual debt service plus kicker interest = $125,576 + $18,000 = $143,576

C. Factor = $960,000 ÷ $143,576 = 6.6864

D. Again, searching the tables in the 20-year row, the factor for 14% is 6.6231 (p. A-7, column 5) which is approximately equal to 6.6864. Therefore, the expected effective yield is nearly 14%.

EFFECT OF FINANCING ON BEFORE-TAX CASH FLOWS

THE BEFORE-TAX CASH FLOW STATEMENT

Since the sources of financing share the NOI, let us look at how the decision is made as to which source—debt or equity—gets how much of the NOI. Essentially, both sources view themselves as investors. As investors, they establish, independently of one another, minimum investment criteria. Their major goal is to minimize risk while maximizing expected return. For the sake of simplicity, we refer to the source of debt financing as the lender and the source of equity as the investor.

The pro forma cash flow statement shown in Table 14-10 will be

---

TABLE 14-10 CASH FLOW PRO FORMA

Gross rental receipts	
15 units × $350 month × 12 months	$81,000
5 units × $300 month × 12 months	
Plus: other income	
$3 unit × 20 units × 12 months	720
Gross potential income	$81,720
Less: vacancy and credit loss (6% of GPI)	(4,903)
Effective gross income	$76,817
Less: operating expenses (38% of GPI)	(31,054)
Net operating income	$45,763
Less: debt service	(42,139)[a]
Before-tax equity cash flow	$ 3,624

[a]$382,500 (loan amount) × 0.110168 (mortgage constant—see tables) = $42,139. Table 14-6 explains this calculation.

used in presenting the lender's and equity investor's investment criteria. Assume that a 20-unit existing apartment house has 15 two-bedroom units ($350 monthly rent) and 5 one-bedroom units ($300 monthly rent). Vending income equals $3 per month per unit. Market analysis indicates a vacancy and credit loss of 6 percent of gross potential income (GPI) and operating expenses of 38 percent of GPI. The asking price is $510,000, and a mortgage loan of $382,500 (75 percent of the purchase price) is available at 10 percent interest for 25 years. The equity investment is $127,500. The before-tax equity cash flow is then $3,624.

With this background, we can now consider the equity perspective of debt financing. Looking to Table 14-10, we can calculate two pertinent return measures: (1) rate of return on total capital (ROR) and (2) rate of return on equity (ROE).

RATE OF RETURN ON TOTAL CAPITAL (ROR)

The **ROR** measures the overall productivity of an income-producing property. The major assumption implied by this rate of return measure is that the project has been financed with equity only; consequently, there is no debt service (remember Part 3). The ROR is sometimes referred to as the overall capitalization rate, or the "free and clear" rate of return. As a profitability measure, the ROR relates market-determined NOI to purchase price (i.e., total capital invested). An investor could compare expected RORs of various projects in an attempt to determine how the market relates NOI to purchase price. The ROR is calculated as follows:

$$ROR = \frac{NOI}{Total\ capital\ invested}$$

For our example in Table 14-10, the ROR is

$$ROR = \frac{\$45,763}{\$510,000} = 8.97\ percent$$

RATE OF RETURN ON EQUITY (ROE)

Return on equity matches before-tax cash flow to equity investment. Since most real estate projects involve debt financing, the rate of return on equity (**ROE**) measures the performance of a project after financing on an equity cash-on-cash basis. When comparing different projects or financing schemes, an investor can use the ROE as an indicator of how financing affects current return. Since the ROE uses before-tax cash flow and the equity invested, it is often referred to as the cash-on-cash return or the equity dividend rate. The ROE is measured as follows:[11]

$$\text{ROE} = \frac{\text{Before-tax equity cash flow}}{\text{Equity investment}}$$

For the example in Table 14-10, the ROE is

$$\text{ROE} = \frac{\$3,624}{\$127,500} = 2.84 \text{ percent}$$

POSITIVE AND NEGATIVE LEVERAGE

The use of borrowed funds to finance a project is called **leverage.** The use of leverage requires a division of the project's net operating income between two claims—debt and equity—and has two effects on the residual (equity) cash flow. First, the use of debt may increase or decrease the percentage return to equity. Second, the use of debt will increase the variability of the cash flow to equity.

The impact of leverage on equity return (ROE) can be analyzed by comparing the ROR with the annual constant (K). The general rule is that if K is greater than ROR, leverage is negative and works against the equity investor by reducing the percentage return to equity. If K is less than ROR, leverage is positive and works for the equity investor by increasing the percentage return to equity.

In Table 14-10, ROR is approximately 9 percent, and K is 11.01 percent (K = annual debt service ÷ original loan amount). Thus, leverage is negative. The inequality $K >$ ROR simply indicates that the cost of financing (K) is greater than the overall productivity of the project (ROR). If an investor pays more for borrowed funds than can be earned on those same funds when invested (i.e., $K >$ ROR), ROE will suffer.

If the financing associated with a particular project results in negative leverage, what can the investor do? The investor can either (1) reduce K by negotiating a lower interest rate or longer term or (2) increase ROR by raising rents, reducing operating expenses, or paying less for the project. Generally, the terms of the financing are market-determined, so little can be done to change K. As far as ROR is concerned, both the rents and operating expenses are market-determined, leaving the offering price as the only variable well within the investor's control.

---

[11] *In Part 7 this calculation will be extended to an after-tax ROE. For a more comprehensive treatment of financial leverage, investment risk, and return, see William Brueggeman and William Fisher,* Real Estate Finance, *8th ed. (Homewood, Ill.: Richard D. Irwin, 1989).*

TABLE 14-11 EXAMPLE OF POSITIVE LEVERAGE

Financing of $70,000, with an annual constant (K) of 11%, is available on a project that costs $100,000 and is expected to generate net operating income of $12,000 per year. What is the expected return to equity?

I. *Unleveraged return*
Annual NOI = $12,000
Total capital invested = $100,000
Percentage unleveraged return (ROR) = $12,000 ÷ $100,000 = 12%

II. *Leveraged return*
Annual NOI = $12,000
Annual debt service = $70,000 × 11% = $7,700
Before-tax equity cash flow = $12,000 − $7,700 = $4,300
Equity investment = $100,000 − $70,000 = $30,000
Leveraged return percentage (ROE) = $4,300 ÷ $30,000 = 14.33%

Note that the ROR is still 12%.

Traditionally, **negative leverage** has been viewed as bad. However, in an inflationary economy where a large part of the total equity return comes from the proceeds from sale and from tax shelter, the issue is not quite as clear-cut. In such cases, investors may be content to give a greater amount of the NOI to the lender (and take lower ROE), knowing that the tax shelter and capital gains will not be shared with the lender. This logic explains why an investor might willingly invest in a project with negative leverage.[12] But the decision should depend on the numbers.

Table 14-11 presents an example of a real estate project that demonstrates **positive leverage.** The ROR represents the rate of return if it is assumed that the investment is unleveraged (i.e., financed entirely with equity). When NOI equals $12,000 and the total capital invested equals $100,000, the ROR is 12 percent. When $70,000 of borrowed funds are used to finance the project, the equity investment falls to $30,000. Given an annual constant (K) of 11 percent, the annual debt service is $7,700 and the before-tax equity cash flow is $4,300. This results in a leveraged return or ROE of 14.33 percent.

Since ROR > K (i.e., 12 percent > 11 percent), this project demonstrates positive leverage. Note also that if the project were financed totally with cash, the ROE would equal the ROR of 12 percent. But since the cost of financing the project (the amount constant K) with debt is less than the ROR of 12 percent, the ROE increases to 14.33 percent.

---

[12]*This description of "cash flow leverage" will be extended to "financial leverage" in Part 7.*

LEVERAGE AND VARIABILITY OF CASH FLOW

Whether positive or negative, leverage increases the variability of the equity cash flow. **Variability of the cash flow** is often equated with the riskiness of the equity position. Remember that debt (in the simple debt-equity distinction) has a prior claim on the property's NOI. If a constant amount of the operating cash flows must be paid to the lender, the impact of any variation in the overall operating cash flows will be felt entirely by the residual (equity) holder. This magnified effect is illustrated in Table 14-12. Let us assume that a considerable amount of new office space opens up in our town and that many of our tenants are induced to leave at the end of their leases with us. We will look at a before-and-after analysis. Outcome 1 in Table 14-12 assumes $12,000 in NOI, whereas Outcome 2 assumes that NOI reaches only $8,000. In both cases, the annual debt service is $7,700 and is not affected by the level of NOI. (The debt service is determined by the terms of the mortgage.) When NOI is $12,000, our ROE is 14.33 percent. But when NOI falls to $8,000, as in Outcome 2, our ROE falls to a very modest 1 percent (i.e., NOI barely covers the debt service).

This example demonstrates that even if positive leverage can be expected, based on market information, if pro forma NOI is not attained the ROE may fall drastically. Note that if we assumed an unleveraged situation and NOI fell to $8,000, the ROE would still decline but not as significantly (from 12 to 8 percent as opposed to from 14.33 to 1 percent

---

TABLE 14-12   LEVERAGED-INDUCED VARIABILITY EXAMPLE

An investment alternative is expected (with equal likelihood) to produce a net operating income of $12,000 or $8,000 per year. The total project cost is $100,000, and a 70% loan is available at 9% interest, 11% annual constant. What is the effect of the debt on the equity return?

	Outcome 1	Outcome 2
I. *Unleveraged:*		
NOI	$ 12,000	$ 8,000
Amount of equity	$100,000	$100,000
Percentage ROE	12%	8%
II. *Leveraged:*		
NOI	$ 12,000	$ 8,000
Interest ($70,000 at 11% K)	7,700	7,700
Return to equity	$ 4,300	$ 300
Amount of equity ($100,000 − $70,000)	$ 30,000	$ 30,000
Percentage ROE	14.33%	1.00%

14-1 LEVERAGE FOR THE FARMER	In a 1977 *Business Week* story, Eugene Smith was hailed as one of the emerging "elite" of sophisticated, millionaire farmers. In a decade, the Indiana farmer and Purdue University graduate had amassed 10,000 acres through leveraged land purchases and rented 4,000 acres more. Smith frequently lectured farm and student groups on his methods, advising operation at 80 percent debt and only 20 percent equity. And during the seventies, when inflation was high, interest was relatively low, and farmland prices were soaring, that kind of leverage worked—capital gains from farmland were about twice what net income was.

But in 1979 interest rates jumped everywhere, especially in rural banks. Farmers who may have paid 9 percent for farm loans in 1979 were paying up to 18 percent a year later. At the same time, farmers' prospects for profit fell because of the 1980 embargo on grain sales to the Soviet Union. A drought later that year slashed yields—and profits—still further. All this left Smith with huge debts and no means of paying the interest on them. In the past, he had been able to deal with occasional cash shortages by quickly selling a parcel of land. But now, because of high costs and poor price prospects, no one was buying.

By the spring of 1982, Smith couldn't borrow enough money to plant a crop. While the interest on his $30 million of debt climbed by $10,000 daily, his net worth continued to fall with land prices—another lesson in the riskiness of using excessive leverage.

Source: Adapted from Meg Cox, "Go-Go Young Farmer Who rode Prices Up Is Laid Low by debt," *Wall Street Journal,* March 11, 1982, pp. 1, 10. Adapted by permission of *The Wall Street Journal,* © Dow Jones & Company, 1982. All rights reserved.

in the leveraged situation). In sum, debt financing can increase the expected returns to the equity investor but at the cost of exposing the equity investor to greater risk. (See Box 14-1.)

ADDITIONAL DEBT AND EQUITY DISTINCTIONS

The definition of winning in real estate involves looking at the residual cash flow (the cash flow generated from the project after the prior claims of the lender and the government). This is a useful model, but at times it oversimplifies the distinction between debt and equity. There are various ways to divide the claims of the different sources of funds other than the simple debt-equity distinction. There can be several levels (priorities) of debt—first lien, second lien, third lien—and then an equity position. There can be a group of equity holders and no debt—but with a preferred (priority) position within the equity group. A lender may participate in the equity return in ways limited only by the ingenuity of the players.

In all these cases, the logic is the same. Each one of the players—lender, lender-investor, equity investor—wants to win; more precisely, each wants more return for less risk. All want to maximize the NOI from the project (the Level One return), and each is in competition with the others when it comes to dividing the NOI among them, (that is, maximizing his or her own Level Two return).

SUMMARY

The mechanics of real estate financing are based on compounding and discounting. The Compound Interest Tables at the end of the book facilitate use of the compounding and discounting formulas shown in this chapter, as do hand-held calculators and personal computers.

From the borrower's perspective, debt affects the equity return in two ways. First, leverage may either increase or decrease the expected return to the equity holder. Second, regardless of whether leverage is positive or negative, the existence of the fixed debt obligation increases the variability of the equity cash flow.

When we talk about financing, it is appropriate to think in terms of the left- and right-hand sides of the balance sheet. The left-hand side is the asset side, which produces certain operating cash flows. The assets listed in the left-hand side are financed through different sources of funds shown on the right-hand (liability) side. These sources of funds have different claims (in terms of priority and amount) on the NOI. Typically, the sources of funds having a *prior* claim expect a *lower* return because they assume less risk. Similarly, the residual equity return is expected to be higher than the prior return of the lender because the equity holder's claim will be satisfied only if and when the prior claim has been met.

IMPORTANT TERMS

Amortization	Opportunity cost
Annuity	Origination fee
Compounding	Positive leverage
Compound interest	Present value
Discounting	ROE (rate of return on equity capital)
Discount points	
Financing	ROR (rate of return on total capital)
Future value	
Leverage (in financing)	Sinking fund accumulation
Mortgage constant	Time value of money
Negative leverage	Variability
Net operating income (NOI)	

REVIEW QUESTIONS

14.1 Why is it important that the sources of financing (debt and equity) understand one another's investment requirements?

14.2 Why is the value of $1 to be received in the future less valuable than $1 to be received today?

14.3 Define and give an example of compound interest.

14.4 What is the difference between the rate of return on total capital and the rate of return on equity?

14.5 If a project has negative leverage, how might the equity investor attempt to correct the situation?

14.6 How does the use of leverage affect the variability of equity cash flow?

14.7 Explain the statement, "The net operating income is essentially shared by the sources of financing."

14.8 What is the present value of a series of *monthly* payments of $250 received for 120 months assuming a 12 percent discount rate?

14.9 What would be the annual installment needed to fully amortize (interest and principal) the following loan: $145,000 original balance at 9.5 percent interest for 25 years?

14.10 What variables can be adjusted to correct negative leverage?

Mortgage Underwriting: The Lender's Perspective

Remember from Chapter 13 that the lender is an intermediary aggregating savers' funds and then allocating them to individuals or corporations who invest in tangible assets. The mortgage lender should be viewed as a special kind of intermediate real estate investor, one having a claim that is senior to the claim of the equity investor, whose position in the real estate decision-making framework was discussed in Chapter 14. The actual source of the lender's return may be in the form of debt service payments, income participations, or equity participations. Regardless of the source of the lender's return, as an investor, the lender wants to earn a return consisting of four elements.

- **Real return** (i.e., compensation for deferred consumption).
- **Inflation premium** (i.e., compensation for the declining value of the dollar).
- **Inflation risk premium** (i.e., compensation for the possibility that the inflation premium was underestimated and that the loan will be paid back in even cheaper dollars than expected).
- **Default risk premium** (i.e., compensation for the possibility that the loan may not be repaid as agreed).

The real return as measured by the difference between Treasury bills and inflation averaged between 1 and 2 percent from 1929 through 1969. Over the last several years, since the deregulation of the early 1980s, the real rate has increased to around 3 or 4 percent. The bigger the required real return to the lender, the bigger the piece of the total pie that the lender is taking and the smaller the piece remaining for the equity investor.

Changes in the level of interest rates usually result mainly from changes in the three premiums. Just as noted in the derivation of a discount rate for use in the income approach to value, the inflation premium will move up and down in accordance with inflationary trends in the economy and will, in general, affect all loans of similar maturity equally. The inflation risk premium varies with the perceived accuracy of the inflation forecast. The default risk premium, on the other hand, is a function of the safety and liquidity of the particular loan. The better the collateral (the higher the quality of the real property asset) and the wealthier the borrower (assuming personal liability on the note), the lower will be the risk premium demanded by the lender.

Mortgage underwriting essentially is the process whereby a lender analyzes a loan to determine the degree of risk involved: that is, the likelihood that interest and principal payments on the loan will not be made promptly and that the loan eventually may not be repaid. Lenders raise the interest rate with the perceived riskiness of the loan. In addition, the more uncertain the estimate of future inflation, the greater the inflation risk premium. The typical lender will attempt to pass this risk back to the saver (the lender's source of funds) by making investments (loans) with the same maturity as his deposits. In this way, the lender is protected, since unexpected increases in inflation will reduce his inflation-adjusted cost of funds by the same amount that they reduce his inflation-adjusted return.

Lenders may adjust the amount of the loan they are willing to extend as well as the interest rate. For example, if a proposed loan is slightly more risky than normal, the lender may be satisfied with just a higher interest rate. If the proposed loan is substantially more risky than normal, the lender may reduce the amount he or she is willing to lend, say, from 80 percent to only 60 percent of the property's value. If the proposed loan is very risky, the lender may simply refuse to make any loan at all. As an intermediary, the lender must charge a high enough return to satisfy the saver (the lender's depositor), who also wants an appropriate return. The lender must then cover his or her own costs and make a profit too. These last two items—lender's cost and profit—that the lender adds to the saver's required return are referred to as the *spread*. Lenders who take more risks usually have more risk-tolerant sources of funds (who want a commensurately higher return); and more risk-tolerant lenders also want a higher spread (Because of the portfolio diversification in the larger lenders, their risk is usually lower than the sum of the risks of their loans, as detailed in Part 7.)

Mortgage underwriting decisions are made on the basis of guidelines that the lender uses to evaluate individual mortgage loan applications. Specific guidelines vary from one type of property to another and among the various types of lending institutions. But the major **underwriting** considerations are common to most lenders. We will discuss these before moving on to consider mortgages, deeds, alternative security agreements, mortgage loan analysis, and alternative mortgage instruments.

<table>
<tr><td>

MAJOR UNDERWRITING CONSIDERATIONS

</td><td>

FIRST LIEN POSITION AND GOOD TITLE

Since the loan will be secured by a particular property, the lender must be sure the borrower has **good title** to the real estate. This will involve an examination of title as described in Chapter 5. In addition, the lender's security interest (in the form of a mortgage or deed of trust) must normally be a **first lien** (i.e., have first priority in the event of a default by the borrower).[1] This can also be confirmed by a title examination that will reveal the existence of any outstanding claims or liens against the property.

</td></tr>
</table>

MARKET ANALYSIS

After an evaluation of legal title, the mortgage lender will be interested in the region's general economic health, as well as the particular urban area's development pattern. Both factors are important in our analytical framework, and the lender's perspective is identical to the perspective we developed in the opening chapters. In essence, the lender looks at regional and urban economic conditions as a means of evaluating the strength of the location of the subject property over the term of the loan.

Normally, the lender will hire an appraiser to estimate market value, and, as explained in Part 3, this valuation will include a market analysis. However, the appraiser's valuation is only an opinion based on his or her forecast of market trends. Changing and unforeseen market trends can still cause the lender problems even after the appraiser's rigorous market analysis. In the middle 1980s, farm productivity rose (more supply), and the U.S. dollar strengthened (less foreign demand), so farmers' returns declined, and so did farm land prices. In the late 1980s, many midwestern farm lenders were in trouble; in fact, the entire federally supported farm credit system (from individual financial institutions to the supporting federal institutions) was in trouble—not because of bad market analysis, but because of changing market conditions. Even after a careful evaluation of market trends (the next step after current market analysis), considerable default risk remains. This is why lenders (1) worry a great deal about the issues discussed in Part 9 and (2) seek safety in diversification as explained below.

---

[1] *Conceptually, a $30,000 second lien behind a $30,000 first lien is no less secure than the second $30,000 of a $60,000 first lien. Still, owing to foreclosure problems and costs, the second $30,000 of a $60,000 first lien is preferred.*

THE PROPERTY AND THE BORROWER

Next the lender will consider an appraisal of the specific property, calculating the proposed loan-to-value ratio and the debt coverage ratios described in detail later in the chapter. The lender will also examine the borrower's own financial position. In the case of owner-occupied property, the borrower's income and assets are a crucial factor in determining the amount of the loan the lender will be willing to make. Even when income-producing property secures the loan, borrower characteristics remain important, for if the lender is forced to foreclose and the property fails to sell at a price high enough to pay off the remaining amount on the note, the lender will seek a **deficiency judgment** against the borrower for the difference. Once obtained, this judgment is good only if the borrower has resources that may be attached.

As explained in Chapter 27, a hazardous waste audit of some type has become a standard feature of larger commercial loans and will probably be common in all mortgage loans in the near future. The property will not only fail to serve as adequate collateral if extensive toxic problems are found, but it may also become a liability (remember it was supposed to be an asset) to the lender. This potential liability is so large and the number of potentially dangerous sites so great that the authors expect continuing significant legislation at both the state and federal levels.

SAFETY AND LIQUIDITY

In general, lenders prefer safer loans. In line with our definition of winning, lenders prefer not only higher interest rates but also lower risk associated with the loan. In lending, two important elements are safety of principal and **liquidity.**

❑ **SAFETY OF PRINCIPAL.** There is a chance that the lender will not get the principal back. This can occur if the borrower fails to repay the loan. In the case of real estate finance, if such a default occurs, the lender can foreclose and force the sale of the mortgaged property.

Mortgage insurance is not the only form of insurance available to protect the lender's interest. In Chapter 5 we noted that title insurance is also available and that it can protect the lender from loss due to a previously undiscovered superior claim (i.e., to a loss resulting from title problems). Fire and casualty insurance is designed to protect the collateral against the elements. As hurricane Hugo and the San Francisco earthquake taught us, it is useful to have insurance to cover specific events that are often excluded from fire and casualty policies. Finally, the lender may require the borrower to take out mortgage life insurance, which will pay off the note in the event of the borrower's death. Each of these forms of insurance supports the ability of the property or the borrower, or both, to pay the loan. They can make up for some deficiencies in either the property or the borrower, but they cannot substitute for rigorous underwriting standards, for costs are usually associated with having to rely on insurance after the property and the borrower fail to meet loan obligations. (In addition, the insurer will insist on rigorous underwriting standards.)

❑ **LIQUIDITY.**   The lender's source of funds may require repayment before the lender's loans (assets) mature. Other things being equal, lenders are more attracted to loans for which there is an active secondary market. The rapid development of the secondary mortgage market during the 1970s contributed greatly to increasing mortgage lender liquidity. Financial institutions can freely sell loans in the secondary mortgage market and increasingly do so to maintain liquidity and reduce the cash flow (but not the income) problems associated with maturity imbalances (substantial short-term deposits financing long-term mortgage loans). Although the financial institutions are more liquid because of the secondary market, upward shifts in interest rates can still cripple their earnings with fixed-rate loans as assets and short-term deposits or liabilities. This is the major reason for a shift toward the variable rate lending explained later in this chapter.

There is not a large active secondary mortgage market to serve the liquidity needs of commercial lenders.[2] Life insurance companies (LICs) and other commercial lenders generally are not as concerned about liquidity, in terms of liquidating mortgages, as are S&L associations, who still are a major factor in residential lending. This is primarily due to the fact that LICs enjoy a relatively stable source of funds (policy premiums), whereas S&Ls are faced with a relatively unstable source of funds (savings deposits).

LENDER PORTFOLIO CONSIDERATIONS

Lenders must look beyond specific loan characteristics to portfolio considerations. If loans are diversified, both by location and by property type, less risk exists in the portfolio. However, it is not always easy to diversify either by property type or geographically because real estate markets are both local and inefficient. This means that market expertise is required in order to make a successful loan, and that expertise is by its

---

[2]*There is some secondary trading in commercial mortgages, but the small volume and lack of a formal market means that lenders still see the commercial loan as relatively liquid. As trading in mortgage securities backed by commercial loans increases, we should see some increase in commercial loan liquidity.*

nature normally localized. Therefore, full diversification often requires more expertise than the lender possesses.

Other portfolio considerations involve loan terms. The lender will not want all or a substantial percentage of its loans maturing at the same time, for this will create problems of reinvestment. The lender will be concerned with balancing the terms of its loans (assets) with the sources of its funds (liabilities) as discussed in Chapter 14. The lender will seek a portfolio of loans that fit with the institution's sources of funds and the stability of those sources.

The winning player in the real estate game knows the needs of all the lenders listed in Chapter 13. With this knowledge, she is able to find the right source of financing for any particular deal. She knows each institution's history, regulatory environment, self-image, and expertise (Level One of the analysis). Inside each institution she knows the individual loan officers and their biases (Level Two of the analysis). If an individual loan officer is personally committed to minority housing, central city renovation, or some other cause, she will be better able to "sell" her institution's loan committee on such a loan. If you want to be a winner, ask for financing from the appropriate institution and deal with a loan officer who has a special interest in your type of project.

MORTGAGES AND DEEDS OF TRUST

A loan made to finance the acquisition or construction of real estate is normally secured by the real estate itself. Whenever a loan has real estate as collateral, the loan is called a **mortgage** or a **deed of trust** depending on the particular state in which the loan is made. The function of both types of instrument is the same, but the way each type carries out the function is somewhat different, as is explained later.

Although the terms *mortgage* and *deed of trust* imply that only a single instrument is executed, in fact, there are two. One is a promissory note, whereby the borrower expressly contracts to repay the loan principal together with interest at a specified rate. The other is the instrument that makes the real estate security for the note. It is the latter instrument that, properly speaking, is either the mortgage or deed of trust.

SECURITY INTEREST

As pointed out in Chapter 5, a mortgage creates a **security interest** in real estate. The mortgagee (lender) has no right to possess or use the real estate by virtue of the mortgage. In "**title theory**" states, the mortgage is viewed as more than just a lien. The title to the mortgaged property is "legally" in the name of the lender. In **lien theory** states, the mortgage simply creates a **lien** (claim) on the real estate to secure the repayment of a debt. In such states, the title is in the name of the borrower. Once the debt is repaid, the lien is canceled or discharged. This distinction, however, is not of great practical significance.

When either a mortgage or a deed of trust has been executed and delivered to the lender, it should immediately be recorded in the local records office. By so doing, the lender gives public notice of its lien on the real estate and so retains priority against subsequent purchasers or claimants.

DISTINCTIONS BETWEEN THE MORTGAGE AND DEED OF TRUST

The mortgage is the instrument that gives the lender the legal right to force foreclosure when the note is not paid. The mortgage is, therefore, tied to the note and specific to the particular piece of property serving as collateral. The foreclosure procedure involves posting notice and eventually an auction sale. The exact mechanics of foreclosure vary from jurisdiction to jurisdiction and usually require the use of legal counsel. Although the details vary from location to location, the basics are simple. The property rights are sold at public auction to the highest bidder. (The lender can bid the amount owed without putting up any new cash, but all other bidders must put up cash). If the property sells for more than the amount of the indebtedness plus the cost of foreclosure, the borrower receives the difference.

In many states, a note and a deed of trust are used as a substitute instrument for the note and mortgage just described. Basically, this is a combination instrument that facilitates the foreclosure procedure. The borrower conveys title to a trustee, who holds the title until the note is paid. In the event of default on the note, the trustee can more easily sell the property at auction.

ELEMENTS OF THE MORTGAGE AND DEED OF TRUST

The mortgage or deed of trust is usually a lengthy document that sets forth the various obligations of the borrower, with respect both to the loan and to the real estate that acts as security. The major elements included are:

- The parties
- Loan amount and repayment period
- Interest rate
- Description of property
- Priority of mortgage
- Prepayment clause
- Due-on-sale clause

- Escrow provision
- Condition of property
- Default clause
- Foreclosure
- Personal liability

❏ **THE PARTIES.**   The mortgage is a two-party instrument, with the borrower (who gives or executes the mortgage) called the **mortgagor** and the lender (who takes the mortgage as security) called the **mortgagee.**

When a deed of trust is used, three parties are involved. The borrower is known as the **trustor,** a third party (usually a trust company or attorney) is the **trustee,** and the lender is the **beneficiary.** In effect, title to the trust deed is split into legal title and equitable title. Whereas the mortgagee in the case of a mortgage holds both kinds of title, in a deed of trust, the legal title is held by a trustee who acts on behalf of the lender who owns the equitable title. The trustee will transfer the security instrument back to the borrower (**deed of reconveyance**) when the debt has been repaid or, alternatively, will act to protect the lender in the event of a default under the terms of the trust deed. The trustee has a power of sale under a deed of trust and hence the ability to cause a nonjudicial action. Such action is much faster to execute and is thus preferable to the lender since the traditional foreclosure process may involve far more time and expense.

❏ **LOAN AMOUNT AND REPAYMENT.**   The note sets forth the amount of the loan and the manner in which it will be repaid.

❏ **INTEREST RATE.**   The note sets forth the contract rate of interest, as well as any other lender fees or participations, and the manner in which interest is to be paid.

❏ **DESCRIPTION OF PROPERTY.**   The real property that is to secure the loan must be precisely described. The legal description and the local address will meet this requirement. If the mortgagor's interest in the real estate is other than that of a fee simple, the exact nature of the interest should be spelled out.

❏ **PRIORITY OF MORTGAGE.**   An owner can execute several mortgages on the same piece of property, each securing a debt to a different lender. In the absence of any agreement among the lenders themselves, the priority of the mortgages is determined by the date of execution and recordation. The mortgage first executed and recorded is the *first* or *senior* mortgage. All others are *junior* loans, being designated as the second mortgage, third mortgage, and so on.

❏ **PREPAYMENT CLAUSE.**   An important clause in any note is that permitting prepayment (early repayment) of the loan under specific terms and conditions (**prepayment clause**). For example, an income property loan might provide that no prepayment may be made for the initial 10 years (lock-in period), with prepayment permitted thereafter at a penalty of 2 percent of the outstanding loan principal. In the case of home mortgages, the borrower is frequently given the right to prepay a portion of the loan (e.g., 20 percent) on the anniversary of the note's execution without penalty, with any additional prepayment permitted only on payment of a penalty.[3]

❏ **DUE-ON-SALE CLAUSE.**   The **due-on-sale** (or "**alienation**") **clause** is a relatively recent innovation having come into general use since the mid-1970s. Found in the note, the purpose of the clause is to permit the lender to **call the loan** (accelerate the maturity date) in the event that the buyer sells the property. This allows the lender to re-qualify the loan for the new buyer. Inclusion of the due-on-sale clause provides the lender with an opportunity to raise the interest rate if the buyer "assumes" the loan. This problem has led some states to question the "consumer impact" of such a clause. (See Box 15-1.)

❏ **ESCROW PROVISION.**   The borrower is often required to pay to the lender each month approximately one-twelfth of the annual amount necessary to pay real estate taxes and insurance premiums. Then the lender makes the payments directly to the taxing authority or insurance company when bills are rendered. This is known as the **escrow provision** because the lender is obligated to hold them separate and apart from its other funds and use them only for the purpose specified.

❏ **CONDITION OF PROPERTY.**   The borrower is usually obligated to (1) maintain the property in good repair, (2) not demolish any improvements without the permission of the lender, and, in general, (3) not permit the occurrence of "waste." Waste constitutes acts or omissions by the owner of real estate that injure it to the detriment of the mortgage lender, which relies on the property as security.

❏ **DEFAULT CLAUSE.**   The **default clause** normally specifies a number of *events of default,* which might include (1) failure to pay interest and principal when due, (2) failure to pay real estate taxes and insurance premiums, and (3) failure to keep the property in good repair. In virtually all cases, the mortgagor is given a period of time within which to

---

[3]*In many jurisdictions the right to repay is assumed, particularly on residential loans. However, many prepayment statutes place some restrictions on this right in the early years of a loan.*

**15-1
DUE-ON-SALE:
CLAUSE
ENFORCEMENT
EXPANDED**

With little or no fanfare, October 15, 1985, marked an important change in the mortgage finance marketplace. Due-on-sale clauses, giving lenders the option to call mortgage loans when the owner sells the property, became enforceable for all conventional loans in all but five states. The controversy surrounding due-on-sale clauses developed when mortgage rates rose rapidly in the early 1980s. Until then, most conventional loans contained due-on-sale clauses, but neither borrowers nor lenders were concerned about their enforcement. In an 18 percent mortgage environment, however, home sellers recognized the value of passing on 9 percent loans to buyers. Meanwhile, lenders wanted the loans to prepay, so that they could reinvest their funds at higher rates.

Some states had laws or judicial decisions restricting due-on-sale clause enforcement for both new and existing mortgages. In June 1982, the United States Supreme Court ruled that federally chartered savings and loans were not subject to these restrictions. Instead, the regulations of the Federal Home Loan Bank Board allowing due-on-sale enforcement applied.

State-chartered lenders remained subject to state restrictions until passage of the Garn–St. Germain Depository Institutions Act in October 1982. At that time, due-on-sale became generally enforceable for *new* originations by all lenders. However, for existing mortgages, the act made exceptions for states with restrictions on due-on-sale enforcement. Creditworthy borrowers could assume loans in those states that were originated or assumed between the time the state enacted the restriction and the time Congress passed the act (the "window" period) for a three-year period ending October 15, 1985. In effect, Garn–St. Germain gave states three years to extend the restrictions on due-on-sale enforcement for window-period loans. Only five states did so: restrictions for single-family loans were extended until October 15, 1987; in Arizona: September 30, 1990, in Minnesota (if the loan was originated, not assumed, during the window-period); and indefinitely in Michigan, New Mexico, and Utah.

Source: "Housing and the Economy," *Freddie Mac Reports* 3:11 (November 1985).

cure the default (e.g., 30 days in the case of a failure to pay interest and principal when due).

If a default is not cured by the mortgagor within the permissible period, the mortgagee has the right to accelerate the payment of the entire loan principal.

❏ **FORECLOSURE.** **Foreclosure** is the legal process by which a mortgagee may cause the property to be sold in a public sale in order to raise cash to pay off a debt due the mortgagee. The details of the foreclosure process and the rights of the individuals involved vary substan-

| 15-2 STATUTORY REDEMPTION | The equitable right of redemption is cut off by a sale under a foreclosure judgment, or decree, for that was the object of the foreclosure suit. After the foreclosure sale, in many states, an entirely different right arises, called the statutory right of redemption. Laws providing for statutory redemption give the mortgagor and other persons interested in the land, or certain classes of such persons, the right to redeem from the sale within a certain period, usually one year, but varying in differing states from two months to two years after sale. |

Most statutory redemption laws were passed in a time when the United States was predominantly agricultural. Most mortgagors were farmers. When the weather was bad, crops failed, and foreclosures followed. It seemed logical to suppose that the next year might bring better weather and good crops. Hence, laws created the statutory redemption period, usually one year, and usually the law was so worded that the mortgagor had the right to possession during that year.

At the expiration of the redemption period, if redemption has not been made, the purchaser at the foreclosure sale receives a deed from the officer who made the sale.

Statutory redemption is usually accompanied by payment to the officer who made the sale of the amount of the foreclosure plus interest. After redemption the mortgagor holds the land free and clear of the mortgage.

In a number of states there is no statutory redemption after sale. Immediately after the foreclosure sale, a deed is given to the purchaser, and he or she thereupon acquires ownership of the land. In states that do not permit redemption after the foreclosure sale, provision is often made for postponing the sale in some way in order to permit the mortgagor to effect redemption or discharge of the mortgage prior to the foreclosure sale.

Source: Robert Kratovil and Raymond J. Werner, *Real Estate Law,* 8th ed. (Englewood Cliffs, N.J.: Prentice-Hall, 1983), p. 386.

tially from state to state as shown in Box 15-2. Two types of foreclosure are common in the United States. **Foreclosure by action and sale** is associated with the mortgage, whereas a **foreclosure by power of sale** is associated with the deed of trust.

In both types, the property securing the loan is sold to the highest bidder at a public sale. The proceeds of sale are applied first to the payment of the unpaid mortgage debt plus unpaid interest and court costs and second to the mortgagor (or any other secured creditor).

❏ **PERSONAL LIABILITY.**   In most kinds of loans, the lender wants the borrower to be personally liable for the loan. **Personal liability** means that the borrower (individual or business entity) agrees that the borrower's other assets[4] stand behind the loan and that, in the event of a default, the lender may through appropriate legal action claim those assets.

A mortgage loan without personal liability is known as a **nonrecourse loan,** because the lender agrees it will seek no recourse against the borrower personally if the debt is unpaid.

ALTERNATIVE SECURITY AGREEMENTS

A number of variations on the basic mortgage (deed of trust) may be useful in particular lending situations. They are briefly described now.

❏ **BLANKET MORTGAGE.** A **blanket mortgage** is a mortgage that covers several properties or a single tract of land that is to be subdivided into individual building lots. In the latter case, the developer pledges the entire tract as collateral for the blanket first mortgage. As the lots are subdivided and sold either to builders or to homeowners, the lender releases the sold lots from the lien of the mortgage in exchange for a partial repayment of the loan. The amount of the repayment, the "release price," is generally 10 to 20 percent above the portion of the loan that would be allocable to the released lot on a strictly pro rata basis to maintain the integrity of the remaining collateral.

❏ **OPEN-END MORTGAGE.** The **open-end mortgage** is so named because the lender may advance additional funds in the future secured by the original mortgage, which thus has an "open end." This type of mortgage is most frequently used in connection with construction loans that are funded as the work progresses. Its major purpose is to eliminate the cost of additional paperwork in the event of a subsequent loan and to prevent future disbursements from being viewed as second mortgages.

❏ **PACKAGE MORTGAGE.** A **package mortgage** has two different meanings in real estate finance.

- A package loan may combine two separate loans into a single loan transaction. An example of this would be as follows. A lender may extend a construction loan to a developer and agree that, on completion of construction, the loan will automatically be converted into a long-term mortgage. The developer then needs negotiate only with a single lender and usually pays only one set of closing costs.

- A package loan may also be a mortgage loan in which the collateral includes not only real estate but other items normally considered

---

[4]As shown in Part 2, some of the borrower's other assets can be protected under homestead exemption and tenancy by the entireties.

**15-3
PURCHASE
MONEY
MORTGAGE TO
REDUCE
BUYER'S
EQUITY**

An important function of the purchase money mortgage may be to close the gap between the sales price and the balance of an existing mortgage that the buyer wishes to take over. For example, the seller may have purchased the property 10 years earlier for a price of $50,000 and obtained a $40,000 mortgage. Now the value of the property may have doubled to $100,000, whereas the mortgage has been amortized down to $30,000, so that the current equity is $70,000. If the first mortgage carries a low interest rate, a buyer will wish to keep the mortgage but is likely to have trouble raising $70,000 in cash. In this kind of situation, the seller may be willing to take back a second lien purchase money mortgage for, say, $35,000, with the loan to run for a certain number of years. The cash downpayment has been cut in half, and the new owner gets to keep the first mortgage that is at lower than current interest rates.[5]

personal property (with the result that the loan can be in a larger amount than otherwise). This type of loan is used to permit a borrower to obtain maximum financing; the additional collateral may include such items as refrigerator, washer, dryer, stove, carpeting, and drapery.

❑ **PURCHASE MONEY MORTGAGE.**   A **purchase money mortgage** is one taken by a seller from a buyer in lieu of purchase money. That is, the seller helps finance the purchase. This type of mortgage may or may not be a first mortgage, depending on whether the property is subject to an existing mortgage. (See Box 15-3.)

❑ **PARTICIPATION MORTGAGE.**   In the case of large-scale development, a single lender may be unable or unwilling to provide all the necessary financing. A **participation mortgage** can be used to bring two or more lenders together to share in the loan. The terms of the participation are set forth in an agreement signed by all the lenders. Each lender is assigned a designated portion of the loan, including a commensurate portion of the collateral, and will receive that portion of the debt service as paid. Frequently, the originating ("lead") lender receives a fee for servicing the loan on behalf of the entire group. (The participation is very different from the lender participation, which was discussed in Chapter 14.)

❑ **WRAPAROUND MORTGAGE.**   A **wraparound mortgage** is a second mortgage that "wraps around" or includes an existing first mort-

---

[5]*The first mortgage must be assumable for this strategy to work.*

15-4

PROFITING ON WRAPAROUNDS

Assume the owner of a property subject to a $1 million first mortgage at 9 percent interest requires an additional $200,000 in financing. Current market mortgage rates are 12 percent, and the first mortgagee is unwilling or unable to refinance the mortgage and increase the loan. (Alternatively, prepayment of the first mortgage might be either barred or subject to heavy penalties.) Since the first lien is at a desirable interest rate, the owner goes to a different lender and negotiates a wraparound loan, which works as follows.

- The new lender advances $200,000 in cash.
- The owner executes a promissory note in favor of the new lender in the face amount of $1.2 million (total of the first mortgage and the new financing).
- The interest rate on the $1.2 million note is 10 percent.
- The owner pays the new lender debt service on the entire $1.2 million loan, the latter then forwarding to the first lender the debt service on the first mortgage.

The new lender ends up receiving a return of 15 percent on his $200,000 ($1,200,000 @ 10 percent = $120,000; $1,000,000 @ 9 percent = $90,000; the difference of $30,000 is a 15 percent return on the $200,000 investment by the wraparound lender). The *upside leverage* results because the new lender is receiving (1) 10 percent on the $200,000 actually advanced plus (2) the 1 percent difference between the 10 percent now being received on the existing $1 million loan and the 9 percent that must be paid to the old lender. At the same time, the owner of the property is able to keep alive the existing first mortgage with its desirable 9 percent interest rate. Consequently, the new owner has obtained the desired total financing at the cost of 10 percent, which is lower than the current market rate of 12 percent.

gage. The face amount of the wraparound mortgage loan is equal to the balance of the existing first mortgage plus the amount of the new (second) mortgage. The wraparound loan typically calls for a higher interest rate on the entire loan than is payable on the existing first mortgage; so the wraparound lender is able to realize a very high return on the new money advanced. (See Box 15-4.)[6] In addition, the wraparound provides an easy way for the second lienholder to be sure the first lienholder is paid.

[6]*Many due-on-sale clauses in the first mortgage effectively preclude this strategy.*

LOAN AMORTIZATION ALTERNATIVES

In our discussion of loan underwriting, the repayment of loan principal and interest is the next consideration. These two items together constitute the **debt service.**

The question of debt service is of crucial importance to the borrower because if will often absorb the largest portion of the cash flow from the property. Since both borrower and lender look to the property's cash flow to provide the funds to service the loan, the amount of the debt service often is a determining factor in setting the amount of the loan itself. Naturally, higher interest rates mean higher debt service (other things being equal), but the term of the loan is also important. The shorter the term, the faster the principal must be repaid and consequently the higher the debt service and vice versa.

From the point of view of loan **amortization,** real estate mortgages fall into three categories.

- No amortization (interest-only or term) loans
- Fully amortizing (self-liquidating) loans
- Partially amortized (balloon) loans

❏ **INTEREST-ONLY OR TERM LOAN.** A **term loan** calls for no amortization during its term—**interest only** is paid. The entire principal becomes due on maturity. From the borrower's point of view, interest-only loans have one significant advantage. Since no part of the cash flow need be set aside for loan reduction, the periodic residual cash flow to the borrower from the property is increased.

The disadvantage of an interest-only loan is that the borrower may be unable to pay the full principal when the loan matures. This may happen because the value of the location has deteriorated, the property has deteriorated, or financing is not readily available, precluding sale or refinancing.

❏ **SELF-LIQUIDATING LOAN.** A **self-liquidating loan** or fully amortized loan is the type of financing usually used for residential mortgages in the United States. In this type of payment, the constant periodic payments are in amounts slightly larger than the interest due at that time. The excess amount goes toward reduction of the loan so that, at the time the loan matures, the entire principal has been paid. (This is the type of loan described in Chapter 14 with the calculation of the mortgage loan constant.)

As time goes by, the borrower is building up additional equity in the property and the lender is obtaining an additional "cushion" against loss in the event of a default. (The lender's "cushion" grows only when market value of the property remains stable or increases and not if the market value decreases.)

❑ **BALLOON LOAN.**   A partially amortized or **balloon loan** calls for some, but not complete, repayment of principal during the loan term. At maturity, the borrower will have a substantial sum (balloon) still to be repaid. A balloon loan represents a compromise between an interest-only loan, which maximizes cash flow to the borrower but increases the risk of principal nonpayment, and a fully amortizing loan (to be discussed next), with its opposite result. (See Box 15-5.)

In a typical loan situation, a borrower may apply for a mortgage loan in a specified amount for a specified term (say, 25 years), with the loan to be fully amortized over its life. The loan request is based on the maximum amount of annual debt service that can be paid while still permitting the borrower to realize a residual cash flow from the property which serves as a "cushion" for the lender.

The lender may agree to the amount of annual debt service but not want to be committed for 25 years. In this situation, the parties may

15-5 **PROBLEMS** **WITH** **"CREATIVE** **FINANCING"**	Beginning in 1979, "creative financing" enabled tens of thousands of home-seekers unable to find long-term financing to buy homes by combining a first mortgage, usually assumed from the seller at the seller's generally low-interest rate, with a short-term, high-interest second mortgage. In most cases, the second mortgage called for interest-only monthly payments until maturity, when the entire principal came due in one "balloon" payment.

The trouble was that the second loans were predicated on several assumptions that turned out to be incorrect. Everyone figured that by the time the balloons came due, in three to five years, interest rates would be considerably lower, mortgage money more plentiful, and housing values up sharply. Borrowers could refinance their homes and pay off the loans comfortably. But by late 1982, when many balloons came due, none of these assumptions had materialized.

As a result, many homeowners were unable to come up with the balloon payments (averaging around $21,000 in 1982) and defaulted on the loans. Many others fell behind in their payments, and most were unable to sell their homes in the depressed market. These developments, according to most authorities, contributed significantly to the concurrent wave of home foreclosures and delinquencies.

The situation hurt not only homeowners but also major lenders, particularly the savings and loan institutions, which faced further financial strains from repossessing and trying to resell foreclosed homes in a poor market.

Source: Adapted from p. 55 of "'Creative Financing' Comes a Cropper," by Thomas J. Murray, with the special permission of *Dun's Business Month* (formerly *Dun's Review*), August 1982, copyright 1982 Dun & Bradstreet Publications Corporation.

agree that the loan will have a 10- or 15-year maturity, with periodic debt service on a 25-year amortization basis. In this way, annual debt service does not fully liquidate the principal at the end of 15 years, and the balance outstanding comes due as a balloon payment.

INCOME PROPERTY LOAN ANALYSIS

Two particular distinctions can be noted when comparing the underwriting of income property loans and ordinary residential loans. First, the terms of a residential mortgage are fairly standardized, but the terms of income property loans are generally much more flexible and open to negotiation. Second, the relative emphasis placed on borrower and property analysis is reversed. Whereas in a residential loan the credit history and the repayment capability of the borrower are the paramount considerations, it is the property that usually constitutes the main security for an income property loan. The reason is that an income property, by definition, will generate cash flow, and this is normally the primary means of paying the debt service on the loan.

At this point, astute readers might notice the similarity between a lender's approach to lending and our organization in this book. You can think of this entire book as how to do a good property analysis. The mortgage lender's "due diligence" (study and analysis) begins with the market (Part 1), is mindful of the partnership with government and the dynamic rules of the game (Part 2), usually involves a formal appraisal (Part 3), considers the long-term marketability and management of the property (Part 4), makes sure that this property loan fits with the lender's source of funds (Part 5), knows that income taxes have a major impact on decision makers (Part 6), uses portfolio approach to risk minimization (Part 7), and worries about competing new developments and emerging trends (Parts 8 and 9).

Having done the appropriate level of property analysis and completed the mortgage loan constant calculations, the lender typically will examine certain key ratios before finalizing terms with the prospective borrower. Before we proceed with a discussion of these ratios, it is important to note two things. First, everything rests on the first-step determination of the ability of the property in its fixed location to satisfy expected consumer needs (i.e., Level One, property analysis). Second, both overall market interest rates (the real return and the inflation premium) and the relative riskiness of this loan (the risk premium) are incorporated through the interest rate and maturity in the mortgage loan constant. Like everyone else, the lender wants a higher return and a lower risk. In this chapter we are looking at financing from the lender's perspective and thus will examine various ratios that lenders use to monitor the riskiness of a loan. For an example of how lenders and equity investors can work together, blurring the traditional debt-equity distinction, see Box 15-6.

15-6
INCOME AND
EQUITY
PARTICIPATION
EXAMPLE

An office-warehouse developer approached a large life insurance company for a commitment to finance a new project. The developer had an appraisal that indicated a market value of $2.7 million. The developer was interested in acquiring a $2 million loan. At the time of the loan application, long-term interest rates were approaching 17.5 percent. The developer knew the income generated from the office-warehouse could not support a 17.5 percent mortgage. However, he felt the project could justify a 13 percent loan. Therefore, the developer was willing to discuss a 13 percent loan with additional interest tied to some agreed-on level of net cash flow plus some percentage of the project's capital appreciation.

After considerable negotiation, the life insurance company proposed the following loan terms.

Loan amount:	$2 million first mortgage
Interest:	13 percent per annum
Term:	360 months
Balloon:	Lender may require that the principal and all accrued interest on the loan be paid in full without penalty in 15 years.
Income kicker:	Lender shall receive 20 percent of the net cash flow within 90 days after the end of each fiscal year as additional interest. Net cash flow is defined as all gross income generated by the project less operating expenses and debt service associated with the 13 percent, $2 million loan.
Equity kicker:	Lender shall receive a cash sum equal to 25 percent of the market value of the mortgaged property in excess of $2.7 million as of the date of the seventh anniversary of the $2 million loan. Market value will be established by a qualified MAI appraiser chosen by the lender. At the option of the borrower, the equity kicker may be payable in cash or by the delivery of a promissory note (optional note) of equal amount bearing interest at the then prevailing prime lending rate plus 2

percent or 13 percent, whichever is greater. The optional note will be interest only with principal payable at the time of the first mortgage balloon. Furthermore, a sum of 25 percent of the market value above the market value established on the seventh anniversary shall be payable to the lender at the time of the first mortgage balloon.

Escrow provisions:

Borrowers shall make monthly deposits on account of real estate taxes and insurance equal to one-twelfth of the estimated annual charges.

Due on sale:

In the event that the borrower (without the written consent of the lender) sells, conveys, or alienates any part or interest in the mortgaged premises, the entire first mortgage plus accrued interest and optional note or 25 percent of market shall be due and payable.

Commitment fee:

Lender shall receive a commitment fee of $20,000 in cash on the acceptance of this commitment.

Commitment standby fee:

Borrower will deposit with lender a commitment standby fee of $40,000 in the form of an irrevocable and unconditional letter of credit or certificate of deposit in favor of the lender upon the issuance of this commitment. Should the loan not be disbursed the lender shall retain the commitment standby fee as additional consideration.

Prepayment privilege:

None during the first 120 months. During each of the subsequent 12-month periods the prepayment charge will be 5 percent, 4 percent, 3 percent, and 2 percent of the outstanding balance at the time of prepayment. No prepayment charge if payment is made during the fourteenth year.

In this introductory text, we discuss only the most common ratios used to monitor risk: the loan-to-value ratio, the debt service coverage ratio, the operating expense ratio, and the breakeven ratio.

LOAN-TO-VALUE RATIO

The **loan-to-value ratio** (LTVR) is an expression of the safety of the principal of the loan based on the value of the collateral. The LTVR is calculated as follows:

$$\text{LTVR} = \frac{\text{Loan amount}}{\text{Project value}}$$

In the yield calculation example, Table 14-9, the loan-to-value ratio is

$$\text{LTVR} = \frac{\$1,000,000}{\$1,200,000} = 83.3 \text{ percent}$$

The lower the LTV, the lower the risk to the lender, for in the case of default, there would exist a greater gap between the outstanding loan balance and project value. However, note that overvaluing the project, through a faulty inflated appraisal, can give the lender a false sense of security. The LTVR will normally decline over the life of the loan as principal payments reduce the loan amount and inflation enhances the property's value. If so, the lender's risk is reduced in later years.

DEBT COVERAGE RATIO

In addition to calculating the yield received for money lent and the safety of principal, lenders wish to measure the risk associated with receiving the return. The **debt coverage ratio** (DCR) helps the lender to evaluate the riskiness of an income property loan, that is, the likelihood of needing to foreclose and then rely on the property's value (the loan to value ratio). Obviously, the lender would prefer never to have to rely on the foreclosure process, so the DCR is typically the most important ratio in commercial lending. It measures the "buffer" or "cushion" between the NOI and the debt service. The debt coverage ratio is calculated as follows:

$$\text{DCR} = \frac{\text{NOI}}{\text{Debt service}}$$

In the yield calculation example in Table 14-9, the debt coverage ratio is the NOI ($150,000) divided by the debt service ($125,576):

$$DCR = \frac{\$150,000}{\$125,576} = 1.19$$

For an average motel project, a lender will be looking for a debt coverage ratio of approximately 1.15 to 1.5. (Most lenders would view this loan as of above-average risk.) Generally, the lower the debt coverage ratio, the higher the risk to the lender and vice versa. Consequently, when lenders perceive that a particular project is high risk, they will require a higher DCR to lessen the riskiness of the loan.

THE MAXIMUM LOAN AMOUNT

The **maximum loan amount** a lender would be willing to provide can be determined by examining the relationship between the expected NOI, desired DCR (assumed here to be 1.5), and the mortgage constant (K). The relationship can be expressed as

$$\text{Maximum loan} = \frac{NOI}{K \cdot DCR}$$

Given the preceding example, the maximum loan would be

$$\text{Maximum loan} = \frac{\$150,000}{0.125576 \times 1.5} = \$796,331$$

Clearly, the request for a \$1 million loan does not meet the lender's hypothesized standards. Why? First, the borrowers want a relatively high loan-to-value ratio loan, 83.3 percent (for reasons that were examined in Chapter 14.) Second, motels are relatively risky, and lenders demand relatively high DCRs (i.e., 1.15 to 1.5). This lender has opted to be on the high side of that range (1.5) because of its own portfolio situation. Would a lender seeking a 1.15 DCR make this loan? The answer to this question is yes, as can be demonstrated by calculating the maximum loan amount using the 1.15 DCR

$$\text{Maximum loan} = \frac{\$150,000}{0.125576 \times 1.15} = \$1,038,695$$

This clearly demonstrates the importance of accurately evaluating the risk associated with a particular loan. By changing the required DCR, the lender can change the accept-reject decision associated with a loan application even though the project's NOI and the terms of the loan (K) have not been changed.

OPERATING EXPENSE RATIO

The lender will be concerned with the relationship between operating expenses and effective gross income. Depending on the property type and market, the lender will establish a guideline **operating expense ratio** (OER). This ratio shows operating expenses as a percentage of effective gross income and should not vary dramatically from the market norm. The operating expense ratio can be calculated as follows.

$$OER = \frac{\text{Operating expenses}}{\text{Effective gross income}}$$

If we assume the effective gross income for the motel in Table 14-9 is $600,000 and the operating expenses are $450,000, the OER will be

$$OER = \frac{\$450,000}{\$600,000} = 75 \text{ percent}$$

BREAKEVEN RATIO

Sometimes referred to as the *default ratio*, the **breakeven ratio** (BER) indicates the percentage of gross potential income that must be collected in order to meet the operating expenses and debt service. The ratio is calculated by dividing the total operating expenses *plus* debt service by the gross potential income. Lenders ordinarily establish some maximum allowable percentage from 70 to 95 percent. The breakeven ratio can be expressed as

$$BER = \frac{\text{Operating expenses + Debt service}}{\text{Gross potential income}}$$

If the motel example in Table 14-9 was expected to generate a gross potential income of $800,000 (less a vacancy of 25 percent equals effective gross income of $600,000) and the annual debt service was $125,576, the BER would be calculated as follows:

$$BER = \frac{\$450,000 + \$125,576}{\$800,000} = 71.9 \text{ percent}$$

This means that operating expenses and debt service consume 71.9 percent of gross potential income, so occupancy (and, therefore, revenue) must be at least 71.9 percent of its maximum attainable, or the property will not generate breakeven cash flow.

We believe in avoiding rules of thumb at all costs. However, to give a

15-7	TYPE OF RATIO	PERCENT
COMMERCIAL MORTGAGE UNDERWRITING GUIDELINES— OFFICE BUILDINGS	Loan-to-value	70–90
	Debt coverage	1.05–1.35
	Operating expense	25–50
	Breakeven	75–95

perspective on the typical levels of these ratios, one institution's commercial mortgage underwriting guidelines in 1990 are summarized in Box 15-7.

LOAN TERMS

The lender is also concerned with other **loan terms.** Can the borrower prepay? If so, is there a prepayment penalty? The lender experiences certain costs in loan origination and expects to receive a return over the term of the loan to cover these origination costs. (The lender's costs usually exceed the loan origination fee.) In addition, if a loan is repaid early, the lender must reinvest the same funds and experience the origination costs again. Finally, if interest rates drop, an existing loan made at a higher interest rate is very attractive to the lender. And in the case of prepayment, the lender would have to reinvest at a lower rate of interest.

Consequently, the lender will typically want some form of compensation if the loan is to be prepaid at an early date. Lenders call this compensation a **prepayment penalty,** and it is usually expressed as a percentage of the outstanding loan balance at the time of repayment. (In many states there are significant legal restrictions on the size and duration of prepayment penalties on some loans.)

Lenders are adversely affected if interest rates rise after they have made a long-term loan. As partial protection against such occurrences, lenders often ask for **escalation clauses** in the loan agreement. An escalation clause states that if the original borrower (owner) sells the property and the new owner assumes the loan, the lender has the right, at that time, to renegotiate the interest rate. Escalation clauses protect the lender to some extent against rises in long-term interest rates.

The real estate decision maker should be clear on the difference between an escalation clause and an acceleration clause. The **accelera-**

tion clause is a clause that states that when debt service payments are missed (default occurs), the entire face amount of the note becomes due, thereby facilitating the foreclosure procedure. This should be carefully distinguished from the escalation clause just described.

Lenders may also want restrictions on the operation of the project, guaranteed levels of maintenance and insurance, and probably the personal liability of the borrower for all or a portion of the loan amount.

ANALYSIS OF THE BORROWER

The lender's analysis of the borrower concentrates on the borrower's past investment history and credit. The borrower's "track record" and reputation are a vital part of the analysis. A series of successful projects ensures, at the very least, a very careful scrutiny of the loan application, whereas past failures significantly reduce the chances for approval. The borrower's credit standing will be based on a credit report, current financial statements, and "the word on the street," that is, what the other players are saying about this prospective borrower. Where available, a Dun & Bradstreet (**D&B**) report will be obtained. Finally, the lender will evaluate the project in light of current business conditions. In the case of new construction, where the lead time may be several years, the lender will make some effort to anticipate where the business cycle will be when the building is ready for rental. It is extremely common in the real estate industry for enthusiastic developers, at the height of a boom, to plan new buildings that will be ready to receive tenants just after the boom has peaked and vacancy rates are beginning to rise.

RESIDENTIAL LOAN ANALYSIS

Home loans are obviously simpler and quicker to underwrite than big commercial loans. Still, in analyzing a residential mortgage loan application (see Figure 15-1), the lender must make decisions in three interrelated areas. If the underwriting process reveals significant problems in any one of the areas, the loan is likely to be rejected. The three areas are (1) property analysis, (2) loan analysis, and (3) borrower analysis.

PROPERTY ANALYSIS

Although the residential lender looks primarily to the credit of the borrower when reaching the loan decision, the real estate that will be the collateral for the loan is obviously also of great importance. Lenders rely primarily on an appraisal as the source of information for the property analysis. The appraiser will do the property analysis, which involves neighborhood analysis and an evaluation of the physical condition of the property.

The undersigned hereby applies to _____ BANK and TRUST COMPANY, _____, for a loan of the amount and upon the terms hereinafter set forth, said loan to be secured by a first mortgage upon the real estate hereinafter described.

_____   _____
Applicant's full name   Full name of wife or husband

Property located at _____ (Street) _____ (City)
Amount of Loan: $_____ for _____ years at _____ per cent interest per annum.
Payments of $_____ monthly.
Is the purpose of the loan to finance the acquisition or construction of a dwelling in which you reside or expect to reside? _____
If not, will the first mortgage secure property which you use or expect to use as your principal residence? _____
If not answered above, please state the purpose of the loan _____

Is the property now mortgaged? _____ If so, to whom? _____
_____ Address _____
Is the property now occupied by owner or rented? _____
Title now stands in the name of _____
Dimensions of land _____ feet front, by depth of _____ feet,
area _____ square feet.
Description of buildings (frame or brick, dwellings, store, etc.) _____

No. of stories high ____ No. of rooms ____ Baths ____ Year in which Building erected ____
Cost of property $_____

Utilities		Roof			Heating System		Fuel		
Water	[ ]	Non-combust. shingles	[ ]		Hot Air	[ ]	Coal	[ ]	No. of
Elec.	[ ]	Wood shingles	[ ]		Hot Water	[ ]	Gas	[ ]	Heaters
Gas	[ ]	Tar and Gravel	[ ]		Steam	[ ]	Oil	[ ]	
Sewer	[ ]	Slate	[ ]				Elec.	[ ]	_____

Assessed Value 19_____   Applicant's Valuation 19_____
Land $_____   Land $_____
Buildings $_____   Buildings $_____
Total $_____   Total $_____
Remarks _____

The undersigned understands that the title of the above described real estate is to be examined and the necessary papers are to be prepared and recorded by the attorney for the mortgagee Bank, all at the expense of the undersigned, and that the closing of the loan is contingent among other things upon the title of the real estate being satisfactory to the Bank. The undersigned agrees to pay the expenses incurred by the Bank in having the title examined and the property inspected, whether this application is accepted or rejected.

FIGURE 15-1   *Residential mortgage loan application*

The estimated market value of the property is critical to the lender's decision as to the size of the loan. The loan-to-value ratio (LTVR) will usually be a percentage of either the appraised value *or* the purchase price of the property, whichever is *lower*. The difference between the loan amount and the price to be paid by the borrower represents the cash equity to be put in the property by the buyer.

LOAN ANALYSIS

In determining the terms of a proposed loan, the lender will consider both its own requirements and the needs of the borrower. The key terms in a residential mortgage loan are briefly discussed in the following paragraphs.

❑ **LOAN-TO-VALUE RATIO.**   The amount of a residential mortgage loan typically is expressed as a percentage of the property's market value at the time the loan is made. This percentage is commonly referred to as the loan-to-value ratio. The ratio for residential mortgages can range anywhere from 50 percent to 95 percent of market value. In any given case, the ratio is a function of several factors.

■ The lender's supply of loanable funds.

■ The borrower's ability or willingness to provide equity.

■ Limitations on LTVRs set by the particular lender or by regulatory agencies to which it is subject. The higher the loan-to-value ratio, the greater the risk to the lender unless the loan is backed by mortgage insurance (more on mortgage insurance in a moment).

❑ **RATE OF INTEREST.**   The rate of interest charged on a residential mortgage loan is a function of current market conditions, LTVR, term of the loan, and financial condition of the borrower. Of these, current market conditions are the most important factor since the lender cannot charge much more or it will lose out to competitors. And it will not charge much less because it would be unnecessarily sacrificing profit. A lender will sometimes offer loans with different LTVRs and different terms. The greater the risk assumed by the lender, the higher will be the interest rate. The type of residential property being financed will also be considered by the lender. Typically, condominium loans have a slightly higher interest rate (perhaps one-eighth to one-fourth percent) than do detached single-family dwellings. Other considerations affecting the interest rate include the age and physical condition of the property and the financial condition of the borrower; however, a lender will often prefer to decline the loan rather than to charge an interest premium to compensate for a large amount of extra risk.

❑ **TERM TO MATURITY.**   The loan term may range anywhere from 15 to 30 years, with the shorter terms customarily utilized for older buildings. The general rule to be observed in any loan, residential or otherwise, is that the term should not exceed the remaining economic life of the improvements. A recent innovation is the yuppie loan. With a two-wage earner family, some borrowers are opting to pay off the loan faster, frequently over 15 years. The advantage to the borrower is less total interest over the life of the loan. If the borrower can handle the higher payments, such a loan definitely reduces the lender's interest rate exposure. As a result, the interest rate charged may be considerably lower, maybe a full 1 percent, for the shorter term loan.

❏ **ORIGINATION AND CLOSING COSTS.**   Origination and closing costs fall into two categories. First, they include actual out-of-pocket expenses that the borrower must pay for a property survey, title insurance, mortgage recording fees, and the like. The second, frequently known as an *origination fee,* is an "up-front" amount, often equal to 1 or 2 percent of the loan, paid to the lender for compensation of overhead costs associated with underwriting the loan.

❏ **MORTGAGE INSURANCE.**   In the case of an FHA-insured mortgage, the lender is completely protected against loss in the event of default. A guarantee from the Veterans Administration, VA, can serve the same function, as explained in Chapter 16.

Private mortgage insurance (PMI) is frequently required on conventional loans (i.e., not government insured) when the LTVR is in excess of 80 percent. PMI, unlike FHA insurance, usually covers only the top 20 percent of the mortgage. Thus, if a 95 percent LTV ratio loan is foreclosed on and sold at a price equal to 80 percent of the original appraised value, the private mortgage insurer will pay the lender the additional 15 percent, and the lender will suffer no actual loss.

BORROWER ANALYSIS

In residential loan underwriting, primary emphasis is placed on the borrower's ability to repay the loan, whereas in income property lending the real estate itself is the primary security. The residential lender will concentrate on three areas in reaching a decision about the borrower's credit standing.

❏ **ABILITY TO PAY.**   A borrower's financial capacity is evaluated by examining the quality and quantity of income available to meet debt service requirements. Quality of income refers to the stability of the income stream—how likely is it that the borrower will become unemployed or lose the assets that provide income? Certain kinds of employment are very stable, for example, professional work and government employment, but other people have jobs that are much less certain, for example, commission salespersons (such as real estate brokers), seasonal workers, and self-employed businesspersons.

A more difficult question arises when a borrower has more than one source of income. At one time, lenders discounted the income provided by a working wife because of the possibility that the wife might leave her job to bear children. This latter consideration has been made irrelevant by passage of the Equal Credit Opportunity Act (**ECOA**). ECOA prohibits a lender from discounting the quality of income because of the borrower's age, sex, national origin, marital status, race, color, religion, or the fact that the borrower's income is derived from welfare or public assistance payments.

❑ **INCOME RATIOS.**   Lenders use income ratios to relate the borrower's ability to make the loan's monthly payments. Income ratios express in percentage terms how much of the borrower's monthly income must be devoted to debt service if the requested loan is granted. The debt service is assumed to include payments covering principal amortization, interest, property taxes, and insurance premiums, and so is referred to as **PITI** (an acronym made up of the first letters of each word). The ratios are used as guidelines only and do not constitute the sole basis for evaluating a loan application.

When a conventional (non-**FHA** or -**VA**) home mortgage is applied for, lenders concentrate on two income ratios in their underwriting process. The first income ratio, which is now in a state of transition, holds that the monthly PITI payment may not exceed 25 or 30 percent of the monthly gross income. The second income ratio requires that PITI *plus* monthly installment payments covering other debts (e.g., automobile, credit cards) should not exceed one-third of the monthly gross income.

With respect to the FHA-insured mortgage loans, underwriting guidelines emphasize two income ratios; these are referred to as the 35 percent rule and the 50 percent rule. The 35 percent rule stipulates that total housing expense (PITI plus monthly utilities and maintenance) should not exceed 35 percent of *net effective income*—that is, gross income less federal income taxes, or what is more generally known as "take home pay." The 50 percent rule states that total monthly obligations should not exceed 50 percent of net effective income. Total monthly obligations include total housing expense plus installment payments on other debt obligations plus withholding for state income taxes plus social security (FICA) payments.

❑ **CREDIT ANALYSIS.**   The final element to be examined is the borrower's credit standing or reputation. The question here is whether the applicant's credit history raises any question about the applicant's commitment to discharge his or her obligations. The lender, with the applicant's permission, will contact a credit bureau for a credit report. The report lists the status of the applicant's various credit accounts, both past and present. The type of each account (open, installment, or revolving) and source of credit (bank, credit card, department store) will be listed. The applicant's customary payment pattern will be treated on a scale that ranges from "pays as agreed" to "turned over to a collection agency."

ALTERNATIVE MORTGAGE INSTRUMENTS

Thus far we have examined the traditional fixed rate loan from the lender's perspective. In recent years, this traditional loan has presented lenders (both commercial and residential) with serious problems related to unexpected increases in inflation, which affect market interest rates. When the rate of inflation reaches 12 percent, a lender's cost of capital rises, and a 25-year loan on the books at 8 percent is very unattractive. As explained in Chapter 13, this problem drove the S&L industry, which was heavily concentrated in long-term fixed rate loans, to the point of insolvency the first time (the late 1970s). As a remedy to this problem, several alternative mortgage instruments have been created. Unfortunately, the solution to the lender's problem often creates new problems for the borrower. Although a full discussion of the pros and cons from both the lender's and the borrower's perspective could make a course in itself, we will at least introduce the basics here.

VARIABLE RATE MORTGAGE (VRM)

Variable rate mortgages (**VRM**s) were the original alternative to the traditional fully amortized constant payment mortgage. The interest rate charged on a VRM is not fixed throughout the term of the loan but rather is tied to a market index such as the prime interest rate or rate on government bonds. As a result, the interest rate on a VRM rises and falls over the term of the loan in response to changes in the market index. The benefits of a VRM generally include the following.

❑ **TO ALLOW OR ENCOURAGE CONTINUED BORROWING DURING HIGH INTEREST RATE PERIODS.**   As a VRM is tied to a market interest rate index, should rates fall during the term of the loan, so would the interest associated with the VRM. Consequently, borrowers may not hesitate to borrow during high interest rate periods and risk being "locked in" to the high rates. Conversely, should market rates rise, so would the interest rate associated with the VRM.

❑ **TO PROTECT LENDERS FROM INTEREST RATE RISK AND CONSEQUENTLY TO ALLOW THEM TO EXCLUDE AN INFLATION RISK PREMIUM WHEN DETERMINING THE ORIGINAL RATE ASSOCIATED WITH A VRM.**   When rates rise in the market, the lender's portfolio return will rise, and when rates fall, the return will fall.

❑ **TO RELIEVE VRM BORROWERS OF PREPAYMENT PENALTY CLAUSES, TO CHARGE THEM A LOWER ORIGINATION FEE, AND TO START THEM AT LOWER ORIGINAL INTEREST RATES.**

A decision must be made indicating how the periodic payments will be altered when the market index fluctuates. This can be done in one of three ways: (1) increase or decrease the monthly payment, (2) lengthen or shorten the term of the loan, and (3) raise or lower the principal balance owed and keep the term constant, resulting in a balloon payment or a refund at maturity.

ADJUSTABLE-RATE MORTGAGE (ARM)

When the Home Loan Bank Board first authorized variable rate mortgages, it required interest rate "caps," that is, ceilings on rate increases. The variable rate concept was the solution to a major lender problem, but it presented a problem for borrowers: payment shock. If interest rates move from 8 to 12 percent, the monthly payment necessary to amortize the original loan over the same 30-year period goes up 40 percent. Clearly, many families did not want to be exposed to such a risk. The high inflation of the late 1970s quickly ran the rates to the ceilings, and from then on the rates were no longer variable. Lenders were again disappointed.

What evolved next was a series of adjustable-rate mortgages (ARMs), which embodied the VRM concept but with more viable caps. One of the more popular ARMs ties the interest rate to a two-year government bond rate with interest rate and payment adjustments every two years. The caps are that the interest rate can rise (or fall) no more than 1 percent at any adjustment period and no more than 5 percent over the life of the loan. Such an ARM gives the lender substantial protection without subjecting the borrower to a potentially devastating payment shock.

In 1984, over 50 percent of the residential loan originations were some form of ARM. In 1985 fixed-rate loans made a comeback as long-term interest rates fell, but clearly ARMs are here to stay as one financing alternative. It is a "hot" area with frequent innovations as suggested in Box 15-8.

GRADUATED PAYMENT MORTGAGE (GPM)

A relatively recent innovation in home mortgages has been the *graduated payment mortgage* (**GMP**) or *flexible payment mortgage* (**FPM**). Each of these creates a changing payment schedule in order to reduce payments in the early years when the borrower's income is low. The early payments may be in the amount of the interest due so that the loan is standing during this period or may be less than the interest due so that a portion of the interest accrues and is added to the outstanding principal.

In later years, the payments are increased sufficiently to pay the accrued interest and make up for the missed amortization in the early years. This makes sure that the loan liquidates at maturity. The main purpose of this type of loan is to allow young persons in the early stages of their earning careers to qualify for home loans.

15-8
ADJUSTABLE
RATE
MORTGAGES
AND THE
MARKET

At times during the 1980s, adjustable-rate mortgages (ARMs) took center stage in the primary mortgage market. They overcame formidable obstacles, including borrower resistance, fierce price-cutting competition, an almost unlimited variety of terms, lender uncertainties, and a resurgence in the popularity of the fixed-rate loan—to emerge as a premier product in the secondary mortgage market.

Mortgage lenders, investors, traders, and secondary market observers now agree that the demand for ARM products in the secondary market is stronger than ever and continues to grow. A snapshot of the ARM market reveals the following:

- Virtually all private ARM investors are thrifts—savings and loans and savings banks—seeking to restructure their portfolios through increased ARM investments. There has been little interest in ARM products from other large mortgage investors such as pension funds and insurance companies.

- The most sought-after ARM product continues to be one-year adjustable loans, particularly those with rate caps of 2 percent per adjustment and of 5 to 6 percent over the life of the loan. The option to convert to a fixed-rate loan is becoming more popular.

Although a few major mortgage bankers are originating and selling a six-month product, most thrifts are aggressively looking for loans that adjust annually. This preference is reflected in the respective yield requirements for the two products. Prices for one-year ARMs have been higher than those for the six-month product, producing yield requirements one-eighth to one-half point higher for the shorter adjustment periods. Three-year ARMs are available in small supplies, but the five-year ARM has almost disappeared.

- The most popular index continues to be Treasury constant maturity, but there is some interest in the popularity of the Eleventh District Federal Home Loan Bank cost of funds index. Some investors outside California, including some in the Midwest and Northeast, began to accept this index when rates were falling because of its traditional lag on the downside.

- Strong investor demand for the ARM product, however, is outstripping supplies for several reasons. Heading the list is the fact that fixed-rate loans are still the product of choice for many borrowers. Fewer ARMs are now available at the steep discounted teaser rates prevalent during late 1984 and early 1985.

- Finally, and perhaps most significant, ARM competition in most markets is fierce. Many lenders are aggressively originating ARM loans for their portfolios and are still offering terms that are difficult for many mortgage bankers to match. Only those mortgage bankers who locate thrift investors willing to cut prices for bulk production can compete effectively in such markets.

Source: Secondary Mortgage Market Analyst, sample copy (Boston: Warren, Gorham, and Lamont).

RENEGOTIABLE (RM) OR ROLLOVER MORTGAGE (ROM)

RMs or **ROM**s were first introduced in Canada. The interest is fixed for a specified period of time, usually from one to three years. At the end of that period, the borrower and lender renegotiate the interest based on prevailing market conditions. If rates have risen, the interest rate on the loan increases, or vice versa. RMs and/or ROMs shift much of the interest rate risk burden to the borrower.

SHARED APPRECIATION MORTGAGE (SAM)

SAMs provide the borrower with a large reduction in the contract rate of interest in exchange for an equity participation. For example, the lender may reduce the contract rate of interest by one-third in exchange for one-third of the capital gain in 5 or 10 years. The SAM mortgage is presumably most attractive to first-time home buyers, but there are still significant problems in both the calculation and payments of the appreciation portion of the total interest charge.

REVERSE ANNUITY MORTGAGE (RAM)

Designed primarily for the elderly, the **RAM** permits homeowners to borrow based on the equity in their current home and use the proceeds to buy a lifetime annuity from a life insurance company. The monthly proceeds from the annuity first go to pay back the RAM, and the remaining annuity payment is paid to the homeowner. The RAM is repaid from the sale of the home on the borrower's death.

GROWING EQUITY MORTGAGE (GEM)

The **GEM** is another variation of the amortization pattern. If interest rates rise, the rate of interest stays fixed, but the maturity shortens and the periodic payment increases accordingly. This means that the borrower's equity increases faster, hence the name GEM. From the lender's perspective, the more rapid amortization lessens the problem of unexpected high inflation. (This represents contractual early payment as distinguished from the optional early payment that is permitted in some form with most of the other loans.)

PRICE-LEVEL-ADJUSTED MORTGAGE (PLAM)

PLAMs have received a great deal of attention in the academic literature. The idea is to have the mortgage balance adjust periodically for price-level changes. With such a loan the lender could charge a lower interest rate since no inflation or inflation risk premium would be needed. As long as the property's value kept pace with the price index, the loan-to-value ratio would remain in the reasonable range.

Most of the alternative mortgage instruments create the problem of a "real payment tilt" for the borrower. As the lender's risk is reduced, the borrower is exposed to the possibility of an increase in required loan payments without any certain increase in rents (commercial loans) or salary (residential loans). The marketplace has not yet decided which, if any, of the alternative mortgage instruments will replace the fixed-rate constant amortization loan as the most popular mortgage instrument. The eventual decision will be based on the relative abilities of each to meet the needs of both lenders and borrowers.

SUMMARY   Clearly, the real estate decision maker must understand the lender's perspective if he or she is to obtain the best possible financing for any given project. Lenders consider many things when evaluating a loan proposal: their own position, the property itself, the security agreement, and the relationship of the loan requested to the projected net operating income of the property or the borrower's income. The lender has a great deal of flexibility in structuring a loan to fit a particular property and buyer. The concepts behind all the alternative mortgage instruments may be used to create a loan that meets the needs of both borrowers and lenders.

IMPORTANT TERMS

Acceleration clause	ECOA
Alienation	Escalation clause
Amortization	Escrow provision (loan)
Balloon loan	FHA
Beneficiary	First lien
Blanket mortgage	Foreclosure
Breakeven ratio	Foreclosure by action and sale
Call the loan	Foreclosure by power of sale
D&B	FPM
Debt coverage ratio (DCR)	GEM
Debt service	Good title
Deed of reconveyance	GPM
Deed of trust	Inflation premium
Default clause	Inflation risk premium
Default risk premium	Interest-only loan (term loan)
Deficiency judgment	Lien
Due-on-sale clause	Lien theory (mortgages)

Liquidity
Loan terms
Loan-to-value ratio (LTVR)
Maximum loan amount
Mortgage
Mortgagee
Mortgagor
Nonrecourse loan
Open-end mortgage
Operating expense ratio
Package mortgage
Participation mortgage
Personal liability
PITI
Points (discount)
Prepayment clause
Prepayment penalty

Purchase money mortgage
RAM
Real return
Risk premium
RM
ROM
SAM
Security interest
Self-liquidating loan
Term loan
Title theory (mortgages)
Trustee
Trustor
Underwriting
VA
VRM
Wraparound mortgage

REVIEW QUESTIONS

15.1   List and define the lender's basic objectives in real estate finance.

15.2   Why are commercial banks and life insurance companies not as concerned with the liquidity of mortgages as are the savings and loans?

15.3   Differentiate between a mortgage and a deed of trust.

15.4   What is the importance of a promissory note with regard to a deficiency judgment?

15.5   What are the differences between a blanket mortgage and package mortgage?

15.6   How might a purchase money mortgage be used to reduce the downpayment required for the purchase of an existing single-family dwelling?

15.7   Under what circumstances might a wraparound mortgage represent an attractive real estate financing alternative for both the buyer and the seller?

15.8   List two ways to reduce the mortgage constant.

15.9   How does the payment of an origination fee affect the effective cost of a real estate loan? Why?

15.10   What factors would a lender consider in evaluating the riskiness of an income property loan?

$\mathcal{T}$HE SECONDARY MORTGAGE MARKETS

INTRODUCTION   Mortgage markets are similar in many ways to the markets for financial assets. For example, the *primary* market for common stocks consists of initial public stock offerings by corporations to raise funds for capital investment. When these shares of stock change hands, or trade, subsequent to their original issuance, they do so in a *secondary* market. For stocks, and to a lesser extent bonds, the secondary markets are highly organized exchanges with a large number of buyers and sellers, and well-publicized performance results. Needless to say, the activities in the secondary market greatly influence the activities in the primary markets. Value and terms of new stock offerings are dictated by current perspectives of investors in the secondary markets.

The mortgage market behaves in much the same way. For example, when lenders originate mortgages according to the process described in Chapters 13 through 15, they do so in the primary mortgage markets. Home purchasers borrow from the array of lenders described in Chapter 13 to finance their housing investments. Prior to the 1970s, mortgage lenders commonly originated these loans and held them in their own portfolios until the underlying collateral (the home) was sold, or the mortgage was repaid for some other reason such as default or maturity of the loan.

In the 1970s, lenders began to package together the loans that they had made in the primary markets, and to sell the packages to other investors who desired the cash flow streams offered by large mortgage pools.[1] Although there is no central market for mortgages like the secondary exchanges for stocks, when mortgages change hands after their

---

[1] *For a good technical summary, see "The Secondary Market in Residential Mortgages," December 1984 (Federal Home Loan Mortgage Corporation, 1776 G Street N.W., Washington, D.C. 20013–7248).*

origination, they do so in the secondary market. Instead of originating to hold mortgages, lending institutions sell loans in the secondary market to gain liquidity. In this way, lenders can receive cash by selling assets that had previously been illiquid portions of their portfolios. For lenders, liquidity means flexibility.

As it has evolved, the secondary mortgage market has grown to the point where nearly 80 percent of all mortgages originated in the first three quarters of 1989 were sold into the secondary market. As investors' needs and requirements have changed, so have the types of mortgages that they have been willing to purchase. Investors purchase shares of the mortgage pools in the form of mortgage-backed securities, which are offered in many varieties. For the most part, the different varieties of mortgage-backed securities alter the pattern of cash flow paid by the owner to make them more desirable to investors.

The remainder of this chapter expands this basic discussion. First, we note the important role of government and quasi-government agencies in supporting the secondary mortgage market. Then we describe the interaction between private sector lenders and investors and their public sector counterparts, highlighting the roles of mortgage bankers. Finally, we look at recent innovations and possible future trends.

PUBLIC POLICY: IMPORTANCE OF THE SECONDARY MORTGAGE MARKETS

Through several administrations, both Republican and Democratic, a central stated goal of federal housing policy has been "to provide a decent home and suitable living environment for every American family" (Preamble to the **Housing Act of 1949**). Although we have not fully achieved this goal, the United States is a world leader in terms of the percentage of owner-occupied housing (65.6 percent per the last major housing census in 1980). For most families, the home is the largest asset; the value of all U.S. residential real estate is substantially greater than the value of all stocks and bonds traded on the New York Stock Exchange.

Given the importance of housing from a public perspective and the importance of financing to housing development (more in Part 8), it is not surprising that government has become involved in housing finance. In fact, the history of government operations in the secondary mortgage market is one of the great federal success stories. (Part 9 will point out several less successful government efforts in the housing field.)

HISTORICAL EVOLUTION OF THE SECONDARY MORTGAGE MARKETS

During and immediately following the Great Depression, the public became convinced that private financial markets alone would not provide all the financing necessary to achieve the national housing policy objective. Up to that time, home loans resembled consumer loans with short-term maturities (say, five years), low loan-to-value ratios (50 percent), and payments that consisted of interest only. Given these loan characteristics, borrowers were forced to sell or refinance for the entire balance of the loan after the five-year maturity.

These restrictive terms existed because the mortgage loan originator—bank, S&L, or other—was concerned with the safety of a loan. Of course, the physical property itself provides good collateral for a loan. However, lenders do not feel perfectly safe lending 100 percent of value. In the first place, appraised values are not considered an exact prediction of selling price. Moreover, subsequent to a loan, properties may be physically damaged or decline in value owing to a general deterioration of the neighborhood. Finally, properties sold in distress, for example, at auction following foreclosure, often fail to bring full market value because of insufficient marketing time.[2]

At the time of the Depression, many lenders faced a significant problem: the interest-only loan balances could no longer be rolled over into new loans. As the money supply contracted, lenders did not have funding available for new loans, and they demanded repayment of the original loan balances. Borrowers at the time could not afford to repay those loans, and many defaulted on their mortgages, turning over their homes to the banks. As the supply of homes increased owing to foreclosure sales, and as demand for homes declined as the banks sharply reduced their mortgage lending activity, the values of homes plummeted. Many argue that this confluence of events pushed the U.S. economy further into the Depression.

Given this experience and given the mortgage instruments of the early 1900s, lenders in the 1930s were unwilling to lend because of the high risk involved. Borrowers were therefore unable to obtain financing. In response to this problem, the government chose not to make loans itself; instead, it chose to induce traditional lenders in the private sector to make larger loans based on higher loan-to-value ratios. The government's strategy was to reduce the risk of lending by providing (1) mortgage loan insurance and (2) mortgage loan guarantees. In addition, also, the government encouraged the use of fully amortizing loans so that borrower equity could increase as the principal was paid down. Reducing the risk of loss with these additional safety features encouraged private lenders to make higher-ratio loans that would enable many more Americans to obtain sufficient financing to buy a home. It is noteworthy that the government sought a solution by facilitating, not replacing, private sector lending. Furthermore, the government established an opportunity for lenders to liquidate their mortgage loans if necessary by selling them into a secondary market. This created a more fluid flow of funds across both institutional and regional boundaries. The percentage of

---

[2]*Furthermore, many would-be borrowers who want to buy real estate do not have ideal borrower characteristics such as sufficient personal wealth and job stability.*

owner-occupied homes rose from under 48 percent in 1930 to over 65 percent in 1980 largely because of federal government support.[3]

The introduction of guarantees and insurance for residential mortgages, and the creation of the beginnings of a secondary mortgage market, greatly changed the funding system in residential finance. The rest of this chapter describes the processes by which these changes have occurred, and the institutions and agencies that have come to play such a pivotal role in the development of the system that currently exists. The only constant in the secondary mortgage market is change. This change results from the changing needs of lenders and borrowers in the primary mortgage market, and from innovations created by issuers and investors in the secondary mortgage market.

MORTGAGE INSURANCE AND GUARANTEES

Guarantees and insurance provided by government and private mortgage insurers reduce the risk of lending for loan originators (primary market). For investors in mortgage-backed securities (the secondary market), further assurance that they will receive their promised cash flows is provided by secondary mortgage market institutions such as the Federal National Mortgage Association (FNMA), the Government National Mortgage Association (GNMA), and the Federal Home Loan Mortgage Corporation (FHLMC).

THE FEDERAL HOUSING ADMINISTRATION (FHA)

The Federal Housing Administration was created by the **National Housing Act of 1934.** This act has been amended several times and currently charges the FHA with the following major objectives.

■ To operate housing loan insurance programs designed to encourage improvement in housing standards and conditions.

■ To facilitate sound home financing on reasonable terms.

■ To exert a stabilizing influence in the mortgage market.

The FHA is not a direct lender of mortgage funds. Neither does it plan or build homes. It insures loans. It also affects both lending terms and building plans, as well as selection of housing sites, by underwriting conditions it sets. Lenders, borrowers, and the property involved must

---

[3]*Federal support for interstate highways and the deductibility of interest were the other two major causes of the dramatic increase in home ownership.*

meet specified qualifications before an FHA-insured loan can be originated.

Currently, the majority of FHA-insured loans are originated under either **Section 203(b)** or **Section 245** of the **National Housing Act.** The Section 203(b) program covers single-family insured loans whereas the Section 245 program covers graduated payment mortgages (as opposed to level payment mortgages).

How is the lender protected on such high-ratio loans? In the case of a default, the lender is entitled to receive from the FHA debentures equivalent to the amount of the debt then unpaid. The interest and principal payments on the debentures are fully guaranteed by the U.S. government. Borrowers are charged a fee to fund the cost of the program.

THE VETERANS ADMINISTRATION (VA)

Created in 1944, the Veterans Administration is authorized to help veterans secure the financing of houses. Guaranteed loans may be made to veterans of World War II or the Korean conflict who have served on active duty for 90 days or more. In addition, other veterans in active service for over 180 days may also qualify, as well as widows of veterans who died in service or as a result of service-connected disabilities. Finally, wives of members of the armed forces who have been listed as missing in action or prisoners of war for 9 days or more are also eligible.

The VA guarantee is an absolute guarantee in which the VA becomes liable for the amount of the existing guarantee on default. The guarantee has always been based on a percentage of the loan with a maximum amount fixed by law. The percentage applies to the loan as an outstanding debt and is decreased by payments or increased by unpaid interest. Any person, firm, association, corporation, state, or federal agency can be an eligible lender under VA legislation. (The VA also provides insurance, but the magnitude of such insured loans is not significant.)

The federal government, through both the Federal Housing Administration (FHA) and the Veterans Administration (VA), has greatly facilitated operation of a viable secondary mortgage market by increasing the safety of mortgage lending. Indirectly, federal mortgage insurance programs have had a significant spillover effect on original lending terms appraisal practices, actual building plans, and uniform loan documentation.

In regard to lending terms, the FHA and VA provide underwriting guidelines to mortgage loan originators. This allows loan originators to package more loans while maintaining an acceptable level of risk. Building requirements as established by the FHA and VA contribute to standardization in the area of construction quality and overall have tended to upgrade the quality of housing pledged as mortgage collateral. The requirement of uniform loan documentation enhances the marketability of such mortgages. These specifications provide for a great deal of homogeneity among such loans. This homogeneity, in turn, makes mortgages associated with the FHA and VA programs marketable throughout the United States.

PRIVATE MORTGAGE INSURERS

Prior to the provision of mortgage insurance by the government in the 1930s, the field was exclusively occupied by private companies. In the Great Depression, these firms either failed or otherwise ceased operations. From the depression period until 1957, mortgage insurance and guarantee underwriting were handled almost exclusively by the FHA and the VA.

In 1957, the Mortgage Guaranty Insurance Corporation (**MGIC**) was organized and licensed by the Wisconsin commissioner of insurance. Since that time additional **private mortgage insurers** have begun operations. Today the Federal National Mortgage Association (**FNMA**) and the Federal Home Loan Mortgage Corporation (**FHLMC**) approve several private mortgage insurance companies (**MICs**) as qualified insurers, making their guarantees acceptable in the secondary conventional loan market. Their guarantees are also accepted by the different regulatory bodies that supervise the mortgage loan originators. (See Table 16-1.)

When a mortgage loan is foreclosed, the policyholder (lender) must first take title to the real property, securing the loans. Once the claim is filed, the MIC can settle in one of two ways. It either accepts title to the real property and pays the insured lender the full amount of the claim, or it pays the percentage of coverage carried by the insured and has no further liability under the policy. (The difference is a matter of how the insurer protects its own position; either way, the lender is satisfied.)

Unlike the FHA (which offers insurance up to 100 percent of the principal amount) or the VA (which provides a guarantee of the top portion of the loan), the MICs offer insurance coverage only up to a maximum of 20 to 25 percent of the loan amount, depending on the loan-to-value ratio and the coverage desired by the lender. However, this 20 to 25 percent is the top or most risky portion of the loan. As the loan-to-value ratio falls below 25 percent, homeowners are less likely to default given the higher level of equity that they have in the property. The limited coverage feature has enabled the MICs to offer their insurance at a lower cost than the FHA and VA programs.

The proportion of total mortgage insurance in force supplied by the MICs has grown steadily since 1957. As shown in Table 16-1, by 1984 the MICs insurance comprised about 69 percent of the total insured loans, although the percentage has fallen since then.

TABLE 16-1 COMPARISON OF PRIVATE VERSUS GOVERNMENT MORTGAGE INSURANCE ON TOTAL MORTGAGE ORIGINATIONS: ONE- TO FOUR-FAMILY HOMES (DOLLARS IN MILLIONS)

YEAR	TOTAL ORIGINATIONS	CONVENTIONAL	FHA	VA	MICs[a]	MIC % OF INSURED ORIGINATIONS
1970	$ 35,587	$ 22,972	$ 8,769	$ 3,846	$ 1,162	8.4
1971	57,789	39,964	10,994	6,830	3,430	16.1
1972	71,820	59,660	8,456	7,748	9,158	36.1
1973	79,125	66,364	5,185	7,578	12,627	49.0
1974	67,508	55,088	4,533	7,889	9,219	42.6
1975	77,913	62,811	6,265	8,837	10,024	40.0
1976	112,786	95,361	6,998	10,424	14,600	45.6
1977	161,974	136,623	10,470	14,881	21,595	46.0
1978	185,036	154,429	14,955	16,027	27,327	47.2
1979	187,088	147,479	20,772	18,838	25,324	39.0
1980	133,762	106,704	14,581	12,102	19,035	41.3
1981	97,278	79,402	10,367	7,509	18,719	51.1
1982	94,919	75,867	11,472	7,580	18,749	59.3
1983	200,445	152,967	28,602	18,876	43,360	48.3
1984	200,464	172,022	16,349	12,093	63,403	68.6
1985	241,681	204,587	23,872	13,222	50,956	54.7
1986	449,987	357,059	62,038	30,890	47,358	40.2
1987	493,074	376,411	81,880	34,783	45,217	24.5

[a]Conventional mortgages insured by private mortgage insurance companies (MICs).
Source: Factbook and Directory, 1985 and 1988 editions, Mortgage Insurance Companies of America; and Federal Home Loan Mortgage Corporation, Secondary Mortgage Markets, various issues.

MARKET MAKERS IN THE SECONDARY MORTGAGE MARKET

Federal mortgage guarantees and insurance were not enough to solve problems of capital availability for home loans. As noted in earlier chapters, many of the largest providers of home mortgage loans faced problems of disintermediation owing to Regulation Q ceilings on the rates they could pay on savings deposits. Money market mutual funds and other investment alternatives earned higher returns than savings deposits, which led rational investors to withdraw their funds from low-yielding deposits. As depositors moved their funds to nonmortgage lenders, the supply of funds available for mortgages declined, affecting the ability of individuals to obtain financing for purchasing homes. Furthermore, as rates increased, the value of low-yielding assets on the books of savings institutions fell. Therefore, savings institutions faced liquidity problems at the same time as their assets were losing value.[4] In the periods of **disintermediation** in the 1970s, the inability of funds to move from institutions that had a great deal of capital (for example, pension funds and life insurance companies in the 1970s and 1980s) to institutions with shortages of capital (such as savings and loans) led to shortages of funds available to the mortgage markets. Similarly, it may be the case that institutions in capital-rich regions have been unable to make investments in capital-poor regions owing to restrictions on the flow of funds. The market makers in the secondary mortgage markets facilitate the flow of funds to alleviate to some extent these geographical and institutional mismatches.

Generally, the secondary mortgage market alleviates these mismatches in the following way.[5] A savings and loan institution in Raleigh, North Carolina, makes loans to borrowers to purchase homes in their local markets. The S&L then combines those mortgages into a pool large enough to elicit some interest among institutions (usually New York investment banks) that sell the mortgage-backed securities to investors. Typical investors in these mortgage-backed securities include other depository institutions (commercial banks and thrift institutions) or the contractual institutions (pension funds and life insurance companies) described in Chapter 13.

Assume a pension fund like the California State Teachers Employee Retirement System purchases a security backed by the entire pool of mortgages. Funds from the pension fund are transferred to the Raleigh S&L, which transfers ownership of the mortgages to the pension fund. Therefore, the original mortgages are taken off the originating lender's books and replaced with cash proceeds from the sale of the mortgages. Since savings and loans, on average, hold 80 percent of their assets in residential mortgages, 80 cents of every dollar of mortgages sold can be released into Raleigh's mortgage market.

Notice that two things are happening in this example. On the one hand, funds are flowing from California to North Carolina in ways that would have been unavailable before a secondary market was established. Similarly, since the funds ultimately come from a pension fund, which has traditionally not been a residential mortgage lender, the institutional mismatch described above is alleviated. The result is a more efficient flow of funds within the mortgage market and more consistent mortgage interest rates across the country. The rest of this chapter provides a more detailed explanation of the workings of the secondary mortgages mar-

---

[4]*This phenomenon is somewhat similar to the logic presented earlier in the discussion of housing markets in the Great Depression. Recall that lenders were unable to make loans owing to a shortage of funds, leading to a major dislocation in housing markets.*

[5]*We will expand on the exact roles of each of the players involved throughout the rest of this chapter. This example is intended to provide a simple explanation of how the secondary market reduces imbalances in the primary market.*

16-1
ODYSSEY OF A
MORTGAGE
LOAN

Each month, a couple in California sends their mortgage check to a local savings and loan association. For them, that is the end of the transaction. In fact, their payment is only the first step in a chain of transactions in a vast new financial network, the mortgage-trading business.

Mortgage interest is one of the biggest monthly cash flows in the U.S. economy, and many new investors want some of it. Barely three months after the couple above had bought their home, their local S&L had already sold off their mortgage. Since then, it has been resold and split up so much that part of the young couple's payments now end up everywhere from an Oklahoma thrift institution to a London bank.

A few years ago, such rapid trading in mortgages barely existed. In 1987, however, $238 billion of mortgages were bundled together and resold as securities, according to Salomon Brothers, Inc. Though down slightly from the 1986 record, that's nearly as much as U.S. companies raised by selling stocks and bonds in 1987.

To show how this new mortgage market works, participants in the odyssey of the couple's mortgage agreed to reconstruct its trek to its final owners. After their application sailed through the income and credit checks, three weeks after applying they got a 30-year loan at 10⅝ percent interest.

First Federal is the sort of neighborhood S&L that might belong in a sentimental Jimmy Stewart movie. It has just 150 employees in seven branches northeast of Los Angeles. Its four-story headquarters building in West Securities, California, sits next to a suburban shopping mall, and its emblem includes a stylized American flag.

In the past five years, however, First Federal has become a savvy seller of mortgages. "Selling off mortgages has let us make another $200 million in mortgage loans that we couldn't have done otherwise," explains the S&L's president.

So, as soon as the couple's mortgage entered its books, First Federal planned to sell it. With little chance of finding investors on its own, First Federal waited until it had several other fixed-rate mortgages on hand. Then, it turned to the quasi-governmental agencies that function as mortgage clearinghouses, bundling up mortgages into standardized pools, providing guarantees against default and reselling them to investors.

The couple's mortgage fit into a standard purchase category for Freddie Mac. Created in 1970 and just a bit player in mortgage markets in its first decade, Freddie Mac bought $77 billion of mortgages from S&Ls, banks, and other lenders last year and earned $301 million. It operates as a middleman, charging lenders a quarter-percentage-point fee for processing a mortgage.

> Along with thousands of other mortgages, the couple's mortgage arrived at
> Freddie Mac's Reston, Virginia, offices one day in mid-December with all the
> fanfare of an oxygen atom entering a room. It was put into Freddie Mac pool No.
> 360018, as part of the $443 million of fixed-rate loans from all over the United
> States.
>
> *Source:* Adapted from "A Loan's Odyssey: How a Home Mortgage Got into a Huge Pool
> That Lured Investors," *Wall Street Journal,* August 17, 1988.

kets and how each of the institutions operates within these markets. (See Box 16-1.)

THE FEDERAL NATIONAL MORTGAGE ASSOCIATION

In the 1930s, as a reaction to the Great Depression, Congress attempted to induce private capital to form national mortgage associations as a secondary market for insured mortgages. Failing in these efforts, Congress authorized the Reconstruction Finance Corporation (**RFC**) to form a subsidiary known as the Federal National Mortgage Association (FNMA or "Fannie Mae").

FNMA started with an initial capitalization of $10 million, and its original purposes were to

- Establish a market for the purchase and sale of first mortgages insured by the FHA, covering newly constructed houses or housing projects.

- Facilitate the construction and financing of economically sound rental housing projects or groups of houses for rent or sale through direct lending on FHA-insured mortgages.

- Make FNMA bonds or debentures available to institutional investors. (This was the source of the financing necessary to achieve the two preceding purposes.)

In 1950, FNMA was transferred from the RFC to the Housing and Home Finance Agency, a forerunner of the Department of Housing and Urban Development (HUD). This move enabled FNMA's activities to be more closely coordinated with the Federal Home Loan Bank (FHLB) as well as with the Federal Housing Administration (FHA).

In 1954, FNMA was rechartered by Congress and commissioned with three separate and distinct activities.

- Secondary market operations in federally insured and guaranteed mortgages.

- Management and liquidating functions (i.e., the management and liquidation of the loans that FNMA had purchased up to that time).

- Special assistance programs (i.e., subsidy programs that the federal government might initiate from time to time).

FNMA was to be administered as though it were a separate corporation with its own assets, liabilities, and borrowing ability.

A major objective of the Charter Act of 1954 was to establish a procedure whereby FNMA would be transformed over time into a privately owned and managed organization. With the passage of the Housing and Urban Development Act of 1968, the assets and liabilities of the secondary market operations were transferred to a private corporation— also known as the Federal National Mortgage Association. As a result, FNMA is now a government-sponsored corporation owned solely by private investors and is listed on the New York Stock Exchange.

The remaining functions of the "old" FNMA (sanctioned under the Charter Act) remained in HUD. To carry out these duties, the Government National Mortgage Association (**GNMA** or "Ginnie Mae") was created.

Today, FNMA (Fannie Mae) is largely run by its board of directors consisting of 15 members—one-third appointed annually by the president of the United States, with the remainder chosen by the common stockholders. Of those chosen by the president at least one appointee must be from each of the home-building, mortgage-lending, and real estate industries.

FNMA raises funds mainly by selling bonds in the capital markets. It then uses these funds to purchase mortgage loans from mortgage lenders (conventionally as well as governmentally insured). This purchase is known as a mandatory delivery commitment, with FNMA promising to buy and the originator promising to sell at posted yields. In addition to its standard purchase programs, Fannie Mae issues commitments and makes purchases on a negotiated basis, that is, one-on-one with loan originators. Since 1983, FNMA has also offered a pass-through guarantee program similar to that provided by GNMA (see the next section).

Through the Federal National Mortgage Association, the government substantially reduces the impact of disintermediation on the real estate industry. When high interest rates for borrowing and interest rate ceilings on certain types of savings accounts combine to cause funds to flow out of key institutions (primarily savings and loans), FNMA can provide liquidity to these institutions by selling bonds in the capital markets and use the funds to buy the existing loans in the institutions' portfolios. Note, however, that although selling old mortgage loans solves the liquidity problem, it does not remove the interest rate risk from the loan originator. When the originator of a loan sells that loan in the secondary market, it must sell at the market rate. If interest rates have risen, the lender is forced to sell its existing loans at a loss.

THE GOVERNMENT NATIONAL MORTGAGE ASSOCIATION

GNMA (or "Ginnie Mae") is a government corporation comprising a branch of HUD. All powers and duties of GNMA are vested in the secretary of Housing and Urban Development, who is authorized to determine Ginnie Mae's general policies, administrative procedures, and officer appointments. Created through Title III of the Federal National Mortgage Association Charter Act of 1968, GNMA is empowered with three functions.

- The special assistance function (old FNMA subsidy function now expanded).

- The management and liquidation of GNMAs own mortgage portfolio. (This portfolio was originally obtained from FNMA in 1968; GNMA differs from the FNMA and FHLMC in that it does not accumulate a portfolio of mortgages—that is, mortgages purchased by GNMA are generally resold within a year.)

- The guaranteeing of specified securities collateralized by specific pools of mortgages (**pass-throughs**).

Under Section 306(g), of the Charter Act, GNMA is authorized "to guarantee the timely payment of principal and interest" on long-term securities backed by self-liquidating pools of mortgages (**mortgage-backed securities**). Currently, only pools comprised of FHA-insured or VA-guaranteed mortgages qualify as collateral for such securities. So Ginnie Mae does not buy mortgages. Rather, it issues guarantees on FHA-VA mortgages that others (such as large S&Ls) package into mortgage pools and sell to investors. The investors receive the principal and interest payments on the individual mortgages. Thus was born the GNMA pass-through security."

The pass-through security has become a very popular form of mortgage loan financing. Each certificate represents a share in a pool of FHA or VA mortgages or both. The pass-through comes in two forms: (1) standard and (2) modified.

Under the standard alternative the total interest and principal collections are "passed-through" to the certificate holders on a monthly basis. Any mortgage delinquencies are immediately replaced in the pool. The standard plan has not enjoyed the same popularity as the modified plan; hence, it is not frequently issued.

The modified pass-through is by far the most popular of all the mortgage-backed securities. Under the modified plan, the investor can have the interest and principal collections passed through less frequently than monthly (say quarterly, semiannually, etc.). Again, principal and interest payments are passed through to the certificate holders whether or not the corresponding mortgage payments have actually been collected. The issuer replaces mortgage delinquencies via mortgage reserve pools.

All mortgage-backed securities have several common characteristics. First, each instrument bears interest at a rate less than the rate borne by the supporting mortgage pool. The differential provides the issuer working capital to cover administrative costs and to guarantee risks. Second, substantial reinvestment risk exists if mortgages are liquidated by the mortgagor-borrower's repayment prior to maturity. Early repayment cuts off the interest income stream representing return on investment to the security holders. If interest rates have fallen since issuance of the securities, investors may not be able to reinvest the prepaid loan proceeds at as high a rate as the certificate rate.[6]

Pass-through securities are actually created by the mortgage loan originator. It makes the loans (FHA or VA) and then applies for the additional GNMA insurance. (It is this insurance that makes the package attractive in the capital markets.) Typically, once the loans are insured, the originator then negotiates with a Wall Street securities firm to sell the pass-throughs just as the firm sells stocks and bonds. As a result, the dentist in Abilene, the college endowment fund manager in Spokane, and the investment club in Albuquerque can all march down to the nearest brokerage firm branch office and buy a participation in a pool of loans originated in Miami. The market for pass-through securities is truly a large, diversified national market. (See Figures 16-1, 16-2, and 16-3.)

THE FEDERAL HOME LOAN MORTGAGE CORPORATION

After creating Fannie Mae and Ginnie Mae, in 1970 Congress produced Freddie Mac. Created by Title III of the Emergency Home Finance Act of 1970, the Federal Home Loan Mortgage Corporation (FHLMC) is a corporate entity whose purpose is to serve as a secondary market for real estate mortgages under the sponsorship of the Federal Home Loan Bank System (FHLBS). Recall that, at the time, FNMA and GNMA provided secondary market support only for FHA and VA mortgages. Thrift institutions, regulated by the Federal Home Loan Banks Board, have traditionally specialized in mortgages that carry private mortgage

---

[6]*Most home loans today pay off before the stated maturity as houses are sold, refinanced, destroyed by fire and not replaced, and so on. Because the exact timing of such early repayments is a function of many things (particularly interest rates and home prices), it is difficult to predict the life of the GNMA security. Remember that principal payments are passed through as received.*

The reader should ponder how this situation affects the yield calculation (for the GNMA security holder) as described in Chapter 13. For a complete discussion of this issue, see Hendershott and Buser, "Spotting Prepayment Premiums," Secondary Mortgage markets (August 1984).

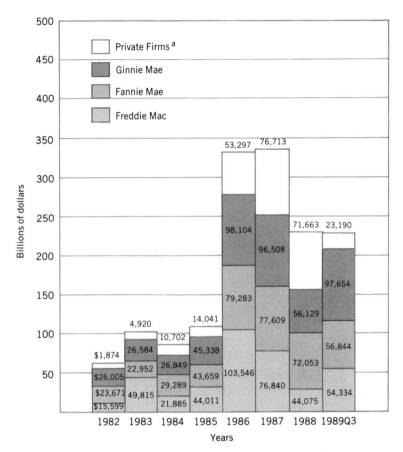

FIGURE 16-1   *Originations of mortgage related securities (millions of dollars)* (*Source:* Federal Home Loan Mortgage Corporation, *Secondary Mortgage Markets, various issues.*

[a] The growth of the private firm proportion of mortgage-related securities issuance is due to the collateralized mortgage obligation issuance by investment banks and commercial banks.

insurance, i.e., conventional mortgages. Freddie Mac was created to assist in the development and maintenance of a secondary market for these conventional mortgages.

FHLMC has three responsibilities.

- To circulate funds from capital-surplus geographical areas to capital-deficit areas.

- To develop new sources of funds during periods of credit stringency.

- To develop new financing instruments to aid in the development of the private secondary mortgage market.

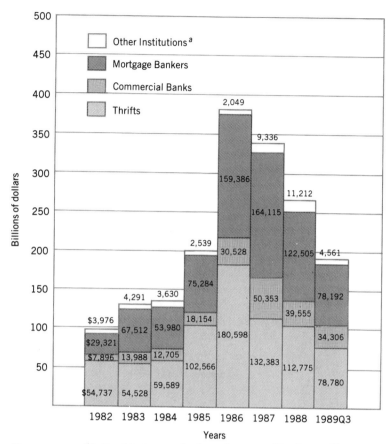

F I G U R E 16-2 *Mortgage sales by major types of lenders (millions of dollars)*
(Source: Federal Home Loan Mortgage Corporation, *Secondary Mortgage*
Markets, various issues.)

*[a]Other institutions include life insurance companies, pension funds, Freddie Mac, Fannie Mae,
Ginnie Mae, federal credit agencies, and state and local credit agencies.*

The Federal Home Loan Mortgage Corporation is controlled by a board
of directors whose members are appointed by the president of the
United States, with the advice and consent of the U.S. Senate, for terms
of four years. FHLMC raises funds by selling pass-through securities
known as guaranteed mortgage certificates (GMC) and mortgage participation certificates (PC). As the secondary market has matured and
become more sophisticated, FHLMC has sought new sources of financing as shown in Box 16-2. Through the 1970s only savings and loans
could use Freddie Mac, but recent legislation has opened this auction to
other qualified mortgage lending institutions as well.

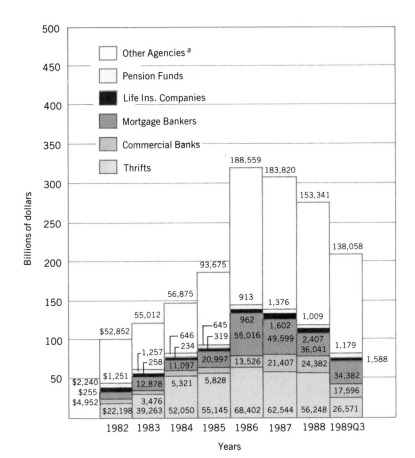

FIGURE 16-3 *Mortgage purchases by major types of investors (millions of dollars) (Source:* Federal Home Loan Mortgage Corporation, *Secondary Mortgage Markets, various issues.)*

[a]This column includes purchases resulting from FNMA and FHLMC swap transactions, and purchases by other federal credit agencies and state and local credit agencies.

THE PRIVATELY GUARANTEED MORTGAGE LOAN PACKAGE SECURITY

Another financial instrument in the mortgage market is the privately guaranteed security (**PG**), issued by many of the larger financial institutions. Mortgage bankers and thrift institutions have been issuing GNMA-guaranteed securities for many years, but the privately guaranteed claim represents an endeavor new with the 1980s.

These securities do not represent the obligation of any governmental agency, nor are they guaranteed by any governmental agency. The securities represent an undivided interest in a pool of conventional mortgages originated and serviced by the issuing financial institution.

Interest and principal payments received by the issuer are passed

16-2
JAPANESE
INVESTORS

TOKYO—Japan has found another safe outlet for its money: U.S. home mortgages.

An increasing number of big Japanese investors are buying up U.S. home mortgages that have been pooled and packaged for sale as interest-bearing instruments known as mortgage-backed securities. As much as 10 percent of new U.S. mortgage securities issued by the Federal National Mortgage Association, or Fannie Mae, and Federal Home Loan Mortgage Corporation, or Freddie Mac, now flow into Japanese hands.

That may not come as a surprise to Americans who have watched the Japanese snap up properties in the United States from golf courses to a stake in Rockefeller Center. But it marks a big change for the Japanese, who shunned mortgage securities after getting burned by a big downturn in interest a few years back.

Evidence of the growing Japanese demand for mortgage securities abounds. Earlier this year, Blackstone Group, a New York investment bank, had no trouble selling out a special $570 million mortgage-securities trust it created for Japanese investors. Industrial Bank of Japan, which claims to be the biggest Japanese buyer of U.S. mortgage securities, says it will more than double its purchases this year, to an amount one official puts at several billion dollars. And a Fannie Mae seminar this week promises to draw hundreds of prospective investors, who can be expected to channel tens of billions of dollars into the market in the next few years.

"Last year, there were only several big investors who were interested," says Kinji Kato, a vice president at the international arm of Nomura Securities Company. "This year, some investors are changing their policies and investing a lot." Ultimately, he says, strong demand could help to drive down interest rates on mortgage securities.

These securities are attractive to Japanese investors for three reasons. First, they are safe. While they aren't backed by the full faith and credit of the U.S. government, as Treasury bonds are, it is widely assumed that the government would support them if necessary. (U.S. Treasury bonds are still the dollar-denominated investment of choice for long-term Japanese investors.) Second, they are liquid. The secondary market in federally backed mortgage securities now exceeds $900 billion, or nearly half of the $2.2 trillion in U.S. residential mortgages issued. Third, they offer high yields. At the moment, some offer as much as 1.6 to 1.8 percentage points over Treasury securities of similar maturities.

Since 1985, Japanese investors have bought nearly 80 percent of the $10 billion in Fannie Mae corporate debt issued to foreigners, money that Fannie Mae uses to buy mortgages from U.S. banks. And Japanese investors took up nearly all of two $200 million Real Estate Mortgage Investment Conduits, a kind of collateralized mortgage obligation, that were offered to foreigners this year.

In addition, further packaging of mortgage-backed securities, such as Blackstone's fund, has reduced the effects of prepayment risk and automatically reinvests monthly payments so institutions don't have to. For years Freddie Mac has offered a so-called participation certificate that guarantees it won't be prepaid for a set number of years, and it offers semiannual payments.

Source: Adapted from "Japanese Warm to U.S. Market in Mortgages," *The Wall Street Journal,* November 1, 1989.

through monthly (as they are received from the mortgagors) to the certificate holders. Any mortgage prepayments are generally passed on to the PG holders in the month following their receipt.

The underlying mortgages are usually insured by private mortgage insurers, somewhat reducing the exposure of the issuing institution that guarantees the overall pool. Generally, only the very large financial institutions are thought capable of issuing such securities, for investor confidence is critical to the success of the offering. The issuer unconditionally guarantees the prompt payment of interest and principal payments to the PG holders. If mortgage collections are insufficient, the issuer reimburses the trustee (a central person operating for all the investors) for the necessary amount and, in so doing, acquires an interest in the underlying mortgages.

The pool of underlying mortgages has the same general characteristics of those pools backing GNMA-guaranteed securities. The mortgages in any one pool bear similar interest rates, cover the same types of dwelling, and have approximately the same maturity. The privately guaranteed pools are now major competitors of the government pools; however, they have experienced some problems as shown in Box 16-3.

SUMMARY OF MARKET MAKERS

As evidenced by the number of institutions participating in the secondary mortgage market, home loan financing has come a long way since the days of the private correspondent system. The FNMA, GNMA, FHLMC, and PG initiatives have opened up a new world to mortgage bankers. Together these devices provide mortgage lenders a variety of placement alternatives.

From a public policy point of view whether these alternatives will provide the level of financing necessary to meet the goal of the decent home and suitable living environment for every American is still an unanswered question. Clearly, they collectively represent a move toward "homogenization" of the capital markets as Richard Marcis suggested (Chapter 13).[7]

[7]*For a further discussion of related issues, see Tucillo, Van Order, and Villani, "Housing and Mortgage Market Policies." HUD Publication, Vol. 9 of the Housing and Community Affairs Series.*

**16-3
PRIVATE
MORTGAGE
SECURITIES
MAY HAVE
ADDED RISKS**

Recent news accounts of private mortgage securities backed by fraudulent loans illustrate the importance of recourse. According to the *Wall Street Journal,* the Bank of America was the trustee and escrow agent on private mortgage securities backed by greatly inflated mortgages. The firm that owned the properties was, in turn, run by a convicted felon. The securities were packaged by a concern apparently run by another convicted felon, and the mortgages were insured by a company that is now insolvent. The bank dismissed five officers for gross negligence.

Normally, the escrow agent or trustee bears little risk in a mortgage securities transaction. The role is simply one of overseeing collections and disbursements. However, the Bank of America recently completed a $133 million settlement with investors in this deal. Although the bank's role is unclear, it appears that investors who purchased the securities relied on the Bank of America's reputation, and the bank has chosen to honor this reliance.

An incident involving Ginnie Mae securities contrasts the risks for private and federally related securities. By providing a full faith and credit federal guarantee on its securities, Ginnie Mae assumes the duty of investigating default risk. Since all Ginnie Maes are backed by FHA/VA mortgages, the agency does not need to investigate the quality of the insurer. However, it must rely on the servicer and the trustee to protect itself against fraud. Indeed, Ginnie Mae recently received a $1.55 million settlement from a mortgage banking firm accused of diverting mortgage insurance proceeds on single-family mortgages. The firm's alleged failure to pass insurance proceeds through to pool investors forced Ginnie Mae to reimburse investors for the diverted payments.

These examples represent some of the risks involved in the mortgage securities industry. The guarantees on federally related mortgage securities protect investors from virtually all such risks. Thus, investors do not need detailed information on the structure of these deals to evaluate these risks. In contrast, investors in private mortgage securities must diligently assess the risks of their investments. For both federally related and private MBSs, such information is of course, important for investors to evaluate prepayment expectations and, therefore, yield on the securities.

Source: Secondary Mortgage Markets (Spring 1985), p. 19.

**THE MORTGAGE
BANKER AND THE
SECONDARY
MORTGAGE
MARKET**

Although participation in the secondary mortgage market is open to most financial institutions, it is only the **mortgage banker** who relies on the secondary market exclusively. Each of the other financial institutions has depository funds of some sort that serve as its primary source of funding. The mortgage banker is the entrepreneur who operates without depository funds. The typical sequence of events for the mortgage banker operating within the secondary mortgage market is as follows:

1. The mortgage banker receives a commitment from FNMA, GNMA, or FHLMC either to purchase or guarantee to investors that they will receive timely payment of principal and interest on mortgages originated by the mortgage banker. Typically, the secondary market agencies stipulate what types of mortgages (i.e., rates, term to maturity, fixed rate or adjustable rate, etc.) they will support through purchase or guarantee. For this, the secondary mortgage market agencies receive a commitment fee.

2. With the commitment, the mortgage banker originates loans in the primary market that meet the criteria set by the secondary market agencies.

3. Once enough loans have been originated to pool into a package large enough to sell in the secondary market, the mortgage banker submits documentation to the agencies to show that the criteria for purchase or guarantee have been met.

4. Satisfied that the mortgages meet the requirements, the agencies will pursue one of many avenues. If FNMA or FHLMC have committed to purchase the loans originated by the mortgage banker, they will take title to the mortgages in exchange for cash. These funds serve as the capital for new loans originated in the primary market by the mortgage banker, starting the cycle over again. On the other hand, if FNMA, GNMA, or FHLMC have committed to guarantee to investors that they will receive timely payments of principal and interest on the mortgages, the agencies will issue certificates to the mortgage banker that can be sold in the secondary market through dealers. Dealers would include investment banks such as Salomon Brothers, Goldman Sachs, and similar institutions.

5. The dealers sell the mortgage-backed securities to investors who wish to receive the cash flows provided by the underlying mortgages. Proceeds from the sale, net of the investment banker's fee, go to the mortgage banker, who then reloans the funds in the local primary mortgage market.

The mortgage banker profits through the successful management of five different cash flows created through this process.

❏ **ORIGINATION FEES.** The **mortgage loan origination** process, often called loan production, involves certain costs to the mortgage banker. As a means of offsetting these costs, a loan origination fee is usually charged to the borrower at the closing, typically 1 percent of the loan amount.

❏ **WAREHOUSING OPERATIONS.** As noted in an earlier chapter, the mortgage banker borrows on a short-term basis from a commercial bank while accumulating mortgage loans. Once the package of loans is accumulated, the mortgage banker sells the entire package. During the period of time that the banker is accumulating loans, interest is paid to the commercial bank for the short-term funds and at the same time collected on the mortgage loans, originated but not yet sold. The difference between the interest paid the commercial bank (short-term) and the interest received on the mortgage loans (long-term) is termed the **warehousing** profit (or loss).

❏ **SERVICING ACTIVITIES.**   Once the loans have been sold to a permanent lender, the mortgage banker typically continues to service the loan (**servicing activities**). In other words, the mortgage banker collects the periodic principal, interest, insurance, and tax payments and forwards them to the permanent lender, insurer, and government, respectively. The mortgage banker charges a fee for this service. Servicing fees are the major profit item for most large mortgage bankers.

❏ **FLOAT.**   As part of the servicing activity, the mortgage banker accumulates funds prior to sending them on to the permanent lender. Depending on who the permanent lender is, the mortgage banker may accumulate principal and interest payments from a few days up to a month. In addition, the mortgage banker will accumulate property tax and insurance (fire and casualty) payments for a period of time before actually paying the local government or the insurance company. Interest is received on these bank balances, which the mortgage banker can trade off against the interest cost of the short-term loan from the commercial bank.

❏ **MARKETING.**   The mortgage banker may experience a gain or loss when the package of loans is sold to the final lender. If market interest rates rise between the date of origination and the date of sale, the loans the mortgage banker is selling are less attractive and must be discounted (i.e., sold at a loss). On the other hand, if market interest rates fall, then the mortgage banker's loans will sell at a premium (i.e., a gain on sale).

The mortgage banker seeks to maximize positive cash flows from the five sources noted above, subject to certain constraints. The first constraint is an overall volume restriction. No more loans can be originated and held than can be financed through equity or credit sources. The mortgage banker must originate and sell loans in a cycle since the absolute dollar amount of loans that can be held in the portfolio is limited.

The second constraint involves interest rate risks. During the period when the mortgage banker is holding long-term loans, fluctuations in mortgage interest rates might very well occur. As noted earlier, if market interest rates go up during this period, the loans the mortgage banker is holding become less valuable, and a marketing loss is experienced on disposition. The mortgage banker does not usually wish to be exposed to an unlimited amount of interest rate risk. As we will see, several of the secondary market alternatives make it possible for the mortgage banker to pass on this risk, but at a definite cost. Through this process, the reader should be able to see how the secondary market supports local real estate markets. At any time, lenders in the primary market can follow the above process, or liquidate loans from their existing loan portfolios, by selling them in the same way or issuing certificates backed by them. New funds from the sale of these mortgages can be used to make new loans or to pursue other investment opportunities. To the extent that investors in FNMA, GNMA, or FHLMC securities are from other regions from where the mortgages were originated, new funds come from literally all over the world to support the local mortgage market. Similarly, if institutions like pension funds and other traditionally nonmortgage investors invest in the mortgage-backed securities, new funds that would not have gone for mortgage lending enter into the mortgage industry, providing a more efficient flow of funds to the housing market. More detail on the operation of mortgage bankers and their relationship to the secondary market agencies is provided in Part 6.

The mortgage banker seeks to maximize cash flows, particularly servicing, subject to the constraints previously mentioned. Traditionally, this has meant maximizing loan originations (and, thus, eventual servicing fees) in the local area and selling them to a permanent lender, often a national financial institution. As we noted earlier, the traditional process, even with mortgage insurance, was not successful in moving the desired level of funds from the private sector into the real estate industry. Consequently, as we have seen, alternative methods of secondary mortgage market financing were established in the public sector. Mortgage bankers, like lenders in the primary market, make extensive use of Fannie Mae and Ginnie Mae to dispose of loan packages in exchange for a fresh infusion of capital.

FNMA AND THE MORTGAGE BANKER

Mortgage bankers use the FNMA purchase commitment to reduce interest rate risk. Through direct purchase or negotiation, mortgage bankers obtain commitments from FNMA to purchase packages of mortgages at any time during a four-month period.

Such commitments, if obtained, enable the banker to do several things. First, the commitment acts as a hedge by allowing the banker to lock in a guaranteed sales price on the mortgage loan portfolio. If market rates rise, the mortgage banker can deliver against the commitment at the yield established at the date the commitment was issued. However, should market interest rates fall, the mortgage banker may be allowed to renege on his or her commitment (depending on whether delivery is optional or mandatory) even though the commitment has been issued and is binding on FNMA. Therefore, the upside return may be unrestricted by the optional commitment, whereas the downside return is hedged.

In addition, the commitments provide the banker with the assurance that the funds will be available, if the banker needs them, to cover promised loans to home buyers (borrowers) as well as to clear up any outstanding bank loans or to originate any new loans. Since these funds are obtained only if the commitment is exercised (i.e., the loans are sold to FNMA), a sophisticated approach combining loan origination, obtaining commitments, and commitment exercise strategy is necessary if mortgage banking is to be as profitable as possible.

GNMA AND THE MORTGAGE BANKER

Commitments from Ginnie Mae securities dealers come in two forms: (1) mandatory and (2) optional. Mortgage bankers ordinarily prefer optional delivery, but it is subject to availability and pricing. Optional delivery allows the mortgage banker to hedge against a rise in rates but to take advantage of a decline, as noted in the description of the Fannie Mae pricing system. Arrangements for delivery usually entail completion of the mortgage loan pool and issuance of the securities by some future date. The mortgage banker arranges for the GNMA guarantee and then, while originating the loans, negotiates an arrangement with securities dealers in New York (or other money centers) to market the pass-through interests. The risk-shifting as well as financing possibilities for the mortgage banker parallel those described in the FNMA section except that negotiation with a dealer replaces the direct purchase or negotiation with FNMA. Within this process, GNMA holds no residential mortgage loans in its portfolio; rather, GNMA ensures that the mortgage-backed security (MBS) investor receives timely payment of principal and interest. This shifting of credit risk from the mortgage banker to GNMA reduces the risk to the MBS investors, and draws new types of institutions and other investors into the mortgage market.

FHLMC AND THE MORTGAGE BANKER

Freddie Mac represents still another opportunity for mortgage bankers to adjust their risk/expected return position. Through the FHLMC commitment programs, mortgage bankers can minimize their exposure to interest rate risk as well as have the assurance that funds will be available to meet liquidity needs. Thus, the FHLMC purchase commitments represent alternatives comparable to those of FNMA and GNMA.

PRIVATE PASS-THROUGHS AND THE MORTGAGE BANKER

Most privately guaranteed pass-throughs (PGs) have been created by large financial institutions operating as mortgage bankers. That is, the largest lenders in the nation with the greatest credibility among investors make mortgage loans, obtain private mortgage insurance, package the loans, and issue and sell securities backed by the loans. The private pass-throughs are not another source of capital for the small mortgage bankers in our illustration; instead, PGs illustrate the scope of mortgage banking operations when major financial institutions create new instruments to obtain funds necessary to satisfy their customers' borrowing needs.

A FINAL LOOK AT THE MORTGAGE BANKER

Historically, the mortgage banker borrowed from a commercial bank, originated a package of mortgage loans, and repaid the commercial bank when it sold the package to a life insurance company. The relative informality of such arrangements has been largely replaced by the more complex operations of a national secondary mortgage market. The fund-generating side of today's large mortgage banking firms is every bit as technically sophisticated as that of the Wall Street bond trader.

MARKET INNOVATIONS AND FUTURE TRENDS

As mentioned earlier in the chapter, the government and quasi-government agencies in the secondary mortgage market support the primary mortgage market by either purchasing mortgages and issuing bonds backed by those mortgages, or by guaranteeing that investors in pass-through securities will receive timely payments of principal and interest. An example of the first type of bond would be FNMA bonds, which pay a stated interest rate for a stated maturity, just like a bond issued by a corporation. At maturity, these bonds pay the stated principal amount. Since they are so similar to straight-corporate bonds, these securities are called mortgage-backed bonds.

The pass-through securities are not quite as simple. As mentioned above, an investor in these securities is guaranteed receipt of timely payment of principal and interest. Therefore, monthly mortgage payments made by individual borrowers are "passed through" to investors who have purchased the rights to receive these cash flows in the form of a mortgage-backed pass-through security. If for some reason the borrower does not make the payment, GNMA will step in and make the scheduled payment to investors and be repaid at a later date when the payment is ultimately made.[8]

---

[8]Note that sometimes repayment to GNMA is made only after the loan has been foreclosed and the house sold.

One risk that an investor takes when purchasing a mortgage-backed security is prepayment risk, which can arise from many sources. American homeowners have become highly mobile, selling homes and paying off their mortgages much more frequently than was the case 15 years ago. Whenever a loan that is part of a pass-through security is paid off, the entire loan balance is paid to the investor. As the typical length of time that households stay in their homes decreases, so does the time that investors receive the guaranteed timely payment of principal and interest.

Another reason why investors may receive principal payments before their scheduled payment is due to refinancing. For example, as interest rates in the early- and mid-1980s dropped from the record highs of 1978–80, many borrowers who had taken out loans with rates as high as 17 percent found that they could reduce their monthly mortgage payment significantly by refinancing. Under refinancing, the borrower simply takes out a new, lower rate mortgage and uses the proceeds to pay off the original higher rate loan. When this happens (as it did for nearly all mortgages originated in the late-1970s and early-1980s), investors in mortgage-backed securities receive the total principal amount upon refinancing. This greatly reduces the maturity of these securities and forces the investors to reinvest the principal they receive at the worst possible time—after interest rates have fallen significantly.

Prepayments for either reason, or for other reasons such as death or divorce, are certain to occur for nearly all mortgages prior to their full 30-year maturities. The investor in a standard mortgage-backed security merely receives the payments of principal as they are made by the borrowers and is forced to reinvest the proceeds. Whether the repayment of principal occurs at 2, 5, 10, or 15 years is completely out of the investor's control, since prepayment is made at the borrower's option. As the discussions in previous chapters show, since interest is paid on the principal amount outstanding at any point in time, the total cash flow payments to investors declines as principal balances are completely paid off. Because of these risks and the uncertainty regarding the length of the period that they will receive payments, investors will pay less for mortgage-backed pass-through securities than they will for bonds with a stated maturity. Conversely, investors will require a higher yield on the mortgage securities.[9]

To reduce these uncertainties, and because many investors have been wary of investing in mortgage-backed securities because they offer a different cash flow stream from straight bonds, investment banks and other institutions have generated a number of extremely innovative se-

---

[9]*Investment banks and many investors have developed highly sophisticated models for forecasting prepayment rates based on original interest rate, the amount of time that has passed since the mortgages were originated, and the demograhic characteristics of the borrowers. These models help determine the appropriate price to pay for the mortgage-backed security.*

curities. A brief sketch of these securities will provide insights into their complexities.

COLLATERALIZED MORTGAGE OBLIGATIONS

Collateralized mortgage obligations (CMOs) are an innovative attempt to manage the prepayments to provide greater certainty to investors regarding when they will receive their principal payments.

Issuers of CMOs separate the security into several *tranches,* or segments. As prepayments are made by the borrowers, they are passed through sequentially to the different tranches. For example, a typical CMO might have a total value of $900 million—that is, there are $900 million of mortgages underlying the CMO. A simple pass-through would pass through payments of principal and interest as long as the mortgage was outstanding on a pro rata basis to investors. As soon as all mortgages were completely paid off, the pass-through would cease to exist.

A CMO with the same original $900 million value would be segmented into three tranches of $300 million each. Holders of securities in the first tranche would expect to receive the earliest prepayments. For example, assume that $100 million of the underlying mortgages were prepaid some time in the first two years. The first tranche would receive all these prepayments, while the other two tranches would receive none of them. Let's also assume that over the next three years, another $200 million of prepayments on the underlying mortgages are made. At the end of the fifth year, a cumulative $300 million of principal prepayments have been made, and they have all gone to the first tranche of the CMO, effectively paying back the amount they originally invested. At that point, they have no further right to receive any cash flows from the CMO.

After the first tranche has been completely paid off, subsequent prepayments are paid to the second tranche until they have received the $300 million in principal that they originally provided. In our example, this might occur between years 6 and 10. After the second tranche has been paid off, the third tranche begins to receive principal payments until the total $900 million of original principal is completely repaid. Typically, this might occur by year 15.

While the investors in CMOs still do not know *exactly* when their principal repayments are going to occur, they at least know a time *range*. For example, investors in the first tranche have a pretty good idea that they will receive all the principal payments within the first five years, so these securities should appeal to investors with a short-term horizon. Similarly, the second tranche investors should reasonably expect to receive their principal payments between years 6 and 10, although there may be some variation depending on the speed of prepayment on the underlying mortgages. These securities appeal to intermediate-term investors. Finally, the third tranche investors know that they will receive only the principal payments that they deserve after both of the other tranches have been completely paid off. Therefore, their securities will be outstanding for a longer period than the first two tranches, and may not begin paying back principal until the tenth year. Ultimate maturity of the third tranche depends on how long the original mortgages remain outstanding.

STRIPPED MORTGAGE-BACKED SECURITIES

Another recent innovation uses the same mortgage principal and interest cash flows but allows investors to "carve up" the mortgage payment. For example, an investment banker separates the mortgage payments received from the borrowers in a mortgage pool into principal and interest components. Investors then buy the rights to receive either the principal, the interest, or both. As long as the borrower continues to pay on his or her mortgage, the investors receive their expected cash flows. If the investor buys both the interest portion and the principal portion, he or she creates a security that looks just like the pass-through security described above. When the investors buy one of the components of the mortgage payment, however, their expected cash flow changes significantly.

Consider the investor who buys only the principal component, or the "principal only" (PO). This investor receives the scheduled monthly payments of principal as long as the borrower continues to make the payments. The investors' stream of cash flow continues until all the mortgages in the pool are paid off. Therefore, as borrowers pay down their mortgage loans, the investors receive their investment payoff. Whenever a principal prepayment is made, the total payment goes through to the investor. Since investors pay a discount to the face value of the mortgages, they would like to receive their PO cash flows as quickly as possible to earn the highest return.

Other investors prefer the "interest only," or IO portion of the borrower's monthly mortgage payment. Since interest on most mortgages is paid based on the balance outstanding, as the balance decreases payments to the IO holders also decrease. Whenever unscheduled payments of principal are made, as in the case of prepayments owing to refinancing or the homeowner moving, the principal amount decreases to zero, and interest payments on the loan cease. Therefore, the investor in the IO receives no more income from that mortgage. Since the IO payments depend greatly on the loan balance still outstanding, and since investors have no control over when their payments will stop, the price of an IO is very much below the face value of the mortgages in the pool underlying the IO. Given the uncertainty about how long they will continue to receive their investment cash flow, IO holders generally prefer to earn the income for as long a period as possible.

COMMERCIAL MORTGAGE-BACKED SECURITIES

Another recent innovation is the development of a commercial mortgage-backed security market, similar to the residential market described thus far in this chapter (see Box 16-4). Investors in commercial mortgage-backed securities (CMBS) receive the scheduled cash flows from a pool of commercial mortgages, much as the investors in a GNMA pass-through receive scheduled principal and interest payments from the underlying residential mortgages. Since there is not the same public policy objective to promote the building and financing of commercial properties as there is for residential properties, government agencies do not provide any type of guarantees or insurance. Therefore, investors have not generated as much interest in these securities. Whereas over 35 percent of outstanding residential mortgages have been securitized, to date only 3 percent of commercial mortgages trade in the secondary mortgage markets. As investors continue to accept securities backed by commercial mortgages, the percentages will increase.

SUMMARY   In this chapter, we describe the secondary market as it evolved over the 1970s and 1980s. A firm grasp of this material is necessary before the student attempts to deal with continuing innovations. Even though the details of changes in FNMA, GNMA, and FHLMC go beyond the scope of this text, the beginning student should be aware that significant changes are rapidly taking place in the secondary mortgage market.

Most of these changes can be traced to a philosophical change on the part of the secondary market makers. As lenders became more creative in attempting to balance their asset maturities to their liability maturities, they were constrained by the secondary market, which wanted a "set of standard products." Although standard fixed-rate loans are still handled by GNMA, FNMA, and FHLMC, the action has been in ARMs and other AMIs. The market makers have decided (1) to let the borrower-consumer decide what products are wanted and (2) then to attempt to accommodate lenders by turning a collection of nonstandard mortgages into instruments that can be financed in the secondary market.

As an example, FNMA experimented with the purchase of 125 different types of ARMs in 1983 alone and now does a significant percentage of its acquisitions on a "negotiated" basis. This means that the FNMA regional offices negotiate a price with the loan originator, and FNMA can then either buy for its own portfolio (the traditional bond financing) or issue mortgage-backed securities with a FNMA guarantee

16-4

THERE IS ALSO A SECONDARY MARKET IN COMMERCIAL MORTGAGES

Today, as in 1982, regulatory forces are driving the creation of a new mortgage-backed securities market.

Remember 1982? The thrift industry, confronted with jolting new regulation and stiff economic pressure, was in a state of disruptive transition. The financial community was undergoing a major restructuring of its asset mix, and the modern-day residential mortgage-backed security (MBS) market was born.

Now it's 1989, and history is repeating itself. Many of the economic and regulatory pressures that led to the creation of today's residential MBS market are back. Only this time, we are experiencing the awakening of a new secondary market—this time, for commercial real estate loans.

We are seeing the first signs that the stage is set for explosive growth in the secondary market for commercial mortgages. The indications are that it is likely to grow steadily during the next several years. According to Joseph Franzetti of Standard and Poor's rating group, only 3 percent of the $700 billion in commercial mortgage debt outstanding has been securitized.

Franzetti concludes that "when the next liquidity crunch emerges in the market for income property finance, securitization will be the best method to meet the needs of institutions."

Conditions are ripe for the creation of the commercial secondary market. All we needed are advance methodologies and automated systems to collect, analyze, and structure information on existing loans in portfolios.

Detailed information can increase the investors's understanding of nongeneric loan pools and help create security structures that meet specific financial requirements. Information can assist in obtaining the most favorable credit ratings for security issues while minimizing required credit enhancement costs.

Lending institutions, investment bankers, and other commercial mortgage market players who have the information and analytical systems ready to carefully inventory their portfolios will be able to take advantage of the many opportunities that always emerge at the beginning of any market that is ready to take off.

Source: Adapted from "The Awakening of the Commercial Secondary Market," *Mortgage Banking Magazine,* November 1989.

that the mortgage originator can then sell in the secondary market (something like the old GNMA). FNMA has also started to deal in conventional second liens and conventional multifamily mortgages.

It is truly an exciting time as government and Wall Street discover more and more mortgage market opportunities. However, the innovations come at a price. The pricing and servicing of the more complex alternative mortgage instruments (AMIs) is very difficult for smaller financial institutions. From the consumer-borrower perspective, we are approaching the limit of what can be understood and evaluated. As a player in the real estate industry, a good way to keep up with new developments is to read publications of the secondary market agencies, like *Secondary Mortgage Markets* published by Freddie Mac.

IMPORTANT TERMS

Disintermediation	National Housing Act of 1934
FHLMC	Pass-throughs (mortgage)
Float	PGs
FNMA	Private mortgage insurers
GNMA	RFC
Housing Act of 1949	Secondary mortgage market
Marketing (in mortgage banking)	Section 203(b) of The National
MGIC	Housing Act
MICs	Section 245 of The National
Mortgage-backed security	Housing Act
Mortgage banker	Servicing activities
Mortgage loan origination	Warehousing operations

REVIEW QUESTIONS

16.1   Distinguish between the primary and secondary mortgage markets.

16.2   What does it mean to refer to the top 20 to 25 percent of a loan as the riskiest?

16.3   What effect did FHA and VA insurance and guarantees have on the secondary mortgage market?

16.4   Distinguish between private and government mortgage insurance. Which generally costs more? Why?

16.5   What are the proper names of Fannie Mae, Ginnie Mae, and Freddie Mac? What is the major function of each?

16.6   How does Fannie Mae raise funds? What problem was the Federal National Mortgage Association created to solve?

16.7   Specify two ways in which Ginnie Mae differs from Fannie Mae; name one way in which they are similar.

16.8   What is a pass-through security? What does the term pass-through refer to?

16.9   Name two ways Wall Street is involved with mortgage banking.

16.10   Explain the warehousing process used by mortgage bankers. Why is the secondary mortgage market so important to mortgage bankers?

REFERENCES   BOOKS

Atterbury, William. *Modern Real Estate Finance.* 3rd ed. New York: Wiley, 1984.

Baker, D. Richard, and Rick Stephan Hayes. *A Guide to Lease Financing.* New York: Wiley, 1981.

Beaton, William R. *Real Estate Finance.* 2nd ed. Englewood Cliffs, N.J.: Prentice-Hall, 1982.

Blew, J. Miller. *Casebook in Real Estate Finance and Development.* Glenview, Ill.: Scott, Foresman, and Co., 1989.

Brealey, Richard A., and Stewart C. Meyers. *Principles of Corporate Finance.* 3rd ed. New York: McGraw–Hill, 1988.

Brueggeman, William B., and Leo D. Stone. *Real Estate Finance.* 8th ed. Homewood, Ill.: Irwin, 1989.

Copeland, Thomas E., and J. Fred Weston. *Financial Theory and Corporate Policy.* 3rd ed. New York: Addison-Wesley Co., 1988.

Dasso, Jerome, and Gerald Kuhn. *Real Estate Finance.* Englewood Cliffs, N.J.: Prentice-Hall, 1983.

Dennis, Marshall. *Mortgage Lending Fundamentals and Practices.* 2nd ed. Reston, Va.: Reston Publishing Co., 1983.

Dougall, Herbert E., and Jack E. Gaumnitz. *Capital Markets and Institutions.* 5th ed. Englewood Cliffs, N.J.: Prentice-Hall, 1986.

Epley, Donald R. *Basic Real Estate Finance and Investment.* 3rd ed. New York: Wiley, 1988.

Henning, Charles, William Pigott, and Robert Haney Scott. *Financial Markets and the Economy.* 5th ed.

Hine, Mary Alice. *Real Estate Finance.* Englewood Cliffs, N.J.: Prentice-Hall, 1978.

Hoagland, Henry E., and Leo D. Stone. *Real Estate Finance.* 8th ed. Homewood, Ill.: Irwin, 1989.

Irwin, Robert. *The New Mortgage Game.* New York: McGraw-Hill, 1982.

Morton, Tan. *Real Estate Finance: A Practical Approach.* Glenview Ill.: Scott, Foresman and Co., 1983.

Ross, Stephen A., and Randolph W. Westerfield. *Corporate Finance.* St. Louis: Times Mirror/Mosby College Publishers, 1988.

Shapiro, Alan C. *Multinational Financial Management.* 3rd ed. Boston: Allyn and Bacon, 1989.

Sirmans, C. F. *Real Estate Finance.* 2nd ed. New York: McGraw-Hill, 1988.

Stegman, Michael A. *Housing Finance and Public Policy.* New York: Van Nostrand Reinhold, 1986.

Stevenson, Eric. *Financing Income—Producing Real Estate.* 2nd ed. New York: McGraw-Hill, 1988.

Sweat, Ray, et al. *Mortgages and Alternate Mortgage Instruments.* New York: Practicing Law Institute, 1981.

Unger, Maurice A. and Ronald W. Melicher. *Real Estate Finance.* 2nd ed. Cincinnati, Ohio: Southwestern, 1984.

Van Horne, James C. *Financial Management and Policy.* 8th ed. Englewood Cliffs, N.J.: Prentice Hall, 1989.

Weidemer, John P. *Real Estate Finance.* 5th ed. Englewood, N.J.: Prentice Hall, 1987.

PERIODICALS

Federal Home Loan Bank Board Journal. Washington, D.C.: Federal Home Loan Bank Board (monthly).

Federal Reserve Bulletin. Washington, D.C.: Board of Governors of the Federal Reserve System (monthly).

Financial Analysis Journal. New York: Financial Analysts Federation (bimonthly).

Financial Management. Tampa, Fla.: Finman Corporation (quarterly).

Housing Finance Review. Philadelphia, Pa.: Whitmore Publishing (quarterly).

The Journal of Real Estate Finance and Economics. Boston: Kluwer Academic Publishers (quarterly).

Mortgage and Real Estate Executives Report. Boston: Warren, Gorham, and Lamont (bimonthly).

Mortgage Banking (formerly *Mortgage Banker*). Washington, D.C.: Mortgage Bankers Association of America (monthly).

Savings and Loan News. Chicago: U.S. League of Savings Associations (monthly).

Savings and Loan Sourcebook. Chicago: U.S. League of Savings Associations (annually).

Secondary Mortgage Markets. Federal Home Loan Mortgage Corporation, Washington, D.C. (quarterly).

NEWSLETTERS

Demand for New Golf Courses at All Time High. Novato, Calif.: Crittenden News Service.

Freddie Mac Reports. Reston, Va.: Freddie Mac (monthly).

National Thrift and Mortgage News. New York: Dorset Group (weekly).

Resolution Trust Reporter. New York: Dorset Group (bimonthly).

TAXATION

$\mathcal{I}$ NCOME AND PROPERTY TAXATION

The first claim on operating cash flows from real estate is that of the government. The government imposes property taxes, which have first priority with respect to the real estate itself; the income taxes it imposes have first priority on the investor's personal cash flow. Because tax revenues and government expenditures play such a large role in our overall economy and in real estate investing as well, we will take a moment here to amplify some of the macroeconomic numbers that were first presented in Chapter 1.

Governmental spending today represents about 20 percent of our gross national product (GNP). This total expenditure on goods and services is made up of approximately $380 billion a year in federal government spending and $587 billion a year in state and local government spending. In actuality, the federal government receives considerably more money than state and municipal governments do. However, a large portion of federal receipts are transferred to the state and local governments and to individuals.

On the ethical side, who should bear what portion of these common costs? On the purely economic side, which economic activities should be encouraged, and which, if any, should be discouraged? Consideration of these policy issues allows the real estate analyst to anticipate and evaluate changes in the tax laws over the investment holding period. Remember that even if a tax law change does not affect how you are taxed on an existing investment (you are "grandfathered in"), it will affect any subsequent owner and, consequently, the price you will receive on sale. Therefore, the astute player is always alert to possible changes in tax law, and part of the forecasting of tax law change comes from evaluating the fairness and economic logic of the current law.

In 1986, the Congress passed the sixth significant tax change (see Box 17-1) for real estate in 10 years (1976, 1978, 1981, 1982, 1984, 1986). Chapter 18 highlights the most recent changes (see Table 18-1);

17-1

THE 1986 TAX REFORM ACT

The 1986 Tax Reform Act embodied what former Senator Russell Long, a long-time member and past chairman of the Senate Finance Committee, called "the most important changes in our tax system in 50 years." The new law enacted the Internal Revenue Code of 1986, a milestone in tax history. More important, it dramatically lowered rates, broadened the tax base, and shifted the tax burden from individuals to corporations.

The substantial reduction in maximum rates for individuals—from 50 percent to 28 percent—accomplished a major goal of the Reagan Administration. When the President was inaugurated, the top rate for individuals was 70 percent; when he retired it was less than half that much. Also, millions of low-income taxpayers came off the tax rolls entirely, and additional millions no longer itemized deductions. For them, the act brought real tax simplification.

For many others, including most businesses, the verdict has not been so clear. Although corporate rates dropped, the combination of a broader base and a new corporate alternative minimum tax was expected to raise $120 billion of new revenues from the corporate sector in the first five years. Most businesses and a substantial number of middle-income and wealthy individuals have also found the new tax system more complex.

When taxes are such a significant factor in a nation's economic life, perhaps it is inevitable that they be highly complex. Still, the tax reform movement started out with simplification as one of its chief goals. The original Treasury Department proposals of November 1984 had in their title the objective of "fairness, simplicity, and economic growth." Six months later, when the President released his proposals to Congress, their entitled mission was "fairness, growth, and simplicity." Simplification had already fallen to third place. By the time the House Ways and Means Committee issued its report in December 1985, simplicity was nowhere to be found in the title.

Source: "Understanding the 1986 Tax Changes" Touche Ross, 1986; 1900 M. Street, NW, Washington, D.C. 20036, 202–955–4243.

and, throughout the remainder of the text, we try to estimate their impact on real estate decision making. Since anticipation of tax law change is a major part of the real estate game, we show the recent evolution of tax law change and describe how real estate taxation should be seen as part of the management of the overall economy. With this history and taking a holistic view, you should be better able to anticipate future tax changes. The 1986 Tax Reform Act did not represent "tax simplification" (as advocates claimed), but we believe that the changes have significantly affected "player motivations" and therefore how the real estate game is played.

Because of the impact of tax laws on after-tax cash flow to real estate projects, tax planning is an essential step for real estate investors, developers, and planners. This chapter concludes with a simple example of how the depreciation deduction creates a tax shelter. It sets the stage for a more detailed treatment of tax laws and their effect on real estate decision makers in the next chapters.

TAXING AUTHORITIES

Although considerable overlap in governmental spending exists, some general categorization is possible. The federal government must pay the costs of the following areas.

- National defense.
- Federal social programs. (See Chapter 27 for real estate-related programs.)
- The ongoing operations of the large federal bureaucracy.
- Interest on the national debt.

State governments must handle the costs of their own operations. In addition, they also make transfer payments to various levels of local governments. County and township government is responsible for a variety of service functions, including highway upkeep, parks, recreation areas, and so on. Municipal governments must bear the cost of operating city services such as fire and police protection, sanitation, and road maintenance as well as the cost of new construction. At all levels, a court system must be maintained. Finally, school districts bear the important responsibility of operating public schools, and special assessment districts, such as water, sewer, and park districts, are responsible for a variety of public benefit projects. The analyst is concerned with how these governmental bodies are financed and whether this financing is adequate to provide the services and infrastructure necessary to proper utilization of the particular real estate interest. On the other hand, the analyst also wants to know how much of the cost must be borne by his project through tax payments.

TYPES OF TAXES

TAXES: REGRESSIVE OR PROGRESSIVE?

A tax may be levied on income, on property, in connection with a transaction (a sales tax), or for benefits received (highway tolls and park fees). A pervasive issue in all tax legislation is whether a particular tax ought to be progressive or regressive. A **progressive** tax is keyed to the ability to pay, with wealthier persons paying relatively more, whereas a **regressive tax** forces the poor to pay a higher percentage of their income in taxes.

Any straight tax on necessary consumption (sales tax on food) is regressive because the poor tend to spend a higher percentage of their income on such items.

In order to raise necessary revenues, the various levels of government are empowered to levy different types of taxes. Taxes can be levied either on the basis of ability to pay (the income tax being the most notable example) or benefits received by the taxpayer (e.g., a highway toll or park fee).

❏ **PERSONAL INCOME TAXES.**   **Personal income taxes** (levied by the federal government as well as most state governments and a few municipalities) are generally considered to be progressive since rates increase in higher income brackets. However, researchers have found that the middle class pays the highest percentage of income in taxes because high-bracket taxpayers have been better able to utilize tax-minimizing and tax-sheltering techniques. Consequently, the income tax system may be progressive up to a certain point but not beyond.

❏ **CORPORATE INCOME TAXES.**   It is more difficult to characterize **corporate income taxes** as progressive or regressive. As the result of the 1986 Internal Revenue Code, a corporate tax rate of 34 percent applies. In addition, for the first time, an alternative minimum tax, with variations in income base, deductions, and exemptions of 20 percent, applies. Thus, at least for small corporations, the corporate income tax may be progressive. For larger corporations, the issue is much more complex and requires an estimate of the corporation's ability to "pass-through" the tax to its customers, employees, or shareholders.

❏ **PROPERTY TAX.**   The **property tax** is the primary revenue tool for funding local governments and school districts. Because the property tax rate is the same for all property, whether of low or high value, the tax can be considered regressive. On the other hand, since owners of higher priced properties, in fact, pay more taxes, the opposite argument can be made if income and property value are related.[1]

❏ **SALES TAX.**   Some state and many municipal governments use the **sales tax.** It is quite clearly regressive when applied to consumer goods and services, for it is a flat percentage of the price, and the poor consume a higher percentage of their incomes. When some basic necessities are exempted, the sales tax is less regressive.

---

[1]*Many states have passed* circuit breaker laws. *These are intended to relieve elderly or low-income homeowners from constantly rising property taxes. When such legislation exists, the property tax becomes progressive to some degree.*

❏ **SOCIAL SECURITY TAX.**   The **Social Security tax** is perhaps the most regressive tax of all, for earned income up to a specified ceiling is taxed at a flat rate, with income above the ceiling not taxed at all.[2]

FEDERAL GOVERNMENT REVENUES AND EXPENDITURES

By considering how much revenue the various types of taxes raise, we can sense who pays for the common costs of government and which economic activities are being encouraged. Federal government revenues in fiscal 1988 ran around $972 billion. Of this total, 42 percent came from personal income taxes, 11 percent from corporate income taxes, and 40 percent from the highly regressive Social Security tax. Indirect and other taxes accounted for the final 7 percent. In total, then, federal tax collection may be only slightly progressive.

Federal government expenditures in fiscal 1988 ran about $1,118 billion, indicating an approximate deficit of $146 billion. Of total federal expenditures, defense represents about 26 percent, of which about two-thirds is for goods and services and one-third is for employee compensation. Other federal purchases of goods and services make up another 8 percent of total expenditures. Transfer payments represent about 39 percent of the total, exceeding Social Security tax collections by a considerable margin. Transfers to state and local government (revenue sharing) make up another 10 percent. (See Box 17-2.) The final 16 percent of federal expenditures is for interest payments on the national debt, which continues to grow at around $200 billion per year, an unfortunate legacy for the future. (See Figures 17-1 and 17-2.)

THE FEDERAL DEFICIT

The continuing annual federal deficits have great social importance in terms of who pays and who benefits from federal tax collections. In a more immediate sense, the annual deficit has a pronounced impact on the supply and demand for funds in the economy. This is particularly important for the real estate industry because, as already noted, real estate is tremendously dependent on debt financing, both for new construction and for purchases of existing property.

"CROWDING OUT" AND INFLATION

A **crowding out** of real estate borrowers can occur when the federal government, considered a risk-free borrower, becomes an important

---

[2]*Numerous other types of taxes exist, including excise taxes, estate and gift taxes, license taxes, and value-added taxes, which are found primarily in Western Europe. An analysis of these types of taxes goes beyond the scope of investigation in this book.*

17-2

THE IMPACT OF CUTS IN FEDERAL REVENUE SHARING

For over a decade, cities across the country have been coping with rising costs and cuts in federal aid. Since the federal Housing and Urban Development Department was established in 1965, cities have counted on federal funds to help finance city programs. But federal aid as a portion of city budgets has been declining since 1978, and recent talk about transferring responsibility for many urban programs from federal to state hands—the so-called new federalism—has many city governments worried.

"I have trouble imagining a rural legislator will give a tinker's damn about mass transit," says one mayor. His feelings are not without foundation. Most state legislatures are dominated by suburban and rural lawmakers. Beset with spending requirements and antitax pressures at the state level, these legislators aren't likely to give cities much financial help.

Trouble with state legislatures can crop up again when cities try to raise money at home; a city frequently must ask permission from its state legislature to levy a tax—and permission isn't always granted. Massachusetts legislators, for example, wouldn't let Boston impose a parking tax because it would have affected suburban commuters. That isn't the only problem with raising city taxes and fees. It isn't popular with city residents either, and mayors hesitate to alienate voters by using this method to make up for lost federal funds. Many cities are limited to the unpopular real estate tax as their main revenue source and they fear that businesses will leave for the suburbs if these taxes rise.

So cities have little choice but to cut spending. State legislators frequently argue that tightening aid will encourage cities to eliminate waste, and some city officials concede that reduced funds will force them to find some efficiencies. But, in addition, many have already cut back services—street cleaning, library hours, recreation programs, and activities for children and the elderly. And they are borrowing from the future by delaying maintenance on structures such as bridges and sewers, leading inevitably to more urban deterioration.

Source: Adapted from William M. Bulkeley, "Trouble Downtown: Cities Fear 'New Federalism' Will Further Pinch Budgets Already Hit by Tighter Government Aid," *The Wall Street Journal,* March 2, 1982, p. 46. Adapted by permission of *The Wall Street Journal,* © Dow Jones & Company, Inc., 1982. All rights reserved.

presence in the financial markets. This crowding out will be most pronounced if the deficit is not *monetized*—in other words, if the Federal Reserve System does not increase the money supply in an amount corresponding to the increased deficit. The Federal Reserve is often unwilling to increase the money supply, for this tends to increase the rate of inflation over the long run.

The usual result in practice is some combination of crowding out

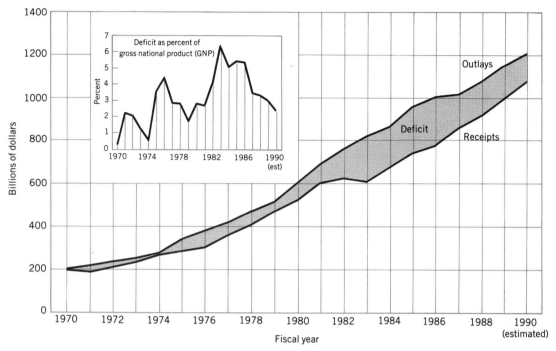

F I G U R E 17-1 *Federal budget receipts and outlays, 1970–90 (Source:* The
Budget of the United States Government, Fiscal Year 1991; Executive Office
of the President, Office of Management and Budget.)

plus monetization (and increased inflation). As long as the federal government continues to run a substantial deficit, both can be expected, and
both have significant implications for the real estate industry, as is noted
throughout this book.

The problem is further complicated by the large trade deficit that
emerged in the mid-1980s, with the United States shifting to a net debtor
nation status in September 1985. To fund the huge deficit, the government has looked to foreign investors, luring them to Treasury bonds
with historically high real rates of interest. (The nominal rate minus
expected inflation equals the expected real rate.) Although this helps
solve the immediate government financing problem, it also helps create
a strong dollar as foreign investors buy dollars to invest in the United
States. The strong dollar hurts U.S. exports by making them more expensive overseas and eventually shifts jobs abroad. As the government
reacts to the resulting trade problem by trying to weaken the dollar and
lower real interest rates, it will eventually be forced to (1) cut the deficit,
(2) allow substantial crowding out, or (3) print more money and rekindle
inflation. The first option will reduce services to real estate, the second

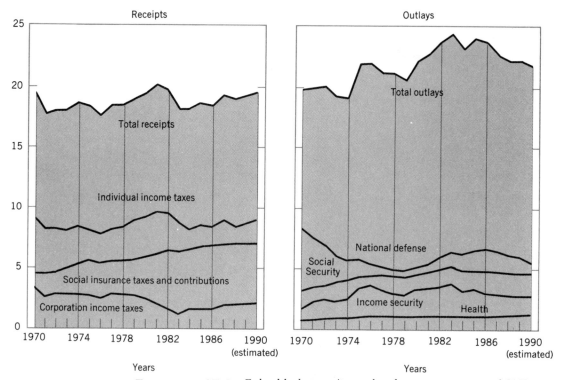

FIGURE 17-2 *Federal budget receipts and outlays as a percentage of GNP, 1970–90 (Source:* The Budget of The United States, Fiscal Year 1991; Executive Office of the President, Office of Management and Budget.)

will reduce the amount of financing available, and the third will increase nominal interest rates. Figuring out what combination of these three things is going to happen is the macroside of forecasting, which must be combined with the microlevel net operating income forecasts discussed in parts 1, 3, and 4 for players to play the real estate game successfully.

STATE AND LOCAL GOVERNMENT REVENUES AND EXPENDITURES

State and local governments collected about $702 billion in fiscal 1988. Of this total, 16 percent was in the form of transfer payments from the federal government. The balance of 84 percent came from direct taxation and was made up of (1) sales taxes (23 percent), (2) property taxes (19 percent), (3) personal income taxes (12 percent), and (4) miscellaneous sources (30 percent). Because the sales tax is clearly a regressive tax and the property tax is at least partly so, it appears that total state and local taxes are generally less progressive than federal taxes.

About 90 percent of state and local expenditures are for the purchase of goods and services. The balance is for transfer payments. Total expenditures amounted to $652 billion in 1988 resulting in a surplus of approximately $50 billion. Historically, state and local governments have generally not been plagued by budget deficits. This has been the case because many state laws expressly prohibit budget deficits. However, during the oil price recession of the mid-1980s, the budgets of many oil states experienced deficits as state revenues fell along with transfer payments from the federal government. (See Figure 17-3.)

REAL PROPERTY TAXATION

Now that we have given you a brief description of the federal, state, and local tax systems, we will move on to the property tax and then the income tax provisions of the Internal Revenue Code that most directly affect real property assets. These two taxes—property and income—have a very direct and substantial effect on the cash flow received by the real estate investor.

The property tax varies form locality to locality and may be relatively insignificant in some places, but in others it may constitute the single largest operating expense. Property taxes are **ad valorem** taxes—that is, they are based on value. Consequently, property taxes are based neither on the ability of the property owner to pay nor directly on the particular benefits received by the owner.

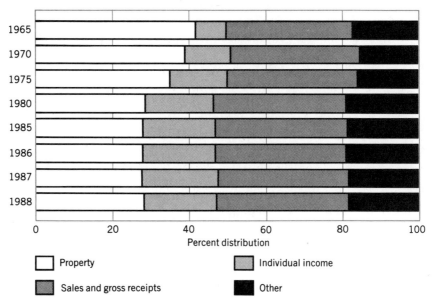

F I G U R E 17-3 *State and local government taxes—percentage distribution by type, 1965–88 (Source:* U.S. Department of Commerce, Bureau of Economic Analysis.)

Real estate taxes are determined by applying *tax rates* to *assessed valuations.* The tax rate is set by the legislature or local governing council. It is often expressed in *mills* (tenths of a cent). For example, a tax rate of 50 mills per $100 is the equivalent of 5 cents per $100 (of assessed valuation). The assessed valuation is the value placed on real (and sometimes personal) property and recorded on the assessment roll of the taxing district. The standard followed in determining assessed valuation, usually specified by law, is the value that would be obtainable for the property in the open market. Assessed valuation may equal 10 percent of such open-market value or a specified fraction thereof (e.g., 50 percent of full value).

The normal procedure for the taxing authority, when establishing the property tax each year, is to determine the total assessed valuation of property within the taxing district (which will change each year as a result of inflation, new construction, property being improved, demolition, etc.). Then the total amount of revenues required to be raised from this source by the taxing district will be divided by the assessed valuation, and the result will be the tax rate for the current year.

CALIFORNIA'S PROPOSITION 13

In 1978, California voters approved Proposition 13, a voter-initiated statute that was a harbinger of a significant "tax revolt" in many parts of the country. Under Proposition 13, California real property taxes were reduced by limiting the maximum property tax rate to 1 percent of "full cash value" of real property and by rolling back assessed property values to 1975–1976 levels, subject only to an annual 2 percent increase. Only when ownership of a property changes may the property be reassessed to reflect its current market value. In addition, the legislature was barred from enacting new property taxes, and local governments could impose "special taxes" only if two-thirds of the voters approved.

There were warnings that passage of the proposition would cause catastrophic rollbacks in social and educational programs. In actuality, the impact of the law has been relatively mild, primarily because the state government, by virtue of a large surplus in state tax collections, was able to transfer funds to local governments to offset most of the lost revenues. In addition, local communities passed new laws imposing fees on services that previously had been free and increasing other fees. Many of these new and increased charges were directed against builders who, in turn, passed their costs along to tenants and purchasers of space.

A number of other states have since passed Proposition 13-like measures, and indications are that local governments will continue to be required to fit budgets to available property tax revenues rather than the other way around.

PUBLIC EDUCATION FINANCING

Another significant trend in real property taxation is that the financing of public education may gradually be transferred to the state from individual school districts. This trend is the result of a number of legal decisions holding that state constitutional provisions are violated when public school financing depends on the assessed valuation of property in the school district. This results in very wide variations in expenditures per student within school districts in a single state. To the extent that the school financing burden is shifted to the state—which normally utilizes taxes other than the property tax to raise revenue—local property taxes may decline. This may also result in a "leveling" of school quality that would have a significant impact on residential property values.

PROPERTY TAX AS A LAND-PLANNING TOOL

Local governments recognize that the property tax is a land-planning tool as well as a means of raising revenue. This is particularly true when the property tax is a significant element of a property's operating expenses and so has a great impact on residual equity cash flows. By giving special property tax relief in such cases, local governments can encourage one land use over another or attract a new industry to the community.

For example, farmers near developing urban areas sometimes find their property taxes rising substantially because of sharp increases in assessed valuations reflecting the market value of their land as development acreage rather than as farmland. As a result, the land must sometimes be sold since it can no longer be used profitably for agricultural purposes. In order to prevent this loss of farmland, some communities follow a practice known as **value in use assessment.** This practice permits farmland to be assessed at a lower value in order to encourage the continuation of agricultural use. (These issues are dealt with in detail in part 9.)

TAX-EXEMPT PROPERTY

A growing problem in many communities is the percentage of property exempt from tax liability because it is used for public, charitable, or religious purposes. This problem comes into sharp focus in cities that have economic bases dominated by government employment. If a major educational institution is located in a state's capital, a very large percentage—perhaps as much as half—of the property within the city may be tax-exempt. This means that the city either must set high tax rates or develop other sources of revenue.

If property taxes are high, then property owners in the district are being taxed at a higher rate than owners in other districts. This may contribute to increased development outside the city limits to avoid the high city taxes. The result can be an eroding city tax base and future city financing difficulties.

PROPERTY TAX: REGRESSIVE OR PROGRESSIVE?

From the point of view of society in general, a key question about the property tax is: Who bears the major tax burden? Is the tax progressive or regressive? Although these questions cannot be answered categorically, a few illustrations offer a clearer perspective on some of the issues involved.

❏ **PROPERTY-RICH AND PROPERTY-POOR DISTRICTS.**   A taxing district with a large number of industrial or business properties or with many high-priced homes will have a very large property base for taxation. Consequently, it can utilize relatively low tax rates to raise a great deal of revenue. By contrast, a taxing district with low-priced homes and no industry will have a difficult time, even with relatively high tax rates, in raising sufficient revenue to provide needed services.

As a result, an expensive home in a relatively poor community may be taxed a larger amount than the same home in a more affluent community. What is even more probable is that the home in the wealthier community would pay the same or somewhat lower taxes, but services would be at a much higher level.

❏ **PASS-THROUGH TO USERS.**   When increases in property taxes can be passed on to tenants of income properties through higher rentals or expense pass-throughs (as may be the case for office buildings and retail stores), the tax tends to be regressive, with final users and consumers shouldering the burden. On the other hand, when competition or rent control statutes prohibit a pass-through of property tax increases, then the consequence is a reduced equity cash flow for the investor.

In such cases, the property tax would be progressive *if* equity holders in the aggregate were wealthier than tenants. On the other hand, if rising taxes forced properties to be abandoned, as has happened in some big, older cities, the more important consequence is that the assessment roll is reduced and less space is available for occupancy.

The progressive-versus-regressive distinction is not totally academic. As cities expand and, through annexation of adjacent areas place more property on their tax rolls, consideration of who bears which common costs is more acutely focused. Newly annexed areas do not necessarily receive the same level of services as are provided in the central city—at least not immediately.

In many cases, local statues allow the taxing authority to phase in the provision of complete city services over a two- to five-year period. On the other hand, certain municipal services are available to people living just beyond the boundaries of the taxing district. Such services include park and recreation facilities, museums, and other cultural facilities that are available to those living outside the taxing district and who pay no property taxes to it. Clearly, both policy and ethical questions must be considered in understanding the constantly changing nature of the property tax.

IMPACT OF PROPERTY TAX ON CASH FLOW

From the perspective of a real estate analyst, property taxes are an important element in projecting future cash flows. Such taxes are often an important expense today and give indications in some jurisdictions of rising in the future. The failure to account for increases in property taxes turned many attractive investments into mistakes during the last decade. Although it is possible that property taxes will increase less rapidly in the future as a result of statutes similar to Proposition 13 in California, this is far from certain.

On the other hand, the real estate analyst is also interested in determining whether the municipality is able to support the level of services required by the populace. Particularly where a project may seek to attract tenants or purchasers from a distance, the quality of public education, fire and police services, sanitation, and the like is an important consideration. At times it is better to pay a little more in property tax than to live in a municipality with low-quality public services.

THE FEDERAL INCOME TAX AND TAX PLANNING

The federal income tax has a major impact on real estate investment decisions and on the benefits to be derived from property ownership. Real estate has always been a tax-favored investment medium. One of the most important goals of the real estate professional is to *structure* a real estate investment package so as to maximize the tax savings for the equity interests.

The balance of this chapter discusses general provisions of the Internal Revenue Code affecting real estate. Chapters 18 and 19 analyze in some detail the tax law provisions that specifically deal with real estate investment.

GOALS OF THE REAL ESTATE DECISION MAKER

In reaching tax decisions, the real estate decision maker usually has as his or her objective to pay as little as possible as late as possible. This basic objective has been accomplished in two ways. The first is **tax deferral**—*deferring* tax liability as far into the future as possible by accelerating all deductible items and by postponing income recognition where feasible. The second is **tax conversion,** that is, *converting* ordinary income into capital gain because capital gains are taxed at a substantially lower rate than ordinary income.

With the tax change in 1986, capital gains income no longer enjoys preferential treatment. However, the distinction between ordinary income and capital gains remains in the Code. Furthermore, it is possible that the large federal deficit may require future increases in tax rates. If this happens, Congress is on record as favoring the reinstitution of preferential treatment for capital gains. Hence, the real estate professional needs to understand the distinction between ordinary income and capital gain. (See Box 17-3.)

ORDINARY INCOME TAX VERSUS CAPITAL GAIN

Ordinary income includes salary, wages, commissions, and profits earned from carrying on a trade or business. Interest, dividends, royalties, and rents also are ordinary income. The tax rate applied to ordinary **taxable income** is progressive (i.e., after the taxpayer has taken permissible deductions and exemptions). By comparison, **capital gains** are profits received from the sale or exchange of capital assets.[3]

The historic justification of the capital gains tax was that capital gains represented the appreciation of property that often had been held for a long period of time. Under our somewhat progressive tax rate structure, it seemed unfair to tax the entire gain as if it had entirely occurred in a single year. Besides, a large portion of the reported long-term gain resulted form inflation, and taxing such "unreal" gains would be unfair.

From a public policy perspective, preferential tax treatment of capital gains income provides an inducement to invest (and consequently to save) and also makes capital more mobile, so that greater overall economic efficiency is achieved. That is, investors are not prohibited from moving toward more attractive investments by a heavy tax on the exchange. Such a tax would make the capital markets less efficient in allocating savings to investment.

---

[3]*The definition in the tax law of a capital asset is complex. Basically, the term includes any property not held for sale in the normal course of business. Thus, investment real estate held for income is a capital asset. However, a developer is considered to be in the business of producing real estate for sale and so would not be eligible for capital gains treatment.*

17-3
HISTORIC TAX
PLANNING: A
MINIPRIMER

Objective: Pay as little as you can as late as you can or

1. Deter tax liabilities to the future and

2. Wherever possible, convert "ordinary" income to a "capital gain," which is effectively taxed at a lower rate.

How: Real estate probably benefits more than any other form of investment from provisions in the tax law that create tax shelters. Why is this so? The Internal Revenue Code contains almost no provisions intentionally designed to benefit real estate. Indeed, the opposite is true. Why, then, is real estate considered a tax-favored industry? The answer is that real estate enjoys a magnified advantage from the basic principles of tax law because of the inherent nature of real estate itself—that is, its immobility, long life, and (usually) high quality that often justifies large nonrecourse financing by third-party lenders and that makes it unnecessary to maintain large cash reserves for renewal and replacement.

The most important of the everyday principles of tax law that favor real estate are as follows:

- The allowance of the deduction for the depreciation of certain business assets.

- The right to depreciate business assets to the extent of their total cost rather than to the extent of the investor's equity (now limited to real estate only).

- The treatment of borrowed money as a transfer of capital and not as a receipt of taxable income.

- The right to elect to report the gain from the sale of property by the installment method.

- The step-up of the tax basis of the assets of the deceased individual to their fair market value on the date of death.

Result: Tax shelter (i.e., after-tax cash flows that are higher than reportable "taxable" income).[a]

---

[a]All five of these principles will be covered in some detail in Chapters 18 and 19.

Since the 1986 Tax Reform Act reduced individual rates from a maximum of 50 percent to a maximum of 28 percent,[4] the authors of the legislation felt that preferential treatment for capital gains was no longer needed. Again, if tax rates rise, or if investment falls dramatically, Con-

---

[4]As explained in Chapter 18, the effective marginal tax rate can be as high as 33 percent under the new law, as personal exemptions are phased out for high-income taxpayers.

gress could well reinstitute preferential capital gains treatment for the reasons cited earlier.

The tax consequences of investing in real estate can be conveniently divided into two categories. The first relates to operating the real estate, and the second to the proceeds on sale or other disposition. In both cases, the bottom-line figure of concern is taxable income or deductible loss. If the bottom line is taxable income, it will be added to any other taxable income of the taxpayer, and the whole will be taxed at the appropriate tax rate. If the result is a deductible tax loss, in certain circumstances the loss will offset certain other taxable income of the taxpayer (as explained in Chapter 18), with the net taxable income then subject to tax.

CALCULATING TAXABLE INCOME (LOSS) FROM REAL ESTATE OPERATIONS

During the period of ownership, the investor's basic tax calculations each year will be as follows.

- *Determine gross income.* First, the investor adds up all rental income, receipts, and other revenues from the property or business operation to determine gross income.

- *Deduct operating expenses.* Next the investor deducts all operating expenses, which include all of the ordinary and necessary expenses in connection with the property, including payroll, real estate taxes maintenance and repair, insurance premiums, legal and accounting fees, advertising and promotion, supplies, and so on. This results in net operating income.

- *Depreciation.* The investor then deducts an amount representing depreciation of the improvements on the property. Depreciation is a special kind of deduction, representing a bookkeeping entry rather than a cash outlay. Because of its crucial importance to real estate investment, it is discussed in detail in Chapter 18.

- *Interest on mortgages.* Also deducted are interest payments on any outstanding loans used to finance the property. Note, however, that loan amortization (repayment of principal) is not deductible for tax purposes since the IRS views amortization not as an expense but as a payment or contribution of capital (investment).

- *Taxable income (loss).* If gross income exceeds all the deductions just listed, the balance remaining is taxable income. If, on the other hand, deductions exceed gross income, the property has shown a taxable loss for the year, which may be used to offset (shelter) other passive income of the investor. (See Chapter 18 for a definition of passive income.)

CALCULATING TAXABLE INCOME (LOSS) ON SALE

When the property is sold or disposed of, the investor must determine whether any gain or loss has been realized. This involves the following calculation:

❏ **SALES PROCEEDS.** First, the amount of sales proceeds must be determined. This normally will be the sales price stated in the contract of sale less any selling costs such as commissions and legal fees. It will include not only the cash paid to the seller, but also the amount of any mortgages of which the buyer is relieved. If consideration other than cash is given for the property, then the fair market value of such property is a part of the sales price.

❏ **ADJUSTED BASIS** (cost). Next, the seller deducts from the sale proceeds the seller's cost or basis. This figure is developed as follows.

- The seller begins with the original cost (cash or property paid plus the amount of any mortgages to which the property was subject when acquired).
- Any capital expenditures made by the seller during the period of ownership are added to this.
- The cumulative depreciation deductions taken by the seller during ownership are subtracted from this.

❏ **GAIN OR LOSS.** If the amount of sales proceeds is larger than the adjusted basis of the seller, a gain has been realized; otherwise, a loss has been realized. The gain or loss will be characterized as capital gain (loss) or ordinary income (loss), depending on whether the property was a capital asset in the hands of the seller.

FORMS OF OWNERSHIP AND INCOME TAXES

In Chapter 4, the most important legal entities used for real estate ownership were discussed. These include, in addition to individual ownership (**sole proprietorship**), the general partnership, limited partnership, regular corporation, and S corporation.[5] They are now briefly reviewed in light of the tax-planning considerations introduced in this chapter. (See Table 17-1.)

---

[5]*S corporations were identified as Subchapter S corporations prior to the Subchapter S Revision Act of 1982.*

TABLE 17-1 COMPARING INVESTMENT VEHICLES

ENTITY CHARACTERISTIC	SOLE PROPRIETORSHIP	GENERAL PARTNERSHIP	CORPORATION	S CORPORATION	LIMITED PARTNERSHIP	REAL ESTATE INVESTMENT TRUST
Ability to raise capital	Limited	Yes	Yes	Yes	Yes	Yes
Limited liability	No	No	Yes	Yes	Yes	Yes
No double taxation	Yes	Yes	No	Yes	Yes	Yes
Income retains its character[a]	Yes	Yes	No	Yes	Yes	Yes
Deduction of losses in excess of the amount of investor capital at risk	Yes	Yes	No	No[b]	Yes[c]	No

[a]Since the 1986 Internal Revenue Code no longer provides for the preferential treatment of capital gains, this becomes an unimportant distinction. However, it is included here to show how the decision maker's investment vehicle preference may have changed under the new act.

[b]Shareholders may carry excess losses forward indefinitely.

[c]Under the 1986 Code the deduction of excess losses now depends on the source of financing as well as the investment vehicle. The limited partnership permits such deductions as long as the at-risk provisions explained in Chapter 18 are met.

INDIVIDUAL OWNERSHIP

All the tax-planning benefits noted in this chapter are available to an individual owner of real estate. In particular, when real property is owned by one or more individuals (in the latter case, as tenants in common, joint tenants, or tenants by the entirety), the individual owners may utilize any loss shown by real property for tax purposes to offset other passive income that would otherwise be taxable.

The major difficulties with individual ownership (sole proprietorship) are two. First, it is often difficult to raise any substantial amount of capital, for none of the forms of individual ownership can easily encompass more than a few people. Furthermore, each individual owner will be fully liable for any debts or obligations in connection with the real property. (Nonrecourse financing is possible insofar as a mortgage is concerned, but the individuals will still be liable for all other obligations of the venture.)

GENERAL PARTNERSHIP

The **general partnership** is really a further extension of the co-ownership entities described in Chapter 4 and mentioned in the preceding paragraph. All the partners in a general partnership share unlimited liability just as does an individual owner, and all have an equal say in management. That is, unanimous consent is required unless the partnership agreement specifies otherwise.

Since the general partnership is not a separate entity for tax purposes, gain and loss are "passed through" the partnership form directly to the individual partners. The individual partners thus retain all the tax benefits that would be available to them as individual or co-owners. Put another way, the general partnership is an *income conduit.*

If the general partnership has no tax or liability advantages over individual or co-ownership, why is it used? Primarily because it is at times a more convenient way for a group of persons to own real estate than co-ownership. For example, the partnership agreement may specify the exact conditions under which the specific joint activity is undertaken.

REGULAR CORPORATION

The regular business **corporation** solves the most serious problem of the preceding entities: that of unlimited liability. When a corporate entity owns real estate, the entity only—and not its individual shareholders—is liable for all obligations. Thus, each individual participant can limit his or her liability to the amount of capital contributed.

Corporations have three other advantages that normally are not present in other multiple-ownership arrangements.

■ Interests in the corporation are freely transferable by the endorsement of stock certificates, with no consent by the corporation required.

■ The corporation, by its charter, may be given very long or perpetual life.

■ Centralized management, through a board of directors, is not only possible but is a requisite of this form of ownership.

The corporation has one major disadvantage. Unlike all other forms of ownership described, it is a separate taxable entity and so cannot pass through losses to the individual shareholders. Alternatively, if the assets of the corporation produce taxable income, a double tax must be paid, once by the corporation at the corporate level and once again to the extent that remaining income is distributed to the shareholders as dividends. Despite this serious limitation, corporations may nevertheless be utilized to own real estate that produces taxable income if

■ The corporation's net income may be distributed to its shareholder-employees in the form of compensation (salaries). Since the compensation is a deductible expense to the corporation, only a single tax is paid at the shareholder-employee level.

■ The corporation is to accumulate the net income or use the net income for other investments so that no dividend distributions are projected. However, the accumulation of income above a certain amount will subject the corporation to a substantial penalty tax.

Under the 1986 Tax Reform Act, however, corporate tax rates are higher than individual tax rates for the first time. Hence, using the corporate form and paying no dividends will now be taxed at a higher rate than using individual ownership. This means that when considering incorporation, the benefit of limited liability must be weighed against more significant tax disadvantages.

LIMITED PARTNERSHIP

Properly designed, the **limited partnership** combines the best features of both the corporate and general partnership form of ownership. Consequently, the limited partnership is the most frequently used vehicle when more than one investor is participating.

The limited partnership contains at least one general partner and one or more limited partners. The one general partner—often the promoter or developer—assumes unlimited liability for the obligations of the project. The limited partners, on the other hand, may lose only the amount of capital contributed to the venture.

At the same time, the limited partnership retains all the tax advantages of the general partnership. That is, all income and losses are passed through directly to the individual partners and no double taxation results.

S CORPORATION

Just as the limited partnership is a partnership with corporate attributes, the **S corporation** is a corporation with partnership attributes. The name derives from the circumstance that this type of corporation is authorized by Subchapter S of the Internal Revenue Code.

An S corporation is limited to 35 shareholders, who may elect to be taxed as though the corporation were a partnership. In other words, for tax purposes, gains and losses are passed through directly to the shareholders as in the case of a partnership. However, for nontax purposes (limited liability and centralized management), the Subchapter S corporation is treated as if it were a true corporation.

In the past, the S corporation was not frequently used for real estate because of the rule that such a corporation could not derive more than 20 percent of its gross receipts from passive investment income, which included, among other things, most residential and commercial rents. However, the Subchapter S Revision Act of 1982 eliminated the passive income test unless an S Corporation had earnings and profits generated in years for which a Subchapter S election was not in effect. Therefore, (1) S Corporations formed after December 31, 1982, and electing in their first taxable year and (2) S Corporations that have been under Subchapter S from the date of incorporation will not have to meet the passive income test. As a result of this change, the S Corporation may be more frequently used in real estate investments in the future.

REAL ESTATE INVESTMENT TRUST

One solution to the tax problems experienced by the corporation was the **real estate investment trust (REIT).** The REITs were a creation of the tax laws in the early 1960s and became the darlings of Wall Street in the late 1960s. They provided a way for the small investor to participate in the benefits of real estate. The REIT is a corporation in every sense of the word except that it pays no tax at the corporate level as long as it meets certain requirements. These requirements are as follows.

☐ **INCOME DISTRIBUTION AND ASSETS.** Ninety-five percent of a REIT's income must be distributed to the beneficial shareholders annually. Furthermore, at least 95 percent of its gross income must come from passive sources, and at least 75 percent must come from real estate (e.g., rents).

❏ **OWNERSHIP.**   The REIT must be owned by 100 or more persons, and not over 50 percent of the ownership can be in the hands of five or fewer persons.

If the REIT meets all these requirements, there is no tax at the trust level. In addition, capital gains income retains its character. Therefore, if the REIT experiences a capital gain, the dividend resulting from that capital gain is taxed at capital gains rates to the beneficial shareholder. However, there is no deduction of REIT losses by shareholders.

As already mentioned, many of the 1970s-style REITs have experienced operating problems owing partially to their own errors, partially to the nature of the market, and partially to the enabling legislation that created them. This legislation significantly limited their flexibility of operations. The idea of the REIT was to provide a passive vehicle for the small investor. Unfortunately, many small investors investing in REIT shares lost their chips in the real estate game. As we will see in Part 7, REITs made a comeback in the mid-1980s with such prestigious properties as Rockefeller Center in New York being syndicated using the REIT form.[6]

SUMMARY   This chapter has set forth as a foundation the basics of property and income taxation. Both the property tax and the income tax are methods of providing the financing necessary to support government operations. Because taxation has such a pronounced impact on cash flow, it is a key part of the real estate game. The decision maker must not only know current tax law, but also have a feel for the historical evolution of tax principles, the social consequences of who bears what part of which common costs, and the economic implications of the different means of

[6]*The 1986 Internal Revenue Code modified the taxation of REITs and their shareholders. A REIT is now subject to a nondeductible 4 percent excise tax if it fails to make distributions to shareholders on a calendar-year basis. This effectively eliminates the economic benefit of the deferral opportunity given under earlier law. The excise tax is not imposed if the REIT distributes an amount equal to the sum of (1) 85 percent of its ordinary income, (2) 95 percent of its net capital gain income (determined on a calendar-year basis), and (3) generally any amount not paid out or subject to corporate tax in the preceding calendar year. In addition, the Act eases the qualification requirements for REITs. Among the changes are (1) easing of the stock ownership tests for the REITs first tax year; (2) allowing REITs to form REIT subsidiaries (corporations), provided the REIT owns 100 percent of the subsidiary's stock; (3) permitting REITs to invest in stock or debt instruments on a temporary basis following receipt of new equity capital, without affecting qualification under the real estate income and asset tests; (4) allowing REITs to provide certain services directly to tenants of their rental properties without having to use an independent contractor; and (5) specifying that income from a "shared appreciation provision" be treated as gain from the sale of secured property. For this purpose, a "shared appreciation provision" is one that entitles a REIT to a portion of the gain realized on the sale or exchange of a secured property.*

The act also liberalizes some of the rules governing distributions from REITs. The changes include (1) modifying the minimum distribution requirement to exclude a portion of noncash income (such as original issue discount) recognized by a REIT; (2) allowing REITs to distribute the full amount of capital gain income to shareholders without requiring that the capital gain be reduced by any net operating loss; and (3) eliminating the penalty tax imposed on deficiency dividends.

raising the necessary revenue. This background aids the decision maker in anticipating changes in tax law over the expected economic life of the real estate asset.

IMPORTANT TERMS

Ad valorem tax

Capital gains

Corporate income tax

Corporation

Crowding out

General partnership

Limited partnership

Ordinary income

Personal income tax

Progressive tax

Property tax

Real Estate Investment Trust (REIT)

Regressive tax

S Corporation

Sales Tax

Social Security Tax

Sole proprietorship

Tax conversion

Tax deferral

Taxable income

Value in use assessment

REVIEW QUESTIONS

17.1 Discuss the difference between regressive and progressive taxation. Why might a general sales tax be considered regressive and an income tax progressive?

17.2 How does the federal deficit relate to "crowding out" real estate borrowers in the national financial markets?

17.3 The United States is at present a net debtor nation, and the government is attempting to fund the huge deficit by luring foreign investors to invest in Treasury bonds. What impact does this have on the strength of the dollar abroad? How does this affect the market for real estate in the United States?

17.4 What services does a municipality normally provide the real estate user?

17.5 Property taxes are often levied on an ad valorem basis. What problems might this cause for property owners?

17.6 What were the major objectives of the 1986 Tax Reform Act?

17.7 How can an economic base that is dominated by government employment affect taxes for property owners and hence possibly property values?

17.8 How is taxable income calculated?

17.9 What is a capital gain, and how is it taxed?

17.10 What is the difference between tax deferral and tax conversion? Which is most desirable to the investor?

REAL ESTATE INCOME TAX DEDUCTIONS

In this chapter and the next, we'll examine specific provisions of the Internal Revenue Code (IRC) affecting real estate investments. We will take the point of view of an equity investor in real estate who is seeking to maximize after-tax equity (residual) cash flow.

The Internal Revenue Code is replete with rules favoring real estate over other forms of investment. However, the Code has been amended so many times in response to political pressures that it is now a complicated patchwork of regulations. Furthermore, the Code is not perfectly clear in all details; what is allowable is sometimes a matter of interpretation. Since an investor almost always seeks to reduce tax liability by any legal means possible, it is essential to understand the distinction between **tax avoidance** and **tax evasion.** Tax avoidance means taking an aggressive approach to minimizing tax liability when interpreting tax law. Tax evasion is fraud; it amounts to the willful concealment or misrepresentation of facts in order to avoid the payment of tax. Tax avoidance is a justifiable economic action; tax evasion is criminal activity that can lead to severe penalties. The line between them is not difficult to draw. A taxpayer who fully and truthfully discloses all pertinent information on a tax return may draw legal conclusions differing from those of the IRS without being guilty of fraud. But when disclosure is either incomplete or untruthful, the line has been overstepped.

This chapter concerns rules governing deductions for depreciation and loan interest. Chapter 19 continues with tax credits and transactions that defer taxes. Although both chapters are somewhat technical, their purpose is not to make the reader a tax expert. Our intention in these chapters is to convey the basic principles of tax law and to alert the reader to tax-planning opportunities, pitfalls, and possible situations requiring expert advice from a tax accountant or attorney. (See Box 18-1.)

18-1

THE ECONOMIC RECOVERY TAX ACT OF 1981, THE TAX EQUITY AND FISCAL RESPONSIBILITY TAX ACT OF 1982, AND THE DEFICIT REDUCTION ACT OF 1984

In 1981, Congress passed the biggest tax cut bill in U.S. history—ERTA, the Economic Recovery Tax Act. Supply-side economics, still enjoying the popularity that had carried it, with Ronald Reagan, into the White House in 1980, dictated that money should be made available to individual and corporate taxpayers to encourage economic growth. ERTA was to accomplish this goal by providing large multiyear tax cuts for individuals and massive tax breaks for businesses. Although the tax cuts were almost three times larger than the accompanying budget cuts, supply-siders maintained that the already large federal budget deficit would not be increased. Instead, the U.S. economy would respond to the tax cuts with a burst of growth that would create new revenues and automatically shrink the deficit.

By later that year, however, this optimistic forecast had not been realized. The business community had not yet responded to the generous ERTA tax cuts by investing in production as it was expected to do. The economy was still in recession, interest rates were still high, and unemployment was still rising. Most lawmakers felt that if the huge federal deficit was not balanced by more cuts in spending or more income, interest rates were likely to remain high, choking off a recovery. To complicate matters, an election year was coming up. Voting for either further spending cuts or higher taxes would not likely help candidates' chances with increasingly disillusioned voters. But voters did not like the deficit either. Something had to be done, and raising taxes was considered by most the better alternative, in part because programs that benefited the poor already had been severely cut back and because many voters seemed to believe the wealthy had been treated too kindly by ERTA. For these same reasons, politics demanded that higher bracket corporations and individuals bear a healthy share of the new tax burden.

The result of Congress's deliberations over all these problems was TEFRA—the Tax Equity and Fiscal Responsibility Act of 1982. The act, its proponents said, was really a tax fairness measure that focused on increasing compliance with both the letter and spirit of tax laws. For instance, it required certain corporations and individuals to pay a minimum tax, thus preventing them from sheltering too much income from taxation. Overall, TEFRA's effect was to rescind some of the tax breaks introduced in ERTA.

Whenever there is a major tax change as in 1981 (with adjustments in 1982), there will be new problems of both fairness and economic logic that arise as the law is used but that were not foreseen when the law was enacted. This was certainly the case in 1984 as we realized certain problems in the 1981 and 1982 legislation. In addition, the continuing huge budget deficits led some to complain that the 1981 cuts had been too generous from a macroeconomic perspective. There were also continuing questions about the overall fairness of the tax laws. The political result was the Deficit Reduction Act of 1984, which had several detailed provisions affecting real estate, most notably, a slightly longer depreciable life and the institution of a present value concept to restrict syndications that were considered abusive. (See Box 18-3.)

DEPRECIATION AS A TAX SHELTER— BACKGROUND

From the very beginning, the federal income tax has been a tax on net income rather than on gross revenue. Obviously, an income tax system requires a set of rules to determine exactly what "taxable income" is. The set of rules contained in the Internal Revenue Code has always recognized that part of the gross income from a business or investment represents the recoupment of capital invested in **wasting assets, that is, assets that gradually lose value over a period of time owing to use, wear and tear, or the action of the elements.** All physical assets of a business or investment with the exception of land are considered depreciable assets. Land, however, is considered to have a permanent life because it is a portion of the earth itself (even though soil or mineral elements in the land may be despoiled or removed).

The concept that taxable income should not include that portion of gross income that represents the using up of depreciable assets is given effect by permitting owners of investment or business assets to take an annual deduction from gross revenue for **depreciation.** Over the years, the allowable depreciation deduction has been modified in various ways—at times to reflect the fact that inflation was pushing the cost of replacement property far above the cost of the original property being depreciated.

For example, if a piece of equipment had a useful life of 15 years and had an original cost of $15,000, the owner could deduct $1,000 a year on his tax return as depreciation. At the end of 15 years, when the equipment was used up, the taxpayer would have recouped $15,000, the original cost, so that he could buy a new piece of equipment. (Salvage value is ignored in this example.) But if the new equipment had gone up in cost, the taxpayer was forced to put up his own money or to borrow money in order to replace the used-up asset. The disparity in original cost and replacement cost was reduced over the years by amendments to the Internal Revenue Code. These amendments speeded up the process of cost recovery through accelerated depreciation and other techniques.

The speedup of depreciation write-offs culminated with the Economic Recovery Tax Act of 1981 (ERTA), when the former system of depreciation deductions was replaced by a new system known as the **Accelerated Cost Recovery System (ACRS).** (In the interests of simplicity, the term "depreciation" will continue to be used synonymously with cost recovery in the following discussion.) The new system came close to being a replacement cost system, for its provisions for shorter useful asset lives and rapid recovery of capital in theory allowed faster recovery of capital in anticipation of higher replacement costs. In the case of real estate, the Accelerated Cost Recovery System often provided a much larger tax shelter than had been available under the former system.

The 1986 Tax Reform Act (see Table 18-1) dramatically reversed the trend toward more rapid depreciation. The useful life of nonresidential

TABLE 18-1 1986 TAX REFORM LEGISLATION PROVISIONS AFFECTING REAL ESTATE

	PRE-1986 TAX REFORM	1986 TAX REFORM ACT PROVISIONS FOR 1987			1986 INTERNAL REVENUE CODE PROVISIONS FOR 1990		
		TAXABLE INCOME BRACKETS			TAXABLE INCOME BRACKETS		
RATES		TAX RATE	JOINT RETURNS	SINGLE INDIVIDUALS	TAX RATE	JOINT RETURNS	SINGLE INDIVIDUALS
Individuals							
Ordinary income and short-term capital gains	14 brackets from 11 to 50%	11%	0–$ 3,000	0–$ 1,800	15%	0–$32,450	0–$19,450
		15%	$ 3,000–$28,000	$ 1,800–$16,800	28%	Over $32,450	Over $19,450
		28%	$28,000–$45,000	$16,800–$27,000			
		35	$45,000–$90,000	$27,000–$54,000			
		38.5	Over–$90,000	Over–$54,000			

15% bracket phases out for certain taxpayers increasing their taxable income by 5% within specified ranges. The phaseout ranges are
Joint returns $78,400–$162,770
Single $47,050–$ 97,620
The alternative minimum tax (ATMT) is extended under the new law and increased to 21%, but, with the elimination of the capital gains preference and accelerated depreciation, the alternative minimum tax is less important for real estate analysis.

	PRE-1986 TAX REFORM	1987	1990
Standard deduction (zero-bracket amount)	Joint return: $3,670 Single: $2,480	Joint return: $3,760 Single: $2,540	Joint return: $5,450 Single: $3,250
Personal exemption	$1,080	$1,900	$2,050 (1990) The personal exemptions phase out for "high-income" taxpayers increases with their taxable income by 5% within the phaseout range.

(continued)

TABLE 18-1   1986 TAX REFORM LEGISLATION PROVISIONS AFFECTING REAL ESTATE

	PRE-1986 TAX REFORM	1986 TAX REFORM ACT PROVISIONS FOR 1987			1986 INTERNAL REVENUE CODE PROVISIONS FOR 1990		
		TAXABLE INCOME BRACKETS			TAXABLE INCOME BRACKETS		
RATES		TAX RATE	JOINT RETURNS	SINGLE INDIVIDUALS	TAX RATE	JOINT RETURNS	SINGLE INDIVIDUALS
						Phaseout begins at the level where the standard deduction phaseout is complete, e.g., $162,770 for joint returns. The dollar amount at which this phaseout ends varies according to the number of exemptions claimed.	
Long-term capital gains	20%	28%			28%		
Corporations *General Rule*							
Ordinary income and short-term capital gains	46% top rate	40%			34%		
Long-term capital gains	28%	34%			34%		
	Individuals subject to 20% alternative minimum tax and corporations subject to add-on 15% minimum tax.				An alternative minimum tax applies, with variations in income base, deductions, and exemptions, to individuals (20%) and corporations (20%).		

	PREVIOUS LAW	1986 INTERNAL REVENUE CODE
Depreciation	Straight line or 175% declining balance useful life, 19 years	Straight line only 27½ years, residential 31½ years, nonresidential

Depreciation Recapture	Gain is treated as ordinary income instead of capital gain if property was depreciated on accelerated method. For residential property, the difference between accelerated and straight-line depreciation is recaptured; for nonresidential, all depreciation is recaptured.	All gain is ordinary because the capital gains rate is repealed.
Investment tax credit	6 to 10%	None
Home mortgage interest	Fully deductible	Principal and second-residence mortgage interest is deductible up to "cap." Per residence cap is (1) lesser of fair market value or basis (cash, mortgage, and improvements) plus (2) mortgage for education or medical expenses.
Other interest deductions	$10,000 plus amount equal to investment income	No deduction for consumer interest. Investment interest deduction limited to amount equal to investment income, excluding interest income. (See "passive activities" discussed later in this chapter.)
Construction period interest and taxes	Capitalized with 10-year amortization	Capitalization and recovery over depreciable life of property.
Passive-loss limitation	Individual losses from investments may reduce income from wages, other sources, and other investments.	Losses and credits from a business activity in which the *individual* taxpayer does not materially participate (e.g., a limited partner or a nonparticipatory, "passive" general partner) *and* from rental activities cannot be deducted against earnings or "portfolio income." Interest deductions from passive activities are treated as passive losses. Disallowance is phased in 1987 to 1991, but only with respect to activities entered into or interests acquired prior to the act's signing date.

(continued)

TABLE 18-1 (CONTINUED)

	PRE-1986 TAX REFORM	1986 TAX REFORM ACT PROVISIONS FOR 1987			1986 INTERNAL REVENUE CODE PROVISIONS FOR 1990	
			TAXABLE INCOME BRACKETS			TAXABLE INCOME BRACKETS
		TAX RATE	JOINT RETURNS	SINGLE INDIVIDUALS	TAX RATE	JOINT RETURNS / SINGLE INDIVIDUALS
RATES						"Portfolio income" includes interest on securities and savings, stock dividends, REIT dividends, "portfolio" capital gains.

"Portfolio income" includes interest on securities and savings, stock dividends, REIT dividends, "portfolio" capital gains.

Disallowed losses and credits are carried forward indefinitely and allowed in full upon disposition of interest in the activity.

Rental activities are treated as nonparticipatory even though the taxpayer does materially participate, but material participants in rental real estate can offset up to $25,000 of other income with rental losses and credits, subject to income phaseouts. Up to $25,000 of low-income housing credits are allowed regardless of whether participation is material, subject to income phaseouts.

Generally, *$25,000 allowance* against nonpassive income *phases out* between $100,000 and $150,000 of income. The phaseout range for rehabilitation and low-income housing credits (the latter for pre-1990 property only) is $200,000 to $250,000.

		The limitation applies beginning in 1987 to individuals, for losses recognized directly or through pass-through entities, and to estates, trusts, certain personal service, and closely held regular corporations. The limitation does *not* apply to widely held regular corporations.
At risk-rule	Real estate activities excepted. Losses deductible in excess of cash investment and recourse debt.	Extended to real estate, but losses not affected to extent of "qualified nonrecourse financing," cash investment, and recourse debt. Qualified nonrecourse financing generally means nonrecourse debt from an unrelated commercial lender or from a related lender, if on same commercially reasonable terms available to unrelated persons.
Rehabilitation tax credits	30-year-old nonresidential: 15% 40-year-old nonresidential: 20% Historic residential and nonresidential structures: 25%	Pre-1936 structures: 10% Certified historic structures: 20% Applies to property placed in service after December 31, 1986.
Low-income rental housing credits	No credit, but other tax incentives.	In lieu of previous incentives: 1. New construction and rehabilitation of existing housing: approximately 9% per year over 10 years. (Present value approximately 70%). 2. New construction and rehabilitation financed with tax-exempt bonds or other federal subsidies: approximately 4% per year for 10 years. (Present value approximately 30%).

(continued)

TABLE 18-1 (CONTINUED)

	PRE-1986 TAX REFORM	1986 TAX REFORM ACT PROVISIONS FOR 1987			1986 INTERNAL REVENUE CODE PROVISIONS FOR 1990		
		TAXABLE INCOME BRACKETS			TAXABLE INCOME BRACKETS		
		TAX RATE	JOINT RETURNS	SINGLE INDIVIDUALS	TAX RATE	JOINT RETURNS	SINGLE INDIVIDUALS
RATES					3. Acquisition costs for certain existing buildings not in service prior to acquisition: 4% per year for 10 years. (Present value approximately 30%.) New credits generally effective for buildings placed in service after 1986.		
Tax-exempt bonds: MRBs		Interest on mortgage revenue bonds is tax-exempt. States can issue up to $700 million in MRBs for housing at prices no greater than 110% of average local price. Program expires December 31, 1987.			MRBs' use restricted: 95% of proceeds must be for first-time buyers and houses at 90% or less of local average price. Incomes of buyers must not exceed 115% of local median income. Termination date extended to December 31, 1992.		
IRBs		Interest on industrial revenue bonds is tax-exempt. Multifamily housing IRBs targeted to moderate- or low-income persons.			Exemption retained. Tighter targeting rules applied and at least 95% of an issue's proceeds must be used for exempt facility and functionally related and subordinate property. Most new rules apply to IRBs issued after August 15, 1986.		

Source: Michelle P. Scott, Esq., Law Department, The Prudential Insurance Co. of America.

property was extended from 19 years to 31.5 years (27.5 for residential property). Perhaps more importantly, the Accelerated Cost Recovery System was eliminated, and now only the straight-line method is allowed.

<table>
<tr><td>

DEPRECIATION DEDUCTIONS AND TAX SHELTER

</td><td>

Buildings and other improvements clearly are wasting assets and, therefore, are a proper subject for cost recovery. In practice, however, well-located and well-maintained real property often has a useful life far longer than the write-off period fixed by the IRS. Thus, the cumulative depreciation deductions taken by a property owner (1) often bear little or no relationship to the true economic decline in the value of the property and (2) will rarely be used to create a cash reserve to purchase replacement property at the end of the recovery period or, indeed, within any foreseeable period.[1]

Because a property owner may take depreciation deductions in excess of the actual decline in economic value of the property, a tax shelter is created. In other words, the property owner may take a tax deduction that is matched neither by a cash outlay nor by any diminution in value of the property. In fact, the property may well be appreciating in value while the investor is depreciating it for tax purposes. Thus, a portion of gross revenue that would otherwise be taxable income is sheltered from tax. (Actually, the tax is merely deferred until a future date, when the property is sold.) Furthermore, the tax shelter created by depreciation deductions is made even more effective because of the way real estate is financed. (See Table 18-2.)

</td></tr>
<tr><td>

COST RECOVERY AND BORROWED CAPITAL

</td><td>

Thus far we have proceeded on the assumption that the capital investment in real estate was all cash from the investor's pocket—that is, a $1 million building represents $1 million in cash. However, as noted in part 5, real estate is seldom purchased for all cash. Because of the immovable, enduring, and insurable quality of real estate, the major portion of its cost can usually be financed.

Since 1976, the tax law has limited the deductions for a loss in certain activities to the amounts for which the taxpayer is **at risk.** Generally, this amount has been the sum of the cash invested, the value of property contributed, and the debt for which the taxpayer is personally liable. All real estate activities were exempt from the at-risk rules until now. Real property is still a major exception to the rules. A taxpayer is treated as at risk in a real estate activity to the extent that qualified third-party non-recourse financing secured by real property is used in the activity. In other words, a taxpayer can still be considered at risk in a real estate

</td></tr>
</table>

---

[1]*One type of property to which this statement may not apply is an industrial plant where technological change as well as other forms of depreciation may require replacement within a measurable period.*

TABLE 18-2   POSITIVE BEFORE-TAX CASH FLOW WITH TAXABLE LOSS

OFFICE BUILDING INVESTMENT

A. Investment Terms		
Purchase price		$1,000,000
First mortgage loan (14% interest; 15% constant; 20 years)	$650,000	
Second mortgage loan (14% interest; no amortization)	150,000	
Cash down	200,000	
B. First-Year Cash-Flow Statement		
Gross rental receipts	$220,000	
Vacancy—5%	(11,000)	
Effective gross income	209,000	
Operating expenses	(84,000)	
Net operating income		$ 125,000
Debt service		
First mortgage	$(97,500)	
Second mortgage	(21,000)	
Less: total debt payments		$ (118,500)
Before-tax cash flow		$ 6,500
C. First-Year Tax (Profit-and-Loss) Statement		
Net operating income		$ 125,000
Interest on first mortgage	$(91,000)	
Interest on second mortgage	(21,000)	
Less: total interest		$ (112,000)
Depreciation (on $800,000, building cost, excluding land)		(25,400)
Taxable income (loss)		($ (12,400)

activity financed with nonrecourse debt, provided the lender is a person or business regularly engaged in the trade or business of lending money. The taxpayer will not be considered at risk if the lender is the person from whom the taxpayer bought the property or a person who receives a fee with respect to the taxpayer's investment in the property. All loans from related parties, however, must be on commercially reasonable terms.[2]

The justification for allowing an owner to depreciate the entire cost

[2]From "Understanding the 1986 Tax Changes," Touche Ross, Washington, D.C., 1986.

without regard to the amount of debt is that eventually the owner will have to amortize the debt obligation and thereby complete his or her investment in the property. In actual practice, of course, real estate mortgages are usually amortized at a very slow pace during the early years of ownership, whereas depreciation deductions are much greater. Owners, therefore, may be able to generate depreciation write-offs that exceed their cash investment.

HOW CASH FLOW IS SHELTERED BY TAX LOSSES

Table 18-2 illustrates how an office building investment can generate a positive before-tax cash flow (dollars in the owner's pocket) and at the same time show a **taxable loss.** There are two outcomes of this taxable loss: (1) since there is no taxable income from the property, all the cash flow is received tax free, and (2) the tax loss from the property may be used to offset other passive income to the investor, and the tax saving so achieved is added to the cash flow from the investment itself.

In Table 18-2, the office building costing $1 million had a land value of $200,000 and thus an original depreciable basis of $800,000. Under the 1986 Internal Revenue Code, the depreciable life is 31.5 years (Table 18-1), and thus first-year depreciation is $25,400 ($800,000 ÷ 31.5).[3] Calculating taxable income as shown in Chapter 17, the investor ends up with a taxable loss of $12,400 despite a positive cash flow of $6,500.

PASSIVE-LOSS LIMITATIONS

Until 1987, the $12,400 loss could be used to offset other income with very few restrictions. Now (as shown in Box 18-2) this loss can no longer easily be used to offset ordinary income (wages) or portfolio income (dividends), but only other **passive income.** Obviously, this reduces the value of the tax shelter where taxable losses were intended to offset other income, especially income from large salaries or dividends. In fact, since the 1986 Internal Revenue Code was enacted, an active business is springing up in providing "income partnerships." These provide passive income so that people invested in the old, now called passive, tax shelters can still use their tax losses by offsetting them against passive gains from the "income partnerships." Without passive income, the tax losses on the old-style tax shelters would go unused.

PASSIVE ACTIVITY DEFINED

Obviously, one key to understanding the 1986 Internal Revenue Code is understanding the new categories of income, especially passive income. The 1986 Code defines a passive activity as any activity involving the conduct of a trade or business in whose operations the taxpayer does not

---

[3]*As illustrated in Part 7, depreciation would have been much greater in 1986 with a 19-year useful life and a 175 percent declining balance rate—($800,000 ÷ 19) × 175% = $73,684!*

18-2
PASSIVE-LOSS
LIMITATION
RULES

The most significant attempt in the 1986 Tax Reform Act to eliminate invest-ments in tax shelters was a provision limiting the ability of individuals to offset losses or credits from "passive" trade or business activities against "active" or "portfolio" income under both the regular tax and the minimum tax. Items of income or loss are assigned to the "passive," "active" or "portfolio" categories by reference to the nature of the activity the taxpayer engaged in to generate the particular item.

Limitation of Passive Losses and Credits

The limitation on **passive losses** does not disallow losses and credits from passive activities but, rather, determines how and when a taxpayer can claim the losses and credits. Losses from a **passive activity** are deductible only against income from that or another passive activity. Unused or "suspended" losses can be carried forward (but not back) indefinitely and can be used to offset passive income realized by the taxpayer in subsequent years. Taxpayers are allowed to apply prior-year suspended passive losses against current-year passive income prior to the application of net operating loss carryovers or other losses from nonpassive activities.

The determination of whether a loss is suspended under the passive-loss limitation is made after the application of the at-risk rules and most other provisions relating to the measurement of taxable income.

Any interest expense and income attributable to a passive activity will generally be subject to the passive-loss limitation and will not be subject to the limitation on investment interest. Interest on debt secured by a taxpayer's principal or second residence will not be subject to the passive-loss limitation.

A taxable disposition by a taxpayer of the entire interest in a passive activity will trigger the recognition of any suspended losses attributable to that activity. The act provides an election for property used in the activity if the basis thereof was reduced by a tax credit. Upon final disposition, the taxpayer may elect to increase the basis of the credit property (by an amount not exceeding the original basis reduction) to the extent the credit has yet to be allowed under the passive-loss rules. Exchanges of a taxpayer's entire interest in an activity in a nonrecognition transaction will not trigger suspended losses.

The passive-loss limitation applies to individuals, estates, trusts, and most personal service corporations (but not to C corporations, that is, the passive-loss limitation does not apply to regular corporations!). A modified form of the rule also applies to closely held corporations. Although these corporations may offset passive losses and credits against active trade or business income, the losses may not be offset against portfolio income earned by the corporation. If an affiliated group of closely held corporations files a consolidated return, the passive-loss rules will be applied on a consolidated basis whereby the passive losses of one group member may be offset against the passive income of another member. The limitation is applied at the shareholder level of S corporations and will focus on the participation of the shareholders in the business activity of the S corporation.

Definition of Passive Activity

A passive activity generally involves the conduct of a trade or business. If the taxpayer investing in that trade or business does not materially participate in the conduct of the activity, the investment is "passive." Whether an activity constitutes a passive activity must be determined separately for each taxpayer holding an interest in the activity and for each separate activity in which a taxpayer holds an interest.

Generally, rental activities with respect to real or personal property will be treated as passive activities without regard to whether the taxpayer materially participates in the activity. However, activities in which substantial services are provided, such as operating a hotel or other transient lodging facility or daily equipment rentals, do not come within this presumption that an activity is passive. In addition, the activities of a dealer in real estate are not generally treated as a rental activity.

The 1986 Code established a conclusive presumption that a taxpayer holding a limited partnership interest in an activity does not materially participate in this activity. Thus, income and losses attributable to a limited partnership interest will be classified as passive (with an exception for oil and gas working interests).

The new passive-loss provisions have increased the number of real estate syndications structured to produce passive-activity income. The real estate in these limited partnerships is purchased with little or no debt. Taxpayers should determine what their present passive income or loss position will be for the current and subsequent years before making any investment decisions about purchases or sales of limited partnership interests or interests in real estate.

Active Income or Loss

Salaries and income or loss from the conduct of a trade or business in which the taxpayer materially participates are classified as "active" under the Code. The material participation of a taxpayer in an activity is determined separately for each year the taxpayer holds an interest in the trade or business. When determining whether an activity (other than a rental activity) conducted by a closely held consolidated group is active, the material participation test is applied on a group basis and will take into account material participation by shareholders. A taxpayer must be involved in the operations of the activity on a regular, continuous, and substantial basis to be a material participant therein. When determining material participation, the performance of management functions is treated no differently from the rendering of physical labor or other types of services. Providing legal, tax, or accounting services to an activity that does not involve the providing of such services, by itself, generally will not be viewed as a material participation in such activity.

Portfolio Income and Expense

The 1986 Code provides that portfolio income is not passive income and thus may not be sheltered by passive losses and credits. Dividends on stock, REIT dividends, interest, royalties, income from annuities, RICs and REMICs (explained in a later chapter), and gain or loss realized on the sale of properties providing such income are portfolio income or losses. However, income attributable to the business of a partnership, or an S corporation, or to a lease of property is not treated as portfolio income. Any portfolio income earned by a passive activity must be accounted for separately from the other items of income or expense relating to the activity. Consequently, dividends and interest earned by a limited partnership must be separately stated and represent portfolio income of the partners.

Portfolio income is reduced by the deductible expenses (other than interest) that are clearly and directly allocable to such income. Interest expenses that are properly allocable to portfolio income also reduce the amount thereof. Such deductions are not attributed to a passive activity.

Source: "The Tax Revolution," Deloitte, Haskins, and Sells, Washington, D.C., 1986.

"materially participate" on a regular and continuous basis. It does not matter whether the taxpayer owns an interest in the activity directly or indirectly, or through a partnership or an S corporation. A limited partnership interest is automatically deemed passive. A working interest in an oil or gas property is not passive, as long as it is held directly or through an entity that does not limit the taxpayer's liability. Thus, general-partner status avoids the passive-loss rules for an oil and gas working interest; limited-partner status does not.

However, *all rental activities are treated as passive,* including real estate, even when the taxpayer participates materially. But an individual can still deduct against nonpassive income up to $25,000 in passive-activity losses attributable to rental real estate activities in which the taxpayer actively participates. The catch, however, is that the $25,000 is phased out at 50 cents on the dollar for taxpayers with adjusted gross incomes of over $100,000.

TAX ON THE SALE OF REAL ESTATE

We have seen that each year during ownership the investor is entitled to exclude from taxable income an amount representing the extent to which the asset was used up or investment was returned during the year. As a result, the investor pays less income tax than he would otherwise. Now what happens when the property finally is disposed of, by sale or otherwise?

On the sale of any capital asset, any gain realized by the seller is subject to tax. The amount of gain is equal to *the difference between the net selling price and the seller's tax basis in the property.* **Tax basis** is equal to original cost plus additional capital investments during the period of ownership minus accumulated depreciation deductions. This is logical since, as far as the investor's tax returns are concerned, the investor treated a portion of the income from the property each year as a return of capital via the depreciation deduction. As a result, when the property is sold, the seller must report as a gain the increase in value over his or her remaining capital in the property (i.e., the investor's remaining tax basis).

DEFERRAL OF TAX

We can see that the depreciation deduction does not let the investor avoid tax. It merely defers the tax until a later date—that is, until the property is sold. Prior to 1987, if the gain realized at sale was taxed at capital gains rates, the investor converted income that otherwise would have been taxed at ordinary income rates into income taxed at the much lower capital gains rate.

THE INTEREST DEDUCTION	In highly leveraged real estate deals, loan interest can provide a large deduction from revenue, reducing taxable income. For interest to be deductible, it must be paid on "true" indebtedness. The debt must be valid and enforceable, and it must be that of the taxpayer. Generally, in real estate transactions, interest is specifically stated as such. However, even when interest is disguised as something different (to avoid the state usury laws, for example), it is still interest if it is paid as compensation for the use or forbearance of money.

On fully amortized home mortgage loans, a portion of each payment consists of deductible interest. However, on many home mortgage loans, an initial loan origination fee is also assessed, usually at the rate of 0.5 to 2 percent of the amount of the loan. This fee is deductible in full by the borrower, if he or she can show that it is a financing fee incurred solely for the use of money as contrasted with a service fee being paid for performance of a service.

Prepaid interest deductions, at one time a popular form of front-end deduction, were dispatched completely by the Tax Reform Act of 1976. Cash-basis taxpayers must now deduct prepaid interest ratably over the period of a loan regardless of when the interest actually is paid—thus conforming to the present rule for interest prepayments by an accrual-basis taxpayer. The new rules cover all types of taxpayers and include interest paid for personal, business, or investment purposes. They also apply to prepaid interest on a wraparound mortgage.

In general, points (additional interest charges paid when a loan is closed beyond the origination fee discussed earlier) must also be de-

18-3
SYNDICATORS
AND THE BIG
DEDUCTION

In the mid-1980s, some very smart people found a new way to create a tax shelter. They would buy a property for $100 million with a cash flow of $10 million in a normal market transaction. They would then sell the property for $170 million with $20 million down and $150 million financed at 6 percent when the market interest was 12 percent.

The new investor had enough cash flow ($10 million) to service the debt ($150 million at 6 percent is $9 million), and at first it looks like a simple situation of below-market financing's creating an artificially high sales price. The creative part is in the new investor's tax position. He or she now has a basis of $170 million in a property originally worth $100 million and correspondingly large depreciation deductions. Syndicators found they could make big money helping investors to reduce their tax liabilities. The government got less, and the syndicators took a portion of the investors' tax savings for their troubles.

Obviously, the IRS could not live with this situation and in the 1984 Act got Congress to toughen certain rules.[a] The 1984 bill extended the original issue discount rules, which require deferred interest to be deducted under the economic accrual method (i.e., smaller deductions in the early years and larger ones in later years), to obligations issued for nontraded property and obligations issued by individuals. The enactment of these provisions means that after 1984 virtually any obligation issued by the syndicated partnership in exchange for property was subject to the original issue discount rules, unless the obligation contained an interest rate equal to at least 110 percent of the applicable federal interest rate, and the interest was payable in full each year (i.e., no deferred interest element). When an obligation issued in exchange for property does not contain the required interest rate or contains a deferred interest element, the interest element and corresponding principal amount of the obligation are re-determined by the IRS, and interest will generally be imputed as follows.

1. The interest rate combined in the obligation is compared to certain test rates equal to 110 percent of the average yield on federal obligations of similar maturities (the "federal rates"). If sufficient interest is not paid annually on a compound basis at least equal to these test rates, interest will be imputed at a rate equal to 120 percent of the applicable federal rates.

2. Interest income (determined as set forth in item 1) will be recognized by the lender, and interest expense (determined as set forth in item 1) will generally be deducted by the borrower on an economic accrual basis regardless of their respective methods of accounting. The federal rates will be adjusted every six months, but the interest rate in effect at the time of the transaction will be used for the entire transaction.

[a]The smart people were playing similar games with lease payments, pushing income recognition into the future. Accrued but unpaid interest and sale/leasebacks with tax-exempt entities completed the syndicators' bag of tricks. The 1984 Act eliminated these angles as well with the same required discounting approach and the disallowance of both "unpaid interest" and "disqualified leases."

ducted over the term of the loan. The one exception to this rule is that points paid by cash-basis taxpayer on a mortgage covering his or her principal residence may be deducted entirely in the year paid provided that the practice of charging points is customary in the locality and the number of points charged the taxpayer does not exceed the normal amount.[4] (Box 18-3.)

CONSTRUCTION PERIOD INTEREST AND PROPERTY TAXES

Before 1976, amounts paid for interest and property taxes attributable to the construction of real property were currently deductible unless the taxpayers elected to capitalize these items as carrying charges, which they would do to the extent that they lacked current income against which to offset the deductions. The Tax Reform Act of 1976 (1976 TRA) required that such interest and taxes be capitalized and amortized over a 10-year period. The first year of the period is the year in which the taxes or interest are paid or incurred; subsequent amortization begins in the year in which the property is placed in service or is available for sale.

The 1976 TRA still allowed deduction of construction interest and property taxes for construction of personal residences and vacation homes. In addition, the rule was to be applicable to low-income housing beginning in 1988; however, the Economic Recovery Tax Act of 1981 permanently exempted low-income housing from the rule. Thus, construction period interest and taxes in connection with personal residences, vacation homes, and low-income housing are immediately deductible by the property owner.

The 1986 Internal Revenue Code requires capitalization of construction period interest and property taxes for all other real estate. However, these costs are now to be amortized over the property's depreciable life, that is, 31½ years for nonresidential and 27½ for residential properties.

INTEREST DEDUCTION LIMITATIONS

Previously, interest deductions on debt incurred to buy or carry property held for investment by noncorporate taxpayers were generally limited to $10,000 a year plus net investment income. Furthermore, all consumer interest was deductible.

CONSUMER INTEREST

Under the 1986 Code, deductions of all nonbusiness interest, including **consumer interest,** are tightened. Interest on debt secured by a principal residence or second home is generally deductible, but only to the extent

---

[4]*The astute student will want to reflect on the relationship of the interest deduction, inflation, and tax shelter. Remember, from Part 5, the three-part lender return—real return, inflation premium, and risk premium. Of the three, only the inflation premium (a form of forced savings) actually generates a tax shelter.*

that the debt does not exceed the original purchase price of the home plus any improvements. This debt limit can be up to the fair market value of the residence if the loans (also secured by the principal or second residence) are for educational or medical expenses. Also, interest associated with the conduct of a trade or business remains deductible.

Generally, consumer interest (on credit cards, car loans, and life insurance policies, for example) becomes nondeductible. However, a taxpayer can still deduct interest on loans used for some consumer purchases. The proceeds of loans secured by a principal residence or second home and taken out for home improvements may be used for any purpose (including investment). Therefore, a taxpayer can deduct interest on "home equity"-type loans even if the proceeds are spent on a car or boat or even to purchase investments such as stock, as long as these loans represent no more than the purchase price plus improvements in the principal and second residences. (If the loan was taken out before August 16, 1986, interest is deductible even if the loan exceeds cost plus improvements.)

INVESTMENT INTEREST

Deductibility of **investment interest,** limited in the past, remains extremely limited. Such interest may still shelter net investment income, but the additional $10,000 offset of other income is no longer allowed. Interest on loans used to buy investments subject to the new passive-loss rules is not considered investment interest, nor is income from such activities to be considered investment income. However, in the transition years from 1987 to 1990, any passive losses allowed by the transition rules will offset investment income.

EFFECTIVE DATE

Regardless of when the loans were made, the new rules pertain to all interest paid or incurred in taxable years after 1986. The new limitations are being phased in, with the new rules becoming fully effective for 1991. For interest deductions eliminated by the new rules, 65 percent will still be allowed in 1987, 40 percent in 1988, 20 percent in 1989, and 10 percent in 1990. The phase-in of limits applies both to consumer interest deductions and loss of the $10,000 other-income offset to investment interest. For loans secured by a principal or second residence, the new provisions apply only to a loan taken out after August 16, 1986. Earlier loans up to the fair market value will still support full interest deductibility.

SUMMARY   Investors and others usually choose to minimize income tax liability by practicing tax avoidance, the use of all legal means to reduce tax liability. Their motive is to maximize after-tax cash flow. Since income tax is

18-4

REAL ESTATE AND "HOBBY LOSSES"

The Internal Revenue Code is honeycombed with tax traps for careless real estate investors. Consider the "hobby loss" trap in Section 183 of the Code. In brief, this section bars deduction of losses from a sideline or secondary business or operation unless the taxpayer can establish that the operation was carried on with the intention of making a profit. If the operation was merely a hobby, then the loss is personal and nondeductible.

Real estate operations often fall afoul of this rule because an investor may be willing to "eat" a string of losses in the course of building up a clientele or in anticipation of selling at a profit sometime in the future. However, if investors are careful to treat the operation as a true business, they often are in a position to deduct losses year after year because they can satisfy the Internal Revenue Service or the courts that their ultimate object is profit.

Consider the case of Mr. Allen, a successful executive, who operated a ski lodge in addition to his main job. The job gave him sufficient income so that he could absorb 12 consecutive annual losses from the lodge. Despite this string of losses, the Tax Court found Allen was in business for a profit, based on these factors.

■ Taxpayer operated the lodge in a businesslike manner. Excellent records were maintained.

■ The purchase, construction, and financing of the lodge resulted from careful planning. Its operation was directed toward obtaining sufficient revenue to realize a profit. The losses resulted not from lack of attention or ability by the taxpayer but were due to changes in the local economy.

■ Most important, the lodge was never used for the taxpayer's personal enjoyment. When he and his family went to the area to ski, they stayed at another facility, where they rented a room on an annual basis. The only time they stayed at the lodge was when they were working on it.

On this basis, the court found that the taxpayer was deriving no personal pleasure or gratification from operating the lodge; therefore, it was a business.

figured on what remains after allowable deductions from gross revenues, taxpayers need to be familiar with the law as it pertains to deductions. (See Box 18-4.)

Depreciation is the most significant deduction in calculating taxable income from real estate, because (1) for real estate it is often a very large deduction, and (2) it is a noncash item (i.e., it does not reduce cash from operations by any actual payment; it does, however, reduce taxable income and thereby reduces tax liability). Depreciation deductions do not avoid tax completely, for the income offset by depreciation is recognized as gain when the property is sold. However, in the meantime tax has been deferred (perhaps for many years).

The rules on depreciation deductions have been changed repeatedly over the years. Because these deductions create large tax shelters for real estate investors, they are subject to political pressure from all sides. It is important to have some familiarity with the current rules in order to seek competent professional tax advice when necessary.

Interest is another potentially large tax deduction. Again, real estate enjoys favored tax treatment in terms of what interest may be deducted; but, there are significant limitations on the deduction of certain types of interest. Based on 1976, 1981, and 1986 tax reforms, all construction period interest (and property taxes) must be capitalized and amortized except that interest paid in connection with the construction of personal residences, vacation homes, and low-income housing.

Deductions from gross revenues reduce income taxes by a percentage of the deduction equivalent to the taxpayer's marginal tax rate, as long as the taxpayer has other passive income. (The higher the tax rate, the more money the deduction saves.) In Chapter 19 we examine tax credits, which reduce income taxes dollar for dollar and consequently represent the most favorable tax treatment of all.

IMPORTANT TERMS

Accelerated Cost Recovery System (ACRS)
Consumer interest
Depreciation
Investment interest
Passive activity
Passive income

Passive loss
Tax avoidance
Tax basis
Tax evasion
Taxable loss
Wasting assets

REVIEW QUESTIONS

18.1   Distinguish between tax evasion and tax avoidance. What is the legal criterion for determining the difference?

18.2   In what way does a depreciation deduction differ from deductions for maintenance, management, property taxes, or interest expense?

18.3   Assume that an individual owns an office building for seven years, during which time the total depreciation taken was $400,000. If the total taxable gain is $700,000 and the investor is in a 28 percent marginal bracket, what is the tax liability at time of sale?

18.4   What is the difference between before-tax cash flow and taxable income?

18.5   Would you rather be eligible for a deduction of $10,000 or a tax credit of $10,000? Why?

18.6   What does "at risk" mean in the tax code? How does real estate get favorable tax treatment with regard to "at-risk" rules?

18.7   What types of property are most likely to cause investment interest limitation problems?

18.8   Did the 1986 Tax Reform Act increase or decrease allowable depreciation?

18.9   Which is favored by the tax law, residential or nonresidential property?

18.10 What does it mean to capitalize construction interest rather than to deduct it? Which is the more favorable tax treatment? Which is allowed today?

*T*ax Credits, Installment Sales, Like-Kind Exchanges, And Other Considerations

This chapter concludes the section on taxation. An overview of income and property taxes in Chapter 17 provided a foundation for the concept of tax planning for real estate investors, who generally seek to maximize after-tax cash flow. Chapter 18 focused on deductions from revenue in the calculation of taxable income or loss. This chapter continues to look at income tax provisions from an investor's point of view. Here we examine two more incentives for capital investment in real estate: the **investment tax credit** and **deferral of taxes on disposition** of real property, as well as a few miscellaneous items.

In earlier chapters we saw how Congress uses the federal tax code to enact public policy as well as to raise revenue. Tax incentives (otherwise known as loopholes) are powerful agents for change. But we have also seen how such incentives are amended or eliminated when one group of taxpayers is perceived to benefit too much at the expense of others—and others have enough political clout to remove the privilege. Public policies, like consumer products and pieces of real estate, are subject to life cycles. The birth, growth, maturity, and decline of federal policies can often be traced in the tax code.

Tax credits are a dollar-for-dollar reduction of the amount a taxpayer owes the IRS. In particular, the rehabilitation tax credit has stimulated the acquisition and remodeling of old buildings that formerly might have been demolished for new construction. This additional financial incentive is accelerating the renewal phase in the life cycle of old buildings throughout the nation.

REHABILITATION TAX CREDIT

Prior to 1978, buildings and their structural components were not eligible for any investment tax credit. In order to provide investors with an incentive to rehabilitate and modernize existing buildings, Congress granted **rehabilitation tax credits** for such expenditures in the Revenue

Act of 1978. In essence, rehabilitation expenses for a nonresidential building at least 20 years old became eligible for the 10 percent investment tax credit plus an additional energy credit. If the rehabilitation was of a certified historic structure, the taxpayer was given an election of either the 10 percent investment credit or a 60-month amortization of the rehabilitation.

The investment credit is intended to be an incentive for capital expenditures by business persons and investors. It is particularly effective by virtue of being a **tax credit** rather than a **tax deduction.** The tax credit reduces the tax liability directly, on a dollar-for-dollar basis, whereas the tax deduction reduces taxable income and so reduces tax liability by a varying percentage, depending on the taxpayer's bracket. A $1 credit reduces tax liability by $1 for every taxpayer who can claim it. A deduction of $1 taken by a taxpayer in the 28 percent tax bracket reduces tax liability by 28 cents, with the reduction declining as the tax bracket declines.

From 1981 through 1986, costs incurred in rehabilitating a building qualified for a credit ranging from 15 to 25 percent, depending on the age of the building and the type of rehabilitation. The credit was 15 percent of qualified rehabilitation expenditures for nonresidential buildings at least 30 years old, 20 percent for nonresidential buildings at least 40 years old, and 25 percent for certified historic structures. The rehabilitation credit was available only if the taxpayer elected the straight-line method of depreciation for the rehabilitation expenditures. For computing the allowable depreciation, the basis of a certified historic structure was reduced by 50 percent of the credit allowed. For all other buildings, the basis was reduced by the full amount of the allowed credit. The credit was available only for a substantial rehabilitation that satisfied a number of criteria, including retaining 75 percent of the external walls.

With the introduction of the 1986 Tax Reform Act, a two-tier investment credit replaced the three-tier credit. The 15 and 20 percent credits were reduced to 10 percent for the rehabilitation of a nonresidential building, and the credit was available only if the building was originally placed in service before 1936. The 25 percent credit for the rehabilitation of a certified historic structure was reduced to 20 percent. The depreciable basis of a certified historic structure must also be reduced by the full amount of the tax credit. (See Box 19-1.) The Act continues to require that there be a substantial rehabilitation. However, the external-walls test is eliminated for certified historic structures but is modified for nonhistoric structures. For nonhistoric rehabilitations, the act generally adopts an additional "internal structural framework" test. There must be a retention of both 75 percent of the existing external walls and 75 percent of the building's internal structural framework. This added internal-structural-framework test is meant to prevent a taxpayer from gutting the inside of the building and still qualifying for the credit.

Even though the rehabilitated building constitutes a passive activity,

19-1 TWENTY PERCENT CERTIFIED HISTORIC REHABILITATION TAX CREDIT	A group of investors buys a 60-year-old solid-brick tobacco warehouse in a historic district; the building is eligible for the 20 percent tax credit if rehabilitation expenses exceed its basis. The warehouse contains approximately 40,000 square feet and has features such as maple floors. The investors think it can be converted to apartments renting to affluent singles and couples. (The location is good.) They project their investment tax credit as follows.	
	Acquisition cost	$200,000
	Land	$40,000
	Building	$160,000
	Rehabilitation expenses	
	(Must exceed basis of $160,000)	
	40,000 square feet × $25 per square foot)	$1,000,000
	Tax credit	
	20% of $1,000,000	$200,000
	Basis calculation	
	Cost	$200,000
	Improvements	$1,000,000
	Historic credit	($200,000)
	Basis after rehabilitation and credit	$1,000,000

the taxpayer may, in certain situations, claim enough rehabilitation credits to offset the tax on up to $25,000 of nonpassive income, regardless of the taxpayer's level of participation. This limited ability to shelter the tax attributable to active or portfolio income phases out for high-income taxpayers.

EFFECTIVE DATE. Generally, the new rules apply for rehabilitated property placed in service after 1986. Exceptions are provided for property placed in service after 1986 if the rehabilitation is completed under a written contract that was binding on March 1, 1986.

COMMENTARY. Because of its limited exemption from the passive activity rules, the rehabilitation credit may provide one of the last opportunities for individuals to shelter up to $25,000 of wages, salary, interest, dividends, and other forms of nonpassive income. Before investing in any rehabilitation project, however, the investor should consider two questions. Will I lose part (or all) of the credit because my income is above the adjusted gross income limit in the year I claim the credit? Even though the credit is partially exempted from the passive-activity rules, will the rehabilitated property generate a passive loss that may be suspended if I do not actively (or, in some cases, materially) participate in the activity?[1]

LOW-INCOME HOUSING CREDITS

Replacing several low-income housing provisions in the prior law, the 1986 Tax Reform Act created a series of new **low-income housing credits.** The Code provides three separate tax credits that may be claimed by owners of certain residential rental projects providing low-income housing. Generally, the act provides the highest credit on expenditures for new construction and rehabilitation of existing structures of each qualifying low-income housing unit. A unique aspect of the credit is that any available credits are claimed annually in the same amounts for 10 years. For example, a taxpayer who is first eligible for the credit for $100,000 of qualifying costs to rehabilitate low-income property, would generally be eligible for a credit for each year for 10 years. First-year credits will generally be prorated to reflect a partial year of qualification. If the credit is prorated, the balance of year one's credit is available in the eleventh year.

If, however, qualifying expenditures are financed with tax-exempt bonds or other federal subsidies (e.g., a federal loan at an interest rate below the applicable federal rate), the Code generally allows a lower credit of such expenditures. Rehabilitation expenditures, in order to qualify for either of these two credits, must at least equal an average of $2,000 per low-income unit.

A third credit for the acquisition cost of each low-income housing unit may generally be claimed for each of 10 years whether or not any rehabilitation or construction work has taken place. The credit for the acquisition cost may generally be claimed only if the property was placed in service more than 10 years before the acquisition.

A project receiving the credit for acquisition cost may also qualify for the credit for rehabilitation expenditures incurred after the property is acquired.

The mandatory targeting, that is, the provisions about tenants to whom units must be rented as a condition of getting the tax credit, is much tougher under the current law than similar provisions under the old law for other housing programs. Therefore, although the developer may be getting 90 percent of qualifying costs back through the tax credit (the present value might be closer to 70 percent), the project is likely to require extensive ongoing operating subsidies from the developer over the 15-year required use period. The extent of this operating subsidy will be a function of the strength of the market, that is, of the rents received from the nontargeted units in the project.

[1]From "Tax Reform—1986," Ernst & Whinney, 1986.

Among other requirements, a low-income housing project qualifies for the credit if it is residential rental property, if the units are used on a nontransient basis, and if a minimum occupancy requirement is met. Hotels, dormitories, nursing homes, hospitals, life-care facilities, and retirement homes do not qualify for the credit. At least 20 percent of a project's units must be occupied by individuals having incomes of 50 percent or less of the area median income (adjusted for family size), or at least 40 percent of the units must be occupied by individuals having incomes of 60 percent or less of area median income (again, adjusted for family size). The taxpayer must irrevocably elect which of the two requirements (the 20 percent or the 40 percent test) will apply to the project. In addition, the gross rent paid by families in units qualifying for the credit cannot exceed 30 percent of the income limitation applicable to the tenants, based on family size.

The 1986 act provides a state volume limitation that gives a state the authority to determine the projects within the state that are eligible for part or all of each credit, other than projects financed with the proceeds of certain tax-exempt private-activity bonds. In general, each state is granted rental housing credits of $1.25 per resident.

Qualified low-income housing projects must comply with these rules for 15 years from the beginning of the year in which the project first qualifies for the credit. If not, some or all of the credit must be recaptured with interest.

Taxpayers wishing to claim the low-income housing credit must certify to the secretary of the treasury certain information pertaining to compliance requirements.

The low-income housing credit is subject to the limitations on the use of the general business credit, but there is no basis reduction for any portion of the credit claimed.

EFFECTIVE DATE.   The credit may be taken on property placed in service after 1986, other than property grandfathered under the depreciation rules, and generally before 1990.

COMMENTARY.   As with the rehabilitation tax credit, the low-income housing credit may provide a limited form of future tax shelter. The credit (but not any loss) is treated as arising from rental real estate activities in which the taxpayer actively participates. Taxpayers, therefore, will be able to shelter up to the credit equivalent of $25,000 of nonpassive income with the low-income housing credit. This limited ability to shelter the tax attributable to nonpassive income phases out for taxpayers with an adjusted gross income (computed without reference to passive losses) between $200,000 and $250,000.[2]

From "Tax Reform—1986," Ernst & Whinney, 1986.

DEFERRING TAX ON SALE OR DISPOSITION OF REAL ESTATE

Under our tax system, the owner of property—real estate or otherwise—may see its value increase year after year while paying no tax on this appreciation during the entire period of ownership. In other words, unrealized appreciation does not constitute taxable income. However, when the property is sold or otherwise disposed of, the owner normally will realize a taxable gain (or loss).

Under certain circumstances, however, an owner of property may defer the payment of tax on gain even beyond the time of disposition. This can prove to be a major tax benefit since funds that otherwise would be required for taxes remain available to the investor for varying lengths of time.

Of these various methods for deferring the payment of tax, two are particularly significant: (1) the **installment sale** and (2) the **tax-free exchange.**

INSTALLMENT SALES

The installment sale method was put into the tax law as an exception to the general principle that the full gain on the sale of real estate must be recognized—and the tax paid—in the year of sale. In an installment sale, the seller can report the gain proportionately over those years during which the purchase price is paid. The purpose of the installment sale method is to enable a seller to avoid a situation where the tax to be paid in any one year is greater than the cash proceeds received by the seller.

For example, property is sold for $50,000, with the seller agreeing to accept $5000 in cash, with the balance of $45,000 represented by a purchase money mortgage payable in nine equal installments during the nine years following the year of the sale. Assume that the seller's basis in the property was $7,000, so that the total gain is $43,000. If the seller's tax bracket was 28 percent, the total tax due is $12,040 (28 percent × $43,000).

If the seller were required to pay the entire tax in the year of sale, he would be out of pocket $7040, for he received only $5000 as a cash payment. However, the seller may elect the installment sale method and so report only one-tenth of his gain in the year of sale. This reduces his tax in the first year to $1,204, leaving him with a cash balance of $3,796. In succeeding years, as each payment is received, the seller will pay a similar amount in tax so that at the end of the payment period, the total tax will equal $12,040.[3]

---

[3]*Under the "proportionate-disallowance" rule, gross profits on dealer installment sales (and on certain sales of business or rental real property) can no longer be deferred to the extent of the ratio of the taxpayer's total indebtedness to total assets. In effect, an allocable portion of the taxpayer's borrowings is considered a collection on installment accounts. For this purpose, the taxpayer's indebtedness consists of*

TAX-FREE EXCHANGES

A provision of the tax law confers on real estate investors a special tax benefit: the right to exchange one parcel of real estate for another without paying any tax on the appreciation of value in the original property. Instead, the gain is "carried over" to the new property *by assuming the old tax basis in the new property.*

This deferral of gain may continue through a whole cycle of exchanges until a property is sold or disposed of in a taxable transaction; at that time, the entire gain, beginning with the original property, is subject to tax.

❏ TAX-FREE EXCHANGES OF INVESTMENT AND BUSINESS PROPERTY.

The first of the two tax-free exchange provisions in the tax law permits investment or business real estate to be exchanged directly (swapped) for property of like kind without payment of tax on any appreciation in value in the original property. The obvious advantage of this tax postponement is that investors can reinvest their full capital into new properties undiminished by tax payments. In effect, investors have the benefit of an interest-free loan from the government. (See Box 19-2.)

By permitting this type of tax-free exchange, Congress sought to minimize the adverse effect of tax payments on the transferability of property. The active movement of property, as already noted, is considered to be beneficial from both a social and an economic point of view. Moreover, it is, practically speaking, very difficult to calculate the gain in such exchanges.

The 1984 Act toughened the law. For the property to be received, it must actually be received within 180 days of the original property transfer or, if earlier, on the due date of the return. Obviously, this restricts flexibility in complex exchanges. And, in a clarifying statement, the Act said that partnerships' interests could not qualify as like-kind property.

❏ TAX-FREE EXCHANGE OF RESIDENTIAL PROPERTY.

The direct swap of property just described may be utilized only for business or investment property. However, Congress has made separate provision for residential properties in the tax law. Any owner of a personal residence may avoid payment of any tax on the appreciation of value if the

---

trade payables, accrued expenses, and all other loans or borrowings, including indebtedness incurred in buying property.

Certain dealers in timeshares or residential lots may elect out of the proportionate-disallowance rule if they pay interest on the resulting tax deferral. Controlled groups are generally treated as one taxpayer for the proportionate-disallowance rule. The rule applies to taxable years ending after 1986 for any installment obligation arising after February 28, 1986, with a three-year phase-in. Nondealers are subject to these rules for sales after August 16, 1986, except for sales of personal use property and certain farm assets. (Source: "Understanding the 1986 Tax Changes," Touche Ross, Washington, D.C., 1986.)

19-2
ADVANTAGES OF A TAX-FREE EXCHANGE

- *Deferring capital gains.* As noted previously, when properties are exchanged, the capital gains tax that would be payable because of any appreciation in the value of the property exchanged is deferred as long as the chain of exchanges is not broken. In theory, the tax may be deferred for many years.

- *Making property more salable.* Often, a prospective buyer lacks sufficient cash and may not be able to get a mortgage from a third party to make up the difference. The seller may then have to take back a large purchase money mortgage, which she may not wish to do for a number of reasons. An exchange means she can take other property of the buyer in lieu of taking back a mortgage. Since the buyer himself may not have property that the seller desires, three-party and even four-party exchanges can be set up.

- *Changing investment strategy.* A tax-free exchange may appeal to investors who, because of age or changes in personal income, wish to adopt a new investment strategy or change the balance of their real estate portfolio. For example, an investor with a high income may want to exchange real estate producing taxable income for raw land with potential for long-term appreciation. Or an investor may wish to change the geographical location of his holdings when faced with retirement or transfer.

- *Raising cash.* An investor who needs cash but cannot mortgage or refinance her existing investment for one reason or another can exchange for property that is more financeable. For example, property that justifies no more than a 60 percent mortgage might be exchanged for property that will support an 80 percent mortgage. Or property carrying a mortgage that bars prepayment could be exchanged for a property with no mortgage or with one that could be easily refinanced.

funds received are reinvested in a new personal residence within two years before or two years after the sale of the old residence.

Tax law requires that in order to qualify for the deferral of the capital gain tax on the sale of a personal residence, the purchase price of the newly purchased residence must be equal to, or greater than, the adjusted sales price of the residence sold. It should be noted that the law does not require that the cash proceeds be reinvested in a more expensive new personal residence in order to qualify for the deferral, only that the price (including the mortgage) be greater. If the purchase price of the new residence is less than the sale price of the old residence, gain is recognized but only to the extent of the difference in price. (See Box 19-3.)

**19-3
TAX-FREE
SALES OF
HOMES**

In addition to the tax-free exchange techniques described in the text, the tax law contains a special provision applicable to homeowners who are 55 years of age or over at the time they sell their residence. Such a homeowner may exclude from gross income all the gain realized, up to a ceiling of $125,000 of gain. The homeowner must have lived in the residence for three out of the previous five years. The tax-free election can be made only once during the owner's lifetime. (If a new residence is purchased, its basis is not reduced by the amount of the one-time exclusion.)

The special provision in the tax law reflects the recognition by Congress that value built up in a residence may be the major private source of retirement income for the elderly. Removing the tax on this gain allows the elderly to move to smaller (possibly rental) quarters and use the proceeds from the sale of their former homes to support themselves.

The most difficult aspect of most tax-free exchanges is **boot.** Any cash other than non-like-kind property or net mortgage reduction that is exchanged with the otherwise like-kind property constitutes boot; and the exchange is taxable to the extent of any boot. Some type of boot is usually required since the properties being exchanged seldom are of exactly the same value with exactly the same amount of existing debt. Hence, in most "tax-free exchanges," some portion of one of the parties' proceeds is taxable.

For example, Al trades a $100,000 warehouse with a $50,000 mortgage (basis of $80,000) to Bill for an office building worth $200,000 with $150,000 in mortgage debt (basis of $70,000). (Note that the equity interests are of equal value.) The exchange is tax-free to Al, but Bill has a net mortgage reduction (boot) of $100,000. Hence, $100,000 of Bill's gain of $130,000 ($200,000 value less $70,000 basis) is taxable.

**VACATION
HOMES**

Section 280A of the Code limits the amount an individual may deduct for expenses attributable to the rental of a vacation home whenever the individual's personal use thereof exceeds the greater of 14 days or 10 percent of the number of days during the year for which the dwelling is rented at a fair rental. Under this limitation, deductions attributable to the rental of a vacation home cannot exceed rental income. Section 280A, however, does not limit deductions for interest or taxes. Disallowed expenses cannot be carried forward for use in future years but are instead lost forever.

The 1986 Internal Revenue Code provides that an individual's rental activities, including the rental of a vacation home, are subject to the passive-loss limitations. It also provides that all qualified interest on first and second residences is fully deductible without limitation. For a vacation home to qualify as a residence, the taxpayer's personal use of the dwelling must be extensive enough to cause the section 280A limitation to apply. Whether a taxpayer should have a vacation home considered a second residence will require careful analysis.[4]

REAL ESTATE MORTGAGE INVESTMENT CONDUITS

The marketplace for mortgage-related investment vehicles grew rapidly during the 1980s, but it needed a mechanism by which to promote activity in these capital markets efficiently. Although a national market for pass-through certificates and pay-through bonds had been established, efforts to create a market for multiple-class mortgage securities were frustrated by the harsh tax consequences that were imposed on them. Indeed, income generated by mortgages (or other debt instruments) owned indirectly through an intermediary entity could be subject to more than one level of taxation (i.e., at the entity level and at the indirect owner level).

Double taxation occurred when the intermediary entity was held to be a corporation or an association taxable as a corporation. Treating the entity as a complete conduit (e.g., a grantor trust) avoided the double-tax problem, but mortgage-backed pass-through securities with multiple maturity structures were not permitted conduit treatment. Treasury regulations provided guidelines to determine whether a particular entity should be classified as a trust, corporation, or some other type of entity.

Problems also arose in calculating original-issue discount (OID) on mortgage-backed pass-through securities. It was unclear how the OID rules applied when the obligation's maturity date could be accelerated (e.g., based on prepayments on home mortgages collateralizing the obligation).

The 1986 Tax Reform Act created an entity called a real estate mortgage investment conduit (**REMIC**), which holds a fixed pool of mortgages and issues multiple classes of interests in itself to investors. A REMIC is not subject to an entity-level tax except in certain prohibited transactions. Solely for purposes of the administrative provisions of the

---

[4]*If the taxpayer is not concerned with the passive-loss rules because of high passive income or eligibility for the $25,000 loss exception, the vacation home/residence classification will never provide an advantage. If the passive-loss rules limit a taxpayer's deductions, choosing to regard the vacation home as a second residence may be advantageous because all the interest can be deducted under the second-residence mortgage exception, as well as the taxes allocable to personal use. (This choice will be more attractive when market softness causes rentals to be low and vacancies high, and operating income is therefore insufficient to offset the interest deduction.) However, this advantage must be offset by the permanent loss, rather than suspension, of certain deductible expenses such as those incurred for insurance, utilities, maintenance, and repairs. (Source: "The Tax Revolution," Deloitte, Haskins and Sells, Washington, D.C., 1986.)*

19-4
TAX-EXEMPT
BONDS

Faced with the accelerating growth of tax-exempt bonds issued each year, the 1986 Tax Reform Act attacked the problem with both scalpel and axe. Two major changes that immediately and significantly limited the issuance of tax-exempts were (1) a large reduction in the volume of industrial development bonds (IDBs) that could be issued, and (2) disallowance to banks of interest deductions on amounts borrowed to carry tax-exempts. Also, a new qualified redevelopment bond was created. Some activities were added and some subtracted for which tax-exempt IDBs may be issued. Tighter arbitrage restrictions apply to all tax-exempt bonds. Except for the arbitrage and reporting rules, the provisions affecting bonds for financing traditional government activities are substantially unchanged. Some tighter restrictions apply to bonds issued to benefit certain organizations. The types of student loan bonds eligible for tax exemption are expanded.

Generally, under previous law, a bond was treated as a government bond if more than 25 percent of the proceeds were used directly or indirectly in a private activity. The current law cuts the 25 percent to 10 percent.

IDB Financing

Facilities for sports events, conventions or trade shows, parking, air or water pollution control, and qualified hydroelectric generating were struck from the list of facilities that could be financed with IDBs. But hazardous-waste treatment facilities were added to the list. Tax-exempt financing for industrial parks are no longer permitted. The Code requires that 95 percent of bond proceeds (previously 90 percent) be spent for the exempt facility. Costs of issuance cannot exceed 2 percent of proceeds and are not included in the 95 percent.

Multifamily Residential Rental Property

The set-asides for low-income residents in multifamily residential real property are (1) 40 percent of the units for persons with income that is 60 percent or less of the area median income or (2) 20 percent of the units for persons with income that is 50 percent of the median or less. The tenant eligibility requirements have to be satisfied annually, based on current income throughout the qualified-project period (generally, the longer of 15 years or when the bonds are redeemed. A special rule applies to "deep rent skewed" projects. Rules are eased when standards are exceeded because income of existing tenants increases. Operators must file an annual certification of compliance.

Sunset Kept for Small IDBs

Under the sunset rule, small-issue IDBs cannot be issued after 1986 unless used to finance manufacturing facilities. Sunset for these facilities was extended to December 31, 1989, and applies to first-time farmers whose previous land ownership was land disposed of while the farmer was insolvent. In addition, first-time farmers can also use up to $62,500 of the proceeds to acquire used agricultural equipment.

Qualified Redevelopment Bonds

New qualified redevelopment bonds have to meet the following requirements:

- At least 95 percent of the proceeds must be used for redevelopment in a designated blighted area.
- Any increased property tax revenues must be used as necessary for debt service.
- The obligations must be issued under state law authorizing such obligations for redevelopment, and a redevelopment plan must be adopted before issuance by the governing body. There are many varied and detailed rules dealing with this new type of bond.

Bonds Issued To Benefit a 501(c)(3) Organization

For a bond issued on behalf of a charitable, religious, or educational institution to qualify for exemption, no more than 5 percent of the proceeds can be used directly or indirectly in any trade or business carried on by a nonexempt person or loaned to any person who is not exempt. Except for hospitals, there is an aggregate $150 million volume limitation for each institution. All property financed with the bonds must be owned by the 51(c)(3) organization or government unit.

Volume Limitations on Private-Activity Bonds

A unified cap took effect August 15, 1986. Included under the new cap are volumes greater than $50 per resident or $150 million per state cap, exempt-facility bonds, small-issue bonds, qualified-redevelopment bonds, student loan bonds, qualified-mortgage bonds, and private-loan bonds. Principal exceptions are qualified 501(c)(3) bonds, certain exempt-facility bonds, and certain refunding bonds.

Arbitrage Restrictions

Reasonable expectation tests no longer protect intentional arbitrage investments. The minor portion exception was reduced to the lesser of 5 percent of proceeds or $100,000, including refunding issues. The temporary-period exception was tightened. Bond yield is determined using original issue discount rules. Limited exceptions to the rebate requirements were extended to bonds issued to finance operations of small government units. Precluded higher-yielding obligations were expanded to annuity contracts and other property held for investment.

Loss of Tax-Exempt Status

If bonds lose their tax-exempt status, the Code denies a deduction for expenditures by nongovernment persons using the property financed with the no-longer-exempt bonds. Included in any disallowed deductions would be interest and the interest element of user charges. Also, 501(c)(3) organizations would realize unrelated business income.

Private Management of Government Activities

So that private management of government activities is not discouraged, the Code spells out guidelines that may be met to avoid a determination that a private person is using the property. At least 50 percent of the payments must be on a fixed-fee basis; the contract, including renewals, must not exceed five years; and the government entity must have the right to terminate the contract after three years.

Depreciation for Tax-Exempt Property

The straight-line method continues to be required for depreciating property financed with tax-exempt bonds. However, some changes have been made. The recovery period for real estate would be 40 years, but for residential rental projects it would be 27½ years. The midpoint of the accelerated depreciation range would be used for personal property—12 years for personal property with no accelerated depreciation midpoint life. Technological equipment and automobiles would be recovered over five years; solid-waste and hazardous-waste disposal facilities over eight years.

Source: "Understanding the 1986 Tax Changes," Touche Ross, Washington, D.C., 1986.

Internal Revenue Code, including IRS filing requirements, a REMIC is treated as a partnership.

Generally, an entity qualifies as a REMIC if substantially all its assets consist of qualified mortgages and permitted investments. A qualified mortgage is any obligation that is principally secured, directly or indirectly, by an interest in real property. There are three types of permitted investments: (1) investment of amounts (mortgage payments) received between distribution dates, called "cash flow investments"; (2) investments made to ensure that funds will be available to meet expenses and to pay holders of regular interests, called "qualified-reserve assets"; and (3) direct investment in property received in connection with either a foreclosure or an abandonment, called "foreclosure property." An entity meeting the specified requirements must elect to be treated as a REMIC on its first partnership information return.

In order to qualify as a REMIC, an entity must have one or more classes of "regular" interests and a single class of "residual" interest. A regular interest has fixed terms upon issuance, unconditionally entitling the holder to receive a specified amount of money. The timing of the distribution may depend on the extent of prepayments on the underlying mortgages. Interest, if any, is earned at a fixed rate on the outstanding balance. A residual interest is any interest other than a regular interest, provided there is only one class of such interest and all distributions are pro rata.

No gain or loss is recognized upon the transfer of property to a REMIC in exchange for either a regular or a residual interest. A transferor of property to the REMIC receives a substituted basis in the REMIC interest. If the substituted basis is less than the fair market value of the REMIC interest, the excess will be included in gross income as original interest discount (OID). If the substituted basis is more than the fair market value of the REMIC interest, the premium will be deducted as amortizable bond premium. The REMIC's basis in property received, however, is equal to the property's fair market value at the time of transfer.

Generally, holders of regular interests in a REMIC are placed on a mandatory accrual method of accounting for income related to their REMIC interests. Regular interests are generally treated as debt instruments for tax purposes. Holders of residual interests are taxed on the net income or loss of the REMIC, after taking into account the amounts treated as interest to the holders of regular interests. This calculation must be done quarterly. In general, the holder of a residual interest is taxed like a holder of a partnership interest. The basis of the residual interest is increased or decreased (but not below zero) by the share of the REMIC's income or loss. Distributions to holders of residual interests are not taxed until they reduce the basis to zero. Any excess is treated as gain from the sale of the interest. Special rules apply to the portion of the net income of a residual interest that exceeds the income that would have been earned by an investment equal to the adjusted issue price of the residual interest at 120 percent of the long-term federal rate. The adjusted issue price for this purpose only will be increased by the undistributed net income of the REMIC for earlier periods. This income cannot be offset by a taxpayer's net operating losses (except for certain thrifts), is subject to full statutory withholding when paid to a foreign investor, and is considered unrelated business income in the hands of a nonprofit organization. Regular and residual interests held by financial institutions are not considered unrelated business income in the hands of a nonprofit organization. Regular and residual interests held by financial institutions are not considered capital assets; thus, any gain or loss from holding such interests would be ordinary. In addition, such interests are generally treated as qualifying real property loans.[5]

SUMMARY   Tax credits that reduce a taxpayer's liability dollar for dollar are powerful incentives for effecting public policy through investment. Tax credits now exist in the tax code encouraging rehabilitation of old buildings, investment in personal property used in a trade or business, and installation of energy-saving devices in both business and residential properties.

[5]From "Tax Reform—1986," Ernst & Whinney, 1986.

Just as tax credits spur investment, deferral of taxes on disposition of real property encourages reinvestment of capital in real estate.

In this section on taxes, we focused on federal income tax as it affects the behavior of investors. As we will see in Chapter 20, tax consequences are an important component of some measures of rate of return.

IMPORTANT TERMS

Boot

Deferral of taxes on disposition

Installment sale

Investment tax credit

Low-income housing credit

Rehabilitation tax credit

REMIC

Tax credit

Tax deduction

Tax-free exchange

REVIEW QUESTIONS

19.1   An investor in the 28 percent tax bracket has a choice between a $1,000 deduction or a $1,000 tax credit. How much will each choice save the investor in taxes?

19.2   How is historic property favored over nonhistoric property in the law on rehabilitation of old buildings?

19.3   What effect would the rehabilitation tax credit have on an investor's basis in the structure?

19.4   Can you depreciate a vacation home?

19.5   Explain how taxes are deferred in an installment sale and a like-kind exchange. Which transaction receives more favorable tax treatment?

19.6   What is a REMIC?

19.7   Describe the new low-income housing credit.

19.8   What is boot?

19.9   How can a home sale be tax-free?

19.10 What is unrealized appreciation? Is it taxable?

REFERENCES   BOOKS

Arnold, Alvin C. *Special Report: Real Estate Investment After the Tax Reform Act of 1986.* Boston: Warren, Gorham, and Lamont, 1987.

Costas, Michael, and Richard D. Harroch. *Private Real Estate Syndications.* New York: Law Journal Seminars Press, 1985.

Douglas, James A., and James Stanislaw. *Real Estate Tax Digest: With Cumulative Supplements.* Boston: Warren, Gorham and Lamont, 1990.

Eustihe, James A., Joel D. Kuntz, Charles S. Lewis, III, and Thomas P. Deering. *The Tax Reform Act of 1986: Analysis and Commentary.* Boston: Warren, Gorham, and Lamont, 1987.

Federal Tax Course 1990. Englewood Cliffs, N.J.: Prentice Hall, 1990.

Kau, James B., and C. F. Sirmans. *Tax Planning for Real Estate Investors.* Englewood Cliffs, N.J.: Prentice-Hall, 1985.

Kaufman, George G., and Kenneth J. Rosen, *The Property Tax Revolt: The Case of Proposition 13.* Cambridge, Mass.: Ballinger, 1981.

Robinson, Gerald J. *Federal Income Taxation of Real Estate.* 5th ed. Boston: Warren, Gorham, and Lamont, 1988 (with supplements).

Smith, James Charles, and Allan J. Samansky. *Federal Taxation of Real Estate.* New York: Law Journal Seminars Press, 1985 (annual updates).

PERIODICALS

The Federal Tax Handbook. Englewood Cliffs, N.J.: Prentice Hall (annually).

Real Estate Accounting and Taxation. Boston: Warren, Gorham, and Lamont (quarterly).

The U.S. Master Tax Guide. New York: Commerce Clearing House (annually).

NEWSLETTERS

Monthly Tax Report. Laventhol and Horwath.

Washington Tax Wire. Laventhol and Horwath (monthly).

INVESTMENT
ANALYSIS

C H A P T E R **2 0**

$\mathcal{P}$RINCIPLES OF INVESTMENT

The next four chapters demonstrate how residual cash flow is determined, how real estate investments are evaluated, and how different players may prefer different levels of risk. In short, Chapters 20–23 are about keeping score and "winning" the real estate game; we then move on to the development section.

This chapter develops a theoretical framework for real estate investment analysis. Chapter 21 follows with a practical framework, which is flexible enough to be used in most investment decision-making situations. Chapter 22 then develops more complex portfolio theory issues; Chapter 23 illustrates how such theories have been used in institutional real estate investment.

OBJECTIVES: BENEFITS, RISKS, AND VALUE

Our goal here is to develop a methodology whereby the decision maker can evaluate the benefits associated with real estate investment. These benefits include (1) cash flow, (2) tax shelter, (3) capital gain, and (4) possibly some nonpecuniary items. The analyst must estimate *expected* benefits associated with a particular investment and then estimate the investment value based on these expectations.

Investment value represents the maximum offering price that a particular investor can justify for a particular project. The *determination of investment value* is highly dependent on the property's characteristics, the financing and tax situation, and the individual investor's institutional or personal situation. It is important to note that the appropriate investment value for a particular property can vary quite a bit. One investor may determine investment value assuming an all-cash purchase, while another investor may assume the extensive use of leverage. As a result, in the bidding process that frequently occurs in the marketplace, the leveraged investor may be willing to pay more (or less) than the all-cash

20-1 INVESTMENT ANALYSIS VERSUS APPRAISAL	Investment analysis should be clearly contrasted with appraisal methodology. Appraisal deals with the estimation of *market value* in terms of a most likely selling price, whereas investment analysis estimates what maximum offering price an *individual purchaser* can justify.

Appraisal market value is a function of the composite of all investors operating in the marketplace. Investment analysis is designed to meet the individual investment criteria of a particular investor and to assist in making specific investment decisions.

Thus, although appraisal concepts can be useful in investment analysis, the decision maker, who must reach specific investment decisions, requires more detailed and individualized techniques of analysis.

investor. A second approach in investment analysis is to measure the *rate of return* provided by a particular project, given assumptions about expected revenues, operating expenses, financing, taxes, and the holding period. Finally, whether one uses either or both of these measures, the objective of investment analysis is to select among *alternative investments*. Since many investment opportunities exist, the investor must be able to evaluate them and choose the investment that best meets the appropriate investment needs. (See Box 20-1 for a distinction between investment analysis and appraisal.)

RISK AND EXPECTED RETURN

The expected return to be received from investment constitutes the inducement to invest. The investor will look at the *riskiness* of an investment (the possibility of adverse results) as well as the *expected return* from the investment. In other words, investors must not only estimate expected returns but must also have some idea about how accurate these estimates are. The more confidence investors have about their estimates, the lower the risk. Based on the aggregate expectations of all investors about investment risk and return, the market allocates savings to investment both directly and through the financial institutions described in Part 5.

INVESTMENT GOALS AND CONSTRAINTS

WEALTH MAXIMIZATION

The major objective of most investors is to maximize wealth. However, this wealth maximization idea means different things to different investors. Some investors are concerned with maximizing current cash flow or tax shelter, or both, whereas others wish to maximize future wealth through capital gain. Still other investors carefully consider the role a particular property may play within a portfolio context. (This view is examined in Chapters 22 and 23.) As a result, certain types of investments are better suited to one particular group of investors than to another.

PECUNIARY AND NONPECUNIARY RETURNS

Note that the return on a real estate project can be pecuniary or nonpecuniary. The **pecuniary return** includes annual cash flow, tax shelter, and gains from sale.

Because real estate plays many roles in our life-style, **nonpecuniary returns** may also be realized. (See Box 20-2.) What might be termed **psychic income** includes such items as (1) self-esteem, (2) ego fulfillment, and (3) a sense of security. Nonpecuniary items are difficult to incorporate in an accounting framework, and we will not attempt to quantify them. However, they must always be in the back of the real

| 20-2 GOALS OTHER THAN WEALTH MAXIMATION | When companies invest in office buildings for their own use, nonpecuniary factors often come into play. The high prices paid for first-rate architectural advice, for example, often produce benefits more psychological than tangible. More and more companies are spending more money for architects and using more care to select them. Although some executives point to profit-related returns from this investment (increased productivity, for example), many consider architecture a way to make a statement about their companies. |

Neighboring skyscrapers built in Manhattan by two competitors—IBM and AT&T—illustrate the point. IBM's 43-story angled tower is futuristic and geometrically precise, reflecting the corporation's image of technological sophistication. AT&T's more controversial "postmodern" building is said by its architects to recall famous historical New York styles but is compared by others to a grandfather clock. AT&T, which paid an extremely high price for the building, had reasons for choosing that sort of style: One executive said, "I was looking for a building that would express to people that here is a business deeply rooted in history, with a great sense of tradition, yet as up-to-date as any of the high-technology companies."[a]

Source: John W. Verity, "The Battle of the Buildings," *Datamation,* July 20, 1982, pp. 40–42; "Architecture as a Corporate Asset," *Business Week,* October 4, 1982, pp. 124–126.
[a]Stanley W. Smith, president of AT&T's construction arm, in "Architecture," p. 126.

estate analyst's mind. All the investor's objectives must be considered to fully understand the marketplace.

INVESTMENT CONSTRAINTS

In pursuing the goal of wealth maximization, investors face a variety of constraints. Among these are (1) legal constraints, (2) cultural constraints, (3) personal constraints, (4) the investor's budget constraints, (5) the amount of risk the investor is willing to assume, and (6) the availability of investment alternatives.

- *Legal constraints* provide the formal rules of the real estate game, and investment decisions are subject to them. For example, assume that a developer feels that an apartment complex can economically and physically be located on a particular undeveloped site if appropriate zoning can be obtained. If the necessary rezoning cannot be obtained, the project will not be pursued as the result of a very real legal constraint.

- *Cultural constraints* go beyond the immediate pressures of the legal rules. For example, there are significant differences in what constitutes acceptable architectural style in different parts of the United States. A Spanish-style apartment complex may be quite appropriate in New Mexico but might be totally out of place in Boston. Architectural style is not legally dictated but may be constrained by cultural attitudes. In addition, the investor may pay, in cash flow terms, for negative externalities that a project generates. This is true even if the externalities are technically legal at the inception of the investment. Society will not tolerate certain social and environmental abuses for a long period of time.

- *Personal constraints* can include ethical constraints on the investor. As a long-run strategy, the investor may want to avoid specific projects because of personal conviction or moral beliefs. For example, although a local liquor store may prove to be an excellent investment in a financial and legal sense, an investor opposed to liquor consumption may avoid such properties. The investor may also have historical familiarity with certain property types and geographic regions; this familiarity will affect his investment decisions. Some investors stick with the kinds of properties they feel comfortable with; others branch out.

- *The investor's budget or amount of capital available for investment* is an obvious constraint. For many investors, this is often a critical factor in limiting the range of potential properties. Terminal wealth (at the end of the game) is a function of how much money the investor starts with as well as the results obtained throughout the investment peri-od. Certain investors are not able to carry negative cash flows, and this limits the "eligible" investors in some markets.

■ *The amount of risk the investor is willing to assume* will influence invest-ment decisions. This will vary from investor to investor and can have a dramatic impact on terminal wealth. Risk and expected return are positively related, so risk avoidance can have a limiting influence on potential wealth creation.

■ *Finally, the availability of investment alternatives* represents an invest-ment constraint. Even if a project is not affected by the constraints just mentioned, there is no guarantee that it will be available for purchase.

Given these constraints, the real estate investment analyst tries to deter-mine (1) investment value based on estimates of the return the project is expected to generate over the holding period and (2) the certainty of receiving the expected returns. Then the investment decision can be made by comparing investment value to the cost or purchase price of the project. If the cost or purchase price is less than or equal to the invest-ment value, the investment *should* be made. Conversely, if the cost or purchase price is *more* than the investment value, the investment should not be made.

ELEMENTS OF INVESTMENT ANALYSIS

TWO-PART RETURN

Return is typically analyzed within an accounting framework that focuses on the source and timing of cash flows. The expected residual cash flow generated by income-producing real estate comes in two parts. First are the annual cash flows to be received throughout the holding period. Second are the capital appreciation or proceeds from sale or disposition of the real estate. This second part of the return captures the change in investment value over time.

Notice that in the above paragraph we have used the term *cash* flow. The explicit assumption has been that return is *cash*. For some investors, however, return must be calculated quarterly or annually throughout the holding period. In such cases, a periodic appraised value of the property will be estimated in lieu of actual proceeds of sale. In this manner, investors calculate the two-part return using actual cash flows from operations plus unrealized (not realized from sale) capital appreciation.

For some investments, as well as for some investors, the periodic cash flows are more important, but for others the proceeds from sale may be more significant. The annual cash flows and proceeds from sale are received at different times over the holding period. Therefore, both of these expected cash flows must be discounted to the single point when the investment is being made.

THE ACCOUNTING FRAMEWORK

In an accounting framework, the two-part real estate return is analyzed based on the following elements.

- Net operating income
- Before-tax cash flow
- After-tax cash flow
- Proceeds from sale
- The time value of money and risk

The net operating income (NOI) is primarily market-determined, assuming good property management, and can be treated as an exogenous variable by the real estate investor. This means that a given project should generate a market-determined NOI, which is independent of the investor (but, of course, dependent on the quality of property management). The NOI goes first to satisfy lenders.[1] Remaining cash flow goes to the equity owner as before-tax cash flow.

Tax savings or liability is accounted for in the determination of after-tax cash flow. It is at this point that the tax shelter benefits associated with income property investment are evidenced. Current tax law as it affects the deductibility of interest and depreciation plus the investor's marginal tax rate interact to determine the after-tax cash flow. For tax-exempt investors like pension plans, the after-tax cash flow is the same as the before-tax cash flow; that is, tax savings or liabilities are zero.

The investment benefits of long-term capital appreciation are also included within the accounting framework. The value of a property at the end of the holding period must be estimated. After-tax proceeds from sale frequently have a significant impact on investment value. In fact, an investment's annual before-tax cash flows received during the holding period frequently contribute very little to the total return, which is often largely a function of tax shelter and appreciation.

THE TIME VALUE OF MONEY

The investor is concerned not only with the size of the expected cash flows but also with their timing. Recall from Part 5 that discounting

---

[1] *Frequently mentioned here is the prior claim of government, represented by the property tax. In our investment analysis this tax is considered an operating expense, and so its payment is reflected in the net operating income figure.*

(present value) is simply the inverse of the compound interest formula and can be used to value future cash flows. Since all the benefits associated with investment in real estate are received over time (i.e., throughout the holding period), the application of the concept of the time value of money is extremely important in investment analysis.

Cash flows of an identical size translate into lower current investment values if they are to be received further into the future. The worth of future cash flows depends not only on *when* they will be received, but also on the *risk* that they will not be received at all. This risk is expressed along with the time value of money in the discount rate. Value and the discount rate are inversely related.

In essence, the process of discounting allows the analyst to reduce all anticipated cash flows to a single point so that an investment decision can be made. This single-point estimate of the value of the expected cash flows incorporates the *time value of money* and *riskiness* in the investment analysis.

TYPES OF RISK

Risk is the possibility of suffering adverse consequences resulting from an investment. (Here we will focus on project- or property-level risk, whereas in Chapters 22 and 23 we will introduce portfolio-level risk.) In this context, there are several types of risk.

- Business and market risk
- Financial risk
- Purchasing power risk
- Liquidity risk

BUSINESS RISK

Business risk reflects the possible unsuccessful operation of the particular project. Business risk is determined by (1) the type of project, (2) its management, and (3) the particular market in which it is located. All these affect the expected operating cash flows from the project.

The possibility that these cash flows will not be sufficient to justify the investment represents the degree of business risk associated with the investment. A regional shopping center fully rented under long-term net leases to triple-A tenants has a lower business risk than a raw land investment that anticipates construction of a motel sometime in the future.

From a practical real estate point of view, business risk is centered in two major areas. The first is *management*. Fixing and collecting rents, properly maintaining and repairing the structure, and controlling operating expenses are major variables in the management area. *Market changes* represent the second area involving business risk. New competition, changes in local demographic characteristics, new roads bypassing a project, and new employers entering the market all affect the business risk associated with a particular project.

FINANCIAL RISK

Financial risk reflects uncertainty about the residual equity return as the result of the use of leverage. The use of debt to finance a property (leverage) can increase the variability of the return to equity. Put another way, financial risk is the potential inability of the project's NOI to cover the required debt service. Such an event is more likely to occur when a high proportion of the purchase price is financed with debt. The less debt that is used in the capital structure, the lower the financial risk.

The fact that lenders offer a variety of variable rate mortgages can also affect financial risk. If market interest rates rise, the debt service associated with many nonfixed-rate mortgages will also rise. As the debt service rises, NOI may not be sufficient to cover the increase. Hence, projects financed with nonfixed-rate mortgages may expose the borrower to greater financial risk.

PURCHASING POWER RISK

Purchasing power risk reflects the fact that inflation may cause the investor to be paid back with less valuable dollars. The expectation of inflation is incorporated in the discount rate, but future rates of inflation may be underestimated. The possibility of higher inflation than was incorporated in the discount rate is the purchasing power risk associated with the investment. Depending on their other investments, some investors may be more worried about purchasing power risk than others. Retired persons with all their wealth in one asset would quite obviously be very concerned about purchasing power risk. This type of risk varies dramatically from project to project. A warehouse leased to IBM at a fixed rate for 20 years is much more susceptible to purchasing power risk than a hotel, which can change its rates daily should there be unexpected inflation.

LIQUIDITY RISK

Liquidity risk relates to the conversion of the investment to cash at some future date. Ideally, an investor wants to be able to sell quickly and without substantially discounting the price below fair market value. The liquidity risk associated with a particular investment is the risk that a quick sale will not be possible or that a significant price reduction will be required to achieve a quick sale.

Real estate is generally considered an **illiquid asset,** not easily convertible to cash without sacrificing price. Consequently, liquidity risk tends to be high for real estate investments.

This liquidity risk leads to a need for balance in the investor's portfolio. For example, the investor should include in the portfolio highly liquid assets, such as government bonds.

EVALUATING RISK

RISK AS VARIANCE

The four types of risk just mentioned can be collectively measured and quantified by estimating the *variance* of the expected equity cash flow. **Variance** measures the dispersion of the expected return around the mean expected return. The variance is an estimate of the possible deviations of the actual return from the expected return. The more variance the investor expects in the equity portion of the return generated by the property, the greater the risk associated with receiving that cash flow.

Many times, investors will estimate the cash flow under varying circumstances in order to analyze the sensitivity of the project's rate of return to changes in rental receipts, vacancy, and operating expenses. **Sensitivity analysis** is an appealing method for estimating risk in the real estate field, for changes frequently occur in many of the elements that affect cash flow.

RISK OF RUIN

Although *variance* is the classic finance definition of risk, in many cases an alternative definition more accurately characterizes the perspective of the investor. This alternative definition is the **risk of ruin.** This is the probability that the expected returns will be less than a minimal acceptable level. For some investors, this might be a return of less than 5 percent; for others, the risk of ruin could be the risk of bankruptcy or the risk of experiencing a negative cash flow. The variance and risk of ruin definitions are similar when expected future returns can be characterized by a normal distribution,[2] that is, when upside and downside fluctuations in returns are equally likely.

---

[2]*The normal distribution is a perfectly symmetric distribution. For an example, note the following:*

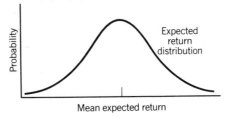

In investment analysis, risk is incorporated in the discount rate used as an estimate of the required rate of return.[3] As will be shown in the next section, the required rate of return involves (1) a real return, (2) an inflation premium, and (3) a risk premium. Unlike the appraisal methodology, no recapture premium is necessary because in investment analysis an indefinitely long or continual return is not assumed, as it is in the appraisal formula $V = NOI/R$.

In investment analysis, a holding period and disposition assumption are made and incorporated into the discounted cash flow analysis. In effect, what is considered is a two-part return.

Positive Correlation Between Risk and Return

Risk and return are thought to be positively correlated. Harry M. Markowitz, the father of modern portfolio theory, stated that the investor seeks to maximize return for given levels of risk or minimize risk for given levels of return. The logic here can be very appealing. The investor expects more compensation if there is a greater chance of adverse financial consequences—that is, the investor wants more return if there is more risk. Investors, in other words, are **risk-averse.**

Even with no risk, however, the investor requires a certain minimum return. This minimum return represents the real return and inflation premium portion of the required rate of return. Government bonds are generally considered to be risk-free[4] and are used as an indication of the return required when there is no risk associated with the receipt of expected cash flows. Beyond this risk-free rate, risk and return are positively correlated. (See Figure 20-1.) If the required rate of return is increased from B to B', the investor must also assume an increase in risk from C to C'.

Risk Aversion

The concept of **risk aversion** is usually proved by using the concept of the *diminishing marginal utility of money.* This implies that, for equal increments in wealth, an investor's utility increases by a smaller amount for each increase. Consider the situation of an investor who has a risky and a riskless alternative; the riskless alternative might be preferred even though a greater return is possible if the risky alternative is chosen.

[3]*An alternative capital market theory, the state preference theory, adjusts the expected cash flows to their certainty equivalent and discounts at a risk-free rate. Although the state preference theory is an appealing idea, utilizing it is not often practical in real-world real estate investment analysis; it would require the investor to make an estimate of the certainty tradeoff in every future period.*

[4]*We mean free of all risk except purchasing power risk (i.e., a misestimate of future inflation).*

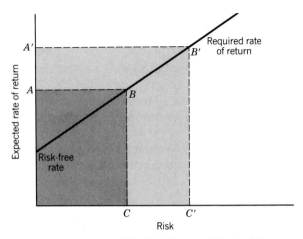

F I G U R E 20-1   *The Risk-Return Relationship*

Assume a riskless government bond paying a certain 8 percent and a riskier apartment house offering equal likelihood (50–50) of either a 10 or a 6 percent return. Both investments have the same expected return of 8 percent, but the risk-averse investor will not be indifferent. The apartment house has a 50 percent chance of returning 2 percent more, and a 50 percent chance of returning 2 percent less, than the expected return. Given the diminishing marginal utility of money, the 2 percent above the expected return of 8 percent is worth less in terms of utility than the 2 percent below the expected return. Therefore, although the outcomes are equally likely, the investor suffers more from the possible loss than he benefits from the possible gain and would prefer the riskless alternative. (See Figure 20-2.)

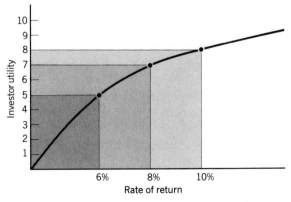

F I G U R E 20-2   *Diminishing Marginal Utility*

REQUIRED RATE OF RETURN

Given all of the risk factors discussed, how does the analyst arrive at the investor's **required rate of return** or the discount rate? There is no perfect methodology, but the following process will allow the analyst to derive a meaningful required rate of return.

❑ **REAL RETURN**   First, the analyst must estimate the required **real return**—that is, the premium the investor wants for deferred consumption. This figure can be estimated from historical data by comparing rates of return on government securities with rates of inflation over long periods of time. Various researchers have put this number at between 2 and 3 percent.

❑ **INFLATION PREMIUM.**   An estimate of the expected rate of inflation over the holding period is then made by subtracting the real return from the current yield on government bonds. If the investor expects to hold an asset for 10 years, she can look at the yield on 10-year government bonds (which are assumed to be free of any risks other than risks associated with inflation) and estimate the market's expectations regarding inflation. The current total bond yield less the 2 to 3 percent real return is a composite of investors' expectations about inflation over a 10-year period and represents the **inflation premium.**

❑ **RISK PREMIUM.**   The risk premium can be estimated by considering an *average risk premium* and an *adjusted risk premium*. The average **risk premium** can be established by looking at the difference between the returns over long periods of time on common stock and the returns on risk-free government securities over the same period of time. A number of studies have put this difference at 4 to 8 percent. (See Box 20-3.)

The average risk premium must then be adjusted for the relative riskiness of the particular project. This adjustment is subjective but can be realistically estimated by an analyst who knows the property, the local market, the financial leverage, and the type of investment vehicle to be used as well as the liquidity needs and personal considerations of the investor. It is possible to make meaningful adjustments to the average risk premium and develop a risk premium appropriate for the particular investment.[5]

The investor's required rate of return or discount rate is simply the sum of the real return, inflation premium, and the risk premium. Note that since the risk premium for different investments will vary, one would expect an investor's required rate of return to vary for different

---

[5]*Once again these factors are (1) business risk, (2) market risk, (3) financial risk, (4) liquidity risk, (5) rule change risk, (6) purchasing power risk, and (7) portfolio risk. The subject investment is evaluated relative to an average risk investment on each of these dimensions to determine its relative risk.*

20-3
**INVESTOR RISK
PREMIUMS**

Two individual investors can evaluate the same real estate investment opportunity and assign different risk premiums in calculating their separate required rates of return. For example, an investment opportunity involved a fourplex in a middle-class neighborhood. The asking price was $180,000. An existing first mortgage could be assumed, and the seller would carry a second mortgage if an investor was willing to put $20,000 down. Each of the units was currently being rented for $425 per month, $1,700 per month total gross rent, and monthly operating expenses amounted to $100 per unit. The financing offered by the seller would require a total of $1,740 per month for principal, interest, taxes, and insurance. Assuming 100 percent occupancy, this would result in a $5,280 negative annual before-tax cash flow.

The first investor was a prominent real estate attorney who owned several other properties in the area. Since the other properties generated a substantial before-tax cash flow, the attorney did not feel the negative cash flow unduly increased the risk of the fourplex. However, the second investor had recently graduated from college and was considering the fourplex as a first investment. The college graduate would have a hard time coming up with the downpayment and feared the impact of a possible vacancy on cash flow. Consequently, the business risk seemed high to the second investor.

As a result of the investors' differing financial and business backgrounds, the risk they perceived to be associated with the fourplex varied. The attorney had a lower required rate of return than the college graduate. When tax benefits and capital appreciation were considered, the expected return from the fourplex *exceeded* the attorney's required rate of return. The college graduate's required rate of return was *higher* than the expected return. The attorney made the investment, but the college graduate did not.

investments. In addition, it would be reasonable to expect different investors to have different risk premiums for the *same* real estate investment. (This second difference is explained more fully in Chapter 22 on portfolio theory.)

USING THE REQUIRED RATE OF RETURN

The concept of a required rate of return is used extensively in real estate investment decision making as will be demonstrated in Chapter 21. As a *minimum* required rate of return, the concept can be used for establishing an investor's **hurdle rate of return.** This is a minimum level of performance concept. That is, if an investment is expected to return the hurdle rate or more, the decision rule will be to invest. Conversely, if the expected rate of return is less than the hurdle rate, the investment will not be made.

As a discount rate, the required rate of return is used to discount expected future cash flows to a present value. Consequently, the concept of a required rate of return will be used extensively in developing the discounted cash flow model in Chapter 21.

SUMMARY   Investment analysis seeks to determine value to the individual investor. Value is a function of the expected returns from a project and the risks associated with those expected returns. A useful methodology in arriving at investment value is the discounted after-tax cash flow technique. In this technique, all the different aspects of risk, as well as the time value of money, are incorporated in the discount rate.

Be careful when using the technique. Anyone can be taught to do the mechanics (i.e., to go through the accounting framework, deduct prior claims, arrive at residual cash flows, and discount these cash flows to a present value). The key in investment analysis is knowledge of the project and the market. Long-run success requires profitable operations, and dependable estimates of operations can only be made by an analyst who has a clear understanding of the marketplace.

IMPORTANT TERMS

Business risk	Real return
Financial risk	Required rate of return
Hurdle rate of return	Risk
Illiquid asset	Risk-averse
Inflation premium	Risk aversion
Liquidity risk	Risk of ruin
Nonpecuniary return	Risk premium
Pecuniary return	Sensitivity analysis
Psychic income	Variance
Purchasing power risk	

REVIEW QUESTIONS

20-1   Outline the major differences between appraisal and investment analysis.

20-2   How would each of the major investment constraints mentioned in the text affect your personal investment in real estate?

20-3   Why is it justified to think of the real estate return as a two-part return?

20-4   How does the time value of money relate to the concept of a two-part return?

20-5   Compare and contrast the concepts of risk as variance and risk as risk of ruin.

20-6   Distinguish between the average risk premium and an adjusted risk premium.

20-7   Why is it reasonable to suggest that risk and return are positively correlated?

20-8   How should nonpecuniary returns or psychic income be incorporated into real estate investment analysis?

20-9   How might it be possible for two investors analyzing the same investment property to derive different discount rates?

20-10   How can the concept of a hurdle rate of return be used by an individual investor?

$\mathcal{T}$HE DISCOUNTED CASH-FLOW MODEL

The purpose of the **discounted cash flow (DCF) model** is to bring together, in an analysis, all the factors that affect the return from a real estate investment. All cash flows are reduced to a single figure, the *present value*. These cash flows include all **cash inflows,** such as rents and proceeds of sale, and all **cash outflows** such as operating expenses, taxes, and debt service. The present value figure represents the value today of the residual equity claim to future cash flows adjusted for both the time value of money and the risk associated with the expected cash flows. The net present value (NPV) is the difference between the present value of the expected inflows and the cost of the project. If the NPV is positive, the investment meets the investor's requirements.

All the cash flows that are used in the DCF model must be estimated from data collected in the marketplace. Estimating the inputs for the model becomes the most difficult portion of investment analysis once the mechanics of the DCF model are mastered. The more accurate the input estimates, the more reliable the DCF model becomes as an aid to decision making. The computer science axiom of "garbage in—garbage out" holds true in the case of DCF real estate investment analysis; the model is only as useful as the accuracy of the input variables allows it to be. Estimates of operating cash flows reflect the analyst's knowledge of existing market conditions and trends and are crucial to successful analysis.

Beyond the operating cash flows, the straightforward accounting framework developed in Chapter 20 takes into account the prior claims of the lender (debt service) and the government (income tax liability, if any) in calculating the after-tax residual cash flow. The real estate analyst must also consider the investor's marginal tax rate, his after-tax required rate of return or discount rate, the expected investment horizon or holding period, and the expected sales price at the end of the holding period.

The investor's marginal tax rate will reflect income earned from other sources as well as the taxable income or loss from the property. The discount rate to be used in turning the expected future cash flows into a present value, discussed in Chapter 20, incorporates a real return, an inflation premium, and risk. The investment horizon or anticipated holding period may be affected by tax planning considerations,[1] market trends, and other factors.

The model presented in this chapter puts all these items together and allows the analyst to look at a complex problem in a logical way. The purpose of the DCF model, then, is to estimate the present value of a particular real estate investment. The estimated present value will then be compared to project cost or purchase price to determine the acceptability of the investment for a *particular* investor.

Obviously, the computer can greatly facilitate the use of the DCF model. In the early 1970s, Steve Pyhrr led a series of academics and practioners in setting up FORTRAN-based mainframe versions of this basic model. In the early 1980s, the low-cost microcomputer made the technology available to a much wider audience. Improved software provided user friendly programs with many neat "bells and whistles" such as RealVAL, created by Jeff Fisher. These micromodels allow the real estate analyst to apply quickly and inexpensively the logic that is developed in this chapter. In the 1990s, increasingly powerful hand-held and laptop computers will allow easy use of DCF analysis in investment decision making. However, the technology may lull some analysts into paying more attention to the process than to developing carefully and thoughtfully the inputs the model requires. So an important caveat is in order. The use of technology should free up more time for the analyst to conduct the important fieldwork necessary to collect accurate forecasts of expected rents, operating expenses, and so on.

THE BASIC DISCOUNTED CASH FLOW MODEL

The preceding chapters should have given you an idea of the skills necessary to derive appropriate data from the marketplace for use in the DCF model. In this chapter, we go through the accounting mechanics and review the sources of information for all the variables incorporated in the model. Although we use as an example a new apartment property, the DCF framework, from both a practical accounting and a theoretical perspective, can be applied to any property.

We will take you through the accounting framework first: gross potential income, less vacancy and collection loss, equals effective gross income, less operating expenses, less major repairs and replacements, equals net operating income. From there we go on to before- and after-tax cash flows, estimated cash proceeds from sale, net present value and

---

[1]*When the debt is amortized, the tax shelter deteriorates over time.*

the investment decision, internal rate of return, and financial ratio and multiplier analysis.

GROSS POTENTIAL INCOME

The starting point of the DCF model is **gross potential income** (GPI). This is the income that is possible if all the space is leased at the projected rent level plus any income from other sources, such as vending income. GPI is estimated by considering the rent received on comparable properties as well as the historic rent, if any, received on the subject property. Furthermore, if the analyst uses the regional and urban economic techniques discussed in part 1, trends may be discovered that help the analyst project potential income over time. The DCF model allows the analyst to project different rent levels at different points in time, thus offering a refinement over the simple $V = NOI/R$ formula presented in Part 3.

Estimates of future rent levels can be presented on an actual (dollar) basis or relative (percentage change) basis. Often the analyst assumes an average rate of rent increase (or decrease) over the investment horizon. When the percentage method is used, the analyst must be careful not to overestimate the rate of increase by failing to realize that the increase will be compounded over time. As a general rule, most would agree that the initial estimates of income (and expenses) should represent the "most likely" outlook. In any event, the analyst must not only estimate revenues but also develop a feeling for the accuracy of the estimate for use in calculating the risk premium incorporated in the discount rate. In attempting to evaluate the risk inherent in the revenue estimate, we often find it useful to look also at a best- and worst-case scenario. After we have fully developed our most likely scenario using the DCF model, we then consider such **sensitivity analyses.**

VACANCY AND COLLECTION LOSS

From the gross potential income figure, the **vacancy allowance and collection loss** estimate is deducted. The vacancy allowance is, again, a function of the property's history, comparables, and market trends. It represents an average vacancy rate for the project being analyzed and in our example is expressed as a percentage of the GPI. In the case of existing multitenant commercial properties, for example, office, retail, or industrial properties, existing lease terms will be explicitly considered. The lease rollover structure will have a significant impact on the analyst's ultimate estimate of the property's present value. In addition, the phenomenon of "free rent" must be considered. Free rent, the ultimate real estate oxymoron, has become commonplace in many overbuilt markets. It occurs when tenants receive a portion of the lease term rent free. For purposes of DCF analysis, the recognition of free rent should occur when provided, that is, on a cash basis. For example, if the free rent is provided up front and no actual rent is collected during the early term of the lease, it should be so reflected in the DCF analysis. The term *net effective income* defines the remaining cash rent collected after "free rent" has been considered.

The vacancy rate is directly related to the property's life cycle. A new property often experiences a relatively high vacancy rate during the rent-up period, then may have few vacancies during its prime, followed by increasing vacancies as it ages. Vacancy is also related to rent levels. It is often possible to trade off rent increases with occupancy levels. Collection losses (i.e., rents due but unpaid) vary from insignificant on some properties to a major item on others, particularly apartment buildings in declining areas. Gross potential income reduced by a vacancy allowance and collection loss allowance equals realized revenues or **effective gross income** (EGI).

Note that the estimate of vacancy and collection losses represents an anticipated average rate for the property being analyzed rather than a current experience. Even if the project is currently 100 percent occupied, a vacancy and collection loss rate should be included against some of the future GPI, for sooner or later (and probably sooner), the investor will experience some actual vacancy and credit losses.

OPERATING EXPENSES

Operating expenses include property management fees, payroll, repairs and maintenance, utilities, security, advertising and promotion, property taxes, and insurance premiums. In practice, each of these expenses would be estimated separately. The DCF example presented here, for convenience of presentation, lumps them together as a percentage of gross possible income. Estimates for each of these items will be based on the operating history of the property, comparables and future trends.

Inflation will affect both operating costs and revenues.[2] However, age will also increase operating expenses. As properties become older, they tend to require more maintenance. Conversely, as a property ages and has higher functional obsolescence, revenues are adversely affected. So although both age and inflation work to increase operating expenses, only inflation increases revenues. The age factor works in the opposite direction. Consequently, it is generally true that operating expenses tend to rise at a more rapid *rate* than revenues over the holding period.

---

[2]*Property subject to long-term leases may have fixed income (because of flat rentals), fixed expenses (because increases are passed through to tenants), or both. Naturally, the analysis should reflect these provisions.*

Property taxes and insurance premiums must also be deducted from gross effective income. In the case of property taxes, current year's taxes are the starting point, but future increases normally can be anticipated, the extent depending on the financial condition of the municipality. Insurance premiums for fire, casualty, and liability coverages should be included.

MAJOR REPAIRS AND REPLACEMENTS

Also to be deducted from gross effective income is the cost of major repairs and replacements anticipated over the holding period. These might include a new roof, new electrical, heating or plumbing systems, or replacement of appliances in an apartment building. Rather than incorporate an average figure each year for these items (as was done in the "stabilized income" concept presented in Chapter 8), the DCF model charges off each individual expenditure in the year for which it is projected. In this way, the time value of money is more accurately reflected.

NET OPERATING INCOME

Realized revenues less operating expenses and major repair items equal NOI, as shown in Table 21-1.[3]

A DISCOUNTED CASH FLOW EXAMPLE

The following real estate investment analysis focuses on a new apartment building where the factors of increasing rentals, leverage, depreciation, investor tax considerations, and price appreciation all have an important bearing on the property's total investment value and rate of return. The property analysis incorporates the following assumptions.

- First-year GPI of $30,000 increases by 3 percent annually (compounded). The building has five units, each with 750 square feet and renting for $500 per month.

- The vacancy and collection loss allowance is 5 percent of GPI.

- Total operating expenses are 40 percent of GPI during the first year of operations, or $12,000. (Each component of operating expenses was analyzed separately to obtain the 40 percent collective figure.)

---

[3] *A standard appraisal would typically end the income analysis at this point, for what follows would not be of concern to the appraiser using the income method in estimating market value. It should be pointed out, however, that many appraisers will use after-financing and after-tax discounted cash flow as a check on their work.*

Thereafter, expenses increase at a rate of 5 percent per year (compounded). This includes property taxes and insurance premiums. No major repairs are anticipated over the next five years.

- The total cost of the project is $160,000. Land is valued at $24,000 and the improvements at $136,000. Since there are 3,750 square feet in the building (750 square feet/unit times 5 units), the square foot cost of the property is $42.66.

- Mortgage debt of $120,000 is available at 12 percent interest, self-liquidating over 25 years. This results in a mortgage constant of approximately 12.75 percent and annual debt service of $15,300.[4]

- The improvements will be depreciated using the straight-line method over 27.5 years.

- Based on an extensive urban land economic analysis, the project value is expected to grow at 4 percent per year (based on the original cost of the project).

- The investor's marginal income is taxed at 28 percent. (See Table 18-1 for the 1986 Internal Revenue Code Provisions for 1990 and the phaseout of personal exemptions for high-income individuals.)

- An annual after-tax return on equity investment of 15 percent is sought over the entire holding period.

- The investor expects to hold the property five years. A $6,000 provision is made for a selling commission and other expenses when the property is sold.

TABLE 21-1   CALCULATION OF NET OPERATING INCOME

	YEAR 1	YEAR 2	YEAR 3	YEAR 4	YEAR 5
A. Gross potential income	$30,000	$30,900	$31,827	$32,782	$33,765
B. Less: vacancy and collection allowance	(1,500)	(1,545)	(1,591)	(1,639)	(1,688)
C. Effective gross income	$28,500	$29,355	$30,236	$31,143	$32,077
D. Less: operating expense	(12,000)	(12,600)	(13,230)	(13,892)	(14,587)
E. Major repairs and replacements	-0-	-0-	-0-	-0-	-0-
F. Net operating income (NOI)	$16,500	$16,755	$17,006	$17,251	$17,490

[4]*The monthly constant, assuming monthly payments in arrears (i.e., paid at the end of each month), is 12.64 percent.*

DEBT SERVICE

NOI is the amount of EGI remaining after deduction of operating expenses and cost of major repairs and replacements. The first claim on this cash is for debt service, which includes payment for interest on the outstanding loan plus an amount for debt reduction (amortization).

As explained in Chapter 15, the debt-service constant is the percentage of the original loan amount required to (1) pay periodic interest on the outstanding loan balance and (2) amortize the loan over its term. The constant can be found quickly by the use of loan amortization tables. As shown in Table 21-2, the portion of each year's constant payment allocable to interest and principal payments is easily calculated once the annual debt-service constant is known. Table 21-2 shows clearly how the interest portion of the debt service *declines* each period, for current interest is based on the outstanding loan balance (not the original principal). Since the total debt service remains constant, the principal repayment (amortization) rises by the same amount as the interest declines. This example assumes a fully amortized mortgage. If a partially amortized or balloon mortgage were being considered, simply adjust the presentation in Table 21-2 to reflect the actual financing.

DEPRECIATION

The annual depreciation schedule for the example is presented in Table 21-3. Since the example property is residential, straight-line depreciation was taken over 27.5 years per the Internal Revenue Code Provisions for 1990. For nonresidential properties, straight-line depreciation may be taken over 31.5 years. As pointed out in Chapter 18, the passivity rules require that investors carefully estimate both passive losses and passive

TABLE 21-2   CALCULATION OF DEBT SERVICE

	YEAR 1	YEAR 2	YEAR 3	YEAR 4	YEAR 5
Mortgage amount	$120,000	$119,100	$118,092	$116,963	$115,698
Interest rate	0.12	0.12	0.12	0.12	0.12
Interest payment	14,400	14,292	14,171	14,035	13,884
Principal payment	900	1,008	1,129	1,265	1,416
Debt service (12.75% constant)[a]	$ 15,300	$ 15,300	$ 15,300	$ 15,300	$ 15,300

Note: *The loan balance at the end of year 5 is ($115,698 − $1416 = $114,282.*
[a] *See Tables p. A-14, column 6.*

TABLE 21-3   CALCULATION OF DEPRECIATION

	YEAR 1	YEAR 2	YEAR 3	YEAR 4	YEAR 5
Depreciable basis	$136,000	$136,000	$136,000	$136,000	$136,000
Depreciation rate	0.0364	0.0364	0.0364	0.0364	0.0364
Annual depreciation	$4950	$4,950	$4,950	$4,950	$4,950

Notes: 1. *The initial depreciable basis is $136,000 (cost of improvements). The 27.5 year straight-line method shown above assumes that the property was purchased in January of the taxable year.*
2. *The accrued depreciation taken after 5 years is $24,750.*

gains. In general, investors are now more interested in investments that generate sufficient passive income to utilize passive losses.

TAXABLE INCOME OR LOSS

Figuring the claim of government in the form of income taxes follows the determination of interest and depreciation expense. NOI less interest and depreciation equals taxable income or loss. Multiplying the taxable income by the investor's *marginal* tax rate gives the annual tax liability associated with the particular investment. The marginal tax rate should be used, and not the average tax rate, for all investment decisions are made at the margin. A tax loss will arise as in our example if the interest and depreciation expense exceeds the net operating income, as shown in Table 21-4.

In the event that the property shows a tax loss, the investor will receive certain benefits from that loss. By offsetting the loss against other passive income, the investor will *shelter income*. Aggregate taxable income will be reduced, and, consequently, the overall tax liability will be less.

TABLE 21-4   TAXABLE INCOME (A CONTINUATION OF TABLE 21.1)

	YEAR 1	YEAR 2	YEAR 3	YEAR 4	YEAR 5
F. NOI	$16,500	$16,755	$17,006	$17,251	$17,490
G. Less: depreciation	(4,950)	(4,950)	(4,950)	(4,950)	(4,950)
H. Less: interest	(14,400)	(14,292)	(14,171)	(14,035)	(13,884)
I. Taxable income (loss)	($2,850)	($2,487)	($2,115)	($1,734)	($1,344)

Note: *Taxable loss declines each year as a result of two factors: rising NOI and declining interest expense.*

The extent of the tax benefit or *tax savings* from any particular loss may be calculated by multiplying the taxable loss times the marginal tax rate as shown on line N of Table 21-5. Therefore, if the taxable loss figure and the marginal tax rate are used, either the tax due or the tax shelter may be calculated. However, the passive-loss rules detailed in Chapter 18 must be examined to make certain that the investor can in fact use passive losses.

BEFORE-TAX CASH FLOW

Depreciation deductions (reflected in taxable income or loss) do not represent an actual cash expense; they are merely a bookkeeping entry. Therefore, they must be added back to the taxable income or loss in order to reflect accurately the before-tax cash flow. On the other hand, principal repayment is not a tax-deductible item (and so is not reflected in the taxable income or loss) but is an actual out-of-pocket cash expense. Therefore, such repayments must be reflected in before-tax income or loss. These calculations are presented in lines J and K of Table 21-5, respectively, with line L showing the before-tax cash flow.

AFTER-TAX EQUITY CASH FLOW

The **equity cash flow after tax** is determined by simply deducting any tax liability or adding any tax savings as in M and N of Table 21-5. In our example, the project is not expected to generate a tax liability during the investment horizon. This means that all the NOI is sheltered. Tax savings are an important feature in our example. Not only does the investor

TABLE 21-5   EQUITY CASH FLOW AFTER TAX (A CONTINUATION OF TABLE 21.4)

	YEAR 1	YEAR 2	YEAR 3	YEAR 4	YEAR 5
I. Taxable income (loss)	($2,850)	($2,487)	($2,115)	($1,734)	($1,344)
J. Plus: depreciation	4,950	4,950	4,950	4,950	4,950
K. Less: principal repaid	(900)	(1,008)	(1,129)	(1,265)	(1,416)
L. Before-tax cash flow	$1,200	$1,455	$1,706	$1,951	$2,190
M. Less: taxes	0	0	0	0	0
N. Plus: tax savings (28% × line I above)	798	696	592	485	376
O. Equity cash flow after tax	$1,998	$2,151	$2,298	$2,436	$2,566

shelter all the income generated by the investment, but passive income earned from other sources is also sheltered. This reduction in aggregate tax liability can be attributed to this investment because without the investment the investor's taxes would be higher by the amount of the tax savings. As a result, the tax savings are added to the before-tax cash flow to yield the equity cash flow after tax, as shown on lines N and O of Table 21-5.

PRESENT VALUE OF AFTER-TAX CASH FLOW

The cash flow to equity calculated earlier represents the first part of the two-part return to equity: the periodic cash flow from operations. These cash flows can be reduced to their present value by using the present value formula:

$$PV = \sum_{n=1}^{N} \frac{CF_n}{(1 + r)^n}$$

If the Compound Interest Tables at the end of this book are used, a present value factor is often easier to work with than the multiplication and division required in the formula. Multiplying the present value factor (associated with the investor's expected after-tax return on equity) by the individual cash flows and summing the product give the present value of the after-tax cash flows to equity for the assumed holding period. Table 21-6 indicates that the total present value of the equity cash flow after tax in our example is $7,541. Obviously, most analysts will use hand calculators or personal computers, thereby eliminating the need to use the tables. As a learning device, we suggest that you use the tables first, then learn to push the buttons.

TABLE 21-6   PRESENT VALUE OF THE EQUITY CASH FLOW AFTER TAX (A CONTINUATION OF TABLE 21.5)

	YEAR 1	YEAR 2	YEAR 3	YEAR 4	YEAR 5
O. Equity cash flow after tax	$1,998	$2,151	$2,298	$2,436	$2,565
Present value factor @ 15%	0.8696	0.7561	0.6575	0.5718	0.4972
P. Present value of equity cash flow after tax[a]	$1,737	$1,626	$1,510	$1,393	$1,275

[a] Total present value of equity cash flow after tax for five years is $7541.

SALES PRICE

The second part of the two-part return on real estate investment requires an assumption about a sale or disposition. Without any better information, it is often reasonable to assume that a future buyer will be willing to pay the same amount per dollar of income generated by the project as the current investor is willing to pay; in other words, that the capitalization rate or the multiplier (see the discussion of the income approach to value in Part 3) will be the same on disposition as on purchase. From the sales price assumption, commissions and closing costs are deducted.

In the example, it was assumed that the market value of the property would increase by 4 percent per year, compounded annually, over the holding period. As shown in Table 21-7, the market value of the project is estimated to be $194,700 at the end of the fifth year. It was further assumed that selling commission, closing costs, or loan prepayment penalties would be $6,000. These are simplifying assumptions; clearly, some marketing costs are incurred in most real estate transactions, and they would directly reduce the proceeds of the sale.

INCOME TAX ON GAIN FROM SALE

Any realized gain on sale of the property is subject to a government claim for income tax. The gain on sale is the sales price (net of commissions and closing costs) less the seller's tax basis. The **tax basis** is the original cost plus capital expenditures during ownership (none in our example) less depreciation taken.

For our example, the calculation of realized gain is shown in Table 21-8, and the tax due on the sale is shown in Table 21-9. In Table 21-8, the total capital gain is calculated by first determining the remaining

---

TABLE 21-7 SALES PRICE

	YEAR 1	YEAR 2	YEAR 3	YEAR 4	YEAR 5
Market value (4% compound growth)	$166,400	$173,056	$179,978	$187,177	$194,700[a]

Note: *Assume that commissions, closing costs, and so on, total $6000.*
[a] *Rounded from $194,664. Sales price projections are typically in round figures.*

TABLE 21-8 CALCULATION OF GAIN ON SALE	
A. Tax basis	
Cost	$160,000
Depreciation taken (Table 21.3)	(24,750)
Remaining tax basis	$135,250
B. Sales price (Table 21.7)	$194,700
Less selling expenses	(6,000)
Adjusted sales price	$188,700
C. Taxable gain	
Adjusted sales price	$188,700
Less: remaining tax basis	(135,250)
Total taxable gain	$53,450

basis. The remaining basis is the difference between the original cost of the project ($160,000) and the depreciation taken during the holding period ($24,750). The resulting remaining basis ($135,250) is then deducted from the adjusted sales price ($188,700) to yield the **total taxable gain** of $53,450.

Once the total gain has been determined, the tax due on the sale can be calculated as in Table 21-9. The total tax on sale is calculated by multiplying the taxable gain by the appropriate tax rate, which results in a total tax on sale liability of $14,966 for our example.

CASH PROCEEDS FROM SALE

The total tax liability and the loan repayment are then subtracted from the net sales price (after commissions and closing costs) to obtain the cash

TABLE 21-9 CALCULATION OF TAX ON SALE	
A. Total taxable gain (Table 21.8)	$53,450
B. Total tax on sale	
(line A × 28%)	$14,966

proceeds from the sale. This figure is discounted to its present value by the same method used to discount the annual cash flows. Table 21-10 shows the present value of the proceeds from sale for our example. The total tax liability ($14,966) and the loan repayment ($114,282) are subtracted from the adjusted sales price ($188,700) to yield the net cash to equity from sale ($59,452). Since this figure will not be received until the end of the holding period, it must be discounted to determine its present value. Therefore, the figure is multiplied by the present value factor at 15 percent (our investor's required after-tax return on equity investment) to yield the present value of the proceeds from sale ($29,559).

NET PRESENT VALUE AND THE INVESTMENT DECISION

The total present value of the equity is the sum of the total present value of the after-tax equity cash flows and the present value of proceeds from sale. If this total present value exceeds the equity cost of the investment, then the **net present value** is said to be *positive,* and the investment decision is to invest.

In our example, the total present value of equity ($37,100) is less than the cost of equity ($40,000), resulting in a negative net present value (Table 21-11). Consequently, the decision would be not to invest. From a practical point of view, the results of the DCF model indicate that the investment does not meet all the financial requirements of the investor. It presents the investor with an investment value, in light of the investor's criteria, of $157,100.

The justified purchase price is the investment value of the project based on the ability of its projected cash flows to satisfy the needs of all the financing parties involved. In other words, the justified price is the value of the debt plus the value of the equity. The value of the equity is the total present value of the equity as shown. The value of the debt is the face amount of the debt (i.e., no discounting is necessary) since the

TABLE 21-10   PRESENT VALUE OF THE CASH PROCEEDS FROM SALE

Adjusted sales price	$188,700
Less: tax on sale (Table 21.9)	(14,966)
Less: loan payoff (Table 21.2)	(114,282)
Net cash to equity from sale	$59,452
Present value factor @ 15%	0.4972
Present value of proceeds from sale	$29,559

TABLE 21-11 THE INVESTMENT DECISION	
Total present value of equity cash flow after tax (Table 21.6)	$7,541
Present value of proceeds from sale (Table 21.10)	$29,559
Total present value of equity	$37,100
Less original equity cost ($160,000 − $120,000)	($40,000)
Net present value	($2,900)
Investment Value	
Value of debt (face amount)	$120,000
Value of equity (from above)	$37,100
Price at which investment is expected to yield exactly 15%	$157,100

investor will pay the required rate of return to the lender in the form of periodic interest. Therefore, adding the present value of the equity cash flow to the face value of the debt gives the justified purchase price. If the investor can buy for less than this price, then more than the investor's required rate of return will be achieved.

To sum up the possible alternative results from DCF analysis:

- *The net present value is zero.* Here, the expected cash flows, when discounted at the required rate (the rate of return sought by the investor), exactly equal the cost of investment. Put another way, the rate of return from the project is exactly equal to the required return. Consequently, the investors will invest because their required return is exactly met.

- *The net present value is positive.* If the expected cash flows, when discounted, exceed the cost of investment, the decision will be to invest.

- *The net present value is negative.* As in our example, the expected cash flows, when discounted, are less than the cost of investment, so that the investor will not receive the desired return and so presumably will not invest at the asking price.

Again, we must remember that the results of the DCF analysis are no better than the urban land economics that underlie the projections shown in the pro formas. We should also add that negotiation plays a big role in real estate investment and that, even though an investment appears to meet the investor's needs (a positive NPV), the investor will probably still try to negotiate an even better price. Conversely, a negative net present value suggests an offer price below the asking price.

PRESENT VALUE
AND THE
INTERNAL RATE
OF RETURN

Instead of using DCF analysis to determine whether discounted cash flows exceed or fall below a desired return, the analyst may seek to establish the precise return from the property. This return is called the **internal rate of return (IRR).** IRR is the discount rate that equates all the project's cash inflows to the outflows. Therefore, IRR measures the yield of the investment. Often this is very important to the investor, who may feel more comfortable with a *yield* or *return* concept rather than merely with the "invest or not invest" decision.

The actual IRR may be calculated by trial-and-error methods. Simply increase or decrease the discount rate as needed to move the net present value toward zero. Once the zero net present value has been straddled by two different discount rates, the analyst knows that the internal rate of return is somewhere between the two discount rates. (The reader can experiment with this trial-and-error method, using the Compound Interest Tables provided at the end of the book.)[5] IRR can also be quickly determined with many calculators.[6]

In our example, the IRR is less than 15 percent since the DFC model yielded a negative net present value using a 15 percent discount rate.

ESTIMATING THE INTERNAL RATE OF RETURN

The present value tables can be used to choose the appropriate discount factors for our example. As already noted, the IRR in this example is less than 15 percent. Choosing 15 and 13 percent as possible discount rates yields the data in Table 21-12.

The present value of the after-tax equity cash flow is $37,100 at 15 percent and $40,200 at 13 percent. Since the cost of equity, $40,000, falls within this range, the IRR for our example is somewhere between 15 and 13 percent. For a more accurate estimate of the IRR, the factors must be interpolated. (See Table 21-13.)

The IRR is then compared with the investor's required rate of return. If the IRR exceeds the required rate of return, the decision is to invest. If the IRR is lower than the required rate of return, the decision would be not to invest. In our example, the IRR of 13.13 percent is less

---

[5]*The internal rate of return and the net present value criteria involve different reinvestment assumptions. On a theoretical basis, they are not interchangeable phrases; yet in the real world, the distinction is seldom made. In a theoretical sense, the two can give different answers in constrained capital-budgeting situations at a point known as* Fisher's Intersection. *Technically, both concepts involve theoretically incorrect reinvestment assumptions. The* financial management rate of return *is an idea similar to the internal rate of return, with a theoretically more valid reinvestment assumption that borrows from duration theory. For a discussion of these items, see Stephen D. Messner and M. Chapman Findlay III, "Real Estate Investment Analysis: IRR Versus FMRR," The Real Estate Appraiser (July-August 1975), pp. 5–20.*

[6]*This entire model is easily computerized. Computer models can incorporate subjective probability distributions as well as simple point estimates as suggested earlier.*

TABLE 21-12   ESTIMATING THE INTERNAL RATE OF RETURN

YEAR	15% PV FACTOR	ECFAT[a]	PV	13% PV FACTOR	ECFAT	PV
1	0.8696	$ 1,998	$ 1,737	0.8850	$ 1,998	$ 1,768
2	0.7561	2,151	1,626	0.7831	2,151	1,684
3	0.6575	2,298	1,510	0.6931	2,298	1,592
4	0.5718	2,436	1,393	0.6133	2,436	1,494
5	0.4972	2,566	1,275	0.5428	2,566	1,392
Sale proceeds	0.4972	59,452	29,559	0.5428	59,452	32,270
Total			$37,100			$40,200

[a] Equity cash flow after tax (Tables 21.5 and 21.10).

than the required rate of return of 15 percent; hence, the investor would not be encouraged to invest. Note that the determination of the required rate of return exactly parallels the determination of the appropriate discount rate.

FURTHER CONSIDERATIONS ABOUT INVESTMENT RETURN

The foregoing model allows the investment analyst to reduce to one figure the numbers associated with the two-part return and compare that figure to the cost. Risk and the time value of money are incorporated in the discount rate. Remember, however, that the model is only as good as the input data—that is, only as good as the analyst's projections of the marketplace. Furthermore, the model may overlook important items in the investment analysis and should always be tested.

**TABLE 21-13   INTERPOLATING THE INTERNAL RATE OF RETURN
(A CONTINUATION OF TABLE 21.12)**

Present value @ 13%	$40,200	Present value @ 13%	$40,200
Present value @ 15%	$37,100	Present value @ IRR	$40,000
Difference	$ 3,100	Difference	$ 200

$$\text{IRR} = 13\% + \frac{200}{3,100}(15\% - 13\%)$$

$$= 13\% + 0.0645\ (2\%)$$

$$= 13\% + 0.0013\%$$

$$= 13.13\%$$

FINANCIAL RATIO AND MULTIPLIER ANALYSIS

One way to test the results of the DCF model is to conduct a simple financial ratio and multiplier analysis. As shown in Table 21-14, the financial ratios include the operating expense ratio, the debt coverage ratio, and the breakeven ratio. The important multipliers include the gross and net income multipliers. Financial ratio and multiplier analysis allows the analyst to compare the expected performance of the subject property (given the assumptions used in the DCF model) to the performance of comparable projects in the marketplace. Such an analysis will reduce the probability of allowing unrepresentative or inaccurate data to bias the DCF and IRR results. Financial ratio and multiplier analysis allow the analyst to verify the accuracy of the DCF and IRR assumptions.

FINANCIAL RATIO ANALYSIS.   The **operating expense ratio (OER)** allows the analyst to evaluate the relationship between a project's rents and expenses. Calculated on the basis of gross potential income, the OER expresses the operating expenses as a percentage of the GPI. If the project's OER is lower than market standards, usually 35 to 50 percent depending on property type, either expected rents may have been overstated or expected operating expenses may have been understated.

TABLE 21-14   FINANCIAL RATIO AND MULTIPLIER ANALYSIS

	YEAR 1	YEAR 5	MARKET STANDARDS
Operating Expense Ratio			
OER = $\dfrac{\text{Operating expenses}}{\text{Gross potential income}}$	$\dfrac{\$12,000}{\$30,000} = 40\%$	$\dfrac{\$14,587}{\$33,765} = 43\%$	35–50%
Debt Coverage Ratio			
DCR = $\dfrac{\text{Net operating income}}{\text{Debt service}}$	$\dfrac{\$16,500}{\$15,300} = 1.07$	$\dfrac{\$17,490}{\$15,300} = 1.14$	1.15–1.50×
Breakeven Ratio			
BER = $\dfrac{\text{Operating expenses + debt service}}{\text{Gross potential}}$	$\dfrac{\$27,300}{\$30,000} = 91\%$	$\dfrac{\$29,887}{\$33,765} = 89\%$	75–90%
Gross Income Multiplier			
GIM = $\dfrac{\text{Market value}}{\text{Gross potential income}}$	$\dfrac{\$160,000}{\$30,000} = 5.33\times$	$\dfrac{\$194,700}{\$33,765} = 5.77\times$	4–6×
Net Income Multiplier			
NIM = $\dfrac{\text{Market value}}{\text{Net operating income}}$	$\dfrac{\$160,000}{\$16,500} = 9.69\times$	$\dfrac{\$194,700}{\$17,490} = 11.13\times$	9–11×

The **debt coverage ratio (DCR)** is a measure of financial risk and indicates the ability of the project to cover debt-service payments. As the DCR moves down toward 1.0, the financial risk increases. The DCR can also be used to evaluate the reasonableness of proposed financing. If the DCR is lower than current industry standards, the DCF analysis may have assumed unrealistically liberal financing.

Breakeven analysis allows the analyst to determine what level of occupancy at the projected rent level must be reached to cover operating expenses and debt service. Lenders also use the **breakeven ratio (BER)** to measure financial risk. The higher the BER, the greater the financial risk (i.e., the possibility that sufficient rent will not be collected to cover operating expenses and debt service).

MULTIPLIER ANALYSIS.   Both the gross income multiplier (GIM) and the net income multiplier (NIM) can help the analyst test the reasonableness of DCF and IRR assumptions. The **gross income multiplier** is the most frequently used. The GIM relates the value of a project to the gross potential income. However, since operating expenses vary widely among different projects, the NIM has gained popularity in recent years. The **net income multiplier** simply relates the net operating income to project value. As in the case of ratio analysis, the multipliers should be compared to the multipliers of projects in the marketplace to test the reasonableness of assumptions used in the DCF and IRR models.

Analysis of Table 21-14 indicates that the OER of 40 percent is in line with market standards. The DCR however, is very low in year 1, but it increases to a nearly acceptable level by year 5.

The first-year DCR of 1.07 could be caused by one of two factors: gross rents are too low or debt service is too high. It may be reasonable to presume that the project may have difficulty carrying the 12 percent, 25-year, $120,000 mortgage. A smaller loan, lower interest, or longer term (or a combination of all three) could reduce the debt service and increase the DCR. As pointed out in Chapter 15, the maximum loan amount can be determined as follows.

$$\text{Maximum loan} = \frac{\text{NOI}}{K \times \text{desired DCR}}$$

Therefore, in our example the maximum loan would be at most

$$\$112,532 = \frac{16,500}{0.1275 \times 1.15}$$

if the loan terms are not changed. This would require an increase in the equity contribution of $7,468. If this change were to be made, the DCF and IRR calculations would need to be adjusted accordingly.

The BER in year 1 of 91 percent exceeds industry standards. A reduction in BER could be effected by a change in financing terms, an increase in rent, or a reduction in operating expenses. Based on the OER, the burden probably falls on the financing.

Both GIM and NIM fall within reasonable ranges. However, both are increasing. This means the analyst assumes that the buyer five years from now will pay more for each dollar of income than the current buyer is paying. When might this be a reasonable assumption?

In summary, whereas both the DCF present value and IRR analyses suggested that the investment should not be made, the financial ratio and multiplier process raised important questions. Specifically, is the risk of the example project out of line with the market? The DCR and BER suggested that it is. The next step in the analysis would be to restructure the offer price and financing and then recalculate the DCF and IRR.

Whenever unusual situations or inconsistencies are noted in the multiplier/ratio analysis suggested in Table 21-14, the assumptions of the model should be analyzed; and, where a revision is warranted, a new net present value and IRR computation should be made.

SUMMARY

The after-tax DCF model is an organized way to evaluate complex investment alternatives. Essentially, DCF is used to calculate a project's value based on the present value of equity and the present value of debt. It is therefore a useful investment decision-making tool. It can also be used on a continuous basis after the initial investment to decide on the appropriate time of disposition. The critical items in using the model are knowledge of the market, an estimation of risk, and an estimation of the time value of money. Many people can learn the accounting mechanics. But since knowledge of the market is more an art than a science, it is important to stress that the decision-making value of DCF and IRR analysis is only as strong as the underlying assumptions made by the analyst.

However, a word of caution is in order. This chapter evaluated one investment opportunity in isolation. When the analysis is expanded to include the investor's entire portfolio (see Chapter 23), then, and only then, can the complete impact of tax law changes and alternative financing terms on individual investors be understood.

IMPORTANT TERMS

Breakeven ratio (BER)	Net income multiplier
Cash inflow	Net present value
Cash outflow	Operating expense ratio (OER)
Debt coverage ratio (DCR)	Operating expenses

Discounted cash flow model
Effective gross income
Equity cash flow after tax
Gross income multiplier (GIM)
Gross potential income (GPI)
Internal rate of return (IRR)

Sensitivity analysis
Tax basis
Tax savings
Taxable gain
Vacancy allowance and collection
  loss

REVIEW QUESTIONS

21.1   How does the discounted cash flow model incorporate the concept of present value?

21.2   What data must be collected in order to calculate the estimated effective gross income for an existing income-producing property?

21.3   What factors does the discounted cash flow model consider that would be ignored in a typical appraisal?

21.4   In the example presented in this chapter, how can net operating income increase each year when gross potential income is rising by only 3 percent per year while operating expenses are increasing by 5 percent per year?

21.5   Again referring to the example in this chapter, why does the tax shelter offered by the project fall in each year of the investment horizon?

21.6   How would an increase in the contract rate of interest affect the taxable income (loss) in Table 21-4?

21.7   In the example in this chapter, would the project be more or less valuable to an investor in the 15 percent marginal tax bracket? Why?

21.8   If an investor reassessed her required rate of return to incorporate a higher inflation premium, what impact would this have on the project's internal rate of return?

21.9   Using the example presented in Tables 21-1 through 21-13, restructure an offer price that would satisfy the investor's requirements. Consider altering the offer price and/or the assumed financing.

21.10 The project depicted in this chapter has an unacceptably low debt coverage ratio and an unacceptably high breakeven ratio. Suggest a way to restructure the debt that will increase the DCR and lower the BER. What influence will your decision have on the required equity and the IRR?

C H A P T E R   **2 2**

R EAL ESTATE AND MODERN PORTFOLIO THEORY

In Chapter 21 we went through the mechanics of discounted cash flow analysis for an individual project. There we considered the project alone, in isolation from any other projects the investor might already hold or consider buying. In this chapter, we go a step further to look at investment decision making based on the interaction of one real estate project with the rest of the investor's real estate portfolio.

INTRODUCTION   Fifteen years ago few real estate practitioners thought much about portfolio theory. It was generally acknowledged that diversification was a good thing, but most deals were done on a project-by-project basis, with little formal analysis of the benefits of portfolio **diversification.** In the early 1970s, pension funds first began to invest in real estate equities.[1] As we will see in this chapter and the next, they have become the major new investment player in many real estate markets, and they have brought with them a portfolio-consciousness in decision making.

Before pension funds got into real estate, most real estate equity portfolios were traditionally structured as collections of individual deals. Constructed one acquisition at a time, these portfolios gave little attention to the potential impact of adding another project to an existing portfolio. Furthermore, a project under consideration was not selected based on a well-developed (i.e., written) portfolio strategy that provided investment guidance. The use and understanding of portfolio diversification were either nonexistent or naive at best; the implicit strategy was that if each individual deal was a "good deal," then portfolio perfor-

---

[1]*For many years, insurance companies, through their general accounts (their own funds invested to payoff future policy claims), had been investing in real estate. However, the entrance of the pension funds, which typically used outside investment mangers rather than manage their own real estate investments, made institutional real estate equity investment "public" for the first time.*

mance would be maximized. At most, the managers of some portfolios established broad allocation categories by property type or geographic region (e.g., the traditional four regions: North, Midwest, South, West). However, such guidelines were not based on modern portfolio theory (MPT).

As a new player in real estate, the pension funds came from a world of stocks and bonds, where portfolio theory was already an established part of the decision-making process. As the pension funds diversified into real estate, they sought to explain their decisions with the same logic they had used in diversifying their portfolio across the broad array of stocks and bonds. But real estate investment counselors, developers, and other players often found the logic of the pension funds alien to their own ways of thinking. Yet the sheer size of the pension funds has forced the real estate industry to address the needs of the pension funds—to change traditional ways of doing business to adapt to the funds' ways.

Modern portfolio theory is consistent with traditional real estate analysis as we describe it throughout this text. Recall that in Chapter 1 we talked about owning the bundle of rights and noted that the bundle of rights was both separable and divisible. In later chapters we discovered that there are many creative ways to structure a transaction to benefit the various claimants of the cash flow best. The better we know a client, the better we can use all the creative possibilities inherent in real estate rights to structure a transaction to suit everyone in the deal. In fact, knowing modern portfolio theory is no more than knowing the mind and the needs of an important client, the pension funds. Even if you do not deal directly with pension funds yourself, you must understand their logic, or you will fail to understand the marketplace. If you do deal directly with them and you fail to acknowledge the importance to them of modern portfolio theory, you are very likely to pay too much, sell too cheap, or finance at too high a cost.

In this chapter and the next, we will probe the logic of this major new institutional player, the pension funds. In Chapter 23 we will see the same logic applied to another major player, one that in the next 10 years may become as big as, if not bigger than, the pension funds. We are referring to large corporations and their corporate fixed-asset managers.

We begin this chapter with a short description of the evolution of institutional real estate investment. We will look quickly at how modern portfolio theory has developed over the last 30 years and at how this theory "fits" in the real estate marketplace. We will then look at where the institutional player is used to finding "investment numbers," that is, the historical numbers that describe the performance of various asset classes. "Investment numbers" include the New York Stock Exchange Index, the Dow-Jones averages, and various other return series. Next we'll learn that the historical data on real estate returns are far less reliable than those on stocks, though still very useful. After we examine the historical record, we will look at academic research, using these data, and see what real estate offers to the institutional investor. Finally, and most important, we will move from past research explaining historical returns to a consideration of future directions. This is the most difficult, yet certainly the most important, part of analyzing portfolio theory. We study its history, not because we believe the future will be an exact replica of the past, but because we seek to learn whatever the past can teach us about being better players in the future.

BACKGROUND: SIX ESSENTIAL LESSONS BEFORE WE START

Table 22-1 lists six essential lessons as a prelude to our study of real estate portfolio theory. First, while portfolio theory is still new to most real estate professionals, it is old hat to the stock and bond people who manage pension fund investments. This means (1) that they have a tremendous amount of human capital invested in the theory and its applications and, therefore, will seek to apply it as they move into the real estate asset class; and (2) that, possibly less obviously, they understand portfolio theory to be qualitative as well as quantitative. In other words, they understand that even for financial assets the theory does not fit the marketplace perfectly and that there are many problems in using the theory to structure an investment portfolio. As an example, a commonly used market risk measure of a stock, its "beta," changes over time, depending on which historical interval analysts use to track the stock's performance in relation to the market. In other words, numbers vary over time; measurements taken at one point in time are not valid for all time. Consequently, as stock and bond people move into real estate portfolio analysis, they will not be intolerant of difficulties; yet they do wish to understand the limits that arise from weakness in the data.

Second, we must always remember that portfolio theory did not become important in real estate because a professor fitted a theory to last

---

TABLE 22-1   ESSENTIAL BACKGROUND LESSONS

1. Portfolio theory is old hat to stock and bond people.
2. Portfolio theory became important in real estate because it has worked well in other markets.
3. Since it is the logic behind most capital allocation models, portfolio theory drives the thinking of the major source of savings in the U.S. economy (pension funds).
4. The theory is both simple and logical.
5. Historical empirical studies are fraught with problems.
6. Moving from empirical ex post studies to real-world applications is a perilous journey.

year's reality. Portfolio theory became important and has remained important because it helps people make better decisions and thus make money. Making money is, of course, the bottom line on Wall Street as well as in this text. So as we go through the theoretical derivations later in the chapter, we need to remember that the theory is useful. If it were not, it would not have survived so long.

Third, portfolio theory is the logic driving the capital allocation models used by the pension funds. In other words, it helps them decide how much to put in real estate, in stocks, in bonds, in venture capital, and in other investment vehicles. Why should we care about pension funds' capital allocations? Well, let's take a look at their size and significance. Pension funds are a major new source of savings in the economy. In 1990, pension funds had total assets of over $2 trillion. By 1995, the Department of Labor estimates that their total assets will be approximately $3 trillion.

Since $3 trillion is a great deal of money, let's break it down and see what it means in the real estate game. If approximately 10 percent of the total were invested in real estate, that would mean $300 billion by 1995. Today pension funds have about $100 billion invested in real estate. So over the next five years they would need to acquire over $200 billion in equity real estate.

Now look at the real estate investment manager, who recommends and executes portfolio strategies for the pension funds. Managers typically receive about 1 percent of assets under management as their fee. (That is investment management, not property management.) One percent of $300 billion is $3.0 billion in fees for a year. Clearly, this is a big incentive to serious players. Furthermore, beyond management fees there are development profits, brokerage profits, appraisal fees, and all the other moneymaking parts of the real estate industry that we have previously covered in the text.

Fourth, portfolio theory is both simple and logical—much more so in theory than in practice, we admit, but it *is* widely practiced despite all difficulties. Those of us who want to be players should make the effort to understand the theory and its practical applications to real estate. In 1970, real estate was a nontraditional investment on Wall Street. But now real estate is no longer outside the mainstream. Wall Street, pension funds, and global investors are in the game, and understanding how they play is important to all players. The competition is smart, and they play hard. If you want to play successfully, you have to be good.

Fifth, as we will see later in this chapter, a variety of empirical studies have attempted to apply portfolio logic in various real estate markets. These studies have been limited in many important ways. Yet, in a world where information is expensive and comparative advantage is possible, the studies are still relevant for what good information they do contain. Furthermore, as leading real estate investment managers and pension funds enhance their research staffs, empirical studies continue to improve. Sixth and last, we repeat that we study the past to prepare for the future. The problem with using the past—that is, using historic numbers (**ex post**)—is that conditions change, and the same numbers may not apply in the future. Yet we estimate future numbers (**ex ante**) based on past experience along with our best estimates of what changes will occur. To the extent that we project future risks and returns, our models are only as good as our underlying assumptions. Moral: study the past, and apply its lessons thoughtfully.

This chapter should prepare you for Chapter 23 in which we will use portfolio logic to understand the players of the game. Modern portfolio theory affords us even more creativity in structuring real estate investment vehicles. As we have seen from the examples given earlier, it can be a very lucrative business.

MODERN PORTFOLIO THEORY—WHAT IS IT?

For as long as anyone can remember, the value of any single project has been defined as a function of expected return and the risk associated with that return. This is clearly traditional real estate analysis; it is the heart of the income approach to value used in appraisal practice. At the portfolio level the technical definition of risk is the variance of the distributions of expected returns.

The expected return and variance of return can be calculated from historical data using the formulas

$$\bar{X} = \frac{\displaystyle\sum_{t=1}^{N} X_t}{N}$$

$$\text{Var}(X) = \frac{\displaystyle\sum_{t=1}^{N} (X_t - \bar{X})^2}{N}$$

and

$$\text{SD}(X) = \sqrt{\text{Var}(X)}$$

where X_t is the observed percentage return over some holding period, typically one year for stocks and bonds, $\bar{X}$ is the mean of the observed returns, $\text{Var}(X)$ is the variance of the observed returns, $\text{SD}(X)$ is the standard deviation of observed returns, and N is the number of observed returns.

TABLE 22-2 BASIC SERIES—TOTAL ANNUAL RETURNS, 1926–1989			
SERIES	GEOMETRIC MEAN	ARITHMETIC MEAN	STANDARD DEVIATION
Common stocks	10.3%	12.4%	20.9%
Small stocks	12.2	17.7	35.3
Long-term corporate bonds	5.2	5.5	8.5
Long-term government bonds	4.6	4.9	8.6
U.S. treasury bills	3.6	3.7	5.5
Inflation	3.1	3.1	4.8

Source: *Ibbotson and Associates, 8 South Michigan Avenue, Suite 700, Chicago, Illinois, 60603, (312) 263–3434.*

Table 22-2 shows the distribution with the expected returns and variances for holding various types of stocks and bonds. As can be seen, the higher the expected or mean return, the higher the variance. This is the well-known tradeoff between risk and return. The key issue in terms of portfolio theory is whether the variability or the variance of the return on a single stock, or for real estate the variance of the return on a single property, is the risk we should be concerned about.

The general approach is to calculate from historical data an expected return and variance of return for every security. From these calculations it would be decided what assets should be chosen on the basis of risk compared to expected return. The basic point of portfolio theory is that this is not enough. It is not enough to consider the risk-return tradeoff of a specific investment. In order to fully understand the risk of an individual asset, we must consider how it interacts with the return on other assets.

In order to understand this, let us consider two individual investments, A and B. The expected return of A is $\bar{X}_A = 12$ percent, and the expected return on B is also 12 percent. In addition, assume that they both have the same standard deviation, $\text{SD}_A = \text{SD}_B = 25$ percent. It would seem that they have the same risk-return tradeoff. But what about a portfolio of the two? What is the expected return and standard deviation of such a portfolio? Suppose we invested 50 percent of our wealth in A and 50 percent in B. The expected return and standard deviation would be

$$\bar{X}_p = 50\% \cdot \bar{X}_A + 50\% \cdot \bar{X}_B$$

and

$$\text{SD}_P = \sqrt{(50\% \cdot \text{SD}_A)^2 + (50\% \cdot \text{SD}_B)^2 + 2 \cdot 50\% \cdot \text{SD}_A \cdot 50\% \cdot \text{SD}_B \cdot r_{AB}}.$$

Note that the expected return of the portfolio is simply a weighted average of the expected returns, but the standard deviation has a rather different form. In particular, there is the term r_{AB}, which is the **correlation coefficient** between A and B. This is a statistical measure of how two things move in relation to each other. It can take on values of 1, -1, or any value in between. Positive values indicate that they move in the same direction, and negative values that they move in opposite directions. Table 22-3 gives the values of the expected return and standard deviation of the portfolio for different values of r_{AB}. As can be seen, the portfolio of A and B has a better risk-return tradeoff than either A or B alone, as long as the correlation coefficient is less than 1. In addition, the benefit from diversification increases as correlation between the two assets decreases.

This increase from diversification as correlation between assets decreases is a key point. In a portfolio, the total return is simply a weighted average of the return on all the assets in the portfolio. However, portfolio risk is *not* simply a weighted average of the risk of the individual projects in the portfolio. In a portfolio, high returns on one project may offset low returns on another project during the same period, so that overall portfolio risk is lowered.

To the traditional stock and bond analyst, this means that a hotel is not necessarily more risky than a warehouse leased for 20 years to IBM. Certainly, the hotel individually would be expected to show more variance in its future returns. However, if these returns are *not* highly correlated with the stocks and bonds already held by the institutional investor, the hotel, when included in the institutional investment portfolio, may contribute less to portfolio risk than the warehouse which, when leased on a long-term basis to a triple-credit tenant, looks a great deal like a bond.

This example points out a unique aspect of real estate with respect to

TABLE 22-3   EXPECTED RETURNS AND STANDARD DEVIATIONS FOR A PORTFOLIO OF A AND B (TWO ASSETS WITH IDENTICAL RETURNS AND VARIANCES) WITH DIFFERENT COVARIANCES

R_{AB}	$\bar{X}_P$	SD_P
+1.0	12%	25%
0.5	12%	22%
0.1	12%	19%
0.0	12%	18%
−.1	12%	17%
−.5	12%	13%
−1.0	12%	0%

diversification. It is clear that diversification can be achieved by having different types of properties in a portfolio. Another way of achieving diversification within real estate may be to focus on a real estate portfolio as a collection of leases. A significant amount of diversification may be obtained by using a mix of different types of leases even within the same property type. This may be a cheaper way of diversifying within real estate and is actually more in keeping with the traditional view of real estate, which tends to emphasize specialization. However, executing a portfolio strategy that is based on lease characteristics may be problematic, if not impossible. As we stress later in this chapter, if a strategy cannot be executed in the field, it is of little use.

Risk, then, must be measured in a portfolio context. This was the point Harry Markowitz made in his pioneering work on portfolio theory begun in 1952. He showed in clear mathematical language how to look at risk in a portfolio context. (See Box 22-1.) Risk and return collectively still determine value; however, since most major investors are diversified, they do not care about the unique risk of any one project but about the risk that a project contributes to their portfolio. This is the perspective that the new players are bringing to their investment in real estate. An important element in all this, in addition to the correlation between real estate projects themselves, is the correlation between real estate and the more traditional assets such as stocks and bonds. To the extent that new players view risk in a portfolio context, they bring a whole new definition of risk to the real estate markets. This can and will have a profound impact on the way real estate assets are valued.

Academics applauded Markowitz's idea, but practitioners found the concept difficult to use. For 50 to 100 assets, doing the math is practical. Above that number, even with computers, the calculations are cumbersome, and the number of correlation coefficients to be estimated is unreasonably large. Remember that institutional portfolios are huge, and managers are faced with an enormous number of potential acquisitions, be they stocks, bonds, other securities, or individual real estate projects. Therefore, though intuitively pleasing and mathematically correct, Markowitz's definition of portfolio risk proved all but impossible to apply on an asset-by-asset basis to large institutional portfolios.

In 1964, William Sharpe made a major advance with what has come to be known as the **capital asset pricing model.** This model is a simplification of Markowitz's idea. Sharpe argues that the only variance that matters to the truly diversified portfolio is the covariance of the individual asset's return with the return of the overall market. Portfolio risk in the capital asset pricing model is the weighted average of the individual assets' betas. **Beta** is a risk measure derived from regressing an asset's historical returns on the historical returns of the market (usually applied to stocks). The mechanics of the theory are described in Box 22-2.

22-1
PORTFOLIO
RISK A LA
MARKOWITZ

Traditional Finance Theory states that the value of a single project is a function of the mean and variance of the expected return. Markowitz dealt with the value of the portfolio of projects using the following formulas.

$$V = \frac{\sum_{N=1}^{N} (X_i - \bar{X})^2}{N}$$

where

V = variance
X_i = total return percentage
$\bar{X}$ = average total return percentage
N = number of periods

The standard deviation is

$$SD = \sqrt{Variance}$$

The covariance is

$$SD_X \cdot SD_Y \cdot \text{correlation of } X \text{ and } Y.$$

Using historical data on the returns of the various possible investment opportunities, the analyst estimates the mean and covariances of the expected future returns. The covariance includes both the standard deviation of the individual securities' returns and the correlation of returns among the different securities.

Points on the **efficient frontier** are the particular portfolios that offer the highest expected return for any given level of portfolio risk, or conversely, the lowest level of risk for any given level of expected return (Figure 22-1). Once the analyst has developed the efficient frontier, the investor can select any point on this frontier based on the amount of risk he wishes to assume.

The more **risk-averse** investor moves logically toward the left on the curve, and the less risk-averse investor toward the right. No investor can do better with any other portfolio than he can with the efficient frontier.

In developing the frontier, remember that the expected return for the portfolio as a whole is simply the weighted average of the return of each of the securities held in the portfolio. Portfolio risk, however, is not an additive function. A formula for the standard deviation of portfolio return is

$$\sigma_i = \sqrt{\sum_{i=1}^{N} X_i^2 \sigma_i^2 + \sum_{i=1}^{N} \sum_{\substack{j=1 \\ i \neq j}}^{N} X_i X_j \sigma_i \sigma_j r_{ij}}$$

$$\sigma_i = \sqrt{\sum_{i=1}^{N} X_i^2 \sigma_i^2 + \sum_{i=1}^{N} \sum_{\substack{j=1 \\ i \neq j}}^{N} X_i X_j \sigma_{ij}}$$

$$= \begin{array}{c} \text{weighted} \\ \text{security} \end{array} + \begin{array}{c} \text{effect of correlation} \\ \text{between securities} \end{array}$$

where

X_i is the percent of the portfolio invested in asset *i*

σ_i is the standard deviation of the expected return of asset *i*

r_{ij} is the correlation of returns between assets *i* and *j*

σ_{ij} is the covariance of *i* and *j*

As you can see, the standard deviation can be broken into two different parts, the unique security risk and the effect of the correlation between securities.[a] In a widely diversified portfolio, the first component approaches zero, thus leaving the second component as the primary measure of risk. In this measure the covariance includes the standard deviation of each security as well as the correlation between the securities. Thus, it is the correlation of returns that becomes the most important item.

Since the correlation coefficient is such an important item, it behooves us to look more closely at this measure. Both the ex ante and ex post calculations of the correlation coefficient follow. The analyst develops the ex post measure from historical securities' returns and then uses this, along with other information, to develop ex ante expectations for the correlation coefficient.

The Correlation Coefficient

The ex ante calculation is

$$r_{ij} = \frac{\sum_{i=1}^{s} P_s \left[R_{is} - E(R_i) \right] \left[R_{js} - E(R_j) \right]}{\sigma_i \sigma_j}$$

where

P_s = probability of outcome *s*

$E(R_i)$ = expected (average) return on asset *i*

R_{is} = return on asset *i* given outcome *s*

σ_i, σ_j = the standard deviations of the expected returns from assets *i* and *j*

the ex post calculation is

$$r_{ij} = \frac{\sum_{i=1}^{N} (R_{it} - \bar{R}_i)(R_{jt} - \bar{R}_j)/N}{\sigma_i \sigma_j}$$

where R_{it} and R_{jt} refer to the historic return on securities i and j during period t, $\bar{R}_i$ and $\bar{R}_j$ are average rates of return earned during the past N periods, and σ_i and σ_j are ex post standard deviations.

[a]Those of you familiar with the capital asset pricing model will quickly recognize the first as the unsystematic component and the second as the systematic component.

Since the capital asset pricing model was intuitively pleasing and at first appeared to be a reasonable approximation of the marketplace, it became the darling of both professors and Wall Street analysts. For the next 14 years after its introduction, both groups tried to force empirical reality to fit the theory. As forcing a fit became increasingly difficult, more doubts about the theory arose. Then in 1978 Richard Roll delivered the final blow when he demonstrated mathematically that the theory was at best untestable.

Unfortunately, there was no ready replacement for what had become the major capital market paradigm, widely used in practice by Wall Street. Lack of a better model, coupled with the reluctance of many people to discard a heavy investment in human capital, has led to the continuing use of the capital asset pricing model,

Moreover, during the 1970s, in search of an alternative capital market paradigm, Steven Ross offered an even more intuitively appealing theory known as the **arbitrage pricing model.** First developed by Ross in 1976 and elaborated by Ross and Roll over the next few years, this theory argues that there is not just one market risk factor but several systematic (common to the market) risk factors, and that investors are paid for bearing risks in each area. Arbitrage pricing theory is particularly appealing when applied to real estate because it says that investors should receive a higher return for greater exposure to risks like unexpected

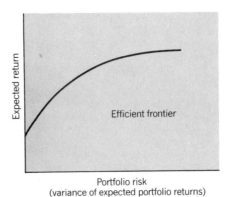

FIGURE 22-1 *The efficient frontier*

<table>
<tr><td>

22-2
THE CAPITAL
ASSET PRICING
MODEL

</td><td>

Capital asset pricing theory involves a simple mean-variance approach to investment analysis. All assets are priced based on their expected return (the mean of that return) and the riskiness associated with that return (defined as the variance associated with incorporating the given expected return in the portfolio). In its discounted cash flow application, the numerator is the expected (most likely) return, and the denominator incorporates a risk premium. The risk premium is similar to that developed in Chapter 20 but also includes a component for portfolio risk.

</td></tr>
</table>

Overall variance in any asset's expected return can be divided into a systematic and an unsystematic component. The systematic component is the amount of the asset's variance that can be explained by the variance of the overall market. The **unsystematic risk** or component is the variance in the individual asset's return that is unique to the particular asset. That is, the security's variance is broken down into two parts: One is a function of the general market, and the other is unique to the particular asset. In a fully diversified portfolio, unique (unsystematic) variances will cancel out in the aggregate. Consequently, only systematic (market-related) risk is important in pricing assets in the capital markets.

A measure of **systematic risk** can be determined by regressing the historical return of any particular asset on the historical returns of the market as a whole. The regression coefficient for that asset is termed its beta.[a] A beta of 1.0 is equal to the market overall (i.e., an investment with a beta of 1.0 moves up or down in value 1 for 1 with the market). A beta of more than 1.0, say, 1.6, represents an aggressive investment that moves up or down in value faster than the market. A beta of less than 1, say 0.8, represents a somewhat defensive investment that moves up more slowly than the market but also declines more slowly.

The higher this beta, the greater the systematic risk associated with the security's return. That is, the higher the beta, the more a particular asset will contribute to the variance of the overall portfolio. (Remember that the investor is concerned with the variance of the total portfolio.)

Figure 22-2 illustrates the typical relationship between return and risk according to the capital asset pricing model. Again, risk and expected return are positively correlated. The higher a particular investment's beta, the greater the investor's required return.

The investor would be particularly attracted to any investment whose returns are negatively correlated with the market. Such negative correlation would be indicated by a negative beta (signifying an investment whose returns generally move in the opposite direction from the market).

Once a particular security's beta is known, in theory the calculation of an appropriate risk premium for use in DCF analysis is straightforward. The appropriate risk premium (now in a portfolio context) is the **market risk premium** (MRP) times beta ($\beta \times$ MRP). MRP is simply the average market return less the risk-free return. This product is then added to the risk-free rate appropriate for the anticipated holding period to obtain the appropriate required rate of return (discount rate).

> Example. *Assume that the stock of a hypothetical company, the U.S. Homebuilders, Inc., has a beta of 1.4. Historically, the average market risk premium has been about 5 percent. (Note that the market risk premium varies, and the most current figure should be used for investment calculations.)*

The **discount rate** to be applied to U.S. Homebuilders' returns (dividends plus appreciation) is the risk-free rate (say, T-bills at 9 percent) plus risk premium (5 percent MRP × 1.4 = 7 percent) = 16 percent.[b]

[a]The beta is typically calculated using historical data and regression analysis

$$R_s = a + \beta_s(\text{MRP})$$

where

R_s = return on investment s (both periodic cash flow and appreciation in value)

a = risk-free rate

β_s = investment's beta

MRP = average market risk premium (historical average market return less the corresponding historical risk-free return)

R_s and MRP are known for each month over a substantial period, say 20 years; a and β_s are then produced through regression analysis.

[b]Theoretically, this application is only the tip of the iceberg. The issues include what returns to measure, how to measure them, and what historic time periods to use. However, an example like this one does help in understanding the model, regardless of emperical uncertainties.

inflation, unexpected changes in the term structure of interest rates, changes in the market risk premium, and unexpected changes in gross national product. The theory is logical, but practical use requires factor analysis, a fairly loose form of multivariate statistics. Unfortunately, factor analysis is so flexible that analysts can come up with almost any number as a risk premium for each factor. In short, even though arbitrage pricing theory is intuitively appealing, its empirical relevance is limited by the fact that everyone seems to arrive at a different set of numbers.

Finally, there is the **options pricing theory.** Though options pricing is not a complete capital market model, it is probably the theory that will

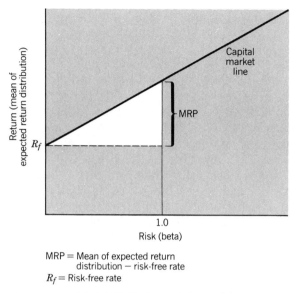

MRP = Mean of expected return
          distribution − risk-free rate
R_f = Risk-free rate

F I G U R E 22-2   *Capital asset price model*

have the greatest impact on real estate investment over the next decade. As we have shown in several places in the text, the option is quite common in real estate investment, and pricing an option can serve as a model for pricing other interests in real estate.

The question has always been, "How do you price the option? What is the option worth?" Black and Sholes developed an options pricing formula; several authors have subsequently contributed to its development. Let us use the simple example of a vacant lot in an industrial park, Lot 15. According to the Black-Sholes formulation, the price of an option on Lot 15 is a function of (1) the current market price of the asset (Lot 15); (2) the exercise price of the asset when sold (as stated in the option contract); (3) the length of the option period; (4) the risk-free interest rate (measured by T-bills of comparable maturity); and, most important, (5) the variance in the price of the asset over the option period (e.g., the day-to-day estimated variation in the market price of Lot 15 over a 90-day option period). This last item is very difficult to measure in real estate. The math underlying this model is well beyond elementary textbooks, but the authors believe that, in the future, as more data become available, options pricing will become much more important in real estate decision making.[2]

---

[2]*For an example of the application of the Black-Sholes pricing formula to real estate options pricing, see* California Real Estate Indictors *(Los Angeles: Housing Real Estate and Urban Studies, Graduate School of Management, University of California, Summer–Fall 1985), pp. 4 and 5.*

LINKING MODERN PORTFOLIO THEORY TO PRACTICE

In practical terms, portfolio strategy, which relies on modern portfolio theory (MPT), represents what many have come to call the "top down" or macro portion of real estate decision making. In contrast, the so-called traditional view of deal-oriented (individual asset) decision making represents the "bottom up" or micro portion of real estate decision making.

The primary role of top down MPT-driven portfolio strategy is to link the real estate portfolio decision to capital market pricing. Specifically, consider the following analogy. The U.S. economy is a subset of the global economy. As such, the U.S. economy fulfills a specific role within the global economy. This role can be clearly identified and measured by the economy's balance of trade and capital flows. The pricing, that is, the interaction between the forces of supply and demand, of goods and services, between two economies has a significant impact on each economy's productive capacity and economic activity. In like manner, individual U.S. markets fulfill a specific role within the U.S. economy. The heavy manufacturing markets of the industrialized Midwest provide certain goods for export to other markets, both foreign and domestic. At the same time, major financial services markets such as New York and San Francisco, for example, fulfill a very different role. However, each individual market's economy, just like the U.S. economy within the global economy, has a balance of trade and capital flows with all other U.S. markets.

Understanding the application of MPT to equity real estate requires a clear understanding of the urban and regional economic differences and similarities between many different local markets. This understanding enables the portfolio strategist to produce a covariance matrix across local markets so that MPT can be brought to bear on the allocation of assets within the portfolio. (Chapters 2 and 3 gave us the base to acquire this understanding.)

The "bottom up" traditional transaction approach brings what many would identify as "the art of deal" to the portfolio. Local market inefficiencies come into play here, and it is at this level that the real estate investment manager has traditionally focused the most attention.

In economic terms, both top down portfolio strategy and bottom up traditional transaction expertise are necessary, and neither is individually sufficient. (See Box 22-3.) That is, you must have excellence in both areas in order to achieve portfolio performance objectives. Simply having a portfolio strategy and not linking it successfully with transactional expertise will not succeed. Conversely, relying solely on expert transactions skills that are not accompanied by a sound portfolio strategy will, in the long term, be equally unsuccessful.

SOURCES OF INVESTMENT RETURNS DATA

Before we look further at portfolio theory in real estate, we need to see where institutional investors obtain data on investment returns. Table 22-4 shows three ways to calculate performance returns. As you can see, the Dow-Jones industrial average is certainly the best known as a price-

22-3
IMPLEMENTING PORTFOLIO STRATEGY

If the primary topic of this book were financial markets from the ivory tower perspective, we would stress that, in terms of applying modern portfolio theory, all that matters is the portfolio level strategy, that is, that transaction skill at the local market level is assumed to be equal across portfolio managers. However, as we have emphasized throughout the book, real estate markets are not as efficient as the stock market. As a result, we stress here that top down equity real estate portfolio strategy is critical, but so are the traditional bottom up skills. Why is this the case? There are two reasons.

First, consider the New York Stock Exchange. If you were standing in the visitors' gallery, you could look down onto the floor of the Exchange and notice the activities of the stock "specialists." Stock specialists "take a position," that is, simultaneously buy and sell for their own account in certain stocks. This helps the stock market appear to offer immediate execution of any transaction. Thus, if you are a stock portfolio manager and want to buy 10,000 shares of IBM, you simply call the trading desk and place your order. When you return from getting a cup of coffee, the trade has been completed and verified.

If you were an equity real estate portfolio manager and wished to increase your portfolio's holdings in regional shopping centers, how would you execute the strategy? Since there are no "regional shopping center specialists," you contact your property acquisition team and notify them of your desire. They search for a willing seller, negotiate the terms of sale, and then (if you are lucky) 9 to 18 months later you close the deal.

Second, what legal rights do you acquire when stock or real estate is purchased? In the stock case, you purchase common stock that gives the right to vote your proxy and affect the composition of the firm's board of directors. Using the IBM case, as a stockholder can you affect IBM's decision to enter the work station market? No. Your influence is limited to voting your proxy and influencing the board of directors who in turn influence management. Now consider real estate. When you buy real estate, what do you get? Often, you get something close to the complete bundle of rights. As the owner of the legal interest, you have the right *and* responsibility for the complete operation of the investment as a business. That is, as owner you are responsible for lease negotiations, capital improvement decisions, and so on, as well as seeing to it that the trash is taken out! In short, in the real estate case, at the property level the owner is responsible for all aspects of property operations.

Consequently, the "value added" by a real estate investment manager is at both the portfolio strategy level and the individual property operation level. Each level of activity is equally essential in terms of portfolio performance.

TABLE 22-4   PERFORMANCE/RETURN INDICES

A. Price-weighted: Dow-Jones Industrials. (It changes and is illogical, but it is still the best known.)

B. Value-weighted: S & P, NYSE, NASDAQ, American, Wilshire 5000, The Russell-NCREIF Property Index.

C. Unweighted price indicators: Fisher, Indicator Digest.

weighted series. A price-weighted series is one in which the weight that any particular security carries in the overall index varies with its price. Thus, the Dow-Jones Industrial Average changes every time there is a stock split. In addition, the actual composition of the index changes as firms merge, are acquired, or go bankrupt. This is really quite illogical; however, it is the oldest and best known overall performance measure.

The most accepted way to calculate an index is the value-weighted series. Here we have the Standard & Poor's (S&P) 500, the New York Stock Exchange Index (NYSE), the American Stock Exchange Index, the NASDAQ Index, the Wilshire Index, and, in real estate, The Russell-NCREIF Property Index. A joint effort of the Frank Russell Company and the National Council of Real Estate Investment Fiduciaries (NCREIF), the Property Index is a quarterly return index for income-producing real estate. It is the standard of the real estate industry and is the real estate index closest to the stock indices most frequently used by the Wall Street banks.

There are also unweighted price indices, such as the Fisher Index, but these are used mainly for academic purposes and need not concern us here. They are presented only for completeness.

Most indices are developed from extensive data bases that New York securities analysts use on a regular basis. Securities analysts have on computer tape or disk the daily, weekly, monthly, and annual returns of a host of securities going back many, many years, along with extensive supplementary information such as earnings per share and dividends per share. As securities analysts move into real estate, they look for similar information. And although the Russell-NCREIF Property Index is now available, the data underlying the Property Index are not yet public. As a result, traditional securities analysts are left wondering how different real estate is from stocks and bonds and whether they can trust what information they do get.

RESEARCH RESULTS TO DATE The many studies listed in the References following Part 7, working from different data bases, have come to some general conclusions regarding real estate as a portfolio asset. These results are summarized in Table 22-5.

T A B L E   2 2 - 5   RESEARCH RESULTS TO DATE
A. Over certain time periods, real estate has offered higher returns and lower portfolio risk (standard deviation of project returns) than stocks or bonds.
B. Real estate has offered an attractive diversification opportunity for those invested in stocks and bonds (a low correlation of real estate returns with stock and bond returns).
C. Real estate has offered an attractive **inflation hedge**, whereas stocks and bonds have not.
D. Diversification benefits can be acheived within the real estate asset class itself. It matters how assets are allocated within the real estate portfolio.

As we look at Table 22-5, real estate seems too good to be true; in fact, that is exactly the conclusion of most stock and bond people looking at real estate research. Over certain time periods, real estate has offered higher returns and lower portfolio risks than have either stocks or bonds. This result appears largely because most of the real estate data bases were constructed beginning in the 1970s, when many real estate markets experienced substantial appreciation. No one expects that much appreciation to be sustained over the long run. Two other explanations of anomalous returns to real estate in comparison with stocks and bonds are that (1) we have failed to measure risk correctly in the past (as discussed earlier in connection with arbitrage pricing theory), and (2) we have underestimated costs, thereby overestimating returns (Roger Ibbotson's new equilibrium theory, discussed briefly in Chapter 23).

The other three findings are more interesting and possibly of longer term significance. Real estate appears to offer attractive diversification opportunities both between real estate and other asset classes and within the asset class itself. Real estate has also offered attractive inflation protection whereas stocks and bonds have not. If these findings hold in the future, we will witness a continuation of significant institutional investment in various real estate markets. Let's discuss each of these research results in turn.

❏ **REAL ESTATE HAS OFFERED HIGHER RETURNS AND LOWER RISK THAN STOCKS AND BONDS.**   Over certain historical periods, real estate has indeed provided investors with superior levels of total return compared to both stocks and bonds. For example, Firstenberg, Ross, and Zisler, in the Spring 1988 article in *The Journal of Portfolio Management,* developed the data presented in Table 22-6. Over other periods, however, the total return advantages are not as attractive. For example, the data presented in Table 22-7 suggest that since 1985, real estate has not fared as well as stocks or bonds.

The bottom line is that real estate returns have been very com-

TABLE 22-6   COMPARATIVE RETURNS 1978–85

	TOTAL RETURN (PCT.)	STANDARD DEVIATION (PCT.)
The Russell-NCREIF Property Index	13.87	2.55
S&P 500	9.71	15.35
Government bonds	7.91	11.50

petitive with the returns of stocks and bonds over the long term. Since real estate is generally a long-lived and illiquid asset, if diversification benefits can be established between real estate and stocks and bonds, then a prudent institutional investor should hold some of each.

❏ **REAL ESTATE PROVIDES ATTRACTIVE DIVERSIFICATION CHARACTERISTICS WITHIN A MIXED-ASSET PORTFOLIO.**   Institutional investors must remember that the diversification characteristics of real estate, when compared to stocks and bonds, make an impressive argument for including 5 to 15 percent (some studies suggest higher levels) of a mixed-asset portfolio in real estate. The primary reason for this recommendation comes from real estate's low correlation with other financial assets. Perhaps no other real estate research topic has met more unanimity. In essence, the literature is in agreement on this result; only the extent of the attractiveness of the correlation is left in question.

❏ **REAL ESTATE OFFERS AN ATTRACTIVE INFLATION HEDGE.** Again, most observers would agree that real estate has been shown to provide an excellent hedge against inflation. The major question concerning this result focuses on its applicability going forward, that is, ex ante. In a world of overbuilt national markets, for example, the office market during 1990, would a bump in **unanticipated inflation** (an increase in the price level not currently reflected in capital market pricing) result in a corresponding increase in capital values? We doubt that. In

TABLE 22-7   COMPARATIVE RETURNS, 1985–89

	TOTAL RETURN (PCT.)	STANDARD DEVIATION (PCT.)
The Russell-NCREIF Property Index	7.00	1.77
S&P 500	20.50	11.16
Government bonds	12.21	8.52

the short run, when markets are severely overbuilt, real estate values will not rise if unanticipated inflation rises. High vacancy rates tend to limit an investor's ability to raise rents and thus hold down prices. However, given equilibrium in the space market, that is, relative balance between space supply and demand, we believe that real estate will continue to provide an attractive inflation hedge.

❏ **DIVERSIFICATION BENEFITS CAN BE ACHIEVED WITHIN THE REAL ESTATE ASSET CLASS ITSELF.**   Some of the earliest commingled real estate fund research indicated that diversification could be achieved within the asset class. Two early reports were Miles and McCue,[3] and Hartzell, Hekman, and Miles.[4] In essence, these reports stated that it mattered how a real estate portfolio was allocated by property type, but it raised questions about the effectiveness of geographic boundaries as effective diversification categories. Geographic boundaries were defined in terms of a broad four-region map that identified the East, South, Midwest, and West as portfolio-level locational categories. Later research by Hartzell, Shulman, and Wurtzebach[5] introduced the concept of **economic location** as a more effective category for portfolio allocation. This work supports the notion that the underlying economic base of a market, not its mere geographic location, makes it unique. Work is continuing in the area, but the trends are clear.

Diversification opportunities clearly exist within the asset class. As a result, institutional investors should understand not only the role of real estate as a mixed-asset diversifier, but also the importance of diversification considerations within the asset class.

CRITICISMS OF REAL ESTATE INVESTMENT RESEARCH

Table 22-8 lists the three primary criticisms of the real estate research described in the previous sections. The first two criticisms (A and B) come from traditional stock and bond people. They argue that the research is based on data from only one manager or on data from government-compiled data such as the price of an agricultural acre of land in Iowa or the average price of a residential house, neither of which is a relevant measure to the pension fund investor buying shopping centers and office buildings. The stock and bond people also complain that the return series are based on appraised values, not on market prices, and are therefore far less reliable.

[3]*Mike E. Miles and Thomas E. McCue, "Commercial Real Estate Returns."* The AREUA Journal *(Fall 1984).*

[4]*David J. Hartzell, John Hekman, and Mike E. Miles, "Diversification Categories in Investment Real Estate."* The AREUEA Journal *(Summer 1986).*

[5]*David J. Hartzell, David G. Shulman, and Charles H. Wurtzebach, "Refining the Analysis of Regional Diversification for Income-Producing Real Estate."* The Journal of Real Estate Research 2, 2 *(Winter 1987).*

TABLE 22-8   PRIMARY CRITICISM OF RESEARCH TO DATE

A. It is idiosyncratic, that is, from only one or a few managers.

or

It is nonproperty-specific; that is, it is an average that smooths returns. (An average always reduces the variance.)

B. It is based not on actual sales from the market but on appraised values.

C. It is all finance; it has lost the "real estate."

The authors recognize that the real estate data are not perfect, and we wish we had access to 30 years of transactions data. However, the quality and the quantity of the data have been improving over the last 15 years. Furthermore, the basic results have not changed as the data have improved. As more data have been collected, we have found that earlier studies have, at the very least, been directionally correct. Recent research by Miles and Webb on developing a Hedonic transactions-based model from the Russell-NCREIF Property Index data indicates that higher variability may exist in the real estate market but not enough to offset the diversification advantages of real estate.

Another criticism (C) comes from traditional real estate analysts. They argue that, in trying to accommodate the new institutional investors, we have lost much of great value. They argue that traditional real estate analysis (location, location, location), construction type, lease term, and so on, are all relevant and that, in attempting to accommodate the new pension fund investor, we have homogenized an asset heterogeneous by definition.

As we said earlier in this chapter, in the final analysis we view the application of modern portfolio theory to real estate to be "a necessary but not sufficient condition." Applying MPT to real estate analysis does not replace, but merely complements, the traditional deal-oriented micro analysis that is an integral part of real estate decision making. Together, both approaches support the validity and discipline of the decision-making process and help to ensure that the client's investment goals and objectives are ultimately understood and met.

SUMMARY   Institutional real estate investment is here to stay and will be a growing influence in most major real estate markets. The people making these investment decisions have a tremendous amount of human capital invested in modern portfolio theory, and this theory will continue to shape their decisions over the coming years. If a major player is using this logic, all serious real estate players must understand it.

When we apply the logic to real estate, our data leave much to be desired. Stock and bond analysts are used to extensive information available at relatively low cost on computer tape and disk. In real estate a variety of return indices have been constructed, none of which is truly comparable to stock indices such as the S&P 500. The best of the real estate data bases is the Russell-NCREIF Property Index, which will be the source of considerable research in the future.

Research results to date suggest that real estate is an attractive investment in and of itself. It provides attractive diversification benefits within a mixed asset context, and within the asset class itself. Research further suggests real estate is an excellent inflation hedge. Although these results would portend a tremendous shift of wealth into real estate, criticism does exist. The main criticisms are that idiosyncratic data have been used and that appraisals rather than market prices establish the total return series. Furthermore, traditional real estate analysts have argued that the new demand for "institutional-type analysis" has caused us to lose sight of traditional factors in real estate value.

All this implies some new directions for institutional investment in real estate. Originally, diversification meant constructing a portfolio with different types of property and different locations. This contradicted the more traditional view of real estate, which emphasized specialization in property type or location. Recent research has introduced the concept of "economic" location as a superior diversification category to mere geography. The evidence now indicates that a better marriage of the institutions and real estate is made if the diversification is obtained not just within real estate but by combining real estate with stocks and bonds.

In the future, we believe that you will see heightened activity in real estate investment research. The major institutional players need it and are now doing a good bit of it themselves. As you will see in the next chapters, the rewards are tremendous for the person who develops an interesting strategic niche in institutional real estate investment.

IMPORTANT TERMS

Arbitrage pricing model	Ex ante
Beta	Ex post
Capital asset pricing model (CAPM)	Inflation hedge
	Market risk premium
Correlation coefficient	Options pricing theory
Discount rate	Risk-averse
Diversification	Systematic risk
Economic location	Unanticipated inflation
Efficient frontier	Unsystematic risk

REVIEW QUESTIONS

22.1   What is the significance of the efficient frontier in portfolio analysis?

22.2   How would you estimate the expected return on a portfolio?

22.3   In order to reduce risk in a portfolio context, one must diversify the portfolio well. What does this mean?

22.4   Using the capital asset pricing model, how would you estimate the risk of a portfolio?

22.5   Explain the difference between systematic and unsystematic risk. Which one or ones is the investor most concerned with? Why?

22.6   Studies have shown that real estate returns have zero correlation or negative correlation with the New York Stock Exchange and the S&P 500 Index. If these indices are assumed to represent a market portfolio, how would the results of these studies assist you in establishing your portfolio?

22.7   Explain the major differences in the capital asset pricing model and the arbitrage pricing model. Discuss the basic problems with each model.

22.8   What is the major problem with adapting the options pricing theory to valuing interests in real property?

22.9   If it is true that risk and return are perfectly correlated, how is it possible for real estate investors to have received higher returns and lower risks than for either stocks or bonds?

22.10   What do we mean when we say "real estate is a good inflation hedge"? If this is true, does this mean the investor's real wealth has increased in inflationary times? Why or why not?

$\mathcal{I}$NSTITUTIONAL REAL ESTATE INVESTMENT

In Chapter 20 we explored the concept of value as a function of the expected return and the risk associated with receiving that expected return. In Chapter 21 we used this simple concept to combine all the material developed in the first 19 chapters into the discounted cash flow model. This discounted cash flow model has traditionally been the way to value real estate on a project-by-project basis. However, in Chapter 22 we noted that stock and bond investors have traditionally also used portfolio theory. They have looked not only at the risk of a particular project alone but at the risk in an entire portfolio of investments that included the particular project. As we mentioned in Chapter 22, the institutional investors have entered the real estate arena in a big way. As a result, portfolio risk becomes a more important concept to all players. In this chapter, we seek to use the portfolio theory introduced in Chapter 22 to see how the real estate game is played by institutional real estate investment managers.

We begin by looking at the aggregate level of activity. We then consider each of the major groups of capital market players, and, finally, the way these people make money by managing wealth. This management function usually involves finding and serving a "strategic niche." In total, it is a creative, entrepreneurial, and potentially very rewarding game.

WHAT IS INVOLVED?
Part 1 of this book developed a basic framework in real estate analysis. As part of that framework, we looked at Ibbotson's world wealth portfolio to get a feel for the relative magnitude of the various assets that comprise the wealth of the world. At this point, being a bit more pragmatic, we need to look at U.S. real estate wealth. Here numbers recently developed by Goldman Sachs, Salomon Brothers, the Bureau of Economic Analysis,

TABLE 23-1 ESTIMATES OF TOTAL U.S. COMMERCIAL REAL ESTATE WEALTH (BILLION DOLLARS)	
Goldman Sachs (1985)	$2.500
Salomon Brothers (1988)	$1.295
Bureau of Economic Analysis (1987)	$4.692
Ibbotson (1984)	$ .652
Stephen Roulac (1988)	$3.492

Source: *Mike Miles, "What is the Value of All U.S. Real Estate?"* Real Estate Review, 20 2, *Summer 1990, p. 69.*

Ibbotson & Associates, and Stephen Roulac are estimates of the value of commercial real estate. Looking at Table 23-1, we see that estimates of U.S. real estate wealth totals vary widely. Although these numbers are estimates, and there may be considerable double counting, the table does show us the magnitude of what has to be invested. And people do this job; some of you who are reading this text will join the players who invest and reinvest our wealth.

Through the capital markets, we continually adjust overall portfolio allocation, that is, the ownership of these assets. Each day's savings are put into those areas that promise the highest return at the lowest risk. The people who organize and constitute the capital markets are the players who determine what America will look like tomorrow. In this introductory real estate text, we are, of course, concerned primarily with the real estate players. But looking at Table 23-1 again, we can see that the real estate players are a major portion of the total capital markets.

THE REAL ESTATE CAPITAL MARKETS PLAYERS

LIFE INSURANCE COMPANY GENERAL ACCOUNTS

The oldest—and still a major—institutional real estate investment player is the life insurance company. Through their general accounts, life insurance companies have developed tremendous portfolios, a good portion of which has always been invested in real estate. Although some of the life insurance companies originally concentrated in residential mortgages, today most have moved toward commercial mortgages and real estate equities. Some of the more aggressive companies, such as the Prudential Realty Group, are developers as well as investors, building product for their own general account and the accounts of pension clients.

SAVINGS AND LOAN ASSOCIATIONS

As mentioned in Part 5, the nation's savings and loans have been significantly deregulated, allowing them to better match their investments to their liabilities. In attempting this matching, the S&Ls moved aggressively from residential to commercial real estate finance. Some of the larger S&Ls have actually taken significant equity positions, although most have concentrated their efforts in commercial mortgages. At the beginning of 1990, it appears that many of the S&Ls have been overly aggressive and underestimated the risks inherent in both construction and permanent lending on the commercial side. The astute student will closely follow important developments in this area. In one such development, the Federal Home Loan Bank Board has organized the Resolution Trust Corporation (RTC) to manage and liquidate "problem loans" acquired from troubled S&Ls. A good many of these are commercial construction loans, and the performance of the new corporation will have a major impact on many real estate markets.

PENSION FUND INVESTMENT MANAGERS

Most pension funds do not manage their own investments. Particularly in the real estate field, they tend to hire outside investment managers.[1] There are three broad groupings of these managers. First are the life insurance companies, which entered the pension fund management area during the 1970s. Major players include the Prudential Realty Group, Aetna Realty Investors, Inc., Cigna Investments, Inc., and Equitable Real Estate Management, Inc. With their extensive experience in real estate investment for their own account, insurance companies applied investment knowledge to servicing the needs of third-party pension funds.

Life companies pioneered the use of separate accounts for pension fund asset management. Under the separate account scheme, asset ownership is held in the name of the life company, with all benefits accruing to the pension participant via an annuity contract. This ownership vehicle allows pension funds to access the financial benefits of real estate ownership without assuming the risks associated with direct property ownership. Separate accounts also allow the pension fund, if it so desires, to delegate complete investment discretion, that is, investment decision-making control, to the investment manager. Traditionally, most pension funds preferred delegating investment discretion to investment managers. However, recent trends have shown more pension plans retaining at least partial investment discretion. Separate accounts can be structured for use in commingled funds (many investors investing in multiple properties) or single-client accounts (one investor investing in a series of properties).

The second group of outside investment managers are the bank trust departments, which manage a significant volume of real estate

---

[1] An excellent history of pension fund real estate investment is provided by Meyer Milnikoff in the Fall 1984 issue of The Journal of the American Real Estate and Urban Economics Association.

investment for pension funds. First Wachovia Corporation, Wells Fargo Realty Advisors, NCNB National Bank, and Bank of Boston represent some of the market leaders. In fact, First Wachovia Corporation (then Wachovia Bank) was the first bank to establish a **commingled real estate investment account** for pension funds in the early 1970s.

Third, independent investment managers also offer their services to pension funds. Some organizations, such as JMB Institutional Realty Corporation and Balcor Institutional Realty Advisors, Inc., entered the pension management business after establishing track records in the public and private syndication business. These firms are generally not affiliated with insurance companies or banks and have markedly increased the level of competition in the business.

Some investment management firms have also been launched by individuals who left other real estate operations. For example, TCW Realty Advisors was founded by individuals previously associated with commercial brokerages, whereas McMahan Real Estate Advisors, Inc., grew out of a real estate consulting operation. Such organizations tend to focus their investment activities in more localized or regional areas and do not generally attempt to offer nationwide investment management services. As of December 31, 1989, the 52 largest pension fund investment managers, including life insurance companies, comprised the National Council of Real Estate Investment Fiduciaries. They, along with the Frank Russell Company, produce a quarterly return series in what is known as the Russell-NCREIF Property Index (See box 23-1). A segment of the fourth-quarter 1989 issue of the NCREIF Real Estate Performance Report is presented in Table 23-2. These historical performance numbers for real estate are needed by portfolio analysts and are derived from the Russell-NCREIF Property Index.

SYNDICATIONS

Syndication has many meanings. In medieval Europe the syndicator was the one who oversaw the village property. In this country, the word **syndication** simply refers to a way to finance a property. The syndicator is the one who brings together a large number of investors, acquires an appropriate property, manages the property over the holding period, and eventually disposes of the property. More complex syndications require a great deal of talent ranging from accounting and tax preparations to property management, negotiation, and financial planning. The syndication business in the United States grew dramatically in the 1980s. However, such offerings declined precipitously when the Tax Reform Act of 1986 eliminated many of the tax benefits associated with syndication.

The major syndication firms such as JMB have grown in size and

23-1

THE RUSSELL-NCREIF PROPERTY INDEX

The Russell-NCREIF Property Index measures the historical performance of income-producing properties owned by commingled funds on behalf of qualified pension and profit-sharing trusts, or owned directly by these trusts and managed on a separate account basis. The starting date for the Index is December 31, 1977. In order to eliminate the effects of mortgage indebtedness on valuation, only unleveraged properties (properties owned free of any debt) are included. The data incorporated in the Index are drawn from the performance of properties managed by voting members of the National Council of Real Estate Investment Fiduciaries (NCREIF).

All properties that qualified for the Index are included. Fourteen managers provided the initial property base for the Index of 234 properties, valued at $587.3 million on December 31, 1977. The property base has been expanded since that time through the addition of properties acquired by all members contributing property data. As of December 31, 1989, 1,222 properties valued at $15.9 billion were included in the Index.

The Index properties are both 100-percent owned and held in joint venture partnerships. The results of the partnership properties are reported as if they were wholly owned, disregarding the effects of any partnership agreements. When an Index property is sold by a participating manager, its historical performance data remain in the Index, net sales proceeds are entered as the final market value in the quarter in which the property is sold, and no further data for that property are added. The Index returns represent an aggregate of individual property returns calculated quarterly before deduction of portfolio management fees.

The rate of return for the properties included in the Index is based on two distinct components of return: (1) net operating income and (2) the change in property market value (appreciation or depreciation). The increase or decrease in market value of any property is determined by real estate appraisal methodology, consistently applied.

The Russell-NCREIF Property Index contains performance data on five major categories of properties: residential apartment complexes; office buildings; retail properties, including regional, community, and neighborhood shopping centers as well as free-standing store buildings; research and development/office facilities; and warehouses.

The Index is also segmented by four geographic regions and eight regional divisions.

Source: The NCREIF Real Estate Performance Report, Fourth Quarter 1989. Published by the National Council of Real Estate Investment Fiduciaries and Frank Russell Company.

TABLE 23-2 RUSSEL-NCREIF PROPERTY INDEX:INCOME-APPRECIATION COMPONENTS, ANNUAL TIME-WEIGHTED RATES OF RETURN, 1978–89

YEAR	INCOME	APPRECIATION	TOTAL RETURN
1978	8.70%	6.70%	15.90%
1979	8.80	11.10	20.60
1980	8.40	9.11	18.07
1981	8.06	8.30	16.85
1982	7.89	1.46	9.44
1983	7.77	5.14	13.21
1984	7.34	5.43	13.07
1985	7.50	2.33	9.96
1986	7.23	−0.73	6.46
1987	7.03	−1.55	5.39
1988	7.03	0.14	7.18
1989	6.71	−0.65	6.02

Note: *The income and appreciation components of return are calculated individually, and thus will not add up to the total annual return due to the effect of cross-compounding.*

TABLE 23-2 (CONTINUED) RUSSEL-NCREIF PROPERTY INDEX: ONE-, THREE-, FIVE-, AND TEN-YEAR TIME-WEIGHTED RATES OF RETURN FOR THE YEAR ENDING 12/31/89

	INCOME	APPRECIATION	TOTAL RETURN
One year	6.71%	−0.65%	6.71%
Three years	6.92	−0.69	6.20
Five years	7.10	−0.10	6.99
Ten years	7.50	2.83	10.48

Source: *Russell-NCREIF Property Index, Fourth Quarter 1989. National Council of Real Estate Fiduciaries.*

become major players in the real estate capital markets. Several of the major syndicators are also pension fund investment managers. For example, LaSalle Advisors Limited, JMB Institutional Realty Corporation, and Balcor Institutional Realty Advisors, Inc., are all members of the National Council of Real Estate Investment Fiduciaries.

In addition to the major public syndications (those registered with the Securities and Exchange Commission), there has been a substantial volume of private syndications. While their volume cannot be measured with precision, private syndications are estimated to be at least as large as the public syndications. Prior to the 1986 Tax Reform Act, public syndicators—and to some extent private syndicators—offered two general types of product. To high-tax-bracket individuals they offered deep tax shelters with substantial leverage and emphasis on tax deductions and investment tax credits; "deep" means $3 to $5 in tax deductions, in early years, for every $1 dollar invested in the syndication. Many of the deep-shelter syndications have proven to be poor investments at best. As over-building resulted in over 20 percent vacancy rates in many markets, the underlying economics of the market simply were not capable of support-ing the extensive leverage used by these syndications. As a result, in the late 1980s and in early 1990, several large public syndicators fell on hard times. These firms included VMS and Fogelman.

Deep shelters have been described by *Barron's* and *Forbes* magazines in many stories focusing on the abuses of syndication. We are pleased to note that the 1986 Tax Reform Act eliminated some of those possibilities for abuse. As a result, public syndicators have shifted dramatically from tax-oriented syndications toward servicing IRAs and Keogh accounts. The authors believe that the volume of private syndications, most of which historically have been tax-oriented, has declined relative to the volume of public syndications during 1986 and that this trend will con-tinue for the next few years.

Looking at Box 23-2 and 23-3, we can see clearly that the real estate investment trust made a comeback among investors only to level off at the end of the 1980s. In Part 6, on taxation, we learned that the real estate investment trust is a good vehicle for investors who are not ori-ented toward tax shelters. (Income is not taxed at the trust level and passes through to the individual; a gain on sale is treated as a capital gain; but losses do not flow through the trust to the individual.) There-fore, the REIT has become more popular as syndicators moved away from deep-tax-shelter syndication toward the tax-exempt community, particularly IRAs and Keoghs. (REITs can be sold in many very small shares, as they would have to be for the IRA market; most other forms of real estate investing require much large chunks of capital.) Still, the limited partnership is the primary vehicle for syndicators and will proba-bly remain so because, as we pointed out in Part 6, it is ideal for passing tax losses through to individual investors.

CORPORATE FIXED ASSET MANAGEMENT

Though often overlooked (by people who didn't read Chapter 12), in the long run the most important real estate capital market player is the corporate fixed asset manager. This corporation officer is responsible for the corporation's fixed assets. Today U.S. corporations have over $3 trillion in fixed assets and own a good portion of the major real estate listed in Table 23-1. As corporations become more cost conscious, it is only logical that they will more aggressively manage the fixed assets that

23-2
REAL ESTATE
INVESTMENT
TRUSTS
EXPERIENCE
HIGH GROWTH

The real estate investment trust (REIT) industry has recently experienced spectacular growth in total REITs formed, dollar volume of public offerings, total assets, and new REIT structures. Some of the variations in new REIT structures have developed along the following dimensions.

- One hundred percent specified versus blind pool
- Existing properties versus development properties
- Finite life versus open-ended
- Distribution of gains versus reinvestment
- Equity versus mortgage
- Leveraged versus unleveraged
- Property type
- Nature of the fee structure

The phoenixlike performance of REITs is due to several factors. The market has come to understand the true factors that troubled the REIT industry in the early 1970s, and REIT shares offer greater liquidity compared to partnership shares. Today's REITs are emphasizing equity or hybrid assets rather than mortgages and deemphasizing tax benefits on the eve of potentially significant tax code changes. Falling interest rates during late 1985 and early 1986 have made REITs more attractive as well as more suitable as tax-free investment funds (e.g., IRA and Keogh funds).

According to the National Association of Real Estate Investment Trusts (NAREIT), more REITs were formed in the first half of 1985 than in the previous four years combined. The growth in total REIT assets increased 50 percent during the first six months of 1985. REIT share prices were up 5.8 percent during the first half of 1985 and up 16 percent over the previous 12 months.

Source: Randall Zisler, *The Goldman Sachs Real Estate Report* (New York: October 1985), p. 9.

comprise the largest portion of their balance sheet. The authors believe that, in the decade ahead, brighter and brighter people will be attracted to corporate fixed asset management as corporations find attractive financing alternatives in their real estate. Already corporations have recognized the pension funds' need to diversify and have begun to package their assets on a **sale-lease-back** basis to the pension funds. In this way, real estate financing becomes an alternative for the corporation seeking cash to grow, along with the traditional sources of new stock issues and new corporate debt.

**23-3
REAL ESTATE
INVESTMENT
TRUSTS SUFFER
DECLINE**

The real estate investment trust (REIT) industry has experienced its longest recession since the inception of the National Association of Real Estate Investment Trusts (NAREIT) Index, in 1972. Equity REITs, as a leading indicator, have for an extended period of time been forecasting lower real estate values. Equity REITs, which had experienced steady appreciation growth between 1975 and 1987, have since experienced steady decline. According to NAREIT, REITs showed a negative return of 3.9 percent for the 12 months ending June 30, 1990.

The REIT industry, however, may have temporarily reached the end of its decline. This expected improvement is based not on any improvement in real estate markets but, instead, on lower interest rates. Lower interest rates make REITs more attractive on a relative yield basis and lower their cost of capital for purposes of acquisitions. Recent problems with real estate markets in general will cause real estate values to be based on a cash flow (yield) basis instead of the potential for capital gains.

The current softness in the REIT market is expected to ease in the 1990s as a result of several factors. The liquidity of REITs, relative to other real estate investment vehicles, will be important to many investors. Older, established REITs with cash balances and open bank lines will be able to capitalize on the current weakness in many real estate markets.

Source: Alex. Brown & Sons, Inc., *Real Estate Stocks Monitor, Second Quarter 1990* (Baltimore, MD: July 1990)

It is essential for us to have a feel for these capital market players if we are to understand what is going on in local real estate markets. The major capital market players have become individually and collectively so large that today no serious local player in the real estate game can ignore their presence. As in Chapter 16, on secondary mortgages, we will attempt to describe the game in general by viewing it as an **entrepreneur** would. In the rest of this chapter, we will describe how the individual, working for the institutional players described earlier, seeks to win the game by using the portfolio theory developed in Chapter 22.

**MAKING MONEY
BY MANAGING
WEALTH**

The different real estate capital market players seek to use modern portfolio theory plus their own entrepreneurial skills to serve a client and thereby win the game themselves. There are two basic ways to do this. The first is to manage investments for one of the major institutions such as the pension funds. As we noted before, the pension funds are huge pools of savings and typically hire outside managers for their real estate investment. In the 1970s, their real estate investing consisted primarily of "naive" diversification. In other words, "There is a lot of real estate out there; therefore, we should have some in our portfolio." In the 1980s, their real estate investing formally began to consider portfolio theory and the correlation of the returns on various real estate assets with the returns on other assets currently held in their portfolio. In the 1990s, the significance of applying portfolio theory to real estate will lead to the application of organizational theory to real estate investment management organizations.

The second major way to make money managing wealth is by consulting. Usually associated with consulting is "deal making." Here we have the investment banks and other individuals and firms seeking to serve their corporate and pension clients with good ideas and the ability to carry out their ideas. For example, an investment banker saw Bank of America's need to improve its net worth and recognized the opportunity to do so by selling the corporate headquarters building in San Francisco. The investment banker persuaded Bank of America, found a buyer, negotiated the transaction, and received a substantial fee for handling the transactions. Another set of investment bankers did the same thing with the Rockefeller Center properties in New York. This was one of the most complex real estate deals ever arranged and included a foreign issue of **zero coupon bonds** and a domestic real estate investment trust. Behind it all was the creative individual who saw the Rockefellers' needs and the potential to meet those needs with real property assets.

On both the asset management side and the consulting–deal-making side, players should be creative. In addition to being creative, they should have interdisciplinary training. As we mentioned in Part 1, real estate has always required interdisciplinary thinking; for players in the major capital markets game, integrating different fields is even more important. The player must be an accountant in order to understand the earnings per share impact on decisions. The player must be financially astute and conversant with modern portfolio theory to show the buyer which property is the ideal portfolio fit. The player must clearly be a marketing expert. In a world that is overbuilt (e.g., more office space than office tenants), putting the tenant in the building is often even more important than building the building. Finally, the player must have a sense of production. Building a "**smart**" **building** (one with electronically controlled security and HVAC—heating, ventilating, air conditioning—and with shared telecommunications) is a far from simple task, as we will see in Part 8. The upshot, as you might expect, is that when creativity and interdisciplinary training are demanded, high salaries are supplied. As real estate capital markets have evolved over the last few years, many of the key players have changed positions between the firms that manage and those that consult.

WAYS TO PLAY OR THE SEARCH FOR A STRATEGIC NICHE

Real estate capital market players offer a variety of services to their clients. The first is portfolio allocation, that is, using the Markowitz model (from Chapter 22) to show an institutional investor how much of its portfolio should be in real estate. As shown in Table 23-3, one analyst believes that real estate with little or no leverage is a good bet for the investor seeking a low-risk or medium portfolio. Remember that in the Markowtiz model the first step is to develop the efficient frontier (the highest returns for each level of risk) and then allow the client to specify the appropriate level of targeted return. If the client wants a high-risk–high-return portfolio, unleveraged real estate might not be as attractive. However, for the more conservative investor, E & D Associates feels that low-leverage real estate is a good bet and should constitute 41 percent of the portfolio.

The largest institutional real estate investment manager is the Prudential Realty Group, managing (including its own large general account real estate) over $50 billion in real estate equity and mortgage investments. PRISA, a separate account for pension funds, celebrated its twentieth anniversary in 1990. Equitable and Aetna also have large interests in real estate, again both in their general accounts and in separate accounts for pension funds. Since these large-scale players have something that approximates an index fund (i.e., one analogous to an S&P 500

TABLE 23-3 PORTFOLIO ALLOCATION IN THE MARKOWITZ FRAMEWORK: USING HISTORICAL DATA FOR THE 1974–88 PERIOD

ASSET CLASS	LOW RISK	MEDIUM RISK	HIGH RISK
T-bills[a]	28%	5%	5%
Stocks[a]	25%	25%	25%
Bonds[a]	20%	20%	20%
International stocks[a]	0%	11%	40%
Real estate[a]	27%	39%	10%
Total	100%	100%	100%
Mean annual return	11.4%	13.5%	15.5%
Standard deviation	5.34%	6.35%	11.89%

Sources of Data for Asset Classes for 1974–88:

T-bills	90-day Treasury bills
Bonds	Salomon Brothers High-Grade Long-Term Bond Index
Stocks	Standard & Poor's 500
International stocks	EAFE Index
Real estate	All separate account properties of a leading investment manager

Note: *The period selected and data sources are critical; longer or shorter periods may yield different results.*
[a] *Minimum 25% in S&P 500, 20% in long-term corporate bonds, 5% in T-bills (cash), and nonminimum in international or real estate.*

stock fund in that it incorporates real estate of all types, sizes, and geographic locations in the United States), other players have searched for a strategic niche—in other words, something that may not be as general but serves some need of a particular client even better. As their competition searches for a strategic niche, these three large life insurance companies have begun to offer yet other funds (investment vehicles) to compete. Aetna, for example, has been very successful with a **participating mortgage fund.**

The game involves using portfolio theory and entrepreneurial skills, as well as basic real estate analysis, to come up with a better way to serve the client. At this date, we do not know who the winners will be. However, we believe the winners will be firms with this combination of characteristics: creativity, deal-making ability, administrative know-how, and a competitive reward system.

❑ **INNOVATION.**   The investment manager must be able to "see" new kinds of deals. The ideal environment not only fosters such innovation, but also protects the innovator from hasty condemnation during the periodic downside stages that are inevitable in such endeavors.

❑ **DEAL MAKING.**   The investment manager must be able to negotiate and to close purchases or sales quickly.

❑ **ADMINISTRATION.**   The investment manager must have plan and budget discipline. He should be organized to have close contact with his ultimate customers and the high level of informal communication often associated with success in such ventures.

❑ **INCENTIVE REWARD FOR PERFORMANCE.**   For displaying or not displaying these characteristics, the investment manager (the individual, not necessarily his firm) should be compensated in a way that rewards good performance and punishes bad performance. Structuring the incentive is not easy because pension funds may make honest men millionaires while flirting with ERISA restrictions regarding risk avoidance and conflict of interest.

Since it seems unlikely that one human being would possess all three ideal qualities, the ideal investment management firm is probably a team. On the other hand, it is difficult for huge organizations to accommodate deal making and innovation. Therefore, we have seen the giant institutions create separate real estate investment groups small enough to play the game aggressively. Each of these groups has its own, at least partially unique, strategy.

Some players seek a strategic niche in different property types, as shown in Box 23-4. They gain a certain comparative advantage in finding, analyzing, acquiring, and managing different types of property. The

23-4
ELEMENTARY
INCOME
PROPERTY
CHARACTERIS-
TICS

A. *Multifamily Residential*

   1. Importance of *location* in determining vacancy and rent levels.

   2. Preferred depreciation method.

   3. Not as liquid as common stocks.

   4. Tenant selection as an important management activity.

B. *Office Buildings*

   1. More sophisticated leases.

   2. Importance of major tenant (draw, financing).

   3. Location and accommodation as possibly more important than the price.

   4. Elevator times.

   5. Possible tenant equity participation.

C. *Warehouses*

   1. Longest economic life because functional obsolescence is minimal.

   2. Ceiling clearance and floor load capacity.

   3. Potential estate-planning tool.

D. *Hotels*

   1. Specialized building + short lease period + high levels of services = greater risk. (Complex logistics in building design may add to construction costs as well as operating costs. Short lease periods increase the risk of vacancy. Services mean more people management and cash control problems.)

   2. Greater risk indicates a need for correspondingly greater potential returns.

   3. Franchises.

   4. Management contracts.

E. *Shopping Centers*

   1. Quality of leases and tenant mix as determinants of the attractiveness.

   2. Ability to contract away cost increases.

   3. Percentage rents as an inflation hedge.

F. *Raw Land*

   1. Greatest risk (except possibly urban redevelopment, which incorporates a greater degree of government involvement along with land investment).

2. Importance of urban and regional analysis—the land use decision has not yet been made.

3. Zoning and rezoning issues.

4. Availability of public services and the timing of new services.

5. The carry problem—how to meet property tax and interest payments during the holding period.

6. New interest limitation deduction.

7. Chain letter effect motivated by the argument that "They aren't making any more of it."

8. Agricultural lands—a whole different dimension.

9. Recreational land developments—yet another dimension.

different types of real estate offer different returns at varying risk exposures, appealing to a range of clients.

The interesting question is which type of real estate is the best diversification for an investor heavily invested in stocks and bonds.

In addition to portfolios created around various types of real property, there are portfolios that concentrate on only one part of the country, such as the Northeast, or on cities with populations between 300,000 and

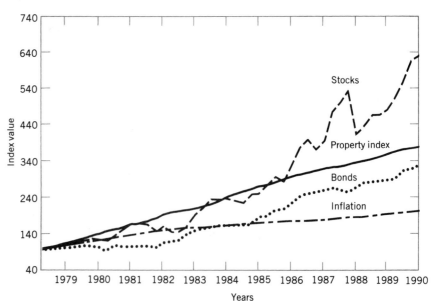

FIGURE 23-1   *Russel-NCREIF property index and alternative investments, January 1, 1979–December 31, 1989*

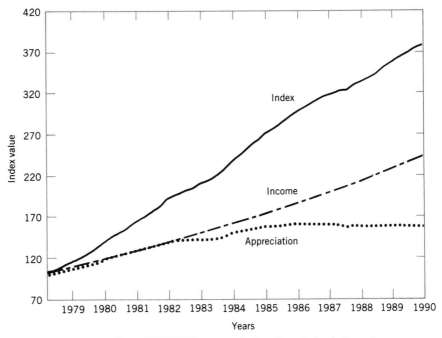

F I G U R E 23-2 *Russel-NCREIF property index. Cumulative index values, January 1, 1979–December 31, 1989*

700,000. Still others are chosen to fit a strategic niche based on certain types of leases, and some consist of development properties. As we have seen throughout the text, there are many different ways to separate the bundle of rights in real estate. Portfolio theory just allows us another way to be creative.

In addition to forming new portfolios, several consultants have come up with new ways to calculate return and new ways to evaluate risks. Roger Ibbotson and friends at the Ibbotson Company in Chicago have proposed "new equilibrium theory" as an explanation of why real estate *appears* to offer superior returns to stocks and bonds (i.e., greater returns for equal levels of risk). He regards investors as pursuing return "net" of all investor costs. In his scenario, each investor translates all risks, taxes, and burdens of illiquidity and obtaining information into costs that reduce "net return." It is the net return, balanced against risk, that determines value. Ibbotson would argue that conventional measures of return have been too high since they have not included all costs to the investor. His is an interesting theory, and it does help explain why real estate returns appear higher than stock and bond returns. Certainly, the real estate investor does face greater information costs and greater difficulty selling than a typical stock and bond investor.

SUMMARY   Real estate capital markets are large in themselves and comprise a significant proportion of the total U.S. capital markets. Some of the players who manage funds, like the life insurance companies, have been around a long time. Others, such as the pension fund investment managers, are quite new. Some, like the deep tax syndicators, are shrinking in size, and others will grow dramatically, particularly those dealing with corporate fixed asset managers.

The game is to make money by managing the investment process: either by taking people's savings and investing it for them or by advising them and structuring deals for them. The winners in this game will be those who design the vehicles that offer clients what they need. Winners will exhibit creativity and entrepreneurship. The game is classic real estate, played for high stakes.

IMPORTANT TERMS

Commingled real estate invest-
  ment account
Entrepreneur
Participating mortgage fund

Sale-lease-back
Smart building
Syndication
Zero coupon bonds

REVIEW QUESTIONS

23.1 What effect has the 1986 Tax Reform Act had on the structure of real estate syndications?

23.2 Why are the REITs regaining popularity in the 1990s?

23.3 Explain the difference between the diversification approach used by pension fund managers in the 1970s and the approach used in the 1990s.

23.4 In addition to measuring only the performance of income-producing properties, the Russell-NCREIF Property Index differs significantly from the NYSE, S&P 500, and others in another important way. What is it?

23.5 For the IRAs and Keoghs, why is the REIT an ownership form preferred to the limited partnership?

23.6 Cite two ways in which real estate capital market players can make money by managing wealth.

23.7 List the characteristics needed by real estate investment managers in order to become winners in the future.

23.8 Why might corporate fixed-asset management represent a rewarding career path?

23.9   Why does investment in income properties provide substantial diversification potential?

23.10   Which institutions are likely to considerably increase their involvement in real estate investment during the 1990–1995 period?

REFERENCES   BOOKS

Alexander, Gordon J., and William F. Sharpe. *Investments.* 4th ed. Englewood Cliffs, N.J.: Prentice Hall, 1990.

Allen, Roger H. *Real Estate Strategy.* 3rd ed. Cincinnati: Southwestern, 1988.

Amling, Frederick. *Investments: An Introduction to Analysis and Management.* 6th ed. Englewood Cliffs: N.J.: Prentice Hall, 1989.

Armfield, W. A. *Investment in Subsidized Housing: Opportunities and Risks.* New York: Pilot Books, 1979.

Beaton, W. R., and T. D. Robertson. *Real Estate Investment.* 2nd ed. Englewood Cliffs, N.J.: Prentice-Hall, 1977.

Case, Fred E. *Investing in Real Estate.* Englewood Cliffs, N.J.: Prentice Hall, 1988.

Cooper, James R., Steven D. Kapplin, Paul D. Lapides, Steven Pyhrr, and Larry Wofford. *Real Estate Investment: Strategy, Analysis, Decision.* 2nd ed. New York: Wiley, 1989.

Creedy, Judith, and Norbert F. Wall. *Real Estate, Investment by Objectives.* New York: McGraw-Hill, 1979.

Greer, Gaylon E., and Michael D. Farrell. *Investment Analysis for Real Estate Decisions.* Hinsdale, Ill.: Dryden Press, 1983.

Lyons, Paul. *Investing in Residential Real Estate.* Reston, Va.: Reston Publishing Co., 1981.

Messner, Stephen D., et al. *Marketing, Investment Real Estate: Finance Taxation Techniques.* 3rd ed. Chicago: Realtors National Marketing Institute of the National Association of Realtors, 1986.

Meyers, Myron. *Foreign Investment in United States Real Estate.* Homewood, Ill.: Dow-Jones-Irwin, 1982.

Miles, Martin J. *Real Estate Investor's Complete Handbook.* Englewood Cliffs, N.J.: Prentice-Hall, 1982.

Reilly, Frank K. *Investment Analysis and Portfolio Management.* 3rd ed. Orlando, Fla.: Dryden Press, 1989.

Reit Fact Book. Washington, D.C.: National Association of Real Estate Investment Trusts Inc., 1990.

Seldin, Maury. *Real Estate Investments for Profit Through Appreciation.* Reston, Va.: Reston Publishing Co., 1980.

Seldin, Maury, and Richard H. Swesnik. *Real Estate Investment Strategy.* 2nd ed. New York: Wiley-Interscience, 1979.

Sirmans, C. F., and Austin, J. Jaffe. *Fundamentals of Real Estate Investment.* Englewood Cliffs, N.J.: Prentice-Hall, 1986.

Unger, Maurice A. *How to Invest in Real Estate.* Rev. ed. New York: McGraw-Hill, 1984.

Wendt, Paul F., and Alan R. Cerf. *Real Estate Investment Analysis and Taxation,* 2nd ed. New York: McGraw-Hill, 1979.

Wiedemer, John P. *Real Estate Investment.* 4th ed. Reston, Va.: Reston Publishing Co., 1988.

NEWSLETTERS AND PERIODICALS

Institutional Real Estate Letter. San Francisco: Institutional Real Estate (monthly).

International Property Report. Scottsdale, Ariz.: International Real Estate Institute.

Investment Research Review. London: Richard Ellis Research (monthly).

Japanese Investment in U.S. Real Estate Review. Phoenix, Ariz.: Mead Ventures (monthly).

Market Profile. New York: Baring Institutional Realty (quarterly).

National Council of Real Estate Investment Fiduciaries. Tacoma, Wash.: Frank Russell Company (quarterly).

National Real Estate Investor. Atlanta, Ga.: Communications Channels, Inc. (monthly)

The Real Estate Securities Journal. Chicago.

REIS Reports. New York (periodic by market).

The Stanger Register. Shrewsbury, N.J.: Stanger and Co. (monthly).

PART **8**

REAL ESTATE
DEVELOPMENT

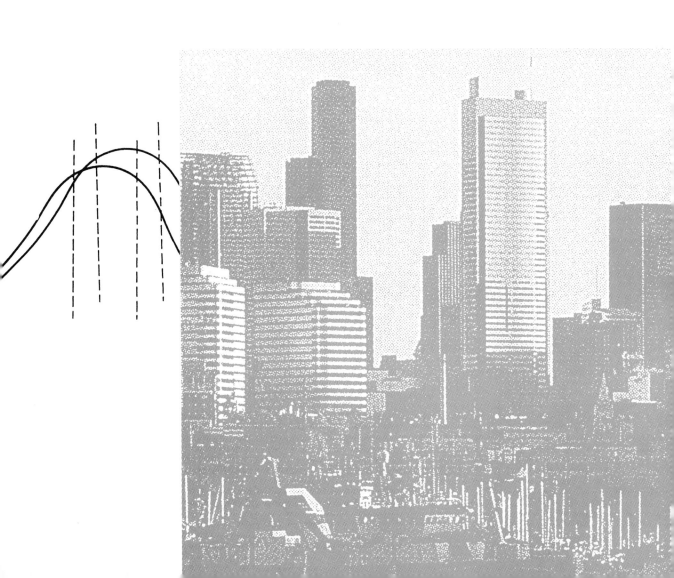

EVELOPMENT: THE PROCESS, THE PLAYERS, AND THE ATMOSPHERE

Real estate development takes place in an extremely dynamic world. Real property development is the crux of the game, offering risks and rewards to the developer, all the other players, the neighbors of the property, and government. Real property development creates the jobs and the constructed space that are so important to our general economy. And it is primarily during development that crucial issues are raised concerning the impact of the physical environment on society. Finally, in terms of the game, real estate development (and redevelopment) is one of the few remaining places where entrepreneurial skill can bring a big return. The developer operates under the same general rules of the game that we have observed throughout the book. The same legal rules set the stage, the same appraisal techniques apply, the same marketing functions are relevant, and the same financial institutions are involved. Therefore, the same analytical framework is appropriate.

Now, however, the investor is buying a pro forma (hypothetical) bottom line. The improved space does not exist, no historic earnings record can be examined, and the investor must be totally forward-looking in approach. Since there is no history (and in the case of more innovative space, few good comparables), the investor's understanding of the marketplace and the needs of the users of space is even more critical.

In the next few chapters we will explore the real property development process. Chapter 24 highlights the participants in the development process and their respective roles. The role of the developer as entrepreneur and decision maker is emphasized, and ten key development decision points are introduced. In addition, since a major aspect of the developer's role focuses on managing the risk associated with development, the concept of risk-control techniques as decision points is presented. In Chapter 25 the real property development process is presented as a series of eight stages. The role of each of the development participants is integrated into an actual development case. In this manner, the analytical framework developed throughout the book is adapted to the real property development process. In Chapter 26 we examine the feasibility study, a key risk-control device in the development process.

THE CREATION OF SPACE

It is the architect's role to translate the developer's ideas into working plans and specifications. John Portman is a well-known architect-turned-developer. As an architect whose ideas could not be fulfilled by existing developers, he became involved in the entrepreneurial effort in order to execute his ideas in bricks and mortar. His work is important in any discussion of the creation of space because he proved that the public would pay (i.e., effective demand exists) for unique and creative space. His idea is that space should be designed for people. An immediate dollars-and-cents accounting concept must be transcended and a look given to the total needs of the human being in designing the constructed physical environment. However, Portman also proved that the market system works and that design itself may not be sufficient to overcome lack of demand and excessive financial risk.

IT BEGINS WITH THE LAND

Before we move on to consider how "dreams" are turned into reality, it is appropriate to look first to the land itself. There are four common development situations. Each presents the developer with different development possibilities. First, "a site looking for a use" is perhaps the most common situation. In this instance, a landowner wants to develop his or her land, or an investor buys land, without first deciding on a particular development plan. Second, there is "a use looking for a site." Here, the developer notes a need in a certain area for a specific kind of constructed space, for example, miniwarehouses. Then the most appropriate site must be found. The third situation represents "capital looking for an investment opportunity." An investor has cash and needs to invest.[1] Finally, the development process might focus on "an existing development." In this case, an existing structure may be converted to a new use or be "redeveloped."

Although all four situations are common in the real world, the second alternative is the most efficient way to turn ideas into reality. The site looking for a use is in some sense putting the cart before the horse. The developer seeks to satisfy needs in society, not pour concrete on every square foot of land. Capital looking for an investment should involve looking at all investment opportunities, not just development. As was seen in the case of the real estate investment trusts (REITs) during the 1970s, searching too hard for too few good deals may result in stretching pro formas and finally in bad investments.

---

[1]*The first three of these four development perspectives come from James A. Graaskamp,* A Guide to Feasibility Analysis *(Chicago: Society of Real Estate Appraisers, 1970), p. 13.*

THE
DEVELOPMENT
PROCESS

The **development process** can be defined as the act of bringing an idea or concept to successful fruition in bricks and mortar (space) with associated services. It is a complex process requiring the coordinated expertise of many professionals. On the investment side, sources of financing must be attracted by the promise of sharing the cash flow generated by development in a manner that properly balances risk and return. The physical construction of the project requires coordination among architects, engineers, and contractors. The public sector, especially local government, must approve the legality of the development in terms of zoning, building codes, and so on. Ultimately and most importantly, user needs must be satisfied. This requires the developer to identify a market segment in which sufficient effective market demand *will* exist for the type of space *to be created.* In short, successful development requires a team effort.

The members of the development team can be viewed as coparticipants even if they do not have a formal partnership relationship. At the same time, they have different goals or reasons for becoming involved in development. To understand the development process, we must know something about these different goals. In addition, we will look at the function of each participant. The interaction of these players provides the dynamic element in the analytical framework first presented in Chapter 1. Before we begin with the developer, let's first look at the setting of the game in the 1990s and the importance of good ideas.

CREATIVITY COMES FROM MANY SOURCES

As the 1990s begin, most real estate markets are overbuilt. It is even more true today than at any point in the past that successful development requires creativity. In an overbuilt market, commodity space is not needed. In fact, with overbuilding comes reduced rents and losses to those who provide commodity space.

Of course, developers, who are by nature optimistic, usually view their location, their idea, and their team as unique. However, the realities of the marketplace in the 1990s have forced even the most optimistic developers to seek niches in which they may create the kind of space that society will need over the decades to come. Ideas for new development come from many sources,[2] but for ease of presentation, we will group them into short-term, long-term, and looking and touching.

Short-term mental stimulation comes from the seemingly endless flow of newsletters that developers digest on a regular basis. Box 24-1 presents highlights of the *Salomon Brothers Quarterly Real Estate Review*

---

[2]*The Urban Land Institute has recently released its first textbook titled* The Real Estate Development Process. *Since there is a considerable overlap of authors between this text and that one, many ideas find their way into both. The interested student is directed toward that ULI publication for considerably more detail on how ideas are generated and defined so as to become successful development projects.*

24-1
Real Estate Market Review— Annual Review and Outlook

Economic Outlook

- The economy will slow to a crawl in the first half of 1990, with the growth in real gross national product (GNP) dwindling to approximately 1 percent. Many local economies will be in recession, but such conditions will not extend nationally. The slowdown will cause the Federal Reserve Board to ease credit sufficiently to resume modest economic growth of 2 to 2½ percent in the second half of 1990. The slow-growth environment will exacerbate the excess capacity problem that now affects most commercial real estate.

Real Estate Equity

- The Frank Russell Company (FRC) Property Index returned an estimated 7.3 percent during 1989, up slightly from 7.2 percent in 1988. At 31.2 percent and 14.4 percent, respectively, the total returns of both the Standard & Poor's 500 Index (S&P 500) and the Salomon Brothers Broad Investment-Grade Bond Index significantly outperformed real estate. The office sector remained the weakest component of the FRC, returning an estimated 4.3 percent while returns of warehouse properties held steady at just under 11 percent and retail properties declined to an estimated 11.6 percent. We anticipate that real estate returns will again approximate 7 percent in 1990.

- We continue to believe that domestic real estate investors will go global in the 1990s. Several U.S. managers obtained investor commitments for international real estate vehicles in 1989.

- Equity real estate investment trusts (REITs) generated a total return of 8.9 percent for 1989, lagging behind the broad stock index's 31.2 percent return. Weak real estate fundamentals limited security issuance to $1.6 billion.

Real Estate Debt

- Default pressures, beginning with thrifts and ascending the credit quality ladder to commercial banks and life insurance companies, are likely to be at well-above-average levels. As the economy gradually improves, so will default experience, albeit with a long lag.

- Lender concern about credit quality has led to a tiering in the debt market, where life insurance companies have carved out distinct clienteles. Large borrowers with strong projects tend to be the biggest institutions' preferred customers, while life insurance companies have consciously elected not to compete for prime customers.

Real Estate Fundamentals

- As the 1980s ended, about half of the real estate industry boomed while the other half witnessed a major correction of excesses bred earlier in the decade. The 1990s will usher in a correction to those sectors hitherto immune to the problems now facing the savings and loan industry, Texas, and single-family housing in the Northeast.

- The overleveraging of several major department store groups and the failure of most department stores to adjust their marketing strategies to the 1980s consumer have called into question the underlying logic of the shopping mall business. Power is shifting to the aggressive merchant within the center, to the detriment of the mall owner.

Regional Economics

- In response to a sluggish economy, the 10 fastest-growing cities will see their absolute gains in employment cut in half in 1990. We expect the 1990 top-ten job-gainers list to include three cities in the Northwest, the strongest region of the country. Washington, D.C., and Seattle, Washington, likely will vie for the lead in job growth.

Source: Salomon Brothers Quarterly Real Estate Review, January 1990.

from January 1990. We use it as an example because it brings together in a professional way many different aspects of the real estate profession. It is, however, only one of the many newsletters that will be described in greater detail in Chapter 26 (Feasibility).

The Realtors put out a monthly economic forecast that also deals with many aspects of the real estate business but focuses on housing. Laventhol and Horwath produce a monthly report on lodging industry trends which is relevant for developers whose projects are in any way connected with the hotel business. Brokerage firms, such as Grubb and Ellis, produce periodic newsletters that focus on projects and areas of their particular interest. Institutional investment advisors, such as Baring Institutional Realty, also produce special reports on projects of interest to them. Consulting firms, such as Kenneth Leventhal, publish monthly newsletters that describe particular characteristics of hot markets. Starting in the 1990s, Kenneth Leventhal believes that Seattle, for example, will be the hottest market in the United States. Developers even read the CPA newsletters because the *CPA Letter,* which comes out monthly, periodically publishes rule changes that are important to the real estate industry. As they enter 1990, the most important rule changes facing accountants involve accounting for troubled bank and life insurance company loans. And, of course, they also include that continual holdover from the 1980s, problems with savings and loan accounting.

Collectively, real estate newsletters are extremely important. Although they don't provide the ideas, they do give developers a fertile background in which ideas can grow. They are, however, only a beginning point, since the newsletters seldom reach beyond the current quarter or year, and the development process extends over a far greater period.

With a firm grip on the immediate situation across markets and products, the developer looks to the library for in-depth analysis of long-term trends. In Part 9, we will talk about the more important trends affecting real estate in the 1990s, but at this juncture, you need to see how long-term research affects the atmosphere in the real estate industry. For that purpose, we will cite two publications that have made a major impact on the development industry over the last decade. The first is *The Nine American Lifestyles,* written by Arnold Mitchell, which is now over 10 years old. Although many other publications deal with the same issue, Mitchell's is probably the most frequently cited study. It develops typologies for different consumer groups from need-driven to outer-directed through inner-directed and, finally, to those described as having an integrated life-style. Throughout American industry, analysis of markets by consumer need was a watchword of the 1980s and is expected to continue to be prominent in the 1990s. From a real estate perspective, knowing the needs of the customer goes far beyond the simple age and income statistics often presented in newspaper articles to understanding what makes the individual happy and what allows the individual to function most successfully. Only with more detailed knowledge of what the consumer wants can all the details of the project, which must be coordinated in the development process, be fully understood and integrated.

While *The Nine American Lifestyles* is an appropriate illustration of an in-depth look at consumer needs, Joel Garreau's "Behold Nine Nations" provides an interesting view of how Americans differ across this large country. This provocative article was originally issued nine years ago and suggested that America was not one nation but, rather, nine nations. Whether we totally agree with the segmentation that flows from "the foundry," the declining industrial nation of the Northeast, through to the "empty quarter" in America's energy belt to "Ectopia" on the West Coast, we cannot quarrel with the fact that in different parts of this country consumers want very different things. As just one example, the Mexican culture so prominent in the Southwest often calls for more spacious retail and smaller rooms in residential development. Successful developers do not depend solely on newsletters: they go to the library and do research on all the different disciplines that affect real estate development. The two publications mentioned here are just a small start. The would-be developer who combines knowledge of the immediate with an in-depth perspective on what makes the country work will thereby develop a foundation for making long-term projections, and that is the essence of successful development.

The third step in promoting creativity, as noted above, involves looking and touching. Successful developers love to work as they travel. In their traveling they are alert to new developments, and with their creative minds they use the stimulation of new sights to create even newer projects. A developer who knows the immediate market context, who has an in-depth understanding of what the consumer wants, and who sees something in another region or country that fits a similar market niche can then design something to fit the market at home. It's not a matter of copying; it's a matter of looking, touching, learning, and then creating something new that will fit a particular customer.

Since real estate is inherently interdisciplinary, the spectrum of ideas that may be acquired from looking and touching is quite broad. For example, a traveler first visiting Asia notices lots of things that look quite unusual from the American perspective. Whether the new sights and appearances involve a technological dimension, as shown in Box 24-2, or a basic land value question, as seen in Box 24-3, travel is an educational experience for the astute developer. Any travel that opens the mind is good, be it to an adjoining American city, to Asia, Europe, or anywhere else where creative people have produced space over time with associated services that satisfy their need.

24-2 TECHNOLOGY AND COST INTERACT IN DIFFERENT WAYS OVER TIME

In Bangkok, the Temple of Dawn is a 200-year-old masterpiece. It is also 254 feet tall. In the nineteenth century, the technology was not available to build, on a cost-efficient basis, anything over three to four stories. (Naturally, cost efficiency was not the primary concern in a religious structure like the Temple of Dawn.) For this reason, Bangkok, like Mexico City, is a sprawling city. Both cities have soil problems which make it difficult and costly to erect skyscrapers. More recently, architects and engineers have found a cost-efficient way to build high rises in both cities. Interestingly, the old landmark of Bangkok, the Temple of Dawn, dominates in style anything built a hundred years later and rivals in scale today's high-rise hotels. Of course, not all that is built is technologically ideal regardless of scale. As Mexico City learned, many of the deaths suffered in their earthquake in 1985 were from their supposedly safer low-rise buildings.

Technology has many dimensions. The traveler in Bangkok can hardly turn around without seeing the rice boats of Thailand, a main source of transportation, moving rice, along with charcoal and fruits and vegetables, from the hinterlands to Bangkok. The rice boats are the workers' permanent homes, so that their housing is found on the river and in the ports, providing security and reducing commuting needs in a very congested city. The technology that provides transportation also provides, as a byproduct, housing because of the high cost of other housing alternatives for these transportation workers.

24-3
ASSESSING
DEVELOPMENT
POTENTIAL

Remember that the developer anticipates not just what the property will lease for when it is completed, but also how it will perform in the marketplace over its entire useful life. Today, in Hong Kong, there is a parcel of land adjacent to and slightly in front of the famous Peninsula Hotel, which in on the Kowloon side looking directly across the water at Hong Kong Island. It serves the tourist trade, which is concentrated on the Peninsula or Kowloon side, and it originally had a spectacular view of the central business district on the island. Over time, fill was brought in directly in front of the hotel, and now a major civic center has been built which obscures a good deal of the view from the lower floors of the Peninsula Hotel. The available development site is next to the civic center and across from the Peninsula, and has the same spectacular view of the island that the Peninsula once enjoyed. It is as fine a site, in terms of location and view, as one will find in the Pacific Rim. Building conditions are difficult on fill dirt, but then difficult building conditions are nothing new in Hong Kong.

The question is, what is this site worth, given only modest restrictions on height? Hong Kong, however, has a potentially more serious restriction than building codes and zoning. It is political control in 1997: control of the city is scheduled to revert to mainland China in that year. As of today (1990), the British in Hong Kong and the mainland Chinese are deadlocked over reforms, and clearly a brain drain is taking place away from Hong Kong to the emerging Pacific Rim financial capitals of Singapore, Vancouver, and the major Australian and New Zealand cities. If mainland China chooses to use Hong Kong as its opening to the Western world, the site we just mentioned is as valuable as any site in the world. On the other hand, if Tiananmen Square is a forecast of future Chinese attitudes and of how the Chinese will run the former British colony after 1997, Hong Kong will cease to function as a world financial center, and the site will be worth precious little. There will be a vast abundance of all types of space available very cheaply surrounding it.

The developer who is meditating on a replacement for Hong Kong should remember that Hong Kong Island itself has the climate, the vegetation, and particularly the views to make even San Francisco worry about its competitiveness. If mainland China doesn't ruin it, this is a world-class city.

PLAYERS   THE DEVELOPER

The developer is the entrepreneur who makes things happen, the quarterback or prime mover of the development process. The developer is first a source of ideas, who translates perceived needs into a concept of space that will satisfy those needs. Next, the developer is the promoter, bringing together the sources of capital, labor, and materials and, at the same time, seeing that the project meets the regulations imposed by one or more levels of government. Once the process is under way, the role of the developer changes into that of a manager who must coordinate the efforts of all the participants in the development process and keep them moving toward a common goal. Finally, it is the developer who must assure that someone supervises the operations of the completed project.

It seems true that developers are born, not made. It takes a unique personality combining great ability with a tremendous drive to function successfully in the development environment. As with John Portman, some developers come from the architectural profession. Others come from contracting, lending, marketing, or other specialized aspects of the real estate development business. Rarely, however, does one begin a professional carrer as a developer. Individuals are hired as participants in the development process, and those with unique talents move on to become the primary decision makers.

The role of the developer changes with changes in the marketplace. During the late 1970s and early 1980s, structural changes in the financial market had the effect of changing the developer's role. As interest rates rose and lenders became interested in becoming joint venture partners, traditional developers found themselves in partnership with lenders rather than as straight borrowers. The impact of lenders becoming active partners with developers has been to decrease the developers' share of the pie and their autonomy on a project. However, in most cases the developer still provides the basic concept of the development, and the lender provides attractive financial and staff support. As the dollar value and physical complexities of project development continue to increase, developers find that trading a "piece of the action" for financial strength can enhance project success.

❏ **THE DEVELOPER'S GOALS.** As the project's prime mover, the developer seeks the maximum possible return with a minimum commitment of time and money. This return consists of the following:

- The development fee, the stated direct compensation for "doing the development."

- Profits on the sale to long-term investors (i.e., sales price less cost to construct).

- Possibly a long-term equity position (for which the developer may or may not put in any cash). To the extent that this is done, the developer's goals are similar to those of the passive investor.

The developer's time commitment is a function of the length of the development period. Although the other equity interests also wish to minimize the time of their involvement, they are not "selling their time," as is the developer. They are involved in only a portion of the development process and are less sensitive to the overall length of the development period.

The developer may also profit through ownership of entities that sell services to the development—insurance agencies, mortgage banking firms, leasing companies, management companies, or even general contracting firms. To the extent that these arrangements are on an arm's-length basis and represent ethical agreements, the developer is simply compensated for performing additional functions. If, on the other hand, all parties to the development agree to unusual compensation for one of the outside activities in which the developer has an interest, then any excess above standard compensation should be considered as an addition to the development fee.

The financial exposure of the developer arises in two different ways. First, the developer expends time and money before being assured that the project will be built (i.e., before the commitment point). For example, the developer may buy an option on a site to tie it up. Naturally, the developer seeks to minimize such expenditures. Second, in addition to the developer's own equity position (both contributed capital and debt on which the developer is personally liable), a certain project cost or a certain initial occupancy level may be guaranteed to the investors or lenders or both. For example, the permanent loan may be funded only when occupancy reaches X percent. As the *primary risk bearer,* the developer's exposure is a time function of his or her direct financial commitment as well as the magnitude of any guarantees and the likelihood of their being called on.

THE JOINT VENTURE PARTNER

Any individual or institution providing the developer with development-period equity funding in return for participation in development profits can be called a **joint venture partner.** (Remember the term "joint venture" is not a precise legal term.) The partner attempts to achieve the maximum possible portion of returns from development based on the minimum possible financial commitment. The partner's return is based primarily on the difference between project value and project cost and, therefore, indirectly on the amount and terms of the debt financing. The joint venturer's equity contribution often bridges a portion of the gap between project cost and available construction debt financing. (The remainder of the gap, if any, must be filled by the developer's equity.) The risk to the joint venture partner is a function of the extent of that contribution, assuming no personal liability, or a function of the amount of debt and the extent of the contribution, in the case of personal liability. In either case, the partner is interested in any downside obligations and the financial as well as operating strength of the developer as these relate to the overall solvency of the project.

THE CONSTRUCTION LENDER

The construction lender is not primarily concerned with the long-term economic viability of the project as long as a permanent loan (takeout) commitment has been obtained. (See Figure 24-1 for sources of development financing.) With such a commitment in hand, the construction lender is assured of being repaid on completion of the project. The construction lender (frequently a commerical bank) has the responsibility of seeing that the developer completes the project on time and on budget according to the plans and specifications. (The time frame is important because the permanent loan commitment usually provides that it will expire by a designated date.) This policing role requires that the construction lender monitor the construction process, a process usually done by a *draw* procedure that involves certification of the degree of completion prior to each payment (draw) under the construction loan.

The construction lender faces the risk that construction costs will exceed the final permanent loan amount, forcing recourse to the equity interests or to the developer to cover the difference. If these others are unable or unwilling to do so, the construction lender has the option of foreclosing or taking a long-term loan position as a remedy. The construction lender weighs these undesirable possibilities against the expected interest return (including origination fees) to be earned by making the loan.

THE PERMANENT LENDER

The permanent lender, like the construction lender, seeks a secure loan while achieving the maximum possible return. Because the permanent lender, unlike the construction lender, has no takeout source, the market value of the completed project is critical since it serves as collateral for the loan. The value of the project will be a function of the expected cash

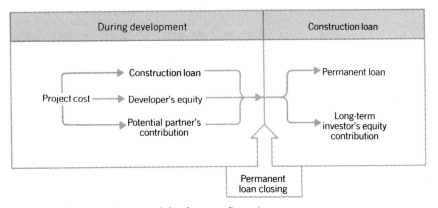

F I G U R E 24-1   *Sources of development financing*

flow generated, market capitalization rates, and the project's expected economic life. The relationship of the loan to the project is commonly expressed in the *loan-to-value ratio* (LTVR) and the *debt coverage ratio* (DCR). (See Part 5.)

The LTVR generally is an indication of the safety of the loan; the lower the LTVR, the lower the lender's risk (because the greater is the equity "cushion"). The DCR is an indication of the project's ability to meet the debt service requirements from net operating income (NOI). The larger the DCR, the lower the risk to the lender (because the greater is the income "cushion").

In addition to charging interest on the permanent loan, long-term lenders frequently receive a form of "contingent" interest. Sometimes referred to as income or equity kickers, these allow the lender to participate in the overall success of the project. **Income kickers** stipulate that the lender will receive a portion of gross income over some minimum. For example, a lender may receive 15 percent of gross rent over the estimated first year pro forma gross rental receipts. In the case of **equity kickers,** the lender participates in a portion of the capital gain received at the time of sale.

As the 1990s begin, the old income and equity kickers are increasingly giving way to fully participating loans and joint ventures. Although many sophisticated bells and whistles are attached to major real estate financing, the general idea of a participating loan extends the concept of income and equity kickers. The lender will usually receive an interest rate on the loan, which is slightly below market, in return for a percentage of the equity cash flows and proceeds from sale or refinancing. The typical participating loan might involve a lender making a loan at 8 percent in a 9 percent market, thus allowing for an acceptable debt service coverage in the early years in a tough market. In return for this lower interest rate, the lender might well receive 50 percent of any equity cash flows and 50 percent of the proceeds from sale or refinancing.

Various institutional lenders will sometimes be involved in the same project. We might find, for example, a more risk-oriented institutional lender taking a joint venture position, with the developer behind the financing of a more conservative institutional investor. In such a situation, the more conservative institutional investor would provide the long-term debt financing described above. The second, more risk-oriented institutional lender would be a joint venture partner of the developer, again as described above.

THE LONG-TERM EQUITY INVESTOR

The long-term equity investor may or may not make an appearance during the development period. The investor may contract to purchase the completed property prior to construction (basing the price on pre-construction value estimates) or wait until the project is completed. If the former, the contract usually will be signed before the commitment point—the time immediately preceding the commencement of construction. Whatever the time of sale, the price is usually not payable until completion, and so the funds are not available to the developer. (However, a purchase commitment prior to construction may substitute for or supplement the permanent loan commitment as a takeout for the construction lender.)

The long-term equity investor usually assumes the role of a **passive investor** during the development period, which does not include the sharing of development period risks. On completion of the project, the investor wants the maximum possible operating period returns (sometimes guaranteed by the developer for an initial period of one or more years) for the least possible price. (The situation here directly parallels the investor position described in Part 7.) These returns will normally be lower than those accruing to development period investors because development period investors assume more risk owing to the uncertainties surrounding the construction and lease-up process.

In the past, construction period tax deductions (primarily for interest and real estate taxes) encouraged early investment by long-term equity interest. However, the Tax Reform Act of 1976 substantially reduced the tax incentive for early investment by requiring all or most of these costs to be capitalized, and the 1981 and 1986 bills extended the amortization periods for these capitalized costs. Consequently, early equity commitments have become more difficult to obtain. However, the developer's incentive for preselling the long-term equity interest remains. The sale enables the developer to avoid or minimize the market risks associated with changing value estimates over the development period. Presale of the equity may also facilitate the procurement of permanent financing.

THE ARCHITECT

As previously mentioned, the architect translates the developer's ideas into working drawings and specifications that guide the construction workers in building the project. The architect typically begins with renderings that are rough sketches of what the project will look like when completed on the chosen site. If these prove to be an accurate reflection of the developer's ideas, the architect moves on to preliminary drawings that are more technical descriptions of the earlier sketches. From preliminary drawings, building cost estimates will be made. (In more sophisticated development situations, operating cost estimates will also be adjusted to reflect specific project construction specifications.)

These building cost estimates are part of the feasibility study, which has a primary role in the decision-making process. If the overall feasibility indicates that the project should be developed (i.e., projected value exceeds estimated cost), the architect will turn the preliminary drawings into final drawings. The architect may also be involved during the actual construction process. Then the architect observes the construction process and verifies to the developer, the lender, or both that the work is being done according to the plans and specifications established in the final drawings.

THE ENGINEER

The engineer most often works with the architect. The architect uses the engineer to ensure that the plans are structurally sound. It is the engineer who is responsible for determining soil-bearing capacity, the depth of footings, stress, and related items. In more complex development situations, an engineer may also be used as a construction manager. On such projects the engineer replaces the architect in supervising the construction process. The construction manager, unlike the architect, is on the construction site continually and serves as the developer's representative or interface with the general contractor.

Architects and engineers are critical to the development process from a safety as well as from a market-risk perspective. Certainly, a structure that lacks "eye appeal" or efficiency in its operations (elevator times, location of bathrooms, etc.) will have a difficult time in the marketplace, possibly even leading the developer to bankruptcy. However, as the MGM fire in Las Vegas and the collapsed hotel catwalk in Kansas City demonstrated, both the financial and *human* loss can be even greater if the architects and engineers fail in their primary duty to deliver a safe physical product.

As buildings became "smarter" in the 1980s, architects and engineers worked more closely together to design particular features, functions, and benefits. The smart building is one that controls its heating, ventilating, and air-conditioning costs as efficiently as possible. Achieving these efficiencies typically involves designing the space as well as the equipment so that different tenants may have different temperatures, and so that in different seasons and at different times of the day, energy is not being wasted. Smart buildings may also have sophisticated security features and sophisticated telecommunication systems.

As we will describe at length in Part 9, the engineer now has a new job on most developments: hazardous waste assessment and, at times, hazardous waste mitigation. This important new twist to the engineer's role involves assessing past uses of the site that could put the proposed development at risk and correcting problems that could jeopardize the proposed development and surrounding sites.

THE CONTRACTORS

The **general contractor** (**GC**) executes a contract with the developer to build the project according to the plans and specifications of the architect and engineer. The GC then retains whatever outside assistance is needed actually to build the project. The general contracting function is basically to subdivide the contract with the developer among different construction firms, which then perform the actual construction work. In other words, the GC will hire excavation crews, concrete crews, a rough carpentry group, mechanical systems firms, a finish carpentry group, and all the other related worker groups involved in the particular job. The GC schedules their work and monitors the quality of that work to ensure that their performance will, in the aggregate, satisfy his contractual obligations to the developer. The **subcontractors** are the individual workers or construction firms retained by the general contractor to do specific portions of the work. Their contract is with the GC, and they look to the general contractor for payment as the work is completed.

REGULATORS

There are numerous regulators of the development process. On the local level, zoning officials ensure compliance with local zoning ordinances. Local building inspectors enforce local building codes. On a regional, state, and national basis, there are a host of additional regulators. Their functions range from environmental and consumer protection to enforcement of antitrust statutes. The regulators enforce the rules of the game. If society's needs are to be met through the private sector development process, the rules must adjust to changing times. In fact, the development process has become so complex that regulators must often be active participants in that process, not merely passive critics, if social goals are to be achieved. These issues are explored more fully in Chapter 27.

LAWYERS

With so many different participants in the development process, it is not surprising that lawyers are often needed. In fact, most of the different participants will have their own lawyer, and the different lawyers will negotiate the contracts that tie the participants together. For example, architects typically want to use what is known as the standard AIA form provided by the American Institute of Architects. This form provides for the contract between the architect and the developer. However, in its latest form, this contract contains many provisions that are far more favorable to the architect than to the developer. For example, in the event of a dispute between the architect and the developer, the form calls for the architect to be the arbitrator of the dispute. Clearly, many developers find such provisions unduly onerous and often have their own lawyer negotiate with the architect's lawyer to arrange a more favorable contract.

FINAL USERS

The description of all the participants in the development process would not be complete without mention of the final users of the space being created. It is anticipation of the needs of these users that leads to the idea that the developer asks the architect to translate into plans and specifications. As is seen in the next chapter, users often contract for space before it is actually completed. In this manner, they can make sure that the finished product will meet their needs. As a result, they may become more than passive participants in the development process. Working through the developer's marketing representative, the final users may interact with the financial and construction representatives of the developer during the actual building of a project.

Before we conclude the discussion of participants in the asset-creation process, we should point out that quite often one individual or institution will fulfill more than one development function. However, we can better evaluate the development environment by considering each function individually, even when the goals and risk perspectives inherent in different functions are combined in a single entity.

DIFFERENT RISK-RETURN PERSPECTIVES
OF PARTICIPANTS

The various measures of return used by the different participants in the development process are derived primarily from anticipated *project cost* and *project value*. These are the two key accounting statements in the feasibility report. The participants need to evaluate different possible combinations of the factors impacting these statements in light of their particular goals in the development process. As is seen in Chapter 26, the feasibility study provides sufficient information for many different participants to make development decisions. (See Figure 24-2.)

PRIMARY
DECISIONS

Since the development decision is, in essence, an investment decision, development analysis encompasses all aspects of the real estate process just as does investment analysis. However, in the development situation, greater uncertainties result from the fact that the space being considered has not yet been created. The developer, the key decision maker on the development team, must make certain primary decisions during the development process.

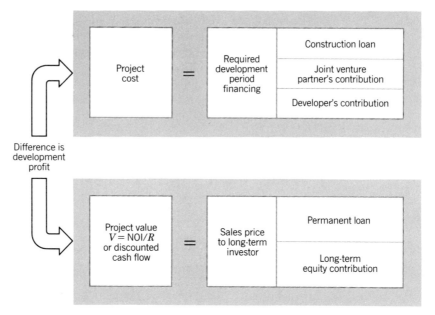

FIGURE 24-2   *Relationship of project cost to project value*

HOW SHOULD THE SITE BE ACQUIRED?

An option or low downpayment time purchase can significantly reduce early capital requirements, though usually with an adverse effect on total land cost. Note that this is not the decision to commit to the development of the proposed project but only the decision as to the best way to "tie up" the land so that it will be available if, on completion of the feasibility study, the developer decides to proceed.

HOW EXTENSIVE SHOULD THE FEASIBILITY STUDY BE?

Estimates of most variables in the development process can be made more accurate by expanding the feasibility study. However, the cost of these studies and the time required to complete them place limits on the extent to which they can be utilized. The feasibility study contains project cost and value estimates that frequently are the basis for the decisions of several participants in the development process.

WHAT TYPES OF FINANCING SHOULD BE OBTAINED?

Should a permanent loan commitment be obtained before initiating construction? Possibly better permanent loan terms could be obtained after construction and lease-up. The commitment fee is an additional expense. However, construction loan terms may suffer if no permanent loan commitment is obtained. There also is the risk that only less advantageous permanent loan terms will be available at the end of the development period. In addition, obtaining a construction loan without first obtaining a permanent commitment may be impossible. (Less advantageous terms would include some combination of a lower loan amount, a shorter loan maturity, a higher interest rate, and more restrictive loan covenants.)

HOW SHOULD THE DEVELOPER DEAL WITH THE GENERAL CONTRACTOR?

How should the construction contract price be established? Who should supervise the construction process? Should the general contractor be bonded? All these questions directly affect the largest single component of development costs: basic construction cost per square foot.

SHOULD A MAJOR TENANT OR TENANTS BE PRESIGNED?

Often rental concessions will be necessary to presign quality tenants. However, such presignings improve the prospects for high initial occupancy and may result in more attractive long-term financing.

SHOULD THE DEVELOPER TAKE IN A JOINT VENTURE PARTNER?

Such a partner would provide needed construction period financing and possibly ease borrowing problems, but the developer might otherwise keep all development profits for himself. It is becoming more common for the lender to require joint venture participation as a condition for the developer's obtaining a long-term loan. The developer would then be concerned with the terms of both the loan and the joint venture agreement.

SHOULD THE DEVELOPER PRESELL THE EQUITY TO PASSIVE INVESTORS?

When there is a presale, the escrowed proceeds might advantageously affect negotiations for a permanent loan commitment. Certainly, such a sale lessens the risk of a decline in expected operating profits during the development period. However, if the developer waits to sell to the eventual investors, rental levels may increase and the completed project may sell at a higher price. The capitalization rate applied to a completed project's NOI would normally be lower because the project would then be real.

SHOULD AN OUTSIDE LEASING AGENT OR SALES FIRM BE USED?

Outside agents reduce the extent of leasing or sales activity required by the development team, but at a monetary cost and with a reduction in developer control of the marketing function. If the developer plans to create a permanent leasing staff for all new projects (and possibly other investors' projects as well), an outside leasing company will not be needed. It tends to be more common, however, for a developer to establish an ongoing relationship with a reputable outside leasing company.

SHOULD AN OUTSIDE MANAGEMENT FIRM BE EMPLOYED?

Leasing and property management functions often interact since most leading leasing companies also have property management divisions. In any case, the concerns here parallel those in the leasing situation described earlier.

With most real estate markets overbuilt as we enter the 1990s, management is clearly more important than ever in the success of the project. As we described in Part 4, the term "asset management" has come of age. From a developer's perspective, lenders now require, as a condition of their involvement with the project, that quality asset management be available. Again, asset management requires more than property management and includes the ability to make strategic decisions involving repositioning the project in the market at later dates and coordinating the project with the particular needs of major corporate users.

WHAT GOVERNMENT APPROVALS WILL BE REQUIRED?

A major element of the construction process today is compliance with local, state, and federal regulations. An environmental impact statement (EIS) may have to be prepared to document the environmental impact of the proposed development. On the local level, the project must comply with zoning regulations and may require approvals pursuant to a master plan. Permits will be required during the construction process, and a **certificate of occupancy (CO)** may be required when the building is completed.

ADDITIONAL DECISION POINTS   Although the preceding issues represent major development decision points, they are by no means the only decision points in the real property development process. As the manager of the development process, the developer is keenly aware of the importance of minimizing development risks. Consequently, several **risk-control techniques** have evolved that can be utilized in the management of the development process. Whenever the developer (or another participant in the development process) considers the use of any of the risk-control techniques described in Box 24-4, a decision point has been reached. The uses of these risk control techniques are more fully developed in Chapter 25.

24-4 RISK-CONTROL TECHNIQUES

A. Initiation and Overview

1. Evaluate honestly the developer's own capabilities and resources.
2. Determine the qualifications of the possible participants in the development—that is, examine their track record, financial strength, and performance capabilities.
3. Coordinate the individuals performing the different activities involved in the real property development process.

B. Government Regulation

1. Coordinate with the city master plan.
2. Increase the frequency of building inspections by city officials.
3. Increase the extent and quality of environmental impact study.

C. Feasibility Analysis.

1. The feasibility study is in itself a risk-control technique. Increased effort in any area of the feasibility analysis can be regarded as a risk-control technique whose purpose is to improve the quality of the estimates of the variables used in development analysis.

D. Site Selection and Land Acquisition

1. The acquisition method can limit exposure prior to the commitment point.
2. Obtain protective warranties in deeds.
3. Include release clauses and subordination agreements in contracts if possible.

E. Site Planning and Design

1. Provide for a review of design plans by operations, marketing, and financial personnel.

2. Check for utility availability and possible city concessions such as property tax relief.

3. Provide for structural warranties in the architect's contract.

4. Check for the possibility of cost sharing through joint venture efforts on site utilities.

F. Financing the Development

1. The construction lender wants a floating rate loan, strict draw procedures, early equity contributions, personal liability of the investors and the developer, and a permanent loan commitment.

2. The permanent lender wants either the interest rate or the principal balance to be adjusted periodically for inflation, a lower loan-to-value ratio, a higher debt service coverage ratio, and the personal liability of the investors.

3. The investors want to make their cash contributions late, avoid cash calls and personal liability, and reduce the equity amount.

4. The developer wants a fixed-rate construction loan, relaxed draw procedures, large contingency provisions, and no personal liability.

5. It is the lawyer's job to assure that whatever gets negotiated among these four parties with conflicting interests in the terms of financing is internally consistent and clear to all parties.

G. Construction

1. The level of construction risk may be affected by performance and payment bonds, retainage, union relations, general contractor participations, architectural supervision and construction management, or a combination of these.

2. When construction management is used, critical path programming may be a useful control device.

H. Leasing

1. Tenant equity participations may help attract quality lead tenants.

2. Tenant mix should be based on the market study.

3. Net leases and expense stops may be used to limit exposure to increases in operating costs.

4. Outside leasing agents may be used to reduce certain leasing risks.

THE TERMINATION OPTION

Since development is a dynamic process, decisions are made in a time sequence. When any variable changes, the developer can reconsider the "go–no go" decision and is therefore at a decision point. As time passes in the process, certain variables that could previously only be estimated become historical facts, and the estimates of other variables change. The project can then be reevaluated on the basis of the new data and estimates revised. Resulting changes in anticipated results could cause the developer to reexamine his or her participation in the development.

24-5 GREAT CITIES DISAPPEAR	We have argued that, for a number of reasons, certain areas create possibilities for people and so will develop as cities. But remember that a great city can also disappear. Testing your knowledge of urban history, what is the largest city that has died in the last 500 years?

If you said Uranium City in northern Saskatchewan, you were right. It did go away as uranium prices dropped, but then again, while a *dynamic* city, it was never truly a *great* city. Similarly, if you thought of the Mayan civilization in Mexico and Central America, you were again correct, but a few hundred years off on your date. Probably the greatest city to decline in the last 500 years is Ayudhaya in Thailand, which fell in 1767. The ancient capital was reportedly home to over 1 million people in the eighteenth century. Before the Burmese wiped it out in war, it was a city greater in size and quite possibly had a higher culture than the London of its day. Today, it stands in ruins much as Carthage, a reminder to us that just as cities can rise, they can also fall.

Beirut today might also be considered a great city lost. Yet when we compare bombed-out Beirut to the lost capital of Thailand, we see that Beirut is still alive even though threatened. Thailand's ancient capital is no more than a few bricks and some poured concrete, an early twentieth-century recreation of what might have been. In fact, so little is known of what once was, and there is so little local appreciation of it, that power lines now run through the heart of the remains of the great capital. There is scant interest in the history as represented by the single sign telling when some of the ancient rulers supposedly built great temples on the site. It is haunting to stand in the ancient capital and think that 300 years ago it was one of the world's great cities.

When a civilization dies quickly, as did the flourishing Mayan civilization of Mexico, something is usually left—at least enough to imagine what life was like. Similarly, in a very dry climate, such as Egypt, we have many reminders of civilizations that rose and fell over thousands of years. In the case of Thailand, the high heat and humidity and the ongoing living needs of the people have left us almost nothing of a great city of over a million people.

Thus, any time movement through the process can represent a decision point in the process.

The complexity of the real property development process indicates the need for a decision model—in other words, a specialized analytical framework unique to the development process. In Chapter 25, such a model, or specialized analytical framework, is developed as a variation on the basic analytical framework used throughout the book. The variation will encompass the dynamic element that is the key to the development process.

SUMMARY   Development is a focal point of the real estate industry, and the developer is the focal point of the development process. Although real estate development is constantly changing, there will always be a need for developers in the traditional sense. That is, even though institutional developers are becoming more common, the developer's role has not significantly changed. The developer is an entrepreneur, promoter, manager, and, in fact, the individual most responsible for the constructed physical environment in which we all live. As such, a developer must be a competent micro manager in all the aspects listed in this chapter. However, don't forget that the developer must also be a big-picture person. For the really big picture, see if you can answer the question posed in Box 24-5.

IMPORTANT TERMS

Certificate of occupancy (CO)	Joint venture partners
Development process	Passive investor
Equity kickers	Risk-control techniques
General contractor (GC)	Subcontractors
Income kickers	

REVIEW QUESTIONS

24.1 What is the role of the developer in the real estate development process?

24.2 What is the major goal of the developer? How is his return generated?

24.3 What are the major risks that a construction lender faces as a participant in the real estate development process?

24.4 How does the income or equity kicker affect the yield of the permanent lender?

24.5   How might a site for development be obtained in order to reduce the capital necessary to get the development under way?

24.6   What factors might a developer consider when deciding to presell the equity interest to passive investors?

24.7   Why might investment in a development situation have more risk than investing in an existing project?

24.8   Should a developer maintain a continual termination option as a realistic decision point after the development process has begun?

24.9   What are the advantages and disadvantages of presigning major tenants in an income-producing property?

24.10   How is the lending position of the permanent lender different from that of the construction lender?

The Development Process

In Chapter 24 we talked about *who does what* in real estate development. This chapter is about *what happens when.* In other words, here we're going to focus on the development process itself. Real estate deals may vary in their particulars, and developers may have very different personal styles, but a certain sequence of activities characterizes the great majority of projects developed.

We can view the real property development process as having eight stages (as shown in Figure 25-1). The flow of activities through the stages represents a typical sequence in real property development. Although this sequence is not followed in all cases, it does provide a very useful framework for analyzing the process; it also creates a structure for evaluating individual projects. Viewing development as a series of stages allows a needed flexibility that is not present in traditional appraisal models. With this perspective the developer/decision maker can review the project at each stage of completion and consider the implications of whether or not to proceed.

The eight-stage framework also contributes to our understanding of how the various development activities interact. The stages interact in two ways. First, some development activities span several different stages, and several different activities will be ongoing during any one stage. For example, the marketing and leasing effort will normally begin very early in the development process, long before the project is ready for occupancy, and will continue until the project has been fully leased. Second, the process is interactive in the sense that the values of certain variables in the process are conditioned by the values of other variables. For instance, the availability of a permanent loan that will be closed at the end of the development period will probably improve the terms of the construction loan initially funded at the beginning of the construction stage.

As we present the eight-stage development model, we will use the

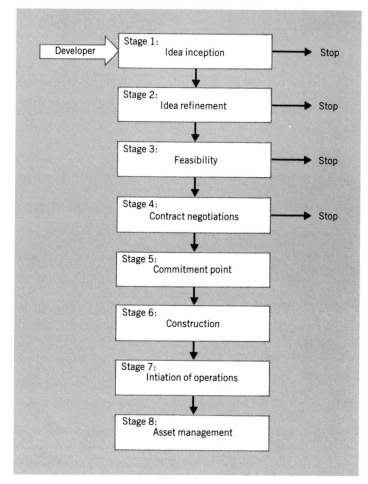

FIGURE 25-1   *The real property development model*

development of an actual garden-office complex to illustrate the different stages. The example is BancFirst Plaza, a luxury suburban office development located in Austin, Texas.

STAGE 1: IDEA INCEPTION   The development process begins with idea inception. In this stage, the developer generates an idea for a particular type of project, that is, space over time with associated services, and considers what project size might be appropriate for a particular urban area. The developer then reflects on the type of tenants who might be interested in the projected space and the possible sources of financing.

This description may sound cut-and-dried, but the reality is far from it. Getting ideas is the most creative aspect of the real estate industry. By reading, looking, and listening, the developer finds new combinations of place, built space, and services to satisfy tomorrow's consumers' needs. When we combine the broad marketing concept (Chapter 9) with the ever longer development process (2 to 10 years from stage 1 to the beginning of stage 8), it can be said that the developer (1) anticipates what *new* space consumers *will* want in the future, (2) finds a way to produce this space and provide associated services (i.e., the production function will extend from land acquisition to people management), and (3) convinces the market that his space (at his price) is the best way to meet their needs. The underlying idea for all of this is generated in stage 1. (Several important future trends are discussed in Part 9.)

THE "PRO FORMA"

To test an interesting idea, the developer will put together a rough cost-and-income pro forma. The **pro forma** will include a preliminary cost and value statement. (See Table 25-1.) The different tenants' needs that must be satisfied and the related construction requirements will be combined on a rough basis to come up with a cost figure. Looking at what rental rate space similar to the projected project presently commands in

---

T A B L E   2 5 - 1   BANCFIRST PLAZA COST-AND-INCOME PRO FORMA

Cost

Land	$1,394,000
Tenant improvements	920,500
Construction costs	3,836,500
Soft costs including developer profits	3,517,500
Total cost	$9,668,500
Less: operating income[a]	1,468,500
Expected Cost	$8,200,000

Value

Gross rental receipts (76,712 sq. ft. × $16.75/ft./yr.)	$1,285,000
Vacancy and bad debts (5%)	(64,250)
Effective gross income	1,220,750
Operating expenses (76,712 sq. ft. × $3.75/ft./yr.)[b]	287,670
Net operating income	$933,080
Capitalized value 10.8%	$8,639,600
Conclusion: Move to stage 2 since value exceeds cost.	

[a] *Income generated during projected 18-month absorption period.*
[b] *Net of costs passed through to tenants.*

the marketplace, the developer will devise a rough estimate of the income stream that the project will generate.

From that income stream, a very rough project value can be established based on current market capitalization rates. The developer compares estimated value to estimated cost, looking for an idea that makes sense. Most don't. The developer will go through this relatively inexpensive process many times, usually discarding the results. When a rough idea does look good at this early stage (i.e., value exceeds cost), the developer moves on to the second stage in the process.

THE BANCFIRST PLAZA EXAMPLE

The developer of BancFirst Plaza felt that Austin, Texas, needed a luxury suburban office development in the Northwest Hills area. (This is an early 1980s development, allowing us to follow the project through design, construction, initial operations, and the first rollover of major tenants.) The plan was to induce a full-service national bank and local office tenants to locate on the site. The location offered excellent access to both downtown and the state capital complex, 10 minutes away by car, plus very close proximity to middle- and upper-income residential neighborhoods. In addition, the site was only 10 minutes by car to the rapidly developing high tech center in north Austin. Such firms as IBM, Texas Instruments, Radian Corporation, Intel, Abbott Labs, and Microcomputer Electronics Corporation were all within easy access to the site.

STAGE 2: IDEA REFINEMENT

When the rare idea passes muster in stage 1, it is refined and tested again in stage 2. (Note that the developer can decide to quit at each of the early stages without much financial pain—see Figure 25-1. Also note that more than money may be a part of the developer's interest in an idea; ego and long-term company strategy may be motivators too, although they should not distort fundamental analysis of the market.)

First, the developer must find a specific location within the given market area. The site must be checked to see that zoning is appropriate or that appropriate rezoning is possible. Furthermore, there must be access to transportation arteries, and required municipal services must be available.

Second, the developer will seek to "tie up" the site. At this early stage in the development process, the developer is leery of committing large sums of money to a tract of land that may not end up being developed. However, doing extensive planning work prior to gaining control of the site can leave the developer in a disadvantageous negotiating position with the landowner. Consequently, the objective at this time may be to arrange for an option on the land or possibly a low downpayment purchase with no personal liability (in economic effect, also an option). In this manner, the site will be available when needed, and present investment will be minimized.

The next step is to determine physical feasibility and prepare an architectural layout. The developer will arrange for soil tests to determine the load-bearing capacity of the ground, examine the grade and configuration of the site, and consider any other unique physical characteristics. The developer's architect determines whether the general type and size of the envisioned project can be placed on the site. For example, the architect will judge whether the number of square feet to be developed will leave sufficient space to meet municipal parking requirements. The building must be put on the land without compromising the overall visual impression of the site or the functioning of the constructed space for the proposed tenant. Appearance and function are important not only to marketability, but also to the developer's relationship with his ever-present partner, government, in all its levels and forms.

Moreover, during the idea refinement stage, the developer will begin to look for general contractors (GCs) who are available to do work in the area. Some very tentative discussion may be initiated with possible tenants, with a view to obtaining the right mix for the project. Potential permanent and construction lenders will be approached to ascertain their general interest in providing loans. Finally, a check of possible sources of equity capital will be made, and the tax ramifications of alternative financing structures will be considered. By the end of idea refinement, the developer has given his idea a location and a physical form, and he has begun to test this refined idea for physical, legal, and financial feasibility. He may also have tied up the land with an option, but so far he has gotten a lot of information at little more than the cost of his own time. If he pursues the idea into stage 3, he will start to spend significantly more money and the cost of quitting will be higher. Thus, in stage 2 the developer needs to use his very best judgment about whether to go ahead, to rework the idea, or to abandon it and start over.

THE BANCFIRST PLAZA EXAMPLE

BancFirst Plaza was the fourth phase in a series of five planned for Greystone Center, a master-planned office-retail project located at the intersection of Greystone Drive and MoPac Boulevard in northwest Austin. (Thus, the site was already a given.) The site seemed ideal for a luxury office development; it was at the intersection of two major arteries and within a reasonable driving distance of a considerable residential population and downtown.

The first phase of Greystone Center was developed in 1978 with the Greystone I office building and restaurant. Since that time the Greystone

Square Shopping Center and Greystone II office building have been completed. The developer considered the best layout for the phase 4 office complex and determined that the planned project should include a full-service bank. This proposed use was not permitted under the current zoning, and the developer had to obtain a variance for bank use, particularly the drive-in facility, which the projected major tenant required, and the projected height. Although the location was adjacent to major transportation arteries, this did not assure "access." The developer still needed permission for a curb cut to move traffic from the site onto the artery.

STAGE 3:
FEASIBILITY

The third stage in the development process is the precommitment stage. At the beginning of this stage, the *formal* feasibility study is begun. (Until now the developer has done his own informal estimates of feasibility.) As will be explained in Chapter 26, varying degrees of market research are possible. In essence, the developer will use regional and urban economic data to study the market prospects for the chosen product (constructed space). Preliminary drawings will be made, trading off an aesthetic market appeal against the cost of the particular project. (The operating cost ramifications of any particular design concept will also be considered.) From the preliminary drawings, more refined construction cost estimates will be made by using such sources as the Dodge Building Cost Calculator and Marshall and Swift.

At this point, discussions with both permanent and construction lenders will become more specific. A developer lacking the necessary contacts may retain a mortgage banker to facilitate these discussions. Based on the costs projected in the preliminary drawings as well as the estimate of market demand for the space, the feasibility study is completed, permitting a more refined cost and value statement to be developed that more rigorously determines the economic viability of the proposed project.

Also part of the feasibility study is a clear statement of all the aspects of the partnership with government. As explained in more detail in Part 9, this will include not only required building permits but also possible impact fees. Most importantly, it will assure that all the necessary public services (water, sewer, etc.) will be available for the project.

The feasibility study is a resource document and should include sufficient data to allow each participant in the process to evaluate objectives in a risk-return perspective. The feasibility study shows overall viability (project value exceeds cost), and it provides much of the data necessary for each of the players to evaluate his own individual cash flows from the project.

If the developer has to pay an architect up-front for preliminary drawings, pay a land planner (if the project is large and contains mixed uses), and pay an outside consultant for the market study and feasibility analysis, then he is beginning to spend significant dollars on this project. He can still quit if the formal feasibility study looks bad, or he can rework the idea to better fit the market. But at this point the price of quitting has grown higher.

THE BANCFIRST PLAZA EXAMPLE

The architect designed the site plan for BancFirst Plaza, emphasizing ease of access and parking as well as visual compatibility with the preceding three phases. The reasonableness of the cost estimates for the center was checked with GCs doing business in the area. The most likely permanent lender was given a rough idea of the design to be sure that nothing in the proposed development created unusual financing problems. Based on the market study, construction cost and value statements similar to those shown in Tables 25-2 and 25-3 were developed.

STAGE 4: CONTRACT NEGOTIATIONS

The fourth stage is the contract stage, at which point written agreements are entered into with all the key participants in the project. On the financial side, a permanent loan commitment will usually be obtained. The permanent lender, relying on the developer's feasibility study as well as on its own analysis and appraisal of the site and project, agrees by this commitment to make a loan if the project is built according to plans and specifications. The developer will then take the permanent loan commitment to a potential construction lender. After convincing the construction lender that the project is likely to be completed on time according to plans and specifications, the developer obtains a construction loan, to be funded in stages as the project is built.

At this point, the developer must decide on how to retain the GC. Should a construction contract be negotiated on a one-to-one basis, or should construction bids be solicited from all interested GCs? Should the architect supervise the construction process, or should a construction manager be hired? Should the general contractor be required to post payment or performance bonds (i.e., should insurance be taken out to assure satisfaction of the GC's contractual obligations)?

In most private (versus government) construction situations, contracts are negotiated because primarily not all the plans are complete when the GC is hired. On the other hand, most government jobs involve bidding. In government projects, plans and specifications are usually fully complete, and, therefore, a bidding process makes sense.

At this stage, the developer must also decide whether to attempt preleasing to major tenants. If major tenants are presigned, financing will be easier to obtain, and smaller tenants will be drawn to the project. On the other hand, major tenants know their value to the developer and

TABLE 25-2   BANCFIRST PLAZA COST/PRO FORMA COST ANALYSIS
81,017 SQ. FT. GROSS—76,712 SQ. FT. RENTABLE—

Hard costs	
Shell	$3,500,000
Land	1,394,000
Tenant finish	920,000
Architect and engineer	191,500
Landscape, sprinkler	160,000
Site work	105,000
On-site utilities	48,500
Off-site construction	22,000
Permits and fees	9,500
Soft costs	
Expenses during lease-up	1,950,000
Construction interest	530,000
Development fee and supervision	200,000
Contingency	411,000
Lease commissions	205,000
Permanent loan points	152,000
Construction loan points	76,000
Legal and accounting	50,000
Promotion and advertising	45,000
Construction loan closing costs	37,500
Permanent loan closing costs	35,000
Appraisal	10,000
Construction period taxes	10,000
Surveying	6,0000
Total cost	$10,068,500
Less: Operating income during lease-up	(1,468,500)
Pro forma cost total	$ 8,600,000

will be able to bargain for a better deal if they are drawn into the process early. In either case, overall leasing parameters, including **tenant allowances** (for tenant finish); common area charges; heating, ventilating, and air-conditioning (HVAC) charges; length of lease; renewal options; and so forth, must be established. This is necessary so that the marketing function may continue without interruption during the construction process.

Finally, a decision on financing the equity must be made. Should a money partner be brought in to share development risks? Should the project be presold to long-term equity investors? What particular investment vehicle would be most advantageous, considering the tax shelter possibilities as well as the risks involved in the particular development?

TABLE 25-3 BANCFIRST PLAZA FIVE-YEAR OPERATING PRO FORMA

Rentable square feet	76,712
Annual fixed expenses	$0.85/sq. ft.
Annual variable expenses	$2.90/sq. ft.
Initial expense stop	$3.75/sq. ft.
Annual expense increase	5%
Annual rent increase	5%

	1985	1986	1987	1988	1989
Average rent per square foot	$16.75	$17,59	$18,47	$19,39	$20.36
Drive through ground lease	$28,000	$29,400	$30,870	$32,414	$34,034
Covered parking income	$9,300	$9,765	$10,253	$10,766	$11,304
Average occupancy	49%	91%	95%	95%	95%
Gross Potential Income	$1,322,226	1,388,337	1,457,754	1,530,642	1,607,174
Less: Vacancy	659,788	127,329	70,832	74,373	78,092
Effective Gross Income	$662,438	1,261,008	1,386,923	1,456,269	1,529,082
Less: Expenses	173,438	280,008	304,893	320,137	336,144
Net Operating Income	$489,000	$981,000	$1,082,030	$1,136,131	$1,192,938

1. "Average rent" in 1985 was based on $16.00 per foot during initial preleasing and on rates being at $17.00 per foot on completion of building.
2. Occupancy was based on initial occupancy of 30 percent in January 1985 and full occupancy within 18 months.
3. The "Expense stop" would increase each year for all leases by the "Annual expense increase."
4. All income sources would increase each year by the "Annual rent increase."

In stage 4, it is *possible* for negotiations not to come to fruition in loan agreements and so forth; if debt and equity monies can't be raised, then the project may still be aborted—with considerable pain—at this late date (see Figure 25-1). But if the developer did his homework in stage 3, he is pretty sure he can bring contracts to fruition in stage 4.

THE BANCFIRST PLAZA EXAMPLE

The developer of BancFirst Plaza entered into a joint venture agreement with a group of investors. The developer acted as the managing general partner, and the investors acted as limited partners. The limited partners were liable only for their initial equity contributions. The developer–general partner was liable for any partnership liabilities required, including negative cash flow, above and beyond the limited partners' equity contributions.

In the event that operating deficits, that is, negative before-tax cash flows, were experienced during lease-up, the developer–general partner planned to finance such deficits via the construction loan. This expectation is indicated in Table 25-2 as expense in the soft-cost category of the pro forma cost analysis. Benefits accruing to the developer–general partner, in addition to operating profits during the lease-up period (beyond pro forma), included a development and supervision fee of $200,000. Once breakeven occupancy was reached, the partnership agreement called for a distribution of cash flow as follows. First, all cash flow would be distributed to the limited partners until their initial equity contributions had been returned; from that point forward, all cash distributions would be allocated 90 percent to limited partners and 10 percent to the general partner. (The limited partners were putting up 100 percent of the equity.)

**STAGE 5:
COMMITMENT
POINT**

The fifth stage of the development process is termed the commitment point. Here the contracts negotiated in stage 4 are signed, or conditions required to make them effective are satisfied. Frequently, contracts negotiated in stage 4 are contingent on other contracts; for example, the permanent loan commitment may be contingent on signing a certain major tenant. Since the developer does not want to be bound under one contract unless all the contracts are in force and because the contracts may, in fact, be contingent on one another, it is frequently necessary to arrange a simultaneous execution of several contracts.

In the fifth stage, the partnership or joint venture agreement is closed (if the developer needs a money partner). Any presale to passive investors is closed. The construction loan is closed, and the permanent commitment fee is paid, binding the permanent lender. The construction contract is signed with the general contractor. Any presigned major tenants execute their leases. Finally, the informal accounting system, in use since successful completion of the pro forma in stage 1, is replaced by a more formal accounting system.

A detailed construction budget is drawn, based on the agreements negotiated earlier. Cash control is maintained through construction loan draw procedures, which will be explained shortly. Time control is established by relating the different contracts in a **PERT** or **CPM** chart. These operations research techniques allow the decision maker to identify and focus on the "critical path." Thus, the greatest attention can be directed at the activities that must be completed before other activities can be begun.

THE BANCFIRST PLAZA EXAMPLE

The construction lender for BancFirst Plaza, a local commercial bank, was willing to commit to a three-year miniperm at prime plus one. Therefore, there was no need to acquire a permanent loan commitment.

The financing plan called for approaching a mortgage broker when BancFirst Plaza was 60 percent leased. At that time, the mortgage broker would arrange an $8.8 million loan. It was expected that the loan would be a nonrecourse, fixed-rate, interest-only loan with a 10-year term. When 60 percent occupancy was reached, the permanent lender would fund the cost of the project except for the tenant finish on the unleased portion of the building. At 90 percent occupancy, full funding would occur.

All the contracts were executed at approximately the same time, so that the construction lender and the general contractor became bound simultaneously. A budget was developed, adhering to the cost statement shown in the feasibility study and tied to the contracts just executed. The construction lender was then ready to begin advancing funds based on this budget. The construction lender took a first lien position in the land through a mortgage executed by the developer.

STAGE 6: CONSTRUCTION

During this period, the structure is built. At this point, the developer's emphasis switches from stressing minimal financing exposure (in the event the project does not go forward) to seeking to reduce the construction time during which he experiences maximum financial exposure. The commitment point is past, and now the developer will be called on to function more as a manager and less as a promoter.

Periodically during construction, the subcontractors submit bills or vouchers for their costs to the general contractor. The developer adds his **soft-dollar costs** (insurance, interest, marketing, etc.) to the **hard-dollar costs** and sends a draw request to the commercial bank. The commercial bank funds the loan according to the loan agreement executed in the previous stage by placing funds in the developer's bank account. The developer writes a check to the GC, and the GC pays the subcontractors.

The construction lender is protected by having the GC's work approved by either the architect or the construction manager in order to make sure that it has been done according to plans and specifications. Furthermore, a portion of the payments due the GC and the subcontractors (perhaps 10 percent) will be withheld. This practice, known as **retainage**, is intended to protect the lender (and developer) against incomplete or defective work. The retained sums are paid after the architect or construction manager certifies that the project has been completed in accordance with the plans and specifications.

The **construction manager**, marketing representative, and financial officer—all members of the development team—work closely together during this stage. The construction manager must be sure that the project is being built according to plans and specifications and on time. The marketing representative must see to it that presigned major tenants are receiving what they expected and any remaining space is being leased or sold. The financial officer is the coordinator between the construction process and the marketing function on one side and sources of financing on the other. That officer transmits the draw request from the construction manager and supervises banking relations. At the same time, he approves adjustments that must be made to reflect the realities of the marketplace as described by the marketing representative.

THE BANCFIRST PLAZA EXAMPLE

The developer of BancFirst Plaza chose to utilize an employee project manager (PM) rather than a construction manager. The developer felt that this would ensure a greater degree of control over the construction process. The PM monitored the progress of the general contractor and approved draw requests, which were forwarded to the controller of the development company. The controller added soft-dollar costs and made a draw request, net of the retainage to be withheld, to the construction lender. The developer's leasing agent handled the construction problems of the major tenants and negotiated the leasing of the smaller offices.

STAGE 7: INITIATION OF OPERATIONS

In the next to last stage of the development process, construction is completed and operating personnel are brought on the scene. Preopening advertising and promotion take place, utilities are connected, municipal requirements such as inspections and certificates of occupancy are satisfied, and the tenants move in.

On the financial side, the permanent loan is closed and the construction loan paid off. Unless the developer is keeping the property as an investment, long-term equity interests take over from the developer (based on a presale contract or a sale after completion), and the formal opening is held.

THE BANCFIRST PLAZA EXAMPLE

The developer of BancFirst Plaza was responsible for leasing and property management, and was also a general partner in the investment partnership. The lease terms were dictated by the market but typically ran from three to five years. Base rent was tied to a 5 percent annual escalation clause. Operating expenses were limited by an expense stop that was adjusted annually with increases passed through to the tenants.

The building was opened, and the first tenant moved in about 14 months after construction began. Lease-up was expected to take about 12 months following construction. As the project was completed, utilities were connected, and a city occupancy permit was obtained.

STAGE 8: ASSET
MANAGEMENT
OVER TIME

Asset management (discussed extensively in Chapters 11 and 12) includes all facets of maintaining, releasing, and repositioning the long-lived real estate asset in the marketplace over its economic life. To do this well in the best of times is a challenge. In today's overbuilt markets, the capacity for quality asset management may be the critical ingredient in financing and initially leasing any new development. We use the Banc-First Plaza example to focus on asset management in a "workout" situation—the kind that has become a distressingly common phenomenon at the beginning of the 1990s.

THE BANCFIRST PLAZA EXAMPLE

As we begin the 1990s, Austin, Texas, is possibly the weakest office market in the world. All the problems of the oil, high tech, and savings and loan industries were compounded in Austin. Today in downtown Austin, most of the major office buildings are owned by lenders. In suburban Austin, most of the buildings are owned by government agencies that have taken over failed lenders.

Typically, BancFirst Plaza's major tenant failed, and the developer defaulted on the loan. Today you can get a three-year lease in the building for operating expenses only. Compare that to the $20.36 per square foot projected for 1989 rent in Table 25-3.

From an asset management perspective, this project represents the worst of all possible worlds. The market is terrible, and the owner is an out-of-town committee that just wants to sell. Obviously, in such an environment it is very difficult to manage, as suggested in Chapters 11 and 12. What this points out is that asset management can include distressed property management as well as major repositionings. The developer needs this skill to be a legitimate player in the 1990s and so does the taxpayer, who is ultimately funding the Resolution Trust Corporation discussed in Chapter 13.

SUMMARY

Development may be the most exciting part of the real estate game. An understanding of all facets of the industry is required to understand fully the dynamics of the creation of space. An organized approach to understanding development is shown in the eight-stage model presented in this chapter. You should remember, however, that development in real life is interactive: multiple activities in each stage of the process and variables in each stage affect other variables in other stages. And as always, the game proceeds at the project level and at the level of the individual players. Before changes in the rules of the game (public policy) are considered, a firm analytical foundation is essential, so a review of previous chapters may be in order at this point.

IMPORTANT TERMS

Construction manager
CPM
Hard-dollar costs
PERT

Pro forma
Retainage
Soft-dollar costs
Tenant allowances

REVIEW QUESTIONS

25.1   It has been suggested that the development process can be viewed as eight interactive stages. How do the various development activities interact?

25.2   List and discuss the eight stages of the development model suggested in Chapter 25.

25.3   What is retainage? How does this practice protect construction lenders?

25.4   What sources of data may be relied on in developing a pro forma operating statement for a new income-producing property? In which of the development stages should these data be collected?

25.5   Why might a developer utilize a land option to gain control of property in the idea refinement stage?

25.6   Why does the developer's role change from one of a promoter to a manager in the construction stage?

25.7   Why might it be advisable to execute the permanent loan commitment and major tenant leases at the same time?

25.8   In what stage is the developer actually committed to the project? Why?

25.9   Why might a developer be willing to offer very attractive lease concessions to an anchor tenant?

25.10 What might be the impact on the value of land adjacent to a new development? What might a developer do to take advantage of the situation?

$\mathcal{L}$ AND USE FEASIBILITY ANALYSIS

In Chapter 24 we noted that real estate development begins with an idea or a need: a site looking for a use or vice versa, or capital looking for an opportunity. Between the idea (stage 1) and the beginning of construction (stage 6) lies a critical step. Someone must formally decide whether the idea is feasible; that is, will it work? As obvious as it sounds, developers and investors sometimes gloss over this critical step in their optimism and their impatience to get moving. But back-of-the-envelope numbers have increasingly given way to sophisticated projections; high stakes and cautious institutional partners dictate formal analysis beyond the initial hunch.

Furthermore, there is increasing recognition that feasibility depends on more than a set of numbers that work. Land use so materially affects the everyday lives of so many people—their health, economic well-being, and social interactions—that land use is not a free choice. In practical terms, real estate development is constrained by many forces—police powers of the state, public opinion, and private legal agreements to name only a few. Land use decisions take place not in a vacuum but in a social and legal system. As the world in which they work becomes more interdependent, real estate participants must recognize the interdependency and take it into account when analyzing a project for feasibility.

Feasibility analysis can be as simple as evaluating a one-year cash flow pro forma or as complex as a multiyear market and economic study. Although the depth of analysis that can be economically justified varies depending on the importance of the decision, the feasibility study should always be developed according to an analytical framework similar to the one described in this chapter. This framework is flexible enough to cover a wide variety of real estate projects, with the level of detail depending on the importance of the decision.

A complete **real estate feasibility analysis** requires a market and economic study undertaken with a clear understanding of the decision environment. The decision environment consists of the motivations and capacities of a myriad of individuals and institutions as well as the general public. The specific group of individuals involved varies from project to project, but the basic theme remains: Land use decisions cannot be made in a vacuum. They are, in fact, public issues. Examined here will be this environment, site and participant relationships, exogenous shocks to the relationship, and related implications for the participants. On this basis, the mechanics of feasibility analysis are presented and a practical framework for analysis is developed.

This chapter really belongs to Professor James A. Graaskamp, the father of feasibility analysis and our personal hero. Although he died in 1988, his ideas will be with us as long as real estate decisions are made. In this edition we have changed a few of his words and updated the examples, but the concepts are his.

Professor Graaskamp said that "a real estate project is feasible when the real estate analyst determines that there is a reasonable likelihood of satisfying explicit objectives when a selected course of action is tested for fit to a context of specific constraints and limited resources." For the normal reader, this is a rather long and tough sentence. In this chapter, we will show how this definition incorporates all the different aspects of the development process we discussed in Chapters 24 and 25. Professor Graaskamp goes beyond the broad marketing view we have used thus far in the text and considers the land a public trust. Thus, his idea not only brings in all of the marketing points made in Chapters 9 and 10, but also goes on to ask about how the developer serves society. All these concepts will be clear as we move through the chapter.

Please don't confuse the appraisals that justified much of the S&L lending of the 1980s with the complete feasibility discussed in this chapter. If all the appraisals of development projects done for S&Ls had included everything Professor Graaskamp suggests should be in a feasibility study, the nation wouldn't be looking at a nearly $200 billion cost to cover insured S&L deposits.

THE LAND USE DECISION ENVIRONMENT

Analysis of the land use decision environment requires a realistic view of the key participants involved. These participants generally include (1) the public sector, (2) developers, investors, and producers, and (3) consumers or users. Any land use decisions affecting a parcel of land will involve interaction among these three parties. This necessary interaction suggests a need for cooperation rather than confrontation; ultimately, the three groups must view themselves not as adversaries but as partners.

The participants must recognize the others' needs and be willing to work within a partnership atmosphere, even though specific goals may differ. Each must survive the short run and prosper over the long run if societal equilibrium in the development field is to be achieved.

SHORT-RUN CONSIDERATIONS—CASH MANAGEMENT

The short-run considerations for each participant revolve around their **cash management cycle.** Developers must be able to meet their short-run cash needs and remain financially solvent in order to complete the development process successfully. This requires them to estimate and control development expenditures accurately, finance the expenditures, and complete the project on time.

The public sector participants are faced with a similar cash management problem. They must also be able to finance or fund public expenditures associated with development. For example, public services to a site must usually be provided. The initial costs of providing such services may exceed the revenue generated by property taxes from the locality. As a result, the municipality's master plan may seek to coordinate growth with the public sector's ability to provide and pay for public services. (This topic is discussed more fully in Part 9.)

Users or consumers of real estate must also operate within a cash management cycle. Owner-occupants and tenants must be able to pay the market price of the real estate they use. In the case of commercial real estate, users must be able to meet monthly rental payments and still earn a profit on their own goods or services. Residential real estate users must be able to pay market prices for real estate services and still meet all other consumption and saving demands.

In the short run, then, land use decisions affecting any site must recognize each participant's cash management needs. This does not suggest that one or two of the participants must cater to the specific needs or demands of the third, but rather that each must be aware of the role and responsibility of each of the others and be prepared to work within a partnership atmosphere.

LONG-RUN CONSIDERATIONS—ECONOMIC AND CULTURAL

Long-run constraints affecting the development participants revolve around the economic and cultural stability of the community within which development occurs. This long-run stability, or societal equilibrium, requires continued communication among the participants. Developers must make a lasting commitment to the community itself. That is, developers have a responsibility to the community to create or produce real estate services that will provide an acceptable environment in the long run. Community involvement and leadership in the political arena may be an example of such a commitment. (An example is developer James Rouse's efforts on behalf of the civic initiative to rejuvenate downtown Baltimore.)

The public sector needs to plan for future growth taking into consideration expected demographic and economic changes. By determining where growth is likely to occur, the public sector is in a better position to encourage responsible development and provide the necessary infrastructure to support future real estate development.

Users or consumers of real estate also participate in, and contribute to, societal equilibrium. This requires an active contribution to the development of local land use policy. Users should support policy decisions made in the public sector that improve the overall attractiveness or economic health of the community, or both. Examples might include support of either an efficient public transportation system or the construction of housing geared to the needs of senior citizens.

Clearly, there are tradeoffs between short- and long-run considerations. The developer has limited resources, and certain public officials face periodic reelection challenges. Short-run pressures cannot be ignored, but neither can they be allowed to totally dominate longer term considerations.

MARKET CONSTRAINTS

In addition to the short- and long-run considerations mentioned, the land use decision environment poses certain constraints that must be recognized and dealt with: Legal constraints; physical constraints; economic constraints; and social constraints.

LEGAL CONSTRAINTS. From a legal perspective, land use decisions revolve around the bundle of rights associated with ownership and the limitations placed on ownership from various sources. The most obvious of these limitations include the government powers of property taxation, police power, and eminent domain. Furthermore, other preexisting interests in property (for example, leasehold interests, easements, and restrictive covenants) can have a significant impact on land use decisions. A careful examination of legal constraints *currently* affecting a property must be included in any land use feasibility analysis.

Legal constraints on a site may change as the site's use changes. This is true for both new development and redevelopment or rehabilitation. For new developments, zoning and building code requirements usually have a significant impact. The feasibility of rehabilitation projects often depends on the requirements of the building code. Sometimes it simply costs too much to bring old structures up to code, especially for uses like restaurants and clubs, where large numbers of people will occupy the building. It is always best to know what will be required before committing too much time and money to an idea. One way is to spend adequate time on a regular basis with city planning officials, zoning administrators, and building inspectors.

PHYSICAL CONSTRAINTS.   Many analysts focus primary attention on the physical dimensions of the site itself, for example, its topography and drainage. But the structure is equally important in a physical sense. Physical constraints like height and size frequently result from legal constraints (zoning), economic constraints (cost considerations), or market demand (floor plans and design features). An analysis of the physical attributes of a property must bring the site and structure together as one unit functioning within a marketplace.

Students without architectural or engineering training often overlook what should be obvious physical constraints. Earlier we mentioned topography and drainage. The configuration of the site can also be very limiting. For example, long, narrow corridors present significant development challenges. And looking beyond the site itself to the immediate physical surroundings, the analyst or decision maker must consider flood plains and prior uses of surrounding sites. She or he should be particularly concerned with any toxic waste problem that may currently exist or may develop in the future on a nearby site. Clearly, past uses of surrounding properties can present physical constraints on the use of the subject site.

ECONOMIC CONSTRAINTS.   To those with a business education, economic constraints often seem the most important limitation. This is because it is very time consuming to gather all the market information suggested in Part 4 and relate it as suggested here to the specific project. This work obviously requires a background in accounting, finance, and taxation. Still, the economic constraints are probably easier to understand than the legal, physical, or social. We live in a capitalistic society, and in order to motivate action, all the required participants must make a profit. This means that after we put together the numbers for the project at Level One, we must also ascertain that at Level Two all the required participants have a positive net present value.

SOCIAL CONSTRAINTS.   Society itself can impose informal rules or constraints on land use. These constraints are dynamic since they change from time to time and from place to place. In some big cities bars are a fixture of residential neighborhoods; in other cities bars are not accepted in residential areas. Housing is another example: the wide incidence of unmarried couples living together has had a significant impact on the acceptability of certain types of development. Today's yuppie residential development designed for sophisticated singles of the hot tub set probably would have had a hard time selling in Topeka 20 years ago. Today, something that used to be considered radical and decidedly "southern California" can find acceptance in neighborhoods around the country. While social constraints clearly evolve over time, they are still very real at any point in time. Consequently, an awareness of social constraints is an important aspect of land use feasibility analysis.

SITE AND PARTICIPANT RELATION- SHIPS

The feasibility study is undertaken subject to the constraints mentioned above and in a very interactive environment. Each participant in the land use decision process interacts with each of the other participants and, of course, with the site itself. These relationships reflect the fact that the participants rely on one another in many ways in an effort to develop a particular site successfully. Responsibilities, decisions, and services contributed or received by each participant must be recognized as the culmination of extensive cooperation among the participants. Figure 26-1 presents a simplified representation of the participants' relationship to each other and to the site. (This figure is a graphic illustration of the practical importance of the land economics concepts initially presented in Chapter 3.)

PUBLIC SECTOR/SITE RELATIONSHIP

The fundamental relationship between the public sector and the site is dominated by the provision of services to the site and the implementation of policy decisions affecting the site, as indicated by number 1 in Figure 26-1. In return, the site represents the basis for levying real estate taxes that finance the many services provided to the site. Services provided by the public sector to the site would normally include police and fire protection, utilities, schools, libraries, roadway maintenance, and so on. Policy decisions affecting the site would include master planning, zoning, building codes, environmental controls, and capital improvement programs, to name a few. The combination of the availability of public services and the implementation of policy decisions may encourage, or even preclude development.

PUBLIC SECTOR/USER RELATIONSHIPS

The relationships between the public sector and the user, as indicated by number 2 in Figure 26-1, concentrate on policy decisions affecting, and services offered to, the user and tax payments and political input directed to the public sector. Services provided directly to the user include

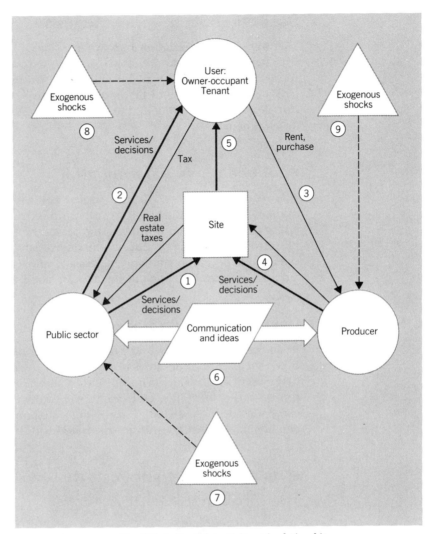

FIGURE 26-1   *Simplified site and participants' relationships*

health facilities, schools, transportation, and recreational facilities. Policy decisions that affect the user might include utility charges, neighborhood zoning decisions, and income taxes. These funds are used to finance public sector operations.

Users also provide, or should provide, a great deal of input to the public sector. Such input is directed to the public sector through the elective process and through direct participation in government. This government participation may be achieved through service on appointed boards and commissions or through lobbying for specific legislation.

USER/PRODUCER RELATIONSHIPS

User and producer relationships are developed through the market system. Rental levels and purchase prices are the result of the interaction of supply and demand for real estate service within the marketplace, as indicated by number 3 in Figure 26-1. Relative increases in profits may stimulate new development, but relative declines would discourage new development.

PRODUCER/SITE RELATIONSHIP

The relationship between the producer and the site is represented by number 4 in Figure 26-1. This relationship is dominated by services and policy decisions of the producer that affect the site and the capital applied to the site by the producer. The services and decisions affecting the site include development concept, design, and actual construction. Capital applied to the site includes materials, labor, and management skill.

USER/SITE RELATIONSHIP

As indicated by number 5 in Figure 26-1, the primary relationship between the user and the site is represented by the net benefits that accrue to the user. These benefits may be either pecuniary or nonpecuniary and represent the utility derived from the site by the user. Pecuniary benefits could include increased sales owing to location or design; nonpecuniary benefits might include prestige associated with the site.

PUBLIC SECTOR/PRODUCER RELATIONSHIP

The relationship between the public sector and the producer is represented by number 6 in Figure 26-1. This relationship is perhaps the least understood and least recognized of all the relationships. With the recent increase of public sector influence in the development process, difficulties have emerged that tend to put the two participants in an adversarial position. The primary relationship between the public sector and the producer includes communication and an exchange of ideas. In general, however, this necessary two-way communication is informal at best and nonexistent at worst. Idea exchange is, in many instances, even less developed than the communication process.

Producers may perceive the public sector as merely representing a series of obstacles to development. The public sector may perceive the producers as being insensitive to larger socioeconomic issues as they pursue profit at all costs. Naturally, neither of these perceptions represents the typical attitude of the participants. In fact, in most cases, the participants are making what at least they consider to be an honest effort to be fair and responsive to the other's needs.

A major problem area in the relationship between the public sector and producers lies in the nature of their day-to-day interaction. In many instances the parties only communicate with one another when a problem arises. For example, a request for a zoning change may require interaction. This site or problem-specific interaction is usually carried out through a fairly well-defined series of official steps. Application is made requesting the zoning change, which is followed by review and recommendation by the public sector. During the process, both parties are aware of the fact that something is at stake. Many times the applicant is requesting something that the public sector does not wish to grant. As a result, the parties are often placed in a direct adversarial position. To remedy this situation producers and the public sector need to develop a parallel communication network or medium devoid of specific confrontation. This might include workshops sponsored by the public sector or by producers. Explanations of city growth management policy and producer involvement in the development of the growth policy can help provide understanding between the two parties.

EXOGENOUS SHOCKS TO THE RELATIONSHIPS AMONG THE PARTICIPANTS

In addition to the relationships among the public sector, producers, and users, potential **exogenous shocks** may affect how each of the participants relates to the site. These shocks are represented as triangles in Figure 26-1. The shocks are external to the participants; that is, the participants can respond or react to the shocks but do not initiate them. At times it is these shocks that cause a crisis precipitating a decision, which itself necessitates a feasibility study. Whether the feasibility study is initiated by shock or by a new idea independent of any shock to the system, it is imperative that the analyst doing the feasibility study be aware of how a shock to the interactive system may affect the various participants in the process.

We don't know what the major shocks will be in the 1990s, but we do expect several to occur. We have only to look to the 1970s and 1980s which produced the multiple oil crises, the S&L collapse, the Japanese financial invasion, and the asbestos cleanup (to name just a few of the major exogenous shocks) to believe that new shocks will come in the 1990s.

EXOGENOUS SHOCKS TO THE PUBLIC SECTOR

Exogenous shocks affecting the public sector's impact on land use decisions can be the result of several factors. Changes in elected officials may cause a change in policy regarding land use decisions. This may come about via appointments to boards and commissions or through a change in support for certain policy attitudes. As elected officials come and go over the years, local government's attitude toward land use policy may change. These changes are usually not controlled by public sector administrators, and therefore, though the employees remain, the policies they must implement may vary.

Changes in key (nonelected) personnel may also cause changes in public sector land use decisions. For example, a new planning department head may recommend new policy guidelines for growth management. Other lower level personnel changes may also cause changes in the implementation of policy; these will also affect feasibility, though probably to a lesser extent.

Citizen support of public sector land use policy could also affect specific programs. This type of exogenous shock does not necessarily bring about changes in personnel but rather changes in attitudes. For example, citizens who desire less government regulation may demand tax cuts. Existing public sector land use policy may require substantial expenditures of public funds generated by either taxes or bond proceeds. Unwillingness to approve tax increases or bond referendums could reduce public sector activity in land use policy areas.

Many of these exogenous shocks are basically outside of the control of the individuals who make up the public sector. Still, public sector land use decisions must respond to such shocks on an almost continuous basis. Policy changes cause difficulties not only for the public sector, but also for producers and users. Producers and users discover that the "rules of the game" have changed as reflected in new land use policies and guidelines.

EXOGENOUS SHOCKS TO USERS

Owner-occupants and tenants are affected by a number of exogenous shocks. The majority of these shocks affect users' ability or willingness to pay for real estate services. Macroeconomic changes that affect general economic activity, employment, and inflation can significantly affect user decisions. Corporate users will plan plant and office expansions based on expectations of future economic growth. If their expectations are jolted by major economic changes, the response to the shock may greatly affect utilization of particular sites. Adverse economic news may cause a reduction in demand, and optimistic news may increase demand.

An additional source of exogenous shocks more directly affects individual users. These microshocks might include job transfers, promotions, loss of job, death, illness, or divorce. Each of these shocks—and many more not listed—can significantly alter personal land use decisions. Again, these shocks cannot normally be controlled, but they elicit a response.

EXOGENOUS SHOCKS TO PRODUCERS

Exogenous shocks that adversely affect producers could develop in the marketplace in general and thus affect all producers, or locally so as to affect an individual producer. Market shocks generally would have relatively the same impact on all producers. These shocks would include the same macroeconomic changes that affect users. Increases in unemployment and inflation can directly affect producers on both the supply and the demand side. In the supply area, inflation increases cost, which must be passed on to the ultimate consumer. On the demand side, unemployment can reduce demand for real estate services.

Microexogenous shocks that might affect individual producers would include such factors as increased competition, major local employer relocations, and producer-employee labor problems. Policy decisions instituted by the public sector may also materially affect a producer's ability to develop a site in a certain manner. These factors would include growth policy, zoning decisions, and local ordinances affecting development. Finally, changes in a producer's financial strength may limit his or her ability to attract adequate financing for future projects. For example, the failure of several projects may have damaged the developer's track record.

The issues just outlined demonstrate the need to develop relationships among the participants that have not traditionally been in evidence. The public sector, producers, and users must realize that they are partners in the growth and development of a community and, therefore, need to establish a framework for the partnership to develop. Because the nature of decisions made by the public sector affecting a particular site (and the organizational form of the public sector), the public sector has the greatest responsibility in developing this partnership.

IMPLICATIONS FOR THE FEASIBILITY STUDY

The foregoing description of participants and their interaction has many implications for the feasibility study. Returning to Graaskamp's definition of feasibility, we immediately see these implications:

1. First, remember that Graaskamp suggests a test for fit between a course of action and explicit objectives. This requires a statement of objectives for all three participants or groups of participants in each of the three areas. The objectives are often unique and personal to individuals. Therefore, at the project level we have the three groups involved, and then within each group we have individual decision makers maximizing their own cash flows (or other interests) at another level. The feasibility study begins with an explicit statement of the objectives of all three primary groups as well as the major Level Two decision makers. It isn't always easy to determine everyone's

objectives, but a feasibility study that doesn't start here is fatally flawed.

2. The course of action that is tested for fit must fit within specific constraints imposed on the development environment. These are in fact the legal, physical, economic, and social constraints described in the preceding section.

3. The idea of limited resources in Graaskamp's definition is broadly construed and thus includes not just capital availability, but people, energy, and image as well. All three primary participants have not only limited capital resources, but also limited people, limited energy, and very real limits on image.

4. The term "satisfaction" in Graaskamp's definition deals not only with the present value derived from discounted cash flow and other tangible financial data, but also with ethical responsibilities. At times, a particular course of action may appear to satisfy one of the three participant groups or even two on a tangible basis. Yet the third will drag his feet because, while there is no tangible problem, there is a feeling that ethical responsibilities are being ignored. Remember that the land is a finite resource, and when the interaction of the three groups produces bad products, people are victims within their own real estate terrarium.

5. The word "likelihood" in Graaskamp's definition makes explicit the importance of risk. All three participant groups face typical risks in any real estate development. The feasibility analyst must make these risks explicit in the beginning so as to be sure that no participant is exposed to what he or she considers undue risk. Otherwise the project is not feasible.

All of this suggested to Graaskamp a six-point framework for feasibility analysis. First, the analyst should begin by clearly stating the objectives of the enterprise for whom the feasibility study is performed. These will be the dominant objectives in the study. However, the feasibility analyst will be mindful of the objectives of all the other participants as well because if their objectives are not met, his client's project will likely not go forward and will not be successful in the long term. Second, Graaskamp believed in identifying opportunities in the market that were consistent with the previously mentioned objectives. In a third step, then, he would segment the market to find specific targets. (In the following section, we will combine his second and third thoughts in describing the role of the market study.)

Graaskamp's fourth point was to identify both the legal and political constraints on the particular development idea. Then he would move on to point five, which was a similar identification of aesthetic and ethical constraints. Notice here the strong connection to the idea of the land as a sacred trust. He would then follow with point six, which was a listing of physical/technical constraints as well as alternative technical solutions to physical problems. Thus, architecture and engineering come in as solutions to the third set of constraints.

Graaskamp suggested putting all the information contained in the first six steps in a financial synthesis. His financial synthesis was always mindful of the cash flow needs, both short and long term, of all three participant groups.

In the following section, we deal with the two most important elements in Graaskamp's framework. We have already dealt with the formal rules of the game and have considered the analyst's aesthetic and ethical responsibilities. Once the objectives of all the participants are known, the chief elements that remain are the market and economic studies followed by the final financial synthesis. Part 7 illustrated the technology most useful for the financial synthesis, that is, the discounted cash flow, while Part 4 gave us the marketing background for the market and economic study. In this chapter, we focus on the specifics of the market and economic study.

ROLE OF THE MARKET STUDY

The **market study** provides all the data necessary to allow the real estate analyst to make an informed investment decision about a specific project. In the economic study the analyst then uses these data for making projections to determine if the proposed project appears to be a viable investment. Based on these studies, the investment decision can be to reject the project, accept it, or modify it.

The market analyst must choose from among the most relevant data sources, depending on the specific situation. In most instances, land use feasibility analysis deals with a specific site, user, and investor-developer. In other words, a large mass of data must be related to a specific situation.

The perspective of the market study will depend on the purpose of the analysis. As we have noted, the analyst is usually faced with one of four scenarios.

- A site in search of a use
- A use in search of a site
- Capital in search of an investment
- An existing development

□ **SITE IN SEARCH OF A USE.** A site in search of a use is the market study perspective of investors in raw land. Often such investors (in some instances speculators) have acquired a particular site to hold for several years and develop or sell in the future. When the time comes to investigate potential feasible uses for the site, market forces may be quite different from what they were when the site was purchased. As a result, the analyst should examine potential uses given the site's legal, physical, economic, and social constraints. (See Box 26-1).

A market study that focuses on a site in search of a use will emphasize the impact of surrounding land uses on the site. That is, surrounding property uses have a significant impact on feasible uses for the site under study. For example, suppose that the owner of a vacant lot is looking for a feasible use. If the adjoining property is the county courthouse, an office building oriented toward lawyers might be appropriate. This would be an example of the location effect (i.e., impact of surrounding land uses on a particular site) affecting the feasibility of a proposed use.

❏   **USE IN SEARCH OF A SITE.**   A use in search of a site is the most common occasion for real estate feasibility analysis today. Large and

---

26-1

FEASIBILITY—A TRUE TALE OF A SITE IN SEARCH OF A USE

In this case the numbers worked; feasibility depended on something more.

A developer bought absolutely the last vacant lot on a one-and-a-half-block commercial strip opposite the campus of a state university with an enrollment of 20,000. He wanted to develop the lot with a fast-food restaurant for Burger King. The problem was that the lot, though commercially zoned, happened to be just inside the town's historic district and next door to a church. A high value was placed on tradition in the community, and public opinion, when outraged, was known to be a potent force. Was a fast-food restaurant feasible on the site?

Yes. Before the developer bought the lot, he knew the *use* was legal; the problem was appearance. Structures proposed for the historic district had to be reviewed by the town's Historic District Commission before a Certificate of Appropriateness would be awarded. Review criteria focused on external features like height, roof line, materials used in exterior walls, and signs. Clearly, the hamburger chain's typical store would never pass.

The burger chain agreed to depart from its usual design. On his second try, the developer came up with drawings that satisfied the town's Historic District Commission. A two-story brick building similar to its neighbors (but with contemporary-sized show windows) now houses the restaurant, less than a three-minute walk from the nearest classrooms and dormitories. It is, incidentally, the only national hamburger chain with representation in the prime block and a half of the central business district.

small users alike frequently are searching for sites that will meet their special needs. Examples of such users include fast-food restaurants, shopping center developers, office developers, oil companies, convenience stores, and so on. All the users have relatively specific requirements that a site must meet before they would consider purchasing. Such requirements might include a minimum traffic count, a specific demographic profile of nearby residents, parking availability, and so on.

The perspective of a use in search of a site usually requires the analyst to locate several sites that, to varying degrees, meet the user's needs. This may include several locations in one city or locations in different cities or regions. The latter would apply for such large-scale uses as a new plant, a corporate headquarters, a hotel, and a regional shopping mall. The market analyst must become familiar with the characteristics of several sites and be able to distinguish their various strengths and weaknesses. This will often require a rank ordering of the investors' site selection criteria. If a perfect site cannot be found (as is usually the case), tradeoffs must be made among various sites. This can often be the most difficult aspect of the site selection process.

❏ **CAPITAL IN SEARCH OF INVESTMENT.**   Feasibility analysis performed for a client in search of an investment usually focuses on the economic study, for investors usually make their investment decisions on the basis of after-tax rates of return. A market study provides the data for making economic projections. If incorrect or misleading data and assumptions are provided, the validity of the economic study is in doubt. It is important that analysts not fall into the trap of merely comparing economic studies. They should also validate the data and confirm the reasonableness of assumptions in the market study.

❏ **AN EXISTING DEVELOPMENT.**   When an existing development is analyzed, the problem is to evaluate accurately the project's position in the market. Is the existing development still competitive? Are current contract rents in line with current market rents? If contract rents have lagged market rents, is the reason improper management, needed repairs and maintenance, or something else? The analyst evaluates the market and how the existing development fits into the market. The analyst should also note changes that have occurred or are occurring to identify trends affecting the development's competitive position in the market.

The four scenarios we have outlined here require somewhat different approaches. Nevertheless, the basic objective is always to provide the data necessary for making an informed decision. Data collection can be organized around five areas: (1) regional (area) analysis, (2) neighborhood analysis, (3) site analysis, (4) demand analysis, and (5) supply analysis. (See Table 26-1.)

TABLE 26-1   OUTLINE OF MARKET AND ECONOMIC FEASIBILITY STUDY

STUDY AND ANALYSIS	DATA SOURCE
I. *Market Study*	
A. Regional and urban analysis	
1. Regional economic activity	Federal Reserve district banks, state real estate research centers
2. Economic base analysis	Major financial institutions
3. Population and income analysis	State economic agencies and U.S. Bureau of the Census
4. Transportation networks	State department of highways
5. Growth and development patterns	Chamber of commerce, regional planning departments
B. Neighborhood analysis	
1. Local economic activity	University bureaus of business research, local chamber of commerce
2. Transportation flows	Major city planning departments
3. Neighborhood competition	Survey of local Realtors and merchants
4. Future competition	Major city planning departments
5. Demographic characteristics	Census tract data
C. Site analysis	
1. Zoning and building codes	Local planning departments and commissions
2. Utilities	Local utility companies
3. Access	Local highway department and transportation offices
4. Size and shape	Plat records, usually at county courthouse
5. Topography	Local and U.S. geodetic surveys and direct soil samples
D. Demand analysis	
1. New Jobs	Primary survey market analysis, trade publications, local newspapers
2. Demographic	U.S. Bureau of the Census
3. Trend analysis	Building permits, starts, and zoning change requests
E. Supply analysis	
1. Vacancy rates and rental levels	Primary survey, local appraisers, leasing agents
2. Starts and building	Building permits, starts, and zoning change requests

TABLE 26-1 (CONTINUED)	
STUDY AND ANALYSIS	**DATA SOURCE**
3. City services	Planning departments and utilities
4. Community planning	Planning department
5. Construction cost and financing	Local builders, financial institutions
I. *Economic Study*	
A. Before-tax cash flow	See discussion in Part 4 on appraisal
1. Gross possible rents	Market survey, appraisers, property managers
2. Vacancy and bad debt	Market survey, appraisers, property managers
3. Operating expenses	Market survey, appraisers, property managers
4. Net operating income	Calculated
5. Debt service	Survey of financial institutions and Federal Reserve Bulletin
B. After-tax discounted cash flow 1. Depreciation 2. Tax liability	See Part 6 on taxation
C. Present value and justified investment price	See Chapter 21
D. Yield or internal rate of return	See Chapter 21
E. Invest—do-not-invest decision	See Chapter 21
F. The Level Two position of all significant decision makers	See Chapter 4

Note: *For a more complete conceptual picture of the market study, see James A. Graaskamp, "Identification and Delineation of Real Estate Market Research," Real Estate Issues (Spring–Summer 1985).*

COMPONENTS OF THE MARKET STUDY

REGIONAL ANALYSIS

The region might be a state, MSA (Metropolitan Statistical Area), county, or city. The key elements of **regional analysis** include the following.

- *Impact of the national economy on the region.* For example, how would a nationwide recession affect the region? What is the role of the region in the national economy?

- *Economic base analysis.* The region is analyzed as a separate economy. What industries dominate the economy? What is their impact on demand for services and eventually demand for space? What does the future of the economic base look like?

- *Population analysis.* Population changes and trends can indicate market strengths and weaknesses. Migration patterns, age, education, mobility, and so on, should be evaluated.

- *Income levels.* Average income of the area, sources of income, unemployment patterns, and new employment opportunities will affect the needs of the area.

- *Transportation.* Does the region act as a transportation hub, or is it isolated? Check highway routes to various markets as well as train, air, and possible water service.

- *Growth or development patterns.* Is the region a growth-oriented area, or has the growth leveled off? Where will future development occur and why?

Like all the components of the feasibility study, the extent of the regional analysis varies with the decision at hand. For a recent example of how a leading investment banker looks at the Boston region, see Box 26-2.

NEIGHBORHOOD ANALYSIS

With the next step the focus narrows. **Neighborhood analysis** should accurately portray the dynamics of the area immediately surrounding the site. Boundaries are sometimes difficult to define. Logical neighborhood boundaries may be defined by use (commercial, residential, etc.). Artificial barriers (highways, parks, etc.) and natural barriers (rivers, soil conditions, etc.) frequently help to outline the neighborhood. The following lists some key characteristics of neighborhood analysis.

❏ **IMPACT OF THE LOCAL ECONOMY ON THE SITE'S NEIGHBORHOOD.**   Analysis of major employers in the area is generally of critical importance. How real estate decisions have been made in the past in the area and how such decisions affected the site may also be of importance.

❏ **TRANSPORTATION FLOWS.**   Traffic in the neighborhood is important. The relevant kind of traffic may be pedestrian, public transportation, or private automobile traffic. Traffic counts and patterns are part of the analysis.

❏ **NEIGHBORHOOD COMPETITION.**   Although many types of real estate projects compete with similar projects throughout the region, often more weight is placed on neighborhood competition. If the neighborhood is becoming saturated with a particular type of property use,

26-2

THE BOSTON OFFICE MARKET: WILL IT SURVIVE THE MASSACHUSETTS MIRACLE?

Recent indicators lead us to believe that a downturn in Boston's office market is currently under way:

- For the first time in seven years, Boston—the seventh largest city in the United States—is losing jobs. Total nonagricultural employment in the metropolitan area actually declined in the 12 months ending September 1989 compared with an average annual increase of 45,000 per year during the 1983–88 period.

- Over the past decade, pressure has been building among many of the nation's office markets as supply has continued to outpace demand. Boston is no exception: the vacancy rate in the greater Boston office market surged from 4 percent in 1980 to 14.4 percent in 1989. Although many proposed projects are unlikely to proceed, the vacancy rate is expected to remain above current levels through 1995.

- During the construction cycle of the 1980s, Boston absorbed an unprecedented amount of new office space. We do not anticipate that this phenomenon will recur in the 1990s.

- Demand for office space in greater Boston in 1989 dropped precipitously from 1988 levels, declining by 61 percent in absolute terms to 2.8 million square feet. Select suburban markets already have reported negative net absorption. A further collapse in demand is imminent.

- Effective rents are being driven to cyclical lows as Boston enters a period marked by heavy concessions. In real terms, rents have dropped by 20 percent since 1985, and net effective rents likely will decline by 15 to 20 percent over the next three years in both the central business district (CBD) and suburbs.

- Income streams for newly constructed office properties no longer appear to offer high returns for the next decade. Buildings with leases expiring in the near term face similar risks.

- Boston-based banks recently have posted substantial increases in nonperforming real estate loans, signaling that mounting problems are not limited to office properties in the greater Boston area.

Source: Salomon Brothers Pamphlet on Bond Market Research, December 13, 1989.

adding more of the same space may be unwise. Alternatively, these may be benefits from agglomeration.

❏ **POTENTIAL FOR FUTURE COMPETITION.** The availability of additional sites for future competitors should always be addressed. Undeveloped land and the way it is zoned should be inventoried. Rezoning or potential demolition of existing structures, or both, can also add to the potential for future competition. Just because a neighborhood is "built out," that is, has a structure on every lot, does not mean that there will never be new competition. Renovation, adaptive reuse, and complete re-development are always possible depending on local economic conditions.

❏ **DEMOGRAPHIC CHARACTERISTICS.** The demographic characteristics of the neighborhood residents are important. Age, marital status, sex, household size, income, and education are parts of the profile. Correspondingly, in an office building feasibility study, a description of all the workers who work in the neighborhood constitutes important demography. Demographic changes occurring over time can alter the feasibility of existing and future developments.

SITE ANALYSIS

The focus narrows again to the subject of the study, the **site analysis.**

❏ **ZONING.** In almost all cities, zoning can be the key to site analysis. If demand exists for a particular use but the proper zoning cannot be obtained, the site cannot be utilized. A site requiring a zoning change is less attractive than a site that is already properly zoned. The number of sites zoned for competitive space is also important.

❏ **UTILITIES.** All developed property requires certain minimum utility connections. Electric, gas, water, and sewer availability can be critical.

❏ **ACCESS.** Lack of access to the site severely limits its potential. The evaluation of accessibility usually focuses on immediate ingress and egress, but often also includes the position of the site relative to local transportation arteries.

❏ **SIZE AND SHAPE.** In many instances, the size and shape of a parcel can limit its attractiveness as a developable site. Parking and site planning requirements can have a significant impact on the success of any project.

❏ **TOPOGRAPHICAL CONSIDERATIONS.** The vegetation, slope, and load-bearing capacity, and so on, of a site can greatly affect developmental potential. Severe slopes may cause runoff problems that could result in flooding and damage the project. Poor drainage and bad subsoil can also be expensive to correct.

DEMAND ANALYSIS

Demand analysis involves evaluation of the market in an effort to estimate the effective demand for a particular real estate project. Demand analysis uses the information gathered in the regional, neighborhood, and site analyses. The objective of demand analysis is to determine the quantity of the particular space over a specified time with certain services that the market will absorb over time and the price at which it will absorb the product. This is an absorption schedule.

The first step is to define the market itself. In some retail operations, this can be as small as a block, whereas in a destination resort it can be worldwide. Once the market is defined, the information gathered above is used to evaluate the various forces that influence demand and then to project and quantify demand over a specified period.

❏ **COMPETITION.**   A survey of the market area must be made to determine existing and planned competition. Such a survey would include the location, rental level or sales price, vacancy, and amenities of each comparable project. (Since the competition is part of supply, this aspect of demand analysis overlaps with supply analysis.)

❏ **DEMOGRAPHIC ANALYSIS.**   The characteristics of the population surrounding the site can indicate consumer preferences in the area. Income, age, and household size are important factors when we are analyzing residential and retail real estate developments. Although less important for office and industrial uses, demographic analysis can indicate available labor pools.

❏ **TREND ANALYSIS.**   After evaluating the site's current market, the analyst will find it necessary to forecast future demand. This is very important because feasibility analysis is a forward-looking process that should help the decision maker evaluate a long-term investment.

SUPPLY ANALYSIS

Supply analysis requires that the analyst examine existing supply and expected future supply. Existing supply can be evaluated by an inventory of the market. The inventory should include current rents, vacancy rates, location, and amenities of each project. *Future* supply (expected additions to the market) can be estimated by examining the following areas.

❏ **VACANCY RATES AND RENTAL TRENDS.**   Current vacancy rates can indicate future needs (e.g., high vacancy indicates that current demand does not equal supply and vice versa). Rising rental rates can make future development at higher prices feasible.

❑ **AVAILABILITY OF GOVERNMENT SERVICES.**   Utilities may again be the key here (i.e., the absence of utilities can severely restrict supply). Transportation and other government services may also affect supply.

❑ **STARTS AND BUILDING PERMITS.**   Construction starts indicate additions to supply in the near future, and recorded building permits indicate projects soon to be built.

❑ **COMPREHENSIVE COMMUNITY PLANNING.**   The attitude and policy of the local planning department may be designed to encourage or discourage certain types of development in specific areas. For example, industrial development may be concentrated in one area and forbidden in another.

❑ **CONSTRUCTION COST TRENDS AND AVAILABLE FINANCING.**   Rapidly rising construction costs can limit future supply if rental rates are not expected to rise. Available financing can be a factor in encouraging or discouraging additions to supply. If interest rates are high, residual cash flow will be adversely affected—thus discouraging construction.

Collectively, the work in demand and supply analysis should be sufficient to enable the decision maker to make the market segmentation and market share calculations described in Part 4. A competent market study brings together all appropriate sources of data into an estimate of what the market will absorb over time and the price at which the product will be absorbed. The absorption schedule also lists the general features, functions, and benefits that are expected to attach to the space over time with services in the marketplace. With this information, the analyst is then able to make decisions on the optimal development plan. In other words, the analyst will now be able to decide the appropriate size as well as features, functions, and benefits of the real estate project under analysis.

Note that the market study describes the need for a particular product in a market (such as apartments), but it is not necessarily specific to the particular project being considered. Going back to Graaskamp's general framework, after the market study is done, the analyst looks at market segmentation and how the specific project will fit in. Ideally, this is an interactive process as the analyst moves from the market study to the economic study (the economic study being, of course, the common term for Graaskamp's financial synthesis of expectations for the particular project). The market study relates to the market in general, whereas the economic study relates to the specific project.

Ideally, the initial design of the project under study is modified during the economic study based on the information from the market study. The economic study allows the analyst to judge the value of different features, functions, and benefits in terms of a given market. The optimal project results when those features, functions, and benefits that the market wants, that is, is willing to pay for, and no others, are incorporated in the final development.

ROLE OF THE ECONOMIC STUDY

In feasibility analysis, the market study is done first, followed by the **economic study.** In the economic study, data collected in the market study are used to evaluate the potential profitability of investment in the proposed development. (As explained above, this is where an understanding of the market is brought to bear on a particular project.) The discounted cash flow model, presented in Chapter 21, is the framework. Just as the market study was designed to evaluate the acceptability of the project in a market sense, the economic study will evaluate the attractiveness of the project in an economic sense. This is a critical part of feasibility analysis. Although there may be significant demand for a particular project as revealed in the market study, the economic study may disclose that market rents are not sufficient to justify the investment.

The economic study can be broken down into three major areas. (1) A cost analysis gives estimated total capital required for the project and the breakdown between land and improvements. (2) A simple single-period, before-tax, cash flow pro forma will be developed. This statement presents the analyst's estimates of what the first year's cash flow statement is likely to be. (3) This pro forma is expanded to an after-tax discounted cash flow present value analysis. This process, as described in Chapter 21, gives the investor a feeling for the project's expected performance over time and an estimated maximum offering price or investment value.

In most feasibility studies, the final financial synthesis (Graaskamp's term) or economic study contains the three elements listed above. The authors suggest, however, that this is an underuse of a technology. Given all the information collected in the market study, the economic study can be used to refine the development idea. Every major feature, function, or benefit of the proposed project should be evaluated independently so that the optimal development plan can move forward. Marketing and feasibility studies are not inexpensive, and their value is not fully realized unless they are used to optimize project design.

THE FINAL PACKAGE   The preceding section described the primary components of the feasibility study. However, the complete feasibility study contains other items as well.

Typically, the feasibility study begins with an executive summary, which brings together the highlights of all the subsequent analysis. Often, the highest level decision makers will read only this three- to five-page summary.

The order of items behind the executive summary vary, though the typical sequence is as follows:

1.   A clear definition of the feasibility assignment. What exactly did the client ask the analyst to do? As part of this section, the analyst will bring to bear all of the primary participants' objectives, but the focus will be on the person paying the bill.

2.   A physical description of the project is essential. This is documented by a variety of maps and possibly design plans and specifications. At the very least, there will be a regional map siting the project as well as a neighborhood map showing competing uses. In most cases, there will also be a description of the proposed physical product, sometimes including architect's renderings.

3.   The market study usually follows with as much detail as the particular decision warrants.

4.   Following the market study is typically a description of the development team. Each of the major players is described, and at least a brief resume is included. As we noted in Chapter 24, the team may vary depending on the project, but in today's world it almost always includes an asset manager.

5.   The economic analysis, which uses the general market data to produce a financial synthesis of the proposed project, follows. Occasionally, Level Two analysis will also be included. However, the formal feasibility study more typically has only level one analysis, leaving the players to do their own Level Two work.

6.   Finally, we have the qualifications of the analyst and a series of disclaimers just in case it doesn't work.

SUMMARY   A market study and an economic study can be combined to provide the real estate decision maker with a complete feasibility analysis. The relationship between the public sector and the developer, too often ignored, is a critical portion of the analysis. This relationship should be carried out as a partnership rather than as an adversarial relationship if the project is to have the maximum chance of success.

In Part 9 we explore further the interaction of the public and private sectors. Our point in this chapter will be expanded there: Real estate development is an activity taking place in a social and legal system—not in isolation. Land use decisions affect so many lives that feasibility is determined by much more than whether the numbers work. Government represents the interests of the people, not only the users of real estate but often developers, investors, and lenders as well.

IMPORTANT TERMS

Cash management cycle
Demand analysis
Economic study
Exogenous shocks
Market constraints
Market study

Neighborhood analysis
Real estate feasibility analysis
Regional analysis
Site analysis
MSA
Supply analysis

REVIEW QUESTIONS

26.1   In what sense is a private decision on land use a public issue?

26.2   How does the cash management cycle affect the behavior and preferences of developers? Of public planners? Of end users of real estate?

26.3   What are the three types of constraints on land use? When might a use be legal but not socially acceptable?

26.4   What accounts for the frequent adversarial relationship between the public sector (government) and producers (developers) in land use decisions?

26.5   In simple terms, give two examples of exogenous shocks to the participants in land use decision making.

26.6   Although a distinction may be made between a market study and an economic study, the two are used together to produce one outcome. What is the outcome?

26.7   What aspects of a region are analyzed in a market study?

26.8   What is the relationship of the cost and value estimates in a feasibility analysis?

26.9   How would you analyze supply in a market you were studying? What might vacancy rates tell you about supply and demand?

26.10 How would you go about estimating *future* competition, not existing competition? How could local government offices help with this estimate?

REFERENCES   BOOKS

Barrett, G. Vincent, and John P. Blair. *How to Conduct Real Estate Market and Feasibility Studies.* New York: Van Nostrand Reinhold, 1982.

Barton-Aschman Associates Staff. *Shared Parking.* Washington, D.C.: Urban Land Institute, 1983.

Black, Thomas J., and Donald E. Priest. *Joint Development: Making the Real Estate Transit Connection.* Washington, D.C.: Urban Land Institute, 1979.

Bollens, Scott A., David R. Godschalk, John Hekman, and Mike E. Miles. *Land Supply Monitoring: A Guide for Improving Public and Private Urban Development Decisions,* Lincoln Institute for Land Policy, 1987.

Casazza, John A. *Condominium Conversions.* Washington, D.C.: Urban Land Institute, 1982.

Cost Effective Site Planning. Washington, D.C.: National Association of Home Builders, 1976.

Cross, Thomas B., and Michelle D. Govin. *Intelligent Buildings: Strategies for Technology and Architecture.* Homewood, Ill.: Dow Jones-Irwin, 1986.

Cushman, Robert F., Michael L. Evans, and Arnold S. Levy. *Professional's Guide to Commercial Property Development.* Homewood, Ill.: Dow Jones-Irwin, 1988.

David, Philip. *Urban Land Development.* Homewood, Ill.: Irwin, 1970.

Fragile Foundations: A Report on America's Public Works. Washington, D.C.: National Council on Public Works Improvement, 1988.

Graaskamp, James. *Fundamentals of Real Estate Development.* The Development Component Series. Washington, D.C.: Urban Land Institute, 1981.

Harrison, Henry S. *House: The Illustrated Guide to Construction Design and Systems.* Chicago: Realtors National Marketing Institute, 1980.

Laventhol and Horwath. *Hotel/Motel Development.* Washington, D.C.: Urban Land Institute, 1984.

McMahan, John W. *Property Development.* 2nd ed. New York: McGraw-Hill, 1989.

Messner, Stephen D., and Bryl Boyce. *Analyzing Real Estate Opportunities—Market and Feasibility Studies.* Englewood Cliffs, N.J.: Prentice-Hall, 1986.

Moore, Colleen G. *Puds in Practice.* Washington, D.C.: Urban Land Institute, 1985.

Nutt-Powell, Thomas E. *Manufactured Homes: Making Sense of a Housing Opportunity.* Boston: Auburn House, 1982.

O'Mara, Paul *Adaptive Use: Development Economics, Process, and Profiles.* Washington, D.C.: Urban Land Institute, 1978.

O'Mara, P. W. *Residential Development Handbook.* 2nd ed. Washington, D.C.: Urban Land Institute, 1980.

O'Mara, Paul W., and Cecil E. Sears. *Rental Housing.* Washington, D.C.: Urban Land Institute, 1984.

Phillippo, Gene. *The Professional Guide to Real Estate Development.* Homewood, Ill: Dow Jones-Irwin, 1976.

Romney, Keith B. *Condominium Development Guide.* 2nd ed. Boston: Warren, Gorham, and Lamont, 1983.

Sigafoos, Robert Alan. *Corporate Real Estate Development.* Lexington, Mass.: Lexington Books, 1976.

Snedcof, Dean. *Smart Buildings and Technology-Enhanced Real Estate,* Vols. I and II. Washington, D.C.: Urban Land Institute, 1985.

Snedcof, Harold R. *Cultural Facilities in Mixed-Use Development.* Washington, D.C.: Urban Land Institute, 1985.

Swesnik, Richard H. *Acquiring and Developing Income-Producing Real Estate.* Reston, Va.: Reston Publishing Co. 1979.

Urban Land Institute. *Downtown Development Handbook.* Washington, D.C.: Urban Land Institute, 1980.

———. *Affordable Community: Adapting Today's Communities to Tomorrow's Needs.* Washington, D.C.: Urban Land Institute, 1982.

———. *Affordable Housing: Twenty Examples from the Private Sector.* Washington, D.C.: Urban Land Institute, 1982.

———. *Approval Process: Recreation and Resort Development Experience.* Washington, D.C.: Urban Land Institute, 1983.

———. *Development Trends.* Washington, D.C.: Urban Land Institute (annually in March.)

———. *Dimensions of Parking.* 2nd ed. Washington, D.C.: Urban Land Institute, 1983.

———. *Dollars and Cents of Shopping Centers: 1990.* Washington, D.C.: Urban Land Institute, 1987.

———. *Downtown Office Growth and the Role of Public Transit.* Washington, D.C.: Urban Land Institute, 1982.

———. *Downtown Retail Development: Conditions for Success and Project Profiles.* Washington, D.C.: Urban Land Institute, 1983.

———. *Housing for a Maturing Population.* Washington, D.C.: Urban Land Institute, 1983.

———. *Housing Supply and Affordability.* Washington, D.C.: Urban Land Institute, 1983.

———. *Industrial Development Handbook.* Washington, D.C.: Urban Land Institute, 1978.

———. *Infill Development Strategies.* Washington, D.C.: Urban Land Institute, 1982.

———. *Institutional Real Estate Strategies.* Washington, D.C.: Urban Land Institute, 1988.

———. *Making Infill Projects Work.* Washington, D.C.: Urban Land Institute, 1985.

———. *Managing Development Through Public/Private Negotiations.* Washington, D.C.: Urban Land Institute, 1985.

———. *Office Development Handbook.* Washington, D.C.: Urban Land Institute, 1982.

———. *Planning and Design of Townhouses and Condominiums.* Washington, D.C.: Urban Land Institute, 1980.

———. *Public Incentives and Financial Techniques.* Washington, D.C.: Urban Land Institute, 1985.

———. *Recreational Development Handbook.* Washington, D.C.: Urban Land Institute, 1981.

———. *Research Parks and Other Ventures: The University/Real Estate Connection.* Washington, D.C.: Urban Land Institute, 1985.

———. *Shopping Center Development Handbook.* 2nd ed. Washington, D.C.: Urban Land Institute, 1985.

———. *Timesharing II.* Washington, D.C.: Urban Land Institute, 1982.

———. *Vested Rights: Balancing Public and Private Development Expectations*. Washington, D.C.: Urban Land Institute, 1982.

———. *Working with the Community: A Developer's Guide*. Washington, D.C.: Urban Land Institute, 1985.

Zeckendorf, William, and Edward McCreary. *Zeckendorf*. New York: Holt, Rinehart and Winston, 1979.

Ventolo, William, Jr. *Residential Construction*. Chicago: Longman Financial Services, 1979.

Williams, Martha R., and William L. Ventob, Jr. *Fundamentals of Real Estate Appraisal*. 2nd ed. Chicago: Real Estate Education Co., 1980.

Wren, Douglas M., and John A. Casazza. *Urban Waterfront Development*. Washington, D.C.: Urban Land Institute, 1983.

PERIODICALS AND SERVICES

American Statistics Index. Washington, D.C.: Congressional Information Service (annually with monthly supplements).

Business Conditions Digest. U.S. Commerce Department (monthly).

Development. Arlington, Va.: National Association of Industrial and Office parks (bimonthly).

Dodge Manual for Building Construction, Pricing, and Scheduling. New York: Dodge Building Cost Services (annually).

Economic Report of the President (annually).

Engineering News-Record. "Annual Report and Forecast" issue (annually, third January issue). Washington, D.C.: Urban Land Institute.

The Federal Reserve Bulletin. Board of Governors of the Federal Reserve System. Washington, D.C. 20551.

House and Home (journal). New York: McGraw-Hill.

The Journal of Real Estate Development. Boston: Federal Research Press (quarterly).

Marshall Valuation Services. Los Angeles: Marshall and Swift Publication Company (monthly).

Rand McNally and Company. *Commercial Atlas and Marketing Guide* (annually). This atlas includes, with each state, census statistics for counties and principal cities or population and also total manufacturing and business statistics. Most of the marketing data are at the front and include statistics by SMA (population, households, total retail sales, sales for shopping goods, passenger car registration, total manufacturing land area).

Savings and Loan Fact Book. Chicago: United States Savings and Loan League (annually).

Site Selection and Industrial Development. Norcross, Ga.: Conway Data (six times a year).

Statistical Abstract of the United States, The Survey of Buying Power. Sales and Marketing Management (annually).

Survey of Current Business. U.S. Commerce Department (monthly).

U.S. Census Bureau. *Construction Reports: Housing Authorized by Building Permits and Public Contracts*. Washington, D.C.: U.S. Government Printing Office (monthly). Housing Completers. (monthly). Housing Starts (monthly). Housing Units Authorized for Demolition (annually). New One-Family Homes

Sold and for Sale (annually). Residential Alterations and Repairs (annually). Value of New Construction Put in Place (monthly).

U.S. Census Bureau. *County Business Patterns*. Washington, D.C.: U.S. Government Printing Office (annually).

U.S. Census Bureau. *Current Government Reports*. Washington, D.C.: U.S. Government Printing Office. Series GG: Construction Expenditures of State and Local Governments. Series GF: Government Employment. Series GF: Government Finance. Series GR: Holdings of Selected Public Retirement Studies. Series GSS: State and Local Government Special Studies. Series GT: Quarterly Summary of State and Local Tax Revenue.

U.S. Census Bureau. *New Residential Construction in Selected Standard Metropolitan Statistical Areas*. [Construction Reports (21), quarterly].

U.S. Lodging Industry: Annual Report on Hotel and Motor Hotel Operations. Philadelphia: Laventhol and Horwath.

U.S. Social and Economic Statistics Administration. *Price Index of One-Family Houses Sold*. Washington, D.C. (Current Construction Reports, quarterly).

P A R T **9**

PUBLIC POLICY
AND PROSPECTS
FOR THE FUTURE

$\mathcal{G}$overnment Involvement

In the last three chapters of this book, we return to this book's central themes: (1) government is always your partner (Chapter 27, Government Involvement); (2) real estate is a long-lived asset in a fixed location, so predicting what society *will* want is the key to success (Chapter 28, Long-Term Trends in Urban Structure and Land Use); and (3) real estate is a wonderful interdisciplinary game that must be analyzed on multiple levels to be fully understood (Chapter 29, New Ways to Play the Real Estate Game). Here we consider the question: Why is government at all levels so intricately involved in the real estate industry? We will also look at how government is involved—on what levels (federal, state, and local) and through what vehicles (legislation, regulation, court decisions, etc.). Finally, we will examine particular areas of concern today: housing, the environment, and hazardous wastes.

From the macroeconomic point of view, the real estate industry is important. As we noted in Chapter 1, over half of all private domestic investment goes into real property development. Over two-thirds of the tangible assets of the country are real property assets. Ten to 15 percent of gross national product (GNP) and a significant portion of national employment are directly related to the real estate industry. Since the government itself represents over 20 percent of GNP and is a major employer, it makes sense that the real estate industry and government might be important to each other.

In addition, real estate services fulfill one of the modern individual's basic needs in terms of both shelter and commerce. People interact continuously with real property, shaping its use and reuse to meet their needs. The exact nature of this interaction varies (e.g., an igloo versus a high-rise apartment), but the underlying idea that real property is used to satisfy basic human needs remains the same.

Although land is one of the resources available to satisfy wants and needs, individuals do not own the land. They own certain rights to use the land (the bundle of rights). These property rights are socially defined; that is, they are determined by the people. When existing laws that define the structure of property rights no longer serve society to its best advantage, the people can change the rules. Since real estate services represent such a basic and important human need, it is only logical to expect that society would be almost constantly tinkering with the rules of the game.

Beyond logical reasons relating to the economic size and importance of the real estate industry, there are historical reasons for government involvement in it. Essentially, public policy has responded to citizens' demands for both a framework to guide real estate development and some vital services needed but not forthcoming from private investment. Local land use planning and growth management offer the framework. Public investments in urban services and infrastructure increase the feasibility of private real estate investments.

PUBLIC POLICY OBJECTIVES

In an economic sense, government policy can generally be said to seek balanced growth, acceptable inflation, low unemployment, and a better quality of life for all. In the pursuit of these general goals, the real estate industry has an important role. Since the industry is so large, its performance has an effect on the overall performance of the economy. In fact, over the past few decades, the real estate industry has been a target of government monetary and fiscal policy aimed at achieving balanced growth and lower inflation. Many times this effort has caused a reduction in the level of activity within the real estate industry or has been at the expense of growth within the industry. For example, during 1974–75 relatively high interest rates in the money markets caused funds to flow out of lending institutions (disintermediation), and this was a major cause of the large downswing in the housing sector of the real estate industry. This contributed to the general slowdown in the economy and eventually helped reduce the rate of inflation. In the early 1980s, following a major change in Federal Reserve policy aimed at targeting money supply growth rather than interest rates, high interest rates again reduced real estate activity. In this case loanable funds were available, but record levels of interest rates made it increasingly difficulty for individuals and projects to qualify for loans.

Today government at all levels is trying to respond appropriately to demands for rapid growth to create wealth and jobs and, at the same time, for controlled growth to conserve resources and preserve important features of the environment. The real estate decision maker should realize that government is trying to achieve a delicate balance among competing and conflicting objectives and is using policy instruments that are rather blunt. No market is completely free because in many instances prices do not accurately reflect society's benefits and costs. Coordination and control are designed to make markets more efficient or to achieve equity goals. Yet intervention may or may not achieve its intended results. These questions—does planning result in a more efficient allocation of resources than market allocation, and is planning fairer to all the people than market allocation?—cannot be answered in the abstract but only with reference to specific policies and decisions. When these questions are approached specifically, answers to them will help us anticipate government action that can cause changes in the "rules of the game." These ideas should be kept in mind as the different government influences on land use decisions are examined.

Remember that the economic rules are politically determined. The 1980, 1984, and 1988 conservative victories gave the Reagan–Bush administrations an impressive mandate for change. As we consider the numerous areas of direct government involvement in real estate decision making, keep in mind the four-point program being pushed from the top of the federal establishment.

1. Reduced government spending—the private sector can do certain things more efficiently.

2. Regulatory reform to reduce the burden of regulation and give more authority to local government. (But not more of the counterproductive lack of regulation that allowed the S & L debacle of the 1980s.)

3. Continued low taxes to spur the private sector. (User fees wherever practical are used to replace general tax revenues.)

4. Tight and stable monetary policy (i.e., limited monetization of federal deficits).[1]

HOW IS GOVERNMENT INVOLVED IN THE REAL ESTATE INDUSTRY?

Throughout this text we have maintained that in real estate government is always your partner. If so, what exactly does this partner do? The answer is seen in four basic areas of law: (1) contracts and agency, (2) ownership, (3) conveyancing, and (4) public policy, particularly in the critical areas of police powers and provision of infrastructure.

The laws of contracts and agency are common throughout American industry, so they have not been the focus of this text. However, you should remember that they are a critical element in the rules of the game. What is a contract? Legally, it is a voluntary manifestation of assent between two

---

[1]*During the second Reagan term and the early Bush years, the Republican leadership advocated a less restrictive Federal Reserve policy as government sought to maintain economic growth in the face of the huge deficits generated by years of expansive federal programs and the tax cuts of the first Reagan term.*

parties that creates, destroys, or modifies a legal relation. What this definition tells us is quite important. Beyond the fact that a contract must be voluntarily entered into, we see that it is something that modifies a legal relationship. And what is a legal relationship? It is the relationship which the government will help one party enforce against another party. If one party to an agreement doesn't uphold his or her end, the other party has redress through the courts. Thus, government is your partner simply because government makes contracts possible by providing enforcement.

The agency concept is also terribly important, as we saw in Part 4 on marketing. The agency relationship establishes a higher than arm's length duty between the principal and the agent. As in breach of contract, if an agent does not adhere to this higher duty, the principal has redress through the courts. Once again, government is your partner, providing the muscle behind the rule. In the real estate industry, contracts and agency relationships are critical. We would not have a modern real estate industry without these two bodies of law.[2]

As we saw in Chapter 4, there are many forms of real estate ownership, but they have one thing in common: what one owns. One does not own the land; one owns *rights to use* the land. What are these rights? Rights in a legal sense are defined as the collection of jural relations that exist among people with regard to things. Property rights are then rights in the land and things that are permanently attached to the land. So how does our partner government fit in? Looking further at the definition of rights, we see that it is the collection of jural relations that exist among people. What this tells us is that they exist at any point in time because they serve the people at that point in time. Whenever the current rules cease to serve the people, they can be changed. They are, after all, jural relations that exist among people. Thus, government is involved because government represents the people who make changes in the rules of the game, including the fundamental rules of ownership.

In the Bible (Leviticus), God is described as giving land to the Jewish people and prescribing rules of ownership. Everywhere else, however, the body politic makes the rules. The point we want to emphasize in this chapter is that these rules can change dramatically, and changes in the rules affect value, as we will see in the next section.

Remember from Chapter 5 that conveyancing means changing ownership from one party to another. If we look at the example of a simple single-family home transaction, we can see all the different ways that government is involved in conveyancing.

---

[2]*Interestingly, when we look back at the Level One/Level Two distinction made earlier in the text and reflect on it for a moment, the importance of the law of contracts and agency becomes clear. Principally through contracts and to some extent through the law of agency, level two players make their claims on the property. The property performs a certain way at level one. However, management companies, joint venture partners, lenders, and the rest, have unique claims on the level one net operating income; those claims are defined by contracts. Level Two exists because of contracts, and contracts are enforceable because of our partner, the government.*

Let's start with a little old lady who is ready to sell her home and move to Florida to work on her golf game. Her first step is to retain a broker to sell the house. She signs a listing agreement (discussed in detail in the marketing section) which is itself a contract and falls under the law of agency. The broker, often with the help of other brokers, locates a buyer, and the buyer and seller negotiate a contract. Once the contract is negotiated, a variety of other things must happen before the closing, where the buyer puts up the cash and the seller provides the deed.

First and foremost, the seller (our little old lady) must prove that she has good title. The buyer will hire an attorney to examine title, as discussed in Chapter 5. The attorney looks at the title records, which are, of course, maintained by government. In those records the attorney traces the history of ownership, not of the land, but of the rights, back through time, to the original sovereign because title originally comes from government. The buyer may well need financing and, if so, arranges it before the closing. How is government involved? Government regulates and insures lenders as well as enforces consumer protection legislation requiring the lender to tell the buyer all the terms of the loan (Part 5).

In even this simple illustration, it is clear that government is everywhere. For real estate players it would not be very difficult to deal with the rules if government's position (i.e., the rules) remained constant. However, as we will see below, the rules are very dynamic, and the potential for conflict is great, as shown in Box 27-1.

BIG CHANGES IN JURAL RELATIONSHIPS

We want to impress on you one more time that *change* matters in property valuation. Change can affect cash flows, and the prospect of change is measured as risk. Changes in the rules can be humorous, as illustrated in Box 27-1, but they are usually more far reaching and serious. Take, for example, the increasing trend of holding landlords responsible for what happens on their properties. Twenty years ago, it was renter beware. Over time, a major shift toward consumer protection has appropriately held the landlord responsible for damages when the property was not maintained in a safe manner. However, looking to the future, we can expect the landlord's responsibilities to become far broader, as illustrated by the two news items in Box 27-2.

AREAS OF GOVERNMENT INVOLVEMENT AND RESPONSIBILITY

THE COURTS

The oldest form of control in the real estate industry is through litigation in the courts. Development in the past often proceeded without prior approval or permission. When a project was started that others felt might be damaging to them as individuals or to the whole community, little could be done except by a lawsuit "after the fact." Any legal remedy

27-1

FOR SALE: A CASTLE, NEEDS SOME WORK, A MERE $8 MILLION

Southampton, N.Y., Estate Is Focus of Legal Battle Pitting Old Money vs. New

When Barry Trupin set out to build his dream castle by the sea, he spared no expense. He bought a $700,000 mansion in this tony beach resort, ripped out the walls, raised the roof, added turrets and towers and created an extravagant French Gothic chateau—complete with indoor waterfall.

But Mr. Trupin forgot one important thing: He forgot about his neighbors, many of them longtime summer residents of prim Southampton—and as rich as he.

"It's an eyesore," complains William Salomon, retired head of Salomon Brothers Inc. referring to the Trupin estate. "Large homes aren't uncommon here," adds Leonard Stern, a developer and publisher. "But he flaunted it. I mean, turrets?"

A Legal Battle

Mr. Trupin committed the ultimate social faux pas. In a land of bluebloods and old money, he had displayed a gaudy nouveau riche excess. "He rushed his fences," sniffs Michael Meehan, a Wall Street executive and summer resident, using a horse riding term that suggests Mr. Trupin was in too much of a hurry. Mr. Trupin, 52 years old, would pay for that. A bitter political and legal battle exploded around the garish estate. The village denied Mr. Trupin a permit to finish construction and eventually ordered him to stop work, driving him and his wife from Southampton. Mr. Trupin sued and now, because of a recent $1.9 million federal jury award in his favor, the village is threatened with financial calamity. The unfinished estate, meanwhile, stands vacant.

The local townspeople—the shopkeepers, teachers, and carpenters who live in Southampton year-round—generally support Mr. Trupin. After all, many got a piece of the $10 million in construction the self-made millionaire sank into his personal San Simeon. Ironically, though, the locals may also be the ultimate victims in this battle between the well-heeled. They will be among those picking up the tab—$3.7 million including legal costs—for the court fight against Mr. Trupin. "It's *our* taxes that are going up," grumbles one local shopkeeper.

A Man's Castle

The road to the Trupin house rolls past some of the more moneyed oceanfront estates on Dune Road, some contemporary, others traditional. Around one turn, the Trupin castle suddenly rises from behind a moat of overgrown weeds. Transformed from a mansion built by Henry Du Pont in 1927, it is a dissonant jumble of turrets, cupolas, and cathedral windows laced with abandoned scaffolding. If the Trupins aimed for French Gothic, they may have achieved something closer to Disney Fantasy.

Inside, the castle, named Dragon's Head, is draped in the eerie quiet of a tomb. Pipes, wiring, and rafters are exposed, an unfinished stairway leads nowhere. But the mark of lavishness is everywhere. A recreated 16th century pub occupies one corner of the ground floor. There are 18 fireplaces, one made of jade; a two-story library; a master bedroom with attached spa; and a total of 30,000 square feet of living space, including five bedrooms for the staff. Mr. Trupin's 20-foot-high indoor waterfall cascades into a saltwater aquarium and pool with underwater rock formations intended for snorkeling. Notably absent: the medieval suit of armor Mr. Trupin bought to complement his castle.

Source: By Roger Lowenstein, *The Wall Street Journal,* Vol. CCXII, No. 15, July 22, 1988, p. 1.

came from the **nuisance concept** under common law—the idea that one property owner could not unduly burden a neighbor's property. As our economy became increasingly interrelated and as real estate development became more complex, litigation after the fact became an unsatisfactory method of control. It was more rational and efficient to require advance permission to avoid conflicting rules.

Advance permission was first evidenced through **districting** (an early form of zoning) in New York City in 1916. Today advance permitting has gone beyond zoning to include subdivision control, planned unit development, and other special use permits. Land and growth management are also used to protect the environment and achieve more efficient overall land use. The courts have generally supported most of these permit systems. Furthermore, the courts, both of their own initiative and through the enforcement of statutory laws, became actively involved in the real estate industry in efforts to prevent discrimination on the basis of both income and race. Remember that the enthusiasm of the courts for different government policy tools goes a long way in determining how effective they will be. Therefore, the decision maker must be aware of both "new rules" and the courts' "interpretation" of these rules.

PUBLIC GOODS

Government has a hand in the real estate industry simply because some goods are more efficiently owned or produced on a common basis. Even the most adamant free enterprise advocate would probably not suggest that highways be individually owned. It has been found to be most efficient to have the government be responsible for certain forms of transportation—specifically roads, waterways, airports, and, in some cases, railroads—and other elements of the **infrastructure** (e.g., provision of water and sewer services) that are essential before significant real estate development can occur.

Energy production, though never a nationalized industry, has always been closely regulated and subsidized by government primarily through the tax code. Many utilities are municipally owned. Recreation areas are

Jerry Warshaw, an Atlanta apartment owner, is being sued in state court in Dekalb County for a million dollars by a tenant raped by a man who broke into her apartment. The tenant contends that Warshaw failed to warn her that the neighborhood is a high crime area.

Mr. Warshaw is also being threatened with a million dollar suit by another woman raped by a man who wandered off the street into an apartment while she was looking at it as a possible rental. He faces four more suits from tenants victimized by other crimes, all committed by third parties. "All this scares me," he says. It scares a lot of landlords these days. Tenants are increasingly suing apartment owners, developers, and management companies in cases that are threatening to broaden landlord liability to more areas than ever before. Some of the suits involve crimes committed by people who walk into buildings and shoot, rape, or burglarize tenants. Others involve mishaps such as attacks on tenants by pets owned by the residents. Some tenants, apartment owners say, may even be concocting accidents in order to sue their landlords.

Source: Wall Street Journal, May 20, 1988, "Tenant Suits May Broaden the Liability of Landlords."

"Get your hands out of your pockets!" police officer Armando Aguilar barks at a dazed-looking man leaning against a trash barrel. The setting is a 54-unit apartment complex in Miami's largely black Liberty City section. Officer Aguilar, a plainclothed member of Miami's street narcotics unit, frisks the man and finds wads of five- and ten-dollar bills. Two envelopes of crack are spotted in the dirt nearby. Ultimately, the officer and his partner, Sergeant Manny Orosa, let the man go. They can't tie him directly to the drugs, but the encounter goes on the record of another culprit, the apartment building where the incident took place. Already, the building's rap sheet is seven inches thick—a two-year total of more than 500 complaints, drug finds, and arrests. That record has made the property a target for one of law enforcement's newest weapons in the war on drugs: tough statutes that make landlords responsible for drug dealing on their properties. Using such laws, the State Attorney's Office in Miami is pressuring the apartment's owner, Brennan Construction Company, to help clean up what resembles a public market place for all kinds of drugs. Among the state's demands: put up a ten foot fence around the property to cut off escape routes, board up empty apartments to eliminate hiding places and turn in suspected drug dealers when they appear at the complex. If Brennan doesn't comply, the state can order the property closed and even torn down. "What we're trying to do is move the drug activity from the building to the street," explains Sergeant Orosa. "Basically, we can deal with the problem in the street."

Source: Wall Street Journal, March 29, 1989, "In War on Narcotics: Tough New Statutes Target Owners of Drug Ridden Properties."

provided by all levels of government. Reservation of land for Native Americans is considered a federal government function. Public education, public hospitals, and prisons are other areas in which it has been most efficient to produce goods jointly. In other words, provision of common goods is a very significant government role that is generally accepted by society, even though there are questions about the extent of this government role.

ENVIRONMENTAL PROTECTION

During the 1960s, the nation became more aware of the need to protect the environment. In the 1970s, this need became more acute as the nation recognized it was moving into an era of limited resources. Previously, certain natural resources were viewed by many to be free goods. That is, in an economic sense, their supply was considered to be unlimited and the assets as renewable. Water and air were the first of such "free" resources to be recognized as limited or scarce. In addition, water and air were clearly public goods. It became the responsibility of government to limit or prohibit activities that infringed on the general public's right to clean air and clean water. This is a very sensitive area since much of the nation's industrial activity pollutes the air and water to some extent. Though it is generally accepted that the government should have a role in protecting the environment, just how clean the air and water should be is a hotly debated topic.

There are tradeoffs. First, individual rights versus public rights are often the centerpiece of environmental questions affecting real estate decision making. The questionable areas usually revolve around limiting or restricting individual rights in order to protect the rights of the public. For example, if a river flows through a property, can the owner expel pollutants into the water that will adversely affect the owners downstream? Do public rights supersede individual rights? Recent trends have generally favored public over individual rights.

Second, a significant tradeoff is economic activity versus environmental protection. The cost and implementation of environmental protection measures can be expensive and time consuming. During periods of slow economic growth, certain environmental protection measures might unduly restrict economic development. At such times, decisions must be made as to what is more important—economic growth or environmental protection.

LAND OWNERSHIP

As we noted in Chapter 1, government owns nearly one-third of all acreage in the 50 states. At an extreme, this land may be used strictly to further the nation's economic interests (note the position of Reagan's first secretary of the interior, James Watt) or, at the other extreme, preserved relatively untouched for future generations (the Sierra Club has enunciated several arguments in this direction). Since a significant portion of the nation's natural resources (oil, coal, timber, water, etc.) are found on government land, the extent to which this public good is utilized will have a significant impact on several aspects of real estate decision making over the next decade. The historical record indicates Congress's aversion to either extreme of uncontrolled resource exploitation or preservation. The federal government has favored conservation—the controlled use of resources and restoration of renewable resources.

THE TAX SYSTEM

Both the production of public goods and the provision of public services require funding. In order for the government to function, certain resources must be committed to the public sector. In Part 6 we described the different types of taxes collected by different levels of government. If government has a clear role or responsibility to provide certain public goods as well as to enforce certain regulations, it just as clearly has a right to raise the necessary capital to do so. The question becomes who should pay for the common goods? The general response, based on fairness, is that users of common goods should bear the incidence of taxes raised for these common goods to the fullest extent possible. Yet government can also use the tax system for redistributive and macroeconomic purposes.

Thus, taxes perform not only a revenue-raising function but also an economic planning and possibly welfare function. The tax laws, drawn by legislatures in response to special-interest lobbying, implicitly encourage certain economic activities and discourage others. The tax code allocates tax subsidies and burdens, which results in the redistribution of income and wealth among individuals and corporate entities. Therefore, the question is broadened when one considers the tradeoffs between goals of fairer taxation or taxation designed to help the general economy.[3]

CONSUMER PROTECTION

As the world has become ever more complex, government has come to provide certain consumer protections as part of its general role of overseeing the public's health and well-being. In the real estate industry, this takes many forms, including licensing salespersons and requiring lenders to disclose fully all the costs associated with financing. In real estate

---

[3]*And does this mean a progressive tax whereby those more able to pay carry a greater share of the load, or a tax on consumption expenditures that might encourage savings and hence investment?*

development and investment, government responsiveness to neighborhood associations and tenant groups has often resulted in limits on the right to use property (e.g., to convert from rental to condominium operation), to earn a market return from property (e.g., rent control), and to invest capital freely (e.g., anti-redlining provisions).

DATA COLLECTION

Data collection has also come to be accepted as a legitimate role of government. In order to assess taxes, the government must have tax rolls, that is, lists of property owners, and estimates of the values of their properties. In order to design programs that serve the needs of the people, the government must collect pertinent information about housing patterns, family income, and so on. As we saw in the feasibility chapter, a significant amount of market data is available from the federal government, which maintains not only results of the national census but also large amounts of regional and national economic information.

HOUSING

One of the basic human needs is shelter. Moreover, a deteriorating physical environment can aggravate social and economic problems and contribute to an increasing incidence of crime and violence. For these reasons, the government has a role in dealing with shelter needs not adequately satisfied in the private market. In the United States, this concern has led to the development of housing programs that range from mortgage insurance and development of secondary mortgage markets to increase the efficiency of housing markets to those that are designed to meet the needs of specific groups. Although performance in these areas is difficult to measure, most would agree that policies and programs to stimulate and stabilize housing markets have been more successful than programs to improve the shelter enjoyed by specific groups—or, not enjoyed by them, in the case of the homeless. The homeless are a particularly difficult group to deal with since there are many different reasons for homelessness, and policy solutions that work for one subgroup may not be effective for another subgroup. As a start, the 1990 census will make the first serious effort to document the number of homeless individuals nationwide.

COORDINATION

Finally, the government, of necessity, has assumed a coordination function. In the private sector, this evolved naturally as the nuisance law concept gave way to advance planning and permitting. In addition to coordinating private sector activities, the government has begun to try to coordinate its own activities. This is possibly an even more difficult problem. Between levels of government and within levels of government, significant conflicts arise that are of both a political and practical nature. Coordinating government activity in our political system is a far from simple task.

These different government functions are implemented by various levels of government. For ease of presentation, we discuss the basic implementation tools according to the level of government primarily responsible. There is considerable overlap, but the distinctions are nonetheless important. Local governments operate in a different political environment from that of the federal government; thus, the same tool applied by a different level of government may be used to achieve very different goals.

LOCAL PLANNING TOOLS

Local governments exercise the powers of taxation and expenditure, regulation (police power), and condemnation (eminent domain). Most land use regulation under the police powers has come at the local level as authorized by state enabling statutes. Essentially, there are three primary regulatory tools: (1) the zoning ordinance, (2) the subdivision ordinance, and (3) the building code. Other important local tools are (4) growth planning programs, (5) expenditures for the provision of public goods, and (6) taxation.

ZONING

Zoning involves the use of both a *map* and a *text*. The subject area is mapped into a series of zones or districts that can be classified as residential, commercial, industrial, and such other categories as may be useful for the particular jurisdiction. In most cities these classifications are subdivided; for example, several types of residential development may be allowed in different zones of the city. The text then describes the specific use allowed in each of these classifications, as well as the bulk and density controls.[4]

The first court test of zoning, in 1926, concerned an ordinance in Euclid, Ohio. An application by Ambler Realty to have property rezoned to multifamily residential from single-family residential was denied. The owner sued, claiming an unfair government taking against which citizens are protected by the Fifth and Fourteenth Amendments to the U.S. Constitution. The case eventually reached the U.S. Supreme Court, which ruled that refusal of a municipal government to rezone, as long as

---

[4]Note that, in addition to municipalities, counties and even states may also have zoning ordinances.

the refusal was logically based, did *not* constitute a taking requiring that the private owner be compensated by the government. Following this decision, the Supreme Court was silent on zoning matters until the 1970s, leaving during that period to the state courts the task of applying the "taking" test. In the 1970s a number of important Supreme Court decisions were rendered. These decisions created standards that restricted the ways municipalities could use zoning ordinances.

The basic idea behind zoning hasn't changed over the years, but the particular circumstances have become considerably more complex. The underlying intent of zoning is to encourage the grouping of "compatible uses" (see Box 27-3) while still keeping the bulk of development decision making in the private sector. In 1987, the U.S. Supreme Court rendered two decisions that clearly set limits on the ability of local governments to use zoning (and building permits) to achieve their objectives at the expense of the property owner.

In *First English Evangelical Church* v. *County of Los Angeles* (First Evangelical), the court held that local government had overstepped its bounds and that temporary takings deserve compensation. Through a series of actions over an extended period of time, local government had prohibited First Evangelical from "all use" of its property, particularly the construction of housing for the disadvantaged. The court's opinion states to all governments that there is a time limit on "temporary" restraints. Government cannot simply delay forever an owner's project. However, just how long government can delay is still an open question, and most developers will still want to work with local governments to expedite projects (see Box 27-4).

The second 1987 decision, *Nollan* v. *California Coastal Commission,* involved a combination of zoning and building permits. Again in California, government held up a building permit for a home that was to replace a small bungalow. The municipality wanted more public access to the beach and tried to force the property owner to dedicate a pathway across the beachfront property before giving him a building permit to which he was otherwise entitled. (Such required dedications are called "exactions.") In this case, the court ruled that the public need for access was not sufficiently closely related to this building permit to allow government to withhold the permit. As in *First Evangelical,* how close is legal isn't specified, but the principle is established that there must be a recognizable connection between the public need and the regulatory act. (This "logical nexus" will appear again later in the chapter when we encounter impact fees.)

SUBDIVISION REGULATION

Subdivision regulation works in conjunction with zoning regulation to accomplish municipal land use objectives. Subdivision ordinances set out

27-3
THE DEFINITION OF "COMPATIBLE BUT NOT BORING UNIFORMITY" VARIES FROM PLACE TO PLACE

The Oriental Hotel in Bangkok sits proudly on the Chaophraya River and is widely regarded as one of the finest, if not the finest, hotels in the world. Recently, an upscale shopping mall has been added to the hotel, showing that Bangkok has not missed out on the trend toward mixed use. On both sides of the Oriental are a variety of residential properties leading to other high-rise hotels like the Shangrila. These smaller residential properties are indeed quite modest. The passenger on the river taxi approaching the Oriental is very likely to see one neighbor washing in the same river that the next neighbor is using as a toilet less than 50 feet away. Certainly, in the United States, such a site would be inconsistent with the ultimate luxury hotel.

In Bangkok, however, the river is the center of life, and, despite its unquestioned filth, it is the heart of Bangkok's unique cosmopolitan, crazy, yet happy life-style. For that reason, the river is the tourist attraction that makes the Oriental, its neighbor the Shangrila, and the other upscale hotels work. Bangkok doesn't worry about zoning. But if it did, Bangkok's definition would clearly be very different from the typical U.S. version, because the Thais want something different from their city. But while desired compatibility varies, rent theory still holds.

What to the Western eye initially appears to be a mishmash of different land uses is really an almost perfect illustration of the rent theory presented in Part 1. In fact, it is a more perfect demonstration of rent theory than is found in most U.S. cities; in the United States the political process has produced zoning regulations that force what the majority believe to be compatible land uses into like areas. Land use on the river in Thailand, on the other hand, is constrained by no similar political process and follows the rule of the dollar, that is, rent theory, a bit more closely. Since the river is the most efficient arm of transportation in a city with truly world-class traffic problems, we would expect the first floor on most riverfront parcels to be devoted to industrial and commercial uses, and that is in fact exactly what one finds. The upper floors are typically residential and more expensive residential at that. This is again logical inasmuch as Thailand is a very hot country even in the cold season and a country where air conditioning is not the norm. The breezes off the water are therefore an amenity sought by residential users, and the more affluent citizens live near the water.

As tourism has replaced rice and light manufacturing as the number one export item from a GNP perspective, hotels have risen along the river, sharing valuable frontage with the first floor industrial/higher level residential buildings. The hotels provide foreigners the opportunity to experience the beauty of the river.

A Westerner might then ask, all right, but what about the very low-income, tenant-made housing found on the river that doesn't even have plumbing? Will rent theory explain that? And again, the answer is yes, if you take a minute to think. The workers in the industrial and commercial uses need space, and land in a city of 6 to 8 million is at a premium. Hence, a room of any type close to work is indeed at a premium. What appears to be no more than a hovel is actually quite desirable worker housing when one looks at the alternatives, which do not enjoy the cool breezes or water access. Workers will therefore pay sufficient rent to justify the residential use of these small spaces in between the commercial uses.

The one land use that rent theory won't explain in Thailand, particularly in Bangkok, is the location of the very beautiful and very frequent Buddhist temples. When you remember that the Buddhist faith teaches that what people must overcome most is desire, and that everything around us is illusion, it is not surprising that the dollar, that is, rent theory, is not particularly useful in explaining the location of Buddhist temples.

minimum standards for the subdivision of land that is to be developed. In most areas, the subdivision cannot be platted (recorded in the title records as a subdivision) unless it meets certain standards.

The logic behind subdivision regulation is that eventually the municipal government expects to assume responsibility for operation and maintenance of streets, sewers, and sometimes utilities. Therefore, it is in the best interest of the public if these facilities meet certain minimum standards so as to be easily integrated at a future date with existing municipal systems. (Subdivision regulations sprang up in response to egregious abuses by speculators in the late 1800s and early 1900s.)

In many areas, the law allows municipalities to control development

27-4 POLICE POWERS VERSUS CONDEMNATION

Note the distinction between accomplishing government goals through zoning and use of the power of eminent domain. Eminent domain requires compensation, but zoning does not. Governments thus find it financially more feasible to use zoning wherever possible. However, from the perspective of private property rights, zoning may involve the loss of rights without compensation.

How much can the government take through zoning before it is, in law, condemning property? In other words, how much can a city accomplish through zoning without paying? The general rule is that government can **downzone** (zone to a less intensive and hence less profitable use) without paying compensation so long as the downzoning is consistent with an overall master plan. However, when the zoning becomes extensive enough to involve the actual taking of an easement (such as air rights around an airport) or to eliminate completely the potential for development, the zoning regulation is not allowed. In such situations eminent domain must be used, and the private owner must be compensated.

that is occurring beyond the city limits—in effect, providing the municipality with **extraterritorial jurisdiction** (ETJ). The ETJ frequently ranges from two to five miles beyond the corporate city limits. Since zoning requirements apply only within the city limits, subdivision requirements may represent the only type of municipal control that can affect development within the ETJ.

While subdivision approval is the planning device used in most residential development situations, the *site plan approval process* provides a similar function for commercial development. In addition to complying with zoning regulations (and, of course, private deed restrictions), the commercial developer typically must receive site plan approval. This involves bringing a physical plan of the proposed development to the appropriate local government body (e.g., the town council) for review of massing (the volume of proposed construction), design, signage, traffic access, and other development items discussed in Part 8.

BUILDING CODES

Building codes are another form of regulation to protect the public health and safety, most particularly to avoid structural defects and fire hazards that can cause injury and loss of life. Building codes in most areas require that inspections be made during the development process to make sure that minimum safety standards are being incorporated in the construction of the project.

Note that, in addition to the laudable goal of protecting public health and safety, building codes have in the past often protected partial monopolies. Certain building codes were written to require not minimum standards but specific materials and construction techniques. In other words, rather than saying that a certain type of multifamily unit must have a 30-minute fire wall between each unit, some building codes stated that a particular material must be used and that it must be installed in a particular way. Those supplying and installing this material were, in some sense, granted a partial monopoly. Furthermore, the incorporation of cost-saving innovations in the construction process has been slowed by such restrictive building codes.

GROWTH PLANNING

As we noted at the outset of this chapter, government at various levels tries to balance economic growth with resources conservation and historic preservation. The trend has been for government to expand its advance planning function in order to guide and manage the development process to a greater extent. The courts are cooperating by showing an increasing willingness to uphold municipal regulation that limits private property rights. Remember that the permitting system overlaps, to some extent, the zoning ordinance. That is, in addition to satisfying the zoning ordinance, the developer must also obtain specified permits. Through the zoning ordinance and the permitting system, growth policy consistent with the master plan may be achieved.[5] Although growth planning may help achieve some worthwhile public causes and objectives, the assorted permitting systems have also become so complex and intertwined that many developers complain that a disproportionate amount of time and effort goes into meeting sometimes conflicting government standards. In growth-planning activities, government must be careful to factor in the strength of the local economy. There is far more need for rigorous planning (and far more political support for such planning) in a rapidly growing local economy. Unfortunately, planning is a long-term process, and no local economy stays hot forever. Hence, communities must balance between what is politically possible immediately and what is needed in the long term.

PROVISION OF PUBLIC GOODS

In addition to direct regulation, government, especially local government, influences land use decisions by making expenditures for public goods. All three levels of government are involved in transportation systems and in the location of their own operating facilities. In providing for these public goods, the various levels of government often use the power of **eminent domain.** As noted in Chapter 5, the power of eminent domain permits government to take private property for a public purpose provided fair value is paid. It would be impossible, for example, to have an efficient national highway system without allowing the government such power.

The most important question in eminent domain cases is the exact amount of fair compensation for property condemned. The three basic approaches to value are utilized; but, in addition to judgmental questions involving the determination of value, timing questions are also important. If the government announces the construction of a major transportation artery, land around that particular location normally will increase in value. The owner of the condemned land is entitled to its value before, not after, the announcement. Similarly, if a government condemns a site as a nuclear power waste dump, surrounding land values are likely to decrease in value, but the landowner is entitled to receive the value of his or her property before the announcement of the proposed use.

Local governments often use the provision of public utilities and services to control the direction of growth. This is based on the assump-

[5]*One of the most far-reaching and imaginative regional master plans is the Year 2000 Plan in Washington, D.C.*

tion that new growth is discouraged in areas where municipal services do not meet the need of new development. Capacity limitation can be the result of existing heavy use (e.g., a sewer main has reached its capacity) or of lack of services (e.g., no sewer system serves a particular area). In either case, the decision to expand or extend service involves high fixed costs. The municipality must examine the tradeoff between the cost involved and the desire to accommodate or encourage growth. This decision can often be very difficult for government to make but very profitable for the private developer if correctly anticipated.

TAXATION

Federal, state, and local governments are able to provide public service, in part because of the power to levy property taxes. In a real estate context, the property tax is not only a revenue but also a land-planning tool.[6] Recall that local government has a first lien on the property for unpaid taxes. When combining high property taxes with rent control, government can, in effect, eliminate residual equity cash flow. This has happened in some parts of New York City, for example. Taxing away the equity value is generally not thought to be wise from either an individual equity standpoint (fairness) or a public benefit perspective. "Abandonment" as seen in the South Bronx is one possible result.[7] On the other hand, the property tax can be used as an effective land-planning tool in relatively free markets. In other words, property taxes can be used to encourage certain types of socially beneficial development.

In the basic property tax scheme, both land and buildings in the taxing district are valued. The total value constitutes the property tax base of the particular taxing authority. A tax rate then is set based on the revenue sought to be raised. One problem with most property tax systems is that vacant land may not be taxed as heavily as improved property. Thus, development is penalized and speculative holding of raw land is encouraged. As municipal governments experience increasing costs for municipal services, they are seeking ways to provide such services more efficiently.

Moreover, reduced federal spending for local infrastructure and state and local tax limitation movements have encouraged localities to examine development fees to raise revenues needed for public goods.

---

[6]As noted in Part 6, the income tax is also an economic planning tool. Specific provisions of the Internal Revenue Code definitely encourage certain types of real estate investment and development.

[7]Clearly, there were many causes of the urban disaster that occurred in the South Bronx as a large functioning city became a slum resembling a war zone. Today, in addition to political, racial, and economic problems, we have a situation in which the net operating income from many buildings is insufficient to pay the property taxes, causing owners simply to abandon their property rights. This abandonment furthers the physical slum as vandals move in and puts more tax pressure on other buildings as the tax base is reduced.

Although on-site fees and land dedication for public facilities, like schools, are common, local governments are experimenting with ways to levy fees on development to mitigate off-site impacts.

❏ **INFILL INCENTIVES.** One serious problem in rapidly developing areas has been "leapfrogging." This occurs when developers skip close-in land to develop property in outlying areas of the municipality. Developers usually leapfrog because land closer to the urban center is often much more expensive. (One reason is that public services are available.) From a public policy standpoint, it is much more desirable for land already serviced by municipal facilities to be developed than outlying areas that require the extension of municipal services. Thus, local governments are concerned with ways to create **infill incentives**—that is, inducements to developers to use land in the central city, thus avoiding urban sprawl and reducing the cost of providing municipal services.

❏ **SITE-VALUE TAXATION.** One possible way to reduce sprawl is **site-value taxation.** In site-value taxation, the property tax base includes land only and ignores any improvements. As a result, the overall tax base is lower, requiring a higher tax rate to achieve the same total revenues. This means that vacant land will be taxed at higher rates than under the standard system and that developed land has a lower tax. Consequently, holders of raw land will see their carrying burden increase—cash outlays will rise even though the land generates little, if any, revenue. Site-value taxation is supposed to encourage, if not force, landowners who hold vacant land to develop their land. Site-value taxation would presumably lessen the attractiveness of land on the fringe of the city and, consequently, help achieve the objective of reducing the cost of providing municipal services.[8]

❏ **VALUE-IN-USE TAXATION.** Another approach to property taxation is **value-in-use taxation.** Under this approach, land is taxed based on its current use rather than its highest and best use. In this way, naturally productive lands in agriculture or forestry have much less potential for development. For example, farmland on the boundary of a major urban area may have significant development potential. Its highest and best use (the use that produces the highest residual value to the land) is most often a development use, not an agricultural use. Under the standard property tax system, the farmer pays taxes based on the value of the land for development. High taxes may force a sellout even though this is not in the public interest. Consequently, many local governments have passed provisions allowing for value-in-use taxation for agriculture

---

[8]*Few major urban areas are currently using site-value taxation, although the idea is part of the literature that is being studied in many cities.*

and, in some cases, for forestry. These provide that as long as the land is used for the specified productive purpose, it will be taxed according to its value in use and not according to its highest and best use.

Consider what might happen from a combination of more restrictive zoning, site-value taxation, and value-in-use taxation. Assume that a city zones a small amount of land for development. Then through site-value taxation, the city seriously encourages the owners of that land to develop it. (In fact, in such situations, the cost of not developing could be prohibitive.) Then, through value-in-use assessment, the government makes it easier for surrounding landowners (farmers) to keep their land in agricultural production. If they allow their land to be rezoned, the property taxes increase very significantly. The combination of these three items would allow the government to determine to a great extent exactly where development would occur. This would certainly help accomplish the purpose of reducing the cost of providing municipal services; however, it would also remove land use decisions from the marketplace. A government official or a public body would make the decisions that the market previously made. The question becomes, "Are the benefits from reduced municipal service costs sufficient to offset the less efficient allocation that would result from removing marketplace controls?"[9]

LOCAL GOVERNMENT PLANNING AND PRIVATE SECTOR DEVELOPMENT WERE SOUL-MATES FROM THE BEGINNING

You have no doubt noticed that all of the local government mechanisms mentioned in the preceding sections are interrelated. Land use decisions are made by players partly on the basis of how each of these government-related factors impacts the bottom line and partly on market projections. Thus, even in the free enterprise system of the United States, planning and regulation are major factors. Interestingly, while there are many "bad marriages" between developers and regulators today, it was in fact the development community that helped spawn the planning profession earlier in this decade.

As we mentioned earlier, the first comprehensive zoning was seen in New York City in 1916. In the following year, the forerunner of what is now the American Planning Association was organized. In 1924, President Herbert Hoover (a conservative Republican) proposed what in 1927 would become the standard city planning enabling act. Force was given to the planning movement when, in 1949 and 1954, Federal Housing Acts provided federal financial support. Statutes had to fit with sup-

[9]*Although removing the development decision from the marketplace and placing it in the hands of a government agency seems very foreign to most Americans, this has, in fact, been done in many, if not most, Western European countries.*

porting plans. So local governments' regulations were financially encouraged to tie to local plans. In 1969, in Ramapo, New York, the first full-growth management plan was enacted. In 1972, in *Golden* v. *Planning Board of Ramapo,* the courts supported growth management as a legitimate government activity.

How was the private sector involved in this history? The impetus for initial land use regulation came from high-quality land developers, who were already using land planning to develop large suburban communities in the last quarter of the nineteenth century. In those relatively wealthy communities, the restrictive deed covenants described in Part 2 worked fairly well. However, in most of the rest of the country, poor development was drowning good development.

Marc Weiss, in his excellent book *Community Builders,* describes old-time land development (and its abuses) in great detail. So-called cut and run salespeople bought large parcels of land, cut it legally into pieces, subdividing it on paper, sold what they could, and then literally ran away. Speculation fever led to great booms and busts in lot sales. This activity resulted in a hodge-podge of ownership with no coherent way to use the land—that is, with subdivisions where planned streets did not meet surrounding streets (if any existed) and where lot ownership was too thin to pay for infrastructure. At the same time, high-quality developers with deeper pockets were putting the infrastructure (roads, water, parks, etc.) in their subdivisions. These developers (as opposed to cut and run speculators) wanted to integrate their developments into the city and to have the city take over the infrastructure. Competition from the cut and run land subdividers made it difficult (1) for the big subdividers to sell their product at the prices they thought they deserved and (2) for the city to financially take over new subdivisions, some of which had considerable infrastructure while others had none. To survive and prosper, the high-quality private developer needed regulations to prevent low-quality land development from both running down his prices and impeding his long-term connection with the city which was so essential to the provision of high-quality infrastructure. In our free enterprise system, there have been many instances, like this one, when one group of private businessmen sought government protections against another group and got it. In this case, land development has become much more orderly in the twentieth century than it was in the nineteenth—and much more complex, time consuming, and expensive.

THE RELATIONSHIP IN THE FINANCING GETS MORE COMPLICATED OVER TIME

With the Reagan/Bush administrations, cost consciousness became a watchword. For a host of reasons, much of the financing of infrastructure is currently moving from the public to the private sector. Some of these reasons include the pressures of rapid growth, deteriorating existing infrastructure, inflating costs, declines in federal assistance, tax revolts, unpopular bond programs, and the inability of local governments in general to pick up the full tab for providing the infrastructure their citizens want.

If, for all these reasons, the push from public to private financing of infrastructure is to continue, and the authors believe it will, then we all must find ways to finance this infrastructure. Infrastructure is a public/private partnership. It would be difficult for the private sector developer to finance all the streets, sewers, water lines, bridges, schools, and parks—the infrastructure—both on site and off site, that supports any new development. On the other hand, without new sources of revenue, it is equally impossible for local government to finance this infrastructure. Thus, the private and public sectors clearly need to work together to find solutions. The last several years have seen three general approaches to the problem, with the third rapidly becoming dominant.

First was the special assessment district. This district raised a general-purpose tax that required authority—that is, a vote from the property owners—to be established. The idea was to tax everyone in the district to provide the amenities and infrastructure desired by the district. This worked well in certain isolated situations where everyone in the district had the same idea of what was needed. In such cases, all owners were willing to pledge their property as collateral for bonds to finance the infrastructure. Unfortunately, in most situations, infrastructure and amenity needs spread beyond the immediate area and over a diverse group of property owners, making concurrence of objectives difficult to obtain.

A second approach became known as exactions. Under this model, a public official, representing the general public, extracts from the developer something in return for permission to develop. In some cities, this meant the dedication of an elementary school site in the case of a large residential development. This logical connection was extended in other cities to much more tenuous but still publicly desirable projects. As we noted in the *Nollan* case earlier in the chapter, a "rational nexus" is needed if the court is to bless such actions. More importantly, exactions are negotiated deals with some people winning and others losing. In such situations the losers often scream, and the winners sometimes reap undue profits. Clearly, something better was needed.

A third option has evolved for financing infrastructure. The impact fee, though unknown 10 years ago, is now well established across the country and is increasingly the financing vehicle of choice. Essentially, the impact fee works as follows. The public sector determines the incremental cost for various infrastructure items, particularly transportation and education, to serve the new development. The developer then pays a fee equal to this incremental impact prior to initiating development. The complexities of impact fees go well beyond the scope of this introductory text. The interested reader should consult a 1988 Urban Land Institute publication by Michael Stegman entitled *Impact Fees* for further information.[10]

FEDERAL CONTROLS

We have just examined some of the controls that are usually enacted by local government (jointly in some cases with state government). Other controls are imposed by the federal government. These controls are at times enforced by the federal government directly and at other times are combined with local and state planning tools and enforced at those levels.

ENVIRONMENTAL PROTECTION

In the 1960s, the general public became more concerned about environmental issues. Reacting to this concern, various levels of government passed statutes requiring certain forms of environmental protection and/or conservation. Most of these statutes involve some type of local land use planning, coupled with a permitting system to ensure the minimization of environmental damage from development. At the national level, the U.S. Environmental Protection Agency (EPA) was created by the National Environmental Policy Act (NEPA). After this, in rapid succession, air, water, and noise amendments to the basic statute were enacted. The specific inclusion of land use plans in these amendments illustrates once again how important land is in the nation's general economic and social framework.

Although environmental legislation may not seem to be directly related to land use, implementation of environmental protection usually requires specific land use controls. In the clean air amendments to NEPA, automobile usage was cited as an indirect but troublesome source of pollution. On this basis, local governments were directed to develop land use plans that would minimize automobile trips and so reduce air pollution.

The water amendments were aimed at both direct and nonpoint sources of water pollution. In addition to requiring all dumping into public waterways to meet certain standards, these amendments cited

---

[10]Note that there is yet another level of regulation in some areas. Florida has recently passed a concurrency requirement. This means that, in addition to the developer meeting zoning and subdivision regulations, plus paying impact fees, the local infrastructure must be sufficient to serve any new development at a desired level. Otherwise, new development is not permitted until it can be shown that new infrastructure is being built concurrently which can handle the new load. Impact fees pay your share, but if that isn't enough to provide the funding needed for the new infrastructure required to meet the desired level of service for the overall area, then you must wait until other developers' impact fees and/or general government revenues are sufficient to fund the required infrastructure.

numerous types of land use (even agricultural) as nonpoint sources of pollution. Where waterways did not meet certain minimum standards, no additional development was permitted that would in any way affect the quality of water. In other words, development was prohibited if the water did not meet a certain standard, even if the new development did less environmental damage than existing development. Last in the EPA trilogy are the noise amendments. These have not received the vigorous federal support given the air and water rules.

For some situations these amendments would support conflicting decisions. For example, a municipality considering a new airport must be concerned with meeting environmental standards. The clean air rules, regarding the automobile as an indirect source of pollution, would support an airport site close to the most populous areas of the city, thus limiting the length of automobile trips. On the other hand, the rules pertaining to noise would point to a site far from the city so that the fewest number of people would be burdened with the earthshaking sounds associated with jet aircraft. This is merely one illustration of possible conflicts arising from the application of several standards in one development decision.

Note also that environmental legislation begins at the federal level but requires local enforcement through local land use planning. The courts have been particularly active in this area as well. Courts have supported and, in some cases, have gone beyond specific enabling legislation to make sure that underlying objectives of the environmental legislation are promoted through local planning and permitting systems.[11]

THE BIGGEST, MOST IMPORTANT CHANGE OF ALL: AMERICA'S ATTITUDE TOWARD HAZARDOUS WASTE

By now everyone knows that asbestos causes lung cancer. Although it is no longer used in construction, asbestos can be found in old buildings across America—in ceiling tiles, in insulation, around steampipes, in acoustical applications, sprayed on walls, and in durable siding and roofing shingles. Multimillion dollar liability suits against asbestos manufacturers helped raise everyone's awareness of the asbestos problem. But as we will see here, asbestos is really only the tip of the iceberg comprising hazardous wastes. Even so, it is a very large tip (see Boxes 27-5 and 27-6). For example, the developer of a 28-story office tower recently spent

[11]*The various amendments to the Environmental Policy Act are certainly not the only pieces of federal legislation involving environmental protection. The U.S. Department of Commerce's floodplain insurance is an attempt to force local areas to move development out of flood-prone areas. It is particularly interesting in that it is implemented partially by financial institutions.*

The U.S. Department of the Interior manages the Coastal Zone Management Program, which affects the coastal areas of some 30 states and involves significant federal funding if the state is willing to plan and closely regulate development in hazardous and fragile areas along coastlines.

27-5
ASBESTOS MAKERS RUN OUT OF BREATHING ROOM

An Illinois Ruling Could Leave Them Liable for Billions More in Damages

A few years back, Chicago school district officials realized they faced a real mess. Cleaning up deadly asbestos fibers in school buildings would mean a $500 million hit. So they sued the nearest deep pocket: asbestos makers. Now, after years of courtroom squabbling, the school system has won a key case that spells big new legal woes for asbestos manufacturers.

On October 25, the Illinois Supreme Court ruled that Chicago and 33 other state school districts can press ahead with lawsuits seeking property damages from such heavy hitters as USG, W. R. Grace, Union Carbide, and GAF. It's the first such ruling from a state's highest court, and it will figure into the legal strategies of plaintiffs' attorneys in similar cases pending nationwide.

More legal sharks appear to be circling. Roughly 30 states soon will launch a massive action against present and former asbestos makers to recover cleanup costs for thousands of public buildings. Says one lawyer close to the upcoming case: "This decision opens a big door for us."

What's emerging is a new wave of legal assaults on the industry. Round one, begun in the early 1970s, centered on personal-injury claims from miners and others who developed deadly lung ailments from inhaling asbestos fibers, now a well-documented carcinogen. Lawsuits helped plunge Manville Corp., once the largest asbestos miner, into bankruptcy court in 1982. Now school systems and public agencies want these companies to pay to remove the stuff. **BIG PRICE.** Small wonder. The Environmental Protection Agency figures that about 20 percent of U.S. buildings contain some asbestos. The total cleanup cost, says the EPA, is a mind-boggling $51 billion. Schools have a special problem: They must pay the piper now. Other buildings must follow asbestos guidelines only when razing a structure. The EPA adopted rules two years ago ordering schools to contain or remove asbestos by July 1989. So far, the Chicago school district's cleanup tab is $40 million.

The Illinois high court ruling gives the district a shot at recouping that money. The court reversed a Chicago trial judge who dismissed the school boards' suits three years ago, concluding that the asbestos wasn't a strong enough risk. The state supreme court disagreed—letting the plaintiffs press a so-called tort suit, alleging product liability and negligence. Industry lawyers had argued that the cases were contractual disputes that turned on economic loss.

The distinction isn't legal hair-splitting. Tort cases, involving negligence, often produce bigger awards and punitive damages. Also, in a contract case, the school boards couldn't sue the well-heeled asbestos manufacturers, only the contractors that installed the asbestos. Such smaller fry make less tempting defendants.

But asbestos makers, with their high-priced legal talent, won't be pushovers in court. On October 13, W. R. Grace and & Co. won a case against a Pittsburgh high school seeking $21 million for cleanup costs. Grace had convinced the jury that the small amounts of asbestos on hand weren't a health hazard. In the Chicago case, school districts must only prove actual harm from the asbestos in the buildings. However, if similar cases go to court in other states, such as South Carolina, with tougher burdens of proof, attorneys may also have to show that manufacturers knew the risks regarding asbestos but sold the material anyway.

Ultimately all buildings with the troublesome fiber will need serious renovation—or special treatment if they are torn down—even when asbestos doesn't pose an immediate danger. That being the case, count on school districts to push on with their legal chase. With their asbestos bills now coming due, they have little choice.

Source: Business Week, November 20, 1989, p. 36.

$300,000 removing the asbestos from six old buildings *before* they could be demolished to make way for the new structure. And this is not an isolated example. Hazardous wastes, from asbestos to leaked fuel to buried chemicals, are probably much more widespread than we imagine.

As the nation has become increasingly concerned with hazardous waste, government at all levels is instituting new policies. *These policies are having a dramatic impact on the real estate industry.* In the very near future, we expect that the environmental audit and hazardous waste clauses written into conveyances will become as standard in the real estate transference process as proving title has been in the past.

Since the nineteenth century, the U.S. economy has been intricately tied to industrial processes and technological development. Today, the Office of Technology Assessment estimates that we produce between 250 and 275 metric tons of hazardous waste annually. The EPA suggests that only about 10 percent of this total is properly disposed of. The governmental response to this problem may have been slow in coming, but it was dramatic in the 1980s.

The original superfund legislation, officially titled the Comprehensive Environmental Response Corporation and Liability Act, or **CERCLA,** was passed in 1980. Significant amendments to this act were passed in 1986, known as the Superfund Amendments and Reauthorization Act (**SARA**). Collectively, these two pieces of legislation establish a potential liability for hazardous waste cleanup, the magnitude of which is unparalleled in American industry.

Probably the best known environmental disaster that led up to this legislation was Love Canal outside Buffalo, New York. The Hooker Electrochemical Company disposed of some 21,800 tons of toxic waste in the canal between 1942 and 1953. In 1953, Hooker sealed the canal with clay, a remedy that at that time was considered adequate to protect the environment from chemical runoff. Some 25 years later, problems began to appear in the form of sludge in basements and on lawns; a residential

27-6
REMOVING
ASBESTOS IS
DIFFICULT,
DANGEROUS
TASK

Removing asbestos from a home or commercial building is not easy.

The process begins by taking samples from various locales in a building. The typical spots to check are piping insulation, around walls, floor and ceiling coverings, and in attics. The samples are tested in laboratories to determine if asbestos is present and to what extent.

If removal is needed, the removal company must first isolate the location to ensure none of the asbestos fibers get into the atmosphere.

That is done by erecting plastic walls around the entrances to the buildings and on all openings, as well as all walls and floors. Several makeshift rooms are then built leading to where the removal process will occur.

The first room is called the "clean room." It is called the clean room because the air is not contaminated with asbestos. Workers enter the room from the outside, deposit their clothing and put on their respirators and disposable uniforms.

Then they enter a second room in which a shower is located. Each time workers leave the work area, they must shower thoroughly.

Workers must go through the three chambers each time they enter or exit, showering and changing clothes each time. The uniforms must be thrown away after each wearing.

Two types of respiratory equipment are most commonly used. One is a rubber face piece that uses filter cartridges to screen the asbestos dust. A second is an air hose connected to an outside air supply.

Inside the work area, the plastic walls have created an air-tight enclosure. Several large fans constantly are in operation, equipped with special filters to collect any dust in the air. The fans create negative air pressure in the work area, thus preventing any contaminated air leaking outside. The filtered air is then exhausted to the outside by the fans.

Source: This short article from the *Raleigh News and Observer,* August 22, 1989, shows why asbestos removal is expensive and time consuming.

neighborhood had developed over the old chemical dump site. (Prior to the residential development, the site had been sold to the local school board for $1.00, which ran an elementary school there.) By 1978, the health problems (high death rates, serious birth defects, etc.) associated with Love Canal were clear to all involved, and the tragedy for individual families was inestimable.

The federal government responded in 1980 with CERCLA. If you like legal language, the references at the end of this section provide plenty of that. The gist of the statute was to make *anyone connected with producing the problem or owning the site of the problem responsible for cleaning it up.* This has dramatic implications: for instance, that someone who is (1) ignorant of the problem, or (2) thought they had done the best possible job disposing of the waste given the technology of the time, is still responsible for the cleanup. In legal terms the liability is *strict, joint and several, and retroactive.* In essence, it doesn't matter who is or was at fault for placing hazardous wastes on the site. The EPA may seek recovery for cleanup from present and/or prior owners of the site, or from others connected with the contaminated site as operator, generator, or transporter of the hazardous waste materials.

Is this a big problem across the United States? No one is yet quite sure how big it is. The Chemical Manufacturers Association estimates there are 4,802 hazardous waste sites across the country, whereas a study done by the EPA estimates more than 50,000. (Interestingly, Love Canal is not one of the hundred worst on either list.) In addition to the sites that have already been identified, given the level of industry and technology in the United States it's probably safe to assume that an even greater number have not been identified. Furthermore, cleanup is not simple or cheap. Sometimes the problem can be encapsulated, but usually some sort of biological treatment or incineration is required for the most hazardous sites—for the worst sites we are talking in the tens of millions of dollars per site for such treatment. Is such expensive potential liability affecting the rules of the game?

In 1976, lenders worried about the environment and talked about the environment but were not absolutely paranoid about it. Today, the rules for a lender are very simple: Don't get involved with a hazardous site. Remember that when a lender can't collect, it hopes to foreclose on the property serving as collateral. However, if that lender comes into the chain of title through foreclosure and becomes responsible for an environmental cleanup, then the property is not positive collateral but a huge liability. Consequently, lenders' basic position is not to get involved. Obviously, this means it's very hard to finance any development connected with a hazardous waste site. Of course, it isn't just lenders who are worried. All property owners are concerned. Major tenants are concerned. Government, your partner, who created the legislation, is concerned, because the federal government itself owns a great many sites contaminated with, among other things, military explosives and other discharges from military installations.

Thus, the problem is real, its magnitude is tremendous, and everyone is concerned. When we examine this problem at Level One and Level Two, we see an interesting twist. At Level One, many otherwise attractive sites will go undeveloped because of problems with the environment. From a societal point of view, we need these sites cleaned up so that they may be used for productive purposes; for this reason, CERCLA and SARA were enacted into law. However, at Level Two we have exactly the opposite incentive. The risk of becoming involved with such a site is tremendous to any individual or financial institution, and that scares people away from working with these sites. Superfund legislation provided for something called *potentially responsible parties* or PRPs. If you are *potentially* responsible, say, as the part-owner, you may be made to clean up the site before it is proven that you are indeed responsible. In fact, the legislation allows the government to come after any "deep pockets" even if several other parties are involved with the site. The "deep pockets" may subsequently bring an action for reimbursement against the other parties but in the meantime may have spent a bundle.

In response to CERCLA and SARA, we are cleaning up some problems, and that's good for society. An individual playing a game, however, usually responds by attempting to avoid the problem by doing an environmental audit before becoming involved. Any significant transfer of real property interests today involves at least a phase one environmental audit. Moreover, real estate conveyances are beginning to include indemnification clauses by which parties hope to recover costs if they actually do get charged for a cleanup. The lender may seek to be indemnified by the borrower, for example, and the buyer by the seller.

❏ **THE ENVIRONMENTAL AUDIT** An environmental audit is a method for identifying environmental liabilities and concerns. It is not hard science. It is a newly evolving process for checking the degree of risk on a site. This effort comprises different intensities usually referred to as Phase 1, Phase 2, and Phase 3.

ENVIRONMENT AUDIT

PHASE	ACTIVITIES	APPROX. COST (1989 $)
I	Inspect the site; check its history of ownership and use; check regulatory agency records; talk to key people.	$1,000–3,500
II	Make limited samples; search for more data and order a geological evaluation; do limited testing of soil and water.	$3,500–10,000
III	Do detailed site investigation that may include exploratory borings, wells, tank tests, modeling, multimedia sampling.	$10,000 and up

Regardless of the level of intensity of the audit, there are three objectives: (1) to identify actual or potential problems from *past* activities, (2) to identify areas of *current* noncompliance (typically someone failing to keep records or maintain adequate standards in an ongoing operation), and (3) to identify areas of potential *future* problems. The third is of course the most difficult, because many substances in use today may prove hazardous at some point in the future.

How does a would-be buyer, for example, decide how far to go in an environmental audit? The scope of the audit will depend on the size and former use of the property, the length of time available to do an audit, the quality of historical records, the level of documentation on existing operations, and the results of simply walking around and looking at the property. Obviously, the price of an environmental audit varies with the level of effort. In turn, the level of effort ought to depend on the amount of money at risk and some notion of probability appropriate to the site. For example, a former wood preservative treatment site ought to raise caution flags in a prudent buyer's brain. A prospective buyer would wonder how the highly toxic wood-treating chemicals had been disposed of and whether any had gotten into the ground water.

A Phase I environmental audit consists of a careful visual examination of the property, a discussion with current owners and surrounding landowners, and a review of available documents, including the title search. The purpose is to see whether any activity on or around the property in the past could have caused contamination of soil and water. What do people look for on site in a Phase I audit? Tell-tale signs are stained or discolored soils, unusual hills, unusual odors, pipes coming out of the ground, or most evil of all, decaying steel barrels. Besides the current owners and neighboring owners, the agencies to consult are the U.S. Environmental Protection Agency, the state EPA, the local health department, the county soil conservation office, the public library, the local newspaper, and anyone else who might possibly be able to help.

If a Phase I audit reveals any problems, an investigator typically proceeds to Phase II, which involves limited soil testing. Of course, it is possible to take 10 samples randomly around the site and to test all of them for *every* imaginable toxic material, but this would be very expensive. Phase I audits give a rough idea of what might be in the soil, so at Phase II a few soil samples are tested for the most *likely* toxic materials, thereby limiting cost.

If problems are found at Phase II, investigators move to Phase III with much more extensive testing and more sophisticated technology. Note that time and money are involved in this progression. Remember the example of the little old lady calling a broker and eventually selling her house, after the seller secured financing and she proved she had good title? Well, in the 1990s the environment audit is one more hurdle that has to be passed before a real estate transaction closes. The buyer has to be convinced that he or she isn't stepping into an environmental problem. This can be expensive and time consuming. Think about buying the single-family home owned for 50 years by the little old lady; there a Phase I audit obviously will suffice. But in the situation of an industrial plant being redeveloped as commercial property, how far should a prudent buyer go?

The following list shows some of the contaminants that may be found on different kinds of real estate, whereas Box 27-5 illustrates the potential liability and Box 27-6 the cleanup hassle.

AGRICULTURAL PROPERTIES	COMMERCIAL PROPERTIES	INDUSTRIAL PROPERTIES
Pesticides	Asbestos	Asbestos
Fuels	PCBs	PCBs
Vehicle and equipment maintenance chemicals (solvents, lubricants)	Radon/Formaldehyde etc.	Fuels
	Fuels	Chemicals
	Chemicals	Paints and solvents
Paints and solvents		

Source: Robert L. Hearn.

URBAN RENEWAL

Urban renewal as conceived in the 1950s was designed to alleviate slum conditions. Essentially, the federal government would provide the bulk of the funds needed to enable local governments to (1) buy up slum properties (under eminent domain if necessary), (2) demolish the slums, and (3) sell the land at below-market prices to private developers. The underlying justification for the program was that the private marketplace could not achieve the rehabilitation of large slum areas without some form of subsidy. Private developers would probably be unable to obtain the necessary financing. And without the power of eminent domain, the possibility was very real that one or more landowners would refuse to sell, thus preventing comprehensive redevelopment. Most important, there could be no assurance that the redeveloped properties would generate sufficient cash flow to permit a satisfactory return on the large investment required.

The program looked good on paper but was, in practice, a relative failure. The unfortunate result was that many poor families were removed from neighborhoods where they had lived for many years without being provided new housing. Consequently, they crowded even more densely into the remaining slums. In later years of the urban renewal program, local government agencies were required to provide adequate housing for evicted persons. Furthermore, revised regulations required that redevelopment of any area provide for at least as much low-income housing as was there originally. These two provisions eliminated some of the abuses of the earlier urban renewal program but greatly increased the cost. Land in the central city that was cleared and free of restrictive government regulations was very valuable to the private developer. However, the private developer would not pay as much for land when development required a certain amount of relatively unprofitable low-income housing. When local governments were forced to resell the land to the private sector at a lower cost and at the same time provide for housing the poor during the intervening period, the cost of urban renewal greatly escalated.

LOW-INCOME HOUSING

Using even more direct methods, the U.S. Department of Housing and Urban Development (HUD) provides loans at below-market interest rates and direct rent subsidies to encourage provision of low-income housing. Changes in the myriad HUD programs occur rapidly, making documentation here very difficult. Our purpose will be to look not at any particular program but rather at the general approaches that HUD has taken.

Under the old 236 program (which in the 1970s replaced the 221(d)(3) program), HUD provided interest subsidies to developers of low-income, multifamily housing. This was done by HUD's paying most of the interest on the mortgage, which was made by an institutional lender such as a savings and loan (S&L) association. Imagining the problems involved is not difficult. For example, what standards should apply to the housing? The developer-investor is likely to prefer to build more luxurious units (which are easier to rent) than many people might deem appropriate for subsidized housing. Furthermore, what income limits should be set in determining who are low-income families? It is not easy to audit the income of a tenant, particularly when family situations are in a state of flux.

Some of these problems were dealt with in later programs designed to provide interest rate subsidies in connection with financing for qualified low-income families to *purchase* single-family homes (235 program). This program was more expensive because the housing cost more. And there were problems in determining who should be chosen to receive subsidy benefits since the government could not afford to provide subsidies to all low-income families.

Other HUD programs have provided for direct rental subsidies to tenants and, at the other extreme, for public housing—ownership by government agencies of units to be rented to low-income families. In total, the various HUD programs have provided jobs and stimulated investment. There are some serious questions, however, as to their long-run cost-effectiveness.

27-7

NEW HOUSING MEASURES TO SUPPORT THE ELDERLY

Housing officials will today endorse measures to encourage young families to live with elderly parents or dependents.

The measures include advancing by two years the allocation of housing to families awaiting rehousing along with elderly parents or elderly dependents.

In the new towns, young families will be allowed to apply with their elderly parents or dependents for two separate flats in the same block.

The measures were drawn up by an inter-departmental working group co-chaired by the then Social Welfare Director, Mrs. Elizabeth Wong Chien Chi-lien, and Deputy Director of Housing, Mr. Fung Tung, to study the question of housing for the elderly.

The group concluded that elderly people should be helped to remain in the community with adequate supportive services.

At present, 697,700 people, or 12.2 percent of the population, are aged 60 or above. The figure is expected to climb to 15.5 percent, or 986,400, by 2001.

Social workers have warned that a crisis could occur if the administration does not strengthen services for the elderly.

Recommendations expected to be passed by the Housing Authority's management and operations committee today include:

- Families awaiting rehousing along with elderly parents should have their housing allocation advanced by two years, provided they have been registered on the waiting list for not less than two years.
- The priority scheme will not be restricted to families with elderly parents, but will be extended to include other dependent elderly relatives.
- A new application scheme to allow young families to apply with their elderly parents, or dependents, for two separate flats in the same public housing block in new towns.
- Young families in new towns should be encouraged to add elderly parents or relatives from public housing or private tenancies to their households, and apply for larger flats.
- Elderly parents or relatives in new towns should be allowed to add children or relatives in old urban estates to their tenancies and apply for transfer to larger flats.
- Elderly family members should be allowed to transfer to estates in new towns where their children or close relatives live, and be permitted to occupy a separate flat if required.
- Close relatives or children of elderly persons to be allowed to transfer from urban areas or other new towns and permitted to occupy separate flats where appropriate and available.

A Housing Authority source said proposals could be implemented immediately and without involving much in the way of additional resources.

Source: Jimmy Leung, "New Housing Measures to Support the Elderly," *South China Morning Post,* Vol. XLVI, No. 11, Thursday, January 11, 1990, p. 2.

Today most of the action in subsidized housing comes under HUD Section 8 program. The interested student should begin there in the search for which programs currently have funding. We say *begin there* because most of the Section 8 programs are still under attack by a budget-conscious administration. However, many of these programs have strong vested constituencies (notably among minorities, the elderly, and the building trades), and Washington budget battles are not easy to predict. In addition to federal policy, remember that there are significant legal issues involved and that the courts' role will also be important. (See Box 27-7.)

Affordable housing tends to be a difficult public policy issue in most highly developed nations. Americans are not alone in grappling with it, as Box 27-8 suggests.

27-8

THE COURTS AND LOW-INCOME HOUSING

In the late 1960s and early 1970s, the courts became concerned about provisions for low-income housing. The U.S. Supreme Court, which chooses which cases it will hear based on the importance of the issues involved, had avoided zoning-related issues for nearly 50 years before the questions of low-income housing and racial discrimination brought zoning back to its attention. In general, the courts have recently taken a very active role, sometimes striking down municipal zoning ordinances on the basis that they restricted the amount of low-income housing that could be constructed.

In some cases, the federal courts moved in a different direction from state courts. This can occur because, unless some federal issue is involved, a state court ruling is not subject to review by the U.S. Supreme Court. The two most publicized and precedent-setting cases in past years have been the *Mount Laurel* and the *Arlington Heights* decisions. In the *Mount Laurel* case, the New Jersey Supreme Court stated that every municipality must make provision in its zoning ordinance for a fair share of the low-income housing that is needed in the region as a whole. Put another way, a municipality could not take a narrow view of its own housing requirements and ignore the needs of the region.

Contrasting with this decision is that of the U.S. Supreme Court in the *Arlington Heights* case. The Court said that mere evidence of segregation (note the implied correlation between low-income housing and racial discrimination) does not, in and of itself, mean that any particular zoning ordinance is discriminatory. The evidence must show that a zoning ordinance was intended to discriminate against particular income or racial groups before the ordinance is invalid. The two cases thus can be clearly distinguished. On the one hand, the absence of zoning for low-income housing is sufficient to strike down restrictive zoning; on the other, intent must be proved. Contrasting decisions within the court system are quite obviously a problem to the real estate industry. However, they seem inevitable under the dual court system in the United States.

SUMMARY Numerous tools are available to governments for use in accomplishing their diverse real estate-related goals. Most of these tools imply some reduction in private property rights. They involve having the federal, state, or local government provide for the public benefit while redistributing costs and benefits among particular private interests. The basic rules of the real estate game include rules made by government at all levels. Furthermore the game is influenced by other, nonregulatory actions of government; therefore, the game cannot be fully understood (or competently played) without an appreciation of government's role in it. Because real property has a long economic life in a fixed location, players cannot ignore the possibility that the basic rules, and more likely the government role, will change over the holding period of the asset. Anticipating changes in the government role is difficult but not impossible. It revolves around two considerations. What is fair, and what makes the game more efficient? Politics are likely to distort these items over the short run, but over the long run these two considerations are the keys to successful decision making.

IMPORTANT TERMS

Building codes
CERCLA
Districting
Downzone
Eminent domain
Environmental Audit
Extraterritorial jurisdiction (ETJ)
Infill incentives

Infrastructure
Nuisance concept
SARA
Site-value taxation
Subdivision taxation
Value-in-use taxation
Zoning

REVIEW QUESTIONS

27.1 Suggest a logical reason why the real estate industry might be a target for government programs and policies.

27.2 In an economic sense, what are the goals of government public policy?

27.3 What is the role of the court system in the area of real estate development?

27.4 Why might the production of "public goods" be handled more efficiently by the public sector as opposed to the private sector?

27.5 How might there develop a conflict between economic activity and environmental protection?

27.6 Under what circumstances might the rights of an individual landowner conflict with the rights of the public?

27.7   Discuss the dual dilemma of what public goods should be produced and who should pay for those public goods.

27.8   What are some potential problems with local governments' accepting compensation from developers for zoning upgrades?

27.9   What is the difference between site-value and value-in-use taxation?

27.10   The National Housing Act of 1949 established as a national goal the provision of "a decent home and suitable living environment for every American." Do you believe this is an achievable goal? If yes, how? If no, why not?

$\mathcal{L}$ONG-TERM TRENDS IN URBAN STRUCTURE AND LAND USE

This chapter attempts to point the way to the future. It is a direct extension of Chapters 2 and 3. We have noted that change is a constant factor in land use and should always be taken into consideration by real estate participants. Successful real estate investment, development, and planning in the 1990s will not be guided by any simple format. However, an understanding of the major structural and regional changes now underway in the economy will help the real estate decision maker avoid the pitfalls and find the new opportunities that will be available in the future. This chapter analyzes some of the important patterns of change in the location of population and employment as well as government's current involvement with land use and real estate. In so doing, the chapter augments earlier theories of urban and regional developing (Part 1) in the light of emerging trends and public policy concerns. Chapter 29 then describes innovative new ways to play the real estate game, given the expected impact of these trends.

THE URBAN PICTURE

The growth of American cities throughout most of our history has created the expectation that the continued expansion and prosperity of large cities is assured. Although the central cities of many older metropolitan areas lost population between 1950 and 1970, the metropolitan areas of these cities continued to grow. However, the 1970s brought a sharp change in this historical trend. A pronounced shift of population away from large cities seems to have occurred.[1] For the first time in our history, the largest cities in the country—those with more than three million residents—lost population. People moved out of these cities faster than they moved in, so that the rate of net outmigration was 6.1

[1]See Table 28-1 for a general frame of reference on the U.S. population.

TABLE 28-1   U.S. POPULATION IN MILLIONS

REGION, DIVISION, AND STATE OR OTHER AREA	1950	1960	1970	1980	1990[a]	2000[a]	2010[a]
United States	*151.3*	*179.3*	*203.3*	*226.5*	*249.9*	*267.7*	*282.0*
Region							
Northeast	39.5	45.7	49.0	49.1	50.9	52.4	53.8
Midwest	44.5	51.6	56.6	58.9	60.3	60.5	59.7
South	47.2	55.0	62.8	75.4	86.6	95.6	103.5
West	20.2	28.0	34.8	43.1	52.2	59.2	65.0
New England							
Maine	0.9	1.0	1.0	1.1	1.2	1.3	1.4
New Hampshire	0.5	0.6	0.7	0.9	1.1	1.4	1.7
Vermont	0.4	0.4	0.4	0.5	0.6	0.6	0.7
Massachusetts	4.7	5.1	5.7	5.7	5.9	6.2	6.4
Rhode Island	0.8	0.9	1.0	0.9	1.0	1.0	1.1
Connecticut	2.0	2.5	3.0	3.1	3.3	3.4	3.5
Middle Atlantic							
New York	14.8	16.8	18.2	17.6	17.9	18.0	18.1
New Jersey	4.8	6.0	7.2	7.4	7.8	8.4	8.8
Pennsylvania	10.5	11.3	11.8	11.9	12.0	12.0	12.0
East North Central							
Ohio	7.9	9.7	10.7	10.8	10.9	10.9	10.8
Indiana	3.9	4.7	5.2	5.5	5.6	5.7	5.7
Illinois	8.7	10.0	11.1	11.4	11.7	11.7	11.6
Michigan	6.3	7.8	8.9	9.2	9.3	9.4	9.3
Wisconsin	3.4	4.0	4.4	4.7	4.9	4.8	4.7
West North Central							
Minnesota	3.0	3.4	3.8	4.0	4.4	4.6	4.6
Iowa	2.6	2.8	2.8	2.9	2.8	2.5	2.3
Missouri	4.0	4.3	4.7	4.9	5.2	5.5	5.7
North Dakota	0.6	0.6	0.6	0.7	0.7	0.6	0.5
South Dakota	0.6	0.7	0.7	0.7	0.7	0.7	0.7
Nebraska	1.3	1.4	1.5	1.6	1.6	1.5	1.4
Kansas	1.9	2.2	2.2	2.4	2.5	2.5	2.5
South Atlantic							
Delaware	0.3	0.4	0.5	0.6	0.7	0.8	0.9
Maryland	2.3	3.1	3.9	4.2	4.8	5.6	6.4
District of Columbia	0.8	0.8	0.8	0.6	0.6	0.6	0.6
Virginia	3.3	4.0	4.7	5.3	6.2	7.3	8.2
West Virginia	2.0	1.9	1.7	2.0	1.8	1.7	1.5
North Carolina	4.0	4.6	5.0	5.9	6.7	7.7	8.7
South Carolina	2.1	2.4	2.6	3.1	3.6	4.0	4.3
Georgia	3.4	4.0	4.6	5.5	6.6	8.0	9.4
Florida	2.8	5.0	6.8	9.7	12.9	16.3	19.7

TABLE 28-1 (CONTINUED)

REGION, DIVISION, AND STATE OR OTHER AREA	1950	1960	1970	1980	1990[a]	2000[a]	2010[a]
East South Central							
Kentucky	2.9	3.0	3.2	3.7	3.7	3.7	3.6
Tennessee	3.3	3.6	3.9	4.6	5.0	5.4	5.7
Alabama	3.0	3.3	3.4	3.9	4.2	4.4	4.5
Mississippi	2.2	2.2	2.2	2.5	2.6	2.8	2.9
West South Central							
Arkansas	1.9	1.8	1.9	2.3	2.4	2.5	2.6
Louisiana	2.7	3.3	3.6	4.2	4.4	4.1	3.9
Oklahoma	2.2	2.3	2.6	3.0	3.2	2.9	2.7
Texas	7.7	9.6	11.1	14.2	17.0	17.8	18.0
Mountain							
Montana	0.6	0.7	0.7	0.8	0.8	0.7	0.7
Idaho	0.6	0.7	0.7	0.9	1.0	1.0	1.0
Wyoming	0.3	0.3	0.3	0.5	0.5	0.4	0.4
Colorado	1.3	1.8	2.2	2.9	3.3	3.4	3.4
New Mexico	0.7	1.0	1.0	1.3	1.5	1.7	1.9
Arizona	0.8	1.3	1.8	2.7	3.7	4.6	5.5
Utah	0.7	0.9	1.0	1.5	1.7	1.8	1.9
Nevada	0.2	0.3	0.5	0.8	1.1	1.4	1.6
Pacific							
Washington	2.4	2.9	3.4	4.1	4.8	5.2	5.4
Oregon	1.5	1.8	2.0	2.6	2.8	2.9	2.9
California	10.6	15.7	20.0	23.7	29.2	34.0	38.0
Alaska	0.1	0.2	0.3	0.4	0.5	0.6	0.7
Hawaii	0.5	0.6	0.8	1.0	1.1	1.4	1.6

[a] From U.S. Bureau of the Census, February 1990 (Series A), p. 25, #1053.

percent during the 1970s. This loss outweighed the natural rate of increase, so that population declined by 1.6 percent. Metropolitan areas as a whole—those with population of at least 50,000—grew more slowly than nonmetropolitan areas for the first time since the Great Depression.

This very important apparent reversal of a long-term trend was short-lived. More rapid population and employment growth in metropolitan areas reestablished the historic pattern. Specifically, a reversal has taken place since 1980 in the growth rates of metropolitan versus nonmetropolitan areas. For the first time this century, nonmetropolitan counties grew faster during the 1970s. But, in the 1980s, this trend reverted to its earlier path. The population in metropolitan areas (essentially all urban centers over 50,000) again grew faster than nonmetropolitan areas. However, this growth rate differential has been concentrated in the South, where metropolitan areas grew twice as fast as nonmetropolitan areas. In contrast, in the Northeast, metropolitan areas grew more slowly relative to nonmetropolitan areas. In the remaining two regions, the metropolitan and nonmetropolitan growth rates were similar: both very low in the Midwest and quite high in the West.

DECENTRALIZATION

The combined influence of economic change and the policies of governments at the federal, state, and local levels have vastly changed the structure of American cities in this century. Until 1920, most of the people living in big metropolitan areas resided in the central city, not the suburbs. The central business district (**CBD**) was the focus of most activity, and as the city grew, the density of population and employment also grew, for workers and businesses had a strong desire to be located as close to the CBD as possible. In Chapter 2 this pattern was identified as the basis of the concentric circle theory of urban growth. Producers needed to be near the major transportation facilities (railroad and ship), and workers for the most part walked to their jobs because inexpensive urban transportation such as buses and autos was not widely available, and streetcars and subways served only parts of the suburbs. The development of the skyscraper and the elevator allowed cities to build up rather than out, and urban America was characterized by the so-called **manufacturing belt** running from New York to Chicago.

After 1920 the cities began to spread out to encompass suburban developments as far as 40 or more miles away from the CBD. Population not only grew faster in the suburbs than in the central city, but population density also decreased in the older neighborhoods. This decrease occurred primarily as the result of increased household income, which brought about a rapid increase in the demand for additional housing. In 1940 over 20 percent of housing units in America had more than one person per room; by 1983 this figure had fallen to less than 3 percent. A corresponding improvement in quality of housing is indicated by the fact that over 40 percent of housing units lacked some or all plumbing facilities in 1940, but today less than 2 percent lack some or all such facilities. The desire of people with rising income to consume more housing meant not only that suburban housing was built with more land per dwelling, but also that the number of people occupying older buildings declined, a trend that continues today to reduce the population of some neighborhoods with little or no reduction in their housing stocks.

The automobile worked with rising incomes to disperse urban population outside center cities. The mobility of the automobile was about as great in the 1930s as it is today, but its effect was not fully felt until higher income made ownership of autos widespread, so that the great shift from public transportation to the car for work trips did not come until after World War II. Today, over 90 percent of urban commuters travel to work by car.

Federal taxes and policies toward housing and transportation have also encouraged millions of people to choose suburban living. The ability of taxpayers to deduct mortgage interest and property taxes from their taxable income makes ownership of a home preferable to renting. Central cities have a large proportion of rental apartments, so the income tax effect has speeded the movement to the suburbs. This effect on the cost of ownership was not so important in the 1930s and 1940s, when most taxpayers were in only the 10 percent tax bracket or lower (i.e., the last dollar of income was taxed at a 10 percent rate). However, the combined effects of inflation and the progressive rate structure pushed home-owners into higher brackets in the 1970s. Therefore, the differential between owning and renting became much greater. In fact, the late 1970s were probably the years of greatest housing price appreciation in the nation's history. As noted in Part 6, the Reagan era started with lower tax rates, and soon thereafter the rates of inflation dropped as well. Consequently, the 1980s were characterized by much slower housing price appreciation with wide differences between regions as these two national trends became less important.

Since the late 1960s the advent of laws making condominiums practical has made apartment living eligible for the benefits of ownership. This change has been partly responsible for the current two-way flow of population in cities. The middle class continues to move to the suburbs, causing the central cities of many urban areas to decline further, but a smaller number of households are moving back into the city to occupy new condominiums as well as rehabilitated apartments and single-family homes. This trend is discussed later in this chapter in the context of changes in demography and the labor force.

The federal government also affected the cost of home ownership in a major way by its support of mortgages available through the Federal Housing Administration (FHA) and the Veterans Administration (VA). By lowering both the downpayment and the monthly carrying costs of a new home, FHA and VA loans made single-family homes available to a wider group of American households. For many years the government favored mostly new construction in the suburbs rather than rental units in the city. This helped to speed dramatically the decentralization of metropolitan areas.

Transportation investment in cities has helped to change the pattern of urban development over the last 30 years. Urban expressways have been built with mostly federal dollars, greatly increasing system capacities and raising off-peak speed. Because of congestion during rush hour, peak load speed has increased only from 25 mph to about 30 mph since 1950, but commuters are able to come into the CBD from greater distances than in the past. These roads were paid for by excise taxes on gas, oil, tires, and the like. So users pay for their highways both during work trips and other trips. Since only a portion of total users are commuters, this means that commuters are paying only part of the cost of the investments that allow them to live farther out in the suburbs, and this underpayment represents another subsidy to suburban development.

Many critics charge that policies fostering **suburbanization** have harmed American cities, making them too spread out and too reliant on the automobile. Worries over the price and future supply of oil after the OPEC price hikes caused this debate to heat up, with some calling for large increases in mass transit investment to relieve urban commuters of the need to drive their cars. This line of thinking also leads to predictions that the trend toward suburbanization will be reversed, with population crowding back into central cities to compensate for the future high cost of gasoline. Will this happen, and should we be increasing our investment in mass transit?

Two things are worth noting in this regard. The first is that the oil crisis of the 1970s did not greatly affect the cost of commuting, and the second is that mass transit is not a very efficient way to move people in today's cities. Commuting costs involve both the material cost of gas, oil, and the depreciation of a car as well as the value of the commuter's time. If time is worth $4 per hour and taking the car to work saves one-half hour per day over using the bus, the price of gasoline must rise substantially before drivers will be willing to switch to public transportation. The price of gasoline has risen but by not nearly that much. Measured either relative to all other prices or relative to the commuter's income, the price of gas has risen less than 50 percent since the early 1970s. In order to eliminate this increase and pay the same for gasoline in real terms, the commuter need only have switched from a traditional American family car, which got 15 miles per gallon on average, to a recent midsize car, which gets at least 50 percent better mileage, or 22.5 miles per gallon. Many commuters have gone further than that and switched to a compact car, getting anywhere from 27 to 35 miles per gallon. Paradoxically, they are now spending less of their take-home pay on gasoline. So it is not likely that suburban urban households will be scrambling for housing closer to the central city on the basis of today's oil prices.

In contrast, the proponents of mass transit (i.e., subway, surface rail, and commuter "heavy rail") argue that it is a more efficient method of transportation than the auto because of its ability to move large numbers of people at a very low cost per person. There are two problems with this argument: First, the cost per commuter on mass transit is critically dependent on how many people use it, and, second, the subway or train ride is only part of the commuter's total trip from home to work. The commuting trip is made up of three parts; residential collection, line haul (a straight run down the expressway or rail line), and downtown distribution. Rail transit is efficient mainly for the line haul function and then only if passenger volume is high, for there is no additional cost from the first passenger on a train until it is full. Mass transit serves the needs of residential collection very poorly because today's cities have extensive, low-density suburbs that would be incredibly costly to cover fully by rail lines. The catch-22 of this situation is that the more you attempt complete coverage of the urban area, the less volume you get on each line, and the more volume you seek, the less coverage you get.

Mass transit has to be viewed in conjunction with buses or autos to perform the residential collection. Its inefficiency for residential collection plus the high capital cost of building subways and rail lines make these forms of mass transit very expensive. Figure 28-1 compares the cost per passenger on **BART** (the Bay Area Rapid Transit System in San Francisco) with the alternatives of bus and auto. BART plus a feeder bus for residential collection are more expensive than the car at all passenger volumes below 20,000 per hour. The only traffic corridors in the country that can provide this volume of passengers are located in New York, Chicago, and Boston. It appears from this and other studies that American commuters are not irrationally devoted to their automobiles; they are simply minimizing their commuting cost by driving. What is surprising to many is that the bus *is* a very efficient form of public transportation. Many transportation experts have suggested subsidizing buses

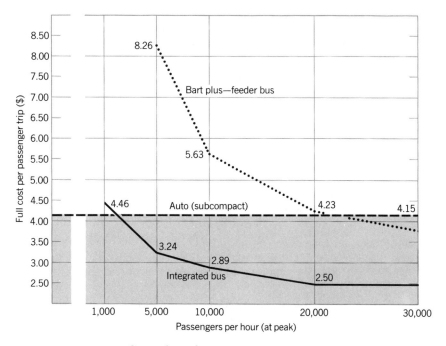

FIGURE 28-1 *Comparison of cost per passenger on BART with costs of auto and bus*

more heavily in order to boost their passenger loads and reduce the cost per passenger, a program that could benefit even small cities.

Are new technologies coming along that will replace the automobile for work trips and change the development pattern of American cities? It does not appear that this will happen any time soon. The technology and economics of transportation have changed very little in the last 40 years. Monorails, magnetic suspension, and computer-controlled highways have received a lot of publicity from time to time, but so far no new technology has come along that has the flexibility of the auto or is less expensive than a bus. Perhaps the next technological breakthrough will be in making batteries light enough and powerful enough to make electric cars and buses feasible. There are some battery-powered buses on the streets of London today, and lighter batteries are now under development. Since higher-cost reserves of crude oil are still available in tar sands, oil shale, and the like, we can expect the internal combustion engine to be around for quite a while. Therefore, our present urban structure, with 90 percent of work trips made by car, probably will not change significantly in the next few decades.

POPULATION COMPOSITION

The pattern of urban development in the 1990s will probably be affected more by the changing composition of households and labor force participation than by government policies toward home ownership, transportation changes, or oil prices. The urban housing picture has never been composed of a single market. Although we sometimes think of home buyers as the married couple with two or more children (a particularly popular image in TV commercials for national brokerage firms), in reality there are a number of quite distinct groups in the market with altogether different demands for space and location. Single-person households and young couples without children in the early years of their careers have in the past occupied mainly rental units located close to the CBD. They are willing to trade off space for proximity to work, paying higher prices per square foot for their housing. Families with children tend to be located farther from the center of the city—the higher is their income. The proportion of working wives is higher among families in which the husband is in the lower end of the income distribution. About twice as many wives of low-income husbands work as wives of high-income husbands. Up to the 1970s, one of the main reasons why low-income families lived closer to the center of the city was that most jobs were located closer to the center than were residences, and the pull of two workers in these families commuting to their jobs led them to demand more proximity to the center. Families in which the husband is a high-income earner may have only one commuter and can gravitate more easily to the outer suburbs, where their higher income can purchase more space at lower prices.

This neat picture of the distribution of households within urban areas may have changed in the 1980s, however. The relative numbers of the different types of households that make up the total market for real estate is changing significantly. Chapter 29 presents some of the highlights of recent population changes. Although total households increased, the stereotyped household composed of a married couple with children at home actually *decreased*. All "family" households did increase, but the most rapidly growing group is the nonfamily household (composed of one or more individuals who are not related). See Table 28-2 for a longer-term perspective on this important shift in population composition.

LABOR FORCE COMPOSITION

When this era is finally named, that name might well be the **Dual-Career Age.** The wage-earning wife is transforming large segments of the American economy, creating the demand for day-care centers, fast-food restaurants, subcompact cars, and Caribbean vacations. The number of wives in the labor force has been increasing steadily for almost 100 years, but in the last two decades the proportion of married women—husband present—who are wage-earners has almost doubled among women aged 20 to 24 and 25 to 34, which are the prime childbearing years. During these same years, the proportion of married men who worked decreased from 94 to 85 percent among those in the 45 to 64 age group, and married men 65 and over cut their participation rate almost in half, from 38 percent to 22 percent.

Over half of the labor force in 1984 was composed of men and women aged 20 to 34, the children of the famous baby boom that followed World War II. This group is the source of most new household formations. In the past they could be expected to marry in their midtwenties and begin having children, buying a house at age 28 to 30. But today these people are delaying marriage or deciding against it altogether; when they marry, they delay having children and then decide to have fewer children or none at all.

What are the housing needs of this large segment of the population? The two-earner families have a higher median income than their single-earner counterparts; and since they have fewer children to support, many of them have considerable purchasing power. But rather than buying a big house in the suburbs, they may want to buy location and convenience. Proximity to work is most important for singles and working couples, and if home is close to work, it also makes it easier for parents to find a day-care center for their young children that is convenient to home and office. So space is being traded off for location; housing is being renovated in older neighborhoods of the central city such as Philadelphia's Nob Hill, New York's Brooklyn Heights, Boston's South End, and Chicago's New Town. In many cities this renewal has

TABLE 28-2   U.S. POPULATION SHIFTS, 1940–89

TYPE OF UNIT	1989 NUMBER	1989 PERCENT	1980	1970	1960	1950	1940
Households							
Total	92,830	100.0	80,776	63,401	52,799	43,544	34,949
Family households	65,837	70.9	59,550	51,456	44,905	38,838	31,491
Married-couple family	52,100	56.1	49,112	44,728	39,254	34,075	26,571
Other family, male householder	2,857	3.1	1,733	1,228	1,228	1,169	1,510
Other family, female householder	10,890	11.7	8,705	5,500	4,422	3,594	3,410
Nonfamily households	26,994	29.1	21,226	11,945	7,895	4,716	3,458
Male householder	11,874	12.8	8,807	4,063	2,716	1,668	1,599
Female householder	15,120	16.3	12,419	7,882	5,179	3,048	1,859
Living alone	22,708	24.5	18,296	10,851	6,896	3,954	2,684
Families							
Total	65,827	100.0	59,550	51,586	45,111	39,303	32,166
Married-couple family	52,100	79.1	49,112	44,755	39,329	34,440	26,971
Other family, male householder	2,847	4.3	1,733	1,239	1,275	1,184	1,559
Other family, female householder	10,890	16.5	8,705	5,591	4,507	3,679	3,616
Unrelated Subfamilies							
Total	473	100.0	360	130	207	465	675
Married couple	49	10.4	20	27	75	365	400
Other, male reference person	26	5.5	36	11	47	15	69
Other, female reference person	298	84.1	304	91	85	85	26
Related Subfamilies							
Total	2,278	100.0	1,150	1,150	1,514	2,402	2,062
Married couple	775	34.0	582	617	871	1,651	1,546
Father–child	103	4.5	45	48	115	113	52
Mother–child	1,400	61.5	512	484	528	638	464
Married Couples							
Total	52,924	100.0	49,714	45,373	40,200	36,091	28,517
With own household	52,100	98.4	49,112	44,728	39,254	34,075	26,571
Without own household	824	1.6	602	645	946	2,016	1,946
Percent without own household	1.6	—	1.2	1.4	2.4	5.6	6.8

T A B L E 2 8 - 2 (CONTINUED)							
	1989						
TYPE OF UNIT	NUMBER	PERCENT	1980	1970	1960	1950	1940
Unrelated Individuals							
Total	34,499	100.0	26,426	14,988	11,092	9,136	9,277
Male	16,115	46.7	11,813	5,693	4,462	4,209	4,942
Female	18,384	53.3	14,613	9,296	6,630	4,927	4,335
Secondary Individuals							
Total	7,505	100.0	5,200	3,043	3,198	4,420	5,819
Male	4,241	56.5	3,006	1,631	1,746	2,541	3,343
Female	3,264	43.5	2,194	1,412	1,451	1,879	2,476

Series P-20, No. 441, issued November 1989.

been synonymous with the process known as **gentrification,** in which rising prices and condominium conversions squeeze out low-income tenants in favor of young professional couples.

Revitalizing inner-city areas has been one of the major goals of municipal government as well as of federal urban renewal programs for several decades. The return of some upper-middle-class households to the city helps to strengthen the tax base and to increase spending in the city, thus creating jobs. But the competition for housing in the most desirable neighborhoods has created a dilemma for these cities. The poor and the elderly, forced out of areas where they may have lived for many years, feel unjustly treated. The issue is social as well as economic; neighborhoods such as Boston's North End, which has long been characterized by its "little Italy" ambience, face a complete change in their ethnic or class makeup. Longtime residents feel they have a right to maintain their neighborhoods in the traditional way. This leads to a feeling that "property rights" to a neighborhood exist. Combined with the fear that displaced residents will not be able to find comparable housing elsewhere, this desire for neighborhood preservation is encouraging the drive for rent control and bans on condominium conversions. City governments are caught between the desire for an improvement in the tax base and the housing needs of older and poorer residents.

Although two-earner families are being drawn closer to the center of the city and are rejuvenating some older neighborhoods, this same development in the labor force is encouraging employers to decentralize in order to be closer to the expanding labor supply in the suburbs. In the past it was mostly the wives of blue-collar and low-income husbands who worked. But today the working wife is a fixture in almost all economic strata. A larger proportion of two-earner families are still concentrated

28-1

THE JOB, THE
CAREER, OR
THE LIFE-STYLE

Obviously, work opportunities have a major impact on where people want to live. However, so does the worker's preferred life-style.

What these motives have to do with cities of the future was highlighted in a discussion between Jim Graaskamp and David Shulman (Salomon Brothers real estate economist). Shulman made the case that the future would see more two-career, not just two-wage-earner, families. He postulated that the largest number of dual-*career* opportunities were usually found only in the largest metropolitan areas. Since the two-career families tended to be the smarter, better educated, and more aggressive, the larger metropolitan areas would continue to grow because of the spinoff effects of high-level inmigration.

In contrast, Graaskamp cited the well-known litany of urban problems: drugs, crime, declining educational systems, ever longer commutes to work, and so on. He then said that Shulman's "best and brightest" young couples would put life-style ahead of immediate job prospects. Since the 1990s would begin the "era of the worker," employers would move the jobs to places where people wanted to live. The result: New York would lose and Madison, Wisconsin, would prosper.

Neither argument is wrong. The world is a complex place, and no one will completely explain tomorrow's city.

in the lower three-fifths of the income distribution, but there are a growing number in the higher economic levels. Today almost every urban neighborhood has a significant proportion of families with two workers, whereas 20 years ago many bedroom suburbs contained primarily one-earner families. The increase in working wives over the last 20 years has provided an attractive supply of labor in the suburbs. Companies have built plants and office buildings outside the central city to take advantage of this source of workers. Studies of the pattern of employment in cities have found that women on average have a shorter commuting trip than men. This is especially true of married workers. Wives with children want to be closer to home and to their children's schools and day-care centers. The pattern that has emerged is one with a higher proportion of male workers in the CBD and relatively more female workers in the suburbs. (See Box 28-1.)

THE CHANGING REGIONAL PATTERN OF DEVELOPMENT

At the same time that urban populations are spreading outward toward the suburbs and moving to smaller cities, significant changes in the regional distribution of population and employment are occurring. In the 1970s the population of the South and West grew over five times faster than that of the Midwest and the Northeast. This was partly due to a rate of natural increase almost twice as high in the growing regions. In addition, the long trend of migration to the industrial areas of the manufacturing belt reversed itself, so that the Northeast and Midwest are now experiencing an outward flow of population.

The economy of most parts of the South and West, or **Sunbelt,** is developing rapidly, which is a major reason for the changing migration flows. This development has raised the incomes in the Sunbelt faster than incomes in the **Frostbelt,** so that these regions today are much closer to equality of income than they were a few decades ago. Figure 28-2 shows how dramatic this convergence has been. In 1929, per capita income in the Southeast was only 53 percent of the national average, but in the Midwest income was 137 percent of the average. By 1977, the gap had narrowed to a range of 86 percent to 111 percent. Today the gap is more between the two coasts and the central United States rather than the Midwest and the South.

The structure of the economy has also changed markedly in the last few decades, which helps to explain some of the population shifts that have occurred. Table 28-3 shows the pattern of employment change that took place between 1960 and 1990. Manufacturing employment has been declining as a percentage of all workers for many decades and is now only about 21 percent of the total. The growth areas in the work force are trade, government, and services, which together increased from 44.2 percent in 1960 to 58.0 percent in 1990. These growing fields

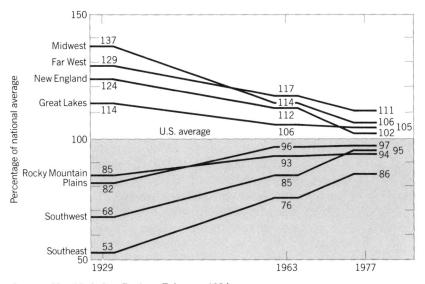

Source: Monthly Labor Review, February 1984.

F I G U R E **28-2** *Index of regional per capita disposable income (U.S. average =*
100)

TABLE 28-3   THE CHANGING STRUCTURE OF EMPLOYMENT, 1960–90

OCCUPATION	PERCENT OF TOTAL EMPLOYMENT		
	1960	1980	1990
Farm	11.5	3.9	3.2
Manufacturing	27.4	21.6	21.9
Durables	15.4	12.9	13.5
Nondurables	12.0	8.6	8.4
Mining	1.2	1.1	1.0
Construction	4.8	4.7	4.8
Trade	18.6	21.8	22.2
Government	13.6	17.0	16.0
Transportation, communication, and public utilities	6.5	5.5	5.2
Services	12.0	18.8	19.8
Finance, insurance, and real estate	4.3	5.5	5.9
Total (in thousands)	61,246	94,231	108,422

Source: U.S. Bureau of Labor Statistics and U.S. Bureau of Economic Analysis.

generally follow the growth pattern of population; that is, the growing cities of the Sunbelt create the demand for trade, government, and service employment. But manufacturing firms are for the most part not tied to local areas. They decide where to build a plant based on considerations of labor force skills, transportation advantages, and their needs for other resources. This makes many manufacturers more footloose in deciding where to locate. In recent years, they have voted heavily with their investment dollars for the Sunbelt and for areas in the Frostbelt outside the traditional manufacturing centers. Table 28-1 shows the pattern of population change by state. The Middle Atlantic and East North Central, which make up the manufacturing belt, continued to lose manufacturing jobs over this period. Manufacturing jobs were gained by Texas, California, Florida, and North Carolina. Although manufacturing is a very slow-growth sector for the country as a whole, it is growing rapidly in the Southeast and the Southwest.

The rapid growth of manufacturing outside the old manufacturing belt represents the reversal of a long trend toward industrial concentration that occurred during the Industrial Revolution. Much of this industry grew up in large urban concentrations whose growth paralleled that of the economy. Urbanization and industrialization were similarly linked in other developed nations. The major reason for these urban-industrial complexes was that related industries, such as fabricated metal, industrial machinery, and transportation equipment, were more efficient because they shared the same labor force skills and other resources, and because they could save together on transportation and communication costs. Wages, rents, taxes, and many other costs were higher in these industrial centers, but higher costs were offset by the higher productivity resulting from the interindustry linkages.

The long trend of population and employment concentration related to manufacturing seems to have come to an end in the United States and many other industrial nations. Countries that had inmigration to their industrial complexes from the beginning of economic development have recently seen a switch to outmigration toward less densely populated areas. Besides the United States these countries include France, Germany, Belgium, Denmark, and Holland. Newer industrial nations such as Japan and Sweden have seen their inmigration come to a halt, whereas countries that are in the early industrial stage such as South Korea and Taiwan are still experiencing inmigration to their industrial complexes.

One of the major forces behind the spreading out of manufacturing in the United States and elsewhere is industrial and economic maturity. Many industries pass through a **life cycle** in which their products are fully developed and standardized, so that they can be turned out in similar form year after year, using automated production processes. Automation means that low-skilled workers and automatic machinery can be used to replace the skilled workers and designers who were needed previously. This makes producers less dependent on the highly developed labor force and specialized firms in the large urban areas. They can reduce their cost of production by locating in smaller cities or rural areas where construction costs, wages, and taxes are lower. In addition, most industries today have a wider range of products, individual products are more complex, and more stages of processing are required. This complexity encourages large companies to build individual plants specializing in particular products, processes, or components. These plants are in cities or regions suited to their particular resource needs.

The relatively standardized production processes are moving out of the older industrial areas, but research and design, engineering, and management tend to remain behind. This division of labor is quite apparent in the field of electronics and related equipment. New product development and highly skilled production such as medical electronics and scientific equipment are concentrated in the Northeast and California; mass-produced components are more dispersed outside the manufacturing belt; and low-skill, labor-intensive parts such as circuit boards are made in low-wage, less-developed countries. The result of this process of dispersion is that manufacturing employment is growing the most slowly in large cities, faster in small cities, and faster still in nonmetropolitan areas.

The changing structure of large cities can be seen most dramatically

TABLE 28-4 EMPLOYMENT IN NEW YORK CITY IN THOUSANDS, 1960 AND 1981			
OCCUPATION	1960	1981	PERCENT CHANGE
Contract construction	124.1	78.9	−36.4
Manufacturing	997.0	486.4	−51.2
Transportation and public utilties	322.7	258.6	−19.9
Trade	762.9	609.0	−20.0
Finance, insurance, and real estate	389.6	460.2	18.1
Service	605.3	912.8	50.8
Government	404.0	503.5	24.6
Total	3607.3	3310.4	−8.2

Source: U.S. Bureau of the Census, *Employment and Earnings,* 1960 and 1981.

in New York, as Table 28-4 demonstrates. From 1960 to 1981, New York City lost about 8 percent of its employment base. But it lost over 50 percent of its manufacturing workers while gaining strongly in government, services, and FIRE (finance, insurance, and real estate). The manufacturing jobs lost were almost all for production workers, as opposed to management and clerical workers. New York remains an important center for business management, and it has increased its role in international trade and finance in the last 20 years. But it has lost its attractiveness as a production location and, consequently, about two-thirds of its production jobs since 1960.

Although the industrial centers of the North are losing manufacturing, the South and West are beginning to look more like the North as they achieve rapid growth in manufacturing, services, and government. There is much less difference in the employment makeup of the major regions today than there was a few decades ago. The question in the minds of many today is whether the Sunbelt is merely catching up with the more developed Frostbelt, or whether the Frostbelt will stagnate, with many of its cities dying and most of its industry fleeing to the Sunbelt. To a great extent the answer to this question depends on the process called reindustrialization.

REINDUSTRIAL-IZATION

In the most generally accepted definition, **reindustrialization** is the process of replacing "old" industries with "new" ones. The meaning of "old" is in the context of technology; when an industry like textiles has reached the stage of development in which the product can be produced with the same widely known process in just about any part of the world, it is an old industry. **Old industries** grow slowly or even shrink in size in the

United States because they face stiff competition from other countries with lower wages. New industries (or industries with technologically new products) do not worry about low-cost foreign competition if they produce a sophisticated product using highly skilled labor and "state-of-the-art" technology. Highly developed countries like the United States, France, and Germany have high wages, so they must rely on their special skills and technological resources to compete in the world economy.

Reindustrialization is the catchword for the process of industrial change that occurs as less developed countries provide more competition in old industries, forcing the United States to specialize more and more in the new industries. This process affects the various regions of the United States in different ways. The Mid-Atlantic and Midwest have a large proportion of the old industries—primarily steel, autos, and rubber. Part of the reason why these regions are growing so slowly in recent years is that their "industry mix" contains so many older industries. The Sunbelt, on the other hand, is growing both because it has "new" industries like electronics and computers and because old industries are building plants there too. The Southeast, for example, is receiving investments in both new industries and such old industries as furniture, textiles, and rubber.

The United States as a whole is reindustrializing, but will the old manufacturing belt be able to follow this path? Its future is clouded by doubt. On the positive side is the example of New England, the first region reindustrialized from declining textile and footwear industries to high-flying computers and instruments. Possibly the Mid-Atlantic and Midwest will follow New England's pattern. Also on the plus side is the fact that the Northeast is still the most important center of research, development, and corporate headquarters, from which new industries may arise. However, the shortcomings of these regions are quite serious in the view of many. They have one of the highest wage structures in the country, so that new industries have shown little interest in setting up shop there. Manufacturing also prefers the Sunbelt today because more land is available, compared with the crowded Northern cities, and because transportation and communication are better, and taxes are lower.

THE MEANING OF REINDUSTRIALIZATION IN A GLOBAL ECONOMY

Although reindustrialization is a serious domestic issue in most advanced economies, it is more properly viewed in a global context. The world, not just one country, is moving from primary employment in agriculture through industrial manufacturing to services. The same issues are important: cost of labor; availability, cost, and reliability of appropriate transportation; technology and worker skills; and the "liveability" of the

28-2
THE GLOBAL
WAY

In the 1970s and 1980s, airports became a dominant feature of intercity commerce. Regular, frequent, high-quality air service was seen as a major prerequisite for corporate locations. Consequently, the domestic hub cities tended to prosper at the expense of less well-served cities. Particularly in the 1980s as the major airlines set up multiple domestic hubs, second-tier cities prospered. For example, the Raleigh-Durham area of North Carolina received a major boost when American Airlines chose it as an eastern hub. As other similar-sized and otherwise comparable cities such as Austin, Texas or Madison, Wisconsin, sought to compete, the American hub gave Raleigh-Durham a major competitive advantage.

Will the domestic hub continue to be as important in the 1990s? Possibly, but with an increasingly global economy, the global gateway, giving easy access to international airline service, may be even more important. Particularly for major corporate headquarters, direct access to Tokyo, London, Paris, and Frankfurt is a very real competitive edge. Not surprisingly, international flights are increasing to smaller cities and are not limited to the big gateways such as New York, Chicago, Los Angeles, and Miami. Yes, even Raleigh-Durham has its direct flight to Paris.

urban area. However, now manufacturing doesn't just move from the Midwest to the Sunbelt. It moves to Japan and then on to South Korea, Thailand, Hong Kong, Singapore, and Taiwan. But not all manufacturing moves—only that part which finds a better industrial location for all the individual reasons discussed in Part 1.

Increasingly, real estate developers are finding tenants as well as financing in a global market. Global relocations have every bit as dramatic an effect on the local economy as domestic moves. However, they involve more complex decisions. Hence, they are often much harder to predict. Cultural differences between any Japanese city and Chicago are much greater than those between Chicago and New York. Cultural differences play a role in global relocation and in how the relocation affects both the receiving and losing urban area.

SUMMARY   Change is occuring at an increasing rate. Real estate changes form with the location, income level, needs, and habits of the people who use it. Concentrations of real estate development shift with the population. Demographics are, therefore, an important area of study for real estate decision makers planning for the future.

This chapter pointed to some of the most significant long-term trends, on a national level, affecting real estate. These trends may or may not continue for the next decade. The important thing to remember, however, is that change is always occurring. An analyst always looks for changes in the environment that will affect real estate both in the short term and the long term. The goal is to evaluate alternatives clearly and adopt logical strategies; this is where we focus our attention in Chapter 29.

IMPORTANT TERMS

BART	Manufacturing belt
CBD	Old industries
Dual-career age	Reindustrialization
Frostbelt	Suburbanization
Gentrification	Sunbelt
Life cycle (industry)	

REVIEW QUESTIONS

28.1   What effect did transportation have on the shape of cities before ownership of automobiles became widespread?

28.2   What government incentives encouraged growth of the suburbs?

28.3   Why is the automobile likely to retain its dominance for work trips for many more years?

28.4   What effects will the changes in the structure of the average household have on the type of housing demanded in the future?

28.5   In the structure of the U.S. economy, what type of employment is declining? What types are increasing?

28.6   What is reindustrialization? Give an example.

28.7   In what way might the strategy of the Northeast to gain jobs parallel the strategy of the United States, France, and Germany to remain competitive in the world economy?

28.8   What recent trend has developed in industrialized nations, including the United States, with regard to population migration and industrial employment? In the United States, whom does this trend affect?

28.9   How has household size changed in the last 30 years? What are some reasons for the change?

28.10   How has the increasing proportion of women in the work force affected the location of offices and plants outside the center cities?

*N*EW WAYS TO PLAY THE REAL ESTATE GAME

In this final section we have returned to the real estate fundamentals. Chapter 27 dealt with government as our continuing partner. In Chapter 28 we looked at long-term trends, remembering that the analyst begins with the history of the subject property, analyzes its current situation in terms of comparable properties in the same marketplace, and then uses past and present conditions to make a forecast, which is primarily a function of observed trends. In this chapter, we move from the Level One analysis in Chapter 28, that is, how have different properties been performing, to a Level Two analysis looking at how individual players are altering their strategies in the ever dynamic real estate game. Finally, in Appendix 29 we go a little beyond the traditional academic approach—out on a limb, in fact. We adjust the trends discussed in Chapter 28 and combine them in strange ways to try to provoke your thinking. We certainly aren't sure about every idea in Appendix 29. However, we *are* sure that in the future there will be players who win not simply by finding a good position for themselves at Level Two, but by creating new and socially useful products at Level One. We also suggest caution as you read Box 29-4. It deals with rules for living. While no one should tell another person how to live his or her life, Mr. Bidwell's rules are interesting.

As you read this chapter, we hope you will think about how each new player or new way of playing the game affects all aspects of the industry that we have discussed in preceding chapters. In an integrated world, no player's action is wholly independent of the actions and reactions of other players. Real estate is not a **zero sum game;** in some situations, however, one player's success may lead to another's failure. In addition, we hope that you will go beyond merely estimating the impact of new players to finding ways yourself to become a creative player in what we believe is the most exciting business on earth.

KEEPING UP WITH CHANGE: YOU CAN START WITH THE PUBLISHED SOURCES

How do you anticipate change? How do you prepare yourself for the future? Since real estate is a broad interdisciplinary subject, you can find many sources of information about recent changes. The successful players in the real estate game begin with the *Wall Street Journal, Forbes, Business Week,* and other business journals, including regional or state magazines. Many also read the great books, both nonfiction and fiction. Almost everyone moving into the 1990s has read *Megatrends, The Zero Sum Society,* and *In Search of Excellence.* But popular fiction is also worth reading because real estate serves one of society's basic needs—shelter—and all parts of the human condition are relevant to the real estate analyst.

Don't panic—everyone knows you can't read *everything.* That being the case, dozens of publishers produce summary information about new events in a host of fields that may interest you. In Table 29-1, we list major newsletters and related publications that can generate ideas for players in the industry. Packaging information for real estate players is a Level Two activity. A player has found that it is difficult for all the other players to keep up with changes, and that player is providing a useful service by summarizing the information. Look carefully at the list of newsletters in Table 29-1, and depending on your chosen field in the industry, pick the two, three, or four that best serve your needs.

CHANGES IN SPECIFICITY OF THE BASIC ANALYTICAL MODEL

One of the most exciting changes affecting all real estate players is the information explosion. It is being felt in the real estate industry in two ways. First, the computer has made it economically feasible to store and retrieve vastly greater amounts of information. For example, major investors today have all the key characteristics of the many leases of any particular property, like a shopping center, stored on disks and available for property management analysis or acquisition and divestiture decisions.

Second, satellites have also made new things possible. (If we can find a Russian rocket in hiding, surely the same technology can allow us to study growth patterns in cities in a more functional way.) Today high-altitude and satellite photography have come of age largely because of the computer. Information from high-altitude cameras is fed into computers, which can then print out fairly detailed maps. Since satellites pass over each point frequently, it is possible for us to see the growth of a city on a week-to-week basis. All of this can be tied to the new census data as indicated in Box 29-1.

TABLE 29-1   REAL ESTATE NEWSLETTERS AND NON ACADEMIC PERIODICALS

TITLE AND FREQUENCY	SOURCE
Asset Manager (quarterly)	Lincoln Graduate Center P.O. Box 12528 San Antonio, Tex. 78212
BOMA Experience and Exchange Report (annually)	Building Owners & Mangement Association 1201 New York Ave., N.W. Suite 300 Washington, D.C. 20005
Carolina Real Estate Journal (bimonthly). Most states and major cities have a similar listing of recent activity.	Shaw Publishing 128 S. Tryon St. Suite 2200 Charlotte, N.C. 28202
California Real Estate Indicators (quarterly)	University of California, Los Angeles Housing, Real Estate and Urban Studies Graduate School of Management 405 Hilgard Ave. Los Angeles, Calif. 90024
Coldwell Banker-Office and Industrial Vacancies (quarterly)	Coldwell Banker Real Estate Consultation Services 533 Fremont Ave. Los Angeles, Calif. 90071
Crittenden News Service, Inc.— Multiple Publications in Real Estate Financing	P.O. Box 1150 Novato, Calif. 94948
Emerging Trends in Real Estate (annually)	Real Estate Research Corporation 72 West Adams St. Chicago, Ill. 60603
Five Easy Ways to Keep Up-to-Date with the Latest State Legislative Developments	Mortgage Bankers Association of America 1125 15th St. N.W. Washington, D.C. 20005–2766
Freddie Mac Reports (monthly)	Freddie Mac 1768 Business Center P.O. Box 4195 Reston, Va. 22090–1716
General Manufacturing Business Climates (annually)	Alexander Grant and Company 1700 Prudential Plaza Chicago, Ill. 60601
Hotel Industry Insights (quarterly)	DRI 24 Hartwell Ave. Lexington, Mass. 02173 (617) 863–5100

TABLE 29-1 (CONTINUED)	
TITLE AND FREQUENCY	SOURCE
Industrial Real Estate Market Survey (semiannually)	Society of Industrial Realtors 777 Fourteenth St. N.W. Washington, D.C. 20005
Institutional Real Estate Letter (monthly)	Institutional Real Estate 160 Folsom St. Suite 203 San Francisco, Calif. 94105
International Property Report	International Real Estate Institute 8383 East Evans Scottsdale, Ariz. 85260
Investment Research Review (monthly) and *Monthly Performance Index*	Richard Ellis Research London
Investor Outlook (quarterly)	Grubb and Ellis Company Commercial Brokerage Group 440 MacArthur Blvd. Suite 740 Newport Beach, Calif. 92660
Japanese Investment in U.S. Real Estate Review (monthly)	Mead Ventures P.O. Box 44952 Phoenix, Ariz. 85064
Landauer Library Letter (monthly)	Landauer Associates 335 Madison Ave. New York, N.Y. 10017
Land Use Digest (monthly)	Urban Land Institute 1090 Vermont Ave. N.W. Washington, D.C. 20005
Land Use Law and Zoning Digest (monthly)	American Planning Association 1313 E. 60th St. Chicago, Ill, 60637
Land Use Planning Report (biweekly)	Business Publishers 951 Pershing Dr. Silver Spring, Md. 20910–4464
Local Economic Growth/Neighborhood Reinvestment Report (monthly)	C D Publications 100 Summit Building 8555 16th St. Silver Spring, Md. 20910–4464
Main Street Journal General Investment Conditions (monthly)	Claremont Economics Institute 143 N. Harvard Ave., Suite E Claremont, Calif. 91711

(Continued)

TABLE 29-1   (CONTINUED)

TITLE AND FREQUENCY	SOURCE
Market Profile (quarterly)	Baring Institutional Realty 335 Madison Ave. New York, N.Y. 10017–4683
The Mortgage and Real Estate Executive's Report (semimonthly)	Warren, Gorham, and Lamont 210 South St. Boston, Mass. 02111
National Mall Monitor (monthly)	Natonal Mall Monitor 2280 U.S. 19 N. Suite 264 Clearwater, Fla. 33575
National Trend of Business Economy/ Limited–Service Lodging Industry (monthly)	Laventhol and Horwath 1845 Walnut St. Philadelphia, Pa. 19103
National Thrift & Mortgage News (weekly)	212 West 35th St. New York, N.Y. 10001–2569
NCREIF Real Estate Performance Report (quarterly)	National Council of Real Estate Investment Fiduciary P.O. Box 1616 Tacoma, Wash. 98401 (206) 572–9500
News Release (monthly)	Federal National Mortgage Association 3900 Wisconsin Ave. N.W. Washington, D.C. 20016
News Release (monthly)	U.S. Department of HUD Office of Public Affairs Washington, D.C. 20410
Outlook for the Economy and Real Estate (monthly)	National Association of Realtors 777 Fourteenth St., N.W. Washington, D.C 20005
PCPS Reporter (monthly)	American Institute of CPAs 1211 Avenue of the Americas New York, N.Y. 10036
Perspectives (quarterly)	Institute of Real Estate Management 430 N. Michigan Ave. P.O. Box 109025 Chicago, Ill. 60610–9025
Publications Catalog (annually)	American Institute of Real Estate Appraisers 430 North Michigan Ave. Chicago, Ill. 60611–4088
Publications Update	World Bank Publications 1818 H St. N.W. Washington, D.C. 20433

TABLE 29-1 (CONTINUED)	
TITLE AND FREQUENCY	**SOURCE**
Quarterly Report (quarterly)	Center for Real Estate and Urban Economics University of California, Berkeley 2680 Bancroft Way, Suite A Berkeley, Calif. 94720
Questor Real Estate Letter (monthly)	Questor Associates 115 Sansome St. San Francisco, Calif. 94104
Real Estate Finance Today (monthly)	Mortgage Bankers Association of America 1125 Fifteenth St. N.W. Washington, D.C. 20005
Real Estate Index Liquidity Fund	Liquidity Fund and S&P 7th Floor 1900 Powell St. Emeryville, Calif. 94608
Real Estate Insight (monthly)	Laventhol and Horwath 919 Third Ave. New York, N.Y. 10022
Real Estate Law Report (monthly)	Warren, Gorham, and Lamont 1633 Broadway New York, N.Y. 10019
Real Estate Leasing Report (monthly)	Federal Research Press 65 Franklin St. Boston, Mass. 02110
Real Estate Market Review (quarterly)	Salomon Brothers Bond Market Research One New York Plaza New York, N.Y. 10004
Real Estate Newsline (monthly)	Laventhol and Company 2049 Century Park East Los Angeles, Calif. 90067
Real Estate Quarterly (quarterly)	National Association of Realtors Economics and Research Division 777 14th St. N.W. Washington, D.C. 20005
Recent Research Results (monthly)	HUD USER P.O. Box 280 Germantown, Md. 20874
REIS Reports (multiple dates)	REIS Reports 250 West 57th St. Suite 1701 New York, N.Y. 10107

(Continued)

TABLE 29-1   (CONTINUED)

TITLE AND FREQUENCY	SOURCE
REIT Report (quarterly)	National Association of Real Estate Investment Trusts 1129 Twentieth St. N.W. Suite 705 Washington, D.C. 20036 (202) 785–8717
1990 Research Catalog (annually)	Urban Land Institute 1090 Vermont Ave., N.W. Washington, D.C. 20005–4962
Resolution Trust Reporter (bimonthly)	Dorset Group 225 West 34th St. Suite 918 New York, N.Y. 10122
Secondary Mortgage Market Analyst (monthly)	Warren, Gorham, and Lamont 210 South St. Boston, Mass. 02111
SG Newsletter (quarterly)	Sonnenblick-Goldman Corporation 1251 Avenue of the Americas New York, N.Y. 10020
SREA Briefs (biweekly)	Society of Real Estate Appraisers 645 N. Michigan Ave. Chicago, Ill. 60611
Strategic Real Estate (monthly)	Laventhol and Company One Market Plaza Stewart Street Tower San Francisco, Calif. 94105
Survey of New Office Space (quarterly)	Cassidy and Pinkard 2000 K St. N.W. Suite 700 Washington, D.C. 20006
Urban and Housing Research Report (monthly)	C D Publications 8555 16 St. Silver Spring, Md. 20910
Urban Edge	World Bank Room S–10–021 Washington, D.C. 20433
Urban Innovation Abroad (monthly)	Council for International Urban Liaison 818 Eighteenth St. N.W. Washington, D.C. 20006

29-1

A TALE OF THE TIGER

For business users, no tiger burns more brightly in the forests of applied demography than a new creature now being released into the marketplace by the Census Bureau. It struggles under the name of Topologically Integrated Geographic Encoding and Referencing—which is why everyone just calls it the **Tiger File.**

The Tiger File amounts to an incredibly detailed map of the U.S. that precisely locates every political subdivision, every street and road (and tells what kind of road it is), every bridge and tunnel—with all the information expressed in digital form that can be stored and manipulated by computers.

This alone will save many companies enormous amounts of money. Using Tiger data and the appropriate software, fleet operators, for example, will be able to see instantly which routes are the fastest and/or most economical to take. Package-delivery outfits will be able to see which drivers are closest to a given pickup point. "The commercial uses of Tiger will outweigh all of the commercial value of census data itself," says the head of one private data-service company.

But that's only the beginning. By merging that 1990 census information into the Tiger File—in effect, putting the people where they belong on the map—other users stand to gain a tool of unparalleled power in the age of niche marketing.

Among other things, companies will be able to pinpoint the location of people whose demographic profile, as reflected in the census data, makes them likely customers. Upon precisely identifying areas rich in untapped prospects, businesses will be able to use a rifle instead of a shotgun in marketing products and services to them. They will also be able to pick the very best spots to open new stores, warehouses and distribution points. Before, customers wanting to combine census and geographic data first had to use printed census maps to put the information into digital form, a job that could consume months and hundreds of thousands of dollars for a single county. Now, with every county in the nation already in computer-ready form, and with prices at rock bottom, customers are flocking to buy the Tiger File even before the 1990 census is taken.

More than 300 concerns had bought such data by year end, and many more are expected. "People are buying like crazy," says Ramala Basu, a geographic specialist at the data-user services division of the Census Bureau.

The price for magnetic tape: $200 for the first county in a given state and only $25 per county beyond that. The bureau also is beginning to release Tiger on compact disks selling for $250; Ms. Basu says all the data from all states will fit on 40 to 45 of them.

Source: Wall Street Journal, Special Section—Census 90, March 9, 1990, p. R31.

THE BASIC
ANALYTICAL
MODEL
CONTINUES TO
EVOLVE TOWARD
A COMPLETE
GEOGRAPHIC
INFORMATION
SYSTEM

Today the data are available to do far more rigorous analysis than has ever been possible before. Evolving software packages such as the ARC INFO package sold by the ESRI Company in Redlands, California, allows Lotus-type analysis in a geographic format, that is, sensitivity analysis on a geographic basis. The hardware and software are available to process the new census and satellite data in new ways. All of this can be integrated with satellite mapping. It is all technically possible, and yet today it is not cost efficient to put all these components together in a complete geographic information system for real estate decision makers. However, more data are becoming available, the software is getting better, the hardware is getting faster and cheaper, and we are all becoming smarter about how to integrate the three. In the next decade the complete GIS (**Geographic Information System**) will become a reality.

Two interesting Level Two activities are involved here. First, someone must package the existing information sources, the software, and the hardware to produce the cost-efficient user friendly information system that decision makers need. Second, someone must figure out how to make better decisions—not old decisions faster—but new decisions with this new technology. Ideally, these decisions should eventually produce better space over time with associated services.

THERE ARE
ALWAYS
OPPORTUNITIES
ON THE
MARKETING
FRONT

In the third edition of this book, we mentioned several new marketing concepts that provided new Level Two opportunities. As we suggested then, changing demographics provided new opportunities to market new types of space to single-parent and single-person households. We talked about the continued segmentation in the hotel industry, with the larger chains capturing an ever greater market share in an ever increasing number of segments. We also talked about the real estate auction and its ability in certain circumstances to market properties in a more cost-efficient manner.

In the 1990s, what will be the great new marketing opportunity? We believe it may well come in the **tenant representation** area. As noted in Chapters 9 and 10, brokerage has served the new real estate industry well for decades. Traditionally, the broker has acted as agent for the seller. In today's overbuilt markets, the opportunities for the smart buyer are tremendous, but of course that means the smart buyer, not the average buyer. As buyers recognize this, they are increasingly hiring their own agents to ferret out the best opportunities, compare the different bells and whistles of different leasing opportunities, and negotiate the best possible deal. Without a doubt, the real estate game is becoming more sophisticated, and it is only natural that both sides should hire high-level marketing talent.

EVEN THE TRADITION-BOUND APPRAISAL FRATERNITY IS INNOVATING RAPIDLY

As we pointed out in Part 3, the appraisal profession has a long history and a significant literature. Over the last 10 years, however, it has received considerable criticism as banks have experienced problem loans and as investors have found the values on their highly leveraged syndications to be less than expected. Although we do not believe that appraisers were the primary culprit in most of these instances, we are pleased to see the innovations.

One set of innovations is being pushed by government agencies. In their role of regulating financial institutions and facilitating the secondary mortgage market, Fannie Mae, Ginnie Mae, and Freddie Mac have tremendous impact on appraisal standards. **Rule 41-b** (originally from the Federal Home Loan Bank Board) is continuing to have a major effect on the appraisal business. Briefly stated, this relatively new rule requires disclosure of more related transactions (comparable sales or leases), reporting a cash or cash-equivalent price, and, most importantly, an estimate by the appraiser of the market's ability to absorb new products. This final requirement is a clear sign that regulators want appraisers to state firmly their estimate of the highest and best use of the subject property. This new rule is pushing appraisers to provide more market analysis, resulting in a better product, and that is a good thing for society.

On the technical side, innovations are coming from both the profession and the university. Mike Robbins, at Denver University, has adapted a traditional agricultural appraisal technique to income property valuation. His variant on the market comparison approach calls for a computerized, two-pass, iterative approach to the appraisal problem. This version of regression analysis rationalizes the multiple components of value in the comparable sales. Although this technique will not be used in every appraisal, it is a brand-new tool for use in more complex appraisal assignments. What it signifies to us is that modern statistical methods and the computer have come of age in the appraisal business. Over the next few years, new thinkers in the appraisal field will make major strides in what has been for decades a tradition-bound industry.

The appraisal fraternity should finally see a merger of its two professional organizations: the American Institute of Real Estate Appraisers and the Society of Real Estate Appraisers. The merger should enhance the profession's ability to provide new guidance in both professional standards and education. These two groups and a host of other appraisal organizations have already joined together to produce a standard commercial appraisal form. Jeff Fisher at Indiana University has been a leader in the effort to bring the kind of standardization to the commercial appraisal product that we have enjoyed for a considerable period of time on the residential side.

With regard to Level Two of the game, we believe there will be a new split in the appraisal profession. Some players will become more efficient at providing the standard product (i.e., an efficiently priced, higher quality version of the standard product). At the same time, other players will deal with unique situations and charge the appropriate premium for an opinion of value in these unusual, hence more difficult, areas.

ON THE FINANCING FRONT, INNOVATIONS ARE COMING ALMOST TOO RAPIDLY

The Reagan administration, in its push for deregulation, opened up many new opportunities in the financial markets. We have alluded to these new opportunities in several of the preceding chapters. As an example of how far deregulation has gone, the Federal Housing Administration stated its intention of eliminating its building standards for single-family and two-family homes. Remember that the FHA originally initiated national standards for home building with the advent of mortgage insurance following the Great Depression. It is a far cry from the National Housing Act of 1934 when the federal government in 1990 says that the market simply no longer needs this type of regulation. Building standards is an area where the federal government has had a tremendous positive impact; if the federal government can now leave the private sector in charge, it will be a major public sector accomplishment.

On the mortgage banking side, together the computer and deregulation have truly changed the industry. Not only is the computer now used to link up by satellite communications various market participants, but it also handles most aspects of mortgage loan origination and processing. The secondary market participants will now accept the transfer of mortgage information involved in secondary market sales by computer disks. From the home buyer-borrower perspective, you can now dial 1–800–CALLPRU and get the latest long-term loan quotes from Prudential Insurance. If you like what you hear, a Prudential operator will take your name and send you a loan application in the mail. Using a local contact point, Prudential can process a loan application faster than your neighborhood savings and loan.

If you combine the regulatory freedom and the technological innovations with the awareness that traditional sources of financing are drying up, you will see all sorts of opportunities in the 1990s and beyond for innovative Level Two players. Clearly, the savings and loans will not be able to provide the same level of financing that they have in the past. Moreover, with the continued problems in commercial banks during 1990, we would expect to see some diminution of that supply as well. Just as government and then the private sector found a way to finance the U.S. single-family home from a broad pool of savings in the general economy through the secondary market innovations of the 1970s and 1980s, new players will find a way to finance not just the residential property, but commercial properties as well, from an expanding global pool of funds. Abroad, someone will find a way to move capital more efficiently from capital-heavy countries to countries with interesting prospects and less capital but some terrific real estate collateral.

GOVERNMENT-INDUCED LEVEL ONE CHANGES CREATE A NUMBER OF LEVEL TWO OPPORTUNITIES

Government's role in real estate (Chapter 27) sets up opportunities for the innovative real estate player. Furthermore, changes in the income tax laws also create opportunities; just as the deep shelter in the 1981 tax act created the real estate syndicator, 1986 changes took away the impetus to form syndicates. Tax changes in the future would be expected to have their own impact on opportunities.

A rather unexplored government area, and yet one that is known to have a tremendous impact on the economy, is that of **infrastructure.** Federal, state, regional, and local governments provide the infrastructure necessary for our economy, and yet there is no complete and accurate accounting for either the quality of service or the condition of the existing infrastructure. We all worry about the ancient sewers in New York; and yet it is Los Angeles, the newer city, that has possibly an even greater problem with crown erosion in the sewers. In the 1990s, someone—maybe an investment banker, maybe a great engineer—will find a way to help society better understand both the benefits of quality infrastructure in terms of the productivity of our society and how to finance the costs. The amount of money is overwhelming, the societal need is great, and the player who finds a way to deal rigorously with the issue certainly shouldn't end up poor.

Without a doubt, the most exciting Level Two opportunity provided by government comes from the **Resolution Trust Corporation.** As we pointed out in Chapter 13, Resolution Trust has an incredibly large portfolio and an almost impossible mission. It must find a way to sell this portfolio without further damaging the local real estate markets. This will require considerable effort and expertise.

From a Level Two perspective, the government traditionally has preferred to use private sector workout specialists, but will now likely do some of the **workouts** itself. What is a competent workout? One that takes an existing, broken real estate concept and produces something in terms of space over time with certain services that the market values. It does all that at a low enough cost that the difference between the final value and the total cost is either positive or as small as possible. The workout industry today is very small in this country, and we see more new jobs here than in any other sector except possibly corporate real estate.

What does it take to do the job? All the real estate fundamentals are required. The interdisciplinary generalist is needed because the workout specialist must deal with construction, financing, marketing—all aspects of real estate. The person must also be tough because the negotiations on a broken property are typically more acrimonious than in other real estate situations. Without doubt, many of the readers of this book, entering the real estate job market in the 1990s, will find opportunities in workouts.

OTHER LEVEL TWO OPPORTUNITIES

CORPORATE REAL ESTATE

As we noted in Chapter 12, corporate America owns the majority of the nation's commercial real estate. Moreover, real estate comprises a major chunk of the typical corporate balance sheet. In the increasingly competitive global economy, CEOs are finding that more active management of their real estate is a very appropriate way to achieve corporate goals. This is the Level One change, and it creates at Level Two a need for more skilled and more entrepreneurial corporate real estate managers. (Refer back to Box 12-6.)

INSTITUTIONAL INVESTMENT

In the first half of Chapter 12, we talked about institutional investors and gave them additional detailed coverage in Chapters 22 and 23. Here we simply remind you that all the new activities at Level One require talent, and that talent has its own set of goals at Level Two. On the investment banking side, what will be the hot new product as we approach the year 2000? Will investment bankers take nonrecourse financing to a reunified Germany and allow Western-style developers to move into Eastern Europe? Or will the real action be in gathering ethnic Chinese savings from the Pacific Rim and reinvesting them in a slowly liberalizing mainland China? The investment banker of the 1980s was the quick-footed leader, and only the one who finds something that is both new and important in the 1990s can command the salary that the investment banker seeks.

Also on the institutional side is the money manager who takes a longer-term view but has very clear Level Two considerations. Thinking back over the preceding material, do you believe that the open-end or the closed-end pension fund account will win? Or will it be some new kind of investment manager, who facilitates direct investments by the pension funds in concern with corporate America? We don't know for sure, but we're sure that at least some of you will make the right call in this area.

URBAN GLOBAL COMPETITIVENESS AND THE ACTIVE LIFE

In considering all the many ingredients that go into making an urban area competitive in the global economy, we should not forget the individual **life-styles** of its leading citizens. Particularly in Western countries, physical fitness and outdoor activities are prized. These activities are not inexpensive in any urban area but are increasingly difficult in certain of the world's leading cities.

For example, Hong Kong reputedly has the second highest retail rents in the world along Nathan Street. For those who tire of Hong Kong's leading sport ("shop till you drop"), golf and tennis are available at the Clearwater Bay Golf and Country Club, which is only 45 minutes from your hotel each way, assuming you encounter no undue traffic problems. With greens fees and cart, golf costs a mere $75 a round. This may seem a bit long and a bit stiff to someone who has enjoyed the nearer and less expensive country clubs of Mobile, Alabama, and yet it is relatively modest compared to what is reputedly the highest retail rent city in the world (Ginza Street in Tokyo). From downtown Tokyo, golf is well over an hour away, and no one plays for anywhere close to $75 per person.

So where is New York? It is certainly closing in on Hong Kong both in terms of rents (for example, Trump Tower on Fifth Avenue), time to the quality golf courses, and price. At some point, the availability of golf (as well as tennis and other popular sports) will have an impact on where the most productive people want to live. Those most productive people in turn will have a major impact on how competitive an urban area is in the global economy.

The active life is just one small aspect of how globalization impacts urban affairs abroad and urban development domestically (see Box 29-2).

GLOBAL TRADING BLOCS AND WHAT DETERMINES COMPETITIVE-NESS

We see three major trading blocs by the year 2000: first, the European Community achieving 1992 unification despite new challenges with the reunited Germany. This trading group has its own culture and will naturally draw on a consumer and worker group from the recently liberalized Eastern European countries.

Second, the **Pacific Rim** will be a similar-sized trading group if mainland China does not open. The **European Community** has about 300 million people, and there are another 100 million in Eastern Europe. In the Pacific Rim Japan has around 100 million plus the tigers, Korea, Taiwan, Singapore, and Hong Kong. Each of these is a very different culture, and yet they share a location and to some extent a heritage. They will draw on Thailand, the Philippines, Indonesia, and Malaysia for additional consumers and workers.

The third trading group is the Americas, led by the United States with 250 million people, with consumers and workers coming from Mexico and South America and resources from Canada.

When you think about it, all three trading groups have some common heritage, are in a similar locale, have a leading country, have their own set of resources, and have their own to-be-industrialized countries.

Of course, anybody could draw their own three, five, or seven trading groups, and there are clear differences among the different countries. In the American trading group, several nationalities will remember

29-2
JAPANESE TRY
NEW TACK ON
U.S. LAND

TOKYO—A couple of years ago, Japanese investors in U.S. real estate went for big-city plums and wouldn't even talk about Florida. Now, they're showing increasing sophistication in shopping for bargains in smaller cities and suburbs.

"There are a quadzillion and one other investments outside major cities," says Paul Shang, managing director at Shearson Lehman Hutton Finance (Japan) Inc.

The shift makes good business sense: Prices in urban centers such as Manhattan and Los Angeles have risen so high that returns can be better elsewhere. Moreover, Japanese corporations are active in all kinds of development projects, which offer bigger potential payoffs than does buying a finished building.

Good Politics

The new pattern also happens to be good politics. Every time a Japanese investor has bought a prominent U.S. hotel or skyscraper, resentment has flared. Japanese investors are increasingly worried that U.S. anger at their shopping spree could boil over and lead to controls on foreign investment.

"A joint venture isn't a disguise, it's just smart," says Henry Cornell, vice president and manager of the real-estate department at Goldman Sachs (Japan) Corp. Still, he adds, "You'd rather have a quiet affair than one where everybody on the block knows about it."

A sample of the last few months' activity shows the range of Japanese investor interest: the New Jersey-based subsidiary of Kajima Corp. bought 445 hectares (one hectare equals 10,000 square meters or 2.741 acres) of industrial land in Cincinnati, Chicago, Memphis and Atlanta; a Tokyo-based kimono maker bought an Orange County, California, resort for $105 million; a small importer planned a $30 million warehouse near Long Beach, California; a partnership of Japanese companies and an Arizona developer bought a 69-hectare golf course in suburban Phoenix; and a leading trading company entered the housing market with the purchase of eight Beverly Hills condominiums for $2 million to $3 million apiece.

Japanese date the start of their most recent investment boom in the U.S. to 1986 when Mitsui Real Estate Development Co.'s New York subsidiary bought the Exxon building in Manhattan for $610 million. Driven abroad by the strong yen and high prices at home, major investors were conservative, but high profile.

They bought such landmark buildings, often at record prices, to establish themselves as serious players in the local market while gaining stable long-term assets.

In the three years since then, a lot has happened. Many analysts agree that the pace of growth slowed in 1989 after new investment in 1988 increased about 30% over new investment in 1987. But estimates of the size of Japanese real-estate holdings in the U.S. vary widely. Analysts put the total as of the end of 1988 anywhere from $10 billion to more than $40 billion.

The latest Japanese to enter the U.S. real-estate market are wealthy small-company owners like Shoji Yokokura, president of Matsubara Construction Co., who sent his eldest son to Los Angeles to establish a U.S. subsidiary of his real-estate development company. The son, Shoyi Yokokura, says, "From the start we borrowed money in dollars from local banks. We use our profits to expand our U.S. company. We do business as Americans."

New Shopping Habits

Such private business owners accounted for about 25% of Japanese overseas real-estate purchases last year, according to Satoshi Yasugi, general manager of corporate services planning at Nomura Securities Co. While about 30 new companies a year have invested in overseas real estate recently, he expects that rate will rise to about 200 companies a year.

Even rich individuals are changing their shopping habits. They still invest overseas because prices at home are prohibitive. But they have moved from picking vacation condominiums in Hawaii to buying shares in real-estate syndications.

"The purpose in such purchases is different from buying a holiday retreat," says Ryoichi Komori, deputy general manager for overseas projects at Haseko Corp., one of the biggest Japanese developers in the U.S. "A lot of individuals in high tax brackets go for syndications. They borrow money and write off the interest charge."

The expanding interest in smaller-scale projects has generated an explosion of new U.S. and Japanese real-estate middlemen. Companies that were never involved in real estate have started divisions to sell to the Japanese. Nomura, for instance, began five months ago to offer important clients free overseas real-estate advice. So far, Nomura has introduced about 70 properties to 100 potential buyers.

GATX Corp. of Chicago, best known for leasing transportation equipment and capital goods, is another example. Three years ago it set aside a corner of its Tokyo office and started trying to put together real-estate transactions for Japanese investors.

Investing in "Second Cities"

At first, it had to struggle simply to get its name in the local papers. Now, says GATX real-estate consultant Kenneth Curtis, Japanese investors are "not just working with Morgan Stanley or Goldman Sachs on the financing of a new office building or refinancing a midtown New York building, which is pretty conservative. Japanese companies now have sufficient understanding to come around to doing our kind of business."

Such business is typical of the current trend toward entering partnerships and investing in so-called second cities. In October 1988, GATX and Japan Leasing USA Inc. financed a $60 million loan to a Chicago-based company to buy shopping centers across the U.S. for leasing, refinancing or reselling. Last June, GATX brought three Japanese companies into a $72.5 million limited partnership to buy retirement communities in San Diego, Indianapolis and Wilmington, Delaware. "You find your niches," says Mr. Curtis.

Japanese are fond of pointing out that they don't go searching for properties to buy, the sellers come to them. Japanese newspapers still regularly feature advertisements selling U.S. condominiums. Real-estate companies with U.S. offices say they receive several approaches from sellers every day. "Not just real-estate brokers, but security companies and merchant bankers are coming to sell the world's real estate to Japan," says an executive at a leading Japanese real-estate company.

"Where Do We Go Next?"

Many Japanese developers and small companies are opening more U.S. offices as well, as a prelude to buying in new areas. Haseko, for example, has five subsidiaries there and aims to set up in 15 states in the future. This year it added Atlanta and San Diego. "Now the question is where do we go next," say Haseko's Mr. Komori. "Washington, D.C.? Seattle?"

But next for some Japanese investors isn't in America at all. Real-estate analysts say the more sophisticated Japanese investor is comparing fluctuating lease rates in New York to London's fixed rates to those in a hot market like Sydney. Adds Nomura's Mr. Yasugi, "Compared with the U.S., London and Paris are more generous and less emotional."

No one expects Japanese investment in the U.S. to cease, but many analysts expect it to slow down as investors get to know other regions better. Already, it looks like Europe faces a repeat of the buying pattern experienced in the U.S. In November, for example, Nippon Life Insurance Co. announced plans to buy a one-third stake in the Forum des Halles shopping complex in the heart of Paris and privately-held syrup-maker Kato Kagaku Co. has been negotiating to buy the home office of British Broadcasting Corp.

Source: Elisabeth Rubinstein, "Japanese Try New Tack on U.S. Land: Investors Increasingly Look Outside Big Cities for Real-Estate Bargains," *The Asian Wall Street Journal*, Vol. XIV, No. 93, Friday, January 12–January 13, 1990, p. 1)

for a long time the U.S. invasion of Panama. Likewise in the Asian group, some people will never forgive Singapore's raiding of Hong Kong for skilled workers in what is clearly an exploitation of Tiananmen Square's impact on Hong Kong's prospects in 1997. However, the real issue is not how you define the trading groups, whether the populations are truly comparable, or whether the resource endowments are appropriate for the year 2000. The real key is figuring out which of the trading groups will be the winners and which will be the losers.

Take two countries in the Pacific and American groups as an example. Thailand is everybody's bet as the next industrialized nation. It is a country of nearly 60 million people with tremendous agricultural productivity. In the American group, it would be comparable in size to

Mexico, or, in agricultural productivity, to Argentina. Why are the Thais driving new cars and motorcycles, all imported, with huge duties, from Japan when the Mexicans and Argentines are living with older vehicles in a continually decaying infrastructure? In Thailand there is construction everywhere; in Argentina there is rampant inflation. Why?

A variety of different explanations have been suggested. One is that 15 years ago Thailand got a handle on population control. Their ability to control family size freed a tremendous energy in the Thai people, so that less time was required at home and more time could be devoted to the community. Of course, there are obvious problems when both spouses are committed to the work force. Still, this is a major advantage over South America where both popular culture and religion still suggest large families, which puts a drain on both the time and savings of the parents.

Another difference in the two situations is how the laws work. Some people have suggested that in South America the law exists to maintain the interest of the propertied group. In other words, the rules are flexible, but they are definitely there to protect the haves against the have nots. Those who have done business on the Mexican border can appreciate the situation.

In Thailand, on the other hand, there appear to be fewer laws, and what laws there are do not protect the entrenched establishment to the same extent as in Mexico. Obviously, the rules in almost any society protect those in the society today, yet in some societies it is easier to move up than in others. In South America the rules may be more constraining.

Once you figure out which countries are going to win and on what basis, you should think about how those successes or failures will impact U.S. metropolitan areas. Different U.S. cities are related in different ways around the globe, so international wins and losses will be recorded at the local level. This is the essence of "Think Globally, Act Locally."

SUMMARY

How do we summarize a host of trends that are expected to provide opportunities to the real estate professional in the future? As we pondered this question, we came on a very wise gentleman in San Francisco, and rather than attempt this summary ourselves, we suggest you look at Mr. Bidwell's suggestions in Box 29-3.

IMPORTANT TERMS

European Economic Community	Resolution Trust Corporation
GIS	Tenant representation
Infrastructure	Tiger File
Life-styles	Workouts
Pacific Rim	Zero sum game

29-3 BIDWELL'S SEMI-IMPORTANT RULES FOR LIVING

If you believe everything you hear about the future is (1) important and (2) about to happen, then you may qualify as the world's most gullible person. Even the professors writing this text don't agree with all the suggestions in this chapter (particularly Appendix 29). We are here to help you think. What follows is a demonstration of how one man has turned this foundation into rules for living with the future. We list these quickly because quite clearly you must adopt them (or not) for yourself based on updated facts, reinterpreted trends, and anticipated reactions to these trends.

- *Rule 1: Only do business with people who are pleasant.* In fact, as you get older, add to that, only people who are fun. After all, people will be the critical resource, and you don't want any unnecessary negatives.

- *Rule 2: Don't get locked in unless you want to be a musician or mathmetician.* If you want to be something else, you can wait until you are over 35. Continued learning is facilitated by a broad educational background.

- *Rule 3: You should measure personal success by a self-defined quality of life.* Otherwise, you will be the victim of the reactionalization process and end up in the wrong neighborhood. More importantly, you'll end up a wimp, which leads to Rule 4.

- *Rule 4: Your self-worth should be measured by what you can give away.* With the breakdown of the traditional political system and a general increase in confusion, it is incumbent upon anyone who wants to have a meaningful life to contribute something to at least the neighborhood in which they live.

- *Rule 5: Education must get better.* You're the first generation of high school graduates to have a poorer education than your parents. Continuing education is a must. With the graduate degree, you're only an average player, and the half life of information is short.

- *Rule 6: Educationally in the future we shouldn't chop things into little boxes.* Breakthroughs come at the interfaces. Your continuing education shouldn't be all in the same field. Real estate is an interdisciplinary field, and the successful player needs an understanding of all the aspects— sociological, psychological, architectural, and historical—as well as business and political.

- *Rule 7: Don't trust economists.* In an information society, you can give it away and still have it. That fact doesn't function well in the old models.

- *Rule 8: Think globally, act locally.* Watch Washington for destabilizing activities but make it happen in your own world, which is probably the neighborhood or the city.

- *Rule 9: It should be wisdom, not information, that we seek.* There's an awful lot of information around but what wins is wisdom. There are already more newsletters in the real estate area than anyone could read on a regular basis. Beyond that, between the telephone and the PC, an incredible array of facts is at your disposal. The trick is developing the conceptual framework that allows you to process this sea of information.

- *Rule 10: Always fully segment your markets.* Don't get trapped into measuring the MSA when you're dealing with a world of neighborhoods. Remember that we all live not in one neighborhood, but in a series of neighborhoods. One is for our work environment, another for our social environment, and possibly many more, depending on the facets of our personality. When you're building space, you're satisfying the needs of people who themselves function in a series of probably overlapping neighborhoods. Going to the census tract is an easy first pass but a possibly misleading one.

- *Rule 11: Overall, expect continued growth in the United States.* It is one of the few countries both developed enough to be comfortable and open enough economically to provide opportunity. Therefore, the best and brightest (and their money) will continue to come. California will remain the harbinger of change. Entrepreneurial immigrant peasants plus a brain-drain toward America will make the United States a very exciting place.

- *Rule 12: Remember that only change is constant, and this will continue to force a search for spiritual certainty, which will in turn have an impact on other aspects of our life-styles.* With people, not capital, the critical resource, this search for meaning will become ever more important to development trends.

- *Rule 13: Don't fool yourself into believing that MBA thinking (adjusting available data) is real thinking.* Even the new accounting rules require more rigor, and the appraisal rules still ignore most of the big issues that we've discussed here. If you're a little right on the future, it can make up for a lot of smaller mistakes. No amount of getting it right in the present time can make up for a major miss on future trends.

- *In the future you need partners—not suppliers, not customers, not acquisition targets—partners.* And these partnerships should not be based on long legal agreements but on reciprocally fair deals oriented toward mutual interest and maintained in an atmosphere of good will (bad news for lawyers).

REVIEW QUESTIONS

29.1   Why is real estate not a zero sum game?

29.2   What is a "complete GIS"?

29.3   Why is tenant representation a growth area?

29.4   What new unions and divisions are occurring in the appraisal fraternity?

29.5   How will deregulation continue to foster change in real estate finance?

29.6   Who will do workouts for the RTC?

29.7   What investment vehicle is most appropriate for institutional investors in the 1990s?

29.8   Are the differences in life-styles across the United States increasing?

29.9   How will Japanese real estate investment strategies change in the 1990s?

29.10 Which is the most powerful global trading block?

APPENDIX 29

$\mathcal{L}$OOKING TO THE FUTURE FOR YOUR FUTURE

INTRODUCTION

Value is created by responding to society's future needs. Regardless of how well we analyze the past, regardless of how well we document the present, appreciation of the *future* and some understanding of it are what count in the real estate business. That understanding is necessary, first, because stages one through eight of our development model take a long time to unfold, and the developer must be able to anticipate the needs of space users far in the future. Second, because real estate is relatively expensive and long-lived, the product will provide space with services for a long time. Tenants will pay for the space if it continues to satisfy their evolving needs. By the time you read this appendix, its contents will already be partially obsolete. However, the point is to stimulate you to think for yourself about the future and the development industry.

The approach is really quite simple. The aspiring real estate player should, first, be aware of market facts. For example, the U.S. Bureau of the Census reports how many people were born each year, and it continuously estimates the size of future population age groups (cohorts). This information is nearly free, and it would be foolish to ignore easily accessible facts.

Second, a player should be able to anticipate probable trends, for example to have seen Houston's collapse coming in the early, not middle, 1980s. Certainly real estate developers and professionals should be better able to grasp the big picture in urban development than the average accountant. Trends projected econometrically, such as worldwide increases in oil consumption, never continue indefinitely. In other words, lines don't continue up forever; the "straight-edge" projection is a dangerous thing. In fact, history teaches that actions usually engender reactions and that growth is cyclical, not linear. Reactions to such trends are usually easier to predict than the commencement of the trend itself. Remember, knowing *when* something will occur is as important as knowing what will occur. The good development idea that comes before its time usually benefits the *second* owner. Once the certain market facts and probable trends are analyzed, reactions to these trends may be anticipated (smaller cars, more energy-efficient buildings, etc).

MARKET FACTS ❑ **INTRODUCTION TO THE FIRST STEP.** Remember that you need to update the facts to your point in time and location as a basis for taking the second step—identifying probable trends and then anticipating reactions that will generate new trends.

The market facts are individually quite straightforward. It is estimating the combined impact of them all that taxes the imagination. As you consider the first set of items that follows, remember, this is the clearest part of the forecast: the things that *have to happen* (1990s teenagers) because of other things that *have already happened* (late 1970s births).

1. *The Rio Grande Syndrome.* According to the United Nations, the world will have twice as many people in 50 years as it does today. More important, however, the projected population growth does not correlate well with projected economic growth, that is, the poor, not the rich, are having most of the babies. On the U.S. border, Mexico continues to experience political and economic turmoil. In 50 years there may well be as many Mexicans as Americans, and the boundary between the two countries is both extensive and shallow. We can no doubt expect continuing immigration from the South—legal and illegal.

2. *Changes in Ethnic Concentrations.* Many recent U.S. population changes have been a function of domestic and international migration. Fertility is below the replacement rate for American whites, so net growth derives from immigrant and non-Caucasian populations. Ports of entry to the United States have shifted from New York, Boston, and Chicago to Miami, Houston, Los Angeles, and San Francisco. Los Angeles County alone added over a million Asian and Hispanic immigrants between 1975 and 1985. In the 1960s, the western United States grew from domestic migration; in the 1980s, it grew from nondomestic migration.

3. *Changes in Population Age Concentration.* The baby bust is due to come of age in the year 2000 when there will be roughly 10 million fewer people age 20 to 35, but lots of young-old, middle-old, and old-old populating our cities. The young-old travel and the old-old huddle. What do the middle-old want? Note that this distinction is not accurately captured by age but more by health. These three groups clearly want different types of constructed space, but how large is each group and how deep is each income level?

4. *The New Internationalization of Labor.* Government import restrictions, high transportation costs, currency instability, and terrorism are all reality, but they have not stopped the new internationalization of labor. Employment opportunities are increasingly generated by a world, rather than national, economy. In such an environment, jobs not only come, but jobs go, based on comparative advantage around the world. Thus, at one point jobs in steel and the automobile industries in the United States were some of the best in the world labor market. Those jobs moved to Japan and then to Korea. Some have now returned to America—but under foreign management. The current Japanese situation is proof that the internationalization of labor is not just an American phenomenon. Even Japan's trade restrictions have not stopped the job flow from Japan into developing Asian countries. Will Korea eventually suffer the same fate that America faced in the 1970s and Japan faces today? What will that mean in terms of the types of industrial space needed in each country in the year 2000?

5. *Distinct National Economies Will Still Exist in a World Economy.* With all this talk of internationalization and the world economy now "driving" most domestic economies, it is important to remember that there is a clear limit on the amount or percentage of gross national spending that can logically be expected to be nondomestic. Furthermore, there will be a "reaction" to the quantity and quality of international influences on local life-styles.

    Today, 12 to 14 percent of GNP in the United States is nondomestic. The upside is probably around 20 percent owing to supply constraints (foreigners already build products here), protectionism, and technology. (VCRs, but not the dentist, are easy to import.)

6. *Smaller Is in.* From 1980 to 1988, the Fortune 500 cut 2 million jobs, while total U.S. employment hit record levels. What does this mean in terms of the need for constructed space?

    Small companies probably want less prestigious spaces and smaller spaces, a point that David Birch at MIT has made for several years. Huge floors (i.e., very large building footprints) that add to the efficiency of office buildings don't speak to this new need, and the cost is substantial to convert newly constructed "efficient" space to a format that is in higher demand.[1]

---

[1] *"Small business" describes a stable category only when the firms are stagnant. And many stagnant small businesses do exist. They usually earn negative economic profits and rent marginal space. The rest are very unstable and are better described by age than by size. New companies, which, like infants, start small, grow for a time. Most fail, some survive and stabilize at modest size, and others, about one in seven, are the growth companies tracked by INC Magazine. Variable sales translate into lower credit ratings. Thus, not only smaller industrial spaces but also flexible spaces are in demand. How will industrial and flex office developers respond to less creditworthy tenants wanting smaller, flexible configurations of space, shorter term leases, and lower rents?*

7. *There Are Other Trends That Mathematically Can't Continue.* In industrialized societies and especially in the United States, there has been a rapid *growth* in female work force participation rates, resulting, we might add, in the growing number of twice unfulfilled women (women employed at less lucrative and less emotionally rewarding jobs that take enough time to make it hard for them to be happy wives and mothers). Here, as in internationalization, there is probably a limit, both in terms of the number of women available and the percentage of those who desire full-time work force participation.

8. *Overall Job Growth Does Not Necessarily Mean There Are More Desirable Jobs.* Quality of job growth will be an important issue. There are many jobs that provide little money, less respect, and few challenges. It's not as much fun running the register at Burger King when you are 30 as it was at 16.

   Note that the urban job has moved toward information processing and services (interestingly, the term "services" includes everything from trash collection to brain surgery), leaving the less educated urban poor out of a job. In fact, some would suggest today's cities encompass three economies: the traditional economy that we study in school; the welfare economy that we hear about on the 6:30 news; and the underground economy that some of you probably have participated in. Reported unemployment in urban areas pertains only to the first, so many of the numbers you hear do not accurately describe the purchasing power of urban dwellers. Still, unemployment in this first traditional economy among urban northeastern blacks without a high school degree went from 7.6 percent in 1969 to 26.2 percent in 1982. Between 1967 and 1982, 12 major northeastern cities lost 1.6 million jobs (1.3 million in manufacturing) while their suburban rings gained 2 million jobs. All this tells the aspiring developer something about the types of space needed and where in the city those spaces will be needed. It also indicates the importance of intracity transportation in determining tomorrow's "right location," as well as suburb-to-suburb transportation.

9. *The Inner City Has a Financial Lock on the Poor.* Land, labor, and in-place capital are not perfectly mobile (or interchangeable) internationally, interregionally, or even inside the city. Again, here it is interesting to note the interaction of public policy with spatial location. Public assistance and committee services tend to keep the poor in the inner city where they have no jobs. When you add the effects of the availability of support systems (welfare office to public transportation) to the cost of housing, the poor are better off financially in the inner city even without a job.[2]

---

[2]*Still, remember what Kasarda says: the three great symbols of U.S. opportunity all involve migration—the Statue of Liberty, the covered wagon, and the underground railroad. Think about the next 20 years. What type of migration is important? Again, in all this, the point is to anticipate change.*

Although many analysts may try to ignore the problems of the inner city, history teaches that these problems will not go away or solve themselves. In particular, Anthony Downs has argued that failing public education in these areas will hurt real estate in the city *and* in the surrounding suburban areas.

10. *Cities Exist Because They Create Opportunities.* The electronic cottage didn't happen, but the global information-based city is a reality. It is still shaped by a combination of (a) economic forces, (b) technological change, (c) accessibility, and (d) composite character.

   What makes a city? Opportunities. Cities grow because they provide opportunities. Think about that and think about pricing in Manhattan today. If the Manhattan opportunity is an alternative to New Jersey, Manhattan is exorbitantly priced. If, on the other hand, as an information-based city, Manhattan is an alternative to Tokyo or London, it is incredibly underpriced as a part of the new world financial belt.

11. *Cities, Neighborhoods, and Relevant Boundaries.* Urban growth has been higher than nonurban growth since the Revolutionary War (except for 1970 through 1978), but the main recent shift in the system has been to the middle. Cities with more than 250,000 people and fewer than 10,000 are shrinking. Those cities between 10,000 and 50,000 grew the fastest, from 18.1 percent of the total population in 1960 to 22.5 percent in 1980.

   This tells us that neighborhoods are the key. Note that the way you hear statistics quoted is not too helpful here. We hear about the metropolitan statistical area (a central city of over 50,000 and 100,000 in the whole area) or primary statistical metropolitan areas (supposedly coherent economic units), and yet this is the wrong measure. Look in your own MSA and you'll probably find areas of growth and areas of decline.

   What then is the right area on which to base statistical analysis? That depends on the concept you're concerned with. The neighborhood that is relevant for employment is different from the neighborhood that is relevant for Little League, which, in turn, is different from the neighborhood that is relevant for the homeowners' association. Each individual lives in a series of neighborhoods, some larger, some smaller, and many overlapping to a greater or lesser extent. The critical item for development is to anticipate the demand for any particular kind of space from the relevant definition of the neighborhood. Since federal statistics are free, it behooves one to start with the county or possibly the census tract, but it is not wise to define all neighborhoods in this manner. Depending on the use of the space, the neighborhood definition will vary considerably.

12. *Cities, Growth, and Culture.* Cities, complex concentrations of population, came into existence, as we just said, because they created oppor-

tunities (originally in Europe, defensive possibilities) and they grow for the same reason. This fact needs to be related to job quality as well as many of the other issues previously discussed. Think about certain key facts. Automobiles started in the cities, where there were roads, mainly as a toy and not as a way to get to work. Urbanization also drove the development of electric power. Only cities had the market size to justify the up-front capital costs. Skyscrapers (the first was the Home Insurance Building in Chicago in 1880) were steel shells that allowed construction over 20 stories (the limit with load-bearing masonry walls).

The facts cited above indicate that something other than economics and technology may be driving the process. American cities have grown in uniquely American ways. Buenos Aires, one of the most beautiful cities in the world, showed very little technological development during its golden age. Why did American cities develop faster and more functionally? There is probably something, or at least there was something, in the American culture that stimulated the urge to make things work. The culture allowed some individuals in that population to develop new and more efficient ways to do things. Some of these, such as the automobile, started as a toy. Others started in a more functional manner. The key point is that something in the culture allowed this concentration of people that came together for one set of opportunities to develop yet other opportunities and to build the most efficient cities that exist in the world today.

Because American urban development has been successful, relative to the rest of the world, it is easy for Americans to become smug about our American culture. This would be a tremendous error. There are many negatives in the American culture, many positives in other cultures, and, most importantly, both the American culture and other cultures are evolving dramatically. Recall our earlier discussion of migration. The American culture changes with new immigrant groups. What type of city will America want and be able to develop in the 1990s and beyond? The Hispanic immigrants are used to a more open and more active downtown, while the Asian immigrant is used to considerably more density. What will work? How will the culture evolve to make it work better in the future? Once you know that, you're on your way to figuring out what type of space will be most useful in the new American cities.

13. *The Sunbelt.* Whether it was due to climate, jobs, life-style, or promotion, the migration trend toward the Sunbelt is more than 100 years old. The great western city of freeways is a case in point. Los Angeles incorporated in 1781 with 10,000 people. There were 50,000 by 1890; 100,000 by 1900; 300,000 by 1910; 600,000 by 1920; and 1.2 million by 1930. In short, the Sunbelt move is not a recent phe-

nomenon, and as in many areas, a more extended view of history can be useful in developing a proper perspective for forecasting.

Of course, the Sunbelt is a very large area with lots of different trends progressing under the one large umbrella. When you think of the Sunbelt (now in a longer time perspective), you may think of the West Coast and then the South. But even the South is a census region that ranges from Texas to Maryland—clearly a huge area. Why has this section of the Sunbelt done well? Quite simple—a benign climate, modern infrastructure, right to work laws, favorable wage rates, low taxes and land costs, upgraded schools, pro-growth committee attitudes, and various other items have boosted the region's attractiveness to both employers and employees. Today, however, the South looks more like the nation. In 1900, U.S. employment was 42 percent primary (agricultural, mining, and the like), 25 percent manufacturing, and 33 percent service (other). These figures were 64, 12, and 24, respectively, for the South. In contrast, by 1984, the United States was 4, 20, and 76 and the South, 5, 18, and 77. Those benefits that attracted people to the South have caused the South to look more like the nation. What does that tell you about the future? This trend still has a way to run, but, like most trends, it eventually precipitates its own end. What you have to figure out is whether that end is 2 or 50 years away.

Within this trend there is a rather stark dichotomy. The leading cities of the South (Washington D.C., Atlanta, Charlotte, etc.) are booming. However, many of the smaller towns are not benefiting from the boom.

14. *Regions Are Not Stable Categories of Economic Growth.* Regions are much more volatile than nations. More is going on *within* than *between* them, as our comment about Washington, D.C., Atlanta, and Charlotte indicates. What matters are the local economies in these regions and how they are linked to the global economy. Greenville-Spartanburg, Columbia, and Charleston, South Carolina, are metro areas in the same region and metro-size category. Yet their futures have little to do with each other in spite of their proximity and other similarities. The Charleston economy will depend on tourism and retirement trends. Greenville-Spartanburg, on the other hand, will rise and fall with nondurable goods manufacturing as will other parts of the United States and elsewhere. Columbia, South Carolina's state capital, relies more on information-based activities. Its fortunes depend more on local forces than they do in the other two metro economies. These areas have more in common with places in other parts of the United States than with each other.

15. *U.S. Residential Development Is Different—Will It Stay That Way?* U.S. residential development is unusual, internationally speaking, in four ways, leading to what some people have called the 60-minute fried

egg phenomenon. First, there is low residential density in this country. In early U.S. history, before 1800, there were no lawns. Land was to be useful. Look at the very old neighborhoods as proof of this point. The suburban ideal didn't come until the nineteenth century, even though today it clearly dominates. Second, there is a high percentage of owner-occupied housing in the United States, in part because of government financial initiatives, in part because of tax incentives, and in part because 97 percent of our homes are the relatively inexpensive stick-built variety. (Europe still uses more expensive masonry walls.)

Third, the socioeconomic distinction between the center city and the suburb is wide and reversed from the rest of the world. In Indian cities, the cleanest drinking water is in the central city. In Mexico, the high-rent retail area and much of the better residential areas are downtown. In most of the rest of the world, the slums are on the periphery. In the United States, the population of the central city has been declining since 1830. Reflecting on previous arguments, something in the American experience uniquely causes us to develop a different kind of city. The wealthy tend to move to the outside of the city where they can enjoy more land; the poor tend to be locked into the central city.

Finally, other cultures seem to value closeness more. Transportation that allows cities to spread out is cheaper and better here. Charlotte, North Carolina, got its first electric trolley in 1893. London, on the other hand, used horses until World War I. At that time, Berlin, Europe's leader, would have been number 22 among U.S. cities in terms of miles of track.

It is important to remember that American government helped all this to happen with investment in highways, the deductibility of interest and property taxes, and, for a while, the willingness of municipalities to pay for new infrastructure.[3] Furthermore, unlike Europe, in the United States speculative land profits were allowed, not legally precluded or taxed away.

In the United States we subsidized public transit and ran it as a business. In Europe, Paris probably has the best transportation system, and it is still two-thirds subsidized. The price and quality of service became separable issues as subsidies grew. Thus, the political economy of our cities was probably easier for a developer to "plug into." However, think about the mega-developments currently planned in Manhattan and the very complex nature of the politics that drive the bottom-line numbers.

16. *The Nuclear Family Appears Terminal.* Ozzie and Harriet don't even make the 5:30 reruns anymore. Today's sitcoms seldom show a fa-

---

[3]*FHA insurance and standardization spurred new construction.*

ther at the office, a mother at home, an older brother who plays football, and a younger sister who cooks. To many of us, this loss does not seem tragic; there are other ways we might want to live besides in a 1950s stereotype. Still, there is much information here for tomorrow's development. The nuclear family wanted a certain type of home, and if most families looked alike, most homes should logically have looked alike. With new types of families, varieties of single-parent families, more individuals living alone, the elderly grouping together in new ways, there would naturally be a need for more different types of housing.

The trend away from the nuclear family started and is most pronounced in the East and in the big cities, but it is real throughout the country. A telling statistic in this area is that real family income is down over the last 10 years, despite the increase in double incomes. Why? Divorce and other separations have overcome the positive influence of the double income.

17. *Fractionalization and the Search for Certainty.* America is a churchgoing nation but hasn't produced a single great theologian. It has also been a while since we had a scholar in the White House. Were Reinhold Niebuhr and Woodrow Wilson exceptions, or will the United States start thinking about who it is as it matures as a nation?

Fractionalization is an interesting concept from a development perspective. Some analysts divide people into two groups: those who believe something beyond themselves (i.e., peace activists, consumer representatives, etc.) and those who don't. In the information explosion we are all experiencing, it is difficult for some to believe. When beliefs are not deeply held, it becomes more important to the individual to choose the right toy or to own the right house to be more like his or her friends. This phenomenon, which is clearly seen in teenagers, leads to a herd effect with greater movement toward the "in-market segment." If you think this idea is a bit heavy for a textbook, hold onto it for a moment and see if it doesn't become important as one of the rules for living that is the goal of this study of rumored facts.

18. *Economic Disenfranchisement.* There is the perception of unfair economic advantage in some groups. While America has been generally happy during the Reagan/Bush years, a significant element of the society has become more economically distant from the rest. Many of today's leaders, workers, and students feel that many of the unemployed deserve no more than they are getting. Not surprisingly, this view is not shared by those in the lower economic groups. When a nation prospers and yet the bottom of the economic ladder fails to benefit from that prosperity, the members of this less fortunate group will find and believe in "unfair" reasons for their conditions.

One need only spend a short amount of time in America's inner cities to verify this perception.

Remember, unemployment understates the underclass. Monthly unemployment asks 160,000 people three questions and lists as unemployed only those who are both unemployed and still seeking a job.

19. *Amenable (i.e., achievable on paper) Does Not Necessarily Mean Politically Doable.* For example, it is clear that older, poorer urban areas could benefit from an influx of the wealthy. However, the political reality favors wealth taxes that in turn lead to a flight of the few wealthy who remain in the area. It's not that people don't understand, that is, that there isn't a public policy that could logically be expected to work. The fact is that politically you can't implement the economically logical policy.

20. *All in All It Ain't Great, But It Ain't All Texas Either.* Texas, the flower of the development world for a decade and a half, is hung up on low oil prices, full prisons, nonreplenishing aquifers, a large proportion of poor elderly, lots of poor folks, the need for bilingual education, a big state deficit, companies with Tesoro-type ethics, and a host of problems that currently seem second only to those of Mexico City.

Still, growth and decay form a natural cycle, and Houston may end up the big winner. Note that Los Angeles was an aircraft-dominated city before World War II; after World War II, in 1947, employment in the aircraft business dropped to 60,000 from a 1943 high of 240,000. However, the Korean War came along, and by 1950, it was back to 240,000. Oil prices may do the same.

Even without an oil price increase, Houston may (we don't personally have a lot of money bet on this) be the city of the future. We know it's a fact that employment has dropped in the Fortune 500, and we have successful small businesses to thank for the overall employment growth that the nation has enjoyed over the last several years. For a small businessperson, Houston provides many things. Retail, industrial, and office space can be had for a fraction of its cost to produce. Furthermore, the city is very open to all kinds of new businesses and will do whatever it can to help. Finally, in Houston employees can live in a $250,000 California-style home for $70,000 or $80,000. When you add it all up, the entrepreneurs may move to Houston. If they do, then at some point in the future, we'll see Houston booming the way Boston boomed from 1985 to 1987.

All of the 20 items mentioned above are in some sense knowable today. They are based on things that have already happened and that will have an impact on the future. As such, they are the basis for our forecast. We must, however, go beyond the rather obvious points mentioned here to try and draw out some things that may be happening. Looking at facts along with probable trends can provide a context in which we can anticipate reactions and develop some rules for living with and in the future.

THE BIG THINGS that MAY BE HAPPENING

These are *not things that are going to happen next year,* but you may need to take action before the whole world agrees that they are actually happening. Once everyone agrees that something is happening, it's probably either been fully priced or someone else has done it. The early bird gets the worm. But then the lead scout is usually the first casualty. Timing is important, and it takes creativity and luck to be first but not early. Whatever action you've taken either fits or doesn't fit. To be a winner in the development business, you need to be a step ahead of the pack but, of course, not pushing the river.

As in the preceding section, the text will list the big things. Your job is not only to comprehend the argument, but also to interpret potential results and, most importantly, to integrate all the different big things that may be happening with the preceding facts so as to come out with a consistent set of rules for the future.

1. *People Are Becoming More Important Relative to Capital.* With the move toward full employment, human resources are becoming the competitive edge. This means that capital availability will not be as critical as the people on your team. In the past, it has often been the person who could bet the money who became the developer. In the future, things may be different. The person who can organize, motivate, and manage the right team may be the developer of the future.

2. *Attention to All Potential Customers Is the Wave of the Future.* Yuppies and dinks are only a trickle, but watch out for the muffs. The *Young Urban Professionals* and the *Double Income* families with *No Kids* are hyped in the press, and certainly most of them have a high percentage of disposal income. Still, the *Mature Urban Failures* are what we see all around us. Not the grisly failure on skid row, but people who live in 2,800-square-foot houses and always thought they belonged in 6,800 square feet. When you think about what kind of space is needed in the society as a whole, it's the muffs, not the yuppies and the dinks, who will create the majority of demand.

The yuppies and the dinks may well lead some trends, but when you look at the total volume of expected new demand, it's largely people who have been semi-successful—mature urban failures in the sense that they don't have the great house and will probably never be president of the company. Still, these are the people who work every day and make society go. They must not only be housed, but they must also have industrial, office, and retail space to work in and be served by. Tomorrow's developer, referring to point one above, will find that a sensitivity to these people's space demands will be critical in a full employment world. In other words, *serious attention to the customer will be needed not only for the high income groups that have always expected it, but also for the large majority of society.*

3. *There Will Be Fewer Middle Managers.* Because of the computer, we are drastically reducing the number of middle managers and shifting from the manager as order giver to the manager as facilitator. The machine allows information to be communicated more efficiently, thus reducing the need for some of the people in the middle. From a real estate perspective, this means fewer midlevel offices. The transition through the corporate ranks will be less important than the shift from employee to quasi-employer, with people who would have been middle managers moving to more entrepreneurial endeavors. Thus, there will be some breaks in the housing link, and the communities of tomorrow should be planned accordingly.

4. *A Different Kind of Neighborhood Homogeneity.* Equal pay for comparable work is coming, but it has nothing to do with being fair or nice to people. It is simply a recognition of item 1 above in the labor market. When the sexes, the races, and various other groups are seen more equally in the work place, they will also be seen more equally in the neighborhood or community that will come to dominate social life in the future. If a short green female works next to you for the same wages, then logically that same short green female should live in the same neighborhood, but only if she wants to. The point here is that the kind of acceptable neighbors in the future will change as employment practices change, so that communities will be less homogeneous across racial and ethnic lines and more homogeneous across employment and income lines and life-style choices.

Here, anticipating the reaction is again the key. We are speaking of integrative forces that tend to pull people together and homogenize life-style. There will almost certainly be "separating" reactions. People have a need to be unique or at least part of unique groups. As old distinctions give way, expect some new "separating" distinctions to emerge.

5. *Child and Parent Care Facilities.* Parenting is coming into the money economy. The majority of the new families are two wage-earners and expect to pay for some nonparental parenting. In the new development world, you had better build in child-care facilities or at least have the space to do it later. In fact, it will probably become common to build in parent-care facilities as well, as more individuals live a longer life and eventually depend more on their children. Having an aged parent at home is, in many respects, similar to having a young

child in that day care is needed. When this is coupled with the idea of greater service to customers as users of constructed space, the new development will have both better child-care facilities and rather elaborate parent-care facilities.

6. *Continuing Education Will Be Increasingly Important.* The high tech Renaissance person who fondly anticipates change is taking over for both the quantitative nerds and the "in-crowd." The half-life of information is short. Ph.Ds. become obsolete at a rapid rate, so continuing education is a wave of the future.

7. *There Will Be Fewer Corporate Types.* The age of self-reliance is coming with lots of entrepreneurs, intrapreneurs, and even stock-owning receptionists. The biggest entrepreneurial explosion since the move off the farm is occurring. In 1985, there were 700,000 new corporations. In the best of the booming 1960s there were never over 100,000 per year. Note that the entrepreneur wants something different at home and in the office from what the corporate man or woman wants. Furthermore, these desires, or at least the financial ability to fulfill them, change appreciably with entrepreneurial success.

8. *"Fun Kids" Will Come Again.* The kids are living in the 1950s, but boredom demands that the Chicago Seven be reincarnated as the L.A. Eleven. The trial marriage is actually a conservative gesture that will create more commitment to the marriage—a reaction against the split families today's kids have grown up in. The mall has become the hangout for the high-consumption teenager. Still, as children react against their parents (today's conservative youth reacting against their hippie parents of the 1960s), you can expect the next generation to react against the conservatism of today's teenagers who will soon become parents.

9. *Unions Will Continue to Decline.* The growth areas of the South and West don't have the family traditions of unionism. In fact, the union concept has less economic validity than it did in earlier years if concern for the worker grows with a full-employment economy. Notice that major national unions are even starting to negotiate work rules on a local basis.

10. *High Touch Comes with High Tech.* In decision making, intuition, hunch, and faith are all getting new respectability. Museums and the arts are more important, and "soft people" can still live very profitably in the new world. From the development perspective, note that some cities are now requiring certain artistic components in new development. Expect this requirement to expand.

11. *The Global Economy Is Coming.* Global economy is more than trade

between nations; it is a move to a one-world economy. We have already seen the sources of financing move offshore. Before long, the search for tenants will follow.

12. *We Are in the Second Jet Age.* The domestic hub will give way to the international gateway as the new growth magnet. It's a natural evolution—water ports to rail to auto to domestic air. Look at what Eastern did for Miami or at what American means to Dallas.

   More important, think about Terminus (now called Atlanta) being the new temporary home of RJR. Several cities have new domestic hubs. However, is this what corporate headquarters want? Notice that Winston-Salem, a beautiful city in the Piedmont of North Carolina, has lost the top management of Piedmont, Hanes, RJR, and even its newspaper, with the Wachovia (its superregional bank) rumored to be moving to Atlanta. Do top executives need the international air connection in the age of a world economy? Possibly the international gateway cities will be home for administrative clusters, while the next tier of cities will be home for the manufacturing cluster that will have to emerge if we are first to end the trade deficit and, then, to pay off the international debt.

13. *Water.* Clean water will be a more critical resource, but the Malthusians are a little bit off. America is short on clean water. In fact, the world, in the more populated areas, is short of clean water. Still, clean water is something that can be made. Just as we will someday find a cure for AIDS, there will be clean water. The question is the price and the source.

   On this note, there is another fact/trend that is less "technically" solvable. All the world's pollution, air and water, ends up in the oceans. Oceans aren't "controlled" by any one nation, yet they are critical to all nations, causing a very difficult political-economic-technical problem.

14. *Tax Change Is Coming.* New taxes are coming, along with a return of the capital gains preference. Note that in 1986 Congress left the capital gains distinction in the code, and through all the debates it was clear that when the maximum rate went above 30 percent, some sort of capital formation incentive was needed. Beyond the easier forecast of an incentive to capital formation are the more difficult calls on "sin taxes," oil import fees, and possibly a national value-added tax. As there is a shift in who bears which part of which social cost with any major tax change, the consumption of and investment in real estate will also change.

15. *A Little Fatter and Happier.* There will be a reaction against the lean-and-mean approach to management because of its long-term impact on corporate growth potential. Corporate managers need to grow

their companies to prosper personally. The ultimate lean-and-mean means no people reserves, no reserve of customer good-will, no R&D, no loss leaders. In the long run, management wants to grow.

16. *High-Growth Industries.* Certain high-growth areas are indicated for the economy in the 1990s, at least according to John Naisbitt (author of *Megatrends*): computers, retailing, leisure, education, health, medical, law, and accounting.

17. *Low-Income Minorities Will Become More Angry.* Wouldn't you, as television continues to show *all races* participating in the good life that is passing you by? Eventually, we can expect increased violence. Where will it be concentrated? In your worst nightmare, think about a major riot in the Wall of Chicago. If you haven't heard about the Wall, drive through Chicago down the interstate and look at the concentration of high-rise ghettos.

    When the violence occurs, television will bring it into every home, and with that violence will come an increased demand by the consumer of real estate space for security. In many respects, only the developer can provide efficiently for enhanced security measures. From alarm systems to lights and open, safer designs, building security in a development is not inexpensive, but it may market very well in the future.

18. *No More Stereotypical American.* WASPs will cease to be a majority in California by the year 2000; in the United States overall, somewhere around 2030. However, the mix will be very different in different regions, implying different types of cities, especially with Hispanic and Asian inmigration. Don't be fooled by census numbers. Remember, the Hispanics were counted as white in the 1970 census and Hispanic in the 1980 census, distorting the reporting trends.

    The truth is in the politics. Twenty-five of 171 cities with a population of over 100,000 in 1970 have over 50 percent nonwhite population. The truth is in the mayor's office as can be seen in the number of major cities that had black mayors in the 1980s: Chicago, Los Angeles, Atlanta, Philadelphia, Washington, D.C., New York City, Detroit. The state of Virginia elected the first black governor in 1989.

19. *Regional Differences Intensify, Reversing the Trend of the 1970s.* The United States will become even more "many nations with many different lifestyles." Values and self-images already vary drastically by region. In each region, there are vertical hierarchies as well, based on income, age (and health), the search for fulfillment, and ethnic group. (Note that not all blacks remain culturally tied to what has traditionally been considered black.) The California "me-first" meritocracy is very different from the old South, which values tradition.

Note that Asians are a dominant new influence in the West and Hispanics in the South. San Diego and Los Angeles may be the bellwethers, with major concentrations of both groups. If the average Asian immigrant is more educated than the Hispanic immigrant, what does that say about significance of class distinctions in different regions of the country?

20. *Inflation.* Inflation is going to be very important, and to be sure we're right, we're going to argue that it is (1) gone for good and (2) certainly coming back. Of course, whichever is true, interest rates will adjust, and that will have a major impact on the development business.

First, inflation is gone for good. The factory utilization rate is only in the low 80 percent range even after a very long expansion. Commercial real estate is vastly oversupplied. American labor is becoming more efficient with the breakdown of old taboos. (For example, paralegals have expanded their work.) There are fewer union workers, and local unions negotiate on work rules. Smaller firms are the ones that are growing, and they tend to be more efficient than the Fortune 500, which are shrinking. High-priced industrial union workers are now willing to take much less as they recognize that the alternative is a much lower paying job. Most important, the 1984–86 tax revisions reduced the incentive to enter into totally tax-motivated transactions. As fewer bright people spend their time trying to beat the tax system, the economy will become more efficient.

On the other hand, just in case you didn't buy the preceding argument, *inflation certainly will come back.* Oil was a big part of the very low inflation numbers in the late 1980s. Eventually, oil prices are going up because of reduced drilling and reduced conservation, as well as the higher risk premium now applied to oil drilling and exploration that the Arabs succeeded in generating with the series of swings in oil prices they manipulated. Today OPEC is producing at around 60 percent of capacity and the non-OPEC world at 98 percent of capacity. Assuming we have approximately 10 million barrels per day of excess capacity today, the supply/demand balance could easily shift. U.S. consumption could be up 2 to 5 million barrels per day in a few years, whereas non-OPEC production will certainly be down 1 to 3 million barrels per day. If the rest of the industrialized world is up 2 to 5 billion with growth in their economies, the net result is no surplus in a rather short period of time. Remember, of course, that it is not when the shortage *actually* gets here that matters; it's when we start *expecting* the shortage.

Some day, in the longer run, reduced domestic agricultural production may have a market impact. Today, everyone argues that we have more agricultural productivity than we will ever need, but you've heard those absolutes before. The correct short-term solution to several political and financial problems is to loosen the money supply. From the need for Third World countries to be able to sell here to pay off their U.S. bank debts to the S&Ls, to the farm credit system, to the small businesses being crowded out of the credit market, to the financing of the deficit, to keeping down interest rates, the short-term solution is the same—to loosen the money supply. Long term, if Washington is not able to exercise the discipline necessary to shut off the spigot, this means more dollars chasing fewer goods.

The cheaper dollar will eventually lead to higher import prices. Furthermore, we continue to have more government and lots of defense; both are less productive users of capital. Productivity gains are more difficult to achieve in a service economy, and, psychologically, we still want to be paid more for doing less. Think about yourself. How much time do you want to spend studying for the final exam in a course? Wouldn't you rather get an A without having to work on it? That's a big problem.

21. *The Church.* The continuing shift in values will cause a decline in the organized church and a more intense search for religious certainty. Neighborhoods may partially replace the organized church as the social focus of individual lives. This argument stems from a combination of the preceding forecasts and clearly says a lot about the kind of development that will be needed in the future.

22. *Indecision.* The U.S. melting pot will become a simmering skillet during a period of rapid change, resulting in indecision at all levels. This will be evident in a declining world leadership role for the United States, the lack of a forceful domestic leader, and more companies called USX. Think about it. How could you name a huge existing company for the great unknown?

23. *Technology.* The focus on improving communications technology is overdone. The linking of machines to machines to create machines is the new technology that will have the greatest impact on life-styles. If you really want to get wild, more important than technological progress will be the proof of Kipling's error (east is east and west is west), which will allow Westerners to accept the Eastern concept that the mind can be physically creative. Ultimately, this means that you will be able to heal yourself as we achieve the integration of mind and body.

24. *Something Must Die.* We are moving from a society oriented toward growth and addition to one oriented toward replacement and substitution. Therefore, when something new comes in, something must die. Examples would be soft drinks killing coffee and chicken hurting beef.

25. *The Merger Wave Will End.* Mergers and acquisitions usually don't work. Experience to date has suggested that most result in negative synergy. Along this line, stock buy-backs are not particularly useful either from a public policy perspective. They clearly raise the break-even point by increasing the leverage ratio, and, all else equal, this has to increase risk. Remember that corporate reorganizations can have a major impact on space markets. When junk bond issuers, like Revco, hit the skids, so do shopping center owners who can't collect the rent from their drug store anchor tenant.

26. *Flexibility Is In.* CEOs are looking for something new from workers: knowledge, decentralized local action, and a global view. Notice that these are all oriented toward increasing flexibility and that the most troublesome asset is the real estate since it is a longer term investment even than R&D in the drug industry.

   Not long ago, the criterion of efficiency required specialized workers to use single-purpose machines to mass produce goods. Now, flexibility requires workers with good basic education to use adaptable, computer-controlled machines to produce specialized goods and services for particular market niches.

27. *Corporations of All Sizes Will Become More Active in Real Estate.* In a world of faster obsolescence, multiple products from multiple markets, and globalization, flexibility is the key. From the corporate perspective a lower breakeven point is the essential element of increased flexibility. For example, in 1982 Harley Davidson was involved in a leveraged buyout, and at that time most analysts saw the last U.S. motorcycle manufacturer headed to an early grave. The Japanese had (1) automated (clever, not expensive automation), (2) reduced the labor force, (3) acquired more productive labor, (4) integrated the computer system, and (5) developed a hands-on organization. While it sounds like *In Search of Excellence,* notice the incentives for Harley-Davidson from these five factors. Don't go with the most expensive automation; lose some workers and reward those remaining more than they had been in the past, possibly in an entrepreneurial manner; eliminate the foremen and use the integrated computer information system; and, finally, make sure that fewer managers are on the factory floor. The new Harley-Davidson management accomplished all these changes and more. For example, inventory control was achieved by getting rid of the person in charge of inventory and the space for storing it. In this way, partnership with suppliers was forced on the company, which was one way of implementing a just-in-time inventory system. The same point can be made in a service industry. The same trend toward a lower breakeven point can be seen from the number of automated teller machines that tripled from 1980 to 1985. More teller machines means

fewer employees and far less bricks and mortar in branch offices. In the 1980s, Wall Street found many innovative ways to finance corporate real estate and thereby expanded the ways in which corporations could seek increased flexibility in their real estate.

REFERENCES   Aaron, Henry. *Shelters and Subsidies: Who Benefits from Housing Policies?* Washington, D.C.: The Brookings Institute, 1972.

American Institute of Planners. *Survey of State Land Use Planning Activity.* Washington, D.C.: Office of Policy Development and Research, HUD, 1976.

Andrews, Richard N. R., ed. *Land in America: Commodity or Natural Resources?* Lexington, Mass.: Lexington Books, 1979.

Barrows, Richard L. *Transfer of Development Rights: A Theoretical and Case Study Analysis of a New Land Use Policy.* Madison, Wis.: Center for Resource Policy Studies, 1976.

Berry, Brian, J. L. *The Open Housing Question: Race and Housing in Chicago 1966–1976.* Cambridge, Mass.: Ballinger, 1979.

Bloom, Allan. *The Closing of the American Mind.* New York: Simon and Schuster, 1987.

Burchell, Robert W., and David Listokin. *Fiscal Impact Handbook: Estimating Local Cost from Revenues of Land Development.* New Brunswick, N.J.: Rutgers University, Center for Urban Policy Research, 1978.

Capra, Fritjof. *The Turning Point.* New York: Bantam Books, 1982.

Christiansen, Kathleen. *Social Impact of Land Development: An Initial Approach for Estimating Impacts of Neighborhood Usages and Perceptions.* Washington, D.C.: Urban Land Institute, 1976.

Downs, Anthony. *Federal Housing Subsidies: How Are They Working?* Lexington, Mass.: D. C. Heath, 1973.

Drucker, Peter. *Innovation and Entrepreneurship.* New York: Harper and Row, 1985.

Egan, John J., et al. *Housing and Public Policy.* Cambridge, Mass.: Ballinger, 1981.

Ervin, David E., et al. *Land Use Control: Evaluation Economic and Political Effects.* Cambridge, Mass.: Ballinger, 1977.

Frieden, Bernard J., and A. P. Solomon. *The Nation's Housing: 1975 to 1985.* Cambridge, Mass.: MIT-Harvard Joint Center for Urban Studies, 1977.

Garreau, Joel. *The Nine Nations of North America.* New York: Avon Books, 1981.

Hagman, Donald G. *Public Planning and Control or Urban and Land Development: Cases and Materials.* St. Paul, Minn.: West, 1980.

Hasen, Niles M. *The Challenge of Urban Growth.* Lexington, Mass.: D. C. Heath, 1975.

International City Managers Association. *The Essential Community: Local Government in the Year 2000.* Washington, D.C.: International City Managers Association, 1980.

Johnson, M. Bruce. *Resolving the Housing Crisis: Government Policy, Decontrol, and the Public Interest.* Cambridge, Mass.: Ballinger, 1982.

Keyes, Dale L. *Land Development and the Natural Environment: Estimating Impacts.* Washington, D.C.: Urban Land Institute, 1976.

Legislative History and Hearings: Superfund, U.S. Congress.

Mitchell, Arnold. *The Nine American Lifestyles.* New York: Macmillan Publishing.

Muller, Thomas. *Economic Impacts of Land Development: Employment, Housing and Property Values.* Washington, D.C.: Urban Land Institute, 1976.

Naisbett, John. *Megatrends.* New York: Warner Books, 1982.

National Realty Committee. *America's Real Estate.* Washington, D.C.: National Realty Committee, 1989.

Nelson, Robert Henry. *Zoning and Property Rights: An Analysis of the American System of Land Use Regulation.* Cambridge, Mass.: MIT Press, 1977.

Peters, Thomas, and Robert Waterman. *In Search of Excellence.* New York: Harper and Row, 1982.

Real Estate Outlook. Washington, D.C.: National Association of Realtors (monthly).

The Return of Comet Halley: Economic Commentary. Chicago: National Association of Realtors.

Rydell, C. Peter, et al. *The Impact of Rent Control on the Los Angeles Housing Market.* Santa Monica, Calif.: Rand Corporation, 1981.

Schaenman, Philip S. *Using an Impact Measurement System to Evaluate Land Development.* Washington, D.C.: Urban Land Institute, 1976.

Schreiber, Gatons, and Richard B. Clemmer. *Economics of Urban Problems.* 3rd ed. Boston: Houghton-Mifflin, 1982.

Stegman, Michael A. *The Dynamics of Rental Housing in New York City.* Piscataway, N.J.: Center for Urban Policy Research, 1982.

Thurow, Lester. *The Zero Sum Society.* New York: Basic Books, 1980.

Zukau, Gary. *The Dancing Wu Li Masters: An Overview of the New Physics.* New York: Bantam Books, 1979.

PERIODICALS

American Institute of Architects (AIA) Journal.

American Institute of Planners Journal.

American Society of Planning Officials (ASPO) Information Report.

Coastal Zone Management Journal. Environment, resources, and law. New York: Crane, Russak and Company.

Environment Reporter. Washington Bureau of National Affairs.

Growth and Change: A Journal of Regional Development. Lexington, Ky.: College of Business and Economics, University of Kentucky.

Housing and Development Reporter. Washington, D.C.: Bureau of National Affairs (weekly).

Journal of Environmental Economics and Management. New York: Academic Press.

Journal of Housing. Washington, D.C.: National Association of Housing and Redevelopment Officials (monthly).

Journal of Regional Science. Philadelphia: Regional Science Research Institute, University of Pennsylvania.

Land Use Digest. Washington, D.C.: Urban Land Institute.

News Release. Washington, D.C.: U.S. Department of Housing and Urban Development (weekly).

Urban Affairs Quarterly. Beverly Hills, Calif.: Sage Publications (Northwestern editor).
The Urban Edge. Washington, D.C.: World Bank Publications (monthly).
Zoning Digest. American Society of Planning Officials.

USEFUL ARTICLES ON HAZARDOUS WASTE

Becker, R. "Environmental Risks and Their Impact on Real Estate." *Real Estate Report,* Real Estate Research Corporation, Vol. 17, No. 4, 1988.
Bhatt, H. G., R. M. Sykes, and T. L. Sweeney. *Management of Toxic and Hazardous Wastes.* Chelsea, Mich.: Lewis Publishers, Inc., 1986.
Brown, Michael. *Laying Waste: The Poisoning of America by Toxic Chemicals.* New York: Pantheon Books, 1980.
Chadd, C. M., and L. L. Bergeson. *Guide to Avoiding Liability for Waste Disposal.* Bureau of National Affairs, 1986.
"The Comprehensive Environmental Response, Compensation and Liability Act of 1980: Is Joint and Several Liability the Answer to Superfund?" *New England Law Review.* Vol. 18:1.
Dubuc, C. E., and W. D. Evans, Jr. "Recent Developments Under CERCLA: Toward a More Equitable Distribution of Liability." *Environmental Law Reporter,* June 1987.
E.P.A. National Priorities List, Supplementary Lists and Supporting Materials. June 1988.
Hall, R. M., R. Watson, J. Davidson, and D. Case. *Hazardous Wastes Handbook.* Rockville, Md.: Government Institutes, Inc., 1984.
Hayes, D. J., and C. B. MacKerron. *Superfund II: A New Mandate.* A Bureau of National Affairs Special Report, 1987.
"Joint and Several Liability Under Superfund: The Plight of the Small Volume Hazardous Waste Contributor." *Wayne Law Review.* Vol. 31: 1057.
Legislative History and Hearings: Superfund. U.S. Congress.
McGregor, G. I. "Landowner Liability for Hazardous Waste." *Journal of Real Estate Development,* Winter 1989.
Mazilow, A. "Property Owners Can Be Liable for Hazardous Waste." *National Real Estate Investor,* November 1986.
Piasecki, B. W., and G. A. David. *America's Future in Toxic Waste Management: Lessons from Europe.* New York: Quorum Books, 1987.
Rich, D. A. "Personal Liability for Hazardous Waste Cleanup: An Examination of CERCLA Section 107." *Environmental Affairs,* Vol. 13: 643.
Rosemarin, C. S. "Reducing the Risk of Environmental Liability in Real Estate Acquisitions." Mimeo, October 12, 1987.
Sullivan, T. F. P., ed. *SUPERFUND: Comprehensive Environmental Response, Compensation, and Liability Act of 1980.* Rockville, Md.: Government Institutes, Inc., 1982.
Vesilind, P. A., and J. Pierce. *Environmental Pollution and Control.* Ann Arbor, Mich.: Ann Arbor Science Publishers, Inc., 1983.

$DS=$

COMPOUND INTEREST TABLES

TABLE A-1. ANNUAL RATE 8 PERCENT

Nominal Annual Interest Rate = 8%   Compounding Periods per Year = 1

Year	Amount of 1 at Compound Interest (Col. 1)	Accumu-lation of 1 per Period (Col. 2)	Sinking Fund Factor (Col. 3)	Present Value Rever-sion of 1 (Col. 4)	Present Value Ordinary Annuity 1 per Period (Col. 5)	Installment to Amortize 1 (Col. 6)	Period
1	1.0800	1.0000	1.000000	0.9259	0.9259	1.0800000	1
2	1.1664	2.0800	0.480769	0.8573	1.7833	0.5607692	2
3	1.2597	3.2464	0.308034	0.7938	2.5771	0.3880335	3
4	1.3605	4.5061	0.221921	0.7350	3.3121	0.3019208	4
5	1.4693	5.8666	0.170456	0.6806	3.9927	0.2504565	5
6	1.5869	7.3359	0.136315	0.6302	4.6229	0.2163154	6
7	1.7138	8.9228	0.112072	0.5835	5.2064	0.1920724	7
8	1.8509	10.6366	0.094015	0.5403	5.7466	0.1740148	8
9	1.9990	12.4876	0.080080	0.5002	6.2469	0.1600797	9
10	2.1589	14.4866	0.069029	0.4632	6.7101	0.1490295	10
11	2.3316	16.6455	0.060076	0.4289	7.1390	0.1400763	11
12	2.5182	18.9771	0.052695	0.3971	7.5361	0.1326950	12
13	2.7196	21.4953	0.046522	0.3677	7.9038	0.1265218	13
14	2.9372	24.2149	0.041297	0.3405	8.2442	0.1212969	14
15	3.1722	27.1521	0.036830	0.3152	8.5595	0.1168295	15
16	3.4259	30.3243	0.032977	0.2919	8.8514	0.1129769	16
17	3.7000	33.7502	0.029629	0.2703	9.1216	0.1096294	17
18	3.9960	37.4502	0.026702	0.2502	9.3719	0.1067021	18
19	4.3157	41.4463	0.024128	0.2317	9.6036	0.1041276	19
20	4.6610	45.7620	0.021852	0.2145	9.8181	0.1018522	20
21	5.0338	50.4229	0.019832	0.1987	10.0168	0.0998322	21
22	5.4365	55.4568	0.018032	0.1839	10.2007	0.0980321	22
23	5.8715	60.8933	0.016422	0.1703	10.3711	0.0964222	23
24	6.3412	66.7648	0.014978	0.1577	10.5288	0.0949780	24
25	6.8485	73.1059	0.013679	0.1460	10.6748	0.0936788	25
26	7.3964	79.9544	0.012507	0.1352	10.8100	0.0925071	26
27	7.9881	87.3508	0.011448	0.1252	10.9352	0.0914481	27
28	8.6271	95.3388	0.010489	0.1159	11.0511	0.0904889	28
29	9.3173	103.9659	0.009619	0.1073	11.1584	0.0896185	29
30	10.0627	113.2832	0.008827	0.0994	11.2578	0.0888274	30
31	10.8677	123.3459	0.008107	0.0920	11.3498	0.0881073	31
32	11.7371	134.2135	0.007451	0.0852	11.4350	0.0874508	32
33	12.6760	145.9506	0.006852	0.0789	11.5139	0.0868516	33
34	13.6901	158.6267	0.006304	0.0730	11.5869	0.0863041	34
35	14.7853	172.3168	0.005803	0.0676	11.6546	0.0858033	35
36	15.9682	187.1021	0.005345	0.0626	11.7172	0.0853447	36
37	17.2456	203.0703	0.004924	0.0580	11.7752	0.0849244	37
38	18.6253	220.3159	0.004539	0.0537	11.8289	0.0845389	38
39	20.1153	238.9412	0.004185	0.0497	11.8786	0.0841851	39
40	21.7245	259.0565	0.003860	0.0460	11.9246	0.0838602	40

TABLE A-2. ANNUAL RATE 9 PERCENT

Nominal Annual Interest Rate = 9%   Compounding Periods per Year = 1

Year	Amount of 1 at Compound Interest (Col. 1)	Accumulation of 1 per Period (Col. 2)	Sinking Fund Factor (Col. 3)	Present Value Reversion of 1 (Col. 4)	Present Value Ordinary Annuity 1 per Period (Col. 5)	Installment to Amortize 1 (Col. 6)	Period
1	1.0900	1.0000	1.000000	0.9174	0.9174	1.0900000	1
2	1.1881	2.0900	0.478469	0.8417	1.7591	0.5684689	2
3	1.2950	3.2781	0.305055	0.7722	2.5313	0.3950548	3
4	1.4116	4.5731	0.218669	0.7084	3.2397	0.3086687	4
5	1.5386	5.9847	0.167092	0.6499	3.8897	0.2570925	5
6	1.6771	7.5233	0.132920	0.5963	4.4859	0.2229198	6
7	1.8280	9.2004	0.108691	0.5470	5.0330	0.1986905	7
8	1.9926	11.0285	0.090674	0.5019	5.5348	0.1806744	8
9	2.1719	13.0210	0.076799	0.4604	5.9952	0.1667988	9
10	2.3674	15.1929	0.065820	0.4224	6.4177	0.1558201	10
11	2.5804	17.5603	0.056947	0.3875	6.8052	0.1469467	11
12	2.8127	20.1407	0.049651	0.3555	7.1607	0.1396507	12
13	3.0658	22.9534	0.043567	0.3262	7.4869	0.1335666	13
14	3.3417	26.0192	0.038433	0.2992	7.7862	0.1284332	14
15	3.5425	29.3609	0.034059	0.2745	8.0607	0.1240589	15
16	3.9703	33.0034	0.030300	0.2519	8.3126	0.1202999	16
17	4.3276	36.9737	0.027046	0.2311	8.5436	0.1170463	17
18	4.7171	41.3013	0.024212	0.2120	8.7556	0.1142123	18
19	5.1417	46.0185	0.021730	0.1945	8.9501	0.1117304	19
20	5.6044	51.1601	0.019546	0.1784	9.1285	0.1095465	20
21	6.1088	56.7645	0.017617	0.1637	9.2922	0.1076166	21
22	6.6586	62.8733	0.015905	0.1502	9.4424	0.1059050	22
23	7.2579	69.5319	0.014382	0.1378	9.5802	0.1043819	23
24	7.9111	76.7898	0.013023	0.1264	9.7066	0.1030226	24
25	8.6231	84.7009	0.011806	0.1160	9.8226	0.1018063	25
26	9.3992	93.3240	0.010715	0.1064	9.9290	0.1007154	26
27	10.2451	102.7231	0.009735	0.0976	10.0266	0.0997349	27
28	11.1671	112.9682	0.008852	0.0895	10.1161	0.0988521	28
29	12.1722	124.1354	0.008056	0.0822	10.1983	0.0980557	29
30	13.2677	136.3075	0.007336	0.0754	10.2737	0.0973364	30
31	14.4618	149.5752	0.006686	0.0691	10.3428	0.0966856	31
32	15.7633	164.0370	0.006096	0.0634	10.4062	0.0960962	32
33	17.1820	179.8003	0.005562	0.0582	10.4644	0.0955617	33
34	18.7284	196.9824	0.005077	0.0534	10.5178	0.0950766	34
35	20.4140	215.7108	0.004636	0.0490	10.5668	0.0946358	35
36	22.2512	236.1247	0.004235	0.0449	10.6118	0.0942351	36
37	24.2538	258.3760	0.003870	0.0412	10.6530	0.0938703	37
38	26.4367	282.6298	0.003538	0.0378	10.6908	0.0935382	38
39	28.8160	309.0665	0.003236	0.0347	10.7255	0.0932356	39
40	31.4094	337.8825	0.002960	0.0318	10.7574	0.0929596	40

TABLE A-3. ANNUAL RATE 10 PERCENT

Nominal Annual Interest Rate = 10%   Compounding Periods per Year = 1

Year	Amount of 1 at Compound Interest (Col. 1)	Accumulation of 1 per Period (Col. 2)	Sinking Fund Factor (Col. 3)	Present Value Reversion of 1 (Col. 4)	Present Value Ordinary Annuity 1 per Period (Col. 5)	Installment to Amortize 1 (Col. 6)	Period
1	1.1000	1.0000	1.000000	0.9091	0.9091	1.1000000	1
2	1.2100	2.1000	0.476190	0.8264	1.7355	0.5761905	2
3	1.3310	3.3100	0.302115	0.7513	2.4869	0.4021148	3
4	1.4641	4.6410	0.215471	0.6830	3.1699	0.3154708	4
5	1.6105	6.1051	0.163797	0.6209	3.7908	0.2637975	5
6	1.7716	7.7156	0.129607	0.5645	4.3553	0.2296074	6
7	1.9487	9.4872	0.105405	0.5132	4.8684	0.2054055	7
8	2.1436	11.4359	0.087444	0.4655	5.3349	0.1874440	8
9	2.3579	13.5795	0.073641	0.4241	5.7590	0.1736405	9
10	2.5937	15.9374	0.062745	0.3855	6.1446	0.1627454	10
11	2.8531	18.5312	0.053963	0.3505	6.4951	0.1539631	11
12	3.1384	21.3843	0.046763	0.3186	6.8137	0.1467633	12
13	3.4523	24.5227	0.040779	0.2897	7.1034	0.1407785	13
14	3.7975	27.9750	0.035746	0.2633	7.3667	0.1357462	14
15	4.1772	31.7725	0.031474	0.2394	7.6061	0.1314738	15
16	4.5950	35.9497	0.027817	0.2176	7.8237	0.1278166	16
17	5.0545	40.5447	0.024664	0.1978	8.0216	0.1246641	17
18	5.5599	45.5992	0.021930	0.1799	8.2014	0.1219302	18
19	6.1159	51.1591	0.019547	0.1635	8.3649	0.1195469	19
20	6.7275	57.2750	0.017460	0.1486	8.5136	0.1174596	20
21	7.4003	64.0025	0.015624	0.1351	8.6487	0.1156244	21
22	8.1403	71.4028	0.014005	0.1228	8.7715	0.1140051	22
23	8.9543	79.5430	0.012572	0.1117	8.8832	0.1125718	23
24	9.8497	88.4973	0.011300	0.1015	8.9847	0.1112998	24
25	10.8347	98.3471	0.010168	0.0923	9.0770	0.1101681	25
26	11.9182	109.1818	0.009159	0.0839	9.1609	0.1091590	26
27	13.1100	121.0999	0.008258	0.0763	9.2372	0.1082576	27
28	14.4210	134.2099	0.007451	0.0693	9.3066	0.1074510	28
29	15.8631	148.6309	0.006728	0.0630	9.3696	0.1067281	29
30	17.4494	164.4940	0.006079	0.0573	9.4269	0.1060792	30
31	19.1943	181.9434	0.005496	0.0521	9.4790	0.1054962	31
32	21.1138	201.1378	0.004972	0.0474	9.5264	0.1049717	32
33	23.2252	222.2516	0.004499	0.0431	9.5694	0.1044994	33
34	25.5477	245.4767	0.004074	0.0391	9.6086	0.1040737	34
35	28.1024	271.0244	0.003690	0.0356	9.6442	0.1036897	35
36	30.9127	299.1268	0.003343	0.0323	9.6765	0.1033431	36
37	34.0040	330.0395	0.003030	0.0294	9.7059	0.1030299	37
38	37.4043	364.0434	0.002747	0.0267	9.7327	0.1027469	38
39	41.1448	401.4478	0.002491	0.0243	9.7570	0.1024910	39
40	45.2593	442.5926	0.002259	0.0221	9.7791	0.1022594	40

TABLE A-4.   ANNUAL RATE 11 PERCENT

Nominal Annual Interest Rate = 11%   Compounding Periods per Year = 1

Year	Amount of 1 at Compound Interest (Col. 1)	Accumu- lation of 1 per Period (Col. 2)	Sinking Fund Factor (Col. 3)	Present Value Rever- sion of 1 (Col. 4)	Present Value Ordinary Annuity 1 per Period (Col. 5)	Installment to Amortize 1 (Col. 6)	Period
1	1.1100	1.0000	1.000000	0.9009	0.9009	1.1100000	1
2	1.2321	2.1100	0.473934	0.8116	1.7125	0.5839336	2
3	1.3676	3.3421	0.299213	0.7312	2.4437	0.4092131	3
4	1.5181	4.7097	0.212326	0.6587	3.1024	0.3223264	4
5	1.6851	6.2278	0.160570	0.5935	3.6959	0.2705703	5
6	1.8704	7.9129	0.126377	0.5346	4.2305	0.2363766	6
7	2.0762	9.7833	0.102215	0.4817	4.7122	0.2122153	7
8	2.3045	11.8594	0.084321	0.4339	5.1461	0.1943211	8
9	2.5580	14.1640	0.070602	0.3909	5.5370	0.1806017	9
10	2.8394	16.7220	0.059801	0.3522	5.8892	0.1698014	10
11	3.1518	19.5614	0.051121	0.3173	6.2065	0.1611210	11
12	3.4985	22.7132	0.044027	0.2858	6.4924	0.1540273	12
13	3.8833	26.2116	0.038151	0.2575	6.7499	0.1481510	13
14	4.3104	30.0949	0.033228	0.2320	6.9819	0.1432282	14
15	4.7846	34.4054	0.029065	0.2090	7.1909	0.1390652	15
16	5.3109	39.1899	0.025517	0.1883	7.3792	0.1355167	16
17	5.8951	44.5008	0.022471	0.1696	7.5488	0.1324715	17
18	6.5436	50.3959	0.019843	0.1528	7.7016	0.1298429	18
19	7.2633	56.9395	0.017563	0.1377	7.8393	0.1275625	19
20	8.0623	64.2028	0.015576	0.1240	7.9633	0.1255756	20
21	8.9492	72.2651	0.013838	0.1117	8.0751	0.1238379	21
22	9.9336	81.2143	0.012313	0.1007	8.1757	0.1223131	22
23	11.0263	91.1479	0.010971	0.0907	8.2664	0.1209712	23
24	12.2392	102.1741	0.009787	0.0817	8.3481	0.1197872	24
25	13.5855	114.4133	0.008740	0.0736	8.4217	0.1187402	25
26	15.0799	127.9988	0.007813	0.0663	8.4881	0.1178126	26
27	16.7386	143.0786	0.006989	0.0597	8.5478	0.1169892	27
28	18.5799	159.8173	0.006257	0.0538	8.6016	0.1162571	28
29	20.6237	178.3972	0.005605	0.0485	8.6501	0.1156055	29
30	22.8923	199.0209	0.005025	0.0437	8.6938	0.1150246	30
31	25.4104	221.9132	0.004506	0.0394	8.7331	0.1145063	31
32	28.2056	247.3236	0.004043	0.0355	8.7686	0.1140433	32
33	31.3082	275.5292	0.003629	0.0319	8.8005	0.1136294	33
34	34.7521	306.8374	0.003259	0.0288	8.8293	0.1132591	34
35	38.5749	341.5896	0.002927	0.0259	8.8552	0.1129275	35
36	42.8181	380.1644	0.002630	0.0234	8.8786	0.1126304	36
37	47.5281	422.9825	0.002364	0.0210	8.8996	0.1123642	37
38	52.7562	470.5106	0.002125	0.0190	8.9186	0.1121254	38
39	58.5593	523.2667	0.001911	0.0171	8.9357	0.1119111	39
40	65.0009	581.8261	0.001719	0.0154	8.9511	0.1117187	40

TABLE A-5.   ANNUAL RATE 12 PERCENT

Nominal Annual Interest Rate = 12%   Compounding Periods per Year = 1

Year	Amount of 1 at Compound Interest (Col. 1)	Accumulation of 1 per Period (Col. 2)	Sinking Fund Factor (Col. 3)	Present Value Reversion of 1 (Col. 4)	Present Value Ordinary Annuity 1 per Period (Col. 5)	Installment to Amortize 1 (Col. 6)	Period
1	1.1200	1.0000	1.000000	0.8929	0.8929	1.1200000	1
2	1.2544	2.1200	0.471698	0.7972	1.6901	0.5916981	2
3	1.4049	3.3744	0.296349	0.7118	2.4018	0.4163490	3
4	1.5735	4.7793	0.209234	0.6355	3.0373	0.3292344	4
5	1.7623	6.3528	0.157410	0.5674	3.6048	0.2774097	5
6	1.9738	8.1152	0.123226	0.5066	4.1114	0.2432257	6
7	2.2107	10.0890	0.099118	0.4523	4.5638	0.2191177	7
8	2.4760	12.2997	0.081303	0.4039	4.9676	0.2013028	8
9	2.7731	14.7757	0.067679	0.3606	5.3282	0.1876789	9
10	3.1058	17.5487	0.056984	0.3220	5.6502	0.1769842	10
11	3.4785	20.6546	0.048415	0.2875	5.9377	0.1684154	11
12	3.8960	24.1331	0.041437	0.2567	6.1944	0.1614368	12
13	4.3635	28.0291	0.035677	0.2292	6.4235	0.1556772	13
14	4.8871	32.3926	0.030871	0.2046	6.6282	0.1508712	14
15	5.4736	37.2797	0.026824	0.1827	6.8109	0.1468242	15
16	6.1304	42.7533	0.023390	0.1631	6.9740	0.1433900	16
17	6.8660	48.8837	0.020457	0.1456	7.1196	0.1404567	17
18	7.6900	55.7497	0.017937	0.1300	7.2497	0.1379373	18
19	8.6128	63.4397	0.015763	0.1161	7.3658	0.1357630	19
20	9.6463	72.0524	0.013879	0.1037	7.4694	0.1338788	20
21	10.8038	81.6987	0.012240	0.0926	7.5620	0.1322401	21
22	12.1003	92.5026	0.010811	0.0826	7.6446	0.1308105	22
23	13.5523	104.6029	0.009560	0.0738	7.7184	0.1295600	23
24	15.1786	118.1552	0.008463	0.0659	7.7843	0.1284634	24
25	17.0001	133.3339	0.007500	0.0588	7.8431	0.1275000	25
26	19.0401	150.3339	0.006652	0.0525	7.8957	0.1266519	26
27	21.3249	169.3740	0.005904	0.0469	7.9426	0.1259041	27
28	23.8839	190.6989	0.005244	0.0419	7.9844	0.1252439	28
29	26.7499	214.5827	0.004660	0.0374	8.0218	0.1246602	29
30	29.9599	241.3327	0.004144	0.0334	8.0552	0.1241437	30
31	33.5551	271.2926	0.003686	0.0298	8.0850	0.1236861	31
32	37.5817	304.8477	0.003280	0.0266	8.1116	0.1232803	32
33	42.0915	342.4294	0.002920	0.0238	8.1354	0.1229203	33
34	47.1425	384.5210	0.002601	0.0212	8.1566	0.1226006	34
35	52.7996	431.6635	0.002317	0.0189	8.1755	0.1223166	35
36	59.1356	484.4631	0.002064	0.0169	8.1924	0.1220641	36
37	66.2318	543.5987	0.001840	0.0151	8.2075	0.1218396	37
38	74.1797	609.8305	0.001640	0.0135	8.2210	0.1216398	38
39	83.0812	684.0101	0.001462	0.0120	8.2330	0.1214620	39
40	93.0510	767.0914	0.001304	0.0107	8.2438	0.1213036	40

TABLE A-6. ANNUAL RATE 13 PERCENT

Nominal Annual Interest Rate = 13%   Compounding Periods per Year = 1

Year	Amount of 1 at Compound Interest (Col. 1)	Accumulation of 1 per Period (Col. 2)	Sinking Fund Factor (Col. 3)	Present Value Reversion of 1 (Col. 4)	Present Value Ordinary Annuity 1 per Period (Col. 5)	Installment to Amortize 1 (Col. 6)	Period
1	1.1300	1.0000	1.000000	0.8850	0.8850	1.1300000	1
2	1.2769	2.1300	0.469484	0.7831	1.6681	0.5994836	2
3	1.4429	3.4069	0.293522	0.6931	2.3612	0.4235220	3
4	1.6305	4.8498	0.206194	0.6133	2.9745	0.3361942	4
5	1.8424	6.4803	0.154315	0.5428	3.5172	0.2843145	5
6	2.0820	8.3227	0.120153	0.4803	3.9975	0.2501532	6
7	2.3526	10.4047	0.096111	0.4251	4.4226	0.2261108	7
8	2.6584	12.7573	0.078387	0.3762	4.7988	0.2083867	8
9	3.0040	15.4157	0.064869	0.3329	5.1317	0.1948689	9
10	3.3946	18.4197	0.054290	0.2946	5.4262	0.1842896	10
11	3.8359	21.8143	0.045841	0.2607	5.6869	0.1758415	11
12	4.3345	25.6502	0.038986	0.2307	5.9176	0.1689861	12
13	4.8980	29.9847	0.033350	0.2042	6.1218	0.1633503	13
14	5.5348	34.8827	0.028667	0.1807	6.3025	0.1586675	14
15	6.2543	40.4175	0.024742	0.1599	6.4624	0.1547418	15
16	7.0673	46.6717	0.021426	0.1415	6.6039	0.1514262	16
17	7.9861	53.7391	0.018608	0.1252	6.7291	0.1486084	17
18	9.0243	61.7251	0.016201	0.1108	6.8399	0.1462009	18
19	10.1974	70.7494	0.014134	0.0981	6.9380	0.1441344	19
20	11.5231	80.9468	0.012354	0.0868	7.0248	0.1423538	20
21	13.0211	92.4699	0.010814	0.0768	7.1016	0.1408143	21
22	14.7138	105.4910	0.009479	0.0680	7.1695	0.1394795	22
23	16.6266	120.2048	0.008319	0.0601	7.2297	0.1383191	23
24	18.7881	136.8315	0.007308	0.0532	7.2829	0.1373083	24
25	21.2305	155.6195	0.006426	0.0471	7.3300	0.1364259	25
26	23.9905	176.8501	0.005655	0.0417	7.3717	0.1356545	26
27	27.1093	200.8406	0.004979	0.0369	7.4086	0.1349791	27
28	30.6335	227.9499	0.004387	0.0326	7.4412	0.1343869	28
29	34.6158	258.5834	0.003867	0.0289	7.4701	0.1338672	29
30	39.1159	293.1992	0.003411	0.0256	7.4957	0.1334106	30
31	44.2010	332.3151	0.003009	0.0226	7.5183	0.1330092	31
32	49.9471	376.5160	0.002656	0.0200	7.5383	0.1326559	32
33	56.4402	426.4631	0.002345	0.0177	7.5560	0.1323449	33
34	63.7774	482.9033	0.002071	0.0157	7.5717	0.1320708	34
35	72.0685	546.6808	0.001829	0.0139	7.5856	0.1318292	35
36	81.4374	618.7493	0.001616	0.0123	7.5979	0.1316162	36
37	92.0243	700.1867	0.001428	0.0109	7.6087	0.1314282	37
38	103.9874	792.2109	0.001262	0.0096	7.6183	0.1312623	38
39	117.5058	896.1983	0.001116	0.0085	7.6268	0.1311158	39
40	132.7815	1013.7041	0.000986	0.0075	7.6344	0.1309865	40

TABLE A-7.   ANNUAL RATE 14 PERCENT

Nominal Annual Interest Rate = 14%   Compounding Periods per Year = 1

Year	Amount of 1 at Compound Interest (Col. 1)	Accumulation of 1 per Period (Col. 2)	Sinking Fund Factor (Col. 3)	Present Value Reversion of 1 (Col. 4)	Present Value Ordinary Annuity 1 per Period (Col. 5)	Installment to Amortize 1 (Col. 6)	Period
1	1.1400	1.0000	1.000000	0.8772	0.8772	1.1400000	1
2	1.2996	2.1400	0.467290	0.7695	1.6467	0.6072897	2
3	1.4815	3.4396	0.290731	0.6750	2.3216	0.4307315	3
4	1.6890	4.9211	0.203205	0.5921	2.9137	0.3432048	4
5	1.9254	6.6101	0.151284	0.5194	3.4331	0.2912835	5
6	2.1950	8.5355	0.117157	0.4556	3.8887	0.2571575	6
7	2.5023	10.7305	0.093192	0.3996	4.2883	0.2331924	7
8	2.8526	13.2328	0.075570	0.3506	4.6389	0.2155700	8
9	3.2519	16.0853	0.062168	0.3075	4.9464	0.2021684	9
10	3.7072	19.3373	0.051714	0.2697	5.2161	0.1917135	10
11	4.2262	23.0445	0.043394	0.2366	5.4527	0.1833943	11
12	4.8179	27.2707	0.036669	0.2076	5.6603	0.1766693	12
13	5.4924	32.0887	0.031164	0.1821	5.8424	0.1711637	13
14	6.2613	37.5811	0.026609	0.1597	6.0021	0.1666091	14
15	7.1379	43.8424	0.022809	0.1401	6.1422	0.1628090	15
16	8.1372	50.9804	0.019615	0.1229	6.2651	0.1596154	16
17	9.2765	59.1176	0.016915	0.1078	6.3729	0.1569154	17
18	10.5752	68.3941	0.014621	0.0946	6.4674	0.1546212	18
19	12.0557	78.9692	0.012663	0.0829	6.5504	0.1526632	19
20	13.7435	91.0249	0.010986	0.0728	6.6231	0.1509860	20
21	15.6676	104.7684	0.009545	0.0638	6.6870	0.1495449	21
22	17.8610	120.4360	0.008303	0.0560	6.7429	0.1483032	22
23	20.3616	138.2970	0.007231	0.0491	6.7921	0.1472308	23
24	23.2122	158.6586	0.006303	0.0431	6.8351	0.1463028	24
25	26.4619	181.8708	0.005498	0.0378	6.8729	0.1454984	25
26	30.1666	208.3327	0.004800	0.0331	6.9061	0.1448000	26
27	34.3899	238.4993	0.004193	0.0291	6.9352	0.1441929	27
28	39.2045	272.8892	0.003664	0.0255	6.9607	0.1436645	28
29	44.6931	312.0937	0.003204	0.0224	6.9830	0.1432042	29
30	50.9502	356.7869	0.002803	0.0196	7.0027	0.1428028	30
31	58.0832	407.7370	0.002453	0.0172	7.0199	0.1424526	31
32	66.2148	465.8202	0.002147	0.0151	7.0350	0.1421468	32
33	75.4849	532.0350	0.001880	0.0132	7.0482	0.1418796	33
34	86.0528	607.5199	0.001646	0.0116	7.0599	0.1416460	34
35	98.1002	693.5727	0.001442	0.0102	7.0700	0.1414418	35
36	111.8342	791.6729	0.001263	0.0089	7.0790	0.1412631	36
37	127.4910	903.5071	0.001107	0.0078	7.0868	0.1411068	37
38	145.3397	1030.9981	0.000970	0.0069	7.0937	0.1409699	38
39	165.6873	1176.3378	0.000850	0.0060	7.0997	0.1408501	39
40	188.8835	1342.0251	0.000745	0.0053	7.1050	0.1407451	40

TABLE A-8. ANNUAL RATE 15 PERCENT

Nominal Annual Interest Rate = 15%   Compounding Periods per Year = 1

Year	Amount of 1 at Compound Interest (Col. 1)	Accumulation of 1 per Period (Col. 2)	Sinking Fund Factor (Col. 3)	Present Value Reversion of 1 (Col. 4)	Present Value Ordinary Annuity 1 per Period (Col. 5)	Installment to Amortize 1 (Col. 6)	Period
1	1.1500	1.0000	1.000000	0.8696	0.8696	1.1500000	1
2	1.3225	2.1500	0.465116	0.7561	1.6257	0.6151163	2
3	1.5209	3.4725	0.287977	0.6575	2.2832	0.4379770	3
4	1.7490	4.9934	0.200265	0.5718	2.8550	0.3502654	4
5	2.0114	6.7424	0.148316	0.4972	3.3522	0.2983156	5
6	2.3131	8.7537	0.114237	0.4323	3.7845	0.2642369	6
7	2.6600	11.0668	0.090360	0.3759	4.1604	0.2403604	7
8	3.0590	13.7268	0.072850	0.3269	4.4873	0.2228501	8
9	3.5179	16.7858	0.059574	0.2843	4.7716	0.2095740	9
10	4.0456	20.3037	0.049252	0.2472	5.0188	0.1992521	10
11	4.6524	24.3493	0.041069	0.2149	5.2337	0.1910690	11
12	5.3503	29.0017	0.034481	0.1869	5.4206	0.1844808	12
13	6.1528	34.3519	0.029110	0.1625	5.5831	0.1791105	13
14	7.0757	40.5047	0.024688	0.1413	5.7245	0.1746885	14
15	8.1371	47.5804	0.021017	0.1229	5.8474	0.1710171	15
16	9.3576	55.7175	0.017948	0.1069	5.9542	0.1679477	16
17	10.7613	65.0751	0.015367	0.0929	6.0472	0.1653669	17
18	12.3755	75.8364	0.013186	0.0808	6.1280	0.1631863	18
19	14.2318	88.2118	0.011336	0.0703	6.1982	0.1613364	19
20	16.3665	102.4436	0.009761	0.0611	6.2593	0.1597615	20
21	18.8215	118.8101	0.008417	0.0531	6.3125	0.1584168	21
22	21.6447	137.6316	0.007266	0.0462	6.3587	0.1572658	22
23	24.8915	159.2764	0.006278	0.0402	6.3988	0.1562784	23
24	28.6252	184.1679	0.005430	0.0349	6.4338	0.1554298	24
25	32.9190	212.7930	0.004699	0.0304	6.4641	0.1546994	25
26	37.8568	245.7120	0.004070	0.0264	6.4906	0.1540698	26
27	43.5353	283.5688	0.003526	0.0230	6.5135	0.1535265	27
28	50.0656	327.1041	0.003057	0.0200	6.5335	0.1530571	28
29	57.5755	377.1697	0.002651	0.0174	6.5509	0.1526513	29
30	66.2118	434.7452	0.002300	0.0151	6.5660	0.1523002	30
31	76.1435	500.9570	0.001996	0.0131	6.5791	0.1519962	31
32	87.5651	577.1005	0.001733	0.0114	6.5905	0.1517328	32
33	100.6998	664.6656	0.001505	0.0099	6.6005	0.1515045	33
34	115.8048	765.3655	0.001307	0.0086	6.6091	0.1513066	34
35	133.1755	881.1703	0.001135	0.0075	6.6166	0.1511349	35
36	153.1519	1014.3458	0.000986	0.0065	6.6231	0.1509859	36
37	176.1247	1167.4977	0.000857	0.0057	6.6288	0.1508565	37
38	202.5434	1343.6224	0.000744	0.0049	6.6338	0.1507443	38
39	232.9249	1546.1657	0.000647	0.0043	6.6380	0.1506468	39
40	267.8636	1779.0906	0.000562	0.0037	6.6418	0.1505621	40

TABLE A-9.   ANNUAL RATE 16 PERCENT

Nominal Annual Interest Rate = 16%   Compounding Periods per Year = 1

Year	Amount of 1 at Compound Interest (Col. 1)	Accumulation of 1 per Period (Col. 2)	Sinking Fund Factor (Col. 3)	Present Value Reversion of 1 (Col. 4)	Present Value Ordinary Annuity 1 per Period (Col. 5)	Installment to Amortize 1 (Col. 6)	Period
1	1.1600	1.0000	1.000000	0.8621	0.8621	1.1600000	1
2	1.3456	2.1600	0.462963	0.7432	1.6052	0.6229630	2
3	1.5609	3.5056	0.285258	0.6407	2.2459	0.4452579	3
4	1.8106	5.0665	0.197375	0.5523	2.7982	0.3573751	4
5	2.1003	6.8771	0.145409	0.4761	3.2743	0.3054094	5
6	2.4364	8.9775	0.111390	0.4104	3.6847	0.2713899	6
7	2.8262	11.4139	0.087613	0.3538	4.0386	0.2476127	7
8	3.2784	14.2401	0.070224	0.3050	4.3436	0.2302243	8
9	3.8030	17.5185	0.057082	0.2630	4.6065	0.2170825	9
10	4.4114	21.3215	0.046901	0.2267	4.8332	0.2069011	10
11	5.1173	25.7329	0.038861	0.1954	5.0286	0.1988607	11
12	5.9360	30.8502	0.032415	0.1685	5.1971	0.1924147	12
13	6.8858	36.7862	0.027184	0.1452	5.3423	0.1871841	13
14	7.9875	43.6720	0.022898	0.1252	5.4675	0.1828980	14
15	9.2655	51.6595	0.019358	0.1079	5.5755	0.1793575	15
16	10.7480	60.9250	0.016414	0.0930	5.6685	0.1764136	16
17	12.4677	71.6730	0.013952	0.0802	5.7487	0.1739522	17
18	14.4625	84.1407	0.011885	0.0691	5.8178	0.1718848	18
19	16.7765	98.6032	0.010142	0.0596	5.8775	0.1701417	19
20	19.4608	115.3797	0.008667	0.0514	5.9288	0.1686670	20
21	24.5745	134.8405	0.007416	0.0443	5.9731	0.1674162	21
22	26.1864	157.4150	0.006353	0.0382	6.0113	0.1663526	22
23	30.3762	183.6014	0.005447	0.0329	6.0442	0.1654466	23
24	35.2364	213.9776	0.004673	0.0284	6.0726	0.1646734	24
25	40.8742	249.2140	0.004013	0.0245	6.0971	0.1640126	25
26	47.4141	290.0883	0.003447	0.0211	6.1182	0.1634472	26
27	55.0004	337.5024	0.002963	0.0182	6.1364	0.1629629	27
28	63.8004	392.5027	0.002548	0.0157	6.1520	0.1625477	28
29	74.0085	456.3032	0.002192	0.0135	6.1656	0.1621915	29
30	85.8499	530.3117	0.001886	0.0116	6.1772	0.1618857	30
31	99.5828	616.1616	0.001623	0.0100	6.1872	0.1616229	31
32	115.5196	715.7474	0.001397	0.0087	6.1959	0.1613971	32
33	134.0027	831.2670	0.001203	0.0075	6.2034	0.1612030	33
34	155.4431	965.2697	0.001036	0.0064	6.2098	0.1610360	34
35	180.3141	1120.7129	0.000892	0.0055	6.2153	0.1608923	35
36	209.1643	1301.0269	0.000769	0.0048	6.2201	0.1607686	36
37	242.6306	1510.1912	0.000662	0.0041	6.2242	0.1606622	37
38	281.4515	1752.8218	0.000571	0.0036	6.2278	0.1605705	38
39	326.4837	2034.2733	0.000492	0.0031	6.2309	0.1604916	39
40	378.7211	2360.7570	0.000424	0.0026	6.2335	0.1604236	40

TABLE A-10.   ANNUAL RATE 20 PERCENT

Nominal Annual Interest Rate = 20%   Compounding Periods per Year = 1

Year	Amount of 1 at Compound Interest (Col. 1)	Accumulation of 1 per Period (Col. 2)	Sinking Fund Factor (Col. 3)	Present Value Reversion of 1 (Col. 4)	Present Value Ordinary Annuity 1 per Period (Col. 5)	Installment to Amortize 1 (Col. 6)	Period
1	1.2000	1.0000	1.000000	0.8333	0.8333	1.2000000	1
2	1.4400	2.2000	0.454545	0.6944	1.5278	0.6545455	2
3	1.7280	3.6400	0.274725	0.5787	2.1065	0.4747253	3
4	2.0736	5.3680	0.186289	0.4823	2.5887	0.3862891	4
5	2.4883	7.4416	0.134380	0.4019	2.9906	0.3343797	5
6	2.9860	9.9299	0.100706	0.3349	3.3255	0.3007057	6
7	3.5832	12.9159	0.077424	0.2791	3.6046	0.2774239	7
8	4.2998	16.4991	0.060609	0.2326	3.8372	0.2606094	8
9	5.1598	20.7989	0.048079	0.1938	4.0310	0.2480795	9
10	6.1917	25.9587	0.038523	0.1615	4.1925	0.2385228	10
11	7.4301	32.1504	0.031104	0.1346	4.3271	0.2311038	11
12	8.9161	39.5805	0.025265	0.1122	4.4392	0.2252650	12
13	10.6993	48.4966	0.020620	0.0935	4.5327	0.2206200	13
14	12.8392	59.1959	0.016893	0.0779	4.6106	0.2168931	14
15	15.4070	72.0351	0.013882	0.0649	4.6755	0.2138821	15
16	18.4884	87.4421	0.011436	0.0541	4.7296	0.2114361	16
17	22.1861	105.9306	0.009440	0.0451	4.7746	0.2094401	17
18	26.6233	128.1167	0.007805	0.0376	4.8122	0.2078054	18
19	31.9480	154.7400	0.006462	0.0313	4.8435	0.2064625	19
20	38.3376	186.6880	0.005357	0.0261	4.8696	0.2053565	20
21	46.0051	225.0256	0.004444	0.0217	4.8913	0.2044439	21
22	55.2061	271.0307	0.003690	0.0181	4.9094	0.2036896	22
23	66.2474	326.2369	0.003065	0.0151	4.9245	0.2030653	23
24	79.4969	392.4843	0.002548	0.0126	4.9371	0.2025479	24
25	95.3962	471.9811	0.002119	0.0105	4.9476	0.2021187	25
26	114.4755	567.3773	0.001762	0.0087	4.9563	0.2017625	26
27	137.3706	681.8528	0.001467	0.0073	4.9636	0.2014666	27
28	164.8447	819.2234	0.001221	0.0061	4.9697	0.2012207	28
29	197.8136	984.0680	0.001016	0.0051	4.9747	0.2010162	29
30	237.3763	1181.8816	0.000846	0.0042	4.9789	0.2008461	30
31	284.8516	1419.2580	0.000705	0.0035	4.9824	0.2007046	31
32	341.8219	1704.1096	0.000587	0.0029	4.9854	0.2005868	32
33	410.1863	2045.9315	0.000489	0.0024	4.9878	0.2004888	33
34	492.2236	2456.1178	0.000407	0.0020	4.9898	0.2004071	34
35	590.6683	2948.3414	0.000339	0.0017	4.9915	0.2003392	35
36	708.8019	3539.0096	0.000283	0.0014	4.9929	0.2002826	36
37	850.5623	4247.8116	0.000235	0.0012	4.9941	0.2002354	37
38	1020.6748	5098.3739	0.000196	0.0010	4.9951	0.2001961	38
39	1224.8098	6119.0487	0.000163	0.0008	4.9959	0.2001634	39
40	1469.7717	7343.8585	0.000136	0.0007	4.9966	0.2001362	40

TABLE A-11. MONTHLY COMPOUNDING 8 PERCENT

Nominal Annual Interest Rate = 8%   Compounding Periods per Year = 12

Year	Amount of 1 at Compound Interest (Col. 1)	Accumulation of 1 per Period (Col. 2)	Sinking Fund Factor (Col. 3)	Present Value Reversion of 1 (Col. 4)	Present Value Ordinary Annuity 1 per Period (Col. 5)	Installment to Amortize 1 (Col. 6)	Period
1	1.0830	12.4499	0.080322	0.9234	11.4958	0.08698843	12
2	1.1729	25.9332	0.038561	0.9526	22.1105	0.04522729	24
3	1.2702	40.5356	0.024670	0.7873	31.9118	0.03133637	36
4	1.3757	56.3499	0.017746	0.7269	40.9619	0.02441292	48
5	1.4898	73.4769	0.013610	0.6712	49.3184	0.02027639	60
6	1.6135	92.0253	0.010867	0.6198	57.0345	0.01753324	72
7	1.7474	112.1133	0.008920	0.5723	64.1593	0.01558621	84
8	1.8925	133.8686	0.007470	0.5284	70.7380	0.01413668	96
9	2.0495	157.4295	0.006352	0.4879	76.8125	0.01301871	108
10	2.2196	182.9460	0.005466	0.4505	82.4215	0.01213276	120
11	2.4039	210.5804	0.004749	0.4160	87.6006	0.01141545	132
12	2.6034	240.5084	0.004158	0.3841	92.3828	0.01082453	144
13	2.8195	272.9204	0.003664	0.3547	96.7985	0.01033074	156
14	3.0535	308.0226	0.003247	0.3275	100.8758	0.00991318	168
15	3.3069	346.0382	0.002890	0.3024	104.6406	0.00955652	180
16	3.5814	387.2092	0.002583	0.2792	108.1169	0.00924925	192
17	3.8786	431.7973	0.002316	0.2578	111.3267	0.00898257	204
18	4.2006	480.0861	0.002083	0.2381	114.2906	0.00874963	216
19	4.5492	532.3830	0.001878	0.2198	117.0273	0.00854501	228
20	4.9268	589.0204	0.001698	0.2030	119.5543	0.00836440	240
21	5.3357	650.3588	0.001538	0.1874	121.8876	0.00820428	252
22	5.7786	716.7881	0.001395	0.1731	124.0421	0.00806178	264
23	6.2582	788.7311	0.001268	0.1598	126.0315	0.00793453	276
24	6.7776	866.6454	0.001154	0.1475	127.8684	0.00782054	288
25	7.3402	951.0264	0.001051	0.1362	129.5645	0.00771816	300
26	7.9494	1042.4111	0.000959	0.1258	131.1307	0.00762598	312
27	8.6092	1141.3806	0.000876	0.1162	132.5768	0.00754280	324
28	9.3238	1248.5646	0.000801	0.1073	133.9121	0.00746759	336
29	10.0976	1364.6447	0.000733	0.0990	135.1450	0.00739946	348
30	10.9357	1490.3595	0.000671	0.0914	136.2835	0.00733765	360
31	11.8434	1626.5085	0.000615	0.0844	137.3347	0.00728148	372
32	12.8264	1773.9579	0.000564	0.0780	138.3054	0.00723038	384
33	13.8910	1933.6454	0.000517	0.0720	139.2016	0.00718382	396
34	15.0439	2106.5870	0.000475	0.0665	140.0292	0.00714137	408
35	16.2926	2293.8826	0.000436	0.0614	140.7933	0.00710261	420
36	17.6448	2496.7236	0.000401	0.0567	141.4989	0.00706719	432
37	19.1093	2716.4004	0.000368	0.0523	142.1504	0.00703480	444
38	20.6954	2954.3102	0.000338	0.0483	142.7520	0.00700516	456
39	22.4131	3211.9665	0.000311	0.0446	143.3075	0.00697800	468
40	24.2734	3491.0080	0.000286	0.0412	143.8204	0.00695312	480

TABLE A-12.   MONTHLY COMPOUNDING 10 PERCENT

Nominal Annual Interest Rate = 10%   Compounding Periods per Year = 12

Year	Amount of 1 at Compound Interest (Col. 1)	Accumulation of 1 per Period (Col. 2)	Sinking Fund Factor (Col. 3)	Present Value Reversion of 1 (Col. 4)	Present Value Ordinary Annuity 1 per Period (Col. 5)	Installment to Amortize 1 (Col. 6)	Period
1	1.1047	12.5656	0.079583	0.9052	11.3745	0.08791589	12
2	1.2204	26.4469	0.037812	0.8194	21.6709	0.04614493	24
3	1.3482	41.7818	0.023934	0.7417	30.9912	0.03226719	36
4	1.4894	58.7225	0.017029	0.6714	39.4282	0.02536258	48
5	1.6453	77.4371	0.012914	0.6078	47.0654	0.02124704	60
6	1.8176	98.1113	0.010193	0.5502	53.9787	0.01852584	72
7	2.0079	120.9504	0.008268	0.4980	60.2367	0.01660118	84
8	2.2182	146.1811	0.006841	0.4508	65.9015	0.01517416	96
9	2.4504	174.0537	0.005745	0.4081	71.0294	0.01407869	108
10	2.7070	204.8450	0.004882	0.3694	75.6712	0.01321507	120
11	2.9905	238.8605	0.004187	0.3344	79.8730	0.01251988	132
12	3.3036	276.4379	0.003617	0.3027	83.6765	0.01195078	144
13	3.6496	317.9501	0.003145	0.2740	87.1195	0.01147848	156
14	4.0317	363.8092	0.002749	0.2480	90.2362	0.01108203	168
15	4.4539	414.4703	0.002413	0.2245	93.0574	0.01074605	180
16	4.9203	470.4363	0.002126	0.2032	95.6113	0.01045902	192
17	5.4355	532.2627	0.001879	0.1840	97.9230	0.01021210	204
18	6.0047	600.5632	0.001665	0.1665	100.0156	0.00999844	216
19	6.6335	676.0156	0.001479	0.1508	101.9099	0.00981259	228
20	7.3281	759.3688	0.001317	0.1365	103.6246	0.00965022	240
21	8.0954	851.4502	0.001174	0.1235	105.1768	0.00950780	252
22	8.9431	953.1737	0.001049	0.1118	106.5819	0.00938246	264
23	9.8796	1065.5490	0.000938	0.1012	107.8537	0.00927182	276
24	10.9141	1189.6915	0.000841	0.0916	109.0050	0.00917389	288
25	12.0569	1326.8333	0.000754	0.0829	110.0472	0.00908701	300
26	13.3195	1478.3356	0.000676	0.0751	110.9906	0.00900977	312
27	14.7142	1645.7022	0.000608	0.0680	111.8446	0.00894098	324
28	16.2550	1830.5946	0.000546	0.0615	112.6176	0.00887960	336
29	17.9571	2034.8470	0.000491	0.0557	113.3174	0.00882477	348
30	19.8374	2260.4876	0.000442	0.0504	113.9508	0.00877572	360
31	21.9146	2509.7558	0.000398	0.0456	114.5242	0.00873178	372
32	24.2094	2785.1256	0.000359	0.0413	115.0433	0.00869238	384
33	26.7444	3089.3302	0.000324	0.0374	115.5131	0.00865703	396
34	29.5449	3425.3889	0.000292	0.0338	115.9384	0.00862527	408
35	32.6386	3796.6375	0.000263	0.0306	116.3234	0.00859672	420
36	36.0563	4206.7606	0.000238	0.0277	116.6719	0.00857105	432
37	39.8319	4659.8289	0.000215	0.0251	116.9873	0.00854793	444
38	44.0028	5160.3394	0.000194	0.0227	117.2729	0.00852712	456
39	48.6105	5713.2599	0.000175	0.0206	117.5314	0.00850836	468
40	53.7007	6324.0784	0.000158	0.0186	117.7654	0.00849146	480

TABLE A-13.   MONTHLY COMPOUNDING 11 PERCENT

Nominal Annual Interest Rate = 11%   Compounding Periods per Year = 12

Year	Amount of 1 at Compound Interest (Col. 1)	Accumulation of 1 per Period (Col. 2)	Sinking Fund Factor (Col. 3)	Present Value Reversion of 1 (Col. 4)	Present Value Ordinary Annuity 1 per Period (Col. 5)	Installment to Amortize 1 (Col. 6)	Period
1	1.1157	12.6239	0.079215	0.8963	11.3146	0.08838166	12
2	1.2448	26.7086	0.037441	0.8033	21.4556	0.04660784	24
3	1.3889	42.4231	0.023572	0.7200	30.5449	0.03273872	36
4	1.5496	59.9562	0.016679	0.6453	38.6914	0.02584552	48
5	1.7289	79.5181	0.012576	0.5784	45.9930	0.02174242	60
6	1.9290	101.3437	0.009867	0.5184	52.5373	0.01903408	72
7	2.1522	125.6949	0.007956	0.4646	58.4029	0.01712244	84
8	2.4013	152.8641	0.006542	0.4164	63.6601	0.01570843	96
9	2.6791	183.1772	0.005459	0.3733	68.3720	0.01462586	108
10	2.9891	216.9981	0.004608	0.3345	72.5953	0.01377500	120
11	3.3351	254.7328	0.003926	0.2998	76.3805	0.01309235	132
12	3.7210	296.8341	0.003369	0.2687	79.7731	0.01253555	144
13	4.1516	343.8072	0.002909	0.2409	82.8139	0.01207527	156
14	4.6320	396.2161	0.002524	0.2159	85.5392	0.01169054	168
15	5.1680	454.6896	0.002199	0.1935	87.9819	0.01136597	180
16	5.7660	519.9296	0.001923	0.1734	90.1713	0.01109000	192
17	6.4333	592.7192	0.001687	0.1554	92.1336	0.01085381	204
18	7.1777	673.9318	0.001484	0.1393	93.8923	0.01065050	216
19	8.0083	764.5423	0.001308	0.1249	95.4687	0.01047464	228
20	8.9350	865.6381	0.001155	0.1119	96.8815	0.01032188	240
21	9.9690	978.4326	0.001022	0.1003	98.1479	0.01018871	252
22	11.1226	1104.2796	0.000906	0.0899	99.2828	0.01007223	264
23	12.4097	1244.6894	0.000803	0.0806	100.3001	0.00997008	276
24	13.8457	1401.3473	0.000714	0.0722	101.2118	0.00988027	288
25	15.4479	1576.1335	0.000634	0.0647	102.0290	0.00980113	300
26	17.2355	1771.1457	0.000565	0.0580	102.7615	0.00973127	312
27	19.2300	1988.7245	0.000503	0.0520	103.4179	0.00966950	324
28	21.4552	2231.4813	0.000448	0.0466	104.0063	0.00961480	336
29	23.9380	2502.3296	0.000400	0.0418	104.5337	0.00956629	348
30	26.7081	2804.5202	0.000357	0.0374	105.0063	0.00952323	360
31	29.7987	3141.6799	0.000318	0.0336	105.4300	0.00948497	372
32	33.2470	3517.8553	0.000284	0.0301	105.8097	0.00945093	384
33	37.0943	3937.5613	0.000254	0.0270	106.1500	0.00942063	396
34	41.3868	4405.8352	0.000227	0.0242	106.4550	0.00939364	408
35	46.1761	4928.2973	0.000203	0.0217	106.7284	0.00936958	420
36	51.5195	5511.2180	0.000181	0.0194	106.9734	0.00934812	432
37	57.4813	6161.5936	0.000162	0.0174	107.1931	0.00932896	444
38	64.1329	6887.2300	0.000145	0.0156	107.3899	0.00931186	456
39	71.5543	7696.8362	0.000130	0.0140	107.5663	0.00929659	468
40	79.8345	8600.1290	0.000116	0.0125	107.7244	0.00928294	480

TABLE A-14. MONTHLY COMPOUNDING 12 PERCENT

Nominal Annual Interest Rate = 12%   Compounding Periods per Year = 12

Year	Amount of 1 at Compound Interest (Col. 1)	Accumulation of 1 per Period (Col. 2)	Sinking Fund Factor (Col. 3)	Present Value Reversion of 1 (Col. 4)	Present Value Ordinary Annuity 1 per Period (Col. 5)	Installment to Amortize 1 (Col. 6)	Period
1	1.1268	12.6825	0.078849	0.8874	11.2551	0.08884879	12
2	1.2697	26.9735	0.037073	0.7876	21.2434	0.04707347	24
3	1.4308	43.0769	0.023214	0.6989	30.1075	0.03321431	36
4	1.6122	61.2226	0.016334	0.6203	37.9740	0.02633384	48
5	1.8167	81.6697	0.012244	0.5504	44.9550	0.02224445	60
6	2.0471	104.7099	0.009550	0.4885	51.1504	0.01955019	72
7	2.3067	130.6723	0.007653	0.4335	56.6485	0.01765273	84
8	2.5993	159.9273	0.006253	0.3847	61.5277	0.01625284	96
9	2.9289	192.8926	0.005184	0.3414	65.8578	0.01518423	108
10	3.3004	230.0387	0.004347	0.3030	69.7005	0.01434709	120
11	3.7190	271.8959	0.003678	0.2689	73.1108	0.01367788	132
12	4.1906	319.0616	0.003134	0.2386	76.1372	0.01313419	144
13	4.7221	372.2090	0.002687	0.2118	78.8229	0.01268666	156
14	5.3210	432.0970	0.002314	0.1879	81.2064	0.01231430	168
15	5.9958	499.5802	0.002002	0.1668	83.3217	0.01200168	180
16	6.7262	575.6220	0.001737	0.1480	85.1988	0.01173725	192
17	7.6131	661.3077	0.001512	0.1314	86.8647	0.01151216	204
18	8.5786	757.8606	0.001320	0.1166	88.3431	0.01131950	216
19	9.6666	866.6588	0.001154	0.1034	89.6551	0.01115386	228
20	10.8926	989.2553	0.001011	0.0918	90.8194	0.01101086	240
21	12.2740	1127.4002	0.000887	0.0815	91.8527	0.01088700	252
22	13.8307	1283.0652	0.000779	0.0723	92.7697	0.01077938	264
23	15.5847	1458.4725	0.000686	0.0642	93.5835	0.01068565	276
24	17.5613	1656.1258	0.000604	0.0569	94.3056	0.01060382	288
25	19.7885	1878.8465	0.000532	0.0505	94.9466	0.01053224	300
26	22.2981	2129.8138	0.000470	0.0448	95.5153	0.01046952	312
27	25.1261	2412.6100	0.000414	0.0398	96.0201	0.01041449	324
28	28.3127	2731.2718	0.000366	0.0353	96.4680	0.01036613	336
29	31.9035	3090.3480	0.000324	0.0313	96.8655	0.01032359	348
30	35.9496	3494.9639	0.000286	0.0278	97.2183	0.01028613	360
31	40.5090	3950.8953	0.000253	0.0247	97.5314	0.01025311	372
32	45.6465	4464.6502	0.000224	0.0219	97.8093	0.01022398	384
33	51.4356	5043.5621	0.000198	0.0194	98.0558	0.01019827	396
34	57.9589	5695.8945	0.000176	0.0173	98.2746	0.01017556	408
35	65.3096	6430.9590	0.000155	0.0153	98.4688	0.01015550	420
36	73.5925	7259.2481	0.000138	0.0136	98.6412	0.01013776	432
37	82.9258	8192.5849	0.000122	0.0121	98.7941	0.01012206	444
38	93.4429	9244.2922	0.000108	0.0107	98.9298	0.01010817	456
39	105.2938	10429.3823	0.000096	0.0095	99.0503	0.01009588	468
40	118.6477	11764.7715	0.000085	0.0084	99.1572	0.01008500	480

TABLE A-15.   MONTHLY COMPOUNDING 13 PERCENT

Nominal Annual Interest Rate = 13%   Compounding Periods per Year = 12

Year	Amount of 1 at Compound Interest (Col. 1)	Accumulation of 1 per Period (Col. 2)	Sinking Fund Factor (Col. 3)	Present Value Reversion of 1 (Col. 4)	Present Value Ordinary Annuity 1 per Period (Col. 5)	Installment to Amortize 1 (Col. 6)	Period
1	1.1380	12.7415	0.078484	0.8787	11.1960	0.08931728	12
2	1.2951	27.2417	0.036708	0.7721	21.0341	0.04754182	24
3	1.4739	43.7433	0.022861	0.6785	29.6789	0.03369395	36
4	1.6773	62.5228	0.015994	0.5962	37.2752	0.02682750	48
5	1.9089	83.8945	0.011920	0.5239	43.9501	0.02275307	60
6	2.1723	108.2161	0.009241	0.4603	49.8154	0.02007411	72
7	2.4722	135.8949	0.007359	0.4045	54.9693	0.01819196	84
8	2.8134	167.3942	0.005974	0.3554	59.4981	0.01680726	96
9	3.2018	203.2415	0.004920	0.3123	63.4776	0.01575359	108
10	3.6437	244.0369	0.004098	0.2744	66.9744	0.01493107	120
11	4.1467	290.4634	0.003443	0.2412	70.0471	0.01427611	132
12	4.7191	343.2983	0.002913	0.2119	72.7471	0.01374625	144
13	5.3704	403.4260	0.002479	0.1862	75.1196	0.01331210	156
14	6.1117	471.8534	0.002119	0.1636	77.2044	0.01295264	168
15	6.9554	549.7260	0.001819	0.1438	79.0362	0.01265242	180
16	7.9154	638.3475	0.001567	0.1263	80.6459	0.01239988	192
17	9.0080	739.2016	0.001353	0.1110	82.0604	0.01217615	204
18	10.2514	853.9769	0.001171	0.0975	83.3033	0.01200433	216
19	11.6664	984.5950	0.001016	0.0857	84.3954	0.01184898	228
20	13.2768	1163.2425	0.000882	0.0753	85.3551	0.01171576	240
21	15.1094	1302.4083	0.000768	0.0662	86.1984	0.01160114	252
22	17.1950	1494.9244	0.000669	0.0582	86.9394	0.01150226	264
23	19.5685	1714.0140	0.000583	0.0511	87.5905	0.01141676	276
24	22.2696	1963.3451	0.000509	0.0449	88.1627	0.01134267	288
25	25.3435	2247.0919	0.000445	0.0395	88.6654	0.01127835	300
26	28.8417	2570.0051	0.000389	0.0347	89.1072	0.01122244	312
27	32.8228	2937.4908	0.000340	0.0305	89.4954	0.01117376	324
28	37.3534	3355.7014	0.000298	0.0268	89.8365	0.01113133	336
29	42.5094	3831.6387	0.000261	0.0235	90.1362	0.01109432	348
30	48.3771	4373.2708	0.000229	0.0207	90.3996	0.01106200	360
31	55.0547	4989.6657	0.000200	0.0182	90.6310	0.01103375	372
32	62.6541	5691.1432	0.000176	0.0160	90.8344	0.01100905	384
33	71.3024	6489.4473	0.000154	0.0140	91.0131	0.01098743	396
34	81.1444	7397.9434	0.000135	0.0123	91.1701	0.01096851	408
35	92.3450	8431.8414	0.000119	0.0108	91.3081	0.01095193	420
36	105.0916	9608.4509	0.000104	0.0095	91.4293	0.01093741	432
37	119.5976	10947.4708	0.000091	0.0084	91.5359	0.01092468	444
38	136.1060	12471.3190	0.000080	0.0073	91.6295	0.01091352	456
39	154.8930	14205.5077	0.000070	0.0065	91.7117	0.01090373	468
40	176.2733	16179.0708	0.000062	0.0057	91.7840	0.01089514	480

TABLE A-16. MONTHLY COMPOUNDING 14 PERCENT

Nominal Annual Interest Rate = 14%   Compounding Periods per Year = 12

Year	Amount of 1 at Compound Interest (Col. 1)	Accumulation of 1 per Period (Col. 2)	Sinking Fund Factor (Col. 3)	Present Value Reversion of 1 (Col. 4)	Present Value Ordinary Annuity 1 per Period (Col. 5)	Installment to Amortize 1 (Col. 6)	Period
1	1.1493	12.8007	0.078120	0.8701	11.1375	0.08978712	12
2	1.3210	27.5132	0.036346	0.7570	20.8277	0.04801288	24
3	1.5183	44.4228	0.022511	0.6586	29.2589	0.03417763	36
4	1.7450	63.8577	0.015660	0.5731	36.5945	0.02732648	48
5	2.0056	86.1951	0.011602	0.4986	42.9770	0.02326825	60
6	2.3051	111.8684	0.008939	0.4338	48.5302	0.02060574	72
7	2.6494	141.3758	0.007073	0.3774	53.3618	0.01874001	84
8	3.0450	175.2899	0.005705	0.3284	57.5655	0.01737150	96
9	3.4998	214.2688	0.004667	0.2857	61.2231	0.01633370	108
10	4.0225	259.0689	0.003860	0.2486	64.4054	0.01552664	120
11	4.6232	310.5595	0.003220	0.2163	67.1742	0.01488666	132
12	5.3136	369.7399	0.002705	0.1882	69.5833	0.01437127	144
13	6.1072	437.7583	0.002284	0.1637	71.6793	0.01395103	156
14	7.0192	515.9348	0.001938	0.1425	73.5029	0.01360490	168
15	8.0675	605.7863	0.001651	0.1240	75.0897	0.01331741	180
16	9.2723	709.0564	0.001410	0.1078	76.4702	0.01307699	192
17	10.6571	827.7490	0.001208	0.0938	77.6713	0.01287476	204
18	12.2486	964.1675	0.001037	0.0816	78.7164	0.01270383	216
19	14.0779	1120.9590	0.000892	0.0710	79.6257	0.01255876	228
20	16.1803	1301.1660	0.000769	0.0618	80.4168	0.01243521	240
21	18.5967	1508.2855	0.000663	0.0538	81.1052	0.01232967	252
22	21.3739	1746.3367	0.000573	0.0468	81.7041	0.01223929	264
23	24.5660	2019.9389	0.000495	0.0407	82.2251	0.01216173	276
24	28.2347	2334.4014	0.000428	0.0354	82.6785	0.01209504	288
25	32.4513	2695.8264	0.000371	0.0308	83.0730	0.01203761	300
26	37.2977	3111.2274	0.000321	0.0268	83.4162	0.01198808	312
27	42.8678	3588.6651	0.000279	0.0233	83.7148	0.01194532	324
28	49.2697	4137.4044	0.000242	0.0203	83.9746	0.01190836	336
29	56.6278	4768.0935	0.000210	0.0177	84.2006	0.01187639	348
30	65.0847	5492.9710	0.000182	0.0154	84.3973	0.01184872	360
31	74.8045	6326.1032	0.000158	0.0134	84.5684	0.01182474	372
32	85.9760	7283.6571	0.000137	0.0116	84.7173	0.01180396	384
33	98.8158	8384.2140	0.000119	0.0101	84.8469	0.01178594	396
34	113.5732	9649.1302	0.000104	0.0088	84.9596	0.01177030	408
35	130.5344	11102.9517	0.000090	0.0077	85.0576	0.01175673	420
36	150.0287	12773.8898	0.000078	0.0067	85.1430	0.01174495	432
37	172.4343	14694.3691	0.000068	0.0058	85.2172	0.01173472	444
38	198.1860	16901.6568	0.000059	0.0050	85.2818	0.01172583	456
39	227.7835	19438.5853	0.000051	0.0044	85.3380	0.01171811	468
40	261.8011	22354.3838	0.000045	0.0038	85.3869	0.01171140	480

TABLE A-17. MONTHLY COMPOUNDING 15 PERCENT

Nominal Annual Interest Rate = 15%   Compounding Periods per Year = 12

Year	Amount of 1 at Compound Interest (Col. 1)	Accumu- lation of 1 per Period (Col. 2)	Sinking Fund Factor (Col. 3)	Present Value Rever- sion of 1 (Col. 4)	Present Value Ordinary Annuity 1 per Period (Col. 5)	Installment to Amortize 1 (Col. 6)	Period
1	1.1608	12.8604	0.077758	0.8615	11.0793	0.09025831	12
2	1.3474	27.7881	0.035987	0.7422	20.6242	0.04848665	24
3	1.5639	45.1155	0.022165	0.6394	28.8473	0.03466533	36
4	1.8154	65.2284	0.015331	0.5509	35.9315	0.02783075	48
5	2.1072	88.5745	0.011290	0.4746	42.0346	0.02378993	60
6	2.4459	115.6736	0.008645	0.4088	47.2925	0.02114501	72
7	2.8391	147.1290	0.006797	0.3522	51.8222	0.01929675	84
8	3.2955	183.6411	0.005445	0.3034	55.7246	0.01794541	96
9	3.8253	226.0226	0.004424	0.2614	59.0865	0.01692434	108
10	4.4402	275.2171	0.003633	0.2252	61.9828	0.01613350	120
11	5.1540	332.3198	0.003009	0.1940	64.4781	0.01550915	132
12	5.9825	398.6021	0.002509	0.1672	66.6277	0.01500877	144
13	6.9442	475.5395	0.002103	0.1440	68.4797	0.01460287	156
14	8.0606	564.8450	0.001770	0.1241	70.0751	0.01427040	168
15	9.3563	668.5068	0.001496	0.1069	71.4496	0.01399587	180
16	10.8604	788.8326	0.001268	0.0921	72.6338	0.01376770	192
17	12.6063	928.5014	0.001077	0.0793	73.6539	0.01357700	204
18	14.6328	1090.6225	0.000917	0.0683	74.5328	0.01341691	216
19	16.9851	1278.8054	0.000782	0.0589	75.2900	0.01328198	228
20	19.7155	1497.2395	0.000668	0.0507	75.9423	0.01316790	240
21	22.8848	1750.7879	0.000571	0.0437	76.5042	0.01307117	252
22	26.5637	2045.0953	0.000489	0.0376	76.9884	0.01298897	264
23	30.8339	2386.7140	0.000419	0.0324	77.4055	0.01291899	276
24	35.7906	2783.2495	0.000359	0.0279	77.7648	0.01285929	288
25	41.5441	3243.5298	0.000308	0.0241	78.0743	0.01280831	300
26	48.2225	3777.8022	0.000265	0.0207	78.3410	0.01276470	312
27	55.9745	4397.9613	0.000227	0.0179	78.5708	0.01272738	324
28	64.9727	5117.8138	0.000195	0.0154	78.7687	0.01269540	336
29	75.4173	5953.3859	0.000168	0.0133	78.9392	0.01266797	348
30	87.5410	6923.2800	0.000144	0.0114	79.0861	0.01264444	360
31	101.6136	8049.0889	0.000124	0.0098	79.2127	0.01262424	372
32	117.9485	9355.8767	0.000107	0.0085	79.3217	0.01260688	384
33	136.9092	10872.7365	0.000092	0.0073	79.4157	0.01259197	396
34	158.9180	12633.4384	0.000079	0.0063	79.4966	0.01257916	408
35	184.4648	14677.1811	0.000068	0.0054	79.5663	0.01256813	420
36	214.1183	17049.4647	0.000059	0.0047	79.6264	0.01255865	432
37	248.5388	19803.1035	0.000050	0.0040	79.6781	0.01255050	444
38	288.4925	22999.4023	0.000043	0.0035	79.7227	0.01254348	456
39	334.8690	26709.5205	0.000037	0.0030	79.7611	0.01253744	468
40	388.7007	31016.0571	0.000032	0.0026	79.7942	0.01253224	480

TABLE A-18.   MONTHLY COMPOUNDING 16 PERCENT

Nominal Annual Interest Rate = 16%   Compounding Periods per Year = 12

Year	Amount of 1 at Compound Interest (Col. 1)	Accumulation of 1 per Period (Col. 2)	Sinking Fund Factor (Col. 3)	Present Value Reversion of 1 (Col. 4)	Present Value Ordinary Annuity 1 per Period (Col. 5)	Installment to Amortize 1 (Col. 6)	Period
1	1.1723	12.9203	0.077398	0.8530	11.0216	0.09073086	12
2	1.3742	28.0664	0.035630	0.7277	20.4235	0.04896311	24
3	1.6110	45.8217	0.021824	0.6207	28.4438	0.03515703	36
4	1.8885	66.6358	0.015007	0.5295	35.2855	0.02834028	48
5	2.2138	91.0355	0.010985	0.4517	41.1217	0.02431806	60
6	2.5952	119.6386	0.008359	0.3853	46.1003	0.02169184	72
7	3.0423	153.1691	0.006529	0.3287	50.3472	0.01986206	84
8	3.5663	192.4760	0.005195	0.2804	53.9701	0.01852879	96
9	4.1807	238.5543	0.004192	0.2392	57.0605	0.01752525	108
10	4.9009	292.5706	0.003418	0.2040	59.6968	0.01675131	120
11	5.7452	355.8923	0.002810	0.1741	61.9457	0.01614317	132
12	6.7350	430.1224	0.002325	0.1485	63.8641	0.01565825	144
13	7.8952	517.1402	0.001934	0.1267	65.5006	0.01526705	156
14	9.2553	619.1487	0.001615	0.1080	66.8965	0.01494845	168
15	10.8497	738.7303	0.001354	0.0922	68.0874	0.01468701	180
16	12.7188	878.9123	0.001138	0.0786	69.1032	0.01447110	192
17	14.9099	1043.2435	0.000959	0.0671	69.9698	0.01429188	204
18	17.4785	1235.8842	0.000809	0.0572	70.7090	0.01414247	216
19	20.4895	1461.7113	0.000684	0.0488	71.3396	0.01401746	228
20	24.0192	1726.4417	0.000579	0.0416	71.8775	0.01391256	240
21	28.1570	2036.7775	0.000491	0.0355	72.3364	0.01382431	252
22	33.0077	2400.5752	0.000417	0.0303	72.7278	0.01374990	264
23	38.6939	2827.0445	0.000354	0.0258	73.0617	0.01368706	276
24	45.3598	3326.9820	0.000301	0.0220	73.3466	0.01363391	288
25	53.1739	3913.0442	0.000256	0.0188	73.5895	0.01358889	300
26	62.3342	4600.0678	0.000217	0.0160	73.7968	0.01355072	312
27	73.0726	5405.4454	0.000185	0.0137	73.9736	0.01351833	324
28	85.6609	6349.5662	0.000157	0.0117	74.1245	0.01349082	336
29	100.4178	7456.3313	0.000134	0.0100	74.2531	0.01346745	348
30	117.7168	8753.7598	0.000114	0.0085	74.3629	0.01344757	360
31	137.9960	10274.6974	0.000097	0.0072	74.4565	0.01343066	372
32	161.7686	12057.6480	0.000083	0.0062	74.5364	0.01341627	384
33	189.6367	14147.7491	0.000071	0.0053	74.6045	0.01340402	396
34	222.3055	16597.9135	0.000060	0.0045	74.6626	0.01339358	408
35	260.6023	19470.1697	0.000051	0.0038	74.7122	0.01338469	420
36	305.4964	22837.2317	0.000044	0.0033	74.7545	0.01337712	432
37	358.1245	26784.3403	0.000037	0.0028	74.7906	0.01337067	444
38	419.8189	31411.4204	0.000032	0.0024	74.8213	0.01336517	456
39	492.1415	36835.6113	0.000027	0.0020	74.8476	0.01336048	468
40	576.9231	43194.2319	0.000023	0.0017	74.8700	0.01335648	480

$\mathcal{G}$ LOSSARY*

A **absorption schedule** The estimated schedule or rate at which properties for sale or lease can be marketed in a given locality; usually used when preparing a forecast of the sales or leasing rate to substantiate a development plan and to obtain financing.

abstract of title A summary of the history of the title to a piece of real estate; it includes all conveyances, liens, or other encumbrances. Its purpose is to determine if the present owner has a marketable title.

Accelerated Cost Recovery System (ACRS) Part of the 1981 tax reform that increased depreciation in early years.

accelerated depreciation A method of depreciation for tax purposes under which a greater amount is written off as an annual deduction each year during the early years of ownership than would be deductible under a straight-line method.

acceleration clause A clause in a mortgage that permits the lender to call the remaining loan balance due and payable in the event the borrower violates the terms of the mortgage (e.g., payments are in default).

accretion The gradual and natural change in land boundaries resulting from flowing water.

accrued depreciation The difference between reproduction cost new or replacement cost new and the present worth of the improvements.

adaptive reuse The process of recycling older buildings into new and profitable uses.

For the student interested in a more comprehensive coverage of real estate terms, see The Dictionary of Real Estate Appraisal, *(Chicago: American Institute of Real Estate Appraisers 2nd ed. 1989).*

ad valorem tax   A tax or duty based on value and levied as a percentage of that value (e.g., 30 mils [3 percent] per dollar of property value).

adverse possession   A method of acquiring title to property by occupying it under a claim of ownership for the period of years specified by the laws of the particular state.

after-tax equity cash flow   The amount of the actual cash returned to the equity interest after deducting from net operating income the amount of any debt service and any tax liability (or adding any tax savings).

agents   Persons who are authorized to represent or act for another person (the principal) in dealing with third parties. A real estate broker is the agent of a person who retains the broker to buy, sell, or lease real estate.

agglomeration economics   The phenomenon that if like-kind activities cluster in an area (agglomeration), profits of each firm will increase because buyers can shop more efficiently.

agreement of sale   A contract between a purchaser and seller of real estate that, to be binding, must identify and specify the purchase price.

air space   The space above the surface of land that is owned by the landowner and that may be sold or leased to others independent of the land itself.

alienability (alienation)   The right to convey rights to real property.

allodial system   A system of individual land ownership in fee simple, which is the basis of real property law in the United States. It contrasts with the feudal system under which land was owned in Europe in the Middle Ages.

amenities   Nonmonetary benefits derived from real property ownership. Amenities generated by a property can be tangible or nontangible.

amortization   The gradual reduction of a debt by means of periodic payments. Full amortization exists when the payments are sufficient to liquidate the loan within the term of the mortgage. Amortization is partial when the payments liquidate a portion, but not all, of the loan principal during the mortgage term. (The mortgage is then known as a balloon mortgage.)

anchor   A major department store, supermarket, or other retail operation that generates the majority of customer traffic in a shopping center.

annual percentage rate (APR)   A term used in the Truth in Lending Act to describe simple annual interest charged to the borrower; the effective yield to the lender.

annuity   A constant periodic payment.

anticipation An appraisal concept that real estate value is created by the expectation of benefits to be received in the future.

apparent agency An agency relationship created by the acts of the principal who gives third persons reason to believe that someone is the agent of the principal.

appraisal A substantiated estimate or opinion of value.

appraiser One who is qualified to estimate the value of real estate.

arbitrage pricing model A financial theory that estimates the expected return of an asset based on several systematic risk factors.

architect One who practices the profession of architecture: a designer of buildings and supervisor of construction. All states require architects to be licensed.

assemblage The joining together under common control of several parcels of land.

asset management A more sophisticated and comprehensive form of property management incorporating institutional and corporate planning perspectives (see Chapter 12).

at-risk provision A provision in the tax law that restricts a taxpayer's loss deductions to the amount of his or her capital invested (i.e., initial capital plus additional assessments).

axial theory A theory that urban areas grow by developing outward around the major transportation arteries from the central business district (the arteries constituting the axes of circles around the urban center).

B balance The theory that the value of a property is determined by the balance or apportionment of the four factors of production (i.e., land, labor, capital, and entrepreneur).

balloon mortgage A mortgage that is only partially amortized and so requires a lump sum (balloon) payment at maturity.

band of investment approach A method of finding an appropriate capitalization rate for appraisal purposes by developing a weighted average of the mortgage rate and the required return on equity. In the finance literature, it is referred to as the weighted average cost of capital.

BART Bay Area Rapid Transit (Northern California).

beneficiary One who receives profit from an estate. Also the lender on the security of a note and deed of trust.

beta As used in finance literature, a measure of systematic risk (i.e., risk that cannot be eliminated or reduced by holding a diversified portfolio).

bid rent curve A graph that maps site rent per square foot to the distance from the central business district.

bilateral contract   A contract that involves the exchange of one promise for another promise.

blanket mortgage   A mortgage covering more than one property.

BOMAI   Building Owners and Managers Association International. A trade association of owners and managers of apartment and office buildings.

boot   Non-like kind property involved in an otherwise tax-free exchange. Boot is taxable.

breakeven ratio   The ratio of debt service and operating expenses to gross income. It can be interpreted as the occupancy level that must be achieved to break even (i.e., before-tax cash flow is zero).

broker   A person who, for a commission, acts as the agent of another in the process of buying, selling, leasing, or managing property rights.

brokerage   The business of a broker that includes all the functions necessary to market property of the seller and represent the seller's (principal's) best interests.

brokerage license   The license to carry on the business of a real estate broker, granted by a state usually on passage of a written examination and satisfaction of other requirements.

builder's method   A method of estimating reproduction cost in which direct costs for labor and materials are added to indirect costs for financing, selling, insurance, and so on, to arrive at the estimated reproduction cost new of the improvement.

building code   State or local ordinance that regulates minimum building and construction standards and is intended to preserve and protect the public's health, safety, and welfare.

building residual approach   A method of valuing improved real estate when the value of the land is known or assumed and the object is to find the value of the building.

built-up method   A method of developing a capitalization rate that involves estimating a safe or riskless return and then adding to it (building it up) returns necessary to compensate an investor for additional risks and burdens associated with the specific investment.

bundle of rights   The rights associated with the ownership of real property consisting primarily of the rights to possession, enjoyment, disposition, and control.

business risk   the hazard of loss that managers of an enterprise assume in attempting to operate it successfully and produce profits over a period of time.

C   **call the loan**   The demand for immediate full payment of a loan.

capital   Money or property invested in an asset for the creation of wealth; alternatively, the surplus of production over consumption.

capital gain Gain from the sale of a capital asset (e.g., real estate).

capital improvement The expenditures that cure or arrest deterioration of property or add new improvements and appreciably prolong its life. By comparison, repairs merely maintain property in an efficient operating condition.

capitalization The process of estimating value by discounting stabilized net operating income by an appropriate rate.

capitalization rate The rate that is used to discount figure income to estimate value. The capitalization rate reflects both the lenders' and the investors' expectations of inflation, risk, and so on.

CAPM Capital asset pricing model. A financial theory that the expected return of an asset is linearly related to a risk-free rate plus a risk premium based on the nondiversifiable (market-related) risk of the asset.

carry The ability of the investor to handle financially and psychologically the burden of carrying costs over a holding period.

carrying costs cash outlays required to continue an investment position. For example, owning raw land that provides no income involves carrying costs for real estate taxes (and interest if financing is used).

cash flow The actual spendable income from a real estate investment. To convert taxable income to cash flow, we must add back the depreciation deduction and then subtract mortgage amortization payments.

cash inflow An investment analysis, all the cash receipts received by the investor (i.e., annual cash flows plus proceeds of sale).

cash management cycle The process of estimating and managing cash needs based on short- and long-run considerations.

cash outflow Expenses (e.g., operating expenses, taxes, and debt service) that must be paid before the equity investor receives a return from the investment.

central business district (CBD) Generally, the main shopping or business area of a town or city and, consequently, the place where real estate values are the highest.

CERCLA The Comprehensive Environmental Response, Compensation, and Liability Act, passed in 1980. This was the original Superfund legislation. See also SARA.

certificate of occupancy (CO) A certificate issued by a zoning board or building department to indicate that a structure complies with the building code and may legally be occupied.

change The appraisal concept that recognizes that economic and social forces are constantly creating change in the environment surrounding a property; and that this change affects the value of the property.

characteristics of value Factors, both property and nonproperty, that are believed to affect value (e.g., size, condition, soil, financing terms, time of sale, etc.).

city In a legal sense, a municipal corporation; in a broader sense, an organized settlement of people subject to a local government that provides services for those who reside there and that raises money by taxation.

close corporation A corporation organized and controlled by a single individual or a small group, such as a family.

color of title An apparently good title, which actually has a defect that is not easily detected (e.g., a title that had been forged).

commercial bank Bank whose primary function is to finance the production, distribution, and sale of goods (i.e., the lending of funds short-term, as distinguished from lending long-term or capital funds).

commercial real estate Improved real estate held for the production of income through leases for commercial or business usage (e.g., office buildings, retail shops, and shopping centers).

commission The payment the broker receives for rendering a service, usually expressed as a percentage of the property sale price.

community center A shopping center with 50,000 to 300,000 square feet, an anchor tenant, and several facilities such as a grocery store, bank, professional offices, clothing or furniture store, and so on.

community property A type of concurrent ownership that exists between spouses residing in certain states and under which each spouse is an equal co-owner of all the property acquired during the marriage, except for certain specified exceptions.

comparable properties In the market data approach, other properties to which the subject property can be compared in order to reach an estimate of market value.

comparative advantage The ability to make an investment that is better than other investments in terms of expected risk and return.

comparative unit method A method used to estimate reproduction or replacement cost of an improvement, whereby the actual costs of similar buildings are divided by the number of cubic or square feet in order to yield a unit cost per cubic foot or per square foot.

competition The appraisal principle that profit tends to encourage competition, but that excess profit encourages ruinous competition (i.e., results in supply exceeding demand).

complementary land use associations Associations between sites that support one another.

compounding (compound interest) Paying interest on interest (i.e., adding earned interest to the principal so that interest is figured on a progressively larger amount). Compounding translates present value into future value.

concentric circle theory A theory that urban growth develops in circles around the central business district.

concurrent ownership Ownership interests in property by more than one person at the same time.

condemnation The taking of real property from an owner for a public purpose under the right of eminent domain on payment of "just" compensation.

condominium A form of joint ownership and control of property by which specified volumes of air space (e.g., apartments) are owned individually while the common elements of the building (e.g., outside walls) are jointly owned.

conformity An appraisal concept that property achieves its maximum value when it is in a neighborhood of compatible land uses and architectural homogeneity.

consideration The promise or performance given by each party to a contract in exchange for the promise or performance of the other. Consideration is a necessary element for a valid contract.

construction cost services published services that provide an estimate of construction costs for different types of properties in different parts of the United States.

construction loan A loan made usually by a commercial bank to a builder to be used for the construction of improvements on real estate and usually running six months to two years.

construction loan draw One of a series of payments made by a lender under a construction loan. The lender seeks to advance only the amount of money already reflected in construction so that, in the event of a default, the value of the partially completed property will at least equal the outstanding loan amount.

construction manager The person responsible for the overall construction project. His or her main objective is seeing that a project is completed as scheduled.

construction period interest Loan interest payable during construction. Unless the property is low-income housing, it cannot be deducted in the year in which it is paid but must be amortized over a ten-year period.

consultant One who provides guidance or advice for a client, usually in consideration of a fixed fee.

consumerism The name given to the movement for legislation to protect the interests of the general public in the purchase of goods and services.

contract   An agreement between two or more persons that is enforceable by the courts.

contract of sale   An agreement between the seller and buyer specifying sales price and all terms of sale.

contract rent   The rents specified in a lease agreement; the actual rent.

contribution   A valuation principle that states that the value of an item depends on how much it contributes to the value of the whole.

control   One of the real property ownership rights that guarantees the right to alter the property physically.

controllable influences on residual cash flow   Property management or other factors that can effectively decrease operating expenses or increase rents, thereby increasing the investor's cash flow.

conversion   A change in the use of real property by altering the improvements.

cooperative   A form of ownership under which a building is owned by a corporation whose stockholders are each entitled to lease a specific unit in the building.

co-ownership   Ownership interests in property by more than one person at the same time.

corporate income tax   An income tax levied on corporations and certain associations treated as corporations.

corporation   A legal entity created for the purpose of carrying on certain activities (usually business for profit).

correlation   A statistical term that refers to the relationship of two or more variables. For example, the number of rooms in a building would be positively correlated with the square footage of the building; and property sales are negatively correlated with mortgage rates.

cost   The price paid for anything.

cost approach   Property value is estimated by subtracting accrued depreciation from reproduction cost new and then adding the value of the land.

cost pro forma   A statement that estimates a proposed project's hard and soft costs based on certain specified assumptions.

counteroffer   When an offeree neither accepts nor rejects an offer but makes an alternative offer to the offeror.

CPM   Certified Property Manager.

CREFs   Commingled real estate funds. Pools of money contributed by a number of investor participants.

crowding out   The effect that occurs when the federal government is financing its deficits and competing with the private sector for funds.

curable depreciation   Physical or functional depreciation in which the cost to cure (i.e., repair or replace) is less than, or equal to, the value added to the property.

D **D&B** Dunn and Bradstreet; company which provides small business credit ratings.

dead land Real estate that, by virtue of its location, lack of access, or topography, is not capable of being developed.

dealer One who buys and sells real estate in the course of normal business.

debt coverage ratio (DCR) The ratio between net operating income and the debt service on outstanding loans. The higher the ratio, the lower the risk to the lender.

debt service Periodic payments on a loan, with a portion of the payment for interest and the balance for repayment (amortization) of principal.

declining balance depreciation A form of accelerated depreciation in which the depreciation rate is applied against a declining balance cost rather than against the original cost.

deed A written instrument that conveys title to real property.

deed of reconveyance A deed from the trustee returning title to the borrower (trustor) to clear a deed of trust.

deed of trust The instrument used in some states (rather than a mortgage) to make real estate security for a debt. It is a three-party instrument among a trustor (borrower), a trustee, and a beneficiary (lender).

default The failure of a party to fulfill a contractual obligation.

default clause Provision in a loan agreement specifying exactly when the borrower has failed to meet his obligations.

default risk premium The extra compensation (interest) required by a lender because the borrower may default, i.e., fail to pay as promised.

defeasible fee Fee simple interest in land that is capable of being terminated on the happening of a specified event; also called a base or qualified fee.

deferral of taxes on disposition The delaying of paying taxes on gains at the time of sale. Usually done through exchanges of like-kind properties or, in the case of the sale of a person's home, by purchasing another home of equal or greater value within a specified time period.

deferred maintenance Maintenance and repairs that are needed but have not been made.

deficiency judgment A personal judgment entered against the mortgagor (borrower) when the amount realized at a foreclosure sale is less than the sum due on the foreclosed mortgage or deed of trust.

degree of uncertainty   The total risk in an investment.

demand analysis   An analysis to determine the quantity of an economic good that can be sold at a specified price, in a given market, and at a particular time.

density   The number of persons or the amount of improved space within a specified unit of land (e.g., an acre). Control of density is one of the primary functions of a zoning ordinance.

Department of Housing and Urban Development (HUD)   A cabinet-level federal department responsible for carrying out national housing programs, including Federal Housing Administration subsidy programs, home mortgage insurance, urban renewal, and urban planning assistance.

depreciation (economic)   Loss in property value. The three types are physical, functional, and locational.

depreciation (tax)   A deductible expense for investment or business property that reflects the presumed "using up" of the asset. Land may not be depreciated.

destination facility   Hospitality facility (motel or hotel) located in a resort city or other area that attracts tourists and others for vacations or other purposes.

developer   One who prepares raw land for improvement by installing roads and utilities, and so on; also used to describe a builder (i.e., one who actually constructs improvements on real estate).

development process   The process of preparing raw land so that it becomes suitable for the erection of buildings; generally involves clearing and grading land and installing roads and utility services.

devise   A transfer of real property under a will. The devisor is the decedent, and the devisee is the recipient.

diminishing marginal utility   The concept that, beyond some point, any further increase in the input of factors of production will decrease the margin between cost and gross income, thus decreasing net income returns.

discounted cash flow model   An estimate of after-tax cash flows and after-tax proceeds from investing in a project, then discounting them to present value to determine the investment value of the property.

discounting   The process of translating future value into present value (i.e., seeking to determine the present value of a dollar to be received at some date in the future); the opposite of compounding. The present value will depend on the discount rate (i.e., the rate at which current funds are expected to earn interest).

discount rate   The rate used to discount future cash flows to determine present value.

disintermediation   The process whereby persons with excess cash invest directly in short-term instruments, such as government paper, instead of depositing the funds in intermediary financial institutions, such as savings and loans.

disposition   The sale or conveyance of real property rights.

diversification   Reduction of risk by investing in many different types of projects.

downside leverage   The reduction in the return on equity by borrowing funds at a cost greater than the free and clear return from the property. In other words, the borrowed funds are earning less than the cost of these funds to the property owner.

downzoning   Changing the zoning classification of property from a higher use to a lower use (e.g., from commercial to residential).

due-on-sale clause   A clause in a mortgage or deed of trust that requires the balance to be paid in full on the sale of the property.

E   **easement**   A nonpossessory interest in land owned by another that gives the holder of the easement the right to use the land for a specific purpose (e.g., a right of way).

easement appurtenant   An easement that is attached to a parcel of land and passes with the land on its conveyance to a subsequent owner.

easement by necessity   An easement created when land is subdivided or separated into more than one parcel without a provision for ingress and egress.

easement by prescription   An easement created by adverse use, openly and continuously for a specified (by state law) period of time.

easement in gross   An easement that is not attached to any parcel of land but is merely a personal right to use the land of another.

ECOA   Equal Credit Opportunity Act, which makes it illegal for a lender to discriminate on the basis of age, sex, religion, race, or marital status.

economic characteristics   Nonphysical property attributes that distinguish real estate from non-real-estate assets (e.g., scarcity, long economic life, modification, and situs).

economic (or locational) depreciation   A loss of value of improved real estate resulting from changes other than those directly occurring to the property itself (e.g., a declining neighborhood).

economic study   A discounted cash flow analysis over the expected holding period to determine the present worth of the project to the investor and the internal rate of return (yield).

effective demand   The desire to buy combined with the ability to pay.

effective gross income (EGI)   Possible gross income from an income property minus an allowance for vacancies and credit loss.

efficient frontier   Points plotted in risk return space that represent the highest expected return for any given level of risk.

efficient market   A market in which all publicly available information is fully and instantaneously reflected in the price of the asset; therefore, no excess returns can be made. The stock market is supposed to be an efficient market.

Ellwood technique   An advanced method of developing a capitalization rate based on the proportion of investment represented by debt and equity and on the expected change in property values over the holding period.

eminent domain   The power of a public authority to condemn and take property for public use on payment of "just compensation."

energy tax credits   A direct reduction of tax liability for investment in certain energy-savings items.

enjoyment   The right of the fee simple interest to be free from interference from prior owners of the property.

environmental audit   An assessment of the environmental aspects of a property's situs. It includes checking both the site's potential impact on surrounding sites and the surrounding site's impact on the subject site as well as the potential hazards from using the subject site in the intended use.

equalization procedure   The adjustment of real property assessments (valuations) within a taxing district in order to achieve a uniform proportion between assessed values and actual cash values of real estate so that all property owners are taxed at an equal rate.

equity cash flow after tax   The net cash flow to the investor after tax considerations; before-tax cash flow minus (or plus) taxes due (or tax savings).

equity kickers   A provision in the loan terms that guarantees the lender a percentage of property appreciation over some specified time period or a percentage of income from the property or both.

ERISA   Employment Retirement Income Security Act. It instructs pension fund managers on their duties and responsibilities in managing a fund.

ERTA   Economic Recovery Tax Act of 1981.

escalation clause   A provision in a lease that permits the landlord to pass through increases in real estate taxes and operating expenses to the tenants, with each tenant paying its pro rata share. Also a mortgage clause that allows the lender to increase the interest rate based on terms of the note.

escheat The reversion of property to the state when a person dies intestate without known heirs.

escrow closing A closing in which proceeds due the seller are escrowed (placed in an account) until all terms of the sales contract are met.

escrow provision An agreement providing that the lender will collect and hold until due (escrow) property taxes and insurance due on mortgaged property.

establishment The urban land economist's term for the basic unit of land use that consists of individuals or groups occupying places of business, residence, government, or assembly.

estate at sufferance The rights of a tenant in real property after the lease expires and the tenant stays without special permission from the landlord.

estate at will An interest in property that arises when the owner leases the property to another and the duration of the lease is at the will of the owner or the tenant.

estate for years The leasehold interest of a tenant in property that automatically renews itself for the period specified in the original lease, until terminated by either tenant or owner.

estate from period to period A leasehold interest in real property that will terminate after a fixed period of time.

ex post After the fact, the opposite of ex ante.

excess profit In appraisal theory, profit that is in excess of that necessary to satisfy the four agents of production. The existence of excess profit will encourage new competition.

exclusive agency An agreement between a real estate broker and a property owner designating the broker as the exclusive agent to sell or lease the subject property. The owner, however, may sell or lease directly without being liable for a commission.

exclusive right of sale An agreement between a real estate broker and a property owner in which the broker is designated as the sole party authorized to sell or lease the subject property. Consequently, if the owner sells or leases directly, a commission is still due the broker.

exogenous The state of being outside or not a part of a particular thing. For example, the quality of a neighborhood is an exogenous factor that affects the value of a particular parcel of property.

exogenous shocks External factors that cannot be controlled (but can be reacted to) and that affect the participants in the real estate process.

expense pass-throughs A provision in a lease that ensures that all increases in expenses will be paid by the tenants.

export base multiplier A mathematical technique used to project employment that will be created by a new industry locating within a particular region.

express easement An easement created by a writing executed by the owner of the land (servient tenement) subject to the easement.

external diseconomies Detriments to the value of property because of nearby activities that are not compatible with the use of the property in question.

external economies Benefits to property from the existence of supporting and like-kind facilities nearby.

externalities Factors external to a parcel of property that affects its value. For example, a noisy or polluted environment is an externality that will depress the value of property.

extraterritorial jurisdiction Jurisdiction that extends subdivision regulations beyond a city's political boundaries.

F **FDIC** Federal Deposit Insurance Corporation. An agency of the federal government that insures deposits of commercial banks.

feasibility study A combination of a market study and economic study that provides the investor with knowledge of the environment in which the project exists and the expected returns from investing in the project.

Federal Reserve System Federal agency charged with managing the national money supply.

fee on condition subsequent Fee simple ownership that *can* be lost should a stated event or condition happen in the future.

fee simple absolute (fee simple) The most extensive interest in land recognized by law; absolute ownership but subject to the limitations of police power, taxation, eminent domain, escheat, and private restrictions of record.

fee simple determinable A fee simple ownership that terminates on the happening (or failure to happen) of a stated condition. Also referred to as a defeasible fee.

FHA Federal Housing Administration. A division of Housing and Urban Development that ensures mortgage loans.

FHLBB Federal Home Loan Bank Board. The administrative agency that charters federal savings and loans and regulates the members of the Federal Home Loan Bank System.

FHLBS Federal Home Loan Bank System. The Federal Home Loan Bank Board, Federal Home Loan Banks, and member financial institutions.

FHLMC Federal Home Loan Mortgage Corporation. Referred to as "Freddie Mac" and supervised by the Federal Home Loan Bank

Board, the FHLMC creates a secondary mortgage market for conventional loans.

fiduciary   One whom the law regards as having a duty toward another by reason of a relationship of trust and confidence.

fiduciary relationship   The relationship between an agent and principal in which the agent has the duty of acting for the benefit of the principal.

filtering   Process in which the wealthy build new homes, selling their old homes to a slightly less affluent group that, in turn, sells its old homes to a yet less affluent group. The process continues, leaving all groups in better housing.

finance charge   The total costs imposed by a lender on the borrower in connection with the extension of credit as defined under the Truth in Lending Act.

financial institutions   Firms that deal in all areas of finance.

financial intermediary   The middleman between savers and borrowers whose primary function is matching sources of funds (savings) with uses of funds (loans).

financial markets   Any "place" where capital assets are bought and sold.

financial risk   In loan underwriting, the risk that a borrower may not be able to repay the loan as scheduled.

financial system   All the individuals, markets, and institutions that aggregate and then allocate capital.

first lien   A lien on real property that has priority over all other (subsequent) liens.

fixture   Personal property becomes a fixture when it is permanently attached to real property.

FLIP   Flexible Loan Insurance Program. A loan in which the borrower's downpayment is placed in an interest-bearing savings account and the principal and interest from the savings used to subsidize (for a period of time) the monthly mortgage payments.

float   When a mortgage loan is serviced, the principal, interest, taxes, and insurance (PITI) held by the mortgage banker until disbursed to the investor who holds the loan.

floor-to-ceiling loan   A mortgage loan that is advanced in two separate portions. The initial portion (the floor) is advanced once certain conditions are met, and the balance (the ceiling) is advanced when other conditions are met.

FNMA   Federal National Mortgage Association. Referred to as "Fannie Mae," the FNMA is a privately owned, government-sponsored agency that buys and sells FHA-insured, VA-guaranteed, and conventional mortgage loans.

foreclosure   The legal process by which a mortgagee, in case of default by a mortgagor, forces a sale of the mortgaged property in order to provide funds to pay off the loan.

foreclosure by action and sale   A foreclosure associated with a mortgage in which the lender must take court action before being able to sell the property held as collateral.

foreclosure by power of sale   A foreclosure associated with a deed of trust in which the trustee can sell the property without going through the court.

FPM   Flexible-payment mortgage. A loan in which the payment varies based on an agreement between the borrower and lender and specified in the mortgage or deed of trust.

fraud   Intentional misrepresentation of a material fact in order to induce another to part with something of value.

freehold estates   The highest quality of rights associated with real property ownership rights.

Frostbelt   The area located in the northcentral part of the United States

FRS   Federal Reserve System.

FSLIC   Federal Savings and Loan Insurance Corporation. Insures the deposits of all savings and loan associations that are members of the FHLBS.

functional depreciation (obsolescence)   The loss of value to improved real estate owing to the fact that the improvements do not provide the same degree of use, or do so less efficiently, than a new structure. Functional depreciation may be curable or incurable.

fundamental analysis   A study of the factors that affect value (e.g., earnings growth, dividend payments, risk, etc.).

fungibles   Goods of a given class or type, any unit of which is as acceptable as another and capable of satisfying an obligation expressed in terms of class. For example, bushels of wheat are fungibles whereas parcels of real estate are not.

G   **gap financing**   Financing provided by a second lender when the first lender advances only the floor portion of a floor-to-ceiling loan (i.e., the second loan fills the gap).

GEM   Growing equity mortgage. The mortgage interest rate is fixed over the life of the loan, but at periodic intervals the payments are increased, with the additional amount going to reduce the remaining balance.

general agent   An agent authorized to conduct all the business of the principal with stipulated limitations.

general contractor (GC)   A person or firm that supervises a construction project under a contract with the owner; also known as the prime contractor (as distinguished from subcontractors).

general partnership Two or more persons associated in a continuing relationship for the purpose of conducting business for a profit.

general warranty deed The highest form of deed a grantor can give a grantee in that the grantor is liable for any title defects that were created during his or her period of ownership and during the periods of all earlier ownerships.

gentrification The process in which rising prices and condominium conversions squeeze out low-income tenants in central cities in favor of high-income tenants.

Geographic Information System (GIS) Any information system that is tied to specific geographical features. Every city's property tax system, which has information on the owner and the property as well as the exact physical location on a map, is a geographic information system.

GNMA Government National Mortgage Association. Referred to as "Ginnie Mae," the GNMA is a government agency, regulated by HUD, which provides a secondary mortgage market for special-assistance loans.

going-concern value The value of property on the assumption that it will continue to be utilized in an existing business.

good title (good and marketable title) A title unencumbered by claims that might prohibit a clean transfer (also referred to as marketable title).

government survey A method of land description that utilizes imaginary grid lines; used primarily in the western United States.

GPM Graduated-payment mortgage. A mortgage in which the payments at the beginning are lower than those of a fixed-payment mortgage. The payments increase periodically to a fixed amount and then remain constant.

gross income multiplier (GIM) approach A rule-of-thumb method for arriving at the value of an income property, which involves applying a multiplier to the gross rental receipts. Choice of the multiplier depends on the type of property, location, and so on.

gross national product (GNP) The sum of all final products of the economy, including both consumption goods and gross investment.

gross potential income (GPI) Gross rental receipts plus nonrental income (e.g., vending machine income).

gross rental receipts (GRR) Maximum rental income that a property would generate if it were fully occupied for the entire fiscal period.

ground rent Rent payable by a tenant to a landlord under a ground lease (i.e., a lease of vacant land).

H **hard-dollar costs** Cash outlays for land, labor, and improvements.

hazardous wastes All materials that have been discarded from their original use and represent a potential health hazard. Some hazardous waste, such as asbestos, is known to cause cancer in certain situations.

heterogeneity The quality of being unique. Every parcel of land is unique because its location cannot be duplicated.

highest-and-best-use principle The property use that at a given point of time is deemed likely to produce the greatest net return in the foreseeable future, whether or not such use is the current use of the property.

hinterland The area surrounding an urban concentration that makes up the market for the services offered at the central location.

hollow shell effect As the city grows outward, the higher income families move to the outer fringe; each income level then moves out to better housing, leaving the inner city to decay.

hospitality facility A facility offering boarding accommodations to the general public and usually providing a wide range of additional services, including restaurants, meeting rooms, and a swimming pool; a hotel or motel.

Housing Act of 1949 The act that established "a decent home and suitable living environment for every American" as a national goal.

HUD The acronym for the Department of Housing and Urban Development.

hurdle rate of return The minimum rate of return acceptable to an investor.

HVAC The acronym for heating, ventilation, and air conditioning.

I **immobility** Not capable of being moved from place to place. Land is both immobile and indestructible; although improvements placed on land can be moved, this is rarely done because of the difficulty and expense involved.

implied agency An agency relationship created by circumstances that gave the agent justified reasons for believing the principal had created an agency.

implied easement An easement created when the owner of a tract of land subjects part of the tract to an easement that benefits the other part, and then conveys one or both parts to other parties so that ownership is divided.

income approach One of the three traditional appraisal methods. In this method, the appraiser seeks the present value of the future flow of income that can be expected from the property. This value is arrived at by projecting a stabilized annual income for the estimated future life of the property and applying an appropriate capitalization rate to this income.

income conduit An entity, typically a partnership, that "passes through" profits and losses directly to the individual participants. This happens because the entity itself is not subject to tax.

income kickers A part of the loan agreement that guarantees the lender will receive a portion of the property's income over some minimum.

increasing and decreasing returns An economic concept that the use of increasingly larger amounts of the factors of production will produce greater net income up to a certain point (the law of increasing returns), but that thereafter further amounts will not produce a commensurate return (the law of decreasing returns).

incurable depreciation Loss in value owing to a feature inherent in the property or in the surrounding area that either is impossible to cure (economic obsolescence) or costs more to cure than the value added to the property.

indemnity clause Provides that one party will stand up for a second party "in a financial sense." Often a corporation will indemnify an employee against personal lawsuits when the employee is working for the corporation.

industrial park A large tract of improved land used for a variety of light industrial and manufacturing uses. Individual sites are either purchased or leased by users.

industrial real estate Improved real estate used for the purpose of manufacturing, processing, or warehousing goods.

industry life cycle The life cycle in which an industry's products are fully developed and standardized so that they can be produced by automated production processes.

infill incentives Public measures, such as tax abatement, that encourage the development of scattered vacant sites in a built-up section of a city.

inflation hedge Prices increasing at the rate of inflation. As a result, there is no decrease in real wealth.

inflation premium The additional or incremental return that must be given to an investor to induce him or her to defer consumption during a period of inflation.

inflation risk premium The extra return (interest) charged to compensate the investor (lender) for the declining value of the dollar (inflation).

infrastructure   The services and facilities provided by a municipality, including roads and highways, water and sewer systems, fire and police protection, parks and recreation, and so on.

inheritance   Benefits obtained from a decedent either by will or by intestate succession.

input/output analysis   A method of analyzing the economy of a region that involves tabulating the data covering major industries in the region to show how an additional dollar spent in any one industry will affect sales in the others.

installment sale   Sale of property in which the purchase price (in whole or in part) is paid in installments to the seller.

Institute of Real Estate Management (IREM)   An affiliate of the National Association of Realtors, whose purpose is to promote professionalism in the field of property management.

institutional factors   All the political, social, and economic entities whose existence affects land use.

institutional investors   Institutions that invest in real or capital assets (e.g., life insurance companies).

institutional lender   A savings bank, savings and loan association, commercial bank, or life insurance company that provides financing for real estate (and other investments).

insurable value   The value of property for insurance purposes, which is based on the cost to replace the improvements; therefore, it is often different from market value.

insurance agent   One who acts as an intermediary between insurers and persons seeking insurance.

interest-only loan (standing loan)   A loan in which payments are for interest only. Since no principal is included in the payment, the loan balance remains the same.

intermediary (financial)   A capital market participant who helps aggregate and allocate savers funds.

internal disintermediation   Depositors at a particular financial institution switching from an existing lower yield account to a new higher yielding account within the same institution.

internal rate of return (IRR)   The discount rate at which investment has zero net present value (i.e., the yield to the investor).

International Council of Shopping Centers (ICSC)   A national trade association for owners, developers, and managers of shopping centers.

Interstate Land Sales Disclosure Act (ILSDA)   A federal statute regulating the interstate sale of home sites and building lots in recreational developments.

intestate   Having left, before dying, no will for the disposition of one's property.

investment interest   Interest paid or accrued on debt incurred to purchase or carry property held for investment.

investment tax credit   A direct reduction of a taxpayer's tax liability equal to a percentage (up to 10 percent) of value of certain types of property.

investor characteristics   Characteristics that constrain the investor in the investment decision (e.g., financial, risk assumption, and personal constraints).

J   **joint and several liability**   A form of liability wherein each party to the liability is individually responsible for his or her own share and potentially the shares of all others involved in the liability.

joint tenancy   A form of concurrent ownership that includes a right of survivorship (i.e., on the death of one joint tenant, title to his or her share passes automatically to the surviving joint tenants).

joint venture   An association of two or more persons or firms to carry on a single business enterprise for profit.

joint venture partners   The individuals or entities who come together to form a joint venture.

L   **land planner**   One who specializes in the art of subdividing land in order to combine maximum utility with such desirable amenities as scenic views and winding roads.

land use succession theory   The premise that real estate, though physically fixed, is economically flexible and responds to changes in the neighborhood life cycle.

law of nuisance   The idea that one property owner cannot use his or her property in a manner damaging to a neighbor's property.

leapfrogging   Land development that skips close-in vacant space for outlying areas, usually because close-in land is too expensive.

lease   A contract that gives the lessor (tenant) the right of possession for a period of time in return for paying rent to the lessee (landlord).

lease concession   A benefit to a tenant to induce him or her to enter into a lease; usually takes the form of one or more month's free rent.

lease expiration schedule   Schedule of leases in a building indicating the dates on which they expire.

leasehold estate   The interest that a tenant holds in property by virtue of a lease; the right of a tenant to use and occupy property pursuant to a lease.

legal capacity　The ability to enter into binding agreements. One who is a minor, of unsound mind, or intoxicated lacks legal capacity to enter into a contract.

legal characteristics　Legal restrictions on property ownership and use.

lessee　One who holds a leasehold estate; a tenant.

lessor　One who grants a leasehold estate; a landlord.

letter of intent　A written "agreement to agree," which often preceeds a formal construct.

leverage (in financing)　The use of borrowed funds in financing a project.

license　The right to go on land owned by another for a specific purpose.

lien　The right to hold property as security until the debt that it secures is paid. A mortgage is one type of lien.

lien theory (mortgages)　A mortgage in which the title remains vested with the owner and the mortgage is considered a lien only against the property.

life estate　An estate that provides control and use of the property during the holder of the estate's lifetime. Upon the holder's death, the property then goes in fee simple to a "remainderman" or reverts to the grantor.

life insurance company　A primary source of permanent (long-term) financing for income properties, such as shopping centers, office buildings, and so on.

life tenant　One who has an estate for life in real property; the measuring life may be his or her own life or the life of a third party designated by the grantor of the life estate.

limitation on excess investment interest　Tax concept created by the 1969 Tax Reform Act that places a limit on the amount of interest that is deductible for certain classes of property.

limited partnership　A partnership that restricts the personal liability of the limited partners to the amount of their investment.

linkage　A relationship between establishments that causes movement of people or goods.

liquidation value　The value realized in the liquidation of a business or of a particular asset. Because liquidation is often distressed selling, liquidation value is ordinarily less than going-concern value.

liquidity　The ability to convert assets into cash quickly without the need to mark the price down substantially below current market values.

liquidity premium　Additional return required for investing in a security that cannot easily be turned into cash.

liquidity risk Risk associated with a slow convertibility of an asset to cash; speeding up conversion may require discounting the price.

listing agreement The contractual relationship between the seller of the property (principal) and the real estate broker (agent).

listing broker The broker who has a contractual agreement with the seller to sell his or her property (i.e., the agent for the seller).

littoral rights Rights of property owners whose land abuts large lakes or an ocean that permits use of the water without restriction.

loan terms All the provisions specified in the loan agreement.

loan-to-value ratio (LTVR) The relationship between the amount of a mortgage loan and the value of the real estate securing it; loan amount divided by market value.

location effect An exogenous factor affecting the value of a particular parcel of property.

location quotient With respect to a particular industry, the relationship between the number of jobs in a particular region and the total number of jobs in the industry nationwide.

low-income housing credit Tax credit associated with investment in low-income housing; designed to encourage investment in low-income housing.

M **maintenance schedule** A detailed listing of all maintenance procedures and the times when they are to be performed.

management contract A contract between the owner of real estate and an individual or firm that undertakes to manage it for a fee.

management plan A plan that outlines the necessary steps to meet the property owner's objectives.

manufacturing belt The area located in the northeast part of the United States extending westward to Chicago.

map A survey of a tract of land, prepared by a surveyor, showing boundaries of individual parcels, roads and highways; also known as a plat.

market The interaction of buying and selling interests in goods, services, or investments.

market constraints Legal, physical, social, and economic constraints that affect the land use decision.

market data approach An appraisal method whereby value of property is established by comparing the subject property with comparable properties that have recently been sold.

market rent The rent that space would command at any given time if not subject to lease.

market risk premium   Additional return for investing in a security that is based on the degree of systematic (market) risk.

market segmentation   Identifying the tenants or buyers and the rent or price levels for the proposed project.

market study   Analyzes general demand for a single type of real estate product for a particular project.

market value   The most probable price expressed in terms of money that a property would bring if exposed for sale in the open market, in an arm's length transaction between a willing seller and a willing buyer, both of whom are knowledgeable concerning the uses of the property.

marketable title   A title to a parcel of real estate that is subject to no question regarding its validity; the type of title to which a purchaser of real estate is entitled unless the contract specifies otherwise.

marketing function   The process of anticipating society's needs and producing or distributing goods and services to satisfy those needs.

marketing process   Methods used to enable, assist, or encourage the sale of property and goods in the marketplace.

marketing study   A study that determines the price or rent that is appropriate in order to market a particular project.

marketing technique   The methods used to make people aware of, and to create a desire for, a particular product.

maturity (of a loan)   The amount of time that the loan will be outstanding.

maximum loan   The largest loan possible given lender criteria such as the loan to value and debt service coverage ratios.

mean variance   An approach to analyzing an investment based on the expected return (the mean of the return) and the risk associated with receiving this return (the variance).

mechanic's lien   A claim that attaches to real estate to protect the right to compensation of one who performs labor or provides materials in connection with construction.

metes and bounds survey   A method of describing land by identifying boundaries through terminal points and degrees of latitude and longitude.

MGIC   Mortgage Guaranty Insurance Corporation. The first privately owned mortgage insurance firm.

MICs   Mortgage insurance companies. Privately owned companies that insure the lender against default.

miniwarehouse   A one-story building subdivided into numerous small cubicles intended to be used as storage by families or small businesses.

modernization Taking corrective measures to bring a property into conformity with changes in style, whether exterior or interior, in order to meet the standards of current demand.

money market The market where short-term money instruments (those that mature within a year) are bought and sold.

mononuclear theories of urban structure The intercity, regional transportation facilities, and associated activities of a community define the nucleus of the urban structure.

mortgage Instrument used in some states (rather than a deed of trust) to make real estate security for a debt. It is a two-party instrument between a mortgagor (borrower) and a mortgagee (lender).

mortgage-backed security A security that is collateralized by one or a package of mortgage loans.

mortgage banker An individual or firm that primarily originates real estate loans and then sells them to institutional lenders and other investors.

mortgage broker An individual or firm, who, for a fee, arranges financing with a permanent lender for a borrower.

mortgage constant Percentage of original loan balance represented by constant periodic mortgage payment.

mortgagee One to whom a mortgage is given as a security for a loan, (i.e., the lender).

mortgage insurance Insurance protecting a mortgage lender in the event of default by a borrower. Usually required on conventional loans with loan-to-value ratios greater than 80 percent.

mortgage loan origination The act of making (creating, originating) a mortgage loan.

mortgagor One who gives a mortgage to secure a loan (i.e., the borrower).

MSA Metropolitan Statistical Area. A county or counties with a central city of at least 50,000 persons or an area of smaller cities clustered together in a single living area with a combined population of 50,000.

multiple listing service (MLS) A selling technique frequently utilized by brokers in a particular locality whereby a listing with any one broker (the listing broker) automatically becomes available to all brokers participating in the service. If a sale is brought about by a broker (the selling broker) other than the listing broker, the commission is divided between the two.

multiple nuclei theory A theory of urban growth in which mini-CBDs are created to provide services to residential areas surrounding the old CBD.

mutual savings bank A banking institution found primarily in the Northeast, in which the majority of the assets are home mortgages and its owners are the depositors.

N **National Association of Realtors® (NAR)** With a membership in excess of 700,000, the largest real estate organization in the country and probably in the world. Members are entitled to use the designation Realtor®, which is a trademarked term owned by the NAR.

National Housing Act of 1934 The act that established the Federal Housing Administration (FHA).

national income The measure in dollars of the total annual production of goods and services in the economy. National income differs from gross national product in that national income is calculated after a provision for depreciation of capital goods.

national wealth A term generally referring to the total real or tangible assets of a country (e.g., land, structures, equipment, inventories, etc.).

negative cash flow A cash deficit during a fiscal period, which requires the investor to raise additional cash either with equity or with new debt.

negative leverage The use of debt financing, which reduces the percentage return to equity because the rate of interest on the debt exceeds the free and clear rate of return on equity.

neighborhood A segment of a city or town having common features that distinguish it from adjoining areas.

neighborhood analysis An analysis of the dynamic environment of the area surrounding the site.

neighborhood center (strip center) A small shopping center (average size 50,000 square feet) with tenants that furnish the daily needs of the area (e.g., supermarkets, drug stores, beauty parlors, etc.).

net income multiplier The ratio of value to net operating income.

net operating income (NOI) The balance of cash remaining after deducting the operating expenses of a property from the gross income generated by the property.

net present value (NPV) The net present value of an investment is the sum of (1) the total present value of the annual after-tax equity cash flows during ownership plus (2) the present value-estimated proceeds from sale less the amount of the equity investment.

nonpecuniary return Nonmonetary benefits derived from ownership.

nonpossessory interest An interest in land other than a fee or leasehold (i.e., an easement, license, or profit).

nonproperty characteristics Attributes that affect property value but are not a part of the property, for example, financing, special conditions or terms of sale that enhance value.

nonraid clause   A clause used to deter the tenant from vacating the premises by deeming it to be a material breech of the lease and causing all unpaid rent to be immediately due and payable.

nonrecourse loan   A loan provision that requires the lender to look only to the security to satisfy the debt and not to the borrower (i.e., the borrower is not personally liable for the debt).

nuisance   A property use or condition that unreasonably interferes with the rights of others to enjoy their property (e.g., establishing a motorcycle track in a residential neighborhood).

O   **offer**   A promise to do something in return for a requested promise to act.

office building   A building leased to tenants for the conduct of business or of a profession, as distinguished from residential, commercial, or retail buildings (although the lower floors of many office buildings are used for commercial purposes).

old industries   An industry in which the product can be produced with the same widely known process in just about any part of the world.

100 percent location   The prime business location of a city and, consequently, the location where retail and office rentals are likely to be at their highest; usually the equivalent of the central business district.

open-end mortgage   A mortgage that is written to permit the lender to make additional advances in the future. This eliminates the need for a new mortgage if the advances are made.

open listing   The offering of a property for sale or lease through a real estate broker with the understanding that the broker has no exclusive agency or right of sale, thus permitting the owner to list the property with as many brokers as he or she wishes.

operating budget   A budget, usually prepared a year in advance, listing projected costs of maintenance and repair for a building.

operating expense ratio   The ratio of total operating expenses to gross revenue.

operating expenses   Expenses directly related to the operation and maintenance of the property, including real estate taxes, maintenance and repair expenses, insurance payments, payroll and management fees, supplies, and utility costs. They do not include debt service on mortgages or depreciation expense.

opportunity cost   The return that might have been realized from alternative uses of capital that has been invested in a particular project. For example, capital invested in real estate incurs an opportunity cost equal to the return it might have earned had it been used to purchase corporate bonds or common stock.

option   The right given by the owner of property (the optionor) to another (the optionee) to purchase or lease the property at a specific price within a set time.

options pricing theory   The theoretical basis for pricing an option.

ordinary income   Compensation, profits, dividends, and all other income other than capital gain.

origination fee   A charge made by the lender at the inception of the loan to cover administrative costs.

overall capitalization rate (OAR)   The ratio of net operating income to value.

P

package mortgage   A mortgage loan that packages what are normally two separate loans (e.g., a construction loan and a permanent loan).

participation mortgage   A single mortgage loan made by several lenders, each putting up a portion of the total.

partnership   An association of two or more persons or entities for the purpose of carrying on an investment or business for profit and for the sharing of both profit and losses.

passive income   One of three categories of taxable income under the 1986 tax reform. Rent is passive income.

passive investor   An investor who seeks no active role in construction or operation but merely seeks to invest funds in order to earn a return. Institutional investors, such as pension funds, are usually passive investors.

pass-through (lease)   A lease provision whereby certain costs flow directly to the tenant (e.g., a pass-through of increases in property taxes on a long-term lease).

pass-through (mortgage)   An investment instrument in which the periodic debt-service payments on a package of mortgage loans is paid out (passed through) to the investors owning the instruments.

pecuniary return   Monetary benefits derived from ownership.

pension fund   An institution that holds assets to be used for the payment of pensions to corporate and government employees, union members, and other groups.

percentage rent   Rent payable under a lease that is equal to a percentage of gross sales or gross revenues received by the tenant. Commonly used in shopping center leases, the percentage rental is usually joined with a minimum rental that the tenant must pay, regardless of the amount of sales volume.

permanent loan commitment   An undertaking by a lender to make a long-term loan on real estate on specified conditions (e.g., the completion of construction of a building).

personal income tax The income tax levied against individuals, as distinguished from the income tax levied against corporations. Members of a partnership are subject to personal income taxes, but the partnership itself is not a taxable entity.

personal liability An agreement (note) between borrower and lender in which the lender will be able to collect (through legal action if necessary) from the borrower when default has occurred and the sale of the collateral was insufficient to cover the amount owed.

personal property All property rights except real property.

PERT Program evaluation and review technique. This technique provides project managers with a flowchart representing construction schedule times. It includes a critical path that indicates the activities that must be completed on time in order not to delay completion time.

PGs Privately guaranteed mortgage securities.

physical depreciation The loss of value suffered by improvements on land resulting from wear and tear, disintegration, and the action of the elements. Physical depreciation may be curable (known as deferred maintenance) or incurable.

PITI Principal, interest, taxes, and insurance.

plat A survey of a tract of land prepared by a surveyor, showing the boundaries of individual parcels, roads, and highways; also known as a map.

points (discount points) An amount charged by the lender at the inception of the loan in order to increase the lender's effective yield. Each point is equal to 1 percent of the loan.

police power The power of a state, which may be delegated to local governments, to enact and enforce laws protecting the public health, morals, safety, and general welfare. Zoning, taxation, subdivision regulation, and licensing of real estate salespersons are examples of the police power.

portfolio A collection of various investments held by an individual or firm.

portfolio risk The expected variance of returns in a portfolio.

positive leverage The use of debt financing that increases the percentage return to equity because the rate of interest on the debt is lower than the free and clear rate of return on equity.

possession One of the bundle of rights that is held by the property owner or leasehold estate (i.e., the right to possess).

possessory or leasehold estate The right of the tenant to occupy the property during the term of the lease.

potential gross income   The expected total revenues if there are zero vacancies.

prepayment clause   A provision in a loan agreement specifying the right of (or prohibition against) the borrower to pay off the loan before maturity.

prepayment penalty   A fee (stated as a percentage of remaining mortgage balance) charged a borrower for the right to pay off a loan early.

prescriptive easement   An easement obtained by adverse possession.

present value   The current value of an income-producing asset that is estimated by discounting all expected future cash flows over the holding period.

price   The amount of money paid for an item.

primary data   Data gathered directly by the market researcher by conducting surveys or making personal observations.

primary financial market   A term used to describe the process whereby new capital is created by the sale of newly issued stocks, bonds, and other investment instruments.

principal   One who retains an agent to act for him or her; also, the amount of money loaned to another.

prior appropriation   The right to use natural water controlled by the state rather than a landowner; usually found in states where water is scarce.

prisoner's dilemma   The theory that the poorest people live on the most expensive land and cannot afford to move.

private mortgage insurers   Privately owned companies that insure the lender against default of the loan by the borrower.

proceeds from sale   The balance remaining to the seller after subtracting from the net sales price the amount of any loan repayment and tax liability.

profit   A right to take part of the soil, minerals, or produce of the land owned by another.

pro forma   A financial statement that projects gross income, operating expenses, and net operating income for a future period (usually one year) based on certain specified assumptions.

progression   An appraisal concept that an inferior property has its value enhanced by association with superior properties.

progressive tax   A tax, such as the federal income tax, whose rate increases in a series of steps as taxable income rises.

promisee   One to whom a promise is made.

promisor   One who makes a promise.

promissory note A written promise by a promisor to pay a sum of money to a promisee. It is a two-party instrument, as distinguished from an order to pay a sum of money, such as a draft or a check, which involves three parties.

property characteristics The physical attributes that describe the property.

property management The management of an individual real estate project, building, or development, including the functions of marketing, leasing, managing, and maintenance.

property manager A person or firm responsible for the operation of improved real estate. Management functions include leasing, managing, and maintenance.

property report An offering statement required to be given to purchasers of development lots regulated under the Interstate Land Sales Disclosure act.

property tax A tax imposed on real estate by municipalities and other local government agencies.

proration A division of taxes, interest, insurance, and so on, so that the seller and buyer each pays the portion covering his or her period of ownership.

psychic income Nonmonetary benefits, such as the pride associated with home ownership.

puffing Exaggerated claims or representations about property by the seller but sufficiently general in nature so that they do not amount to a fraudulent misstatement of fact.

purchase money mortgage A mortgage that is taken by a seller from a buyer in lieu of purchase money (i.e., the seller helps finance the purchase).

purchasing power risk In investment analysis, the risk that the purchasing power of invested capital will erode through inflation; also known as the inflation risk. The investor may be paid back with less valuable dollars.

Q **quantity survey method** The most comprehensive method of estimating reproduction cost of improved real estate. It involves identifying the quantity and quality of all materials used in the improvement as well as the amount of labor involved and the application of unit cost figures to the results.

quitclaim deed A deed in which the grantor makes no warranties to the grantee. In essence the grantor is saying, "Whatever rights I have in this property are yours."

R **RAM** Reverse annuity mortgage. A mortgage loan is made against a home that is paid for in order to provide an annuity to the borrower. At the death of the borrower (or sale of the property), the loan is paid in full.

rate of return (ROR) The percentage relationship between net operating income and the total capital invested.

"ready, willing, and able" A phrase used in the absence of a specific agreement between the parties, whereby the traditional rule of law permits a broker to claim his or her commission as soon as he or she presents a buyer "ready, willing, and able" to buy on the terms offered by the seller.

real estate broker Anyone who acting for valuable consideration, sells, buys, rents, or exchanges real estate or, in fact, attempts to do any of these things.

real estate feasibility analysis An analysis that includes a market study *and* investment analysis to determine whether a project is economically feasible to a specific investor.

Real Estate Investment Trust (REIT) An ownership entity that provides limited liability, no tax at the entity level, and liquidity. Ownership evidenced by shares of beneficial interest which are similar to shares of common stock.

real estate licensing examination An examination given by a state to those who wish to become licensed real estate brokers or salespersons.

real estate market The interaction of buying and selling interests in real estate. Real estate markets have traditionally been a series of local markets because real estate is immobile and requires local management. However, this is gradually changing, with real estate markets becoming national and even international.

real property The rights, interests, and benefits inherent in the ownership of real estate; frequently thought of as a bundle of rights; often used synonymously with the term "real estate."

real return The return required by an investor to induce him or her to refrain from immediate consumption and utilize his or her capital for investment purposes.

Realtor® A member of the National Association of Realtors®.

recapture premium For any investment that will not produce income in perpetuity, the capital must be recouped over the life of the investment. The rate of such recoupment is the recapture premium.

reconciliation of value The process of determining the value of the property based on the three estimates of value (market, cost, and income) and the appropriateness of each.

recreational land development A tract of land that has been divided into building lots and that may or may not be improved with buildings.

redlining The identification of a specific geographic area for the purpose of making loans or lending terms more difficult; a pattern of discriminatory lending.

refinancing Exchanging existing financing for new financing.

regeneration The changing of a neighborhood that results in new developing or rehabilitation of older properties.

regional analysis A study that analyzes population trends, income levels, growth patterns, and economic analysis of a specified region.

regional center The largest of the three categories of shopping centers (300,000 square feet +); it will have two or more anchor tenants with up to 100 or more small retail stores.

regional economics The application of economic concepts in a regional context.

regression An appraisal concept that the value of a superior property is affected adversely by association with inferior properties.

regressive tax A tax, such as the FICA (Social Security) tax, which declines as a percentage when total income increases beyond a certain level.

rehabilitation The restoration of a property to satisfactory condition without changing the plan, form, or style of a structure.

rehabilitation tax credit A direct reduction of an investor's tax liability for modernizing or rehabilitating existing buildings. The credit (as a percentage of the dollar investment) varies based on age and type of structure.

reindustrialization The process of replacing "old industries" with "new ones"; new technologies bring about reindustrialization.

release price The amount of a mortgage loan that must be repaid in order to have a portion of the mortgaged premises released from the mortgage lien.

remainderman One who will become entitled to an estate in property in the future after the termination of an existing estate (e.g., the person entitled to a fee simple interest after termination of an existing life estate).

REMIC Real Estate Mortgage Investment Conduit.

rentable area The measurement of leased space that excludes any space, such as elevator shafts, not actually available to the tenant.

rental achievement requirement A condition in a floor-to-ceiling loan commitment that a specified portion of a building must be rented before the total loan is advanced.

rent schedule   A listing of all rents due on a property.

rent theory   A theory that in an agricultural society a city's structure is determined by (1) land value or site rent and (2) transportation cost.

replacement cost   The cost of creating a building or improvement having equivalent utility to an existing improvement, on the basis of current prices and using current standards of material and design.

replacement reserve   A fund that is set aside for making replacements of properties with short useful lives, such as furniture, carpeting, and refrigerators.

reproduction cost new   The cost of creating a building or improvement in exact replica of an existing structure, on the basis of current prices, while using the same or closely similar materials.

required rate of return   The minimum rate of return an investment must produce in order to induce an individual to invest. Also known as hurdle rate of return.

rescission   The cancellation of an agreement, either by mutual consent of the parties or by judgment of a court.

resident manager   One who actually resides on the site of the property that he or she manages.

residential energy tax credit   A direct reduction of tax liability to homeowners for (1) qualified energy conservation expenditures (e.g., insulation, etc.) and (2) qualified renewable energy source expenditures (up to a maximum amount).

Resolution Trust Corporation (RTC)   A federal government organization created to liquidate properties that have come into federal hands as part of the S&L collapse of the 1980s.

RESPA   Real Estate Settlements Procedures Act. A law that requires any lender that receives funds from a federal agency to disclose within 24 hours of closing, all costs incurred in the loan.

restrictive covenant   A limitation contained in a deed that restricts or regulates the use of the real property (e.g., a restriction that the land may be used for residential use only).

retainage   A portion of the amount due under a construction contract that is withheld by the owner until the job is completed in accordance with plans and specifications; usually a percentage of the total contract price.

RFC   Reconstruction Finance Corporation. An agency of the government that became HUD.

right of reentry   The right of the holder of the residual interest in a property held in fee on condition subsequent.

right of survivorship   The surviving owner or concurrent owners of real property automatically receive the interests of a deceased concurrent owner.

riparian rights The rights of an owner of property abutting water to access and use of the water as long as the use does not interfere with the quality or quantity available to other riparian owners.

risk The possibility that returns on an investment or loan will not be as high as expected.

risk-averse investor An investor who would prefer a lower return on his or her investment rather than investing in a risky asset.

risk aversion The tendency or desire of most persons to avoid risk. One's degree of risk aversion determines the risk premium that one will build into a required rate of return.

risk-control techniques Steps in the development or construction process at which the developer is able either to discontinue the operation or to modify it in light of new circumstances.

risk of ruin The probability a firm will be insolvent (i.e., bankrupt). Also the probability that an investor will receive less than the required rate of return.

risk premium The return required by an investor to compensate him or her for the risk that his or her capital will not be recouped over the life of the investment.

RM Renegotiable mortgage. A loan in which the borrower agrees to renegotiate the loan terms at some specified period.

ROE Rate of return on equity capital. The ratio of before-tax cash flow to investor's equity in the property.

ROM Rollover mortgage, which is another term for a renegotiable mortgage.

ROR Rate of return on total capital. This is another term for the overall rate (OAR) and is the ratio of NOI to value or sales price.

Rule 41b An appraisal ruling by federal lending agencies that has had a dramatic impact on the appraisal profession. It requires better comparables as well as an estimate of feasibility for projects involving ongoing development.

S **sales comparison approach** One of three basic approaches to appraisal (formally called the market approach).

sale-lease-back Transaction where the owner sells a property then leases it (back) from the new owner.

sales or leasing schedule Schedule that estimates the number of expected sales or leases during specified time intervals.

salesperson In real estate, one who is employed by a broker but is licensed only as a salesperson. In most states, it is necessary to be a salesperson for a specified period of time before qualifying to be a broker.

sales tax   A tax levied on purchases of goods and services. Despite its name, it is a tax paid by purchasers and not sellers.

SAM   Shared appreciation mortgage. A loan in which the lender gives the borrower a lower interest rate mortgage in return for a percentage of the appreciation of the property over some specified time period.

SARA   Amendments to CERCLA passed in 1986 and officially titled Superfund Amendments and Reauthorization Act. Collectively, CERCLA and SARA provide the legislative guidance for what constitutes hazardous waste.

Savings and Loan (S&L) Association   A type of savings institution that is the primary source of financing for one- to four-family homes. Most S&Ls are mutual (nonstock) institutions.

scarcity   One of the factors required for an object to have value, in that each parcel of land is unique and certain parcels are more desirable than others.

S Corporation   A small-business corporation that qualifies under the Internal Revenue Code and that can pass through profits and losses directly to its shareholders.

sealed-bid procedure   A sales process in which all prospective buyers submit their offers (bids) in a sealed envelope; the property then goes to the highest bid.

secondary data   Data gathered from existing studies.

secondary financial markets   Term used to describe the process whereby previously originated financial claims are bought and sold.

secondary mortgage market   The market in which existing mortgages are bought and sold.

Section 203(b) of the National Housing Act   The section covering FHA insurance on traditional, fully amortizing loans.

Section 245 of the National Housing Act   The section covering FHA insurance on graduated payment mortgages.

Section 38 property   Tangible personal property used in a trade or business.

sector theory   A theory holding that residential concentrations in an urban area develop according to cultural as well as economic factors.

security interest   The legal interest in real estate represented by a mortgage (i.e., an interest created for the purpose of securing a loan).

self-liquidating loan   A loan that will be completely repaid at maturity by reason of amortization payments during its life.

selling broker   A broker other than a listing broker who brings about a sale and whose commission from the sale is divided with the listing broker.

sensitivity analysis   A method for determining variations in the rate of return on an investment in accordance with changes in a single factor (e.g., how much will the rate of return change if operating expenses rise 10 percent?).

services   Utilities, maintenance, security, and other functions provided by the manager of the property.

servicing activities   The collection (and distribution) of PITI on mortgage loans (i.e., collection from borrowers and distribution to lenders, insurers, and taxing authorities).

shift share   A method of analyzing the economic growth in a particular region by comparing it with the economic growth of the nation.

shopping center   Integrated and self-contained shopping area, mostly in the suburbs; shopping centers are generally considered the blue chips of real estate investment.

sinking fund   A fund of monies periodically set aside for the purpose of debt repayment together with the interest earned by such monies.

site analysis   A study of the physical and legal characteristics of a site.

site rent   The rent paid for a site under a specified use, less the rent it could command in an agricultural use.

site valuation taxation   Property tax base includes land value only and ignores the improvement; therefore, the overall tax base is lower, but tax rates are higher in order to achieve the same total revenues.

situs   The total urban environment in which a specific urban land use on a specific land parcel functions and with which it interacts at a specific time or more simply location.

situs theory   An explanation of urban activity which focuses on how a property interacts with all surrounding properties.

smart building   A structure containing sophisticated technology to control the operating systems (HVAC) and possibly special telecommunications equipment.

Social Security tax   A tax on all income up to a specified amount.

soft-dollar costs   Cash outlays for interest, origination fees, appraisals, and other third-party charges associated with real estate development.

sole proprietorship   A business operated by an individual, as distinguished from a partnership or corporation.

space   Area provided the tenant or property owner (e.g., office space, warehouse space, apartment, condominium, etc.).

space over time with services   A given unit of space for a specified period of time and including items such as utilities, maintenance, and so on.

spatial order of the economy   The study of the geographic allocation of resources.

spatial plane   Surface area of the earth.

special agent   An agent authorized to perform one or more specific acts for the principal and no other acts. A real estate broker normally is a special agent.

special-purpose property   A property that has been developed for a special purpose or use (e.g., a restaurant, motel, etc.) and that is generally considered riskier than other real estate because it is not easily converted to other uses.

special warranty deed   Same as a general warranty deed *except* the grantor is liable only if the problem arose through the actions of the grantor or during his or her period of ownership.

stabilized net operating income   Net operating income from property that differs from the actual historical income in that nonrecurring or unusual items of income and expense have been eliminated. The object is to show as closely as possible the true future earning power of the property.

standby fee   A fee charged to a borrower to induce the lender to remain willing to lend over a specified period on preestablished terms at the borrower's option.

standing loan   A loan that calls for no amortization payments during its life (i.e., the entire loan will come due at maturity).

State Board of Equalization   A state agency that adjusts the assessments from each separate tax district in the state to compensate for differences in fractions of full value that are utilized by different districts.

statute of frauds   A type of statue in effect in every state that seeks to prevent frauds and perjuries by providing that certain types of contracts will not be enforceable in a court unless they are in writing. Included under the statutes are contracts for the sale of land.

straight-line depreciation   A method of depreciation whereby an equal amount is taken as a deduction each year over the useful life of the asset being depreciated.

subcontractor   An individual or company that performs a specific job for a construction project (e.g., electrical work) pursuant to an agreement with the general contractor.

subdivision regulation   A form of municipal ordinance that regulates the development and design of subdivisions, including such matters as the dedication (donation) of land for streets, parks, and schools, provision of utility services, and requirements for building lines and lot sizes.

subject property   The property being spoken about or for which a value is being sought.

substitution   An appraisal concept to the effect that when several goods with substantially the same utility are available, the one with the lowest price attracts the greatest demand.

subsurface rights Ownership rights in the area beneath the surface of the earth to its center. Important because it defines the owner of oil, coal, or gas under the ground.

suburbanization The movement of development to the suburbs created by an overflow effect of cities and by the automobile, which improved accessibility to the inner city.

Sunbelt The area located in the south and southwestern part of the United States.

supply analysis An inventory of the market in terms of rent levels, vacancy rates, location, and amenities.

supply and demand An appraisal and economic concept that says that increasing the supply or decreasing the demand for a thing tends to affect its price adversely, whereas decreasing the supply or increasing the demand tends to increase the price.

surplus productivity In appraisal, the term given to the net real property income remaining after the costs of labor, capital, and coordination have been paid.

survey The process of measuring and establishing the boundaries of real property.

surveyor A real estate professional trained in the science of determining the precise location of a tract of land in relation to the surface of the earth.

syndicate A group of individuals who join together for the purpose of investment. The term "syndicate" has no specific legal significance.

synergistic The act of combining two or more items of value and creating a product whose total value is greater than the sum of its parts.

systematic risk The amount of variance that can be explained by the variance of the overall market.

T **takeout commitment** The term used to describe the permanent loan commitment for a project to be constructed.

tax avoidance The legal right of a taxpayer to utilize all provisions of the tax code in order to minimize tax liability.

tax basis Original cost of the property plus additional capital investments during the period of ownership, minus accrued depreciation deductions.

tax conversion A form of tax avoidance that enables the taxpayer to convert ordinary income to more favorably taxed capital gain (e.g., the use of straight-line depreciation). This occurs when ordinary income tax rates exceed capital gain tax rates.

tax credit   A direct reduction of the tax liability (on a dollar-for-dollar basis).

tax deduction   An item that reduces taxable income (e.g., interest on a mortgage) and reduces tax liability by a varying percentage.

tax deferral   A form of tax avoidance by which the taxpayer is enabled to delay the payment of tax on income from a current year to a future year.

tax-deferred exchange (tax-free exchange)   A swap of investment or business real estate that permits the exchangor to defer the payment of tax on any appreciation in value of the property exchanged.

tax evasion   The wilful concealment or misrepresentation of facts in order to avoid the payment of tax.

tax-preference income   A certain type of income that is subject to the add-on minimum tax.

tax savings   The dollar benefit to an investor as a result of deductions or losses realized for tax purposes.

tax shelter   Any deduction or credit against income that is available to a taxpayer and that increases cash flow to the taxpayer because taxes are lower. The primary source of tax shelter in real estate is the depreciation deduction for improved property.

taxable gain   The amount of gain realized on the sale of an asset that is subject to tax either as ordinary income or as capital gain; net sales price less tax basis.

taxable income   Income subject to tax after appropriate deductions and exemptions have been applied to the taxpayer's gross income.

taxable loss   Negative taxable income that is used to offset income from other sources, decreasing the tax liability of an individual (or investor).

tenancy by the entirety   A form of concurrent ownership that can exist only between husband and wife and includes the right of survivorship.

tenancy in common   A form of concurrent ownership under which each tenant in common may sell or devise his or her interest (i.e., no right of survivorship exists).

tenant   One who rents from another.

tenant allowance   A cash payment made by the developer to a tenant (usually in an income property) to enable the tenant, rather than the developer, to complete the interior work for the leased premises.

tenant mix   The combination of various types of tenants that compete with and complement each other.

terrarium   An enclosure where behavior can be observed.

time   Period in which the tenant has a leasehold interest (which is finite) or the owner has a fee simple interest (which is indefinite).

time sharing   The division of ownership or use of a resort unit or apartment on the basis of time periods (e.g., a resort unit may be used for two weeks by each owner).

time value of money   The idea that a dollar received today is worth more than a dollar received at some future date; the rationale behind compounding (for future value) or discounting (for present value).

title   Evidence of ownership of real property; often used synonymously with the term "ownership" to indicate a person's right to possess, use, and dispose of property.

title closing   The actual transfer of title.

title company   A company that examines titles to real estate, determines whether they are valid, whether any limitations on the title exist, and, for a premium, insures the validity of the title to the owner or lender.

title examiner   One who is trained in the art of examining public land records in order to ascertain whether the present owner of property has good title.

title insurance   Insurance issued by a title company that insures the validity of the title; can be issued to the owner or lender.

title theory (mortgages)   A mortgage in which title to the mortgaged real property vests in the lender.

topography   The shape or contours of the surface of the site (e.g., steep, level, gently rolling, etc.).

trade breakdown method   A method of estimating reproduction cost in which direct cost for labor and materials are added to indirect costs for financing, selling, insurance, and so on, to arrive at the estimated reproduction cost new of the improvement on the site.

transferability   The right to transfer property from one owner to another without legal constraints.

transient facility   Hospitality facility (hotel or motel) that caters primarily to guests in transit from one location to another.

transshipment points   Locations where transportation modes change (e.g., a harbor where ship cargoes are transferred to trucks and railroad cars).

trust   An arrangement under which legal title to property is held by one person under an agreement to administer the property for the benefit of another (the beneficiary) who holds equitable title.

trustee   The one accepting something in trust (e.g., a third party who acts as "middleman" between borrower, trustor, and lender, beneficiary, by holding title to the property in trust until the loan is paid in full).

trustor   The one who puts something in trust (e.g., a borrower who signs a deed of trust).

Truth in Lending Act   A federal law under which lenders are required to make advance disclosure to borrowers of the amount and type of finance charges incurred in connection with the loan.

two-part return   Term that reflects the fact that the overall return to a real estate investor normally consists of (1) cash flows during the period of ownership and (2) proceeds from ultimate sale of property.

U   **unanticipated inflation**   An unexpected decline in the purchasing power of a dollar.

underwriting   The process of analyzing a loan to determine the creditworthiness of the borrower and the strength of the collateral.

unilateral contract   A contract involving the exchange of a promise for performance of an act.

unsystematic risk   A risk that is unique to an investment; therefore, it can be eliminated through diversification.

upside leverage   The method of increasing the return on equity (cash invested) by borrowing funds at a cost lower than the free and clear return from the property. Thus, the borrower is earning more on the borrowed funds than their interest cost. Also called positive leverage.

upzoning   A change in the zoning classification of property from a lower use to a higher use (e.g., from residential to commercial).

urban economics   Economic concepts applied in the context of a particular urban area.

use effect   The effect the site itself has on surrounding activity.

useful life   The period over which a business or investment asset is expected to have economic value and hence the period over which it must be depreciated.

utility   One of the elements of value.

V   **VA**   Veterans Administration. The VA guarantees loans that are made to eligible veterans.

vacancy allowance and collection (or credit) loss   An amount subtracted from gross possible income to allow for vacancies or loss in income owing to nonpayment of rent.

value   In general, the amount of money that can be obtained in exchange for a thing. Value in this sense is also known as market value or value in exchange. A property may also have a value in use (i.e., it may be worth something to one who utilizes the property even though no identifiable market demand exists).

value in use assessment   A method of real property taxation under which land is taxed on the basis of its existing use rather than on its highest and best use; often used to prevent onerous taxation of farmland that would otherwise be taxed on the basis of its suitability for development.

variable rate mortgage (VRM) A mortgage carrying an interest rate that may move either up or down, depending on the movements of an outside standard (e.g., the Treasury bond rate) to which the interest rate is tied.

variability Change in a thing (e.g., as cash flows).

variance In general, the difference between expected results and actual results. Statistically, the term "variance" refers to the square of the standard deviation. Variance can be used as a measure of risk.

W **warehouse** A building that is used for the storage of goods or merchandise and that may be either owner-occupied or leased to one or more tenants.

warehousing operations The methods used by mortgage bankers to fund the loans they originate. The mortgage banker obtains a line of credit from a lender (usually a commercial bank) to generate loans. The loans are held until there is a sufficient volume to sell in the secondary market, at which time the line of credit is repaid.

wasting asset Assets that gradually lose value over a period of time to use, wear and tear, or the action of the elements.

wraparound mortgage A form of secondary financing in which the face amount of the second (wraparound) loan is equal to the balance of the first loan plus the amount of the new financing. Because the interest rate on the wraparound loan is normally greater than on the original first mortgage, upside leverage is achieved on the new lender's return.

Z **zero coupon bonds** A bond with no payments until maturity.

zoning The ordinance by which local governments assign land uses (e.g., residential, commercial, or industrial) to appropriate districts in accordance with a master plan. Zoning also regulates lot size and height and bulk of buildings.

 NDEX